GREAT BOOKS OF THE WESTERN WORLD

GREAT BOOKS
OF THE WESTERN WORLD

ROBERT MAYNARD HUTCHINS, *EDITOR IN CHIEF*

54.

FREUD

The Major Works of
Sigmund Freud

WILLIAM BENTON, *Publisher*

ENCYCLOPÆDIA BRITANNICA, INC.

CHICAGO · LONDON · TORONTO · GENEVA · SYDNEY · TOKYO · MANILA

The following works in this edition are reprinted
by arrangement with the publishers listed below:

THE AMERICAN JOURNAL OF PSYCHOLOGY, for *The Origin And Development
Of Psycho-Analysis.*

GEORGE ALLEN & UNWIN LTD., London, for *The Interpretation Of Dreams.*

LIVERIGHT PUBLISHING CORPORATION, New York, and GEORGE ALLEN & UNWIN
LTD., London, for *A General Introduction To Psycho-Analysis.* Copyright,
1920, 1935, by Edward L. Bernays.

THE HOGARTH PRESS, London, for *Beyond The Pleasure Principle; Group
Psychology And The Analysis Of The Ego; The Ego And The Id; Inhibitions,
Symptoms And Anxiety; Civilization And Its Discontents,* Copyright, 1930,
by Jonathan Cape and Harrison Smith; and the following chapters from
Collected Papers, Vol. II: *The Sexual Enlightenment Of Children, The Future
Prospects Of Psycho-Analytic Therapy, Observations On "Wild" Psycho-
Analysis:* Vol. IV: *On Narcissism, Instincts And Their Vicissitudes, Repres-
sion, The Unconscious, And Thoughts For The Times On War And Death.*

W. W. NORTON & COMPANY, INC., New York, and THE HOGARTH PRESS, London,
for *New Introductory Lectures On Psycho-Analysis.* Copyright, 1939, by
Sigmund Freud.

Selected Papers on Hysteria
Copyright, 1919, by Dr. William A. White.
Renewed, 1947, by Dr. A. A. Brill.

THE UNIVERSITY OF CHICAGO

The Great Books
is published with the editorial advice of the faculties
of The University of Chicago

©

1952
BY ENCYCLOPÆDIA BRITANNICA, INC.
NINETEENTH PRINTING, 1971
COPYRIGHT UNDER INTERNATIONAL COPYRIGHT UNION

Library of Congress Catalog Card Number: 55-10360
International Standard Book Number: 0-85229-163-9

BIOGRAPHICAL NOTE

SIGMUND FREUD, 1856–1939

FREUD was born May 6, 1856, at Freiburg in what is now Czechoslovakia. When he was four, the family moved to Vienna, and his father continued his trade as a small merchant. While following the usual course of studies at the *Gymnasium,* where for seven years he was first in his class, Freud was attracted by Darwin's theories to the study of science. Although he had no "particular predilection for the career of a physician," Freud later noted that "it was upon hearing Goethe's beautiful essay *On Nature* . . . just before I left school that I decided to become a medical student." In 1873 he entered the University of Vienna, where, he records in his autobiographical sketch, he experienced the effects of anti-Semitic prejudice.

While pursuing his medical studies, Freud began experimental investigation by studying the nervous system of the fish in the physiological laboratory of Ernst Brücke. After taking his medical degree in 1881, financial reasons compelled him to become an interne at the General Hospital. With the little spare time he had as an interne, he pursued research at the Institute of Cerebral Anatomy on the subject of nervous diseases. The publication of several monographs on cerebral paralysis in children won him the post of lecturer in neuropathology at the university, and in 1885 he was awarded a traveling fellowship to advance his studies. Having become interested the previous year in Breuer's treatment of hysteria by hypnosis, during which the patient was induced to recollect his past, Freud now chose to pursue such investigation under Charcot, the neurologist, at the Sorbonne. Freud studied with him several months and was strengthened in his determination to take the then revolutionary step of investigating hysteria from a psychological point of view. Before returning home in 1886, he spent a few months at a children's clinic in Berlin and made extensive observations of the nervous disorders of children.

Upon his return to Vienna, Freud married and to provide for a rapidly increasing family, established himself as a specialist in nervous diseases. In the first years of his practice his principal technique "aside from haphazard psycho-therapeutic methods" was hypnotic suggestion. He resumed his friendship with Breuer and in collaboration with him published in 1895 the *Studies in Hysteria.* The partnership was dissolved after the book was completed, and soon afterwards Freud took the decisive step of replacing hypnotism by the method of "free association." Largely as a result of his extensive clinical practice, he turned to the analysis of dreams, and in 1900 provided the first statement of his doctrine in the *Interpretation of Dreams.*

Except for his brief collaboration with Breuer, Freud for more than a decade "stood completely isolated" from the medical world, and his theories, when not completely ignored, were the object of ridicule. It was not until 1902 that several young doctors began to gather around him with the intention of learning and practising psycho-analysis, and from this group grew the Viennese Psycho-Analytic Society. Although his *Psychopathology of Everyday Life* (1904) received more favorable public notice, the opposition to his theories increased as soon as he began publishing his views on the sexual life of children. His work, however, soon began to receive international attention from the medical profession. The Burgholzli Clinic in Zürich, in 1906, was the first institution outside of Austria to adopt the method of psycho-analysis. By 1908 Freud had colleagues throughout Europe, including Adler, Brill, Ferenczi, Ernest Jones, Jung, Sadger, and Stekel, and in that year the first International Congress of Psycho-Analysis was held at Salzburg. In the following year, at the invitation of Clark University, Freud visited the United States and gave five lectures on his discoveries. which were later published as the *Origin and Development of Psycho-Analysis.* With the establishment of the International Psycho-Analytic Association in 1910 Freud devoted his efforts with increasing success to the development of the psycho-analytic movement. Disagreement later led to a severance of relations between Freud and several of his closest associates, including Adler, Stekel, Rank, and Jung, but Freud was the acknowledged founder of psycho-analysis and the leader of the movement.

After 1912 Freud gave most of his time to directing the Psycho-Analytic Society, editing its various journals, and writing many monographs. Although his clinical practice was not as extensive as in previous years, he still remained active as an analyst, and his records of the case-histories of his patients cover almost fifty years. At the University of Vienna during the two winter sessions between 1915 and 1917, he again explained his theories before a general public, as he had in the United States, in lectures afterwards published as the *General Introduction to Psycho-Analysis*.

Until the end of the first World War Freud was mainly occupied with special problems concerning the unconscious, and it was not until 1920 that he began to deal with the more general problems raised by his studies, particularly with the factors making for what he called repression. In 1920 he published *Beyond the Pleasure Principle*, and three years later the *Ego and the Id*. As early as 1913 Freud had attempted in *Totem and Taboo* "to make use of the newly discovered findings of analysis in order to investigate the origin of religions and morality." He now "returned to the cultural problems which had fascinated me long before," and published *The Future of an Illusion* (1927), *Civilization and its Discontents* (1929), and *Moses and Monotheism* (1939), which was his last book.

With the award of the Goethe Prize in 1930, when he was also given the freedom of the city of Vienna, Freud reached what he described as "the climax of my life as a citizen." But soon afterwards, Freud notes, "the boundaries of our country narrowed, and the nation would know of us no more." Upon the Nazi invasion of Austria in 1938, Freud's books were burned, the *Psychoanalytische Verlag*, directed by his son, was destroyed, and his passport confiscated. For years Freud had lived in virtual seclusion, largely because of the development of a cancer of the mouth which caused him great pain. He was finally allowed to leave Austria in 1938 after the payment of a large ransom. With his wife, a nephew, and his daughter, Anna, he went to England, where another of his sons lived. He died on September 23, 1939, in Hampstead, London.

General Contents

The Origin and Development of Psycho-Analysis

FIRST LECTURE [1]

LADIES AND GENTLEMEN: It is a new and somewhat embarrassing experience for me to appear as lecturer before students of the New World. I assume that I owe this honour to the association of my name with the theme of psycho-analysis, and consequently it is of psycho-analysis that I shall aim to speak. I shall attempt to give you in very brief form an historical survey of the origin and further development of this new method of research and cure.

Granted that it is a merit to have created psycho-analysis, it is not my merit. I was a student, busy with the passing of my last examinations, when another physician of Vienna, Dr. Joseph Breuer, made the first application of this method to the case of an hysterical girl (1880-82). We must now examine the history of this case and its treatment, which can be found in detail in *Studien über Hysterie* later published by Dr. Breuer and myself.

But first one word. I have noticed, with considerable satisfaction, that the majority of my hearers do not belong to the medical profession. Now do not fear that a medical education is necessary to follow what I shall have to say. We shall now accompany the doctors a little way, but soon we shall take leave of them and follow Dr. Breuer on a way which is quite his own.

Dr. Breuer's patient was a girl of twenty-one, of a high degree of intelligence. She had developed in the course of her two years' illness a series of physical and mental disturbances which well deserved to be taken seriously. She had a severe paralysis of both right extremities, with anaesthesia, and at times the same affection of the members of the left side of the body; disturbance of eye-movements, and much impairment of vision; difficulty in maintaining the position of the head, an intense *Tussis nervosa*, nausea when she attempted to take nourishment, and at one time for several weeks a loss of the power to drink, in spite of tormenting thirst.

Her power of speech was also diminished, and this progressed so far that she could neither speak nor understand her mother tongue; and, finally, she was subject to states of "absence," of confusion, delirium, alteration of her whole personality. These states will later claim our attention.

When one hears of such a case, one does not need to be a physician to incline to the opinion that we are concerned here with a serious injury, probably of the brain, for which there is little hope of cure and which will probably lead to the early death of the patient. The doctors will tell us, however, that in one type of cases with just as unfavourable symptoms, another, far more favourable, opinion is justified. When one finds such a series of symptoms in the case of a young girl, whose vital organs (heart, kidneys) are shown by objective tests to be normal, but who has suffered from strong emotional disturbances, and when the symptoms differ in certain finer characteristics from what one might logically expect, in a case like this the doctors are not too much disturbed. They consider that there is present no organic lesion of the brain, but that enigmatical state known since the time of the Greek physicians as hysteria, which can simulate a whole series of symptoms of various diseases. They consider in such a case that the life of the patient is not in danger and that a restoration to health will probably come about of itself. The differentiation of such an hysteria from a severe organic lesion is not always very easy. But we do not need to know how a differential diagnosis of this kind is made; you may be sure that the case of Breuer's patient was such that no skillful physician could fail to diagnose an hysteria. We may also add a word here from the history of the case. The illness first appeared while the patient was caring for her father, whom she tenderly loved, during the severe illness which led to his death, a task which she was compelled to abandon because she herself fell ill.

So far it has seemed best to go with the doctors, but we shall soon part company with them.

[1] These lectures were delivered at Clark University in 1909.

I

You must not think that the outlook of a patient with regard to medical aid is essentially bettered when the diagnosis points to hysteria rather than to organic disease of the brain. Against the serious brain diseases medical skill is in most cases powerless, but also in the case of hysterical affections the doctor can do nothing. He must leave it to benign nature, when and how his hopeful prognosis will be realized.[1] Accordingly, with the recognition of the disease as hysteria, little is changed in the situation of the patient, but there is a great change in the attitude of the doctor. We can observe that he acts quite differently toward hystericals than toward patients suffering from organic diseases. He will not bring the same interest to the former as to the latter, since their suffering is much less serious and yet seems to set up the claim to be valued just as seriously.

But there is another motive in this action. The physician, who through his studies has learned so much that is hidden from the laity, can realize in his thought the causes and alterations of the brain disorders in patients suffering from apoplexy or dementia, a representation which must be right up to a certain point, for by it he is enabled to understand the nature of each symptom. But before the details of hysterical symptoms, all his knowledge, his anatomical-physiological and pathological education, desert him. He cannot understand hysteria. He is in the same position before it as the layman. And that is not agreeable to any one, who is in the habit of setting such a high valuation upon his knowledge. Hystericals, accordingly, tend to lose his sympathy; he considers them persons who overstep the laws of his science, as the orthodox regard heretics; he ascribes to them all possible evils, blames them for exaggeration and intentional deceit, "simulation," and he punishes them by withdrawing his interest.

Now Dr. Breuer did not deserve this reproach in this case; he gave his patient sympathy and interest, although at first he did not understand how to help her. Probably this was easier for him on account of those superior qualities of the patient's mind and character to which he bears witness in his account of the case.

His sympathetic observation soon found the means which made the first help possible. It had been noticed that the patient, in her states of "absence," of psychic alteration, usually mumbled over several words to herself. These seemed to spring from associations with which her thoughts were busy. The doctor, who was able to get these words, put her in a sort of hypnosis and repeated them to her over and over, in order to bring up any associations that they might have. The patient yielded to his suggestion and reproduced for him those psychic creations which controlled her thoughts during her "absences," and which betrayed themselves in these single spoken words. These were fancies, deeply sad, often poetically beautiful, day dreams, we might call them, which commonly took as their starting point the situation of a girl beside the sick-bed of her father. Whenever she had related a number of such fancies, she was, as it were, freed and restored to her normal mental life. This state of health would last for several hours, and then give place on the next day to a new "absence," which was removed in the same way by relating the newly created fancies. It was impossible not to get the impression that the psychic alteration which was expressed in the "absence" was a consequence of the excitations originating from these intensely emotional fancy-images. The patient herself, who at this time of her illness strangely enough understood and spoke only English, gave this new kind of treatment the name "talking cure," or jokingly designated it as "chimney sweeping."

The doctor soon hit upon the fact that through such cleansing of the soul more could be accomplished than a temporary removal of the constantly recurring mental clouds. Symptoms of the disease would disappear when in hypnosis the patient could be made to remember the situation and the associative connexions under which they first appeared, provided free vent was given to the emotions which they aroused. "There was in the summer a time of intense heat, and the patient had suffered very much from thirst; for, without any apparent reason, she had suddenly become unable to drink. She would take a glass of water in her hand, but as soon as it touched her lips she would push it away as though suffering from hydrophobia. Obviously for these few seconds she was in her absent state. She ate only fruit, melons and the like, in order to relieve this tormenting thirst. When this had been going on about six weeks, she was talking one day in hypnosis about her English governess, whom she disliked, and finally told, with every sign of disgust, how she had come into the room of the governess, and how that lady's little dog, that she abhorred, had drunk out of a glass. Out of respect for the

[1] I know that this view no longer holds today, but in the lecture I take myself and my hearers back to the time before 1880. If things have become different since that time it has been largely due to the work the history of which I am sketching.

conventions, the patient had remained silent. Now, after she had given energetic expression to her restrained anger, she asked for a drink, drank a large quantity of water without trouble, and woke from hypnosis with the glass at her lips. The symptom thereupon vanished permanently."[1]

Permit me to dwell for a moment on this experience. No one had ever cured an hysterical symptom by such means before, or had come so near understanding its cause. This would be a pregnant discovery if the expectation could be confirmed that still other, perhaps the majority of symptoms, originated in this way and could be removed by the same method. Breuer spared no pains to convince himself of this and investigated the pathogenesis of the other more serious symptoms in a more orderly way. Such was indeed the case; almost all the symptoms originated in exactly this way, as remnants, as precipitates, if you like, of affectively toned experiences, which for that reason we later called *psychic traumata*. The nature of the symptoms became clear through their relation to the scene which caused them. They were, to use the technical term, *determined* (*determiniert*) by the scene whose memory traces they embodied, and so could no longer be described as arbitrary or enigmatical functions of the neurosis.

Only one variation from what might be expected must be mentioned. It was not always a single experience which occasioned the symptom, but usually several, perhaps many similar, repeated traumata coöperated in this effect. It was necessary to repeat the whole series of pathogenic memories in chronological sequence, and, of course, in reverse order, the last first and the first last. It was quite impossible to reach the first and often most essential trauma directly, without first clearing away those coming later.

You will, of course, want to hear me speak of other examples of the causation of hysterical symptoms beside this of inability to drink on account of the disgust caused by the dog drinking from the glass. I must, however, if I hold to my program, limit myself to very few examples. Breuer relates, for instance, that his patient's visual disturbances could be traced back to external causes, in the following way: "The patient, with tears in her eyes, was sitting by the sick-bed when her father suddenly asked her what time it was. She could not see distinctly, strained her eyes to see, brought the watch near her eyes so that the dial seemed very large (*macropia* and *strabismus conv.*), or else she tried

[1] *Studien über Hysterie*, 2d ed., p. 26.

hard to suppress her tears, so that the sick man might not see them."[2]

All the pathogenic impressions sprang from the time when she shared in the care of her sick father. "Once she was watching at night in the greatest anxiety for the patient, who was in a high fever, and in suspense, for a surgeon was expected from Vienna, to operate on the patient. Her mother had gone out for a little while, and Anna sat by the sick-bed, her right arm hanging over the back of her chair. She fell into a revery and saw a black snake emerge, as it were, from the wall and approach the sick man as though to bite him. (It is very probable that several snakes had actually been seen in the meadow behind the house, that she had already been frightened by them, and that these former experiences furnished the material for the hallucination.) She tried to drive off the creature, but was as though paralyzed. Her right arm, which was hanging over the back of the chair, had "gone to sleep," become anaesthetic and paretic, and as she was looking at it, the fingers changed into little snakes with deaths-heads. (The nails.) Probably she attempted to drive away the snake with her paralyzed right hand, and so the anaesthesia and paralysis of this member formed associations with the snake hallucination. When this had vanished, she tried in her anguish to speak, but could not. She could not express herself in any language, until finally she thought of the words of an English nursery song, and thereafter she could think and speak only in this language."[3] When the memory of this scene was revived in hypnosis, the paralysis of the right arm, which had existed since the beginning of the illness, was cured and the treatment ended.

When, a number of years later, I began to use Breuer's researches and treatment on my own patients, my experiences completely coincided with his. In the case of a woman of about forty, there was a tic, a peculiar smacking noise which manifested itself whenever she was labouring under any excitement, without any obvious cause. It had its origin in two experiences which had this common element, that she attempted to make no noise, but that by a sort of counter-will this noise broke the stillness. On the first occasion, she had finally after much trouble put her sick child to sleep, and she tried to be very quiet so as not to awaken it. On the second occasion, during a ride with both her children in a thunderstorm, the horses took fright, and she

[2] *Ibid.*, p. 30.
[3] *Ibid.*, p. 31 [see also p. 25 below.]

carefully avoided any noise for fear of frightening them still more.[1] I give this example instead of many others which are cited in the *Studien über Hysterie*.

Ladies and gentlemen, if you will permit me to generalize, as is indispensable in so brief a presentation, we may express our results up to this point in the formula: *Our hysterical patients suffer from reminiscences.* Their symptoms are the remnants and the memory symbols of certain (traumatic) experiences.

A comparison with other memory symbols from other sources will perhaps enable us better to understand this symbolism. The memorials and monuments with which we adorn our great cities are also such memory symbols. If you walk through London you will find before one of the greatest railway stations of the city a richly decorated Gothic pillar—Charing Cross. One of the old Plantagenet kings, in the thirteenth century, caused the body of his beloved queen Eleanor to be borne to Westminster, and had Gothic crosses erected at each of the stations where the coffin was set down. Charing Cross is the last of these monuments, which preserve the memory of this sad journey.[2] In another part of the city, you will see a high pillar of more modern construction, which is merely called "the Monument." This is in memory of the great fire which broke out in the neighborhood in the year 1666, and destroyed a great part of the city. These monuments are memory symbols like the hysterical symptoms; so far the comparison seems justified. But what would you say to a Londoner who today stood sadly before the monument to the funeral of Queen Eleanor, instead of going about his business with the haste engendered by modern industrial conditions, or rejoicing with the young queen of his own heart? Or to another, who before "the Monument" bemoaned the burning of his loved native city, which long since has arisen again so much more splendid than before?

Now hystericals and all neurotics behave like these two unpractical Londoners, not only in that they remember the painful experiences of the distant past, but because they are still strongly affected by them. They cannot escape from the past and neglect present reality in its favour. This fixation of the mental life on the pathogenic traumata is an essential, and practically a most significant characteristic of the neurosis. I will willingly concede the objection which you are probably formulating, as you think over the history of Breuer's patient. All her traumata originated at the time when she was caring for her sick father, and her symptoms could only be regarded as memory symbols of his sickness and death. They correspond to mourning, and a fixation on thoughts of the dead so short a time after death is certainly not pathological, but rather corresponds to normal emotional behavior. I concede this: there is nothing abnormal in the fixation of feeling on the trauma shown by Breuer's patient. But in other cases, like that of the tic that I have mentioned, the occasions for which lay ten and fifteen years back, the characteristic of this abnormal clinging to the past is very clear, and Breuer's patient would probably have developed it, if she had not come under the "cathartic treatment" such a short time after the traumatic experiences and the beginning of the disease.

We have so far only explained the relation of the hysterical symptoms to the life history of the patient; now by considering two further factors which Breuer observed, we may get a hint as to the processes of the beginning of the illness and those of the cure. With regard to the first, it is especially to be noted that Breuer's patient in almost all pathogenic situations had to suppress a strong excitement, instead of giving vent to it by appropriate words and deeds. In the little experience with her governess' dog, she suppressed, through regard for the conventions, all manifestations of her very intense disgust. While she was seated by her father's sickbed, she was careful to betray nothing of her anxiety and her painful depression to the patient. When, later, she reproduced the same scene before the physician, the emotion which she had suppressed on the occurrence of the scene burst out with especial strength, as though it had been pent up all along. The symptom which had been caused by that scene reached its greatest intensity while the doctor was striving to revive the memory of the scene, and vanished after it had been fully laid bare. On the other hand, experience shows that if the patient is reproducing the traumatic scene to the physician, the process has no curative effect if, by some peculiar chance, there is no development of emotion. It is apparently these emotional processes upon which the illness of the patient and the restoration to health are dependent. We feel justified in regarding *emotion* as a quantity

---

[1] *Ibid.*, pp. 43-46. [See also p. 25 below.] A selection from this book, augmented by several later treatises on hysteria, lies before me, in an English translation by Dr. A. A. Brill, of New York. It bears the title, *Selected Papers on Hysteria and Other Psychoneuroses*, 1909.

[2] Or rather the later copy of such a monument. The name "Charing" is itself, as Dr. E. Jones tells me, derived from the words *chère reine*.

which may become increased, derived and displaced. So we are forced to the conclusion that the patient fell ill because the emotion developed in the pathogenic situation was prevented from escaping normally, and that the essence of the sickness lies in the fact that these *imprisoned (eingeklemmt)* emotions undergo a series of abnormal changes. In part they are preserved as a lasting charge and as a source of constant disturbance in psychical life; in part they undergo a change into unusual bodily innervations and inhibitions, which present themselves as the physical symptoms of the case. We have coined the name *hysterical conversion* for the latter process. Part of our mental energy is, under normal conditions, conducted off by way of physical innervation and gives what we call *the expression of emotions*. Hysterical conversion exaggerates this part of the course of a mental process which is emotionally coloured; it corresponds to a far more intense emotional expression, which finds outlet by new paths. If a stream flows in two channels, an overflow of one will take place as soon as the current in the other meets with an obstacle.

You see that we are in a fair way to arrive at a purely psychological theory of hysteria, in which we assign the first rank to the affective processes. A second observation of Breuer compels us to ascribe to the altered condition of consciousness a great part in determining the characteristics of the disease. His patient showed many sorts of mental states, conditions of "absence," confusion and alteration of character, besides her normal state. In her normal state she was entirely ignorant of the pathogenic scenes and of their connection with her symptoms. She had forgotten those scenes, or at any rate had dissociated them from their pathogenic connection. When the patient was hypnotized, it was possible, after considerable difficulty, to recall those scenes to her memory, and by this means of recall, the symptoms were removed. It would have been extremely perplexing to know how to interpret this fact, if hypnotic practice and experiments had not pointed out the way. Through the study of hypnotic phenomena, the conception, strange though it was at first, has become familiar, that in one and the same individual several mental groupings are possible, which may remain relatively independent of each other, *know nothing* of each other, and which may cause a splitting of consciousness along lines which they lay down. Cases of such a sort, known as *double personality (double conscience)*, occasionally appear spontaneously.

If, in such a division of personality, consciousness remains constantly bound up with one of the two states, this is called the *conscious* mental state, and the other the *unconscious*. In the well-known phenomena of so-called post hypnotic suggestion, in which a command given in hypnosis is later executed in the normal state as though by an imperative suggestion, we have an excellent basis for understanding how the unconscious state can influence the conscious, although the latter is ignorant of the existence of the former. In the same way it is quite possible to explain the facts in hysterical cases. Breuer came to the conclusion that the hysterical symptoms originated in such peculiar mental states, which he called *hypnoidal states (hypnoide Zustände)*. Experiences of an emotional nature, which occur during such hypnoidal states, easily become pathogenic, since such states do not present the conditions for a normal draining off of the emotion of the exciting processes. And as a result there arises a peculiar product of this exciting process, that is, the symptom, and this is projected like a foreign body into the normal state. The latter has, then, no conception of the significance of the hypnoidal pathogenic situation. Where a symptom arises, we also find an amnesia, a memory gap, and the filling of this gap includes the removal of the conditions under which the symptom originated.

I am afraid that this portion of my treatment will not seem very clear, but you must remember that we are dealing here with new and difficult views, which perhaps could not be made much clearer. This all goes to show that our knowledge in this field is not yet very far advanced. Breuer's idea of the hypnoidal states has, moreover, been shown to be superfluous and a hindrance to further investigation, and has been dropped from present conceptions of psycho-analysis. Later I shall at least suggest what other influences and processes have been disclosed besides that of the hypnoidal states, to which Breuer limited the causal moment.

You have probably also felt, and rightly, that Breuer's investigations gave you only a very incomplete theory and insufficient explanation of the phenomena which we have observed. But complete theories do not fall from Heaven, and you would have had still greater reason to be distrustful, had any one offered you at the beginning of his observations a well-rounded theory, without any gaps; such a theory could only be the child of his speculations and not the fruit of an unprejudiced investigation of the facts.

SECOND LECTURE

LADIES AND GENTLEMEN: At about the same
time that Breuer was using the "talking-cure"
with his patient, M. Charcot began in Paris,
with the hystericals of the Salpetrière, those researches which were to lead to a new understanding of the disease. These results were, however, not yet known in Vienna. But when about
ten years later Breuer and I published our preliminary communication on the psychic mechanism of hysterical phenomena, which grew out
of the cathartic treatment of Breuer's first patient, we were both of us under the spell of
Charcot's investigations. We made the pathogenic experiences of our patients, which acted
as psychic traumata, equivalent to those physical traumata whose influence on hysterical paralyses Charcot had determined; and Breuer's
hypothesis of hypnoidal states is itself only an
echo of the fact that Charcot had artificially reproduced those traumatic paralyses in hypnosis.

The great French observer, whose student I
was during the years 1885–86, had no natural
bent for creating psychological theories. His
student, P. Janet, was the first to attempt to
penetrate more deeply into the psychic processes of hysteria, and we followed his example,
when we made the mental splitting and the dissociation of personality the central points of our
theory. Janet propounds a theory of hysteria
which draws upon the principal theories of heredity and degeneration which are current in
France. According to his view, hysteria is a
form of degenerative alteration of the nervous
system, manifesting itself in a congenital *weakness* of the function of psychic synthesis. The
hysterical patient is from the start incapable of
correlating and unifying the manifold of his
mental processes, and so there arises the tendency to mental dissociation. If you will permit
me to use a banal but clear illustration, Janet's
hysterical reminds one of a weak woman who
has been shopping, and is now on her way home,
laden with packages and bundles of every description. She cannot manage the whole lot with
her two arms and her ten fingers, and soon she
drops one. When she stoops to pick this up, another breaks loose, and so it goes on.

Now it does not agree very well with this assumed mental weakness of hystericals that
there can be observed in hysterical cases, besides the phenomena of lessened functioning,
examples of a partial increase of functional capacity, as a sort of compensation. At the time
when Breuer's patient had forgotten her moth-

er-tongue and all other languages save English,
her control of English attained such a level that
if a German book was put before her she could
give a fluent, perfect translation of its contents
at sight. When later I undertook to continue on
my own account the investigations begun by
Breuer, I soon came to another view of the origin of hysterical dissociation (or splitting of
consciousness). It was inevitable that my views
should diverge widely and radically, for my
point of departure was not, like that of Janet,
laboratory researches, but attempts at therapy.
Above everything else, it was practical needs
that urged me on. The cathartic treatment, as
Breuer had made use of it, presupposed that the
patient should be put in deep hypnosis, for only
in hypnosis was available the knowledge of his
pathogenic associations which were unknown
to him in his normal state. Now hypnosis, as a
fanciful, and so to speak, mystical, aid, I soon
came to dislike; and when I discovered that, in
spite of all my efforts, I could not hypnotize by
any means all of my patients, I resolved to give
up hypnotism and to make the cathartic method
independent of it.

Since I could not alter the psychic state of
most of my patients at my wish, I directed my
efforts to working with them in their normal
state. This seems at first sight to be a particularly senseless and aimless undertaking. The
problem was this: to find out something from
the patient that the doctor did not know and
the patient himself did not know. How could
one hope to make such a method succeed? The
memory of a very noteworthy and instructive
proceeding came to my aid, which I had seen
in Bernheim's clinic at Nancy. Bernheim showed
us that persons put in a condition of hypnotic
somnambulism, and subjected to all sorts of experiences, had only apparently lost the memory
of those somnambulic experiences, and that
their memory of them could be awakened even
in the normal state. If he asked them about
their experiences during somnambulism, they
said at first that they did not remember, but if
he persisted, urged, assured them that they did
know, then every time the forgotten memory
came back.

Accordingly, I did this with my patients.
When I had reached in my procedure with them
a point at which they declared that they knew
nothing more, I would assure them that they
did know, that they must just tell it out, and I
would venture the assertion that the memory
which would emerge at the moment that I laid
my hand on the patient's forehead would be the

right one. In this way I succeeded, without hypnosis, in learning from the patient all that was necessary for a construction of the connection between the forgotten pathogenic scenes and the symptoms which they had left behind. This was a troublesome and in its length an exhausting proceeding, and did not lend itself to a finished technique. But I did not give it up without drawing definite conclusions from the data which I had gained. I had substantiated the fact that the forgotten memories were not lost. They were in the possession of the patient, ready to emerge and form associations with his other mental content, but hindered from becoming conscious, and forced to remain in the unconscious by some sort of a force. The existence of this force could be assumed with certainty, for in attempting to drag up the unconscious memories into the consciousness of the patient, in opposition to this force, one got the sensation of his own personal effort striving to overcome it. One could get an idea of this force, which maintained the pathological situation, from the resistance of the patient.

It is on this idea of *resistance* that I based my theory of the psychic processes of hystericals. It had been found that in order to cure the patient it was necessary that this force should be overcome. Now with the mechanism of the cure as a starting point, quite a definite theory could be constructed. These same forces, which in the present situation as resistances opposed the emergence of the forgotten ideas into consciousness, must themselves have caused the forgetting, and repressed from consciousness the pathogenic experiences. I called this hypothetical process *repression* (*Verdrängung*) and considered that it was proved by the undeniable existence of resistance.

But now the question arose: what were those forces, and what were the conditions of this repression, in which we were now able to recognize the pathogenic mechanism of hysteria? A comparative study of the pathogenic situations, which the cathartic treatment has made possible, allows us to answer this question. In all those experiences, it had happened that a wish had been aroused, which was in sharp opposition to the other desires of the individual, and was not capable of being reconciled with the ethical, æsthetic and personal pretensions of the patient's personality. There had been a short conflict, and the end of this inner struggle was the repression of the idea which presented itself to consciousness as the bearer of this irreconcilable wish. This was, then, repressed from con-

sciousness and forgotten. The incompatibility of the idea in question with the *ego* of the patient was the motive of the repression, the ethical and other pretensions of the individual were the repressing forces. The presence of the incompatible wish, or the duration of the conflict, had given rise to a high degree of mental pain; this pain was avoided by the repression. This latter process is evidently in such a case a device for the protection of the personality.

I will not multiply examples but will give you the history of a single one of my cases, in which the conditions and the utility of the repression process stand out clearly enough. Of course, for my purpose I must abridge the history of the case and omit many valuable theoretical considerations. It is that of a young girl, who was deeply attached to her father, who had died a short time before, and in whose care she had shared—a situation analogous to that of Breuer's patient. When her older sister married, the girl grew to feel a peculiar sympathy for her new brother-in-law, which easily passed with her for family tenderness. This sister soon fell ill and died, while the patient and her mother were away. The absent ones were hastily recalled, without being told fully of the painful situation. As the girl stood by the bedside of her dead sister, for one short moment there surged up in her mind an idea, which might be framed in these words: "Now he is free and can marry me." We may be sure that this idea, which betrayed to her consciousness her intense love for her brother-in-law, of which she had not been conscious, was the next moment consigned to repression by her revolted feelings. The girl fell ill with severe hysterical symptoms, and, when I came to treat the case, it appeared that she had entirely forgotten that scene at her sister's bedside and the unnatural, egoistic desire which had arisen in her. She remembered it during the treatment, reproduced the pathogenic moment with every sign of intense emotional excitement, and was cured by this treatment.[1]

Perhaps I can make the process of repression, and its necessary relation to the resistance of the patient, more concrete by a rough illustration, which I will derive from our present situation.

Suppose that here in this hall and in this audience, whose exemplary stillness and attention I cannot sufficiently commend, there is an individual who is creating a disturbance, and, by his ill-bred laughing, talking, by scraping his feet, distracts my attention from my task. I explain

[1] See *Selected Papers on Hysteria*, p. 53 below.

that I cannot go on with my lecture under these conditions, and thereupon several strong men among you get up and, after a short struggle, eject the disturber of the peace from the hall. He is now *repressed,* and I can continue my lecture. But in order that the disturbance may not be repeated, in case the man who has just been thrown out attempts to force his way back into the room, the gentlemen who have executed my suggestion take their chairs to the door and establish themselves there as a *resistance,* to keep up the repression. Now, if you transfer both locations to the psyche, calling this *consciousness,* and the outside the *unconscious,* you have a tolerably good illustration of the process of repression.

We can see now the difference between our theory and that of Janet. We do not derive the psychic fission from a congenital lack of capacity on the part of the mental apparatus to synthesize its experiences, but we explain it dynamically by the conflict of opposing mental forces, we recognize in it the result of an active striving of each mental complex against the other.

New questions at once arise in great number from our theory. The situation of psychic conflict is a very frequent one; an attempt of the ego to defend itself from painful memories can be observed everywhere, and yet the result is not a mental fission. We cannot avoid the assumption that still other conditions are necessary, if the conflict is to result in dissociation. I willingly concede that with the assumption of *repression* we stand, not at the end, but at the very beginning of a psychological theory. But we can advance only one step at a time, and the completion of our knowledge must await further and more thorough work.

Now do not attempt to bring the case of Breuer's patient under the point of view of repression. This history cannot be subjected to such an attempt, for it was gained with the help of hypnotic influence. Only when hypnosis is excluded can you see the resistances and repressions and get a correct idea of the pathogenic process. Hypnosis conceals the resistances and so makes a certain part of the mental field freely accessible. By this same process the resistances on the borders of this field are heaped up into a rampart, which makes all beyond inaccessible.

The most valuable things that we have learned from Breuer's observations were his conclusions as to the connection of the symptoms with the pathogenic experiences or psychic traumata, and we must not neglect to evaluate this result

properly from the standpoint of the repression-theory. It is not at first evident how we can get from the repression to the creation of the symptoms. Instead of giving a complicated theoretical derivation, I will return at this point to the illustration which I used to typify repression.

Remember that, with the ejection of the rowdy and the establishment of the watchers before the door, the affair is not necessarily ended. It may very well happen that the ejected man, now embittered and quite careless of consequences, gives us more to do. He is no longer among us, we are free from his presence, his scornful laugh, his half-audible remarks, but in a certain sense the repression has miscarried, for he makes a terrible uproar outside, and by his outcries and by hammering on the door with his fists interferes with my lecture more than before. Under these circumstances it would be hailed with delight if possibly our honoured president, Dr. Stanley Hall, should take upon himself the rôle of peacemaker and mediator. He would speak with the rowdy on the outside, and then turn to us with the recommendation that we let him in again, provided he would guarantee to behave himself better. On Dr. Hall's authority we decide to stop the repression, and now quiet and peace reign again. This is, in fact, a fairly good presentation of the task devolving upon the physician in the psycho-analytic therapy of neuroses. To say the same thing more directly: we come to the conclusion, from working with hysterical patients and other neurotics, that they have not fully succeeded in repressing the idea to which the incompatible wish is attached. They have, indeed, driven it out of consciousness and out of memory, and apparently saved themselves a great amount of psychic pain, *but in the unconscious the suppressed wish still exists,* only waiting for its chance to become active, and finally succeeds in sending into consciousness, instead of the repressed idea, a disguised and unrecognizable surrogate-creation (*Ersatzbildung*), to which the same painful sensations associate themselves that the patient thought he was rid of through his repression. This surrogate of the suppressed idea—the symptom—is secure against further attacks from the defenses of the ego, and instead of a short conflict there originates now a permanent suffering. We can observe in the symptom, besides the tokens of its disguise, a remnant of traceable similarity with the originally repressed idea; the way in which the surrogate is built up can be discovered during the psycho-analytic treatment of the patient, and for his cure the symptom must be traced back over the same route to the repressed idea. If this repressed material is once more made part of the conscious mental functions—a process which supposes the overcoming of considerable resistance—the psychic conflict which then arises, the same which the patient wished to avoid, is made capable of a happier termination, under the guidance of the physician, than is offered by repression. There are several possible suitable decisions which can bring conflict and neurosis to a happy end; in particular cases the attempt may be made to combine several of these. Either the personality of the patient may be convinced that he has been wrong in rejecting the pathogenic wish, and he may be made to accept it either wholly or in part; or this wish may itself be directed to a higher goal which is free from objection, by what is called sublimation (*Sublimierung*); or the rejection may be recognized as rightly motivated, and the automatic and therefore insufficient mechanism of repression be reinforced by the higher, more characteristically human, mental faculties: one succeeds in mastering his wishes by conscious thought.

Forgive me if I have not been able to present more clearly these main points of the treatment which is today known as *psycho-analysis*. The difficulties do not lie merely in the newness of the subject.

Regarding the nature of the unacceptable wishes, which succeed in making their influence felt out of the unconscious, in spite of repression; and regarding the question of what subjective and constitutional factors must be present for such a failure of repression and such a surrogate or symptom creation to take place, we will speak in later remarks.

THIRD LECTURE

LADIES AND GENTLEMEN: It is not always easy to tell the truth, especially when one must be brief, and so today I must correct an incorrect statement that I made in my last lecture.

I told you how, when I gave up using hypnosis, I pressed my patients to tell me what came into their minds that had to do with the problem we were working on; I told them that they would remember what they had apparently forgotten, and that the thought which irrupted into consciousness (*Einfall*) would surely embody the memory for which we were seeking. I claimed that I substantiated the fact that the first idea of my patients brought the right clew and could be shown to be the forgotten continuation of the memory. Now this is not always so; I represent-

ed it as being so simple only for purposes of abbreviation. In fact, it would only happen the first time that the right forgotten material would emerge through simple pressure on my part. If the experience was continued, ideas emerged in every case which could not be the right ones, for they were not to the purpose, and the patients themselves rejected them as incorrect. Pressure was of no further service here, and one could only regret again having given up hypnosis. In this state of perplexity I clung to a prejudice which years later was proved by my friend C. G. Jung of the University of Zürich and his pupils to have a scientific justification. I must confess that it is often of great advantage to have prejudices. I put a high value on the strength of the determination of mental processes, and I could not believe that any idea which occurred to the patient, which originated in a state of concentrated attention, could be quite arbitrary and out of all relation to the forgotten idea that we were seeking. That it was not identical with the latter could be satisfactorily explained by the hypothetical psychological situation. In the patients whom I treated there were two opposing forces: on the one hand the conscious striving to drag up into consciousness the forgotten experience which was present in the unconscious; and on the other hand the resistance which we have seen, which set itself against the emergence of the suppressed idea or its associates into consciousness. In case this resistance was nonexistent or very slight, the forgotten material could become conscious without disguise (*Enstellung*). It was then a natural supposition that the disguise would be the more complete, the greater the resistance to the emergence of the idea. Thoughts which broke into the patient's consciousness, instead of the ideas sought for, were accordingly made up just like symptoms; they were new, artificial, ephemeral surrogates for the repressed ideas, and differed from these just in proportion as they had been more completely disguised under the influence of the resistances. These surrogates must, however, show a certain similarity with the ideas which are the object of our search, by virtue of their nature as symptoms; and when the resistance is not too intensive, it is possible from the nature of these irruptions to discover the hidden object of our search. This must be related to the repressed thought as a sort of allusion, as a statement of the same thing in *indirect* terms.

We know cases in normal psychology in which analogous situations to the one which we have assumed give rise to similar experiences. Such a case is that of wit. By my study of psycho-analytic technique I was necessarily led to a consideration of the problem of the nature of wit. I will give one example of this sort, which, too, is a story that originally appeared in English.

The anecdote runs:[1] Two unscrupulous business men had succeeded by fortunate speculations in accumulating a large fortune, and then directed their efforts to breaking into good society. Among other means they thought it would be of advantage to be painted by the most famous and expensive artist of the city, a man whose paintings were considered as events. The costly paintings were first shown at a great soirée and both hosts led the most influential connoisseur and art critic to the wall of the salon on which the portraits were hung, to elicit his admiring judgment. The critic looked for a long time, looked about as though in search of something, and then merely asked, pointing out the vacant space between the two pictures, "And where is the Saviour?"

I see that you are all laughing over this good example of wit, which we will now attempt to analyse. We understand that the critic means to say: "You are a couple of malefactors, like those between whom the Saviour was crucified." But he does not say this, he expresses himself instead in a way that at first seems not to the purpose and not related to the matter in hand, but which at the next moment we recognize as an *allusion* to the insult at which he aims, and as a perfect surrogate for it. We cannot expect to find in the case of wit all those relations that our theory supposes for the origin of the irruptive ideas of our patients, but it is my desire to lay stress on the similar motivation of wit and irruptive idea. Why does not the critic say directly what he has to say to the two rogues? Because, in addition to his desire to say it straight out, he is actuated by strong opposite motives. It is a proceeding which is liable to be dangerous to offend people who are one's hosts, and who can call to their aid the strong arms of numerous servants. One might easily suffer the same fate that I used in the previous lecture to illustrate repression. On this ground, the critic does not express the particular insult directly, but in a disguised form, as an allusion with omission. The same constellation comes into play, according to our hypothesis, when our patient produces the irruptive idea as a surrogate for the forgotten idea which is the object of the quest.

Ladies and gentlemen, it is very useful to designate a group of ideas which belong together and have a common emotive tone, according to the custom of the Zürich school (Bleuler, Jung and others), as a *complex*. So we can say that if we set out from the last memories of the patient to look for a repressed complex, that we have every prospect of discovering it, if only the patient will communicate to us a sufficient number of the ideas which come into his head. So we let the patient speak along any line that he desires, and cling to the hypothesis that nothing can occur to him except what has some indirect bearing on the complex that we are seeking. If this method of discovering the repressed complexes seems too circumstantial, I can at least assure you that it is the only available one.

In practising this technique, one is further bothered by the fact that the patient often stops, is at a standstill, and considers that he has nothing to say; nothing occurs to him. If this were really the case and the patient were right, our procedure would again be proven inapplicable. Closer observation shows that such an absence of ideas never really occurs, and that it only appears to when the patient holds back or rejects the idea which he perceives, under the influence of the resistance, which disguises itself as critical judgment of the value of the idea. The patient can be protected from this if he is warned in advance of this circumstance, and told to take no account of the critical attitude. He must say anything that comes into his mind, fully laying aside such critical choice, even though he may think it unessential, irrelevant, nonsensical, especially when the idea is one which is unpleasant to dwell on. By following this prescription we secure the material which sets us on the track of the repressed complex.

These irruptive ideas, which the patient himself values little, if he is under the influence of the resistance and not that of the physician, are for the psychologist like the ore, which by simple methods of interpretation he reduces from its crude state to valuable metal. If one desires to gain in a short time a preliminary knowledge of the patient's repressed complexes, without going into the question of their arrangement and associations, this examination may be conducted with the help of the association experiments, as Jung[2] and his pupils have perfected them. This procedure is to the psychologist what qualitative analysis is to the chemist: it may be dispensed with in the therapy of neurotic pa-

---

[1] See also *Wit and Its Relation to the Unconscious.*

[2] Jung, C. G., *Diagnostische Assoziationsstudien*, vol. I, 1906.

tients, but is indispensable in the investigations of the psychoses, which have been begun by the Zürich school with such valuable results.

This method of work, with whatever comes into the patient's head when he submits to psycho-analytic treatment, is not the only technical means at our disposal for the widening of consciousness. Two other methods of procedure serve the same purpose: the interpretation of his dreams and the evaluation of acts which he bungles or does without intending to (*Fehl-und Zufallshandlungen*).

I might say, esteemed hearers, that for a long time I hesitated whether, instead of this hurried survey of the whole field of psycho-analysis, I should not rather offer you a thorough consideration of the analysis of dreams; a purely subjective and apparently secondary motive decided me against this. It seemed rather an impropriety that in this country, so devoted to practical pursuits, I should pose as *interpreter of dreams,* before you had a chance to discover what significance the old and despised art can claim.

Interpretation of dreams is in fact the *via regia* to the interpretation of the unconscious, the surest ground of psycho-analysis and a field in which every worker must win his convictions and gain his education. If I were asked how one could become a psycho-analyst, I should answer, through the study of his own dreams. With great tact all opponents of the psycho-analytic theory have so far either evaded any criticism of *The Interpretation of Dreams* or have attempted to pass over it with the most superficial objections. If, on the contrary, you will undertake the solution of the problems of dream life, the novelties which psycho-analysis present to your thoughts will no longer be difficulties.

You must remember that our nightly dream productions show the greatest outer similarity and inner relationship to the creations of the insane, but on the other hand are compatible with full health during waking life. It does not sound at all absurd to say that whoever regards these normal sense illusions, these delusions and alterations of character as matter for amazement instead of understanding, has not the least prospect of understanding the abnormal creations of diseased mental states in any other than the lay sense. You may with confidence place in this lay group all the psychiatrists of today. Follow me now on a brief excursion through the field of dream problems.

In our waking state we usually treat dreams with as little consideration as the patient treats the irruptive ideas which the psycho-analyst demands from him. It is evident that we reject them, for we forget them quickly and completely. The slight valuation which we place on them is based, with those dreams that are not confused and nonsensical, on the feeling that they are foreign to our personality, and, with other dreams, on their evident absurdity and senselessness. Our rejection derives support from the unrestrained shamelessness and the immoral longings which are obvious in many dreams. Antiquity, as we know, did not share this light valuation of dreams. The lower classes of our people today stick close to the value which they set on dreams; they, however, expect from them, as did the ancients, the revelation of the future. I confess that I see no need to adopt mystical hypotheses to fill out the gaps in our present knowledge, and so I have never been able to find anything that supported the hypothesis of the prophetic nature of dreams. Many other things, which are wonderful enough, can be said about them.

And first, not all dreams are so foreign to the character of the dreamer, are incomprehensible and confused. If you will undertake to consider the dreams of young children from the age of a year and a half on, you will find them quite simple and easy to interpret. The young child always dreams of the fulfilment of wishes which were aroused in him the day before and were not satisfied. You need no art of interpretation to discover this simple solution, you only need to inquire into the experiences of the child on the day before (the "dream day"). Now it would certainly be a most satisfactory solution of the dream-riddle, if the dreams of adults, too, were the same as those of children, fulfilments of wishes which had been aroused in them during the dream day. This is actually the fact; the difficulties which stand in the way of this solution can be removed step by step by a thorough analysis of the dream.

There is, first of all, the most weighty objection that the dreams of adults generally have an incomprehensible content, which shows wishfulfilment least of anything. The answer is this: these dreams have undergone a process of disguise, the psychic content which underlies them was originally meant for quite different verbal expression. You must differentiate between the *manifest dream-content,* which we remember in the morning only confusedly, and with difficulty clothe in words which seem arbitrary, and the *latent dream-thoughts,* whose presence in the unconscious we must assume. This distortion of the dream (*Traumentstellung*) is the same process which has been revealed to you in the investigations of the creations (*symptoms*) of hysterical subjects; it points to the fact that the same opposition of psychic forces has its share in the creation of dreams as in the creation of symptoms.

The manifest dream-content is the disguised surrogate for the unconscious dream-thoughts, and this disguising is the work of the defensive forces of the ego, of the resistances. These prevent the repressed wishes from entering consciousness during the waking life, and even in the relaxation of sleep they are still strong enough to force them to hide themselves by a sort of masquerading. The dreamer, then, knows just as little the sense of his dream as the hysterical knows the relation and significance of his symptoms. That there are latent dream-thoughts and that between them and the manifest dream-content there exists the relation just described —of this you may convince yourselves by the analysis of dreams, a procedure the technique of which is exactly that of psycho-analysis. You must abstract entirely from the apparent connection of the elements in the manifest dream and seek for the irruptive ideas which arise through free association, according to the psycho-analytic laws, from each separate dream element. From this material the latent dream-thoughts may be discovered, exactly as one divines the concealed complexes of the patient from the fancies connected with his symptoms and memories. From the latent dream-thoughts which you will find in this way, you will see at once how thoroughly justified one is in interpreting the dreams of adults by the same rubrics as those of children. What is now subtituted for the manifest dream-content is the real sense of the dream, is always clearly comprehensible, associated with the impressions of the day before, and appears as the fulfilling of an unsatisfied wish. The manifest dream, which we remember after waking, may then be described as a *disguised* fulfilment of *repressed* wishes.

It is also possible by a sort of synthesis to get some insight into the process which has brought about the disguise of the unconscious dream-thoughts as the manifest dream-content. We call this process *dream-work* (*Traumarbeit*). This deserves our fullest theoretical interest, since here as nowhere else we can study the unsuspected psychic processes which are existent in the unconscious, or, to express it more exactly, *between* two such separate systems as the conscious and the unconscious. Among these newly discovered psychic processes, two, condensation (*Verdichtung*), and displacement or transvaluation, change of psychic accent (*Verschiebung*), stand out most prominently. Dream-work is a special case of the reaction of different mental groupings on each other, and as such is the consequence of psychic fission. In all essential points it seems identical with the work of disguise, which changes the repressed complex in the case of failing repression into symptoms.

You will furthermore discover by the analysis of dreams, most convincingly your own, the unsuspected importance of the rôle which impressions and experiences from early childhood exert on the development of men. In the dream life, the child, as it were, continues his existence in the man, with a retention of all his traits and wishes, including those which he was obliged to allow to fall into disuse in his later years. With irresistible might it will be impressed on you by what processes of development, of repression, sublimation, and reaction there arises out of the child, with its peculiar gifts and tendencies, the so-called normal man, the bearer and partly the victim of our painfully acquired civilization. I will also direct your attention to the fact that we have discovered from the analysis of dreams that the unconscious makes use of a sort of symbolism, especially in the presentation of sexual complexes. This symbolism in part varies with the individual, but in part is of a typical nature, and seems to be identical with the symbolism which we suppose to lie behind our myths and legends. It is not impossible that these latter creations of the people may find their explanation from the study of dreams.

Finally, I must remind you that you must not be led astray by the objection that the occurrence of anxiety-dreams (*Angsttraüme*), contradicts our idea of the dream as a wish-fulfilment. Apart from the consideration that anxiety-dreams also require interpretation before judgment can be passed on them, one can say quite generally that the anxiety does not depend in such a simple way on the dream-content as one might suppose without more knowledge of the facts and more attention to the conditions of neurotic anxiety. Anxiety is one of the ways in which the ego relieves itself of repressed wishes which have become too strong, and so is easy to explain in the dream, if the dream has gone too far towards the fulfilling of the objectionable wish.

You see that the investigation of dreams was justified by the conclusions which it has given us concerning things otherwise hard to understand. But we came to it in connection with the psycho-analytic treatment of neurotics. From what has been said, you can easily understand how the interpretation of dreams, if it is not made too difficult by the resistance of the patient, can lead to a knowledge of the patient's concealed and repressed wishes and the complexes which he is nourishing. I may now pass to that group of everyday mental phenomena whose study has become a technical help for psycho-analysis.

These are the bungling of acts (*Fehlhandlungen*) among normal men as well as among neurotics, to which no significance is ordinarily attached; the forgetting of things which one is supposed to know and at other times really does know (for example, the temporary forgetting of proper names); mistakes in speaking (*Versprechen*), which occur so frequently; analogous mistakes in writing (*Verschreiben*) and in reading (*Verlesen*), the automatic execution of purposive acts in wrong situations (*Vergreifen*), and the loss or breaking of objects, etc. These are trifles, for which no one has ever sought a psychological determination, which have passed unchallenged as chance experiences, as consequences of absent-mindedness, inattention, and similar conditions. Here, too, are included the acts and gestures executed without being noticed by the subject, to say nothing of the fact that he attaches no psychic importance to them; as playing and trifling with objects, humming melodies, handling one's person and clothing and the like.[1]

These little things, the bungling of acts, like the symptomatic and chance acts (*Symptom- und Zufallshandlungen*) are not so entirely without meaning as is generally supposed by a sort of tacit agreement. They have a meaning, generally easy and sure to interpret from the situation in which they occur, and it can be demonstrated that they either express impulses and purposes which are repressed, hidden if possible from the consciousness of the individual, or that they spring from exactly the same sort of repressed wishes and complexes which we have learned to know already as the creators of symptoms and dreams.

It follows that they deserve the rank of symptoms, and their observation, like that of dreams, can lead to the discovery of the hidden complexes of the psychic life. With their help one will usually betray the most intimate of his secrets. If these occur so easily and commonly among people in health, with whom repression

[1] This subject is also discussed in *The Psychopathology of Everyday Life*.

has on the whole succeeded fairly well, this is due to their insignificance and their inconspicuous nature. But they can lay claim to high theoretic value, for they prove the existence of repression and surrogate creations even under the conditions of health. You have already noticed that the psycho-analyst is distinguished by an especially strong belief in the determination of the psychic life. For him there is in the expressions of the psyche nothing trifling, nothing arbitrary and lawless, he expects everywhere a widespread motivation, where customarily such claims are not made; more than that, he is even prepared to find a manifold motivation of these psychic expressions, while our supposedly inborn causal need is satisfied with a single psychic cause.

Now, keeping in mind the means which we possess for the discovery of the hidden, forgotten, repressed things in the soul life; the study of the irruptive ideas called up by free association, the patient's dreams, and his bungled and symptomatic acts; and adding to these the evaluation of other phenomena which emerge during the psycho-analytic treatment, on which I shall later make a few remarks under the heading of *transfer* (*Übertragung*), you will come with me to the conclusion that our technique is already sufficiently efficacious for the solution of the problem of how to introduce the pathogenic psychic material into consciousness, and so to do away with the suffering brought on by the creation of surrogate symptoms.

The fact that by such therapeutic endeavours our knowledge of the mental life of the normal and the abnormal is widened and deepened can, of course, only be regarded as an especial attraction and superiority of this method.

I do not know whether you have gained the impression that the technique through whose arsenal I have led you is a peculiarly difficult one. I consider that, on the contrary, for one who has mastered it, it is quite adapted for use. But so much is sure, that it is not obvious, that it must be learned no less than the histological or the surgical technique.

You may be surprised to learn that in Europe we have heard very frequently judgments passed on psycho-analysis by persons who knew nothing of its technique and had never practised it, but who demanded scornfully that we show the correctness of our results. There are among these people some who are not in other things unacquainted with scientific methods of thought, who, for example, would not reject the result of a microscopical research because it cannot be confirmed with the naked eye in anatomical preparations, and who would not pass judgment until they had used the microscope. But in matters of psycho-analysis circumstances are really more unfavourable for gaining recognition. Psycho-analysis will bring the repressed in mental life to conscious acknowledgment, and every one who judges it is himself a man who has such repressions, perhaps maintained only with difficulty. It will consequently call forth the same resistances from him as from the patient, and this resistance can easily succeed in disguising itself as intellectual rejection, and bring forward arguments similar to those from which we protect our patients by the basic principles of psycho-analysis. It is not difficult to substantiate in our opponents the same impairment of intelligence produced by emotivity which we may observe every day with our patients. The arrogance of consciousness, which, for example, rejects dreams so lightly, belongs—quite generally—to the strongest protective apparatus which guards us against the breaking through of the unconscious complexes, and as a result it is hard to convince people of the reality of the unconscious, and to teach them anew what their conscious knowledge contradicts.

FOURTH LECTURE

LADIES AND GENTLEMEN: At this point you will be asking what the technique which I have described has taught us of the nature of the pathogenic complexes and repressed wishes of neurotics.

One thing in particular: psycho-analytic investigations trace back the symptoms of disease with really surprising regularity to impressions from the sexual life, show us that the pathogenic wishes are of the nature of erotic impulse-components (*Triebkomponente*), and necessitate the assumption that to disturbances of the erotic sphere must be ascribed the greatest significance among the aetiological factors of the disease. This holds of both sexes.

I know that this assertion will not willingly be credited. Even those investigators who gladly follow my psychological labors, are inclined to think that I overestimate the aetiological share of the sexual moments. They ask me why other mental excitations should not lead to the phenomena of repression and surrogate-creation which I have described. I can give them this answer; that I do not know why they should not do this, I have no objection to their doing it, but experience shows that they do not possess such a significance, and that they merely support the effect of the sexual moments, without being able to supplant them. This conclusion was not a theoretical postulate; in the *Studien über Hysterie*, published in 1895 with Dr. Breuer, I did not stand on this ground. I was converted to it when my experience was richer and had led me deeper into the nature of the case. Gentlemen, there are among you some of my closest friends and adherents, who have travelled to Worcester with me. Ask them, and they will tell you that they all were at first completely skeptical of the assertion of the determinative significance of the sexual aetiology, until they were compelled by their own analytic labors to come to the same conclusion.

The conduct of the patients does not make it any easier to convince one's self of the correctness of the view which I have expressed. Instead of willingly giving us information concerning their sexual life, they try to conceal it by every means in their power. Men generally are not candid in sexual matters. They do not show their sexuality freely, but they wear a thick overcoat —a fabric of lies—to conceal it, as though it were bad weather in the world of sex. And they are not wrong; sun and wind are not favourable in our civilized society to any demonstration of sex life. In truth, no one can freely disclose his erotic life to his neighbor. But when your patients see that in your treatment they may disregard the conventional restraints, they lay aside this veil of lies, and then only are you in a position to formulate a judgment on the question in dispute. Unfortunately, physicians are not favoured above the rest of the children of men in their personal relationship to the questions of the sex life. Many of them are under the ban of that mixture of prudery and lasciviousness which determines the behavior of most *Kulturmenschen* in affairs of sex.

Now to proceed with the communication of our results. It is true that, in another series of cases, psycho-analysis at first traces the symptoms back not to the sexual, but to banal traumatic experiences. But the distinction loses its significance through other circumstances. The work of analysis which is necessary for the thorough explanation and complete cure of a case of sickness does not stop in any case with the experience of the time of onset of the disease, but in every case it goes back to the adolescence and the early childhood of the patient. Here only do we hit upon the impressions and circumstances which determine the later sickness. Only the childhood experiences can give the explanation for the sensitivity to later traumata and only when these memory traces, which almost always are forgotten, are discovered and made conscious, is the power developed to banish the symptoms. We arrive here at the same conclusion as in the investigation of dreams—that it is the incompatible, repressed wishes of childhood which lend their power to the creation of symptoms. Without these the reactions upon later traumata discharge normally. But we must consider these mighty wishes of childhood very generally as sexual in nature.

Now I can at any rate be sure of your astonishment. Is there an infantile sexuality? you will ask. Is childhood not rather that period of life which is distinguished by the lack of the sexual impulse? No, gentlemen, it is not at all true that the sexual impulse enters into the child at puberty, as the devils in the gospel entered into the swine. The child has his sexual impulses and activities from the beginning, he brings them with him into the world, and from these the so-called normal sexuality of adults emerges by a significant development through manifold stages. It is not very difficult to observe the expressions of this childish sexual activity; it needs rather a certain art to overlook them or to fail to interpret them.[1]

As fate would have it, I am in a position to call a witness for my assertions from your own midst. I show you here the work of one, Dr. Sanford Bell, published in 1902 in the *American Journal of Psychology*. The author was a fellow of Clark University, the same institution within whose walls we now stand. In this thesis, entitled "A Preliminary Study of the Emotion of Love between the Sexes," which appeared three years before my *Three Contributions to the Theory of Sex* the author says just what I have been saying to you: "The emotion of sex love . . . does not make its appearance for the first time at the period of adolescence as has been thought." He has, as we should say in Europe, worked by the American method, and has gathered not less than 2,500 positive observations in the course of fifteen years, among them 800 of his own. He says of the signs by which this amorous condition manifests itself: "The unprejudiced mind, in observing these manifestations in hundreds of couples of children, cannot escape referring them to sex origin. The most exacting mind is satisfied when to these observations are added the confessions of those who have as children experienced the emotion to a marked degree of intensity, and whose memories of childhood

are relatively distinct." Those of you who are unwilling to believe in infantile sexuality will be most astonished to hear that among those children who fell in love so early not a few are of the tender ages of three, four, and five years.

It would not be surprising if you should believe the observations of a fellow-countryman rather than my own. Fortunately, a short time ago, from the analysis of a five-year-old boy who was suffering from anxiety, an analysis undertaken with correct technique by his own father,[2] I succeeded in getting a fairly complete picture of the bodily expressions of the impulse and the mental productions of an early stage of childish sexual life. And I must remind you that my friend, Dr. C. G. Jung, read you a few hours ago in this room an observation on a still younger girl who from the same cause as my patient —the birth of a little child in the family—betrayed certainly almost the same secret excitement, wish, and complex-creation. Accordingly, I am not without hope that you may feel friendly toward this idea of infantile sexuality that was so strange at first. I might also quote the remarkable example of the Zürich psychiatrist, E. Bleuler, who said a few years ago openly that he faced my sexual theories incredulous and bewildered, and since that time by his own observations had substantiated them in their whole scope.[3] If it is true that most men, medical observers and others, do not want to know anything about the sexual life of the child, the fact is capable of explanation only too easily. They have forgotten their own infantile sexual activity under the pressure of education for civilization and do not care to be reminded now of the repressed material. You will be convinced otherwise if you begin the investigation by a self-analysis, by an interpretation of your own childhood memories.

Lay aside your doubts and let us evaluate the infantile sexuality of the earliest years.[4] The sexual impulse of the child manifests itself as a very complex one, it permits of an analysis into many components, which spring from different sources. It is entirely disconnected from the function of reproduction which it is later to serve. It permits the child to gain different sorts of pleasure sensations, which we include, by the analogues and connections which they show, under the term sexual pleasures. The great source

---

[1] Compare *Three Contributions to the Theory of Sex.*

[2] *Analysis of a Phobia in a five-year-old boy,* in *Collected Papers,* Vol. III.
[3] Bleuler, "Sexuelle Abnormitäten der Kinder," *Jahrbuch der Schweizer Gesellschaft für Schulgesundheitspflege,* IX, 1908.
[4] *Three Contributions to the Theory of Sex.*

of infantile sexual pleasure is the auto-excitation of certain particularly sensitive parts of the body; besides the genitals are included the rectum and the opening of the urinary canal, and also the skin and other sensory surfaces. Since in this first phase of child sexual life the satisfaction is found on the child's own body and has nothing to do with any other object, we call this phase after a word coined by Havelock Ellis, that of *auto-eroticism*. The parts of the body significant in giving sexual pleasure we call *erogenous zones*. The thumb-sucking (*Ludeln*) or passionate sucking (*Wonnesaugen*) of very young children is a good example of such an auto-erotic satisfaction of an erogenous zone. The first scientific observer of this phenomenon, a specialist in children's diseases in Budapest by the name of Lindner, interpreted these rightly as sexual satisfaction and described exhaustively their transformation into other and higher forms of sexual gratification.[1] Another sexual satisfaction of this time of life is the excitation of the genitals by masturbation, which has such a great significance for later life and, in the case of many individuals, is never fully overcome. Besides this and other auto-erotic manifestations, we see very early in the child the impulse-components of *sexual pleasure*, or, as we may say, of the *libido*, which presupposes a second person as its object. These impulses appear in opposed pairs, as active and passive. The most important representatives of this group are the pleasure in inflicting pain (sadism) with its passive opposite (masochism) and active and passive exhibition-pleasure (*Schaulust*). From the first of these later pairs splits off the curiosity for knowledge, as from the latter the impulse toward artistic and theatrical representation. Other sexual manifestations of the child can already be regarded from the viewpoint of object-choice, in which the second person plays the prominent part. The significance of this was primarily based upon motives of the impulse of self-preservation. The difference between the sexes plays, however, in the child no very great rôle. One may attribute to every child, without wronging him, a bit of the homosexual disposition.

The sexual life of the child, rich but dissociated, in which each single impulse goes about the business of arousing pleasure independently of every other, is later correlated and organized in two general directions, so that by the close of puberty the definite sexual character of the individual is practically finally determined. The single impulses subordinate themselves to the

[1] *Jahrbuch f. Kinderheilkunde*, 1879.

overlordship of the genital zone, so that the whole sexual life is taken over into the service of procreation, and their gratification is now significant only so far as they help to prepare and promote the true sexual act. On the other hand, object-choice prevails over auto-eroticism, so that now in the sexual life all components of the sexual impulse are satisfied in the loved person. But not all the original impulse-components are given a share in the final shaping of the sexual life. Even before the advent of puberty certain impulses have undergone the most energetic repression under the impulse of education, and mental forces like shame, disgust, and morality are developed, which, like sentinels, keep the repressed wishes in subjection. When there comes, in puberty, the high tide of sexual desire it finds dams in this creation of reactions and resistances. These guide the outflow into the so-called normal channels, and make it impossible to revivify the impulses which have undergone repression.

The most important of these repressed impulses are coprophilism, that is, the pleasure in children connected with the excrements; and, further, the tendencies attaching themselves to the persons of the primitive object-choice.

Gentlemen, a sentence of general pathology says that every process of development brings with it the germ of pathological dispositions in so far as it may be inhibited, delayed, or incompletely carried out. This holds for the development of the sexual function, with its many complications. It is not smoothly completed in all individuals, and may leave behind either abnormalities or disposition to later diseases by the way of later falling back, or *regression*. It may happen that not all the partial impulses subordinate themselves to the rule of the genital zone. Such an impulse which has remained disconnected brings about what we call a perversion, which may replace the normal sexual goal by one of its own. It may happen, as has been said before, that the auto-eroticism is not fully overcome, as many sorts of disturbances testify. The originally equal value of both sexes as sexual objects may be maintained and an inclination to homosexual activities in adult life result from this, which, under suitable conditions, rises to the level of exclusive homosexuality. This series of disturbances corresponds to the direct inhibition of development of the sexual function, it includes the perversions and the general *infantilism* of the sex life that are not seldom met with.

The disposition to neuroses is to be derived in

another way from an injury to the development of the sex life. The neuroses are related to the perversions as the negative to the positive; in them we find the same impulse-components as in perversions, as bearers of the complexes and as creators of the symptoms; but here they work out from the unconscious. They have undergone a repression, but in spite of this they maintain themselves in the unconscious. Psycho-analysis teaches us that overstrong expression of the impulse in very early life leads to a sort of fixation (*Fixirung*), which then offers a weak point in the articulation of the sexual function. If the exercise of the normal sexual function meets with hindrances in later life, this repression, dating from the time of development, is broken through at just that point at which the infantile fixation took place.

You will now perhaps make the objection: "But all that is not sexuality." I have used the word in a very much wider sense than you are accustomed to understand it. This I willingly concede. But it is a question whether you do not rather use the word in much too narrow a sense when you restrict it to the realm of procreation. You sacrifice by that the understanding of perversions; of the connection between perversion, neurosis, and normal sexual life; and have no means of recognizing, in its true significance, the easily observable beginning of the somatic and mental sexual life of the child. But however you decide about the use of the word, remember that the psycho-analyst understands sexuality in that full sense to which he is led by the evaluation of infantile sexuality.

Now we turn again to the sexual development of the child. We still have much to say here, since we have given more attention to the somatic than to the mental expressions of the sexual life. The primitive object-choice of the child, which is derived from his need of help, demands our further interest. It first attaches to all persons to whom he is accustomed, but soon these give way in favor of his parents. The relation of the child to his parents is, as both direct observation of the child and later analytic investigation of adults agree, not at all free from elements of sexual accessory-excitation (*Miterregung*). The child takes both parents, and especially one, as an object of his erotic wishes. Usually he follows in this the stimulus given by his parents, whose tenderness has very clearly the character of a sex manifestation, though inhibited so far as its goal is concerned. As a rule, the father prefers the daughter, the mother the son; the child reacts to this situation, since, as

son, he wishes himself in the place of his father, as daughter, in the place of the mother. The feelings awakened in these relations between parents and children, and, as a resultant of them, those among the children in relation to each other, are not only positively of a tender, but negatively of an inimical sort. The complex built up in this way is destined to quick repression, but it still exerts a great and lasting effect from the unconscious. We must express the opinion that this with its ramifications presents the *nuclear complex* of every neurosis, and so we are prepared to meet with it in a not less effectual way in the other fields of mental life. The myth of King Œdipus, who kills his father and wins his mother as a wife is only the slightly altered presentation of the infantile wish, rejected later by the opposing barriers of incest. Shakespeare's tale of Hamlet rests on the same basis of an incest complex, though better concealed. At the time when the child is still ruled by the still unrepressed nuclear complex, there begins a very significant part of his mental activity which serves sexual interest. He begins to investigate the question of where children come from and guesses more than adults imagine of the true relations by deduction from the signs which he sees. Usually his interest in this investigation is awakened by the threat to his welfare through the birth of another child in the family, in whom at first he sees only a rival. Under the influence of the partial impulses which are active in him he arrives at a number of *infantile sexual theories*, as that the same male genitals belong to both sexes, that children are conceived by eating and born through the opening of the intestine, and that sexual intercourse is to be regarded as an inimical act, a sort of overpowering.

But just the unfinished nature of his sexual constitution and the gaps in his knowledge brought about by the hidden condition of the feminine sexual canal, cause the infant investigator to discontinue his work as a failure. The facts of this childish investigation itself as well as the infant sex theories created by it are of determinative significance in the building of the child's character, and in the content of his later neuroses.

It is unavoidable and quite normal that the child should make his parents the objects of his first object-choice. But his *libido* must not remain fixed on these first chosen objects, but must take them merely as a prototype and transfer from these to other persons in the time of definite object-choice. The breaking loose (*Ablösung*) of the child from his parents is thus a problem impossible to escape if the social virtue of the young individual is not to be impaired. During the time that the repressive activity is making its choice among the partial sexual impulses and later, when the influence of the parents, which in the most essential way has furnished the material for these repressions, is lessened, great problems fall to the work of education, which at present certainly does not always solve them in the most intelligent and economic way.

Gentlemen, do not think that with these explanations of the sexual life and the sexual development of the child we have too far departed from psycho-analysis and the cure of neurotic disturbances. If you like, you may regard the psycho-analytic treatment only as a continued education for the overcoming of childhood-remnants (*Kindheitsresten*).

FIFTH LECTURE

LADIES AND GENTLEMEN : With the discovery of infantile sexuality and the tracing back of the neurotic symptoms to erotic impulse-components we have arrived at several unexpected formulae for expressing the nature and tendencies of neurotic diseases. We see that the individual falls ill when in consequence of outer hindrances or inner lack of adaptability the satisfaction of the erotic needs in the sphere of reality is denied. We see that he then flees to sickness, in order to find with its help a surrogate satisfaction for that denied him. We recognize that the symptoms of illness contain fractions of the sexual activity of the individual, or his whole sexual life, and we find in the turning away from reality the chief tendency and also the chief injury of the sickness. We may guess that the resistance of our patients against the cure is not a simple one, but is composed of many motives. Not only does the ego of the patient strive against the giving up of the repression by which it has changed itself from its original constitution into its present form, but also the sexual impulses may not renounce their surrogate satisfaction so long as it is not certain that they can be offered anything better in the sphere of reality.

The flight from the unsatisfying reality into what we call, on account of its biologically injurious nature, disease, but which is never without an individual gain in pleasure for the patient, takes place over the path of regression, the return to earlier phases of the sexual life, when satisfaction was not lacking. This regression is seemingly a twofold one, a *temporal*, in

so far as the *libido* or erotic need falls back to a temporally earlier stage of development, and a *formal*, since the original and primitive psychic means of expression are applied to the expression of this need. Both sorts of regression focus in childhood and have their common point in the production of an infantile condition of sexual life.

The deeper you penetrate into the pathogenic of neurotic diseases, the more the connexion of neuroses with other products of human mentality, even the most valuable, will be revealed to you. You will be reminded that we men, with the high claims of our civilization and under the pressure of our repressions, find reality generally quite unsatisfactory and so keep up a life of fancy in which we love to compensate for what is lacking in the sphere of reality by the production of wish-fulfilments. In these phantasies is often contained very much of the particular constitutional essence of personality and of its tendencies, repressed in real life. The energetic and successful man is he who succeeds by dint of labour in transforming his wish fancies into reality. Where this is not successful, in consequence of the resistance of the outer world and the weakness of the individual, there begins the turning away from reality. The individual takes refuge in his satisfying world of fancy. Under certain favourable conditions it still remains possible for him to find another connecting link between these fancies and reality, instead of permanently becoming a stranger to it through the regression into the infantile. If the individual who is displeased with reality is in possession of that *artistic talent* which is still a psychological riddle, he can transform his fancies into artistic creations. So he escapes the fate of a neurosis and wins back his connection with reality by this roundabout way.[1] Where this opposition to the real world exists, but this valuable talent fails or proves insufficient, it is unavoidable that the *libido*, following the origin of the fancies, succeeds by means of regression in revivifying the infantile wishes and so producing a neurosis. The neurosis takes, in our time, the place of the cloister, in which were accustomed to take refuge all those whom life had undeceived or who felt themselves too weak for life. Let me give at this point the main result at which we have arrived by the psycho-analytic investigation of neurotics, namely, that neuroses have no peculiar psychic content of their own, which is not also to be found in healthy states; or as C. G.

[1] *Cf.* Otto Rank, *Der Künstler, Ausätze zu einer Sexual-Psychologie,* 56 pp., Heller & Co., Vienna, 1907.

Jung has expressed it, neurotics fall ill of the same complexes with which we sound people struggle. It depends on quantitative relationships, on the relations of the forces wrestling with each other, whether the struggle leads to health, to a neurosis, or to compensatory overfunctioning (*Überleistung*).

Ladies and gentlemen, I have still withheld from you the most remarkable experience which corroborates our assumptions of the sexual impulse-forces of neurotics. Every time that we treat a neurotic psycho-analytically, there occurs in him the so-called phenomenon of *transfer* (*Übertragung*), that is, he applies to the person of the physician a great amount of tender emotion, often mixed with enmity, which has no foundation in any real relation, and must be derived in every respect from the old wish-fancies of the patient, which have become unconscious. Every fragment of his emotive life, which can no longer be called back into memory, is accordingly lived over by the patient in his relations to the physician, and only by such a living over of them in the *transfer* is he convinced of the existence and the power of these unconscious sexual excitations. The symptoms, which, to use a simile from chemistry, are the precipitates of earlier love experiences (in the widest sense), can only be dissolved in the higher temperature of the experience of transfer and transformed into other psychic products. The physician plays in this reaction, to use an excellent expression of S. Ferenczi,[1] the rôle of a *catalytic ferment*, which temporarily attracts to itself the affection which has become free in the course of the process.

The study of transfer can also give you the key to the understanding of hypnotic suggestion, which we at first used with our patients as a technical means of investigation of the unconscious. Hypnosis showed itself at that time to be a therapeutic help, but a hindrance to the scientific knowledge of the real nature of the case, since it cleared away the psychic resistances from a certain field, only to pile them up in an unscalable wall at the boundaries of this field. You must not think that the phenomenon of transfer, about which I can unfortunately say only too little here, is created by the influence of the psycho-analytic treatment. The transfer arises spontaneously in all human relations and in the relations of the patient to the physician; it is everywhere the especial bearer of therapeutic influences, and it works the stronger the

less one knows of its presence. Accordingly, psycho-analysis does not create it; it merely discloses it to consciousness, and avails itself of it, in order to direct the psychic processes to the wished-for goal. But I cannot leave the theme of transfer without stressing the fact that this phenomenon is of decisive importance to convince not only the patient, but also the physician. I know that all my adherents were first convinced of the correctness of my views through their experience with transfer, and I can very well conceive that one may not win such a surety of judgment so long as he makes no psycho-analysis, and so has not himself observed the effects of transfer.

Ladies and gentlemen, I am of the opinion that there are, on the intellectual side, two hindrances to acknowledging the value of the psycho-analytic viewpoint: first, the fact that we are not accustomed to reckon with a strict determination of mental life, which holds without exception, and second, the lack of knowledge of the peculiarities through which unconscious mental processes differ from these conscious ones with which we are familiar. One of the most widespread resistances against the work of psycho-analysis with patients as with persons in health reduces to the latter of the two moments. One is afraid of doing harm by psycho-analysis, one is anxious about calling up into consciousness the repressed sexual impulses of the patient, as though there were danger that they could overpower the higher ethical strivings and rob him of his cultural acquisitions. One can see that the patient has sore places in his soul life, but one is afraid to touch them, lest his suffering be increased. We may use this analogy. It is, of course, better not to touch diseased places when one can only cause pain. But we know that the surgeon does not refrain from the investigation and reinvestigation of the seat of illness, if his invasion has as its aim the restoration of lasting health. Nobody thinks of blaming him for the unavoidable difficulties of the investigation or the phenomena of reaction from the operation, if these only accomplish their purpose and gain for the patient a final cure by temporarily making his condition worse. The case is similar in psycho-analysis; it can lay claim to the same things as surgery; the increase of pain which takes place in the patient during the treatment is very much less than that which the surgeon imposes upon him, and especially negligible in comparison with the pains of serious illness. But the consequence which is feared, that of a disturbance of the cultural character by the

[1] S. Ferenczi, "Introjektion und Übertragung," *Jahrbuch f. Psychoanal. u. Psychopath. Forschungen*. Vol. I, No. 2, 1909.

impulse which has been freed from repression, is wholly impossible. In relation to this anxiety we must consider what our experiences have taught us with certainty, that the somatic and mental power of a wish, if once its repression has not succeeded, is incomparably stronger when it is unconscious than when it is conscious, so that by being made conscious it can only be weakened. The unconscious wish cannot be influenced, is free from all strivings in the contrary direction, while the conscious is inhibited by those wishes which are also conscious and which strive against it. The work of psycho-analysis, accordingly, presents a better substitute, in the service of the highest and most valuable cultural strivings, for the repression which has failed.

Now what is the fate of the wishes which have become free by psycho-analysis, by what means shall they be made harmless for the life of the individual? There are several ways. The general consequence is that the wish is consumed during the work by the correct mental activity of those better tendencies which are opposed to it. The repression is supplanted by a condemnation carried through with the best means at one's disposal. This is possible, since for the most part we have to abolish only the effects of earlier developmental stages of the ego. The individual for his part only repressed the useless impulse, because at that time he was himself still incompletely organized and weak; in his present maturity and strength he can, perhaps, conquer without injury to himself that which is inimical to him. A second issue of the work of psychoanalysis may be that the revealed unconscious impulses can now arrive at those useful applications which, in the case of undisturbed development, they would have found earlier. The extirpation of the infantile wishes is not at all the ideal aim of development. The neurotic has lost, by his repressions, many sources of mental energy whose contingents would have been very valuable for his character building and his life activities. We know a far more purposive process of development, the so-called *sublimation* (*Sublimirung*), by which the energy of infantile wish-excitations is not secluded, but remains capable of application, while for the particular excitations, instead of becoming useless, a higher, eventually no longer sexual, goal is set up. The components of the sexual instinct are especially distinguished by such a capacity for the sublimation and exchange of their sexual goal for one more remote and socially more valuable. To the contributions of the energy won in such a way for the functions of our mental life we probably owe the highest cultural consequences. A repression taking place at an early period excludes the sublimation of the repressed impulse; after the removal of the repression the way to sublimation is again free.

We must not neglect, also, to glance at the third of the possible issues. A certain part of the suppressed libidinous excitation has a right to direct satisfaction and ought to find it in life. The claims of our civilization make life too hard for the greater part of humanity, and so further the aversion to reality and the origin of neuroses, without producing an excess of cultural gain by this excess of sexual repression. We ought not to go so far as to fully neglect the original animal part of our nature; we ought not to forget that the happiness of individuals cannot be dispensed with as one of the aims of our culture. The plasticity of the sexual-components, manifest in their capacity for sublimation, may cause a great temptation to accomplish greater culture-effects by a more and more far reaching sublimation. But just as little as with our machines we expect to change more than a certain fraction of the applied heat into useful mechanical work, just as little ought we to strive to separate the sexual impulse in its whole extent of energy from its peculiar goal. This cannot succeed, and if the narrowing of sexuality is pushed too far it will have all the evil effects of a robbery.

I do not know whether you will regard the exhortation with which I close as a presumptuous one. I only venture the indirect presentation of my conviction, if I relate an old tale, whose application you may make yourselves. German literature knows a town called Schilda, to whose inhabitants were attributed all sorts of clever pranks. The wiseacres, so the story goes, had a horse, with whose powers of work they were well satisfied, and against whom they had only one grudge, that he consumed so much expensive oats. They concluded that by good management they would break him of his bad habit, by cutting down his rations by several stalks each day, until he had learned to do without them altogether. Things went finely for a while, the horse was weaned to one stalk a day, and on the next day he would at last work without fodder. On the morning of this day the malicious horse was found dead; the citizens of Schilda could not understand why he had died. We should be inclined to believe that the horse had starved, and that without a certain ration of oats no work could be expected from an animal.

Selected Papers on Hysteria

Contents: Selected Papers on Hysteria

Selected Papers on Hysteria

CHAPTER 1

THE PSYCHIC MECHANISM OF HYSTERICAL PHENOMENA[1] (Preliminary Communication)

ACTUATED by a number of accidental observations, we have investigated over a period of years the different forms and symptoms of hysteria for the purpose of discovering the cause and the process which first provoked the phenomena in question, and which in a great many of our cases frequently appeared years before. In the great majority of cases we did not succeed in elucidating this starting point from the mere history, no matter how detailed it might have been, partly because we had to deal with experiences about which discussion was disagreeable to the patients, but mainly because they really could not recall anything. Often they had no inkling of the causal connection between the causative process and the pathological phenomenon. It was generally necessary to hypnotize the patients and reawaken the memory of the time in which the symptom first appeared, but we thus succeeded in exposing that connection in a most precise and convincing manner.

This method of examination in a great number of cases has furnished us with results which seem to be of theoretical as well as of practical value.

It is of *theoretical value* because it has shown us that, in the determination of the pathology of hysteria, the accidental factor plays a much greater part than is generally known and recognized. It is quite evident that in *traumatic* hysteria it is the accident which evokes the syndrome. Moreover, in hysterical crises, if the patients state that in each attack they hallucinate the same process which evoked the first attack, here, too, the causal connection seems quite clear. But the situation is more obscure in the other phenomena.

Our experiences have shown us *that the most varied symptoms which pass as spontaneous, or, as it were, as idiopathic attainments of hysteria, stand in just as stringent connection with the causal trauma as the transparent phenomena*

[1] Written in collaboration with Joseph Breuer. *Neurologische Zentralblatt*, 1893, Nos. 1 and 2; later published in *Studien über Hysterie*, 1895.

mentioned. To such causal factors we are able to refer neuralgias as well as the different kind of anesthesias, often of years' duration, contractures and paralyses, hysterical attacks and epileptiform convulsions, which every observer has taken for real epilepsy, *petit-mal* and tic-like affections, persistent vomiting and anorexia, even up to the refusal of nourishment, all kinds of visual disturbances, constantly recurring visual hallucinations, and similar affections. The disproportion between the hysterical symptom of years' duration and the former cause is the same as the one we are regularly accustomed to see in the traumatic neurosis. Very often they are experiences of childhood which have established more or less intensive morbid phenomena for all succeeding years.

The connection is often so clear that it is perfectly manifest how the causal event produced just this and no other phenomenon. It is quite clearly determined by the cause. Thus, let us take the most banal example: if a painful affect originates while eating, and is repressed, it may produce nausea and vomiting, and then continue for months as an hysterical symptom. The following examples will illustrate what we mean:

A very distressed young girl, while anxiously watching at a sick-bed, fell into a dreamy state, had terrifying hallucinations, and her right arm, which was at the time hanging over the back of the chair, became numb. This resulted in a paralysis, contracture and anaesthesia of that arm. She wanted to pray, but could find no words, but finally succeeded in uttering an English children's prayer. Later, on developing a very grave and most complicated hysteria, she spoke, wrote, and understood only English, whereas her native tongue was incomprehensible to her for a year and a half.

A very sick child finally fell asleep. The mother exerted all her will power to make no noise to awaken it, but because she resolved to do so, she emitted a clicking sound with her tongue (hysterical counter-will). This was later repeated on another occasion when she wished to be absolutely quiet, and developed into a tic, which in the form of tongue clicking accompanied every excitement for years.

A very intelligent man was present while his brother was anaesthetized and his ankylosed hip stretched. At the moment when the joint yielded and crackled, he perceived severe pain in his own hip, which continued for almost a year.

In other cases the connection is not so simple, there being only, as it were, a symbolic relation between the cause and the pathological phenomenon, just as in the normal dream. Thus, psychic pain may result in neuralgia, or the affect of moral disgust may cause vomiting. We have studied patients who were wont to make the most prolific use of such symbolization. In still other cases, such a determination is at first sight incomprehensible, yet in this group we find the typical hysterical symptoms, such as hemianaesthesia, contraction of the visual field, epileptiform convulsions, and similar symptoms. The explanation of our views concerning this group must be deferred for a more detailed discussion of the subject.

Such observations seem to demonstrate the pathogenic analogy between simple hysteria and traumatic neurosis, and justify a broader conception of "traumatic hysteria." The active aetiological factor in traumatic neurosis is really not the insignificant bodily injury, but the affect of the fright; that is, the *psychic trauma.* In an analogous manner, our investigations show that the causes of many, if not of all, cases of hysteria can be designated as psychic traumas. Every experience which produces the painful affect of fear, anxiety, shame, or of psychic pain may act as a trauma. Whether an experience becomes of traumatic importance naturally depends on the person affected, as well as on the condition which will be mentioned later. In ordinary hysterias we frequently find, instead of one large trauma, many partial traumas, grouped causes which can be of traumatic significance only when summarized, and which belong together insofar as they form small fragments of the sorrowful tale. In still other cases, a connection with a real efficacious event, or with a period of time of special excitability, raises seemingly indifferent situations to traumatic dignity, which they would not have attained otherwise, but which they retain ever after.

But the causal connexion of the causative psychic trauma with the hysterical phenomena does not mean that the trauma, as an *agent provocateur,* would release the symptom, which would then become independent and continue as such. On the contrary, we must maintain that the psychic trauma of the memory of the same acts like a foreign body which even long

after its penetration must be considered as an agent of the present, the proof of which we see in a most remarkable phenomenon, which at the same time adds to our discoveries a distinctly practical interest.

We found, at first to our greatest surprise, that the *individual hysterical symptoms immediately disappeared without returning if we succeeded in thoroughly awakening the memories of the causal process with its accompanying affect, and if the patient circumstantially discussed the process in the most detailed manner and gave verbal expression to the affect.* Recollections without affects are almost utterly useless. The psychic process which originally elapsed must be reproduced as vividly as possible so as to bring it back into the *statum nascendi,*[1] and then thoroughly "talked out." If it concerns such irritating manifestations as convulsions, neuralgias, and hallucinations, they are once more brought to the surface with their full intensity, and they then vanish forever. Functional attacks like paralyses and anaesthesias likewise disappear, but naturally without any appreciable distinctness of their momentary aggravation.[2]

It would be quite reasonable to suspect that one deals here with an unintentional suggestion. The patient expects to be relieved of his suffering and it is this expectation and not the discussion that is the effectual factor. But this is not so. The first observation of this kind, in which a most complicated case of hysteria was analysed and the individual causal symptoms separately abrogated, occurred in the year 1881, that is, in a *pre-suggestive* period. It was brought about through a spontaneous auto-hypnosis of the patient and caused the examiner the greatest surprise.

In reversing the sentence: *cessante causa cessat effectus,*[3] we may conclude from this observation that the causal process continues to act

---

[1] Condition of birth. —Ed.

[2] The possibility of such a therapy was clearly recognized by Delboeuf and Binet, as is shown by the accompanying quotations. Delboeuf, *Le magnétisme animal* (Paris, 1889): "After this, one will understand how the hypnotizer helps the cure. He puts the patient back into the condition in which the disease manifested itself and fights by word the same disease as it is being re-born." Binet, *Les altérations de la personalité* (1892), p. 243: ". . . Perhaps one will see that by this mental trick taking the patient back to the very moment when the symptom first appeared, the patient is made more receptive to curative suggestion." In the interesting book of Janet, *L'Automatism psychologique* (Paris, 1899), we find the description of a cure brought about in a hysterical girl by a process similar to our method.

[3] The cause stopping, the effect is stopped.

in some way even after years, not indirectly by means of a chain of causal links, but directly as a provoking cause, just perhaps as in the wakeful consciousness where the memory of a psychic pain may later call forth tears. In other words: *The hysteric suffers mostly from reminiscences.*[1]

II

It would seem at first rather strange that long-forgotten experiences should exert so intensive an influence, and that their recollections should not be subject to the decay into which all our memories sink. We will perhaps gain some understanding of these facts by the following examinations.

The blurring or loss of an affect of memory depends on a great many factors. In the first place, it is of great consequence whether there was an energetic reaction to the affectful experience or not. By *reaction* we here understand a whole series of voluntary or involuntary reflexes, ranging from crying to an act of revenge, through which, according to experience, affects are discharged. If the success of this reaction is of sufficient strength, it results in the disappearance of a great part of the affect. Language attests to this fact of daily observation in such expressions as "to give vent to one's feeling," to be "relieved by weeping," etc. If the reaction is suppressed, the affect remains united with the memory. An insult retaliated, be it only in words, is differently recalled than one that had to be taken in silence. Language also recognizes this distinction between the psychic and physical results, and designates most characteristically the silently endured suffering as *grievance*. The reaction of an injured person to a trauma has really only then a perfect "cathartic" effect if it is expressed in an adequate reaction like revenge. But man finds a substitute for this action in speech through which help the affect can well-nigh be ab-reacted (*abreagirt*).[2] In other

cases, talking in the form of deploring and giving vent to the torments of the secret (confession) is in itself an adequate reflex. If such reaction does not result through deeds, words, or in the most elementary case through weeping, the memory of the occurrence retains above all an affective accentuation.

The ab-reaction, however, is not the only form of discharge at the disposal of the normal psychic mechanism of the healthy person who has experienced a psychic trauma. The memory of the trauma, even where it has not been ab-reacted, enters into the great complex of the associations. It joins the other experiences which are perhaps antagonistic to it, and thus undergoes correction through other ideas. For example, after an accident the memory of the danger and (dimmed) repetition of the fright is accompanied by the recollection of the further course, the rescue and the consciousness of present security. The memory of a grievance may be corrected by a rectification of the state of affairs by reflecting upon one's own dignity and similar things. A normal person is in this way capable of dissipating the accompanying affect by means of association.

In addition, there appears that general blurring of impressions, that fading of memories which we call *forgetting*, and which above all wears out the affective ideas no longer active.

It follows from our observations that those memories which become the causes of hysterical phenomena have been preserved for a long time with wonderful freshness and with their perfect emotional tone. As a further striking and a later realizable fact, we have to mention that the patients do not perhaps have the same control of these as of their other memories of life. On the contrary, *these experiences are either completely lacking from the memory of the patients in their usual psychic state, or at most exist in greatly abridged form.* Only after the patients are questioned in the hypnotic state do these memories appear with the undiminished vividness of fresh occurrences.

Thus, one of our patients in a hypnotic state reproduced with hallucinatory vividness throughout half a year everything that excited her during an acute hysteria on the same days of the preceding year. Her mother's diary, which was unknown to the patient, proved the faultless accuracy of the reproductions. Partly in hypnosis and partly in spontaneous attacks, another patient lived through with hallucinatory distinctness all experiences of a hysterical psychosis which she went through ten years be-

---

[1] We are unable to distinguish in this preliminary contribution what there is new in this content, and what can be found in such other authors as Moebius and Strümpell, who present similar views on hysteria. The greatest similarity to our theoretic and therapeutic accomplishments we accidentally found in some published observations of Benedict, which we shall discuss later on.

[2] The German *abreagiren* has no exact English equivalent. It will therefore, be rendered throughout the text by *ab-react;* the literal meaning is to *react away* or to *react off.* It is the act of giving vent in speech and action to repressed experiences, and thereby disburdening one's self of their unconscious influences. It has different shades of meaning, from *defence reaction* to *emotional catharsis*, which can be discerned from the context.—Tr.

fore, and for the greatest part of which she had been amnesic until its reappearance. Also, some individual memories of aetiological importance showed surprising integrity and sentient force of fifteen to twenty-five years' duration, and on their return exerted the full affective force of new experiences.

The reason for this we can seek only in the fact that these memories occupy an exceptional position in all the above-mentioned relations, as far as vividness is concerned. For it *was really shown that these memories correspond to traumas which were not sufficiently ab-reacted,* and on closer investigation of the reasons for this hindrance, we can find at least two series of determinants through which the reaction to the trauma was omitted.

To the first group we add those cases in which the patient had not reacted to psychic traumas because the nature of the trauma precluded a reaction, or because social relations made the reaction impossible, or because it concerned things which the patient wished to forget and which he, therefore, intentionally inhibited and repressed from his conscious memory. It is just such painful things which are found in the hypnotic state as the basis of hysterical phenomena (hysterical delirium of saints, nuns, abstinent women, and well-bred children).

The second series of determinants is not conditioned by the content of the memories, but by the psychic states with which the corresponding experiences in the patient have united. As a cause of hysterical symptoms, one finds in hypnosis even ideas which are insignificant in themselves, but which owe their preservation to the fact that they originated during a severe paralyzing affect like fright, or directly in abnormal psychic conditions, as in the semihypnotic twilight states of day-dreaming in auto-hypnosis, and similar states. Here, it is the nature of these conditions which makes a reaction to the incident impossible.

To be sure, both determinants can naturally unite, and, as a matter of fact, they often do. This is the case when a trauma, in itself effectual, occurs in a state of a severely paralyzing affect, or from a transformed consciousness. But it may also happen that the psychic trauma evokes in many persons one of these abnormal states which in turn makes the reaction impossible.

What is common to both groups of determinants is the fact that those psychic traumas which are not adjusted by reaction are also prevented from adjustment by associative elaboration. In the first group it is the resolution of the patient which strives to forget the painful experiences and in this way, if possible, to exclude them from association; in the second group the associative elaboration does not succeed because between the normal and pathological state of consciousness, in which these ideas originated, there is no productive associative relationship. We shall soon have occasion to discuss more fully these relationships.

Hence, we can say *that the reason why the pathogenically formed ideas retain their freshness and affective force is because they are not subject to the normal fading through ab-reaction and through reproduction in states of uninhibited association.*

III

When we discussed the conditions which, according to our experience, are decisive in the development of hysterical phenomena from psychic traumas, we were forced to speak of abnormal states of consciousness in which such pathogenic ideas originate, and we had to emphasize the fact that the recollection of the effectual psychic trauma is not to be found in the normal memory of the patient, but in the hypnotized memory. The more we occupied ourselves with these phenomena the more certain became our convictions *that the splitting of consciousness, so striking in the familiar classical cases of double consciousness, exists rudimentarily in every hysteria, and that the tendency to this dissociation, and with it the appearance of abnormal states of consciousness which we comprise as* hypnoid, *is the basic phenomenon of this neurosis.* In this view we agree with Binet and Janet, though we had no experience with their remarkable findings in anaesthetic patients.

Hence, to the often cited axiom, "Hypnosis is artificial hysteria," we should like to add another: "The existence of hypnoid states is the basis and determination of hysteria." These hypnoid states agree in all their diversities among themselves and with hypnosis in the one point, namely that the ideas arising in them are very intensive, but are excluded from associative relations with the rest of the content of consciousness. These hypnoid states are associable among themselves, and their ideation may thus attain various high degrees of psychic organization. In other respects the nature of these states and the degree of their exclusiveness differ from the rest of the conscious processes, as do the various states of hypnosis, which range from light somnolence to somnambulism, and from perfect memory to absolute amnesia.

If such hypnoid states have already existed before the manifest disease, they prepare the soil upon which the affect establishes the pathogenic memories with their resulting somatic manifestations. This behavior corresponds to hysteria, based on a predisposition. But our observations show that a severe trauma (like a traumatic neurosis) or a severe suppression (perhaps of a sexual affect) may bring about a splitting of ideas even in persons without predispositions. This represents the mechanism of the psychically acquired hysteria. Between these two extremes we have a series in which the facility of dissociation in a particular individual and the magnitude of the affective trauma vary inversely.

We are unable to say anything new as to the determination of the predisposed hypnoid states. We presume that they often develop from "reveries," which are so frequent even in normal persons, for which, for example, feminine handwork offers so much opportunity. The questions why "the pathological associations" formed in such states are so firm, and why they exert a stronger influence on the somatic processes than other ideas, are all indissolubly linked with the problem of the effectiveness of hypnotic suggestions in general. Our experiences in this matter do not show us anything new; but they rather throw light on the contradiction between the statement, "Hysteria is a psychosis," and the fact that among hysterics one may meet persons of the clearest intellects, the strongest wills, greatest principles, and of the subtlest minds. In these cases, such characteristics hold true only in the person's waking thought; in his hypnotic state he is alienated just as we all are in our dreams. Yet, whereas our dream psychoses do not influence our waking state, the products of hypnotic states are projected into the waking state as hysterical phenomena.

IV

Almost the same assertions that we have advanced about hysterical symptoms we may also repeat concerning hysterical attacks. As is known, we have Charcot's schematic description of the *major* hysterical attack, which in complete form shows four phases: (1) The epileptoid, (2) the major movements, (3) the *attitudes passionelles* (hallucinatory phase),

and (4) the concluding delirium. By shortening or prolonging the attack, and by isolating the individual phases, Charcot obtained all those forms of the hysterical attack, which are really observed more frequently than the complete *grande attaque*.

Our tentative explanation refers to the third phase, the *attitudes passionelles*. Wherever it is prominent, it contains the hallucinatory reproduction of a memory which was significant for the hysterical onset. It is the memory of a major trauma, the χατ' εξοχήν of the so-called traumatic hysteria, or of a series of partial traumas belonging together as they are found at the basis of the ordinary hysteria. Or, finally the attack may bring back those occurrences which, because of their encounter with a factor of a special predisposition, have become raised to traumas.

But there are also other attacks which ostensibly consist only of motor phenomena and lack the *passionelle* phase. If it is possible during such an attack of general twitching, cataleptic rigidity, or an *attaque de sommeil,* to put one's self *en rapport* with the patient, or still better, if one succeeds in evoking the attack in a hypnotic state, it will then be found that here, too, the root of it is the memory of a psychic trauma, or of a series of traumas which make themselves otherwise prominent in an hallucinatory phase. Thus, a little girl had suffered for years from attacks of general convulsions, which could be, and were, taken for epilepsy. For differential diagnostic reasons she was hypnotized and she immediately lapsed into one of her attacks. On being asked what she saw, she said, "The dog, the dog is coming," and it actually turned out that the first attack of this kind appeared after she was pursued by a mad dog. The success of the therapy then verified our diagnostic decision.

An official, who became hysterical as a result of ill treatment by his employer, suffered from attacks during which he fell to the floor raging furiously without uttering a word or displaying any hallucinations. The attack was provoked in a state of hypnosis, and he then stated that he lived through the scene during which his employer insulted him in the street and struck him with his cane. A few days later he came to me complaining that he had the same attack, but it was shown in the hypnosis this time that he went through the scene which was really connected with the onset of his disease, it was the scene in the court room, when he was unable to get satisfaction for the ill treatment which he received, etc.

The memories which appear in hysterical attacks, or which can be awakened in them, correspond in all other respects to the causes which we have found as the basis of continuous hysterical symptoms. Like these, they refer to psychic traumas which were prevented from adjustment through ab-reaction or through associative elaboration; like these, they were absent entirely or in their essential components in the total memory of normal consciousness, and showed themselves as parts of the ideation content of hypnoid states of consciousness with restricted associations. Finally they were also amenable to the therapeutic test. Our observations have often taught us that a memory which has hitherto provoked attacks becomes incapable of it when it is brought to reaction and associative correction in a hypnotic state.

The motor phenomena of the hysterical attack can in part be interpreted as the memory of general forms of reaction of the accompanying affect (like the fidgeting of the whole body to which the infant already resorts), in part as a direct motor expression of this memory, and in other parts they, like the hysterical stigmata in the permanent symptoms, elude this explanation.

A special estimation of the hysterical attack is obtained if one also takes into account the fact that in hysteria there are groups of ideas which originated in hypnoid states, which are excluded from associative activity with the rest, but are associable among themselves and thus represent a more or less highly organized rudimentary second consciousness, a *condition seconde*. A persistent hysterical symptom, therefore, corresponds to an impingement of this second state upon a bodily innervation otherwise controlled by the normal consciousness. But an hysterical attack gives evidence of a higher organization of this second state and, if of recent origin, signifies a moment in which this hypnoid consciousness has gained control of the whole existence, that is, we have an acute hysteria; but if it is a recurrent attack containing a memory, we simply have a repetition of the same. Charcot has already given utterance to the thought that the hysterical attack must be the rudiment of a *condition seconde*. During the attack, the control of the whole bodily innervation passes over to the hypnoid consciousness. As familiar experiences show, the normal consciousness is not always entirely repressed by it; it may even perceive the motor phenomenon of the attack while the psychic processes of the same escape all knowledge of it.

The typical course of a grave hysteria, as is well known, is as follows: At first an ideation is formed in the hypnoid state, which, after sufficient growth, gains control in a period of *acute hysteria* of the bodily innervation and the existence of the patient, and creates permanent symptoms and attacks, and with the exception of some residuum then ends in recovery. If the normal personality can regain the upper hand, all that has survived the hypnoid ideation content then returns in hysterical attacks, and now and then it brings the person back into similar states which are again amenable to influences and eligible for traumas. Frequently a sort of equilibrium is then established between the psychic groups which are united in the same person; attack and normal life go hand in hand without influencing each other. The attack then comes spontaneously just as memories are wont to come, but just like memories it can also be provoked by the laws of association. The provocation of the attack results either through stimulating a hysterogenic zone or through a new experience which by similarity recalls the pathogenic experience. We hope to be able to show that there is no essential difference between the apparently two diverse determinants, and that in both cases a hyperæsthetic memory is touched. In other cases, this equilibrium shows a marked lability; the attack appears as a manifestation of the hypnoidal remnant of consciousness, as often as the normal person becomes exhausted and functionally incapacitated. We cannot disregard the fact that in such cases the attack becomes stripped of its original significance and may return as a contentless motor reaction.

It remains a task for future investigation to discover what conditions are decisive in determining whether an hysterical individuality should manifest itself in attacks, in persistent symptoms, or in a mingling of both.

V

We can now understand in what manner the psycho-therapeutic method propounded by us exerts its curative effect. *It abrogates the efficacy of the original non-ab-reacted ideas by affording an outlet to their strangulated affects through speech. It brings them to associative correction by drawing them into normal consciousness (in mild hypnosis) or by eliminating them through medical suggestion in the same way as in somnambulism with amnesia.*

We maintain that the therapeutic gain obtained by applying this process is quite significant. To be sure, we do not cure the hysteria insofar as it represents a predisposition, for we really do not block the way for the recurrence of hypnoid states. Nor is our procedure capable of preventing the replacement of the laboriously abrogated phenomena by new ones. But once this acute stage has run its course and its remnants continue as permanent hysterical symptoms and attacks, our radical method can frequently remove them forever, and herein it seems to surpass the efficacy of direct suggestion, as practised at present by psycho-therapists.

If, by disclosing the psychic mechanisms of hysterical phenomena, we have taken a step forward on the path so successfully started by Charcot with his explanation and experimental imitation of hystero-traumatic paralysis, we are well aware that in so doing we have only advanced our knowledge in the mechanisms of hysterical symptoms and not in the subjective causes of hysteria. We have grazed only the aetiology of hysteria, and can only throw light on the causes of the acquired forms, i.e., on the significance of the accidental factors of the neurosis.

CHAPTER 2

CASE HISTORY OF MISS LUCIE R[1]

TOWARDS the end of 1892, a friendly colleague recommended to me a young lady whom he had been treating for chronic recurrent purulent rhinitis. It was later found that the obstinacy of her trouble was caused by a caries of the ethmoid. She finally complained of new symptoms which this experienced physician could no longer refer to local affections. She had lost all perception of smell and was almost constantly bothered by one or two subjective sensations of smell. This she found very irksome. In addition to this she was depressed in spirits, weak, and complained of a heavy head, loss of appetite, and an incapacity for work.

This young lady visited me from time to time during my office hours—she was a governess in the family of a factory superintendent living in the suburbs of Vienna. She was an English lady of rather delicate constitution, anemic, and, with the exception of her nasal trouble, was in good health. Her first statements concurred with those of her physician.

[1] Breuer u. Freud, *Studien über Hysterie* (1895), Case III.

She suffered from mild depression and lassitude, and was tormented by subjective sensations of smell. Of hysterical signs, she showed a quite distinct general analgesia without tactile impairment, the fields of vision showed no narrowing on coarse testing with the hand. The nasal mucous membrane was totally analgesic and reflexless. Tactile sensation was absent, and the perception of this sense organ was abolished for specific as well as for other stimuli, such as ammonia or acetic acid. The purulent nasal catarrh was just then in a period of improvement.

On first attempting to understand this case we felt that subjective sensations of smell must represent recurrent hallucinations interpreting persistent hysterical symptoms, that the mild depression was perhaps the affect belonging to the trauma, and that there must have been an episode during which the present subjective sensations were objective. This episode must have been the trauma, the symbols of which recurred in her memory as sensations of smell. Perhaps it would have been more correct to consider the recurring hallucinations of smell with the accompanying depression as equivalents of hysterical attacks. For the nature of recurrent hallucinations really makes them unsuitable for the rôle of chronic symptoms, which was hardly the question in this rudimentary case. But it was absolutely necessary that the subjective sensations of smell should show a specialization that could correspond to a very definite and real objective origin.

This expectation was soon fulfilled, for on being asked what odour troubled her most she stated that it was an odour of burned pastry. I could then assume that the odour of burned pastry really occurred in the traumatic event. It is quite unusual to select sensations of smell as memory symbols of traumas, but it is quite obvious why these were here selected. She was afflicted with purulent rhinitis, hence the nose and its perceptions were in the foreground of her attention. All I knew about the life of the patient was that she took care of two children whose mother died a few years ago from a grave and acute disease.

As a starting point of the analysis, I decided to use the "odour of burned pastry". I will now relate the history of this analysis. It could have occurred under more favourable conditions, but, as a matter of fact, what should have taken place in one session was extended over a number of them. She could only visit me during my office hours, during which I could devote to her but little of my time. One single conversation had to be extended for over a week as her duties did not permit her to come to me often from such a distance, so that the conversation was frequently broken off and resumed at the next session.

On attempting to hypnotize Miss Lucie R, she did not lapse into the somnambulic state. I, therefore, was obliged to forego somnambulism, and the analysis was made while she was in a state which did not perhaps differ much from the normal.

I feel obliged to express myself more fully about the point of the technique of my procedure. While visiting the Nancy clinics in 1889, I heard Dr. Liébault, the old master of hypnotism, say: "Yes, if we had the means to put everybody into the somnambulic state, hypnotism would then be the most powerful therapeutic agent." In Bernheim's clinic it almost seemed that such an art really existed, and that it could be learned from Bernheim. But as soon as I tried to practise it on my own patients, I noticed that at least my powers were quite limited in this respect. Whenever a patient did not sink into the somnambulic state after one or two attempts, I possessed no means to force him into it. However, the percentage of somnambulists in my experience was far below that claimed by Bernheim.

Thus, I had the choice either to refrain from using the cathartic method in most of the cases suitable for it, or to venture the attempt without somnambulism by using hypnotic influence in light or even doubtful cases. It made no difference of what degree (following the accepted scales of hypnotism) the hypnotism was, which did not correspond to somnambulism, for every line of suggestibility is independent of the other, and nothing prejudices the evocation of catalepsy, automatic movements, and similar phenomena, for the purpose of facilitating the awakening of forgotten recollections. I soon relinquished the habit of deciding the degree of hypnotism, as in a great number of cases it incited the patient's resistance and clouded the confidence which I needed for the more important psychic work. Moreover, in mild grades of hypnotism I soon tired of hearing, after the assurance and command, "You will sleep, sleep now!" such protests as, "But, Doctor, I am not sleeping." I was forced to bring in the very delicate distinction, saying, "I do not mean the usual sleep, I mean the hypnotic—you see, you are hypnotized, you cannot open your eyes"; or, "I really don't

want you to sleep." I am convinced that many of my colleagues who use psycho-therapy know how to get out of such difficulties more skilfully than I, they can, therefore, act differently. I, however, believe that if through the use of a word one can so frequently become embarrassed, it is better to avoid the word and the embarrassment. Wherever the first attempt did not produce either somnambulism or a degree of hypnotism with pronounced bodily changes, I dropped the hypnosis and demanded only "concentration," I ordered the patient to lie on his back and close his eyes as a means of attaining this "concentration." With little effort I obtained as profound a degree of hypnotism as was possible.

But as I gave up the use of somnambulism, I perhaps deprived myself of that prerequisite without which the cathartic method seemed inapplicable. For the latter is based on the assumption that in the altered state of consciousness the patients have at their disposal recollections and associations which do not apparently exist in their normal conscious state, and that wherever there is no somnambulic broadening of consciousness, it must also be impossible to bring about those causal relations which the patient gives the doctor as something unknown to him, that is, those pathogenic recollections "which are lacking from the memory of the patients in their usual psychic states or only exist in a most condensed state" (Preliminary Communication).

My memory helped me out of this embarrassment. I myself saw Bernheim demonstrate that the recollections of somnambulism are only manifestly forgotten in the waking state and can be readily reproduced by some urging, accompanied by hand pressure, which is supposed to mark another conscious state. He, for instance, imparted to a somnambulist the negative hallucination that he was no longer present, and then attempted to make himself noticeable to her by the most manifold and inconsiderate attacks, but was unsuccessful. After the patient was awakened, he asked her what he did to her during the time that she thought he was not there. She replied, very much astonished, that she knew nothing, but he did not stop there, he insisted that she would recall everything, and placed his hand on her forehead so that she should recall things, and behold, she finally related all that she did not apparently perceive in the somnambulic state, and about which she ostensibly knew nothing in the waking state.

This astonishing and instructive experiment was my model. I decided to proceed on the supposition that my patients knew everything that was of any pathogenic significance, and that all that was necessary was to force them to impart it. Whenever I reached a point where to my questions, "Since when have you had this symptom?" or "Where does it come from?" I received the answer, "I really don't know this," I proceeded as follows: I placed my hand on the patient's forehead or took her head between my hands and said, "Through the pressure of my hands it will come into your mind; the moment that I stop the pressure you will see something before you, or something will flash through your mind which you must note; it is that which we are seeking. Well, what have you seen or what came into your mind?"

On applying this method for the first time (it was not in the case of Miss Lucie R) I was surprised to find just what I wanted, and I may say that it has since hardly ever failed me; it always showed me how to proceed in my investigations and enabled me to do all such analyses without somnambulism. Gradually, I became so bold that when a patient would answer "I see nothing," or "Nothing came into my mind," I insisted that it was impossible, that he probably had the right thought, but that he did not believe it and repudiated it, that I would repeat the procedure as often as he wished, and that every time he would see the same thing. Indeed, I was always right; the patients had not as yet learned to let their criticism rest. They repudiated the emerging recollection or fancy because they considered it as a useless, intruding disturbance, but after they imparted it, it was always shown that it was the right one. Occasionally, after forcing a communication by pressing the head three or four times, I got such an answer as "Yes, I was aware of it the first time, but did not wish to say it," or, "I hoped that it would not be this."

By this method it was far more laborious to broaden the alleged narrowed consciousness than by investigating in the somnambulic state, but it made me independent of somnambulism and afforded me an insight into the motives which are frequently decisive for the "forgetting" of recollections. I am in a position to assert that this forgetting is often intentional and desired, but it is always only *manifestly* successful.

It appeared to me even more remarkable that apparently long-forgotten numbers and dates can be reproduced by a similar process, thus demonstrating an unexpected faithfulness of memory.

The insignificant choice which one has in searching for numbers and dates especially allows us to take to our aid the familiar axiom of the theory of aphasia, namely, that recognition is a lesser accomplishment of memory than spontaneous recollection.

Hence, to a patient who is unable to recall in what year, month, or day a certain event took place, enumerate the years during which it might have occurred as well as the names of the twelve months and the thirty-one days of the month, and assure him that at the right number or name his eyes will open themselves or that he will feel which number is the correct one. In most cases the patients really decide on a definite date and frequently enough (as in the case of Mrs. Cecilia N) it could be ascertained from existing notes of that time that the date was correctly recognized. At other times and in different patients it was shown from the connection of the recollected facts that the dates thus found were incontestable. A patient, for instance, after a date was found by enumerating for her the dates, remarked, "This is my father's birthday," and added, "Of course, I expected this episode (about which we spoke) because it was my father's birthday."

I can only lightly touch upon this theme. The conclusion which I wish to draw from all these experiences is that the pathogenic important experiences with all their concomitant circumstances are faithfully retained in memory, even where they seem forgotten, as when the patient seems unable to recall them.[1]

[1] As an example of the technique mentioned above, that is, of investigating in a non-somnambulic state or where consciousness is not broadened, I will relate a case which I analyzed recently. I treated a woman of thirty-eight who suffered from an anxiety neurosis (agoraphobia, fear of death, etc.). Like many patients of that type, she had a disinclination to admit that she acquired this disease in her married state and was quite desirous of referring it back to her early youth. She informed me that at the age of seventeen when she was in the street of her small city she had the first attack of vertigo, anxiety, and faintness, and that these attacks recurred at times up to a few years ago when they were replaced by her present disease. I thought that the first attacks of vertigo, in which the anxiety was only blurred, were hysterical, and decided to analyze the same. All she knew was that she had the first attack when she went out to make purchases in the main street of her city.—"What purchases did you wish to make?"—"Various things, I believe it was for a ball to which I was invited."—"When was the ball to take place?"—"I believe two days later."—"Something must have happened a few days before this which excited you and which made an impression on you."—"But I don't know, it is now twenty-one years."—"That does not matter, you will recall it. I

After this long but unavoidable digression, I now return to the history of Miss Lucie R. As aforesaid, she did not sink into somnambulism when an attempt was made to hypnotize her, but lay calmly in a degree of mild suggestibility, her eyes constantly closed, the features immobile, the limbs without motion. I asked her whether she remembered on what occasion the smell perception of burned pastry originated.—"Oh, yes, I know it well. It was about two months ago, two days before my birthday. I was with the children (two girls) in the schoolroom playing and teaching them to cook, when a letter just left by the letter-carrier was brought in. From its postmark and handwriting, I recognized it as one sent to me by my mother from Glasgow and I wished to open it and read it. The children then came running over, pulled the letter out of my hand and exclaimed, 'No, you must not read it now; it is probably a congratulatory letter for your birthday and we will keep it for you until then.' While the children were thus playing, there was a sudden diffusion of an intense odour. The children forgot the pastry which they were cooking, and it burned. Since then, I have been troubled by this odour; it is really always present, but is more marked during emotional excitement."

"Do you see this scene distinctly before you?"—"As clearly as I experienced it."— "What was there in it that so excited you?"— "I was touched by the affection which the children displayed towards me."—"But weren't they always so affectionate?"—"Yes, but I just got the letter from my mother."—"I can't understand in what way the affection of the little ones and the letter from the mother contrasted, a thing which you appear to intimate."—"I had the intention of going to my mother and my heart became heavy at the thought of leaving those dear children."—"What was the matter with your mother? Was she lonesome that she wanted you, or was she sick just then and you expected some news?"—"No, she is delicate, but not really sick, and has a companion with her."—"Why then were you obliged to leave the children?"—"This house had become unbearable to me. The housekeeper, the cook, and the French maid seemed to be under the impression that I was too proud for my position. They united in intriguing against me and told the grandfather of the children all sorts of things about me, and when I complained to both gentlemen, I did not receive the support which I expected. I then tendered my resignation to the master (father of the children), but he was very friendly, asking me to reconsider it for two weeks before taking any definite steps. It was while I was in that state of

will exert some pressure on your head and when I stop it, you will either think of or see something which I want you to tell me." I went through this procedure, but she remained quiet.—"Well, has nothing come into your mind?"—"I thought of something, but that can have no connection with it."—"Just say it."—"I thought of a young girl who is dead, but she died when I was eighteen, that is, a year later."—"Let us adhere to this. What was the matter with your friend?"—"Her death affected me very much, because I was very friendly with her. A few weeks before another young girl died, which attracted a great deal of attention in our city, but then I was only seventeen years old."—"You see, I told you that the thought obtained under the pressure of the hands can be relied upon. Well, now, can you recall the thought that you had when you became dizzy in the street?"—"There was no thought, it was vertigo."—"That is quite impossible, such conditions are never without accompanying ideas. I will press your hand again and you will think of it. Well, what came to your mind?"—"I thought, 'Now I am the third.'"—"What do you mean?"—"When I became dizzy, I must have thought, 'Now I will die like the other two.'"—"That was then the idea, during the attack you thought of your friend, her death must have made a great impression on you." —"Yes, indeed, I recall now that I felt dreadful when I heard of her death, to think that I should go to a ball while she lay dead, but I anticipated so much pleasure at the ball and was so occupied with the invitation that I did not wish to think of this sad event." (Notice here the intentional repression from consciousness which caused the reminiscences of her friend to become pathogenic.)

The attack was now in a measure explained, but I still needed the occasional factor which just then provoked this recollection, and accidentally I formed a happy supposition about it.—"Can you recall through which street you passed at that time?"—"Surely, the main street with its old houses, I can see it now."— "And where did your friend live?"—"In the same street. I had just passed her house and was two houses farther when I was seized with the attack."—"Then it was the house which you passed that recalled your dead friend, and the contrast which you then did not wish to think about, that took possession of you."

Still, I was not satisfied; perhaps there was something else which provoked or strengthened the hysterical disposition in a hitherto normal girl. My suppositions were directed to the menstrual indisposition as an appropriate factor, and I asked, "Do you know when during that month you had your menses?"— She became indignant: "Do you expect me to know that? I only know that I had them very rarely and irregularly. When I was seventeen, I only had them once."—"Well, let us enumerate the days, months, etc., so as to find when it occurred."—She decided with certainty on a month and wavered between two days preceding a date which accompanied a fixed holiday.—"Does that in any way correspond with the time of the ball?"—She answered quietly: "The ball was on this holiday. And now I recall that the only menses which I had had during the year occurred just when I had to go to the ball. It was the first invitation to a ball that I had received."

The combination of the events can now be readily constructed and the mechanism of this hysterical attack readily viewed. To be sure, the result was gained after painstaking labour. It necessitated on my side full confidence in the technique and in the individual leading ideas, in order to reawaken such details of forgotten experiences after twenty-one years in a skeptical and really awakened patient. But then everything coincided.

indecision that the incident occurred. I thought that I would leave the house, but have remained."—"Aside from the attachment of the children, is there anything particular which attracts you to them?"—"Yes, my mother is distantly related to their mother, and when the latter was on her death-bed, I promised her to do my utmost to be a mother to them, and this promise I broke when I offered my resignation."

The analysis of the subjective sensation of smell seemed complete. It was once objective and intimately connected with an experience, a small scene, in which contrary affects conflicted, sorrow at forsaking the children, and the mortification which despite all, urged her to this decision. Her mother's letter naturally recalled the motives of this decision because she thought of returning to her mother. The conflict of the affects raised this factor to a trauma, and the sensation of smell, which was connected with it, remained as its symbol. The only thing to be explained was the fact that out of all the sensory perceptions of that scene, the perception of smell was selected as the symbol, but I was already prepared to use the chronic nasal affliction as an explanation. On being directly questioned, she stated that just at that time she suffered from a severe coryza and could scarcely smell anything, but in her excitement she perceived the odour of burned pastry; it penetrated the organically motivated anosmia.

As plausible as this sounded, it did not satisfy me; there was no acceptable reason why this series of excitement and this conflict of affects should have led to hysteria. Why did it not remain on a normal psychological basis? In other words, what justified the conversion under discussion? Why did she not recall the scenes themselves instead of the sensations connected with them which she preferred as symbols for her recollection? Such questions might seem superfluous and irrelevant when dealing with old hysterics in whom the mechanism of conversion is habitual, but this girl acquired hysteria for the first time through this trauma, or at least through this slight distress.

From the analysis of similar cases I already knew that in the process of hysterical development one psychic determinant is indispensable; namely, that some idea must *intentionally be repressed from consciousness* and excluded from associative elaboration.

In this intentional repression I also find the reason for the conversion of the sum of excitement, be it partial or total. The sum of excitement which is not to enter into psychic association more readily finds the wrong road to bodily innervation. The reason for the repression itself could only be a disagreeable feeling, the incompatibility of one of the repressible ideas with the ruling ideational-mass of the ego. The repressed idea then avenges itself by becoming pathogenic.

From this I concluded that Miss Lucie R had lapsed into that moment of hysterical conversion, which must have been one of the prerequisites of that trauma which she intentionally wished to leave in the dark, and which she took pains to forget. On considering her attachment for the children and her sensitiveness towards the other persons of the household, there remained but one interpretation which I was bold enough to impart to her. I told her that I did not believe that all these things were simply due to her affection for the children, but that I thought that she was rather in love with her master, perhaps unwittingly, that she really nurtured the hope of taking the place of the mother, and it was for that reason that she became so sensitive towards the servants with whom she had lived peacefully for years. She feared lest they would notice something of her hope and scoff at her.

She answered in her laconic manner: "Yes, I believe it is so."—"But if you knew that you were in love with the master, why did you not tell me so?"—"But I did not know it, or rather, I did not wish to know it. I wished to crowd it out of my mind, never to think of it, and of late I have been successful."[1]

"Why did you not wish to admit it to yourself? Were you ashamed because you loved a man?"—"Oh, no, I am not unreasonably prudish; one is certainly not responsible for one's own feelings. I only felt chagrined because it

[1] Another and better description of this peculiar state, in which one knows something and at the same time does not know it. I could never obtain. It can apparently be understood only if one has found himself in such a state. I have at my disposal a very striking recollection of this kind which I can vividly see. If I make the effort to recall what passed through my mind at that time my output seems very poor. I saw at that time something which was not at all appropriate to my expectations, and I was not in the least diverted from my definite purpose by what I saw when, as a matter of fact, this perception should have deflected me from my purpose. I did not become conscious of this contradiction nor did I notice anything of the affect of the repulsion which was undoubtedly responsible for the fact that this perception did not attain any psychic validity. I was struck with that blindness in seeing eyes, which one admires so much in mothers towards their daughters, in husbands towards their wives, and in rulers towards their favourites.

was my employer in whose service I was and in whose house I lived, and toward whom I could not feel as independent as towards another. What is more, I am a poor girl and he is a rich man of a prominent family, and if anybody should have had any inkling about my feelings, they would have ridiculed me."

After this I encountered no resistances in elucidating the origin of this affection. She told me that the first years of her life in that house were passed uneventfully. She fulfilled her duties without thinking about unrealizable wishes. One day, however, the serious and very busy, and hitherto very reserved master engaged her in conversation about the exigencies of rearing the children. He became milder and more cordial than usual, he told her how much he counted on her in the bringing up of his orphaned children, and looked at her rather peculiarly. It was in this moment that she began to love him, and gladly occupied herself with the pleasing hopes which she conceived during that conversation. However, as this was not followed by anything else, and, despite her waiting and persevering, no other confidential heart-to-heart talk followed, she decided to crowd it out of her mind. She quite agreed with me that the look which she noticed during the conversation was probably intended for the memory of his deceased wife. She was also perfectly convinced that her love was hopeless.

After this conversation I expected a decided change in her condition, but for a time it did not take place. She continued depressed and moody—a course of hydrotherapy which I prescribed for her at the same time refreshed her somewhat in the morning. The odour of burned pastry did not entirely disappear; though it became rarer and feebler, it appeared, as she said, only when she was very much excited.

The continuation of this memory symbol led me to believe that besides the principal scene it also represented many smaller, side traumas and I, therefore, investigated everything that might have been in any way connected with the scene of the burned pastry. We thus passed through the theme of family friction, the behaviour of the grandfather and others, and with that the sensation of burned odour gradually disappeared. Just then there was a lengthy interruption occasioned by a new nasal affliction, which led to the discovery of the caries of the ethmoid.

On her return, she informed me that she received many Christmas presents from both gentlemen as well as from the household servants, as if they were trying to appease her and wipe away the recollection of the conflicts of the last months. These frank advances made no impression on her.

On questioning her on another occasion about the odour of burned pastry, she stated that it had entirely disappeared, but instead she was now bothered by another and similar odour like the smoke of a cigar. This odour really existed before; it was only concealed by the odour of the pastry, but now it appeared as such.

I was not very much pleased with the success of my treatment. What occurred here is what a mere symptomatic treatment is generally blamed for, namely, that it removes one symptom only to make room for another. Nevertheless, I immediately set forth to remove this new memory symbol by analysis.

This time I did not know whence this subjective sensation of smell originated, nor on what important occasion it was objective. On being questioned, she said, "They constantly smoke at home; I really don't know whether the smell which I feel has any particular significance." I then proposed that she should try to recall things under the pressure of my hands. I have already mentioned that her recollections were plastically vivid, that she was of the "visual type." Indeed, under the pressure of my hands a picture came into her mind—at first, only slowly and fragmentarily. It was the dining room in which she waited with the children for the arrival of the gentlemen from the factory for dinner.—"Now we are all at the table, the gentlemen, the French maid, the housekeeper, the children, and I. It is the same as usual."—"Just keep on looking at that picture. It will soon become developed and specialized."—"Yes, there is a guest, the chief accountant, an old gentleman, who loves the children like his own grandchildren, but he dines with us so frequently that it is nothing unusual."—"Just have patience, keep on looking at the picture, something will certainly happen."—"Nothing happens. We leave the table, the children take leave and go with us to the second floor as usual."—"Well?"— "There really is something unusual here. I now recognize the scene. As the children leave, the chief accountant attempts to kiss them, but my master jumps up and shouts at him, 'Don't kiss the children!' I then experienced a stitch in the heart, and, as the gentlemen were smoking, this odour remained in my memory."

This, therefore, was the second, deeper seated

scene, which acted as a trauma, and left the memory symbol. But why was this scene so effective? I then asked her which scene happened first, this one or the one of the burned pastry—"The last scene happened first by almost two months."—"Why did you feel the stitch at the father's interference? The reproof was not meant for you."—"It was really not right to rebuke an old man in such a manner, who was a dear friend and a guest; it could have been said more calmly."—"Then you were really affected by your master's impetuosity? Were you perhaps ashamed of him, or did you think, 'If he could become so impetuous towards an old friend and guest over such a trifle, how would he act towards me if I were his wife?' "—"No, that is not it."—"But still it was about his impetuosity?"—"Yes, about the kissing of the children, he never liked that." Under the pressure of my hands there emerged a still older scene, which was the real effective trauma and which bestowed on the scene of the chief accountant the traumatic affectivity.

A few months before, a lady friend visited the house and on leaving kissed both children on the lips. The father, who was present, controlled himself and said nothing to the lady, but when she left, he was very angry at the unfortunate governess. He said that he held her responsible for this kissing; that it was her duty not to tolerate it; that she was neglecting her duties in allowing such things, and that, if it ever happened again, he would entrust the education of his children to someone else. This occurred while she believed herself loved, and waited for a repetition of that serious and friendly talk. This episode shattered all her hopes. She thought: "If he can upbraid and threaten me on account of such a trifle, of which I am entirely innocent, I must have been mistaken; he never entertained any tenderer feelings towards me, else he would have been more considerate."—It was evidently this painful scene that came to her as the father reprimanded the chief accountant for attempting to kiss the children.

On being visited by Miss Lucie R two days after the last analysis, I had to ask her what pleasant things happened to her. She looked as though transformed, she smiled, and held her head aloft. For a moment I thought that after all I probably mistook the situations, and that the governess of the children had now become the bride of her master. But she soon dissipated all my suppositions by saying, "Nothing new has happened. You really do not know me. You have always seen me while I was sick and depressed. Usually I am always cheerful. On awaking yesterday morning my burden was gone and since then I have felt well."—"What do you think of your chances in the house?" —"I am perfectly clear about that. I know that I have none, and I am not going to be unhappy about it."—"Will you now be able to get along with the others in the house?"—"I believe so, because most of the trouble was due to my sensitiveness."—"Do you still love the master?"—"Certainly I love him, but that does not bother me much. One can think and feel as one wishes."

I now examined her nose and found that the pain and the reflex sensations had almost completely disappeared. She could distinguish odours, but she was uncertain when they were very intense. What part the nasal trouble played in the anosmia, I must leave undecided.

The whole treatment extended over a period of nine weeks. Four months later I accidentally met the patient at one of our summer resorts—she was cheerful and stated that her health continued to be good.

EPICRISIS

I would not like to underestimate the aforesaid case even though it only represents a minor and light hysteria with but few symptoms. On the contrary, it seems to me instructive that even such a slight neurotic affliction should require so many psychic determinants, and, on more exhaustive consideration of this history, I am tempted to put it down as an illustration of that form of hysteria which even persons not burdened by heredity may acquire, if they have the *suitable* experiences for it. It should be well noted that I do not speak of a hysteria which may be independent of all predisposition; such form probably does not exist, but we speak of such a predisposition only after the person became hysterical, as nothing pointed to it before. A neuropathic disposition as commonly understood is something different. It is determined even before the disease by a number of hereditary burdens, or by a sum of individual psychic abnormalities. As far as I know, none of these two factors could be demonstrated in the case of Miss Lucie R. Her hysteria may, therefore, be called acquired, and by and large presupposes nothing more than a very marked susceptibility to acquire hysteria, a characteristic about which we know scarcely anything. In such cases the greatest emphasis lies in the nature of the trauma and naturally in connection with the reaction of the person to the trauma. It is an indispensable condition for the acquisition of hysteria that there should arise a relation of incompatibility between the ego and an idea that comes in contact with it. I hope to be able to show in another place how a variety of neurotic disturbances originate from the different procedures which the *ego* pursues in order to free itself from that incompatibility. The hysterical form of defence, for which a special adaptation is required, consists in a conversion of the excitement into physical innervation. The gain brought about by this process consists in the crowding out of the unbearable idea from the ego consciousness, which then contains instead the physical reminiscences produced by conversion—in our case the subjective sensation of smell—and suffers from the affect which more or less distinctly connects itself with these reminiscences. The situation thus produced can no longer be changed, for the resistance which would have striven for the adjustment of the affect was eliminated through repression and conversion. Thus, the mechanism producing hysteria corresponds on the one hand to an act of moral faintheartedness, on the other hand it presents itself as a protective process at the command of the ego. There are many cases in which it must be admitted that the defence against the increased excitement through the production of hysteria may actually have been most expedient, but more frequently one will naturally come to the conclusion that a greater measure of moral courage would have been of more advantage to the individual.

Accordingly, the real traumatic moment is that in which the conflict thrusts itself upon the ego and the latter decides to banish the incompatible idea. Such banishment does not annihilate the opposing idea, but merely crowds it into the unconscious. When this process occurs for the first time, it forms a nucleus, or a point of crystallization, for the formation of a new psychic group, separated from the ego, around which, in the course of time, everything collects which is in accord with the opposing idea. The splitting of consciousness in such cases of acquired hysteria is thus desired and intentional, and is often initiated by at least one arbitrary act. But as a matter of fact, something different happens than the individual expects; he would like to eliminate an idea as though it never came to pass, but he only succeeds in isolating it psychically.

The traumatic factor in the history of our patient corresponds to the scene created by her master on account of the kissing of the children. For the time being this scene remained without any palpable effects, perhaps it initiated the depression and sensitiveness, but I leave this open; the hysterical symptoms, however, commenced later in moments which can be designated as *auxiliary,* and which may be characterized by the fact that in them there was a simultaneous inter-fusion of both separated groups just as in the broadened somnambulic consciousness. The first of these factors in which the conversion took place in Miss Lucie R was the scene at the table when the chief accountant attempted to kiss the children. The traumatic memory helped along, and she acted as though she had not entirely banished her attachment for her master. In other cases we find that these different factors coalesce and the conversion occurs directly under the influence of the trauma.

The second auxiliary factor repeated almost precisely the mechanism of the first. A strong impression transitorily re-established the unity of consciousness, and the conversion took the same route that was opened to it the first time. It is interesting to note that the symptom which occurred second concealed the first, so that the latter could not be distinctly perceived until the former was eliminated. The reversal of the succession of events, to which also the analysis had to be adapted, seemed quite remarkable. In a whole series of cases I found that the symptoms which came later covered the first, and only the last thing in the analysis contained the key to the whole.

The therapy here consisted in forcing the union of the dissociated psychic groups with the ego consciousness. It is remarkable that the success did not run parallel with the accomplished work, the cure resulted suddenly only after the last part was accomplished.

CHAPTER 3

Case History of Miss Elisabeth von R[1]

In the fall of 1892 I was requested by a friendly colleague to examine a young lady who had been suffering from pains in her legs for over two years, so that she walked badly. He also added to his request that he had diagnosed the case as hysteria, though none of the usual symptoms of the neurosis could be found. He stated that he knew very little of the family, but that

[1] Breuer u. Freud, *Studien über Hysterie* (1895), Case V.

the last few years had brought them much misfortune and little pleasure. First the patient's father died, then the mother underwent a serious operation on her eyes, and soon thereafter a married sister succumbed to a chronic cardiac affection following childbirth. Our patient had taken an active part in all the afflictions, especially in the nursing of the sick.

I made no further progress in the case after I had seen the twenty-four-year-old patient for the first time. She seemed intelligent and psychically normal, and bore her affliction with a cheerful mien, thus vividly recalling the *belle indifference* of hysterics. She walked with the upper part of her body bent forward, but without any support; her walk did not correspond to any known pathological gait, and it was in no way strikingly bad. She complained only of severe pains and of early fatigue in walking as well as standing, so that after a brief period she had to seek rest in which the pains diminished, but by no means disappeared. The pain was of an indefinite nature—one could assume it to be a painful fatigue. The seat of the pain was quite extensive, but indefinitely circumscribed on the superficial surface of the right thigh. It was from this area that the pains radiated and were of the greatest intensity. Here, too, the skin and muscles were especially sensitive to pressure and pinching, while needle pricks were rather indifferently perceived. The same hyperalgesia of the skin and muscles was demonstrable not only in this area, but over almost the entire surface of both legs. The muscles were perhaps more painful than the skin, but both kinds of pains were unmistakably most pronounced over the thighs. The motor power of the legs was not diminished, the reflexes were of average intensity, and, as all other symptoms were lacking, there was no basis for the assumption of a serious organic affection. The disease developed gradually during two years and changed considerably in its intensity.

I did not find it easy to determine the diagnosis, but for two reasons I concluded to agree with my colleague. First, because it was rather strange that such a highly intelligent patient should not be able to give anything definite about the character of her pains. A patient suffering from an organic pain, if it is not accompanied by any nervousness, will be able to describe it definitely and calmly; it may perhaps be lancinating, appear at certain intervals, and extend from this to that location, or in his opinion it may be evoked by this or

that influence. The neurasthenic[1] in describing his pain gives the impression as being occupied with some difficult mental problem, something far beyond his powers. His features are tense and distorted as though under the domination of a painful affect, his voice becomes shriller, he struggles for expression, he rejects all designations that the physician makes for his pains, even though they are undoubtedly afterwards found to be correct. He is ostensibly of the opinion that language is too poor to give expression to his feelings. These sensations are something unique, they never existed before, so that they cannot be exhaustively described. It is for this reason that he never tires of constantly adding new details, and, when he has to stop, he is distinctly controlled by the impression that he was unsuccessful in making himself understood to the physician. All this is due to the fact that his pains absorb his whole attention. In the case of Miss von R, we had just the opposite behaviour, and we had to conclude from this that she attributed sufficient significance to the pain, but that her attention was concentrated on something else of which the pains were only the accompanying phenomena, perhaps on thoughts and sensations which were connected with pain.

A still greater determination for the conception of the pain must, however, be found in a second factor. If we irritate a painful area in a patient suffering from an organic disease or neurasthenia, his physiognomy will show a definite expression of discomfort or of physical pain, the patient winces, refuses to be examined, and assumes a defensive attitude. But if anyone pinched or pressed Miss von R's hyperalgesic skin or muscles of her legs, her face assumed a peculiar expression approaching nearer pleasure than pain, she cried out and—I had to think of a perhaps pleasurable tickling—her face reddened, she threw her head backward, closed her eyes, and her body bent backward; all this was not very distinct, but sufficiently marked so that it could only agree with the conception that her affliction was a hysteria and that the irritation touched a hysterogenic zone.

Her mien was not adequate to the pain, which the pinching of the muscles and skin were supposed to excite. It probably harmonized better with the contents of the thoughts which were behind the pain and which were evoked in the patient through a stimulation of those parts of

[1] A hypochondriac afflicted with anxiety neurosis. —Tr.

the body associated with them. I have repeatedly observed similar significant expression from stimulation of hyperalgesic zones in unmistakable cases of hysteria. The other gestures evidently corresponded to the slightest suggestion of an hysterical attack.

We could not at that time find any explanation for the unusual localization of the hysterogenic zone. That the hyperalgesia chiefly concerned the muscles, gave material for reflection. The most frequent affliction which could produce diffuse and local pressure sensitiveness of the muscles is rheumatic infiltration, or common chronic muscular rheumatism; of its aptitude to mask nervous ailments I have spoken. The consistency of the painful muscles in Miss von R did not contradict this assumption, as there were many hard cords in the muscle masses, which seemed to be especially sensitive. There was probably also an organic change in the muscles, in the assumed sense, upon which the neurosis leaned, and the significance of which was markedly exaggerated by the neurosis.

The therapeutic procedure was, therefore, based on the assumption of a mixed affection. We recommended systematic massage and faradization of the sensitive muscles, regardless of the pain it produced, and in order to remain in contact with the patient, I treated her legs by means of strong Franklin sparks. To her question whether she should force herself to walk, we answered decidedly in the affirmative.

We thus attained a slight improvement. She particularly liked the painful shocks of the "influence machine," and the stronger they were, the more they seemed to remove her pains. My colleague, meanwhile, prepared the soil for the psychic treatment, and, when after four weeks of this sham treatment I proposed it and explained to the patient the procedures and its effects, I found a ready understanding and only a slight resistance.

The work which I then began turned out to be the most arduous undertaking that ever fell to my lot, and the difficulty of giving an account of this work ranks well with the obstacles that had to be overcome. For a long time, too, I did not understand the connection between the history of the disease and the affliction, which should really have been caused and determined by this series of events.

When one undertakes a cathartic treatment, he at first asks himself whether the patient understands the origin and cause of her suffering. If that is so, one does not need any special technique to cause her to reproduce the history of her ailment. The interest shown in her, the understanding which we foreshadow, the hope of recovery extended to her, all these induce the patient to give up her secrets. In the case of Miss Elisabeth, it seemed probably right from the very beginning that she was conscious of the reasons for her suffering, that she had only a secret but no foreign body in consciousness. On looking at her one had to think of the poet's words: "That mask indicates a hidden meaning."[1]

At first I could, therefore, dispense with hypnosis, reserving it, however, for future use should conditions arise in the course of the confession for which explanation the memory would not suffice. Thus, in this first complete analysis of an hysteria which I had undertaken I attained a process of treatment which I later raised to a method and intentionally used as a process of clearing stratum by stratum the pathogenic psychic material, which we were pleased to compare with the technique of excavating a buried city. At first I let the patient relate what was known to her, paying careful attention wherever a connection remained enigmatic, or where a link in the chain of causation seemed to be lacking. Later, I penetrated into the deeper strata of memory by using for those locations hypnotic investigations or a similar technique. The presupposition of the whole work was naturally based on the expectation that a perfect and sufficient determination could be demonstrated. The methods of the deeper investigation will soon be discussed.

The history which Miss Elisabeth gave was quite dull and was woven of manifold painful experiences. During this recital she was not in a hypnotic state; I merely asked her to lie down and keep her eyes closed. I, however, made no objection if from time to time she opened her eyes, changed her position, or sat up. Whenever she entered more deeply into a part of her history, she seemed to lapse spontaneously into a condition resembling a hypnotic state. She then remained motionless and kept her eyes firmly closed.

I shall now reproduce the results of the most superficial stratum of her memory. As the youngest of three daughters she spent her youth with her parents, to whom she was devotedly attached, on their estate in Hungary. Her mother's health was frequently disturbed by an affliction of the eyes, as well as by a nervous ail-

[1] It will be shown that I was, nevertheless, mistaken.

ment. It thus happened that she became especially and devotedly attached to her jovial and broadminded father, who was wont to say that his daughter took the place of both a son and friend with whom he could exchange thoughts. As much as the girl gained in mental stimulation in consequence of this intercourse, it did not escape the father that her psychic constitution deviated from that ideal which one so much desires to see in a girl. Jocosely he called her "pert and disputatious." He warned her against being too confident in her judgments, against her tendencies to tell the truth regardless of everybody, and expressed his opinion that she would find it difficult to get a husband. As a matter of fact, she was very discontented with her girlhood; she was filled with ambitious plans, she wished to study or to obtain a musical education, and revolted at the thought of being forced to give up her ambitions and sacrifice her freedom of judgment for the sake of marriage. Meanwhile, she was proud of her father, of the regard and social position of her family, and jealously guarded everything connected with these matters. The indifference with which she treated her mother and older sisters, as will be shown, was considered by her parents to be due to the blunter side of her character.

The age of the girls impelled the family to move into the metropolis, where for a time Elisabeth enjoyed a richer and gayer social life. But then came the calamity which destroyed the happiness of the home. The father either concealed or overlooked a chronic cardiac affection, and one day he was brought home in an unconscious state after the first attack of œdema of the lungs. This was followed by an illness of one and a half years, during which Elisabeth took the most prominent part in nursing him. She slept in her father's room, awoke at night at his call, watched over him faithfully during the day, and forced herself to appear cheerful while he went through a hopeless condition with amiable resignation. The beginning of her affection must have been connected with this period of her nursing, for she could recall that during the last half year of this care she had to remain in bed on one occasion for a day and a half on account of severe pain in her right leg. She maintained, however, that these pains soon passed away and excited neither worry nor attention. As a matter of fact, it was not before two years after the death of her father that she began to feel sick and unable to walk on account of pain.

The void which her father left in the life of this family consisting of four women, the social solitude, the cessation of so many relations which promised stimulation and pleasure, the increased infirmity of the mother, all these beclouded the patient's emotional attitude, but simultaneously aroused a warm desire that the family might soon find a substitute for the lost happiness, and impelled her to concentrate her entire devotion and care on the surviving mother. At the end of the year of mourning, the eldest sister married a talented and ambitious man of notable position, who seemed to have been destined for a great future by virtue of his mentality, but who, however, soon developed a morbid sensitiveness and egotistic perseveration of moods, and dared to show his disregard for the old lady in the family circle. That was more than Elisabeth could endure. She felt it her duty to take up the cudgels against her brother-in-law whenever he gave occasion for it, whereas the other women took lightly the outburst of his excited temperament. She felt it a painful disillusionment that the reconstruction of the old family happiness could be impeded by such a disturbance, and she could not forgive her married sister because, due to feminine docility, the latter firmly avoided espousing either cause. Thus, a whole series of scenes remained in Elisabeth's memory which were connected with a number of partially unuttered grievances against her first brother-in-law. But her greatest grievance against him was the fact that for the sake of a prospective promotion he moved his small family to a distant city in Austria, and thus helped to increase her mother's isolation. On this occasion Elisabeth distinctly felt her inability and helplessness to afford her mother a substitute for her lost happiness, as well as the impossibility of following out the resolution she made on the occasion of her father's death.

The marriage of the second sister seemed more promising for the future welfare of the family. The second brother-in-law, although not of the same mental calibre as the first, was a man after the heart of delicate ladies, and his behaviour reconciled Elisabeth to the institution of marriage and to the sacrifices it entailed. What is more, the second couple remained near her mother, and the child of this brother-in-law and the second sister became Elisabeth's pet. Unfortunately, the year during which the child was born was clouded by another event. The visual affliction of the mother demanded many weeks' treatment in a dark room, in which Elisabeth participated. Following this, an operation proved necessary and the excitement connected with this occurred at the same time as the first brother-in-law made preparations to move. Finally, the operation, having been skilfully performed, proved successful, and the three families met at a summer resort. There Elisabeth, exhausted by the worries of the past months, had the first opportunity to recuperate from the effects of the suffering and anxiety to which the family had been subjected since the death of her father.

But just during this sojourn in the summer resort, Elisabeth became ill with pain and weakness. These pains, which had been noticeable for a short while some time previously, manifested themselves severely for the first time after taking a warm bath at a small spa. A long walk, actually half a day's hike a few days previously, was thought to have had some connection with the onset of the pains, so that it was quite easy to gain the impression that Elisabeth at first became "fatigued," and then "caught cold."

From now on Elisabeth became the patient in the family. Following the advice of the physician, she spent the rest of the summer in Bad Gastein, whither she went with her mother, but not without having a new worriment to think about. The second sister was again pregnant, and the information as to her condition was quite unfavorable, so that Elisabeth could hardly decide to take the journey to Gastein. After barely two weeks at Gastein both mother and sister were recalled because things were not well with the patient at home.

An agonizing journey, which for Elisabeth was full of pain and anxious expectations, was followed by certain signs at the railroad station which forbode the worst, and then, on entering the sickroom, they were confronted with the reality—that they had arrived too late to take leave of the dying one.

Elisabeth not only suffered from the loss of this sister, whom she dearly loved, but almost as much from the thoughts instigated by her death, and from the changes which it entailed. The sister had succumbed to heart trouble, which was aggravated by the pregnancy.

The idea then came to her mind that heart trouble was the paternal inheritance of the family. It was then recalled that in her early girlhood the deceased went through an attack of chorea with a slight heart affection. The members of the family then blamed themselves and the physicians for permitting the marriage, and they could not help reproaching the

unfortunate widower for endangering his wife's health through two successive pregnancies without any pause. The sad thought that, after the rare conditions for a happy marriage had been found, this happiness should have terminated in this way, constantly occupied Elisabeth's mind. Moreover, she again saw everything go to pieces that she had planned for her mother. The widowed brother-in-law was inconsolable and withdrew from his wife's family. It seemed that his own family, from whom he was estranged during his short and happy married life, took advantage of the opportunity to draw him back into their own circle. There was no way of maintaining the former union; out of regard for his unmarried sister-in-law, it would have seemed improper to live together with his mother-in-law, and as he refused to relinquish his child, the only legacy of the deceased to the two ladies, they accused him for the first time of heartlessness. Finally, and this was not the least painful, Elisabeth received some definite information concerning a disagreement between the two brothers-in-law, the cause of which she could only surmise. It seemed that the widower made some financial demands, which the other brother-in-law considered unjustifiable; indeed, in view of the mother's recent sorrow, he could only designate it as a wicked extortion. This then was the history of the ambitious and lovable young woman. Resentful of her fate, embittered over the failure of her little plans to restore the family lustre; of those dear to her, some were dead, some away, and some estranged—without any inclination to seek refuge in the love of a strange man, she lived thus for a year and a half away from almost all social relations nursing her mother and her pains.

If one could forget greater suffering, and wished to read one's self into the psychic life of a girl, one could hardly deny Miss Elisabeth a sincere human sympathy. But what about the physician's interest in this sorrowful tale and its relation to her painful and weak gait; what about the prospects of explaining and curing this case by the knowledge which we may perhaps obtain from these psychic traumas?

For the physician the confession of this patient was at first a great disappointment. For, to be sure, it was a history composed of banal mental shocks, from which we could neither explain why the patient became afflicted with hysteria, nor how the hysteria assumed the form of the painful abasia. It explained neither the causation nor the determination of the hysteria in question. We could perhaps assume that the patient had formed an association between her psychically painful impressions and bodily pains, which she accidentally perceived simultaneously, and that now she utilized in her memory the physical sensation as a symbol for the psychic. What motives she had for this substitution and in what moment this came about remained unexplained. To be sure, these were questions whose nature was not hitherto familiar to physicians. For it was customary to content one's self with the information that the patient was constitutionally hysterical, and that under the intensive pressure of any kind of excitement she could develop hysterical symptoms.

This confession offered even less for the explanation than for the treatment of the case. One could not conceive what beneficial influence Miss Elisabeth could derive from recounting sad, familiar family experiences of the past years to a stranger, who could give her in return only moderate sympathy, nor could one observe any improvement after the confession. During the first period of the treatment the patient never failed to repeat to her physician: "I continue to feel ill, I have the same pains as before," and when she accompanied this by a crafty and malicious glance, I could perhaps recall the words which old Mr. von R was wont to say about his favourite daughter: "She is frequently pert and disputatious," but after all I had to confess that she was right.

Had I given up the patient at this stage of the psychic treatment, the case of Miss Elisabeth von R would have been of no importance whatever for the theory of hysteria. But I continued my analysis because I felt sure that an understanding of the causation, as well as the determination, of the hysterical symptoms could be gained from the deeper strata of consciousness.

I, therefore, decided to put the direct question to the broadened consciousness of the patient as to what psychic impression was connected with the origin of the pain in the legs.

For this purpose the patient should have been put into deep hypnosis. But fortunately I was forced to realize that all my procedures in that direction could not put the patient in any other state of consciousness than that in which she gave me her confession. Still, I was very pleased that this time she abstained from triumphantly remonstrating with the words: "You see I really do not sleep. I cannot be hypnotized." In such despair I conceived the idea of making use of the trick of pressing the head,

the origin of which I have thoroughly discussed in the preceding observation of Miss Lucie. This was done by requesting the patient unfailingly to inform me of whatever appeared before her mind's eye or flashed through her memory at the moment of the pressure. She was silent for a long time, and then admitted that on my pressure she thought of an evening in which a young man had accompanied her home from some social affair, of the conversation that passed between them, and of her feelings on returning home to nurse her father.

With this first mention of the young man a new shaft was opened, the content of which I then gradually brought out. We dealt here rather with a secret, for, with the exception of a mutual friend, no one knew anything of the relationship and the hopes connected with it. It concerned the son of an old friendly family, who formerly lived in the neighbourhood.

The young man, being an orphan, attached himself with great devotion to her father, who guided him in his career, and this veneration for the father was naturally extended to the ladies of the family. Numerous reminiscences of joint readings, exchange of views, and remarks which had been repeated to her, marked the gradual growth of her conviction that he loved and understood her, and that a marriage with him would not impose upon her the sacrifice that she feared. Unhappily, he was only slightly older than she, and as yet far from independent. She, however, firmly resolved to wait for him.

With the serious illness of her father, and the necessity of nursing him, these relations became less frequent. The evening, which she recalled first, really marked the height of her feelings, but even then there was no exchange of ideas between them on the subject. It was only at the urging of her family that she consented to leave the sick-bed that evening and attend the social affair where she was to meet him. She wished to hasten home early, but she was forced to remain, and only yielded on his promising to accompany her home. At no time had she entertained such a tender regard for him as during this walk, but after returning home at a late hour in this blissful state and finding the condition of her father aggravated, she bitterly reproached herself for having sacrificed so much for her own amusement. It was the last time that she left her sick father for a whole evening, and thereafter she saw her friend only rarely. After the death of her father, he seemed to hold himself aloof out of respect for her sorrow, and business affairs later took him to other regions. Gradually, she came to the realization that his interest in her was suppressed by other feelings and that he was lost to her. This failure of her first love pained her as often as she thought of it.

In this relationship and in the above mentioned scene to which it led, I had to seek the causation of the first hysterical pain. A conflict, or a state of incompatibility, arose through the contrast between the happiness which she had not at that time denied herself and the sad condition in which she found her father upon her arrival home. As a result of this conflict, the erotic ideas were repressed from the associations and the affect connected with them was utilized in aggravating or reviving a simultaneously (or somewhat previously) existing physical pain. It was, thus, the mechanism of a *conversion for the purpose of defence*, as I have shown circumstantially in another place.[1]

To be sure, we have room here for all kinds of observations. I must stress the fact that I did not succeed in demonstrating from her memory that the conversion took place at the time of her returning home. I therefore investigated for similar experiences which might have occurred while she was nursing her father, and I evoked a number of scenes, among which was one during which she had to jump out of bed with bare feet in a cold room to respond to the repeated calls of her father. I was inclined to attribute to this factor a certain significance, for in addition to complaining of pain in her legs, she also complained of tormenting sensations of coldness. Nevertheless, here, too, I could not with certainty lay hold of the scene which could be designated as the scene of conversion. This led me to admit that there was some gap in the explanation, until I recalled that the hysterical pains in the legs were really not present at the time she nursed her father. From her memory she recalled only a single attack of pain lasting a few days, to which at that time she paid no attention. I then directed my attention to the first appearance of the pains. Here I was successful in awakening a definite memory. Just at that time a relative visited her; she could not receive him because she was ill in bed, and he had the misfortune to find her ill on another occasion two years later. But the search for the psychic motive of these first pains failed as often as it was repeated. I believed that I could assume that

these first pains were due to a slight rheumatic attack and really *had no psychic basis*, and I could also discover that this organic trouble was the model for the later hysterical imitation, at all events that it occurred *before* the scene of being accompanied home. That these mild organic pains should have continued for some time without her paying much attention to them was quite possible, when we consider the nature of the situation. The obscurity resulting from this, namely, that the analysis pointed to a conversion of psychic excitement into bodily pain at a time when such pain was certainly not perceived and not recalled—this problem I hope to be able to solve in later considerations and by other examples.[2]

With the discovery of the motive for the first conversion, we began a second more fruitful period of the treatment. In the first place, very soon afterward, the patient surprised me with the statement that she now knew why the pains always radiated from that definite location on the right thigh, and were most painful there. This was the exact place upon which her father's leg rested every morning while she changed the bandages of his badly swollen leg. That occurred hundreds of times, and, strange to say, she did not think of this connection until today. She thus gave me the desired explanation for the origin of an *atypical* hysterogenic zone. Furthermore, during our analysis, her painful legs always "joined in the discussion." I mean the following remarkable state of affairs: The patient was as a rule free from pain when we began our work, but as soon as I evoked some recollection by question or by pressure of the head, she at first reported some pain, usually of a very vivid nature, and then winced and placed her hand on the painful area. This awakened pain remained constant as long as the patient was dominated by the recollection, reaching its height when she was about to utter the essential and critical part of her communication, and disappeared with the last words of the statement. I gradually learned to use this awakened pain as a compass. Whenever she became mute, but still claimed to have pains, I knew that she had not told me everything, and urged her to continue the confession until the pain was "spoken away." Then only did I awaken a new recollection.

During this period of "ab-reaction" the patient's condition showed such a striking improvement both somatically and psychically

---

[1] "The Defence-Neuro-Psychoses" (1894), p. 81 ff. below.

[2] I can neither exclude nor prove that this pain, especially of the thighs, was of a *neurasthenic* nature.

that I used to remark half jokingly that during each treatment I carried away a certain number of pain motives, and that when I had cleaned them all out, she would be well. She soon reached a stage during which she had no pain most of the time, she consented to walk a great deal and to give up her hitherto self-imposed isolation. During the analysis, I followed up now the spontaneous fluctuations of her condition, and now some fragments of her sorrowful tale, which I felt was not sufficiently exhausted. In this work I made some interesting discoveries, the principles of which I could later verify in other patients.

In the first place, it was found that the spontaneous fluctuations never occurred unless provoked associatively by the events of the day. On one occasion she heard of an illness in the circle of her acquaintances, which recalled to her a detail in the illness of her father. On another occasion the child of her deceased sister visited her, and its resemblance to its mother recalled many painful incidents. On still another occasion it was a letter from her absent sister showing distinctly the influence of the inconsiderate brother-in-law, and this awakened a pain which made her crave to relate a family scene not reported before.

As she never reproduced the same pain motives twice, we seemed to be justified in the expectation that the stock would in time become exhausted, and I did not in any way prevent her from getting into situations conducive to evoking new memories which had not yet come to the surface. Thus, for example, I asked her to visit the grave of her sister, or I urged her to go in society where she was apt to meet her youthful friend, who happened to be in the city.

In this manner I obtained an insight into the mode of origin of a hysteria, which could be designated as *monosymptomatic*. I found, for example, that the right leg became painful during our hypnosis when we dealt with memories relating to the nursing of her father, to her young friend, and to other things which occurred during the first part of the pathogenic period; while the pain in the left leg appeared as soon as I evoked the memory of her lost sister, of both brothers-in-law, in brief, of any impression relating to the second half of the history. My attention having been called to this by this constant behaviour, I went further in my investigations and gained the impression that the detailization went perhaps still further and that every new psychic cause of painful

feeling might have some connection with a differently located pain area in the legs. The original painful location on the right thigh referred to the nursing of her father, and as the result of new traumas the painful area then grew by apposition, so that, strictly speaking, we had here not one single physical symptom connected with multiform psychic memory complexes, but a multiplicity of similar symptoms which on superficial examination seemed to be fused into one. To be sure, I have not followed out the demarcations of the individual psychic causes corresponding to the pain zones, for I found that the patient's attention was turned away from these relations.

But my interest was further directed to the mode of construction of the whole symptom-complex, of the abasia, upon this painful zone, and with this view in mind, I asked such questions as this: "What is the origin of the pains in walking, standing, or lying?" She answered these questions partially uninfluenced, partially under the pressure of my hand. We thus obtained two results. In the first place, she grouped all the scenes connected with painful impressions according to their occurrence, sitting, standing, etc. Thus, for example, she *stood* at the door when her father was brought home with his cardiac attack, and in her fright remained as though rooted to the spot. To this first quotation, "fright while *standing*," she connected more recollections up to the overwhelming scene when she again *stood* as if pinned near the death-bed of her sister. The whole chain of reminiscences should justify the connection of the pains with the standing up and could also serve as an association proof, except that one must be mindful of the fact that in all these events another factor must be demonstrated, that which had directed the attention—and consequently the conversion—precisely, to the standing (walking, sitting, etc.). The explanation for this direction of attention could hardly be sought in other connections than in the fact that walking, standing, and lying are connected with functions and conditions of those members which here bore the painful zones; namely, the legs. We could then easily understand the connection between the astasia-abasia and the first scene of conversion in this history.

Among the scenes which, according to this review, had made the *walking* painful, one became most prominent. It referred to a walk she had taken in a large company at the watering place, which apparently lasted too long. The deeper circumstances of this occurrence revealed themselves only hesitatingly and left many a riddle unsolved. She was in an especially good humour and gladly joined the circle of friendly persons; it was a lovely day, not too warm; her mother remained at home, her older sister had already departed, the younger one felt indisposed, but did not wish to mar her pleasure. The husband of the second sister at first declared that he would remain at home with his wife, but finally went along for her (Elisabeth's) sake. This scene seemed to have a great deal to do with the first appearance of the pains, for she recalled that she returned home from the walk very fatigued and with severe pains. She could not, however, say definitely whether she had perceived the pains before this. I took for granted that if she had suffered any pain she would hardly have resolved to enter upon this long walk. On being questioned whence the pains originated on this walk, she answered rather indefinitely that the contrast between her solitude and the married happiness of her sick sister, of which she was constantly reminded by the behaviour of her brother-in-law, was painful to her.

Another scene, closely related to the former in point of time, played a part in connection with the pains on *sitting*. It was a few days later, her sister and brother-in-law had already departed and she found herself in a tense and longing mood. She arose in the morning and ascended to the top of a small hill, which they were frequently wont to visit together, and which afforded a very pretty view. There she sat down on a stone bench and gave free play to her thoughts. Her thoughts again revolved on her lonesomeness, the fate of her family, and she now frankly admitted that she entertained the eager wish to become as happy as her sister. After this morning's meditation, she returned home with severe pains. In the evening of the same day she took the bath after which the pains definitely appeared and continued persistently.

We could further ascertain with great certainty that the pains on walking and standing diminished in the beginning *on lying down*. Only after she heard of her sister's illness and left Gastein in the evening, spending a sleepless night in the sleeping car, tormented simultaneously by worrying over her sister and by violent pains—it was only then that the pains appeared for the first time while she was lying down, and throughout that time, *lying down* was even more painful than walking or standing.

In this way the painful sphere grew by apposition, first, because every new pathogenically affecting theme occupied a new region of the legs; second, every one of the impressionable scenes left a trace because it produced lasting, always more cumulative, cathexes[1] of the different functions of the legs, thus connecting these functions with the sensations of pain. There was unmistakably, however, still a third mechanism which furthered the production of atasia-abasia. When the patient finished the recitation of a whole series of events with the plaint that she then perceived pain on *"standing alone,"* and when in another series, referring to the unfortunate attempt of bringing about new conditions in the family, she was not tired of repeating that the painful part of it was the feeling of her helplessness, the sensation that she *"could make no headway,"* I then had to think that her reflections, too, influenced the formation of the abasia, and I had to assume that she directly sought a *symbolic* expression for her painfully accentuated thoughts and had found it in the aggravation of her pains. That somatic symptoms of hysteria could originate through such symbolization we have already asserted in our preliminary communication, and I shall give some examples of conclusive evidence in the epicrisis to this history. In Miss Elisabeth von R, the psychic mechanism of the symbolization was not in the foreground, it had not produced the abasia, but everything pointed to the fact that the already existing abasia had in this way undergone a considerable reinforcement. Accordingly, this abasia, as I encountered it in the stage of development, could not only be compared to a psychically associative paralysis of function, but also to a symbolic paralysis of function.

Before I continue with the history of my patient I will add something about her behaviour during the second period of the treatment. Throughout this whole analysis I made use of the method of evoking pictures and ideas by pressing her head, a method, therefore, which would be inapplicable without the full cooperation and voluntary attention of the patient. At times her behaviour left nothing to be desired, and at such periods it was really surprising how promptly and how infallibly the individual scenes belonging to one theme succeeded each other in chronological order. It was as if she read from a large picture-book, the pages of which passed in review before her

[1] *Cathexis* means a sum of energy or affect which invests an idea or an act.

eyes. At other times there seemed to be inhibitions, the nature of which I could not at that time surmise. When I applied pressure, she maintained that nothing came into her mind; I repeated the pressure and told her to wait, but still nothing would come. At first, when such obstinacy manifested itself, I determined to discontinue the work and to try again later, as the day seemed unpropitious. Two observations, however, caused me to change my procedure. Firstly, because such failure of this method occurred only when I found Elisabeth cheerful and free from pain and never when she had a bad day; secondly, because she frequently made assertions of seeing nothing after the lapse of a long pause during which her tense and absorbed mind betrayed to me some inner psychic process. I, therefore, decided to assume that the method never failed, that under the pressure of my hands Elisabeth had each time perceived some idea or had seen some picture, but that she was not always ready to impart it to me and attempted to suppress what was conjured up. I could think of two motives for such concealment; either Elisabeth subjected the idea that came to her mind to an unjustified criticism, thinking it not sufficiently important or unfit as an answer to the question, or she feared to say it because that statement was too disagreeable to her. I, therefore, proceeded as if I were perfectly convinced of the reliability of my technique. Whenever she asserted that nothing came into her mind, I did not let that pass. I assured her that something must have come to her, but that perhaps she was not attentive enough, that I was quite willing to repeat the pressure. I also told her not to entertain any doubts concerning the correctness of the idea which presented itself to her mind, be it suitable or not, and I ended by saying that I knew well that something did come which she concealed from me and that, as long as she would continue to do so, she would not get rid of her pains. Through such urging I came to the realization that no pressure remained unsuccessful. I then had to assume that I correctly recognized the state of affairs, and, indeed, I won perfect confidence in my technique through this analysis. It often happened that she did not make a statement until after the third pressure, and then added, "Why I could have told you that the first time."—"Indeed, why did you not say it?"—"I thought that it was not correct," or "I thought that I could avoid it, but it recurred each time." During

this difficult work I began to attach a profounder significance to the resistance[1] which the patient showed in the reproduction of her recollections, and I carefully noted these occasions in which it was especially striking.

I now come to the description of the third period of our treatment. The patient felt better; she was psychically unburdened and less restrained in her behaviour; but the pains were manifestly not removed, and reappeared from time to time with the old severity. The imperfect cure went hand in hand with the imperfect analysis; as yet, I did not know in what moment and through what mechanisms the pains originated. During the reproduction of the most manifold scenes of the second period and the observation of the patient's resistance towards the reproduction, I had a definite suspicion which I did not dare use as a basis for my action. An accidental observation turned the issue. While working with the patient one day, I heard the steps of a man in the adjacent room and a rather pleasant voice asking some questions. My patient immediately arose, requesting me to discontinue the treatment for the day because she heard her brother-in-law, who had just arrived, asking for her. Before this disturbance she was free from pains, but now she betrayed by her mien and gait the sudden appearance of violent pains. This strengthened my suspicion, and I decided to elicit the decisive explanation.

I therefore questioned her again concerning the circumstances and causes of the first appearance of the pains. Her thoughts were directed to the summer resort in that watering place where she had been before making the journey to Gastein. A number of scenes were reproduced which had already been treated less exhaustively. They recalled her frame of mind at that time, the exhaustion following the worriment about her mother's vision, and the nursing of her mother during the time of the operation, and her final despair at being unable as a lonesome girl to enjoy or accomplish anything in life. Until then she felt strong enough to dispense with the help of a man, but now she was overcome by a feeling of her womanly weakness, a yearning for love in which, to put it in her own words, her "obdurate self began to soften." In such humour, the happy marriage of her younger sister made the profoundest

[1] The mechanisms of resistance, which the author now counts among the great pillars of psycho-analytic technique, are mentioned here for the first time.—Tr.

impression on her. She thought how affectionately he cared for her, how they understood each other by a mere glance, and how sure they seemed to be of each other. It was truly regrettable that the second pregnancy followed so closely upon the first; her sister knew that this was the cause of her suffering, but how willingly she endured it, and all because he was the cause of it. The brother-in-law did not at first wish to participate in the walk which was so intimately connected with Elisabeth's pain; he preferred to remain home with his sick wife, but the latter urged him with a glance to go because she thought that it would give Elisabeth pleasure. Elisabeth remained with him throughout the whole walk; they spoke about the most varied and intimate things; she found herself in thorough accord with all he said, and she became overwhelmed with a desire to possess a man like him. This was followed by a scene a few days later, when, on the morning after their departure, she visited the point commanding the beautiful view which had been their favourite walk. There she seated herself upon a stone and again dreamed of her sister's happiness and of a man like her brother-in-law who could engage her affections. When she arose, she had pains which again disappeared, and only in the afternoon after having taken the warm bath did they reappear, remaining ever since. I attempted to investigate the thoughts which occupied her mind while taking the bath, but all I could obtain was that the bathroom recalled her absent sister because she had lived in the same house.

For some time the state of affairs must have been clear to me. The patient seemed absorbed in painfully-sweet recollections, so that she was wholly unconscious of the drift of her thoughts and continued to reproduce her reminiscences. She spoke of the time in Gastein, the worry connected with the expectations of the letter, finally the information of her sister's illness, the long wait until the evening when she could finally leave Gastein, the journey with its tormenting uncertainties during a sleepless night—all these remarks were accompanied by a violent aggravation of the pain. I asked her if during the journey she thought of the sad possibility which she afterward found realized. She answered that she carefully avoided the thought, but that in her opinion, her mother expected the worst from the very beginning. This was followed by the reminiscences of her arrival in Vienna—the impressions which she received from the relatives at the station, the

short journey from Vienna to the neighbouring summer resort where her sister lived, the arrival in the evening, the hasty walk through the garden to the door of the little garden pavilion—the silence in the house, the oppressive darkness, the fact of not having been received by the brother-in-law. She then recalled standing before the bed seeing the deceased, and in the moment of the awful certainty that the beloved sister had died without having taken leave of them and without having her last days eased through their nursing—in that very moment another thought flashed through Elisabeth's brain, which now peremptorily repeated itself. The thought, which flashed like dazzling lightning through the darkness, was, "Now he is free again, and I can become his wife."

Of course, now everything was clear. The analyst's effort was richly repaid. The ideas of *defence* against an unbearable idea, the origin of hysterical symptoms through conversion of psychic into physical excitement, the formation of a separate psychic group by an act of the will, which led to the defence—all these were in that moment palpably presented before my eyes. Thus, and thus alone, did things happen here. This girl entertained an affectionate regard for her brother-in-law, against the acceptance of which into her consciousness her whole moral being struggled. She succeeded in sparing herself the painful consciousness that she was in love with her sister's husband by creating for herself instead bodily pains, and at the moment when this certainty wished to thrust itself into her consciousness (while she walked with him, during that morning reverie, in the bath, and before her sister's bed) her pains originated through a successful conversion into the somatic. At the time she came under my care, the isolation from her awareness of the group of ideas referring to this love affair had already been accomplished, else I believe that she would never have agreed to this mode of treatment. The resistance with which she repeatedly opposed the reproduction of the traumatically effective scenes really corresponded to the energy with which the unbearable idea had been crowded out from the associations.

For the therapist there now came a sorry time. The effect of the resumption of that repressed idea was crushing for the poor child. When I summed up the whole situation with these prosaic words: "You were really for a long time in love with your brother-in-law," she complained of the most horrible pains; she made another despairing effort to reject the explanation, saying that it was not true, that I suggested it to her, it could not be, she was incapable of such baseness, and that she would never forgive herself for it. It was quite easy to prove to her that her own information allowed no other interpretation, but it took a long time before the two reasons that I offered for consolation, namely, that one is not responsible for one's feelings, and that her behaviour, her sickness under those circumstances, was sufficient proof of her moral nature —I say it took a long time before these consolations made an impression on her.

I was now forced to pursue more than one course in order to alleviate the patient. In the first place, I wished to give her the opportunity to rid herself by ab-reaction of the material long since accumulated. We investigated the first impressions of the relations with her brother-in-law, the beginning of those unconsciously kept affectionate regards. We found here all those little indications and forebodings which on retrospection showed a fully developed passion. In his first visit to the house, he mistook her for his destined bride and greeted her before he greeted her older and more homely sister. One evening they entertained each other so vivaciously and seemed to understand each other so well that the bride interrupted them with this half serious remark: "You two, indeed, would have suited each other very nicely." On another occasion, while at a social gathering where none knew of the engagement, the conversation drifted to the young man, and a young lady indiscreetly remarked about a blemish in his figure, a juvenile joint affliction. The bride herself remained calm, while Elisabeth flew into a passion, and with an ardour which even she herself could not afterwards understand, defended the straight form of her future brother-in-law. While we worked our way through these reminiscences, it became clear to Elisabeth that her affection for her brother-in-law had slumbered in her for a long time, perhaps since the beginning of their relations, and had concealed itself so long under the mask of a mere kinsmanlike affection, as only her very delicate family feeling would allow.

This ab-reaction benefited her much, but I was able to give her still more relief by taking a friendly interest in her present state of affairs. With this object in view I sought an interview with Mrs. von R, whom I found to be an intelligent and refined lady, whose courage to face life, however, was somewhat impaired through the last misfortunes. From her I learned that the accusation of rude extortion, which the older brother-in-law had brought against the widower, and which was so painful to Elisabeth, had to be retracted on closer investigation. The character of the young man remained untarnished; it was merely a misunderstanding, an easily conceived difference of opinion concerning the valuation of money that could arise between the merchant, to whom money is only a working tool, and the official—that is all there was to this seemingly so painful incident. I begged the mother to give Elisabeth all explanations that she might hereafter need, and to offer her in the future that opportunity for unburdening her mind to which I had accustomed her.

Naturally I was also anxious to know what chance there was for the fulfilment of the girl's present conscious wish. Here things were less favourable! The mother stated that for some time she had had an inkling of Elisabeth's affections for her brother-in-law; of course, she did not know that it had existed during the lifetime of her sister. Whoever saw them both in friendly intercourse—of late, to be sure, only seldom—could entertain no doubt of the girl's anxiety to please him. However, neither she, the mother, nor the advisers of the family, showed any particular inclination to bring about a matrimonial union between the two. The health of the young man had not been very good and had received a setback through the death of his beloved wife, and it was not at all certain that he had sufficiently recovered from the shock to enter into a new marriage. It was quite probable that this was the reason for his reserve, perhaps also because he was not sure of his position and wished to avoid all obvious gossip. With such a reserve on both sides, the solution for which Elisabeth was yearning was likely to fail.

I informed the girl of everything that I had heard from her mother and had the satisfaction of seeing her benefited by the explanation concerning the money affair. On the other hand, I urged her to bear calmly the uncertainties of her future which could not be dismissed. The advancing summer forced us to bring the treatment to an end. She now felt better, and, since we had discussed the causes to which the pain could be traced, she no longer complained of pain. We both felt that the work had been finished, although I felt that the ab-reaction of the suppressed love was really not as complete as it should have been. I regarded her as cured and urged her to continue independently the solution after the way had been cleared for it, to which she agreed. She left with her mother for a summer resort where they were to join the older sister and her family.

I still have something more to report about the further course of Miss Elisabeth von R's disease. A few weeks after our parting I received a despairing letter from her mother, informing me that, at the first attempt to draw Elisabeth into a conversation about her love affairs, she became very excited and refused to talk, and since then had suffered from violent pains. She was very indignant at my having betrayed her confidence and was perfectly inaccessible, so that the treatment seemed a complete failure. She wished to know what was to be done, for of me she would hear nothing. I made no reply. It was to be expected that after she had been relieved from my discipline she would make another attempt to reject her mother's interference and return to her reserve. I was, however, quite certain that everything would adjust itself, and that my efforts had not been in vain. Two months later they returned to Vienna and the colleague to whom I was grateful for the case informed me that Elisabeth was perfectly well, and that her behaviour was normal although occasionally she had slight pains. Since then she has repeatedly sent me similar messages, each time promising to visit me, which she has never done. This is quite characteristic of the personal relationship formed during such treatment. My colleague assured me that she could be considered cured. The relation of the brother-in-law to the family had not been changed.

In the spring of 1894 I was informed that she would be present at a private ball to which I could gain access. I did not let the opportunity escape me and saw my former patient gliding along in a rapid dance. Since then, following her own inclination, she married a stranger.

EPICRISIS

I have not always been a psycho-therapist, but like other neuro-pathologists I was educated to methods of focal diagnoses and electrical prognosis, so that even I myself am struck by the fact that the case histories which I am writing read like novels and, as it were, dispense with the serious features of the scientific character. Yet, I must console myself with the fact that the nature of the subject is ap-

parently more responsible for this issue than my own predilection. Focal diagnosis and electrical reactions are really not important in the study of hysteria, whereas a detailed discussion of the psychic processes, as one is wont to hear it from the poet, and the application of a few psychological formulæ, allows one to gain an insight into the course of events of hysteria. Such case histories should be considered like psychiatrical ones, but they have the advantage over the latter in the fact that they give the intimate connection between the history of the disease and the morbid symptoms, a thing for which we are still looking in vain in the histories of other psychoses.[1]

With the description of the treatment I endeavoured to interweave the explanations which I gave about the case of Miss Elisabeth von R, and it will perhaps not be superfluous to summarize here the essential features. I have discussed the character of the patient and the features which repeat themselves in so many hysterics, and which we really cannot consider as degenerative. I mentioned the talent, the ambition, the moral sensitiveness, the immense yearning for love, which found its gratification in the family, the independence of her nature reaching beyond the womanly ideal, which manifested itself largely in obstinacy, pugnaciousness, and shut-in-ness. According to the information of my colleague, no hereditary taints could be shown on either side of the family. Her mother, to be sure, suffered for years from some indefinite neurotic depression, but her brothers and sisters, her father and his family, belonged to the even-tempered and not to the nervous, type. There was no serious case of psychosis in any near relatives.

Her nature was influenced by painful emotions, the foremost of which was the debilitating influence of a long attendance upon her beloved sick father.

That nursing of the sick plays such a significant rôle in the histories of hysterias has its good reasons. A number of effective factors, which one finds here, are quite obvious; thus, the disturbance of the physical health through interrupted sleep, neglect of nourishment, and the reaction of a constantly gnawing worriment on the vegatative functions. The most important factor, however, is in my estimation to be found elsewhere. He whose mind is occupied

---

[1] This situation no longer obtains in present-day psychiatry. Beginning with the Zurich School under the stimulation of Bleuler, the descriptive psychiatry of Kraepelin long ago gave way to the interpretative psychiatry of the present.—Tr.

with the hundred different tasks of nursing which succeed each other continuously for weeks and months, gets into the habit, on the one hand, of suppressing all signs of his own emotions, and on the other hand, his attention is soon turned away from his own impressions because he has neither the time nor the strength to do them justice. Thus, the nurse accumulates in himself an overabundance of affective impressions which he or she barely perceives clearly enough; at any rate, they are not dissipated by ab-reaction; that is, he or she creates for himself the material for a *retention hysteria*. If the patient recovers, these impressions naturally lose their value, but if he dies and one goes into a period of mourning during which only that which refers to the deceased seems of value, the impressions waiting for discharge appear in turn, and, after a brief pause of exhaustion, the hysteria, the germ of which originated during the nursing, bursts forth.

The same fact of subsequent adjustment to traumas accumulated during nursing is occasionally also encountered where the general impression of being sick does not ensue, but where the mechanism of hysteria, nevertheless, can be noticed. Thus, I have known a highly gifted but slightly nervous lady whose whole personality suggests the hysteric, yet she never became a burden to the doctor and was never forced to interrupt the exercise of her duties. This lady had nursed three or four of her dear ones until they died, which caused her each time a complete physical exhaustion, yet these sad duties have never made her sick. However, shortly after the death of the patient she begins her work of reproduction, in which she reviews the scenes of the disease, and of the death. Each day—one might say, at her leisure—she goes over again every impression, crying over it, and consoling herself. Such adjustment continues through her daily occupations without any confusion of the two activities. Everything passes before her chronologically. Whether the memory work of one day precisely corresponded to a day of the past, I am unable to say. I presume that it depends on the leisure which is left to her by the current affairs of the household.

Aside from this "after crying," which follows these demises after short intervals, this lady periodically observed the anniversaries of the various catastrophies, and here her vivid visual reproductions and her affective manifestations follow faithfully the dates. Thus, for example,

I found her in tears, and, on sympathetic inquiry as to what occurred on that day, she half irritably remarked, "Nothing on that day except that Professor N was again here and gave us to understand that things were hopeless— at that time I had no time to cry." She referred to the last illness of her husband, who died three years before. It would have been very interesting to know whether she always repeated the same scenes on these recurring anniversaries, or whether, as I suppose, in the interest of my theory, other details presented themselves each time for ab-reaction. I was, however, unable to find anything definite about this; the wise and courageous woman was ashamed of the intensity with which those reminiscences acted upon her.[1]

I repeat that this woman was not sick and that subsequent ab-reaction, despite all resemblance, is still not a hysterical process; one may ask why after one nursing there results a hysteria and after another none. It cannot lie in

---

[1] To my surprise, I once discovered that such subsequent ab-reaction—through other impressions than nursing—may form the content of an otherwise enigmatic neurosis. It was the case of a pretty girl of nineteen, Miss Matilda H, whom I first saw with an incomplete paralysis of the legs, and months later I was again called because her character had changed. She was depressed and tired of living, lacked all consideration of her mother, and was irritable and unapproachable. The whole picture of the patient did not seem to me to be that of an ordinary melancholia. She could easily be put into a somnambulic state, and I made use of this peculiarity to impart to her each time commands and suggestions to which she listened in her profound sleep and responded with profuse tears, but which, however, caused but little change in her condition. One day while hypnotized she became talkative and informed me that the reason for her depression was the breaking of her betrothal many months before. She stated that, on closer acquaintance with her fiancé, the things displeasing to her and her mother became more and more evident in him. On the other hand, the material advantages of the engagement were too tangible to make the decision of a rupture easy; thus, both of them hesitated for a long time. She then lapsed into a condition of indecision in which she allowed everything to pass apathetically and finally her mother pronounced for her the decisive "no." Shortly afterwards she awoke as from a dream and began to occupy herself fervently with the thoughts about the broken betrothal, she began to weigh the pros and cons, a process which she continued for some time. She continued to live in that time of doubt, and entertained daily the moods and the thoughts, which would have been appropriate for that day. The irritability against her mother could only be explained by circumstances that existed at that time. Next to this mental activity she found her present life a mere phantom, just like a dream. I did not again succeed in getting the girl to talk—I continued my exhortations during deep somnambulism. I saw her each time burst into tears without, however, receiving any answer from her. But one day, it was near the anniversary of the engagement, the whole state of depression disappeared. This was attributed to the success of my great hypnotic cure.

the personal predisposition, for the lady whom I have here in mind showed it in the most prolific manner.

I now return to Miss Elisabeth von R. While nursing her father, there occurred for the first time an hysterical symptom in the form of a pain in a definite location on the right thigh. The mechanism of this symptom is fully explained on an analytic basis. It occurred in a moment during which the ideas of her duties towards her sick father came into conflict with the content of her erotic yearning, which she then entertained. Under vivid self-reproach, she decided in favour of the former and created for herself the hysterical pain. According to the conception explained by the theory of conversion in hysteria, the process could be described as follows: She repressed the erotic idea from her consciousness and changed the sum of the affect into somatic sensations of pain. Whether this first conflict occurred only once, or repeated itself, is not clear. The latter is more probable. Quite a similar conflict—of a higher moral significance, and even better demonstrated by the analysis—repeated itself after years and led to the aggravation of the same pain and to its dissemination beyond its original limits. Again, it was an erotic idea which came into conflict with all her moral conceptions, for her affection for her brother-in-law, both during the life and after the death of her sister, and the thought that she should yearn just for this man, was very disagreeable to her. This analysis gives detailed information about this conflict which represents the pivotal point in the history of her malady. The patient's affection for her brother-in-law might have begun to germinate long ago, but in favour of its development was the physical exhaustion from the recent nursing, and her moral exhaustion from years of disillusionment, which then began to break down her reserve and caused her to confess to herself the need of the love of a man. During a relationship which extended over weeks (in that summer resort), this erotic desire attained full development simultaneously with the pain, and analysis shows that during that time the patient was in a special psychic state, which, in conjunction with the desire and pain, seems to afford an understanding of the process in the sense of the conversion theory.

I must place reliance on the statement that the patient's affection for her brother-in-law, intensive as it was, was not *clearly known* to her except on certain rare occasions, and then

only momentarily. If that were not so, she would have become conscious of the incompatibility between this desire and her moral ideas, and would have had to endure the same mental agonies which I saw her suffer after our analysis. Her reminiscences gave us no information concerning such suffering (these she spared herself), and as a result, the love itself did not become clear to her. At that time, as well as during the analysis, her love for her brother-in-law existed in the form of a foreign body in her consciousness without entering into any relationship with her other ideation. In reference to this love there existed the peculiar condition of knowing and simultaneously not knowing; it was the condition of the split-off psychic group. When we assert that this love was not *clearly known* to her, we mean exactly what we say. We do not mean a lower quality or a lesser degree of consciousness, but a separation of the free associative mental process from the rest of the ideational content.

How did it happen that such an intensively accentuated group of ideas could be kept so isolated? For generally the rôle of an idea in the associations actually increases with the size of its affect.

This question can be answered if we take into account two facts which we can use as if proven: (1) That the hysterical pain originated simultaneously with the formation of these separate psychic groups, (2) that the patient exerted great resistance against the attempt to bring about the association between the separate psychic groups and the rest of the content of consciousness, and, when the union was nevertheless effected, she felt excessive psychic pain. Our conception of hysteria brings together these two factors with the fact of the splitting of consciousness, by asserting that (2) contains the indication of the *motive* for the splitting of consciousness, while (1) shows the *mechanism* of the same. The motive was that of *defense*, or the striving of the whole ego to get into harmony with this ideation group, and the mechanism was that of *conversion;* that is, instead of psychic pains which she spared herself, there appeared physical pains. A transformation was thus initiated which resulted in a *gain* insofar as the patient had escaped an unbearable psychic state; to be sure, this gain was obtained at the cost of a psychic anomaly, a splitting of consciousness and physical suffering, the pains, upon which an astasia-abasia was constructed.

To be sure, I can give no directions as to how one can produce in himself such a conversion. Apparently it is not done as one intentionally performs an arbitrary action; it is a process which takes place in a person under the impulse of the motive of defense, if he has a tendency for it in his organization, or if it is brought about by temporary modifications.

One has the right to examine the theory more closely and ask: "What is it then that becomes transformed into physical pains?" The cautious reply will be: "Something out of which psychic pains could have and should have been formed." If one wishes to venture further and attempt a kind of algebraic formulation of the ideational mechanism, one might perhaps attribute to the ideational complex of this desire (which remained unconscious) a certain amount of affect and designate the latter quality as the thing converted. A direct deduction of this conception would be that through such conversion the "unconscious love" forfeits so much of its intensity that it becomes reduced to a weak idea, and its existence as a separate psychic group is made possible only through this weakening. However, the present case is not capable of throwing light on this delicate matter. It probably corresponds only to an imperfect conversion. From other cases it seems quite probable that there are also perfect conversions, and that in these the unbearable idea actually becomes *repressed,* as only an idea of very little intensity could be repressed. After an associative union has been reestablished, the patients assure us that since the origin of the hysterical symptoms their unbearable ideas had never occupied their minds.

I have stated above that on certain occasions, though only transitorily, the patient consciously recognized the love for her brother-in-law. Such a moment occurred when, for example, at the death-bed of her sister the thought flashed through her mind, "Now he is free and I can become his wife." I must discuss the significance of these factors for the conception of the whole neurosis. However, I think that in the assumption of a *defence hysteria* there is already the requisite that at least one such moment should have occurred. For consciousness really does not know in advance when such an unbearable idea will present itself. For the unbearable idea, which is later excluded with its appendage for the formation of a separate psychic group, must have been originally in the mental activity, else there would have

been no conflict to lead to its exclusion.[1] Just such moments should be designated as *traumatic*. It is in them that the conversion takes place and results in the splitting of consciousness and the hysterical symptoms. Everything tends to show that in Miss Elisabeth von R there were a number of such moments (the scenes of the walking, morning meditation, bath, and at the bedside of her sister), and perhaps new moments of this kind also occurred during the treatment. The multiplicity of such traumatic moments is made possible by the fact that an experience, similar to the one which first initiated the unbearable idea, introduces new emotions to the separated psychic groups and thus transitorily abolishes the success of the conversion. The ego is forced to occupy itself with this suddenly reinforced and flared-up idea, and must later restore the former state through new conversions. Miss Elisabeth, who was in constant relation with her brother-in-law, must have been particularly exposed to the appearance of new traumas. A case whose traumatic history has been finished in the past would have been more desirable for this discussion.

I must now occupy myself with the point which I have designated as a difficulty for the understanding of this case history. On the analytical basis, I assumed that the first conversion took place in the patient while she nursed her father, at the time when her duties as a nurse came into conflict with her erotic yearnings, and that this process was the model for the later ones which led to the outbreak of the disease in the Alpine spa. But, according to the patient's statement, she had *not at all suffered from any pains and weakness* at the time of the nursing and the period following it, which I designated as the *first period.* To be sure, during the illness of her father she was once bedridden for a few days with pains in her legs, but it is doubtful whether this attack already belonged to the hysteria. A causal relation between these first pains and any psychic impressions could not be demonstrated by analysis; it is possible, even probable, that at that time we dealt with a common rheumatic muscular pain. But if we should assume that this first attack of pain was the result of an hysterical conversion in consequence of the rejection of erotic thoughts which then existed, the fact, nevertheless, remains that the pains

---

[1] It is different in a hypnoid hysteria. Here the content of the separate psychic groups may never have been in the ego consciousness.

disappeared after a few days, so that the patient actually behaved differently than she seemed to show during the analysis. During the reproduction of the so-called first period, all her statements concerning the illness and death of her father, the impressions relating to her first brother-in-law, etc., all these were accompanied by manifestations of pain, while at the time she really experienced these impressions she felt no pains. Is this not a contradiction which is likely to diminish considerably the confidence in the explanatory value of such an analysis?

I believe that I can explain the contradiction by assuming that the pains—the product of the conversion—did not originate while the patient experienced the impressions during the first period, but subsequently, that is, in the second period when the patient reproduced these impressions in her mind. The conversion did not follow the fresh impressions, but the memories of the same. I even believe that such a process is not at all unusual in hysteria and regularly participates in creating hysterical symptoms. Nevertheless, as such an assertion does not seem plausible, I shall attempt to make it more credible by citing other experiences.

During a similar analysis, it once happened that a new hysterical symptom was formed during the treatment, so that I could attempt its removal on the day after its origin.

I will describe the essential features of the history of this patient. They are simple, but not without interest.

Miss Rosalia H, twenty-three years old, who for a number of years made great efforts to educate herself as a singer, complained that her beautiful voice did not obey her in certain notes. She felt choking and tightening sensations in the throat, so that the tones sounded strained, and her teacher could, therefore, not yet permit her to appear in public. Although this imperfection affected only her middle notes, it could not be explained on the basis of a defect of her vocal organs, for at times this disturbance did not show itself and her teacher was very pleased with her, but at other times, the slightest excitement, seemingly without provocation, evoked the choking sensation, and prevented free expansion of the voice. It was not difficult to recognize in this annoying sensation an hysterical conversion. Whether there was really a contracture of certain muscles of the vocal chords could not be veri-

fied.[1] In the hypnotic analysis, which I undertook with this girl, I found out the following concerning her vicissitudes and the ailments occasioned through them. She became an orphan at an early age and was brought up by her aunt, who had many children and she had to share the life of a most unfortunate family existence. The husband of this aunt, seemingly a pathological personality, abused his wife and children in the most brutal manner, and what especially pained her was his unconcealed sexual preference for the servant and nurse girls in the house. This became even more obnoxious as the children grew older. When her aunt died, Rosalia became the protectress of the orphaned children, who were harassed by their father. She took her duties seriously, fought through all conflicts, and had to exert her greatest efforts to suppress the manifestations of her contempt for her uncle. It was then that the choking sensation in her throat originated. Whenever she was compelled to swallow an affront, whenever she had to remain silent on hearing a provoking accusation, she perceived a scratching in her throat, the tightening and failure of her voice; in brief, she had all the localized sensations in her larynx and pharynx which now disturbed her in singing. It was conceivable that she sought the possibility of making herself independent in order to escape the excitement and the painful impressions which were daily occurrences in her uncle's house. An efficient music teacher took an unselfish interest in her, assuring her that her voice entitled her to choose the profession of singing. She began secretly to take lessons of him, and because she often went for her lessons with the choking sensation in her throat, following some violent scene in the house, a connection was formed between the singing and the hysterical paresthesia for which a way was prepared by the sensitiveness of the vocal organs during singing. The apparatus of which she should have had free control was filled

[1] I had under observation another case in which a contracture of the masseters made it impossible for the artist to sing. The young lady in question, through painful experiences in the family, was forced to go on the stage. While rehearsing in Rome, in great excitement, she suddenly perceived the sensation of being unable to close her opened mouth and sank fainting to the floor. The physician, who was called, closed her jaws forcibly, but since that time the patient had been unable to open her jaws more than a finger's breadth and had to give up her newly chosen profession. When she came under my care, many years later, the motives for that excitement apparently had been over for some time, for massage in a light hypnosis sufficed to open her mouth widely. The lady has since then sung in public.

with the remnants of innervation from those numerous scenes of suppressed excitement. Since then she has left her uncle's house and has moved to another city, so as to be away from the family, but her ailments were not benefited by it. No other hysterical symptoms were discovered in this pretty and unusually bright girl.

I endeavoured to cure this *retention-hysteria* by a reproduction of all the exciting impressions and by subsequent ab-reaction. I afforded her the opportunity of railing against her uncle in long speeches and of telling him the bare truth to his face, etc. The treatment benefited her, but unfortunately she lived here under quite unfavourable conditions. She had no luck with her relatives. She was the guest of another uncle who treated her with friendliness, but just for that reason she incurred the displeasure of her aunt. The latter believed that her husband evinced too marked an interest in his niece and made it a point of opposing the girl's stay in Vienna. She, herself, in her youth was obliged to relinquish a desire of becoming an artist and was now jealous of her niece because she had the opportunity to develop her talent, not considering that it was not mere desire, but a wish to become independent, which led her niece to take this step. Rosalia felt so uncomfortable in the house that she, for instance, did not dare to sing or play the piano when her aunt was within hearing distance, and carefully avoided either singing or playing anything for her aged uncle—her mother's brother—whenever her aunt was home. While I was endeavouring to efface the traces of the old excitements, new ones originated through these relations with her hosts, and finally interfered with the success of my treatment, and prematurely interrupted the cure.

One day the patient came to me with a new symptom hardly twenty-four hours old. She complained of a disagreeable prickling sensation in the fingertips, which had manifested itself every few hours since the day before, and forced her to make very peculiar jerky movements. I could not see the attack; otherwise, I would have guessed the cause from seeing the motions of the fingers, but I immediately endeavoured to trace through hypnotic analysis the causation of this symptom (it was really a minor hysterical attack). As the whole thing existed only for a short time, I hoped to be able to explain it and quickly remove it. To my surprise, she reproduced, without any hesitation in chronological order, a whole row of scenes beginning in her early childhood. All these had perhaps the same characteristics in the fact that she had suffered an injustice without defense, something which could make her fingers jerk; for example, scenes like the one of being forced to hold out her hand in school while the teacher struck it with a ruler. But they were all banal causes, to which I would have gladly opposed the right to enter into the aetiology of hysterical symptoms. It was different, however, with one scene of her early girlhood, which was connected with the others. The bad uncle who suffered from rheumatism asked her to massage his back. She did not dare refuse him. He was in bed while she was doing it and he suddenly threw off the covers, jumped up, and attempted to grab her and throw her down. She naturally stopped the massage and in a moment escaped and locked herself in her own room. She evidently did not like to recall this experience and could not say whether she had seen anything when the man suddenly exposed himself. The sensations in the fingers could be explained as due to the suppressed impulse to punish him, or it might simply have originated from the fact that she was at that time massaging him. Only after this scene did she begin to talk about the one which she experienced yesterday after which the sensitiveness and jerkiness of the fingers appeared as a recurring memory symbol. The uncle with whom she now lived begged her to play something for him. She sat at the piano and accompanied herself singing, believing that her aunt was out. Suddenly she appeared in the doorway, Rosalia jumped up, closed the piano, and flung away the sheet of music. We can guess what memories came to her mind, and the train of thought which she tried to ward off at that moment, for the exasperation brought on by the unjust accusation should have really urged her to leave the house, but on account of her illness she was forced to remain in Vienna and had no other shelter. The movement of the fingers which I saw during the reproduction of this scene resembled a continuous jerking, as if one literally and figuratively would reject something like throwing away a sheet of music or rejecting an unreasonable demand.

She was quite positive in her assurance that she did not perceive the symptom before, that it was not caused by the scenes previously related. Was there anything else to be assumed except that the scene experienced yesterday had in the first place awakened the recollection of a former similar content, and that it then developed into a memory symbol for the whole group of recollections? The conversion was, on the one hand, furnished with newly experienced affects, and, on the other, with recollected affects.

When we consider this state of affairs, we must admit that in the origin of hysterical symptoms such a process is the rule rather than the exception. Whenever I seek for the determinants of such states, I frequently find not a single but a group of similar traumatic motives.[1] In some of these cases it could be ascertained that this particular symptom had already existed for a short time after the first trauma and then subsided, but reappeared after the next trauma and became fixed. Yet, no real distinction can be made between those of temporary appearance and those which remained entirely latent causations. In a large majority of cases, it was also found that the first trauma had left no symptoms, while a later trauma of the same kind produced a symptom for the origin of which the cooperation of the former motives could not be dispensed with, and for the solution of which it required a consideration of all the motives. Translating this into the language of conversion theory, this undeniable fact of the summation of traumas and the erstwhile latency of the symptoms simply means that the conversion can be brought about from a fresh, as well as from a remembered, affect, and this assumption fully explains the contradiction which seems to exist in the history and analysis of Miss Elisabeth von R.

For there is no question that normal persons continue to carry in their consciousness a large number of ideas with unadjusted affects. The assertion which I have just defended merely approximates the behaviour of hysteria to that of the normal. It is apparently reduced to a quantitative factor; it is simply a question of *how many* such affective strains an organization can endure. Even an hysterical person will be able to retain a certain amount in an adjusted state, but if, through a summation of similar motives, it increases beyond the individual's endurance, the impetus for conversion is formed. It is, therefore, no singular theory but almost a postulate to say that the formation of hysterical symptoms may also be brought about at the cost of recollected affects.

I have now occupied myself with the *motive*

and *mechanism* of this case of hysteria; it still remains to discuss the *determination* of the hysterical symptoms. Why should just the pains in the legs have been selected to represent the psychic pains? The circumstances of the case point to the fact that this somatic pain was not created by the neurosis, but was merely utilized, aggravated, and retained by it. I will add that, in most of the cases of hysterical algias into which I have been able to gain an insight, the conditions were similar, that is, there was to begin with always a real organically founded pain. It is always the most common, the most widespread, pain of humanity that seem to be most frequently called upon to play a part in hysteria. Among the most common are the periosteal and the neuralgic pains of the teeth, headaches which originate from so many different sources, and not in a lesser degree the so often mistaken rheumatic pains of the muscles. The first attack of pain which Miss Elisabeth von R had while she nursed her father I consider to have been organically determined, for I received no information when I investigated for its psychic motive, and I admit that I am inclined to attribute differential diagnostic significance to my methods of evoking hidden memories, if they are carefully applied. This original rheumatic pain[2] became the memory symbol for her painful psychic excitements, and as far as I can see, for more than one reason. First, and principally, because it existed in consciousness almost simultaneously with the other excitements, and, second, because it was, or could be connected in many ways with the ideation content of that time. At all events, it was perhaps a remote consequence of the nursing, of her want of exercise, and of the poor nutrition entailed by her duties. But this hardly became clear to the patient, and what is more important is that she had to perceive it during important moments of the nursing, as, for example, when she jumped out of bed in the cold room to respond to her father's call. Even more decisive for the direction taken by the conversion must have been the other manner of associative connection, namely, the fact that for many days one of her painful legs came in contact with the swollen leg of her father during the changing of the bandages. The location on the right leg distinguished by this contact henceforth remained the focus and starting point of the pains; it was an artificial

[1] Compare here the nice examples of Mrs. Emmy in case II of *Studien über Hysterie*, 1895.

[2] But perhaps spinal neurasthenic?

hysterogenic zone, the origin of which can be plainly seen in this case.

If anyone should be surprised at the associative connection between physical pain and psychic affect, thinking it to be too manifold and artificial, I should answer that such surprise is just as unfair as to be surprised over the fact that "just the richest people in the world possess most of the money." Where prolific connections do not exist, there is naturally no formation of hysterical symptoms, and conversion does not find its way. I can also state that, in reference to determinations, the case of Miss Elisabeth von R belongs to the simpler ones. In the case of Mrs. Cecilia M, particularly, I had to solve the most intricate knots of this kind.

I have already discussed in the case history how the astasia-abasia of our patient was built up on those pains after a definite path was opened to the conversion. But, there, too, I have expressed the opinion that the patient created or aggravated the disturbance of function through symbolization. For her dependence and helplessness to change anything in the circumstances, she found a somatic expression in the astasia-abasia, and the expressions "to make no headway," "to have no support," etc., formed the bridge for this new act of conversion. I will endeavour to support this conception by other examples.

Conversion on the basis of coincidence in otherwise existing associative connections seems to exert the least claims on the hysterical predisposition; on the other hand, conversion through symbolization seems to require a higher grade of hysterical modification, a fact also demonstrated in Miss Elisabeth von R in the later stages of her hysteria. The nicest examples of symbolization I have observed in Mrs. Cecilia M, whom I can call my most difficult and most instructive case. I have already mentioned that unfortunately this case history does not lend itself to detailed reproduction.

Among other things Mrs. Cecilia M also suffered from a most violent facial neuralgia, which appeared suddenly two or three times during the year and persisted for from five to ten days, resisting every remedy, and then ceased as if cut off. It limited itself to the second and third branches of the trigeminus, and as there was undoubtedly an excess of urates in the urine, and as a not very "clear acute rheumatism" played a certain part in the patient's history, it was reasonable to assume that we dealt with a gouty neuralgia. This

opinion was also shared by the consulting physicians who saw every attack. The neuralgia was treated by the methods in vogue, such as electric penciling, alkaline waters and purgatives, but it always remained uninfluenced until it found it convenient to make room for another symptom. In former years—the neuralgia was fifteen years old—the teeth were accused of preserving it and were condemned to extraction, and one fine morning, under narcosis the execution of seven of the culprits took place.[1] This did not run so smoothly, as the teeth were so firm that most of the roots were left behind. This cruel operation was followed by neither temporary nor permanent relief. At that time the neuralgia raged for months. Even while under my care, whenever she had neuralgia, the dentist was called and he always declared he found diseased roots. He started to get ready for an extraction, but usually he was soon interrupted, for the neuralgia suddenly ceased, and with it the desire for the dentist. During the intervals, the teeth did not ache at all. One day, just while another attack was raging, I put the patient into a hypnotic condition and placed an energetic interdiction on the pains, and from that moment they ceased. I then began to doubt the genuineness of this neuralgia.

About a year after this hypnotic remedial success, the condition of Mrs. Cecilia M took a new and surprising turn. There suddenly appeared other states than those that had been characteristic of the last years, but after some reflection the patient declared that all these conditions had existed before and were really scattered over the long period of her disease (thirty years). Indeed, a surprising abundance of hysterical incidents were unrolled which the patient was able to localize correctly in the past, and soon the frequently very entangled mental connections, which determined the sequence of these incidents, became recognizable. It was like a series of pictures with an explanatory text. Pitres, on describing his *délire ecmnésique*,[2] must have had in mind a similar case. The way such an hysterical condition belonging to the past was reproduced was

---

[1] It is remarkable how history repeats itself. Lest there should be some misunderstanding, I wish to remind the reader that the above was written in 1893, and the theory of focal infection, especially of the teeth, was brought out as something new in psychiatry only about ten years ago.—TR.

[2] A delirium in which the events of a period of time are forgotten, although prior events are remembered.—ED.

most remarkable. In the first place, while the patient was in the best of condition, there appeared a pathological mood of special colouring, which was regularly mistaken by the patient and was referred to a banal occurrence of the last hours. This increasing obnubilation of consciousness was followed by hysterical symptoms, such as hallucinations, pains, convulsions, and long declamations, and finally an event of the past attached itself to this hallucinatory manifestation which could explain the initial mood and determine the occasional symptoms. With this last part of the attack lucidity returned, the symptoms disappeared as if by magic, and good health again existed—until the next attack, which was half a day later. Usually I was called at the height of this condition. I induced hypnosis, evoked a reproduction of the traumatic events, and by artificial aid I curtailed the attack. Having gone through with the patient many hundreds of such cycles, I obtained the most instructive explanations concerning the determinants of hysterical symptoms. The joint observation with Breuer of this remarkable case was also the chief motive for the publication of our "Preliminary Communication."

In this connection, it finally also came to the reproduction of the facial neuralgias, which I myself had still treated as actual attacks. I was desirous of knowing whether we would find here a psychic causation. When I attempted to evoke the traumatic scene, the patient soon imagined herself in a period during which she felt marked psychic sensitiveness against her husband. She related a conversation with him and a remark that he made which annoyed her very much. She then suddenly grasped her cheek, crying aloud with pain, and said, "That was like a slap in the face." With this, both the attack and the pain came to an end.

There is no doubt that here, too, we dealt with a symbolization. She had felt as if she really received a slap in the face. Now everybody will ask how the sensation of "a slap in the face" can lead to the manifestation of a trigeminal neuralgia, to its limiting itself to the second and third branches, and to its being aggravated on opening the mouth, and on mastication (not on talking).

The following day the neuralgia reappeared, but this time it could be solved by the reproduction of another scene, the content of which equally showed a supposed insult. This process continued for nine days, and from the result it seemed that for years irritations, especially

through words, produced new attacks of this facial neuralgia by way of symbolization.

But finally we also succeeded in reproducing the first attack of the neuralgia which occurred more than fifteen years before. Here, there was no symbolization, but a conversion through coincidence. It was a painful sight which recalled to her mind a reproach, and this caused her to repress another series of thoughts. We had here, then, a case of conflict and defense, and the origin of the neuralgia in this moment could not be further explained if we did not wish to assume that she suffered at that time from slight toothache or facial pains, a thing not improbable, as she was then in the first months of pregnancy.

The result of the explanation showed that this neuralgia became the mark of a definite psychic excitement through the usual road of conversion, but that it could be awakened later through associative accusations from mental life and symbolic conversions. It was really the same procedure as we encountered in Miss Elisabeth von R.

I will now introduce another example which will illustrate the efficacy of symbolization under other determinants. On one occasion Mrs. Cecilia M was tormented by a violent pain in her right heel; she had stinging sensations on every step, which made walking impossible. The analysis conducted us to a time when the patient was in a foreign sanitarium. For eight days she kept to her room, and for the first time the house physician was to take her to the dining room. The pain came on while the patient took the physician's arm on leaving the room. It disappeared during the reproduction of this scene while she remarked that at that time she feared lest she would not make the "proper impression" on this strange society *rechte Auftreten* equals *proper stepping*.

This seems a striking, almost comical, example for the origin of hysterical symptoms through symbolization by means of a verbal expression. But closer investigation of the circumstances of that moment favours another conception. The patient suffered at that time from actual pains in her feet on account of which she remained in bed, and we can only assume that the fear, which obsessed her on taking the first steps, produced from the simultaneously existing pains the one symbolically appropriate symptom in the right heel, in order to form it into a psychic algia and to assist it to maintain itself for a long time.

Notwithstanding the fact that the mechanism of symbolization in these examples seems to be pushed into second rank, which certainly agrees with the rule, I have still other examples at my disposal which seem to demonstrate the origin of hysterical symptoms through symbolization only. One of the best is the following example which again refers to Mrs. Cecilia M. At the age of fifteen she once lay in bed watched by her austere grandmother. The girl suddenly cried out, complaining of having perceived a pain in the forehead between the eyes, which thereafter continued for weeks. On analysing this pain, which was reproduced after almost thirty years, she stated that her grandmother gazed at her so "piercingly" that it seemed as if her look penetrated deeply into her brain. She was really afraid of being looked upon suspiciously by this old lady. On reproducing this thought she burst into loud laughter and the pain ceased. Here I find nothing other than the mechanism of symbolization which in a way stands midway between the mechanism of *auto-suggestion* and that of *conversion.*

The study of Mrs. Cecilia M gave me the opportunity to gather a collection of such symbolizations. A whole series of physical sensations, which were otherwise looked upon as organically determined, were of psychic origin, or at least lent themselves to psychic interpretation. A certain number of her experiences were accompanied by a piercing sensation in the region of the heart ("I felt a stitch in my heart"). The piercing headache of hysteria was undoubtedly, in her case, to be interpreted as a mental pain ("something sticks in my head"), and it disappeared each time when the problem in question was solved. The sensation of the hysterical aura in the throat, when it manifested itself during an annoyance, ran parallel with the thought, "I have to swallow that." There was a whole series of parallel running sensations and ideas, in which it was now the sensation evoking the idea as an interpretation, and now the idea which produced the sensation by symbolization, and not seldom it remained obscure which of the two elements was the primary one.

In no other patient was I able to find such a prolific application of symbolization. To be sure, Mrs. Cecilia M was quite an unusual person, of a special artistic temperament, whose highly developed sense of form manifested itself in producing very beautiful poems. I maintain, however, that if an hysteric creates through symbolization a somatic sensation for an emotionally accentuated idea, it is due less to individual and arbitrary things than one supposes. When during an offending harangue she takes literally such phrases as "stitch in the heart" or "slap in the face," and perceives them as real occurrences, she practises no facetious misuse, but only revives the sensations to which these phrases owe their existence. For how does it happen that in speaking of an aggrieved person we use such expressions as "he experienced a 'stitch in his heart,' " if the mortification was not actually companied by a precordial sensation that could be so interpreted and recognized? Is it not probable that the phrase, "to swallow something," applied to an unreturned insult, really originates from the sensation of innervation appearing in the pharynx when one forces back his speech, thus preventing a reaction to the insult? All these sensations and innervations belong to the "expression of the emotions," which, as Darwin taught us, originally consisted of sensible and expedient actions; at present most of them may be so weakened that their verbal expression seems to us like a figurative transformation, but very probably all this was once meant literally, and hysteria is justified in reconstructing the original literal sense for its stronger innervation. Indeed, perhaps it is improper to say that it creates such sensations through symbolization, perhaps it has not taken the usage of speech as a model, but like it draws it from a common source.[1]

CHAPTER 4

THE PSYCHO-THERAPY OF HYSTERIA[2]

IN our "Preliminary Communication" we have stated that, while investigating the aetiology of hysterical symptoms, we have also discovered a therapeutic method which we consider of practical significance. *"We found, at first to our greatest surprise, that the individual hys-*

[1] In conditions of profounder psychic changes, we apparently find a symbolic stamp of the more artificial usage of language in the form of emblematic pictures and sensations. There was a time in Mrs. Cecilia M during which every thought was changed into an hallucination, and which solution frequently afforded great humor. She at that time complained to me of being troubled by the hallucination that both her physicians, Breuer and I, were hanged in the garden on two nearby trees. The hallucination disappeared after the analysis revealed the following origin: The evening before, Breuer refused her request for a certain drug. She then placed her hopes on me, but found me just as inflexible. She was angry at both of us, and in her affect she thought, "They are worthy of each other, the one is a *pendant* of the other!"

[2] Breuer u. Freud, *Studien über Hysterie,* 1895.

terical symptoms immediately disappeared without returning if we succeeded in thoroughly awakening the memories of the causal process with its accompanying affect, and if the patient circumstantially discussed the process in the most detailed manner and gave verbal expression to the affect" (p. 26).

We furthermore attempted to explain how our psycho-therapeutic method acts: "It abrogates the efficacy of the original non-ab-reacted ideas by affording an outlet to their strangulated affects through speech. It brings them to associative correction by drawing them into normal consciousness (in mild hypnosis) or by eliminating them through medical suggestion in the same way as in somnambulism with amnesia" (p. 30).

Although the essential features of this method have been enumerated in the preceding pages, a repetition is unavoidable, and I shall now attempt to show connectedly how far-reaching this method is, its superiority over others, its technique, and its difficulties.

I

I, for my part, may state that I can firmly adhere to the "Preliminary Communication," but I must confess that in the years that have elapsed since then, and after continuous occupation with the problems touched on there, new viewpoints obtruded themselves on me, as a result of which the former material underwent at least a partial change in grouping and conception. It would be unjust to impute too much of the responsibility for this development to my honored friend, J. Breuer. The responsibility for the following elucidations, therefore, rests preponderately upon me.

In attempting to use Breuer's method for treating hysterical symptoms in a great number of patients by investigation and ab-reaction in hypnosis, I encountered two obstacles, the pursuit of which led me to change the technique, as well as the conception. (1) Not all persons were hypnotizable who undoubtedly showed hysterical symptoms, and in whom there most probably existed the same psychic mechanisms. (2) I had to take an attitude towards the question of what essentially characterizes hysteria, and in what it differs from other neuroses.

How I overcame the first difficulty, and what it taught me, I will show later. I will first state what position I have taken in my daily practise towards the second problem. It is very difficult to examine a case of neurosis before it

has been subjected to a thorough analysis, such as would result only through the application of Breuer's method. But before we have such a thorough knowledge we are obliged to decide upon the diagnosis and kind of treatment. Hence, the only thing left to me was to select such cases for the cathartic method which could, for the time being, be diagnosed as hysteria, and which showed some or many stigmata, or the characteristic symptoms, of hysteria. Yet, it sometimes happened that, in spite of the diagnosis of hysteria, the therapeutic results were very poor, and even the analysis revealed nothing of importance. At other times I attempted to treat cases which no one took for hysteria by Breuer's method, and I found that I could influence them, and even cure them. Such, for example, was my experience with obsessions, the real obsessions of Westphal's type, in cases which did not show a single feature of hysteria. Thus, the psychic mechanism revealed in the "Preliminary Communication" could not, therefore, be pathognomonic of hysteria. Nor could I, for the sake of this mechanism, throw so many neuroses into the same pot with hysteria. Out of all the instigated doubts I finally seized upon a plan to treat all the other neuroses in question just like hysteria, to investigate the aetiology and form of psychic mechanisms, and to leave the decision for the justification of the diagnosis of hysteria to the outcome of this investigation.

It thus happened that proceeding from Breuer's methods I occupied myself mostly with the aetiology and the mechanism of the neuroses. After a relatively brief period I was fortunate in obtaining useful results. First, I became impressed with the cognition that, if one may speak of a causation through which neuroses would be acquired, the aetiology must be sought in sexual factors. This agrees with the findings that, generally speaking, various sexual factors may also produce various pictures of neurotic diseases. And depending on the amount of confirmation of the latter relation, one could now also venture to utilize the aetiology for the characteristics of the neuroses, and build up a sharp line of demarcation between the morbid pictures of the neuroses. If the aetiological characters constantly agreed with the clinical, then this was really justified.

In this way it was found that neurasthenia really corresponds to a monotonous morbid picture in which, as shown by analysis, psychic mechanisms play no part. From neurasthenia we sharply distinguished the compulsion neurosis (obsessions, doubts, phobias), the neurosis of genuine obsessions in which we can recognize a complicated psychic mechanism, an aetiology resembling the one of hysteria, and a far-reaching possibility of its reduction by psychotherapy. On the other hand, it seemed to me absolutely imperative to separate from neurasthenia a neurotic symptom complex which depends on a totally divergent, indeed, strictly speaking, on a contrary aetiology, the partial symptoms of this complex have already been recognized by E. Hecker[1] as having a common character. They are either symptoms, or equivalents, or rudiments of *anxiety manifestations,* and it is for that reason, in order to distinguish this complex from neurasthenia, that I have called it *anxiety neurosis.* I maintained that it originates from an accumulation of physical tension, which is in turn of sexual origin. This neurosis, too, has no psychic mechanism, but regularly influences the psychic life, so that among its regular manifestations we have "anxious expectations," phobias, hyperesthesias to pain, and other symptoms. This anxiety neurosis, as I take it, certainly corresponds in part to the neurosis called hypochondria, which in some features resembles hysteria and neurasthenia. Yet, I cannot consider the demarcation of this neurosis in the existing works as correct, and moreover, I find that the usefulness of the name *hypochondria* is impaired by its close relation to the symptom of *nosophobia.*

After I had thus constructed for myself the simple picture of neurasthenia, anxiety neuroses, and obsessions, I turned my attention to the commonly occurring cases of neuroses which enter into consideration in the diagnosis of hysteria. I now had to say to myself that it would not do to mark a neurosis as hysterical on the whole, merely because its symptom complex evinced some hysterical features. I could readily explain this practice by the fact that hysteria is the oldest, the most familiar, and the most striking neurosis under consideration, but it was an abuse nonetheless to put so many characteristics of perversion and degeneration under the caption of hysteria. Whenever an hysterical symptom, such as anaesthesia or a characteristic attack, could be discovered in a complicated case of psychic degeneration, the whole thing was called *hysteria,* and hence one could naturally find united under this same trade mark the worst and most contradictory features. As certain as this diagnosis was incorrect, it was also certain that our classification must be made on neurotic lines, and, as we knew neurasthenia, anxiety neurosis, and similar conditions in the pure state, there was no need of overlooking them in combination.

It seemed, therefore, that the following conception was more warrantable: The neuroses usually occurring are generally to be designated as *mixed.* Neurasthenia and anxiety neurosis can be found without effort in pure forms, and most frequently in young persons. Pure cases of hysteria and compulsion neurosis are rare; they are usually combined with an anxiety neurosis. This frequent occurrence of mixed neuroses is due to the fact that their aetiological factors are frequently mixed, now only accidentally, and now in consequence of a causal relation between the processes which give rise to the aetiological factors of the neuroses. This can be sustained and proven in the individual cases without any difficulty. But it follows from this that for the purpose of examination it is hardly possible to take hysteria out of its association with the sexual neuroses, that hysteria, as a rule, presents only one side, one aspect of the complicated neurotic case, and that only, as it were, in the borderline case can it be found and treated as an isolated neurosis. In a series of cases we can perhaps say *a potiori fit denominatio.*[2]

I shall now examine the cases reported to see whether they speak in favour of my view of the clinical dependence of hysteria. Breuer's patient, Anna O,[3] seems to contradict this and exemplifies a pure hysterical disease. Yet, this case, which became so fruitful for the knowledge of hysteria, was never considered by its observer under the guise of a sexual neurosis and hence cannot at present be utilized as such. When I began to analyse the second patient, Mrs. Emmy von N, the idea of a sexual neurosis on an hysterical basis was far from my mind. I had just returned from the Charcot school, and considered the connection of hysteria with the sexual theme as a sort of insult—just as my patients were wont to do. But when I now review my notes on this case, there is absolutely no doubt that I have to consider it as a severe case of anxiety neurosis with anxious expectations and phobias, due to sexual abstinence, which was combined with hysteria.

---

[1] E. Hecker, *Zentralblatt für Nervenheilkunde,* December, 1893.

[2] The name is taken from the stronger aspect.—ED.

[3] Case I in Breuer and Freud, *Studien über Hysterie,* 1895 [translated by A. A. Brill, Nervous & Mental Disease Pub. Co., New York, 1936].

The third case, Miss Lucie R.,[1] could perhaps more than any other be called a borderline case of pure hysteria. It is a short episodic hysteria based on an unmistakably sexual aetiology, which would correspond to an anxiety neurosis in an over-ripe, amorous girl, whose love was too rapidly awakened through a misunderstanding. Yet, the anxiety neurosis either could not be demonstrated or had escaped me. Case IV, Katharina, is really a model of what I have called *virginal anxiety;* it is a combination of an anxiety neurosis and hysteria, the former creates the symptoms, while the latter repeats them and works with them. At all events, it is a typical case of many juvenile neuroses called *hysteria.* Case V, Miss Elisabeth von R.,[2] was again not investigated as a sexual neurosis. I could only suspect that there was a spinal neurasthenia at its basis, but I could not confirm it. I must, however, add that since then pure hysterias have become still rarer in my experience. That in grouping together these four cases of hysteria I could disregard in the discussion the decisive factors of sexual neuroses, was due to the fact that they were older cases in which I had not as yet carried out the intentional and urgent investigation for the neurotic sexual subsoil. Moreover, the reason for my reporting four instead of twelve cases of hysteria, the analyses of which would confirm our claims of the psychic mechanism of hysterical phenomena, is due to one circumstance, namely, that the analysis reveals these cases simultaneously as sexual neuroses, though there is no doubt that any diagnostician would have denied them the name *hysteria.* However, the discussion of such sexual neuroses would have overstepped the limits of our joint publication.

I do not wish to be misunderstood and give the impression that I refuse to accept hysteria as an independent neurotic affection, that I conceive it only as a psychic manifestation of the anxiety neurosis, that I ascribe it to only "ideogenous" symptoms, and that I attribute the somatic symptoms, like hysterogenic points and anaesthesias to the anxiety neuroses. None of these statements are true. I believe that hysteria, purified of all admixtures, can be treated independently in every respect except in therapy. For in the treatment we deal with a practical purpose, namely, we have to do away with the whole diseased state, and if hysteria occurs in most cases as a component of a mixed neurosis, the case merely resembles a mixed infection, where the task is to preserve life and not merely to combat the effect of one inciting cause of the disease.

I, therefore, find it important to separate the hysterical part in the pictures of the mixed neuroses from neurasthenia, anxiety neurosis, etc., for after this separation I can express concisely the therapeutic value of the cathartic method. Similarly I would venture to assert that—principally—it can readily dispose of any hysterical symptom, whereas, as can be easily understood, it is perfectly powerless in the presence of neurasthenic phenomena, and can only seldom and only through detours, influence the psychic results of anxiety neurosis. Its therapeutic efficacy in the individual case will depend on whether or not the hysterical components of the morbid picture can claim a practical and significant position in comparison to the other neurotic components.

Still another limitation is placed on the efficacy of the cathartic method, which we have already mentioned in our "Preliminary Communication." It does not influence the causal determinations of hysteria, and hence it cannot prevent the origin of new symptoms in the place of those removed. Hence, on the whole, I must claim a prominent place for our therapeutic method in the realm of a therapy of neuroses, but I would caution against attaching any importance to it, or putting it into practice outside of this connection. As I am unable to give here a *therapy of neuroses* as would be required by the practicing physician, the preceding statements are put on a level with a deferred reference to some later communication; still, for purposes of discussion and elucidation, I can add the following remarks:

1. I do not claim that I have actually removed all the hysterical symptoms which I have undertaken to influence by the cathartic method, but I believe that the obstacles were due to the personal circumstances of the cases, and not to the general principles. In passing sentence, these cases of failure may be left out of consideration, just as the surgeon puts aside all cases who die as a result of narcosis, hemorrhage, accidental sepsis, etc., when deciding upon a new technique. Later, when I will again consider the difficulties and drawbacks of this method, I will again discuss the failures of such origin.

2. The cathartic method does not become valueless simply because it is a *symptomatic* and not a *causal* therapy. For a causal therapy is really in most cases only prophylactic; it

stops the further progress of the injury, but it does not necessarily remove the products which have already resulted from it. It requires, as a rule, a second agent to solve the latter task, and in cases of hysteria the cathartic method is really insurpassable for this purpose.

3. Where a period of hysterical production, or an acute hysterical paroxysm, has been overcome, and the only remnant manifestations left are hysterical symptoms, the cathartic method fulfills all indications, and achieves a full and lasting success. Such a favourable constellation for the therapy rarely results in the realm of the sexual life, in consequence of the marked fluctuations in the intensity of the sexual need and the complications of the required determination for a sexual trauma. Here the cathartic method accomplishes all that is required of it, for the physician cannot possibly change an hysterical constitution. He must rest content if he can remove the disease for which such a constitution shows a tendency, and which can arise through the assistance of external determinants. He must be satisfied if the patient will again be able to function. Moreover, he need not despair of the future, even if he considers the possibility of a relapse, for he knows the main character of the aetiology of the neuroses, namely that their origin is mostly *overdetermined,* and that many factors must cooperate to produce this result. He can hope that this cooperation will not take place very soon, even if some of the aetiological factors remained in force.

It may be argued that in such subsided cases of hysteria the remaining symptoms would spontaneously disappear without anything else; but this can be answered by stating that such spontaneous cures very often terminate neither rapidly nor fully, and that the cure will be extraordinarily advanced by the treatment. Whether the cathartic treatment cures only that which is capable of spontaneous recovery, or incidentally also that which would not cease spontaneously, that question may surely be left open for the present.

4. Wherever we encounter an acute hysteria during the most acute production of hysterical symptoms, and the consecutive overwhelming of the ego by the morbid products (hysterical psychosis), even the cathartic method will change little in the expression and course of the disease. One finds himself in the same position to the neurosis as the doctor to an acute infectious disease. The aetiological factors have exerted a sufficient amount of affect for some time past, which is now beyond the reach of influence, and, now that it has passed the interval of incubation, it comes to the surface. The affection cannot be warded off; it has to run its course; but meanwhile one must bring about the most favourable conditions for the patient. If during such an acute period one can remove the morbid products, the newly formed hysterical symptoms, it may be expected that their places will be taken by new ones. The physician will not be spared the depressing impression of fruitless effort, the enormous expenditure of exertion, and the disappointment of the relatives to whom the idea of the necessary duration of time of an acute neurosis is hardly as familiar as in the analogous case of an acute infectious disease; these, and many other things, will probably largely impede the consequent application of the cathartic method in the assumed case. Nevertheless, it still remains to be considered whether, even in an acute hysteria, the frequent removal of the morbid products does not exercise a curative influence by supporting the normal ego, which is occupied with the defense, and thus preventing it from merging into a psychosis or into ultimate confusion.

That the cathartic method can accomplish something, even in an acute hysteria, and that it can even reduce the new productions of the morbid symptoms quite practically and noticeably, is undoubtedly evident from the case of Anna O, in which Breuer first learned this psycho-therapeutic method.

5. Where we deal with chronic, progressive hysterias with moderate or continued productions of hysterical symptoms, we feel most the lack of a causally effective therapy, but we also learn to value the importance of the cathartic method as a symptomatic remedy. We then have to deal with an injury produced by a chronically acting aetiology. We have to strengthen the capacity of resistance of the nervous system of our patient, and we must bear in mind that the existence of an hysterical symptom signifies a weakening of resistance of the nervous system, and represents a predisposing factor. From the mechanism of monosymptomatic hysteria we know that a new hysterical symptom generally originates as an addition to, and as an analogy of, one already in existence. The location once penetrated represents the weak spot which can be penetrated again. The already split-off psychic group plays the part of the provoking crystal from which a formerly omitted crystallization emanates with

great facility. To remove the already existing symptoms, to do away with the psychic alterations lying at their bases, is to return to the patients the full measure of their resistance capacity, with which they are successfully able to resist the noxious influences. One can do a great deal for the patient by such long continued watchfulness and occasional "chimney-sweeping."

6. I still have to mention the apparent contradiction between the admission that not all hysterical symptoms are psychogenic, and the assertion that they can all be removed by psycho-therapeutic procedures. The solution lies in the fact that some of these non-psychogenic symptoms, though they represent morbid symptoms, as for instance, the stigmata, need, nevertheless, not to be designated as *affections*. It is, therefore, practically unimportant if they outlast the successful treatment. Other symptoms of a similar nature seem to be pulled along indirectly by some psychogenic symptoms, for indirectly they really depend on some psychic causation.

I shall now speak of those difficulties and inconveniences of our therapeutic method which are not evident from the preceding case histories or from the following remarks concerning the technique of the method. I will rather enumerate and indicate them than go into details. The process is toilsome and wearisome for the physician; it presupposes in him a profound interest for psychological occurrences, and yet also a personal sympathy for the patient. I could not imagine myself entering deeply into the psychic mechanism of an hysteria in a person who would impress me as common and disagreeable, and who would not, on closer acquaintanceship, be able to awaken in me human sympathy; whereas I can treat a tabetic or a rheumatic patient regardless of such personal interest. No less demanding are the requisites on the patient's side. The method is especially inapplicable in a person below a certain level of intelligence, and it becomes extremely difficult wherever there is any tinge of mental deficiency. It requires the full consent, the full attention of the patients, but, above all, their confidence, for the analysis regularly leads to the inmost and most secretly guarded psychic processes. A large proportion of the patients suitable for such treatment withdraw from the physician as soon as they get an inkling whither this investigation tends. The physician remains a stranger to them. In others who have determined to give themselves up to the physician and bestow their confidence upon him, something only voluntarily given, but never demanded; in all those I say it is hardly avoidable that the personal relation to the physician should not become unduly prominent, at least for some time. Indeed, it seems as if such an influence exerted by the physician is a condition under which alone a solution of the problem is possible. I do not believe that it makes any essential difference in this state of affairs whether one resorts to hypnosis or has to avoid or substitute for it. Yet, fairness demands that we emphasize the fact that, although these inconveniences are inseparable from our method, they, nevertheless, cannot be charged to it. On the contrary, it is very obvious that they are conditioned in the presuppositions of the neuroses destined to be cured, and that they are interwoven in every medical activity which intensively concerns itself with the patient, and produce in him a psychic change. I could see no harm or danger in the application of hypnosis, even in these cases where it was used excessively. The causes for the harm produced lay elsewhere and deeper. When I review the therapeutic efforts of those years since the communications of my honoured teacher and friend, J. Breuer, gave me the cathartic method, I believe that I have more often produced good than harm, and brought about some things which could not have been produced by any other therapeutic means. On the whole it was, as expressed in the "Preliminary Communication," a "distinct therapeutic gain."

I must mention still another advantage from the application of this method. No severe case of complicated neurosis, with either an excessive or slight tinge of hysteria, can better be explained than by subjecting it to an analysis by Breuer's method. In making this analysis, I find that whatever shows the hysterical mechanism disappears first, while the rest of the manifestations I meanwhile learn to interpret and trace back to their aetiology. I thus gain the essential factors indicated by the instrument of the therapy of the neurosis in question. When I think of the ordinary differences between my opinion of a case of neurosis *before* and *after* such an analysis, I am almost tempted to maintain that the analysis is indispensable for the knowledge of a neurotic disease. Moreover, I have made it a practice of applying the cathartic psycho-therapy in acute cases in conjunction with a Weir-Mitchell rest cure. This advantage lies in the fact that, on the one side, I avoid the very disturbing intrusion of new psychic impressions which may be produced during psycho-therapy; on the other hand, I exclude the monotony of the Weir-Mitchell treatment, during which the patient frequently merges into harmful reveries.

II

I will now add to my former observations that in attempting to use Breuer's method in greater latitude I encountered the difficulty that although I made the diagnosis of hysteria, and the probabilities spoke in favour of the prevalence of the psychic mechanism described by us, yet a number of the patients could not be hypnotized. But as hypnosis was necessary to broaden consciousness in order to find the pathogenic reminiscences which do not exist in the ordinary consciousness, I was, therefore, forced either to give up such patients or to bring about this broadening by other means.

The reason why one person is hypnotizable and another not, I could no more explain than others, and hence, I could not start on a causal way towards the removal of the difficulties. I also observed that in some patients the obstacle was still more marked; they even refused to submit to hypnosis. The idea then occurred to me that both cases might be identical, and that in both it might merely signify an unwillingness. Those who entertain psychic doubts against hypnotism are not hypnotizable; it makes no difference whether they express their unwillingness or not. It is not fully clear to me whether I can firmly adhere to this view or not.

I was, therefore, forced to dispense with hypnotism and yet, obtain the pathogenic reminiscences. I attained this in the following manner:

On asking my patients during our first interview whether they remembered the first motive for the symptom in question, some said that they knew nothing, while others thought of something which they designated as an indistinct recollection, yet were unable to pursue it. I then followed Bernheim's example of forcibly awakening apparently forgotten impressions from somnambulism.[1] I assured them that they did know it, and that they would recall it, etc., and in this way some thought of something, while in others the recollections went even further. I urged still more, I ordered the patient to lie down and voluntarily shut his eyes so as to "concentrate" his mind, and I then discovered that without any hypnosis there emerged new and retrospective reminiscences

[1] Cf. p. 32 above.

which probably belonged to our theme. Through such experiences, I gained the impression that through urging alone it would really be possible to bring to light the definitely existing pathogenic series of ideas; and as this urging necessitated much exertion on my part, and showed me that I had to overcome a resistance, I therefore formulated this whole state of affairs into the following theory: *Through my psychic work I had to overcome a psychic force in the patient which opposed the pathogenic idea from becoming conscious* (remembered). A new insight seemed to have revealed itself to me when it occurred to me that this must really be the same psychic force which assisted in the origin of the hysterical symptom, and which at that time prevented the pathogenic idea from becoming conscious. What kind of force could here be assumed as effective; and what motive could have brought it into activity? I could easily formulate an opinion, for I already had some complete analyses at my disposal, in which I found examples of pathogenic, forgotten, and repressed ideas. From these I could judge the general character of such ideas. They were altogether of a painful nature adapted to provoke the affects of shame, of reproach, of psychic pain, or the feeling of injury; they were altogether of that kind which one would have liked not to experience and preferred to forget.

From all these there resulted the thought of defence, as if spontaneously. Indeed, it is generally admitted by all psychologists that the acceptance of a new idea (acceptance in the sense of belief, admission of reality) depends on the mode and drift of the ideas already united in the ego, and for the process of censorship, to which the newly arrived idea is subjected, special technical names have been created. An idea entered into the patient's ego which proved to be unbearable and evoked a force of repulsion on the part of the ego, the object of which was a *defence* against this unbearable idea. This defence actually succeeded and the idea concerned was crowded out of consciousness and out of memory, so that its psychic trace could not apparently be found; yet, this trace must have existed. When I made the effort to direct the attention to it, I felt the same force as a *resistance* which showed itself as a *repulsion* in the genesis of the symptom. If I could now make it probable that the idea became pathogenic in consequence of the exclusion and repression, the chain would seem complete. In many epicrises of our histories, and in a small work concerning the defense neuropsychoses (1894), I have attempted to indicate the psychological hypotheses with the help of which this connection, as well as the fact of conversion, could be made clear.

Hence, a psychic force, the repugnance of the ego, has originally crowded the pathogenic idea from the association, and now opposed its return into the memory. The *not knowing* of the hysterics was really a—more or less conscious—*not willing to know,* and the task of the therapist was to overpower this association resistance by psychic labour. Such accomplishment is, above all, brought about by *urging;* that is, by applying a psychic force in order to direct the patient's attention to the ideas that one wishes to trace. It does not, however, stop here, but, as I will show, it assumes new forms in the course of the analysis, and calls to aid more psychic forces.

I shall above all still linger at the urging. One cannot go very far with such simple assurances as, "You do know it, just say it," or, "It will soon come to your mind." After a few sentences the thread breaks, even in the patient who is in a state of concentration. We must not, however, forget that we deal everywhere here with a quantitative comparison, with the struggle between motives of diverse force and intensity. The urging by a strange and inexperienced physician does not suffice to overcome *association resistance* in a grave hysteria. One must think of more forceful means.

Here, I utilize in the first place a small technical artifice. I inform the patient that in the next moment I will exert pressure on his forehead, I assure him that during this pressure he will see some reminiscence in the form of a picture, or some thought will occur to him, and I obligate him to communicate to me this picture or this thought, no matter what it might be. He must not keep it to himself because he may think that it is not the desired or the right thing, or because it is too disagreeable to say. There should be neither criticism nor reservation because of affect or underestimation. Only thus could we find the things desired, and only thus have we unfailingly found them. I then exerted pressure for a few seconds on the forehead of the patient lying in front of me, and, after ceasing it, I asked in a calm tone, as if any disappointment was out of the question, "What have you seen?" or "What occurred to your mind?"

This method[1] taught me a great deal and led me to the goal every time. Of course, I know that I can substitute this pressure on the forehead by any other sign, or any other physical influence, but as the patient lies before me, the pressure on the forehead, or the grasping of his head between my two hands, is the most suggestive and most convenient thing that I could undertake for this end. To explain the efficacy of this artifice, I may perhaps say that it corresponds to a "momentary, reinforced hypnosis"; but the mechanism of hypnosis is so enigmatical to me that I would not like to refer to it as an explanation.[2] I rather think that the advantage of the process lies in the fact that through it I dissociated the attention of the patient from his conscious quest and reflection, in brief, from everything upon which his will could manifest itself. The fact that under the pressure of my hand there always appeared that which I was looking for taught me that the supposedly forgotten pathogenic ideas always lie ready, close by, and are attainable through easily approachable associations, all that is necessary is to clear away some obstacle. This obstacle again seems to be the person's will, and different persons learn in different ways how to discard their wilfulness and to assume a perfectly objective attitude towards the psychic processes within them.

It is not always a *forgotten* reminiscence which comes to the surface under the pressure of the hand; in the rarest cases the real pathogenic reminiscences can be superficially discovered. More frequently an idea comes to the surface which is a link between the first idea and the desired pathogenic idea of the association chain, or it is an idea forming the starting point of a new series of thoughts and reminiscences, at the end of which is the pathogenic idea. The pressure, therefore, has really not revealed the pathogenic idea, which, if torn from its connection without any preparation, would be incomprehensible; but it has shown the way to it, and indicated the direction towards which the investigation must proceed. The idea which is at first awakened through the pressure may correspond to a familiar reminiscence which was never repressed. If the connection becomes torn on the road to the

---

[1] The author has discarded this pressure procedure after only a short trial.—Tr.

[2] The solution of this problem was later found by the author and his pupils. Cf. here *Group Psychology and the Analysis of the Ego,* p. 688 below; and Ferenczi's *Contributions to Psycho-analysis,* Chapter II (Badger, Boston, 1916).—Tr.

pathogenic idea, all that is necessary for the reproduction of a new orientation and connection is a repetition of the procedure, that is, of the pressure.

In still other cases the pressure of the hand awakens a reminiscence well known to the patient, which appearance, however, causes him surprise because he has forgotten its relation to the original idea. In the further course of the analysis this relation becomes clear. From all these results of the pressure, one receives a delusive impression of a superior intelligence outside of the patient's consciousness, which systematically holds a large psychic material for definite purposes, and has provided an ingenious arrangement for its return into consciousness. I presume, however, that this unconscious second intelligence is really only apparent.

In every complicated analysis one works repeatedly, nay continuously, with the help of this procedure (pressure on the forehead), which leads us from the place where the patient's wakeful reconductions became interrupted, it shows us the way to reminiscences which remained known, and calls our attention to connections which have sunk into forgetfulness. It also evokes and connects memories which have for years been withdrawn from association, though they can still be recognized as memories; and finally, as the highest performance of reproduction, it causes the appearance of thoughts which the patient never wishes to recognize as his own, which he does not remember, although he admits that they are inexorably required by the connection, and is convinced that precisely these ideas will cause the termination of the analysis and the cessation of the symptoms.

I will now attempt to give a series of examples which will show the excellent achievements of this procedure. I treated a young lady who suffered for six years from an intolerable and protracted nervous cough, which apparently was nurtured by very common catarrh, but must have had its strong psychic motives. Every other remedy had long since shown itself powerless, and I therefore attempted to remove the symptom by psycho-analysis. All that she could remember was that the nervous cough began at the age of fourteen while she boarded with her aunt. She remembered absolutely no psychic excitement during that time, and did not believe that there was a motive for her suffering. Under the pressure of my hand, she at first recalled a large dog. She then recognized the memory picture; it was her aunt's dog, which was attached to her, and used to accompany her everywhere, and without any further aid it occurred to her that this dog died and that the children buried it solemnly; and on the return from this funeral her cough appeared. I asked her why she began to cough, and the following thought occurred to her: "Now I am all alone in this world; no one loves me here; this animal was my only friend, and now I have lost it." She then continued her story. "The cough disappeared when I left my aunt, but reappeared a year and a half later."—"What was the reason for it?"—"I do not know." I again exerted some pressure on the forehead and she recalled the news of her uncle's death, during which the cough again manifested itself, and also recalled a train of thought similar to the former. The uncle was apparently the only one in the family who sympathized with her and loved her. That was, therefore, the pathogenic idea: People do not love her, everybody else is preferred; she really does not deserve to be loved, etc. To the idea of love there clung something which caused a marked resistance to the communication. The analysis was interrupted before this explanation was obtained.

Some time ago I attempted to relieve an elderly lady of her anxiety attacks, which, considering their characteristic qualities, were hardly suitable for such treatment. Since her menopause she had become extremely religious, and always received me as if I were the Devil—she was always armed with a small ivory crucifix which she hid in her hand. Her attacks of anxiety, which bore a hysterical character, could be traced to her early girlhood and were supposed to have originated from the application of an iodine preparation to reduce a moderate swelling of the thyroid. I naturally repudiated this origin and sought to substitute it by another which was in better harmony with my views concerning the aetiology of neurotic symptoms. To the first question for an impression of her youth, which would stand in causal connection to the attacks of anxiety, there appeared the reminiscences of reading a so-called devotional book wherein piously enough there was some mention of the sexual processes. The passage in question made an impression on this girl, which was contrary to the intention of the author. She burst into tears and flung the book away. That was before the first attack of anxiety. The next reminiscence referred to her brother's teacher, who showed her great respect and for whom she entertained a warmer feeling. This reminiscence culminated in the reproduction of an evening in her parents' home during which they all sat around the table with the young man, and delightfully enjoyed themselves in a lively conversation. During the night following this evening, she was awakened by the first attack of anxiety which surely had more to do with some resistance against a sensual feeling than perhaps with the coincidental use of iodine. In what other way could I have succeeded in revealing in this obstinate patient, prejudiced against me and every worldly remedy, such a connection contrary to her own opinion and assertion?

On another occasion I had to deal with a young happily married woman who, as early as in the first years of her girlhood, was found every morning for some time in a state of lethargy, with rigid limbs, opened mouth, and protruding tongue. Similar attacks, though not so marked, recurred at the present time on awakening. A deep hypnosis could not be produced, so that I began my investigation in a state of concentration, and assured her during the first pressure that she would see something that would be directly connected with the cause of her condition during her childhood. She acted calmly and willingly, she again saw the residence in which she had passed her early girlhood—her room, the position of the bed, the grandmother who lived with them at the time, and one of her governesses whom she dearly loved. Then there was a succession of small scenes in these rooms and among these quite indifferent persons, the conclusion of which was the leavetaking of the governess, who married from the home. I did not know what to start with these reminiscences; I could not bring about any connection between them and the aetiology of the attacks. To be sure, the various circumstances were recognized as having occurred at the same time as the attacks first appeared.

Before I could continue the analysis, I had occasion to talk to a colleague who, in former years, was my patient's family physician. From him I obtained the following explanation: At the time that he treated the mature and physically well-developed girl for these first attacks, he was struck by the excessive affection in the relations between her and the governess. He became suspicious and caused the grandmother to watch these relations. After a short while the old lady informed him that the governess was wont to pay nightly visits to the child's bed, and that quite regularly after such visits the child was found in the morning in an attack. She did not hesitate to bring about the quiet removal of this corruptress of youth. The children, as well as the mother, were made to believe that the governess left the house in order to get married.

The treatment, which was above all successful, consisted in informing the young woman of the explanations given to me.

Occasionally the explanations which one obtains by the pressure procedure follow in very remarkable form, and under circumstances which make the assumption of an unconscious intelligence appear even more alluring. Thus, I recall a lady who suffered for years from obsessions and phobias, and who referred the origin of her trouble to her childhood, but could mention nothing to which it could have been attributed. She was frank and intelligent, and evinced only a very slight conscious resistance. I will add here that the psychic mechanism of obsessions is very closely related to that of hysterical symptoms, and that the technique of the analysis in both is the same.

On asking the lady whether she had seen or recalled anything under the pressure of my hand, she answered, "Neither, but a word suddenly occurred to me."—"A single word?"—"Yes, but it is too foolish."—"Just tell it."—"Teacher."—"Nothing more?"—"No." I exerted pressure a second time, and again a single word flashed through her mind: "Shirt." I now observed that we dealt with a new mode of replying, and by repeated pressure I evoked the following apparently senseless series of words: Teacher—shirt—bed—city—wagon. I asked, "What does all that mean?" She reflected for a moment, and it then occurred to her that "it can only refer to this one incident which now comes to my mind. When I was ten years old, my older sister of twelve had a violent emotional attack one night and had to be bound, put in a wagon and taken to the city. I remember distinctly that it was the teacher who overpowered her and accompanied her to the asylum."

We then continued this manner of investigation, and received from our oracle another series of words which, though we could not altogether interpret them, could nevertheless be used as a continuation of the story and as an appendix to a second. The significance of this reminiscence was soon clear. The reason why her sister's illness made such an impression on her was because they both shared a common secret. They slept in the same room, and one night they both submitted to a sexual assault by a certain man. In discovering this sexual trauma of early youth, we revealed not only the origin of the first obsession, but also the trauma which later acted pathogenically.

The peculiarity of this case lies only in the appearance of single catch-words, which we had to elaborate into sentences, for the seeming irrelevance and incoherence in these oracle-like words generally occur in all ideas and scenes as a result of pressure. On further investigation it is regularly found that seemingly disconnected reminiscences are connected by intimate streams of thought, and that they lead quite directly to the desired pathogenic factor.

I therefore recall with pleasure a case of analysis in which my confidence in the results of this method was very splendidly justified. A very intelligent, and apparently very happy, young woman consulted me for persistent pain in her abdomen, which yielded to no treatment. I found that the pain was located in the abdominal wall and was due to palpable muscular hardening, and I therefore ordered local treatment.

After months I again saw the patient who said that "the pain had disappeared after taking the treatment and remained away a long time, but it has now reappeared as a nervous pain. I recognize it by the fact that I do not perceive it now on motion as before, but only during certain hours, as for example, in the morning on awakening, and during certain excitements." The patient's diagnosis was quite correct. It was now important to discover the cause of this pain, but in this she could not assist me in her uninfluenced state. When I asked her in a state of concentration and under the pressure of my hand whether anything occurred to her, or whether she saw anything, she began to describe her visual pictures. She saw something like a sun with rays, which I naturally had to assume to be a phosphene produced by pressure on the eyes. I expected that the needful pictures would follow, but she continued to see stars of a peculiar pale blue light, like moonlight, etc., and I believed that she merely saw glittering, shining, and twinkling spots before her eyes. I was already prepared to add this attempt to the failures, and I was thinking how I could quietly withdraw from this affair, when my attention was called to one of the manifestations which she described. She saw a big, black, inclined cross, the edges of which were surrounded with a subdued moon-like light, in which all the pictures thus far seen were shining, and upon the cross beam there flickered a little flame that was apparently no longer a phosphene. I continued to listen. She saw numerous pictures in the same light, peculiar signs resembling somewhat Sanscrit. She also saw figures like triangles, among which there was one big triangle, and again the cross. I now thought of an allegorical interpretation, and asked, "What does this cross mean?"—"It is probably meant to interpret pain," she answered. I argued, saying that, "By *cross* one usually understands a moral burden," and asked her what was hidden behind that pain. She could not explain that and continued looking. She saw a sun with golden rays which she interpreted as God, the primitive force; she then saw a gigantic lizard which she examined quizzically, but without fear; then a heap of snakes, then another sun, but with mild silvery rays, and in front of it, between her own person and this source of light, there was a barrier which concealed from her the center of the sun.

I knew for some time that we dealt here with allegories, and I immediately asked for an explanation of the last picture. Without reflecting she answered: "The sun is perfection, the ideal, and the barrier represents my weakness and failings which stand between me and the ideal."—"Indeed, do you reproach yourself? Are you dissatisfied with yourself?"—"Yes." —"Since when?"—"Since I became a member of the Theosophical Society and read the writings edited by it. I have always had a poor opinion of myself."—"What was it that made the last, strongest impression upon you?"—"A translation from the Sanscrit, which now appears in serial numbers." A minute later I was initiated into her mental conflicts, and into her self-reproaches. She related a slight incident which gave occasion for a reproach, and in which, as a result of an inciting conversion, the former organic pain at first appeared. The pictures, which I had at first taken for phosphenes, were symbols of occultistic streams of thought, perhaps plain emblems from the title pages of occultistic books.

Thus far, I have warmly praised the achievements of the pressure procedure, and have entirely neglected the aspect of the defence or the resistance, so that I certainly must have given the impression that by means of this small artifice one is placed in a position to become master of the psychic resistances to the cathartic method. But to believe this would be a gross mistake. Such advantages do not exist in the treatment so far as I can see; here, as everywhere else, a great change requires much effort. The pressure procedure is nothing but a trick serving to surprise for awhile the defensive ego; in all graver cases, it soon recalls its intentions and continues its resistance.

I need only recall the various forms in which this resistance manifests itself. At first, the pressure experiment usually fails the first or second time. The patient then expresses himself disappointedly, saying, "I believed that some idea would occur to me, but I only thought how anxious I was for it, but nothing came." Such attitudes assumed by the patient are not yet to be counted as a resistance; we usually answer to that, "You were really too anxious, the second time things will come." And they really come. It is remarkable how completely the patients—even the most tractable and the most intelligent—can forget the agreement into which they have previously entered. They have promised to tell everything that occurs to them, be it intimately related to them or not, be it agreeable to say or not; that is, they are to tell everything without any choice or influence of criticism or affect. Yet, they do not keep their promise; it is apparently beyond their powers. The work repeatedly stops, they continue to assert that this time nothing came to their mind. One need not believe them, and one must always assume, and also say that they hold back something because they believe it to be unimportant, or perceive it as painful. One must insist, and assume an assured attitude until one really hears something. The patient then usually adds, "I could have told you that the first time."—"Why did you not say it?"—"I could not believe that this could be it. Only after it returned repeatedly have I decided to tell it," or, "I had hoped that it would not be just that, that I could save myself saying it, but only after it could not be repressed have I noticed that I could not avoid it." Thus, the patient subsequently betrays the motives of a resistance which he did not at first wish to admit. He apparently could do nothing but offer resistances.

It is remarkable under what subterfuges these resistances are frequently hidden. "I am distracted today; the clock or the piano playing in the next room disturbs me," they say. I became accustomed to answer to that, "Not at all, you simply struck something that you are not willing to say. That does not help you at all. Just stick to it." The longer the pause between the pressure of my hand and the utterance of the patient, the more suspicious I become, and the more it is to be feared that the patient arranges what comes to his mind, and distorts it in the reproduction. The most important explanations are frequently ushered in as superfluous accessories, just as the princes of the opera who are dressed as beggars. "Something now occurred to me, but it has nothing to do with it. I only tell it to you because you wish to know everything." With this introduction we usually obtain the long desired solution. I always listen when I hear a patient talk so lightly of an idea. That the pathogenic idea should appear of so little importance on its reappearance is a sign of the successful defence. One can infer from this of what the process of defence consisted. Its object was to make a weak out of a strong idea, that is, to rob it of its affect.

Among other signs, the pathogenic memories can also be recognized by the fact that they are designated by the patient as unessential, despite the fact that they are uttered with resistance. There are also cases where the patient seeks to disavow the recollections, even while they are being reproduced, with such remarks as these: "Now something occurred to me, but apparently you talked it into me"; or "I know what you expect to this question, you surely think that I thought of this and that." An especially clever way of shifting responsibility is found in the following expression: "Now something really occurred to me, but it seems to me as if I added it, and that it is not a reproduced thought." In all these cases I remain inflexibly firm; I admit none of these distinctions, but I explain to the patient that these are only forms and subterfuges of the resistance against the reproduction of a recollection which in spite of all we are forced to recognize.

One generally experiences less trouble in the reproduction of pictures than thoughts. Hysterical patients, who are usually visual, are easier to manage than patients suffering from obsessions. Once the picture emerges from the memory, we can hear the patient state that, as he proceeds to describe it, it proportionately fades away and becomes indistinct; the patient wears it out, so to speak, by transforming it into words. We then orient ourselves through the memory picture itself in order to find the direction towards which the work should be continued. We say to the patient, "Just look again at the picture, has it disappeared?"—"As a whole, yes, but I still see this detail."—"Then this must have some meaning; you will either see something new, or this remnant will remind you of something." When the work is finished, the visual field becomes free again, and a new picture can be called forth; but at other times such a picture, in spite of its having been described, remains persistently before the inner eye of the patient, and I take this as a sign that he still has something important to tell me concerning its theme. As soon as this has been accomplished, the picture disappears like a wandering spirit returning to rest.

It is naturally of great value for the progress of the analysis to carry our point with the patient, otherwise we have to depend on what he thinks it proper to impart. It therefore will be pleasant to hear that the pressure procedure never failed except in a single case which I shall discuss later, but which I can now characterize by the fact that there was a special motive for the resistance. To be sure, it may happen under certain conditions that the procedure may be applied without bringing anything to light; as, for example, we may ask for the further aetiology of a symptom when the same has already been exhausted; or we may investigate for the psychic geneology of a symptom, perhaps a pain, which really is of somatic origin. In these cases the patient equally insists that nothing occurred to him, and he is right. We should strive to avoid doing an injustice to the patient by making it a general rule not to lose sight of his features while he calmly lies before us during the analysis. One can then learn to distinguish, without any difficulty, the psychic calm in the real non-appearance of a reminiscence from the tension and emotional signs under which the patient labours in trying to disavow the emerging reminiscences with the object of defence. The differential diagnostic application of the pressure procedure is really based on such experiences.

We can thus see that, even with the help of pressure procedure, the task is not an easy one. The only advantage gained is the fact that we have learned from the results of this method in which direction to investigate, and what things we have to force upon the patient. For some cases this suffices, for it is essentially a question of finding the secret and telling it to the patient, so that he is then usually forced to relinquish his resistance. In other cases, more is necessary; here the surviving resistance of the patient manifests itself by the fact that the connections become torn, the solutions do not appear and the recalled pictures come indis-

tinctly and incompletely. On reviewing, at a later period, the earlier results of an analysis, we are often surprised at the distorted aspects of all the occurrences and scenes which we have snatched from the patient. It usually lacks the essential part, the relations to the person or to the theme, and for that reason the picture remained incomprehensible. I will now give one or two examples showing the effects of such a censorship during the first appearance of the pathogenic memories. The patient sees the upper part of a female body on which a loose covering fits carelessly; only much later he adds to this torso the head, and thereby betrays a person and a relationship. Or, he relates a reminiscence of his childhood about two boys whose forms are very indistinct, and to whom a certain mischievousness was attributed. It required many months and considerable progress in the course of the analysis before he again saw this reminiscence and recognized one of the children as himself and the other as his brother. What means have we now at our disposal to overcome this continued resistance?

We have but few, yet we have almost all those by which one otherwise exerts a psychic influence on the other. In the first place, we must remember that psychic resistance, especially of long continuance, can only be broken slowly, gradually, and with much patience. We can also count on the intellectual interest which manifests itself in the patient after a brief period of the analysis. On explaining and imparting to him the knowledge of the marvelous world of psychic processes, which we have gained only through such analysis, we obtain his collaboration and cause him to view himself with the objective interest of the investigator, and we thus drive back the resistance which rests on an affective basis. But finally—and this remains the strongest motive force—after the motives for the defence have been discovered, we must make the attempt to reduce them or even substitute them by stronger ones. Here, the possibility of expressing the therapeutic activity in formulae ceases. One does as well as he can as an explainer where ignorance has produced shyness, as a teacher, as a representative of a freer and superior philosophy of life, and as a confessor, who through the continuance of his sympathy and his respect imparts, so as to say, absolution after the confession. One endeavours to do something humane for the patient as far as the range of one's own personality and the measure of sympathy which one can set apart for the case allows. It is an indispensable prerequisite for such psychic activities to have approximately discovered the nature of the case and the motives of the defence that are here effective. Fortunately the technique of urging and the pressure procedure take us just so far. The more we have solved such enigmas the easier will we discover new ones, and the earlier will we be able to manage the actual curative psychic work. For it is well to bear in mind that, although the patient can rid himself of an hysterical symptom only after reproducing and uttering under emotion its causal pathogenic impressions, yet the therapeutic task merely consists in inducing him to do it, and once the task has been accomplished, there remains nothing for the doctor to correct or abolish. All the contrary suggestions necessary have already been employed during the struggle carried on against the resistance. The case may be compared to the unlocking of a closed door, where, as soon as the doorknob has been pressed downward, no other difficulties are encountered in opening the door.

Among the intellectual motives employed for the overcoming of the resistance one can hardly dispense with one affective factor, that is, the personal equation of the doctor, and in a number of cases this alone is enough to break the resistance. The conditions here do not differ from those found in any other branch of medicine, and one should not expect any therapeutic method fully to disclaim the cooperation of this personal factor.

III

In view of the discussions in the preceding section concerning the difficulty of my technique, which I have unreservedly exposed—I have really collected them from my most difficult cases, though it will often be easier work— in view, then, of this state of affairs, everybody will wish to ask whether it would not be more suitable, instead of all these tortures, to apply one's self more energetically to hypnosis, or to limit the application of the cathartic method only to such cases as can be put into deep hypnosis. To the latter proposition I should have to answer that the number of patients available for my skill would shrink considerably; but to the former advice I will advance the supposition that, even where hypnosis could be produced, the resistance would not be very much lessened. My experiences in this respect are not particularly extensive, so that I am unable to go beyond this supposition, but wherever I achieved a cathartic cure in the

hypnotic state, I found that the work devolved upon me was not less than in the state of mere concentration. I have only recently finished such a treatment, during course of which I caused the disappearance of an hysterical paralysis of the legs. The patient merged into a state, psychically very different from the conscious, and somatically distinguished by the fact that she was unable to open her eyes or rise without my ordering her to do so; and still I never had a case showing greater resistance than this one. I placed no value on these physical signs, and, towards the end of the ten months' treatment, they really became imperceptible. The state of the patient on which we worked has, therefore, lost nothing of its psychic pecularities, such as the ability to recall the unconscious, and its very peculiar relation to the person of the physician. To be sure, in the history of Mrs. Emmy von N, I have described an example of a cathartic cure accomplished in a profound somnambulism in which the resistance played almost no part. But nothing that I obtained from this woman would have required any special effort; I obtained nothing that she could not have told me in her waking state after a longer acquaintanceship and some personal regard. The real causes of her disease, which were surely identical with the causes of her relapses after my treatment, I have never found—it was my first attempt in this therapy—and when I once asked her accidentally for a reminiscence which contained a fragment of the erotic, I found her just as resistive and unreliable in her statements as any one of my later non-somnambulic patients. This patient's resistance, even in the somnambulic state, against other requirements and exactions I have already discussed in her history. Since I have witnessed cases which, even in deep somnambulism, were absolutely refractory therapeutically despite their obedience in everything else, I really have become skeptical as to the value of hypnosis for the facilitation of the cathartic treatment. A case of this kind I have in brief reported[1] and could still add others. Besides, I admit that even this experience fell badly short of my need for a quantitative relation between cause and effect in the psychic spheres.

In our discussion thus far, the idea of resistance has thrust itself to the foreground. I have shown how, in the therapeutic work, one is led to the conception that hysteria originates

---

[1] See *Studien über Hysterie*, 1895, p. 85.

through the repression of an unbearable idea as a motive of defence, that the repressed idea remains as a weak (mildly intensive) reminiscence, and that the affect snatched from it is used for a somatic innervation, that is, for conversion of the excitement. By virtue of its repression the idea becomes the cause of morbid symptoms, that is, pathogenic. A hysteria showing this psychic mechanism may be designated by the name of *defence-hysteria*, but both Breuer and myself have repeatedly spoken of two kinds of hysterias which we have named *hypnoid-* and *retention-hysteria*. The first to reveal itself to us was really the hypnoid-hysteria, for which I can mention no better example than Breuer's case of Miss Anna O. For this form of hysteria Breuer gives an essentially different psychic mechanism than for the form which is characterized by conversion. Here the idea becomes pathogenic through the fact that it is conceived in a peculiar psychic state, having remained from the very beginning external to the ego. It, therefore, needs no psychic force to keep it away from the ego, and it need not awaken any resistance when, with the help of the somnambulic psychic authority, it is initiated into the ego. The history of Anna O really shows nothing of such a resistance.

I hold this distinction as so essential that it has readily induced me to adhere to the formation of the hypnoid-hysteria. It is, however, remarkable that in my own experience I encountered no genuine hypnoid-hysteria; whatever I treated changed itself into a defence hysteria. Not that I have never dealt with symptoms which manifestly originated in separated conscious states, and, therefore, were excluded from being accepted into the ego. I encountered this also in my own cases, but I could show that the so-called hypnoid state owed its separation to the fact that a split-off psychic group originated before through defence. In brief, I cannot suppress the suspicion that hypnoid and defence hysteria meet somewhere at their roots, and that the defence is the primary thing; but I know nothing about it.

Equally uncertain is at present my opinion concerning the retention-hysteria in which the therapeutic work is also supposed to follow without any resistance. I had a case which I took for a typical retention-hysteria, and I was pleased with the anticipation of an easy and certain success, but this success failed to come, easy as the work really was. I, therefore, presume, and again with all caution appropriate to ignorance, that in retention-hysteria, too, we can find at its basis a fragment of defence, which has thrust the whole process into hysteria. Let us hope that new experiences will soon decide whether I am running into the danger, of one-sidedness and error, in my tendency to spread the conception of defence for the whole of hysteria.

Thus far I have dealt with the difficulties and technique of the cathartic method. I would now like to add a few indications to show how one does an analysis with this technique. For me this is a very interesting theme, but I do not expect that it will excite similar interest in others who have not practised such analyses. Properly speaking, we shall again deal with technique, but this time with those difficulties concerning which the patient cannot be held responsible, and which must in part be the same in a hypnoid- and a retention-hysteria as in the defence-hysteria which I have in mind as a model. I start with this last fragment of discussion with the hope, that the psychic peculiarities to be revealed here might sometimes attain a certain value as raw material for ideational dynamics.

The first and strongest impression which one gains from such an analysis is surely the fact that the pathogenic psychic material, apparently forgotten and not at the disposal of the ego, which plays no rôle in the association and in memory, still lies ready in some manner and, what is more, in proper and good order. All that is necessary is to remove the resistances blocking the way. Barring that, everything is known as well as we know anything at all. The proper connections of the individual ideas among themselves and with the non-pathogenic, which are frequently remembered, are present; they have been produced in their time and retained in memory. The pathogenic psychic material appears as the property of an intelligence which is not necessarily inferior to the normal ego. The semblance of a second personality is often most delusively produced. Whether this impression is justified, whether the arrangement of the psychic material resulting after the adjustment is not transferred back into the period of the disease—these are questions, which I do not like to consider in this place. One cannot certainly describe the experiences gained from such analyses more easily and more clearly than by placing one's self in the position which one may take for a survey after the whole thing has been completed.

The situation is usually not so simple as one

represents it in special cases, as, for example, in a single case in which a symptom originates through a large trauma. We frequently deal not with a single hysterical symptom, but with a number of such, which are partially independent of one another and partially connected. We must not expect a single traumatic reminiscence, and as its nucleus one single pathogenic idea, but we must be ready to assume a series of partial traumas and concatenations of pathogenic mental streams. The monosymptomatic traumatic hysteria is, as it were, an elementary organism, a single being in comparison to the complicated structure of a grave hysterical neurosis, as we generally encounter it.

The psychic material of such hysteria presents itself as a multi-dimensional formation of at least *triple stratification.* I hope to be able to justify soon this figurative expression. First of all there is a nucleus of such reminiscences (either experiences or mental streams) in which the traumatic moment culminated, or in which the pathogenic idea has found its purest formation. Around this *nucleus* we often find an incredibly rich mass of other memory material which we have to elaborate in the analysis in the triple arrangement mentioned before. In the first place, there is an unmistakable *linear chronological* arrangement, which takes place within every individual theme. As an example of this, I can only cite the arrangement in Breuer's analysis of Anna O. The theme is that of becoming deaf, of not hearing, which then becomes differentiated according to seven determinants, and under each heading there were from ten to one hundred single reminiscences in chronological order. It read like an abstract from an orderly kept archive. The analysis of my patient Emmy von N contained similar memory fascicles though not so fully described, but they formed part of every analysis. They always appeared in chronological order which was as definitely reliable as the serial sequences of the days of the week or the names of the months in psychically normal individuals. They increased the work of the analysis through the peculiarity of reversing the series of their origin in the reproduction; the freshest and the most recent occurrence of the accumulation occurred first, so to speak, as a "wrapper," and the one with which the series really began gave the impression of the conclusion.

The grouping of similar reminiscences in a multiplicity of linear stratifications, as represented in a bundle of documents, in a package, etc., I have designated as the formation of a *theme.* These themes now show a second form of arrangement. I cannot express it differently than by saying that they are *concentrically stratified around the pathogenic nucleus.* It is not difficult to say what determines these strata, and according to what decreasing or increasing magnitude this arrangement follows. They are *layers of equal resistance* tending toward the nucleus, *accompanied by zones of similar alteration of consciousness* into which the individual themes extend. The most peripheral layers contain those reminiscences (or fascicles) of the different themes, which can readily be recalled and which were always perfectly conscious. The deeper one penetrates the more difficult it becomes to recognize the emerging reminiscences, until one strikes those near the nucleus which the patient disavows, even at the reproduction.

As we shall hear later, it is the peculiarity of the concentric stratification of the pathogenic psychic material which gives to the course of such an analysis its characteristic features. We must now mention the third and most essential arrangement concerning which a general statement can hardly be made. It is the arrangement according to the content of thought, the connection which reaches the nucleus through the logical threads, which might in each case correspond to a special irregular and manifoldly devious road. This arrangement has a dynamic character in contradistinction to both morphological stratifications mentioned before. Whereas, in a specially formed scheme the latter would be represented by rigid, arched, and straight lines, the course of the logical concatenation would have to be followed with a wand, over the most tortuous route, from the superficial into the deep layers and back, generally, however, progressing from the peripheral to the central nucleus, and touching thereby all stations; that is, its movement is similar to the zigzag movement of the knight in the solution of a chess problem.

I shall still adhere for a moment to the last comparison in order to call attention to a point in which it does not do justice to the qualities of the thing compared. The logical connection corresponds not only to a zigzag-like devious line, but rather to a ramifying and especially to a converging system of lines. It has a junction in which two or more threads meet, only to proceed thence united, and, as a rule, many threads running independently, or here and there connected by by-paths, open into the nucleus. To put it in different words, it is very remarkable how frequently *a symptom is manifoldly determined, that is overdetermined.*

I will introduce one more complication, and then my effort to illustrate the organization of the pathogenic psychic material will be achieved. It can happen that we may deal with more than one single nucleus in the pathogenic material, as, for example, when we have to analyze a second hysterical outbreak having its own aetiology, but which is still connected with the first outbreak of an acute hysteria which has been overcome years before. It can readily be imagined what strata and streams of thought must be added in order to produce a connection between the two pathogenic nuclei.

I will still add a few observations to the given picture of the organization of the pathogenic material. We have said of this material that it behaves like a foreign body, and that the therapy also acts like the removal of a foreign body from the living tissues. We are now in position to consider the shortcomings of this comparison. A foreign body does not enter into any connection with the layers of tissue surrounding it, although it changes them and produces in them a reactive inflammation. On the other hand, our pathogenic psychic group does not allow itself to be cleanly shelled out from the ego, its outer layers radiate in all directions into the parts of the normal ego, and really belong to the latter as much as to the pathogenic organization. The boundaries between both become purely conventional in the analysis, being placed now here, now there, and in certain locations no demarcation is possible. The inner layers become more and more estranged from the ego without showing a visible beginning of the pathogenic boundaries. The pathogenic organization really does not behave like a foreign body, but rather like an infiltration. The infiltrate must, in this comparison, be assumed to be the resistance. Indeed, the therapy does not consist in extirpating something—psychotherapy cannot do that at present—but it causes a melting of the resistance, and thus opens the way for the circulation into a hitherto closed territory.

(I make use here of a series of comparisons all of which have only a very limited resemblance to my theme, and do not even agree among themselves. I am aware of that, and I am not in danger of over-estimating their value; but, as it is my intention to illustrate the many sides of a most complicated and not as yet depicted idea, I, therefore, take the liberty of dealing also in the following pages with comparisons which are not altogether free from objections.)

If, after a thorough adjustment, one could show to a third party the pathogenic material in its present recognized, complicated and multidimensional organization, he would justly propound the question: "How could such a camel go through the needle's eye?" Indeed, one does not speak unjustly of a "narrowing of consciousness." The term gains in sense and freshness for the physician who accomplishes such an analysis. Only one single reminiscence can enter into the ego-consciousness; the patient, occupied in working his way through this one, sees nothing of that which follows, and forgets everything that has already wedged its way through. If the conquest of this one pathogenic reminiscence strikes against impediments, as, for example, if the patient does not let up the resistance against it, but wishes to repress or distort it, the strait is, so to speak, blocked; the work comes to a standstill, it cannot advance, and the one reminiscence in the breach confronts the patient until he takes it up into the breadth of his ego. The whole spatially extended mass of the pathogenic material is thus drawn through a narrow fissure and reaches consciousness as if disjointed into fragments or strips. It is the task of the psychotherapist to put it together again into the conjectured organization. He who desires still more comparisons may think here of a Chinese puzzle.

If one is about to begin an analysis in which one may expect such an organization of the pathogenic material, the following results of experience may be useful: *It is perfectly hopeless to attempt to make any direct headway towards the nucleus of the pathogenic organization.* Even if it could be guessed, the patient would still not know how to start with the explanation given to him, nor would it change him psychically.

There is nothing left to do but follow up the periphery of the pathogenic psychic formation. One begins by allowing the patient to relate and recall what he knows, during which one can already direct his attention, and may even overcome slight resistances. Whenever a new way is opened, it can be expected that the patient will follow it for some distance without any new resistance.

After having worked for a while in such manner, a cooperating activity is usually manifested in the patient. A number of reminiscences now occur to him without any need of questioning or setting him a task. A way has thus been opened into an inner stratum, within which the patient now spontaneously disposes of the material of equal resistance. It is well to allow him to reproduce for a while without influencing him; of course, he is unable to reveal important connections, but he may be allowed to clear things within the same stratum. The things which he thus reproduces often seem disconnected, but they give up the material which is later revived by the recognized connections.

One has to guard here in general against two things. If the patient is checked in the reproduction of the inflowing ideas, something is apt to be *buried* which must be uncovered later with great effort. On the other hand, one must not overestimate his *unconscious intelligence,* and one must now allow it to direct the whole work. If I should wish to schematize the mode of labour, I could perhaps say that one should himself undertake the opening of the inner strata and the advancement in the radial direction, while the patient should take care of the peripheral extension.

The advancement is brought about by the fact that the resistance is overcome in the manner indicated above. As a rule, however, one must at first solve another problem. One must obtain a piece of a logical thread by which direction alone one can hope to penetrate into the interior. One should not expect that the voluntary information of the patient, the material which is mostly in the superficial strata, will make it easy for the analyst to recognize its deep-seated locations, and to which points the desired connections of thought are attached. On the contrary, just this is cautiously concealed, the patient's assertion sounds as if perfect and firm in itself. One is at first confronted, as it were, by a wall which shuts off every view and gives no suggestion of anything hidden behind it.

If, however, one views with a critical eye the assertion obtained from the patient without much effort and resistance, one will unmistakably discover it in gaps and damages. Here the connection is visibly interrupted and scantily supplemented by the patient through phrases which convey only insufficient information. There one strikes against a motive which in a normal person would be designated as flimsy. The patient refuses to recognize these gaps when his attention is called to them. The physician, however, does well to seek under these weak points access to the material of the deeper layers and hope to discover just here the threads of the connection, which he traces by the pressure procedure. One, therefore, tells the patient, "You are mistaken, what you assert can have nothing to do with the thing in question; here we will have to strike against something which will occur to you under the pressure of my hand."

The hysterical stream of thought, even if it reaches into the unconscious, may be expected to show the same logical connections and sufficient motivations as those that would be expected in a normal individual. A looseness of these relationships does not lie within the sphere of the neurosis. If the association of ideas of neurotics, and especially of hysterics, makes a different impression, if the relation of the intensities of different ideas does not seem to be explainable here on psychological determinants alone, we know that such manifestations are due to the existence of *concealed unconscious motives.* Such secret motives may be expected, wherever such a deviation in the connection, or a transgression from the normally justified motivations can be demonstrated.

One must naturally free himself from the theoretical prejudice that one has to deal with abnormal brains of *dégénerés* and *deséquilibrés,* in whom the freedom of overthrowing the common psychological laws of the association of ideas is a stigma, or in whom a preferred idea without any motive may grow intensively excessive, and another without psychological motives may remain indestructible. Experience shows the contrary in hysteria; as soon as the hidden—often unconsciously remaining — motives have been revealed and brought to account, there remains nothing in the hysterical mental stream that is enigmatical and anomalous.

Thus, by retracing the breaches of the patient's first statements, which are often hidden by "false connections," one gets hold of a part of the logical thread at the periphery, and thereafter continues the route by the pressure procedure.

Very seldom do we succeed in working our way into the inner strata by the same thread, usually it breaks on the way and yields either no experience, or one which cannot be explained or be continued despite all efforts. In such a case we soon learn how to protect ourselves from the obvious confusion. The expression of the patient must decide whether one really reached an end or encountered a case needing no psychic explanation, or whether it is the enormous resistance that halts the work. If the latter cannot be overcome soon, it may be assumed that the thread has been followed into a stratum which is, as yet, impenetrable. One lets it fall in order to grasp another thread, which may, perhaps, be followed up just as far. If one had followed all the threads into this stratum, if the nodes have been reached through which no single isolated thread can be followed, it is well to think of seizing anew the resistances on hand.

One can readily imagine how complicated such a work may become. By constantly overcoming the resistance, one pushes his way into the inner strata, gaining knowledge concerning the accumulative themes and passing threads found in this layer; one examines as far as he can advance with the means at hand, and thus gains first information concerning the content of the next stratum; the threads are dropped, taken upon again, and followed until they reach the juncture; they are always retrieved, and by following a memory fascicle one reaches some by-way which finally opens again. In this manner it is finally possible to leave the stratifications and advance directly on the main road to the nucleus of the pathogenic organization. With this the fight is won, but not finished. One has to follow up the other threads and exhaust the material; but now the patient again helps energetically, for his resistance has mostly been broken.

In these later stages of the work it is of advantage if one can surmise the connection and tell it to the patient before it has been revealed to him. If the conjecture is correct, the course of the analysis is accelerated, but even an incorrect hypothesis helps, for it urges the patient to participate and elicits from him energetic refutation, thus revealing that he surely knows better.

One, thereby, becomes astonishingly convinced *that it is not possible to press upon the patient things which he apparently does not know, or to influence the results of the analysis by exciting his expectations.* I have not succeeded a single time in altering or falsifying the reproductions of memory or the connections of events by my predictions; had I succeeded it surely would have been revealed in the end by a contradiction in the construction. If anything occurred as I predicted, the correctness of my conjecture was always attested to by numerous trustworthy reminis-

cences. Hence, one must not fear to express his opinion to the patient concerning the connections which are to follow; it does no harm.

Another observation which I had occasion to see again and again refers to the patient's independent reproductions. It can be asserted that not a single reminiscence comes to the surface during such an analysis which has no significance. An interposition of irrelevant memory pictures which has no connection with the important associations does not really occur. An exception not contrary to the rule may be postulated for those reminiscences which, though in themselves unimportant, are indispensable as intercalations, since the associations between two closely related reminiscences pass over them. As mentioned above, the period during which a reminiscence abides in the narrow pass of the patient's consciousness is directly proportionate to its significance. A picture which does not disappear requires further consideration; a thought which cannot be abolished must be followed further. A reminiscence never recurs if it has been adjusted, a picture spoken away cannot be seen again. However, if that does happen, it can be definitely expected that the second time the picture will be joined by a new content of thought, that the idea will contain a new inference which will show that no perfect adjustment has taken place. On the other hand, a recurrence of different intensities, at first vaguely, then quite plainly, often occurs, but it does not, however, contradict the assertion just advanced.

If one of the tasks of the analysis is to remove a symptom (pains, symptoms like vomiting, sensations and contractures) which is capable of aggravation or recurrence, the symptom shows during the work the interesting and not undesirable phenomenon of *joining in the discussion.* The symptom in question reappears, or appears with greater intensity, as soon as one penetrates into the region of the pathogenic organization containing the aetiology of this symptom, and it continues to accompany the work with characteristic and instructive fluctuations. The intensity of the same (let us say of a nausea) increases the deeper one penetrates into its pathogenic reminiscences; it reaches its height shortly before the latter has been expressed, and suddenly subsides or disappears completely for a while after it has been fully expressed. If through resistance the patient delays the expression, the tension of the sensation of nausea becomes unbearable, and if the expression cannot be forced, vomiting actually sets in. One thus gains a plastic impression of the fact that the vomiting takes the place of a psychic action (here, that of speaking) just as was asserted in the conversion theory of hysteria.

These fluctuations of intensity on the part of the hysterical symptom recur as often as one of its new and pathogenic reminiscences is attacked; the symptom remains, as it were, all the time on *the order of the day*. If it is necessary to drop for a while the thread upon which this symptom hangs, the symptom, too, merges into obscurity in order to emerge again at a later period of the analysis. This play continues until, through the completion of the pathogenic material, there occurs a definite adjustment of this symptom.

Strictly speaking, the hysterical symptom does not behave here differently than a memory picture or a reproduced thought which is evoked by the pressure of the hand. Here, as there, the adjustment necessitates the same obsessing obstinacy of recurrence in the memory of the patient. The difference lies only in the apparent spontaneous appearance of the hysterical symptom, whereas one readily recalls having himself provoked the scenes and ideas. But in reality the *memory symbols* run in an uninterrupted series from the unchanged *memory remnants* of affectual experiences and thinking-acts to the hysterical symptoms.

The phenomenon of *joining in the discussion* of the hysterical symptom during the analysis carries with it a practical inconvenience to which the patient should be reconciled. It is quite impossible to undertake the analysis of a symptom in one stretch or to divide the pauses in the work in such a manner as precisely to coincide with the resting points in the adjustment. Furthermore, the interruption which is categorically dictated by the accessory circumstances of the treatment, like the late hour, etc., often occurs in the most awkward locations, just when some critical point could be approached or when a new theme comes to light. These are the same inconveniences which every newspaper reader experiences in reading the daily fragments of his newspaper romance, when, immediately after the decisive speech of the heroine, or after the report of a shot, etc., he reads, "To be continued." In our case, the raked-up, but unabolished theme, the symptom at first strengthened but not yet explained, remains in the patient's psyche, and troubles him perhaps more than before. But the patient must understand this, as it cannot be differently arranged. Indeed, there are patients who during such an analysis are unable to get rid of the theme once touched; they are obsessed by it even during the interval between two treatments, and, as they are unable to advance alone with the adjustment, they suffer more than before. Such patients, too, finally learn to wait for the doctor, postponing all interest which they have in the adjustment of the pathogenic material for the hours of the treatment, and they then begin to feel freer during the intervals.

The general condition of the patient during such an analysis seems also worthy of consideration. For a while it remains uninfluenced by the treatment, expressing the former effective factors, but then a moment comes in which the patient is "seized," and his interest becomes chained, and from that time his general condition becomes more and more dependent on the condition of the work. Whenever a new explanation is gained and an important contribution in the chain of the analysis is reached, the patient feels relieved and experiences a presentiment of the approaching deliverance, but at each standstill of the work, at each threatening entanglement, the psychic burden, which oppresses him, grows, and the unhappy sensation of his incapacity increases. To be sure, both conditions are only temporary, for the analysis continues, disdaining to boast of a moment of well-being, and continues regardlessly over the period of gloominess. One is generally pleased if it is possible to substitute the spontaneous fluctuations in the patient's condition by such as one himself provokes and understands, just as one prefers to see in place of the spontaneous discharge of the symptoms that order of the day which corresponds to the state of the analysis.

Usually the deeper one penetrates into the above described layers of the psychic structure, the more obscure and difficult the work will at first become. But once the nucleus is reached, light ensues and there is no more fear that a strong gloom will overcast the condition of the patient. However, the reward of the labour, the cessation of symptoms of the disease can be expected only when the full analysis of every individual symptom has been accomplished; indeed, where the individual symptoms are connected through many junctures, one is not even encouraged by partial successes during the work. By virtue of the great number of existing causal connections every unadjusted pathogenic idea acts as a motive for the complete creation of the neurosis, and only with the last word of the analysis does the whole picture of the disease disappear, very similarly to the behaviour of the individually reproduced reminiscence.

If a pathogenic reminiscence or a pathogenic connection which was previously withdrawn from the ego-consciousness is revealed by the work of the analysis and inserted into the ego, one can observe in the psychic personality which was thus enriched the many ways in which it gave utterance to its gain. Especially does it frequently happen that, after the patients have been painstakingly forced to a certain knowledge, they say: "Why I have known that all the time, I could have told you that before." Those who have more insight recognize this afterwards as a self-deception and accuse themselves of ingratitude. In general, the position that the ego takes towards the new acquisition depends upon the stratum of the analysis from which the latter originates. Whatever belongs to the outermost layers is recognized without any difficulty, for it always remained in the possession of the ego, and the only thing that was new to the ego was its connection with the deeper layers of the pathogenic material. Whatever is brought to light from these deeper layers also finds appreciation and recognition, but frequently only after long hesitation and reflection. Of course, visual memory pictures are here more difficult to deny than reminiscences of mere streams of thought. Not very seldom the patient will at first say, "It is possible that I thought of that, but I cannot recall it," and only after a longer familiarity with this assumption recognition will appear. He then recalls and even verifies by side associations that he once really had this thought. During the analysis, I make it a point of considering the value of an emerging reminiscence independently of the patient's recognition. I am not tired of repeating that we are obliged to accept everything that we bring to light with our means. Should there be anything unreal or incorrect in the material thus revealed, the connection will later teach us to separate it. I may add that I rarely ever have occasion subsequently to withdraw the recognition from a reminiscence which I had preliminarily admitted. In spite of the deceptive appearance of an urgent contradiction, whatever came to the surface finally proved itself correct.

Those ideas which originate in the deepest layer, and from the nucleus of the pathogenic organization, are recognized by the patient as reminiscences only with the greatest difficulty. Even after everything is accomplished, when the patients are overcome by the logical force and are convinced of the curative effect accompanying the emergence of this idea—I say even if the patients themselves assume that they have thought "so and so," they often add, "but to *recall* that I have thought so, I cannot." One readily comes to an understanding with them by saying that these were *unconscious thoughts*. But how should we note this state of affairs in our own psychological views? Should we pay no heed to the patient's demurring recognition, which has no motive after the work has been completed; should we assume that it is really a question of thoughts which never occurred, and for which there was only a possibility of existence, so that the therapy consisted in the consummation of a psychic act which at that time was omitted? It is obviously impossible to state anything about it, that is, to state anything concerning the condition of the pathogenic material previous to the analysis, before one has thoroughly explained his psychological views, especially concerning the essence of consciousness. It is, however, a fact worthy of reflection that in such analyses one can follow a stream of thought from the conscious into the unconscious (that is, absolutely not recognized as a reminiscence), thence draw it for some distance through consciousness, and again see it end in the unconscious; and yet this alteration of the "psychic elucidation" would change nothing in it, in its logic, and in the connection of its single parts. Should I, then, have this stream of thought freely before me, I could not conjecture what part was, and what part was not, recognized by the patient as a reminiscence. In a measure, I see only the points of the stream of thought that merge into the unconscious, just the reverse of that which has been claimed concerning our normal psychic processes.

I have still another theme to treat which plays an undesirably great part in the work of such a cathartic analysis. I have already admitted the possibility that the pressure procedure may fail, and despite all assurance and urging it may evoke no reminiscences. I also stated that two possibilities are to be considered: there is really nothing to evoke, in the place where we investigate—that can be recognized by the perfectly calm expression of the patient—or, we have struck against a resistance to be overcome only at some future time. We are confronted with a new layer into which we cannot as yet penetrate, and this can again be read from the drawn and psychic exertion of the patient's expression. A third cause may be possible which also indicates an obstacle, not from within, but externally. This cause occurs when the relation of the patient to the physician is disturbed, and signifies the worst obstacle that can be encountered. One can expect this in every more serious analysis.

I have already alluded to the important rôle falling to the personality of the physician in the creation of motives which are to overcome the psychic force of the resistance. In not a few cases, especially in women and where we deal with explanations of erotic streams of thoughts, the cooperation of the patients becomes a personal sacrifice which must be recompensed by some kind of a substitute for love. The great effort and the patient friendliness of the physician must suffice for such substitutes. If this relation of the patient to the physician is disturbed, the readiness of the patient's collaboration fails; if the physician desires information concerning the next pathogenic idea, the patient is confronted by the consciousness of the unpleasantness which has accumulated in her against the physician. As far as I have discovered, this obstacle occurs in three principal cases.

1. In personal estrangement, if the patient believes herself slighted, disparaged, and insulted, or if she hears unfavourable accounts concerning the physician and his methods of treatment. This is the least serious case. This obstacle can readily be overcome by discussion and explanation, although the sensitiveness and the suspicion of hysterics can occasionally manifest itself in unimaginable dimensions.

2. If the patient is seized with the fear that she is becoming too dependent on her physician, that in his presence she loses her independence and could even become sexually dependent upon him; this case is more significant because it is less determined individually. The occasion for this obstacle lies in the nature of the therapeutic distress. The patient has now a new motive for resistance which manifests itself not only in a certain reminiscence, but at each attempt of the treatment. Whenever the pressure procedure is started, the patient usually complains of headache. Her new motive for the resistance remains for the most part unconscious, and she manifests it by a newly created hysterical symptom. The headache signifies the aversion towards being influenced.

3. If the patient fears lest the painful ideas emerging from the content of the analysis would be transferred to the physician. This happens frequently, and, indeed, in many analyses it is a regular occurrence. The transference to the physician occurs through false connections. I must here give an example. The origin of a certain hysterical symptom in one of my hysterical patients was the wish she entertained years ago, which was immediately banished into the unconscious, that the man with whom she at that time conversed would heartily grasp her and force a kiss on her. After the ending of a session, such a wish occurred to the patient in reference to me. She was horrified and spent a sleepless night, and at the next session, although she did not refuse the treatment she was totally unfit for the work. After I had discovered the obstacle and removed it, the work continued. The wish that so frightened the patient appeared as the next pathogenic reminiscence, that is, as the one now required by the logical connection. It came about in the following manner: The content of the wish at first appeared in the patient's consciousness which would have transferred this wish into the past. Through the associative force prevailing in her consciousness, the existing wish became connected with my own person, with which the patient could naturally occupy herself, and in this *mésalliance*—which I call a false connection—the same affect awakened which originally forced the patient to banish this clandestine wish. Now that I have discovered this, I can presuppose in every similar claim on my personality that this is another transference and false connection. It is remarkable how the patient falls a victim to deception on every new occasion.

No analysis can be brought to an end if one does not know how to meet the resistances resulting from the causes mentioned. The way can be found if one bears in mind that the new symptom produced after the old model should be treated like the old symptoms. In the first place, it is necessary to make the patient conscious of the obstacle. In one of my patients, in whom I had cause to assume an unconscious idea like the one mentioned above in 2, I met it for the first time with an unexpected attack. I told her that there must have originated some obstacle, and then pressed her head. She then said, surprisingly, "I see you sitting here on the chair, but that is nonsense, what can that mean?" But now I could explain it.

In another patient, the obstacle did not usually show itself directly on pressure, but I could always demonstrate it by taking the patient back to the moment in which it originated. The pressure procedure never failed to bring back this moment. By discovering and demonstrating the obstacle, the first difficulty was removed, but a greater one still remained. The difficulty lay in inducing the patient to give information where there was an obvious personal relation and where the third person coincided with the physician. At first I was very much annoyed about the increase of this psychic work until I had learned to see the lawful part of this whole process, and I then also noticed that such a transference does not cause any considerable increase in the work. The work of the patient remained the same; she perhaps had to overcome the painful affect of having entertained such a wish, and it seemed to be the same for the success whether she took this psychic repulsion as a theme of the work in the historical case or in the recent case with me. The patients also gradually learned to see that in such transferences to the person of the physician they generally dealt with a force or a deception which disappeared when the analysis was accomplished. I believe, however, that if I should have delayed in making clear to them the nature of the obstacle, I would have given them a new, though a milder, hysterical symptom for another spontaneously developed.

I now believe that I have sufficiently indicated how such analyses should be executed, and the experiences gained from them. They perhaps make some things appear more complicated than they are, for many things really result by themselves during such work. I have not enumerated the difficulties of the work in order to give the impression that in view of such requirements it does not pay the physician or patient to undertake a cathartic analysis except in the rarest cases. However, in my medical activities I am influenced by contrary suppositions. To be sure, I am unable to formulate the most definite indications for the application of the therapeutic method discussed here without entering into the valuation of the more significant and more comprehensive theme of the therapy of the neuroses in general. I have often compared the cathartic psycho-therapy to surgical measures, and designated my cures as psycho-therapeutic operations; the analogies follow the opening of a pus pocket, the curetting of a carious location, etc. Such an analogy finds its justification, not so much in the removal of the morbid material as in the production of better curative conditions for the issue of the process.

When I promised my patients help and relief through the cathartic method, I was often obliged to hear the following objections: "You say, yourself, that my suffering has probably much to do with my own relation and destinies. You cannot change any of that. In what manner, then, can you help me?" To this I could always answer: "I do not doubt at all that it would be easier for fate than for me to remove your sufferings, but you will be convinced that much will be gained if we succeed in transforming your hysterical misery into everyday unhappiness, against which you will be better able to defend yourself with a restored nervous system."

CHAPTER 5

THE DEFENCE-NEURO-PSYCHOSES: A TENTATIVE PSYCHOLOGICAL THEORY OF ACQUIRED HYSTERIA, MANY PHOBIAS AND OBSESSIONS, AND CERTAIN HALLUCINATORY PSYCHOSES[1]

AFTER an exhaustive study of many nervous patients afflicted with phobias and obsessions, a tentative explanation of these symptoms forced itself upon me, which happily helped me later to conjecture the origin of such morbid ideas in other new cases, and I therefore believe it worthy of reporting and further examination. Simultaneously with this *psychological theory of phobias and obsessions*, the examination of these patients resulted in a contribution to the theory of hysteria, or rather to a change of it, which seems to imply an important and common character of hysteria as well as the aforementioned neuroses. Furthermore I had the opportunity to look into the psychological mechanism of a form of indubitable psychic malady and found that my attempted observation shows an intelligible connection between this psychosis and the two neuroses mentioned. At the conclusion of this theme, I shall describe the corroborative hypothesis which I utilized in all three cases.

I

I am beginning with that change which seems to be necessary for the theory of the hysterical neuroses.

That the symptom-complex of hysteria, as far as it can be understood, justifies the assumption of a splitting of consciousness with

---

[1] *Neurologisches Zentralblatt* (1894), 10-11.

the formation of separate psychic groups, has been generally recognized since the interesting works of P. Janet, J. Breuer, and others. Less understood are the opinions concerning the origin of this splitting of consciousness and concerning the rôle played by this character in the structure of the hysterical neuroses.

According to Janet's[1] theory, the splitting of consciousness is a primary feature of the hysterical alteration. It is due to a congenital weakness of the capacity for psychic synthesis, and to a narrowing of the *field of consciousness* (*champ du conscience*) which as a psychic stigma confirms the degeneration of hysterical individuals.

In contradistinction to Janet's views, which in my opinion admit the most manifold objections, are those advocated by J. Breuer in our joint communication. According to Breuer, the "basis and determination" of hysteria is the occurrence of peculiar dream-like conscious states with a narrowed association capacity, for which he proposed the name *hypnoid states*. The splitting of consciousness is secondary and acquired, and originates because the ideas emerging in the hypnoid states are isolated from associative communication with the rest of consciousness.

I can now demonstrate two other extreme forms of hysteria in which it is impossible to show that the splitting of consciousness is primary in the sense of Janet. In the first of these forms I could repeatedly show that the splitting of the content of consciousness was an arbitrary act of the patient, that is, it was initiated through an exertion of the will, the motive of which can be stated. I naturally do not maintain that the patient intended to produce a splitting of his consciousness; the patient's intention was different, but instead of attaining its aim it produced a splitting of consciousness.

In the third form of hysteria, as we have demonstrated by psychic-analysis of intelligent patients, the splitting of consciousness plays only an insignificant and perhaps really no rôle. This includes those cases in which there had been no reaction to the traumatic stimulus and which were then adjusted and cured by ab-reaction. They are the pure *retention hysterias*.

In connection with the phobias and obsessions, I have only to deal here with the second form of hysteria which for reasons to be presently explained I will designate as *defence hysteria* and thus distinguish it from the hypnoid

[1] *Etat mental des hystériques*, Paris, 1893 and 1894. "*Quelques définitions récentes de l'hystérie*," Arch. de. Neurol., 1893, XXXV-VI.

and retention hysterias. Preliminarily I am able to call my cases of defence-hysteria *acquired* hysterias, for they show neither marked hereditary taints nor any degenerative stigmata.

In those patients whom I have analyzed, there existed psychic health until the moment in which a case of incompatibility occurred in their ideation, that is, until there appeared an experience, idea, or feeling which evoked such a painful affect that the person decided to forget it because he did not trust his own ability to remove the resistance between the unbearable ideas and his ego.

Such incompatible ideas originate in the feminine sex on the basis of sexual experiences and feelings. With all desired precision, the patients recall their efforts of defence, their intention "to push it away," not to think of it, to repress it. As appropriate examples I can easily cite the following cases from my own experience: A young lady reproached herself because, while nursing her sick father, she thought of a young man who made a slight erotic impression on her; a governess fell in love with her employer and decided to crowd it out of her mind because it was incompatible with her pride, etc.

I am unable to maintain that the exertion of the will, in crowding such thoughts out of one's mind, is a pathological act, nor am I able to state whether and how the intentional forgetting succeeds in these persons who remain well under the same psychic influences. I only know that in the patients whom I analyzed such a *forgetting* was unsuccessful and led to either hysteria, obsession, or a hallucinatory psychosis. The ability to produce, by the exertion of the will, one of these states which are connected with the splitting of consciousness, is to be considered as the expression of a pathological predisposition, but it need not necessarily be identified with personal or hereditary *degeneration*.

From the road leading from the patient's exertion of the will to the origin of a neurotic symptom I formed a concept which in the current psychological abstractions may be expressed as follows: The task assumed by the defensive ego to treat the incompatible idea as *non arrivée* can not be directly accomplished. The memory trace as well as the affect adhering to the idea are here and can not be exterminated. The task can, however, be brought to an approximate solution if it is possible to change the strong idea into a weak one and to take away the affect or sum of excitement which adheres to it. The weak idea will then exert almost no claims on the association work; but the separated sum of excitement will have to be utilized in another direction.

Thus far the processes are the same as in hysteria, in phobias and obsessions, but from now on their ways part. The unbearable idea in hysteria is rendered harmless because the sum of excitement is transformed into physical manifestations, a process for which I would like to propose the term *conversion*.

The conversion may be total or partial, and follows that motor or sensory innervation which is either ultimately or more loosely connected with the traumatic experience. In this way the ego succeeds in freeing itself from opposition, but instead it becomes burdened with a memory symbol which remains in consciousness as an unadjusted motor innervation, or as a constantly recurring hallucinatory sensation similar to a parasite. It thus remains fixed until a conversion takes place in the opposite direction. The memory symbol of the repressed idea does not perish, but from now on forms the nucleus for a second psychic group.

I will follow up this view of the psycho-physical processes in hysteria with a few more words. If such a nucleus for an hysterical splitting is once formed in a *traumatic moment*, it then increases in other moments which might be designated as *auxiliary traumatic* as soon as a newly formed similar impression succeeds in breaking through the barrier formed by the will and in adding new affects to the weakened idea, and in forcing for a while the associative union of both psychic groups until a new conversion produces a defence. The condition thus attained in hysteria, in regard to the distribution of the excitement, proves to be unstable in most cases. As shown by the familiar contrast of the attacks and the persistent symptoms, the excitement which was pushed on a false path (in the bodily innervation) now and then returns to the idea from which it was discharged and forces the person to associative elaboration or to adjustment in hysterical attacks. The effect of Breuer's cathartic method consists in the fact that it consciously reconducts the excitement from the physical into the psychic spheres and then forces an adjustment of the contradiction through intellectual work, and a discharge of the excitement through speech.

If the splitting of consciousness in acquired hysteria is due to an act of volition, we can explain with surprising simplicity the remarkable fact that hypnosis regularly broadens the narrowed consciousness of hysteria, and causes the split off psychic groups to become accessible. For we know that it is peculiar to all sleeplike states to remove that distribution of excitement which depends on the *will* of the conscious personality.

We accordingly recognize that the characteristic element of hysteria is not the splitting of consciousness but the ability of conversion, and, as an important part of the hitherto unknown disposition of hysteria, we can mention the psycho-physical adaptation for the transference of a great sum of excitement into bodily innervation.

The adaptation does not in itself exclude psychic health, and leads to hysteria only in event of a psychic incompatibility or accumulation of excitement. With this turn, we—Breuer and I —come near to the familiar definitions of hysteria of Oppenheim[1] and Strümpel,[2] and deviate from Janet,[3] who assigns to the splitting of consciousness too great a rôle in the characteristics of hysteria. The description here given can lay claim to the fact that it explains the connection between the conversion and the hysterical splitting of consciousness.

II

If there is no adaptation for conversion in a predisposed person, and an effort is nevertheless made to separate an unbearable idea from its affect for the purpose of defence, the affect must then remain in the psychic sphere. The weakened idea remains apart from all association in consciousness, but its freed affect attaches itself to other not in themselves unbearable ideas, which on account of this "false" connection become obsessions. This is in brief the psychological theory of the obsessions and phobias concerning which I have spoken above.

I shall now state what parts demanded in this theory can be directly demonstrated and

[1] Oppenheim: Hysteria is an exaggerated expression of emotion. But the "expression of emotion" represents that amount of psychic excitement which normally experiences conversion.

[2] Strümpel: The disturbance of hysteria lies in the psycho-physical, there where the physical and psychical are connected with each other.

[3] Janet, in the second chapter of his spirited essay, *Quelques définitions*, etc., has treated the objection that the splitting of consciousness belongs also to the psychoses and the so-called psychaesthenia, but in my opinion he has not satisfactorily solved it. It is essentially this objection which urged him to call hysteria a form of degeneration. But through no characteristic is he able to separate sufficiently the hysterical splitting of consciousness from the psychopathic, etc.

what parts I have supplemented. Besides the end product of the process the obsession, we can in the first place directly demonstrate the source from which the affect in the false connection originates. In all cases that I have analyzed, it was the sexual life that has furnished a painful affect of precisely the same character as the one attached to the obsession. It is not theoretically excluded that this affect could not occasionally originate in other spheres, but I must say that thus far I have found no other origin. Moreover, one can readily understand that it is precisely the sexual life which furnishes the most manifold occasions for the appearance of unbearable ideas.

Moreover, the exertion of the will, the attempt at defence, upon which this theory lays stress is demonstrated by the most unequivocal utterances of the patients. At least in a number of cases the patients themselves inform us that the phobia or obsession appeared only after the exertion of the will manifestly gained its point. "Something very disagreeable happened to me once and I have exerted all my power to push it away, not to think of it. When I have finally succeeded, I have gotten the other thing instead, which I have not lost since." With these words a patient verified the main points of the theory here developed.

Not all who suffer from obsessions are so clear concerning the origin of the same. As a rule when we call the patient's attention to the original idea of a sexual nature, we receive the following answer: "It could not have come from that. Why, I have not thought much about it. For a moment I was frightened, then I distracted myself, and since then it has not bothered me." In this so frequent objection we have the proof that the obsession represents a compensation or substitute for the unbearable sexual idea, and that it has taken its place in consciousness.

Between the patient's exertion of the will which succeeds in repressing the unacceptable sexual idea and the appearance of the obsession, which, though in itself of little intensity, is here furnished with an inconceivably strong affect, there is a yawning gap which the theory here developed will fill. The separation of the sexual idea from its affect and the connection of the latter with another suitable but not unbearable idea—these are processes which take place unconsciously which we can only presume but not prove by any clinico-psychological analysis. Perhaps it would be more correct to say that these are not really processes of a psychic nature but physical processes of which the psychic result so presents itself that the expressions "separation of the idea from its affect and false connection of the latter," seem actual occurrences.

Besides the cases evincing in turn the sexual unbearable idea and the obsession, we find a series of others in which there are simultaneously obsessions and painfully accentuated sexual ideas. It will not do very well to call the latter *sexual obsessions;* they lack the essential character of obsessions in proving themselves fully justified, whereas the painfulness of the ordinary obsession is a problem for the doctor as well as the patient. From the amount of insight that could be obtained in such cases, it seems that we deal here with a continued defence against sexual ideas which are constantly renewed, a work heretofore not accomplished.

As long as the patients are aware of the sexual origin of their obsessions, they often conceal them. If they complain, they generally express surprise that this affect is behind the symptoms, that they are afraid, and that they have certain impulses, etc. To the experienced physician, however, the affect appears justified and intelligible; and the only thing he finds peculiar is the connection of such an affect with an idea unworthy of it. In other words, the affect of the obsession appears to him as one dislocated or transposed, and, if he has accepted the observations laid down here, he can in many cases retranslate obsessions into the sexual.

Any idea which either through its character may be combinable with an affect of such quality, or which bears a certain relation to the unbearable by virtue of which it seems a suitable substitute for it, may be used for the secondary connection of the freed affect. Thus, for example, freed anxiety, the sexual origin of which can not be recalled, attaches itself to the common primary phobias of man for animals, thunderstorms, darkness, etc., or to things which are unmistakably in some way associated with the sexual, such as urination, defecation, pollutions, and infections.

The advantage gained by the ego in the transposition of the affect for the purpose of defence is considerably less than in the hysterical conversion of psychic excitement into somatic innervation. The affect under which the ego has suffered remains now as ever unchanged and undiminished, but the unbearable idea is suppressed and excluded from memory. The repressed ideas again form the nucleus of a second psychic group which I believe can be accessible without having recourse to hypnotism. That in the phobias and obsessions there appear none of the striking symptoms which in hysteria accompany the formation of an independent psychic group, is due to the fact that in the former case the whole transformation remains in the psychic sphere, while the somatic innervation experiences no change.

What I have here said concerning obsessions I will explain by some examples which are probably of a typical nature:

1. A young girl suffers from obsessive reproaches. If she reads anything in the newspapers about counterfeiters, she conceives the thought that she, too, made counterfeit money; if a murder was anywhere committed by an unknown assassin, she anxiously asked herself whether she had not committed this crime. At the same time she is perfectly aware of the absurdity of these obsessive reproaches. For a time the consciousness of her guilt has gained such a power over her that her judgment was suppressed, and she accused herself before her relatives and physician of having really committed all these crimes (Psychosis through simple aggravation — overwhelming psychosis — *Uberwältigungs-psychose*). A thorough examination revealed the source of the origin of this guilty conscience. Accidentally incited by a sensual feeling, she allowed herself to be allured by a friend to masturbate. She practiced it for years with the full consciousness of her wrongdoing, and under the most violent but useless self-reproaches. The girl was cured after a few months' treatment and strict watching.

2. Another girl suffered from the fear of getting sudden desires of micturition and of being forced to wet herself. This began after such a desire had really forced her to leave a concert hall during the performance. This phobia had gradually caused her to become quite incapable of any enjoyment and social relationship. She felt secure only when she knew that there was a toilet nearby to which she could repair unobserved. An organic suffering which might have justified this lack of confidence of the control of the bladder was excluded. At home among quiet surroundings and during the night there was no such desire to micturate. Detailed examination showed that the desire to micturate appeared for the first time under the following conditions: A gentleman to whom she was not indifferent took a seat in the concert hall not far from her. She began to think and to picture to herself how she would sit near

him as his wife. In this erotic reverie she experienced that physical feeling which must be compared to an erection in the man, and which in her—I do not know whether it is general—ended in a slight desire to micturate. She now became extremely frightened over her otherwise accustomed sexual sensation, because she had determined to overcome this as well as every desire, and in the next moment the affect transposed itself to the accompanying desire to micturate and forced her to leave the hall after a very painful struggle. In her life she was so prudish that she experienced an intensive horror for all things sexual, and could not conceive the thought of ever marrying; on the other hand she was sexually so hyperesthetic that during every erotic revery, which she gladly entertained, there appeared sensual feeling. The erection was always accompanied by the desire to micturate, and up to the time of the scene in the concert hall it had made no impression on her. The treatment led to an almost complete control of the phobia.

3. A young woman who had only one child after five years of married life complained of obsessive impulses to throw herself from the window or balcony, and of fears lest at the sight of a sharp knife she might kill her child. She admitted that the marriage relations were seldom practised and then only with caution against conception; but she added that she did not miss this as she was not of a sensual nature. I then ventured to tell her that at the sight of a man she conceives erotic ideas, and that she therefore lost confidence in herself and imagined herself a depraved person fit for anything. The retranslation of the obsession into the sexual was successful; weeping, she soon admitted her long concealed marital misery, and then mentioned painful ideas of an unchanged sexual character such as the often recurring sensation of something forcing itself under her skirts.

I have made use of such experiences in the therapy of phobias and obsessions, and, despite the patient's resistances, I have redirected the attention to the repressed sexual ideas, and wherever feasible I have blocked the sources from which the same originated. To be sure, I cannot maintain that all phobias and obsessions originate in the manner here revealed; first, my experience, in proportion to the abundance of these neuroses, embraces only a limited amount, and second, I, myself, know that these *psychasthenic* symptoms (according to Janet's designation) are not all of the same value.[1] Thus, for instance, there are pure hysterical phobias. But I believe that the mechanism of the displacement of the affect will be demonstrated in the greater part of the phobias and obsessions, and I must assert that these neuroses, which are found just as often isolated as combined with hysteria and neurasthenia, are not to be thrown together with the ordinary neurasthenia for which fundamental symptom a psychic mechanism is not at all to be assumed.

III

In both cases thus far considered, the defence of the unbearable idea was brought about by the separation of the same from its affect; the idea, though weakened and isolated, remained in consciousness. There exists, however, a far more energetic and more successful form of defence wherein the ego misplaces the unbearable idea with its affect, and behaves as though the unbearable idea had never approached the ego. But at the moment when this is brought about, the person suffers from a psychosis which can only be classified as an *hallucinatory confusion*. A single example will explain this assertion. A young girl gives her first impulsive love to a man who she firmly believed reciprocated it. As a matter of fact she was mistaken; the young man had other motives for visiting her. It was not long before she was disappointed; at first she defended herself against it by converting hysterically the corresponding experience, and thus came to believe that he would come some day to ask her in marriage; but in consequence of the imperfect conversion and the constant pressure of new painful impressions, she felt unhappy and ill. She finally expected him with the greatest tension on a definite day, it was the day of a family reunion. The day passes but he did not come. After all the trains on which he could have come have passed she suddenly merged into an hallucinatory confusion. She thought that he did come, she heard his voice in the garden, and hastened down in her nightgown to receive him. For two months thereafter she lived in a happy dream, the content of which was that he was as before (before the time of the painfully defended disappointment). The hysteria and

[1] The group of typical phobias, for which agoraphobia is a prototype, cannot be reduced to the psychic mechanisms here developed. Furthermore, the mechanism of agoraphobia deviates in one decisive point from that of the real obsessions and from phobias based on such. Here there is no repressed idea from which the affect of fear has been separated. The fear of this phobia has another origin.

depression were thus conquered; during her sickness she never mentioned anything about the last period of doubt and suffering; she was happy as long as she was left undisturbed, and was excited only when a regulation of her environment prevented her from accomplishing something which she thought quite natural as a result of her blissful dream. This psychosis, unintelligible as it was in its time, was revealed ten years later through hypnotic analysis.

The fact to which I call attention is this: That the content of such an hallucinatory psychosis consists in directly bringing into prominence that idea which was threatened by the motive of the disease. One is, therefore, justified in saying that through its flight into the psychosis the ego defended the unbearable idea; the process through which this has been brought about withdraws itself from self perception as well as from the psychological-clinical analysis. It is to be considered as the expression of a higher grade of a pathological predisposition, and can perhaps be explained as follows: The ego tears itself away from the unbearable idea, but, as it hangs inseparably together with a part of reality, the ego while accomplishing this performance also detaches itself wholly or partially from reality. The latter is, in my opinion, the condition under which hallucinatory vividness is decreed to particular ideas, and hence after a very successful defence the person finds himself in an hallucinatory confusion.

I have but very few analyses of such psychoses at my disposal; but I believe that we deal with a very frequent type of psychic illness. For analogous examples such as the mother who, becoming sick after the loss of her child, continues to rock in her arms a piece of wood, or the jilted bride who in full dress expects her bridegroom, can be seen in every mental hospital.

It will perhaps not be superfluous to mention that the three forms of defence here considered, and hence the three forms of disease to which this defence leads, may be united in the same person. The simultaneous occurrence of phobias and hysterical symptoms, so frequently observed in practice, really belong to those factors which impede a pure separation of hysteria from other neuroses and force the formation of a *mixed neurosis*. To be sure, the hallucinatory confusion is not frequently compatible with the continuation of hysteria and not as a rule with obsessions; but on the other hand it is not rare that a defense psychosis should episodically break through the course of an hysteria or mixed neurosis.

In conclusion I will mention in a few words the subsidiary idea of which I have made use in this discussion of the defence neuroses. It is the idea that there is something to distinguish in all psychic functions (amount of affect, sum of excitement), that all qualities have a quantity though we have no means to measure the same—it is something that can be increased, diminished, displaced, and discharged, and that extends over the memory traces of the ideas perhaps like an electric charge over the surface of the body.

This hypothesis, which also underlies our theory of *ab-reaction* (" Preliminary Communication"), can be used in the same sense as the physicist uses the assumption of the current of electric fluid. It is preliminarily justified through its usefulness in the comprehension and elucidation of diverse psychic states.

CHAPTER 6

On the Right To Separate from Neurasthenia a Definite Symptom-Complex as "Anxiety Neurosis" (*Angstneurose*)[1]

It is difficult to assert anything of general validity concerning neurasthenia as long as this term is allowed to express all that for which Beard used it. I believe that neuropathology can only gain by an attempt to separate from the actual neurosis all those neurotic disturbances the symptoms of which are on the one hand more firmly connected among themselves than to the typical neurasthenic symptoms, such as headache, spinal irritation, dyspepsia with flatulence and constipation, and which on the other hand show essential differences from the typical neurasthenic neurosis in their aetiology and mechanism. If we accept this plan, we will soon gain quite a uniform picture of neurasthenia. We will soon be able to differentiate—sharper than we have hitherto succeeded—from the real neurasthenia the different pseudo-neurasthenias, such as the organically determined nasal reflex neurosis, the neurotic disturbances of cachexias and arteriosclerosis, the early stages of progressive paralysis, and of some psychoses. Furthermore, following the proposition of Moebius, some *status nervosi* of hereditary degenerates will be set aside and we will also find reasons for ascribing to melancholia, some of the neuroses which are now called neurasthenia, especially those of an intermittent or periodic nature. But we force the way into the most marked changes if we decide to separate from neurasthenia that symptom-complex which I shall hereafter describe and which especially fulfills the conditions formulated above. The symptoms of this complex are clinically more related to one another than to the real neurasthenic symptoms, that is, they frequently appear together and substitute one another in the course of the disease, and both the aetiology as well as the mechanism of this neurosis differs basically from the aetiology and the mechanism of the real neurasthenia which remains after such a separation.

I call this symptom-complex *anxiety neurosis* (*Angstneurose*) because the sum of its components can be grouped around the main symptom of anxiety, because each individual symptom shows a definite relation to anxiety. I believed that I was original in this conception of the symptoms of anxiety neurosis until an interesting lecture by E. Hecker[2] fell into my hand. In this lecture I found the description of the same interpretation with all the desired clearness and completeness. To be sure, Hecker does not separate the equivalents or rudiments of the attack of anxiety from neurasthenia as I intend to do; but this is apparently due to the fact that neither here nor there has he taken into account the diversity of the aetiological determinants. With the knowledge of the latter difference, every obligation to designate the anxiety neurosis by the same name as the real neurasthenia disappears, for the only object of arbitrary naming is to facilitate the formulation of general assertions.

I. *Clinical Symptomatology of Anxiety Neurosis*

What I call *anxiety neurosis* can be observed in complete or rudimentary development, either isolated or in combination with other neuroses. The cases which are in a measure complete, and at the same time isolated, are naturally those which especially corroborate the impression that the anxiety neurosis possesses clinical independence. In other cases we are confronted with the task of selecting and separating from a symptom-complex which corresponds to a *mixed neurosis,* all those symptoms which do not belong to neurasthenia, hysteria, etc., but to the anxiety neurosis.

[1] First published in the *Neurologisches Zentralblatt,* 1895, No. 2.

[2] E. Hecker, "Über larvierte und abortive Angstzustände bei Neurasthenie," *Zentralblatt für Nervenheilkunde,* December, 1893.— Anxiety is made particularly prominent among the chief symptoms of neurasthenia by Kaan, *Der neurasthenische Angstaffekt bei Zwangsvorstellungen und der primordiale Grübelzwang,* Vienna, 1893.

The clinical picture of the anxiety neurosis comprises the following symptoms:

1. *General Irritability.* This is a frequent nervous symptom, common as such as to many nervous states. I mention it here because it constantly occurs in the anxiety neurosis and is of theoretical importance. For increased irritability always points to an accumulation of excitement or to an inability to tolerate such accumulation, hence to an absolute or relative accumulation of excitement. The expression of this increased irritability through an auditory hyperesthesia is especially worth mentioning; it is an over sensitiveness for noises, which symptom is certainly to be explained by the congenital intimate relationship between auditory impressions and fright. Auditory hyperesthesia is frequently found as a cause of insomnia, of which more than one form belongs to anxiety neurosis.

2. *Anxious Expectation.* I cannot explain better the condition that I have in mind than by this name and by some appended examples. Thus a woman who suffers from anxious expectation thinks of influenza-pneumonia whenever her husband, who is afflicted with a catarrhal condition, has a coughing spell; and in her mind she sees a passing funeral procession. If on her way home she sees two persons standing together in front of her house, she cannot refrain from the thought that one of her children fell out of the window; if she hears the bell ring, she thinks that someone is bringing her mournful tidings, etc.; yet in none of these cases is there any special reason for exaggerating a mere possibility.

Anxious expectation naturally reflects itself constantly in the normal, and embraces all that is designated as "uneasiness, and a tendency to a pessimistic conception of things," but as often as possible it goes beyond such a plausible uneasiness, and it is frequently recognized as a part of constraint even by the patient himself. For one form of anxious expectation, namely, that which refers to one's own health, we can reserve the old name of *hypochondria*. Hypochondria does not always run parallel with the height of the general anxious expectation; as a preliminary stipulation it requires the existence of paresthesias and annoying somatic sensations. Hypochondria is thus the form preferred by the genuine neurasthenics whenever they merge into the anxiety neurosis, a thing which frequently happens.

As a further manifestation of anxious expectation, we may mention the frequent tendency observed in morally sensitive persons to pangs of conscience, scrupulosity, and pedantry, which varies, as it were, from the normal to its aggravation as doubting mania.

Anxious expectation is the most essential symptom of the neurosis; it also clearly shows a part of its theory. It can perhaps be said that we have here a quantum of freely floating anxiety which controls the choice of ideas by expectation and is forever ready to unite itself with any suitable ideation.

3. This is not the only way in which anxiousness, usually latent but constantly lurking in consciousness, can manifest itself. On the contrary it can also suddenly break into consciousness, without being aroused by the issue of an idea, and thus provoke an attack of anxiety. Such an attack of anxiety consists either of the anxious feeling alone without any associated idea, or of the nearest interpretation of the termination of life, such as the idea of sudden death or threatening insanity; or the feeling of anxiety becomes mixed with some paresthesia (similar to the hysterical aura); or finally the anxious feeling may be combined with a disturbance of one or many somatic functions, such as respiration, cardiac activity, vasomotor innervation, and glandular activity. From this combination the patient renders especially prominent now this and now the other factor. He complains of "heartspasms," "heavy breathing," "profuse perspiration," "inordinate appetite," etc., and in his description the feeling of anxiety is put to the background or it is rather vaguely described as "feeling badly," "uncomfortably," etc.

4. What is interesting and of diagnostic significance is the fact that the amount of admixture of these elements in the attack of anxiety varies extraordinarily, and that almost any accompanying symptom can alone constitute the attack as well as the anxiety itself. Accordingly there are rudimentary attacks of anxiety, and equivalents for the attack of anxiety, probably all of equal significance in showing a profuse and hitherto little appreciated richness in forms. A more thorough study of these larvated states of anxiety (Hecker) and their diagnostic division from other attacks should soon become the necessary work for neuro-pathologists.

I now add a list of those forms of attacks of anxiety with which I am acquainted. There are attacks:

(a) With disturbances of heart action, such as palpitation with transitory arrythmia, with longer continued tachycardia up to grave states of heart weakness, the differentiation of which from organic heart affection is not always easy; among such we have the pseudo-angina pectoris, a delicate diagnostic sphere!

(b) With disturbances of respiration, many forms of nervous dyspnoea, asthma-like attacks, etc. I assert that even these attacks are not always accompanied by conscious anxiety;

(c) Of profuse perspiration, often nocturnal;

(d) Of trembling and shaking which may readily be mistaken for hysterical attacks;

(e) Of inordinate appetite, often combined with dizziness;

(f) Of diarrhea appearing in the form of attacks;

(g) Of locomotor dizziness;

(h) Of so-called congestions, embracing all that was called vasomotor neurasthenia; and,

(i) Of paresthesias (these are seldom without anxiety or a similar discomfort).

5. Very frequently the nocturnal frights (*pavor nocturnus*) of adults usually combined with anxiety, dyspnea, perspiration, etc., are nothing other than a variety of the attack of anxiety. This disturbance determines a second form of insomnia in the sphere of the anxiety neurosis. Moreover, I became convinced that even the *pavor nocturnus* of children evinces a form belonging to the anxiety neurosis. The hysterical tinge and the connection of the fear with the reproduction of appropriate experience or dream, makes the *pavor nocturnus* of children appear as something peculiar, but it also occurs alone without a dream or a recurring hallucination.

6. *Vertigo.* In its lightest forms better designated as *dizziness,* assumes a prominent place in the group of symptoms of anxiety neurosis. In its severer forms the attack of vertigo, with or without fear, belongs to the gravest symptoms of the neurosis. The vertigo of the anxiety neurosis is neither a rotatory dizziness nor is it confined to certain planes or lines like Menier's vertigo. It belongs to the locomotor or coordinating vertigo, like the vertigo in paralysis of the ocular muscles; it consists in a specific feeling of discomfort which is accompanied by sensations of a heaving ground, sinking legs, of the impossibility to continue in an upright position, and at the same time there is a feeling that the legs are as heavy as lead, they shake, or give away. This vertigo never leads to falling. On the other hand, I would like to state that such an attack of vertigo may also be substituted by a profound attack of syncope. Other fainting-like states in the anxiety neurosis seem to depend on a cardiac collapse.

The vertigo attack is frequently accompanied by the worst kind of anxiety and is often combined with cardiac and respiratory disturbances. Vertigo of elevations, mountains, and precipices, can also be frequently observed in anxiety neurosis; moreover, I do not know whether we are still justified in recognizing a vertigo *a stomacho laeso.*[1]

7. On the basis of the chronic anxiousness (anxious expectation) on the one hand, and the tendency to vertiginous attacks of anxiety on the other, there develop two groups of typical phobias; the first refers to the general physiological menaces, while the second refers to locomotion. To the first group belong the fear of snakes, thunderstorms, darkness, vermin, etc., as well as the typical moral overscrupulousness, and the forms of doubting-mania. Here the available fear is merely used to strengthen those aversions which are instinctively implanted in every human being. But usually a compulsively acting phobia is formed only after a reminiscence is added to an experience in which this fear could manifest itself; as, for example, after the patient has experienced a storm in the open air. To attempt to explain such cases as mere continuations of strong impressions is incorrect. What makes these experiences significant and their reminiscences durable is, after all, only the fear which could at that time appear and can also appear today. In other words, such impressions remain forceful only in persons with *anxious expectations.*

The other group contains agoraphobia with all its accessory forms, all of which are characterized by their relation to locomotion. As a determination of the phobia, we frequently find a precedent attack of vertigo; I do not think that it can always be postulated. Occasionally, after a first attack of vertigo without fear, we see that though locomotion is always accompanied by the sensations of vertigo, it remains possible without any restrictions, but as soon as fear attaches itself to the attack of vertigo, locomotion fails, under the conditions of being alone, narrow streets, etc.

The relation of these phobias to the phobias of obsessions, which mechanism I discussed above,[2] is as follows: The agreement lies in the fact that, here as there, an idea becomes obsessive through its connection with an available affect. The mechanism of displacement of the affect therefore holds true for both kinds

---

[1] From upset stomach.—Ed.
[2] *The Defence-Neuro-Psychoses,* p. 81 ff. above.

of phobias. But in phobias of the anxiety neurosis, this affect is (1) a monotonous one, it is always one of anxiety; (2) it does not originate from a repressed idea, and on psychological analysis it proves itself not further reducible, nor can it be attacked through psycho-therapy. The mechanism of substitution does not, therefore, hold true for the phobias of anxiety neurosis.

Both kinds of phobias (or obsessions) often occur side by side, though the atypical phobias which depend on obsessions need not necessarily develop on the basis of anxiety neurosis. A very frequent, ostensibly complicated, mechanism appears if the content of an original simple phobia of anxiety neurosis is substituted by another idea, the substitution is then subsequently added to the phobia. The *protective measures* originally employed in combating the phobia are most frequently used as substitutions. Thus, for example, from the effort to provide oneself with counter evidence that one is not crazy, contrary to the assertion of the hypochondriacal phobia, there results a reasoning mania. The hesitations, doubts, and the many repetitions of the *folie du doute* originate from the justified doubt concerning the certainty of one's own stream of thoughts, for, through the compulsive-like idea one is surely conscious of so obstinate a disturbance, etc. It may therefore be claimed that many syndromes of compulsion neurosis, like *folie du doute* and similar ones, can clinically, if not notionally, be attributed to anxiety neurosis.[1]

8. The digestive functions in anxiety neurosis are subject to very few but characteristic disturbances. Sensations like nausea and sickly feeling are not rare, and the symptom of inordinate appetite, alone or with other congestions, may serve as a rudimentary attack of anxiety. As a chronic alteration analogous to the anxious expectations, one finds a tendency to diarrhea which has occasioned the queerest diagnostic mistakes. If I am not mistaken it is this diarrhea to which Moebius[2] has recently called attention in a small article. I believe, moreover, that Peyer's[3] reflex diarrhea, which he attributes to a disease of the prostrate, is nothing other than the diarrhea of anxiety neurosis. The deceptive reflex relation is due to the fact that the same factors which are active in the origin of such prostatic affections also come into play in the aetiology of anxiety neurosis.

The behaviour of the gastro-intestinal function in anxiety neurosis shows a sharp contrast to the influence of this same function in neurasthenia. Mixed cases often show the familiar "fluctuations between diarrhea and constipation." The desire to urinate in anxiety neurosis is analogous to the diarrhea.

9. The paresthesias which accompany the attack of vertigo or anxiety are interesting because they associate themselves into a firm sequence, similar to the sensations of the hysterical aura. But, in contrast to the hysterical aura, I find these associated sensations atypical and changeable. Another similarity to hysteria is shown by the fact that in anxiety neurosis a kind of conversion[4] into bodily sensations, as, for example, into rheumatic muscles, takes place which otherwise can be overlooked at one's pleasure. A large number of so-called rheumatics, who are moreover demonstrable as such, really suffer from an anxiety neurosis. Besides this aggravation of the sensation of pain, I have observed in a number of cases of anxiety neurosis a tendency towards hallucinations which could not be explained as hysterical.

10. Many of the so-called symptoms which accompany or substitute for the attack of anxiety also appear in a chronic manner. They are then still less discernible, for the anxious feeling accompanying them appears more indistinct than in the attack of anxiety. This especially holds true for the diarrhea, vertigo, and paresthesias. Just as the attack of vertigo can be substituted for by an attack of syncope, so can the chronic vertigo be substituted for by the continuous feeling of feebleness, lassitude, etc.

II. *The Occurrence and Aetiology of Anxiety Neurosis*

In some cases of anxiety neurosis, no aetiology can readily be ascertained. It is noteworthy that in such cases it is seldom difficult to demonstrate a marked hereditary taint.

Where we have reason to assume that the neurosis is acquired we can find by careful and laborious examination that the aetiologically effective factors are based on a series of injuries and influences from the sexual life. These at first appear to be of a varied nature but easily display the common character which explains their homogeneous effect on the nervous sys-

---

[1] *"Obsessions and Phobias"* (1895), *Collected Papers,* I.

[2] Moebius, *Neuropathologische Beiträge* (1894), Book 2.

[3] Peyer, *Die nervösen Affektionen des Darmes,* Vienna Clinic, January, 1893.

[4] See *The Defence-Neuro-Psychoses,* p. 81 ff. above.

tem. They are found either alone or with other banal injuries to which a reinforcing affect can be attributed. This sexual aetiology of anxiety neurosis can be demonstrated so preponderately often that I venture for the purpose of this brief communication to set aside all cases of a doubtful or different aetiology.

For the more precise description of the aetiological determinations under which anxiety neurosis occurs, it will be advisable to treat separately those occurring in men and those occurring in women. Anxiety neurosis appears in women—disregarding their predisposition—in the following cases:

(a) As virginal fear or anxiety in adults. A number of unequivocal observations showed me that an anxiety neurosis, which is almost typically combined with hysteria, can be evoked in maturing girls, at the first encounter with the sexual problem, that is, at the sudden revelation of the things hitherto veiled, by either seeing the sexual act, or by hearing or reading something of that nature;

(b) As fear in the newly married. Young women who remain anaesthetic during the first cohabitation not seldom merge into an anxiety neurosis which disappears after the anaesthesia is displaced by the normal sensation. As most young women remain undisturbed through such a beginning anaesthesia, the production of this fear requires determinants which I will mention;

(c) As fear in women whose husbands suffer from *ejaculatio precox* or from diminished potency; and,

(d) In those whose husbands practice *coitus interruptus* or *reservatus*. These cases go together, for on analyzing a large number of examples one can easily be convinced that they only depend on whether the woman attained gratification during coitus or not. In the latter case, one finds the determinant for the origin of anxiety neurosis. On the other hand the woman is spared from the neurosis if the husband afflicted by *ejaculatio precox* can repeat the congress with better results immediately thereafter. The *congressus reservatus* by means of the condom is not injurious to the woman if she is quickly excited and the husband is very potent; in other cases, the noxiousness of this kind of preventive measure is not inferior to the others. *Coitus interruptus* is almost regularly injurious; but for the woman it is injurious only if the husband practices it regardlessly, that is, if he interrupts coitus as soon as he comes near ejaculating without concerning

himself about the termination of the excitement of his wife. On the other hand if the husband waits until his wife is gratified, the coitus has the same significance for the latter as a normal one; but then the husband becomes afflicted with an anxiety neurosis. I have collected and analyzed a number of cases which furnished the material for the above statements.

(e) As fear in widows and intentional abstainers, not seldom in typical combination with obsessions; and,

(f) As fear in the *climacterium* during the last marked enhancement of the sexual desire.

The cases (c), (d), and (e) contain the determinants under which the anxiety neurosis originates in the female sex, most frequently and most independently of hereditary predisposition. I will endeavour to demonstrate in these—curable, acquired—cases of anxiety neurosis that the discovered sexual injuries really represent the aetiological factors of the neurosis. But before proceeding I will mention the sexual determinants of anxiety neurosis in men. I would like to formulate the following groups, every one of which finds its analogy in women:

(a) Fear of the intentional abstainers; this is frequently combined with symptoms of defence (obsessions, hysteria). The motives which are decisive for intentional abstinence carry along with them the fact that a number of hereditarily burdened eccentrics, etc., belong to this category.

(b) Fear in men with frustrated excitement (during the engagement period), persons who out of fear for the consequences of sexual relations satisfy themselves with handling or looking at the woman. This group of determinants which can moreover be transferred to the other sex—engagement periods, relations with sexual forbearance—furnish the purest cases of the neurosis.

(c) Fear in men who practice *coitus interruptus*. As observed above, *coitus interruptus* injures the woman if it is practiced regardless of the woman's gratification; it becomes injurious to the man if, in order to bring about the gratification in the woman, he voluntarily controls the coitus by delaying the ejaculation. In this manner we can understand why it is that, in couples who practice *coitus interruptus*, it is usually only one of them who becomes afflicted. Moreover the *coitus interruptus* only rarely produces in man a pure anxiety neurosis; usually it is a mixture of the same with neurasthenia.

(d) Fear in men *in senium*. There are men

who show a *climacterium* like women, and merge into an anxiety neurosis at the time when their potency diminishes and their libido increases.

Finally I must add two more cases holding true for both sexes:

(e) Neurasthenics merge into anxiety neurosis in consequence of masturbation as soon as they refrain from this manner of sexual gratification. These persons have especially made themselves unfit to bear abstinence.

What is important for the understanding of the anxiety neurosis is the fact that any noteworthy development of the same occurs only in men who remain potent, and in non-anesthetic women. In neurasthenics, who on account of masturbation have markedly injured their potency, anxiety neurosis as a result of abstinence occurs but rarely and limits itself usually to hypochondria and light chronic dizziness. The majority of women are really to be considered as *potent;* a real impotent, that is, a real anesthetic woman, is also inaccessible to anxiety neurosis, and bears strikingly well the injuries cited above.

How far we are perhaps justified in assuming constant relations between individual aetiological factors and individual symptoms from the complex of anxiety neurosis, I do not care to discuss here.

(f) The last of the aetiological determinants to be mentioned seems, in the first place, really not to be of a sexual nature. Anxiety neurosis originates in both sexes through overwork, exhaustive exertion, as, for instance, after sleepless nights, nursing the sick, and even after serious illness.

The main objection to my formulation of a sexual aetiology of anxiety neurosis will probably be based on the argument that such abnormal relations of the sexual life exist very frequently, that they will be found wherever one will look for them, and that their occurrence in cases of anxiety neurosis does not therefore demonstrate the aetiology of this neurosis. It may also be argued that the number of persons practicing *coitus interruptus*, etc., is incomparably greater than those who are burdened with anxiety neurosis, and that the overwhelming number of the former are quite well in spite of this injury.

To this I can answer that we certainly need not expect a rare aetiological factor in the neuroses, especially in anxiety neurosis, which everyone concedes are enormously frequent. Moreover, this very finding really fulfills a

pathological postulate, if an aetiological examination shows that the aetiological factor can be more frequently demonstrated than its effect, for the latter requires still other determinants (predisposition, summation of the specific aetiology, reinforcement through other banal injuries); and furthermore, the detailed analysis of suitable cases of anxiety neurosis show quite unequivocally the significance of the sexual factor. I shall, however, confine myself here to the aetiological factor of *coitus interruptus*, and will render prominent obvious individual experiences.

1. As long as anxiety neurosis in young women is not yet constituted but appears in fragments and again spontaneously disappears, it can be shown that every such shift of the neurosis depends on a coitus lacking gratification. Two days after such behaviour, and, in persons of little resistance, the day after, there regularly appears the attack of anxiety or vertigo to which all the other symptoms of the neurosis attach themselves; they abate again on rarer marital relations. An unexpected journey of the husband, a sojourn in the mountains causing a separation of the married couple, does good; the benefit from a course of gynecological treatment is due to the fact that, during its continuation, the marriage relations are stopped. It is noteworthy that the success of a local treatment is only transitory, the neurosis reappears in the mountain resort if the husband joins his wife for his own vacation. If, in a not as yet constituted neurosis, a physician aware of this aetiology causes a substitution of the *coitus interruptus* by normal relations, there results a therapeutic proof of the assertion here formulated. The anxiety disappears and does not return unless there be a new or similar cause.

2. In the anamnesis of many cases of anxiety neurosis, we find in both men and women a striking fluctuation in the intensity of the appearances in both the coming and going of the whole condition. This year was almost wholly good, the following was terrible, etc.; on one occasion the improvement occurred after a definite treatment which, however, failed to produce a response at the next attack. If we inform ourselves about the number and the sequence of the children, and compare this marriage chronicle with the peculiar course of the neurosis, the result of the simple solution shows that the periods of improvement or well-being corresponded with the pregnancies of the woman during which, naturally, the occasions for

preventive relations were unnecessary. The treatment which benefited the husband, be it Father Kneip's or hydrotherapy, was the one which he had taken after his wife was pregnant.

3. From the anamnesis of patients, we often find that the symptoms of the anxiety neurosis are relieved at a certain time by another neurosis, perhaps a neurasthenia which has supplanted it. It can then be regularly demonstrated that, shortly before this change of the picture, there occurred a corresponding change in the form of sexual injury.

Whereas such experiences, which can be augmented at pleasure, plainly obtrude upon the physician the sexual aetiology for a certain category of cases, other cases which would have otherwise remained incomprehensible can at least without gainsaying be solved and classified by the key of the sexual aetiology. We refer to those numerous cases in which everything exists that has been found in the former category, such as the appearance of anxiety neurosis on the one hand, and the specific factor of *coitus interruptus* on the other, but yet something else slips in, namely, a long interval between the assumed aetiology and its effect, and perhaps other aetiological factors of a nonsexual nature. We have, for example, a man who was seized with an attack of palpitation on hearing of his father's death, and who since that time suffered from an anxiety neurosis. The case cannot be understood, for up to that time this man was not nervous. The death of the father, well advanced in years, did not occur under any peculiar circumstances, and it must be admitted that the expected natural death of an aged father does not belong to those experiences which are wont to make a healthy adult sick. The aetiological analysis will perhaps seem clearer if I add that out of regard for his wife this man practiced *coitus interruptus* for eleven years. At all events the manifestations are precisely the same as those appearing in other persons after a short sexual injury of this nature, and without the intervention of another trauma. The same judgment may be pronounced in the case of a woman who merges into an anxiety neurosis after the death of her child, or in the case of the student who becomes disturbed by an anxiety neurosis while preparing for his final state examination. I find that here, as there, the effect is not explained by the reported aetiology. One must not necessarily *overwork* himself studying, and a healthy mother is wont to react to the death of her child with normal grief. But,

above all, I would expect that the overworked student would acquire a cephalasthenia, and that the mother, in our example, an hysteria. That both became afflicted with anxiety neurosis causes me to attach importance to the fact that the mother lived for eight years in marital *coitus interruptus*, and that the student entertained for three years a warm love affair with a "respectable" girl whom he was not allowed to impregnate.

These examples tend to show that where the specific sexual injury of the *coitus interruptus* is in itself unable to provoke an anxiety neurosis, it at least predisposes to its acquisition. The anxiety neurosis then comes to light as soon as the effect of another banal injury enters into the latent effect of the specific factor. The former can quantitatively substitute the specific factor but not supplant it qualitatively. The specific factor always remains that which determines the form of neurosis. I hope to be able to prove to a greater extent this theory for the aetiology of the neurosis.

Furthermore, the last discussions contain the not in itself improbable assumption that a sexual injury like *coitus interruptus* asserts itself through summation. The time required before the effect of this summation becomes visible depends upon the predisposition of the individual and the former burdening of his nervous system. The individuals who bear *coitus interruptus* manifestly without disadvantage really become predisposed by it to the disturbance—anxiety neurosis—which can at any time burst forth spontaneously or after a banal, otherwise inadequate, trauma, just as the chronic alcoholic finally develops a cirrhosis or another disease by summation, or, under the influence of a fever, merges into a delirium.

III. *Addenda to the Theory of Anxiety Neurosis*

The following discussions claim nothing but the value of a first tentative experiment, which judgment should not influence the acceptance of the facts mentioned above. The estimation of this *theory of anxiety neurosis* is rendered still more difficult by the fact that it merely corresponds to a fragment of a more comprehensive representation of the neuroses.

The facts hitherto expressed concerning the anxiety neurosis already contain some starting points for an insight into the mechanism of this neurosis. In the first place, it contains the assumption that we deal with an accumulation of excitement, and then the very important fact that the anxiety underlying the manifestations of the neurosis is not of psychic derivation. Such, for example, would exist if we found as a basis for the anxiety neurosis a justified fright happening once or repeatedly which has since supplied the source of the preparedness for the anxiety neurosis. But this is not the case; a former fright can perhaps cause an hysteria or a traumatic neurosis but never an anxiety neurosis. As the *coitus interruptus* is rendered so prominent among the causes of anxiety neurosis, I have thought at first that the source of the continuous anxiety was perhaps the repeated fear during the sexual act lest the technique will fail and conception follow. But I have found that this state of mind of the man or woman during the *coitus interruptus* plays no part in the origin of anxiety neurosis, that the women who are really indifferent to the possibilities of conception are just as exposed to the neurosis as those who are trembling at the possibility of it; it all depends on which person suffers the loss of sexual gratification.

Another starting point presents itself in the as yet unmentioned observation that in a whole series of cases the anxiety neurosis goes along with the most distinct diminution of the sexual libido or the psychic desire, so that, on revealing to the patients that their affliction depends on *insufficient gratification,* they regularly reply that this is impossible as just now their whole desire is extinguished. The indications that we deal with an accumulation of excitement, that the anxiety which probably corresponds to such accumulated excitement is of somatic origin, so that somatic excitement becomes accumulated, and, furthermore, that this somatic excitement is of a sexual nature, and that it is accompanied by a decreased psychic participation in the sexual processes—all these indications, I say, favour the expectation that the mechanism of the anxiety neurosis is to be found in the deviation of the somatic sexual excitement from the psychic, and in the abnormal utilization of this excitement.

This conception of the mechanism of anxiety neurosis will become clearer if one accepts the following view concerning the sexual process in man. In the sexually mature male organism, the somatic sexual excitement is—probably continuously—produced, and this becomes a periodic stimulus for the psychic life. To make our conceptions clearer we will add that this somatic sexual excitement manifests itself as a pressure on the wall of the seminal vesicle which is provided with nerve endings. This visceral excitement thus becomes continuously increased, but not before attaining a certain height is it able to overcome the resistances of the intercalated conduction as far as the cortex, and manifest itself as psychic excitement. Then the group of sexual ideas existing in the psyche becomes endowed with energy and results in a psychic state of libidinal tension which is accompanied by an impulse to remove this tension. Such psychic unburdening is possible only in one way which I wish to designate as specific or adequate action. This adequate action for the male sexual impulse consists of a complicated spinal reflex-act which results in the unburdening of those nerve endings, and of all psychically formed preparations for the liberation of this reflex. Anything else except the adequate action would be of no avail, for after the somatic sexual excitement has once reached the liminal value, it continuously changes into psychic excitement; that must by all means occur which frees the nerve endings from their heavy pressure, and thus abolish the whole somatic excitement existing at the time and allow the subcortical conduction to reestablish its resistance.

I will desist from presenting in a similar manner more complicated cases of the sexual process. I will merely formulate the statement that this scheme can essentially be transferred to the woman, despite the problem of the perplexity, artificial retardation, and stunting of the female sexual impulse. In the woman, too, it can be assumed that there is a somatic sexual excitement, and a state in which this excitement becomes psychic, evoking libido and the impulse to specific action accompanied by the sensual feeling. But we are unable to state what analogy there may be in the woman to the unburdening of the seminal vesicles.

We can bring into the bounds of this representation of the sexual process the aetiology of actual neurasthenia as well as of anxiety neurosis. Neurasthenia always originates whenever the adequate (action) unburdening is replaced by a less adequate one, like the normal coitus under the most favourable conditions, by a masturbation or spontaneous pollution; while anxiety neurosis is produced by all factors which impede the psychic elaboration of the somatic sexual excitement. The manifestations of anxiety neurosis are brought about by the fact that the somatic sexual excitement diverted from the psyche expends itself subcortically in not at all adequate reactions.

I will now attempt to test the aetiological determinants suggested before in order to see whether they show the common character formulated by me. As the first aetiological factor in the man, I have mentioned intentional abstinence. Abstinence consists in foregoing the specific action which results from libido. Such foregoing may have two consequences, first the somatic excitement accumulates, second, which is more important, it then becomes diverted to another route where there is more chance for discharge than through the psyche. It will then finally diminish the libido and the excitement will manifest itself subcortically as anxiety. Where the libido does not become diminished, or the somatic excitement is expended in pollutions, or where it really becomes exhausted in consequence of repulsion, everything else except anxiety neurosis is formed. In this manner, abstinence leads to anxiety neurosis. But abstinence is also the active process in the second aetiological group of frustrated excitement. The third case, that of the very considerate *coitus reservatus,* acts through the fact that it disturbs the psychic preparedness for the sexual discharge by establishing beside the subjugation of the sexual affect another distracting psychic task. Through this psychic distraction, too, the libido gradually disappears, and the further course is then the same as in the case of abstinence. The anxiety in old age (*climacterium of men*) requires another explanation. Here the libido does not diminish, but, just as in the *climacterium* of women, such an increase takes place in the somatic excitement that the psyche shows itself relatively insufficient for the subjugation of the same.

The subsummation of the aetiological determinants in the woman, under the aspect mentioned, does not afford any greater difficulties. The case of the virginal fear is especially clear. Here the group of ideas with which the somatic sexual excitement should combine are not as yet sufficiently developed. In anaesthetically newly married women, the anxiety appears only if the first cohabitations awakened a sufficient amount of somatic excitement. Where the local signs of such excitability (like spontaneous feelings of excitement, desire to micturate, etc.) are lacking, the anxiety, too, stays away. The case of *ejaculatio precox* or *coitus interruptus* is explained similarly to that in the man by the fact that the libido gradually disappears in the psychically ungratified act, whereas the excitement thereby evoked is subcortically expended. The formation of an estrangement between the somatic and psychic in the discharge of the sexual excitement succeeds quicker in the woman than in the man and is more difficult to remove. The case of widowhood or voluntary abstinence, as well as the case of *climacterium,* adjusts itself in the woman as in the man, but in the case of abstinence there surely is in addition the intentional repression of the sexual ideas, for an abstinent woman struggling with temptation must often decide to suppress it. The abhorrence perceived by an elderly woman during her menopause against the immensely increased libido can have a similar effect.

The two aetiological determinants mentioned last can also be classified without any difficulty.

The tendency to anxiety of the masturbator who becomes neurasthenic is explained by the fact that such persons easily merge into the state of abstinence, after they have so long been accustomed to afford a discharge—to be sure an inadequate one—for every little quantity of somatic excitement. Finally the last case, the origin of anxiety neurosis through a severe illness (overwork, exhaustive nursing, etc.), aided by the efficacy of *coitus interruptus* readily permits this free interpretation: Through deviation, the psyche becomes here insufficient for the subjugation of the somatic sexual excitement, a task which continuously devolves upon it. We know how deeply the libido can sink under the same conditions, and we have here a nice example of a neurosis which *although not of a sexual aetiology still evinces a sexual mechanism.*

The conception here developed represents the symptoms of anxiety neurosis in a measure as a *substitute* for the omitted specific action of sexual excitement. As a further corroboration of this I recall that also in normal coitus the excitement extends itself in respiratory acceleration, palpitation, perspiration, congestion, etc. In the corresponding attack of anxiety of our neurosis, we have before us the dyspnoea, the palpitation, etc., of the coitus in an isolated and aggravated manner.

It can still be asked why the nervous system merges into a peculiar affective state of anxiety under the circumstances of psychic inadequacy for the subjugation of the sexual excitement. A hint to the answer is as follows: The psyche merges into the affect of anxiety, when it perceives itself unfit to adjust *an externally approaching* task (danger) by a corresponding reaction; it merges into the neurosis of anxiety, when it finds itself unable to equalize the endogenously original (sexual) excitement. *The psyche, therefore, behaves as if projecting this excitement externally.* The affect and the neurosis corresponding to it stand in close relationship to each other, the first is the reaction to an exogenous, the latter the reaction to an analogous endogenous excitement. The affect is a rapidly passing state, the neurosis is chronic, because the exogenous excitement acts like a stroke happening but once, while the endogenous acts like a constant force. *The nervous system reacts in the neurosis against an inner source of excitement, just as it does in the corresponding affect against an analogous external one.*

IV. *The Relations to Other Neuroses*

A few observations still remain to be mentioned on the relations of anxiety neurosis to the other neuroses in reference to occurrence and inner relationship.

The purest cases of anxiety neurosis are also usually the most pronounced. They are found in potent young individuals with a uniform aetiology, and where the disease is not of long standing.

To be sure, the symptoms of anxiety are found more frequently as a simultaneous and common occurrence with those of neurasthenia, hysteria, compulsive ideas, and melancholia. If, on account of such clinical mixtures, one hesitates in recognizing anxiety neurosis as an independent unity, he will also have to abandon the laboriously acquired separation of hysteria and neurasthenia.

For the analysis of the *mixed neuroses* I can advocate the following proposition: *Where a mixed neurosis exists, an involvement of many specific aetiologies can be demonstrated.*

Such a multiplicity of aetiological factors determining a mixed neurosis can only come about accidentally, if the activities of a newly formed injury are added to those already existing. Thus, for example, a woman who was at all times a hysteric begins to practice *coitus reservatus* at a certain period of her married life, and adds an anxiety neurosis to her hysteria; a man who had masturbated and become neurasthenic becomes engaged and excites himself with his fiancée so that a fresh anxiety neurosis allies itself to his neurasthenia.

The multiplicity of aetiological factors in other cases is not accidental; one of them has brought the other into activity. Thus, a woman, with whom her husband practices *coitus reservatus* without regard to her gratification,

finds herself forced to finish the tormenting excitement following such an act with masturbation, as a result of which she shows an anxiety neurosis with symptoms of neurasthenia. Under the same noxiousness another woman has to contend with lewd pictures against which she wishes to defend herself, and in this way the *coitus interruptus* will cause her to acquire obsessions along with the anxiety neurosis. Finally, a third woman, as a result of *coitus interruptus,* loses her affection for her husband and forms another which she secretly guards, and as a result she evinces a mixture of hysteria and anxiety neurosis.

In a third category of mixed neuroses the connection of the symptoms is of a still more intimate nature, as the same aetiological determinants regularly and simultaneously evoke both neuroses. Thus, for example, the sudden sexual explanation which we have found in virginal fear always produces hysteria, too; most causes of intentional abstinence connect themselves in the beginning with actual obsessions; and it seems to me that the *coitus interruptus* of men can never provoke a pure anxiety neurosis, but always a mixture of the same with neurasthenia, etc.

It follows from this discussion that the aetiological determinants of the occurrence must moreover be distinguished from the specific aetiological factors of neurasthenia. The first factors, as, for example, *coitus interruptus,* masturbation, and abstinence, are still ambiguous, and can each produce different neuroses; and it is only the aetiological factors abstracted from them, like the inadequate unburdening, psychic insufficiency, and defence with substitution, that have an unambiguous and specific relation to the aetiology of the individual great neuroses.

In its intrinsic property, anxiety neurosis shows the most interesting agreements and differences when compared with the other great neuroses, particularly when compared with neurasthenia and hysteria. With neurasthenia it shares one main character, namely, that the source of excitement, the cause of the disturbance, lies in the somatic rather than in the psychic sphere, as in the case of hysteria and compulsion neurosis. For the rest we can recognize a kind of contrast between the symptoms of neurasthenia and anxiety neurosis, which can be expressed in the catchwords *accumulation* and *impoverishment of excitement.* This contrast does not hinder the two neuroses from combining with each other, but shows itself in the fact that the most extreme forms in both cases are also the purest.

When compared with hysteria, anxiety neurosis shows in the first place a number of agreements in the symptomatology, the valuation of which is still unsettled. The appearance of the manifestations as persistent symptoms or attacks, the aura-like grouped paresthesias, the hyperesthesias and pressure points can be found in certain substitutes for the anxiety attack, as in dyspnoea and palpitation, the aggravation of the perhaps organically determined pains (by conversion)—these and other joint features lead to the supposition that some things which are ascribed to hysteria can with full authority be fastened to anxiety neurosis. But if we enter into the mechanism of both neuroses, as far as it can at present be penetrated, we find aspects which make it appear that the anxiety neurosis is really the somatic counterpart to hysteria. Here as there we have accumulation and excitement, on which is perhaps based the similarity of the aforementioned symptoms; here as there we have a psychic insufficiency which results from abnormal somatic processes; and here as there we have instead of a psychic elaboration a deviation of the excitement into the somatic. The difference only lies in the fact that the excitement, in which displacement the neurosis manifests itself, is purely somatic (somatic sexual excitement) in anxiety neurosis, while in hysteria it is psychic (evoked through a conflict). Hence it is not surprising that hysteria and anxiety neurosis lawfully combine with each other, as in the virginal fear or in the sexual hysteria, and that hysteria simply borrows a number of symptoms from anxiety neurosis, etc. This intimate relationship between anxiety neurosis and hysteria furnishes us with a new argument for demanding the separation of anxiety neurosis from hysteria, for, if this be denied, one will also be unable to maintain the so painstakingly acquired distinction between neurasthenia and hysteria, so indispensable for the theory of the neuroses.

CHAPTER 7

FURTHER OBSERVATIONS ON THE DEFENCE-NEURO-PSYCHOSES[1]

UNDER the caption of *Defence-Neuro-Psychoses* I have comprised hysteria, obsessions, as well as certain cases of acute hallucinatory confusion. All these affections evince one common aspect in the fact that their symptoms originated through the psychic mechanism of (unconscious) defence, that is, through the attempt to repress an unbearable idea which appeared in painful contrast to the ego of the patient. I was also able to explain and exemplify by cases reported in the preceding chapters in what sense this psychic process of *defence* or *repression* is to be understood. I have also discussed the laborious but perfectly reliable method of psycho-analysis of which I make use in my examinations, and which at the same time serves as a therapy.

My experiences during the last two years have strengthened my predilection for making the defence the essential point in the psychic mechanism of the neuroses mentioned, and on the other hand have permitted me to give a clinical foundation to the psychological theory. To my surprise, I have discovered some simple but sharply circumscribed solutions for the problem of the neuroses which I shall provisionally briefly report in the following pages. It would be inconsistent with this manner of reporting to add to the assertions the required proofs, but I hope to be able to fulfill this obligation in a comprehensive discussion.

1. *The* Specific *Aetiology of Hysteria*

That the symptoms of hysteria become comprehensible only through a reduction to *traumatically* effective experiences, and that these psychic traumas refer to the sexual life, has already been asserted by Breuer and me in former publications. What I have to add today as a uniform result of thirteen analyzed cases of hysteria concerns, on the one hand, the nature of these sexual traumas, and on the other, the period of life in which they occurred. An experience occurring at any period of life, touching in any way the sexual life, and then becoming pathogenic through the liberation and suppression of a painful affect, is not sufficient for the causation of hysteria. It must on the contrary belong to the sexual traumas of early childhood (the period of life before puberty), and its content must consist in a real irritation of the genitals (coitus-like processes).

This specific determination of hysteria—sexual passivity in pre-sexual periods—I have found fulfilled in all analyzed cases of hysteria (among which were two men). To what extent the determination of the accidental aetiological factor diminishes the requirement of the hereditary predisposition needs only to be intimated. We can, moreover, understand the dis-

[1] *Neurologisches Zentralblatt*, (1896), No. 10.

proportionately greater frequency of hysteria in the female sex, as even in childhood this sex is more subject to sexual assaults.

The objection most frequently advanced against this result may be to the purport that sexual assaults on little children occur too frequently to give an aetiological value to its verification, or that such experiences must remain ineffectual just because they concern a sexually undeveloped being; and that one must moreover be careful not to obtrude upon the patient through the examination such alleged reminiscences, or believe in the romances which they themselves fabricate. To the latter objections, I hold out the request that no one should really judge with great certainty this obscure realm unless he has made use of the only method which can clear it up (the method of psychoanalysis for bringing to consciousness the hitherto unconscious).[1] The essential point in the first doubts is settled by the observation that it really is not the experiences themselves that act traumatically, but their revival as reminiscences after the individual has entered into sexual maturity.

My thirteen cases of hysteria were throughout of the graver kind, they were all of long duration, and some had undergone a lengthy and unsuccessful hospital treatment. Every one of the infantile traumas which the analysis revealed for their severe cases had to be designated as severe sexual injuries; some of them were indeed abominable. Among the persons who were guilty of such serious abuse we have in the first place nurses, governesses, and other servants to whom children are left much too carelessly; then in regrettable frequency come the teachers; but in seven of the thirteen cases we dealt with innocent childish offenders, mostly brothers who for years entertained sexual relations with their younger sisters. The course of events always resembled some of the cases which could with certainty be tracked, namely, that the boy had been abused by a person of the feminine sex, thus awakening in him prematurely the libido, and that after a few years he repeated in sexual aggression on his sister the same procedures to which he himself was subjected.

I must exclude active masturbation from the list of sexual injuries of early childhood as being pathogenic for hysteria. That it is so very frequently found associated with hysteria

is due to the fact that masturbation in itself is more frequently the result of abuse or seduction than one supposes. It not seldom happens that both members of a childish pair later in life become afflicted by a defence neurosis, the brother by obsessions and the sister by hysteria, which naturally gives the appearance of a familial neurotic predisposition. This pseudo-heredity is now and then solved in a surprising manner. I have had under observation a brother, sister, and a somewhat older cousin. The analysis which I have undertaken with the brother showed me that he suffered from reproaches for being the cause of his sister's malady; he himself was corrupted by his cousin, concerning whom it was known in the family that he fell a victim to his nurse.

I can not definitely state up to what age sexual damage occurs in the aetiology of hysteria, but I doubt whether sexual passivity can cause repression after the eighth and tenth year unless qualified for it by previous experiences. The lower limit reaches as far as memory in general, that is, to the delicate age of one and one-half or two years (two cases)! In a number of my cases the sexual trauma (or the number of traumas) occurred during the third and fourth year of life. I myself would not lend credence to this peculiar discovery if it were not for the fact that the later development of the neurosis furnished it with full trustworthiness. In every case there are a number of morbid symptoms, habits, and phobias, which are only explainable by returning to those youthful experiences, and the logical structure of the neurotic manifestation makes it impossible to reject the faithfully retained memories of childhood. Except through psycho-analysis, it is of no avail to ask a hysterical patient about these infantile traumas; their remnants can only be found in the morbid symptoms and not in conscious memory.

All the experiences and excitements which prepare the way for, or occasion the outburst of, hysteria in the period of life after puberty evidently act through the fact that they awaken the memory remnants of those infantile traumas which do not become conscious but lead to the liberation of affect and repression. It is quite in harmony with this rôle of the later traumas not to be subject to the strict limitation of the infantile traumas, but that both in intensity and quality they can vary from an actual sexual assault to a mere approximation of the sexual, such as perceiving the sexual acts

---

[1] I myself surmise that the so frequently fabricated assaults of hysterical persons are obsessional confabulations emanating from the memory traces of infantile traumas.

of others, or receiving information concerning sexual processes.[1]

In my first communication on the defence neuro-psychoses, I failed to explain how the exertion of a hitherto healthy individual to forget such traumatic happenings would result in the real intentional repression, and thus open the door for the defence neurosis. It can not depend on the nature of the experience, as other persons remain unaffected despite the same motives. Hysteria cannot therefore be fully explained by the effect of the trauma, and we are forced to admit that the capacity for hysteria already existed before the trauma.

This indefinite hysterical predisposition can now wholly or partially be substituted by the posthumous effect of the infantile sexual trauma. The *repression* of the memory of a painful sexual experience of maturer years can take place only in persons in whom this experience can bring into activity the memory remnants of an infantile trauma.[2]

The prerequisite of obsessions is also a sexual infantile experience, but of a different nature than that of hysteria. The aetiology of both defense neuro-psychoses now shows the following relation to the aetiology of both simple neuroses, neurasthenia and anxiety neurosis. As I have shown above, both the latter neuroses are direct results of the sexual *noxae* alone, while both defence neuroses are the direct results of sexual *noxae* which acted before the appearance of sexual maturity; that is, they are the results of the psychic memory remnants of those *noxae*. The actual causes producing neurasthenia and anxiety neurosis simultaneously play the rôle of inciting causes of the defence neuroses, and, on the other hand, the specific causes of the defence neuroses, the infantile traumas, may simultaneously prepare the soil for the later developing neurasthenia. Finally it not seldom happens that the existence of a neurasthenia or anxiety neurosis is only preserved by continued recollection of an infantile trauma rather than by actual sexual injuries.

II. *The Essence and Mechanism of Compulsion Neurosis*

Sexual experiences of early childhood have the same significance in the aetiology of the compulsion neurosis as in hysteria; still we no longer deal here with sexual passivity but with pleasurably accomplished aggressions, and with pleasurably experienced participation in sexual acts; that is, we deal here with sexual activity.[3] It is due to this difference in the aetiological relations that the masculine sex seems to be preferred in the compulsion neurosis.

In all my cases of compulsion neurosis I have found besides *a sub-soil of hysterical symptoms* which could be traced to a pleasurable action of sexual passivity from a precedent scene. I presume that this coincidence is a lawful one, and that premature sexual aggression always presupposes an experience of seduction. But I am unable to present as yet a complete description of the aetiology of the compulsion neurosis. I only believe that the final determination as to whether a hysteria or compulsion neurosis should originate on the basis of infantile traumas depends on the temporal relation of the development of the libido.

The essence of the compulsion neurosis may be expressed in the following simple formula: *Obsessions are always transformed* reproaches *returning from the repression which always refer to a pleasurably accomplished sexual action of childhood.* In order to elucidate this sentence, it will be necessary to describe the typical course of compulsion neurosis.

In a first period—period of childish unmo-

---

[1] In an article on the anxiety neurosis (*Neurologisches Zentralblatt* [1895],) [See p. 91 above] I stated that "an anxiety neurosis which can almost typically be combined with hysteria can be evoked in maturing girls at the first encounter with the sexual problem." I know today that the occasion in which such virginal anxiety breaks out does not really correspond to the first encounter with sexuality, but that in such persons there was in childhood a precedent experience of sexual passivity which memory was awakened at the "first encounter."

[2] A psychological theory of repression ought also to inform us why only ideas of a sexual content can be repressed. It may be formulated as follows: It is known that ideas of a sexual content produce exciting processes in the genitals resembling the actual sexual experience. It may be assumed that this somatic excitement becomes transformed into psychic excitement. As a rule the effect referred to is much stronger at the time of its occurrence than at the recollection of it. But if the sexual experience takes place during the time of sexual immaturity and the recollection of it is awakened during or after maturity, the recollection then acts disproportionately more exciting than the previous experience, for puberty has in the meantime incomparably increased the reactive capacity of the sexual apparatus. But such an inverse proportion between the real experience and the meaning of it seems to contain the psychological determination of repression. Through the retardation of pubescence, in contrast to the psychic function, the sexual life offers the only existing possibility for that reversal of the relative efficacy. *The infantile traumas subsequently act like fresh experiences, but they are then unconscious.* Deeper psychological discussions I will have to postpone for another time. Moreover, I call attention to the fact that the here considered time of sexual maturity does not coincide with puberty, but occurs before the same (eight to ten years).

[3] These theories of passive and active sexual traumas have later been given up by the author.—TR.

rality—the events containing the seeds of the later neurosis take place. In the earliest childhood there appear at first the experiences of sexual seduction which later makes the repression possible, and this is followed by the actions of sexual aggressions against the other sex which later manifest themselves as actions of reproach.

This period is brought to an end by the appearance of the—often self-ripened—sexual maturity. A reproach then attaches itself to the memory of that pleasurable action, and the connection with the initial experience of passivity makes it possible—often only after conscious and recollected effort—to repress it and replace it by a *primary symptom of defence.* The third period, that of apparent healthiness but really of *successful defence,* begins with the symptoms of scrupulousness, shame and diffidence.

The next period of the disease is characterized by *the return of the repressed reminiscences,* hence, by the failure of the defence. But it remains undecided whether the awakening of it is more frequently accidental and spontaneous, or whether it appears in consequence of actual sexual disturbances, that is, as additional influences of the same. But the revived reminiscences and the reproaches formed from them never enter into consciousness unchanged. What becomes conscious as an obsession and obsessive affect, and substitutes the pathogenic memory in the conscious life, are compromise formations between the repressed and the repressing ideas.

In order to describe clearly and probably convincingly the processes of repression, the return of the repression, and the formation of the pathological ideas of compromise, we would have to decide upon very definite hypotheses concerning the substratum of the psychic occurrence and consciousness. As long as we wish to avoid it, we will have to rest content with the following rather figuratively understood observations. Depending on whether the memory content of the reproachful action alone forces an entrance into consciousness or whether it takes with it the accompanying reproachful affect, we have two forms of compulsion neurosis. The first represents the typical obsessions, the content of which attracts the patient's attention; only an indefinite displeasure is perceived as an affect, whereas, for the content of the obsession, the only suitable affect would be one of reproach. The content of the obsession is doubly distorted when compared to the content of the infantile compulsive act. First, something actual replaces the past experience, and, second, the sexual is substituted by an analogous non-sexual experience. These two changes are the results of the constant tendency to repression still in force which we will attribute to the *ego.* The influence of the revived pathogenic memory is shown by the fact that the content of the obsession is still partially identical with the repressed, or can be traced to it by a correct stream of thought. If, with the help of the psycho-analytic method, we reconstruct the origin of one individual obsession, we find that one actual impression instigated two diverse streams of thought, and that the one which passed over the repressed memory, though incapable of consciousness and correction, proves to be just as correctly formed, logically, as the other. If the results of the two psychic operations disagree, the contradiction between the two may never be brought to logical adjustment, but, as a compromise between the resistance and the pathological result of thought, an apparently absurd obsession enters into consciousness, beside the normal result of the thought. If both streams of thought yield the same result, they reinforce each other so that the normally gained result of thought now behaves psychically like an obsession. *Wherever neurotic compulsion manifests itself psychically,* it *originates from repression.* The obsessions have, as it were, a psychical course of compulsion which is due, not to their own validity, but to the source from which they originate, or to the source which furnishes a part of their validity.

A second form of compulsion neurosis results if the repressed reproach and not the repressed content of memory forces a replacement in the conscious psychic life. Through a psychic admixture, the affect of the reproach can change itself into any other affect of displeasure, and if this occurs there is nothing to hinder the substituting affect from becoming conscious. Thus the *reproach* (of having performed in childhood some sexual actions) may be easily transformed into *shame* (if some one else becomes aware of it), into *hypochondriacal anxiety* (because of the physical harmful consequences of those reproachful acts), into *social anxiety* (fearing punishment from others), into *religious anxiety,* into *delusions of observation* (fear of betraying those actions to others), into *fear of temptations* (justified distrust in one's own moral ability of resistance), etc. Besides, the memory content of the reproachful action may also be represented in consciousness, or it may be altogether concealed, which makes the diagnosis very difficult. Many cases which on superficial examination are taken as ordinary (neurasthenic) hypochondria often belong to this group of *compulsive affects;* the very frequently so-called *periodic neurasthenia* or *periodic melancholia* especially seem to be explained by compulsive affects or obsessions, a recognition not unimportant therapeutically.

Beside these compromise symptoms which signify the return of the repression and hence a failure of the originally achieved defence, the compulsion neurosis forms a series of other symptoms of a totally different origin. The ego really tries to defend itself against those descendants of the initial repressed reminiscence, and in this conflict of defence it produces symptoms which may be comprehended as *secondary defence*. These are throughout *protective measures* which have performed good service in the struggle carried on against the obsessions and the obsessing affects. If these helps in the conflict of the defense really succeed in repressing anew the symptoms of return obtruding themselves on the ego, the compulsion then transmits itself on the protective measures themselves and produces a third form of the *compulsion neurosis*, the *compulsive action*. These are never primary; they never contain anything else but a defence, never an aggression. Psycho-analysis shows that, despite their peculiarity, they can always be fully explained by reduction to the compulsive reminiscence which they oppose.[1]

[1] One example instead of many: An eleven-year-old boy has obsessively arranged for himself the following ceremonial before going to bed: He could not fall asleep unless he related to his mother most minutely all experiences of the day; not the smallest scrap of paper or any other rubbish was allowed in the evening on the carpet of his bedroom. The bed had to be moved close to the wall, three chairs had to stand in front of it, and the pillows had to lie in just such a position. In order to fall asleep he had to kick with both legs a number of times, and then he had to lie on the side. This was explained as follows: Years before, while putting this pretty boy to sleep, the servant girl made use of this opportunity to lay over him and assault him sexually. When this reminiscence was later awakened by a recent experience, it made itself known to consciousness by the compulsion in the above mentioned ceremonial, which sense could really be surmised and the details verified by psycho-analysis. The chairs before the bed which was close to the wall—so that no one could have access to it; the arrangement of the pillows in a definite manner—so that they should be differently arranged than they were on that evening; the motion with the legs—to kick away the person lying on him; sleeping on the side—because during that scene he lay on his back; the detailed confession to his mother—because in consequence of the prohibition of his seductress he concealed from his mother this and other sexual experiences; finally, keeping the floor of his bedroom clean—because this was the main

The secondary defence of the obsessions can be brought about by a forcible deviation to other thoughts of possibly contrary content; hence, in case of success, there is a *compulsive reasoning*, regularly concerning abstract and *transcendental* subjects, because the repressed ideas always occupied themselves with sensuousness. Or the patient tries to become master of every compulsive idea through logical labour and by appealing to his conscious memory; this leads to *compulsive thinking and examination* and to *doubting mania*. The priority of the perception before the memory in these examinations at first induces and then forces the patient to collect and preserve all objects with which he comes in contact. The secondary defence against the compulsive affects results in a greater number of defensive measures which are capable of being transformed into compulsive actions. These can be grouped according to their tendency. We may have *measures of penitence* (irksome ceremonial and observation of numbers), of *prevention* (diverse phobias, superstition, pedantry, aggravation of the primary symptom of scrupulousness), measures of *fear of betrayal* (collecting papers, shyness), and measures of *becoming unconscious* (dipsomania). Among these compulsive acts and impulses, the phobias play the greatest part as limitations of the patient's existence.

There are cases in which we can observe how the compulsion becomes transferred from the idea or affect to the measure, and other cases in which the compulsion oscillates between the returning symptoms of secondary defence. But there are also cases in which no obsessions are really formed, but the repressed reminiscence immediately becomes replaced by the apparent primary defensive measure. Here that stage is attained at a bound which otherwise ends the course of the compulsion neurosis only after the conflict of the defence. Grave cases of this affection end either with a fixation of ceremonial actions, general doubting mania, or in an existence of eccentricity conditioned by phobias.

That the obsessions and everything derived from them are not believed is probably due to the fact that the defence symptom of *scrupulousness* was formed during the first repression and gained compulsive validity. The certainty of having lived morally throughout the whole period of the successful defence makes it impossible to give credence to the reproach which the obsession really involves. Only transitorily

———
reproach which he had to hear from his mother up to that time.

during the appearance of a new obsession, and now and then in melancholic exhaustive states of the ego, do the morbid symptoms of the return also enforce the belief. The *compulsion* of the psychic formations here described has in general nothing to do with the recognition through belief, and is not to be mistaken for that factor which is designated as *strength* or *intensity* of an idea. Its main characteristic lies in its inexplicableness through psychic activities of conscious ability, and this character undergoes to change whether the idea to which the compulsion is attached is stronger or weaker, more or less intensively *elucidated, supplied with energy,* etc.

The reason for the unassailableness of the obsession or its derivative is due only to its connection with the repressed memory of early childhood, for as soon as we succeed in making it conscious, for which the psycho-therapeutic methods already seem quite sufficient, the compulsion, too, becomes detached.

III. *Analysis of a Case of Chronic Paranoia*

For some length of time I entertained the idea that paranoia also—or the group of cases belonging to paranoia—is a defence psychosis, that is, like hysteria and obsessions it originates from the repression of painful reminiscences, and that the form of its symptoms is determined by the content of the repression. A special way or mechanism of repression must be peculiar to paranoia, perhaps just as in hysteria which brings about the repression by way of conversion into bodily innervation, and perhaps like obsessions in which a substitution is accomplished (displacement along certain associative categories). I observed many cases which seemed to favour this interpretation, but I had not found any which demonstrated it until a few months ago when, through the kindness of Dr. J. Breuer, I subjected to psycho-analysis, with therapeutic aims, an intelligent woman of 32, whom no one will be able to refuse to designate as a chronic paranoiac. I report here some explanations gained in this work, because I have no prospects of studying paranoia except in very isolated examples, and because I think it possible that these observations may instigate a psychiatrist for whom conditions are more favourable to give due justice to the element of defence in the present animated discussion on the nature and psychic mechanism of paranoia. It is of course far from my thoughts to wish to show from the following single observation anything but that this case

is a defence-psychosis, and that in the group of *paranoia* there may be still others of a similar nature.

Mrs. P, thirty-two years old, married three years. She is the mother of a two-year-old child, and does not descend from nervous parents; but her sister and brother, whom I know, are also neurotic. It was doubtful whether she was not transitorily depressed and mistaken in her judgment in the middle of her twentieth year. During the last years she was healthy and capacitated until she evinced the first symptoms of the present illness, six months after the birth of her child. She became secluded and suspicious, showing a disinclination towards social relations with the relatives of her husband, and complained that the neighbours in the little town now behaved towards her in a rather impolite and regardless manner. Gradually these complaints grew in intensity; she thought that there was something against her, though she had no notion what it could be. But there was no doubt that all the relatives and friends denied her respect, and did everything to aggravate her. She was trying very hard to find out whence this came but could not discover anything. Some time later she complained that she was watched, that her thoughts were guessed, and that everything that happened in her house was known. One afternoon she suddenly conceived the thought that she was watched during the evening while undressing. After that, she applied while undressing the most complicated precautionary measures. She slipped into her bed in the darkness and undressed only under cover. As she avoided all social relations, and took but little nourishment, and was very depressed, she was sent in the summer of 1895 to a hydrotherapeutic institute. There new symptoms appeared and reinforced those already existing. As early as the spring, while she was alone with the servant girl, she suddenly perceived a sensation in her lap, and thought that the servant girl then had an unseemly thought. This sensation became more frequent in the summer, it was almost continuous, and she felt her genitals "as if one feels a heavy hand." She then began to see pictures which frightened her; they were hallucinations of female nakedness, especially an exposed woman's lap with hair; occasionally she also saw male genitals. The picture of the hairy lap and the organic sensation in the lap usually came conjointly. The pictures became very aggravating, as she regularly perceived them when she was in the company of a woman, and the thought accompanying them was that she sees the woman in an indecent exposure, and that in the same moment the woman sees the same picture of her! Simultaneously with these visual hallucinations, which, after their first appearance in the hospital, disappeared again for many months, she began to be troubled with voices which she did not recognize and could not explain. When she was in the street she heard, "This is Mrs. P.—Here she goes.—Where does she go?" Every one of her movements and actions were commented upon. Occasionally she heard threats and reproaches. All these symptoms became worse when she was in society, or even in the street; she therefore hesitated about going out; she also stated that she experienced nausea at the thought of food, and as a result she became reduced in vitality.

I obtained all this from her when she came under my care in the winter of 1895. I have presented the details of this case in order to give the impression that we really deal here with a very common form of chronic paranoia, the diagnosis of which will agree with the details of the symptoms and the patient's behaviour to be described later. At that time she either concealed from me the delusions for the interpretation of the hallucinations, or they really had not as yet occurred. Her intelligence was undiminished. It was reported to me as peculiar that she made a number of rendezvous with her brother who lived in the neighbourhood, in order to confide something to him, but she never told him anything. She never spoke about her hallucinations, and, towards the end, she did not say much about the aggravations and persecutions from which she suffered.

What I shall report about this patient concerns the aetiology of the case and the mechanism of the hallucinations. I discovered the aetiology by applying Breuer's method, exactly as in hysteria, for the investigation and removal of the hallucinations. I started with the presupposition, that, just as in the two other defence-neuroses known to me, this paranoia, too, must contain unconscious thoughts and repressed reminiscences which had to be brought to consciousness, in the same manner as in the others, by overcoming a certain resistance. The patient immediately corroborated this expectation by behaving during the analysis exactly like a hysteric, and under attention to the pressure of my hand she reproduced thoughts which she could not remember having had, which she at first could not understand, and which con-

tradicted her expectations. The occurrence of important unconscious ideas was therefore also demonstrated in a case of paranoia, and I could hope to reconduct the compulsion of paranoia to repression. It was only peculiar that the assertions which originated in the unconscious were usually heard inwardly or hallucinated by her as her voices.

Concerning the origin of the visual hallucinations, or at least the vivid pictures, I discovered the following: The picture of the female lap occurred almost always together with the organic sensation in the lap. The latter, however, was more constant and often occurred without the picture.

The first pictures of feminine laps appeared in the hydro-therapeutic institute a few hours after she had actually seen a number of women naked in the bath house. They were therefore only simple reproductions of a real impression. It may be assumed that these impressions repeated themselves because something of great interest was connected with them. She stated that she was at that time ashamed of these women, and that, since she recalled it, she is ashamed of having been seen naked. Having been obliged to look upon this shame as something compulsive, I concluded that, according to the mechanism of defence, an experience must have here been repressed in which she was not ashamed, and I requested her to allow those reminiscences to emerge which belonged to the theme of shame. She promptly reproduced a series of scenes from her seventh to her eighth year, during which, while bathing before her mother, her sister, and her physician, she was ashamed of her nakedness. This series, however, reached back to a scene in her sixth year when she undressed in the children's room before going to sleep without feeling ashamed of her brother who was present. On questioning her, it was found that there were a number of such scenes, and that for years the brothers and sisters were in the habit of showing themselves naked to one another before retiring. I now understood the significance of the sudden thought of being watched on going to sleep. It was an unchanged fragment of the old reproachful reminiscence, and she was now trying to make up in shame what she lost as a child.

The supposition that we dealt here with an *amour* of childhood, so frequent in the aetiology of hysteria, was strengthened by the further progress of the analysis, which also showed simultaneous solutions for individual frequently recurring details in the picture of paranoia. The beginning of her depression commenced at the time of a disagreement between her husband and her brother on account of which the latter no longer visited her. She was always much attached to this brother and missed him very much at this time. Besides this, she spoke about an experience in the history of her disease during which for the first time "everything became clear," that is, during which she became convinced that her assumption about being generally despised and intentionally annoyed was true. She gained this assurance during a visit of her sister-in-law, who in the course of conversation dropped the words, "If such a thing should happen to me I would not mind it." Mrs. P at first took this utterance unsuspectingly, but when her visitor left her it seemed to her that these words contained a reproach, meaning that she was in the habit of taking serious matters lightly, and since that hour she was sure that she was a victim of common slander. On asking her why she felt justified in referring those words to herself, she answered that the tone in which her sister-in-law spoke convinced her of it—to be sure subsequently. (This is really a characteristic detail of paranoia.) I now urged her to recall her sister-in-law's conversation before the accusing utterance, and it was found that she related that in her father's home there were all sorts of difficulties with the brothers, and added the wise remark, "In every family many things happen which one would rather keep under cover, and that if such a thing should happen to her she would take it lightly." Mrs. P had to acknowledge that her depression was connected with the sentences before the last utterance. As she repressed both sentences which could recall her relations with her brother and retained only the last meaningless one, she was forced to connect with it the feeling of being reproached by her sister-in-law; but inasmuch as the contents of this sentence offered absolutely no basis for such assumption she disregarded it and laid stress on the tone with which the words were pronounced. It is probably a typical illustration of the fact that the misinterpretations of paranoia depend on repression.

In a surprising manner it also explains her peculiar behaviour in making appointments with her brother and then refusing to tell him anything. Her explanation was that she thought that if she only looked at him he must understand her suffering, as he knew the cause of it.

As this brother was really the only person who could know anything about the aetiology of her disease, it followed that she acted from a motive which, though she did not consciously understand, seemed perfectly justified as soon as a new sense was put on it from the unconscious.

I then succeeded in causing her to reproduce different scenes, the culminating points of which were the sexual relations with her brother, at least from her sixth to her tenth year. During this work of reproduction, the organic sensation in the lap "joined in the discussion," precisely as regularly observed in the analysis of memory remnants of hysterical patients. The picture of a naked female lap (but now reduced to childish proportions and without hair) immediately appeared or stayed away in accordance with the occurrence of the scene in question in full light or in darkness. The disgust for eating, too, was explained by a repulsive detail of these actions. After we had gone through this series, the hallucinatory sensations and picture disappeared without having thus far returned.[1]

I have thus learned that these hallucinations were nothing other than fragments from the content of the repressed experiences of childhood, that is, symptoms of the return of the repressed material.

I now turned to the analysis of the voices. Here it must before all be explained why such different remarks as, "Here goes Mrs. P.—She now looks for apartments," etc., could be so painfully perceived, and how these harmless sentences managed to become distinguished by hallucinatory enforcement. To begin with, it was clear that these "voices" could not be hallucinatory reproduced reminiscences like the pictures and sensations, but rather thoughts which "became loud."

She heard the voices for the first time under the following circumstances. With great tension she read the pretty story, *The Heiterethei*, by O. Ludwig, and noticed that while reading she was preoccupied with obtruding thoughts. Immediately after, she took a walk on the highway, and suddenly, while passing a peasant's cottage, the voices told her, "That is how the house of the Heiterethei looked! Here is the well, and here is the bush! How happy she was in all her poverty!" The voices then repeated

[1] When the meagre success of this treatment was later removed by an exacerbation, she did not again see the offensive pictures of strange genitals, but she had the idea that strangers saw her genitals as soon as they were behind her.

whole paragraphs of what she had just read, but it remained incomprehensible why house, bush, and well of the Heiterethei, and just such indifferent and most irrelevant passages of the romance should have obtruded themselves upon her attention with pathological strength. The analysis showed that while reading she at the same time entertained extraneous thoughts, and that she was excited by totally different passages of the book. Against this material analogy between the couple of the romance and herself and her husband, the reminiscence of intimate things of her married life and family secrets—against all these there arose a repressive resistance because they were connected with her sexual shyness by very simple and demonstrable streams of thought, and finally resulted in the awakening of old experiences of childhood. In consequence of the censorship exercised by the repression, the harmless and idyllic passages, connected with the objectionable ones by contrast and vicinity, became reinforced in consciousness, enabling them to become audible. For example, the first repressed thought referred to the slander to which the secluded heroine was subjected by her neighbours. She readily found in this an analogy to herself. She, too, lived in a small place, had no intercourse with anybody and considered herself despised by her neighbours. The suspicion against the neighbours was founded on the fact that in the beginning of her married life she was obliged to content herself with a small apartment. The wall of the bedroom, near which stood the nuptial bed of the young couple, adjoined the neighbour's room. With the beginning of her marriage there awakened in her a great sexual shyness. This was apparently due to an unconscious awakening of some reminiscences of childhood of having played husband and wife. She was very careful lest the neighbours might hear through the adjacent wall either words or noises, and this shyness changed into suspicion against the neighbours.

The voices, therefore, owed their origin to the repression of thoughts which in the last analysis really signified reproaches on the occasion of an experience analogous to the infantile trauma; they were accordingly symptoms of the return of the repression, but at the same time they were results of a compromise between the resistance of the ego and the force of the returning repression, which in this case produced a distortion beyond recognition. On other occasions when analyzing voices in Mrs. P, the distortion was less marked, still the words heard always showed a character of diplomatic uncertainty. The annoying allusion was generally deeply hidden, the connection of the individual sentences was masked by a strange expression, unusual forms of speech, etc., characteristics generally common to the auditory hallucinations of paranoiacs, and in which I noticed the remnant of the compromise distortion. The expression, "There goes Mrs. P; she is looking for apartments in the street," signified, for example, the threat that she will never recover, for I promised her that after the treatment she would be able to return to the little city where her husband was employed. She rented temporary quarters in Vienna for a few months.

On some occasions Mrs. P also perceived more distinct threats, for example, concerning the relatives of her husband, the restrained expression of which still continued to contrast with the grief which such voices caused her. Considering all that we otherwise know of paranoiacs, I am inclined to assume a gradual relaxation of that resistance which weakens the reproaches, so that finally the defence fails completely and the original reproach, the insulting word, which one wished to save himself, returns in unchanged form. I do not, however, know whether this is a constant course, whether the censor of the expressions of reproach can not from the beginning stay away, or persist to the end.

The only thing left is to utilize the explanations gained in this case of paranoia for a comparison of paranoia with compulsion neurosis. Here, as there, the repression was shown to be the nucleus of the psychic mechanism, and in both cases the repression is a sexual experience of childhood. The origin of every compulsion in this paranoia is in the repression, and the symptoms of paranoia allow a similar classification as the one found justified in compulsion neurosis. Some symptoms also originate from the primary defence, among which are all delusions of distrust, suspicion, and persecution by others. In compulsion neurosis the initial reproach became repressed through the formation of the primary symptom of defence: *self-distrust*. Moreover, the reproach was recognized as justified, and, for the purpose of adjustment, the validity acquired by the scrupulousness during the normal interval now guards against giving credence to the returning reproach in the form of an obsession. By the formation of the defence-symptom of *distrust in others,* the reproach in paranoia is repressed in a way which may be designated as *projection;* the reproach is also deprived of recognition, and as a retaliation there is no protection against the returning reproaches contained in the delusions.

The other symptoms in my case of paranoia are, therefore, to be designated as symptoms of the return of the repression, and as in the compulsion neurosis they show the traces of the compromise which alone permits an entrance into consciousness. Such are the delusions of being observed while undressing, the visual hallucination, the perceptual hallucinations, and the hearing of voices. The memory content existing in the delusion mentioned is almost unchanged and appears only uncertain through utterance. The return of the repression into visual pictures comes nearer to the character of hysteria than to the character of compulsion neurosis; still, hysteria is wont to repeat its memory symbols without modification, whereas the paranoiac memory hallucination undergoes a distortion similar to that in compulsion neurosis. An analogous modern picture takes the place of the one repressed (instead of a child's lap, it was the lap of a woman upon which the hair were particularly distinct because they were absent in the original impression). Quite peculiar to paranoia, but no further elucidated in this comparison, is the fact that the repressed reproaches return as loud thoughts; this must yield to a double distortion: (1) a censor, which either leads to a replacement through other associated thoughts or to a concealment by indefinite expressions, and (2) the reference to modern which is merely analogous to the old thoughts.

The third group of symptoms found in compulsion neurosis, the symptoms of the secondary defence, cannot exist as such in paranoia, for no defence asserts itself against the returning systems which really find credence. As a substitute for this, we find in paranoia another source of symptom formation; the delusions (symptom of return) reaching consciousness through the compromise, make great demands on the mental work of the ego before they can be unconditionally accepted. As they themselves are not to be influenced, the ego must adapt itself to them, and hence the combining delusional formation, the *delusion of interpretation* which results in the *transformation of the ego,* corresponds here to the symptoms of secondary defence of compulsion neurosis. In this respect my case was imperfect, as it did not at that time show any attempt at interpretation; this only appeared later. I do not doubt, however, that if psycho-analysis were also applied to that stage of paranoia, another important result would be established. It would probably be found that even the so-called *weakness of memory* in paranoiacs is tendentious, that is, it depends on the repression and serves its purpose. Subsequently even those non-pathogenic memories which stand in opposition to the transformation of the ego become repressed and replaced; this, the symptoms of return imperatively demand.

CHAPTER 8
ON PSYCHO-THERAPY.[1]

GENTLEMEN: It is almost eight years since, at the request of your deceased chairman, Professor von Reder, I had the pleasure of speaking in your midst on the subject of hysteria. Shortly before (1895), I had published the *Studies in Hysteria* together with Dr. J. Breuer, and, on the basis of a new knowledge for which we are thankful to this investigator, I have attempted to introduce a new way of treating the neuroses. Fortunately, I can say that the endeavours of our *Studies* have met with success, that the ideas which they advance concerning the effects of psychic traumas through the restraining of affects, as well as the concept of the hysterical symptoms as a displacement of excitement from the psychic to the physical—ideas for which we have coined the terms *abreaction* and *conversion* are today generally known and understood. In German-speaking countries one cannot find any descriptions of hysteria in which these facts are not more or less recognized. There is no psychiatrist who does not now at least take some note of these theories. And yet, as long as they were new, these theories and these terms must have sounded strange enough.

I can not however, say the same about the therapeutic procedure which we have proposed together with our theory. It still struggles for recognition. This may have its special reasons. The technique of the procedure was at that time still rudimentary. I was unable to give those indications to the medical reader of our book which would enable him to accomplish this treatment. But there were surely other causes of a general nature. To many physicians, psycho-therapy even today appears as a product of modern mysticism. In comparison to our

[1] Lecture delivered before the Vienna College of Physicians, on December 12, 1904.

physico-chemical remedies, the application of which is based on physiological insight, psychotherapy appears quite unscientific and unworthy of the interest of a true scientist. You will, therefore, allow me to speak to you on the subject of psycho-therapy in order to point out what part of this verdict can be designated as unjust or erroneous.

In the first place, let me remind you that psycho-therapy is not a modern therapeutic procedure. On the contrary, it is one of the oldest in medicine. In Lëwenfeld's instructive work *(Lehrbuch der gesamten Psychotherapie)*, you can find that the methods utilized in primitive and ancient medicine were mostly of a psycho-therapeutic nature. In order to cure a patient, he was transferred into a state of *credulous expectation* which acts in a similar manner even today. Even after the doctors found other remedial agents, psycho-therapeutic endeavours never disappeared from this or that branch of medicine.

Secondly, I call your attention to the fact that we doctors really can not abandon psychotherapy, if only because another very important party in the treatment—namely, the patient—has no intention of abandoning it. You know how much we owe to the Nancy school (Liébault, Bernheim) for these explanations. Without our intention, an independent factor from the patient's psychic disposition enters into the activity of every remedial agent introduced by physicians, which, though mostly favourable, often also acts inhibitingly. We have learned to apply to this factor the word *suggestion,* and Moebius taught us that the failures of some of our remedies are to be ascribed to the disturbing influences of this very powerful factor. You doctors, all of you, constantly practise psycho-therapy, even when you do not know it, or do not intend it, but with one disadvantage—you leave entirely to the patient the psychic factors of your influence. It then becomes uncontrollable; it can not be divided into doses and hence can not be increased. Is it not justifiable on the part of the doctor to master this factor, to make intentional use of it, to direct and enforce it? It is nothing but that, that scientific psycho-therapy expects of you.

In the third place, gentlemen, I wish to call your attention to a well-known fact, namely, that certain maladies and particularly the psycho-neuroses, are more accessible to psychic influences than to any other remedies. It is no modern talk, but a dictum of old physicians,

that these diseases are not cured by the drug, but by the doctor—to wit, by the personality of the physician in so far as he exerts a psychic influence. I am well aware, gentlemen, that you are impressed with the idea which the esthete Vischer, in his parody on *Faust (Faust, der Tragödie, III Teil)*, endowed with this classical expression: "I know that the psychical often acts on the moral."

But would it not be more adequate and frequently more correct to influence the moral part of the person with the moral, that is, with psychic means?

There are many ways and means of psychotherapy. All methods are good which produce the aim of the therapy. Our usual consolation, "You will soon be well again," with which we are so generous to our patients, corresponds to one of these psycho-therapeutic methods, only that on gaining a profounder insight into the neuroses we are not forced to limit ourselves to this consolation alone. We have developed the technique of hypnotic suggestion, of psycho-therapy through diversion, through practice, and through the evocation of serviceable affects. I do not disdain any of them, and would practise them all under suitable conditions. That I have in reality restricted myself to a single therapeutic procedure, to the method called by Breuer *cathartic,* which I prefer to call *analytic,* is simply due to subjective motives which guided me. Having participated in the elaboration of this therapy, I feel it a personal duty to devote myself to its investigation, and to the final development of its technique. I maintain that the analytic method of psycho-therapy is one which acts most penetratingly, and carries farthest; through it one can produce the most prolific changes in the patient. If I relinquish for a moment the therapeutic point of view, I can assert that it is the most interesting, and that it alone teaches us something concerning the origin and the connection of the morbid manifestations. Owing to insights which it opens into the mechanism of the psychic malady, it can even lead us beyond itself, and show us the way to still other kinds of therapeutic influences.

Allow me now to correct some errors, and furnish some explanations concerning this cathartic or analytic method of psycho-therapy.

(a) I notice that this method is often mistaken for the hypnotic suggestive treatment. I notice this by the fact that quite frequently colleagues, whose confidant I am not by any means, send patients to me, refractory patients, of course, with the request that I should hypnotize them. Now, for eight years I have not practised hypnotism (individual cases excepted) as a therapeutic aim, and hence I return the patients with the advice that he who relies on hypnosis should do it himself. In truth, the greatest possible contrast exists between the suggestive and the analytic techniques, that contrast which the great Leonardo da Vinci has expressed for the arts in the formulae *per via di porre* and *per via di levare*. Said Leonardo, "the art of painting works *per via di porre*, that is to say, by placing little heaps of paint where they have not been before on the uncoloured canvas; sculpturing, on the other hand, works *per via di levare*, that is to say, it takes away from the stone as much as covers the surface of the statute therein contained." Quite similarly, gentlemen, the suggestive technique acts *per via di porre;* it does not concern itself about the origin, force, and significance of the morbid symptoms, but puts on something, to wit, the suggestion, which it expects will be strong enough to prevent the pathogenic idea from expression. On the other hand, the analytic therapy does not wish to put on anything, or introduce anything new, but to take away, and extract, and for this purpose it concerns itself with the genesis of the morbid symptoms and the psychic connection of the pathogenic idea, the removal of which is its aim. This manner of investigation has considerably furthered our understanding. I have so early given up the technique of suggestion, and with it hypnosis, because I despaired of making the suggestion as strong and persistent as would be necessary for a lasting cure. In all grave cases I noticed that the suggestions which were put on crumbled off again, and then the disease, on replacing it, reappeared. Besides, I charge this technique with concealing from us the psychic play of forces. It does not permit us to recognize the resistance with which the patients adhere to their malady, with which they also strive against recovery, and which alone can give us an understanding of their behaviour in life.

(b) It seems to me that a very widespread mistake among my colleagues is the idea that the technique of the investigation of the causes of the disease and the removal of its manifestations by this investigation is easy and self-evident. I concluded this from the fact that, of the many who interest themselves in my therapy and express a definite opinion on the same, no one has yet asked me how I do it. There can only be one reason for it; they believe there is nothing to ask, that it is a matter of course. I occasionally also hear with surprise that, in this or that division of a hospital, a young interne is requested by his chief to undertake a *psycho-analysis* with a hysterical woman. I am convinced that he would not entrust him with the examination of an extirpated tumor without previously assuring himself that he is acquainted with histological technique. Likewise I am informed that this or that colleague has made appointments with a patient for psychic treatment, whereas I am certain that he does not know the technique of such a treatment. He must, therefore, expect that the patient will bring him her secrets, or he seeks salvation in some kind of a confession or confidence. I should not wonder if the patient thus treated would be harmed rather than benefited. The mental instrument is really not at all easy to play. On such occasions I can not help but think of the speech of a world-renowned neurotic, who really never came under a doctor's treatment, and only lived in the fancy of the poet. I mean Prince Hamlet of Denmark. The king has sent the two courtiers, Rosencrantz and Guildenstern, to investigate him and rob him of his secret. While he defended himself, pipes were brought on the stage. Hamlet took a pipe and requested one of his tormentors to play on it, saying that it is as easy to play as to lie. The courtier hesitated because he knew no touch of it, and, as he could not be moved to attempt to play the pipe, Hamlet finally burst forth: "Why, look you now, how unworthy a thing you make of me! You would play upon me; you would seem to know my stops; you would pluck out the heart of my mystery; you would sound me from my lowest note to the top of my compass; and there is much music, excellent voice, in this little organ, yet you cannot make it speak. 'Sblood! do you think I am easier to be played on than a pipe? Call me what instrument you will; though you can fret me, you cannot play upon me."[1]

(c) You will have surmised from some of my observations that the analytic cure contains qualities which are far from an ideal therapy. *Tuto, cito, incunde;*[2] the investigation and examination do not really mean rapidity of success, and the allusion to the resistance has prepared you for the expectation of inconveniences. Certainly, the psycho-analytic method

---

[1] Act III, scene 2.
[2] Entirely, quickly, agreeably.—ED.

makes high claims on the patient as well as the physician. From the first, it requires the sacrifice of perfect candour, it takes up much of his time, and is therefore also expensive; for the physician it also means the loss of much time, and, due to the technique which he has to learn and practise, it is quite laborious. I even find it quite justified to employ more suitable remedies as long as there is a prospect to achieve something with them. It comes to this point only: if we gain by the more laborious and cumbersome procedure considerably more than by the short and easy one, the first is justified despite everything. Just think, gentlemen, by how much the Finsen therapy of lupus is more inconvenient and expensive than the formerly used cauterization and scraping, and yet it means great progress, merely because it achieves more, it actually cures the lupus radically. I do not really wish to carry through the comparison, but psycho-analysis can claim for itself a similar privilege. In reality, I could develop and test my therapeutic method in grave and in the gravest of cases only; my material at first consisted of patients who tried everything unsuccessfully, and had spent years in asylums. I hardly gained enough experience to be able to tell you how my therapy behaves in those lighter, episodically appearing diseases which we see cured under the most diverse influences, and also spontaneously. The psycho-analytic method was created for patients who are permanently incapacitated, and its triumph is to make a gratifying number of such permanently capacitated. Against this success, all expense is insignificant. We can not conceal from ourselves what we were wont to disavow to the patient, namely, that the significance of a grave neurosis for the individual subjected to it is not less than any cachexia or any of the generally feared maladies.

(d) In view of the many practical limitations which I have encountered in my work, I can hardly definitely enumerate the indications and contra-indications of this treatment. However, I will attempt to discuss with you a few points:

1. The former value of the person should not be overlooked in the disease, and you should refuse a patient who does not possess a certain degree of education, and whose character is not in a measure reliable. We must not forget that there are also healthy persons who are good for nothing, and that if they only show a mere touch of the neurosis, one is only too ready to blame the disease for incapacitating such inferior persons. I maintain that the neurosis does not in any way stamp its bearer as a *dégénéré,* but that frequently enough it is found in the same individual associated with the manifestations of degeneration. The analytic psychotherapy is, therefore, no procedure for the treatment of neuropathic degeneration; on the contrary it is limited by it. It is also not to be applied in persons who are not prompted by their own suffering to seek treatment, but subject themselves to it by order of their relatives. The characteristic feature upon which the usefulness of the psycho-analytic treatment depends, the educability, we will still have to consider from another point of view.

2. If one wishes to take a safe course, he should limit his selection to persons of a normal state, for, in psycho-analytic procedures, it is from the normal that we seize upon the morbid. Psychoses, confusional states, and marked (I might say toxic) depressions, are unsuitable for analysis, at least as it is practised today. I do not think it at all impossible that, with the proper changes in the procedure, it will be possible to disregard this contra-indication, and thus claim a psycho-therapy for the psychoses.

3. The age of the patient also plays a part in the selection for the psycho-analytic treatment. Persons near or over the age of fifty lack, on the one hand, the plasticity of the psychic processes upon which the therapy depends (old people are no longer educable), and, on the other hand, the material which has to be elaborated, and the duration of the treatment, is immensely increased. The earliest age limit is to be individually determined; youthful persons, even before puberty, are excellent subjects for analysis.

4. One should not attempt psycho-analysis when it is a question of rapidly removing a threatening manifestation, as, for example, in the case of an hysterical anorexia.

You have now gained the impression that the sphere of application of the analytic psychotherapy is a very limited one, for you really heard me enumerate nothing but contra-indications. Nevertheless, there remain sufficient cases and morbid states, such as all chronic forms of hysteria with remnant manifestations, the extensive realm of compulsive states, abulias, etc., on which this therapy can be tried.

It is pleasing that particularly the worthiest and highest developed persons can thus be most helped. Where the analytic psycho-therapy has accomplished but little, one can cheerfully assert that any other treatment would have certainly resulted in nothing.

(e) You will surely wish to ask me about the possibility of doing harm through the application of psycho-analysis. To this I will reply that, if you will judge justly, you will meet this procedure with the same critical good-feeling as you have met our other therapeutic methods; and doing this, you will have to agree with me that a rationally executed analytic treatment entails no dangers for the patient. One who, like a layman, is accustomed to ascribe to the treatment everything occurring during the disease, will probably judge differently. It is really not so long since our hydro-therapeutic institutes met with similar opposition. Thus one who was advised to go to such a place became thoughtful because he had an acquaintance who entered the institute as nervous and there became insane. As you may surmise, we dealt with cases of initial paresis who in the first stages could still be sent for hydro-therapeutic help, and who there merged into the irresistible course leading to manifest insanity. For the layman, the water was the cause and author of this sad transformation. Where it is a question of unfamiliar influences, even doctors are not free from such mistaken judgment. I recall having once attempted to treat a woman by psycho-therapy who passed a great part of her existence by alternating between mania and melancholia. I begun to treat her at the end of a melancholia, and everything seemed to go well for two weeks, but in the third week she was again merging into a mania. It was surely a spontaneous alternation of the morbid picture, for two weeks is no time in which anything can be accomplished by psycho-therapy; but the prominent—now deceased —physician who saw the case with me could not refrain from remarking that this change must have been due to the psycho-therapy. I am quite convinced that he would have been more critical under different conditions.

(f) In conclusion, gentlemen, I must say to myself that it will not do to lay claim to your attention so long in favour of the analytic psycho-therapy without telling you of what this treatment consists, and on what it is based. To be sure I can only indicate it, as I have to be brief. This therapy is founded on the understanding that unconscious ideas—or rather the unconsciousness of certain psychic processes —are the main causes of morbid symptoms. We share this conviction with the French school (Janet), which, moreover, by gross schematization reduces the hysterical symptom to an unconscious *idée fixe*. Do not fear now that we will thus merge too far into this obscurest philosophy. Our unconscious is not quite the same as that of the philosophers, and, what is more, most philosophers wish to know nothing of the *psychical unconscious*. But if you will put yourselves in our position, you will understand that the interpretation of this unconscious in patients' psychic life, into the conscious, must result in a correction of their deviation from the normal, and in an abrogation of the compulsion controlling their psychic life. For the conscious will reaches as far as the conscious psychic processes, and every psychic compulsion is substantiated by the unconscious. You need never fear that the patient will be harmed by the emotions produced in entering from his unconscious into consciousness, for you can theoretically readily understand that the somatic and affective activity of the emotions which become conscious can never become as great as those of the unconscious. For we only control all our emotions by directing upon them our highest psychic activities, and they are connected with consciousness.

We can still choose another point of view for the understanding of the psycho-analytic treatment. The revealing and interpreting of the unconscious takes place under constant resistance on the part of the patient. The emerging of the unconscious is connected with displeasure, and owing to this displeasure it is continuously repulsed by the patient. It is upon this conflict in the patient's psychic life that we encroach; and, if we succeed in prevailing upon him to accept something (for motives of better insight) which he has thus far repulsed (repressed) on account of the automatic adjustment of displeasure, we have achieved in him a piece of educational work. For it is really an education if we can induce a person to leave his bed early in the morning despite his unwillingness to do so. As such an after training for the overcoming of inner resistances, you can conceive the psycho-analytic treatment in quite a general manner.

But in no sphere of the nervous patients is such an after training as essential as in the psychic elements of the sexual life. For nowhere have culture and education produced as much harm as here, and it is here, as experience will show you, that the controlling aetiologies of the neuroses are found. The other aetiological element, the constitutional contribution, is really given to us as something immutable. But this gives rise to an important demand on the doctor. Not only must he be of unblemished character—"morality is really a matter of course" as the principal person in Theodor Vischer's *Auch Einer* used to say—but he must have overcome in his own personality the mixture of lewdness and prudishness with which so many others are wont to meet the sexual problems.

This is perhaps the place for another observation. I know that the emphasis which I laid on the sexual rôle in the origin of the psychoneuroses has become widely known. But I also know that restriction and nearer determinations are of little use with the great public; the multitude has little room in its memory, and generally retains from a statement the bare nucleus, thus creating for itself an easily remembered extreme. The same might also have happened to some physicians whose faint notion of my theory is that I trace back the neurosis in the last place to sexual privation. Of such there is surely no dearth under the vital conditions of our society. But, if that assumption were true, would it not seem obvious that, in order to avoid the roundabout way of the psychic treatment and tend directly towards the cure, we should directly recommend sexual activity as the remedy? I really do not know what could induce me to suppress such conclusions if they were justified. But the state of affairs is quite different. Sexual need or privation is merely one of the factors playing a part in the mechanism of the neurosis, and if it alone existed the result would not be a disease but a dissipation. The other equally indispensable factor, which one is only too ready to forget, is the sexual repugnance of neurotics, their inability to love; it is that psychic feature which I have designated as *repression*. It is only from the conflict between the two strivings that the neurotic malady originates, and it is for this reason that the advice for sexual activity can really only seldom be designated as good in cases of psychoneuroses.

Allow me to conclude with this guarded remark. Let us hope that, with an interest for psychotherapy, purified of all hostile prejudice, you will help us to do some good in the treatment of the severe cases of psychoneuroses.

CHAPTER 9

My Views on the Rôle of Sexuality in the Aetiology of the Neurosis[1]

I am of the opinion that my theory on the aetiological significance of the sexual factor in

[1] From Löwenfeld, *Sexualleben und Nervenleiden*, 4th ed., 1906.

the neuroses can be best appreciated by following its development. I will by no means make any effort to deny that it passed through an evolution during which it underwent a change. My colleagues can find the assurance in this admission that this theory is nothing other than the result of continued and painstaking experiences. In contradistinction to this, whatever originates from speculation can certainly appear complete at one go and continue unchanged.

Originally the theory had reference only to the morbid pictures comprehended as *neurasthenia*, in which I found two types which occasionally appeared pure, and which I described as *actual neurasthenia* and *anxiety neurosis*. For it was always known that sexual factors could play a part in the causation of these forms, but they were found neither regularly effective, nor did we think of conceding to them a precedence over other aetiological influences. I was above all surprised at the frequency of coarse disturbances in the *vita sexualis* of nervous patients. The more I was in quest of such disturbances during which I remembered that all men conceal the truth in things sexual, and the more skilful I became in continuing the examination despite the incipient negation, the more regularly such disease-forming factors were discovered in the sexual life, until it seemed to me that they were but little short of universal. But one must from the first be prepared for similar frequent occurrences of sexual irregularities under the stress of the social relations of our society, and one could therefore remain in doubt as to what part of the deviation from the normal sexual function is to be considered as a morbid cause. I could, therefore, only place less value on the regular demonstration of sexual *noxae* than on other experiences which appeared to me to be less equivocal. It was found that the form of the malady, be it neurasthenia or anxiety neurosis, shows a constant relation to the form of the sexual injury. In the typical cases of neurasthenia, we could always demonstrate masturbation or accumulated pollutions, while in anxiety neurosis we could find such factors as *coitus interruptus,* frustrated excitement, etc. The factor of insufficient discharge of generated libido seemed to be common to both. Only after this experience, which is easy to gain and very often confirmed, had I the courage to claim for the sexual influences a prominent place in the aetiology of the neurosis. It also happened that the mixed forms of neurasthenia and anxiety neurosis, occurring so often, showed the admixture of the aetiologies accepted for both, and that such a bipartition in the form of the manifestations of the neurosis seemed to accord well with the polar characters of sexuality (male and female).

At the same time, while I assigned to sexuality this significance in the origin of the simple neurosis, I still professed for the psychoneuroses (hysteria and obsessions) a purely psychological theory in which the sexual factor was no differently considered than any other emotional sources. Together with J. Breuer, and in addition to observations which he had made on his hysterical patients fully a decade before, I have studied the mechanism of the origin of hysterical symptoms by the awakening of memories in hypnotic states. We obtained information which permitted us to cross the bridge from Charcot's traumatic hysteria to the common non-traumatic hysteria. We reached the conception that the hysterical symptoms are permanent results of psychic traumas, and that the amount of affect belonging to them was pushed away from conscious elaboration by special determinations, thus forcing an abnormal road into bodily innervation. The terms *strangulated affect, conversion,* and *ab-reaction,* comprise the distinctive characteristics of this conception.

In the close relations of the psycho-neuroses to the simple neuroses, which can go so far that the diagnostic distinction is not always easy for the inexperienced, it could happen that the cognition gained from one sphere has also taken effect in the other. Leaving such influences out of the question, the deep study of the psychic traumas also leads to the same results. If by the *analytic* method we continue to trace the psychic traumas from which the hysterical symptoms are derived, we finally reach to experiences which belong to the patient's childhood and concern his sexual life. This can be found even in such cases where a banal emotion of a non-sexual nature has occasioned the outburst of the disease. Without taking into account these sexual traumas of childhood, we could neither explain the symptoms, find their determination intelligible, nor guard against their recurrence. The incomparable significance of sexual experiences in the aetiology of the psychoneuroses seems therefore firmly established, and this fact remains until today one of the main supports of our theory.

If we represent this theory by saying that the course of the life long hysterical neurosis lies in the sexual experiences of early childhood, which are usually trivial in themselves, it surely would sound strange enough. But if we take cognizance of the historical development of the theory, and transfer the main content of the same into the sentence: "Hysteria is the expression of a special behaviour of the sexual function of the individual, and that this behaviour was already decisively determined by the first effective influences and experiences of childhood," we will perhaps be poorer in a paradox, but richer in a motive for directing our attention to a hitherto very neglected and most significant after-effect of infantile impressions in general.

As I reserve the question whether the aetiology of hysteria (and compulsion neurosis) is to be found in the sexual infantile experiences for a later more thorough discussion, I now return to the construction of the theory expressed in some small preliminary publications in the years 1895-1896.[1] The bringing into prominence of the assumed aetiological factors permitted us at the time to contrast the common neuroses, which are maladies with an actual aetiology, with the psychoneuroses which aetiology was in the first place to be sought in the sexual experiences of remote times. The theory culminates in the sentence: *In a normal* vita sexualis *no neurosis is possible.*

If I still consider today this sentence as correct, it is really not surprising that after ten years' labour on the knowledge of these relations I passed a good way beyond my former point of view, and that I now think myself in a position to correct by detailed experience the imperfections, the displacements, and the misconceptions, from which this theory then suffered. By chance my former rather meagre material furnished me with a great number of cases in which infantile histories, sexual seduction by grown-up persons or older children, played the main role. I overestimated the frequency of these (otherwise not to be doubted) occurrences, the more so because I was then in no position to distinguish definitely the deceptive memories of hysterical patients concerning their childhood from the traces of the real processes, whereas I have since then learned to explain many a seduction-fancy as an attempt at defence against the reminiscences of their own sexual activity (infantile masturbation). The emphasis laid on the *traumatic* element of the infantile sexual experience disappeared with

---

[1] See chapter 7 above and "The Aetiology of Hysteria," *Collected Papers,* I.

this explanation, and it remained obvious that the infantile sexual activities (be they spontaneous or provoked) dictate the course of the later sexual life after maturity. The same explanation, which really corrects the most significant of my original errors, perforce also changed the conception of the mechanism of the hysterical symptoms. These no longer appeared as direct descendants of repressed memories of infantile sexual experiences, but between the symptoms and the infantile impressions there slipped in the fancies (confabulations of memory) of the patients which were mostly produced during the years of puberty and which, on the one hand, are raised from, and over, the infantile memories, and, on the other hand, are immediately transformed into symptoms. Only after the introduction of the element of hysterical fancies did the structure of the neurosis and its relation to the life of the patient become transparent. It also resulted in a veritable surprising analogy between these unconscious hysterical fancies and the romances which became conscious as delusions in paranoia.

After this correction, the *infantile sexual traumas* were in a sense supplanted by the *infantilism of sexuality*. A second modification of the original theory was not remote. With the accepted frequency of seduction in childhood, there also disappeared the enormous emphasis of the accidental influences of sexuality to which I wished to shift the main rôle in the causation of the disease without, however, denying constitutional and hereditary factors. I even hoped to solve thereby the problem of the selection of the neurosis, that is, to decide by the details of the sexual infantile experience, the form of the psychoneurosis into which the patient may merge. Though with reserve, I thought at that time that passive behaviour during these scenes results in the specific predisposition for hysteria, while active behaviour results in compulsion neurosis. This conception I was later obliged to disclaim completely, though some facts of the supposed connection between passivity and hysteria, and activity and compulsion neurosis, can be maintained to some extent. With the disappearance of the accidental influences of experiences, the elements of constitution and heredity had to regain the upper hand, but, differing from the view generally in vogue, I placed the *sexual constitution* in place of the general neuropathic predisposition. In my recent work, *Three Contributions to the Theory of Sex*,[1] I have at-

[1] First published in 1905.

tempted to discuss the varieties of this sexual constitution, the components of the sexual impulse in general, and its origin from the contributory sources of the organism.

Still in connection with the changed conception of the *sexual infantile traumas,* the theory continued to develop in a course which was already indicated in the publications of 1894-1896. Even before sexuality was installed in its proper place in the aetiology, I had already stated as a condition for the pathogenic efficaciousness of an experience that the latter must appear to the ego as unbearable and thus evoke an exertion for defence. To this defence I have traced the psychic splitting—or, as it was then called, the splitting of consciousness—of hysteria. If the defence succeeded, the unbearable experience with its resulting affect was expelled from consciousness and memory; but under certain conditions the thing expelled, which was now unconscious, developed its activity, and, with the aid of the symptoms and their adhering affect, it returned into consciousness, so that the disease corresponded to a failure of the defence. This conception had the merit of entering into the play of the psychic forces, and hence approximated the psychic processes of hysteria to the normal, instead of shifting the characteristic of the neurosis into an enigmatic and no-further-analyzable disturbance.

Further inquiries among persons who remained normal furnished the unexpected result that the sexual histories of their childhood need not differ essentially from the infantile life of neurotics, and that especially the rôle of seduction is the same in the former, so the accidental influences receded still more in comparison to the factors of *repression* (which I began to use instead of *defence*). It really does not depend on the sexual excitements which an individual experiences in his childhood, but above all on his reactions towards these experiences, and whether these impressions responded with *repression* or not. It could be shown that spontaneous sexual manifestations of childhood were frequently interrupted in the course of development by an act of repression. The sexual maturity of neurotic individuals thus regularly brings with it a fragment of *sexual repression* from childhood, which manifests itself in the requirements of real life. Psycho-analysis of hysterical individuals shows that the malady is the result of the conflict between the libido and the sexual repression, and that their symptoms have the value of a compromise between both psychic streams.

Without a comprehensive discussion of my conception of repression, I could not explain any further this part of the theory. It suffices to refer here to my *Three Contributions to the Theory of Sex*, where I have made an attempt to throw some light on the somatic processes in which the essence of sexuality is to be sought. I have stated there that the constitutional predisposition of the child is more irregularly multifarious than one would expect, that it deserves to be called *polymorphous-perverse*, and that from this predisposition the so-called normal behaviour of the sexual functions results, through a repression of certain components. By referring to the infantile character of sexuality, I could form a simple connection between normal, perversions, and neurosis. The normal resulted through the repression of certain partial impulses and components of the infantile predisposition, and through the subordination of the rest under the primacy of the genital zones for the service of the function of procreation. The perversions corresponded to disturbances of this connection due to a superior compulsive-like development of some of the partial impulses; while the neurosis could be traced to a marked repression of the libidinous strivings. As almost all perversive impulses of the infantile predisposition are demonstrable as forces of symptom formation in the neurosis, in which, however, they exist in a state of repression, I could designate the neurosis as the *negative* of the perversion.

I think it worth emphasizing that with all changes my ideas on the aetiology of the psychoneuroses still never disavowed or abandoned two points of view, to wit, the estimation of *sexuality* and *infantilism*. In other respects we have in place of the accidental influences the constitutional factors, and instead of the pure psychologically intended *defence* we have the organic *sexual repression*. Should anybody ask where a cogent proof can be found for the asserted aetological significance of sexual factors in the psychoneuroses, and argue that, since an outburst of these diseases can result from the most banal emotions, and even from somatic causes, a specific aetiology in the form of special experiences of childhood must therefore be disavowed; I mention as an answer for all these arguments the psycho-analytic investigation of neurotics as the source from which the disputed conviction emanates. If one only makes use of this method of investigation, he will discover that the *symptoms represent the whole or a partial sexual manifes-*

tation of the patient, from the sources of the normal or perverse partial impulses of sexuality. Not only does a good part of the hysterical symptomatology originate directly from the manifestations of the sexual excitement, not only are a series of erogenous zones, reinforcing infantile attributes, raised in the neurosis to the importance of genitals, but even the most complicated symptoms become revealed as the converted representations of fancies having a sexual situation as a content. He who can interpret the language of hysteria can understand that the neurosis only deals with the repressed sexuality. One should, however, understand the sexual function in its proper sphere as circumscribed by the infantile predisposition. Where a banal emotion has to be added to the causation of the disease, the analysis regularly shows that the sexual components of the traumatic experience, which are never missing, have exercised the pathogenic effect.

We have unexpectedly advanced from the question of the causation of the psychoneuroses to the problem of its nature. If we wish to take cognizance of what we have discovered by psycho-analysis, we can only say that the nature of these maladies lies in disturbances of the sexual processes, in those processes of the organism which determine the formation and utilization of the sexual libido. We can hardly avoid imagining these processes in the last place as chemical, so that we can recognize in the so-called actual neuroses the somatic effects of disturbances in the sexual metabolism, while in the phychoneuroses we recognize besides the psychic effects of the same disturbances. The resemblance of the neuroses to the manifestations of intoxication and abstinence following certain alkaloids, and to Basedow's and Addison's diseases, obtrudes itself clinically without any further ado, and, just as these two diseases should no more be described as *nervous diseases,* so will the genuine neuroses soon have to be removed from this class, despite their nomenclature.

Everything that can exert harmful influences in the processes serving the sexual function, therefore, belongs to the aetiology of the neurosis. In the first place we have the noxae directly affecting the sexual functions insofar as they are accepted as injuries by the sexual constitution which is changeable through culture and breeding. In the second place, we have all the different noxae and traumas which may also injure the sexual processes by injuring the organism as a whole. But we must not forget that the aetiological problem of the neuroses is at least as complicated as in the causation of any other disease. One single pathogenic influence almost never suffices; it mostly requires a multiplicity of aetiological factors reinforcing one another, and which can not be brought in contrast to one another. It is for that reason that the state of neurotic illness is not sharply separated from the normal. The disease is the result of a summation, and the measure of the aetiological determinations can be completed from any one part. To seek the aetiology of the neurosis exclusively in heredity, or in the constitution, would be no less one-sided than to attempt to raise to the aetiology the accidental influences of sexuality alone, even though the explanations show that the nature of this malady lies only in a disturbance of the sexual processes of the organism.

CHAPTER 10
HYSTERICAL FANCIES AND THEIR RELATIONS TO BISEXUALITY[1]

THE delusional formations of paranoiacs containing the greatness and sufferings of their own ego, which manifest themselves quite typically in almost monotonous forms, are universally familiar. Furthermore, through numerous communications we became acquainted with the peculiar organizations by means of which certain perverts put into operation their sexual gratifications, be it in fancy or reality. On the other hand, it may sound rather novel to some to hear that quite analogous psychic formations regularly appear in all psychoneuroses, especially in hysteria, and that these so-called hysterical fancies show important relations to the causation of neurotic symptoms.

Of the same source and of the normal prototype are all these fantastic creations, so-called reveries of youth, which have already gained a certain consideration in the literature, though not a sufficient one.[2] They are perhaps equally frequent in both sexes; in girls and women they seem to be wholly of an erotic nature, while in men they are of an erotic or ambitious nature. Yet, even in men, the importance of the erotic factor is not to be put in the second place, for on examining more closely the reveries of men

we generally learn that all these heroic acts are accomplished, that all these successes are acquired, in order to please a woman and to be preferred to other men.[3] These fancies are wish gratifications which emanate from privation and longing. They are justly named *day dreams*, for they give the key for the understanding of night dreams in which the nucleus of the dream formation is produced by just such complicated, disfigured day fancies which are misunderstood by the conscious psychic judgment.[4]

These day dreams are garnished with great interest, are cautiously nurtured and coyly guarded, as if they were numbered among the most intimate estates of personality. On the street, however, the day dreamer can be readily recognized by a sudden, as if absent-minded, smile, by talking to himself, or by a running-like acceleration of his gait wherein he designates the acme of the imaginary situation.

All hysterical attacks which I have been thus far able to examine proved to be of such involuntary incursions of day dreams. Observation leaves no doubt that such fancies may exist as unconscious or conscious, and whenever they become unconscious they may also become pathogenic, that is, they may express themselves in symptoms and attacks. Under favourable conditions it is possible for consciousness to seize such unconscious fancies. One of my patients, whose attention I have called to her fancies, narrated that once while in the street she suddenly found herself in tears, and rapidly reflecting over the cause of her weeping the fancy became clear to her. She fancied herself in delicate relationship with a piano virtuoso familiar in the city, but whom she did not know personally. In her fancy she bore him a child (she was childless), and he then deserted her, leaving her and her child in misery. At this passage of the romance she burst into tears.

The unconscious fancies are either from the first unconscious, having been formed in the unconscious, or, which is more frequently the case, they were once conscious fancies, day dreams, and were then intentionally forgotten, merging into the unconscious by *repression*. Their content then either remained the same or underwent a transformation, so that the present unconscious fancy represents a descendant of the once conscious one. The unconscious fancy stands in a very important relation to the sexual life of the person; it is really identical with that fancy which helped it towards sexual grat-

---

[1] *Zeitschrift für Sexualwissenschaft, herausgegeben von Hirschfeld, I, 1908.*
[2] Compare Breuer and Freud, *op. cit.*; P. Janet, *Névroses et ideés fixes, I* ("*Les rêveries subconscientes*"), 1898; Havelock Ellis, *Sexual Impulse and Modesty;* Freud, *Interpretation of Dreams;* A. Pick, "*Über pathologische Träumerei und ihre Beziehungen zur Hysterie,*" *Jahrbuch für Psychiatrie und Neurologie,* XIV, 1896.

[3] H. Ellis similarly expresses himself, *op. cit.*
[4] Compare Freud, *Interpretation of Dreams.*

ification during a period of masturbation. The masturbating act (in the broader sense the onanistic) then consisted of two parts, the evocation of the fancy, and the active performance of self-gratification at the height of the same. This combination is familiarly in itself a kind of soldering.[1] Originally this action was a purely auto-erotic undertaking for the pleasure obtained from a certain so-called *erogenous* part of the body. Later this action blended with a wish presentation from the sphere of object-love, and served for a partial realization of the situation in which this fancy culminated. If, then, the person forgoes in this manner the masturbo-fantastic gratification, the action remains undone; the fancy, however, changes from a conscious to an unconscious one. If no other manner of sexual gratification occurs, if the person remains abstinent and does not succeed in sublimating his libido, that is, in diverting the sexual excitement to a higher aim, we then have the conditions for the refreshment of the unconscious fancy. It then grows exuberantly and with all the force of the desire for love, at least a fragment of its content becomes a morbid symptom.

The unconscious fancies are then the nearest psychical first steps of a whole series of hysterical symptoms. The hysterical symptoms are nothing other than unconscious fancies brought to light by *conversion*, and, insofar as they are somatic symptoms, they are frequently enough taken from the spheres of the sexual feelings and motor innervations which originally accompanied the former still conscious fancies. In this way the disuse of onanism is really made retrogressive, and the final aim of the whole pathological process, the restoration of the primary sexual gratification, though it never becomes perfect, in a manner always achieves a certain resemblance.

The interest of him who studies hysteria turns directly from the symptoms to the fancies from which the former originate. The technique of psycho-analysis gives the means of finding out from the symptoms these unconscious fancies, and of bringing them back to the patient's consciousness. In this way it was found that the unconscious fancies of hysterics perfectly correspond in content to the consciously performed gratification situations of perverts. Those who lack examples of such nature need only recall the historical achievements of the Roman Caesars, whose frenzies were naturally only conditioned by the unrestricted potency of the fancy-creator. The delusional formations of paranoiacs are the same, but they are phantasies which immediately become conscious, and are borne by the sado-masochistic components of the sexual instinct. Complete counterparts of these can also be found in certain unconscious phantasies of hysterics. It is a familiar, practically important fact, that hysterics express their phantasies not as symptoms but as conscious realization, and in this way they feign and commit murders, assaults, and sexual aggressions.

All that can be found out about the sexuality of the psychoneurotic can be ascertained by psycho-analytic investigation, which leads from the obtrusive symptoms to the hidden unconscious phantasies. It also furnishes the fact of this small preliminary communication which is to be reported here.

Probably because of the difficulties which stand in the way of the effort of the unconscious phantasies to express themselves, the relation of the phantasies to the symptoms is not simple but rather manifoldly complicated.[2] As a rule, i.e., in a fully developed and long standing neurosis, a symptom does not correspond to one unconscious phantasy, but to a number of such, and indeed not in arbitrary but in lawful combination. To be sure, in the beginning of the disease all these complications are not yet developed.

For the sake of general interest, I pass over the connection of this communication and add a series of formulæ which strive progressively to exhaust the nature of hysteria. They do not contradict one another but correspond partly to more complete and sharper conceptions, and partly to the application of different points of view.

1. The hysterical symptom is the memory symbol of certain effective (traumatic) impressions and experiences.

2. The hysterical symptom is the associative return of this traumatic experience, or a substitute produced by *conversion*.

3. The hysterical symptom—like all other psychic formations—is the expression of a wish realization.

4. The hysterical symptom is the realization of one of the unconscious phantasies, serving as a wish fulfillment.

5. The hysterical symptom serves as a sexual gratification, and represents a part of the

---

[1] Cf. *Three Contributions to the Theory of Sex.*

[2] The same holds true for the relation between the *latent* thoughts of the dream and the elements of the *manifest* content of the dream. See the Chapter on the "Dream Work" in the author's *Interpretation of Dreams*, p. 252, below.

sexual life of the individual (corresponding to one of the components of his sexual impulse).

6. The hysterical symptom corresponds to the return of one form of the sexual gratification, which was real in infantile life but had been repressed since then.

7. The hysterical symptom results as a compromise between two opposing affects or impulses, one of which strives to bring to realization a partial impulse, or a component of the sexual constitution, while the other strives to suppress the same.

8. The hysterical symptom may represent diverse unconscious non-sexual impulses, but can not dispense with the sexual meaning.

It is the seventh among these determinants, which expresses most exhaustively the nature of the hysterical symptom as a realization of an unconscious phantasy, and it is the eighth which evaluates in fitting manner the significance of the sexual factor. Some of the preceding formulæ are contained as first steps in this formula.

In view of these relations between symptoms and phantasies, one can readily reach from the psycho-analysis of the symptoms to the knowledge of the components of the sexual impulse controlling the individual, just as I have shown in the *Three Contributions to the Theory of Sex*. But in some cases this examination gives rather unexpected results. It shows that many symptoms can not be solved by one unconscious sexual phantasy or by a series of phantasies in which the most significant and most primitive is of a sexual nature, but that in order to solve the symptoms two sexual phantasies are required, one of the masculine and one of the feminine character, so that one of these phantasies corresponds to a homosexual impulse. The theory expressed in formula seven is in no way affected by this novelty, so that an hysterical symptom necessarily corresponds to a compromise between a libidinal and a repressed emotion, but, besides that, it can correspond to a union of two libidinal phantasies of contrary sex characters.

I refrain from giving examples for this theory. Experience has taught me that short analyses compressed into the form of an abstract can never make the vivid impression for which they were intended. The communication of fully analyzed cases must, however, be reserved for another place.

I therefore content myself with the fact of formulating the theory and elucidating its meaning.

9. An hysterical symptom is the expression, on the one hand, of a masculine, and, on the other hand, of a feminine unconscious sexual phantasy.

I expressly observe that I am unable to adjudge to this theory the same general validity that I claimed for the other formulæ. As far as I can see, it neither fits into all symptoms of a single case, nor into all cases. On the contrary, it is not difficult to find cases in which the contrary sexual emotions have found separate symptomatic expression, so that the symptoms of hetero- and homosexuality can be as sharply distinguished from each other as the phantasies hidden behind them. Nevertheless, the relation claimed in the ninth formula occurs frequently enough, and wherever it is found it is of sufficient importance to merit a special formulation. It seems to signify the highest stage of complexity which the determination of hysterical symptoms can attain, and can only be expected in a long-standing neurosis, wherein a great amount of organization has taken place.[1]

The demonstrable bisexual significance of hysterical symptoms in many cases is indeed an interesting confirmation of the assertion formulated by me that the supposed bisexual predisposition of man can be especially recognized in psychoneurotics by means of psychoanalysis.[2] Quite an analogous process from the same sphere is that in which the masturbator in his conscious phantasies attempts to live through in his imagination the fancied situations of both the man and the woman. Other counterparts are found in certain hysterical crises in which the patients play both rôles lying at the basis of sexual phantasies; thus, for example, one of the cases under my observation pressed his garments to his body with one arm (as a woman), and with the other arm attempted to tear them off (as a man). This contradictory simultaneity determines, for the most part, the incomprehensiveness of the situation otherwise so plastically represented in the attack, and is excellently suited for the concealment of the affective unconscious phantasy.

In psycho-analytical treatment, it is very important to be prepared for the bisexual meaning of a symptom. It should not be at all surprising or misleading when a symptom remains

---

[1] Indeed, J. Sadger, who recently discovered the theory in question, independently of psycho-analysis, claims for it a general validity ("*Die Bedeutung der psychoanalytische Methode nach Freud*," *Zentralbl. f. Nerv. u. Psych.*, No. 229).

[2] Freud, *Three Contributions to the Theory of Sex*.

apparently undiminished in spite of the fact that one of its sexual determinants is already solved. It may still be based on the unsuspected contrary sexual element. Moreover during the treatment of such cases we can observe how the patient makes use of this convenience. While analyzing one of the sexual meanings, he continually switches his thoughts into the sphere of the contrary meaning, as if onto an adjacent track.

The Sexual Enlightenment of Children [1]

An Open Letter to Dr. M. Furst, Editor of
Soziale Medizin und Hygiene

DEAR SIR: When you ask me for an expression of opinion on the matter of sexual enlightenment for children, I assume that what you want is the independent opinion of an individual physician whose professional work offers him special opportunities for studying the subject, and not a regular conventional treatise dealing with all the mass of literature that has grown up around it. I am aware that you have followed my scientific efforts with interest, and that, unlike many other colleagues, you do not dismiss my ideas without a hearing because I regard the psycho-sexual constitution and certain noxae in the sexual life as the most important causes of the neurotic disorders that are so common. My *Three Contributions to the Theory of Sex,* in which I describe the components of which the sexual instinct is made up, and the disturbances which may occur in its development into the function of sexuality, has recently received favourable mention in your journal.

I am, therefore, to answer the questions whether children may be given any information at all in regard to the facts of sexual life, and at what age and in what way this should be done. Now let me confess at the outset that discussion with regard to the second and third points seems to me perfectly reasonable, but that to my mind it is quite inconceivable how the first of these questions could ever be the subject of debate. What can be the aim of withholding from children, or let us say from young people, this information about the sexual life of human beings? Is it a fear of arousing interest in such matters prematurely, before it spontaneously stirs in them? Is it a hope of retarding by concealment of this kind the development of the sexual instinct in general, until such time as it can find its way into the only channels open to it in the civilized social order? Is it supposed that children would show no interest or understanding for the facts and riddles of sexual life if they were not prompted to do so by outside influence? Is it regarded as possible that the knowledge withheld from them will not reach them in other ways? Or is it genuinely and seriously intended that later on they should consider everything connected with sex as something despicable and abhorrent from which their parents and teachers wish to keep them apart as long as possible?

I am really at a loss to say which of these can be the motive for the customary concealment from children of everything connected with sex. I only know that these arguments are one and all equally foolish, and that I find it difficult to pay them the compliment of serious refutation. I remember, however, that in the letters of that great thinker and friend of humanity, Multatuli, I once found a few lines which are more than adequate as an answer.[2]

"To my mind it seems that certain things are altogether too much wrapped in mystery It is well to keep the fantasies of children pure, but their purity will not be preserved by ignorance. On the contrary, I believe that concealment leads a girl or boy to suspect the truth more than ever. Curiosity leads to prying into things which would have roused little or no interest if they were talked of openly without any fuss. If this ignorance could be maintained, I might be more reconciled to it, but that is impossible; the child comes into contact with other children, books fall into his hands which lead him to reflect, and the mystery with which things he has already surmised are treated by his parents actually increases his desire to know more. Then this desire that is only incompletely and secretly satisfied gives rise to excitement and corrupts his imagination, so that the child is already a sinner while his parents still believe he does not know what sin is."

I do not know how the case could be better stated, though perhaps one might amplify it. It is surely nothing else but habitual prudery and a guilty conscience in themselves about sexual matters which causes adults to adopt this attitude of mystery towards children; possibly, however, a piece of theoretical ignorance on their part, to be counteracted only by fresh information, is also responsible. It is commonly

[1] *Collected Papers,* II; first published in *Soziale Medizin und Hygiene,* Vol. II, 1907; reprinted in *Sammlung,* Zweite Folge.

[2] Multatuli, *Briefe* (1906), I, 26.

believed that the sexual instinct is lacking in
children, and only begins to arise in them when
the sexual organs mature. This is a grave error,
equally serious from the point of view both of
theory and of actual practice. It is so easy to
correct it by observation that one can only
wonder how it can ever have arisen. As a matter of fact, the new-born infant brings sexuality with it into the world; certain sexual
sensations attend its development while at the
breast and during early childhood, and only
very few children would seem to escape some
kind of sexual activity and sexual experiences
before puberty. A more complete exposition of
this statement can be found in my *Three Contributions to the Theory of Sex*, to which reference has been made above. The reader will
learn that the specific organs of reproduction
are not the only portions of the body which
are a source of pleasurable sensation, and that
Nature has stringently ordained that even stimulation of the genitals cannot be avoided during infancy. This period of life, during which a
certain degree of directly sexual pleasure is produced by the stimulation of various cutaneous
areas (erotogenic zones), by the activity of certain biological impulses and as an accompanying excitation during many affective states, is
designated by an expression introduced by
Havelock Ellis as the period of auto-erotism.
Puberty merely brings about attainment of the
stage at which the genitals acquire supremacy
among all the zones and sources of pleasure,
and in this way presses erotism into the service
of reproduction, a process which naturally can
undergo certain inhibitions; in the case of
those persons who later on become perverts
and neurotics this process is only incompletely
accomplished. On the other hand, the child is
capable long before puberty of most of the
mental manifestations of love: for example,
tenderness, devotion, and jealousy. Often
enough the connection between these mental
manifestations and the physical sensation of
sexual excitation is so close that the child cannot be in doubt about the relation between the
two. To put it briefly, the child is long before
puberty a being capable of mature love, lacking
only the ability for reproduction; and it may
be definitely asserted that the mystery which
is set up withholds him only from intellectual
comprehension of achievements for which he
is psychically and physically prepared.

The intellectual interest of a child in the
riddle of sexual life, his desire for knowledge,
finds expression at an earlier period of life than
is usually suspected. If they have not often
come across such cases as I am about to mention, parents must either be afflicted with
blindness in regard to this interest in their
children, or, when they cannot overlook it,
must make every effort to stifle it. I know a
splendid boy, now four years old, whose intelligent parents abstain from forcibly suppressing
one side of the child's development. Little
Herbert, who has certainly not been exposed
to any seducing influence from servants, has
for some time shown the liveliest interest in
that part of his body which he calls his "weewee-maker." When only three years old he
asked his mother, "Mamma, have you got a
weewee-maker, too?" His mother answered,
"Of course, what did you think?" He also asked
his father the same question repeatedly. At
about the same age he was taken to a barn and
saw a cow milked for the first time. "Look,
milk is coming out of the weewee-maker!" he
called in surprise. At the age of three and three-
quarters he was well on the way to establish
correct categories by means of his own independent observation. He saw how water is run
off from a locomotive and said, "See, the engine is making weewee, but where is its weewee-maker?" Later on he added thoughtfully,
"Dogs and horses have weewee-makers, but
tables and chairs don't have them." Recently he
was watching his little sister of one week old
being bathed, and remarked, "Her weewee-
maker is still tiny; it will get bigger when she
grows." (I have heard of this attitude towards
the problem of sex difference in other boys of
the same age.) I must expressly assert that
Herbert is not a sensual child nor even morbidly disposed; in my opinion, since he has
never been frightened or oppressed with a sense
of guilt, he gives expression quite ingenuously
to what he thinks.

The second great problem which exercises
a child's mind—probably at a rather later date
—is that of the origin of children, and is usually aroused by the unwelcome arrival of a
baby brother or sister. This is the oldest and
most burning question that assails immature
humanity; those who understand how to interpret myths and legends can detect it in the
riddle which the Theban Sphinx set to Oedipus.
The answers usually given to children in the
nursery wound the child's frank and genuine
spirit of investigation, and generally deal the
first blow at his confidence in his parents; from
this time onwards he commonly begins to mistrust grown-up people and keeps to himself

what interests him most. The following letter may show how torturing this very curiosity may become in older children; it was written by a motherless girl of eleven and a half who had been puzzling over the problem with her younger sister.

DEAR AUNT MALI: Please will you be so kind as to write and tell me how you got Chris or Paul. You must know because you are married. We were arguing about it yesterday, and we want to know the truth. We have nobody else to ask. When are you coming to Salzburg? You know, Aunt Mali, we simply can't imagine how the stork brings babies. Trudel thought the stork brings them in a shirt. Then we want to know, too, how the stork gets them out of the pond, and why one never sees babies in ponds. And please will you tell me, too, how you know beforehand when you are going to have one. Please write and tell me *all* about it. Thousands of kisses from all of us.

Your inquiring niece,

LILY

I do not think that this touching request brought the two sisters the information they wanted. Later on the writer developed the neurosis that arises in unanswered unconscious questions—obsessive speculating.

I do not think that there is even one good reason for denying children the information which their thirst for knowledge demands. To be sure, if it is the purpose of educators to stifle the child's power of independent thought as early as possible, in order to produce that "good behaviour" which is so highly prized, they cannot do better than deceive children in sexual matters and intimidate them by religious means. The stronger characters will, it is true, withstand these influences; they will become rebels against the authority of their parents and later against every other form of authority. When children do not receive the explanations for which they turn to their elders, they go on tormenting themselves in secret with the problem, and produce attempts at solution in which the truth they have guessed is mixed up in the most extraordinary way with grotesque inventions; or else they whisper confidences to each other which, because of the sense of guilt in the youthful inquirers, stamp everything sexual as horrible and disgusting. These infantile sexual theories are well worth collecting and examining. After these experiences children usually lose the only proper attitude to sexual questions, many of them never to find it again.

It would seem that the overwhelming majority of writers, both men and women, who have dealt with the question of explaining sexual matters to children have expressed themselves in favour of enlightenment. The clumsiness, however, of most of their proposals how and when this enlightenment should be carried out leads one to conclude that they have not found it very easy to venture this admission. As far as my knowledge of the literature goes, the charming letter of explanation which a certain Frau Emma Eckstein gives as written to her ten-year-old boy stands out conspicuously.[1] The customary method is obviously not the right one. All sexual knowledge is kept from children as long as possible, and then on one single occasion an explanation, which is even then only half the truth and generally comes too late, is proffered them in mysterious and solemn language. Most of the answers to the question, "How can I tell my children?" make such a pitiful impression, at least upon me, that I should prefer parents not to concern themselves with the explanation at all. It is much more important that children should never get the idea that one wants to make more of a secret of the facts of sexual life than of any other matter not suited to their understanding. To ensure this it is necessary that from the very beginning everything sexual should be treated like everything else that is worth knowing about. Above all, schools should not evade the task of mentioning sexual matters; lessons about the animal kingdom should include the great facts of reproduction, which should be given their due significance, and emphasis should be laid at the same time on the fact that man shares with the higher animals everything essential to his organization. Then, if the atmosphere of the home does not make for suppression of all reasoning, something similar to what I once overheard in a nursery would probably occur oftener. A small boy said to his little sister, "How can you think the stork brings babies! You know that man is a mammal, do you suppose that storks bring other mammals their young, too?" In this way, the curiosity of children will never become very intense, for at each stage in its inquiries it will find the satisfaction it needs. Explanations about the specific circumstances of human sexuality and some indication of its social significance should be provided before the child is eleven years old.[2] The age of confirmation would be a more

[1] Emma Eckstein, *Die Sexualfrage in der Erziehung des Kindes,* 1904.
[2] The original has also: *Am Schlusse des Volksschulunterrichtes und vor Eintritt in die Mittelschule.* —TR.

suitable time than any other at which to instruct the child, who already has full knowledge of the physical facts involved, in those social obligations which are bound up with actual gratification of this instinct. A gradual and progressive course of instruction in sexual matters such as this, at no period interrupted, in which the school takes the initiative, seems to me to be the only method of giving the necessary information that takes into consideration the development of the child and thus successfully avoids ever-present dangers.

I consider it a most significant advance in the science of education that in France, in place of the catechism, the State should have introduced a primer which gives the child his first instruction in his position as a citizen and in the ethical obligations which will be his in time to come. The elementary instruction provided there, however, is seriously deficient in that it includes no reference to sexual matters. Here is the omission which stands in such need of attention on the part of educators and reformers. In those countries which leave the education of children either wholly or in part in the hands of the priesthood, the method urged would of course not be practicable. No priest will ever admit the identity in nature of man and beast, since to him the immortality of the soul is a foundation for moral training which he cannot forgo. Here again we clearly see the unwisdom of putting new wine into old bottles, and perceive the impossibility of carrying through a reform in one particular without altering the foundations of the whole system.

The Future Prospects of Psycho-Analytic Therapy[1]

AN ADDRESS DELIVERED BEFORE THE SECOND
INTERNATIONAL PSYCHO-ANALYTICAL CON-
GRESS AT NUREMBERG IN 1910

SINCE the objects for which we are assembled
here today are mainly practical, I shall choose
a practical theme for my introductory address
and appeal to your interest in medical, not in
scientific, matters. I can imagine what your
opinion about the success of our therapy probably is, and I assume that most of you have
already passed through the two stages which all
beginners go through, that of enthusiasm at the
unexpected increase in our therapeutic achievements, and that of depression at the magnitude
of the difficulties which stand in the way of our
efforts. Whichever of these stages in development, however, each of you may happen to be
going through at the moment, my intention today is to show you that we have by no means
come to the end of our resources for combating the neuroses, and that we may expect a
substantial improvement in our therapeutic
prospects before very long.

This improvement will come, I think, from
three sources:

1. From internal progress.
2. From increased prestige.
3. From the general effect of our work.

1. Under "internal progress" I understand
advances (a) in our analytical knowledge, (b)
in our technique.

(a) Advances in our knowledge. We are, of
course, still a long way from knowing all that
is required for an understanding of the unconscious minds of our patients. Now it is clear
that every advance in our knowledge means an
increase in the power of our therapy. As long
as we understood nothing, we accomplished
nothing; the more we understand the more we
shall achieve. At its beginning, psycho-analytic
treatment was inexorable and exhaustive.
The patient had to say everything himself, and
the physician's part consisted of urging him
on incessantly. Today things have a more
friendly air. The treatment is made up of two
parts: out of what the physician infers and tells

[1] *Collected Papers*, II; first published in *Zentralblatt*, Vol. I, 1910; reprinted in *Sammlung*, 3rd Series.

the patient, and out of the patient's work of
assimilation, of *working through,* what he hears.
The mechanism of our curative method is indeed quite easy to understand; we give the patient the conscious idea of what he may expect
to find (*bewusste Erwartungsvorstellung*), and
the similarity of this with the repressed unconscious one leads him to come upon the latter
himself. This is the intellectual help which
makes it easier for him to overcome the resistances between conscious and unconscious. Incidentally, I may remark that it is not the only
mechanism made use of by the analytic method; you all know that far more powerful one
which lies in the use of the *transference.* I intend soon to undertake an exposition of these
various factors, which are so important for an
understanding of the cure, in a practice of
psycho-analysis. And, further, in speaking to
you I need not rebut the objection that the way
in which we practise the method today obscures its testimony to the correctness of our
hypotheses; you will not forget that this evidence is to be found elsewhere, and that a
therapeutic procedure cannot be performed in
the same way as a theoretical investigation.

Now let me refer briefly to various fields in
which we both have much to learn that is new
and do actually make new discoveries daily.
First of all, there is the matter of symbolism
in dreams and in the unconscious—a fiercely
contested subject, as you know! It is no small
credit to our colleague, W. Stekel, that, indifferent to all the objections of our opponents,
he has undertaken a study of dream-symbols.
In this there is indeed much still to learn; my
Interpretation of Dreams, which was written
in 1899, awaits important amplification from
researches into symbolism.

I will say a few words about one of the
symbols that has lately been recognized. Not
long ago it came to my knowledge that a psychologist whose views are not too distant from
ours had remarked to one of us that we undoubtedly overestimate the hidden sexual significance of dreams; his most frequent dream
was of going upstairs, and there could certainly
be nothing sexual about that. Our attention be-

ing thus drawn to it, we began to study the incidence of stairs, steps and ladders in dreams,
and soon could establish the fact that stairs
and such things are certainly a symbol of coitus. The underlying element which the two
things have in common is not difficult to discover; one climbs an acclivity in rhythmic
movements, accompanied by increasing breath-
lessness, and in a few rapid leaps can be down
again. Thus the rhythm of coitus reappears in
climbing steps. We will not forget to adduce
the usages of speech in this connection. It
shows us that *mounting* is used quite simply
as a symbol for the sexual act. In German, one
says, "the man is a *Steiger, nachsteigen*". In
French, the steps of a stair are called
marches; un vieux marcheur, ein alter Steiger
both mean an old profligate. The dream-material from which these newly recognized symbols
are derived will in due time be put before you
by the committee we are about to form for collecting and studying symbols. An account of
another interesting symbol, of the idea of *rescue* and its changes in significance, will appear
in the second volume of our *Jahrbuch*. However, I must break off here or I shall not reach
my other points.

Every one of you will know from his own
experience the total change in one's attitude to
a new case when once one has thoroughly mastered the structure of some typical cases of illness. Assuming now that we had narrowly defined the regular elements in the composition of
the various forms of neurosis, just as we have
already succeeded in doing for hysterical symptom-formation, how much more assured we
should be in our prognoses! Just as an obstetri-
cian knows by examining the placenta whether
it has been completely expelled or whether noxious fragments of it still remain, so we should
be able, independently of the success of the
cure and the patient's present condition, to say
whether the work had been completely carried
to an end or whether we had to expect relapses
and fresh onsets of illness.

(*b*) I will hasten on to the innovations in the
field of technique, where indeed nearly everything still awaits definitive settlement, and
much is only now beginning to come clear.
There are now two aims in psycho-analytic
technique: to save the physician effort and to
open up for the patient the freest access to his
unconscious. You know that our technique has
been transformed in important respects. At the
time of the cathartic treatment we set ourselves the aim of elucidating the symptoms,
then we turned away from the symptoms to
discovering the *complexes,* to use Jung's indispensable word; now, however, our work is
aimed directly at finding out and overcoming
the *resistances,* and we can with justification
rely on the complexes coming to light as soon as
the resistances have been recognized and removed. Some of you have since shown a desire
to formulate and classify these resistances. Now
I beg you to examine your material and see
whether you can confirm the following statement: In male patients the most important resistances to the treatment seem to be derived
from the father-complex and to express themselves in fear of the father, and in defiance and
incredulity towards him.

Other innovations in technique relate to the
physician himself. We have begun to consider
the *counter-transference,* which arises in the
physician as a result of the patient's influence
on his unconscious feelings, and have nearly
come to the point of requiring the physician
to recognize and overcome this counter-transference in himself. Now that a larger number
of people have come to practise psycho-analysis and mutually exchange their experiences,
we have noticed that every analyst's achievement is limited by what his own complexes and
resistances permit, and consequently we require that he should begin his practice with a
self-analysis and should extend and deepen this
constantly while making his observations on
his patients. Anyone who cannot succeed in this
self-analysis may without more ado regard
himself as unable to treat neurotics by analysis.

We are also now coming to the opinion that
the analytic technique must undergo certain
modifications according to the nature of the
disease and the dominating instinctual trends
in the patient. Our therapy was, in fact, first
designed for conversion-hysteria; in anxiety-
hysteria (phobias) we must alter our procedure
to some extent. The fact is that these patients
cannot bring out the material necessary for
resolving the phobia so long as they feel protected by retaining their phobic condition. One
cannot, of course induce them to give up their
protective measures and work under the influence of anxiety from the beginning of the
treatment. One must, therefore, help them by
interpreting their unconscious to them until
they can make up their minds to do without
the protection of their phobia and expose themselves to a now comparatively moderate degree
of anxiety. Only when they have done so does
the material necessary for achieving solution of

the phobia become accessible. Other modifications of technique which seem to me not yet ready for discussion will be required in the treatment of obsessional neurosis. In this connection very important questions arise, which are not yet elucidated: how far the instincts involved in the conflict in the patient are to be allowed some gratification during the treatment, and what difference it then makes whether these impulses are active (sadistic) or passive (masochistic)in nature.

I hope you have received the impression that, when all that can at present be merely glimpsed is known and when we have established all the improvements in technique to which deeper experience with our patients must lead us, then our medical practice will reach a degree of precision and certainty of success which is not to be had in all medical specialties.

2. I said that we had much to expect from the increase in prestige which must accrue to us as time goes on. I need hardly say much to you about the importance of authority. Only very few civilized persons are capable of existing without reliance on others or are even capable of coming to an independent opinion. You cannot exaggerate the intensity of man's inner irresolution and craving for authority. The extraordinary increase in the neuroses since the power of religion has waned may give you some indication of it. The impoverishment of the ego due to the tremendous effort in repression demanded of every individual by culture may be one of the principal causes of this state of things.

Hitherto the weight of authority with its enormous *suggestive* force has been against us. All our therapeutic successes have been achieved in spite of this suggestion; it is surprising that any success was to be had at all in the circumstances. I will not let myself go to to the extent of describing to you the agreeable things that happened during the time when I alone represented psycho-analysis. I know that when I assured my patients that I knew how to relieve them permanently of their sufferings they looked round my modest abode, thought of my want of fame and honours, and regarded me like a man who possesses an infallible system in a gambling-place, of whom people say that if he could do what he professes he would look very different. Nor was it really at all pleasant to operate on people's minds while colleagues whose duty it was to assist took a pleasure in spitting into the field of operation, and while at the first signs of blood or restlessness in him the patient's relatives threatened one. An operation may surely cause reactions; in surgery we became used to that long ago. Nobody believed in me, in fact, just as even today very few believe in us; under such conditions many an attempt was bound to fail. To estimate the increase in our therapeutic capacities that will ensue when general recognition is accorded us, you should think of the different positions of gynæcologists in Turkey and in the West. All that a woman's physician may do there is to feel the pulse of an arm which is stretched out to him through a hole in the wall. And his curative results are in proportion to the inaccessibility of their object; our opponents in the West wish to restrict our access over our patients' minds to something very similar. But now that the force of public opinion drives sick women to the gynæcologist, he has become their helper and saviour. Now do not say that, even if the weight of public opinion comes to our aid and so much increases our successes, that will in no way prove the validity of our hypotheses. Suggestion is supposed to be able to do anything, and our successes would then be results of suggestion and not of psycho-analysis. Public opinion is at present suggesting hydropathic cures, diet cures, electricity cures for nervous persons, but that does not enable these measures to remove the neuroses. It will be seen whether psycho-analytic treatment can accomplish more than they.

But now, to be sure, I must damp the ardour of your expectations. The community will not hasten to grant authority to us. It is bound to offer resistance to us, for we adopt a critical attitude towards it; we accuse it of playing a great part itself in causing the neuroses. Just as we make any single person our enemy by discovering what is repressed in him, so the community cannot respond with sympathy to a relentless exposure of its injurious effects and deficiencies; because we destroy illusions, we are accused of endangering ideals. It seems, therefore, that the state of things from which I expect such great advantages for our therapeutic results will never arrive. And yet the situation is not so hopeless as one might think at the present time. Powerful though the feelings and the self-interest of men may be, yet intellect is a power too. It has not, perhaps, the power that makes itself felt immediately, but one that is all the more certain in the end. The most mordant verities are heard at last, after the interests they injure and the emotions they rouse have exhausted their frenzy. It has always been so, and the unwelcome truths which we psycho-analysts have to tell the world will undergo the same fate. Only it will not come very quickly; we must be able to wait.

3. Finally, I have to explain to you what I mean by the "general effect" of our work, and how I come to set my hopes on it. This consists in a very remarkable therapeutic constellation which could, perhaps, not be repeated anywhere else and which will appear strange to you too at first, until you recognize in it something you have long been familiar with. You know, of course, that the psychoneuroses are substitutive gratifications of instincts, the existence of which one is forced to deny to oneself and others. Their capacity to exist depends on this distortion and disguise. When the riddle they hold is solved, and the solution accepted by the sufferers, these diseases will no longer be able to exist. There is hardly anything quite like it in medicine; in fairy-tales you hear of evil spirits whose power is broken when you can tell them their names which they have kept secret.

Now in place of a single sick person put the whole community of persons liable to neuroses, persons ill and persons well; in place of the acceptance of the solution in the first put a general recognition in the second; and a little reflection will show you that this substitution cannot alter the result at all. The success which the therapy has with individuals must appear in the many too. Diseased people cannot let their various neuroses become known—their apprehensive overanxiousness which is to conceal their hatred, their agoraphobia which betrays disappointed ambition, their actions which represent self-reproaches for evil intentions and precautions against them—when all their relatives and every stranger from whom they wish to conceal their thoughts and felings know the general meaning of these symptoms, and when they themseves know that the manifestations of their disease produce nothing which others cannot instantly understand. The affect, however, will not be merely that they will conceal their symptoms—a design, by the way, which would be impossible to execute; for this concealment will destroy the purpose of the illness. Disclosure of the secret will have attacked, at its most sensitive point, the *aetiological equation* from which the neuroses descend, will have made the *advantage through illness* illusory, and, consequently, in the end, nothing can come of the changed situation

brought about by the indiscretions of physicians but an end of producing these illnesses.

If this hope seems utopian to you, you may remember that certain neurotic phenomena have already been dispelled by this means, although only in quite isolated instances. Think how common hallucinations of the Virgin Mary were in peasant girls in former times. So long as such a phenomenon brought a flock of believers and resulted, perhaps, in a chapel being built on the sacred spot, the visionary state of these maidens was inaccessible to influence. Today even the priesthood has changed its attitude to such things; it allows police and medical men to visit the seer, and since then the Virgin appears very seldom. Or allow me to study the same processes, that I have been describing as taking place in the future, in an analogous situation which is on a smaller scale and consequently, more easily appreciated. Suppose that a number of ladies and gentlemen in good society had planned a picnic at an inn in the forest one day. The ladies make up their minds that if one of them wants to relieve a natural need she will say aloud that she is going to pick flowers; but a wicked fellow hears of this secret and has printed on the programme which is sent round to the whole party—"If the ladies wish to retire, they are requested to say that they are going to pick flowers." Of course, after this, no lady will think of availing herself of this flowery pretext, and other freshly devised formulas of the same kind will be seriously compromised by it. What will be the result? The ladies will own up to their natural needs without shame and none of the men will take exception to it. Let us return to the serious aspect of our problem. A number of people who find life's conflicts too difficult to solve have taken flight into neurosis and in this way won an unmistakable, although in the end too costly, advantage through illness. What would these people have to do if their flight into illness were barred by the indiscreet revelations of psycho-analysis? They would have to be honest, own up to the instincts that are at work in them, face the conflict, fight for what they want or go without, and the tolerance from the community which is bound to ensue as a result of psycho-analytical knowledge would help them in their task.

Let us remember, however, that it is not for us to advance upon life as fanatical hygienists or therapeutists. We must admit that this ideal prevention of all neurotic illness would not be advantageous to every individual. A good number of those who now take flight into illness would not support the conflict under the conditions we have assumed, but would rapidly succumb or would commit some outrage which would be worse than if they themselves fell ill of a neurosis. The neuroses have, in fact, their biological function as defensive measures and their social justification; the *advantage through illness* that they provide is not always a purely subjective one. Is there one of you who has not at some time caught a glimpse behind the scenes in the causation of a neurosis and had to allow that it was the least of the evils possible in the circumstances? And should one really require such sacrifices in order to exterminate the neuroses, while the world is all the same full of other inextinguishable miseries?

Should we, therefore, abandon our efforts to explain the hidden meaning of neurotic manifestations, regarding it as dangerous to the individual and harmful to the interest of society; should we give up drawing the practical conclusion from a piece of scientific insight? No; I think that, nevertheless, our duty lies in the other direction. The *advantage through illness* provided by the neuroses is indeed on the whole and in the end detrimental to the individual as well as to society. The distress that our work of revelation may cause will affect but a few. The change to a more honest and honourable attitude in the world in general will not be bought too dearly by these sacrifices. But above all, all the energies which are today consumed in the production of neurotic symptoms, to serve the purposes of a world of phantasy out of touch with reality, will, even if they cannot at once be put to uses in life, help to strengthen the outcry for those changes in our civilization from which alone we can hope for beter things for our descendants.

I will let you go, therefore, with the assurance that you do your duty in more than one sense by treating your patients psycho-analytically. You are not merely working in the service of science by using the only and irreplaceable opportunity for discovering the secrets of the neuroses; you are not only giving your patients the most efficacious remedy for their sufferings available at the present time; but you are contributing your share to that enlightenment of the many from which we expect to gain the authority of the community in general and thus to achieve the most far-reaching prophylaxis against neurotic disorders.

Observations on "Wild" Psycho-Analysis[1]

A FEW days ago an elderly lady, under the protection of a female friend, called upon me for a consultation, complaining of anxiety-states. She was in the second half of the forties, fairly well preserved, and had obviously not yet finished with her womanhood. A divorce from her last husband had been the occasion exciting the anxiety-states; but the anxiety had become greatly intensified, according to her account, since she had consulted a young physician in the suburb she lived in, for he had informed her that her sexual desires were the cause of her anxiety. He said that she could not tolerate the loss of intercourse with her husband, and so there were only three ways by which she could recover her health—she must either return to her husband, or take a lover, or satisfy herself. Since then she had been convinced that she was incurable, for she would not return to her husband, and the other two alternatives were repugnant to her moral and religious feelings. She had come to me, however, because the doctor had said that I was responsible for this new opinion, and that she had only to come and ask me to confirm what he said, and I should tell her that this and nothing else was the truth. The friend who was with her, a still older, pinched and unhealthy-looking woman, then implored me to assure the patient that the doctor was mistaken. It could not possibly be true, for she herself had been a widow for many years, and had remained respectable without suffering from anxiety.

I will not dwell on the awkward predicament in which I was placed by this visit, but instead will consider the conduct of the practitioner who sent this lady to me. First, however, it will be as well to adopt a cautious attitude, which may possibly not be superfluous—indeed we will hope so. Long experience has taught me—as it may others—not to accept straight away as true what patients, especially nervous patients, relate about their physician. A neurologist not only easily becomes the object of many of the patient's hostile feelings, whatever method of treatment he employs; he must also sometimes resign himself to accepting responsibility, by a kind of projection, for the buried repressed wishes of his nervous

[1] *Collected Papers*, II; first published in *Zentralblatt*, Vol. I, 1910; reprinted in *Sammlung*, Dritte Folge.

patients. That such accusations, then, nowhere find more credence than among other physicians is a melancholy but a significant circumstance.

I have some grounds, therefore, for hoping that this lady gave me a tendenciously distorted account of what her physician had said, and that I do a man who is unknown to me an injustice by connecting my remarks about "wild" psycho-analysis with this incident. But all the same, by doing so I may perhaps prevent others from acting wrongly towards their patients.

Let us suppose, therefore, that her medical practitioner spoke to the patient exactly as she reported of him. Everyone will at once vouchsafe the criticism that if a physician holds it necessary to discuss the question of sexuality with a woman he must do so with tact and consideration. Compliance with this demand, however, coincides with carrying out certain of the *technical* regulations of psycho-analysis; moreover, the physician in question was ignorant of a number of the *scientific* principles of psycho-analysis or had misapprehended them, and thus showed how little understanding of its nature and purposes he had in fact acquired.

We will begin with the second of these, with his scientific errors. His advice to the lady shows clearly in what sense he understands the expression *sexual life*—in the popular sense, namely, in which by sexual needs nothing is meant but the need for coitus or analogous acts producing orgasm and emission of sexual secretions. The physician cannot have been unaware, however, that psycho-analysis is commonly reproached with having extended the connotation of the term *sexual* far beyond its usual range. The fact is undisputed; whether it may justly be used as a reproach shall not be discussed here. In psycho-analysis the term *sexuality* comprises far more; it goes lower and also higher than the popular sense of the word. This extension is justified genetically; we reckon as belonging to *sexual life* all expressions of tender feeling, which spring from the source of primitive sexual feelings, even when those feelings have become inhibited in regard to their original sexual aim or have exchanged this aim for another which is no longer sexual. For this reason we prefer to speak of *psycho-sexuality*, thus laying stress on the point that the mental factor should not be overlooked or under-estimated. We use the word *sexuality* in the same comprehensive sense as that in which the German language uses the word *lieben* (to love). And we have long known that a mental lack of satisfaction with all its consequences can exist where there is no lack of normal sexual intercourse; as therapeutists, too, we have constantly to remember that the unsatisfied sexual trends (the substitutive satisfactions of which in the form of nervous symptoms we have to combat) can often find only very inadequate outlet in coitus or other sexual acts.

Anyone not sharing this psycho-analytical point of view has no right to call to his aid psycho-analytical theories concerned with the aetiological significance of sexuality. By emphasizing exclusively the somatic factor in sexuality he certainly simplifies the problem greatly, but he alone must bear the responsibility for what he does.

A second and equally gross misunderstanding is discernible behind the physician's advice. It is true that psycho-analysis puts forward lack of sexual satisfaction as the cause of nervous disorders. But does it not also go much further than this? Is its teaching to be ignored as too complicated when it declares that nervous symptoms arise from a conflict between two forces—on the one hand, the libido (which is for the most part excessive), and on the other, a too severe aversion from sexuality or a repression? No one who remembers this second factor, which is by no means secondary in importance, can ever believe that sexual satisfaction in itself constitutes a remedy of general reliability for the sufferings of neurotics. A good number of nervous persons are, indeed, either in the actual circumstances or altogether incapable of satisfaction. If they were capable of it, if they were without their inner resistances, the strength of the instinct itself would point the way to satisfaction for them even though no physician recommended it. What is the good, therefore, of advice such as that supposed to have been given to this lady by her physician?

Even if it could be justified scientifically, it is not advice that she can carry out. If she had had no inner resistances against onanism or against a liaison, she would, of course, have adopted one of these measures long before. Or does the physician think that a woman of over forty has never heard of such a thing as taking a lover, or does he overestimate his influence so much as to think that she could never decide upon such a step without medical recommendation?

All this seems very simple, and yet it must be admitted that there is one factor which often complicates the issue in forming a judgment. Some nervous states which we call the *actual* neuroses, such as typical neurasthenia and pure forms of anxiety-neurosis, obviously depend on the physical factor in sexual life, and we have no certain knowledge of the part played in them by the mental factor and by repression. In such cases it is natural that the physician should first consider some *actual* therapy, some alteration in the physical sexual way of life, and he does so with perfect justification if his diagnosis is correct. The lady who consulted the young physician complained chiefly of anxiety-states, and so he probably assumed that she was suffering from an *anxiety-neurosis*, and felt justified in recommending an actual therapy to her. Again a convenient misapprehension! A person suffering from anxiety is not for that reason necessarily suffering from anxiety-neurosis; a diagnosis of it cannot be based on its name; one has to know what manifestations are comprised in an anxiety-neurosis, and be able to distinguish it from other pathological states in which anxiety appears. My impression was that the lady in question was suffering from anxiety-hysteria, and the whole value of such nosographical distinctions, one which quite justifies them, lies in the fact that they indicate a different aetiology and a different therapy. No one who took into consideration the possibility of anxiety-hysteria in this case would have fallen into the error of neglecting the mental factors, as this physician did with his three alternatives.

Oddly enough, the three therapeutic alternatives of this would-be psycho-analyst leave no room for—psycho-analysis! This woman can only be cured of her anxiety by returning to her husband, or by satisfying her needs by onanism or with a lover. And where does analytic treatment come in, the treatment which we regard as the first remedy in anxiety-states?

This brings us to the *technical* errors to be remarked in the way that, according to our assumption, this physician proceeded. The idea that a neurotic is suffering from a sort of ignorance, and that if one removes this ignorance by telling him facts (about the causal connection of his illness with his life, about his experiences in childhood, and so on) he must recover, is an idea that has long been superseded, and one derived from superficial appearances. The pathological factor is not his ignorance in itself, but the root of this ignorance in his *inner resistances;* it was they that first called this ignorance into being, and they still maintain it now. In combating these resistances lies the task of the therapy. Telling the patient what he does not know because he has repressed it is only one of the necessary preliminaries in the therapy. If knowledge about his unconscious were as important for the patient as the inexperienced in psycho-analysis imagine, it would be sufficient to cure him for him to go to lectures or read books. Such measures, however, have as little effect on the symptoms of nervous disease as distributing menu-cards in time of famine has on people's hunger. The analogy goes even further than its obvious application, too; for describing his unconscious to the patient is regularly followed by intensification of the conflict in him and exacerbation of his symptoms.

Since, however, psycho-analysis cannot dispense with making this disclosure to patients, it prescribes that two conditions are to be fulfilled before it is done. First, by preparatory work, the repressed material must have come very near to the patient's thoughts, and secondly, he must be sufficiently firmly attached by an affective relationship to the physician (transference) to make it impossible for him to take fresh flight again.

Only when these two conditions are fulfilled is it possible to recognize and to overcome the resistances which have led to the repression and the ignorance. Psycho-analytic measures, therefore, cannot possibly dispense with a fairly long period of contact with the patient, and attempts to bully the patient during his first consultation by brusquely telling him the hidden things one infers behind his story are technically reprehensible; they mostly lead to their own doom, too, by inspiring in the patient a hearty dislike for the physician and putting an end to any further influence.

Besides all this, one may sometimes make a false inference, and one is never in a position to discover the whole truth. In psycho-analysis these exact technical precautions take the place of a vague demand, implying a peculiar talent, for "medical tact."

It is not enough, therefore, for a physician to know a little of what psycho-analysis has discovered; he must also have familiarized himself with its technique if he wishes his medical practice to be guided by a psycho-analytic point of view. This technique is even today not to be learnt from books, and it is certainly not to be discovered independently without great sacrifices of time, labour and success. It is to be learnt, like other medical measures, from those who are already proficient in it. In forming a judgment on the incident that I took as a starting-point for these remarks, therefore, it is a matter of some significance that I do not know the physician who is said to have given the lady such advice and have never before heard his name.

Neither for myself nor for my friends and co-workers is it pleasant to claim in this way a monopoly in the use of psycho-analytic technique. But in face of the danger to patients and to the cause of psycho-analysis which one foresees in this "wild" psycho-analysis, we have no other choice. In the spring of 1910 we founded an International Psycho-Analytical Association, in which the members admit their participation by allowing publication of their names, in order to be able to repudiate responsibility for what is done by those who do not belong to us and yet call their methods "psychoanalysis." For as a matter of fact, "wild" analysts of this kind do more harm to the cause of psycho-analysis than to individual patients. I have often found that a clumsy feat of a similar kind led to good results in the end, although it first produced an exacerbation of the patient's condition. Not always, but still often. When he has abused the physician enough and feels impervious enough to any further influence of the kind, his symptoms give way, or he decides to take some step leading to recovery. The final improvement then "comes of itself," or is ascribed to some entirely harmless treatment by another physician to whom the patient turned afterwards. In the case of the lady whose complaint against her doctor we have heard, I should say that, in spite of all, the wild psycho-analyst did more for her than some highly respected authority who might have told her she was suffering from a *vasomotor neurosis.* He did force her attention to the real cause of her trouble, or in that direction, and in spite of all her struggles, that cannot be without some favourable results. But he has done himself harm and helped to intensify the prejudices which patients feel, owing to their natural resistances, against the ways of psycho-analysts. And this can be avoided.

The Interpretation of Dreams

Flectere si nequeo superos, Acheronta movebo.

Contents: The Interpretation of Dreams

The Interpretation of Dreams

FOREWORD TO THE THIRD ENGLISH EDITION

IN 1909 G. Stanley Hall invited me to Clark University, in Worcester, to give the first lectures on psycho-analysis. In the same year Dr. Brill published the first of his translations of my writings, which were soon followed by further ones. If psycho-analysis now plays a rôle in American intellectual life, or if it does so in the future, a large part of this result will have to be attributed to this and other activities of Dr. Brill's.

His first translation of *The Interpretation of Dreams* appeared in 1913. Since then much has taken place in the world, and much has been changed in our views about the neuroses. This book, with the new contribution to psychology which surprised the world when it was published (1900), remains essentially unaltered. It contains, even according to my present-day judgment, the most valuable of all discoveries it has been my good fortune to make. Insight such as this falls to one's lot but once in a lifetime. FREUD

Vienna, March 15, 1931

PREFACE TO THE THIRD (GERMAN) EDITION

WHEREAS there was a space of nine years between the first and second editions of this book, the need of a third edition was apparent when little more than a year had elapsed. I ought to be gratified by this change; but if I was unwilling previously to attribute the neglect of my work to its small value, I cannot take the interest which is now making its appearance as proof of its quality.

The advance of scientific knowledge has not left *The Interpretation of Dreams* untouched. When I wrote this book in 1899 there was as yet no "sexual theory," and the analysis of the more complicated forms of the psychoneuroses was still in its infancy. The interpretation of dreams was intended as an expedient to facilitate the psychological analysis of the neuroses; but since then a profounder understanding of the neuroses has contributed towards the comprehension of the dream. The doctrine of dream-interpretation itself has evolved in a direction which was insufficiently emphasized in the first edition of this book. From my own experience, and the works of Stekel and other writers,[1] I have since learned to appreciate more accurately the significance of symbolism in dreams (or rather, in unconscious thought). In the course of years, a mass of data has accumulated which demands consideration. I have endeavored to deal with these innovations by interpolations in the text and footnotes. If these additions do not always quite adjust themselves to the framework of the treatise, or if the earlier text does not everywhere come up to the standard of our present knowledge, I must beg indulgence for this deficiency, since it is only the result and indication of the increasingly rapid advance of our science. I will even venture to predict the directions in which further editions of this book—should there be a demand for them—may diverge from previous editions. Dream-interpretation must seek a closer union with the rich material of poetry, myth, and popular idiom, and it must deal more faithfully than has hitherto been possible with the relations of dreams to the neuroses and to mental derangement.

Herr Otto Rank has afforded me valuable assistance in the selection of supplementary examples, and has revised the proofs of this edition. I have to thank him and many other colleagues for their contributions and corrections.

Vienna, 1911

PREFACE TO THE SECOND (GERMAN) EDITION

THAT there should have been a demand for a second edition of this book—a book which cannot be described as easy to read—before the completion of its first decade is not to be explained by the interest of the professional circles to which I was addressing myself. My psychiatric colleagues have not, apparently, attempted to look beyond the astonishment which may at first have been aroused by my novel conception of the dream; and the professional philosophers, who are anyhow accustomed to disposing of the dream in a few sentences—mostly the same—as a supplement to the states of consciousness, have evidently failed to realize that precisely in this connection it was possible to make all manner of deductions, such as must lead to a fundamental modification of our

[1] Omitted in subsequent editions.

psychological doctrines. The attitude of the scientific reviewers was such as to lead me to expect that the fate of the book would be to fall into oblivion; and the little flock of faithful adherents, who follow my lead in the therapeutic application of psycho-analysis, and interpret dreams by my method, could not have exhausted the first edition of this book. I feel, therefore, that my thanks are due to the wider circle of cultured and inquiring readers whose sympathy has induced me, after the lapse of nine years, once more to take up this difficult work, which has so many fundamental bearings.

I am glad to be able to say that I found little in the book that called for alteration. Here and there I have interpolated fresh material, or have added opinions based on more extensive experience, or I have sought to elaborate individual points; but the essential passages treating of dreams and their interpretation, and the psychological doctrines to be deduced therefrom, have been left unaltered; subjectively, at all events, they have stood the test of time. Those who are acquainted with my other writings (on the aetiology and mechanism of the psychoneuroses) will know that I never offer unfinished work as finished, and that I have always endeavoured to revise my conclusions in accordance with my maturing opinions; but as regards the subject of the dream-life, I am able to stand by my original text. In my many years' work upon the problems of the neuroses I have often hesitated, and I have often gone astray; and then it was always the interpretation of dreams that restored my self-confidence. My many scientific opponents are actuated by a wise instinct when they decline to follow me into the region of oneirology.

Even the material of this book, even my own dreams, defaced by time or superseded, by means of which I have demonstrated the rules of dream-interpretation, revealed, when I came to revise these pages, a continuity that resisted revision. For me, of course, this book has an additional subjective significance, which I did not understand until after its completion. It reveals itself to me as a piece of my self-analysis, as my reaction to the death of my father, that is, to the most important event, the most poignant loss in a man's life. Once I had realized this, I felt that I could not obliterate the traces of this influence. But to my readers the material from which they learn to evaluate and interpret dreams will be a matter of indifference.

Where an inevitable comment could not be fitted into the old context, I have indicated by square brackets that it does not occur in the first edition.[1]

Berchtesgaden, 1908

INTRODUCTORY NOTE

IN this volume I have attempted to expound the methods and results of dream-interpretation; and in so doing I do not think I have overstepped the boundary of neuro-pathological science. For the dream proves on psychological investigation to be the first of a series of abnormal psychic formations, a series whose succeeding members—the hysterical phobias, the obsessions, the delusions—must, for practical reasons, claim the attention of the physician. The dream, as we shall see, has no title to such practical importance, but for that very reason its theoretical value as a typical formation is all the greater, and the physician who cannot explain the origin of dream-images will strive in vain to understand the phobias and the obsessive and delusional ideas, or to influence them by therapeutic methods.

But the very context to which our subject owes its importance must be held responsible for the deficiencies of the following chapters. The abundant lacunae in this exposition represent so many points of contact at which the problem of dream-formation is linked up with the more comprehensive problems of psychopathology; problems which cannot be treated in these pages, but which, if time and powers suffice and if further material presents itself, may be elaborated elsewhere.

The peculiar nature of the material employed to exemplify the interpretation of dreams has made the writing even of this treatise a difficult task. Consideration of the methods of dream-interpretation will show why the dreams recorded in the literature on the subject, or those collected by persons unknown to me, were useless for my purpose; I had only the choice between my own dreams and those of the patients whom I was treating by psychoanalytic methods. But this later material was inadmissible, since the dream-processes were undesirably complicated by the intervention of neurotic characters. And if I relate my own dreams I must inevitably reveal to the gaze of strangers more of the intimacies of my psychic life than is agreeable to me, and more than seems fitting in a writer who is not a poet but a scientific investigator. To do so is painful, but unavoidable; I have submitted to the necessity, for otherwise I could not have

_____
[1] Omitted in subsequent editions.

demonstrated my psychological conclusions. Sometimes, of course, I could not resist the temptation to mitigate my indiscretions by omissions and substitutions; but wherever I have done so the value of the example cited has been very definitely diminished. I can only express the hope that my readers will understand my difficult position, and will be indulgent; and further, that all those persons who are in any way concerned in the dreams recorded will not seek to forbid our dream-life at all events to exercise freedom of thought!

I. THE SCIENTIFIC LITERATURE OF DREAM-PROBLEMS (UP TO 1900)

IN the following pages I shall demonstrate that there is a psychological technique which makes it possible to interpret dreams, and that on the application of this technique every dream will reveal itself as a psychological structure, full of significance, and one which may be assigned to a specific place in the psychic activities of the waking state. Further, I shall endeavour to elucidate the processes which underlie the strangeness and obscurity of dreams, and to deduce from these processes the nature of the psychic forces whose conflict or cooperation is responsible for our dreams. This done, my investigation will terminate, as it will have reached the point where the problem of the dream merges into more comprehensive problems, and to solve these we must have recourse to material of a different kind.

I shall begin by giving a short account of the views of earlier writers on this subject, and of the status of the dream-problem in contemporary science; since in the course of this treatise I shall not often have occasion to refer to either. In spite of thousands of years of endeavour, little progress has been made in the scientific understanding of dreams. This fact has been so universally acknowledged by previous writers on the subject that it seems hardly necessary to quote individual opinions. The reader will find, in the works listed at the end of this work, many stimulating observations, and plenty of interesting material relating to our subject, but little or nothing that concerns the true nature of the dream, or that solves definitely any of its enigmas. The educated layman, of course, knows even less of the matter.

The conception of the dream that was held in prehistoric ages by primitive peoples, and the influence which it may have exerted on the formation of their conceptions of the universe, and of the soul, is a theme of such great interest that it is only with reluctance that I refrain from dealing with it in these pages. I will refer the reader to the well-known works of Sir John Lubbock (Lord Avebury), Herbert Spencer, E. B. Tylor, and other writers; I will only add that we shall not realize the importance of these problems and speculations until we have completed the task of dream-interpretation that lies before us.

A reminiscence of the concept of the dream that was held in primitive times seems to underlie the evaluation of the dream which was current among the peoples of classical antiquity.[1] They took it for granted that dreams were related to the world of the supernatural beings in whom they believed, and that they brought inspirations from the gods and demons. Moreover, it appeared to them that dreams must serve a special purpose in respect of the dreamer; that, as a rule, they predicted the future. The extraordinary variations in the content of dreams, and in the impressions which they produced on the dreamer, made it, of course, very difficult to formulate a coherent conception of them, and necessitated manifold differentiations and group-formations, according to their value and reliability. The valuation of dreams by the individual philosophers of antiquity naturally depended on the importance which they were prepared to attribute to manticism in general.

In the two works of Aristotle in which there is mention of dreams, they are already regarded as constituting a problem of psychology. We are told that the dream is not god-sent, that it is not of divine but of demonic origin. For nature is really demonic, not divine; that is to say, the dream is not a supernatural revelation, but is subject to the laws of the human spirit, which has, of course, a kinship with the divine. The dream is defined as the psychic activity of the sleeper, inasmuch as he is asleep. Aristotle was acquainted with some of the characteristics of the dream-life; for example, he knew that a dream converts the slight sensations perceived in sleep into intense sensations ("one imagines that one is walking through fire, and feels hot, if this or that part of the body becomes only

---

[1] The following remarks are based on Büchsenschütz's careful essay, *Traum und Traumdeutung im Altertum* (Berlin, 1868).

quite slightly warm"), which led him to conclude that dreams might easily betray to the physician the first indications of an incipient physical change which escaped observation during the day.[1]

As has been said, those writers of antiquity who preceded Aristotle did not regard the dream as a product of the dreaming psyche, but as an inspiration of divine origin, and in ancient times the two opposing tendencies which we shall find throughout the ages in respect of the evaluation of the dream-life were already perceptible. The ancients distinguished between the true and valuable dreams which were sent to the dreamer as warnings, or to foretell future events, and the vain, fraudulent, and empty dreams whose object was to misguide him or lead him to destruction.

Gruppe[2] speaks of such a classification of dreams, citing Macrobius and Artemidorus: "Dreams were divided into two classes; the first class was believed to be influenced only by the present (or the past), and was unimportant in respect of the future; it included the ἐνύκνια (insomnia), which directly reproduce a given idea or its opposite; e.g., hunger or its satiation; and the φαντάσματα, which elaborate the given idea phantastically, as e.g. the nightmare, ephialtes. The second class of dreams, on the other hand, was determinative of the future. To this belonged:

1. Direct prophecies received in the dream (χρηματισμός, oraculum);
2. the foretelling of a future event (ὅραμα, visio);
3. the symbolic dream, which requires interpretation (ὄνειρος, somnium).

This theory survived for many centuries."

Connected with these varying estimations of the dream was the problem of "dream-interpretation." Dreams in general were expected to yield important solutions, but not every dream was immediately understood, and it was impossible to be sure that a certain incomprehensible dream did not really foretell something of importance, so that an effort was made to replace the incomprehensible content of the dream by something that should be at once comprehensible and significant. In later antiquity Artemidorus of Daldis was regarded as the greatest authority on dream-interpretation.

His comprehensive works must serve to compensate us for the lost works of a similar nature.[3] The pre-scientific conception of the dream which obtained among the ancients was, of course, in perfect keeping with their general conception of the universe, which was accustomed to project as an external reality that which possessed reality only in the life of the psyche. Further, it accounted for the main impression made upon the waking life by the morning memory of the dream; for in this memory the dream, as compared with the rest of the psychic content, seems to be something alien, coming, as it were, from another world. It would be an error to suppose that the theory of the supernatural origin of dreams lacks followers even in our own times; for quite apart from pietistic and mystical writers—who cling, as they are perfectly justified in doing, to the remnants of the once predominant realm of the supernatural until these remnants have been swept away by scientific explanation—we not infrequently find that quite intelligent persons, who in other respects are averse from anything of a romantic nature, go so far as to base their religious belief in the existence and co-operation of superhuman spiritual powers on the inexplicable nature of the phenomena of dreams (Haffner). The validity ascribed to the dream-life by certain schools of philosophy— for example, by the school of Schelling—is a distinct reminiscence of the undisputed belief in the divinity of dreams which prevailed in antiquity; and for some thinkers the mantic or prophetic power of dreams is still a subject of debate. This is due to the fact that the explanations attempted by psychology are too inadequate to cope with the accumulated material, however strongly the scientific thinker may feel that such superstitious doctrines should be repudiated.

To write a history of our scientific knowledge of the dream-problem is extremely difficult, because, valuable though this knowledge may be in certain respects, no real progress in a definite direction is as yet discernible. No

---

[1] The relationship between dreams and disease is discussed by Hippocrates in a chapter of his famous work.

[2] *Griechische Mythologie und Religionsgeschichte*, p. 390.

[3] For the later history of dream-interpretation in the Middle Ages consult Diepgen, and the special investigations of M. Förster, Gotthard, and others. The interpretation of dreams among the Jews has been studied by Amoli, Amram, and Lowinger, and recently, with reference to the psycho-analytic standpoint, by Lauer. Details of the Arabic methods of dream-interpretation are furnished by Drexl, F. Schwarz, and the missionary Tfinkdji. The interpretation of dreams among the Japanese has been investigated by Miura and Iwaya, among the Chinese by Secker, and among the Indians by Negelein.

real foundation of verified results has hitherto been established on which future investigators might continue to build. Every new author approaches the same problems afresh, and from the very beginning. If I were to enumerate such authors in chronological order, giving a survey of the opinions which each has held concerning the problems of the dream, I should be quite unable to draw a clear and complete picture of the present state of our knowledge on the subject. I have therefore preferred to base my method of treatment on themes rather than on authors, and in attempting the solution of each problem of the dream I shall cite the material found in the literature of the subject.

But as I have not succeeded in mastering the whole of this literature—for it is widely dispersed, and interwoven with the literature of other subjects—I must ask my readers to rest content with my survey as it stands, provided that no fundamental fact or important point of view has been overlooked.

Until recently most authors have been inclined to deal with the subjects of sleep and dreams in conjunction, and together with these they have commonly dealt with analogous conditions of a psycho-pathological nature, and other dream-like phenomena, such as hallucinations, visions, etc. In recent works, on the other hand, there has been a tendency to keep more closely to the theme, and to consider, as a special subject, the separate problems of the dream-life. In this change I should like to perceive an expression of the growing conviction that enlightenment and agreement in such obscure matters may be attained only by a series of detailed investigations. Such a detailed investigation, and one of a special psychological nature, is expounded in these pages. I have had little occasion to concern myself with the problem of sleep, as this is essentially a physiological problem, although the changes in the functional determination of the psychic apparatus should be included in a description of the sleeping state. The literature of sleep will therefore not be considered here.

A scientific interest in the phenomena of dreams as such leads us to propound the following problems, which to a certain extent, interdependent, merge into one another.

A. *The Relation of the Dream to the Waking State*

The naïve judgment of the dreamer on waking assumes that the dream—even if it does not come from another world—has at all events transported the dreamer into another world. The old physiologist, Burdach, to whom we are indebted for a careful and discriminating description of the phenomena of dreams, expressed this conviction in a frequently quoted passage (p. 474): "The waking life, with its trials and joys, its pleasures and pains, is never repeated; on the contrary, the dream aims at relieving us of these. Even when our whole mind is filled with one subject, when our hearts are rent by bitter grief, or when some task has been taxing our mental capacity to the utmost, the dream either gives us something entirely alien, or it selects for its combinations only a few elements of reality; or it merely enters into the key of our mood, and symbolizes reality." J. H. Fichte (I. 541) speaks in precisely the same sense of supplementary dreams, calling them one of the secret, self-healing benefits of the psyche. L. Strümpell expresses himself to the same effect in his *Natur und Entstehung der Träume*, a study which is deservedly held in high esteem. "He who dreams turns his back upon the world of waking consciousness" (p. 16); "In the dream the memory of the orderly content of waking consciousness and its normal behaviour is almost entirely lost" (p. 17); "The almost complete and unencumbered isolation of the psyche in the dream from the regular normal content and course of the waking state . . ." (p. 19).

Yet the overwhelming majority of writers on the subject have adopted the contrary view of the relation of the dream to waking life. Thus Haffner (p. 19): "To begin with, the dream continues the waking life. Our dreams always connect themselves with such ideas as have shortly before been present in our consciousness. Careful examination will nearly always detect a thread by which the dream has linked itself to the experiences of the previous day." Weygandt (p. 6) flatly contradicts the statement of Burdach. "For it may often be observed, apparently indeed in the great majority of dreams, that they lead us directly back into everyday life, instead of releasing us from it." Maury (p. 56) expresses the same idea in a concise formula: *'Nous rêvons de ce que nous avons vu, dit, desiré, ou fait.'*[1] Jessen, in his *Psychologie*, published in 1855 (p. 530), is rather more explicit: "The content of dreams is always more or less determined by the per-

[1] We dream of what we have seen, said, desired, or done.—ED.

sonality, the age, sex, station in life, education and habits, and by the events and experiences of the whole past life of the individual."

The philosopher, I. G. E. Maas, adopts the most unequivocal attitude in respect of this question (Über die Leidenschaften, 1805): "Experience corroborates our assertion that we dream most frequently of those things toward which our warmest passions are directed. This shows us that our passions must influence the generation of our dreams. The ambitious man dreams of the laurels which he has won (perhaps only in imagination), or has still to win, while the lover occupies himself, in his dreams, with the object of his dearest hopes. . . . All the sensual desires and loathings which slumber in the heart, if they are stimulated by any cause, may combine with other ideas and give rise to a dream; or these ideas may mingle in an already existing dream."[1]

The ancients entertained the same idea concerning the dependence of the dream-content on life. I will quote Radestock (p. 139): "When Xerxes, before his expedition against Greece, was dissuaded from his resolution by good counsel, but was again and again incited by dreams to undertake it, one of the old, rational dream-interpreters of the Persians, Artabanus, told him, and very appropriately, that dream-images for the most part contain that of which one has been thinking in the waking state."

In the didactic poem of Lucretius, On the Nature of Things (IV. 962), there occurs this passage:
"*Et quo quisque fere studio devinctus adhaeret, aut quibus in rebus multum sumus ante morati atque in ea ratione fuit contenta magis mens, in somnis eadem plerumque videmur obire; causidici causas agere et componere leges, induperatores pugnare ac proelia obire,*" . . . etc., etc.[2]
Cicero (De Divinatione, II. LXVII) says, in a similar strain, as does also Maury many centuries later: "*Maximeque 'reliquiae' rerum earum moventur in animis et agitantur, de quibus vigilantes aut cogitavimus aut egimus.*"[3]
The contradiction between these two views concerning the relation between dream life and

waking life seems indeed irresolvable. Here we may usefully cite the opinion of F. W. Hildebrandt (1875), who held that on the whole the peculiarities of the dream can only be described as "a series of contrasts which apparently amount to contradictions" (p. 8). "The first of these contrasts is formed by the *strict isolation or seclusion* of the dream from true and actual life on the one hand, and on the other hand by the continuous encroachment of the one upon the other, and the constant dependence of the one upon the other. The dream is something absolutely divorced from the reality experienced during the waking state; one may call it an existence hermetically sealed up and insulated from real life by an unbridgeable chasm. It frees us from reality, blots out the normal recollection of reality, and sets us in another world and a totally different life, which fundamentally has nothing in common with real life. . . ." Hildebrandt then asserts that in falling asleep our whole being, with its forms of existence, disappears "as through an invisible trapdoor." In one's dream one is perhaps making a voyage to St. Helena in order to offer the imprisoned Napoleon an exquisite vintage of Moselle. One is most affably received by the ex-emperor, and one feels almost sorry when, on waking, the interesting illusion is destroyed. But let us now compare the situation existing in the dream with the actual reality. The dreamer has never been a wine-merchant, and has no desire to become one. He has never made a sea-voyage, and St. Helena is the last place in the world that he would choose as the destination of such a voyage. The dreamer feels no sympathy for Napoleon, but on the contrary a strong patriotic aversion. And lastly, the dreamer was not yet among the living when Napoleon died on the island of St. Helena; so that it was beyond the realms of possibility that he should have had any personal relations with Napoleon. The dream-experience thus appears as something entirely foreign, interpolated between two mutually related and successive periods of time.

"Nevertheless," continues Hildebrandt, "the apparent contrary is just as true and correct. I believe that side by side with this seclusion and insulation there may still exist the most intimate interrelation. We may therefore justly say: Whatever the dream may offer us, it derives its material from reality, and from the psychic life centered upon this reality. However extraordinary the dream may seem, it can never detach itself from the real world, and its

---

[1] Communicated by Winterstein to the Zentralblatt für Psychoanalyse.
[2] And whatever be the pursuit to which one clings with devotion, whatever the things on which we have been occupied much in the past, the mind being thus more intent upon that pursuit, it is generally the same things that we seem to encounter in dreams; pleaders to plead their cause and collate laws, generals to contend and engage battle.—ED.
[3] And especially the "remnant" of our waking thoughts and deeds move and stir within the soul.—ED.

most sublime as well as its most ridiculous constructions must always borrow their elementary material either from that which our eyes have beheld in the outer world, or from that which has already found a place somewhere in our waking thoughts; in other words, it must be taken from that which we have already experienced, either objectively or subjectively."

B. *The Material of Dreams—Memory in Dreams*

That all the material composing the content of a dream is somehow derived from experience, that it is reproduced or *remembered* in the dream—this at least may be accepted as an incontestable fact. Yet it would be wrong to assume that such a connection between the dream-content and reality will be easily obvious from a comparison between the two. On the contrary, the connection must be carefully sought, and in quite a number of cases it may for a long while elude discovery. The reason for this is to be found in a number of peculiarities evinced by the faculty of memory in dreams; which peculiarities, though generally observed, have hitherto defied explanation. It will be worth our while to examine these characteristics exhaustively.

To begin with, it happens that certain material appears in the dream-content which cannot be subsequently recognized, in the waking state, as being part of one's knowledge and experience. One remembers clearly enough having dreamed of the thing in question, but one cannot recall the actual experience or the time of its occurrence. The dreamer is therefore in the dark as to the source which the dream has tapped, and is even tempted to believe in an independent productive activity on the part of the dream, until, often long afterwards, a fresh episode restores the memory of that former experience, which had been given up for lost, and so reveals the source of the dream. One is therefore forced to admit that in the dream something was known and remembered that cannot be remembered in the waking state.[1]

Delbœuf relates from his own experience an especially impressive example of this kind. He saw in his dream the courtyard of his house covered with snow, and found there two little lizards, half-frozen and buried in the snow. Being a lover of animals he picked them up, warmed them, and put them back into the hole

in the wall which was reserved especially for them. He also gave them a few fronds of a little fern which was growing on the wall, and of which he knew they were very fond. In the dream he knew the name of the plant; *Asplenium ruta muralis*. The dream continued returning after a digression to the lizards, and to his astonishment Delbœuf saw two other little lizards falling upon what was left of the ferns. On turning his eyes to the open fields he saw a fifth and a sixth lizard making for the hole in the wall, and finally the whole road was covered by a procession of lizards, all wandering in the same direction.

In his waking state Delbœuf knew only a few Latin names of plants, and nothing of any *Asplenium*. To his great surprise he discovered that a fern of this name did actually exist, and that the correct name was *Asplenium ruta muraria*, which the dream had slightly distorted. An accidental coincidence was of course inconceivable; yet where he got his knowledge of the name *Asplenium* in the dream remained a mystery to him.

The dream occurred in 1862. Sixteen years later, while at the house of one of his friends, the philosopher noticed a small album containing dried plants, such as are sold as souvenirs to visitors in many parts of Switzerland. A sudden recollection came to him: he opened the herbarium, discovered therein the *Asplenium* of his dream, and recognized his own handwriting in the accompanying Latin name. The connection could now be traced. In 1860, two years before the date of the lizard dream, one of his friend's sisters, while on her wedding-journey, had paid a visit to Delbœuf. She had with her at the time this very album, which was intended for her brother, and Delbœuf had taken the trouble to write, at the dictation of a botanist, the Latin name under each of the dried plants.

The same good fortune which gave this example its unusual value enabled Delbœuf to trace yet another portion of this dream to its forgotten source. One day in 1877 he came upon an old volume of an illustrated periodical, in which he found the whole procession of lizards pictured, just as he had dreamt of it in 1862. The volume bore the date 1861, and Delbœuf remembered that he had subscribed to the journal since its first appearance.

That dreams have at their disposal recollections which are inaccessible to the waking state is such a remarkable and theoretically important fact that I should like to draw attention

[1] Vaschide even maintains that it has often been observed that in one's dreams one speaks foreign languages more fluently and with greater purity than in the waking state.

to the point by recording yet other *hypermne-sic* dreams. Maury relates that for some time the word *Mussidan* used to occur to him during the day. He knew it to be the name of a French city, but that was all. One night he dreamed of a conversation with a certain person, who told him that she came from Mussidan, and, in answer to his question as to where the city was, she replied: "Mussidan is the principal town of a district in the department of Dordogne." On waking, Maury gave no credence to the information received in his dream; but the gazetteer showed it to be perfectly correct. In this case the superior knowledge of the dreamer was confirmed, but it was not possible to trace the forgotten source of this knowledge.

Jessen (p. 55) refers to a very similar incident, the period of which is more remote. "Among others we may here mention the dream of the elder Scaliger (Hennings, l.c., p. 300), who wrote a poem in praise of the famous men of Verona, and to whom a man named Brugnolus appeared in a dream, complaining that he had been neglected. Though Scaliger could not remember that he had heard of the man, he wrote some verses in his honour, and his son learned subsequently that a certain Brugnolus had at one time been famed in Verona as a critic."

A hypermnesic dream, especially remarkable for the fact that a memory not at first recalled was afterwards recognized in a dream which followed the first, is narrated by the Marquis d'Hervey de St. Denis[1]: "I once dreamed of a young woman with fair golden hair, whom I saw chatting with my sister as she showed her a piece of embroidery. In my dream she seemed familiar to me; I thought, indeed, that I had seen her repeatedly. After waking, her face was still quite vividly before me, but I was absolutely unable to recognize it. I fell asleep again; the dream-picture repeated itself. In this new dream I addressed the golden-haired lady and asked her whether I had not had the pleasure of meeting her somewhere. 'Of course,' she replied; 'don't you remember the bathing-place at Pornic?' Thereupon I awoke, and I was then able to recall with certainty and in detail the incidents with which this charming dream-face was connected."

The same author[2] recorded that a musician of his acquaintance once heard in a dream a melody which was absolutely new to him. Not until many years later did he find it in an old collection of musical compositions, though still he could not remember ever having seen it before.

I believe that Myers has published a whole collection of such hypermnesic dreams in the *Proceedings of the Society for Psychical Research*, but these, unfortunately, are inaccessible to me. I think everyone who occupies himself with dreams will recognize, as a very common phenomenon, the fact that a dream will give proof of the knowledge and recollection of matters of which the dreamer, in his waking state, did not imagine himself to be cognizant. In my analytic investigations of nervous patients, of which I shall speak later, I find that it happens many times every week that I am able to convince them, from their dreams, that they are perfectly well acquainted with quotations, obscene expressions, etc., and make use of them in their dreams, although they have forgotten them in their waking state. I shall here cite an innocent example of dream-hypermnesia, because it was easy to trace the source of the knowledge which was accessible only in the dream.

A patient dreamed amongst other things (in a rather long dream) that he ordered a *kontuszówka* in a café, and after telling me this he asked me what it could be, as he had never heard the name before. I was able to tell him that *kontuszówka* was a Polish liqueur, which he could not have invented in his dream, as the name had long been familiar to me from the advertisements. At first the patient would not believe me, but some days later, after he had allowed his dream of the café to become a reality, he noticed the name on a signboard at a street corner which for some months he had been passing at least twice a day.

I have learned from my own dreams how largely the discovery of the origin of individual dream-elements may be dependent on chance. Thus, for some years before I had thought of writing this book, I was haunted by the picture of a church tower of fairly simple construction, which I could not remember ever having seen. I then suddenly recognized it, with absolute certainty, at a small station between Salzburg and Reichenhall. This was in the late nineties, and the first time I had travelled over this route was in 1886. In later years, when I was already busily engaged in the study of dreams, I was quite annoyed by the frequent recurrence of the dream-image of a certain peculiar locality. I saw, in definite orientation to my own person—on my left—a dark space in

[1] See Vaschide, p. 232.
[2] Vaschide, p. 233

which a number of grotesque sandstone figures stood out. A glimmering recollection, which I did not quite believe, told me that it was the entrance to a beer-cellar; but I could explain neither the meaning nor the origin of this dream-picture. In 1907 I happened to go to Padua, which, to my regret, I had been unable to visit since 1895. My first visit to this beautiful university city had been unsatisfactory. I had been unable to see Giotto's frescoes in the church of the Madonna dell' Arena: I set out for the church, but turned back on being informed that it was closed for the day. On my second visit, twelve years later, I thought I would compensate myself for this disappointment, and before doing anything else I set out for Madonna dell' Arena. In the street leading to it, on my left, probably at the spot where I had turned back in 1895, I discovered the place, with its sandstone figures, which I had so often seen in my dream. It was, in fact, the entrance to a restaurant garden.

One of the sources from which dreams draw material for reproduction—material of which some part is not recalled or utilized in our waking thoughts—is to be found in childhood. Here I will cite only a few of the authors who have observed and emphasized this fact:

Hildebrandt (p. 23): "It has already been expressly admitted that a dream sometimes brings back to the mind, with a wonderful power of reproduction, remote and even forgotten experiences from the earliest periods of one's life."

Strümpell (p. 40): "The subject becomes more interesting still when we remember how the dream sometimes drags out, as it were, from the deepest and densest psychic deposits which later years have piled upon the earliest experiences of childhood, the pictures of certain persons, places and things, quite intact, and in all their original freshness. This is confined not merely to such impressions as were vividly perceived at the time of their occurrence, or were associated with intense psychological values, to recur later in the dream as actual reminiscences which give pleasure to the waking mind. On the contrary, the depths of the dream-memory rather contain such images of persons, places, things and early experiences as either possessed but little consciousness and no psychic value whatsoever, or have long since lost both, and therefore appear totally strange and unknown, both in the dream and in the waking state, until their early origin is revealed."

Volkelt (p. 119): "It is especially to be remarked how readily infantile and youthful reminiscences enter into our dreams. What we have long ceased to think about, what has long since lost all importance for us, is constantly recalled by the dream."

The control which the dream exercises over material from our childhood, most of which, as is well known, falls into the lacunae of our conscious memory, is responsible for the production of interesting hypermnesic dreams, of which I shall cite a few more examples.

Maury relates (p. 92) that as a child he often went from his native city, Meaux, to the neighbouring Trilport, where his father was superintending the construction of a bridge. One night a dream transported him to Trilport and he was once more playing in the streets there. A man approached him, wearing a sort of uniform. Maury asked him his name, and he introduced himself, saying that his name was C, and that he was a bridge-guard. On waking, Maury, who still doubted the actuality of the reminiscence, asked his old servant, who had been with him in his childhood, whether she remembered a man of this name. "Of course," was the reply; "he used to be watchman on the bridge which your father was building then."

Maury records another example, which demonstrates no less clearly the reliability of the reminiscences of childhood that emerge in our dreams. M. F., who as a child had lived in Montbrison, decided, after an absence of twenty-five years, to visit his home and the old friends of his family. The night before his departure he dreamt that he had reached his destination, and that near Montbrison he met a man whom he did not know by sight, and who told him that he was M. F., a friend of his father's. The dreamer remembered that as a child he had known a gentleman of this name, but on waking he could no longer recall his features. Several days later, having actually arrived at Montbrison, he found once more the locality of his dream, which he had thought was unknown to him, and there he met a man whom he at once recognized as the M. F. of his dream, with only this difference, that the real person was very much older than his dream-image.

Here I might relate one of my own dreams, in which the recalled impression takes the form of an association. In my dream I saw a man whom I recognized, while dreaming, as the doctor of my native town. His face was not distinct, but his features were blended with those of one of my schoolmasters, whom I still meet from time to time. What association there was between the two persons I could not discover on waking, but upon questioning my mother concerning the doctor I learned that he was a one-eyed man. The schoolmaster, whose image in my dream obscured that of the physician, had also only one eye. I had not seen the doctor for thirty-eight years, and as far as I know I had never thought of him in my waking state, although a scar on my chin might have reminded me of his professional attentions.

As though to counterbalance the excessive part which is played in our dreams by the impressions of childhood, many authors assert that the majority of dreams reveal elements drawn from our most recent experiences. Robert (p. 46) even declares that the normal dream generally occupies itself only with the impressions of the last few days. We shall find, indeed, that the theory of the dream advanced by Robert absolutely requires that our oldest impressions should be thrust into the background, and our most recent ones brought to the fore. However, the fact here stated by Robert is correct; this I can confirm from my own investigations. Nelson, an American author, holds that the impressions received in a dream most frequently date from the second day before the dream, or from the third day before it, as though the impressions of the day immediately preceding the dream were not sufficiently weakened and remote.

Many authors who are unwilling to question the intimate connection between the dream-content and the waking state have been struck by the fact that the impressions which have intensely occupied the waking mind appear in dreams only after they have been to some extent removed from the mental activities of the day. Thus, as a rule, we do not dream of a beloved person who is dead while we are still overwhelmed with sorrow (Delage). Yet Miss Hallam, one of the most recent observers, has collected examples which reveal the very opposite behaviour in this respect, and upholds the claims of psychological individuality in this matter.

The third, most remarkable, and at the same time most incomprehensible, peculiarity of memory in dreams is shown in the selection of the material reproduced; for here it is not, as in the waking state, only the most significant things that are held to be worth remembering, but also the most indifferent and insignificant details. In this connection I will quote those authors who have expressed their surprise in the most emphatic language.

Hildebrandt (p. 11): "For it is a remarkable fact that dreams do not, as a rule, take their elements from important and far-reaching events, or from the intense and urgent interests of the preceding day, but from unimportant incidents, from the worthless odds and ends of recent experience or of the remoter past. The most shocking death in our family, the impressions of which keep us awake long into the night, is obliterated from our memories until the first moment of waking brings it back to us with distressing force. On the other hand, the wart on the forehead of a passing stranger, to whom we did not give a moment's thought once he was out of sight, finds a place in our dreams."

Strümpell (p. 39) speaks of "cases in which the analysis of a dream brings to light elements which, although derived from the experiences of yesterday or the day before yesterday, were yet so unimportant and worthless for the waking state that they were forgotten soon after they were experienced. Some experiences may be the chance-heard remarks of other persons, or their superficially observed actions, or, fleeting perceptions of things or persons, or isolated phrases that we have read, etc."

Havelock Ellis (p. 727): "The profound emotions of waking life, the questions and problems on which we spend our chief voluntary mental energy, are not those which usually present themselves at once to dream-consciousness. It is, so far as the immediate past is concerned, mostly the trifling, the incidental, the 'forgotten' impressions of daily life which reappear in our dreams. The psychic activities that are awake most intensely are those that sleep most profoundly."

It is precisely in connection with these characteristics of memory in dreams that Binz (p. 5) finds occasion to express dissatisfaction with the explanations of dreams which he himself had favoured: "And the normal dream raises similar questions. Why do we not always dream of mental impressions of the day before, instead of going back, without any perceptible reason, to the almost forgotten past, now lying far behind us? Why, in a dream, does consciousness so often revive the impression of indifferent memory-pictures, while the cerebral cells that bear the most sensitive records of experience remain for the most part inert and numb, unless an acute revival during the waking state has quite recently excited them?"

We can readily understand how the strange preference shown by the dream-memory for the indifferent and therefore disregarded details of daily experience must commonly lead us altogether to overlook the dependence of dreams on the waking state, or must at least make it difficult for us to prove this dependence in any individual case. Thus it happened that in the statistical treatment of her own and her friend's dream, Miss Whiton Calkins found that 11 per cent of the entire number showed no relation to the waking state. Hildebrandt was certainly correct in his assertion that all our dream-images could be genetically explained if we devoted enough time and material to the tracing of their origin. To be sure, he calls this "a most tedious and thankless job. For most often it would lead us to ferret out all sorts of psychically worthless things from the remotest corners of our storehouse of memories, and to bring to light all sorts of quite indifferent events of long ago from the oblivion which may have overtaken them an hour after their occurrence." I must, however, express my regret that this discerning author refrained from following the path which at first sight seemed so unpromising, for it would have led him directly to the central point of the explanation of dreams.

The behaviour of memory in dreams is surely most significant for any theory of memory whatsoever. It teaches us that "nothing which we have once psychically possessed is ever entirely lost" (Scholz, p. 34); or as Delbœuf puts it, *"que toute impression, même la plus insignificante, laisse une trace inaltérable, indéfiniment susceptible de reparaître au jour"*;[1] a conclusion to which we are urged by so many other pathological manifestations of mental life. Let us bear in mind this extraordinary capacity of the memory in dreams, in order the more keenly to realize the contradiction which has to be put forward in certain dream-theories to be mentioned later, which seek to explain the absurdities and incoherences of dreams by a partial forgetting of what we have known during the day.

It might even occur to one to reduce the phenomenon of dreaming to that of remembering, and to regard the dream as the manifestation of a reproductive activity, unresting even at night, which is an end in itself. This would

seem to be in agreement with statements such as those made by Pilcz, according to which definite relations between the time of dreaming and the contents of a dream may be demonstrated, inasmuch as the impressions reproduced by the dream in deep sleep belong to the remote past, while those reproduced towards morning are of recent origin. But such a conception is rendered improbable from the outset by the manner in which the dream deals with the material to be remembered. Strümpell rightly calls our attention to the fact that repetitions of experiences do not occur in dreams. It is true that a dream will make a beginning in that direction, but the next link is wanting; it appears in a different form, or is replaced by something entirely novel. The dream gives us only fragmentary reproductions; this is so far the rule that it permits of a theoretical generalization. Still, there are exceptions in which an episode is repeated in a dream as completely as it can be reproduced by our waking memory. Delbœuf relates of one of his university colleagues that a dream of his repeated, in all its details, a perilous drive in which he escaped accident as if by miracle. Miss Calkins mentions two dreams the contents of which exactly reproduced an experience of the previous day, and in a later chapter I shall have occasion to give an example that came to my knowledge of a childish experience which recurred unchanged in a dream.[2]

C. *Dream-Stimuli and Sources*

What is meant by dream-stimuli and dream-sources may be explained by a reference to the popular saying: "Dreams come from the stomach." This notion covers a theory which conceives the dream as resulting from a disturbance of sleep. We should not have dreamed if some disturbing element had not come into play during our sleep, and the dream is the reaction against this disturbance.

The discussion of the exciting causes of dreams occupies a great deal of space in the literature of dreams. It is obvious that this problem could have made its appearance only after dreams had become an object of biological investigation. The ancients, who conceived of dreams as divine inspirations, had no need

---

[1] That every impression, even the most insignificant, leaves an ineradicable mark, indefinitely capable of reappearing by day.—ED.

[2] From subsequent experience I am able to state that it is not at all rare to find in dreams reproductions of simple and unimportant occupations of everyday life, such as packing trunks, preparing food in the kitchen, etc., but in such dreams the dreamer himself emphasizes not the character of the recollection but its "reality"—"I really did this during the day."

to look for stimuli; for them a dream was due to the will of divine or demonic powers, and its content was the product of their special knowledge and intention. Science, however, immediately raised the question whether the stimuli of dreams were single or multiple, and this in turn led to the consideration whether the causal explanation of dreams belonged to the region of psychology or to that of physiology. Most authors appear to assume that disturbance of sleep, and hence dreams, may arise from various causes, and that physical as well as mental stimuli may play the part of dream-excitants. Opinions differ widely in preferring this or the other factor as the cause of dreams, and in classifying them in the order of importance.

Whenever the sources of dreams are completely enumerated they fall into the following four categories, which have also been employed in the classification of dreams: (1) external (objective) sensory stimuli; (2) internal (subjective) sensory stimuli; (3) internal (organic) physical stimuli; (4) purely psychical sources of excitation.

1. *External sensory stimuli*

The younger Strümpell, the son of the philosopher, whose work on dreams has already more than once served us as a guide in considering the problems of dreams, has, as is well known, recorded his observations of a patient afflicted with general anaesthesia of the skin and with paralysis of several of the higher sensory organs. This man would laps into sleep whenever the few remaining sensory paths between himself and the outer world were closed. When we wish to fall asleep we are accustomed to strive for a condition similar to that obtaining in Strümpell's experiment. We close the most important sensory portals, the eyes, and we endeavour to protect the other senses from all stimuli or from any change of the stimuli already acting upon them. We then fall asleep, although our preparations are never wholly successful. For we can never completely insulate the sensory organs, nor can we entirely abolish the excitability of the sensory organs themselves. Tnat we may at any time be awakened by intenser stimuli should prove to us "that the mind has remained in constant communication with the external world even during sleep." The sensory stimuli that reach us during sleep may easily become the source of dreams.

There are a great many stimuli of this nature, ranging from those unavoidable stimuli which are proper to the state of sleep or occasionally admitted by it, to those fortuitous stimuli which are calculated to wake the sleeper. Thus a strong light may fall upon the eyes, a noise may be heard, or an odour may irritate the mucous membranes of the nose. In our unintentional movements during sleep we may lay bare parts of the body, and thus expose them to a sensation of cold, or by a change of position we may excite sensations of pressure and touch. A mosquito may bite us, or a slight nocturnal mischance may simultaneously attack more than one sense-organ. Observers have called attention to a whole series of dreams in which the stimulus ascertained on waking and some part of the dream-content corresponded to such a degree that the stimulus could be recognized as the source of the dream.

I shall here cite a number of such dreams, collected by Jessen (p. 527), which are traceable to more or less accidental objective sensory stimuli. Every noise indistinctly perceived gives rise to corresponding dream-representations; the rolling of thunder takes us into the thick of battle, the crowing of a cock may be transformed into human shrieks of terror, and the creaking of a door may conjure up dreams of burglars breaking into the house. When one of our blankets slips off us at night we may dream that we are walking about naked, or falling into water. If we lie diagonally across the bed with our feet extending beyond the edge, we may dream of standing on the brink of a terrifying precipice, or of falling from a great height. Should our head accidentally get under the pillow we may imagine a huge rock overhanging us and about to crush us under its weight. An accumulation of semen produces voluptuous dreams, and local pains give rise to ideas of suffering ill-treatment, of hostile attacks, or of accidental bodily injuries. . . .

"Meier (*Versuch einer Erklärung des Nachtwandelns*, Halle, 1758, p. 33) once dreamed of being attacked by several men who threw him flat on the ground and drove a stake into the earth between his first and second toes. While imagining this in his dream he suddenly awoke and felt a piece of straw sticking between his toes. The same author, according to Hemmings (*Von den Traumen und Nachtwandlern*, Weimar, 1784, p. 258), "dreamed on another occasion, when his nightshirt was rather too tight round his neck, that he was being hanged. In his youth Hoffbauer dreamed of having fallen from a high wall, and found, on waking, that the bedstead had come apart, and that he had actually fallen on to the floor. . . . Gregory relates that he once applied a hot-water bottle to his feet, and dreamed of taking a trip to the summit of Mount Etna, where he found the heat of the soil almost unbearable. After having a blister applied to his head, another man dreamed of being scalped by Indians; still another, whose shirt was damp, dreamed that he was dragged through a stream. An attack of gout caused a patient to believe that he was in the hands of the Inquisition, and suffering the pains of torture (Macnish)."

The argument that there is a resemblance between the dream-stimulus and the dream-content would be confirmed if, by a systematic induction of stimuli, we should succeed in producing dreams corresponding to these stimuli. According to Macnish such experiments had already been made by Giron de Buzareingues. "He left his knee exposed and dreamed of travelling on a mail-coach by night. He remarked, in this connection, that travellers were well aware how cold the knees become in a coach at night. On another occasion he left the back of his head uncovered, and dreamed that he was taking part in a religious ceremony in the open air. In the country where he lived it was customary to keep the head always covered except on occasions of this kind."

Maury reports fresh observation on self-induced dreams of his own. (A number of other experiments were unsuccessful.)

1. He was tickled with a feather on his lips and on the tip of his nose. He dreamed of an awful torture, viz., that a mask of pitch was stuck to his face and then forcibly torn off, bringing the skin with it.

2. Scissors were whetted against a pair of tweezers. He heard bells ringing, then sounds of tumult which took him back to the days of the Revolution of 1848.

3. Eau de Cologne was held to his nostrils. He found himself in Cairo, in the shop of Johann Maria Farina. This was followed by fantastic adventures which he was not able to recall.

4. His neck was lightly pinched. He dreamed that a blister was being applied, and thought of a doctor who had treated him in childhood.

5. A hot iron was brought near his face. He dreamed that *chauffeurs*[1] had broken into the house, and were forcing the occupants to give up their money by thrusting their feet into braziers. The Duchesse d'Abrantés, whose sec-

retary he imagined himself to be then entered the room.

6. A drop of water was allowed to fall on to his forehead. He imagined himself in Italy, perspiring heavily, and drinking the white wine of Orvieto.

7. When the light of a candle screened with red paper was allowed to fall on his face, he dreamed of thunder, of heat, and of a storm at sea which he once witnessed in the English Channel.

Hervey, Weygandt, and others have made attempts to produce dreams experimentally.

Many have observed the striking skill of the dream in interweaving into its structure sudden impressions from the outer world, in such a manner as to represent a gradually approaching catastrophe (Hildebrandt). "In former years," this author relates, "I occasionally made use of an alarm-clock in order to wake punctually at a certain hour in the morning. It probably happened hundreds of times that the sound of this instrument fitted into an apparently very long and connected dream, as though the entire dream had been especially designed for it, as though it found in this sound its appropriate and logically indispensable climax, its inevitable denouement."

I shall presently have occasion to cite three of these alarm-clock dreams in a different connection.

Volkelt (p. 68) relates: "A composer once dreamed that he was teaching a class, and was just explaining something to his pupils. When he had finished he turned to one of the boys with the question: 'Did you understand me?' The boy cried out like one possessed 'Oh, ja!' Annoyed by this, he reprimanded his pupil for shouting. But now the entire class was screaming 'Orja,' then 'Eurjo,' and finally 'Feuerjo.' He was then aroused by the actual fire alarm in the street."

Garnier (*Traité des facultés de l'âme*, 1865), on the authority of Radestock, relates that Napoleon I, while sleeping in a carriage, was awakened from a dream by an explosion which took him back to the crossing of the Tagliamento and the bombardment of the Austrians, so that he started up, crying, "We have been undermined."

The following dream of Maury's has become celebrated: He was ill in bed; his mother was sitting beside him. He dreamed of the Reign of Terror during the Revolution. He witnessed some terrible scenes of murder, and finally he himself was summoned before the Tribunal.

---

[1] *Chauffeurs* were bands of robbers in the Vendée who resorted to this form of torture.

There he saw Robespierre, Marat, Fouquier-Tinville, and all the sorry heroes of those terrible days; he had to give an account of himself, and after all manner of incidents which did not fix themselves in his memory, he was sentenced to death. Accompanied by an enormous crowd, he was led to the place of execution. He mounted the scaffold; the executioner tied him to the plank, it tipped over, and the knife of the guillotine fell. He felt his head severed from his trunk, and awakened in terrible anxiety, only to find that the head-board of the bed had fallen, and had actually struck the cervical vertebrae just where the knife of the guillotine would have fallen.

This dream gave rise to an interesting discussion, initiated by Le Lorrain and Egger in the *Revue Philosophique,* as to whether, and how, it was possible for the dreamer to crowd together an amount of dream-content apparently so large in the short space of time elapsing between the perception of the waking stimulus and the moment of actual waking.

Examples of this nature show that objective stimuli occurring in sleep are among the most firmly-established of all the sources of dreams; they are, indeed, the only stimuli of which the layman knows anything whatever. If we ask an educated person who is not familiar with the literature of dreams how dreams originate, he is certain to reply by a reference to a case known to him in which a dream has been explained after waking by a recognized objective stimulus. Science, however, cannot stop here, but is incited to further investigation by the observation that the stimulus influencing the senses during sleep does not appear in the dream at all in its true form, but is replaced by some other representation, which is in some way related to it. But the relation existing between the stimulus and the resulting dream is, according to Maury, *"une affinité quelconque mais qui n'est pas unique et exclusive"*[1] (p. 72). If we read, for example, three of Hildebrandt's "alarm-clock dreams," we shall be compelled to ask why the same casual stimulus evoked so many different results, and why just these results and no others.

(P. 37): "I am taking a walk on a beautiful spring morning. I stroll through the green meadows to a neighbouring village, where I see numbers of the inhabitants going to church, wearing their best clothes and carrying their hymn-books under their arms. I remember that

it is Sunday, and that the morning service will soon begin. I decide to attend it, but as I am rather overheated I think I will wait in the churchyard until I am cooler. While reading the various epitaphs, I hear the sexton climbing the church-tower, and I see above me the small bell which is about to ring for the beginning of service. For a little while it hangs motionless; then it begins to swing, and suddenly its notes resound so clearly and penetratingly that my sleep comes to an end. But the notes of the bell come from the alarm-clock."

"A second combination. It is a bright winter day; the streets are deep in snow. I have promised to go on a sleigh-ride, but I have to wait some time before I am told that the sleigh is at the door. Now I am preparing to get into the sleigh. I put on my furs, the foot-warmer is put in, and at last I have taken my seat. But still my departure is delayed. At last the reins are twitched, the horses start, and the sleigh bells, now violently shaken, strike up their familiar music with a force that instantly tears the gossamer of my dream. Again it is only the shrill note of my alarm-clock."

"Yet a third example. I see the kitchen-maid walking along the passage to the dining-room, with a pile of several dozen plates. The porcelain column in her arms seems to me to be in danger of losing its equilibrium. 'Take care,' I exclaim, 'you will drop the whole pile!' The usual retort is naturally made—that she is used to such things, etc. Meanwhile I continue to follow her with my anxious gaze, and behold, at the threshold the fragile plates fall and crash and roll across the floor in hundreds of pieces. But I soon perceive that the endless din is not really a rattling but a true ringing, and with this ringing the dreamer now becomes aware that the alarm-clock has done its duty."

The question why the dreaming mind misjudges the nature of the objective sensory stimulus has been answered by Strümpell, and in an almost identical fashion by Wundt; their explanation is that the reaction of the mind to the stimulus attacking sleep is complicated and confused by the formation of illusions. A sensory impression is recognized by us and correctly interpreted—that is, it is classed with the memory-group to which it belongs according to all previous experience if the impression is strong, clear, and sufficiently prolonged, and if we have sufficient time to submit it to those mental processes. But if these conditions are not fulfilled we mistake the object which gives

[1] A sort of relation which is, however, neither unique nor exclusive.—ED.

rise to the impression, and on the basis of this impression we construct an illusion. "If one takes a walk in an open field and perceives indistinctly a distant object, it may happen that one will at first take it for a horse." On closer inspection the image of a cow, resting, may obtrude itself, and the picture may finally resolve itself with certainty into a group of people sitting on the ground. The impressions which the mind receives during sleep from external stimuli are of a similarly indistinct nature; they give rise to illusions because the impression evokes a greater or lesser number of memory-images, through which it acquires its psychic value. As for the question, in which of the many possible spheres of memory the corresponding images are aroused, and which of the possible associative connections are brought into play, that—to quote Strümpell again—is indeterminable, and is left, as it were, to the caprices of the mind.

Here we may take our choice. We may admit that the laws of dream-formation cannot really be traced any further, and so refrain from asking whether or not the interpretation of the illusion evoked by the sensory impression depends upon still other conditions; or we may assume that the objective sensory stimulus encroaching upon sleep plays only a modest rôle as a dream-source, and that other factors determine the choice of the memory-image to be evoked. Indeed, on carefully examining Maury's experimentally produced dreams, which I have purposely cited in detail, one is inclined to object that his investigations trace the origin of only one element of the dreams, and that the rest of the dream-content seems too independent and too full of detail to be explained by a single requirement, namely, that it must correspond with the element experimentally introduced. Indeed, one even begins to doubt the illusion theory, and the power of objective impressions to shape the dream, when one realizes that such impressions are sometimes subjected to the most peculiar and farfetched interpretations in our dreams. Thus M. Simon tells of a dream in which he saw persons of gigantic stature[1] seated at a table, and heard distinctly the horrible clattering produced by the impact of their jaws as they chewed their food. On waking he heard the clatter of a horse's hooves as it galloped past his window. If in this case the sound of the horse's hooves had revived ideas from the memory-sphere of *Gulliver's Travels*, the sojourn with the giants of Brobdingnag, and the virtuous horse-like creatures—as I should perhaps interpret the dream without any assistance on the author's part— ought not the choice of a memory-sphere so alien to the stimulus to be further elucidated by other motives?

2. *Internal (subjective) sensory stimuli*

All objections to the contrary notwithstanding, we must admit that the rôle of the objective sensory stimuli as producers of dreams has been indisputably established, and if, having regard to their nature and their frequency, these stimuli seem perhaps insufficient to explain all dream-pictures, this indicates that we should look for other dream-sources which act in a similar fashion. I do not know where the idea first arose that together with the external sensory stimuli the internal (subjective) stimuli should also be considered, but as a matter of fact this has been done more or less explicitly in all the more recent descriptions of the aetiology of dreams. "I believe," says Wundt (p. 363), "that an important part is played in dream-illusions by those subjective sensations of sight and hearing which are familiar to us in the waking state as a luminous chaos in the dark field of the vision, and a ringing, buzzing, etc., of the ears, and in especial, subjective irritations of the retina. This explains the remarkable tendency of dreams to delude the eyes with numbers of similar or identical objects. Thus we see outspread before our eyes innumerable birds, butterflies, fishes, coloured beads, flowers, etc. Here the luminous dust in the dark field of vision has assumed fantastic forms, and the many luminous points of which it consists are embodied in our dreams in as many single images, which, owing to the mobility of the luminous chaos, are seen as moving objects. This is perhaps the reason of the dream's decided preference for the most varied animal forms, for owing to the multiplicity of such forms they can readily adapt themselves to the subjective luminous images."

The subjective sensory stimuli as a source of dreams have the obvious advantage that, unlike objective stimuli, they are independent of external accidents. They are, so to speak, at the disposal of the interpretation whenever they are required. But they are inferior to the

---

[1] Gigantic persons in a dream justify the assumption that the dream is dealing with a scene from the dreamer's childhood. This interpretation of the dream as a reminiscence of *Gulliver's Travels* is, by the way, a good example of how an interpretation should not be made. The dream-interpreter should not permit his own intelligence to operate in disregard of the dreamer's impressions.

objective sensory stimuli by the fact that their claim to the rôle of dream-inciters—which observation and experiment have established in the case of objective stimuli—can in their case be verified with difficulty or not at all. The main proof of the dream-inciting power of subjective sensory stimuli is afforded by the so-called hypnogogic hallucinations, which have been described by Johann Müller as "phantastic visual manifestations." They are those very vivid and changeable pictures which with many people occur constantly during the period of falling asleep, and which may linger for a while even after the eyes have been opened. Maury, who was very subject to these pictures, made a thorough study of them, and maintained that they were related to or rather identical with dream-images. This had already been asserted by Johann Müller. Maury maintains that a certain psychic passivity is necessary for their origin; that it requires a relaxation of the intensity of attention (p. 59). But one may perceive a hypnogogic hallucination in any frame of mind if one falls into such a lethargy for a moment, after which one may perhaps wake up, until this oft-repeated process terminates in sleep. According to Maury, if one wakes up shortly after such an experience, it is often possible to trace in the dream the images which one has perceived before falling asleep as hypnogogic hallucinations (p. 134). Thus Maury on one occasion saw a series of images of grotesque figures with distorted features and curiously dressed hair, which obtruded themselves upon him with incredible importunity during the period of falling asleep, and which, upon waking, he recalled having seen in his dream. On another occasion, while suffering from hunger, because he was subjecting himself to a rather strict diet, he saw in one of his hypnogogic states a plate, and a hand armed with a fork taking some food from the plate. In his dream he found himself at a table abundantly supplied with food, and heard the clatter of the diner's forks. On yet another occasion, after falling asleep with strained and painful eyes, he had a hypnogogic hallucination of microscopically small characters, which he was able to decipher, one by one, only with a great effort; and on waking from sleep an hour later he recalled a dream in which there was an open book with very small letters, which he was obliged to read through with laborious effort.

Not only pictures, but auditory hallucinations of words, names, etc., may also occur hypnogogically, and then repeat themselves in the dream, like an overture announcing the principal motif of the opera which is to follow.

A more recent observer of hypnogogic hallucinations, G. Trumbull Ladd, follows the same lines as Johann Müller and Maury. By dint of practice he succeeded in acquiring the faculty of suddenly arousing himself, without opening his eyes, two to five minutes after gradually falling asleep. This enabled him to compare the disappearing retinal sensations with the dream-images remaining in his memory. He assures us that an intimate relation between the two can always be recognized, inasmuch as the luminous dots and lines of light spontaneously perceived by the retina produce, so to speak, the outline or scheme of the psychically perceived dream-images. For example, a dream in which he saw before him clearly printed lines, which he read and studied, corresponded with a number of luminous spots arranged in parallel lines; or, to express it in his own words: The clearly printed page resolved itself into an object which appeared to his waking perception like part of an actual printed page seen through a small hole in a sheet of paper, but at a distance too great to permit of its being read. Without in any way underestimating the central element of the phenomenon, Ladd believes that hardly any visual dream occurs in our minds that is not based on material furnished by this internal condition of retinal irritability. This is particularly true of dreams which occur shortly after falling asleep in a dark room, while dreams occurring in the morning, near the period of waking, receive their stimulus from the objective light penetrating the eye in a brightly-lit room. The shifting and infinitely variable character of the spontaneous luminous excitations of the retina exactly corresponds with the fitful succession of images presented to us in our dreams. If we attach any importance to Ladd's observations, we cannot underrate the productiveness of this subjective source of stimuli; for visual images, as we know, are the principal constituents of our dreams. The share contributed by the other senses, excepting, perhaps, the sense of hearing, is relatively insignificant and inconstant.

3. Internal (organic) physical stimuli

If we are disposed to look for the sources of dreams not outside but inside the organism, we must remember that almost all our internal organs, which in a state of health hardly remind us of their existence, may, in states of excitation—as we call them—or in disease, become a source of the most painful sensations, and must therefore be put on a par with the external excitants of pain and sensation. Strümpell, for example, gives expression to a long-familiar experience when he declares that "during sleep the psyche becomes far more deeply and broadly conscious of its coporality than in the waking state, and it is compelled to receive and to be influenced by certain stimulating impressions originating in parts of the body, and in alterations of the body, of which it is unconscious in the waking state." Even Aristotle declares it to be quite possible that a dream may draw our attention to incipient morbid conditions which we have not noticed in the waking state (owing to the exaggerated intensity of the impressions experienced in the dream[1]; and some medical authors, who certainly did not believe in the prophetic nature of dreams, have admitted the significance of dreams, at least in so far as the predicting of disease is concerned. [Cf. M. Simon, p. 31, and many earlier writers.[2]])

Even in our days there seems to be no lack of authenticated examples of such diagnostic achievements on the part of dreams. Thus Tissié cites from Artigues (*Essai sur la valeur séméiologique des Rêves*) the history of a woman of forty-three, who, during several years of apparently perfect health, was troubled with anxiety-dreams, and in whom a medical examination subsequently revealed an incipient affection of the heart, to which she presently succumbed.

Serious derangements of the internal organs clearly excite dreams in quite a number of persons. The frequency of anxiety-dreams in diseases of the heart and lungs has been generally realized; indeed, this function of the dream-life is emphasized by so many writers that I

shall here content myself with a reference to the literature of the subject (Radestock, Spitta, Maury, M. Simon, Tissié). Tissié even believes that the diseased organs impress upon the dream-content its characteristic features. The dreams of persons suffering from diseases of the heart are generally very brief, and end in a terrified awakening; death under terrible circumstances almost always find a place in their content. Those suffering from diseases of the lungs dream of suffocation, of being crushed, and of flight, and a great many of them are subject to the familiar nightmare —which, by the way, Börner has succeeded in inducing experimentally by lying on the face and covering the mouth and nostrils. In digestive disturbances the dream contains ideas from the sphere of gustatory enjoyment and disgust. Finally, the influence of sexual excitement on the dream-content is obvious enough in everyone's experience, and provides the strongest confirmation of the whole theory of dream-instigation by organic sensation.

Moreover, if we study the literature of dreams it becomes quite evident that some writers (Maury, Weygandt) have been led to the study of dream-problems by the influence their own pathological state has had on the content of their dreams.

The enlargement of the number of dream-sources by such undeniably established facts is, however, not so important as one might be led to suppose; for dreams are, after all, phenomena which occur in healthy persons—perhaps in all persons, and every night—and a pathological state of the organs is evidently not one of the indispensable conditions. For us, however, the question is not whence particular dreams originate, but rather: what is the exciting cause of ordinary dreams in normal people?

But we have only to go a step farther to find a source of dreams which is more prolific than any of those mentioned above, and which promises indeed to be inexhaustible. If it is established that the bodily organs become, in sickness, an exciting source of dreams, and if we admit that the mind, when diverted during sleep from the outer world, can devote more of its attention to the interior of the body, we may readily assume that the organs need not necessarily become diseased in order to permit stimuli, which in one way or another grow into dream-images, to reach the sleeping mind. What in the waking state we vaguely perceive as a general sensation, perceptible by its quality alone—a sensation to which, in the opinion

---

[1] Cf. above, p. 137.

[2] In addition to the diagnostic valuation of dreams (*e.g.*, by Hippocrates) mention must also be made of their therapeutic significance in antiquity.

Among the Greeks there were dream oracles, which were vouchsafed to patients in quest of recovery. The patient betook himself to the temple of Apollo or Aesculapius; there he was subjected to various ceremonies, bathed, rubbed and perfumed. A state of exaltation having been thus induced, he was made to lie down in the temple on the skin of a sacrificial ram. He fell asleep and dreamed of remedies, which he saw in their natural form, or in symbolic images which the priests afterwards interpreted.

For further references concerning the remedial dreams of the Greeks, *cf.* Lehmann, i, 74; Bouché-Leclerq; Hermann, *Gottesd. Altert. d. Gr.*, § 41; *Privataltert.* § 38, 16; Böttinger in Sprengel's *Beitr. z. Gesch. d. Med.*, ii, p. 163, et seq.; W. Lloyd, *Magnetism and Mesmerism in Antiquity*, London, 1877; Döllinger, *Heidentum und Judentum*, p. 130.

of physicians, all the organic systems contribute their share—this general sensation would at night attain a greater potency, and, acting through its individual components, would constitute the most prolific as well as the most usual source of dream-representations. We should then have to discover the laws by which organic stimuli are translated into dream-representations.

This theory of the origin of dreams is the one most favoured by all medical writers. The obscurity which conceals the essence of our being—the *"moi splanchnique"* as Tissié terms it—from our knowledge, and the obscurity of the origin of dreams, correspond so closely that it was inevitable that they should be brought into relation with one another. The theory according to which the organic sensations are responsible for dreams has, moreover, another attraction for the physician, inasmuch as it favours the aetiological union of the dream with mental derangement, both of which reveal so many points of agreement in their manifestations, since changes in the general organic massive sensation and in the stimuli emanating from the internal organs are also considered to have a far-reaching significance as regards the origin of the psychoses. It is therefore not surprising that the organic stimulus theory can be traced to several writers who have propounded this theory independently.

A number of writers have followed the train of thought developed by Schopenhauer in 1851. Our conception of the universe has its origin in the recasting by the intellect of the impressions which reach it from without in the moulds of time, space and causality. During the day the stimuli proceeding from the interior of the organism, from the sympathetic nervous system, exert at most an unconscious influence on our mood. At night, however, when the overwhelming effect of the impressions of the day is no longer operative, the impressions that surge upward from within are able to force themselves on our attention—just as in the night we hear the rippling of the brook that was drowned in the clamour of the day. But how else can the intellect react to these stimuli than by transforming them in accordance with its own function into things which occupy space and time and follow the lines of causality?—and so a dream originates. Thus Scherner, and after him Volkelt, endeavoured to discover the more intimate relations between physical sensations and dream-pictures; but we shall reserve the discussion of this point for our chapter on the theory of dreams.

As a result of a singularly logical analysis, the psychiatrist Krauss referred the origin of dreams, and also of deliria and delusions, to the same element, namely, to organically determined sensations. According to him, there is hardly any part of the organism which might not become the starting-point of a dream or a delusion. Organically determined sensations, he says, "may be divided into two classes: (1) general sensations—those affecting the whole system; (2) specific sensations—those that are immanent in the principal systems of the vegetative organism, and which may in turn be subdivided into five groups: (*a*) the muscular, (*b*) the pneumatic, (*c*) the gastric, (*d*) the sexual, (*e*) the peripheral sensations (p. 33 of the second article)."

The origin of the dream-image from physical sensations is conceived by Krauss as follows: The awakened sensation, in accordance with some law of association, evokes an idea or image bearing some relation to it, and combines with this idea or image, forming an organic structure, towards which, however, the consciousness does not maintain its normal attitude. For it does not bestow any attention on the sensation, but concerns itself entirely with the accompanying ideas; and this explains why the facts of the case have been so long misunderstood (p. 11 ff.). Krauss even gives this process the special name of "transubstantiation of the sensations into dream-images" (p. 24).

The influence of organic physical stimuli on the formation of dreams is today almost universally admitted, but the question as to the nature of the law underlying this relation is answered in various ways, and often obscurely. On the basis of the theory of physical excitation the special task of dream-interpretation is to trace back the content of a dream to the causative organic stimulus, and if we do not accept the rules of interpretation advanced by Scherner, we shall often find ourselves confronted by the awkward fact that the organic source of excitation reveals itself only in the content of the dream.

A certain agreement, however, appears in the interpretation of the various forms of dreams which have been designated as "typical," because they recur in so many persons with almost the same content. Among these are the well-known dreams of falling from a height, of the dropping out of teeth, of flying, and of embarrassment because one is naked or scantily clad. This last type of dream is said to be caused simply by the dreamer's perception, felt in his sleep, that he has thrown off the bed-clothes and is uncovered. The dream that one's teeth are dropping out is explained by "dental irritation," which does not, however, of necessity imply a morbid condition of irritability in the teeth. According to Strümpell, the flying dream is the adequate image employed by the mind to interpret the quantum of stimulus emanating from the rising and sinking of the pulmonary lobes when the cutaneous sensation of the thorax has lapsed into insensibility. This latter condition causes the sensation which gives rise to images of hovering in the air. The dream of falling from a height is said to be due to the fact that an arm falls away from the body, or a flexed knee is suddenly extended, after unconsciousness of the sensation of cutaneous pressure has supervened, whereupon this sensation returns to consciousness, and the transition from unconsciousness to consciousness embodies itself psychically as a dream of falling (Strümpell, p. 118). The weakness of these fairly plausible attempts at explanation clearly lies in the fact that without any further elucidation they allow this or that group of organic sensations to disappear from psychic perception, or to obtrude themselves upon it, until the constellation favourable for the explanation has been established. Later on, however, I shall have occasion to return to the subject of typical dreams and their origin.

From a comparison of a series of similar dreams, M. Simon endeavoured to formulate certain rules governing the influence of organic sensations on the nature of the resulting dream. He says (p. 34): "If during sleep any organic apparatus, which normally participates in the expression of an affect, for any reason enters into the state of excitation to which it is usually aroused by the affect, the dream thus produced will contain representations which harmonize with that affect."

Another rule reads as follows (p. 35): "If, during sleep, an organic apparatus is in a state of activity, stimulation, or disturbance, the dream will present ideas which correspond with the nature of the organic function performed by that apparatus."

Mourly Vold has undertaken to prove the supposed influence of bodily sensation on the production of dreams by experimenting on a single physiological territory. He changed the positions of a sleeper's limbs, and compared the resulting dreams with these changes. He recorded the following results:

1. The position of a limb in a dream corresponds approximately to that of reality, i.e., we dream of a static condition of the limb which corresponds with the actual condition.

2. When one dreams of a moving limb it always happens that one of the positions occurring in the execution of this movement corresponds with the actual position.

3. The position of one's own limb may in the dream be attributed to another person.

4. One may also dream that the movement in question is impeded.

5. The limb in any particular position may appear in the dream as an animal or monster, in which case a certain analogy between the two is established.

6. The behaviour of a limb may in the dream incite ideas which bear some relation or other to this limb. Thus, for example, if we are using our fingers we dream of numerals.

Results such as these would lead me to conclude that even the theory of organic stimulation cannot entirely abolish the apparent freedom of the determination of the dream-picture which will be evoked.[1]

4. *Psychic sources of excitation*

When considering the relation of dreams to waking life, and the provenance of the material of dreams, we learned that the earliest as well as the most recent investigators are agreed that men dream of what they do during the day, and of the things that interest them in the waking state. This interest, continued from waking life into sleep, is not only a psychic bond, joining the dream to life, but it is also a source of dreams whose importance must not be underestimated, and which, taken together with those stimuli which become active and of interest during sleep, suffices to explain the origin of all dream-images. Yet we have also heard the very contrary of this asserted; namely, that dreams bear the sleeper away from the interests of the day, and that in most cases we do not dream of things which have occupied our attention during the day until after they have lost, for our waking life, the stimulating force of belonging to the present. Hence in the analysis of dream-life we are reminded at every step that it is inadmissible to frame general rules without making provision for qualifications by introducing such terms as "frequently," "as a

[1] See below for a further discussion of the two volumes of records of dreams since published by this writer.

rule," "in most cases," and without being prepared to admit the validity of exceptions.

If interest during the waking state, together with the internal and external stimuli that occur during sleep, sufficed to cover the whole aetiology of dreams, we should be in a position to give a satisfactory account of the origin of all the elements of a dream; the problem of the dream-sources would then be solved, leaving us only the task of discriminating between the part played by the psychic and that played by the somatic dream-stimuli in individual dreams. But as a matter of fact no such complete solution of a dream has ever been achieved in any case, and everyone who has attempted such a solution has found that components of the dream—and usually a great many of them —are left whose source he is unable to trace. The interests of the day as a psychic source of dreams are obviously not so influential as to justify the confident assertion that every dreamer continues the activities of his waking life in his dreams.

Other dream-sources of a psychic nature are not known. Hence, with the exception perhaps of the explanation of dreams given by Scherner, to which reference will be made later on, all the explanations found in the literature of the subject show a considerable hiatus whenever there is a question of tracing the images and ideas which are the most characteristic material of dreams. In this dilemma the majority of authors have developed a tendency to belittle as far as possible the share of the psychic factor, which is so difficult to determine, in the evocation of dreams. To be sure, they distinguish as major divisions the nerve-stimulus dream and the association-dream, and assert that the latter has its source exclusively in reproduction (Wundt, p. 365), but they cannot dismiss the doubt as to "whether they appear without any impulsion from organic stimuli" (Volkelt, p. 127). And even the characteristic quality of the pure association-dream disappears. To quote Volkelt (p. 118): "In the association-dream proper, there is no longer any question of such a stable nucleus. Here the loose grouping penetrates even to the very centre of the dream. The imaginative life, already released from the control of reason and intellect, is here no longer held together by the more important psychical and physical stimuli, but is left to its own uncontrolled and confused divagations." Wundt, too, attempts to belittle the psychic factor in the evocation of dreams by asserting that "the phantasms of the dream are perhaps unjustly

regarded as pure hallucinations. Probably most dream-representations are really illusions, inasmuch as they emanate from the slight sensory impressions which are never extinguished during sleep" (p. 359, *et seq.*). Weygandt has adopted this view, and generalizes upon it. He asserts that "the most immediate causes of all dream-representations are sensory stimuli to which reproductive associations then attach themselves" (p. 17). Tissié goes still further in suppressing the psychic sources of excitation (p. 183): "*Les rêves d'origine absolument psychique n'existent pas*",[1] and elsewhere (p. 6), "*Les pensées de nos rêves nous viennent de dehors....*"[2]

Those writers who, like the eminent philosopher Wundt, adopt a middle course, do not hesitate to assert that in most dreams there is a cooperation of the somatic stimuli and psychic stimuli which are either unknown or are identified with the interests of the day.

We shall learn later that the problem of dream-formation may be solved by the disclosure of an entirely unsuspected psychic source of excitation. In the meanwhile we shall not be surprised at the over-estimation of the influence of those stimuli which do not originate in the psychic life. It is not merely because they alone may easily be found, and even confirmed by experiment, but because the somatic conception of the origin of dreams entirely corresponds with the mode of thought prevalent in modern psychiatry. Here, it is true, the mastery of the brain over the organism is most emphatically stressed; but everything that might show that the psychic life is independent of demonstrable organic changes, or spontaneous in its manifestations, is alarming to the contemporary psychiatrist, as though such an admission must mean a return to the old-world natural philosophy and the metaphysical conception of the nature of the soul. The distrust of the psychiatrist has placed the psyche under tutelage, so to speak; it requires that none of the impulses of the psyche shall reveal an autonomous power. Yet this attitude merely betrays a lack of confidence in the stability of the causal concatenation between the physical and the psychic. Even where on investigation the psychic may be recognized as the primary cause of a phenomenon, a more profound comprehension of the subject will one

[1] Dreams do not exist whose origin is totally psychic.—ED.

[2] The thoughts of our dreams come from outside.— ED.

day succeed in following up the path that leads to the organic basis of the psychic. But where the psychic must, in the present state of our knowledge, be accepted as the terminus, it need not on that account be disavowed.

D. *Why Dreams Are Forgotten After Waking*

That a dream *fades away* in the morning is proverbial. It is, indeed, possible to recall it. For we know the dream, of course, only by recalling it after waking; but we very often believe that we remember it incompletely, that during the night there was more of it than we remember. We may observe how the memory of a dream which in the morning was still vivid fades in the course of the day, leaving only a few trifling remnants. We are often aware that we have been dreaming, but we do not know of what we have dreamed; and we are so well used to this fact—that the dream is liable to be forgotten—that we do not reject as absurd the possibility that we may have been dreaming even when, in the morning, we know nothing either of the content of the dream or of the fact that we have dreamed. On the other hand, it often happens that dreams manifest an extraordinary power of maintaining themselves in the memory. I have had occasion to analyse, with my patients, dreams which occurred to them twenty-five years or more previously, and I can remember a dream of my own which is divided from the present day by at least thirty-seven years, and yet has lost nothing of its freshness in my memory. All this is very remarkable, and for the present incomprehensible.

The forgetting of dreams is treated in the most detailed manner by Strümpell. This forgetting is evidently a complex phenomenon; for Strümpell attributes it not to a single cause, but to quite a number of causes.

In the first place, all those factors which induce forgetfulness in the waking state determine also the forgetting of dreams. In the waking state we commonly very soon forget a great many sensations and perceptions because they are too slight to remember, and because they are charged with only a slight amount of emotional feeling. This is true also of many dream-images; they are forgotten because they are too weak, while the stronger images in their neighbourhood are remembered. However, the factor of intensity is in itself not the only determinant of the preservation of dream-images; Strümpell, as well as other authors (Calkins), admits that dream-images are often rapidly for-

gotten although they are known to have been vivid, whereas, among those that are retained in the memory, there are many that are very shadowy and unmeaning. Besides, in the waking state one is wont to forget rather easily things that have happened only once, and to remember more readily things which occur repeatedly. But most dream-images are unique experiences,[1] and this peculiarity would contribute towards the forgetting of all dreams equally. Of much greater significance is a third cause of forgetting. In order that feelings, representations, ideas and the like should attain a certain degree of memorability, it is important that they should not remain isolated, but that they should enter into connections and associations of an appropriate nature. If the words of a verse of poetry are taken and mixed together, it will be very difficult to remember them. "Properly placed, in a significant sequence, one word helps another, and the whole, making sense, remains and is easily and lastingly fixed in the memory. Contradictions, as a rule, are retained with just as much difficulty and just as rarely as things that are confused and disorderly." Now dreams, in most cases, lack sense and order. Dream-compositions, by their very nature, are insusceptible of being remembered, and they are forgotten because as a rule they fall to pieces the very next moment. To be sure, these conclusions are not entirely consistent with Radestock's observation (p. 168), that we most readily retain just those dreams which are most peculiar.

According to Strümpell, other factors, deriving from the relation of the dream to the waking state, are even more effective in causing us to forget our dreams. The forgetfulness of dreams manifested by the waking consciousness is evidently merely the counterpart of the fact already mentioned, namely, that the dream hardly ever takes over an orderly series of memories from the waking state, but only certain details of these memories, which it removes from the habitual psychic connections in which they are remembered in the waking state. The dream-composition, therefore, has no place in the community of the psychic series which fill the mind. It lacks all mnemonic aids. "In this manner the dream-structure rises, as it were, from the soil of our psychic life, and floats in psychic space like a cloud in the sky, quickly dispelled by the first breath of re-

[1] Periodically recurrent dreams have been observed repeatedly. Compare the collection made by Chabaneix.

awakening life" (p. 87). This situation is accentuated by the fact that on waking the attention is immediately besieged by the inrushing world of sensation, so that very few dream-images are capable of withstanding its force. They fade away before the impressions of the new day like the stars before the light of the sun.

Finally, we should remember that the fact that most people take but little interest in their dreams is conducive to the forgetting of dreams. Anyone who for some time applies himself to the investigation of dreams, and takes a special interest in them, usually dreams more during that period than at any other; he remembers his dreams more easily and more frequently.

Two other reasons for the forgetting of dreams, which Bonatelli (cited by Benini) adds to those adduced by Strümpell, have already been included in those enumerated above; namely, (1) that the difference of the general sensation in the sleeping and the waking state is unfavourable to mutual reproduction, and (2) that the different arrangement of the material in the dream makes the dream untranslatable, so to speak, for the waking consciousness.

It is therefore all the more remarkable, as Strümpell himself observes, that, in spite of all these reasons for forgetting the dream, so many dreams are retained in the memory. The continual efforts of those who have written on the subject to formulate laws for the remembering of dreams amount to an admission that here, too, there is something puzzling and unexplained. Certain peculiarities relating to the remembering of dreams have attracted particular attention of late; for example, the fact that the dream which is believed to be forgotten in the morning may be recalled in the course of the day on the occasion of some perception which accidentally touches the forgotten content of the dream (Radestock, Tissié). But the whole recollection of dreams is open to an objection which is calculated greatly to depreciate its value in critical eyes. One may doubt whether our memory, which omits so much from the dream, does not falsify what it retains.

This doubt as to the exactness of the reproduction of dreams is expressed by Strümpell when he says: "It may therefore easily happen that the waking consciousness involuntarily interpolates a great many things in the recollection of the dream; one imagines that one

has dreamt all sorts of things which the actual dream did not contain."

Jessen (p. 547) expresses himself in very decided terms: "Moreover, we must not lose sight of the fact, hitherto little heeded, that in the investigation and interpretation of coherent and logical dreams we almost always take liberties with the truth when we recall a dream to memory. Unconsciously and unintentionally we fill up the gaps and supplement the dream-images. Rarely, and perhaps never, has a connected dream been as connected as it appears to us in memory. Even the most truth-loving person can hardly relate a dream without exaggerating and embellishing it in some degree. The human mind so greatly tends to perceive everything in a connected form that it intentionally supplies the missing links in any dream which is in some degree incoherent."

The observations of V. Eggers, though of course independently conceived, read almost like a translation of Jessen's words:

". . . L'observation des rêves a ses difficultés spéciales et le seul moyen d'éviter toute erreur en pareille matière est de confier au papier sans le moindre retard ce que l'on vient d'éprouver et de remarquer; sinon, l'oubli vient vite ou total ou partiel; l'oubli total est sans gravité; mais l'oubli partiel est perfide: car si l'on se met ensuite à raconter ce que l'on n'a pas oublié, on est exposé à compléter par imagination les fragments incohérents et disjoints fourni par la mémoire . . . on devient artiste à son insu, et le récit, périodiquement répété s'impose à la créance de son auteur, qui, de bonne foi, le présente comme un fait authentique, dûment établi selon les bonnes méthodes. . . ."[1]

Similarly Spitta, who seems to think that it is only in the attempt to reproduce the dream that we bring order and arrangement into loosely associated dream-elements—"turning juxtaposition into concatenation; that is, adding the process of logical connection which is absent in the dream."

Since we can test the reliability of our mem-

[1] . . . The observation of dreams has its special difficulties, and the only way to avoid all error in such matter is to put on paper without the least delay what has just been experienced and noticed; otherwise, totally or partially the dream is quickly forgotten; total forgetting is without seriousness; but partial forgetting is treacherous: for, if one then starts to recount what has not been forgotten, one is likely to supplement from the imagination the incoherent and disjointed fragments provided by the memory . . . . unconsciously one becomes an artist, and the story, repeated from time to time, imposes itself on the belief of its author, who, in good faith, tells it as authentic fact, regularly established according to proper methods. . . .—ED.

ory only by objective means, and since such a test is impossible in the case of dreams, which are our own personal experience, and for which we know no other source than our memory, what value do our recollections of our dreams possess?

E. *The Psychological Peculiarities of Dreams*

In our scientific investigation of dreams we start with the assumption that dreams are a phenomenon of our own psychic activity; yet the completed dream appears to us as something alien, whose authorship we are so little inclined to recognize that we should be just as willing to say "A dream came to me," as "I dreamed." Whence this "psychic strangeness" of dreams? According to our exposition of the sources of dreams, we must assume that it is not determined by the material which finds its way into the dream-content, since this is for the most part common both to dream-life and waking life. We might ask ourselves whether this impression is not evoked by modifications of the psychic processes in dreams, and we might even attempt to suggest that the existence of such changes is the psychological characteristic of dreams.

No one has more strongly emphasized the essential difference between dream-life and waking life and drawn more far reaching conclusions from this difference than G. Th. Fechner in certain observations contained in his *Elemente der Psychophysik* (Part II, p. 520). He believes that "neither the simple depression of conscious psychic life under the main threshold," nor the distraction of the attention from the influences of the outer world, suffices to explain the peculiarities of dream-life as compared with waking life. He believes, rather, that the arena of dreams is other than the arena of the waking life of the mind. "If the arena of psychophysical activity were the same during the sleeping and the waking state, the dream, in my opinion, could only be a continuation of the waking ideational life at a lower degree of intensity, so that it would have to partake of the form and material of the latter. But this is by no means the case."

What Fechner really meant by such a transposition of the psychic activity has never been made clear, nor has anybody else, to my knowledge, followed the path which he indicates in this remark. An anatomical interpretation in the sense of physiological localization in the brain, or even a histological stratification of the cerebral cortex, must of course be excluded.

The idea might, however, prove ingenious and fruitful if it could refer to a psychical apparatus built up of a number of successive and connected systems.

Other authors have been content to give prominence to this or that palpable psychological peculiarity of the dream-life, and even to take this as a starting-point for more comprehensive attempts at explanation.

It has been justly remarked that one of the chief peculiarities of dream-life makes its appearance even in the state of falling asleep, and may be defined as the sleep-heralding phenomenon. According to Schleiermacher (p. 351), the distinguishing characteristic of the waking state is the fact that its psychic activity occurs in the form of ideas rather than in that of images. But the dream thinks mainly in visual images, and it may be noted that with the approach of sleep the voluntary activities become impeded in proportion as involuntary representations make their appearance, the latter belonging entirely to the category of images. The incapacity for such ideational activities as we feel to be deliberately willed, and the emergence of visual images, which is regularly connected with this distraction—these are two constant characteristics of dreams, and on psychological analysis we are compelled to recognize them as essential characteristics of dream-life. As for the images themselves—the hypnogogic hallucinations—we have learned that even in their content they are identical with dream-images.[1]

Dreams, then, think preponderantly, but not exclusively, in visual images. They make use also of auditory images, and, to a lesser extent, of the other sensory impressions. Moreover, in dreams, as in the waking state, many things are simply thought or imagined (probably with the help of remnants of verbal conceptions). Characteristic of dreams, however, are only those elements of their contents which behave like images, that is, which more closely resemble perceptions than mnemonic representations. Without entering upon a discussion of the nature of hallucinations—a discussion familiar to every psychiatrist—we may say, with every well-informed authority, that the dream hallucinates—that is, that it replaces thoughts by hallucinations. In this respect visual and acoustic im-

[1] Silberer has shown by excellent examples how in the state of falling asleep even abstract thoughts may be changed into visible plastic images, which, of course, express them. (*Jahrbuch*, Bleuler-Freud, vol. i, 1900.) I shall return to the discussion of his findings later on.

pressions behave in the same way. It has been observed that the recollection of a succession of notes heard as we are falling asleep becomes transformed, when we have fallen asleep, into a hallucination of the same melody, to give place, each time we wake, to the fainter and qualitatively different representations of the memory, and resuming, each time we doze off again, its hallucinatory character.

The transformation of an idea into a hallucination is not the only departure of the dream from the more or less corresponding waking thought. From these images the dream creates a situation; it represents something as actually present; it dramatizes an idea, as Spitta (p. 145) puts it. But the peculiar character of this aspect of the dream-life is completely intelligible only if we admit that in dreaming we do not as a rule (the exceptions call for special examination) suppose ourselves to be thinking, but actually experiencing; that is, we accept the hallucination in perfectly good faith. The criticism that one has experienced nothing, but that one has merely been thinking in a peculiar manner—dreaming—occurs to us only on waking. It is this characteristic which distinguishes the genuine dream from the day-dream, which is never confused with reality.

The characteristics of the dream-life thus far considered have been summed up by Burdach (p. 476) as follows: "As characteristic features of the dream we may state (a) that the subjective activity of our psyche appears as objective, inasmuch as our perceptive faculties apprehend the products of phantasy as though they were sensory activities . . . (b) that sleep abrogates our voluntary action; hence falling asleep involves a certain degree of passivity. . . . The images of sleep are conditioned by the relaxation of our powers of will."

It now remains to account for the credulity of the mind in respect to the dream-hallucinations which are able to make their appearance only after the suspension of certain voluntary powers. Strümpell asserts that in this respect the psyche behaves correctly and in conformity with its mechanism. The dream-elements are by no means mere representations, but true and actual experiences of the psyche, similar to those which come to the waking state by way of the senses (p. 34). Whereas in the waking state the mind thinks and imagines by means of verbal images and language, in dreams it thinks and imagines in actual perceptual images (p. 35). Dreams, moreover, reveal a spatial consciousness, inasmuch as in dreams, just as in the waking state, sensations and images are transposed into outer space (p. 36). It must therefore be admitted that in dreams the mind preserves the same attitude in respect of images and perceptions as in the waking state (p. 43). And if it forms erroneous conclusions in respect of these images and perceptions, this is due to the fact that in sleep it is deprived of that criterion which alone can distinguish between sensory perceptions emanating from within and those coming from without. It is unable to subject its images to those tests which alone can prove their objective reality. Further, it neglects to differentiate between those images which can be exchanged at will and those in respect of which there is no free choice. It errs because it cannot apply the law of causality to the content of its dreams (p. 58). In brief, its alienation from the outer world is the very reason for its belief in its subjective dream-world.

Delbœuf arrives at the same conclusion through a somewhat different line of argument. We believe in the reality of dream-pictures because in sleep we have no other impressions with which to compare them; because we are cut off from the outer world. But it is not because we are unable, when asleep, to test our hallucinations that we believe in their reality. Dreams can make us believe that we are applying such tests—that we are touching, say, the rose that we see in our dream; and yet we are dreaming. According to Delbœuf there is no valid criterion that can show whether something is a dream or a waking reality, except— and that only pragmatically—the fact of waking. "I conclude that all that has been experienced between falling asleep and waking is a delusion, if I find on waking that I am lying undressed in bed" (p. 84). "I considered the images of my dream real while I was asleep on account of the unsleeping mental habit of assuming an outer world with which I can contrast my ego."[1]

[1] Haffner, like Delbœuf, has attempted to explain the act of dreaming by the alteration which an abnormally introduced condition must have upon the otherwise correct functioning of the intact psychic apparatus; but he describes this condition in somewhat different terms. He states that the first distinguishing mark of dreams is the abolition of time and space, i.e., the emancipation of the representation from the individual's position in the spatial and temporal order. Associated with this is the second fundamental character of dreams, the mistaking of the hallucinations, imaginations, and phantasy-combinations for objective perceptions. "The sum-total of the higher psychic functions, particularly the formation of concepts, judgments, and conclusions on the one hand, and free self-determination on the other hand, combine

If the turning-away from the outer world is accepted as the decisive cause of the most conspicuous characteristics of our dreams, it will be worth our while to consider certain subtle observations of Burdach's, which will throw some light on the relation of the sleeping psyche to the outer world, and at the same time serve to prevent our over-estimating the importance of the above deductions. "Sleep," says Burdach, "results only under the condition that the mind is not excited by sensory stimuli . . yet it is not so much a lack of sensory stimuli that conditions sleep as a lack of interest in them;[1] some sensory impressions are even necessary in so far as they serve to calm the mind; thus the miller can fall asleep only when he hears the clatter of his mill, and he who finds it necessary, as a matter of precaution, to burn a light at night, cannot fall asleep in the dark" (p. 457).

"During sleep the psyche isolates itself from the outer world, and withdraws from the periphery. . . . Nevertheless, the connection is not entirely broken; if one did not hear and feel during sleep, but only after waking, one would assuredly never be awakened at all. The continuance of sensation is even more plainly shown by the fact that we are not always awakened by the mere force of the sensory impression, but by its relation to the psyche. An indifferent word does not arouse the sleeper, but if called by name he wakes . . . so that even in sleep the psyche discriminates between sensations. . . . Hence one may even be awakened by the obliteration of a sensory stimulus, if this is related to anything of im-

with the sensory phantasy-images, and at all times have these as a substratum. These activities too, therefore, participate in the erratic nature of the dream-representations. We say they participate, for our faculties of judgment and will are in themselves unaltered during sleep. As far as their activity is concerned, we are just as shrewd and just as free as in the waking state. A man cannot violate the laws of thought; that is, even in a dream he cannot judge things to be identical which present themselves to him as opposites. He can desire in a dream only that which he regards as a good (*sub ratione boni*). But in this application of the laws of thought and will the human intellect is led astray in dreams by confusing one notion with another. Thus it happens that in dreams we formulate and commit the greatest of contradictions, while, on the other hand, we display the shrewdest judgment and arrive at the most logical conclusions, and are able to make the most virtuous and sacred resolutions. The lack of orientation is the whole secret of our flights of phantasy in dreams, and the lack of critical reflection and agreement with other minds is the main source of the reckless extravagances of our judgments, hopes and wishes in dreams" (p. 18).

[1] Compare with this the element of *"Désintérêt,"* in which Claparède (1905) finds the mechanism of falling falling asleep.

agined importance. Thus one man wakes when the nightlight, is extinguished, and the miller when his mill comes to a standstill; that is, waking is due to the cessation of a sensory activity, and this presupposes that the activity has been perceived, but has not disturbed the mind, its effect being indifferent, or actually reassuring" (p. 46, etc.).

Even if we are willing to disregard these by no means trifling objections, we must yet admit that the qualities of dream-life hitherto considered, which are attributed to withdrawal from the outer world, cannot fully account for the strangeness of dreams. For otherwise it would be possible to reconvert the hallucinations of the dream into mental images, and the situations of the dream into thoughts, and thus to achieve the task of dream-interpretation. Now this is precisely what we do when we reproduce a dream from memory after waking, and no matter whether we are fully or only partially successful in this retranslation, the dream still remains as mysterious as before.

Furthermore, all writers unhesitatingly assume that still other and profounder changes take place in the plastic material of waking life. Strümpell seeks to isolate one of these changes as follows: (p. 17) "With the cessation of active sensory perception and of normal consciousness, the psyche is deprived of the soil in which its feelings, desires, interests, and activities are rooted. Those psychic states, feelings, interests, and valuations, which in the waking state adhere to memory-images, succumb to an obscuring pressure, in consequence of which their connection with these images is severed; the perceptual images of things, persons, localities, events and actions of the waking state are, individually, abundantly reproduced, but none of these brings with it its psychic value. Deprived of this, they hover in the mind dependent on their own resources . . ."

This annihilation of psychic values, which is in turn referred to a turning away from the outer world, is, according to Strümpell, very largely responsible for the impression of strangeness with which the dream is coloured in our memory.

We have seen that the very fact of falling asleep involves a renunciation of one of the psychic activities—namely, the voluntary guidance of the flow of ideas. Thus the supposition obtrudes itself (though it is in any case a natural one) that the state of sleep may extend even to the psychic functions. One or another of these functions is perhaps entirely suspended;

we have now to consider whether the rest continue to operate undisturbed, whether they are able to perform their normal work under the circumstances. The idea occurs to us that the peculiarities of the dream may be explained by the restricted activity of the psyche during sleep, and the impression made by the dream upon our waking judgment tends to confirm this view. The dream is incoherent; it reconciles, without hesitation, the worst contradictions; it admits impossibilities; it disregards the authoritative knowledge of the waking state, and it shows us as ethically and morally obtuse. He who should behave in the waking state as his dreams represent him as behaving would be considered insane. He who in the waking state should speak as he does in his dreams, or relate such things as occur in his dreams, would impress us as a feeble-minded or muddle-headed person. It seems to us, then, that we are merely speaking in accordance with the facts of the case when we rate psychic activity in dreams very low, and especially when we assert that in dreams the higher intellectual activities are suspended or at least greatly impaired.

With unusual unanimity (the exceptions will be dealt with elsewhere) the writers on the subject have pronounced such judgments as lead immediately to a definite theory or explanation of dream-life. It is now time to supplement the résumé which I have just given by a series of quotations from a number of authors —philosophers and physicians—bearing upon the psychological characteristics of the dream.

According to Lemoine, the *incoherence* of the dream-images is the sole essential characteristic of the dream.

Maury agrees with him (*Le Sommeil*, p. 163): *"Il n'y a pas des rêves absolument raisonnables et qui ne contiennent quelque incohérence, quelque absurdité."*[1]

According to Hegel, quoted by Spitta, the dream lacks any intelligible objective coherence.

Dugas says: *"Les rêve, c'est l'anarchie psychique, affective et mentale, c'est le jeu des fonctions livrées à elles-mêmes et s'exerçant sans contrôle et sans but; dans le rêve l'esprit est un automate spirituel."*[2]

[1] There are no dreams which are absolutely reasonable which do not contain some incoherence, some absurdity.—Ed.

[2] The dream is psychic anarchy, emotional and intellectual, the playing of functions, freed of themselves and performing without control and without end; in the dream, the mind is a spiritual automaton.—Ed.

"The relaxation, dissolution, and promiscuous confusion of the world of ideas and images held together in waking life by the logical power of the central ego" is conceded even by Volkelt (p. 14), according to whose theory the psychic activity during sleep appears to be by no means aimless.

The absurdity of the associations of ideas which occur in dreams can hardly be more strongly stigmatized than it was by Cicero (*De Divinatione*, II. lxxi): *"Nihil tam praepostere, tam incondite, tam monstruose cogitari potest, quod non possimus somniare."*[3]

Fechner says (p. 522): "It is as though the psychological activity of the brain of a reasonable person were to migrate into that of a fool."

Radestock (p. 145): "It seems indeed impossible to recognize any stable laws in this preposterous behaviour. Withdrawing itself from the strict policing of the rational will that guides our waking ideas, and from the processes of attention, the dream, in crazy sport, whirls all things about in kaleidoscopic confusion."

Hildebrandt (p. 45): "What wonderful jumps the dreamer permits himself, for instance, in his chain of reasoning! With what unconcern he sees the most familiar laws of experience turned upside down! What ridiculous contradictions he is able to tolerate in the order of nature and of society, before things go too far, and the very excess of nonsense leads to an awakening! Sometimes we quite innocently calculate that three times three make twenty; and we are not in the least surprised if a dog recites poetry to us, if a dead person walks to his grave, or if a rock floats on the water. We solemnly go to visit the duchy of Bernburg or the principality of Liechtenstein in order to inspect its navy; or we allow ourselves to be recruited as a volunteer by Charles XII just before the battle of Poltava."

Binz (p. 33), referring to the theory of dreams resulting from these impressions, says: "Of ten dreams nine at least have an absurd content. We unite in them persons or things which do not bear the slightest relation to one another. In the next moment, as in a kaleidoscope, the grouping changes to one, if possible, even more nonsensical and irrational than before; and so the shifting play of the drowsy brain continues, until we wake, put a hand to our forehead, and ask ourselves whether we

[3] There is no imaginable thing too absurd, too involved, or too abnormal for us to dream about.—Ed.

still really possess the faculty of rational imagination and thought."

Maury, *Le Sommeil* (p. 50) makes, in respect of the relation of the dream-image to the waking thoughts, a comparison which a physician will find especially impressive: *"La production de ces images que chez l'homme éveillé fait le plus souvent naître la volonté, correspond, pour l'intelligence, à ce que sont pour la motilité certains mouvements que nous offrent la chorée et les affections paralytiques. . . ."*[1] For the rest, he considers the dream *"toute une série de dégradations de la faculté pensante et raisonnante"*[2] (p. 27).

It is hardly necessary to cite the utterances of those authors who repeat Maury's assertion in respect of the higher individual psychic activities.

According to Strümpell, in dreams—and even, of course, where the nonsensical nature of the dream is not obvious—all the logical operations of the mind, based on relations and associations, recede into the background (p. 26). According to Spitta (p. 148) ideas in dreams are entirely withdrawn from the laws of causality; while Radestock and others emphasize the feebleness of judgment and logical inference peculiar to dreams. According to Jodl (p. 123), there is no criticism in dreams, no correcting of a series of perceptions by the content of consciousness as a whole. The same author states that "All the activities of consciousness occur in dreams, but they are imperfect, inhibited, and mutually isolated." The contradictions of our conscious knowledge which occur in dreams are explained by Stricker and many others on the ground that facts are forgotten in dreams, or that the logical relations between ideas are lost (p. 98), etc., etc.

Those authors who, in general, judge so unfavourably of the psychic activities of the dreamer nevertheless agree that dreams do retain a certain remnant of psychic activity. Wundt, whose teaching has influenced so many other investigators of dream-problems, expressly admits this. We may ask, what are the nature and composition of the remnants of normal psychic life which manifest themselves in dreams? It is pretty generally acknowledged that the reproductive faculty, the memory, seems to be the least affected in dreams; it may,

indeed, show a certain superiority over the same function in waking life (see above, p. 141), even though some of the absurdities of dreams are to be explained by the forgetfulness of dream-life. According to Spitta, it is the sentimental life of the psyche which is not affected by sleep, and which thus directs our dreams. By sentiment (*Gemüt*) he means "the constant sum of the emotions as the inmost subjective essence of the man" (p. 84).

Scholz (p. 37) sees in dreams a psychic activity which manifests itself in the "allegorizing interpretation" to which the dream-material is subjected. Siebeck (p. 11) likewise perceives in dreams a "supplementary interpretative activity" of the psyche, which applies itself to all that is observed and perceived. Any judgment of the part played in dreams by what is presumed to be the highest psychical function, i.e., consciousness, presents a peculiar difficulty. Since it is only through consciousness that we can know anything of dreams, there can be no doubt as to its being retained. Spitta, however, believes that only *consciousness* is retained in the dream, but not *self-consciousness*. Delbœuf confesses that he is unable to comprehend this distinction.

The laws of association which connect our mental images hold good also for what is represented in dreams; indeed, in dreams the dominance of these laws is more obvious and complete than in the waking state. Strümpell (p. 70) says: "Dreams would appear to proceed either exclusively in accordance with the laws of pure representation, or in accordance with the laws of organic stimuli accompanied by such representations; that is, without being influenced by reflection, reason, aesthetic taste, or moral judgment." The authors whose opinions I here reproduce conceive the formation of the dream somewhat as follows: The sum of sensory stimuli of varying origin (discussed elsewhere) that are operative in sleep at first awaken in the psyche a number of images which present themselves as hallucinations (according to Wundt, it is more correct to say "as illusions," because of their origin in external and internal stimuli). These combine with one another in accordance with the known laws of association, and, in accordance with the same laws, they in turn evoke a new series of representations (images). The whole of this material is then elaborated as far as possible by the still active remnant of the thinking and organizing faculties of the psyche (cf. Wundt and Weygandt). Thus far, however, no one has been

---

[1] The production of those images which, in the waking man, most often excite the will, correspond, for the mind, to those which are, for the motility, certain movements that offer St. Vitus' dance and paralytic affections. . . .—ED.

[2] A whole series of degradations of the faculty of thinking and reasoning.—ED.

successful in discerning the motive which would decide what particular law of association is to be obeyed by those images which do not originate in external stimuli.

But it has been repeatedly observed that the associations which connect the dream-images with one another are of a particular kind, differing from those found in the activities of the waking mind. Thus Volkelt (p. 15): "In dreams the ideas chase and seize upon one another on the strength of accidental similarities and barely perceptible connections. All dreams are pervaded by casual and unconstrained associations of this kind." Maury attaches great value to this characteristic of the connection of ideas, for it allows him to draw a closer analogy between the dream-life and certain mental derangements. He recognizes two main characteristics of "deliria": " (1) *une action spontanée et comme automatique de l'esprit; (2) une association vicieuse et irrégulière des idées*"[1] (p. 126). Maury gives us two excellent examples from his dreams, in which the mere similarity of sound decides the connection between the dream-representations. Once he dreamed that he was on a pilgrimage (*pèlerinage*) to Jerusalem, or to Mecca. After many adventures he found himself in the company of the chemist Pelletier; the latter, after some conversation, gave him a galvanized shovel (*pelle*) which became his great broadsword in the next portion of the dream (p. 137). In another dream he was walking along a highway where he read the distances on the kilometre-stones; presently he found himself at a grocer's who had a large pair of scales; a man put *kilogramme* weights into the scales, in order to weigh Maury; the grocer then said to him: "You are not in Paris, but on the island *Gilolo*." This was followed by a number of pictures, in which he saw the flower *lobelia*, and then General *Lopez*, of whose death he had read a little while previously. Finally he awoke as he was playing a game of *lotto*.[2]

We are, indeed, quite well aware that this low estimate of the psychic activities of the dream has not been allowed to pass without contradiction from various quarters. Yet here contradiction would seem rather difficult. It is not a matter of much significance that one of the depreciators of dream-life, Spitta (p. 118),

should assure us that the same psychological laws which govern the waking state rule the dream also, or that another (Dugas) should state: "*Le rêve n'est pas déraison ni même irraison pure*,"[3] so long as neither of them has attempted to bring this opinion into harmony with the psychic anarchy and dissolution of all mental functions in the dream which they themselves have described. However, the possibility seems to have dawned upon others that the madness of the dream is perhaps not without its method—that it is perhaps only a disguise, a dramatic pretence, like that of Hamlet, to whose madness this perspicacious judgment refers. These authors must either have refrained from judging by appearances, or the appearances were, in their case, altogether different.

Without lingering over its superficial absurdity, Havelock Ellis considers the dream as "an archaic world of vast emotions and imperfect thoughts," the study of which may acquaint us with the primitive stages of the development of mental life. J. Sully (p. 362) presents the same conception of the dream in a still more comprehensive and penetrating fashion. His statements deserve all the more consideration when it is added that he, perhaps more than any other psychologist, was convinced of the veiled significance of the dream. "Now our dreams are a means of conserving these successive personalities. When asleep we go back to the old ways of looking at things and of feeling about them, to impulses and activities which long ago dominated us." A thinker like Delbœuf asserts—without, indeed, adducing proof in the face of contradictory data, and hence without real justification—"*Dans le sommeil, hormis la perception, toutes les facultés de l'esprit, intelligence, imagination, mémoire, volonté, moralité, restent intactes dans leur essence; seulement, elles s'appliquent à des objets imaginaires et mobiles. Le songeur est un acteur qui joue à volonté les fous et les sages, les bourreaux et les victimes, les nains et les géants, les démons et les anges*"[4] (p. 222). The Marquis Hervey,[5] who is flatly contradicted by Maury, and whose essay I have been unable to obtain despite all my efforts, appears emphati-

---

[1] (1) An action of the mind spontaneous and as though automatic; (2) a defective and irregular association of ideas.—ED.

[2] Later on we shall be able to understand the meaning of dreams like these which are full of words with similar sounds or the same initial letters.

[3] The dream is neither pure derangement nor pure irrationality.—ED.

[4] In sleep, excepting perception, all the faculties of the mind—intellect, imagination, memory, will, morality—remain intact in their essence; only, they are applied to imaginary and variable objects. The dreamer is an actor who plays at will the mad and the wise, executioner and victim, dwarf and giant, devil and angel.—ED.

[5] Hervey de St. Denys.

cally to protest against the under-estimation of the psychic capacity in the dream. Maury speaks of him as follows (p. 19): *"M. le Marquis Hervey prête à l'intelligence durant le sommeil toute sa liberté d'action et d'attention, et il ne semble faire consister le sommeil que dans l'occlusion des sens, dans leur fermeture au monde extérieur; en sorte que l'homme qui dort ne se distingue guère, selon sa manière de voir, de l'homme qui laisse vaguer sa pensée en se bouchant les sens; toute la différence qui sépare alors la pensée ordinaire du celle du dormeur c'est que, chez celui-ci, l'idée prend une forme visible, objective, et ressemble, à s'y méprendre, à la sensation déterminée par les objets extérieurs; le souvenir revêt l'apparence du fait présent."*[1]

Maury adds, however, *"qu'il y a une différence de plus et capitale à savoir que les facultés intellectuelles de l'homme endormi n'offrent pas l'équilibre qu'elles gardent chez l'homme éveillé."*[2]

In Vaschide, who gives us fully information as to Hervey's book, we find that this author expresses himself as follows, in respect to the apparent incoherence of dreams: *"L'image du rêve est la copie de l'idée. Le principal est l'idée; la vision n'est pas qu'accessoire. Ceçi établi, il faut savoir suivre la marche des idées, il faut savoir analyser le tissu des rêves; l'incohérence devient alors compréhensible, les conceptions les plus fantasques deviennent des faits simples et parfaitement logiques"*[3] (p. 146). And (p. 147): *"Les rêves les plus bizarres trouvent même une explication des plus logiques quand on sait les analyser."*[4]

[1] The Marquis Hervey attributes to the intelligence during sleep all its freedom of action and attention, and he seems to make sleep consist only of the shutting of the senses, of their closing to the outside world; except for his manner of seeing, the man asleep is hardly distinguishable from the man who allows his mind to wander while he obstructs his senses; the whole difference, then, between ordinary thought and that of the sleeper, is that with the latter the idea takes an objective and visible shape, which resembles, to all appearances, sensation determined by exterior objects; memory takes on the appearance of present fact.—ED.

[2] That there is a further and important difference in that the mental faculties of the sleeping man do not offer the equilibrium which they keep in the waking state.—ED.

[3] The image in a dream is a copy of an idea. The main thing is the idea; the vision is only accessory. This established, it is necessary to know how to follow the progression of ideas, how to analyse the texture of the dreams; incoherence then is understandable, the most fantastic concepts become simple and perfectly logical facts.—ED.

[4] Even the most bizarre dreams find a most logical explanation when one knows how to analyse them.—ED.

J. Stärke has drawn attention to the fact that a similar solution of the incoherence of dreams was put forward in 1799 by an old writer, Wolf Davidson, who was unknown to me (p. 136): "The peculiar leaps of our imaginings in the dream-state all have their cause in the laws of association, but this connection often occurs very obscurely in the soul, so that we frequently seem to observe a leap of the imagination where none really exists."

The evaluation of the dream as a psychic product in the literature of the subject varies over a very wide scale; it extends from the extreme of under-estimation, as we have already seen, through premonitions that it may have a value as yet unrevealed, to an exaggerated over-estimation, which sets the dream-life far above the capacities of waking life. In his psychological characterization of dream-life, Hildebrandt, as we know, groups it into three antinomies, and he combines in the third of these antinomies the two extreme points of this scale of values (p. 19): "It is the contrast between, on the one hand, an enhancement, an increase of potentiality, which often amounts to virtuosity, and on the other hand a decided diminution and enfeeblement of the psychic life, often to a sub-human level."

"As regards the first, who is there that cannot confirm from his own experience the fact that in the workings and weavings of the genius of dreams, there are sometimes exhibited a profundity and sincerity of emotion, a tenderness of feeling, a clearness of view, a subtlety of observation and a readiness of wit, such as we should have modestly to deny that we always possessed in our waking life? Dreams have a wonderful poetry, an apposite allegory, an incomparable sense of humour, a delightful irony. They see the world in the light of a peculiar idealization, and often intensify the effect of their phenomena by the most ingenious understanding of the reality underlying them. They show us earthly beauty in a truly heavenly radiance, the sublime in its supremest majesty, and that which we know to be terrible in its most frightful form, while the ridiculous becomes indescribably and drastically comical. And on waking we are sometimes still so full of one of these impressions that it will occur to us that such things have never yet been offered to us by the real world."

One might here ask oneself: do these depreciatory remarks and these enthusiastic praises really refer to the self-same phenomenon? Have some writers overlooked the foolish and others the profound and sensitive dreams? And if both kinds of dreams do occur—that is, dreams that merit both these judgments—does it not seem idle to seek a psychological characterization of the dream? Would it not suffice to state that everything is possible in the dream, from the lowest degradation of the psychic life to its flight to heights unknown in the waking state? Convenient as such a solution might be, it has this against it: that behind the efforts of all the investigators of dreams there seems to lurk the assumption that there is in dreams some characteristic which is universally valid in its essential features, and which must eliminate all these contradictions.

It is unquestionably true that the mental capacities of dreams found readier and warmer recognition in the intellectual period now lying behind us, when philosophy rather than exact natural science ruled the more intelligent minds. Statements like that of Schubert, to the effect that the dream frees the mind from the power of external nature, that it liberates the soul from the chains of sensory life, together with similar opinions expressed by the younger Fichte[1] and others, who represent dreams as a soaring of the mind to a higher plane—all these seem hardly conceivable to us today; they are repeated at present only by mystics and devotees.[2] With the advance of a scientific mode of thought a reaction took place in the estimation of dreams. It is the medical writers who are most inclined to underrate the psychic activity in dreams, as being insignificant and valueless; while philosophers and unprofessional observers—amateur psychologists—whose contributions to the subject in especial must not be overlooked, have for the most part, in agreement with popular belief, laid emphasis on the psychological value of dreams. Those who are inclined to underrate the psychic activity of dreams naturally show a preference for the somatic sources of excitation in the aetiology of the dream; those who admit that the dreaming mind may retain the greater part of its waking faculties naturally have no motive for denying the existence of autonomous stimulations.

Among the superior accomplishments which one may be tempted, even on a sober compari-son, to ascribe to the dream-life, that of memory is the most impressive. We have fully discussed the by no means rare experiences which prove this superiority. Another privilege of the dream-life, often extolled by the older writers—namely, the fact that it can overstep the limitations of time and space—is easily recognized as an illusion. This privilege, as Hildebrandt remarks, is merely illusory; dreams disregard time and space only as does waking thought, and only because dreaming is itself a form of thinking. Dreams are supposed to enjoy a further advantage in respect of time—to be independent of the passage of time in yet another sense. Dreams like Maury's dream of his execution (p. 147 above) seem to show that the perceptual content which the dream can compress into a very short space of time far exceeds that which can be mastered by our psychic activity in its waking thoughts. These conclusions have, however, been disputed. The essays of Le Lorrain and Egger on *The Apparent Duration of Dreams* gave rise to a long and interesting discussion, which in all probability has not yet found the final explanation of this profound and delicate problem.[3]

That dreams are able to continue the intellectual activities of the day and to carry them to a point which could not be arrived at during the day, that they may resolve doubts and problems, and that they may be the source of fresh inspiration in poets and composers, seems, in the light of numerous records, and of the collection of instances compiled by Chabaneix, to be proved beyond question. But even though the facts may be beyond dispute, their interpretation is subject to many doubts on wider grounds.[4]

Finally, the alleged divinatory power of the dream has become a subject of contention in which almost insuperable objections are confronted by obstinate and reiterated assertions. It is, of course, right that we should refrain from denying that this view has any basis whatever in fact, since it is quite possible that a number of such cases may before long be explained on purely natural psychological grounds.

F. *The Ethical Sense in Dreams*

For reasons which will be intelligible only after a consideration of my own investigations of dreams, I have isolated from the psychology of

---

[1] Cf. Haffner and Spitta.

[2] That brilliant mystic, Du Prel, one of the few writers for the omission of whose name in earlier editions of this book I should like to apologize, has said that, so far as the human mind is concerned, it is not the waking state but dreams which are the gateway to metaphysics (*Philosophie der Mystik*, p. 59).

[3] For the further literature of the subject, and a critical discussion of these problems, the reader is referred to Tobowolska's dissertation (Paris, 1900).

[4] Compare Havelock Ellis's criticism in *The World of Dreams*, p. 268.

the dream the subsidiary problem as to whether and to what extent the moral dispositions and feelings of waking life extend into dream-life. The same contradictions which we were surprised to observe in the descriptions by various authors of all the other psychic activities will surprise us again here. Some writers flatly assert that dreams know nothing of moral obligations; others as decidedly declare that the moral nature of man persists even in his dream-life.

Our ordinary experience of dreams seems to confirm beyond all doubt the correctness of the first assertion. Jessen says (p. 553): "Nor does one become better or more virtuous during sleep; on the contrary, it seems that conscience is silent in our dreams, inasmuch as one feels no compassion and can commit the worst crimes, such as theft, murder, and homicide, with perfect indifference and without subsequent remorse."

Radestock (p. 146) says: "It is to be noted that in dreams associations are effected and ideas combined without being in any way influenced by reflection, reason, aesthetic taste, and moral judgment; the judgment is extremely weak, and ethical indifference reigns supreme."

Volkelt (p. 23) expresses himself as follows: "As every one knows, dreams are especially unbridled in sexual matters. Just as the dreamer himself is shameless in the extreme, and wholly lacking in moral feeling and judgment, so likewise does he see others, even the most respected persons, doing things which, even in his thoughts, he would blush to associate with them in his waking state."

Utterances like those of Schopenhauer, that in dreams every man acts and talks in complete accordance with his character, are in sharpest contradiction to those mentioned above. R. Ph. Fischer[1] maintains that the subjective feelings and desires, or affects and passions, manifest themselves in the wilfulness of the dream-life, and that the moral characteristics of a man are mirrored in his dreams.

Haffner says (p. 25): "With rare exceptions ... a virtuous man will be virtuous also in his dreams; he will resist temptation, and show no sympathy for hatred, envy, anger, and all other vices; whereas the sinful man will, as a rule, encounter in his dreams the images which he has before him in the waking state."

Scholz (p. 36): "In dreams there is truth;

despite all camouflage of nobility or degradation, we recognize our own true selves. ... The honest man does not commit a dishonouring crime even in his dreams, or, if he does, he is appalled by it as by something foreign to his nature. The Roman emperor who ordered one of his subjects to be executed because he dreamed that he had cut off the emperor's head was not far wrong in justifying his action on the ground that he who has such dreams must have similar thoughts while awake. Significantly enough, we say of things that find no place even in our intimate thoughts: 'I would never even dream of such a thing.'"

Plato, on the other hand, considers that they are the best men who only dream the things which other men do.

Plaff,[2] varying a familiar proverb, says: "Tell me your dreams for a time and I will tell you what you are within."

The little essay of Hildebrandt's from which I have already taken so many quotations (the best-expressed and most suggestive contribution to the literature of the dream-problem which I have hitherto discovered), takes for its central theme the problem of morality in dreams. For Hildebrandt, too, it is an established rule that the purer the life, the purer the dream; the impurer the life, the impurer the dream.

The moral nature of man persists even in dreams. "But while we are not offended or made suspicious by an arithmetical error, no matter how obvious, by a reversal of scientific fact, no matter how romantic, or by an anachronism, no matter how ridiculous, we nevertheless do not lose sight of the difference between good and evil, right and wrong, virtue and vice. No matter how much of that which accompanies us during the day may vanish in our hours of sleep, Kant's categorical imperative dogs our steps as an inseparable companion, of whom we cannot rid ourselves even in our slumber. ... This can be explained only by the fact that the fundamental element of human nature, the moral essence, is too firmly fixed to be subjected to the kaleidoscopic shaking-up to which phantasy, reason, memory, and other faculties of the same order succumb in our dreams" (p. 45, etc.).

In the further discussion of the subject we find in both these groups of authors remarkable evasions and inconsequences. Strictly speaking, all interest in immoral dreams should be at an

---

[1] *Grundzüge des Systems der Anthropologie.* Erlangen, 1850 (quoted by Spitta).

[2] *Das Traumleben und seine Deutung,* 1868 (cited by Spitta, p. 192).

end for those who assert that the moral personality of the individual falls to pieces in his dreams. They could as coolly reject all attempts to hold the dreamer responsible for his dreams, or to infer from the immorality of his dreams that there is an immoral strain in his nature, as they have rejected the apparently analogous attempt to prove from the absurdity of his dreams the worthlessness of his intellectual life in the waking state. The others, according to whom the categorical imperative extends even into the dream, ought to accept *in toto* the notion of full responsibility for immoral dreams; and we can only hope that their own reprehensible dreams do not lead them to abandon their otherwise firm belief in their own moral worth.

As a matter of fact, however, it would seem that although no one is positively certain just how good or how bad he is, he can hardly deny that he can recollect immoral dreams of his own. That there are such dreams no one denies; the only question is: how do they originate? So that, in spite of their conflicting judgments of dream-morality, both groups of authors are at pains to explain the genesis of the immoral dream; and here a new conflict arises, as to whether its origin is to be sought in the normal functions of the psychic life, or in the somatically conditioned encroachments upon this life. The nature of the facts compels both those who argue for and those who argue against moral responsibility in dream-life to agree in recognizing a special psychic source for the immorality of dreams.

Those who maintain that morality continues to function in our dream-life nevertheless refrain from assuming full responsibility for their dreams. Haffner says (p. 24): "We are not responsible for our dreams, because that basis which alone gives our life truth and reality is withdrawn from our thoughts and our will. Hence the wishes and actions of our dreams cannot be virtuous or sinful." Yet the dreamer is responsible for the sinful dream in so far as indirectly he brings it about. Thus, as in waking life, it is his duty, just before going to sleep, morally to cleanse his mind.

The analysis of this admixture of denial and recognition of responsibility for the moral content of dreams is carried much further by Hildebrandt. After arguing that the dramatic method of representation characteristic of dreams, the condensation of the most complicated processes of reflection into the briefest periods of time, and the debasement and confusion of the imaginative elements of dreams, which even

he admits must be allowed for in respect of the immoral appearance of dreams, he nevertheless confesses that there are the most serious objections to flatly denying all responsibility for the lapses and offenses of which we are guilty in our dreams.

(P. 49): "If we wish to repudiate very decisively any sort of unjust accusation, and especially one which has reference to our intentions and convictions, we use the expression: 'We should never have dreamt of such a thing.' By this, it is true, we mean on the one hand that we consider the region of dreams the last and remotest place in which we could be held responsible for our thoughts, because there these thoughts are so loosely and incoherently connected with our real being that we can, after all, hardly regard them as our own; but inasmuch as we feel impelled expressly to deny the existence of such thoughts even in this region, we are at the same time indirectly admitting that our justification would not be complete unless it extended even thus far. And I believe that here, although unconsciously, we are speaking the language of truth."

(P. 52): "No dream-action can be imagined whose first beginnings have not in some shape already passed through the mind during our waking hours, in the form of wish, desire, or impulse." Concerning this original impulse we must say: The dream has not discovered it— it has only imitated and extended it; it has only elaborated into dramatic form a scrap of historical material which it found already existing within us; it brings to our mind the words of the Apostle—that he who hates his brother is a murderer. And though, after we wake, being conscious of our moral strength, we may smile at the whole widely elaborated structure of the depraved dream, yet the original material out of which we formed it cannot be laughed away. One feels responsible for the transgressions of one's dreaming self; not for the whole sum of them, but yet for a certain percentage. "In short, if in this sense, which can hardly be impugned, we understand the words of Christ, that out of the heart come evil thoughts, then we can hardly help being convinced that every sin committed in our dreams brings with it at least a vague minimum of guilt."

Thus Hildebrandt finds the source of the immorality of dreams in the germs and hints of evil impulses which pass through our minds during the day as mental temptations, and he does not hesitate to include these immoral elements in the ethical evaluation of the personality. These same thoughts, and the same evaluation of these thoughts, have, as we know, caused devout and holy men of all ages to lament that they were wicked sinners.[1]

The general occurrence of these contrasting thoughts in the majority of men, and even in other regions than the ethical, is of course established beyond a doubt. They have sometimes been judged in a less serious spirit. Spitta quotes a relevant passage from A. Zeller (Article "Irre," in the Allgemeine Encyklopädie der Wissenschaften, Ersch and Grüber, p. 144): "An intellect is rarely so happily organized as to be in full command of itself at all times and seasons, and never to be disturbed in the lucid and constant processes of thought by ideas not merely unessential, but absolutely grotesque and nonsensical; indeed, the greatest thinkers have had cause to complain of this dream-like, tormenting and distressing rabble of ideas, which disturbs their profoundest contemplations and their most pious and earnest meditations."

A clearer light is thrown on the psychological meaning of these contrasting thoughts by a further observation of Hildebrandt's, to the effect that dreams permit us an occasional glimpse of the deepest and innermost recesses of our being, which are generally closed to us in our waking state (p. 55). A recognition of this fact is betrayed by Kant in his Anthropology, when he states that our dreams may perhaps be intended to reveal to us not what we are but what we might have been if we had had another upbringing; and by Radestock (p. 84), who suggests that dreams disclose to us what we do not wish to admit to ourselves, and that we therefore unjustly condemn them as lying and deceptive. J. E. Erdmann asserts: "A dream has never told me what I ought to think of a person, but, to my great surprise, a dream has more than once taught me what I do really think of him and feel about him." And J. H. Fichte expresses himself in a like manner: "The character of our dreams gives a far truer reflection of our general disposition than anything that we can learn by self-observation in the waking state." Such remarks as this of Benini's call our attention to the fact

that the emergence of impulses which are foreign to our ethical consciousness is merely analogous to the manner, already familiar to us, in which the dream disposes of other representative material: "Certe nostre inclinazioni che si credevano soffocate e spente da un pezzo, si ridestano; passioni vecchie e sepolte revivono; cose e persone a cui non pensiamo mai, ci vengono dinanzi" (p. 149). Volkelt expresses himself in a similar fashion: "Even ideas which have entered into our consciousness almost unnoticed, and which, perhaps, it has never before called out of oblivion, often announce their presence in the mind through a dream" (p 105). Finally, we may remember that according to Schleiermacher the state of falling asleep is accompanied by the appearance of undesired imaginings.

We may include in such "undesired imaginings" the whole of that imaginative material the occurrence of which surprises us in immoral as well as in absurd dreams. The only important difference consists in the fact that the undesired imaginings in the moral sphere are in opposition to our usual feelings, whereas the others merely appear strange to us. So far nothing has been done to enable us to reconcile this difference by a profounder understanding.

But what is the significance of the emergence of undesired representations in dreams? What conclusions can the psychology of the waking and dreaming mind draw from these nocturnal manifestations of contrasting ethical impulses? Here we find a fresh diversity of opinion, and also a different grouping of the authors who have treated of the subject. The line of thought followed by Hildebrandt, and by others who share his fundamental opinion, cannot be continued otherwise than by ascribing to the immoral impulses, even in the waking state, a latent vitality, which is indeed inhibited from proceeding to action, and by asserting that during sleep something falls away from us which, having the effect of an inhibition, has kept us from becoming aware of the existence of such impulses. Dreams, therefore, reveal the true, if not the whole, nature of the dreamer, and are one means of making the hidden life of the psyche accessible to our understanding. It is only on such hypotheses that Hildebrandt can attribute to the dream the rôle of a monitor who calls our attention to the secret mischief in the soul, just as, according to the physicians, it may announce a hitherto unobserved physical disorder. Spitta, too, must

---

[1] It is not uninteresting to consider the attitude of the Inquisition to this problem. In the Tractatus de Officio sanctissimae Inquisitionis of Thomas Careña (Lyons edit., 1659) one finds the following passage: "Should anyone utter heresies in his dreams, the inquisitors shall consider this a reason for investigating his conduct in life, for that is wont to return in sleep which occupies a man during the day" (Dr. Ehniger, St. Urban, Switzerland).

be influenced by this conception when he refers, for example, to the stream of excitations which flow in upon the psyche during puberty, and consoles the dreamer by assuring him that he has done all that is in his power to do if he has led a strictly virtuous life during his waking state, if he has made an effort to suppress the sinful thoughts as often as they arise, and has kept them from maturing and turning into action. According to this conception, we might designate as "undesired imaginings" those that are *suppressed* during the day, and we must recognize in their emergence a genuine psychic phenomenon.

According to certain other authors, we have no right to draw this last inference. For Jessen (p. 360) the undesired ideas and images, in the dream as in the waking state, and also in the delirium of fever, etc., possess "the character of a voluntary activity laid to rest, and of a procession, to some extent mechanical, of images and ideas evoked by inner impulses." An immoral dream proves nothing in respect of the psychic life of the dreamer except that he has somehow become cognizant of the imaginative content in question; it is certainly no proof of a psychic impulse of his own mind. Another writer, Maury, makes us wonder whether he, too, does not ascribe to the dream-state the power of dividing the psychic activity into its components, instead of aimlessly destroying it. He speaks as follows of dreams in which one oversteps the bounds of morality: *"Ce sont nos penchants qui parlent et qui nous font agir, sans que la conscience nous retienne, bien que parfois elle nous avertisse. J'ai mes défauts et mes penchants vicieux; à l'état de veille, je tâche de lutter contre eux, et il m'arrive assez souvent de n'y pas succomber. Mais dans mes songes j'y succombe toujours, ou pour mieux dire j'agis par leur impulsion, sans crainte et sans remords. . . . Evidemment les visions qui se déroulent devant ma pensée, et qui constituent le rêve, me sont suggérées par les incitations que je ressens et que ma volonté absente ne cherche pas à refouler."*[1]—*Le Sommeil* (p. 113).

If one believed in the power of the dream to reveal an actually existing, but suppressed or concealed, immoral disposition of the dreamer, one could not express one's opinion more emphatically than in the words of Maury (p. 115): *"En rêve l'homme se révèle donc tout entier à soi-même dans sa nudité et sa misère natives. Dès qu'il suspend l'exercice de sa volonté, il dévient le jouet de toutes les passions contre lesquelles, à l'état de veille, la conscience, le sentiment d'honneur, la crainte nous défendent."*[2] In another place he makes the striking assertion (p. 462): *"Dans le rêve, c'est surtout l'homme instinctif que se révèle. . . . L'homme revient pour ainsi dire à l'état de nature quand il rêve; mais moins les idées acquises ont pénétré dans son esprit, plus 'les penchants en desaccord' avec elles conservent encore sur lui d'influence dans le rêve."*[3] He then mentions, as an example, that his own dreams often reveal him as a victim of just those superstitions which he has most vigorously attacked in his writings.

The value of all these acute observations is, however, impaired in Maury's case, because he refuses to recognize in the phenomena which he has so accurately observed anything more than a proof of the *automatisme psychologique* which in his own opinion dominates the dreamlife. He conceives this automatism as the complete opposite of psychic activity.

A passage in Stricker's *Studien über das Bewusstsein* reads: "Dreams do not consist purely and simply of delusions; for example, if one is afraid of robbers in a dream, the robbers indeed are imaginary, but the fear is real." Our attention is here called to the fact that the affective development of a dream does not admit of the judgment which one bestows upon the rest of the dream-content, and the problem then arises: What part of the psychic processes in a dream may be real? That is to say, what part of them may claim to be enrolled among the psychic processes of the waking state?

G. Dream-Theories and the Function of the Dream

A statement concerning the dream which seeks to explain as many as possible of its ob-

---

[1] Our tendencies speak and make us act, without being restrained by our conscience, although it sometimes warns us. I have my faults and vicious tendencies; awake I try to fight against them, and often enough I do not succumb to them. But in my dreams I always succumb, or, rather, I act at their direction, without fear or remorse. . . . Evidently, the visions which unfold in my thoughts, and which constitute the dream, are suggested by the stimuli which I feel and which my absent will does not try to repel.—ED.

[2] In a dream, a man is totally revealed to himself in his naked and wretched state. As he suspends the exercise of his will, he becomes the toy of all the passions from which, when awake, our conscience, horror, and fear defend us.—ED.

[3] In a dream, it is above all the instinctive man who is revealed. . . . Man returns, so to speak, to the natural state when he dreams; but the less acquired ideas have penetrated into his mind, the more his "tendencies to disagreement" with them keep their hold on him in his dreams.—Ed.

served characteristics from a single point of view, and which at the same time defines the relation of the dream to a more comprehensive sphere of phenomena, may be described as a theory of the dream. The individual theories of the dream will be distinguished from one another by their designating as essential this or that characteristic of dreams, and relating thereto their data and their explanations. It is not absolutely necessary that we should deduce from the theory of the dream a function, i.e., a use or any such similar rôle, but expectation, being as a matter of habit teleologically inclined, will nevertheless welcome those theories which afford us some insight into a function of dreams.

We have already become acquainted with many conceptions of the dream, which in this sense are more or less deserving of the name of dream-theories. The belief of the ancients that dreams were sent by the gods in order to guide the actions of man was a complete theory of the dream, which told them all that was worth knowing about dreams. Since dreams have become an object of biological research we have a greater number of theories, some of which, however, are very incomplete.

Provided we make no claim to completeness, we might venture on the following rough grouping of dream-theories, based on their fundamental conception of the degree and mode of the psychic activity in dreams:—

1. Theories, like those of Delbœuf, which allow the full psychic activity of the waking state to continue in our dreams. Here the psyche does not sleep; its apparatus remains intact; but under the conditions of the sleeping state, which differ from those of the waking state, it must in its normal functioning give results which differ from those of the waking state. As regards these theories, it may be questioned whether their authors are in a position to derive the distinction between dreaming and waking thought entirely from the conditions of the sleeping state. Moreover, they lack one possible access to a function of dreams; one does not understand to what purpose one dreams— why the complicated mechanism of the psychic apparatus should continue to operate even when it is placed under conditions to which it does not appear to be adapted. There are only two purposeful reactions in the place of the reaction of dreaming: to sleep dreamlessly, or to wake when affected by disturbing stimuli.

2. Theories which, on the contrary, assume for the dream a diminution of the psychic activity, a loosening of connections, and an impoverishment of the available material. In accordance with these theories, one must assume for sleep a psychological character entirely different from that given by Delbœuf. Sleep encroaches widely upon the psyche; it does not consist in the mere shutting it off from the outer world; on the contrary, it enters into its mechanism, and makes it for the time being unserviceable. If I may draw a comparison from psychiatry, I would say that the first group of theories construes the dream like a paranoia, while the second represents it as a type of mental deficiency or amentia.

The theory that only a fragment of the psychic activity paralysed by sleep finds expression in dreams is that by far the most favoured by medical writers, and by scientists in general. In so far as one may presuppose a general interest in dream-interpretation, one may indeed describe it as the most popular theory of dreams. It is remarkable how nimbly this particular theory avoids the greatest danger that threatens every dream-interpretation; that is, shipwreck on one of the contrasts incorporated in dreams. Since this theory regards dreams as the result of a partial waking (or, as Herbart puts it in his *Psychologie über den Traum,* "a gradual, partial, and at the same time very anomalous waking"), it is able to cover the whole series, from the inferior activities of dreams, which betray themselves by their absurdity, to fully concentrated intellectual activity, by a series of states of progressive awakening, ending in complete wakefulness.

Those who find the physiological mode of expression indispensable, or who deem it more scientific, will find this theory of dreams summarized in Binz's description (p. 43):—

"This state (of torpor), however, gradually comes to an end in the hours of early morning. The accumulated products of fatigue in the albumen of the brain gradually diminish. They are slowly decomposed, or carried away by the constantly flowing blood-stream. Here and there individual groups of cells can be distinguished as being awake, while around them all is still in a state of torpidity. The *isolated work of the individual groups* now appears before our clouded consciousness, which is still powerless to control other parts of the brain, which govern the associations. Hence the pictures created, which for the most part correspond to the objective impressions of the immediate past, combine with one another in a wild and uncontrolled fashion. As the number of brain-cells set free constantly increases, the irrationality of the dream becomes constantly less."

The conception of the dream as an incomplete, partial waking state, or traces of the influence of this conception, will of course be found in the works of all the modern physiologists and philosophers. It is most completely represented by Maury. It often seems as though this author conceives the state of being awake or asleep as susceptible of shifting from one anatomical region to another; each anatomical region seeming to him to be connected with a definite psychic function. Here I will merely suggest that even if the theory of partial waking were confirmed, its finer superstructure would still call for exhaustive consideration.

No function of dreams, of course, can emerge from this conception of the dream-life. On the contrary, Binz, one of the chief proponents of this theory, consistently enough denies that dreams have any status or importance. He says (p. 357): "All the facts, as we see them, urge us to characterize the dream as a *physical* process, in all cases useless, and in many cases definitely morbid."

The expression *physical* in reference to dreams (the word is emphasized by the author) points, of course, in more than one direction. In the first place, it refers to the aetiology of dreams, which was of special interest to Binz, as he was studying the experimental production of dreams by the administration of drugs. It is certainly in keeping with this kind of dream-theory to ascribe the incitement to dreaming, whenever possible, exclusively to somatic origins. Presented in the most extreme form the theory is as follows: After we have put ourselves to sleep by the banishment of stimuli, there would be no need to dream, and no reason for dreaming until the morning, when the gradual awakening through the fresh invasion of stimuli might be reflected in the phenomenon of dreaming. But, as a matter of fact, it is not possible to protect our sleep from stimuli; like the germs of life of which Mephistopheles complained, stimuli come to the sleeper from all directions—from without, from within, and even from all those bodily regions which never trouble us during the waking state. Thus our sleep is disturbed; now this, now that little corner of the psyche is jogged into the waking state, and the psyche functions for a while with the awakened fraction, yet is thankful to fall asleep again. The dream is the reaction to the disturbance of sleep caused by the stimulus, but it is, when all is said, a purely superfluous reaction.

The description of the dream—which, after all, remains an activity of the psychic organ—as a physical process has yet another connotation. So to describe it is to deny that the dream has the *dignity* of a psychic process. The old simile of "the ten fingers of a person ignorant of music running over the keyboard of an instrument" perhaps best illustrates in what esteem the dream is commonly held by the representatives of exact science. Thus conceived, it becomes something wholly insusceptible of interpretation. How could the ten fingers of a player ignorant of music perform a musical composition?

The theory of partial wakefulness did not escape criticism even by the earlier writers. Thus Burdach wrote in 1830: "If we say that dreaming is a partial waking, then, in the first place, neither the waking nor the sleeping state is explained thereby; secondly, this amounts only to saying that certain powers of the mind are active in dreams while others are at rest. But such irregularities occur throughout life. . . ." (p. 482).

The prevailing dream-theory which conceives the dream as a "physical" process finds a certain support in a very interesting conception of the dream which was first propounded by Robert in 1866, and which is seductive because it assigns to the dream a function or a useful result. As the basis of his theory Robert takes two objectively observable facts which we have already discussed in our consideration of dream-material (p. 144 above). These facts are: (1) that one very often dreams about the most insignificant impressions of the day; and (2) that one rarely carries over into the dream the absorbing interests of the day. Robert asserts as an indisputable fact that those matters which have been fully settled and solved never evoke dreams, but only such as lie incompleted in the mind, or touch it merely in passing (p. 10). "For this reason we cannot usually explain our dreams, since their causes are to be found *in sensory impressions of the preceding day which have not attained sufficient recognition on the part of the dreamer.*" The condition permitting an impression to reach the dream is, therefore, that this impression has been disturbed in its elaboration, or that it was too insignificant to lay claim to such elaboration.

Robert therefore conceives the dream "as a physical process of elimination which in its psychic reaction reaches the consciousness." *Dreams are eliminations of thoughts nipped in the bud.* "A man deprived of the capacity for dreaming would in time become mentally unbalanced, because an immense number of unfinished and unsolved thoughts and superficial impressions would accumulate in his brain, under the pressure of which all that should be incorporated in the memory as a completed whole would be stifled." The dream acts as a safety-valve for the over-burdened brain. *Dreams possess a healing and unburdening power* (p. 32).

We should misunderstand Robert if we were to ask him how representation in the dream could bring about an unburdening of the mind. The writer apparently concluded from these two peculiarities of the dream-material that during sleep such an elimination of worthless impressions is effected *somehow* as a somatic process; and that dreaming is not a special psychic process, but only the information which we receive of such elimination. Moreover, elimination is not the only thing that takes place in the mind during sleep. Robert himself adds that the stimuli of the day are likewise elaborated, and "what cannot be eliminated from the undigested thought-material lying in the mind *is bound up into a completed whole by mental clues borrowed from the imagination,* and is thus enrolled in the memory as a harmless phantasy-picture" (p. 23).

But it is in his criticism of the sources of dreams that Robert is most flatly opposed to the prevailing theory. Whereas according to this theory there would be no dream if the external and internal sensory stimuli did not repeatedly wake the mind, according to Robert the impulse to dream lies in the mind itself. It lies in the overloading of the mind, which demands discharge, and Robert considers, quite consistently, that those causes conditioning the dream which depend on the physical condition assume a subordinate rank, and could not incite dreams in a mind which contained no material for dream-formation derived from the waking consciousness. It is admitted, however, that the phantasy-images originating in the depths of the mind may be influenced by nervous stimuli (p. 48). Thus, according to Robert, dreams are not, after all, wholly dependent on the somatic element. Dreaming is, of course, not a psychic process, and it has no place among the psychic processes of the waking state; it is a nocturnal somatic process in the apparatus of mental activity, and has a function to perform, viz., to guard this apparatus against excessive strain, or, if we may be allowed to change the comparison, to cleanse the mind.

Another author, Yves Delage, bases his theory on the same characteristics of the dream—characteristics which are perceptible in the selection of the dream-material, and it is instructive to observe how a trifling twist in the conception of the same things gives a final result entirely different in its bearings.

Delage, having lost through death a person very dear to him, found that we either do not dream at all of what occupies us intently during the day, or that we begin to dream of it only after it is overshadowed by the other interests of the day. His investigations in respect of other persons corroborated the universality of this state of affairs. Concerning the dreams of newly-married people, he makes a comment which is admirable if it should prove to be generally true: *"S'ils ont été fortement épris, presque jamais ils n'ont rêvé l'un de l'autre avant le mariage ou pendant la lune de miel; et s'ils ont rêvé d'amour c'est pour être infidèles avec quelque personne indifférente ou odieuse."*[1] But of what does one dream? Delage recognizes that the material of our dreams consists of fragments and remnants of impressions, both from the last few days and from earlier periods. All that appears in our dreams, all that we may at first be inclined to consider the creation of the dream-life, proves on closer investigation to be unrecognized reproduction, *"souvenir inconscient."* But this representative material reveals one common characteristic; it originates from impressions which have probably affected our senses more forcibly than our mind, or from which the attention has been deflected soon after their occurrence. The less conscious, and at the same time the stronger an impression, the greater the prospect of its playing a part in our next dream.

These two categories of impressions—the insignificant and the undisposed-of—are essentially the same as those which were emphasized by Robert, but Delage gives them another significance, inasmuch as he believes that these impressions are capable of exciting dreams not because they are indifferent, but because they are not disposed of. The insignificant impressions also are, in a sense, not fully disposed of; they, too, owing to their character of new impressions, are *"autant de ressorts tendus,"*[2]

---

[1] If they are very much in love, they have almost never dreamed of each other before the marriage or during the honeymoon; and if they have dreamed of love, it was to be unfaithful with someone unimportant or distasteful.—ED.

[2] So many taut lines.—ED.

which will be relaxed during sleep. Still more entitled to a rôle in the dream than a weak and almost unnoticed impression is a vivid impression which has been accidentally retarded in its elaboration, or intentionally repressed. The psychic energy accumulated during the day by inhibition or suppression becomes the mainspring of the dream at night. In dreams psychically suppressed material achieves expression.[1]

Unfortunately Delage does not pursue this line of thought any farther; he is able to ascribe only the most insignificant rôle in our dreams to an independent psychic activity, and thus, in his theory of dreams, he reverts to the prevailing doctrine of a partial slumber of the brain: *"En somme le rêve est le produit de la pensée errante, sans but et sans direction, se fixant successivement sur les souvenirs, qui ont gardé assez d'intensité pour se placer sur sa route et l'arrêter au passage, établissant entre eux un lien tantôt faible et indécis, tantôt plus fort et plus serré, selon que l'activité actuelle du cerveau est plus ou moins abolie par le sommeil."*[2]

3. In a third group we may include those dream-theories which ascribe to the dreaming mind the capacity for and propensity to special psychic activities, which in the waking state it is able to exert either not at all or imperfectly. In most cases the manifestation of these activities is held to result in a useful function of dreams. The evaluations of dreams by the earlier psychologists fall chiefly within this category. I shall content myself, however, with quoting in their stead the assertion of Burdach, to the effect that dreaming "is the natural activity of the mind, which is not limited by the power of the individuality, nor disturbed by self-consciousness, nor directed by self-determination, but is the vitality of the sensible focus indulging in free play" (p. 486).

Burdach and others evidently consider this

revelling in the free use of its own powers as a state in which the mind refreshes itself and gathers fresh strength for the day's work; something, indeed, after the fashion of a vacation. Burdach therefore cites with approval the admirable words in which the poet Novalis lauds the power of the dream: "The dream is a bulwark against the regularity and commonplace character of life, a free recreation of the fettered phantasy, in which it intermingles all the images of life and interrupts the constant seriousness of the adult by the joyful play of the child. Without the dream we should surely grow old earlier, so that the dream may be considered, if not precisely as a gift from above, yet as a delightful exercise, a friendly companion on our pilgrimage to the grave."

The refreshing and healing activity of dreams is even more impressively described by Purkinje (p. 456). "The productive dreams in particular would perform these functions. These are the unconstrained play of the imagination, and have no connection with the events of the day. The mind is loth to continue the tension of the waking life, but wishes to relax it and recuperate from it. It creates, in the first place conditions opposed to those of the waking state. It cures sadness by joy, worry by hope and cheerfully distracting images, hatred by love and friendliness, and fear by courage and confidence; it appeases doubt by conviction and firm belief, and vain expectation by realization. Sleep heals many sore spots in the mind, which the day keeps continually open, by covering them and guarding them against fresh irritation. On this depends in some degree the consoling action of time." We all feel that sleep is beneficial to the psychic life, and the vague surmise of the popular consciousness is apparently loth to surrender the notion that dreaming is one of the ways in which sleep bestows its benefits.

The most original and most comprehensive attempt to explain dreaming as a special activity of the mind, which can freely unfold itself only in the sleeping state, is that made by Scherner in 1861. Scherner's book is written in a heavy and bombastic style and is inspired by an almost intoxicated enthusiasm for the subject, which is bound to repel us unless it can carry us away with it. It places so many difficulties in the way of an analysis that we gladly resort to the clearer and conciser presentation of Scherner's theories made by the philosopher Volkelt: "From these mystical conglomerations, from all these outbursts of splendour and radiance, there indeed flashes and shines an

---

[1] A novelist, Anatole France, expresses himself to a similar effect (*Le Lys Rouge*): "*Ce que nous voyons la nuit ce sont les restes malheureux que nous avons négligé dans la veille. Le rêve est souvent la revanche des choses qu'on méprise ou le reproche des êtres abandonnés.*" [What we see at night are the unhappy relics that we neglected while awake. The dream is often the revenge of things scorned or the reproach of beings deserted.—ED

[2] In short, the dream is the product of wandering thought, without end or direction, successively fixing on memories which have retained sufficient intensity to put themselves in the way and block the passage, establishing between themselves a connection sometimes weak and loose, sometimes stronger and closer, according to whether the actual work of the brain is more or less suppressed by sleep.—ED.

ominous semblance of meaning; but the path of the philosopher is not illumined thereby." Such is the criticism of Scherner's exposition by one of his own followers.

Scherner is not one of those writers for whom the mind carries its undiminished faculties into the dream-life. He even explains how, in our dreams, the centrality and spontaneous energy of the ego become enervated; how cognition, feeling, will, and imagination are transformed by this decentralization; how the remnant of these psychic forces has not a truly intellectual character, but is rather of the nature of a mechanism. But, on the other hand, that activity of the psyche which may be described as *phantasy,* freed from all rational governance, and hence no longer strictly controlled, rises to absolute supremacy in our dreams. To be sure, it borrows all its building-material from the memory of the waking state, but with this material it builds up structures which differ from those of the waking state as day differs from night. In our dreams it reveals itself as not only reproductive but also *productive.* Its peculiarities give the dream-life its singular character. It shows a preference for the *unlimited,* the *exaggerated,* the *prodigious;* but by its liberation from the inhibiting categories of thought, it gains a greater flexibility and agility, and indulges in pleasurable turns. It is excessivly sensitive to the delicate emotional stimuli of the mind, to its stirring and disturbing affects, and it rapidly recasts the inner life into an external, plastic visibility. The dream-phantasy *lacks the language of concepts.* What it wishes to say it must express in visible form; and since in this case the concept does not exert an inhibitory control, it depicts it in all the fulness, power, and breadth of visible form. But hereby its language, plain though it is, becomes cumbersome, awkward, and prolix. Plain speaking is rendered especially difficult by the fact that it dislikes expressing an object by its actual image, but prefers to select an *alien image,* if only the latter is able to express that particular aspect of the object which it is anxious to represent. Such is the *symbolizing activity* of the phantasy. . . . It is, moreover, very significant that the dream-phantasy reproduces objects not in detail, but only in outline, and in the freest possible manner. Its paintings, therefore, are like light and brilliant sketches. The dream-phantasy, however, does not stop at the mere representation of the object, but feels an internal urge to implicate the dream-ego to some extent with the object, and thus to give rise to action. The visual dream, for example, depicts gold coins lying in the street; the dreamer picks them up, rejoices, and carries them away.

According to Scherner, the material upon which the dream-phantasy exerts its artistic activity consists preponderantly of the organic sensory stimuli which are so obscure during the day (cf. p. 151 above); hence it is that the over-fantastic theory of Scherner, and perhaps too matter-of-fact theories of Wundt and other physiologists, though otherwise diametrically opposed to each other, are in perfect agreement in their assumptions with regard to dream-sources and dream-stimuli. But whereas, according to the physiological theory, the psychic reaction to the inner physical stimuli becomes exhausted with the arousing of any of the ideas appropriate to these stimuli (as these ideas then, by way of association, call to their aid other ideas, so that on reaching this stage the chain of psychic processes appears to terminate), according to Scherner, on the other hand, the physical stimuli merely supply the psyche with material which it may utilize in fulfilling its phantastic intentions. For Scherner dream-formation begins where, according to the views of other writers, it comes to an end.

What the dream-phantasy does with the physical stimuli cannot, of course, be regarded as purposeful. The phantasy plays a tantalizing game with them, and represents the organic source of the stimuli of the dream in question by any sort of plastic symbolism. Indeed, Scherner holds—though here Volkelt and others differ from him—that the dream-phantasy has a certain favourite symbol for the organism as a whole: namely, the house. Fortunately, however, for its representations, it does not seem to limit itself to this material; it may also employ a whole series of houses to designate a single organ; for example, very long streets of houses for the intestinal stimulus. In other dreams particular parts of the house may actually represent particular regions of the body, as in the headache-dream, when the ceiling of the room (which the dream sees covered with disgusting toad-like spiders) represents the head.

Quite apart from the symbol of the house, any other suitable object may be employed to represent those parts of the body which excite the dream. "Thus the breathing lungs find their symbol in the flaming stove with its windy roaring, the heart in hollow chests and baskets, the bladder in round, ball-shaped, or simply hollow objects. The man's dreams, when due to the sexual stimulus, make the dreamer find in the street the upper portion of a clarinet, or the mouthpiece of a tobacco-pipe, or, again, a piece of fur. The clarinet and tobacco-pipe represent the approximate form of the male sexual organ, while the fur represents the pubic hair. In the sexual dreams of the female, the tightness of the closed thighs may be symbolized by a narrow courtyard surrounded by houses, and the vagina by a very narrow, slippery and soft footpath, leading through the courtyard, upon which the dreamer is obliged to walk, in order perhaps to carry a letter to a man" (Volkelt, p. 39). It is particularly noteworthy that at the end of such a physically stimulated dream the phantasy, as it were, unmasks itself by representing the exciting organ or its function unconcealed. Thus the "tooth-excited dream" usually ends with the dreamer taking a tooth out of his mouth.

The dream-phantasy may, however, direct its attention not merely to the form of the exciting organ, but may even make the substance contained therein the object of symbolization. Thus, for example, the dream excited by the intestinal stimuli may lead us through muddy streets, the dream due to stimuli from the bladder to foaming water. Or the stimulus as such, the nature of its excitation, and the object which it covets, are represented symbolically. Or, again, the dream-ego enters into a concrete association with the symbolization of its own state; as, for example, when in the case of painful stimuli we struggle desperately with vicious dogs or raging bulls, or when in a sexual dream the dreamer sees herself pursued by a naked man. Disregarding all the possible prolixity of elaboration, a phantastic symbolizing activity remains as the central force of every dream. Volkelt, in his fine and enthusiastic essay, attempted to penetrate still further into the character of this phantasy, and to assign to the psychic activity thus recognized its position in a system of philosophical ideas, which, however, remains altogether too difficult of comprehension for anyone who is not prepared by previous training for the intuitive comprehension of philosophical modes of thought.

Scherner attributes no useful function to the activity of the symbolizing phantasy in dreams. In dreams the psyche plays with the stimuli which are offered to it. One might conjecture that it plays in a mischievous fashion. And we might be asked whether our detailed consideration of Scherner's dream-theory, the arbitrariness of which, and its deviation from the rules of all forms of research are only too obvious, can lead to any useful results. We might fitly reply that to reject Scherner's theory without previous examination would be imposing too arrogant a veto. This theory is based on the impressions produced by his dreams on a man who paid close attention to them, and who would appear to be personally very well equipped for tracing obscure psychic phenomena. Furthermore, it treats of a subject which (though rich in its contents and relations) has for thousands of years appeared mysterious to humanity, and to the elucidation of which science, strictly so called, has, as it confesses, contributed nothing beyond attempting—in uncompromising opposition to popular sentiment—to deny its content and significance. Finally, let us frankly admit that it seems as though we cannot very well avoid the phantastical in our attempts to explain dreams. We must remember also that there is such a thing as a phantasy of ganglion cells; the passage cited (p. 87) from a sober and exact investigator like Binz, which describes how the dawn of awakening floods the dormant cell-masses of the cerebral cortex, is not a whit less fanciful and improbable than Scherner's attempts at interpretation. I hope to be able to demonstrate that there is something real underlying these attempts, though the phenomena which he describes have been only vaguely recognized, and do not possess the character of universality that should entitle them to be the basis of a theory of dreams. For the present, Scherner's theory of dreams, in contrast to the medical theory, may perhaps lead us to realize between what extremes the explanation of dream-life is still unsteadily vacillating.

H. *The Relation between Dreams and Mental Diseases*

When we speak of the relation of dreams to mental derangement, we may mean three different things: (1) aetiological and clinical relations, as when a dream represents or initiates a psychotic condition, or occurs subsequently to such a condition; (2) changes which the dream-life undergoes in cases of mental disease; (3) inner relations between dreams and psychoses, analogies which point to an intimate relationship. These manifold relations between the two series of phenomena were in the early days of medical science—and are once more at the present time—a favourite theme of medical writers, as we may learn from the literature on the subject collated by Spitta, Radestock, Maury, and Tissié. Recently Sante de Sanctis has directed his attention to this relationship.[1] For the purposes of our discussion it will suffice merely to glance at this important subject.

As to the clinical and aetiological relations between dreams and the psychoses, I will report the following observations as examples: Hohnbaum asserts (see Krauss) that the first attack of insanity is frequently connected with a terrifying anxiety-dream, and that the predominating idea is related to this dream. Sante de Sanctis adduces similar observations in respect of paranoiacs, and declares the dream to be, in some of them, "la vraie cause déterminante de la folie."[2] The psychosis may come to life quite suddenly, simultaneously with the dream that contains its effective and delusive explanation, or it may develop slowly through subsequent dreams that have still to struggle against doubt. In one of de Sanctis's cases an intensively moving dream was accompanied by slight hysterical attacks, which, in their turn, were followed by an anxious melancholic state. Féré (cited by Tissié) refers to a dream which was followed by hysterical paralysis. Here the dream is presented as the aetiology of mental derangement, although we should be making a statement equally consistent with the facts were we to say that the first manifestation of the mental derangement occurred in the dream-life, that the disorder first broke through in the dream. In other instances, the morbid symptoms are included in the dream-life, or the psychosis remains confined to the dream-life. Thus Thomayer calls our attention to anxiety-dreams which must be conceived as the equivalent of epileptic attacks. Allison has described cases of nocturnal insanity (see Radestock), in which the subjects are apparently perfectly well in the day-time, while hallucinations, fits of frenzy, and the like regularly make their appearance at night. De Sanctis and Tissié record similar observations (the equivalent of a paranoic dream in an alcoholic, voices accusing a wife of infidelity). Tissié records many observations of recent date in which behaviour of a pathological character (based on delusory hypotheses, obsessive impulses) had their origin in dreams. Guislain describes a case in which sleep was replaced by an intermittent insanity.

We cannot doubt that one day the physician will concern himself not only with the psychology, but also with the psycho-pathology of dreams.

In cases of convalescence from insanity, it is often especially obvious that while the functions may be healthy by day the dream-life may still partake of the psychosis. Gregory is said to have been the first to call attention to such cases (see Krauss). Macario (cited by Tissié) gives an account of a maniac who, a week after his complete recovery, once more experienced in dreams the flux of ideas and the unbridled impulses of his disease.

Concerning the changes which the dream-life undergoes in chronic psychotics, little research has been undertaken as yet. On the other hand, early attention was given to the inner relationship between dreams and mental disturbances, a relationship which is demonstrated by the complete agreement of the manifestations occurring in each. According to Maury, Cabanis, in his Rapports du Physique et du Moral, was the first to call attention to this relationship; he was followed by Lélut, J. Moreau, and more particularly the philosopher Maine de Biran. The comparison between the two is of course older still. Radestock begins the chapter in which he deals with the subject by citing a number of opinions which insist on the analogy between insanity and dreaming. Kant says somewhere: "The lunatic is a dreamer in the waking state." According to Krauss, "Insanity is a dream in which the senses are awake." Schopenhauer terms the dream a brief insanity, and insanity a long dream. Hagen describes delirium as a dream-life which is inducted not by sleep but by disease. Wundt, in his Physiologische Psychologie, declares: "As a matter of fact we ourselves may in dreams experience almost all the manifestations which we observe in the asylums for the insane."

The specific points of agreement in consequence of which such a comparison commends itself to our judgment are enumerated by Spitta, who groups them (very much as Maury has done) as follows: "(1) Suspension, or at least retardation of self-consciousness, and consequently ignorance of the condition as such, the impossibility of astonishment, and a lack of moral consciousness. (2) Modified perception of the sensory organs; that is, perception is as a rule diminished in dreams, and greatly enhanced in insanity. (3) Mutual combination of ideas exclusively in accordance with the laws of association and reproduction, hence automatic series-formations: hence again a lack of proportion in the relations between ideas (ex-

[1] Among the more recent authors who have occupied themselves with these relations are: Féré, Ideler, Laségue, Pichon, Régis Vespa, Giessler, Kazodowsky, Pachantoni, and others.

[2] The real determining cause of the madness.—ED.

aggerations, phantasms); and the results of all this: (4) Changes in—for example, inversions of—the personality, and sometimes of the idiosyncrasies of the character (perversities)."

Radestock adds a few additional data concerning the analogous nature of the material of dreams and of mental derangement: "The greatest number of hallucinations and illusions are found in the sphere of the senses of sight and hearing and general sensation. As in dreams, the fewest elements are supplied by the senses of smell and taste. The fever-patient, like the dreamer, is assailed by reminiscences from the remote past; what the waking and healthy man seems to have forgotten is recollected in sleep and in disease." The analogy between dreams and the psychoses receives its full value only when, like a family resemblance, it is extended to the subtler points of mimicry, and even the individual peculiarities of facial expression.

"To him who is tortured by physical and mental sufferings the dream accords what has been denied him by reality, to wit, physical well-being, and happiness; so, too, the insane see radiant images of happiness, eminence, and wealth. The supposed possession of estates and the imaginary fulfilment of wishes, the denial or destruction of which have actually been a psychic cause of the insanity, often form the main content of the delirium. The woman who has lost a dearly beloved child experiences in her delirium the joys of maternity; the man who has suffered reverses of fortune deems himself immensely wealthy; and the jilted girl sees herself tenderly beloved."

(This passage from Radestock is an abstract of a brilliant exposition of Griesinger's (p. 111), which reveals, with the greatest clarity, *wish-fulfilment* as a characteristic of the imagination common to dreams and to the psychoses. My own investigations have taught me that here is to be found the key to a psychological theory of dreams and of the psychoses.)

"Absurd combinations of ideas and weakness of judgment are the main characteristics of the dream and of insanity." The *over-estimation* of one's own mental capacity, which appears absurd to sober judgment, is found alike in both, and the *rapid flux of imaginings* in the dream corresponds to the *flux of ideas* in the psychoses. Both are devoid of any *measure of time*. The *splitting of the personality* in dreams, which, for instance, distributes one's own knowledge between two persons, one of whom, the strange person, corrects one's own ego in

the dream, entirely corresponds with the well-known splitting of the personality in hallucinatory paranoia; the dreamer, too, hears his own thoughts expressed by strange voices. Even the constant delusive ideas find their analogy in the stereotyped and recurring pathological dream (*rêve obsédant*). After recovering from delirium, patients not infrequently declare that the whole period of their illness appeared to them like an uncomfortable dream; indeed, they inform us that sometimes during their illness they have suspected that they were only dreaming, just as often happens in the sleep-dream.

In view of all this, it is not surprising that Radestock should summarize his own opinion, and that of many others, in the following words: "Insanity, an abnormal morbid phenomenon, is to be regarded as an enhancement of the periodically recurring normal dream-state" (p. 228).

Krauss attempted to base the relationship between the dream and insanity upon their aetiology (or rather upon the sources of excitation), thus, perhaps, making the relationship even more intimate than was possible on the basis of the analogous nature of the phenomena manifested. According to him, the fundamental element common to both is, as we have already learned, the organically conditioned sensation, the sensation of physical stimuli, the general sensation arising out of contributions from all the organs (cf. Peisse, cited by Maury, p. 52).

The undeniable agreement between dreams and mental derangement, extending even to characteristic details, constitutes one of the strongest confirmations of the medical theory of dream-life, according to which the dream is represented as a useless and disturbing process, and as the expression of a diminished psychic activity. One cannot expect, for the present, to derive the final explanation of the dream from the psychic derangements, since, as is well known, our understanding of the origin of the latter is still highly unsatisfactory. It is very probable, however, that a modified conception of the dream must also influence our views regarding the inner mechanism of mental disorders, and hence we may say that we are working towards the explanation of the psychoses when we endeavour to elucidate the mystery of dreams.

ADDENDUM 1909

I shall have to justify myself for not extending my summary of the literature of dream-problems to cover the period between the first appearance of this book and the publication of the second edition. This justification may not seem very satisfactory to the reader; none the less, to me it was decisive. The motives which induced me to summarize the treatment of dreams in the literature of the subject have been exhausted by the foregoing introduction; to have continued this would have cost me a great deal of effort and would not have been particularly useful or instructive. For the interval in question—a period of nine years—has yielded nothing new or valuable as regards the conception of dreams, either in actual material or in novel points of view. In most of the literature which has appeared since the publication of my own work the latter has not been mentioned or discussed; it has, of course, received the least attention from the so-called "research-workers on dreams," who have thus afforded a brilliant example of the aversion to learning anything new so characteristic of the scientist. *"Les savants ne sont pas curieux,"* [1] said the scoffer Anatole France. If there were such a thing in science as the right of revenge, I in my turn should be justified in ignoring the literature which has appeared since the publication of this book. The few reviews which have appeared in the scientific journals are so full of misconceptions and lack of comprehension that my only possible answer to my critics would be a request that they should read this book over again—or perhaps merely that they should read it!

In the works of those physicians who make use of the psycho-analytic method of treatment a great many dreams have been recorded and interpreted in accordance with my directions. In so far as these works go beyond the confirmation of my own assertions, I have noted their results in the context of my exposition. A supplementary bibliography at the end of this volume comprises the most important of these new publications. The comprehensive work on the dream by Sante de Sanctis, of which a German translation appeared soon after its publication, was produced simultaneously with my own, so that I could not review his results, nor could he comment upon mine. I am sorry to have to express the opinion that this laborious work is exceedingly poor in ideas, so poor that one could never divine from it the possibility of the problems which I have treated in these pages.

I can thing of only two publications which

touch on my own treatment of the dream-problems. A young philosopher, H. Swoboda, who has ventured to extend W. Fliess's discovery of biological periodicity (in series of twenty-three and twenty-eight days) to the psychic field, has produced an imaginative essay,[2] in which, among other things, he has used this key to solve the riddle of dreams. Such a solution, however, would be an inadequate estimate of the significance of dreams. The material content of dreams would be explained by the coincidence of all those memories which, on the night of the dream, complete one of these biological periods for the first or the nth time. A personal communication of the author's led me to assume that he himself no longer took this theory very seriously. But it seems that I was mistaken in this conclusion: I shall record in another place some observations made with reference to Swoboda's thesis, which did not, however, yield convincing results. It gave me far greater pleasure to find by chance, in an unexpected quarter, a conception of the dream which is in complete agreement with the essence of my own. The relevant dates preclude the possibility that this conception was influenced by reading my book: I must therefore hail this as the only demonstrable concurrence with the essentials of my theory of dreams to be found in the literature of the subject. The book which contains the passage that I have in mind was published (in its second edition) in 1910, by Lynkeus, under the title *Phantasien eines Realisten.*[3]

ADDENDUM 1914

The above *apologia* was written in 1909. Since then, the state of affairs has certainly undergone a change; my contribution to the "interpretation of dreams" is no longer ignored in the literature of the subject. But the new situation makes it even more impossible to continue the foregoing summary. *The Interpretation of Dreams* has evoked a whole series of new contentions and problems, which have been expounded by the authors in the most varied fashions. But I cannot discuss these works until I have developed the theories to which their authors have referred. Whatever has appeared to me as valuable in this recent literature I

[1] The learned are not inquisitive.—ED.

[2] H. Swoboda, *Die Perioden des Menschlichen Organismus,* 1904.

[3] Cf. *Josef Popper-Lynkeus und die Theorie des Traumes* (1923) in vol. xi of my *Gesammelten Schriften.*

have accordingly reviewed in the course of the following exposition.

II. THE METHOD OF DREAM INTERPRETATION

The Analysis of a Specimen Dream

THE epigraph on the title-page of this volume indicates the tradition to which I prefer to ally myself in my conception of the dream. I am proposing to show that dreams are capable of interpretation; and any contributions to the solution of the problems which have already been discussed will emerge only as possible by-products in the accomplishment of my special task. On the hypothesis that dreams are susceptible of interpretation, I at once find myself in disagreement with the prevailing doctrine of dreams—in fact, with all the theories of dreams, excepting only that of Scherner, for *to interpret a dream* is to specify its *meaning*, to replace it by something which takes its position in the concatenation of our psychic activities as a link of definite importance and value. But, as we have seen, the scientific theories of the dream leave no room for a problem of dream-interpretation; since, in the first place, according to these theories, dreaming is not a psychic activity at all, but a somatic process which makes itself known to the psychic apparatus by means of symbols. Lay opinion has always been opposed to these theories. It asserts its privilege of proceeding illogically, and although it admits that dreams are incomprehensible and absurd, it cannot summon up the courage to deny that dreams have any significance. Led by a dim intuition, it seems rather to assume that dreams have a meaning, albeit a hidden one; that they are intended as a substitute for some other thought-process, and that we have only to disclose this substitute correctly in order to discover the hidden meaning of the dream.

The unscientific world, therefore, has always endeavoured to *interpret* dreams, and by applying one or the other of two essentially different methods. The first of these methods envisages the dream-content as a whole, and seeks to replace it by another content, which is intelligible and in certain respects analogous. This is symbolic dream-interpretation; and of course it goes to pieces at the very outset in the case of those dreams which are not only unintelligible but confused. The construction which the biblical Joseph placed upon the dream of Pharaoh furnishes an example of this method. The seven fat kine, after which came seven lean ones that devoured the former, were a symbolic substitute for seven years of famine in the land of Egypt, which according to the prediction were to consume all the surplus that seven fruitful years had produced. Most of the artificial dreams contrived by the poets [1] are intended for some such symbolic interpretation, for they reproduce the thought conceived by the poet in a guise not unlike the disguise which we are wont to find in our dreams.

The idea that the dream concerns itself chiefly with the future, whose form it surmises in advance—a relic of the prophetic significance with which dreams were once invested—now becomes the motive for translating into the future the meaning of the dream which has been found by means of symbolic interpretation.

A demonstration of the manner in which one arrives at such a symbolic interpretation cannot, of course, be given. Success remains a matter of ingenious conjecture, of direct intuition, and for this reason dream-interpretation has naturally been elevated into an art which seems to depend upon extraordinary gifts. [2] The second of the two popular methods of dream-interpretation entirely abandons such claims. It might be described as the *cipher method*, since it treats the dream as a kind of secret code in which every sign is translated into another sign of known meaning, according to an established key. For example, I have dreamt of a letter, and also of a funeral or the like; I consult a "dream-book," and I find that "letter" is to be translated by "vexation" and "funeral" by "engagement." It now remains to establish a connection, which I am again to assume as pertaining to the future, by means of the rigmarole which I have deciphered. An interesting variant of this cipher procedure, a variant in which its character of purely me-

---

[1] In a novel *Gradiva*, by the poet W. Jensen, I chanced to discover several fictitious dreams, which were perfectly correct in their construction, and could be interpreted as though they had not been invented, but had been dreamt by actual persons. The poet declared, upon my inquiry, that he was unacquainted with my theory of dreams. I have made use of this agreement between my investigations and the creations of the poet as a proof of the correctness of my method of dream-analysis (*Der Wahn und die Träume* in W. Jensen's *Gradiva*, vol. i of the *Schriften zur angewandten Seelenkunde*, 1906, edited by myself, *Ges. Schriften*, vol. ix).

[2] Aristotle expressed himself in this connection by saying that the best interpreter of dreams is he who can best grasp similarities. For dream-pictures, like pictures in water, are disfigured by the motion (of the water), so that he hits the target best who is able to recognize the true picture in the distorted one (Büchsenschütz, p. 65).

chanical transference is to a certain extent corrected, is presented in the work on dream-interpretation by Artemidoros of Daldis[1]. Here not only the dream-content, but also the personality and social position of the dreamer are taken into consideration, so that the same dream-content has a significance for the rich man, the married man, or the orator, which is different from that which applies to the poor man, the bachelor, or, let us say, the merchant. The essential point, then, in this procedure is that the work of interpretation is not applied to the entirety of the dream, but to each portion of the dream-content severally, as though the dream were a conglomerate in which each fragment calls for special treatment. Incoherent and confused dreams are certainly those that have been responsible for the

invention of the cipher method.[2]

The worthlessness of both these popular methods of interpretation does not admit of discussion. As regards the scientific treatment of the subject, the symbolic method is limited in its application, and is not susceptible of a general exposition. In the cipher method everything depends upon whether the *key*, the dream-book, is reliable, and for that all guarantees are lacking. So that one might be tempted to grant the contention of the philosophers and psychiatrists, and to dismiss the problem of dream-interpretation as altogether fanciful.[3]

I have, however, come to think differently. I have been forced to perceive that here, once more, we have one of those not infrequent cases where an ancient and stubbornly retained popular belief seems to have come nearer to the truth of the matter than the opinion of modern science. I must insist that the dream actually does possess a meaning, and that a scientific method of dream-interpretation is possible. I arrived at my knowledge of this method in the following manner:

For years I have been occupied with the resolution of certain psycho-pathological structures—hysterical phobias, obsessional ideas, and the like—with therapeutic intentions. I have been so occupied, in fact, ever since I heard the significant statement of Joseph

---

[1] Artemidoros of Daldis, born probably in the beginning of the second century of our calendar, has furnished us with the most complete and careful elaboration of dream-interpretation as it existed in the Graeco-Roman world. As Gompertz has emphasized, he ascribed great importance to the consideration that dreams ought to be interpreted on the basis of observation and experience, and he drew a definite line between his own art and other methods, which he considered fraudulent. The principle of his art of interpretation is, according to Gompertz, identical with that of magic: *i.e.*, the principle of association. The thing dreamed meant what it recalled to the memory—to the memory, of course, of the dream-interpreter! This fact—that the dream may remind the interpreter of various things, and every interpreter of different things—leads, of course, to uncontrollable arbitrariness and uncertainty. The technique which I am about to describe differs from that of the ancients in one essential point, namely, in that it imposes upon the dreamer himself the work of interpretation. Instead of taking into account whatever may occur to the dream-interpreter, it considers only what occurs to the dreamer in connection with the dream-element concerned. According to the recent records of the missionary, Tfinkdjit (*Anthropos*, 1913), it would seem that the modern dream-interpreters of the Orient likewise attribute much importance to the co-operation of the dreamer. Of the dream-interpreters among the Mesopotamian Arabs this writer relates as follows: "*Pour interpréter exactement un songe les oniromanciens les plus habiles s'informent de ceux qui les consultent de toutes les circonstances qu'ils regardent nécessaires pour la bonne explication. . . . En un mot, nos oniromanciens ne laissent aucune circonstance leur échapper et ne donnent l'interprétation désirée avant d'avoir parfaitement saisi et reçu toutes les interrogations désirables.*" [To interpret a dream exactly, the most practised interpreters of dreams learn from those who consult them all circumstances which they regard as necessary for a good explanation. . . . . In a word, our interpreters allow no circumstance to be overlooked and do not give the desired interpretation before perfectly taking and apprehending all desirable questions.] Among these questions one always finds demands for precise information in respect to near relatives (parents, wife, children) as well as the following formula: *habistine in hoc nocte copulam conjugalem ante vel post somnium?* [Did you this night have conjugal copulation before or after the dream?] "*L'idée dominante dans l'interprétation des songes consiste à expliquer le rêve par son opposé.*" [The dominant idea in the interpretation of dreams consists in explaining the dream by its opposite.]

[2] Dr. Alfred Robitsek calls my attention to the fact that Oriental dream-books, of which ours are pitiful plagiarisms, commonly undertake the interpretation of dream-elements in accordance with the assonance and similarity of words. Since these relationships must be lost by translation into our language, the incomprehensibility of the equivalents in our popular "dream-books" is hereby explained. Information as to the extraordinary significance of puns and the play upon words in the old Oriental cultures may be found in the writings of Hugo Winckler. The finest example of a dream-interpretation which has come down to us from antiquity is based on a play upon words. Artemidoros relates the following (p. 225): "But it seems to me that Aristandros gave a most happy interpretation to Alexander of Macedon. When the latter held Tyros encompassed and in a state of siege, and was angry and depressed over the great waste of time, he dreamed that he saw a Satyr dancing on his shield. It happened that Aristandros was in the neighbourhood of Tyros, and in the escort of the king, who was waging war on the Syrians. By dividing the word Satyros into σά and τύρος, he induced the king to become more aggressive in the siege. And thus Alexander became master of the city." (Σὰ Τύρος=Thine is Tyros.) The dream, indeed, is so intimately connected with verbal expression that Ferenczi justly remarks that every tongue has its own dream-language. A dream is, as a rule, not to be translated into other languages.

[3] After the completion of my manuscript, a paper by Stumpf came to my notice which agrees with my work in attempting to prove that the dream is full of meaning and capable of interpretation. But the interpretation is undertaken by means of an allegorizing symbolism, and there is no guarantee that the procedure is generally applicable.

Breuer, to the effect that in these structures, regarded as morbid symptoms, solution and treatment go hand in hand.[1] Where it has been possible to trace a pathological idea back to those elements in the psychic life of the patient to which it owed its origin, this idea has crumbled away, and the patient has been relieved of it. In view of the failure of our other therapeutic efforts, and in the face of the mysterious character of these pathological conditions, it seemed to me tempting, in spite of all the difficulties, to follow the method initiated by Breuer until a complete elucidation of the subject had been achieved. I shall have occasion elsewhere to give a detailed account of the form which the technique of this procedure has finally assumed, and of the results of my efforts. In the course of these psycho-analytic studies, I happened upon the question of dream-interpretation. My patients, after I had pledged them to inform me of all the ideas and thoughts which occurred to them in connection with a given theme, related their dreams, and thus taught me that a dream may be interpolated in the psychic concatenation, which may be followed backwards from a pathological idea into the patient's memory. The next step was to treat the dream itself as a symptom, and to apply to it the method of interpretation which had been worked out for such symptoms.

For this a certain psychic preparation on the part of the patient is necessary. A twofold effort is made, to stimulate his attentiveness in respect of his psychic perceptions, and to eliminate the critical spirit in which he is ordinarily in the habit of viewing such thoughts as come to the surface. For the purpose of self-observation with concentrated attention it is advantageous that the patient should take up a restful position and close his eyes; he must be explicitly instructed to renounce all criticism of the thought-formations which he may perceive. He must also be told that the success of the psycho-analysis depends upon his noting and communicating everything that passes through his mind, and that he must not allow himself to suppress one idea because it seems to him unimportant or irrelevant to the subject, or another because it seems nonsensical. He must preserve an absolute impartiality in respect to his ideas; for if he is unsuccessful in finding the desired solution of the dream, the obsessional idea, or the like, it will be because he permits himself to be critical of them.

[1] *Studien über Hysterie*, 1895. [Compare page 26 above.]

I have noticed in the course of my psychoanalytical work that the psychological state of a man in an attitude of reflection is entirely different from that of a man who is observing his psychic processes. In reflection there is a greater play of psychic activity than in the most attentive self-observation; this is shown even by the tense attitude and the wrinkled brow of the man in a state of reflection, as opposed to the mimic tranquillity of the man observing himself. In both cases there must be concentrated attention, but the reflective man makes use of his critical faculties, with the result that he rejects some of the thoughts which rise into consciousness after he has become aware of them, and abruptly interrupts others, so that he does not follow the lines of thought which they would otherwise open up for him; while in respect of yet other thoughts he is able to behave in such a manner that they do not become conscious at all—that is to say, they are suppressed before they are perceived. In self-observation, on the other hand, he has but one task—that of suppressing criticism; if he succeeds in doing this, an unlimited number of thoughts enter his consciousness which would otherwise have eluded his grasp. With the aid of the material thus obtained—material which is new to the self-observer—it is possible to achieve the interpretation of pathological ideas, and also that of dream-formations. As will be seen, the point is to induce a psychic state which is in some degree analogous, as regards the distribution of psychic energy (mobile attention), to the state of the mind before falling asleep—and also, of course, to the hypnotic state. On falling asleep the *undesired ideas* emerge, owing to the slackening of a certain arbitrary (and, of course, also critical) action, which is allowed to influence the trend of our ideas; we are accustomed to speak of fatigue as the reason of this slackening; the emerging undesired ideas are changed into visual and auditory images. In the condition which it utilized for the analysis of dreams and pathological ideas, this activity is purposely and deliberately renounced, and the psychic energy thus saved (or some part of it) is employed in attentively tracking the undesired thoughts which now come to the surface—thoughts which retain their identity as ideas (in which the condition differs from the state of falling asleep). *Undesired ideas are thus changed into desired ones.*

There are many people who do not seem to find it easy to adopt the required attitude toward the apparently "freely rising" ideas, and to renounce the criticism which is otherwise applied to them. The "undesired ideas" habitually evoke the most violent resistance, which seeks to prevent them from coming to the surface. But if we may credit our great poet-philosopher Friedrich Schiller, the essential condition of poetical creation includes a very similar attitude. In a certain passage in his correspondence with Körner (for the tracing of which we are indebted to Otto Rank), Schiller replies in the following words to a friend who complains of his lack of creative power: "The reason for your complaint lies, it seems to me, in the constraint which your intellect imposes upon your imagination. Here I will make an observation, and illustrate it by an allegory. Apparently it is not good—and indeed it hinders the creative work of the mind—if the intellect examines too closely the ideas already pouring in, as it were, at the gates. Regarded in isolation, an idea may be quite insignificant, and venturesome in the extreme, but it may acquire importance from an idea which follows it; perhaps, in a certain collocation with other ideas, which may seem equally absurd, it may be capable of furnishing a very serviceable link. The intellect cannot judge all these ideas unless it can retain them until it has considered them in connection with these other ideas. In the case of a creative mind, it seems to me, the intellect has withdrawn its watchers from the gates, and the ideas rush in pell-mell, and only then does it review and inspect the multitude. You worthy critics, or whatever you may call yourselves, are ashamed or afraid of the momentary and passing madness which is found in all real creators, the longer or shorter duration of which distinguishes the thinking artist from the dreamer. Hence your complaints of unfruitfulness, for you reject too soon and discriminate too severely" (letter of December 1, 1788).

And yet, such a withdrawal of the watchers from the gates of the intellect, as Schiller puts it, such a translation into the condition of uncritical self-observation, is by no means difficult.

Most of my patients accomplish it after my first instructions. I myself can do so very completely, if I assist the process by writing down the ideas that flash through my mind. The quantum of psychic energy by which the critical activity is thus reduced, and by which the intensity of self-observation may be increased, varies considerably according to the subject-matter upon which the attention is to be fixed.

The first step in the application of this procedure teaches us that one cannot make the dream as a whole the object of one's attention, but only the individual components of its content. If I ask a patient who is as yet unpractised: "What occurs to you in connection with this dream?" he is unable, as a rule, to fix upon anything in his psychic field of vision. I must first dissect the dream for him; then, in connection with each fragment, he gives me a number of ideas which may be described as the *thoughts behind* this part of the dream. In this first and important condition, then, the method of dream-interpretation which I employ diverges from the popular, historical and legendary method of interpretation by symbolism and approaches more nearly to the second or *cipher method*. Like this, it is an interpretation in detail, not *en masse;* like this, it conceives the dream, from the outset, as something built up, as a conglomerate of psychic formations.

In the course of my psycho-analysis of neurotics I have already subjected perhaps more than a thousand dreams to interpretation, but I do not wish to use this material now as an introduction to the theory and technique of dream-interpretation. For quite apart from the fact that I should lay myself open to the objection that these are the dreams of neuropaths, so that the conclusions drawn from them would not apply to the dreams of healthy persons, there is another reason that impels me to reject them. The theme to which these dreams point is, of course, always the history of the malady that is responsible for the neurosis. Hence every dream would require a very long introduction, and an investigation of the nature and aetiological conditions of the psychoneuroses, matters which are in themselves novel and exceedingly strange, and which would therefore distract attention from the dream-problem proper. My purpose is rather to prepare the way, by the solution of the dream-problem, for the solution of the more difficult problems of the psychology of the neuroses. But if I eliminate the dreams of neurotics, which constitute my principal material, I cannot be too fastidious in my treatment of the rest. Only those dreams are left which have been incidentally related to me by healthy persons of my acquaintance, or which I find given as examples in the literature of dream-life. Unfortunately, in all these dreams I am deprived of the analysis without which I cannot find the meaning of the dream. My mode of procedure is, of course, less easy than that of the popular cipher method, which translates the given dream-content by reference to an established key; I, on the contrary, hold that the same dream-content may conceal a different meaning in the case of different persons, or in different connections. I must, therefore, resort to my own dreams as a source of abundant and convenient material, furnished by a person who is more or less normal, and containing references to many incidents of everyday life. I shall certainly be confronted with doubts as to the trustworthiness of these *self-analyses* and it will be said that arbitrariness is by no means excluded in such analyses. In my own judgment, conditions are more likely to be favourable in self-observation than in the observation of others; in any case, it is permissible to investigate how much can be accomplished in the matter of dream-interpretation by means of self-analysis. There are other difficulties which must be overcome in my own inner self. One has a comprehensible aversion to exposing so many intimate details of one's own psychic life, and one does not feel secure against the misinterpretations of strangers. But one must be able to transcend such considerations. *"Tout psychologiste,"* writes Delbœuf, *"est obligé de faire l'aveu même de ses faiblesses s'il croît par là jeter du jour sur quelque problème obscur."*[1] And I may assume for the reader that his initial interest in the indiscretions which I must commit will very soon give way to an exclusive engrossment in the psychological problems elucidated by them.[2]

I shall therefore select one of my own dreams for the purpose of elucidating my method of interpretation. Every such dream necessitates a preliminary statement; so that I must now beg the reader to make my interests his own for a time, and to become absorbed, with me, in the most trifling details of my life; for an interest in the hidden significance of dreams imperatively demands just such a transference.

PRELIMINARY STATEMENT

In the summer of 1895 I had treated psychoanalytically a young lady who was an intimate friend of mine and of my family. It will be understood that such complicated relations may excite manifold feelings in the physician, and especially the psychotherapist. The personal interest of the physician is greater, but his authority less. If he fails, his friendship with the patient's relatives is in danger of being undermined. In this case, however, the treatment ended in partial success; the patient was cured of her hysterical anxiety, but not of all her somatic symptoms. At that time I was not yet quite sure of the criteria which denote the final cure of an hysterical case, and I expected her to accept a solution which did not seem acceptable to her. In the midst of this disagreement, we discontinued the treatment for the summer holidays. One day a younger colleague, one of my most intimate friends, who had visited the patient—Irma—and her family in their country residence, called upon me. I asked him how Irma was, and received the reply: "She is better, but not quite well." I realize that these words of my friend Otto's, or the tone of voice in which they were spoken, annoyed me. I thought I heard a reproach in the words, perhaps to the effect that I had promised the patient too much, and—rightly or wrongly—I attributed Otto's apparent taking sides against me to the influence of the patient's relatives, who, I assumed, had never approved of my treatment. This disagreeable impression, however, did not become clear to me, nor did I speak of it. That same evening I wrote the clinical history of Irma's case, in order to give it, as though to justify myself, to Dr. M, a mutual friend, who was at that time the leading personality in our circle. During the night (or rather in the early morning) I had the following dream, which I recorded immediately after waking.[3]

DREAM OF JULY 23—24, 1895

A great hall—a number of guests, whom we are receiving—among them Irma, whom I immediately take aside, as though to answer her letter, and to reproach her for not yet accepting the "solution." I say to her: "If you still have pains, it is really only your own fault."—She answers: "If you only knew what pains I have now in the throat, stomach, and abdomen—I am choked by them." I am startled, and look at her. She looks pale and puffy. I think that after all I must be overlooking some organic affection. I take her to the window and look into her throat. She offers some resistance to this, like a woman who has a set of false teeth. I

---

[1] Every psychologist is obliged to admit even his own weaknesses, if he thinks by that he may throw light on a difficult problem.—ED.

[2] However, I will not omit to mention, in qualification of the above statement, that I have practically never reported a complete interpretation of a dream of my own. And I was probably right not to trust too far to the reader's discretion.

[3] This is the first dream which I subjected to an exhaustive interpretation.

think, surely, she doesn't need them.—The mouth then opens wide, and I find a large white spot on the right, and elsewhere I see extensive grayish-white scabs adhering to curiously curled formations, which are evidently shaped like the turbinal bones of the nose.— I quickly call Dr. M, who repeats the examination and confirms it.. . .Dr. M looks quite unlike his usual self; he is very pale, he limps, and his chin is clean-shaven.. . .Now my friend Otto, too, is standing beside her, and my friend Leopold percusses her covered chest, and says "She has a dullness below, on the left," and also calls attention to an infiltrated portion of skin on the left shoulder (which I can feel, in spite of the dress).. . .M says: "There's no doubt that it's an infection, but it doesn't matter; dysentery will follow and the poison will be eliminated.".. .We know, too, precisely how the infection originated. My friend Otto, not long ago, gave her, when she was feeling unwell, an injection of a preparation of propyl...propyls...propionic acid...trimethylamin (the formula of which I see before me, printed in heavy type).. . .One doesn't give such injections so rashly...Probably, too, the syringe was not clean.

This dream has an advantage over many others. It is at once obvious to what events of the preceding day it is related, and of what subject it treats. The preliminary statement explains these matters. The news of Irma's health which I had received from Otto, and the clinical history, which I was writing late into the night, had occupied my psychic activities even during sleep. Nevertheless, no one who had read the preliminary report, and had knowledge of the content of the dream, could guess what the dream signified. Nor do I myself know. I am puzzled by the morbid symptoms of which Irma complains in the dream, for they are not the symptoms for which I treated her. I smile at the nonsensical idea of an injection of propionic acid, and at Dr. M's attempt at consolation. Towards the end the dream seems more obscure and quicker in tempo than at the beginning. In order to learn the significance of all these details I resolve to undertake an exhaustive analysis.

Analysis

The hall—a number of guests, whom we are receiving. We were living that summer at *Bellevue,* an isolated house on one of the hills adjoining the Kahlenberg. This house was orig-inally built as a place of entertainment, and therefore has unusually lofty, hall-like rooms. The dream was dreamed in *Bellevue,* a few days before my wife's birthday. During the day my wife had mentioned that she expected several friends, and among them Irma, to come to us as guests for her birthday. My dream, then, anticipates this situation: It is my wife's birthday, and we are receiving a number of people, among them Irma, as guests in the large hall of *Bellevue.*

I reproach Irma for not having accepted the "solution." I say, "If you still have pains, it is really your own fault." I might even have said this while awake; I may have actually said it. At that time I was of the opinion (recognized later to be incorrect) that my task was limited to informing patients of the hidden meaning of their symptoms. Whether they then accepted or did not accept the solution upon which success depended—for that I was not responsible. I am grateful to this error, which, fortunately, has now been overcome, since it made life easier for me at a time when, with all my unavoidable ignorance, I was expected to effect successful cures. But I note that, in the speech which I make to Irma in the dream, I am above all anxious that I shall not be blamed for the pains which she still suffers. If it is Irma's own fault, it cannot be mine. Should the purpose of the dream be looked for in this quarter?

Irma's complaints—pains in the neck, abdomen, and stomach; she is choked by them. Pains in the stomach belonged to the symptom-complex of my patient, but they were not very prominent; she complained rather of qualms and a feeling of nausea. Pains in the neck and abdomen and constriction of the throat played hardly any part in her case. I wonder why I have decided upon this choice of symptoms in the dream; for the moment I cannot discover the reason.

She looks pale and puffy. My patient had always a rosy complexion. I suspect that here another person is being substituted for her.

I am startled at the idea that I may have overlooked some organic affection. This, as the reader will readily believe, is a constant fear with the specialist who sees neurotics almost exclusively, and who is accustomed to ascribe to hysteria so many manifestations which other physicians treat as organic. On the other hand, I am haunted by a faint doubt—I do not know whence it comes—whether my alarm is altogether honest. If Irma's pains are indeed of organic origin, it is not my duty to cure them. My treatment, of course, removes only hysterical pains. It seems to me, in fact, that I wish to find an error in the diagnosis; for then I could not be reproached with failure to effect a cure.

I take her to the window in order to look into her throat. She resists a little, like a woman who has false teeth. I think to myself, she does not need them. I had never had occasion to inspect Irma's oral cavity. The incident in the dream reminds me of an examination, made some time before, of a governess who at first produced an impression of youthful beauty, but who, upon opening her mouth, took certain measures to conceal her denture. Other memories of medical examinations, and of petty secrets revealed by them, to the embarrassment of both physician and patient, associate themselves with this case.—"She surely does not need them," is perhaps in the first place a compliment to Irma; but I suspect yet another meaning. In a careful analysis one is able to feel whether or not the *arrière-pensées* which are to be expected have all been exhausted. The way in which Irma stands at the window suddenly reminds me of another experience. Irma has an intimate woman friend of whom I think very highly. One evening, on paying her a visit, I found her at the window in the position reproduced in the dream, and her physician, the same Dr. M, declared that she had a diphtheritic membrane. The person of Dr. M and the membrane return, indeed, in the course of the dream. Now it occurs to me that during the past few months I have had every reason to suppose that this lady too is hysterical. Yes, Irma herself betrayed the fact to me. But what do I know of her condition? Only the one thing, that like Irma in the dream she suffers from hysterical choking. Thus, in the dream I have replaced my patient by her friend. Now I remember that I have often played with the supposition that this lady, too, might ask me to relieve her of her symptoms. But even at the time I thought it improbable, since she is extremely reserved. She *resists*, as the dream shows. Another explanation might be that *she does not need it;* in fact, until now she has shown herself strong enough to master her condition without outside help. Now only a few features remain, which I can assign neither to Irma nor to her friend; pale, puffy, false teeth. The false teeth led me to the governess; I now feel inclined to be satisfied with bad teeth. Here another person, to whom these features

may allude, occurs to me. She is not my patient, and I do not wish her to be my patient, for I have noticed that she is not at her ease with me, and I do not consider her a docile patient. She is generally pale, and once, when she had not felt particularly well, she was puffy.[1] I have thus compared my patient Irma with two others, who would likewise resist treatment. What is the meaning of the fact that I have exchanged her for her friend in the dream? Perhaps that I wish to exchange her; either her friend arouses in me stronger sympathies, or I have a higher regard for her intelligence. For I consider Irma foolish because she does not accept my solution. The other woman would be more sensible, and would thus be more likely to yield. *The mouth then opens readily;* she would tell more than Irma.[2]

What I see in the throat: a white spot and scabby turbinal bones. The white spot recalls diphtheria, and thus Irma's friend, but it also recalls the grave illness of my eldest daughter two years earlier, and all the anxiety of that unhappy time. The scab on the turbinal bones reminds me of my anxiety concerning my own health. At that time I frequently used cocaine in order to suppress distressing swellings in the nose, and I had heard a few days previously that a lady patient who did likewise had contracted an extensive necrosis of the nasal mucous membrane. In 1885 it was I who had recommended the use of cocaine, and I had been gravely reproached in consequence. A dear friend, who had died before the date of this dream, had hastened his end by the misuse of this remedy.

I quickly call Dr. M, who repeats the examination. This would simply correspond to the position which M occupied among us. But the word *quickly* is striking enough to demand a special examination. It reminds me of a sad medical experience. By continually prescribing a drug (sulphonal), which at that time was still considered harmless, I was once responsible for a condition of acute poisoning in the

---

[1] The complaint of pains in the abdomen, as yet unexplained, may also be referred to this third person. It is my own wife, of course, who is in question; the abdominal pains remind me of one of the occasions on which her shyness became evident to me. I must admit that I do not treat Irma and my wife very gallantly in this dream, but let it be said, in my defence, that I am measuring both of them against the ideal of the courageous and docile female patient.

[2] I suspect that the interpretation of this portion has not been carried far enough to follow every hidden meaning. If I were to continue the comparison of the three women, I should go far afield. Every dream has at least one point at which it is unfathomable; a central point, as it were, connecting it with the unknown.

case of a woman patient, and hastily turned for assistance to my older and more experienced colleague. The fact that I really had this case in mind is confirmed by a subsidiary circumstance. The patient, who succumbed to the toxic effects of the drug, bore the same name as my eldest daughter. I had never thought of this until now; but now it seems to me almost like a retribution of fate—as though the substitution of persons had to be continued in another sense: this Matilda for that Matilda; an eye for an eye, a tooth for a tooth. It is as though I were seeking every opportunity to reproach myself for a lack of medical conscientiousness.

Dr. M is pale; his chin is shaven, and he limps. Of this so much is correct, that his unhealthy appearance often arouses the concern of his friends. The other two characteristics must belong to another person. An elder brother living abroad occurs to me, for he, too, shaves his chin, and if I remember him rightly, the M of the dream bears on the whole a certain resemblance to him. And some days previously the news arrived that he was limping on account of an arthritic affection of the hip. There must be some reason why I fuse the two persons into one in my dream. I remember that, in fact, I was on bad terms with both of them for similar reasons. Both had rejected a certain proposal which I had recently made them.

My friend Otto is now standing next to the patient, and my friend Leopold examines her and calls attention to a dulness low down on the left side. My friend Leopold also is a physician, and a relative of Otto's. Since the two practice the same specialty, fate has made them competitors, so that they are constantly being compared with one another. Both of them assisted me for years, while I was still directing a public clinic for neurotic children. There, scenes like that reproduced in my dream had often taken place. While I would be discussing the diagnosis of a case with Otto, Leopold would examine the child anew and make an unexpected contribution towards our decision. There was a difference of character between the two men like that between Inspector Brasig and his friend Karl. Otto was remarkably prompt and alert; Leopold was slow and thoughtful, but thorough. If I contrast Otto and the cautious Leopold in the dream I do so, apparently, in order to extol Leopold. The comparison is like that made above between the disobedient patient Irma and her friend, who

was believed to be more sensible. I now become aware of one of the tracks along which the association of ideas in the dream proceeds: from the sick child to the children's clinic. Concerning the dulness low on the left side, I have the impression that it corresponds with a certain case of which all the details were similar, a case in which Leopold impressed me by his thoroughness. I thought vaguely, too, of something like a metastatic affection, but it might also be a reference to the patient whom I should have liked to have in Irma's place. For this lady, as far as I can gather, exhibited symptoms which imitated tuberculosis.

An infiltrated portion of skin on the left shoulder. I know at once that this is my own rheumatism of the shoulder, which I always feel if I lie awake long at night. The very phrasing of the dream sounds ambiguous: *Something which I can feel, as he does, in spite of the dress.* "Feel on my own body" is intended. Further, it occurs to me how unusual the phrase *infiltrated portion of skin* sounds. We are accustomed to the phrase: "an infiltration of the upper posterior left"; this would refer to the lungs, and thus, once more, to tuberculosis.

In spite of the dress. This, to be sure, is only an interpolation. At the clinic the children were, of course, examined undressed; here we have some contrast to the manner in which adult female patients have to be examined. The story used to be told of an eminent physician that he always examined his patients through their clothes. The rest is obscure to me; I have, frankly, no inclination to follow the matter further.

Dr. M says: "It's an infection, but it doesn't matter; dysentery will follow, and the poison will be eliminated." This, at first, seems to me ridiculous; nevertheless, like everything else, it must be carefully analysed; more closely observed it seems after all to have a sort of meaning. What I had found in the patient was a local diphtheritis. I remember the discussion about diphtheritis and diphtheria at the time of my daughter's illness. Diphtheria is the general infection which proceeds from local diphtheritis. Leopold demonstrates the existence of such a general infection by the dulness, which also suggests a metastatic focus. I believe, however, that just this kind of metastasis does not occur in the case of diphtheria. It reminds me rather of pyaemia.

It doesn't matter is a consolation. I believe it fits in as follows: The last part of the dream has yielded a content to the effect that the patient's sufferings are the result of a serious organic affection. I begin to suspect that by this I am only trying to shift the blame from myself. Psychic treatment cannot be held responsible for the continued presence of a diphtheritic affection. Now, indeed, I am distressed by the thought of having invented such a serious illness for Irma, for the sole purpose of exculpating myself. It seems so cruel. Accordingly, I need the assurance that the outcome will be benign, and it seems to me that I made a good choice when I put the words that consoled me into the mouth of Dr. M. But here I am placing myself in a position of superiority to the dream; a fact which needs explanation.

But why is this consolation so nonsensical?

Dysentery. Some sort of far-fetched theoretical notion that the toxins of disease might be eliminated through the intestines. Am I thereby trying to make fun of Dr. M's remarkable store of far-fetched explanations, his habit of conceiving curious pathological relations? Dysentery suggests something else. A few months ago I had in my care a young man who was suffering from remarkable intestinal troubles; a case which had been treated by other colleagues as one of "anaemia with malnutrition." I realized that it was a case of hysteria; I was unwilling to use my psycho-therapy on him, and sent him off on a sea-voyage. Now a few days previously I had received a despairing letter from him; he wrote from Egypt, saying that he had had a fresh attack, which the doctor had declared to be dysentery. I suspect that the diagnosis is merely an error on the part of an ignorant colleague, who is allowing himself to be fooled by the hysteria; yet I cannot help reproaching myself for putting the invalid in a position where he might contract some organic affection of the bowels in addition to his hysteria. Furthermore, dysentery sounds not unlike diphtheria, a word which does not occur in the dream.

Yes, it must be the case that with the consoling prognosis, *Dysentery will develop, etc.*, I am making fun of Dr. M, for I recollect that years ago he once jestingly told a very similar story of a colleague. He had been called in to consult with him in the case of a woman who was very seriously ill, and he felt obliged to confront his colleague, who seemed very hopeful, with the fact that he found albumen in the patient's urine. His colleague, however, did not allow this to worry him, but answered calmly: *That does not matter*, my dear sir;

the albumen will soon be excreted!" Thus I can no longer doubt that this part of the dream expresses derision for those of my colleagues who are ignorant of hysteria. And, as though in confirmation, the thought enters my mind: "Does Dr. M know that the appearances in Irma's friend, his patient, which gave him reason to fear tuberculosis, are likewise due to hysteria? Has he recognized this hysteria, or has he allowed himself to be fooled?"

But what can be my motive in treating this friend so badly? That is simple enough: Dr. M agrees with my solution as little as does Irma herself. Thus, in this dream I have already revenged myself on two persons: on Irma in the words, *If you still have pains, it is your own fault*, and on Dr. M in the wording of the nonsensical consolation which has been put into his mouth.

We know precisely how the infection originated. This precise knowledge in the dream is remarkable. Only a moment before this we did not yet know of the infection, since it was first demonstrated by Leopold.

My friend Otto gave her an injection not long ago, when she was feeling unwell. Otto had actually related during his short visit to Irma's family that he had been called in to a neighbouring hotel in order to give an injection to someone who had been suddenly taken ill. Injections remind me once more of the unfortunate friend who poisoned himself with cocaine. I had recommended the remedy for internal use only during the withdrawal of morphia; but he immediately gave himself injections of cocaine.

With a preparation of propyl . . . propyls . . . propionic acid. How on earth did this occur to me? On the evening of the day after I had written the clinical history and dreamed about the case, my wife opened a bottle of liqueur labelled "Ananas,"[1] which was a present from our friend Otto. He had, as a matter of fact, a habit of making presents on every possible occasion; I hope he will some day be cured of this by a wife.[2] This liqueur smelt so strongly of fusel oil that I refused to drink it. My wife suggested: "We will give the bottle to the servants," and I, more prudent, objected, with the philanthropic remark: "They shan't be

---

[1] "Ananas," moreover, has a remarkable assonance with the family name of my patient Irma.
[2] In this the dream did not turn out to be prophetic. But in another sense it proved correct, for the "unsolved" stomach pains, for which I did not want to be blamed, were the forerunners of a serious illness, due to gall-stones.

poisoned either." The smell of fusel oil (amyl . . .) has now apparently awakened my memory of the whole series: propyl, methyl, etc., which furnished the preparation of propyl mentioned in the dream. Here, indeed, I have effected a substitution: I dreamt of propyl after smelling amyl; but substitutions of this kind are perhaps permissible, especially in organic chemistry.

Trimethylamin. In the dream I see the chemical formula of this substance—which at all events is evidence of a great effort on the part of my memory—and the formula is even printed in heavy type, as though to distinguish it from the context as something of particular importance. And where does trimethylamin, thus forced on my attention, lead me? To a conversation with another friend, who for years has been familiar with all my germinating ideas, and I with his. At that time he had just informed me of certain ideas concerning a sexual chemistry, and had mentioned, among others, that he thought he had found in trimethylamin one of the products of sexual metabolism. This substance thus leads me to sexuality, the factor to which I attribute the greatest significance in respect of the origin of these nervous affections which I am trying to cure. My patient Irma is a young widow; if I am required to excuse my failure to cure her, I shall perhaps do best to refer to this condition, which her admirers would be glad to terminate. But in what a singular fashion such a dream is fitted together! The friend who in my dream becomes my patient in Irma's place is likewise a young widow.

I surmise why it is that the formula of trimethylamin is so insistent in the dream. So many important things are centered about this one word: trimethylamin is an allusion, not merely to the all-important factor of sexuality, but also to a friend whose sympathy I remember with satisfaction whenever I feel isolated in my opinions. And this friend, who plays such a large part in my life: will he not appear yet again in the concatenation of ideas peculiar to this dream? Of course; he has a special knowledge of the results of affections of the nose and the sinuses, and has revealed to science several highly remarkable relations between the turbinal bones and the female sexual organs. (The three curly formations in Irma's throat.) I got him to examine Irma, in order to determine whether her gastric pains were of nasal origin. But he himself suffers from suppurative rhinitis, which gives me concern, and to this per-

haps there is an allusion in pyaemia, which hovers before me in the metastasis of the dream.

One doesn't give such injections so rashly. Here the reproach of rashness is hurled directly at my friend Otto. I believe I had some such thought in the afternoon, when he seemed to indicate, by word and look, that he had taken sides against me. It was, perhaps: "How easily he is influenced; how irresponsibly he pronounces judgment." Further, the above sentence points once more to my deceased friend, who so irresponsibly resorted to cocaine injections. As I have said, I had not intended that injections of the drug should be taken. I note that in reproaching Otto I once more touch upon the story of the unfortunate Matilda, which was the pretext for the same reproach against me. Here, obviously, I am collecting examples of my conscientiousness, and also of the reverse.

Probably too the syringe was not clean. Another reproach directed at Otto, but originating elsewhere. On the previous day I happened to meet the son of an old lady of eighty-two, to whom I am obliged to give two injections of morphia daily. At present she is in the country, and I have heard that she is suffering from phlebitis. I immediately thought that this might be a case of infiltration caused by a dirty syringe. It is my pride that in two years I have not given her a single infiltration; I am always careful, of course, to see that the syringe is perfectly clean. For I am conscientious. From the phlebitis I return to my wife, who once suffered from thrombosis during a period of pregnancy, and now three related situations come to the surface in my memory, involving my wife, Irma, and the dead Matilda, whose identity has apparently justified my putting these three persons in one another's places.

I have now completed the interpretation of the dream.[1] In the course of this interpretation I have taken great pains to avoid all those notions which must have been suggested by a comparison of the dream-content with the dream-thoughts hidden behind this content. Meanwhile the *meaning* of the dream has dawned upon me. I have noted an intention which is realized through the dream, and which must have been my motive in dreaming. The dream fulfills several wishes, which were awakened within me by the events of the previous

[1] Even if I have not, as might be expected, accounted for everything that occurred to me in connection with the work of interpretation.

evening (Otto's news, and the writing of the clinical history). For the result of the dream is that it is not I who am to blame for the pain which Irma is still suffering, but that Otto is to blame for it. Now Otto has annoyed me by his remark about Irma's imperfect cure; the dream avenges me upon him, in that it turns the reproach upon himself. The dream acquits me of responsibility for Irma's condition, as it refers this condition to other causes (which do, indeed, furnish quite a number of explanations). The dream represents a certain state of affairs, such as I might wish to exist; *the content of the dream is thus the fulfilment of a wish; its motive is a wish.*

This much is apparent at first sight. But many other details of the dream become intelligible when regarded from the standpoint of wish-fulfilment. I take my revenge on Otto, not merely for too readily taking sides against me, in that I accuse him of careless medical treatment (the injection), but I revenge myself also for the bad liqueur which smells of fusel oil, and I find an expression in the dream which unites both these reproaches: the injection of a preparation of propyl. Still I am not satisfied, but continue to avenge myself by comparing him with his more reliable colleague. Thereby I seem to say: "I like him better than you." But Otto is not the only person who must be made to feel the weight of my anger. I take my revenge on the disobedient patient, by exchanging her for a more sensible and more docile one. Nor do I pass over Dr. M's contradiction; for I express, in an obvious allusion, my opinion of him: namely, that his attitude in this case is that of an ignoramus (*Dysentery will develop, etc.*). Indeed, it seems as though I were appealing from him to someone better informed (my friend, who told me about trimethylamin), just as I have turned from Irma to her friend, and from Otto to Leopold. It is as though I were to say: Rid me of these three persons, replace them by three others of my own choice, and I shall be rid of the reproaches which I am not willing to admit that I deserve! In my dream the unreasonableness of these reproaches is demonstrated for me in the most elaborate manner. Irma's pains are not attributable to me, since she herself is to blame for them, in that she refuses to accept my solution. They do not concern me, for being as they are of an organic nature, they cannot possibly be cured by psychic treatment. Irma's sufferings are satisfactorily explained by her widowhood (trimethylamin!); a state which I cannot al-

ter. Irma's illness has been caused by an incautious injection administered by Otto, an injection of an unsuitable drug, such as I should never have administered. Irma's complaint is the result of an injection made with an unclean syringe, like the phlebitis of my old lady patient, whereas my injections have never caused any ill effects. I am aware that these explanations of Irma's illness, which unite in acquitting me, do not agree with one another; that they even exclude one another. The whole plea —for this dream is nothing else—recalls vividly the defence offered by a man who was accused by his neighbour of having returned a kettle in a damaged condition. In the first place, he had returned the kettle undamaged; in the second place it already had holes in it when he borrowed it; and in the third place, he had never borrowed it at all. A complicated defence, but so much the better; if only one of these three lines of defence is recognized as valid, the man must be acquitted.

Still other themes play a part in the dream, and their relation to my non-responsibility for Irma's illness is not so apparent: my daughter's illness, and that of a patient with the same name; the harmfulness of cocaine; the affection of my patient, who was traveling in Egypt; concern about the health of my wife; my brother, and Dr. M; my own physical troubles, and anxiety concerning my absent friend, who is suffering from suppurative rhinitis. But if I keep all these things in view, they combine into a single train of thought, which might be labelled: Concern for the health of myself and others; professional conscientiousness. I recall a vaguely disagreeable feeling when Otto gave me the news of Irma's condition. Lastly, I am inclined, after the event, to find an expression of this fleeting sensation in the train of thoughts which forms part of the dream. It is as though Otto had said to me: "You do not take your medical duties seriously enough; you are not conscientious; you do not perform what you promise." Thereupon this train of thought placed itself at my service, in order that I might give proof of my extreme conscientiousness, of my intimate concern about the health of my relatives, friends and patients. Curiously enough, there are also some painful memories in this material, which confirm the blame attached to Otto rather than my own exculpation. The material is apparently impartial, but the connection between this broader material, on which the dream is based, and the more limited theme from which emerges the wish to be innocent of Irma's illness, is, nevertheless, unmistakable.

I do not wish to assert that I have entirely revealed the meaning of the dream, or that my interpretation is flawless.

I could still spend much time upon it; I could draw further explanations from it, and discuss further problems which it seems to propound. I can even perceive the points from which further mental associations might be traced; but such considerations as are always involved in every dream of one's own prevent me from interpreting it farther. Those who are overready to condemn such reserve should make the experiment of trying to be more straightforward. For the present I am content with the one fresh discovery which has just been made: If the method of dream-interpretation here indicated is followed, it will be found that dreams do really possess a meaning, and are by no means the expression of a disintegrated cerebral activity, as the writers on the subject would have us believe. *When the work of interpretation has been completed the dream can be recognized as a wish fulfilment.*

III. THE DREAM AS WISH-FULFILMENT

WHEN, after passing through a narrow defile, one suddenly reaches a height beyond which the ways part and a rich prospect lies outspread in different directions, it is well to stop for a moment and consider whither one shall turn next. We are in somewhat the same position after we have mastered this first interpretation of a dream. We find ourselves standing in the light of a sudden discovery. The dream is not comparable to the irregular sounds of a musical instrument, which, instead of being played by the hand of a musician, is struck by some external force; the dream is not meaningless, not absurd, does not presuppose that one part of our store of ideas is dormant while another part begins to awake. It is a perfectly valid psychic phenomenon, actually a wish-fulfilment; it may be enrolled in the continuity of the intelligible psychic activities of the waking state; it is built up by a highly complicated intellectual activity. But at the very moment when we are about to rejoice in this discovery a host of problems besets us. If the dream, as this theory defines it, represents a fulfilled wish, what is the cause of the striking and unfamiliar manner in which this fulfilment is expressed? What transformation has occurred in our dream-thoughts before the manifest dream, as we remember it on waking, shapes

itself out of them? How has this transformation taken place? Whence comes the material that is worked up into the dream? What causes many of the peculiarities which are to be observed in our dream-thoughts; for example, how is it that they are able to contradict one another? Is the dream capable of teaching us something new concerning our internal psychic processes and can its content correct opinions which we have held during the day? I suggest that for the present all these problems be laid aside, and that a single path be pursued. We have found that the dream represents a wish as fulfilled. Our next purpose should be to ascertain whether this is a general characteristic of dreams, or whether it is only the accidental content of the particular dream (the dream about Irma's injection) with which we have begun our analysis; for even if we conclude that every dream has a meaning and psychic value, we must nevertheless allow for the possibility that this meaning may not be the same in every dream. The first dream which we have considered was the fulfilment of a wish; another may turn out to be the realization of an apprehension; a third may have a reflection as its content; a fourth may simply reproduce a reminiscence. Are there, then dreams other than wish-dreams; or are there none but wish-dreams?

It is easy to show that the wish-fulfilment in dreams is often undisguised and easy to recognize, so that one may wonder why the language of dreams has not long since been understood. There is, for example, a dream which I can evoke as often as I please, experimentally, as it were. If, in the evening, I eat anchovies, olives, or other strongly salted foods, I am thirsty at night, and therefore I wake. The waking, however, is preceded by a dream, which has always the same content, namely, that I am drinking. I am drinking long draughts of water; it tastes as delicious as only a cool drink can taste when one's throat is parched; and then I wake, and find that I have an actual desire to drink. The cause of this dream is thirst, which I perceive when I wake. From this sensation arises the wish to drink, and the dream shows me this wish as fulfilled. It thereby serves a function, the nature of which I soon surmise. I sleep well, and am not accustomed to being waked by a bodily need. If I succeed in appeasing my thirst by means of the dream that I am drinking, I need not wake up in order to satisfy that thirst. It is thus a *dream of convenience.* The dream takes the place of action, as elsewhere in life. Unfortunately, the need of water to quench the thirst cannot be satisfied by a dream, as can my thirst for revenge upon Otto and Dr. M, but the intention is the same. Not long ago I had the same dream in a somewhat modified form. On this occasion I felt thirsty before going to bed, and emptied the glass of water which stood on the little chest beside my bed. Some hours later, during the night, my thirst returned, with the consequent discomfort. In order to obtain water, I should have had to get up and fetch the glass which stood on my wife's bed-table. I thus quite appropriately dreamt that my wife was giving me a drink from a vase; this vase was an Etruscan cinerary urn, which I had brought home from Italy and had since given away. But the water in it tasted so salt (apparently on account of the ashes) that I was forced to wake. It may be observed how conveniently the dream is capable of arranging matters. Since the fulfilment of a wish is its only purpose, it may be perfectly egoistic. Love of comfort is really not compatible with consideration for others. The introduction of the cinerary urn is probably once again the fulfilment of a wish; I regret that I no longer possess this vase; it, like the glass of water at my wife's side, is inaccessible to me. The cinerary urn is appropriate also in connection with the sensation of an increasingly salty taste, which I know will compel me to wake.[1]

Such convenience-dreams came very frequently to me in my youth. Accustomed as I had always been to working until late at night, early waking was always a matter of difficulty. I used then to dream that I was out of bed and standing at the wash-stand. After a while I could no longer shut out the knowledge that I was not yet up; but in the meantime I had continued to sleep. The same sort of lethargy-dream was dreamed by a young colleague of mine, who appears to share my propensity for sleep. With him it assumed a particularly amusing form. The landlady with whom he was lodging in the neighbourhood of the hospital had strict orders to wake him every morning at a given hour, but she found it by no means easy to carry out his orders. One morning sleep was especially sweet to him. The woman called into his room: "Herr Pepi, get up; you've got to go to the hospital." Whereupon the sleeper dreamt of a room in the hospital, of a bed in which he was lying, and of a chart pinned over his head, which read as follows: "Pepi M, medical student, 22 years of age." He told himself in the dream: "If I am already at the hospital, I don't have to go there," turned over, and slept on. He had thus frankly admitted to himself his motive for dreaming.

Here is yet another dream of which the stimulus was active during sleep: One of my women patients, who had been obliged to undergo an unsuccessful operation on the jaw, was instructed by her physicians to wear by day and night a cooling apparatus on the affected cheek; but she was in the habit of throwing it off as soon as she had fallen asleep. One day I was asked to reprove her for doing so; she had again thrown the apparatus on the floor. The patient defended herself as follows: "This time I really couldn't help it; it was the result of a dream which I had during the night. In the dream I was in a box at the opera, and was taking a lively interest in the performance. But Herr Karl Meyer was lying in the sanatorium and complaining pitifully on account of pains in his jaw. I said to myself, 'Since I haven't the pains, I don't need the apparatus either'; that's why I threw it away." The dream of this poor sufferer reminds me of an expression which comes to our lips when we are in a disagreeable situation: "Well, I can imagine more amusing things!" The dream presents these "more amusing things!" Herr Karl Meyer, to whom the dreamer attributed her pains, was the most casual acquaintance of whom she could think.

It is quite as simple a matter to discover the wish-fulfilment in several other dreams which I have collected from healthy persons. A friend who was acquainted with my theory of dreams, and had explained it to his wife, said to me one day: "My wife asked me to tell you that she dreamt yesterday that she was having her menses. You will know what that means." Of course I know: if the young wife dreams that she is having her menses, the menses have

---

[1] The facts relating to dreams of thirst were known also to Weygandt, who speaks of them as follows: "It is just this sensation of thirst which is registered most accurately of all; it always causes a representation of quenching the thirst. The manner in which the dream represents the act of quenching the thirst is manifold, and is specified in accordance with some recent recollection. A universal phenomenon noticeable here is the fact that the representation of quenching the thirst is immediately followed by disappointment in the inefficacy of the imagined refreshment." But he overlooks the universal character of the reaction of the dream to the stimulus. If other persons who are troubled by thirst at night awake without dreaming beforehand, this does not constitute an objection to my experiment, but characterizes them as persons who sleep less soundly. Cf. Isaiah, 29. 8.

stopped. I can well imagine that she would have liked to enjoy her freedom a little longer, before the discomforts of maternity began. It was a clever way of giving notice of her first pregnancy. Another friend writes that his wife had dreamt not long ago that she noticed milk-stains on the front of her blouse. This also is an indication of pregnancy, but not of the first one; the young mother hoped she would have more nourishment for the second child than she had for the first.

A young woman who for weeks had been cut off from all society because she was nursing a child who was suffering from an infectious disease dreamt, after the child had recovered, of a company of people in which Alphonse Daudet, Paul Bourget, Marcel Prévost and others were present; they were all very pleasant to her and amused her enormously. In her dream these different authors had the features which their portraits give them. M. Prévost, with whose portrait she is not familiar, looked like the man who had disinfected the sickroom the day before, the first outsider to enter it for a long time. Obviously the dream is to be translated thus: "It is about time now for something more entertaining than this eternal nursing."

Perhaps this collection will suffice to prove that frequently, and under the most complex conditions, dreams may be noted which can be understood only as wish-fulfilments, and which present their content without concealment. In most cases these are short and simple dreams, and they stand in pleasant contrast to the confused and overloaded dream-compositions which have almost exclusively attracted the attention of the writers on the subject. But it will repay us if we give some time to the examination of these simple dreams. The simplest dreams of all are, I suppose, to be expected in the case of children whose psychic activities are certainly less complicated than those of adults. Child psychology, in my opinion, is destined to render the same services to the psychology of adults as a study of the structure or development of the lower animals renders to the investigation of the structure of the higher orders of animals. Hitherto but few deliberate efforts have been made to make use of the psychology of the child for such a purpose.

The dreams of little children are often simple fulfilments of wishes, and for this reason are, as compared with the dreams of adults, by no means interesting. They present no problem to be solved, but they are invaluable as affording proof that the dream, in its inmost essence, is the fulfilment of a wish. I have been able to collect several examples of such dreams from the material furnished by my own children.

For two dreams, one that of a daughter of mine, at that time eight and a half years of age, and the other that of a boy of five and a quarter, I am indebted to an excursion to Hallstatt, in the summer of 1896. I must first explain that we were living that summer on a hill near Aussee, from which, when the weather was fine, we enjoyed a splendid view of the Dachstein. With a telescope we could easily distinguish the Simony hut. The children often tried to see it through the telescope— I do not know with what success. Before the excursion I had told the children that Hallstatt lay at the foot of the Dachstein. They looked forward to the outing with the greatest delight. From Hallstatt we entered the valley of Eschern, which enchanted the children with its constantly changing scenery. One of them, however, the boy of five, gradually became discontented. As often as a mountain came into view, he would ask: "Is that the Dachstein?" whereupon I had to reply: "No, only a foot-hill." After this question had been repeated several times he fell quite silent, and did not wish to accompany us up the steps leading to the waterfall. I thought he was tired. But the next morning he came to me, perfectly happy, and said: "Last night I dreamt that we went to the Simony hut." I understood him now; he had expected, when I spoke of the Dachstein, that on our excursion to Hallstatt he would climb the mountain, and would see at close quarters the hut which had been so often mentioned when the telescope was used. When he learned that he was expected to content himself with foot-hills and a waterfall he was disappointed, and became discontented. But the dream compensated him for all this. I tried to learn some details of the dream; they were scanty. "You go up steps for six hours," as he had been told.

On this excursion the girl of eight and a half had likewise cherished wishes which had to be satisfied by a dream. We had taken with us to Hallstatt our neighbour's twelve-year-old boy; quite a polished little gentleman, who, it seemed to me, had already won the little woman's sympathies. Next morning she related the following dream: "Just think, I dreamt that Emil was one of the family, that he said 'papa' and 'mamma' to you, and slept at our house, in the big room, like one of the boys. Then mamma came into the room and threw a handful of big bars of chocolate, wrapped in blue and green paper, under our beds." The girl's brothers, who evidently had not inherited an understanding of dream-interpretation, declared, just as the writers we have quoted would have done: "That dream is nonsense." The girl defended at least one part of the dream, and from the standpoint of the theory of the neuroses it is interesting to learn which part it was that she defended: "That Emil was one of the family was nonsense, but that about the bars of chocolate wasn't." It was just this latter part that was obscure to me, until my wife furnished the explanation. On the way home from the railway-station the children had stopped in front of a slot-machine, and had wanted exactly such bars of chocolate, wrapped in paper with a metallic lustre, such as the machine, in their experience, provided. But the mother thought, and rightly so, that the day had brought them enough wish-fulfilments, and therefore left this wish to be satisfied in the dream. This little scene had escaped me. That portion of the dream which had been condemned by my daughter I understood without any difficulty. I myself had heard the well-behaved little guest enjoining the children, as they were walking ahead of us, to wait until "papa" or "mamma" had come up. For the little girl the dream turned this temporary relationship into a permanent adoption. Her affection could not as yet conceive of any other way of enjoying her friend's company permanently than the adoption pictured in her dream, which was suggested by her brothers. Why the bars of chocolate were thrown under the bed could not, of course, be explained without questioning the child.

From a friend I have learned of a dream very much like that of my little boy. It was dreamed by a little girl of eight. Her father, accompanied by several children, had started on a walk to Dornbach, with the intention of visiting the Rohrer hut, but had turned back, as it was growing late, promising the children to take them some other time. On the way back they passed a signpost which pointed to the Hameau. The children now asked him to take them to the Hameau, but once more, and for the same reason, they had to be content with the promise that they should go there some other day. Next morning the little girl went to her father and told him, with a satisfied air: "Papa, I dreamed last night that you were with us at the Rohrer hut, and on the Hameau."

Thus, in the dream her impatience had anticipated the fulfilment of the promise made by her father.

Another dream, with which the picturesque beauty of the Aussee inspired my daughter, at that time three and a quarter years of age, is equally straightforward. The little girl had crossed the lake for the first time, and the trip had passed too quickly for her. She did not want to leave the boat at the landing, and cried bitterly. The next morning she told us: "Last night I was sailing on the lake." Let us hope that the duration of this dream-voyage was more satisfactory to her.

My eldest boy, at that time eight years of age, was already dreaming of the realization of his fancies. He had ridden in a chariot with Achilles, with Diomedes as charioteer. On the previous day he had shown a lively interest in a book on the myths of Greece which had been given to his elder sister.

If it can be admitted that the talking of children in their sleep belongs to the sphere of dreams, I can relate the following as one of the earliest dreams in my collection: My youngest daughter, at that time nineteen months old, vomited one morning, and was therefore kept without food all day. During the night she was heard to call excitedly in her sleep: "Anna F(r)eud, St'awbewy, wild st'awbewy, om'lette, pap!" She used her name in this way in order to express the act of appropriation; the menu presumably included everything that would seem to her a desirable meal; the fact that two varieties of strawberry appeared in it was a demonstration against the sanitary regulations of the household, and was based on the circumstance, which she had by no means overlooked, that the nurse had ascribed her indisposition to an over-plentiful consumption of strawberries; so in her dream she avenged herself for this opinion which met with her disapproval.[1]

When we call childhood happy because it does not yet know sexual desire, we must not forget what a fruitful source of disappointment and renunciation, and therefore of dream-stimulation, the other great vital impulse may be

[1] The dream afterwards accomplished the same purpose in the case of the child's grandmother, who is older than the child by about seventy years. After she had been forced to go hungry for a day on account of the restlessness of her floating kidney, she dreamed, being apparently translated into the happy years of her girlhood, that she had been asked out, invited to lunch and dinner, and had at each meal been served with the most delicious titbits.

for the child.[1] Here is a second example. My nephew, twenty-two months of age, had been instructed to congratulate me on my birthday, and to give me a present of a small basket of cherries, which at that time of the year were scarce, being hardly in season. He seemed to find the task a difficult one, for he repeated again and again: "Cherries in it," and could not be induced to let the little basket go out of his hands. But he knew how to indemnify himself. He had, until then, been in the habit of telling his mother every morning that he had dreamt of the "white soldier," an officer of the guard in a white cloak, whom he had once admired in the street. On the day after the sacrifice on my birthday he woke up joyfully with the announcement, which could have referred only to a dream: *"He [r] man eaten all the cherries!"*[2]

What animals dream of I do not know. A proverb, for which I am indebted to one of my pupils, professes to tell us, for it asks the question: "What does the goose dream of?" and answers: "Of maize." [3] The whole theory that the dream is the fulfilment of a wish is contained in these two sentences.[4]

We now perceive that we should have reached our theory of the hidden meaning of dreams by the shortest route had we merely consulted the vernacular. Proverbial wisdom, it is true, often speaks contemptuously enough of dreams—it apparently seeks to justify the scientists when it says that "dreams are bubbles"; but in colloquial language the dream is predominantly the gracious fulfiller of wishes. "I should never have imagined that in my wildest dreams," we exclaim in delight if we find that the reality surpasses our expectations.

IV. DISTORTION IN DREAMS

IF I now declare that wish-fulfilment is the meaning of *every* dream, so that there cannot

children, see also von Hug-Hellmuth, Putnam, Raalte, Spielrein, and Tausk; others by Banchieri, Busemann, Doglia, and especially Wigam, who emphasizes the wish-fulfilling tendency of such dreams. On the other hand, it seems that dreams of an infantile type reappear with especial frequency in adults who are transferred into the midst of unfamiliar conditions. Thus Otto Nordenskjöld, in his book, *Antarctic* (1904, vol. i, p. 336), writes as follows of the crew who spent the winter with him: "Very characteristic of the trend of our inmost thoughts were our dreams, which were never more vivid and more numerous. Even those of our comrades with whom dreaming was formerly exceptional had long stories to tell in the morning, when we exchanged our experiences in the world of phantasy. They all had reference to that outside world which was now so far removed from us, but they often fitted into our immediate circumstances. An especially characteristic dream was that in which one of our comrades believed himself back at school, where the task was assigned to him of skinning miniature seals, which were manufactured especially for purposes of instruction. Eating and drinking constituted the pivot around which most of our dreams revolved. One of us, who was especially fond of going to big dinner-parties, was delighted if he could report in the morning 'that he had had a three-course dinner.' Another dreamed of tobacco, whole mountains of tobacco; yet another dreamed of a ship approaching on the open sea under full sail. Still another dream deserves to be mentioned: The postman brought the post and gave a long explanation of why it was so long delayed; he had delivered it at the wrong address, and only with great trouble was he able to get it back. To be sure, we were often occupied in our sleep with still more impossible things, but the lack of phantasy in almost all the dreams which I myself dreamed, or heard others relate, was quite striking. It would certainly have been of great psychological interest if all these dreams could have been recorded. But one can readily understand how we longed for sleep. That alone could afford us everything that we all most ardently desired." I will continue by a quotation from Du Prel (p. 231): "Mungo Park, nearly dying of thirst on one of his African expeditions, dreamed constantly of the well-watered valleys and meadows of his home. Similarly Trenck, tortured by hunger in the fortress of Magdeburg, saw himself surrounded by copious meals. And George Back, a member of Franklin's first expedition, when he was on the point of death by starvation, dreamed continually and invariably of plenteous meals."

[3] A Hungarian proverb cited by Ferenczi states more explicitly that "the pig dreams of acorns, the goose of maize." A Jewish proverb asks: "Of what does the hen dream?"—"Of millet" (*Sammlung jüd. Sprichw. u. Redensarten.*, edit. by Bernstein, 2nd ed., p. 116).

[4] I am far from wishing to assert that no previous writer has ever thought of tracing a dream to a wish. (Cf. the first passages of the next chapter.) Those interested in the subject will find that even in antiquity the physician Herophilos, who lived under the First Ptolemy, distinguished between three kinds of dreams: dreams sent by the gods; natural dreams—those which come about whenever the soul creates for itself an image of that which is beneficial to it, and will come to pass; and mixed dreams — those which originate spontaneously from the juxtaposition of images, when we see that which we desire. From the examples collected by Scherner, J. Stärcke cites a dream which was described by the author himself as a wish-fulfilment (p. 239). Scherner says: "The phantasy immediately fulfills the dreamer's wish, simply because this existed vividly in the mind." This dream belongs to the "emotional dreams." Akin to it are dreams due to "masculine and feminine erotic longing," and to "irritable moods." As will readily be seen, Scherner does not ascribe to the wish any further significance for the dream than to any other psychic condition of the waking state; least of all does he insist on the connection between the wish and the essential nature of the dream.

[1] A more searching investigation into the phychic life of the child teaches us, of course, that sexual motives, in infantile forms, play a very considerable part, which has been too long overlooked, in the psychic activity of the child. This permits us to doubt to some extent the happiness of the child, as imagined later by adults. Cf. *Three Contributions to the Theory of Sex*.

[2] It should be mentioned that young children often have more complex and obscure dreams, while, on the other hand, adults, in certain circumstances, often have dreams of a simple and infantile character. How rich in unsuspected content the dreams of children no more than four or five years of age may be is shown by the examples in my "Analysis of a Phobia in a five-year-old Boy," *Collected Papers*, III, and Jung's "Experiences Concerning the Psychic Life of the Child," translated by Brill, *American Journal of Psychology*. April, 1910. For analytically interpreted dreams of

be any dreams other than wish-dreams, I know beforehand that I shall meet with the most emphatic contradiction. My critics will object: "The fact that there are dreams which are to be understood as fulfilments of wishes is not new, but has long since been recognized by such writers as Radestock, Volkelt, Purkinje, Griesinger and others.[1] That there *can* be no other dreams than those of wish-fulfilments is yet one more unjustified generalization, which, fortunately, can be easily refuted. Dreams which present the most painful content, and not the least trace of wish-fulfilment, occur frequently enough. The pessimistic philosopher, Eduard von Hartmann, is perhaps most completely opposed to the theory of wish-fulfilment. In his *Philosophy of the Unconscious,* Part II (Stereotyped German edition, p. 344), he says: 'As regards the dream, with it all the troubles of waking life pass over into the sleeping state; all save the one thing which may in some degree reconcile the cultured person with life—scientific and artistic enjoyment. . . .' But even less pessimistic observers have emphasized the fact that in our dreams pain and disgust are more frequent than pleasure (Scholz, p. 33; Volkelt, p. 80, *et al.*). Two ladies, Sarah Weed and Florence Hallam, have even worked out, on the basis of their dreams, a numerical value for the preponderance of distress and discomfort in dreams. They find that 58 per cent of dreams are disagreeable, and only 28.6 positively pleasant. Besides those dreams that convey into our sleep the many painful emotions of life, there are also anxiety-dreams, in which this most terrible of all the painful emotions torments us until we wake. Now it is precisely by these anxiety-dreams that children are so often haunted (cf. Debacker on *Pavor nocturnus*); and yet it was in children that you found the wish-fulfilment dream in its most obvious form."

The anxiety-dream does really seem to preclude a generalization of the thesis deduced from the examples given in the last chapter, that dreams are wish-fulfilments, and even to condemn it as an absurdity.

Nevertheless, it is not difficult to parry these apparently invincible objections. It is merely necessary to observe that our doctrine is not based upon the estimates of the obvious dream-content, but relates to the thought-content, which, in the course of interpretation, is found

to lie behind the dream. Let us compare and contrast the *manifest* and the *latent dream-content*. It is true that there are dreams the manifest content of which is of the most painful nature. But has anyone ever tried to interpret these dreams—to discover their latent thought-content? If not, the two objections to our doctrine are no longer valid; for there is always the possibility that even our painful and terrifying dreams may, upon interpretation, prove to be wish fulfilments.[2]

In scientific research it is often advantageous, if the solution of one problem presents difficulties, to add to it a second problem; just as it is easier to crack two nuts together instead of separately. Thus, we are confronted not only with the problem: How can painful and terrifying dreams be the fulfilments of wishes? but we may add to this a second problem which arises from the foregoing discussion of the general problem of the dream: Why do not the dreams that show an indifferent content, and yet turn out to be wish-fulfilments, reveal their meaning without disguise? Take the exhaustively treated dream of Irma's injection: it is by no means of a painful character, and it may be recognized, upon interpretation, as a striking wish-fulfilment. But why is an interpretation necessary at all? Why does not the dream say directly what it means? As a matter of fact, the dream of Irma's injection does not at first produce the impression that it represents a wish of the dreamer's as fulfilled. The reader will not have received this impression, and even I myself was not aware of the fact until I had undertaken the analysis. If we call this peculiarity of dreams—namely, that they need elucidation — the phenomenon of distortion in dreams, a second question then arises: What is the origin of this distortion in dreams?

If one's first thoughts on this subject were

---

[1] Already Plotinus, the neo-Platonist, said: "When desire bestirs itself, then comes phantasy, and presents to us, as it were, the object of desire" (Du Prel, p. 276).

[2] It is quite incredible with what obstinacy readers and critics have excluded this consideration and disregarded the fundamental differentiation between the manifest and the latent dream-content. Nothing in the literature of the subject approaches so closely to my own conception of dreams as a passage in J. Sully's essay, *Dreams as a Revelation* (and it is not because I do not think it valuable that I allude to it here for the first time): "It would seem then, after all, that dreams are not the utter nonsense they have been said to be by such authorities as Chaucer, Shakespeare, and Milton. The chaotic aggregations of our night-fancy have a significance and communicate new knowledge. Like some letter in cipher, the dream-inscription when scrutinized closely loses its first look of balderdash and takes on the aspect of a serious, intelligible message. Or, to vary the figure slightly, we may say that, like some palimpsest, the dream discloses beneath its worthless surface-characters traces of an old and precious communication" (p. 364).

consulted, several possible solutions might suggest themselves: for example, that during sleep one is incapable of finding an adequate expression for one's dream-thoughts. The analysis of certain dreams, however, compels us to offer another explanation. I shall demonstrate this by means of a second dream of my own, which again involves numerous indiscretions, but which compensates for this personal sacrifice by affording a thorough elucidation of the problem.

Preliminary Statement

In the spring of 1897 I learnt that two professors of our university had proposed me for the title of *Professor Extraordinarius* (assistant professor). The news came as a surprise to me, and pleased me considerably as an expression of appreciation on the part of two eminent men which could not be explained by personal interest. But I told myself immediately that I must not expect anything to come of their proposal. For some years past the Ministry had disregarded such proposals, and several colleagues of mine, who were my seniors and at least my equals in desert, had been waiting in vain all this time for the appointment. I had no reason to suppose that I should fare any better. I resolved, therefore, to resign myself to disappointment. I am not, so far as I know, ambitious, and I was following my profession with gratifying success even without the recommendation of a professorial title. Whether I considered the grapes to be sweet or sour did not matter, since they undoubtedly hung too high for me.

One evening a friend of mine called to see me; one of those colleagues whose fate I had regarded as a warning. As he had long been a candidate for promotion to the professorate (which in our society makes the doctor a demigod to his patients), and as he was less resigned than I, he was accustomed from time to time to remind the authorities of his claims in the hope of advancing his interests. It was after one of these visits that he called on me. He said that this time he had driven the exalted gentleman into a corner, and had asked him frankly whether considerations of religious denomination were not really responsible for the postponement of his appointment. The answer was: His Excellency had to admit that in the present state of public opinion he was not in a position, etc. "Now at least I know where I stand," my friend concluded his narrative, which told me nothing new, but which was cal-

culated to confirm me in my resignation. For the same denominational considerations would apply to my own case.

On the morning after my friend's visit I had the following dream, which was notable also on account of its form. It consisted of two thoughts and two images, so that a thought and an image emerged alternately. But here I shall record only the first half of the dream, since the second half has no relation to the purpose for which I cite the dream.

I. *My friend R is my uncle—I have a great affection for him.*

II. *I see before me his face, somewhat altered. It seems to be elongated; a yellow beard, which surrounds it, is seen with peculiar distinctness.*

Then follow the other two portions of the dream, again a thought and an image, which I omit.

The interpretation of this dream was arrived at in the following manner:

When I recollected the dream in the course of the morning, I laughed outright and said, "The dream is nonsense." But I could not get it out of my mind, and I was pursued by it all day, until at last, in the evening, I reproached myself in these words: "If in the course of a dream-interpretation one of your patients could find nothing better to say than 'That is nonsense,' you would reprove him, and you would suspect that behind the dream there was hidden some disagreeable affair, the exposure of which he wanted to spare himself. Apply the same thing to your own case; your opinion that the dream is nonsense probably signifies merely an inner resistance to its interpretation. Don't let yourself be put off." I then proceeded with the interpretation.

R is my uncle. What can that mean? I had only one uncle, my uncle Joseph.[1] His story, to be sure, was a sad one. Once, more than thirty years ago, hoping to make money, he allowed himself to be involved in transactions of a kind which the law punishes severely, and paid the penalty. My father, whose hair turned grey with grief within a few days, used always to say that uncle Joseph had never been a bad man, but, after all, he was a simpleton. If, then, my friend R is my uncle Joseph, that is

[1] It is astonishing to see how my memory here restricts itself—in the waking state!—for the purposes of analysis. I have known five of my uncles and loved and honoured one of them. But at the moment when I overcame my resistance to the interpretation of the dream, I said to myself: "I have only one uncle, the one who is intended in the dream."

equivalent to saying: "R is a simpleton." Hardly credible, and very disagreeable! But there is the face that I saw in the dream, with its elongated features and its yellow beard. My uncle actually had such a face—long, and framed in a handsome yellow beard. My friend R was extremely swarthy, but when black-haired people begin to grow grey they pay for the glory of their youth. Their black beards undergo an unpleasant change of colour, hair by hair; first they turn a reddish brown, then a yellowish brown, and then definitely grey. My friend R's beard is now in this stage; so, for that matter, is my own, a fact which I note with regret. The face that I see in my dream is at once that of my friend R and that of my uncle. It is like one of those composite photographs of Galton's; in order to emphasize family resemblances Galton had several faces photographed on the same plate. No doubt is now possible; it is really my opinion that my friend R is a simpleton—like my uncle Joseph.

I have still no idea for what purpose I have worked out this relationship. It is certainly one to which I must unreservedly object. Yet it is not very profound, for my uncle was a criminal, and my friend R is not, except in so far as he was once fined for knocking down an apprentice with his bicycle. Can I be thinking of this offence? That would make the comparison ridiculous. Here I recollect another conversation, which I had some days ago with another colleague, N; as a matter of fact, on the same subject. I met N in the street; he, too, has been nominated for a professorship, and having heard that I had been similarly honoured he congratulated me. I refused his congratulations, saying: "You are the last man to jest about the matter, for you know from your own experience what the nomination is worth." Thereupon he said, though probably not in earnest: "You can't be sure of that. There is a special objection in my case. Don't you know that a woman once brought a criminal accusation against me? I need hardly assure you that the matter was put right. It was a mean attempt at blackmail, and it was all I could do to save the plaintiff from punishment. But it may be that the affair is remembered against me at the Ministry. You, on the other hand, are above reproach." Here, then, I have the criminal, and at the same time the interpretation and tendency of my dream. My uncle Joseph represents both of my colleagues who have not been appointed to the professorship—the one as a simpleton, the other as a criminal.

Now, too, I know for what purpose I need this representation. If denominational considerations are a determining factor in the postponement of my two friends' appointment, then my own appointment is likewise in jeopardy. But if I can refer the rejection of my two friends to other causes, which do not apply to my own case, my hopes are unaffected. This is the procedure followed by my dream: it makes the one friend R, a simpleton, and the other, N, a criminal. But since I am neither one nor the other, there is nothing in common between us. I have a right to enjoy my appointment to the title of professor, and have avoided the distressing application to my own case of the information which the official gave to my friend R.

I must pursue the interpretation of this dream still farther; for I have a feeling that it is not yet satisfactorily elucidated. I still feel disquieted by the ease with which I have degraded two respected colleagues in order to clear my own way to the professorship. My dissatisfaction with this procedure has, of course, been mitigated since I have learned to estimate the testimony of dreams at its true value. I should contradict anyone who suggested that I really considered R a simpleton, or that I did not believe N's account of the blackmailing incident. And of course I do not believe that Irma has been made seriously ill by an injection of a preparation of propyl administered by Otto. Here, as before, what the dream expresses is only my *wish that things might be so*. The statement in which my wish is realized sounds less absurd in the second dream than in the first; it is here made with a skilful use of actual points of support in establishing something like a plausible slander, one of which one could say that "there is something in it." For at that time my friend R had to contend with the adverse vote of a university professor of his own department, and my friend N had himself, all unsuspectingly, provided me with material for the calumny. Nevertheless, I repeat, it still seems to me that the dream requires further elucidation.

I remember now that the dream contained yet another portion which has hitherto been ignored by the interpretation. After it occurred to me that my friend R was my uncle, I felt in the dream a great affection for him. To whom is this feeling directed? For my uncle Joseph, of course, I have never had any feelings of affection. R has for many years been a dearly loved friend, but if I were to go to him and express my affection for him in terms approaching the degree of affection which I felt in the dream, he would undoubtedly be surprised. My affection, if it was for him, seems false and exaggerated, as does my judgment of his intellectual qualities, which I expressed by merging his personality in that of my uncle; but exaggerated in the opposite direction. Now, however, a new state of affairs dawns upon me. The affection in the dream does not belong to the latent content, to the thoughts behind the dream; it stands in opposition to this content; it is calculated to conceal the knowledge conveyed by the interpretation. Probably this is precisely its function. I remember with what reluctance I undertook the interpretation, how long I tried to postpone it, and how I declared the dream to be sheer nonsense. I know from my psycho-analytic practice how such a condemnation is to be interpreted. It has no informative value, but merely expresses an affect. If my little daughter does not like an apple which is offered her, she asserts that the apple is bitter, without even tasting it. If my patients behave thus, I know that we are dealing with an idea which they are trying to *repress*. The same thing applies to my dream. I do not want to interpret it because there is something in the interpretation to which I object. After the interpretation of the dream is completed, I discover what it was to which I objected; it was the assertion that R is a simpleton. I can refer the affection which I feel for R not to the latent dream-thoughts, but rather to this unwillingness of mine. If my dream, as compared with its latent content, is disguised at this point, and actually misrepresents things by producing their opposites, then the manifest affection in the dream serves the purpose of the misrepresentation; in other words, the distortion is here shown to be intentional—it is a means of *disguise*. My dream-thoughts of R are derogatory, and so that I may not become aware of this the very opposite of defamation—a tender affection for him—enters into the dream.

This discovery may prove to be generally valid. As the examples in Chapter III have demonstrated, there are, of course, dreams which are undisguised wish-fulfilments. Wherever a wish-fulfilment is unrecognizable and disguised there must be present a tendency to defend oneself against this wish, and in consequence of this defence the wish is unable to express itself save in a distorted form. I will try to find a parallel in social life to this occurrence in the inner psychic life. Where in social life can a similar misrepresentation be found? Only where two persons are concerned, one of whom possesses a certain power while the other has to act with a certain consideration on account of this power. The second person will then distort his psychic actions; or, as we say, he will *mask* himself. The politeness which I practise every day is largely a disguise of this kind; if I interpret my dreams for the benefit of my readers, I am forced to make misrepresentations of this kind. The poet even complains of the necessity of such misrepresentation: *Das Beste, was du wissen kannst, darfst du den Buben doch nicht sagen:* "The best that thou canst know thou mayst not tell to boys."

The political writer who has unpleasant truths to tell to those in power finds himself in a like position. If he tells everything without reserve, the Government will suppress them—retrospectively in the case of a verbal expression of opinion, preventively if they are to be published in the Press. The writer stands in fear of the censorship; he therefore moderates and disguises the expression of his opinions. He finds himself compelled, in accordance with the sensibilities of the censor, either to refrain altogether from certain forms of attack, or to express himself in allusions instead of by direct assertions; or he must conceal his objectionable statement in an apparently innocent disguise. He may, for instance, tell of a *contretemps* between two Chinese mandarins, while he really has in mind the officials of his own country. The stricter the domination of the censorship, the more thorough becomes the disguise, and, often enough, the more ingenious the means employed to put the reader on the track of the actual meaning.

The detailed correspondence between the phenomena of censorship and the phenomena of dream-distortion justifies us in presupposing similar conditions for both. We should then assume that in every human being there exist, as the primary cause of dream-formation, two psychic forces (tendencies or systems), one of which forms the wish expressed by the dream, while the other exercises a censorship over this dream-wish, thereby enforcing on it a distortion. The question is: What is the nature of the authority of this second agency by virtue of which it is able to exercise its censorship? If we remember that the latent dream-thoughts are not conscious before analysis, but that the manifest dream-content emerging from them is consciously remembered, it is not a far-fetched assumption that admittance to the consciousness is the prerogative of the second agency. Nothing can reach the consciousness from the first system which has not previously passed the second instance; and the second instance lets nothing pass without exercising its rights, and forcing such modifications as are pleasing to itself upon the candidates for admission to consciousness. Here we arrive at a very definite conception of the *essence* of consciousness; for us the state of becoming conscious is a special psychic act, different from and independent of the process of becoming fixed or represented, and consciousness appears to us as a sensory organ which perceives a content proceeding from another source. It may be shown that psycho-pathology simply cannot dispense with these fundamental assumptions. But we shall reserve for another time a more exhaustive examination of the subject.

If I bear in mind the notion of the two psychic instances and their relation to the consciousness, I find in the sphere of politics a perfectly appropriate analogy to the extraordinary affection which I feel for my friend R, who is so disparaged in the dream-interpretation. I refer to the political life of a State in which the ruler, jealous of his rights, and an active public opinion are in mutual conflict. The people, protesting against the actions of an unpopular official, demand his dismissal. The autocrat, on the other hand, in order to show his contempt for the popular will, may then deliberately confer upon the official some exceptional distinction which otherwise would not have been conferred. Similarly, my second instance, controlling the access to my consciousness, distinguishes my friend R with a rush of extraordinary affection, because the wish-tendencies of the first system, in view of a particular interest on which they are just then intent, would like to disparage him as a simpleton.[1]

---

[1] Such hypocritical dreams are not rare, either with me or with others. While I have been working at a certain scientific problem, at quite short intervals, by a somewhat confusing dream which has as its content a reconciliation with a friend dropped long ago. After three or four attempts I finally succeeded in grasping the meaning of this dream. It was in the nature of an encouragement to give up the remnant of consideration still surviving for the person in question, to make myself quite free from him, but it hypocritically disguised itself in its antithesis. I have recorded a "hypocritical Oedipus dream" in which the hostile feelings and death-wishes of the dream-thoughts were replaced by manifest tenderness (*"Typisches Beispiel eines verkappten Oedipusträumes." Zentralblatt für Psychoanalyse,* Vol. I,

We may now perhaps begin to suspect that dream-interpretation is capable of yielding information concerning the structure of our psychic apparatus which we have hitherto vainly expected from philosophy. We shall not, however, follow up this trail, but shall return to our original problem as soon as we have elucidated the problem of dream-distortion. The question arose, how dreams with a disagreeable content can be analysed as wish-fulfillments. We see now that this is possible where a dream-distortion has occurred, when the disagreeable content serves only to disguise the thing wished for. With regard to our assumptions respecting the two psychic instances, we can now also say that disagreeable dreams contain, as a matter of fact, something which is disagreeable to the second instance, but which at the same time fulfills a wish of the first instance. They are wish-dreams in so far as every dream emanates from the first instance, while the second instance behaves towards the dream only in a defensive, not in a constructive manner.[2] Were we to limit ourselves to a consideration of what the second instance contributes to the dream we should never understand the dream, and all the problems which the writers on the subject have discovered in the dream would have to remain unsolved.

That the dream actually has a secret meaning, which proves to be a wish-fulfillment, must be proved afresh in every case by analysis. I will therefore select a few dreams which have painful contents, and endeavour to analyse them. Some of them are dreams of hysterical subjects, which therefore call for a long preliminary statement, and in some passages an examination of the psychic processes occurring in hysteria. This, though it will complicate the presentation, is unavoidable.

When I treat a psychoneurotic patient analytically, his dreams regularly, as I have said, become a theme of our conversations. I must therefore give him all the psychological explanations with whose aid I myself have succeeded in understanding his symptoms. And here I encounter unsparing criticism, which is perhaps no less shrewd than that which I have to expect from my colleagues. With perfect uniformity, my patients contradict the doctrine that dreams are the fulfillments of wishes. Here

---

No. I-II [1910]). Another class of hypocritical dreams will be recorded in another place (see Chap. vi, "The Dream-Work").

[2] Later on we shall become acquainted with cases in which, on the contrary, the dream expresses a wish of this second instance.

are several examples of the sort of dream-material which is adduced in refutation of my theory.

"You are always saying that a dream is a wish fulfilled," begins an intelligent lady patient. "Now I shall tell you a dream in which the content is quite the opposite, in which a wish of mine is not fulfilled. How do you reconcile that with your theory? The dream was as follows: *I want to give a supper, but I have nothing available except some smoked salmon. I think I will go shopping, but I remember that it is Sunday afternoon, when all the shops are closed. I then try to ring up a few caterers, but the telephone is out of order. Accordingly I have to renounce my desire to give a supper.*"

I reply, of course, that only the analysis can decide the meaning of this dream, although I admit that at first sight it seems sensible and coherent and looks like the opposite of a wish-fulfilment. "But what occurrence gave rise to this dream?" I ask. "You know that the stimulus of a dream always lies among the experiences of the preceding day."

Analysis

The patient's husband, an honest and capable meat salesman, had told her the day before that he was growing too fat, and that he meant to undergo treatment for obesity. He would rise early, take physical exercise, keep to a strict diet, and above all accept no more invitations to supper. She proceeds jestingly to relate how her husband, at a *table d'hôte*, had made the acquaintance of an artist, who insisted upon painting his portrait, because he, the painter, had never seen such an expressive head. But her husband had answered in his downright fashion, that while he was much obliged, he would rather not be painted; and he was quite convinced that a bit of a pretty girl's posterior would please the artist better than his whole face.[1] She is very much in love with her husband, and teases him a good deal. She has asked him not to give her any caviar. What can that mean?

As a matter of fact, she had wanted for a long time to eat a caviar sandwich every morning, but had grudged the expense. Of course she could get the caviar from her husband at once if she asked for it. But she has, on the contrary, begged him not to give her any cav-

iar, so that she might tease him about it a little longer.

(To me this explanation seems thin. Unconfessed motives are wont to conceal themselves behind just such unsatisfying explanations. We are reminded of the subjects hypnotized by Bernheim, who carried out a post-hypnotic order, and who, on being questioned as to their motives, instead of answering: "I do not know why I did that," had to invent a reason that was obviously inadequate. There is probably something similar to this in the case of my patient's caviar. I see that in waking life she is compelled to invent an unfulfilled wish. Her dream also shows her the non-fulfillment of her wish. But why does she need an unfulfilled wish?)

The ideas elicited so far are insufficient for the interpretation of the dream. I press for more. After a short pause, which corresponds to the overcoming of a resistance, she reports that the day before she had paid a visit to a friend of whom she is really jealous because her husband is always praising this lady so highly. Fortunately this friend is very thin and lanky, and her husband likes full figures. Now of what did this thin friend speak? Of course, of her wish to become rather plumper. She also asked my patient: "When are you going to invite us again? You always have such good food."

Now the meaning of the dream is clear. I am able to tell the patient: "It is just as though you had thought at the moment of her asking you that: 'Of course, I'm to invite you so that you can eat at my house and get fat and become still more pleasing to my husband! I would rather give no more suppers!' The dream then tells you that you cannot give a supper, thereby fulfilling your wish not to contribute anything to the rounding out of your friend's figure. Your husband's resolution to accept no more invitations to supper in order that he may grow thin teaches you that one grows fat on food eaten at other people's tables." Nothing is lacking now but some sort of coincidence which will confirm the solution. The smoked salmon in the dream has not yet been traced.— "How did you come to think of salmon in your dream?"—"Smoked salmon is my friend's favourite dish," she replied. It happens that I know the lady, and am able to affirm that she grudges herself salmon just as my patient grudges herself caviar.

This dream admits of yet another and more exact interpretation—one which is actually necessitated only by a subsidiary circumstance.

[1] To sit for the painter.
Goethe: *And if he has no backside,*
How can the nobleman sit?

The two interpretations do not contradict one another, but rather dovetail into one another, and furnish an excellent example of the usual ambiguity of dreams, as of all other psychopathological formations. We have heard that at the time of her dream of a denied wish the patient was impelled to deny herself a real wish (the wish to eat caviar sandwiches). Her friend, too, had expressed a wish, namely, to get fatter, and it would not surprise us if our patient had dreamt that this wish of her friend's—the wish to increase in weight—was not to be fulfilled. Instead of this, however, she dreamt that one of her own wishes was not fulfilled. The dream becomes capable of a new interpretation if in the dream she does not mean herself, but her friend, if she has put herself in the place of her friend, or, as we may say, has *identified* herself with her friend.

I think she has actually done this, and as a sign of this identification she has created for herself in real life an unfulfilled wish. But what is the meaning of this hysterical indentification? To elucidate this a more exhaustive exposition is necessary. Identification is a highly important motive in the mechanism of hysterical symptoms; by this means patients are enabled to express in their symptoms not merely their own experiences, but the experiences of quite a number of other persons; they can suffer, as it were, for a whole mass of people, and fill all the parts of a drama with their own personalities. It will here be objected that this is the well-known hysterical imitation, the ability of hysterical subjects to imitate all the symptoms which impress them when they occur in others, as though pity were aroused to the point of reproduction. This, however, only indicates the path which the psychic process follows in hysterical imitation. But the path itself and the psychic act which follows this path are two different matters. The act itself is slightly more complicated than we are prone to believe the imitation of the hysterical to be; it corresponds to an unconscious end-process, as an example will show. The physician who has, in the same ward with other patients, a female patient suffering from a particular kind of twitching, is not surprised if one morning he learns that this peculiar hysterical affection has found imitators. He merely tells himself: The others have seen her, and have imitated her; this is psychic infection. Yes, but psychic infection occurs somewhat in the following manner: As a rule, patients know more about one another than the physician knows

about any one of them, and they are concerned about one another when the doctor's visit is over. One of them has an attack to-day: at once it is known to the rest that a letter from home, a recrudescence of lovesickness, or the like, is the cause. Their sympathy is aroused, and although it does not emerge into consciousness they form the following conclusion: "If it is possible to suffer such an attack from such a cause, I too may suffer this sort of an attack, for I have the same occasion for it." If this were a conclusion capable of becoming conscious, it would perhaps express itself in *dread* of suffering a like attack; but it is formed in another psychic region, and consequently ends in the realization of the dreaded symptoms. Thus identification is not mere imitation, but an assimilation based upon the same aetiological claim; it expresses a *just like*, and refers to some common condition which has remained in the unconscious.

In hysteria, identification is most frequently employed to express a sexual community. The hysterical woman identifies herself by her symptoms most readily—though not exclusively—with persons with whom she has had sexual relations, or who have had sexual intercourse with the same persons as herself. Language takes cognizance of this tendency: two lovers are said to be "one." In hysterical phantasy, as well as in dreams, identification may ensue if one simply thinks of sexual relations; they need not necessarily become actual. The patient is merely following the rules of the hysterical processes of thought when she expresses her jealousy of her friend (which, for that matter, she herself admits to be unjustified) by putting herself in her friend's place in her dream, and identifying herself with her by fabricating a symptom (the denied wish). One might further elucidate the process by saying: In the dream she puts herself in the place of her friend, because her friend has taken her own place in relation to her husband, and because she would like to take her friend's place in her husband's esteem.[1]

The contradiction of my theory of dreams on the part of another female patient, the most intelligent of all my dreamers, was solved in a simpler fashion, though still in accordance with the principle that the non-fulfilment of one

[1] I myself regret the inclusion of such passages from the psycho-pathology of hysteria, which, because of their fragmentary presentation, and because they are torn out of their context, cannot prove to be very illuminating. If these passages are capable of throwing any light upon the intimate relations between dream and the psycho-neurosis, they have served the intention with which I have included them.

wish signified the fulfilment of another. I had one day explained to her that a dream is a wish-fulfilment. On the following day she related a dream to the effect that she was travelling with her mother-in-law to the place in which they were both to spend the summer. Now I knew that she had violently protested against spending the summer in the neighbourhood of her mother-in-law. I also knew that she had fortunately been able to avoid doing so, since she had recently succeeded in renting a house in a place quite remote from that to which her mother-in-law was going. And now the dream reversed this desired solution. Was not this a flat contradiction of my theory of wish-fulfilment? One had only to draw the inferences from this dream in order to arrive at its interpretation. According to this dream, I was wrong; *but it was her wish that I should be wrong, and this wish the dream showed her as fulfilled.* But the wish that I should be wrong, which was fulfilled in the theme of the country house, referred in reality to another and more serious matter. At that time I had inferred, from the material furnished by her analysis, that something of significance in respect to her illness must have occurred at a certain time in her life. She had denied this, because it was not present in her memory. We soon came to see that I was right. Thus her wish that I should prove to be wrong, which was transformed into the dream that she was going into the country with her mother-in-law, corresponded with the justifiable wish that those things which were then only suspected had never occurred.

Without an analysis, and merely by means of an assumption, I took the liberty of interpreting a little incident in the life of a friend, who had been my companion through eight classes at school. He once heard a lecture of mine, delivered to a small audience, on the novel idea that dreams are wish-fulfilments. He went home, dreamt *that he had lost all his lawsuits*—he was a lawyer—and then complained to me about it. I took refuge in the evasion: "One can't win all one's cases"; but I thought to myself: "If, for eight years, I sat as *primus* on the first bench, while he moved up and down somewhere in the middle of the class, may he not naturally have had the wish, ever since his boyhood, that I too might for once make a fool of myself?"

Yet another dream of a more gloomy character was offered me by a female patient in contradiction of my theory of the wish-dream. This patient, a young girl, began as follows:

"You remember that my sister has now only one boy, Charles. She lost the elder one, Otto, while I was still living with her. Otto was my favourite; it was I who really brought him up. I like the other little fellow, too, but, of course, not nearly as much as his dead brother. Now I dreamt last night that I *saw Charles lying dead before me. He was lying in his little coffin, his hands folded; there were candles all about; and, in short, it was just as it was at the time of little Otto's death, which gave me such a shock.* Now tell me, what does this mean? You know me—am I really so bad as to wish that my sister should lose the only child she has left? Or does the dream mean that I wish that Charles had died rather than Otto, whom I liked so much better?"

I assured her that this latter interpretation was impossible. After some reflection, I was able to give her the interpretation of the dream, which she subsequently confirmed. I was able to do so because the whole previous history of the dreamer was known to me.

Having become an orphan at an early age, the girl had been brought up in the home of a much older sister, and had met, among the friends and visitors who frequented the house, a man who made a lasting impression upon her affections. It looked for a time as though these barely explicit relations would end in marriage, but this happy culmination was frustrated by the sister, whose motives were never completely explained. After the rupture the man whom my patient loved avoided the house; she herself attained her independence some time after the death of little Otto, to whom, meanwhile, her affections had turned. But she did not succeed in freeing herself from the dependence due to her affection for her sister's friend. Her pride bade her avoid him, but she found it impossible to transfer her love to the other suitors who successively presented themselves. Whenever the man she loved, who was a member of the literary profession, announced a lecture anywhere, she was certain to be found among the audience; and she seized every other opportunity of seeing him unobserved. I remembered that on the previous day she had told me that the Professor was going to a certain concert, and that she too was going, in order to enjoy the sight of him. This was on the day before the dream; and the concert was to be given on the day on which she told me the dream. I could now easily see the correct interpretation, and I asked her whether she could think of any particular event which had occurred after Otto's death. She replied immediately: "Of course; the Professor returned then, after a long absence, and I saw him once more beside little Otto's coffin." It was just as I had expected. I interpreted the dream as follows: "If now the other boy were to die, the same thing would happen again. You would spend the day with your sister; the Professor would certainly come to offer his condolences, and you would see him once more under the same circumstances as before. The dream signifies nothing more than this wish of yours to see him again— a wish against which you are fighting inwardly. I know that you have the ticket for today's concert in your bag. Your dream is a dream of impatience; it has anticipated by several hours the meeting which is to take place to-day."

In order to disguise her wish she had obviously selected a situation in which wishes of the sort are commonly suppressed—a situation so sorrowful that love is not even thought of. And yet it is entirely possible that even in the actual situation beside the coffin of the elder, more dearly loved boy, she had not been able to suppress her tender affection for the visitor whom she had missed for so long.

A different explanation was found in the case of a similar dream of another patient, who in earlier life had been distinguished for her quick wit and her cheerful disposition, and who still displayed these qualities, at all events in the free associations which occurred to her during treatment. In the course of a longer dream, it seemed to this lady that she saw her fifteen-year-old daughter lying dead before her in a box. She was strongly inclined to use this dream-image as an objection to the theory of wish-fulfilment, although she herself suspected that the detail of the box must lead to a different conception of the dream[1] For in the course of the analysis it occurred to her that on the previous evening the conversation of the people in whose company she found herself had turned on the English word *box,* and upon the numerous translations of it into German such as *Schachtel* (box), *Loge* (box at the theatre), *Kasten* (chest), *Ohrfeige* (box on the ear), etc. From other components of the same dream it was now possible to add the fact that the lady had guessed at the relationship between the English word "box" and the German *Büchse,* and had then been haunted by the recollection that *Büchse* is used in vulgar parlance to denote the female genitals. It was therefore possible, treating her knowledge of topographical anatomy with a certain indulgence, to assume that the child in the box signified a child in the mother's womb. At this stage of the explanation she no longer denied that the picture in the dream actually corresponded with a wish of hers. Like so many other young women, she was by no means happy on finding that she was pregnant, and she had confessed to me more than once the wish that her child might die before its birth; in a fit of anger, following a violent scene with her husband, she had even struck her abdomen with her fists, in order to injure the child within. The dead child was therefore, really the fulfilment of a wish, but a wish which had been put aside for fifteen years, and it is not surprising that the fulfilment of the wish was no longer recognized after so long an interval. For there had been many changes in the meantime.

The group of dreams (having as content the death of beloved relatives) to which belong the last two mentioned will be considered again under the head of "Typical Dreams." I shall then be able to show by new examples that in spite of their undesirable content all these dreams must be interpreted as wish-fulfilments. For the following dream, which again was told me in order to deter me from a hasty generalization of my theory, I am indebted, not to a patient, but to an intelligent jurist of my acquaintance. *"I dream,"* my informant tells me, *"that I am walking in front of my house with a lady on my arm. Here a closed carriage is waiting; a man steps up to me, shows me his authorization as a police officer, and requests me to follow him. I ask only for time in which to arrange my affairs."* The jurist then asks me: "Can you possibly suppose that it is my wish to be arrested?"—"Of course not," I have to admit. "Do you happen to know upon what charge you were arrested?"—"Yes; I believe for infanticide."—"Infanticide? But you know that only a mother can commit this crime upon her new-born child?"—"That is true."[2]—"And under what circumstances did you dream this? What happened on the evening before?"—"I would rather not tell you— it is a delicate matter."—"But I need it, otherwise we must forgo the interpretation of the dream."—"Well, then, I will tell you. I spent

---

[1] As in the dream of the deferred supper and the smoked salmon.

[2] It often happens that a dream is told incompletely, and that a recollection of the omitted portions appears only in the course of the analysis. These portions, when subsequently fitted in, invariably furnish the key to the interpretation. Cf. Chapter VII, on forgetting of dreams.

the night, not at home, but in the house of a lady who means a great deal to me. When we awoke in the morning, something again passed between us. Then I went to sleep again, and dreamt what I have told you."—"The woman is married?"—"Yes."—"And you do not wish her to conceive?"—"No; that might betray us."—"Then you do not practice normal coitus?"—"I take the precaution to withdraw before ejaculation."—"Am I to assume that you took this precaution several times during the night, and that in the morning you were not quite sure whether you had succeeded?"—"That might be so."—"Then your dream is the fulfilment of a wish. By the dream you are assured that you have not begotten a child, or, what amounts to the same thing, that you have killed the child. I can easily demonstrate the connecting-links. Do you remember, a few days ago we were talking about the troubles of matrimony, and about the inconsistency of permitting coitus so long as no impregnation takes place, while at the same time any preventive act committed after the ovum and the semen meet and a foetus is formed is punished as a crime? In this connection we recalled the medieval controversy about the moment of time at which the soul actually enters into the foetus, since the concept of murder becomes admissible only from that point onwards. Of course, too, you know the gruesome poem by Lenau, which puts infanticide and birth-control on the same plane."—"Strangely enough, I happened, as though by chance, to think of Lenau this morning."—"Another echo of your dream. And now I shall show you yet another incidental wish-fulfilment in your dream. You walk up to your house with the lady on your arm. So you take her home, instead of spending the night at her house, as you did in reality. The fact that the wish-fulfilment, which is the essence of the dream, disguises itself in such an unpleasant form, has perhaps more than one explanation. From my essay on the aetiology of anxiety neurosis, you will see that I note *coitus interruptus* as one of the factors responsible for the development of neurotic fear. It would be consistent with this if, after repeated coitus of this kind, you were left in an uncomfortable frame of mind, which now becomes an element of the composition of your dream. You even make use of this uncomfortable state of mind to conceal the wish-fulfilment. At the same time, the mention of infanticide has not yet been explained. Why does this crime, which is peculiar to females, occur to you?"—"I will confess to you that I was involved in such an affair years ago. I was responsible for the fact that a girl tried to protect herself from the consequences of a *liaison* with me by procuring an abortion. I had nothing to do with the carrying out of her plan, but for a long time I was naturally worried in case the affair might be discovered."—"I understand. This recollection furnished a second reason why the supposition that you had performed *coitus interruptus* clumsily must have been painful to you."

A young physician, who heard this dream related in my lecture-room, must have felt that it fitted him, for he hastened to imitate it by a dream of his own, applying its mode of thinking to another theme. On the previous day he had furnished a statement of his income; a quite straightforward statement, because he had little to state. He dreamt that an acquaintance of his came from a meeting of the tax commission and informed him that all the other statements had passed unquestioned, but that his own had aroused general suspicion, with the result that he would be punished with a heavy fine. This dream is a poorly disguised fulfilment of the wish to be known as a physician with a large income. It also calls to mind the story of the young girl who was advised against accepting her suitor because he was a man of quick temper, who would assuredly beat her after their marriage. Her answer was: "I wish he *would* strike me!" Her wish to be married was so intense that she had taken into consideration the discomforts predicted for this marriage; she had even raised them to the plane of a wish.

If I group together the very frequent dreams of this sort, which seem flatly to contradict my theory, in that they embody the denial of a wish or some occurrence obviously undesired, under the head of *counter-wish-dreams*, I find that they may all be referred to two principles, one of which has not yet been mentioned, though it plays a large part in waking as well as dream-life. One of the motives inspiring these dreams is the wish that I should appear in the wrong. These dreams occur regularly in the course of treatment whenever the patient is in a state of resistance; indeed, I can with a great degree of certainty count on evoking such a dream once I have explained to the patient my theory that the dream is a wish-fulfilment.[1] Indeed, I have reason to expect that many of

[1] Similar *counter-wish-dreams* have been repeatedly reported to me within the last few years, by those who attend my lectures, as their reaction to their first encounter with the *wish-theory* of dreams.

my readers will have such dreams, merely to fulfil the wish that I may prove to be wrong. The last dream which I shall recount from among those occurring in the course of treatment once more demonstrates this very thing. A young girl who had struggled hard to continue my treatment, against the will of her relatives and the authorities whom they had consulted, dreamt the following dream: *At home she is forbidden to come to me any more. She then reminds me of the promise I made her to treat her for nothing if necessary, and I tell her: "I can show no consideration in money matters."*

It is not at all easy in this case to demonstrate the fulfilment of a wish, but in all cases of this kind there is a second problem, the solution of which helps also to solve the first. Where does she get the words which she puts into my mouth? Of course, I have never told her anything of the kind; but one of her brothers, the one who has the greatest influence over her, has been kind enough to make this remark about me. It is then the purpose of the dream to show that her brother is right; and she does not try to justify this brother merely in the dream; it is her purpose in life and the motive of her illness.

A dream which at first sight presents peculiar difficulties for the theory of wish-fulfilment was dreamed by a physician (Aug. Stärcke) and interpreted by him: *"I have and see on the last phalange of my left forefinger a primary syphilitic affection."*

One may perhaps be inclined to refrain from analysing this dream, since it seems clear and coherent, except for its unwished-for content. However, if one takes the trouble to make an analysis, one learns that *primary affection* reduces itself to *prima affectio* (first love), and that the repulsive sore, in the words of Stärcke, proves to be "the representative of wish-fulfilments charged with intense emotion." [1]

The other motive for counter-wish-dreams is so clear that there is a danger of overlooking it, as happened in my own case for a long time. In the sexual constitution of many persons there is a masochistic component, which has arisen through the conversion of the aggressive, sadistic component into its opposite. Such people are called *ideal* masochists if they seek pleasure not in the bodily pain which may be inflicted upon them, but in humiliation and psychic chastisement. It is obvious that such persons may have counter-wish-dreams and disagreeable dreams, yet these are for them

nothing more than wish-fulfilments, which satisfy their masochistic inclinations. Here is such a dream: A young man, who in earlier youth greatly tormented his elder brother, toward whom he was homosexually inclined, but who has since undergone a complete change of character, has the following dream, which consists of three parts: (1) *He is "teased" by his brother.* (2) *Two adults are caressing each other with homosexual intentions.* (3) *His brother has sold the business the management of which the young man had reserved for his own future.* From this last dream he awakens with the most unpleasant feelings; and yet it is a masochistic wish-dream, which might be translated: It would serve me right if my brother were to make that sale against my interests. It would be my punishment for all the torments he has suffered at my hands.

I hope that the examples given above will suffice—until some further objection appears —to make it seem credible that even dreams with a painful content are to be analysed as wish-fulfilments. [2] Nor should it be considered a mere matter of chance that, in the course of interpretation, one always happens upon subjects about which one does not like to speak or think. The disagreeable sensation which such dreams arouse is of course precisely identical with the antipathy which would, and usually does, restrain us from treating or discussing such subjects—an antipathy which must be overcome by all of us if we find ourselves obliged to attack the problem of such dreams. But this disagreeable feeling which recurs in our dreams does not preclude the existence of a wish; everyone has wishes which he would not like to confess to others, which he does not care to admit even to himself. On the other hand, we feel justified in connecting the unpleasant character of all these dreams with the fact of dream-distortion, and in concluding that these dreams are distorted, and that their wish-fulfilment is disguised beyond recognition, precisely because there is a strong revulsion against—a will to repress—the subject-matter of the dream, or the wish created by it. Dream-distortion, then, proves in reality to be an act of censorship. We shall have included everything which the analysis of disagreeable dreams has brought to light if we reword our formula thus: *The dream is the (disguised) fulfilment of a (suppressed, repressed) wish.* [3]

---

[1] *Zentralblatt für Psychoanalyse,* Jahrg. II, 1911-12.

[2] I will here observe that we have not yet disposed of this theme; we shall discuss it again later.

[3] A great contemporary poet, who, I am told, will hear nothing of psycho-analysis and dream-inter-

Now there still remain to be considered, as a particular sub-order of dreams with painful content, the anxiety-dreams, the inclusion of which among the wish-dreams will be still less acceptable to the uninitiated. But I can here deal very cursorily with the problem of anxiety-dreams; what they have to reveal is not a new aspect of the dream-problem; here the problem is that of understanding neurotic anxiety in general. The anxiety which we experience in dreams is only apparently explained by the dream-content. If we subject that content to analysis, we become aware that the dream-anxiety is no more justified by the dream-content than the anxiety in a phobia is justified by the idea to which the phobia is attached. For example, it is true that it is possible to fall out of a window, and that a certain care should be exercised when one is at a window, but it is not obvious why the anxiety in the corresponding phobia is so great, and why it torments its victims more than its cause would warrant. The same explanation which applies to the phobia applies also to the anxiety-dream. In either case, the anxiety is only *fastened on to* the idea which accompanies it, and is derived from another source.

pretation, has nevertheless derived from his own experience an almost identical formula for the nature of the dream: "Unauthorized emergence of suppressed yearnings under false features and names" (C. Spitteler, "*Meine frühesten Erlebnisse,*" in *Süddeutsche Monatshefte,* October, 1913).

I will here anticipate by citing the amplification and modification of this fundamental formula propounded by Otto Rank: "On the basis of and with the aid of repressed infantile-sexual material, dreams regularly represent as fulfilled current, and as a rule also erotic, wishes in a disguised and symbolic form" (*Ein Traum, der sich selbst deutet*).

Nowhere have I said that I have accepted this formula of Rank's. The shorter version contained in the text seems to me sufficient. But the fact that I merely mentioned Rank's modification was enough to expose psycho-analysis to the oft-repeated reproach that it asserts that *all dreams have a sexual content*. If one understands this sentence as it is intended to be understood, it only proves how little conscientiousness our critics are wont to display, and how ready our opponents are to overlook statements if they do not accord with their aggressive inclinations. Only a few pages back I mentioned the manifold wish-fulfilments of children's dreams (to make an excursion on land or water, to make up for an omitted meal, etc.). Elsewhere I have mentioned dreams excited by thirst and the desire to evacuate, and mere comfort- or convenience-dreams. Even Rank does not make an absolute assertion. He says "as a rule also erotic wishes," and this can be completely confirmed in the case of most dreams of adults.

The matter has, however, a different aspect if we employ the word *sexual* in the sense of *Eros*, as the word is understood by psycho-analysts. But the interesting problem of whether all dreams are not produced by *libidinal* motives (in opposition to *destructive* ones) has hardly been considered by our opponents.

On account of this intimate relation of dream-anxiety to neurotic anxiety, the discussion of the former obliges me to refer to the latter. In a little essay on *Anxiety Neurosis,*[1] written in 1895, I maintain that neurotic anxiety has its origin in the sexual life, and corresponds to a libido which has been deflected from its object and has found no employment. The accuracy of this formula has since then been demonstrated with ever-increasing certainty. From it we may deduce the doctrine that anxiety-dreams are dreams of sexual content, and that the libido appertaining to this content has been transformed into anxiety. Later on I shall have an opportunity of confirming this assertion by the analysis of several dreams of neurotics. In my further attempts to arrive at a theory of dreams I shall again have occasion to revert to the conditions of anxiety-dreams and their compatibility with the theory of wish-fulfilment.

V. THE MATERIAL AND SOURCES OF DREAMS

HAVING realized, as a result of analysing the dream of Irma's injection, that the dream was the fulfilment of a wish, we were immediately interested to ascertain whether we had thereby discovered a general characteristic of dreams, and for the time being we put aside every other scientific problem which may have suggested itself in the course of the interpretation. Now that we have reached the goal on this one path, we may turn back and select a new point of departure for exploring dream-problems, even though we may for a time lose sight of the theme of wish-fulfilment, which has still to be further considered.

Now that we are able, by applying our process of interpretation, to detect a *latent* dream-content whose significance far surpasses that of the *manifest* dream-content, we are naturally impelled to return to the individual dream-problems, in order to see whether the riddles and contradictions which seemed to elude us when we had only the manifest content to work upon may not now be satisfactorily solved.

The opinions of previous writers on the relation of dreams to waking life, and the origin of the material of dreams, have not been given here. We may recall however three peculiarities of the memory in dreams, which have been often noted, but never explained:

1. That the dream clearly prefers the impressions of the last few days (Robert, Strümpell, Hildebrandt; also Weed-Hallam);

[1] See p. 87 above.

2. That it makes a selection in accordance with principles other than those governing our waking memory, in that it recalls not essential and important, but subordinate and disregarded things;

3. That it has at its disposal the earliest impressions of our childhood, and brings to light details from this period of life, which, again, seem trivial to us, and which in waking life were believed to have been long since forgotten.[1]

These peculiarities in the dream's choice of material have, of course, been observed by previous writers in the manifest dream content.

A. Recent and Indifferent Impressions in the Dream

If I now consult my own experience with regard to the origin of the elements appearing in the dream-content, I must in the first place express the opinion that in every dream we may find some reference to the experiences of the *preceding day*. Whatever dream I turn to, whether my own or somone else's, this experience is always confirmed. Knowing this, I may perhaps begin the work of interpretation by looking for the experience of the preceding day which has stimulated the dream; in many cases this is indeed the quickest way. With the two dreams which I subjected to a close analysis in the last chapter (the dreams of Irma's injection, and of the uncle with the yellow beard) the reference to the preceding day is so evident that it needs no further elucidation. But in order to show how constantly this reference may be demonstrated, I shall examine a portion of my own dream-chronicle. I shall relate only so much of the dreams as is necessary for the detection of the dream-source in question.

1. *I pay a call at a house to which I gain admittance only with difficulty, etc., and meanwhile I am keeping a woman waiting for me.*

Source: A conversation during the evening with a female relative to the effect that she would have to wait for a remittance for which she had asked, until . . . etc.

2. *I have written a monograph on a species (uncertain) of plant.*

Source: In the morning I had seen in a bookseller's window a *monograph* on the genus Cyclamen.

3. *I see two women in the street, mother and daughter, the latter being a patient.*

Source: A female patient who is under treatment had told me in the evening what difficulties her *mother* puts in the way of her continuing the treatment.

4. *At S and R's bookshop I subscribe to a periodical which costs 20 florins annually.*

Source: During the day my wife has reminded me that I still owe her *20 florins* of her weekly allowance.

5. *I receive a communication from the Social Democratic Committee, in which I am addressed as a member.*

Source: I have received simultaneous *communications* from the Liberal Committee on Elections and from the president of the Humanitarian Society, of which latter I am actually a member.

6. *A man on a steep rock rising from the sea, in the manner of Böcklin.*

Source: Dreyfus on Devil's Island; also news from my relatives in *England*, etc.

The question might be raised, whether a dream invariably refers to the events of the preceding day only, or whether the reference may be extended to include impressions from a longer period of time in the immediate past. This question is probably not of the first importance, but I am inclined to decide in favour of the exclusive priority of the day before the dream (the dream-day). Whenever I thought I had found a case where an impression two or three days old was the source of the dream, I was able to convince myself after careful investigation that this impression had been remembered the day before; that is, that a demonstrable reproduction on the day before had been interpolated between the day of the event and the time of the dream; and further, I was able to point to the recent occasion which might have given rise to the recollection of the older impression. On the other hand, I was unable to convince myself that a regular interval of biological significance (H. Swoboda gives the first interval of this kind as eighteen hours) elapses between the dream-exciting daytime impression and its recurrence in the dream.

I believe, therefore, that for every dream a dream-stimulus may be found among those experiences "on which one has not yet slept."

Havelock Ellis, who has likewise given attention to this problem, states that he has not been able to find any such periodicity of reproduction in his dreams, although he has

---

[1] It is evident that Robert's idea—that the dream is intended to rid our memory of the useless impressions which it has received during the day—is no longer tenable if indifferent memories of our childhood appear in our dreams with some degree of frequency. We should be obliged to conclude that our dreams generally perform their prescribed task very inadequately.

looked for it. He relates a dream in which he found himself in Spain; he wanted to travel to a place called *Daraus, Varaus,* or *Zaraus.* On awaking he was unable to recall any such place-names, and thought no more of the matter. A few months later he actually found the name Zaraus; it was that of a railway-station between San Sebastian and Bilbao, through which he had passed in the train eight months (250 days) before the date of the dream.

Thus the impressions of the immediate past (with the exception of the day before the night of the dream) stand in the same relation to the dream-content as those of periods indefinitely remote. The dream may select its material from any period of life, provided only that a chain of thought leads back from the experiences of the day of the dream (the *recent* impressions) of that earlier period.

But why this preference for recent impressions? We shall arrive at some conjectures on this point if we subject one of the dreams already mentioned to a more precise analysis. I select the

Dream of the Botanical Monograph

I have written a monograph on a certain plant. The book lies before me; I am just turning over a folded coloured plate. A dried specimen of the plant, as though from a herbarium, is bound up with every copy.

Analysis

In the morning I saw in a bookseller's window a volume entitled *The Genus Cyclamen,* apparently a monograph on this plant.

The cyclamen is my wife's favorite flower. I reproach myself for remembering so seldom to bring her flowers, as she would like me to do. In connection with the theme of giving her flowers, I am reminded of a story which I recently told some friends of mine in proof of my assertion that we often forget in obedience to a purpose of the unconscious, and that forgetfulness always enables us to form a deduction about the secret disposition of the forgetful person. A young woman who has been accustomed to receive a bouquet of flowers from her husband on her birthday misses this token of affection on one of her birthdays, and bursts into tears. The husband comes in, and cannot understand why she is crying until she tells him: "Today is my birthday." He claps his hand to his forehead, and exclaims: "Oh, forgive me, I had completely forgotten it!" and proposes to go out immediately in order to get her flowers. But she refuses to be consoled, for she sees in her husband's forgetfulness a proof that she no longer plays the same part in his thoughts as she formerly did. This Frau L met my wife two days ago, told her that she was feeling well, and asked after me. Some years ago she was a patient of mine.

Supplementary facts: I did once actually write something like a monograph on a plant, namely, an essay on the coca plant, which attracted the attention of K. Koller to the anaesthetic properties of cocaine. I had hinted that the alkaloid might be employed as an anaesthetic, but I was not thorough enough to pursue the matter farther. It occurs to me, too, that on the morning of the day following the dream (for the interpretation of which I did not find time until the evening) I had thought of cocaine in a kind of day-dream. If I were ever afflicted with glaucoma, I would go to Berlin, and there undergo an operation, incognito, in the house of my Berlin friend, at the hands of a surgeon whom he would recommend. The surgeon, who would not know the name of his patient, would boast, as usual, how easy these operations had become since the introduction of cocaine; and I should not betray the fact that I myself had a share in this discovery. With this phantasy were connected thoughts of how awkward it really is for a physician to claim the professional services of a colleague. I should be able to pay the Berlin eye specialist, who did not know me, like anyone else. Only after recalling this day-dream do I realize that there is concealed behind it the memory of a definite event. Shortly after Koller's discovery, my father contracted glaucoma; he was operated on by my friend Dr. Koenigstein, the eye specialist. Dr. Koller was in charge of the cocaine anaesthetization, and he made the remark that on this occasion all the three persons who had been responsible for the introduction of cocaine had been brought together.

My thoughts now pass on to the time when I was last reminded of the history of cocaine. This was a few days earlier, when I received a *Festschrift,* a publication in which grateful pupils had commemorated the jubilee of their teacher and laboratory director. Among the titles to fame of persons connected with the laboratory I found a note to the effect that the discovery of the anaesthetic properties of cocaine had been due to K. Koller. Now I suddenly become aware that the dream is connected with an experience of the previous evening. I had just accompanied Dr. Koenig-stein to his home, and had entered into a discussion of a subject which excites me greatly whenever it is mentioned. While I was talking with him in the entrance-hall Professor Gärtner and his young wife came up. I could not refrain from congratulating them both upon their *blooming* appearance. Now Professor Gärtner is one of the authors of the *Festschrift* of which I have just spoken, and he may well have reminded me of it. And Frau L, of whose birthday disappointment I spoke a little way back, had been mentioned, though of course in another connection, in my conversation with Dr. Koenigstein.

I shall now try to elucidate the other determinants of the dream-content. A *dried specimen* of the plant accompanies the monograph, as though it were a *herbarium*. And herbarium reminds me of the Gymnasium. The director of our Gymnasium once called the pupils of the upper classes together, in order that they might examine and clean the Gymnasium herbarium. Small insects had been found—*book-worms*. The director seemed to have little confidence in my ability to assist, for he entrusted me with only a few of the pages. I know to this day that there were crucifers on them. My interest in botany was never very great. At my preliminary examination in botany I was required to identify a crucifer, and failed to recognize it; had not my theoretical knowledge come to my aid, I should have fared badly indeed. Crucifers suggest composites. The artichoke is really a composite, and in actual fact one which I might call my *favourite flower*. My wife, more thoughtful than I, often brings this favourite flower of mine home from the market.

I see the monograph which I have written lying before me. Here again there is an association. My friend wrote to me yesterday from Berlin: "I am thinking a great deal about your dream-book. I see it lying before me, completed, and I turn the pages." How I envied him this power of vision! If only I could see it lying before me, already completed!

The folded coloured plate. When I was a medical student I suffered a sort of craze for studying monographs exclusively. In spite of my limited means, I subscribed to a number of the medical periodicals, whose *coloured plates* afforded me much delight. I was rather proud of this inclination to thoroughness. When I subsequently began to publish books myself, I had to draw the plates for my own treatises,

and I remember one of them turned out so badly that a well-meaning colleague ridiculed me for it. With this is associated, I do not exactly know how, a very early memory of my childhood. My father, by the way of a jest, once gave my elder sister and myself a book containing *coloured plates* (the book was a narrative of a journey through Persia) in order that we might destroy it. From an educational point of view this was hardly to be commended. I was at the time five years old, and my sister less than three, and the picture of us two children blissfully tearing the book to pieces (I should add, like an *artichoke*, leaf by leaf), is almost the only one from this period of my life which has remained vivid in my memory. When I afterwards became a student, I developed a conspicuous fondness for collecting and possessing books (an analogy to the inclination for studying from monographs, a hobby alluded to in my dream-thoughts, in connection with cyclamen and artichoke). I became a *book-worm* (cf. *herbarium*). Ever since I have been engaged in introspection I have always traced this earliest passion of my life to this impression of my childhood: or rather, I have recognized in this childish scene a screen or concealing memory for my subsequent bibliophilia.[1] And of course I learned at an early age that our passions often become our misfortunes. When I was seventeen, I ran up a very considerable account at the bookseller's, with no means with which to settle it, and my father would hardly accept it as an excuse that my passion was at least a respectable one. But the mention of this experience of my youth brings me back to my conversation with my friend Dr. Koenigstein on the evening preceding the dream; for one of the themes of this conversation was the same old reproach—that I am much too absorbed in my *hobbies*.

For reasons which are not relevant here I shall not continue the interpretation of this dream, but will merely indicate the path which leads to it. In the course of the interpretation I was reminded of my conversation with Dr. Koenigstein, and, indeed, of more than one portion of it. When I consider the subjects touched upon in this conversation, the meaning of the dream immediately becomes clear to me. All the trains of thought which have been started—my own inclinations, and those of my wife, the cocaine, the awkwardness of securing medical treatment from one's own colleagues,

[1] Cf. *The Psycho-pathology of Everyday Life.*

my preference for monographical studies, and my neglect of certain subjects, such as botany —all these are continued in and lead up to one branch or another of this widely-ramified conversation. The dream once more assumes the character of a justification, of a plea for my rights (like the dream of Irma's injection, the first to be analysed); it even continues the theme which that dream introduced, and discusses it in association with the new subject-matter which has been added in the interval between the two dreams. Even the dream's apparently indifferent form of expression at once acquires a meaning. Now it means: "I am indeed the man who has written that valuable and successful treatise (on cocaine)," just as previously I declared in self-justification: "I am after all a thorough and industrious student"; and in both instances I find the meaning: "I can allow myself this." But I may dispense with the further interpretation of the dream, because my only purpose in recording it was to examine the relation of the dream-content to the experience of the previous day which arouses it. As long as I know only the manifest content of this dream, only one relation to any impression of the day is obvious; but after I have completed the interpretation, a second source of the dream becomes apparent in another experience of the same day. The first of these impressions to which the dream refers is an indifferent one, a subordinate circumstance. I see a book in a shop window whose title holds me for a moment, but whose contents would hardly interest me. The second experience was of great psychic value; I talked earnestly with my friend, the eye specialist, for about an hour; I made allusions in this conversation which must have ruffled the feelings of both of us, and which in me awakened memories in connection with which I was aware of a great variety of inner stimuli. Further, this conversation was broken off unfinished, because some acquaintances joined us. What, now, is the relation of these two impressions of the day to one another, and to the dream which followed during the night?

In the manifest dream-content I find merely an allusion to the indifferent impression, and I am thus able to reaffirm that the dream prefers to take up into its content experiences of a non-essential character. In the dream-interpretation, on the contrary, everything converges upon the important and justifiably disturbing event. If I judge the sense of the dream in the only correct way, according to

the latent content which is brought to light in the analysis, I find that I have unwittingly lighted upon a new and important discovery. I see that the puzzling theory that the dream deals only with the worthless odds and ends of the day's experiences has no justification; I am also compelled to contradict the assertion that the psychic life of the waking state is not continued in the dream, and that hence, the dream wastes our psychic energy on trivial material. The very opposite is true; what has claimed our attention during the day dominates our dream-thoughts also, and we take pains to dream only in connection with such matters as have given us food for thought during the day.

Perhaps the most immediate explanation of the fact that I dream of the indifferent impression of the day, while the impression which has with good reason excited me causes me to dream, is that here again we are dealing with the phenomenon of dream-distortion, which we have referred to as a psychic force playing the part of a censorship. The recollection of the monograph on the genus cyclamen is utilized as though it were an *allusion* to the conversation with my friend, just as the mention of my patient's friend in the dream of the deferred supper is represented by the allusion *smoked salmon*. The only question is: by what intermediate links can the impression of the monograph come to assume the relation of allusion to the conversation with the eye specialist, since such a relation is not at first perceptible? In the example of the deferred supper, the relation is evident at the outset; *smoked salmon*, as the favourite dish of the patient's friend, belongs to the circle of ideas which the friend's personality would naturally evoke in the mind of the dreamer. In our new example we are dealing with two entirely separate impressions, which at first glance seem to have nothing in common, except indeed that they occur on the same day. The monograph attracts my attention in the morning: in the evening I take part in the conversation. The answer furnished by the analysis is as follows: Such relations between the two impressions as do not exist from the first are established subsequently between the idea-content of the one impression and the idea-content of the other. I have already picked out the intermediate links emphasized in the course of writing the analysis. Only under some outside influence, perhaps the recollection of the flowers missed by Frau L, would the idea of the monograph on the cyclamen have attached itself to the idea that the cyclamen is my wife's favourite flower. I do not believe that these inconspicuous thoughts would have sufficed to evoke a dream.

> There needs no ghost, my lord, come
> from the grave
> To tell us this,

as we read in Hamlet. But behold! in the analysis I am reminded that the name of the man who interrupted our conversation was *Gärtner* (gardener), and that I thought his wife looked *blooming;* indeed, now I even remember that one of my female patients, who bears the pretty name of *Flora*, was for a time the main subject of our conversation. It must have happened that by means of these intermediate links from the sphere of botanical ideas the association was effected between the two events of the day, the indifferent one and the stimulating one. Other relations were then established, that of cocaine for example, which can with perfect appropriateness form a link between the person of Dr. Koenigstein and the botanical monograph which I have written, and thus secure the fusion of the two circles of ideas, so that now a portion of the first experience may be used as an allusion to the second.

I am prepared to find this explanation attacked as either arbitrary or artificial. What would have happened if Professor Gärtner and his blooming wife had not appeared, and if the patient who was under discussion had been called, not Flora, but Anna? And yet the answer is not hard to find. If these thought-relations had not been available, others would probably have been selected. It is easy to establish relations of this sort, as the jocular questions and conundrums with which we amuse ourselves suffice to show. The range of wit is unlimited. To go a step farther: if no sufficiently fertile associations between the two impressions of the day could have been established, the dream would simply have followed a different course; another of the indifferent impressions of the day, such as come to us in multitudes and are forgotten, would have taken the place of the monograph in the dream, would have formed an association with the content of the conversation, and would have represented this in the dream. Since it was the impression of the monograph and no other that was fated to perform this function, this impression was probably that most suitable for the purpose. One need not, like Lessing's *Hänschen Schlau*, be astonished that "only the rich people of the world possess the most money."

Still the psychological process by which, according to our exposition, the indifferent experience substitutes itself for the psychologically important one seems to us odd and open to question. In a later chapter we shall undertake the task of making the peculiarities of this seemingly incorrect operation more intelligible. Here we are concerned only with the result of this process, which we were compelled to accept by constantly recurring experiences in the analysis of dreams. In this process it is as though, in the course of the intermediate steps, a *displacement* occurs—let us say, of the psychic accent—until ideas of feeble potential, by taking over the charge from ideas which have a stronger initial potential, reach a degree of intensity which enables them to force their way into consciousness. Such displacements do not in the least surprise us when it is a question of the transference of affective magnitudes or of motor activities. That the lonely spinster transfers her affection to animals, that the bachelor becomes a passionate collector, that the soldier defends a scrap of coloured cloth—his flag—with his life-blood, that in a love-affair a clasp of the hands a moment longer than usual evokes a sensation of bliss, or that in *Othello* a lost handkerchief causes an outburst of rage—all these are examples of psychic displacements which to us seem incontestable. But if, by the same means, and in accordance with the same fundamental principles, a decision is made as to what is to reach our consciousness and what is to be withheld from it—that is to say, what we are to think—this gives us the impression of morbidity, and if it occurs in waking life we call it an *error* of thought. We may here anticipate the result of a discussion which will be undertaken later, namely, that the psychic process which we have recognized in dream-displacement proves to be not a morbidly deranged process, but one merely differing from the normal, one of a more *primary* nature.

Thus we interpret the fact that the dream-content takes up remnants of trivial experiences as a manifestation of *dream-distortion* (by displacement), and we thereupon remember that we have recognized this dream-distortion as the work of a censorship operating between the two psychic instances. We may therefore expect that dream-analysis will constantly show us the real and psychically significant source of the dream in the events of the day, the memory of which has transferred its accentuation to some indifferent memory. This conception is in complete opposition to Robert's theory, which consequently has no further value for us. The fact which Robert was trying to explain simply does not exist; its assumption is based on a misunderstanding, on a failure to substitute the real meaning of the dream for its apparent meaning. A further objection to Robert's doctrine is as follows: If the task of the dream were really to rid our memory, by means of a special psychic activity, of the slag of the day's recollections, our sleep would perforce be more troubled, engaged in more strenuous work, than we can suppose it to be, judging by our waking thoughts. For the number of the indifferent impressions of the day against which we should have to protect our memory is obviously immeasurably large; the whole night would not be long enough to dispose of them all. It is far more probable that the forgetting of the indifferent impressions takes place without any active interference on the part of our psychic powers.

Still, something cautions us against taking leave of Robert's theory without further consideration. We have left unexplained the fact that one of the indifferent impressions of the day—indeed, even of the previous day—constantly makes a contribution to the dream-content. The relations between this impression and the real source of the dream in the unconscious do not always exist from the outset; as we have seen, they are established subsequently, while the dream is actually at work, as though to serve the purpose of the intended displacement. Something, therefore, must necessitate the opening up of connections in the direction of the recent but indifferent impression; this impression must possess some quality that gives it a special fitness. Otherwise it would be just as easy for the dream-thoughts to shift their accentuation to some inessential component of their own sphere of ideas.

Experiences such as the following show us the way to an explanation: If the day has brought us two or more experiences which are worthy to evoke a dream, the dream will blend the allusion of both into a single whole: it obeys *a compulsion to make them into a single whole.* For example: One summer afternoon I entered a railway carriage in which I found two acquaintances of mine who were unknown to one another. One of them was an influential colleague, the other a member of a distinguished family which I had been attending in my professional capacity. I introduced the two gentlemen to each other; but during the long journey they conversed with each other through me, so that I had to discuss this or that topic now with one, now with the other. I asked my colleague to recommend a mutual acquaintance who had just begun to practise as a physician. He replied that he was convinced of the young man's ability, but that his undistinguished appearance would make it difficult for him to obtain patients in the upper ranks of society. To this I rejoined: "That is precisely why he needs recommendation." A little later, turning to my other fellow-traveller, I inquired after the health of his aunt—the mother of one of my patients—who was at this time prostrated by a serious illness. On the night following this journey I dreamt that the young friend whom I had asked one of my companions to recommend was in a fashionable drawing-room, and with all the bearing of a man of the world was making—before a distinguished company, in which I recognized all the rich and aristocratic persons of my acquaintance—a funeral oration over the old lady (who in my dream had already died) who was the aunt of my second fellow-traveller. (I confess frankly that I had not been on good terms with this lady.) Thus my dream had once more found the connection between the two impressions of the day, and by means of the two had constructed a unified situation.

In view of many similar experiences, I am persuaded to advance the proposition that a dream works under a kind of compulsion which forces it to combine into a unified whole all the sources of dream-stimulation which are offered to it.[1] In a subsequent chapter (on the function of dreams) we shall consider this impulse of combination as part of the process of condensation, another primary psychic process.

I shall now consider the question whether the dream-exciting source to which our analysis leads us must always be a recent (and significant) event, or whether a subjective experience—that is to say, the recollection of a psychologically significant event, a train of thought—may assume the rôle of a dream-stimulus. The very definite answer, derived from numerous analyses, is as follows: The stimulus of the dream may be a subjective transaction, which has been made recent, as it were, by the mental activity of the day.

[1] The tendency of the dream at work to blend everything present of interest into a single transaction has already been noticed by several authors, for instance, by Delage and Delbœuf.

And this is perhaps the best time to summarize in schematic form the different conditions under which the dream-sources are operative.

The source of a dream may be:

(a) A recent and psychologically significant event which is directly represented in the dream.[1]

(b) Several recent and significant events, which are combined by the dream in a single whole.[2]

(c) One or more recent and significant events, which are represented in the dream-content by allusion to a contemporary but indifferent event.[3]

(d) A subjectively significant experience (recollection, train of thought), which is constantly represented in the dream by allusion to a recent but indifferent impression.[4]

As may be seen, in dream-interpretation the condition is always fulfilled that one component of the dream-content repeats a recent impression of the day of the dream. The component which is destined to be represented in the dream may either belong to the same circle of ideas as the dream-stimulus itself (as an essential or even an inessential element of the same), or it may originate in the neighbourhood of an indifferent impression, which has been brought by more or less abundant associations into relation with the sphere of the dream-stimulus. The apparent multiplicity of these conditions results merely from the *alternative*, that a *displacement has or has not occurred*, and it may here be noted that this alternative enables us to explain the contrasts of the dream quite as readily as the medical theory of the dream explains the series of states from the partial to the complete waking of the brain cells.

In considering this series of sources we note further that the psychologically significant but not recent element (a train of thought, a recollection) may be replaced for the purposes of dream-formation by a recent but psychologically indifferent element, provided the two following conditions are fulfilled: (1) the dream-content preserves a connection with things recently experienced; (2) the dream-stimulus is still a psychologically significant

event. In one single case (a) both these conditions are fulfilled by the same impression. If we now consider that these same indifferent impressions, which are utilized for the dream as long as they are recent, lose this qualification as soon as they are a day (or at most several days) older, we are obliged to assume that the very freshness of an impression gives it a certain psychological value for dream-formation, somewhat equivalent to the value of emotionally accentuated memories or trains of thought. Later on, in the light of certain psychological considerations, we shall be able to divine the explanation of this importance of *recent* impressions in dream formation.[5]

Incidentally our attention is here called to the fact that at night, and unnoticed by our consciousness, important changes may occur in the material comprised by our ideas and memories. The injunction that before making a final decision in any matter one should sleep on it for a night is obviously fully justified. But at this point we find that we have passed from the psychology of dreaming to the psychology of sleep, a step which there will often be occasion to take.

At this point there arises an objection which threatens to invalidate the conclusions at which we have just arrived. If indifferent impressions can find their way into the dream only so long as they are of recent origin, how does it happen that in the dream-content we find elements also from earlier periods of our lives, which, at the time when they were still recent, possessed, as Strümpell puts it, no psychic value, and which, therefore, ought to have been forgotten long ago; elements, that is, which are neither fresh nor psychologically significant?

This objection can be disposed of completely if we have recourse to the results of the psychoanalysis of neurotics. The solution is as follows: The process of shifting and rearrangement which replaces material of psychic significance by material which is indifferent (whether one is dreaming or thinking) has already taken place in these earlier periods of life, and has since become fixed in the memory. Those elements which were originally indifferent are in fact no longer so, since they have acquired the value of psychologically significant material. That which has actually remained indifferent can never be reproduced in the dream.

From the foregoing exposition the reader may rightly conclude that I assert that there are no indifferent dream-stimuli, and therefore

---

[1] The dream of Irma's injection; the dream of the friend who is my uncle.
[2] The dream of the funeral oration delivered by the young physician.
[3] The dream of the botanical monograph.
[4] The dreams of my patients during analysis are mostly of this kind.

[5] Cf. Chap. VII on "transference."

no guileless dreams. This I absolutely and unconditionally believe to be the case, apart from the dreams of children, and perhaps the brief dream-reactions to nocturnal sensations. Apart from these exceptions, whatever one dreams is either plainly recognizable as being psychically significant, or it is distorted and can be judged correctly only after complete interpretation, when it proves, after all, to be of psychic significance. The dream never concerns itself with trifles; we do not allow sleep to be disturbed by trivialities.[1] Dreams which are apparently guileless turn out to be the reverse of innocent, if one takes the trouble to interpret them; if I may be permitted the expression, they all show "the mark of the beast." Since this is another point on which I may expect contradiction, and since I am glad of an opportunity to show dream-distortion at work, I shall here subject to analysis a number of *guileless dreams* from my collection.

I

An intelligent and refined young woman, who in real life is distinctly reserved, one of those people of whom one says that "still waters run deep," relates the following dream: *"I dreamt that I arrived at the market too late, and could get nothing from either the butcher or the greengrocer woman."* Surely a guileless dream, but as it has not the appearance of a real dream I induce her to relate it in detail. Her report then runs as follows: *She goes to the market with her cook, who carries the basket. The butcher tells her, after she has asked him for something: "That is no longer to be obtained," and wants to give her something else, with the remark: "That is good, too." She refuses, and goes to the greengrocer woman. The latter tries to sell her a peculiar vegetable, which is bound up in bundles, and is black in colour. She says: "I don't know that, I won't take it."*

The connection of the dream with the preceding day is simple enough. She had really gone to the market too late, and had been unable to buy anything. *The meatshop was already closed*, comes into one's mind as a description of the experience. But wait, is not that a very vulgar phrase which—or rather, the opposite of which—denotes a certain negative

lect with regard to man's clothing? The dreamer has not used these words; she has perhaps avoided them; but let us look for the interpretation of the details contained in the dream.

When in a dream something has the character of a spoken utterance—that is, when it is said or heard, not merely thought, and the distinction can usually be made with certainty—then it originates in the utterances of waking life, which have, of course, been treated as raw material, dismembered, and slightly altered, and above all removed from their context.[2] In the work of interpretation we may take such utterances as our starting-point. Where, then, does the butcher's statement, *That is no longer to be obtained*, come from? From myself; I had explained to her some days previously "that the oldest experiences of childhood are *no longer to be obtained* as such, but will be replaced in the analysis by *transferences* and dreams." Thus, I am the butcher, and she refuses to accept these transferences to the present of old ways of thinking and feeling. Where does her dream utterance, *I don't know that, I won't take it*, come from? For the purposes of the analysis this has to be dissected. *I don't know that* she herself had said to her cook, with whom she had a dispute on the previous day, but she had then added: *Behave yourself decently*. Here a displacement is palpable; of the two sentences which she spoke to her cook, she included the insignificant one in her dream; but the suppressed sentence, *Behave yourself decently!* alone fits in with the rest of the dream-content. One might use the words to a man who was making indecent overtures, and had neglected "to close his meat-shop." That we have really hit upon the trail of the interpretation is proved by its agreement with the allusions made by the incident with the greengrocer woman. A vegetable which is sold tied up in bundles (a longish vegetable, as she subsequently adds), and is also black: what can this be but a dream-combination of asparagus and black radish? I need not interpret asparagus to the initiated; and the other vegetable, too (think of the exclamation: "Blacky, save yourself!"), seems to me to point to the sexual theme at which we guessed in the beginning, when we wanted to replace the story of the dream by "the meat-shop is closed." We are not

---

[1] Havelock Ellis, a kindly critic of *The Interpretation of Dreams*, writes in *The World of Dreams* (p. 169): "From this point on, not many of us will be able to follow F." But Mr. Ellis has not undertaken any analyses of dreams, and will not believe how unjustifiable it is to judge them by the manifest dream-content.

[2] Cf. what is said of speech in dreams in the chapter on "The Dream-Work." Only one of the writers on the subject—Delbœuf—seems to have recognized the origin of the speeches heard in dreams; he compares them with *clichés*.

here concerned with the full meaning of the dream; so much is certain, that it is full of meaning and by no means guileless.[1]

II

Another guileless dream of the same patient, which in some respects is a pendant to the above. *Her husband asks her: "Oughtn't we to have the piano tuned?" She replies: "It's not worth while, the hammers would have to be rebuffed as well."* Again we have the reproduction of an actual event of the preceding day. Her husband had asked her such a question, and she had answered it in such words. But what is the meaning of her dreaming it? She says of the piano that it is a *disgusting* old box which has a bad tone; it *belonged* to her husband before they were married,[2] etc., but the key to the true solution lies in the phrase: *It isn't worth while*. This has its origin in a call paid yesterday to a woman friend. She was asked to take off her coat, but declined, saying: "Thanks, it isn't worth while, I must go in a moment." At this point I recall that yesterday, during the analysis, she suddenly took hold of her coat, of which a button had come undone. It was as though she meant to say: "Please don't look in, it isn't worth while." Thus *box* becomes *chest*, and the interpretation of the dream leads to the years when she was growing out of her childhood,. when she began to be dissatisfied with her figure. It leads us back, indeed, to earlier periods, if we take into consideration the *disgusting* and the *bad tone,* and remember how often in allusions and in dreams the two small hemispheres of the female body take the place—as a substitute and an antithesis—of the large ones.

III

I will interrupt the analysis of this dreamer in order to insert a short, innocent dream which

was dreamed by a young man. *He dreamt that he was putting on his winter overcoat again; this was terrible.* The occasion for this dream is apparently the sudden advent of cold weather. On more careful examination we note that the two brief fragments of the dream do not fit together very well, for what could be terrible about wearing a thick or heavy coat in cold weather? Unfortunately for the innocency of this dream, the first association, under analysis, yields the recollection that yesterday a lady had confidentially confessed to him that her last child owed its existence to the splitting of a condom. He now reconstructs his thoughts in accordance with this suggestion: A thin condom is dangerous, a thick one is bad. The condom is a "pullover" (*Ueberzieher* = literally *pullover*), for it is pulled over something: and *Ueberzieher* is the German term for a light overcoat. An experience like that related by the lady would indeed be terrible for an unmarried man.

We will now return to our other innocent dreamer.

IV

She puts a candle into a candlestick; but the candle is broken, so that it does not stand up. The girls at school say she is clumsy; but she replies that it is not her fault.

Here, too, there is an actual occasion for the dream; the day before she had actually put a candle into a candlestick; but this one was not broken. An obvious symbolism has here been employed. The candle is an object which excites the female genitals; its being broken, so that it does not stand upright, signifies impotence on the man's part (*it is not her fault*). But does this young woman, carefully brought up, and a stranger to all obscenity, know of such an application of the candle? By chance she is able to tell how she came by this information. While paddling a canoe on the Rhine, a boat passed her which contained some students, who were singing rapturously, or rather yelling: "When the Queen of Sweden, behind closed shutters, with the candles of Apollo. . . ."

She does not hear or else understand the last word. Her husband was asked to give her the required explanation. These verses are then replaced in the dream-content by the innocent recollection of a task which she once performed *clumsily* at her boarding-school, because of the *closed shutters*. The connection between the theme of masturbation and that of impotence is clear enough. *Apollo* in the latent dream-con-

---

[1] For the curious, I may remark that behind the dream there is hidden a phantasy of indecent, sexually provoking conduct on my part, and of repulsion on the part of the lady. If this interpretation should seem preposterous, I would remind the reader of the numerous cases in which physicians have been made the object of such charges by hysterical women, with whom the same phantasy has not appeared in a distorted form as a dream, but has become undisguisedly conscious and delusional. With this dream the patient began her psycho-analytical treatment. It was only later that I learned that with this dream she repeated the initial trauma in which her neurosis originated, and since then I have noticed the same behaviour in other persons who in their childhood were victims of sexual attacks, and now, as it were, wish in their dreams for them to be repeated.

[2] A substitution by the opposite, as will be clear after analysis.

tent connects this dream with an earlier one in which the virgin Pallas figured. All this is obviously not innocent.

V

Lest it may seem too easy a matter to draw conclusions from dreams concerning the dreamer's real circumstances, I add another dream originating with the same person, which once more appears innocent. *"I dreamt of doing something,"* she relates, *"which I actually did during the day, that is to say, I filled a little trunk so full of books that I had difficulty in closing it. My dream was just like the actual occurrence."* Here the dreamer herself emphasizes the correspondence between the dream and the reality. All such criticisms of the dream, and comments on the dream, although they have found a place in the waking thoughts, properly belong to the latent dream-content, as further examples will confirm. We are told, then, that what the dream relates has actually occurred during the day. It would take us too far afield to show how we arrive at the idea of making use of the English language to help us in the interpretation of this dream. Suffice it to say that it is again a question of a little box (cf. p. 202, the dream of the dead child in the box) which has been filled so full that nothing can go into it.

In all these "innocent" dreams the sexual factor as the motive of the censorship is very prominent. But this is a subject of primary significance, which we must consider later.

B. *Infantile Experiences as the Source of Dreams*

As the third of the peculiarities of the dream-content, we have adduced the fact, in agreement with all other writers on the subject (excepting Robert), that impressions from our childhood may appear in dreams, which do not seem to be at the disposal of the waking memory. It is, of course, difficult to decide how seldom or how frequently this occurs, because after waking the origin of the respective elements of the dream is not recognized. The proof that we are dealing with impressions of our childhood must thus be adduced objectively, and only in rare instances do the conditions favour such proof. The story is told by A. Maury, as being particularly conclusive, of a man who decides to visit his birthplace after an absence of twenty years. On the night before his departure he dreams that he is in a totally unfamiliar locality, and that he there meets a strange man with whom he holds a conversation. Subsequently, upon his return home, he is able to convince himself that this strange locality really exists in the vicinity of his home, and the strange man in the dream turns out to be a friend of his dead father's, who is living in the town. This is, of course, a conclusive proof that in his childhood he had seen both the man and the locality. The dream, moreover, is to be interpreted as a dream of impatience, like the dream of the girl who carries in her pocket the ticket for a concert, the dream of the child whose father had promised him an excursion to the Hameau (p. 192), and so forth. The motives which reproduce just these impressions of childhood for the dreamer cannot, of course, be discovered without analysis.

One of my colleagues, who attended my lectures, and who boasted that his dreams were very rarely subject to distortion, told me that he had sometime previously seen, in a dream, *his former tutor in bed with his nurse,* who had remained in the household until his eleventh year. The actual location of this scene was realized even in the dream. As he was greatly interested, he related the dream to his elder brother, who laughingly confirmed its reality. The brother said that he remembered the affair very distinctly, for he was six years old at the time. The lovers were in the habit of making him, the elder boy, drunk with beer whenever circumstances were favourable to their nocturnal intercourse. The younger child, our dreamer, at that time three years of age, slept in the same room as the nurse, but was not regarded as an obstacle.

In yet another case it may be definitely established, without the aid of dream-interpretation, that the dream contains elements from childhood—namely, if the dream is a so-called *perennial* dream, one which, being first dreamt in childhood, recurs again and again in adult years. I may add a few examples of this sort to those already known, although I have no personal knowledge of perennial dreams. A physician, in his thirties, tells me that a yellow lion, concerning which he is able to give the precisest information, has often appeared in his dream-life, from his earliest childhood up to the present day. This lion, known to him from his dreams, was one day discovered *in natura,* as a long-forgotten china animal. The young man then learned from his mother that the lion had been his favourite toy in early childhood, a fact which he himself could no longer remember.

If we now turn from the manifest dream-content to the dream-thoughts which are revealed only on analysis, the experiences of childhood may be found to recur even in dreams whose content would not have led us to suspect anything of the sort. I owe a particularly delightful and instructive example of such a dream to my esteemed colleague of the "yellow lion." After reading Nansen's account of his polar expedition, he dreamt that he was giving the intrepid explorer electrical treatment on an ice-floe for the sciatica of which the latter complained! During the analysis of this dream he remembered an incident of his childhood, without which the dream would be wholly unintelligible. When he was three or four years of age he was one day listening attentively to the conversation of his elders; they were talking of exploration, and he presently asked his father whether exploration was a bad illness. He had apparently confounded *Reisen* (journey, trips) with *Reissen* (gripes, tearing pains), and the derision of his brothers and sisters prevented his ever forgetting the humiliating experience.

We have a precisely similar case when, in the analysis of the dream of the monograph on the genus cyclamen, I stumble upon a memory, retained from childhood, to the effect that when I was five years old my father allowed me to destroy a book embellished with coloured plates. It will perhaps be doubted whether this recollection really entered into the composition of the dream-content, and it may be suggested that the connection was established subsequently by the analysis. But the abundance and intricacy of the associative connections vouch for the truth of my explanation: cyclamen—favourite flower—favourite dish—artichoke; to pick to pieces like an artichoke, leaf by leaf (a phrase which at that time one heard daily, *à propos* of the dividing up of the Chinese empire); herbarium—bookworm, whose favourite food is books. I can further assure the reader that the ultimate meaning of the dream, which I have not given here, is most intimately connected with the content of the scene of childish destruction.

In another series of dreams we learn from analysis that the very wish which has given rise to the dream, and whose fulfilment the dream proves to be, has itself originated in childhood, so that one is astonished to find that *the child with all his impulses survives in the dream*.

I shall now continue the interpretation of a dream which has already proved instructive: I refer to the dream in which my friend R is my uncle. We have carried its interpretation far enough for the wish-motive—the wish to be appointed professor—to assert itself palpably; and we have explained the affection felt for my friend R in the dream as the outcome of opposition to, and defiance of, the two colleagues who appear in the dream-thoughts. The dream was my own; I may, therefore, continue the analysis by stating that I did not feel quite satisfied with the solution arrived at. I knew that my opinion of these colleagues, who were so badly treated in my dream-thoughts, would have been expressed in very different language in my waking life; the intensity of the wish that I might not share their fate as regards the appointment seemed to me too slight fully to account for the discrepancy between my dream-opinion and my waking opinion. If the desire to be addressed by another title were really so intense, it would be proof of a morbid ambition, which I do not think I cherish, and which I believe I was far from entertaining. I do not know how others who think they know me would judge me; perhaps I really was ambitious; but if I was, my ambition has long since been transferred to objects other than the rank and title of *Professor extraordinarius*.

Whence, then, the ambition which the dream has ascribed to me? Here I am reminded of a story which I heard often in my childhood, that at my birth an old peasant woman had prophesied to my happy mother (whose first-born I was) that she had brought a great man into the world. Such prophecies must be made very frequently; there are so many happy and expectant mothers, and so many old peasant women, and other old women who, since their mundane powers have deserted them, turn their eyes toward the future; and the prophetess is not likely to suffer for her prophecies. Is it possible that my thirst for greatness has originated from this source? But here I recollect an impression from the later years of my childhood, which might serve even better as an explanation. One evening, at a restaurant on the Prater, where my parents were accustomed to take me when I was eleven or twelve years of age, we noticed a man who was going from table to table and, for a small sum, improvising verses upon any subject that was given him. I was sent to bring the poet to our table, and he showed his gratitude. Before asking for a subject he threw off a few rhymes about myself, and told us that if he could trust his inspiration I should probably one day become a minister. I can still distinctly remember the impression produced by this second prophecy. It was in the days of the "bourgeois Ministry"; my father had recently brought home the portraits of the bourgeois university graduates, Herbst, Giskra, Unger, Berger and others, and we illuminated the house in their honour. There were even Jews among them; so that every diligent Jewish schoolboy carried a ministerial portfolio in his satchel. The impression of that time must be responsible for the fact that until shortly before I went to the university I wanted to study jurisprudence, and changed my mind only at the last moment. A medical man has no chance of becoming a minister. And now for my dream: It is only now that I begin to see that it translates me from the sombre present to the hopeful days of the bourgeois Ministry, and completely fulfils what was then my youthful ambition. In treating my two estimable and learned colleagues, merely because they are Jews, so badly, one as though he were a simpleton and the other as though he were a criminal, I am acting as though I were the Minister; I have put myself in his place. What a revenge I take upon his Excellency! He refuses to appoint me *Professor extraordinarius*, and so in my dream I put myself in his place.

In another case I note the fact that although the wish that excites the dream is a contemporary wish it is nevertheless greatly reinforced by memories of childhood. I refer to a series of dreams which are based on the longing to go to Rome. For a long time to come I shall probably have to satisfy this longing by means of dreams, since, at the season of the year when I should be able to travel, Rome is to be avoided for reasons of health.[1] Thus I once dreamt that I saw the Tiber and the bridge of Sant' Angelo from the window of a railway carriage; presently the train started, and I realized that I had never entered the city at all. The view that appeared in the dream was modelled after a well-known engraving which I had casually noticed the day before in the drawing-room of one of my patients. In another dream someone took me up a hill and showed me Rome half shrouded in mist, and so distant that I was astonished at the distinctness of the view. The content of this dream is too rich to be fully reported here. The mo-

tive, "to see the promised land afar," is here easily recognizable. The city which I thus saw in the mist is Lübeck; the original of the hill is the Gleichenberg. In a third dream I am at last in Rome. To my disappointment the scenery is anything but urban: it consists of *a little stream of black water, on one side of which are black rocks, while on the other are meadows with large white flowers. I notice a certain Herr Zucker (with whom I am superficially acquainted), and resolve to ask him to show me the way into the city.* It is obvious that I am trying in vain to see in my dream a city which I have never seen in my waking life. If I resolve the landscape into its elements, the white flowers point to Ravenna, which is known to me, and which once, for a time, replaced Rome as the capital of Italy. In the marshes around Ravenna we had found the most beautiful water-lilies in the midst of black pools of water; the dream makes them grow in the meadows, like the narcissi of our own Aussee, because we found it so troublesome to cull them from the water. The black rock so close to the water vividly recalls the valley of the Tepl at Karlsbad. *Karlsbad* now enables me to account for the peculiar circumstance that I ask Herr Zucker to show me the way. In the material of which the dream is woven I am able to recognize two of those amusing Jewish anecdotes which conceal such profound and, at times, such bitter worldly wisdom, and which we are so fond of quoting in our letters and conversation. One is the story of the *constitution;* it tells how a poor Jew sneaks into the Karlsbad express without a ticket; how he is detected, and is treated more and more harshly by the conductor at each succeeding call for tickets; and how, when a friend whom he mets at one of the stations during his miserable journey asks him where he is going, he answers: "To Karlsbad—if my constitution holds out." Associated in memory with this is another story about a Jew who is ignorant of French, and who has express instructions to ask in Paris for the Rue Richelieu. Paris was for many years the goal of my own longing, and I regarded the satisfaction with which I first set foot on the pavements of Paris as a warrant that I should attain to the fulfilment of other wishes also. Moreover, asking the way is a direct allusion to Rome, for, as we know, "all roads lead to Rome." And further, the name Zucker (sugar)again points to Karlsbad, whither we send persons afflicted with the *constitutional* disease, diabetes (*Zuckerkrankheit,* sugar-

---

[1] I long ago learned that the fulfilment of such wishes only called for a little courage, and I then became a zealous pilgrim to Rome.

disease). The occasion for this dream was the proposal of my Berlin friend that we should meet in Prague at Easter. A further association with sugar and diabetes might be found in the matters which I had to discuss with him.

A fourth dream, occurring shortly after the last-mentioned, brings me back to Rome. I see a street corner before me, and am astonished that so many German placards should be posted there. On the previous day, when writing to my friend, I had told him, with truly prophetic vision, that Prague would probably not be a comfortable place for German travellers. The dream, therefore, expressed simultaneously the wish to meet him in Rome instead of in the Bohemian capital, and the desire, which probably originated during my student days, that the German language might be accorded more tolerance in Prague. As a matter of fact, I must have understood the Czech language in the first years of my childhood, for I was born in a small village in Moravia, amidst a Slav population. A Czech nursery rhyme, which I heard in my seventeenth year, became, without effort on my part, so imprinted upon my memory that I can repeat it to this day, although I have no idea of its meaning. Thus in these dreams also there is no lack of manifold relations to the impressions of my early childhood.

During my last Italian journey, which took me past Lake Trasimenus, I at length discovered, after I had seen the Tiber, and had reluctantly turned back some fifty miles from Rome, what a reinforcement my longing for the Eternal City had received from the impressions of my childhood. I had just conceived a plan of travelling to Naples via Rome the following year when this sentence, which I must have read in one of our German classics, occurred to me: [1] "It is a question which of the two paced to and fro in his room the more impatiently after he had conceived the plan of going to Rome—Assistant Headmaster Winckelmann or the great General Hannibal." I myself had walked in Hannibal's footsteps; like him I was destined never to see Rome; and I too had gone to Campania when all were expecting him in Rome. Hannibal, with whom I had achieved this point of similarity, had been my favourite hero during my years at the Gymnasium; like so many boys of my age, I bestowed my sympathies in the Punic war not on the Romans, but on the Carthaginians.

Moreover, when I finally came to realize the consequences of belonging to an alien race, and was forced by the anti-Semitic feeling among my class-mates to take a definite stand, the figure of the Semitic commander assumed still greater proportions in my imagination. Hannibal and Rome symbolized, in my youthful eyes, the struggle between the tenacity of the Jews and the organization of the Catholic Church. The significance for our emotional life which the anti-Semitic movement has since assumed helped to fix the thoughts and impressions of those earlier days. Thus the desire to go to Rome has in my dream-life become the mask and symbol for a number of warmly cherished wishes, for whose realization one had to work with the tenacity and single-mindedness of the Punic general, though their fulfilment at times seemed as remote as Hannibal's life-long wish to enter Rome.

And now, for the first time, I happened upon the youthful experience which even to-day still expresses its power in all these emotions and dreams. I might have been ten or twelve years old when my father began to take me with him on his walks, and in his conversation to reveal his views on the things of this world. Thus it was that he once told me the following incident, in order to show me that I had been born into happier times than he: "When I was a young man, I was walking one Saturday along the street in the village where you were born; I was well-dressed, with a new fur cap on my head. Up comes a Christian, who knocks my cap into the mud, and shouts, 'Jew, get off the pavement!'"—"And what did you do?"—"I went into the street and picked up the cap," he calmly replied. That did not seem heroic on the part of the big, strong man who was leading me, a little fellow, by the hand. I contrasted this situation, which did not please me, with another, more in harmony with my sentiments—the scene in which Hannibal's father, Hamilcar Barcas, made his son swear before the household altar to take vengeance on the Romans.[2] Ever since then Hannibal has had a place in my phantasies.

I think I can trace my enthusiasm for the Carthaginian general still further back into my childhood, so that it is probably only an instance of an already established emotional relation being transferred to a new vehicle. One of the first books which fell into my childish hands

---

[1] The writer in whose works I found this passage was probably Jean Paul Richter.

[2] In the first edition of this book I gave here the name "Hasdrubal," an amazing error, which I explained in my *Psycho-pathology of Everyday Life*.

after I learned to read was Thiers' *Consulate and Empire*. I remember that I pasted on the flat backs of my wooden soldiers little labels bearing the names of the Imperial marshals, and that at that time Masséna (as a Jew, Menasse) was already my avowed favourite.[1] This preference is doubtless also to be explained by the fact of my having been born, a hundred years later, on the same date. Napoleon himself is associated with Hannibal through the crossing of the Alps. And perhaps the development of this martial ideal may be traced yet farther back, to the first three years of my childhood, to wishes which my alternately friendly and hostile relations with a boy a year older than myself must have evoked in the weaker of the two playmates.

The deeper we go into the analysis of dreams, the more often are we put on the track of childish experiences which play the part of dream-sources in the latent dream-content.

We have learned that dreams very rarely reproduce memories in such a manner as to constitute, unchanged and unabridged, the sole manifest dream-content. Nevertheless, a few authentic examples which show such reproduction have been recorded, and I can add a few new ones, which once more refer to scenes of childhood. In the case of one of my patients a dream once gave a barely distorted reproduction of a sexual incident, which was immediately recognized as an accurate recollection. The memory of it had never been completely lost in the waking life, but it had been greatly obscured, and it was revivified by the previous work of analysis. The dreamer had at the age of twelve visited a bedridden schoolmate, who had exposed himself, probably only by a chance movement in bed. At the sight of the boy's genitals he was seized by a kind of compulsion, exposed himself, and took hold of the member of the other boy who, however, looked at him in surprise and indignation, whereupon he became embarrassed and let it go. A dream repeated this scene twenty-three years later, with all the details of the accompanying emotions, changing it, however, in this respect, that the dreamer played the passive instead of the active rôle, while the person of the schoolmate was replaced by a contemporary.

As a rule, of course, a scene from childhood is represented in the manifest dream-content only by an allusion, and must be disentangled from the dream by interpretation. The citation of examples of this kind cannot be very convincing, because any guarantee that they are really experiences of childhood is lacking; if they belong to an earlier period of life, they are no longer recognized by our memory. The conclusion that such childish experiences recur at all in dreams is justified in psychoanalytic work by a great number of factors, which in their combined results appear to be sufficiently reliable. But when, for the purposes of dream-interpretation, such references to childish experiences are torn out of their context, they may not perhaps seem very impressive, especially where I do not even give all the material upon which the interpretation is based. However, I shall not let this deter me from giving a few examples.

I

With one of my female patients all dreams have the character of *hurry;* she is hurrying so as to be in time, so as not to miss her train, and so on. In one dream *she has to visit a girl friend; her mother had told her to ride and not walk; she runs, however, and keeps on calling.* The material that emerged in the analysis allowed one to recognize a memory of childish romping, and, especially for one dream, went back to the popular childish game of rapidly repeating the words of a sentence as though it was all one word. All these harmless jokes with little friends were remembered because they replaced other less harmless ones.[2]

II

The following dream was dreamed by another female patient: *She is in a large room in which there are all sorts of machines; it is rather like what she would imagine an orthopaedic institute to be. She hears that I am pressed for time, and that she must undergo treatment along with five others. But she resists, and is unwilling to lie down on the bed—or whatever it is—which is intended for her. She stands in a corner, and waits for me to say "It is not true." The others, meanwhile, laugh at her, saying it is all foolishness on her part. At the same time, it is as though she were called upon to make a number of little squares.*

The first part of the content of this dream is an allusion to the treatment and to the transference to myself. The second contains an

---

[1] The Jewish descent of the Marshal is somewhat doubtful.

[2] In the original this paragraph contains many plays on the word *Hetz* (hurry, chase, scurry, game, etc.).—TR.

allusion to a scene of childhood; the two portions are connected by the mention of the bed.
The orthopaedic institute is an allusion to one
of my talks, in which I compared the treatment, with regard to its duration and its nature, to an orthopaedic treatment. At the beginning of the treatment I had to tell her that
for the present I had little time to give her,
but that later on I would devote a whole hour
to her daily. This aroused in her the old sensitiveness, which is a leading characteristic of
children who are destined to become hysterical.
Their desire for love is insatiable. My patient
was the youngest of six brothers and sisters
(hence, *with five others*), and as such her
father's favourite, but in spite of this she
seems to have felt that her beloved father devoted far too little time and attention to her.
Her waiting for me to say *It is not true* was
derived as follows: A little tailor's apprentice
had brought her a dress, and she had given
him the money for it. Then she asked her husband whether she would have to pay the money
again if the boy were to lose it. To tease her,
her husband answered "Yes" (the *teasing* in
the dream), and she asked again and again,
and *waited for him to say "It is not true."* The
thought of the latent dream-content may now
be construed as follows: Will she have to pay
me double the amount when I devote twice as
much time to her?—a thought which is stingy
or *filthy* (the uncleanliness of childhood is
often replaced in dreams by greed for money;
the word *filthy* here supplies the bridge). If
all the passage referring to her waiting until I
say *It is not true* is intended in the dream as a
circumlocution for the word *dirty, the stand-
ing-in-the-corner and not lying-down-on-the-
bed* are in keeping with this word, as component parts of a scene of her childhood in which
she had soiled her bed, in punishment for
which *she was put into the corner*, with a warning that papa would not love her any more,
whereupon her brothers and sisters laughed at
her, etc. The little squares refer to her young
niece, who showed her the arithmetical trick
of writing figures in nine squares (I think) in
such a way that on being added together in
any direction they make fifteen.

III

Here is a man's dream: *He sees two boys tuss-
ling with each other; they are cooper's boys,
as he concludes from the tools which are lying
about; one of the boys has thrown the other
down; the prostrate boy is wearing ear-rings*
*with blue stones. He runs towards the assail-
ant with lifted cane, in order to chastise him.
The boy takes refuge behind a woman, as
though she were his mother, who is standing
against a wooden fence. She is the wife of a
day-labourer, and she turns her back to the
man who is dreaming. Finally she turns about
and stares at him with a horrible look, so that
he runs away in terror; the red flesh of the
lower lid seems to stand out from her eyes.*

This dream has made abundant use of trivial occurrences from the previous day, in the
course of which he actually saw two boys in
the street, one of whom threw the other down.
When he walked up to them in order to settle
the quarrel, both of them took to their heels.
Cooper's boys—this is explained only by a
subsequent dream, in the analysis of which he
used the proverbial expression: *"To knock the
bottom out of the barrel."* Ear-rings with blue
stones, according to his observation, are worn
chiefly by *prostitutes*. This suggests a familiar
doggerel rhyme about two boys: "The other
boy was called Marie": that is, he was a girl.
The woman standing by the fence: after the
scene with the two boys he went for a walk
along the bank of the Danube and, taking advantage of being alone, urinated *against a
wooden fence*. A little farther on a respectably
dressed, elderly lady smiled at him very pleasantly and wanted to hand him her card with
her address.

Since, in the dream, the woman stood as he
had stood while urinating, there is an allusion
to a woman urinating, and this explains the
horrible look and the prominence of the red
flesh, which can only refer to the genitals
gaping in a squatting posture; seen in childhood, they had appeared in later recollection
as *proud flesh*, as a *wound*. The dream unites
two occasions upon which, as a little boy, the
dreamer was enabled to see the genitals of
little girls, once by throwing the little girl
down, and once while the child was *urinating*;
and, as is shown by another association, he had
retained in his memory the punishment administered or threatened by his father on account
of these manifestations of sexual curiosity.

IV

A great mass of childish memories, which have
been hastily combined into a phantasy, may
be found behind the following dream of an
elderly lady: *She goes out in a hurry to do
some shopping. On the Graben she sinks to
her knees as though she had broken down. A*

number of people collect around her, especially cab-drivers, but no one helps her to get up. She makes many vain attempts; finally she must have succeeded, for she is put into a cab which is to take her home. A large, heavily laden basket (something like a market-basket) is thrown after her through the window.

This is the woman who is always harassed in her dreams; just as she used to be harassed when a child. The first situation of the dream is apparently taken from the sight of a fallen horse; just as *broken down* points to horse-racing. In her youth she was a rider; still earlier she was probably also a *horse*. With the idea of falling down is connected her first childish reminiscence of the seventeen-year-old son of the hall porter, who had an epileptic seizure in the street and was brought home in a cab. Of this, of course, she had only heard, but the idea of epileptic fits, of *falling down,* acquired a great influence over her phantasies, and later on influenced the form of her own hysterical attacks. When a person of the female sex dreams of falling, this almost always has a sexual significance; she becomes a *fallen woman,* and, for the purpose of the dream under consideration, this interpretation is probably the least doubtful, for she falls in the Graben, the street in Vienna which is known as the concourse of prostitutes. The *market-basket* admits of more than one interpretation; in the sense of refusal (German, *Korb* = basket = snub, refusal) it reminds her of the many snubs which she at first administered to her suitors and which, she thinks, she herself received later. This agrees with the detail: *no one will help her up,* which she herself interprets as *being disdained.* Further, the *market-basket* recalls phantasies which have already appeared in the course of analysis, in which she imagines that she has married far beneath her station and now goes to the market as a market-woman. Lastly, the market-basket might be interpreted as the mark of a *servant.* This suggests further memories of her childhood—of a *cook* who was discharged because she stole; she, too, *sank to her knees* and begged for mercy. The dreamer was at that time twelve years of age. Then emerges a recollection of a chamber-maid, who was dismissed because she had an affair with the coachman of the household, who, incidentally, married her afterwards. This recollection, therefore, gives us a clue to the cab-drivers in the dream (who, in opposition to the reality, do not stand by the fallen woman). But there still remains to be explained the throwing of the basket; in particular, why it is thrown *through the window?* This reminds her of the forwarding of luggage by rail, to the custom of *Fensterln*[1] in the country, and to trivial impressions of a summer resort, of a gentleman who threw some blue plums into the window of a lady's room, and of her little sister, who was frightened because an idiot who was passing looked in at the window. And now, from behind all this emerges an obscure recollection from her tenth year of a nurse in the country to whom one of the men-servants made love (and whose conduct the child may have noticed), and who was sent packing, thrown out, together with her lover (in the dream we have the expression: *thrown into*); an incident which we have been approaching by several other paths. The luggage or box of a servant is disparagingly described in Vienna as "seven plums." "Pack up your seven plums and get out!"

My collection, of course, contains a plethora of such patients' dreams, the analysis of which leads back to impressions of childhood, often dating back to the first three years of life, which are remembered obscurely, or not at all. But it is a questionable proceeding to draw conclusions from these and apply them to dreams in general, for they are mostly dreams of neurotic, and especially hysterical, persons; and the part played in these dreams by childish scenes might be conditioned by the nature of the neurosis, and not by the nature of dreams in general. In the interpretation of my own dreams, however, which is assuredly not undertaken on account of grave symptoms of illness, it happens just as frequently that in the latent dream-content I am unexpectedly confronted with a scene of my childhood, and that a whole series of my dreams will suddenly converge upon the paths proceeding from a single childish experience. I have already given examples of this, and I shall give yet more in different connections. Perhaps I cannot close this chapter more fittingly than by citing several dreams of my own, in which recent events and long-forgotten experiences of my childhood appear together as dream-sources.

I. After I have been travelling, and have

[1] *Fensterln* is the custom, now falling into disuse, found in rural districts of the German Schwarzwald, of lovers who woo their sweethearts at their bedroom windows, to which they ascend by means of a ladder, enjoying such intimacy that the relation practically amounts to a trial marriage. The reputation of the young woman never suffers on account of *Fensterln,* unless she becomes intimate with too many suitors.—TR.

gone to bed hungry and tired, the prime necessities of life begin to assert their claims in sleep, and I dream as follows: *I go into a kitchen in order to ask for some pudding. There three women are standing, one of whom is the hostess; she is rolling something in her hands, as though she were making dumplings. She replies that I must wait until she has finished* (not distinctly as a speech). *I become impatient, and go away affronted. I want to put on an overcoat; but the first I try on is too long. I take it off, and am somewhat astonished to find that it is trimmed with fur. A second coat has a long strip of cloth with a Turkish design sewn into it. A stranger with a long face and a short, pointed beard comes up and prevents me from putting it on, declaring that it belongs to him. I now show him that it is covered all over with Turkish embroideries. He asks: "How do the Turkish (drawings, strips of cloth . . .) concern you?" But we soon become quite friendly.*

In the analysis of this dream I remember, quite unexpectedly, the first novel which I ever read, or rather, which I began to read from the end of the first volume, when I was perhaps thirteen years of age. I have never learned the name of the novel, or that of its author, but the end remains vividly in my memory. The hero becomes insane, and continually calls out the names of the three women who have brought the greatest happiness and the greatest misfortune into his life. Pélagie is one of these names. I still do not know what to make of this recollection during the analysis. Together with the three women there now emerge the three Parcae, who spin the fates of men, and I know that one of the three women, the hostess in the dream, is the mother who gives life, and who, moreover, as in my own case, gives the child its first nourishment. Love and hunger meet at the mother's breast. A young man—so runs an anecdote—who became a great admirer of womanly beauty, once observed, when the conversation turned upon the handsome wet-nurse who had suckled him as a child, that he was sorry that he had not taken better advantage of his opportunities. I am in the habit of using the anecdote to elucidate the factor of retrospective tendencies in the mechanism of the psychoneuroses. One of the Parcae, then, is rubbing the palms of her hands together, as though she were making dumplings. A strange occupation for one of the Fates, and urgently in need of explanation! This explanation is furnished by another and earlier memory of my childhood. When I was six years old, and receiving my first lessons from my mother, I was expected to believe that we are made of dust, and must, therefore, return to dust. But this did not please me, and I questioned the doctrine. Thereupon my mother rubbed the palms of her hands together—just as in making dumplings, except that there was no dough between them—and showed me the blackish scales of *epidermis* which were thus rubbed off, as a proof that it is of dust that we are made. Great was my astonishment at this demonstration *ad oculos,* and I acquiesced in the idea which I was later to hear expressed in the words: "Thou owest nature a death."[1] Thus the women to whom I go in the kitchen, as I so often did in my childhood when I was hungry and my mother, sitting by the fire, admonished me to wait until lunch was ready, are really the Parcae. And now for the dumplings! At least one of my teachers at the University—the very one to whom I am indebted for my *histological* knowledge (*epidermis*)—would be reminded by the name *Knödl* (*Knödl* means dumpling), of a person whom he had to prosecute for *plagiarising* his writings. Committing a plagiarism, taking anything one can lay hands on, even though it belongs to another, obviously leads to the second part of the dream, in which I am treated like the *overcoat thief* who for some time plied his trade in the lecture-halls. I have written the word *plagiarism*—without definite intention—because it occurred to me, and now I see that it must belong to the latent dream-content and that it will serve as a bridge between the different parts of the manifest dream-content. The chain of associations — *Pélagie* — *plagiarism* — *plagiostomi*[2] (sharks)—*fish-bladder*—connects the old novel with the affair of Knödl and the overcoats (German: *Überzieher* = pullover, overcoat or condom), which obviously refer to an appliance appertaining to the technique of sex. This, it is true, is a very forced and irrational connection, but it is nevertheless one which I could not have established in waking life if it had not already been established by the dream-work. Indeed, as though nothing were sacred to this impulse to enforce associations, the beloved name, *Brücke* (bridge of words, see above),

---

[1] Both the affects pertaining to these childish scenes—astonishment and resignation to the inevitable—appeared in a dream of slightly earlier date, which first reminded me of this incident of my childhood.

[2] I do not bring in the plagiostomi arbitrarily; they recall a painful incident of disgrace before the same teacher.

now serves to remind me of the very institute in which I spent my happiest hours as a student, wanting for nothing. "So will you at the *breasts* of Wisdom every day more pleasure find"), in the most complete contrast to the desires which plague me (German: *plagen*) while I dream. And finally, there emerges the recollection of another dear teacher, whose name once more sounds like something edible (*Fleischl—Fleisch* = meat—like *Knödl* = dumplings), and of a pathetic scene in which the scales of epidermis play a part (mother—hostess), and mental derangement (the novel), and a remedy from the Latin pharmacopeia (*Küche* = kitchen) which numbs the sensation of *hunger*, namely, cocaine.

In this manner I could follow the intricate trains of thought still farther, and could fully elucidate that part of the dream which is lacking in the analysis; but I must refrain, because the personal sacrifice which this would involve is too great. I shall take up only one of the threads, which will serve to lead us directly to one of the dream-thoughts that lie at the bottom of the medley. The stranger with the long face and pointed beard, who wants to prevent me from putting on the overcoat, has the features of a tradesman of Spalato, of whom my wife bought a great deal of *Turkish* cloth. His name was *Popović*, a suspicious name, which even gave the humorist Stettenheim a pretext for a suggestive remark: "He told me his name, and blushingly shook my hand."[1] For the rest, I find the same misuse of names as above in the case of *Pélagie, Knödl, Brücke, Fleischl*. No one will deny that such playing with names is a childish trick; if I indulge in it the practice amounts to an act of retribution, for my own name has often enough been the subject of such feeble attempts at wit. Goethe once remarked how sensitive a man is in respect to his name, which he feels that he fills even as he fills his skin; Herder having written the following lines on his name:

Der du von Göttern abstammst, von
  Gothen oder vom Kote.
So seid ihr Götterbilder auch zu Staub.

[*Thou who art born of the gods, of the*
  Goths, or of the mud.
Thus are thy godlike images even
  dust.]

I realize that this digression on the misuse of names was intended merely to justify this complaint. But here let us stop. . . . The pur-

chase at Spalato reminds me of another purchase at Cattaro, where I was too cautious, and missed the opportunity of making an excellent bargain. (Missing an opportunity at the breast of the wet-nurse; see above.) One of the dream-thoughts occasioned by the sensation of hunger really amounts to this: We should let nothing escape; we should take what we can get, even if we do a little wrong; we should never let an opportunity go by; life is so short, and death inevitable. Because this is meant even sexually, and because desire is unwilling to check itself before the thought of doing wrong, this philosophy of *carpe diem* has reason to fear the censorship, and must conceal itself behind a dream. And so all sorts of counter-thoughts find expression, with recollections of the time when *spiritual nourishment* alone was sufficient for the dreamer, with hindrances of every kind and even threats of disgusting sexual punishments.

II. A second dream requires a longer preliminary statement:

I had driven to the Western Station in order to start on a holiday trip to the Aussee, but I went on to the platform in time for the Ischl train, which leaves earlier. There I saw Count Thun, who was again going to see the Emperor at Ischl. In spite of the rain he arrived in an open carriage, came straight through the entrance-gate for the local trains, and with a curt gesture and not a word of explanation he waved back the gatekeeper, who did not know him and wanted to take his ticket. After he had left in the Ischl train, I was asked to leave the platform and return to the waiting-room; but after some difficulty I obtained permission to remain. I passed the time noting how many people bribed the officials to secure a compartment; I fully intended to make a complaint—that is, to demand the same privilege. Meanwhile I sang something to myself, which I afterwards recognized as the aria from *The Marriage of Figaro*:

If my lord Count would tread a measure,
    tread a measure,
  Let him but say his pleasure,
  And I will play the tune.

(Possibly another person would not have recognized the tune.)

The whole evening I was in a high-spirited, pugnacious mood; I chaffed the waiter and the cab-driver, I hope without hurting their feelings; and now all kinds of bold and revolutionary thoughts came into my mind, such as

[1] *Popo*="backside," in German nursery language.

would fit themselves to the words of Figaro, and to memories of Beaumarchais' comedy, of which I had seen a performance at the *Comédie Française*. The speech about the great men who have taken the trouble to be born; the seigneurial right which Count Almaviva wishes to exercise with regard to Susanne; the jokes which our malicious Opposition journalists make on the name of Count Thun (German, *thun*=do), calling him Graf Nichtsthun, Count-Do-Nothing. I really do not envy him; he now has a difficult audience with the Emperor before him, and it is I who am the real Count-Do-Nothing, for I am going off for a holiday. I make all sorts of amusing plans for the vacation. Now a gentleman arrives whom I know as a Government representative at the medical examinations, and who has won the flattering nickname of "the Governmental bedfellow" (literally, *by-sleeper*) by his activities in this capacity. By insisting on his official status he secured half a first-class compartment, and I heard one guard say to another: "Where are we going to put the gentleman with the first-class half-compartment?" A pretty sort of favouritism! I am paying for a whole first-class compartment. I did actually get a whole compartment to myself, but not in a through carriage, so there was no lavatory at my disposal during the night. My complaints to the guard were fruitless; I revenged myself by suggesting that at least a hole be made in the floor of this compartment, to serve the possible needs of passengers. At a quarter to three in the morning I wake, with an urgent desire to urinate, from the following dream:

A crowd, a students' meeting. . . . A certain Count (Thun or Taaffe) is making a speech. Being asked to say something about the Germans, he declares, with a contemptuous gesture, that their favourite flower is coltsfoot, and he then puts into his buttonhole something like a torn leaf, really the crumpled skeleton of a leaf. I jump up, and I jump up,[1] but I am surprised at my implied attitude. Then, more indistinctly: *It seems as though this were the vestibule (Aula); the exits are thronged, and one must escape. I make my way through a suite of handsomely appointed rooms, evidently ministerial apartments, with furniture of a colour between brown and violet, and at last I come to a corridor in which a housekeeper, a fat, elderly woman, is seated. I try to avoid speaking to her, but she apparently thinks I have a right to pass this way, because she asks whether she shall accompany me with the lamp. I indicate with a gesture, or tell her, that she is to remain standing on the stairs, and it seems to me that I am very clever, for after all I am evading detection. Now I am downstairs, and I find a narrow, steeply rising path, which I follow.*

Again indistinctly: *It is as though my second task were to get away from the city, just as my first was to get out of the building. I am riding in a one-horse cab, and I tell the driver to take me to a railway station. "I can't drive with you on the railway line itself," I say, when he reproaches me as though I had tired him out. Here it seems as though I had already made a journey in his cab which is usually made by rail. The stations are crowded; I am wondering whether to go to Krems or to Znaim, but I reflect that the Court will be there, and I decide in favour of Graz or some such place. Now I am seated in the railway carriage, which is rather like a tram, and I have in my buttonhole a peculiar long braided thing, on which are violet-brown violets of stiff material, which makes a great impression on people.* Here the scene breaks off.

I am once more in front of the railway station, but I am in the company of an elderly gentleman. I think out a scheme for remaining unrecognized, but I see this plan already being carried out. Thinking and experiencing are here, as it were, the same thing. He pretends to be blind, at least in one eye, and I hold before him a male glass urinal (which we have to buy in the city, or have bought). I am thus a sick-nurse, and have to give him the urinal because he is blind. If the conductor sees us in this position, he must pass us by without drawing attention to us. At the same time the position of the elderly man, and his urinating organ, is plastically perceived. Then I wake with a desire to urinate.

The whole dream seems a sort of phantasy, which takes the dreamer back to the year of revolution, 1848, the memory of which had been revived by the jubilee of 1898, as well as by a little excursion to Wachau, on which I visited *Emmersdorf*, the refuge of the student leader Fischof,[2] to whom several features of the manifest dream-content might refer. The association of ideas then leads me to

---

[1] This repetition has crept into the text of the dream, apparently through absent-mindedness, and I have left it because analysis shows that it has a meaning.

[2] This is an error and not a slip, for I learned later that the Emmersdorf in Wachau is not identical with the refuge of the revolutionist Fischof, a place of the same name.

England, to the house of my brother, who used in jest to twit his wife with the title of Tennyson's poem *Fifty Years Ago,* whereupon the children were used to correct him: *Fifteen Years Ago.* This phantasy, however, which attaches itself to the thoughts evoked by the sight of Count Thun, is, like the façade of an Italian church, without organic connection with the structure behind it, but unlike such a façade it is full of gaps, and confused, and in many places portions of the interior break through. The first situation of the dream is made up of a number of scenes, into which I am able to dissect it. The arrogant attitude of the Count in the dream is copied from a scene at my school which occurred in my fifteenth year. We had hatched a conspiracy against an unpopular and ignorant teacher; the leading spirit in this conspiracy was a schoolmate who since that time seems to have taken Henry VIII of England as his model. It fell to me to carry out the *coup d'état,* and a discussion of the importance of the Danube (German, *Donau*) to Austria (Wachau!) was the occasion of an open revolt. One of our fellow-conspirators was our only aristocratic schoolmate—he was called "the giraffe" on account of his conspicuous height—and while he was being reprimanded by the tyrant of the school, the professor of the *German* language, he stood just as the Count stood in the dream. The explanation of the *favourite* flower, and the putting into a buttonhole of something that must have been a flower (which recalls the orchids which I had given that day to a friend, and also a rose of Jericho) prominently recalls the incident in Shakespeare's historical play which opens the civil wars of the *Red* and the *White* Roses; the mention of Henry VIII has paved the way to this reminiscence. Now it is not very far from roses to red and white carnations. (Meanwhile two little rhymes, the one German, the other Spanish, insinuate themselves into the analysis: *Rosen, Tulpen, Nelken, alle Blumen welken,*[1] and *Isabelita, no llores, que se marchitan las flores.*[2] The Spanish line occurs in *Figaro.*) Here in Vienna white carnations have become the badge of the *Anti-Semites,* red ones of of the *Social Democrats.* Behind this is the recollection of an anti-Semitic challenge during a railway journey in beautiful Saxony (Anglo-Saxon). The third scene contributing to the formation of the first situation in the dream dates from my early stu-

dent days. There was a debate in a *German* students' club about the relation of philosophy to the general sciences. Being a green youth, full of materialistic doctrines, I thrust myself forward in order to defend an extremely one-sided position. Thereupon a sagacious older fellow-student, who has since then shown his capacity for leading men and organizing the masses, and who, moreover, bears a name belonging to the animal kingdom, rose and gave us a thorough dressing-down; he too, he said, had herded swine in his youth, and had then returned repentant to his father's house. *I jumped up* (as in the dream), became *piggishly rude,* and retorted that since I knew he had herded *swine,* I *was not surprised* at the tone of his discourse. (In the dream I am *surprised at* my German Nationalistic feelings.) There was a great commotion, and an almost general demand that I should retract my words, but I stood my ground. The insulted student was too sensible to take the advice which was offered him, that he should send me a *challenge,* and let the matter drop.

The remaining elements of this scene of the dream are of more remote origin. What does it mean that the Count should make a scornful reference to coltsfoot? Here I must question my train of associations. Coltsfoot (German: *Huflattich*), *Lattice* (lettuce), *Salathund* (the dog that grudges others what he cannot eat himself). Here plenty of opprobrious epithets may be discerned: *Gir-affe* (German: *Affe*=monkey, ape), *pig, sow, dog;* I might even arrive, by way of the name, at *donkey,* and thereby pour contempt upon an academic professor. Furthermore, I translate coltsfoot (*Huflattich*) —I do not know whether I do so correctly— by *pisse-en-lit.* I get this idea from Zola's *Germinal,* in which some children are told to bring some dandelion salad with them. The dog— *chien*—has a name sounding not unlike the verb for the major function (*chier,* as *pisser* stands for the minor one). Now we shall soon have the indecent in all its three physical categories, for in the same *Germinal,* which deals with the future revolution, there is a description of a very peculiar contest, which relates to the production of the gaseous excretions known as *flatus.*[3] And now I cannot but observe how the way to this *flatus* has been prepared a long while since, beginning with the *flowers,* and proceeding to the Spanish rhyme of *Isabelita,* to *Ferdinand* and *Isabella,* and, by way of Henry VIII,

---

[1] Roses, tulips, and carnations, flowers all will wither.
[2] Do not cry, little Isabella because your flowers have faded.

[3] Not in *Germinal,* but in *La Terre*—a mistake of which I became aware only in the analysis. Here I would call attention to the identity of letters in *Huflattich* and *Flatus.*

to English history at the time of the Armada, after the victorious termination of which the English struck a medal with the inscription: *Flavit et dissipati sunt,* for the storm had scattered the Spanish fleet.[1] I had thought of using this phrase, half jestingly, as the title of a chapter on "Therapy," if I should ever succeed in giving a detailed account of my conception and treatment of hysteria.

I cannot give so detailed an interpretation of the second scene of the dream, out of sheer regard for the censorship. For at this point I put myself in the place of a certain eminent gentleman of the revolutionary period, who had an adventure with an eagle (German: *Adler*) and who is said to have suffered from incontinence of the bowels, *incontinentia alvi,* etc.; and here I believe that I *should not be justified* in passing the censorship, even though it was an *aulic* councillor (*aula, consiliarius aulicus*) who told me the greater part of this history. The suite of rooms in the dream is suggested by his Excellency's private saloon carriage, into which I was able to glance; but it means, as it so often does in dreams, a woman.[2] The personality of the housekeeper is an ungrateful allusion to a witty old lady, which ill repays her for the good times and the many good stories which I have enjoyed in her house. The incident of the lamp goes back to *Grillparzer,* who notes a charming experience of a similar nature, of which he afterwards made use in *Hero and Leander* (the *waves* of the *sea* and of love— the Armada and the *storm*).

I must forego a detailed analysis of the two remaining portions of the dream; I shall single out only those elements which lead me back to the two scenes of my childhood for the sake of which alone I have selected the dream. The reader will rightly assume that it is sexual material which necessitates the suppression; but he may not be content with this explanation. There are many things of which one makes no secret to oneself, but which must be treated as secrets in addressing others, and here we are concerned not with the reasons which induce me to conceal the solution, but with the motive of the inner censorship which conceals the real con-

tent of the dream even from myself. Concerning this, I will confess that the analysis reveals these three portions of the dream as impertinent boasting, the exuberance of an absurd megalomania, long ago suppressed in my waking life, which, however, dares to show itself, with individual ramifications, even in the manifest dream-content (*it seems to me that I am a cunning fellow*), making the high-spirited mood of the evening before the dream perfectly intelligible. Boasting of every kind, indeed; thus, the mention of Graz points to the phrase: "What price Graz?" which one is wont to use when one feels unusually wealthy. Readers who recall Master Rabelais's inimitable description of the life and deeds of Gargantua and his son Pantagruel will be able to enroll even the suggested content of the first portion of the dream among the boasts to which I have alluded. But the following belongs to the two scenes of childhood of which I have spoken: I had bought a *new* trunk for this journey, the colour of which, a *brownish violet,* appears in the dream several times (violet-brown violets of a stiff cloth, on an object which is known as a *girl-catcher*— the furniture in the ministerial chambers). Children, we know, believe that one *attracts people's attention with anything new.* Now I have been told of the following incident of my childhood; my recollection of the occurrence itself has been replaced by my recollection of the story. I am told that at the age of two I still used occasionally to wet my bed, and that when I was reproved for doing so I *consoled* my father by promising to buy him a beautiful *new red* bed in N (the nearest large town). Hence, the interpolation in the dream, that we *had bought the urinal in the city or had to buy it;* one must keep one's promises. (One should note, moreover, the association of the male urinal and the woman's trunk, *box.*) All the megalomania of the child is contained in this promise. The significance of dreams of urinary difficulties in the case of children has already been considered in the interpretation of an earlier dream (cf. the dream on p. 208). The psycho-analysis of neurotics has taught us to recognize the intimate connection between wetting the bed and the character trait of ambition.

Then, when I was seven or eight years of age another domestic incident occurred which I remember very well. One evening, before going to bed, I had disregarded the dictates of discretion, and had satisfied my needs in my parents' bedroom, and in their presence. Reprimanding

---

[1] An unsolicited biographer, Dr. F. Wittels, reproaches me for having omitted the name of Jehovah from the above motto. The English medal contains the name of the Diety, in Hebrew letters, on the background of a cloud, and placed in such a manner that one may equally well regard it as part of the picture or as part of the inscription.

[2] *Frauenzimmer,* German, *Zimmer*-room, is appended to *Frauen*-woman, in order to imply a slight contempt. —TR.

me for this delinquency, my father remarked: "That boy will never amount to anything." This must have been a terrible affront to my ambition, for allusions to this scene recur again and again in my dreams, and are constantly coupled with enumerations of my accomplishments and successes, as though I wanted to say: "You see, I have amounted to something after all." This childish scene furnishes the elements for the last image of the dream, in which the rôles are interchanged, of course for the purpose of revenge. The elderly man obviously my father, for the blindness in one eye signifies his one-sided glaucoma,[1] is now urinating before me as I once urinated before him. By means of the glaucoma I remind my father of cocaine, which stood him in good stead during his operation, as though I had thereby fulfilled my promise. Besides, I make sport of him; since he is blind, I must hold the *glass* in front of him, and I delight in allusions to my knowledge of the theory of hysteria, of which I am proud.[2]

[1] Another interpretation: He is one-eyed like Odin, the father of the gods—Odin's consolation. The consolation in the childish scene: I will buy him a new bed.

[2] Here is some more material for interpretation: Holding the urine-glass recalls the story of a peasant (illiterate) at the optician's, who tried on now one pair of spectacles, now another, but was still unable to read.—(Peasant-catcher—girl-catcher in the preceding portion of the dream.)—The peasants' treatment of the feeble-minded father in Zola's *La Terre.*—The tragic atonement, that in his last days my father soiled his bed like a child; hence, I am his nurse in the dream.—"Thinking and experiencing are here, as it were, identical"; this recalls a highly revolutionary closet drama by Oscar Panizza, in which God, the Father, is ignominiously treated as a palsied greybeard. With Him will and deed are one, and in the book he has to be restrained by His archangel, a sort of Ganymede, from scolding and swearing, because His curses would immediately be fulfilled.—Making plans is a reproach against my father, dating from a later period in the development of the critical faculty, much as the whole rebellious content of the dream, which commits *lèse majesté* and scorns authority, may be traced to a revolt against my father. The sovereign is called the father of his country (*Landesvater*), and the father is the first and oldest, and for the child the only authority, from whose absolutism the other social authorities have evolved in the course of the history of human civilization (in so far as mother-right does not necessitate a qualification of this doctrine). — The words which occurred to me in the dream, "thinking and experiencing are the same thing," refer to the explanation of hysterical symptoms, with which the male urinal (glass) is also associated.—I need not explain the principle of *Gschnas* to a Viennese; it consists in constructing objects of rare and costly appearance out of trivial, and preferably comical and worthless material—for example, making suits of armour out of kitchen utensils, wisps of straw and *Salzstangeln* (long rolls), as our artists are fond of doing at their jolly parties. I had learned that hysterical subjects do the same thing; besides what really happens to them, they unconsciously conceive for themselves horrible or extravagantly fantastic incidents,

If the two childish scenes of urination are, according to my theory, closely associated with the desire for greatness, their resuscitation on the journey to the Aussee was further favoured by the accidental circumstance that my compartment had no lavatory, and that I must be prepared to postpone relief during the journey, as actually happened in the morning when I woke with the sensation of a bodily need. I suppose one might be inclined to credit this sensation with being the actual stimulus of the dream; I should, however, prefer a different explanation, namely, that the dream-thoughts first gave rise to the desire to urinate. It is quite unusual for me to be disturbed in sleep by any physical need, least of all at the time when I woke on this occasion—a quarter to four in the morning. I would forestall a further objection by remarking that I have hardly ever felt a desire to urinate after waking early on other journeys made under more comfortable circumstances. However, I can leave this point undecided without weakening my argument.

Further, since experience in dream-analysis has drawn my attention to the fact that even from dreams the interpretation of which seems at first sight complete, because the dream-sources and the wish-stimuli are easily demonstrable, important trains of thought proceed which reach back into the earliest years of childhood, I had to ask myself whether this characteristic does not even constitute an essential condition of dreaming. If it were permissible to generalize this notion, I should say that every dream is connected through its manifest content with recent experiences, while through its latent content it is connected with the most remote experiences; and I can actually show in the analysis of hysteria that these remote experiences have in a very real sense remained *recent* right up to the present. But I still find it very difficult to prove this conjecture; I shall have to return to the probable rôle in dream-formation of the earliest experiences of our childhood in another connection (chapter VII).

Of the three peculiarities of the dream-mem-

which they build up out of the most harmless and commonplace material of actual experience. The symptoms attach themselves primarily to these phantasies, not to the memory of real events, whether serious or trivial. This explanation had helped me to overcome many difficulties, and afforded me much pleasure. I was able to allude to it by means of the dream-element "male urine-glass," because I had been told that at the last *Gschnas* evening a poison-chalice of Lucretia Borgia's had been exhibited, the chief constituent of which had consisted of a glass urinal for men, such as is used in hospitals.

ory considered above, one—the preference for the unimportant in the dream-content—has been satisfactorily explained by tracing it back to dream-distortion. We have succeeded in establishing the existence of the other two peculiarities—the preferential selection of recent and also of infantile material—but we have found it impossible to derive them from the motives of the dream. Let us keep in mind these two characteristics, which we still have to explain or evaluate; a place will have to be found for them elsewhere, either in the discussion of the psychology of the sleeping state, or in the consideration of the structure of the psychic apparatus—which we shall undertake later after we have seen that by means of dream-interpretation we are able to glance as through an inspection-hole into the interior of this apparatus.

But here and now I will emphasize another result of the last few dream-analyses. The dream often appears to have several meanings; not only may several wish-fulfilments be combined in it, as our examples show, but one meaning or one wish-fulfilment may conceal another, until in the lowest stratum one comes upon the fulfilment of a wish from the earliest period of childhood; and here again it may be questioned whether the word *often* at the beginning of this sentence may not more correctly be replaced by *constantly*.[1]

C. The Somatic Sources of Dreams

If we attempt to interest a cultured layman in the problems of dreams, and if, with this end in view, we ask him what he believes to be the source of dreams, we shall generally find that he feels quite sure he knows at least this part of the solution. He thinks immediately of the influence exercised on the formation of dreams by a disturbed or impeded digestion ("Dreams come from the stomach"), an accidental position of the body, a trifling occurrence during sleep. He does not seem to suspect that even after all these factors have been duly considered something still remains to be explained.

In the introductory chapter we examined at

length the opinion of scientific writers on the rôle of somatic stimuli in the formation of dreams, so that here we need only recall the results of this inquiry. We have seen that three kinds of somatic stimuli will be distinguished: the objective sensory stimuli which proceed from external objects, the inner states of excitation of the sensory organs, having only a subjective reality, and the bodily stimuli arising within the body; and we have also noticed that the writers on dreams are inclined to thrust into the background any psychic sources of dreams which may operate simultaneously with the somatic stimuli, or to exclude them altogether. In testing the claims made on behalf of these somatic stimuli we have learned that the significance of the objective excitation of the sensory organs—whether accidental stimuli operating during sleep, or such as cannot be excluded from the dormant relation of these dream-images and ideas to the internal bodily stimuli and confirmed by experiment; that the part played by the subjective sensory stimuli appears to be demonstrated by the recurrence of hypnagogic sensory images in dreams; and that, although the broadly accepted relation of these dream-images and ideas to the internal bodily stimuli cannot be exhaustively demonstrated, it is at all events confirmed by the well-known influence which an excited state of the digestive, urinary and sexual organs exercises upon the content of our dreams.

Nerve stimulus and *bodily stimulus* would thus be the anatomical sources of dreams; that is, according to many writers, the sole and exclusive sources of dreams.

But we have already considered a number of doubtful points, which seem to question not so much the correctness of the somatic theory as its adequacy.

However confident the representatives of this theory may be of its factual basis—especially in respect of the accidental and external nerve-stimuli, which may without difficulty be recognized in the dream-content—nevertheless they have all come near to admitting that the rich content of ideas found in dreams cannot be derived from the external nerve-stimuli alone. In this connection Miss Mary Whiton Calkins tested her own dreams, and those of a second person, for a period of six weeks, and found that the element of external sensory perception was demonstrable in only 13.2 per cent and 6.7 per cent of these dreams respectively. Only two dreams in the whole collection could be referred to organic sensations. These statis-

[1] The stratification of the meanings of dreams is one of the most delicate but also one of the most fruitful problems of dream-interpretation. Whoever forgets the possibility of such stratification is likely to go astray and to make untenable assertions concerning the nature of dreams. But hitherto this subject has been only too imperfectly investigated. So far, a fairly orderly stratification of symbols in dreams due to urinary stimulus has been subjected to a thorough evaluation only by Otto Rank.

tics confirm what a cursory survey of our own experience would already have led us to suspect.

A distinction has often been made between *nerve-stimulus dreams* which have already been thoroughly investigated, and other forms of dreams. Spitta, for example, divided dreams into nerve-stimulus dreams and association-dreams. But it was obvious that this solution remained unsatisfactory unless the link between the somatic sources of dreams and their ideational content could be indicated.

In addition to the first objection, that of the insufficient frequency of the external sources of stimulus, a second objection presents itself, namely, the inadequacy of the explanations of dreams afforded by this category of dream-sources. There are two things which the representatives of this theory have failed to explain: firstly, why the true nature of the external stimulus is not recognized in the dream, but is constantly mistaken for something else; and secondly, why the result of the reaction of the perceiving mind to this misconceived stimulus should be so indeterminate and variable. We have seen that Strümpell, in answer to these questions, asserts that the mind, since it turns away from the outer world during sleep, is not in a position to give the correct interpretation of the objective sensory stimulus, but is forced to construct illusions on the basis of the indefinite stimulation arriving from many directions. In his own words (*Die Natur und Entstehung der Träume,* p. 108).

"When by an external or internal nerve-stimulus during sleep a feeling, or a complex of feelings, or any sort of psychic process arises in the mind, and is perceived by the mind, this process calls up from the mind perceptual images belonging to the sphere of the waking experiences, that is to say, earlier perceptions, either unembellished, or with the psychic values appertaining to them. It collects about itself, as it were, a greater or lesser number of such images, from which the impression resulting from the nerve-stimulus receives its psychic value. In this connection it is commonly said, as in ordinary language we say of the waking procedure, that the mind *interprets* in sleep the impressions of nervous stimuli. The result of this interpretation is the so-called *nerve-stimulus dream*—that is, a dream the components of which are conditioned by the fact that a nerve-stimulus produces its psychical effect in the life of the mind in accordance with the laws of reproduction."

In all essential points identical with this doc-

trine is Wundt's statement that the concepts of dreams proceed, at all events for the most part, from sensory stimuli, and especially from the stimuli of general sensation, and are therefore mostly phantastic illusions—probably only to a small extent pure memory-conceptions raised to the condition of hallucinations. To illustrate the relation between dream-content and dream-stimuli which follows from this theory, Strümpell makes use of an excellent simile. It is "as though the ten fingers of a person ignorant of music were to stray over the keyboard of an instrument." The implication is that the dream is not a psychic phenomenon, originating from psychic motives, but the result of a physiological stimulus, which expresses itself in psychic symptomatology because the apparatus affected by the stimulus is not capable of any other mode of expression. Upon a similar assumption is based the explanation of obsessions which Meynert attempted in his famous simile of the dial on which individual figures are most deeply embossed.

Popular though this theory of the somatic dream-stimuli has become, and seductive though it may seem, it is none the less easy to detect its weak point. Every somatic dream-stimulus which provokes the psychic apparatus in sleep to interpretation by the formation of illusions may evoke an incalculable number of such attempts at interpretation. It may consequently be represented in the dream-content by an extraordinary number of different concepts.[1] But the theory of Strümpell and Wundt cannot point to any sort of motive which controls the relation between the external stimulus and the dream-concept chosen to interpret it, and therefore it cannot explain the "peculiar choice" which the stimuli "often enough make in the course of their productive activity" (Lipps, *Grundtatsachen des Seelenlebens,* p. 170). Other objections may be raised against the fundamental assumption behind the theory of illusions—the assumption that during sleep the mind is not in a condition to recognize the real nature of the objective sensory stimuli. The old physiologist Burdach shows us that the mind is quite capable even during sleep of a correct interpretation of the

[1] I would advise everyone to read the exact and detailed records (collected in two volumes) of the dreams experimentally produced by Mourly Vold in order to convince himself how little the conditions of the experiments help to explain the content of the individual dream, and how little such experiments help us towards an understanding of the problems of dreams.

sensory impressions which reach it, and of reacting in accordance with this correct interpretation, inasmuch as he demonstrates that certain sensory impressions which seem important to the individual may be excepted from the general neglect of the sleeping mind (as in the example of nurse and child), and that one is more surely awakened by one's own name than by an indifferent auditory impression; all of which presupposes, of course, that the mind discriminates between sensations, even in sleep. Burdach infers from these observations that we must not assume that the mind is incapable of interpreting sensory stimuli in the sleeping state, but rather *that it is not sufficiently interested in them.* The arguments which Burdach employed in 1830 reappear unchanged in the works of Lipps (in the year 1883), where they are employed for the purpose of attacking the theory of somatic stimuli. According to these arguments the mind seems to be like the sleeper in the anecdote, who, on being asked, "Are you asleep?" answers "No," and on being again addressed with the words: "Then lend me ten florins," takes refuge in the excuse: "I am asleep."

The inadequacy of the theory of somatic dream-stimuli may be further demonstrated in another way. Observation shows that external stimuli do not oblige me to dream, even though these stimuli appear in the dream-content as soon as I begin to dream—supposing that I do dream. In response to a touch or pressure-stimulus experienced while I am asleep, a variety of reactions are at my disposal. I may overlook it, and find on waking that my leg has become uncovered, or that I have been lying on an arm; indeed, pathology offers me a host of examples of powerfully exciting sensory and motor stimuli of different kinds which remain ineffective during sleep. I may perceive the sensation during sleep, and through my sleep, as it were, as constantly happens in the case of pain stimuli, but without weaving the pain into the texture of a dream. And thirdly, I may wake up in response to the stimulus, simply in order to avoid it. Still another, fourth, reaction is possible: namely, that the nerve-stimulus may cause me to dream; but the other possible reactions occur quite as frequently as the reaction of dream-formation. This, however, would not be the case *if the incentive to dreaming did not lie outside the somatic dream-sources.*

Appreciating the importance of the above-mentioned lacunae in the explanation of dreams by somatic stimuli, other writers—Scherner, for example, and, following him, the philosopher Volkelt—endeavoured to determine more precisely the nature of the psychic activities which cause the many-coloured images of our dreams to proceed from the somatic stimuli, and in so doing they approached the problem of the essential nature of dreams as a problem of psychology, and regarded dreaming as a psychic activity. Scherner not only gave a poetical, vivid and glowing description of the psychic peculiarities which unfold themselves in the course of dream-formation, but he also believed that he had hit upon the principle of the method the mind employs in dealing with the stimuli which are offered to it. The dream, according to Scherner, in the free activity of the phantasy, which has been released from the shackles imposed upon it during the day, strives to represent symbolically the nature of the organ from which the stimulus proceeds. Thus there exists a sort of dream-book, a guide to the interpretation of dreams, by means of which bodily sensations, the conditions of the organs, and states of stimulation, may be inferred from the dream-images. "Thus the image of a cat expressed extreme ill-temper; the image of pale, smooth pastry the nudity of the body. The human body as a whole is pictured by the phantasy of the dream as a house, and the individual organs of the body as parts of the house. In *toothache-dreams* a vaulted vestibule corresponds to the mouth, and a staircase to the descent from the pharynx to the oesophagus; in the *headache-dream* a ceiling covered with disgusting toad-like spiders is chosen to denote the upper part of the head." "Many different symbols are employed by our dreams for the same organ: thus the breathing lung finds its symbol in a roaring stove, filled with flames, the heart in empty boxes and baskets, and the bladder in round, bag-shaped or merely hollow objects. It is of particular significance that at the close of the dream the stimulating organ or its function is often represented without disguise and usually on the dreamer's own body. Thus the *toothache-dream* commonly ends by the dreamer drawing a tooth out of his mouth." It cannot be said that this theory of dream-interpretation has found much favour with other writers. It seems, above all, extravagant; and so Scherner's readers have hesitated to give it even the small amount of credit to which it is, in my opinion, entitled. As will be seen, it tends to a revival of dream-interpretation by means of *symbolism,* a method employed by the ancients; only the province from which the interpretation is to be derived is restricted to the human body. The lack of a scientifically comprehensible technique of interpretation must seriously limit the applicability of Scherner's theory. Arbitrariness in the interpretation of dreams would appear to be by no means excluded, especially since in this case also a stimulus may be expressed in the dream-content by several representative symbols; thus even Scherner's follower Volkelt was unable to confirm the representation of the body as a house. Another objection is that here again the dream-activity is regarded as a useless and aimless activity of the mind, since, according to this theory, the mind is content with merely forming phantasies around the stimulus with which it is dealing, without even remotely attempting to abolish the stimulus.

Scherner's theory of the symbolization of bodily stimuli by the dream is seriously damaged by yet another objection. These bodily stimuli are present at all times, and it is generally assumed that the mind is more accessible to them during sleep than in the waking state. It is therefore impossible to understand why the mind does not dream continuously all night long, and why it does not dream every night about all the organs. If one attempts to evade this objection by positing the condition that special excitations must proceed from the eye, the ear, the teeth, the bowels, etc., in order to arouse the dream-activity, one is confronted with the difficulty of proving that this increase of stimulation is objective; and proof is possible only in a very few cases. If the dream of flying is a symbolization of the upward and downward motion of the pulmonary lobes, either this dream, as has already been remarked by Strümpell, should be dreamt much oftener, or it should be possible to show that respiration is more active during this dream. Yet a third alternative is possible—and it is the most probable of all—namely, that now and again special motives are operative to direct the attention to the visceral sensations which are constantly present. But this would take us far beyond the scope of Scherner's theory.

The value of Scherner's and Volkelt's disquisitions resides in their calling our attention to a number of characteristics of the dream-content which are in need of explanation, and which seem to promise fresh discoveries. It is quite true that symbolizations of the bodily organs and functions do occur in dreams: for example, that water in a dream often signifies a desire to urinate, that the male genital organ may be represented by an upright staff, or a pillar, etc. With dreams which exhibit a very animated field of vision and brilliant colours, in contrast to the dimness of other dreams, the interpretation that they are "dreams due to visual stimulation" can hardly be dismissed, nor can we dispute the participation of illusion-formation in dreams which contain noise and a medley of voices. A dream like that of Scherner's, that two rows of fair handsome boys stood facing one another on a bridge, attacking one another, and then resuming their positions, until finally the dreamer himself sat down on a bridge and drew a long tooth from his jaw; or a similar dream of Volkelt's, in which two rows of drawers played a part, and which again ended in the extraction of a tooth; dream-formations of this kind, of which both writers relate a great number, forbid our dismissing Scherner's theory as an idle invention without seeking the kernel of truth which may be contained in it. We are therefore confronted with the task of finding a different explanation of the supposed symbolization of the alleged dental stimulus.

Throughout our consideration of the theory of the somatic sources of dreams, I have refrained from urging the argument which arises from our analyses of dreams. If, by a procedure which has not been followed by other writers in their investigation of dreams, we can prove that the dream possesses intrinsic value as psychic action, that a wish supplies the motive of its formation, and that the experiences of the previous day furnish the most obvious material of its content, any other theory of dreams which neglects such an important method of investigation—and accordingly makes the dream appear a useless and enigmatical psychic reaction to somatic stimuli—may be dismissed without special criticism. For in this case there would have to be—and this is highly improbable—two entirely different kinds of dreams, of which only one kind has come under our observation, while the other kind alone has been observed by the earlier investigators. It only remains now to find a place in our theory of dreams for the facts on which the current doctrine of somatic dream-stimuli is based.

We have already taken the first step in this direction in advancing the thesis that the dream-work is under a compulsion to elaborate into a unified whole all the dream-stimuli which are simultaneously present (p. 211 above). We have seen that when two or more experiences capable of making an impression on the mind have been left over from the previous day, the wishes that result from them are united into one dream; similarly, that the impressions possessing psychic value and the indifferent experiences of the previous day unite in the dream-material, provided that connecting ideas between the two can be established. Thus the dream appears to be a reaction to everything which is simultaneously present as actual in the sleeping mind. As far as we have hitherto analysed the dream-material, we have discovered it to be a collection of psychic remnants and memory-traces, which we were obliged to credit (on account of the preference shown for recent and for infantile material) with a character of psychological actuality, though the nature of this actuality was not at the time determinable. We shall now have little difficulty in predicting what will happen when to these actualities of the memory fresh material in the form of sensations is added during sleep. These stimuli, again, are of importance to the dream because they are actual; they are united with the other psychic actualities to provide the material for dream-formation. To express it in other words, the stimuli which occur during sleep are elaborated into a wish-fulfilment, of which the other components are the psychic remnants of daily experience with which we are already familiar. This combination, however, is not inevitable; we have seen that more than one kind of behaviour toward the physical stimuli received during sleep is possible. Where this combination is effected, a conceptual material for the dream-content has been found which will represent both kinds of dream-sources, the somatic as well as the psychic.

The nature of the dream is not altered when somatic material is added to the psychic dream-sources; it still remains a wish-fulfilment, no matter how its expression is determined by the actual material available.

I should like to find room here for a number of peculiarities which are able to modify the significance of external stimuli for the dream. I imagine that a co-operation of individual, physiological and accidental factors, which depend on the circumstances of the moment, determines how one will behave in individual cases of more intensive objective stimulation during sleep; habitual or accidental profundity of sleep, in conjunction with the intensity of the stimulus, will in one case make it possible so to suppress the stimulus that it will not disturb the sleeper, while in another case it will force the sleeper to wake, or will assist the

attempt to subdue the stimulus by weaving it into the texture of the dream. In accordance with the multiplicity of these constellations, external objective stimuli will be expressed more rarely or more frequently in the case of one person than in that of another. In my own case, since I am an excellent sleeper, and obstinately refuse to allow myself to be disturbed during sleep on any pretext whatever, this intrusion of external causes of excitation into my dreams is very rare, whereas psychic motives apparently cause me to dream very easily. Indeed, I have noted only a single dream in which an objective, painful source of stimulation is demonstrable, and it will be highly instructive to see what effect the external stimulus had in this particular dream.

I am riding a gray horse, at first timidly and awkwardly, as though I were merely carried along. Then I meet a colleague, P, also on horseback, and dressed in rough frieze; he is sitting erect in the saddle; he calls my attention to something (probably to the fact that I have a very bad seat). Now I begin to feel more and more at ease on the back of my highly intelligent horse; I sit more comfortably, and I find that I am quite at home up here. My saddle is a sort of pad, which completely fills the space between the neck and the rump of the horse. I ride between two vans, and just manage to clear them. After riding up the street for some distance, I turn round and wish to dismount, at first in front of a little open chapel which is built facing on to the street. Then I do really dismount in front of a chapel which stands near the first one; the hotel is in the same street; I might let the horse go there by itself, but I prefer to lead it thither. It seems as though I should be ashamed to arrive there on horseback. In front of the hotel there stands a page-boy, who shows me a note of mine which has been found, and ridicules me on account of it. On the note is written, doubly underlined, "Eat nothing," and then a second sentence (indistinct): something like "Do not work"; at the same time a hazy idea that I am in a strange city, in which I do no work.

It will not at once be apparent that this dream originated under the influence, or rather under the compulsion, of a pain-stimulus. The day before, however, I had suffered from boils, which made every movement a torture, and at last a boil had grown to the size of an apple at the root of the scrotum, and had caused me the most intolerable pains at every step; a feverish lassitude, lack of appetite, and the hard work which I had nevertheless done during the day, had conspired with the pain to upset me. I was not altogether in a condition to discharge my duties as a physician, but in view of the nature and the location of the malady, it was possible to imagine something else for which I was most of all unfit, namely riding. Now it is this very activity of riding into which I am plunged by the dream; it is the most energetic denial of the pain which imagination could conceive. As a matter of fact, I cannot ride; I do not dream of doing so; I never sat on a horse but once—and then without a saddle—and I did not like it. But in this dream I ride as though I had no boil on the perineum; or rather, *I ride, just because I want to have none.* To judge from the description, my saddle is the poultice which has enabled me to fall asleep. Probably, being thus comforted, I did not feel anything of my pain during the first few hours of my sleep. Then the painful sensations made themselves felt, and tried to wake me; whereupon the dream came and said to me, soothingly: "Go on sleeping, you are not going to wake! You have no boil, for you are riding on horseback, and with a boil just there no one could ride!" And the dream was successful; the pain was stifled, and I went on sleeping.

But the dream was not satisfied with "suggesting away" the boil by tenaciously holding fast to an idea incompatible with the malady (thus behaving like the hallucinatory insanity of a mother who has lost her child, or of a merchant who has lost his fortune). In addition, the details of the sensation denied and of the image used to suppress it serve the dream also as a means to connect other material actually present in the mind with the situation in the dream, and to give this material representation. I am riding on a *gray* horse—the colour of the horse exactly corresponds with the *pepper-and-salt* suit in which I last saw my colleague P in the country. I have been warned that highly seasoned food is the cause of boils, and in any case it is preferable as an aetiological explanation to *sugar,* which might be thought of in connection with furunculosis. My friend P likes to *ride the high horse* with me ever since he took my place in the treatment of a female patient, in whose case I had performed great feats (*Kunststücke:* in the dream I sit the horse at first sideways, like a trick-rider, *Kunstreiter*), but who really, like the horse in the story of the Sunday equestrian, led me wherever she wished. Thus the horse comes to be a symbolic representation of a lady patient (in the dream it is *highly intelligent*). *I feel quite at home* refers to the position which I occupied in the patient's household until I was replaced by my colleague P. "I thought you were safe in the saddle up there," one of my few well-wishers among the eminent physicians of the city recently said to me, with reference to the same household. And it was a *feat* to practise psychotherapy for eight to ten hours a day, while suffering such pain, but I know that I cannot continue my peculiarly strenuous work for any length of time without perfect physical health, and the dream is full of dismal allusions to the situation which would result if my illness continued (the note, such as neurasthenics carry and show to their doctors): *Do not work, do not eat.* On further interpretation I see that the dream-activity has succeeded in finding its way from the wish-situation of riding to some very early childish quarrels which must have occurred between myself and a nephew, who is a year older than I, and is now living in England. It has also taken up elements from my journeys in Italy: the street in the dream is built up out of impressions of Verona and Siena. A still deeper interpretation leads to sexual dream-thoughts, and I recall what the dream-allusions to that beautiful country were supposed to mean in the dream of a female patient who had never been to Italy (*to Italy,* German: *gen Italien=Genitalien=genitals*); at the same time there are references to the house in which I preceded my friend P as physician, and to the place where the boil is located.

In another dream, I was similarly successful in warding off a threatened disturbance of my sleep; this time the threat came from a sensory stimulus. It was only chance, however, that enabled me to discover the connection between the dream and the accidental dream-stimulus, and in this way to understand the dream. One midsummer morning in a Tyrolese mountain resort I woke with the knowledge that I had dreamed: *The Pope is dead.* I was not able to interpret this short, non-visual dream. I could remember only one possible basis of the dream, namely, that shortly before this the newspapers had reported that His Holiness was slightly indisposed. But in the course of the morning my wife asked me: "Did you hear the dreadful tolling of the church bells this morning?" I had no idea that I had heard it, but now I understood my dream. It was the reaction of my need for sleep to the noise by which the pious Tyroleans were trying to wake me. I avenged myself on them by the conclusion which formed the content of my dream, and continued to sleep, without any further interest in the tolling of the bells.

Among the dreams mentioned in the previous chapters there are several which might serve as examples of the elaboration of so-called nerve-stimuli. The dream of drinking in long draughts is such an example; here the somatic stimulus seems to be the sole source of the dream, and the wish arising from the sensation —thirst—the only motive for dreaming. We find much the same thing in other simple dreams, where the somatic stimulus is able of itself to generate a wish. The dream of the sick woman who throws the cooling apparatus from her cheek at night is an instance of an unusual manner of reacting to a pain-stimulus with a wish-fulfilment; it seems as though the patient had temporarily succeeded in making herself analgesic, and accompanied this by ascribing her pains to a stranger.

My dream of the three Parcae is obviously a hunger-dream, but it has contrived to shift the need for food right back to the child's longing for its mother's breast, and to use a harmless desire as a mask for a more serious one that cannot venture to express itself so openly. In the dream of Count Thun we were able to see by what paths an accidental physical need was brought into relation with the strongest, but also the most rigorously repressed impulses of the psychic life. And when, as in the case reported by Garnier, the First Consul incorporates the sound of an exploding infernal machine into a dream of battle before it causes him to wake, the true purpose for which alone psychic activity concerns itself with sensations during sleep is revealed with unusual clarity. A young lawyer, who is full of his first great bankruptcy case, and falls asleep in the afternoon, behaves just as the great Napoleon did. He dreams of a certain G. Reich in *Hussiatyn,* whose acquaintance he has made in connection with the bankruptcy case, but *Hussiatyn* (German: *husten,* to cough) forces itself upon his attention still further; he is obliged to wake, only to hear his wife—who is suffering from bronchial catarrh—violently coughing.

Let us compare the dream of Napoleon I— who, incidentally, was an excellent sleeper— with that of the sleepy student, who was awakened by his landlady with the reminder that he had to go to the hospital, and who thereupon dreamt himself into a bed in the hospital, and then slept on, the underlying reasoning being as follows: If I am already in the hospital, I needn't get up to go there. This is obviously a convenience-dream; the sleeper frankly admits to himself his motive in dreaming; but he thereby reveals one of the secrets of dreaming in general. In a certain sense, all dreams are *convenience-dreams;* they serve the purpose of continuing to sleep instead of waking. *The dream is the guardian of sleep, not its disturber.* In another place we shall have occasion to justify this conception in respect to the psychic factors that make for waking; but we can already demonstrate its applicability to the objective external stimuli. Either the mind does not concern itself at all with the causes of sensations during sleep, if it is able to carry this attitude through as against the intensity of the stimuli, and their significance, of which it is well aware; or it employs the dream to deny these stimuli; or, thirdly, if it is obliged to recognize the stimuli, it seeks that interpretation of them which will represent the actual sensation as a component of a desired situation which is compatible with sleep. The actual sensation is woven into the dream *in order to deprive it of its reality.* Napoleon is permitted to go on sleeping; it is only a dream-memory of the thunder of the guns at Arcole which is trying to disturb him.[1]

The wish to sleep, to which the conscious ego has adjusted itself, and which (together with the dream-censorship and the "secondary elaboration" to be mentioned later) represents the ego's contribution to the dream, must thus always be taken into account as a motive of dream-formation, and every successful dream is a fulfilment of this wish. The relation of this general, constantly present, and unvarying sleep-wish to the other wishes of which now one and now another is fulfilled by the dream-content, will be the subject of later consideration. In the wish to sleep we have discovered a motive capable of supplying the deficiency in the theory of Strümpell and Wundt, and of explaining the perversity and capriciousness of the interpretation of the external stimulus. The correct interpretation, of which the sleeping mind is perfectly capable, would involve active interest, and would require the sleeper to wake; hence, of those interpretations which are possible at all, only such are admitted as are acceptable to the dictatorial censorship of the sleep-wish. The logic of dream situations would run, for example: "It is the nightingale, and not the lark." For if it is the lark, love's night

---

[1] The two sources from which I know of this dream do not entirely agree as to its content.

is at an end. From among the interpretations of the stimulus which are thus admissible, that one is selected which can secure the best connection with the wish-impulses that are lying in wait in the mind. Thus everything is definitely determined, and nothing is left to caprice. The misinterpretation is not an illusion, but—if you will—an excuse. Here again, as in substitution by displacement in the service of the dream-censorship, we have an act of deflection of the normal psychic procedure.

If the external nerve-stimuli and the inner bodily stimuli are sufficiently intense to compel psychic attention, they represent—that is, if they result in dreaming at all, and not in waking—a fixed point for dream-formation, a nucleus in the dream-material, for which an appropriate wish-fulfilment is sought, just as (see above) mediating ideas between two psychical dream-stimuli are sought. To this extent it is true of a number of dreams that the somatic element dictates the dream-content. In this extreme case even a wish that is not actually present may be aroused for the purpose of dream-formation. But the dream cannot do otherwise than represent a wish in some situation as fulfilled; it is, as it were, confronted with the task of discovering what wish can be represented as fulfilled by the given sensation. Even if this given material is of a painful or disagreeable character, yet it is not unserviceable for the purposes of dream-formation. The psychic life has at its disposal even wishes whose fulfilment evokes displeasure, which seems a contradiction, but becomes perfectly intelligible if we take into account the presence of two sorts of psychic instance and the censorship that subsists between them.

In the psychic life there exist, as we have seen, *repressed* wishes, which belong to the first system, and to whose fulfilment the second system is opposed. We do not mean this in a historic sense—that such wishes have once existed and have subsequently been destroyed. The doctrine of *repression*, which we need in the study of psychoneuroses, asserts that such repressed wishes still exist, but simultaneously with an inhibition which weighs them down. Language has hit upon the truth when it speaks of the *suppression* (sub-pression, or pushing under) of such impulses. The psychic mechanism which enables such suppressed wishes to force their way to realization is retained in being and in working order. But if it happens that such a suppressed wish is fulfilled, the vanquished inhibition of the second system (which is ca-

pable of consciousness) is then expressed as discomfort. And, in order to conclude this argument: If sensations of a disagreeable character which originate from somatic sources are present during sleep, this constellation is utilized by the dream-activity to procure the fulfilment—with more or less maintenance of the censorship—of an otherwise suppressed wish.

This state of affairs makes possible a certain number of anxiety-dreams, while others of these dream-formations which are unfavourable to the wish-theory exhibit a different mechanism. For the anxiety in dreams may of course be of a psychoneurotic character, originating in psycho-sexual excitation, in which case, the anxiety corresponds to repressed libido. Then this anxiety, like the whole anxiety-dream, has the significance of a neurotic symptom, and we stand at the dividing-line where the wish-fulfilling tendency of dreams is frustrated. But in other anxiety-dreams the feeling of anxiety comes from somatic sources (as in the case of persons suffering from pulmonary or cardiac trouble, with occasional difficulty in breathing), and then it is used to help such strongly suppressed wishes to attain fulfilment in a dream, the dreaming of which from psychic motives would have resulted in the same release of anxiety. It is not difficult to reconcile these two apparently contradictory cases. When two psychic formations, an affective inclination and a conceptual content, are intimately connected, either one being actually present will evoke the other, even in a dream; now the anxiety of somatic origin evokes the suppressed conceptual content, now it is the released conceptual content, accompanied by sexual excitement, which causes the release of anxiety. In the one case, it may be said that a somatically determined affect is psychically interpreted; in the other case, all is of psychic origin, but the content which has been suppressed is easily replaced by a somatic interpretation which fits the anxiety. The difficulties which lie in the way of understanding all this have little to do with dreams; they are due to the fact that in discussing these points we are touching upon the problems of the development of anxiety and of repression.

The general aggregate of bodily sensation must undoubtedly be included among the dominant dream-stimuli of internal bodily origin. Not that it is capable of supplying the dream-content; but it forces the dream-thoughts to make a choice from the material destined to serve the purpose of representation in the dream-content, inasmuch as it brings within easy reach that part of the material which is adapted to its own character, and holds the rest at a distance. Moreover, this general feeling, which survives from the preceding day, is of course connected with the psychic residues that are significant for the dream. Moreover, this feeling itself may be either maintained or overcome in the dream, so that it may, if it is painful, veer round into its opposite.

If the somatic sources of excitation during sleep—that is, the sensations of sleep—are not of unusual intensity, the part which they play in dream-formation is, in my judgment, similar to that of those impressions of the day which are still recent, but of no great significance. I mean that they are utilized for the dream-formation if they are of such a kind that they can be united with the conceptual content of the psychic dream-source, but not otherwise. They are treated as a cheap ever-ready material, which can be used whenever it is needed, and not as valuable material which itself prescribes the manner in which it must be utilized. I might suggest the analogy of a connoisseur giving an artist a rare stone, a piece of onyx, for example, in order that it may be fashioned into a work of art. Here the size of the stone, its colour, and its markings help to decide what head or what scene shall be represented; while if he is dealing with a uniform and abundant material such as marble or sandstone, the artist is guided only by the idea which takes shape in his mind. Only in this way, it seems to me, can we explain the fact that the dream-content furnished by physical stimuli of somatic origin which are not unusually accentuated does not make its appearance in all dreams and every night.[1]

Perhaps an example which takes us back to the interpretation of dreams will best illustrate my meaning. One day I was trying to understand the significance of the sensation of being inhibited, of not being able to move from the spot, of not being able to get something done, etc., which occurs so frequently in dreams, and is so closely allied to anxiety. That night I had the following dream: *I am very incompletely dressed, and I go from a flat on the groundfloor up a flight of stairs to an upper story. In doing this I jump up three stairs at a time, and I am glad to find that I can mount the stairs so quickly. Suddenly I notice that a servant-maid is coming down the stairs—that is, towards me. I am ashamed, and try to hurry away, and now comes this feeling of being inhibited; I am glued to the stairs, and cannot move from the spot.*

Analysis: The situation of the dream is taken from an every-day reality. In a house in Vienna I have two apartments, which are connected only by the main staircase. My consultation-rooms and my study are on the raised ground-floor, and my living-rooms are on the first floor. Late at night, when I have finished my work downstairs, I go upstairs to my bedroom. On the evening before the dream I had actually gone this short distance with my garments in disarray—that is, I had taken off my collar, tie and cuffs; but in the dream this had changed into a more advanced, but, as usual, indefinite degree of undress. It is a habit of mine to run up two or three steps at a time; moreover, there was a wish-fulfilment recognized even in the dream, for the ease with which I run upstairs reassures me as to the condition of my heart. Further, the manner in which I run upstairs is an effective contrast to the sensation of being inhibited, which occurs in the second half of the dream. It shows me—what needed no proof—that dreams have no difficulty in representing motor actions fully and completely carried out; think, for example, of flying in dreams!

But the stairs up which I go are not those of my own house; at first I do not recognize them; only the person coming towards me informs me of their whereabouts. This woman is the maid of an old lady whom I visit twice daily in order to give her hypodermic injections; the stairs, too, are precisely similar to those which I have to climb twice a day in this old lady's house.

How do these stairs and this woman get into my dream? The shame of not being fully dressed is undoubtedly of a sexual character; the servant of whom I dream is older than I, surly, and by no means attractive. These questions remind me of the following incident: When I pay my morning visit at this house I am usually seized with a desire to clear my throat; the sputum falls on the stairs. There is no spittoon on either of the two floors, and I consider that the stairs should be kept clean not at my expense, but rather by the provision of a spittoon. The housekeeper, another elder-

---

[1] Rank has shown, in a number of studies, that certain awakening-dreams provoked by organic stimuli (dreams of urination and ejaculation) are especially calculated to demonstrate the conflict between the need for sleep and the demands of the organic need, as well as the influence of the latter on the dream-content.

ly, curmudgeonly person, but, as I willingly admit, a woman of cleanly instincts, takes a different view of the matter. She lies in wait for me, to see whether I shall take the liberty referred to, and, if she sees that I do, I can distinctly hear her growl. For days thereafter, when we meet she refuses to greet me with the customary signs of respect. On the day before the dream the housekeeper's attitude was reinforced by that of the maid. I had just finished my usual hurried visit to the patient when the servant confronted me in the ante-room, observing: "You might as well have wiped your shoes today, doctor, before you came into the room. The red carpet is all dirty again from your feet." This is the only justification for the appearance of the stairs and the maid in my dream.

Between my leaping upstairs and my spitting on the stairs there is an intimate connection. Pharyngitis and cardiac troubles are both supposed to be punishments for the vice of smoking, on account of which vice my own housekeeper does not credit me with excessive tidiness, so that my reputation suffers in both the houses which my dream fuses into one.

I must postpone the further interpretation of this dream until I can indicate the origin of the typical dream of being incompletely clothed. In the meantime, as a provisional deduction from the dream just related, I note that the dream-sensation of inhibited movement is always aroused at a point where a certain connection requires it. A peculiar condition of my motor system during sleep cannot be responsible for this dream-content, since a moment earlier I found myself, as though in confirmation of this fact, skipping lighty up the stairs.

D. Typical Dreams

Generally speaking, we are not in a position to interpret another person's dream if he is unwilling to furnish us with the unconscious thoughts which lie behind the dream-content, and for this reason the practical applicability of our method of dream-interpretation is often seriously restricted.[1] But there are dreams which exhibit a complete contrast to the individual's customary liberty to endow his dream-world with a special individuality, there-

[1] The statement that our method of dream-interpretation is inapplicable when we have not at our disposal the dreamer's association-material must be qualified. In one case our work of interpretation is independent of these associations: namely, when the dreamer makes use of *symbolic* elements in his dream. We then employ what is, strictly speaking, a second *auxiliary* method of dream-interpretation. (See below).

by making it inaccessible to an alien understanding: there are a number of dreams which almost every one has dreamed in the same manner, and of which we are accustomed to assume that they have the same significance in the case of every dreamer. A peculiar interest attaches to these typical dreams, because, no matter who dreams them, they presumably all derive from the same sources, so that they would seem to be particularly fitted to provide us with information as to the sources of dreams.

With quite special expectations, therefore, we shall proceed to test our technique of dream-interpretation on these typical dreams, and only with extreme reluctance shall we admit that precisely in respect of this material our method is not fully verified. In the interpretation of typical dreams we as a rule fail to obtain those associations from the dreamer which in other cases have led us to comprehension of the dream, or else these associations are confused and inadequate, so that they do not help us to solve our problem.

Why this is the case, and how we can remedy this defect in our technique, are points which will be discussed in a later chapter. The reader will then understand why I can deal with only a few of the group of typical dreams in this chapter, and why I have postponed the discussion of the others.

(a) THE EMBARRASSMENT-DREAM OF NAKEDNESS

In a dream in which one is naked or scantily clad in the presence of strangers, it sometimes happens that one is not in the least ashamed of one's condition. But the dream of nakedness demands our attention only when shame and embarrassment are felt in it, when one wishes to escape or to hide, and when one feels the strange inhibition of being unable to stir from the spot, and of being utterly powerless to alter the painful situation. It is only in this connection that the dream is typical; otherwise the nucleus of its content may be involved in all sorts of other connections, or may be replaced by individual amplifications. The essential point is that one has a painful feeling of shame, and is anxious to hide one's nakedness, usually by means of locomotion, but is absolutely unable to do so. I believe that the great majority of my readers will at some time have found themselves in this situation in a dream.

The nature and manner of the exposure is usually rather vague. The dreamer will say, perhaps, "I was in my chemise," but this is rarely a clear image; in most cases the lack of clothing is so indeterminate that it is described in narrating the dream by an alternative: "I was in my chemise or my petticoat." As a rule the deficiency in clothing is not serious enough to justify the feeling of shame attached to it. For a man who has served in the army, nakedness is often replaced by a manner of dressing that is contrary to regulations. "I was in the street without my sabre, and I saw some officers approaching," or "I had no collar," or "I was wearing checked civilian trousers," etc.

The persons before whom one is ashamed are almost always strangers, whose faces remain indeterminate. It never happens, in the typical dream, that one is reproved or even noticed on account of the lack of clothing which causes one such embarrassment. On the contrary, the people in the dream appear to be quite indifferent; or, as I was able to note in one particularly vivid dream, they have stiff and solemn expressions. This gives us food for thought.

The dreamer's embarrassment and the spectator's indifference constitute a contradiction such as often occurs in dreams. It would be more in keeping with the dreamer's feelings if the strangers were to look at him in astonishment, or were to laugh at him, or be outraged. I think, however, that this obnoxious feature has been displaced by wish-fulfilment, while the embarrassment is for some reason retained, so that the two components are not in agreement. We have an interesting proof that the dream which is partially distorted by wish-fulfilment has not been properly understood; for it has been made the basis of a fairy-tale familiar to us all in Andersen's version of *The Emperor's New Clothes,* and it has more recently received poetical treatment by Fulda in *The Talisman*. In Andersen's fairy-tale we are told of two impostors who weave a costly garment for the Emperor, which shall, however, be visible only to the good and true. The Emperor goes forth clad to this invisible garment, and since the imaginary fabric serves as a sort of touchstone, the people are frightened into behaving as though they did not notice the Emperor's nakedness.

But this is really the situation in our dream. It is not very venturesome to assume that the unintelligible dream-content has provided an incentive to invent a state of undress which gives meaning to the situation present in the memory. This situation is thereby robbed of its original meaning, and made to serve alien ends.

But we shall see that such a misunderstanding of the dream-content often occurs through the conscious activity of a second psychic system, and is to be recognized as a factor of the final form of the dream; and further, that in the development of obsessions and phobias similar misunderstandings—still, of course, within the same psychic personality—play a decisive part. It is even possible to specify whence the material for the fresh interpretation of the dream is taken. The impostor is the dream, the Emperor is the dreamer himself, and the moralizing tendency betrays a hazy knowledge of the fact that there is a question, in the latent dream-content, of forbidden wishes, victims of repression. The connection in which such dreams appear during my analysis of neurotics proves beyond a doubt that a memory of the dreamer's earliest childhood lies at the foundation of the dream. Only in our childhood was there a time when we were seen by our relatives, as well as by strange nurses, servants and visitors, in a state of insufficient clothing, and at that time we were not ashamed of our nakedness.[1] In the case of many rather older children it may be observed that being undressed has an exciting effect upon them, instead of making them feel ashamed. They laugh, leap about, slap or thump their own bodies; the mother, or whoever is present, scolds them, saying: "Fie, that is shameful—you mustn't do that!" Children often show a desire to display themselves; it is hardly possible to pass through a village in country districts without meeting a two-or three-year-old child who lifts up his or her blouse or frock before the traveller, possibly in his honour. One of my patients has retained in his conscious memory a scene from his eighth year, in which, after undressing for bed, he wanted to dance into his little sister's room in his shirt, but was prevented by the servant. In the history of the childhood of neurotics, exposure before children of the opposite sex plays a prominent part; in paranoia, the delusion of being observed while dressing and undressing may be directly traced to these experiences; and among those who have remained perverse, there is a class in whom the childish impulse is accentuated into a symptom: the class of *exhibitionists*.

This age of childhood, in which the sense of shame is unknown, seems a paradise when we look back upon it later, and paradise itself is

---

[1] The child appears in the fairy-tale also, for there a little child suddenly cries out: "But he hasn't anything on at all!"

nothing but the mass-phantasy of the childhood of the individual. This is why in paradise men are naked and unashamed, until the moment arrives when shame and fear awaken; expulsion follows, and sexual life and cultural development begin. Into this paradise dreams can take us back every night; we have already ventured the conjecture that the impressions of our earliest childhood (from the prehistoric period until about the end of the third year) crave reproduction for their own sake, perhaps without further reference to their content, so that their repetition is a wish-fulfilment. Dreams of nakedness, then, are *exhibition-dreams*.[1]

The nucleus of an exhibition-dream is furnished by one's own person, which is seen not as that of a child, but as it exists in the present, and by the idea of scanty clothing which emerges indistinctly, owing to the superimposition of so many later situations of being partially clothed, or out of consideration for the censorship; to these elements are added the persons in whose presence one is ashamed. I know of no example in which the actual spectators of these infantile exhibitions reappear in a dream; for a dream is hardly ever a simple recollection. Strangely enough, those persons who are the objects of our sexual interest in childhood are omitted from all reproductions, in dreams, in hysteria or in obsessional neurosis; paranoia alone restores the spectators, and is fanatically convinced of their presence, although they remain unseen. The substitute for these persons offered by the dream, the *number of strangers* who take no notice of the spectacle offered them, is precisely the *counter-wish* to that single intimately-known person for whom the exposure was intended. "*A number of strangers*," moreover, often occur in dreams in all sorts of other connections; as a *counter-wish* they always signify a secret.[2] It will be seen that even that restitution of the old state of affairs that occurs in paranoia complies with this counter-tendency. One is no longer alone; one is quite positively being watched; but the spectators are *a number of strange, curiously indeterminate people*.

Furthermore, repression finds a place in the exhibition-dream. For the disagreeable sensation of the dream is, of course, the reaction on the part of the second psychic instance to the fact that the exhibitionistic scene which has been condemned by the censorship has nevertheless succeeded in presenting itself. The only way to avoid this sensation would be to refrain from reviving the scene.

In a later chapter we shall deal once again with the feeling of inhibition. In our dreams it represents to perfection *a conflict of the will, a denial*. According to our unconscious purpose, the exhibition is to proceed; according to the demands of the censorship, it is to come to an end.

The relation of our typical dreams to fairy-tales and other fiction and poetry is neither sporadic nor accidental. Sometimes the penetrating insight of the poet has analytically recognized the process of transformation of which the poet is otherwise the instrument, and has followed it up in the reverse direction; that is to say, has traced a poem to a dream. A friend has called my attention to the following passage in G. Keller's *Der Grüne Heinrich:* "I do not wish, dear Lee, that you should ever come to realize from experience the exquisite and piquant truth in the situation of Odysseus, when he appears, naked and covered with mud, before Nausicaä and her playmates! Would you like to know what it means? Let us for a moment consider the incident closely. If you are ever parted from your home, and from all that is dear to you, and wander about in a strange country; if you have seen much and experienced much; if you have cares and sorrows, and are, perhaps, utterly wretched and forlorn, you will some night inevitably dream that you are approaching your home; you will see it shining and glittering in the loveliest colours; lovely and gracious figures will come to meet you; and then you will suddenly discover that you are ragged, naked, and covered with dust. An indescribable feeling of shame and fear overcomes you; you try to cover yourself, to hide, and you wake up bathed in sweat. As long as humanity exists, this will be the dream of the care-laden, tempest-tossed man, and thus Homer has drawn this situation from the profoundest depths of the eternal nature of humanity."

What are the profoundest depths of the eternal nature of humanity, which the poet commonly hopes to awaken in his listeners, but these stirrings of the psychic life which are rooted in that age of childhood, which subsequently becomes prehistoric? Childish wishes,

---

[1] Ferenczi has recorded a number of interesting dreams of nakedness in women which were without difficulty traced to the infantile delight in exhibitionism, but which differ in many features from the *typical* dream of nakedness discussed above.

[2] For obvious reasons the presence of *the whole family* in the dream has the same significance.

now suppressed and forbidden, break into the dream behind the unobjectionable and permissibly conscious wishes of the homeless man, and it is for this reason that the dream which is objectified in the legend of Nausicaä regularly develops into an anxiety-dream.

My own dream of hurrying upstairs, which presently changed into being glued to the stairs, is likewise an exhibition-dream, for it reveals the essential ingredients of such a dream. It must therefore be possible to trace it back to experiences in my childhood, and the knowledge of these should enable us to conclude how far the servant's behaviour to me (i.e., her reproach that I had soiled the carpet) helped her to secure the position which she occupies in the dream. Now I am actually able to furnish the desired explanation. One learns in a psychoanalysis to interpret temporal proximity by material connection; two ideas which are apparently without connection, but which occur in immediate succession, belong to a unity which has to be deciphered; just as an *a* and a *b*, when written in succession, must be pronounced as one syllable, *ab*. It is just the same with the interrelations of dreams. The dream of the stairs has been taken from a series of dreams with whose other members I am familiar, having interpreted them. A dream included in this series must belong to the same context. Now, the other dreams of the series are based on the memory of a nurse to whom I was entrusted for a season, from the time when I was still at the breast to the age of two and a half, and of whom a hazy recollection has remained in my consciousness. According to information which I recently obtained from my mother, she was old and ugly, but very intelligent and thorough; according to the inferences which I am justified in drawing from my dreams, she did not always treat me quite kindly, but spoke harshly to me when I showed insufficient understanding of the necessity for cleanliness. Inasmuch as the maid endeavoured to continue my education in this respect, she is entitled to be treated, in my dream, as an incarnation of the prehistoric old woman. It is to be assumed, of course, that the child was fond of his teacher in spite of her harsh behaviour.[1]

[1] A supplementary interpretation of this dream: To spit (*spucken*) on the stairs, since *spuken* (to haunt) is the occupation of spirits (cf. English, "spook"), led me by a free translation to *espirit d'escalier*. "Stair-wit" means unreadiness at repartee, (*Schlagfertigkeit* = literally: "readiness to hit out") with which I really have to reproach myself. But was the nurse deficient in *Schlagfertigkeit*?

(b) DREAMS OF THE DEATH OF BELOVED PERSONS

Another series of dreams which may be called typical are those whose content is that a beloved relative, a parent, brother, sister, child, or the like, has died. We must at once distinguish two classes of such dreams: those in which the dreamer remains unmoved, and those in which he feels profoundly grieved by the death of the beloved person, even expressing this grief by shedding tears in his sleep.

We may ignore the dreams of the first group; they have no claim to be reckoned as typical. If they are analysed, it is found that they signify something that is not contained in them, that they are intended to mask another wish of some kind. This is the case in the dream of the aunt who sees the only son of her sister lying on a bier (p. 201). The dream does not mean that she desires the death of her little nephew; as we have learned, it merely conceals the wish to see a certain beloved person again after a long separation—the same person whom she had seen after as long an interval at the funeral of another nephew. This wish, which is the real content of the dream, gives no cause for sorrow, and for that reason no sorrow is felt in the dream. We see here that the feeling contained in the dream does not belong to the manifest, but to the latent dream-content, and that the affective content has remained free from the distortion which has befallen the conceptual content.

It is otherwise with those dreams in which the death of a beloved relative is imagined, and in which a painful affect is felt. These signify, as their content tells us, the wish that the person in question might die; and since I may here expect that the feelings of all my readers and of all who have had such dreams will lead them to reject my explanation, I must endeavour to rest my proof on the broadest possible basis.

We have already cited a dream from which we could see that the wishes represented as fulfilled in dreams are not always current wishes. They may also be bygone, discarded, buried and repressed wishes, which we must nevertheless credit with a sort of continued existence, merely on account of their reappearance in a dream. They are not dead, like persons who have died, in the sense that we know death, but are rather like the shades in the Odyssey which awaken to a certain degree of life so soon as they have drunk blood. The dream of the dead child in the box (p. 202) contained a wish that had been present fifteen years earlier, and which had at that time been frankly admitted as real. Further—and this, perhaps, is not unimportant from the standpoint of the theory of dreams—a recollection from the dreamer's earliest childhood was at the root of this wish also. When the dreamer was a little child—but exactly when cannot be definitely determined—she heard that her mother, during the pregnancy of which she was the outcome, had fallen into a profound emotional depression, and had passionately wished for the death of the child in her womb. Having herself grown up and become pregnant, she was only following the example of her mother.

If anyone dreams that his father or mother, his brother or sister, has died, and his dream expresses grief, I should never adduce this as proof that he wishes any of them dead *now*. The theory of dreams does not go as far as to require this; it is satisfied with concluding that the dreamer has wished them dead at some time or other during his childhood. I fear, however, that this limitation will not go far to appease my critics; probably they will just as energetically deny the possibility that they ever had such thoughts, as they protest that they do not harbour them now. I must, therefore, reconstruct a portion of the submerged infantile psychology on the basis of the evidence of the present.[1]

Let us first of all consider the relation of children to their brothers and sisters. I do not know why we presuppose that it must be a loving one, since examples of enmity among adult brothers and sisters are frequent in everyone's experience, and since we are so often able to verify the fact that this estrangement originated during childhood, or has always existed. Moreover, many adults who today are devoted to their brothers and sisters, and support them in adversity, lived with them in almost continuous enmity during their childhood. The elder child ill-treated the younger, slandered him, and robbed him of his toys; the younger was consumed with helpless fury against the elder, envied and feared him, or his earliest impulse toward liberty and his first revolt against injustice were directed against his oppressor. The parents say that the children do not agree, and cannot find the reason for it. It is not difficult to see that the character even of a well-behaved child is not the character we should wish to find in an adult. A child is absolutely egois-

tical; he feels his wants acutely, and strives remorselessly to satisfy them, especially against his competitors, other children, and first of all against his brothers and sisters. And yet we do not on that account call a child *wicked*—we call him *naughty;* he is not responsible for his misdeeds, either in our own judgment or in the eyes of the law. And this is as it should be; for we may expect that within the very period of life which we reckon as childhood, altruistic impulses and morality will awake in the little egoist, and that, in the words of Meynert, a secondary ego will overlay and inhibit the primary ego. Morality, of course, does not develop simultaneously in all its departments, and furthermore, the duration of the amoral period of childhood differs in different individuals. Where this morality fails to develop we are prone to speak of *degeneration;* but here the case is obviously one of arrested development. Where the primary character is already overlaid by the later development it may be at least partially uncovered again by an attack of hysteria. The correspondence between the so-called hysterical character and that of a naughty child is positively striking. The obsessional neurosis, on the other hand, corresponds to a super-morality, which develops as a strong reinforcement against the primary character that is threatening to revive.

Many persons, then, who now love their brothers and sisters, and who would feel bereaved by their death, harbour in their unconscious hostile wishes, survivals from an earlier period, wishes which are able to realize themselves in dreams. It is, however, quite especially interesting to observe the behaviour of little children up to their third and fourth year towards their younger brothers or sisters. So far the child has been the only one; now he is informed that the stork has brought a new baby. The child inspects the new arrival, and expresses his opinion with decision: "The stork had better take it back again!"[2]

I seriously declare it as my opinion that a child is able to estimate the disadvantages which he has to expect on account of a newcomer. A connection of mine, who now gets on

---

[1] Cf. also "Analysis of a Phobia in a Five-year-old Boy," *Collected Papers,* III; and "On the Sexual Theories of Children," *Ibid.,* II.

[2] Hans, whose phobia was the subject of the analysis in the above-mentioned publication, cried out at the age of three and a half, while feverish, shortly after the birth of a sister: "But I don't want to have a little sister." In his neurosis, eighteen months later, he frankly confessed the wish that his mother should drop the child into the bath while bathing it, in order that it might die. With all this, Hans was a good-natured, affectionate child, who soon became fond of his sister, and took her under his special protection.

very well with a sister, who is four years her junior, responded to the news of this sister's arrival with the reservation: "But I shan't give her my red cap, anyhow." If the child should come to realize only at a later stage that its happiness may be prejudiced by a younger brother or sister, its enmity will be aroused at this period. I know of a case where a girl, not three years of age, tried to strangle an infant in its cradle, because she suspected that its continued presence boded her no good. Children at this time of life are capable of a jealousy that is perfectly evident and extremely intense. Again, perhaps the little brother or sister really soon disappears, and the child once more draws to himself the whole affection of the household; then a new child is sent by the stork; is it not natural that the favourite should conceive the wish that the new rival may meet the same fate as the earlier one, in order that he may be as happy as he was before the birth of the first child, and during the interval after his death?[1] Of course, this attitude of the child towards the younger brother or sister is, under normal circumstances, a mere function of the difference of age. After a certain interval the maternal instincts of the older girl will be awakened towards the helpless new-born infant.

Feelings of hostility towards brothers and sisters must occur far more frequently in children than is observed by their obtuse elders.[2]

In the case of my own children, who followed one another rapidly, I missed the opportunity of making such observations, I am now retrieving it, thanks to my little nephew, whose undisputed domination was disturbed after fifteen months by the arrival of a feminine rival. I hear, it is true, that the young man behaves very chivalrously toward his little sister, that he kisses her hand and strokes her; but in spite

of this I have convinced myself that even before the completion of his second year he is using his new command of language to criticize this person, who, to him, after all, seems superfluous. Whenever the conversation turns upon her he chimes in, and cries angrily: "Too (l)ittle, too (l)ittle!" During the last few months, since the child has outgrown this disparagement, owing to her splendid development, he has found another reason for his insistence that she does not deserve so much attention. He reminds us, on every suitable pretext: "She hasn't any teeth."[3] We all of us recollect the case of the eldest daughter of another sister of mine. The child, who was then six years of age, spent a full half-hour in going from one aunt to another with the question: "Lucie can't understand that yet, can she?" Lucie was her rival—two and a half years younger.

I have never failed to come across this dream of the death of brothers or sisters, denoting an intense hostility, e.g., I have met it in all my female patients. I have met with only one exception, which could easily be interpreted into a confirmation of the rule. Once, in the course of a sitting, when I was explaining this state of affairs to a female patient, since it seemed to have some bearing on the symptoms under consideration that day, she answered, to my astonishment, that she had never had such dreams. But another dream occurred to her, which presumably had nothing to do with the case—a dream which she had first dreamed at the age of *four*, when she was the youngest child, and had since then dreamed repeatedly. "*A number of children, all her brothers and sisters with her boy and girl cousins, were romping about in a meadow. Suddenly they all grew wings, flew up, and were gone.*" She had no idea of the significance of this dream; but we can hardly fail to recognize it as a dream of the death of all the brothers and sisters, in its original form, and but little influenced by the censorship. I will venture to add the following analysis of it: on the death of one out of this large number of children—in this case the children of two brothers were brought up together as brothers and sisters—would not our dreamer, at that time not yet four years of age, have asked some wise, grown-up person: "What becomes of children when they are dead?" The answer would probably have been: "They grow

---

[1] Such cases of death in the experience of children may soon be forgotten in the family, but psycho-analytical investigation shows that they are very significant for a later neurosis.

[2] Since the above was written, a great many observations relating to the originally hostile attitude of children toward their brothers and sisters, and toward one of their parents, have been recorded in the literature of psycho-analysis. One writer, Spitteler, gives the following peculiarly sincere and ingenious description of this typical childish attitude as he experienced it in his earliest childhood: "Moreover, there was now a second Adolf. A little creature whom they declared was my brother, but I could not understand what he could be for, or why they should pretend he was a being like myself. I was sufficient unto myself: what did I want with a brother? And he was not only useless, he was also even troublesome. When I plagued my grandmother, he too wanted to plague her; when I was wheeled about in the baby-carriage he sat opposite me, and took up half the room, so that we could not help kicking one another."

[3] The three-and-a-half-year-old Hans embodied his devastating criticism of his little sister in these identical words (*loc. cit.*). He assumed that she was unable to speak on account of her lack of teeth.

wings and become angels." After this explanation, all the brothers and sisters and cousins in the dream now have wings, like angels and—this is the important point—they fly away. Our little angel-maker is left alone: just think, the only one out of such a crowd! That the children romp about a meadow, from which they fly away, points almost certainly to butterflies—it is as though the child had been influenced by the same association of ideas which led the ancients to imagine Psyche, the soul, with the wings of a butterfly.

Perhaps some readers will now object that the inimical impulses of children toward their brothers and sisters may perhaps be admitted, but how does the childish character arrive at such heights of wickedness as to desire the death of a rival or a stronger playmate, as though all misdeeds could be atoned for only by death? Those who speak in this fashion forget that the child's idea of *being dead* has little but the word in common with our own. The child knows nothing of the horrors of decay, of shivering in the cold grave, of the terror of the infinite Nothing, the thought of which the adult, as all the myths of the hereafter testify, finds so intolerable. The fear of death is alien to the child; and so he plays with the horrid word, and threatens another child: "If you do that again, you will die, just like Francis died"; at which the poor mother shudders, unable perhaps to forget that the greater proportion of mortals do not survive beyond the years of childhood. Even at the age of eight, a child returning from a visit to a natural history museum may say to her mother: "Mamma, I do love you so; if you ever die, I am going to have you stuffed and set you up here in the room, so that I can always, always see you!" So different from our own is the childish conception of being dead.[1]

Being dead means, for the child, who has been spared the sight of the suffering that precedes death, much the same as *being gone*, and ceasing to annoy the survivors. The child does not distinguish the means by which this absence is brought about, whether by distance, or estrangement, or death.[2] If, during the child's prehistoric years, a nurse has been dismissed, and if his mother dies a little while later, the two experiences, as we discover by analysis, form links of a chain in his memory. The fact that the child does not very intensely miss those who are absent has been realized, to her sorrow, by many a mother, when she has returned home from an absence of several weeks, and has been told, upon inquiry: "The children have not asked for their mother once." But if she really departs to "that undiscovered country from whose bourne no traveller returns," the children seem at first to have forgotten her, and only *subsequently* do they begin to remember their dead mother.

While, therefore, the child has its motives for desiring the absence of another child, it is lacking in all those restraints which would prevent it from clothing this wish in the form of a death-wish; and the psychic reaction to dreams of a death-wish proves that, in spite of all the differences of content, the wish in the case of the child is after all identical with the corresponding wish in an adult.

If, then, the death-wish of a child in respect of his brothers and sisters is explained by his childish egoism, which makes him regard his brothers and sisters as rivals, how are we to account for the same wish in respect of his parents, who bestow their love on him, and satisfy his needs, and whose preservation he ought to desire for these very egoistical reasons?

Towards a solution of this difficulty we may be guided by our knowledge that the very great majority of dreams of the death of a parent refer to the parent of the same sex as the dreamer, so that a man generally dreams of the death of his father, and a woman of the death of her mother. I do not claim that this happens constantly; but that it happens in a great majority of cases is so evident that it requires explanation by some factor of general significance.[3] Broadly speaking, it is as though a sexual preference made itself felt at an early age,

---

[1] To my astonishment, I was told that a highly intelligent boy of ten, after the sudden death of his father, said: "I understand that father is dead, but I can't see why he does not come home to supper." Further material relating to this subject will be found in the section *"Kinderseele,"* edited by Frau Dr. von Hug-Hellmuth, in *Imago* Vol. i-v, 1912-18.

[2] The observation of a father trained in psycho-analysis was able to detect the very moment when his very intelligent little daughter, age four, realized the difference between *being away* and *being dead*. The child

was being troublesome at table, and noted that one of the waitresses in the *pension* was looking at her with an expression of annoyance. "Josephine ought to be dead," she thereupon remarked to her father. "But why dead?" asked the father, soothingly. "Wouldn't it be enough if she went away?" "No," replied the child, "then she would come back again." To the uncurbed self-love (*narcissism*) of the child, every inconvenience constitutes the crime of *lèse majesté*, and, as in the Draconian code, the child's feelings prescribe for all such crimes the one invariable punishment.

[3] The situation is frequently disguised by the intervention of a tendency to punishment, which, in the form of a moral reaction, threatens the loss of the beloved parent.

as though the boy regarded his father, and the girl her mother, as a rival in love—by whose removal he or she could but profit.

Before rejecting this idea as monstrous, let the reader again consider the actual relations between parents and children. We must distinguish between the traditional standard of conduct, the filial piety expected in this relation, and what daily observation shows us to be the fact. More than one occasion for enmity lies hidden amidst the relations of parents and children; conditions are present in the greatest abundance under which wishes which cannot pass the censorship are bound to arise. Let us first consider the relation between father and son. In my opinion the sanctity with which we have endorsed the injunctions of the Decalogue dulls our perception of the reality. Perhaps we hardly dare permit ourselves to perceive that the greater part of humanity neglects to obey the fifth commandment. In the lowest as well as in the highest strata of human society, filial piety towards parents is wont to recede before other interests. The obscure legends which have been handed down to us from the primeval ages of human society in mythology and folklore give a deplorable idea of the despotic power of the father, and the ruthlessness with which it was exercised. Kronos devours his children, as the wild boar devours the litter of the sow; Zeus emasculates his father[1] and takes his place as ruler. The more tyrannically the father ruled in the ancient family, the more surely must the son, as his appointed successor, have assumed the position of an enemy, and the greater must have been his impatience to attain to supremacy through the death of his father. Even in our own middle-class families the father commonly fosters the growth of the germ of hatred which is naturally inherent in the paternal relation, by refusing to allow the son to be a free agent or by denying him the means of becoming so. A physician often has occasion to remark that a son's grief at the loss of his father cannot quench his gratification that he has at last obtained his freedom. Fathers, as a rule, cling desperately to as much of the sadly antiquated *potestas patris familias*[2] as still survives in our modern society, and the

poet who, like Ibsen, puts the immemorial strife between father and son in the foreground of his drama is sure of his effect. The causes of conflict between mother and daughter arise when the daughter grows up and finds herself watched by her mother when she longs for real sexual freedom, while the mother is reminded by the budding beauty of her daughter that for her the time has come to renounce sexual claims.

All these circumstances are obvious to everyone, but they do not help us to explain dreams of the death of their parents in persons for whom filial piety has long since come to be unquestionable. We are, however, prepared by the foregoing discussion to look for the origin of a death-wish in the earliest years of childhood.

In the case of psychoneurotics, analysis confirms this conjecture beyond all doubt. For analysis tells us that the sexual wishes of the child—in so far as they deserve this designation in their nascent state—awaken at a very early age, and that the earliest affection of the girl-child is lavished on the father, while the earliest infantile desires of the boy are directed upon the mother. For the boy the father, and for the girl the mother, becomes an obnoxious rival, and we have already shown, in the case of brothers and sisters, how readily in children this feeling leads to the death-wish. As a general rule, sexual selection soon makes its appearance in the parents; it is a natural tendency for the father to spoil his little daughters, and for the mother to take the part of the sons, while both, so long as the glamour of sex does not prejudice their judgment, are strict in training the children. The child is perfectly conscious of this partiality, and offers resistance to the parent who opposes it. To find love in an adult is for the child not merely the satisfaction of a special need; it means also that the child's will is indulged in all other respects. Thus the child is obeying its own sexual instinct, and at the same time reinforcing the stimulus proceeding from the parents, when its choice between the parents corresponds with their own.

The signs of these infantile tendencies are for the most part over-looked; and yet some of them may be observed even after the early years of childhood. An eight-year-old girl of my acquaintance, whenever her mother is called away from the table, takes advantage of her absence to proclaim herself her successor. "Now I shall be Mamma; Karl, do you want some more vegetables? Have some more, do,"

---

[1] At least in some of the mythological accounts. According to others, emasculation was inflicted only by Kronos on his father Uranos.

With regard to the mythological significance of this motive, cf. Otto Rank's *Der Mythus von der Geburt des Helden*, in No. v of *Schriften zur angew. Seelenkunde* (1909), and *Das Inzestmotiv in Dichtung und Sage* (1912), chap. ix, 2.

[2] Authority of the father.—ED.

etc. A particularly clever and lively little girl, not yet four years of age, in whom this trait of child psychology is unusually transparent, says frankly: "Now mummy can go away; then daddy must marry me, and I will be his wife." Nor does this wish by any means exclude the possibility that the child may most tenderly love its mother. If the little boy is allowed to sleep at his mother's side whenever his father goes on a journey, and if after his father's return he has to go back to the nursery, to a person whom he likes far less, the wish may readily arise that his father might always be absent, so that he might keep his place beside his dear, beautiful mamma; and the father's death is obviously a means for the attainment of this wish; for the child's experience has taught him that *dead* folks, like grandpapa, for example, are always absent; they never come back.

While such observations of young children readily accommodate themselves to the interpretation suggested, they do not, it is true, carry the complete conviction which is forced upon a physician by the psycho-analysis of adult neurotics. The dreams of neurotic patients are communicated with preliminaries of such a nature that their interpretation as wish-dreams becomes inevitable. One day I find a lady depressed and weeping. She says: "I do not want to see my relatives any more; they must shudder at me." Thereupon, almost without any transition, she tells me that she has remembered a dream, whose significance, of course, she does not understand. She dreamed it when she was four years old, and it was this: *A fox or a lynx is walking about the roof; then something falls down, or she falls down, and after that, her mother is carried out of the house—dead;* whereat the dreamer weeps bitterly. I have no sooner informed her that this dream must signify a childish wish to see her mother dead, and that it is because of this dream that she thinks that her relatives must shudder at her, than she furnishes material in explanation of the dream. "Lynx-eye" is an opprobrious epithet which a street boy once bestowed on her when she was a very small child; and when she was three years old a brick or tile fell on her mother's head, so that she bled profusely.

I once had occasion to make a thorough study of a young girl who was passing through various psychic states. In the state of frenzied confusion with which her illness began, the patient manifested a quite peculiar aversion for her mother; she struck her and abused her whenever she approached the bed, while at the same period she was affectionate and submissive to a much older sister. Then there followed a lucid but rather apathetic condition, with badly disturbed sleep. It was in this phase that I began to treat her and to analyse her dreams. An enormous number of these dealt, in a more or less veiled fashion, with the death of the girl's mother; now she was present at the funeral of an old woman, now she saw herself and her sister sitting at a table, dressed in mourning; the meaning of the dreams could not be doubted. During her progressive improvement hysterical phobias made their appearance, the most distressing of which was the fear that something had happened to her mother. Wherever she might be at the time, she had then to hurry home in order to convince herself that her mother was still alive. Now this case, considered in conjunction with the rest of my experience, was very instructive; it showed, in polyglot translations, as it were, the different ways in which the psychic apparatus reacts to the same exciting idea. In the state of confusion, which I regard as an overthrow of the second psychic instance by the first instance, at other times suppressed, the unconscious enmity towards the mother gained the upper hand, and found physical expression; then, when the patient became calmer, the insurrection was suppressed, and the domination of the censorship restored, and this enmity had access only to the realms of dreams, in which it realized the wish that the mother might die; and, after the normal condition had been still further strengthened, it created the excessive concern for the mother as a hysterical counter-reaction and defensive phenomenon. In the light of these considerations, it is no longer inexplicable why hysterical girls are so often extravagantly attached to their mothers.

On another occasion I had an opportunity of obtaining a profound insight into the unconscious psychic life of a young man for whom an obsessional neurosis made life almost unendurable, so that he could not go into the streets, because he was tormented by the fear that he would kill everyone he met. He spent his days in contriving evidence of an alibi in case he should be accused of any murder that might have been committed in the city. It goes without saying that this man was as moral as he was highly cultured. The analysis—which, by the way, led to a cure—revealed, as the basis of this distressing obsession, murderous impulses in respect of his rather overstrict father—impulses which, to his astonishment, had consciously expressed themselves when he was seven years old, but which, of course, had originated in a much earlier period of his childhood. After the painful illness and death of his father, when the young man was in his thirty-first year, the obsessive reproach made its appearance, which transferred itself to strangers in the form of this phobia. Anyone capable of wishing to push his own father from a mountain-top into an abyss cannot be trusted to spare the lives of persons less closely related to him; he therefore does well to lock himself into his room.

According to my already extensive experience, parents play a leading part in the infantile psychology of all persons who subsequently become psychoneurotics. Falling in love with one parent and hating the other forms part of the permanent stock of the psychic impulses which arise in early childhood, and are of such importance as the material of the subsequent neurosis. But I do not believe that psychoneurotics are to be sharply distinguished in this respect from other persons who remain normal —that is, I do not believe that they are capable of creating something absolutely new and peculiar to themselves. It is far more probable— and this is confirmed by incidental observations of normal children—that in their amorous or hostile attitude toward their parents, psychoneurotics do no more than reveal to us, by magnification, something that occurs less markedly and intensively in the minds of the majority of children. Antiquity has furnished us with legendary matter which corroborates this belief, and the profound and universal validity of the old legends is explicable only by an equally universal validity of the above-mentioned hypothesis of infantile psychology.

I am referring to the legend of King Oedipus and the *Oedipus Rex* of Sophocles. Oedipus, the son of Laius, king of Thebes, and Jocasta, is exposed as a suckling, because an oracle had informed the father that his son, who was still unborn, would be his murderer. He is rescued, and grows up as a king's son at a foreign court, until, being uncertain of his origin, he, too, consults the oracle, and is warned to avoid his native place, for he is destined to become the murderer of his father and the husband of his mother. On the road leading away from his supposed home he meets King Laius, and in a sudden quarrel strikes him dead. He comes to Thebes, where he solves the riddle of the Sphinx, who is barring the way to the city, whereupon he is elected king by the grateful Thebans, and is rewarded with the hand of Jocasta. He reigns for many years in peace and honour, and begets two sons and two daughters upon his unknown mother, until at last a plague breaks out—which causes the Thebans to consult the oracle anew. Here Sophocles' tragedy begins. The messengers bring the reply that the plague will stop as soon as the murderer of Laius is driven from the country. But where is he?

> *Where shall be found,*
> *Faint, and hard to be known, the trace of the*
> *ancient guilt?*

The action of the play consists simply in the disclosure, approached step by step and artistically delayed (and comparable to the work of a psycho-analysis) that Oedipus himself is the murderer of Laius, and that he is the son of the murdered man and Jocasta. Shocked by the abominable crime which he has unwittingly committed, Oedipus blinds himself, and departs from his native city. The prophecy of the oracle has been fulfilled.

The *Oedipus Rex* is a tragedy of fate; its tragic effect depends on the conflict between the all-powerful will of the gods and the vain efforts of human beings threatened with disaster; resignation to the divine will, and the perception of one's own impotence is the lesson which the deeply moved spectator is supposed to learn from the tragedy. Modern authors have therefore sought to achieve a similar tragic effect by expressing the same conflict in stories of their own invention. But the playgoers have looked on unmoved at the unavailing efforts of guiltless men to avert the fulfilment of curse or oracle; the modern tragedies of destiny have failed of their effect.

If the *Oedipus Rex* is capable of moving a modern reader or playgoer no less powerfully than it moved the contemporary Greeks, the only possible explanation is that the effect of the Greek tragedy does not depend upon the conflict between fate and human will, but upon the peculiar nature of the material by which this conflict is revealed. There must be a voice within us which is prepared to acknowledge the compelling power of fate in the *Oedipus*, while we are able to condemn the situations occurring in *Die Ahnfrau* or other tragedies of fate as arbitrary inventions. And there actually is a motive in the story of King Oedipus which explains the verdict of this inner voice. His fate moves us only because it might have been our own, because the oracle laid upon us before our birth the very curse which rested upon him. It may be that we were all destined to direct our first sexual impulses toward our mothers, and our first impulses of hatred and violence toward our fathers; our dreams convince us that we were. King Oedipus, who slew his father Laius and wedded his mother Jocasta, is nothing more or less than a wish-fulfilment—the fulfilment of the wish of our childhood. But we, more fortunate than he, in so far as we have not become psychoneurotics, have since our childhood succeeded in withdrawing our sexual impulses from our mothers, and in forgetting our jealousy of our fathers. We recoil from the person for whom this primitive wish of our chilhood has been fulfilled with all the force of the repression which these wishes have undergone in our minds since childhood. As the poet brings the guilt of Oedipus to light by his investigation, he forces us to become aware of our own inner selves, in which the same impulses are still extant, even though they are suppressed. The antithesis with which the chorus departs:

. . . Behold, this is Oedipus,
Who unravelled the great riddle, and was first in power,
Whose fortune all the townsmen praised and envied;
See in what dread adversity he sank!

—this admonition touches us and our own pride, we who, since the years of our childhood, have grown so wise and so powerful in our own estimation. Like Oedipus, we live in ignorance of the desires that offend morality, the desires that nature has forced upon us and after their unveiling we may well prefer to avert our gaze from the scenes of our childhood.[1]

In the very text of Sophocles' tragedy there is an unmistakable reference to the fact that the Oedipus legend had its source in dream-material of immemorial antiquity, the content of which was the painful disturbance of the child's relations to its parents caused by the first impulses of sexuality. Jocasta comforts Oedipus—who is not yet enlightened, but is troubled by the recollection of the oracle—by an allusion to a dream which is often dreamed, though it cannot, in her opinion, mean anything:

For many a man hath seen himself in dreams
His mother's mate, but he who gives no heed
To suchlike matters bears the easier life.

The dream of having sexual intercourse with one's mother was as common then as it is to-day with many people, who tell it with indignation and astonishment. As may well be imagined, it is the key to the tragedy and the complement to the dream of the death of the father. The Oedipus fable is the reaction of phantasy to these two typical dreams, and just as such a dream, when occurring to an adult, is experienced with feelings of aversion, so the content of the fable must include terror and self-chastisement. The form which it subsequently assumed was the result of an uncomprehending secondary elaboration of the material, which sought to make it serve a theological intention.[2] The attempt to reconcile divine omnipotence with human responsibility must, of course, fail with this material as with any other.

Another of the great poetic tragedies, Shakespeare's *Hamlet*, is rooted in the same soil as *Oedipus Rex*. But the whole difference in the psychic life of the two widely separated periods of civilization, and the progress, during the course of time, of repression in the emotional life of humanity, is manifested in the differing treatment of the same material. In *Oedipus Rex* the basic wish-phantasy of the child is brought to light and realized as it is in dreams; in *Hamlet it* remains repressed, and we learn of its existence—as we discover the relevant facts in a neurosis—only through the inhibitory effects which proceed from it. In the more modern drama, the curious fact that it is possible to remain in complete uncertainty as to the character of the hero has proved to be quite consistent with the over-powering effect of the tragedy. The play is based upon Hamlet's hesitation in accomplishing the task of revenge assigned to him; the text does not give the cause or the motive of this hesitation, nor have the manifold attempts at interpretation succeeded in doing so. According to the still pre-

---

[1] None of the discoveries of psycho-analytical research has evoked such embittered contradiction, such furious opposition, and also such entertaining acrobatics of criticism, as this indication of the incestuous impulses of childhood which survive in the unconscious. An attempt has even been made recently, in defiance of all experience, to assign only a *symbolic* significance to incest. Ferenczi has given an ingenious reinterpretation of the Oedipus myth, based on a passage in one of Schopenhauer's letters, in *Imago*, i, (1912). The Oedipus complex, which was first alluded to here in *The Interpretation of Dreams*, has through further study of the subject, acquired an unexpected significance for the understanding of human history and the evolution of religion and morality. See *Totem and Taboo*.

[2] Cf. the dream-material of exhibitionism, pp. 238-9.

vailing conception, a conception for which Goethe was first responsible, Hamlet represents the type of man whose active energy is paralyzed by excessive intellectual activity: "Sicklied o'er with the pale cast of thought." According to another conception, the poet has endeavoured to portray a morbid, irresolute character, on the verge of neurasthenia. The plot of the drama, however, shows us that Hamlet is by no means intended to appear as a character wholly incapable of action. On two separate occasions we see him assert himself: once in a sudden outburst of rage, when he stabs the eavesdropper behind the arras, and on the other occasion when he deliberately, and even craftily, with the complete unscrupulousness of a prince of the Renaissance, sends the two courtiers to the death which was intended for himself. What is it, then, that inhibits him in accomplishing the task which his father's ghost has laid upon him? Here the explanation offers itself that it is the peculiar nature of this task. Hamlet is able to do anything but take vengeance upon the man who did away with his father and has taken his father's place with his mother—the man who shows him in realization the repressed desires of his own childhood. The loathing which should have driven him to revenge is thus replaced by self-reproach, by conscientious scruples, which tell him that he himself is no better than the murderer whom he is required to punish. I have here translated into consciousness what had to remain unconscious in the mind of the hero; if anyone wishes to call Hamlet an hysterical subject I cannot but admit that this is the deduction to be drawn from my interpretation. The sexual aversion which Hamlet expresses in conversation with Ophelia is perfectly consistent with this deduction—the same sexual aversion which during the next few years was increasingly to take possession of the poet's soul, until it found its supreme utterance in *Timon of Athens*. It can, of course, be only the poet's own psychology with which we are confronted in *Hamlet;* and in a work on Shakespeare by Georg Brandes (1896) I find the statement that the drama was composed immediately after the death of Shakespeare's father (1601)—that is to say, when he was still mourning his loss, and during a revival, as we may fairly assume, of his own childish feelings in respect of his father. It is known, too, that Shakespeare's son, who died in childhood, bore the name of Hamnet (identical with Hamlet). Just as *Hamlet* treats of the relation of the son to his parents, so

Macbeth, which was written about the same period, is based upon the theme of childlessness. Just as all neurotic symptoms, like dreams themselves, are capable of hyper-interpretation, and even require such hyper-interpretation before they become perfectly intelligible, so every genuine poetical creation must have proceeded from more than one motive, more than one impulse in the mind of the poet, and must admit of more than one interpretation. I have here attempted to interpret only the deepest stratum of impulses in the mind of the creative poet.[1]

With regard to typical dreams of the death of relatives, I must add a few words upon their significance from the point of view of the theory of dreams in general. These dreams show us the occurrence of a very unusual state of things; they show us that the dream-thought created by the repressed wish completely escapes the censorship, and is transferred to the dream without alteration. Special conditions must obtain in order to make this possible. The following two factors favour the production of these dreams: first, this is the last wish that we could credit ourselves with harbouring; we believe such a wish "would never occur to us even in a dream"; the dream-censorship is therefore unprepared for this monstrosity, just as the laws of Solon did not foresee the necessity of establishing a penalty for patricide. Secondly, the repressed and unsuspected wish is, in this special case, frequently met half-way by a residue from the day's experience, in the form of some *concern* for the life of the beloved person. This anxiety cannot enter into the dream otherwise than by taking advantage of the corresponding wish; but the wish is able to mask itself behind the concern which has been aroused during the day. If one is inclined to think that all this is really a very much simpler process, and to imagine that one merely continues during the night, and in one's dream, what was begun during the day, one removes the dreams of the death of those dear to us

---

[1] These indications in the direction of an analytical understanding of *Hamlet* were subsequently developed by Dr. Ernest Jones, who defended the above conception against others which have been put forward in the literature of the subject (*The Problem of Hamlet and the Oedipus Complex,* [1911]). The relation of the material of Hamlet to the myth of the birth of the hero has been demonstrated by O. Rank. Further attempts at an analysis of *Macbeth* will be found in my essay on "Some Character Types Met with in Psycho-Analytic Work," *Collected Papers,* IV., in L. Jekels's "Shakespeare's Macbeth," in *Imago,* v. (1918) and in *"The Oedipus Complex as an Explanation of Hamlet's Mystery: a Study in Motive"* (American Journal of Psychology [1910], vol. xxi).

out of all connection with the general explanation of dreams, and a problem that may very well be solved remains a problem needlessly.

It is instructive to trace the relation of these dreams to anxiety-dreams. In dreams of the death of those dear to us the repressed wish has found a way of avoiding the censorship—and the distortion for which the censorship is responsible. An invariable concomitant phenomenon, then, is that painful emotions are felt in the dream. Similarly, an anxiety-dream occurs only when the censorship is entirely or partially overpowered, and on the other hand, the overpowering of the censorship is facilitated when the actual sensation of anxiety is already present from somatic sources. It thus becomes obvious for what purpose the censorship performs its office and practises dream-distortion; it does so *in order to prevent the development of anxiety or other forms of painful affect.*

I have spoken in the foregoing sections of the egoism of the child's psyche, and I now emphasize this peculiarity in order to suggest a connection, for dreams too have retained this characteristic. All dreams are absolutely egoistical; in every dream the beloved ego appears, even though in a disguised form. The wishes that are realized in dreams are invariably the wishes of this ego; it is only a deceptive appearance if interest in another person is believed to have evoked a dream. I will now analyse a few examples which appear to contradict this assertion.

I

A boy not yet four years of age relates the following dream: *He saw a large garnished dish, on which was a large joint of roast meat; and the joint was suddenly—not carved—but eaten up. He did not see the person who ate it.*[1]

Who can he be, this strange person, of whose luxurious repast the little fellow dreams? The experience of the day must supply the answer. For some days past the boy, in accordance with the doctor's orders, had been living on a milk diet; but on the evening of the dream-day he had been naughty, and, as a punishment, had

been deprived of his supper. He had already undergone one such hunger-cure, and had borne his deprivation bravely. He knew that he would get nothing, but he did not even allude to the fact that he was hungry. Training was beginning to produce its effect; this is demonstrated even by the dream, which reveals the beginnings of dream-distortion. There is no doubt that he himself is the person whose desires are directed toward this abundant meal, and a meal of roast meat at that. But since he knows that this is forbidden him, he does not dare, as hungry children do in dreams (cf. my little Anna's dream about strawberries, p. 192), to sit down to the meal himself. The person remains anonymous.

II

One night I dream that I see on a bookseller's counter a new volume of one of those collectors' series, which I am in the habit of buying (monographs on artistic subjects, history, famous artistic centres, etc.). *The new collection is entitled "Famous Orators" (or Orations), and the first number bears the name of Dr. Lecher.*

On analysis it seems to me improbable that the fame of Dr. Lecher, the long-winded speaker of the German Opposition, should occupy my thoughts while I am dreaming. The fact is that a few days ago I undertook the psychological treatment of some new patients, and am now forced to talk for ten to twelve hours a day. Thus I myself am a long-winded speaker.

III

On another occasion I dream that a university lecturer of my acquaintance says to me: *"My son, the myopic."* Then follows a dialogue of brief observations and replies. A third portion of the dream follows, in which I and my sons appear, and so far as the latent dream-content is concerned, the father, the son, and Professor M, are merely lay figures, representing myself and my eldest son. Later on I shall examine this dream again, on account of another peculiarity.

IV

The following dream gives an example of really base, egoistical feelings, which conceal themselves behind an affectionate concern:

My friend Otto looks ill; his face is brown and his eyes protrude.

Otto is my family physician, to whom I owe a debt greater than I can ever hope to repay, since he has watched for years over the health

[1] Even the large, over-abundant, immoderate and exaggerated things occurring in dreams may be a childish characteristic. A child wants nothing more intensely than to grow big, and to eat as much of everything as grown-ups do; a child is hard to satisfy; he knows no such word as *enough* and insatiably demands the repetition of whatever has pleased him or tasted good to him. He learns to practise moderation, to be modest and resigned, only through training. As we know, the neurotic also is inclined to immoderation and excess.

of my children, has treated them successfully when they have been ill, and, moreover, has given them presents whenever he could find any excuse for doing so. He paid us a visit on the day of the dream, and my wife noticed that he looked tired and exhausted. At night I dream of him, and my dream attributes to him certain of the symptoms of Basedow's disease. If you were to disregard my rules for dream-interpretation you would understand this dream to mean that I am concerned about the health of my friend, and that this concern is realized in the dream. It would thus constitute a contradiction not only of the assertion that a dream is a wish-fulfilment, but also of the assertion that it is accessible only to egoistical impulses. But will those who thus interpret my dream explain why I should fear that Otto has Basedow's disease, for which diagnosis his appearance does not afford the slightest justification? My analysis, on the other hand, furnishes the following material, deriving from an incident which had occurred six years earlier. We were driving—a small party of us, including Professor R—in the dark through the forest of N, which lies at a distance of some hours from where we were staying in the country. The driver, who was not quite sober, overthrew us and the carriage down a bank, and it was only by good fortune that we all escaped unhurt. But we were forced to spend the night at the nearest inn, where the news of our mishap aroused great sympathy. A certain gentleman, who showed unmistakable symptoms of *morbus Basedowii*—the brownish colour of the skin of the face and the protruding eyes, but no goitre—placed himself entirely at our disposal, and asked what he could do for us. Professor R answered in his decisive way, "Nothing, except lend me a nightshirt." Whereupon our generous friend replied: "I am sorry, but I cannot do that," and left us.

In continuing the analysis, it occurs to me that Basedow is the name not only of a physician but also of a famous pedagogue. (Now that I am wide awake, I do not feel quite sure of this fact.) My friend Otto is the person whom I have asked to take charge of the physical education of my children—especially during the age of puberty (hence the nightshirt) in case anything should happen to me. By seeing Otto in my dream with the morbid symptoms of our above-mentioned generous helper I clearly mean to say: "If anything happens to me, he will do just as little for my children as Baron L did for us, in spite of his amiable offers."

The egoistical flavour of this dream should now be obvious enough.[1]

But where is the wish-fulfilment to be found in this? Not in the vengeance wreaked on my friend Otto (who seems to be fated to be badly treated in my dreams), but in the following circumstance: Inasmuch as in my dream I represented Otto as Baron L, I likewise identified myself with another person, namely, with Professor R; for I have asked something of Otto, just as R asked something of Baron L at the time of the incident I have described. And this is the point. For Professor R has gone his way independently, outside academic circles, just as I myself have done, and has only in his later years received the title which he had earned long before. Once more, then, I want to be a professor! The very phrase *in his later years* is a wish-fulfilment, for it means that I shall live long enough to steer my boys through the age of puberty myself.

Of other typical dreams, in which one flies with a feeling of ease or falls in terror, I know nothing from my own experience, and whatever I have to say about them I owe to my psychoanalyses. From the information thus obtained one must conclude that these dreams also reproduce impressions made in childhood—that is, that they refer to the games involving rapid motion which have such an extraordinary attraction for children. Where is the uncle who has never made a child fly by running with it across the room with outstretched arms, or has never played at falling with it by rocking it on his knee and then suddenly straightening his leg, or by lifting it above his head and suddenly pretending to withdraw his supporting hand? At such moments children shout with joy, and insatiably demand a repetition of the performance, especially if a little fright and dizziness

[1] While Dr. Ernest Jones was delivering a lecture before an American scientific society, and was speaking of egoism in dreams, a learned lady took exception to this unscientific generalization. She thought the lecturer was entitled to pronounce such a verdict only on the dreams of Austrians, but had no right to include the dreams of Americans. As for herself, she was sure that all her dreams were strictly altruistic.

In justice to this lady with her national pride it may, however, be remarked that the dogma: "the dream is wholly egoistic" must not be misunderstood. For inasmuch as everything that occurs in preconscious thinking may appear in dreams (in the content as well as the latent dream-thoughts) the altruistic feelings may possibly occur. Similarly, affectionate or amorous feelings for another person, if they exist in the unconscious, may occur in dreams. The truth of the assertion is therefore restricted to the fact that among the unconscious stimuli of dreams one very often finds egoistical tendencies which seem to have been overcome in the waking state.

are involved in the game; in after years they repeat their sensations in dreams, but in dreams they omit the hands that held them, so that now they are free to float or fall. We know that all small children have a fondness for such games as rocking and see-sawing; and if they see gymnastic performances at the circus their recollection of such games is refreshed.[1] In some boys a hysterical attack will consist simply in the reproduction of such performances, which they accomplish with great dexterity. Not infrequently sexual sensations are excited by these games of movement, which are quite neutral in themselves.[2] To express the matter in a few words: the *exciting* games of childhood are repeated in dreams of flying, falling, reeling and the like, but the voluptuous feelings are now transformed into anxiety. But, as every mother knows, the excited play of children often enough culminates in quarrelling and tears.

I have therefore good reason for rejecting the explanation that it is the state of our dermal sensations during sleep, the sensation of the movements of the lungs, etc., that evokes dreams of flying and falling. I see that these very sensations have been reproduced from the memory to which the dream refers—and that they are, therefore, dream-content and not dream-sources.

I do not for a moment deny, however, that I am unable to furnish a full explanation of this series of typical dreams. Precisely here my material leaves me in the lurch. I must adhere to the general opinion that all the dermal and kinetic sensations of these typical dreams are awakened as soon as any psychic motive of whatever kind has need of them, and that they are neglected when there is no such need of them. The relation to infantile experiences seems to be confirmed by the indications which

I have obtained from the analyses of psycho-neurotics. But I am unable to say what other meanings might, in the course of the dreamer's life, have become attached to the memory of these sensations—different, perhaps, in each individual, despite the typical appearance of these dreams—and I should very much like to be in a position to fill this gap with careful analyses of good examples. To those who wonder why I complain of a lack of material, despite the frequency of these dreams of flying, falling, tooth-drawing, etc., I must explain that I myself have never experienced any such dreams since I have turned my attention to the subject of dream-interpretation. The dreams of neurotics which are at my disposal, however, are not all capable of interpretation, and very often it is impossible to penetrate to the farthest point of their hidden intention; a certain psychic force which participated in the building up of the neurosis, and which again becomes active during its dissolution, opposes interpretation of the final problem.

(c) The Examination-Dream

Everyone who has received his certificate of matriculation after passing his final examination at school complains of the persistence with which he is plagued by anxiety-dreams in which he has failed, or must go through his course again, etc. For the holder of a university degree this typical dream is replaced by another, which represents that he has not taken his doctor's degree, to which he vainly objects, while still asleep, that he has already been practising for years, or is already a university lecturer or the senior partner of a firm of lawyers, and so on. These are the ineradicable memories of the punishments we suffered as children for misdeeds which we had committed—memories which were revived in us on the *dies irae, dies illa*[3] of the gruelling examination at the two critical junctures in our careers as students. The *examination-anxiety* of neurotics is likewise intensified by this childish fear. When our student days are over, it is no longer our parents or teachers who see to our punishment; the inexorable chain of cause and effect of later life has taken over our further education. Now we dream of our matriculation, or the examination for the doctor's degree—and who has not been faint-hearted on such occasions?—whenever we fear that we may be punished by some unpleasant result because we have done something carelessly or wrongly, because we have

---

[1] Psycho-analytic investigation has enabled us to conclude that in the predilection shown by children for gymnastic performances, and in the repetition of these in hysterical attacks, there is, besides the pleasure felt in the organ, yet another factor at work (often unconscious): namely, a memory-picture of sexual intercourse observed in human beings or animals.

[2] A young colleague, who is entirely free from nervousness, tells me, in this connection: "I know from my own experience that while swinging, and at the moment at which the downward movement was at its maximum, I used to have a curious feeling in my genitals, which, although it was not really pleasing to me, I must describe as a voluptuous feeling." I have often heard from patients that the first erections with voluptuous sensations which they can remember to have had in boyhood occurred while they were climbing. It is established with complete certainty by psycho-analysis that the first sexual sensations often have their origin in the scufflings and wrestlings of childhood.

[3] Day of wrath.—ED.

not been as thorough as we might have been—in short, whenever we feel the burden of responsibility.

For a further explanation of examination-dreams I have to thank a remark made by a colleague who had studied this subject, who once stated, in the course of a scientific discussion, that in his experience the examination-dream occurred only to persons who had passed the examination, never to those who had flunked. We have had increasing confirmation of the fact that the anxiety-dream of examination occurs when the dreamer is anticipating a responsible task on the following day, with the possibility of disgrace; recourse will then be had to an occasion in the past on which a great anxiety proved to have been without real justification, having, indeed, been refuted by the outcome. Such a dream would be a very striking example of the way in which the dream-content is misunderstood by the waking instance. The exclamation which is regarded as a protest against the dream: "But I am already a doctor," etc., would in reality be the consolation offered by the dream, and should, therefore, be worded as follows: "Do not be afraid of the morrow; think of the anxiety which you felt before your matriculation; yet nothing happened to justify it, for now you are a doctor," etc. But the anxiety which we attribute to the dream really has its origin in the residues of the dream-day.

The tests of this interpretation which I have been able to make in my own case, and in that of others, although by no means exhaustive, were entirely in its favour.[1] For example, I failed in my examination for the doctor's degree in medical jurisprudence; never once has the matter worried me in my dreams, while I have often enough been examined in botany, zoology, and chemistry, and I sat for the examinations in these subjects with well-justified anxiety, but escaped disaster, through the clemency of fate, or of the examiner. In my dreams of school examinations, I am always examined in history, a subject in which I passed brilliantly at the time, but only, I must admit, because my good-natured professor—my one-eyed benefactor in another dream—did not overlook the fact that on the examination-paper which I returned to him I had crossed out with my fingernail the second of three questions, as a hint that he should not insist on it. One of my patients, who withdrew before the matriculation examination, only to pass it later, but

[1] See also pp. 261-2.

failed in the officer's examination, so that he did not become an officer, tells me that he often dreams of the former examination, but never of the latter.

W. Stekel, who was the first to interpret the *matriculation dream,* maintains that this dream invariably refers to sexual experiences and sexual maturity. This has frequently been confirmed in my experience.

VI. THE DREAM-WORK

ALL other previous attempts to solve the problems of dreams have concerned themselves directly with the manifest dream-content as it is retained in the memory. They have sought to obtain an interpretation of the dream from this content, or, if they dispensed with an interpretation, to base their conclusions concerning the dream on the evidence provided by this content. We, however, are confronted by a different set of data; for us a new psychic material interposes itself between the dream-content and the results of our investigations: the *latent* dream-content, or dream-thoughts, which are obtained only by our method. We develop the solution of the dream from this latent content, and not from the manifest dream-content. We are thus confronted with a new problem, an entirely novel task—that of examining and tracing the relations between the latent dream-thoughts and the manifest dream-content, and the processes by which the latter has grown out of the former.

The dream-thoughts and the dream-content present themselves as two descriptions of the same content in two different languages; or, to put it more clearly, the dream-content appears to us as a translation of the dream-thoughts into another mode of expression, whose symbols and laws of composition we must learn by comparing the origin with the translation. The dream-thoughts we can understand without further trouble the moment we have ascertained them. The dream-content is, as it were, presented in hieroglyphics, whose symbols must be translated, one by one, into the language of the dream-thoughts. It would of course, be incorrect to attempt to read these symbols in accordance with their values as pictures, instead of in accordance with their meaning as symbols. For instance, I have before me a picture-puzzle (rebus)—a house, upon whose roof there is a boat; then a single letter; then a running figure, whose head has been omitted, and so on. As a critic I might be tempted to judge this composition and its elements to be nonsensical. A boat is out of place on the roof of a house, and a headless man cannot run; the man, too, is larger than the house, and if the whole thing is meant to represent a landscape the single letters of the alphabet have no right in it, since they do not occur in nature. A correct judgment of the picture-puzzle is possible only if I make no such objections to the whole and its parts, and if, on the contrary, I take the trouble to replace each image by a syllable or word which it may represent by virtue of some allusion or relation. The words thus put together are no longer meaningless, but might constitute the most beautiful and pregnant aphorism. Now a dream is such a picture-puzzle, and our predecessors in the art of dream-interpretation have made the mistake of judging the *rebus* as an artistic composition. As such, of course, it appears nonsensical and worthless.

A. *Condensation*

The first thing that becomes clear to the investigator when he compares the dream-content with the dream-thoughts is that a tremendous *work of condensation* has been accomplished. The dream is meagre, paltry and laconic in comparison with the range and copiousness of the dream-thoughts. The dream, when written down, fills half a page; the analysis, which contains the dream-thoughts, requires six, eight, twelve times as much space. The ratio varies with different dreams; but in my experience it is always of the same order. As a rule, the extent of the compression which has been accomplished is under-estimated, owing to the fact that the dream-thoughts which have been brought to light are believed to be the whole of the material, whereas a continuation of the work of interpretation would reveal still further thoughts hidden in the dream. We have already found it necessary to remark that one can never be really sure that one has interpreted a dream completely; even if the solution seems satisfying and flawless, it is always possible that yet another meaning has been manifested by the same dream. Thus the *degree of condensation* is —strictly speaking—indeterminable. Exception may be taken—and at first sight the objection seems perfectly plausible—to the assertion that the disproportion between dream-content and dream-thoughts justifies the conclusion that a considerable condensation of psychic material occurs in the formation of dreams. For we often have the feeling that we have been dreaming a great deal all night, and have then forgotten most of what we have dreamed. The dream

which we remember on waking would thus *appear* to be merely a remnant of the total dream-work, which would surely equal the dream-thoughts in range if only we could remember it completely. To a certain extent this is undoubtedly true; there is no getting away from the fact that a dream is most accurately reproduced if we try to remember it immediately after waking, and that the recollection of it becomes more and more defective as the day goes on. On the other hand, it has to be recognized that the impression that we have dreamed a good deal more than we are able to reproduce is very often based on an illusion, the origin of which we shall explain later on. Moreover, the assumption of a condensation in the dream-work is not affected by the possibility of forgetting a part of dreams, for it may be demonstrated by the multitude of ideas pertaining to those individual parts of the dream which do remain in the memory. If a large part of the dream has really escaped the memory, we are probably deprived of access to a new series of dream-thoughts. We have no justification for expecting that those portions of the dream which have been lost should likewise have referred only to those thoughts which we know from the analysis of the portions which have been preserved.[1]

In view of the very great number of ideas which analysis elicits for each individual element of the dream-content, the principal doubt in the minds of many readers will be whether it is permissible to count everything that subsequently occurs to the mind during analysis as forming part of the dream-thoughts—in other words, to assume that all these thoughts have been active in the sleeping state, and have taken part in the formation of the dream. Is it not more probable that new combinations of thoughts are developed in the course of analysis, which did not participate in the formation of the dream? To this objection I can give only a conditional reply. It is true, of course, that separate combinations of thoughts make their first appearance during the analysis; but one can convince oneself every time this happens that such new combinations have been established only between thoughts which have already been connected in other ways in the dream-thoughts; the new combinations are, so to speak, corollaries, short-circuits, which are

---

[1] References to the condensation in dreams are to be found in the works of many writers on the subject. Du Prel states in his *Philosophie der Mystik* that he is absolutely certain that a condensation-process of the succession of ideas had occurred.

made possible by the existence of other, more fundamental modes of connection. In respect of the great majority of the groups of thoughts revealed by analysis, we are obliged to admit that they have already been active in the formation of the dream, for if we work through a succession of such thoughts, which at first sight seem to have played no part in the formation of the dream, we suddenly come upon a thought which occurs in the dream-content, and is indispensable to its interpretation, but which is nevertheless inaccessible except through this chain of thoughts. The reader may here turn to the dream of the botanical monograph, which is obviously the result of an astonishing degree of condensation, even though I have not given the complete analysis.

But how, then, are we to imagine the psychic condition of the sleeper which precedes dreaming? Do all the dream-thoughts exist side by side, or do they pursue one another, or are there several simultaneous trains of thought, proceeding from different centres, which subsequently meet? I do not think it is necessary at this point to form a plastic conception of the psychic condition at the time of dream-formation. But let us not forget that we are concerned with *unconscious* thinking, and that the process may easily be different from that which we observe in ourselves in deliberate contemplation accompanied by consciousness.

The fact, however, is irrefutable that dream-formation is based on a process of condensation. How, then, is this condensation effected?

Now, if we consider that of the dream-thoughts ascertained only the most restricted number are represented in the dream by means of one of their conceptual elements, we might conclude that the condensation is accomplished by means of omission, inasmuch as the dream is not a faithful translation or projection, point by point, of the dream-thoughts, but a very incomplete and defective reproduction of them. This view, as we shall soon perceive, is a very inadequate one. But for the present let us take it as a point of departure, and ask ourselves: If only a few of the elements of the dream-thoughts make their way into the dream-content, what are the conditions that determine their selection?

In order to solve this problem, let us turn our attention to those elements of the dream-content which must have fulfilled the conditions for which we are looking. The most suitable material for this investigation will be a dream to whose formation a particularly intense condensation has contributed. I select the dream, cited on page 207, of the botanical monograph.

I

Dream-content: *I have written a monograph upon a certain (indeterminate) species of plant. The book lies before me. I am just turning over a folded coloured plate. A dried specimen of the plant is bound up in this copy, as in a herbarium.*

The most prominent element of this dream is the *botanical monograph*. This is derived from the impressions of the dream-day; I had actually seen a *monograph on the genus Cyclamen* in a bookseller's window. The mention of this genus is lacking in the dream-content; only the monograph and its relation to botany have remained. The *botanical monograph* immediately reveals its relation to the *work on cocaine* which I once wrote; from cocaine the train of thought proceeds on the one hand to a *Festschrift*, and on the other to my friend, the oculist, Dr. *Koenigstein*, who was partly responsible for the introduction of cocaine as a local anaesthetic. Moreover, Dr. Koenigstein is connected with the recollection of an interrupted conversation I had had with him on the previous evening, and with all sorts of ideas relating to the remuneration of medical and surgical services among colleagues. This conversation, then, is the actual dream-stimulus; the monograph on cyclamen is also a real incident, but one of an indifferent nature; as I now see, the *botanical monograph* of the dream proves to be a *common mean* between the two experiences of the day, taken over unchanged from an indifferent impression, and bound up with the psychically significant experience by means of the most copious associations.

Not only the combined idea of the *botanical monograph*, however, but also each of its separate elements, *botanical* and *monograph*, penetrates farther and farther, by manifold associations, into the confused tangle of the dream-thoughts. To *botanical* belong the recollections of the person of Professor Gärtner (German: *Gärtner = gardener*), of his *blooming* wife, of my patient, whose name is *Flora*, and of a lady concerning whom I told the story of the forgotten *flowers. Gärtner*, again, leads me to the laboratory and the conversation with *Koenigstein;* and the allusion to the two female patients belongs to the same conversation. From the lady with the flowers a train of thoughts branches off to the favourite flowers of my wife, whose other branch leads to the title of the hastily seen monograph. Further, *botanical* recalls an episode at the Gymnasium, and a university examination; and a fresh subject—that of my hobbies—which was broached in the above-mentioned conversation, is linked up, by means of what is humorously called my *favourite flower*, the artichoke, with the train of thoughts proceeding from the forgotten flowers; behind *artichoke* there lies, on the one hand, a recollection of Italy, and on the other a reminiscence of a scene of my childhood, in which I first formed an acquaintance—which has since then grown so intimate—with books. *Botanical*, then, is a veritable nucleus, and, for the dream, the meeting-point of many trains of thought; which, I can testify, had all really been brought into connection by the conversation referred to. Here we find ourselves in a thought-factory, in which, as in *The Weaver's Masterpiece*:

> *The little shuttles to and fro*
> *Fly, and the threads unnoted flow;*
> *One throw links up a thousand threads.*

Monograph in the dream, again, touches two themes: the one-sided nature of my studies, and the costliness of my hobbies.

The impression derived from this first investigation is that the elements *botanical* and *monograph* were taken up into the dream-content because they were able to offer the most numerous points of contact with the greatest number of dream-thoughts, and thus represented *nodal points* at which a great number of the dream-thoughts met together, and because they were of *manifold* significance in respect of the meaning of the dream. The fact upon which this explanation is based may be expressed in another form: Every element of the dream-content proves to be *over-determined*—that is, it appears several times over in the dream-thoughts.

We shall learn more if we examine the other components of the dream in respect of their occurrence in the dream-thoughts. The *coloured plate* refers (cf. the analysis on p. 208) to a new subject, the criticism passed upon my work by colleagues, and also to a subject already represented in the dream—my hobbies—and, further, to a memory of my childhood, in which I pull to pieces a book with coloured plates; the *dried specimen* of the plant relates to my experience with the herbarium at the Gymnasium, and gives this memory particular

emphasis. Thus I perceive the nature of the relation between the dream-content and dream-thoughts: Not only are the elements of the dream determined several times over by the dream-thoughts, but the individual dream-thoughts are represented in the dream by several elements. Starting from an element of the dream, the path of the association leads to a number of dream-thoughts; and from a single dream-thought to several elements of the dream. In the process of dream-formation, therefore, it is not the case that a single dream-thought, or a group of dream-thoughts, supplies the dream-content with an abbreviation of itself as its representative, and that the next dream-thought supplies another abbreviation as its representative (much as representatives are elected from among the population); but rather that the whole mass of the dream-thoughts is subjected to a certain elaboration, in the course of which those elements that receive the strongest and completest support stand out in relief; so that the process might perhaps be likened to election by the *scrutin du liste*. Whatever dream I may subject to such a dissection, I always find the same fundamental principle confirmed—that the dream-elements have been formed out of the whole mass of the dream-thoughts, and that every one of them appears, in relation to the dream-thoughts, to have a multiple determination.

It is certainly not superfluous to demonstrate this relation of the dream-content to the dream-thoughts by means of a further example, which is distinguished by a particularly artful intertwining of reciprocal relations. The dream is that of a patient whom I am treating for claustrophobia (fear of enclosed spaces). It will soon become evident why I feel myself called upon to entitle this exceptionally clever piece of dream-activity:

II. "A Beautiful Dream"

The dreamer is driving with a great number of companions in X-street, where there is a modest hostelry (which is not the case). A theatrical performance is being given in one of the rooms of the inn. He is first spectator, then actor. Finally the company is told to change their clothes, in order to return to the city. Some of the company are shown into rooms on the ground floor, others to rooms on the first floor. Then a dispute arises. The people upstairs are annoyed because those downstairs have not yet finished changing, so that they cannot come down. His brother is upstairs; he is downstairs; and he is angry with his brother because they are so hurried. (This part obscure.) *Besides, it was already decided, upon their arrival, who was to go upstairs and who down. Then he goes alone up the hill towards the city, and he walks so heavily, and with such difficulty, that he cannot move from the spot. An elderly gentleman joins him and talks angrily of the King of Italy. Finally, towards the top of the hill, he is able to walk much more easily.*

The difficulty experienced in climbing the hill was so distinct that for some time after waking he was in doubt whether the experience was a dream or the reality.

Judged by the manifest content, this dream can hardly be eulogized. Contrary to the rules, I shall begin the interpretation with that portion to which the dreamer referred as being the most distinct.

The difficulty dreamed of, and probably experienced during the dream—difficulty in climbing, accompanied by dyspnoea—was one of the symptoms which the patient had actually exhibited some years before, and which, in conjunction with other symptoms, was at the time attributed to tuberculosis (probably hysterically simulated). From our study of exhibition-dreams we are already acquainted with this sensation of being inhibited in motion, peculiar to dreams, and here again we find it utilized as material always available for the purposes of any other kind of representation. The part of the dream-content which represents climbing as difficult at first, and easier at the top of the hill, made me think, while it was being related, of the well-known masterly introduction to Daudet's *Sappho*. Here a young man carries the woman he loves upstairs; she is at first as light as a feather, but the higher he climbs the more she weighs; and this scene is symbolic of the progress of their relation, in describing which Daudet seeks to admonish young men not to lavish an earnest affection upon girls of humble origin and dubious antecedents.[1] Although I knew that my patient had recently had a love-affair with an actress, and had broken it off, I hardly expected to find that the interpretation which had occurred to me was correct. The situation in Sappho is actually the *reverse* of that in the dream; for in the dream climbing was difficult at the first and easy later on; in the novel the symbolism is

pertinent only if what was at first easily carried finally proves to be a heavy burden. To my astonishment, the patient remarked that the interpretation fitted in very well with the plot of a play which he had seen the previous evening. The play was called *Rund um Wien* (*Round about Vienna*), and treated of the career of a girl who was at first respectable, but who subsequently lapsed into the *demimonde*, and formed relations with highly-placed lovers, thereby *climbing*, but finally she *went downhill* faster and faster. This play reminded him of another, entitled *Von Stufe zu Stufe* (*From Step to Step*), the poster advertising which had depicted *a flight of stairs.*

To continue the interpretation: The actress with whom he had had his most recent and complicated affair had lived in X-street. There is no inn in this street. However, while he was spending part of the summer in Vienna for the sake of this lady, he had lodged (German: *abgestiegen = stopped,* literally *stepped off*) at a small hotel in the neighbourhood. When he was leaving the hotel, he said to the cab-driver: "I am glad at all events that I didn't get any vermin here!" (Incidentally, the dread of vermin is one of his phobias.) Whereupon the cab-driver answered: "How could anybody stop there! That isn't a hotel at all, it's really nothing but a *pub!*"

The *pub* immediately reminded him of a quotation:

> *Of a wonderful host*
> *I was lately a guest.*

But the host in the poem by Uhland is an *apple-tree.* Now a second quotation continues the train of thought:

> Faust *(dancing with the young witch)*
> A lovely dream once came to me;
> I then beheld an apple-tree,
> And there two fairest apples shone:
> They lured me so, I *climbed thereon.*
>
> The Fair One
> Apples have been desired by you,
> Since first in Paradise they grew;
> And I am moved with joy to know
> That such within my garden grow.[2]

There is not the slightest doubt what is meant by the apple-tree and the apples. A beautiful bosom stood high among the charms by which the actress had bewitched our dreamer.

Judging from the context of the analysis, we had every reason to assume that the dream

---

[1] In estimating the significance of this passage we may recall the meaning of dreams of climbing stairs, as explained in the chapter on Symbolism.

[2] *Faust* I, 4128-35.

referred to an impression of the dreamer's childhood. If this is correct, it must have referred to the wet-nurse of the dreamer, who is now a man of nearly thirty years of age. The bosom of the nurse is in reality an inn for the child. The nurse, as well as Daudet's *Sappho*, appears as an allusion to his recently abandoned mistress.

The (elder) brother of the patient also appears in the dream-content; he is *upstairs,* while the dreamer himself is *downstairs.* This again is an inversion, for the brother, as I happen to know, has lost his social position, while my patient has retained his. In relating the dream-content, the dreamer avoided saying that his brother was upstairs and that he himself was downstairs. This would have been to obvious an expression, for in Austria we say that a man is *on the ground floor* when he has lost his fortune and social position, just as we say that he has *come down.* Now the fact that at this point in the dream something is represented as inverted must have a meaning; and the inversion must apply to some other relation between the dream-thoughts and the dream-content. There is an indication which suggests how this inversion is to be understood. It obviously applies to the end of the dream, where the circumstances of climbing are the *reverse* of those described in *Sappho.* Now it is evident what inversion is meant: In *Sappho* the man carries the woman who stands in a sexual relation to him; in the dream-thoughts, conversely, there is a reference to a woman carrying a man; and, as this could occur only in childhood, the reference is once more to the nurse who carries the heavy child. Thus the final portion of the dream succeeds in representing Sappho and the nurse in the same allusion.

Just as the name *Sappho* has not been selected by the poet without reference to a Lesbian practise, so the portions of the dream in which people are busy *upstairs* and *downstairs, above* and *beneath,* point to fancies of a sexual content with which the dreamer is occupied, and which, as suppressed cravings, are not unconnected with his neurosis. Dream-interpretation itself does not show that these are fancies and not memories of actual happenings; it only furnishes us with a set of thoughts and leaves it to us to determine their actual value. In this case real and imagined happenings appear at first as of equal value—and not only here, but also in the creation of more important psychic structures than dreams. A large company, as we already know, signifies a secret. The

brother is none other than a representative, drawn into the scenes of childhood by *fancying backwards,* of all of the subsequent rivals for women's favours. Through the medium of an experience indifferent in itself, the episode of the gentleman who talks angrily of the King of Italy refers to the intrusion of people of low rank into aristocratic society. It is as though the warning which Daudet gives to young men were to be supplemented by a similar warning applicable to a suckling child.[1]

In the two dreams here cited I have shown by italics where one of the elements of the dream recurs in the dream-thoughts, in order to make the multiple relations of the former more obvious. Since, however, the analysis of these dreams has not been carried to completion, it will probably be worth while to consider a dream with a full analysis, in order to demonstrate the manifold determination of the dream-content. For this purpose I shall select the dream of Irma's injection (see p. 183). From this example we shall readily see that the condensation-work in the dream-formation has made use of more means than one.

The chief person in the dream-content is my patient Irma, who is seen with the features which belong to her waking life, and who therefore, in the first instance, represents herself. But her attitude, as I examine her at the window, is taken from a recollection of another person, of the lady for whom I should like to exchange my patient, as is shown by the dream-thoughts. Inasmuch as Irma has a diphtheritic membrane, which recalls my anxiety about my eldest daughter, she comes to represent this child of mine, behind whom, connected with her by the identity of their names, is concealed the person of the patient who died from the effects of poison. In the further course of the dream the significance of Irma's personality changes (without the alteration of her image as it is seen in the dream): she becomes one of the children whom we examine in the public dispensaries for children's diseases, where my friends display the differences in their mental capacities. The transition was obviously effected by the idea of my little daughter. Owing to her unwillingness to open her mouth, the same Irma constitutes an allusion to another

[1] The fantastic nature of the situation relating to the dreamer's wet-nurse is shown by the circumstance, objectively ascertained, that the nurse in this case was his mother. Further, I may call attention to the regret of the young man in the anecdote related on p. 222 above (that he had not taken better advantage of his opportunities with his wet-nurse) as the probable source of his dream.

lady who was examined by me, and, also in the same connection, to my wife. Further, in the morbid changes which I discover in her throat I have summarized allusions to quite a number of other persons.

All these people whom I encounter as I follow up the associations suggested by *Irma* do not appear personally in the dream; they are concealed behind the dream-person *Irma*, who is thus developed into a collective image, which, as might be expected, has contradictory features. Irma comes to represent these other persons, who are discarded in the work of condensation, inasmuch as I allow anything to happen to her which reminds me of these persons, trait by trait.

For the purposes of dream-condensation I may construct a *composite person* in yet another fashion, by combining the actual features of two or more persons in a single dream-image. It is in this fashion that the Dr. M of my dream was constructed; he bears the name of Dr. M, and he speaks and acts as Dr. M does, but his bodily characteristics and his malady belong to another person, my eldest brother; a single feature, paleness, is doubly determined, owing to the fact that it is common to both persons. Dr. R, in my dream about my uncle, is a similar composite person. But here the dream-image is constructed in yet another fashion. I have not united features peculiar to the one person with the features of the other, thereby abridging by certain features the memory-picture of each; but I have adopted the method employed by Galton in producing family portraits; namely, I have superimposed the two images, so that the common features stand out in stronger relief, while those which do not coincide neutralize one another and become indistinct. In the dream of my uncle the *fair beard* stands out in relief, as an emphasized feature, from a physiognomy which belongs to two persons, and which is consequently blurred; further, in its reference to growing grey the beard contains an allusion to my father and to myself.

The construction of collective and composite persons is one of the principal methods of dream-condensation. We shall presently have occasion to deal with this in another connection.

The notion of *dysentery* in the dream of Irma's injection has likewise a multiple determination; on the one hand, because of its paraphasic assonance with diphtheria, and on the other because of its reference to the patient whom I sent to the East, and whose hysteria had been wrongly diagnosed.

The mention of *propyls* in the dream proves again to be an interesting case of condensation. Not *propyls* but *amyls* were included in the dream-thoughts. One might think that here a simple displacement had occured in the course of dream-formation. This is in fact the case, but the displacement serves the purposes of the condensation, as is shown from the following supplementary analysis: If I dwell for a moment upon the word *propylen* (German) its assonance with the word *propylaeum* suggests itself to me. But a *propylaeum* is to be found not only in Athens, but also in Munich. In the latter city, a year before my dream, I had visited a friend who was seriously ill, and the reference to him in *trimethylamin*, which follows closely upon *propyls*, is unmistakable.

I pass over the striking circumstance that here, as elsewhere in the analysis of dreams, associations of the most widely differing values are employed for making thought-connections as though they were equivalent, and I yield to the temptation to regard the procedure by which *amyls* in the dream-thoughts are replaced in the dream-content by *propyls* as a sort of plastic process.

On the one hand, here is the group of ideas relating to my friend Otto, who does not understand me, thinks I am in the wrong, and gives me the liqueur that smells of amyls; on the other hand, there is the group of ideas—connected with the first by contrast—relating to my Berlin friend who does understand me, who would always think that I was right, and to whom I am indebted for so much valuable information concerning the chemistry of sexual processes.

What elements in the *Otto* group are to attract my particular attention are determined by the recent circumstances which are responsible for the dream; *amyls* belong to the element so distinguished, which are predestined to find their way into the dream-content. The large group of ideas centering upon *William* is actually stimulated by the contrast between William and Otto, and those elements in it are emphasized which are in tune with those already stirred up in the *Otto* group. In the whole of this dream I am continually recoiling from somebody who excites my displeasure towards another person with whom I can at will confront the first; trait by trait I appeal to the friend as against the enemy. Thus *amyls* in the *Otto* group awakes recollections in the other group, also belonging to the region of chemistry; *trimethylamin,* which receives support from several quarters, finds its way into the dream-content. *Amyls,* too, might have got into the dream-content unchanged, but it yields to the influence of the *William* group, inasmuch as out of the whole range of recollections covered by this name an element is sought out which is able to furnish a double determination for *amyls. Propyls* is closely associated with *amyls;* from the *William* group comes Munich with its propylaeum. Both groups are united in *propyls—propylaeum.* As though by a compromise, this intermediate element then makes its way into the dream-content. Here a common mean which permits of a multiple determination has been created. It thus becomes palpable that a multiple determination must facilitate penetration into the dream-content. For the purpose of this mean-formation a displacement of the attention has been unhesitatingly effected from what is really intended to something adjacent to it in the associations.

The study of the dream of Irma's injection has now enabled us to obtain some insight into the process of condensation which occurs in the formation of dreams. We perceive, as peculiarities of the condensing process, a selection of those elements which occur several times over in the dream-content, the formation of new unities (composite persons, mixed images), and the production of common means. The purpose which is served by condensation, and the means by which it is brought about, will be investigated when we come to study in all their bearings the psychic processes at work in the formation of dreams. Let us for the present be content with establishing the fact of dream-condensation as a relation between the dream-thoughts and the dream-content which deserves attention.

The condensation-work of dreams becomes most palpable when it takes words and means as its objects. Generally speaking, words are often treated in dreams as things, and therefore undergo the same combinations as the ideas of things. The results of such dreams are comical and bizarre word-formations.

1. A colleague sent an essay of his, in which he had, in my opinion, overestimated the value of a recent physiological discovery, and had expressed himself, moreover, in extravagant terms. On the following night I dreamed a sentence which obviously referred to this essay: "That is a truly norekdal style." The solution of this word-formation at first gave me some difficulty; it was unquestionably formed as a parody of the superlatives *colossal, pyramidal;* but it was not easy to say where it came from. At last the monster fell apart into the two names *Nora* and *Ekdal,* from two well-known plays by Ibsen. I had previously read a newspaper article on Ibsen by the writer whose latest work I was now criticizing in my dream.

2. One of my female patients dreams that *a man with a fair beard and a peculiar glittering eye is pointing to a sign-board attached to a tree which reads: uclamparia—wet.*[1]

Analysis.—The man was rather authoritative-looking, and his peculiar glittering eye at once recalled the church of San Paolo, near Rome, where she had seen the mosaic portraits of the Popes. One of the early Popes had a golden eye (this is really an optical illusion, to which the guides usually call attention). Further associations showed that the general physiognomy of the man corresponded with her own clergyman (pope), and the shape of the fair beard recalled her doctor (myself), while the stature of the man in the dream recalled her father. All these persons stand in the same relation to her; they are all guiding and directing the course of her life. On further questioning, the golden eye recalled gold—money—the rather expensive psycho-analytic treatment, which gives her a great deal of concern. Gold, moreover, recalls the gold cure for alcoholism —Herr D, whom she would have married, if it had not been for his clinging to the disgusting alcohol habit—she does not object to anyone's taking an occasional drink; she herself sometimes drinks beer and liqueurs. This again brings her back to her visit to San Paolo (*fuori la mura*) and its surroundings. She remembers that in the neighbouring monastery of the *Tre Fontane* she drank a liqueur made of *eucalyptus* by the Trappist monks of the monastery. She then relates how the monks transformed this malarial and swampy region into a dry and wholesome neighbourhood by planting numbers of *eucalyptus* trees. The word *uclamparia* then resolves itself into *eucalyptus* and *malaria,* and the word *wet* refers to the former swampy nature of the locality. Wet also suggests dry. *Dry* is actually the name of the man whom she would have married but for his over-indulgence in alcohol. The peculiar name of *Dry* is of Germanic origin (*drei*=three) and hence, alludes to the monastery of the Three (*drei*) Fountains. In talking of Mr. Dry's habit she used the strong expression: "He could drink a

[1] Given by translator, as the author's example could not be translated.

fountain." Mr. Dry jocosely refers to his habit by saying: "You know I must drink because I am always *dry*" (referring to his name). The *eucalyptus* refers also to her neurosis, which was at first diagnosed as *malaria*. She went to Italy because her attacks of anxiety, which were accompanied by marked rigors and shivering, were thought to be of malarial origin. She bought some eucalyptus oil from the monks, and she maintains that it has done her much good.

The condensation *uclamparia—wet* is, therefore, the point of junction for the dream as well as for the neurosis.

3. In a rather long and confused dream of my own, the apparent nucleus of which is a sea-voyage, it occurs to me that the next port is *Hearsing*, and next after that *Fliess*. The latter is the name of my friend in B, to which city I have often journeyed. But *Hearsing* is put together from the names of the places in the neighbourhood of Vienna, which so frequently end in "ing": *Hietzing, Liesing, Moedling* (the old Medelitz, *meae deliciae*, my joy; that is, my own name, the German for *joy* being *Freude*), and the English *hearsay*, which points to calumny, and establishes the relation to the indifferent dream-stimulus of the day—a poem in *Fliegende Blätter* about a slanderous dwarf, Sagter Hatergesagt (Saidhe Hashesaid). By the combination of the final syllable *ing* with the name *Fliess*, *Vlissingen* is obtained, which is a real port through which my brother passes when he comes to visit us from England. But the English for *Vlissingen* is *Flushing*, which signifies *blushing*, and recalls patients suffering from *erythrophobia* (fear of blushing), whom I sometimes treat, and also a recent publication of Bechterew's, relating to this neurosis, the reading of which angered me.[1]

[1] The same analysis and synthesis of syllables—a veritable chemistry of syllables—serves us for many a jest in waking life. "What is the cheapest method of obtaining silver? You go to a field where silver-berries are growing and pick them; then the berries are eliminated and the silver remains in a free state." [Translator's example]. The first person who read and criticized this book made the objection—with which other readers will probably agree—that "the dreamer often appears too witty." That is true, so long as it applies to the dreamer; it involves a condemnation only when its application is extended to the interpreter of the dream. In waking reality I can make very little claim to the predicate *witty;* if my dreams appear witty, this is not the fault of my individuality, but of the peculiar psychological conditions under which the dream is fabricated, and is intimately connected with the theory of wit and the comical. The dream becomes witty because the shortest and most direct way to the expression of its thoughts is barred for it; the dream is under constraint. My readers may convince themselves that the dreams of my patients give the impression of being quite as witty (at least,

4. Upon another occasion I had a dream which consisted of two separate parts. The first was the vividly remembered word *Autodidasker:* the second was a faithful reproduction in the dream-content of a short and harmless fancy which had been developed a few days earlier, and which was to the effect that I must tell Professor N, when I next saw him: "The patient about whose condition I last consulted you is really suffering from a neurosis, just as you suspected." So not only must the newly-coined *Autodidasker* satisfy the requirement that it should contain or represent a compressed meaning, but this meaning must have a valid connection with my resolve—repeated from waking life—to give Professor N due credit for his diagnosis.

Now *Autodidasker* is easily separated into *author* (German, *Autor*), *autodidact*, and *Lasker*, with whom is associated the name *Lasalle*. The first of these words leads to the occasion of the dream—which this time is significant. I had brought home to my wife several volumes by a well-known author who is a friend of my brother's, and who, as I have learned, comes from the same neighbourhood as myself (J. J. David). One evening she told me how profoundly impressed she had been by the pathetic sadness of a story in one of David's novels (a story of wasted talents), and our conversation turned upon the signs of talent which we perceive in our own children. Under the influence of what she had just read, my wife expressed some concern about our children, and I comforted her with the remark that precisely such dangers as she feared can be averted by training. During the night my thoughts proceeded farther, took up my wife's concern for the children, and interwove with it all sorts of other things. Something which the novelist had said to my brother on the subject of marriage showed my thoughts a by-path which might lead to representation in the dream. This path led to Breslau; a lady who was a very good friend of ours had married and gone to live there. I found in Breslau *Lasker* and *Lasalle*, two examples to justify the fear lest our boys should be ruined by women, examples which enabled me to represent simultaneously two ways of influencing a man to his undoing.[2] The

in intention), as my own, and even more so. Nevertheless, this reproach impelled me to compare the technique of wit with the dream-work.

[2] Lasker died of progressive paralysis; that is, of the consequences of an infection caught from a woman (syphilis); Lasalle, also a syphilitic, was killed in a duel which he fought on account of the lady whom he had been courting.

Cherchez la femme, by which these thoughts may be summarized, leads me, if taken in another sense, to my brother, who is still unmarried and whose name is *Alexander*. Now I see that *Alex*, as we abbreviate the name, sounds almost like an inversion of *Lasker*, and that this fact must have contributed to send my thoughts on a *détour* by way of Breslau.

But the playing with names and syllables in which I am here engaged has yet another meaning. It represents the wish that my brother may enjoy a happy family life, and this in the following manner: In the novel of artistic life, *L'Œuvre*, which, by virtue of its content, must have been in association with my dream-thoughts, the author, as is well-known, has incidentally given a description of his own person and his own domestic happiness, and appears under the name of *Sandoz*. In the metamorphosis of his name he probably went to work as follows: *Zola*, when inverted (as children are fond of inverting names) gives *Aloz*. But this was still too undisguised; he therefore replaced the syllable *Al*, which stands at the beginning of the name Alexander, by the third syllable of the same name, *sand*, and thus arrived at *Sandoz*. My *autodidasker* originated in a similar fashion.

My phantasy—that I am telling Professor N that the patient whom we have both seen is suffering from a neurosis—found its way into the dream in the following manner: Shortly before the close of my working year, I had a patient in whose case my powers of diagnosis failed me. A serious organic trouble—possibly some alterative degeneration of the spinal cord—was to be assumed, but could not be conclusively demonstrated. It would have been tempting to diagnose the trouble as a neurosis, and this would have put an end to all my difficulties, but for the fact that the sexual anamnesis, failing which I am unwilling to admit a neurosis, was so energetically denied by the patient. In my embarrassment I called to my assistance the physician whom I respect most of all men (as others do also), and to whose authority I surrender most completely. He listened to my doubts, told me he thought them justified, and then said: "Keep on observing the man, it is probably a neurosis." Since I know that he does not share my opinions concerning the aetiology of the neuroses, I refrained from contradicting him, but I did not conceal my scepticism. A few days later I informed the patient that I did not know what to do with him, and advised him to go to someone else. Thereupon, to my great astonishment, he began to beg my pardon for having lied to me; he had felt so ashamed; and now he revealed to me just that piece of sexual aetiology which I had expected, and which I found necessary for assuming the existence of a neurosis. This was a relief to me, but at the same time a humiliation; for I had to admit that my consultant, who was not disconcerted by the absence of anamnesis, had judged the case more correctly. I made up my mind to tell him, when next I saw him, that he had been right and I had been wrong.

This is just what I do in the dream. But what sort of a wish is fulfilled if I acknowledge that I am mistaken? This is precisely my wish; I wish to be mistaken as regards my fears—that is to say, I wish that my wife, whose fears I have appropriated in my dream-thoughts, may prove to be mistaken. The subject to which the fact of being right or wrong is related in the dream is not far removed from that which is really of interest to the dream-thoughts. We have the same pair of alternatives, of either organic or functional impairment caused by a woman, or actually by the sexual life—either tabetic paralysis or a neurosis—with which latter the nature of Lasalle's undoing is indirectly connected.

In this well-constructed (and on careful analysis quite transparent) dream, Professor N appears not merely on account of this analogy, and my wish to be proved mistaken, or the associated references to Breslau and to the family of our married friend who lives there, but also on account of the following little dialogue which followed our consultation: After he had acquitted himself of his professional duties by making the above-mentioned suggestion, Dr. N proceeded to discuss personal matters. "How many children have you now?"—"Six." —A thoughtful and respectful gesture.—"Girls, boys?"—"Three of each. They are my pride and my riches."—"Well, you must be careful; there is no difficulty about the girls, but the boys are a difficulty later on as regards their upbringing." I replied that until now they had been very tractable; obviously this prognosis of my boys' future pleased me as little as his diagnosis of my patient, whom he believed to be suffering only from a neurosis. These two impressions, then, are connected by their contiguity, by their being successively received; and when I incorporate the story of the neurosis into the dream, I substitute it for the conversation on the subject of upbringing, which is even more closely connected with the dream-thoughts, since it touches so closely upon the anxiety subsequently expressed by my wife. Thus, even my fear that N may prove to be right in his remarks on the difficulties to be met with in bringing up boys is admitted into the dream-content, inasmuch as it is concealed behind the representation of my wish that I may be wrong to harbour such apprehensions. The same phantasy serves without alteration to represent both the conflicting alternatives.

Examination-dreams present the same difficulties to interpretation that I have already described as characteristic of most typical dreams. The associative material which the dreamer supplies only rarely suffices for interpretation. A deeper understanding of such dreams has to be accumulated from a considerable number of examples. Not long ago I arrived at a conviction that reassurances like "But you already are a doctor," and so on, not only convey a consolation but imply a reproach as well. This would have run: "You are already so old, so far advanced in life, and yet you still commit such follies, are guilty of such childish behaviour." This mixture of self-criticism and consolation would correspond with the examination-dreams. After this it is no longer surprising that the reproaches in the last analysed examples concerning *follies* and *childish behaviour* should relate to repetitions of reprehensible sexual acts.

The verbal transformations in dreams are very similar to those which are known to occur in paranoia, and which are observed also in hysteria and obsessions. The linguistic tricks of children, who at a certain age actually treat words as objects, and even invent new languages and artificial syntaxes, are a common source of such occurrences both in dreams and in the psychoneuroses.

The analysis of nonsensical word-formations in dreams is particularly well suited to demonstrate the degree of condensation effected in the dream-work. From the small number of the selected examples here considered it must not be concluded that such material is seldom observed or is at all exceptional. It is, on the contrary, very frequent, but, owing to the dependence of dream interpretation on psychoanalytic treatment, very few examples are noted down and reported, and most of the analyses which are reported are comprehensible only to the specialist in neuropathology.

When a spoken utterance, expressly distinguished as such from a thought, occurs in a dream, it is an invariable rule that the dream-speech has originated from a remembered speech in the dream-material. The wording of the speech has either been preserved in its entirety or has been slightly altered in expression; frequently the dream-speech is pieced together from different recollections of spoken remarks; the wording has remained the same, but the sense has perhaps become ambiguous, or differs from the wording. Not infrequently the dream-speech serves merely as an allusion to an incident in connection with which the remembered speech was made.[1]

B. *The Work of Displacement*

Another and probably no less significant relation must have already forced itself upon our attention while we were collecting examples of dream-condensation. We may have noticed that these elements which obtrude themselves in the dream-content as its essential components do not by any means play this same part in the dream-thoughts. As a corollary to this, the converse of this statement is also true. That which is obviously the essential content of the dream-thoughts need not be represented at all in the dream. The dream is, as it were, *centred elsewhere;* its content is arranged about elements which do not constitute the central point of the dream-thoughts. Thus, for example, in the dream of the botanical monograph the central point of the dream-content is evidently the element *botanical;* in the dream-thoughts, we are concerned with the complications and conflicts resulting from services rendered between colleagues which place them under mutual obligations; later on with the reproach that I am in the habit of sacrificing too much time to my hobbies; and the element *botanical* finds no place in this nucleus of the dream-thoughts, unless it is loosely connected with it by antithesis, for botany was never among my favourite subjects. In the Sappho-dream of my patient, ascending and descending, being upstairs and down, is made the central point; the dream, however, is concerned with the danger of sexual relations with persons of *low* degree; so that only one of the elements of the dream-

[1] In the case of a young man who was suffering from obsessions, but whose intellectual functions were intact and highly developed, I recently found the only exception to this rule. The speeches which occurred in his dreams did not originate in speeches which he had heard or had made himself, but corresponded to the undistorted verbal expression of his obsessive thoughts, which came to his waking consciousness only in an altered form.

thoughts seems to have found its way into the dream-content, and this is unduly expanded. Again, in the dream of my uncle, the fair beard, which seems to be its central point, appears to have no rational connection with the desire for greatness which we have recognized as the nucleus of the dream-thoughts. Such dreams very naturally give us an impression of a *displacement*. In complete contrast to these examples, the dream of Irma's injection shows that individual elements may claim the same place in dream-formation as that which they occupy in the dream-thoughts. The recognition of this new and utterly inconstant relation between the dream-thoughts and the dream-content will probably astonish us at first. If we find, in a psychic process of normal life, that one idea has been selected from among a number of others, and has acquired a particular emphasis in our consciousness, we are wont to regard this as proof that a peculiar psychic value (a certain degree of interest) attaches to the victorious idea. We now discover that this value of the individual element in the dream-thoughts is not retained in dream-formation, or is not taken into account. For there is no doubt which of the elements of the dream-thoughts are of the highest value; our judgment informs us immediately. In dream-formation the essential elements, those that are emphasized by intensive interest, may be treated as though they were subordinate, while they are replaced in the dream by other elements, which were certainly subordinate in the dream-thoughts. It seems at first as though the psychic intensity[1] of individual ideas were of no account in their selection for dream-formation, but only their greater or lesser multiplicity of determination. One might be inclined to think that what gets into the dream is not what is important in the dream-thoughts, but what is contained in them several times over; but our understanding of dream-formation is not much advanced by this assumption; to begin with, we cannot believe that the two motives of multiple determination and intrinsic value can influence the selection of the dream otherwise than in the same direction. Those ideas in the dream-thoughts which are most important are probably also those which recur most frequently, since the individual dream-thoughts radiate from them as centres. And yet the dream may reject these intensely emphasized and extensively reinforced

[1] The psychic intensity or value of an idea—the emphasis due to interest—is of course to be distinguished from perceptual or conceptual intensity.

elements, and may take up into its content other elements which are only extensively reinforced.

This difficulty may be solved if we follow up yet another impression received during the investigation of the over-determination of the dream-content. Many readers of this investigation may already have decided, in their own minds, that the discovery of the multiple determination of the dream-elements is of no great importance, because it is inevitable. Since in analysis we proceed from the dream-elements, and register all the ideas which associate themselves with these elements, is it any wonder that these elements should recur with peculiar frequency in the thought-material obtained in this manner? While I cannot admit the validity of this objection, I am now going to say something that sounds rather like it: Among the thoughts which analysis brings to light are many which are far removed from the nucleus of the dream, and which stand out like artificial interpolations made for a definite purpose. Their purpose may readily be detected; they establish a connection, often a forced and far-fetched connection, between the dream-content and the dream-thoughts, and in many cases, if these elements were weeded out of the analysis, the components of the dream-content would not only not be over-determined, but they would not be sufficiently determined. We are thus led to the conclusion that multiple determination, decisive as regards the selection made by the dream, is perhaps not always a primary factor in dream-formation, but is often a secondary product of a psychic force which is as yet unknown to us. Nevertheless, it must be of importance for the entrance of the individual elements into the dream, for we may observe that, in cases where multiple determination does not proceed easily from the dream-material, it is brought about with a certain effort.

It now becomes very probable that a psychic force expresses itself in the dream-work which, on the one hand, strips the elements of the high psychic value of their intensity and, on the other hand, by *means of over-determination*, creates new significant values from elements of slight value, which new values then make their way into the dream-content. Now if this is the method of procedure, there has occurred in the process of dream-formation a *transference and displacement of the psychic intensities* of the individual elements, from which results the textual difference between the dream-content and the thought-content. The process which we here assume to be operative is actually the most essential part of the dream-work; it may fitly be called *dream-displacement. Dream-displacement and dream-condensation* are the two craftsmen to whom we may chiefly ascribe the structure of the dream.

I think it will be easy to recognize the psychic force which expresses itself in dream-displacement. The result of this displacement is that the dream-content no longer has any likeness to the nucleus of the dream-thoughts, and the dream reproduces only a distorted form of the dream-wish in the unconscious. But we are already acquainted with dream-distortion; we have traced it back to the censorship which one psychic instance in the psychic life exercises over another. Dream-displacement is one of the chief means of achieving this distortion. *Is fecit, cui profuit.*[1] We must assume that dream-displacement is brought about by the influence of this censorship, the endopsychic defence.[2]

The manner in which the factors of displacement, condensation and over-determination in-

[1] "The doer gained."

[2] Since I regard the attribution of dream-distortion to the censorship as the central point of my conception of the dream, I will here quote the closing passage of a story, *Träumen wie Wachen,* from *Phantasien eines Realisten,* by Lynkeus (Vienna, second edition [1900]), in which I find this chief feature of my doctrine reproduced:

"Concerning a man who possesses the remarkable faculty of never dreaming nonsense. . . ."

"Your marvellous faculty of dreaming as if you were awake is based upon your virtues, upon your goodness, your justice, and your love of truth; it is the moral clarity of your nature which makes everything about you intelligible to me."

"But if I really give thought to the matter," was the reply, "I almost believe that all men are made as I am, and that no one ever dreams nonsense! A dream which one remembers so distinctly that one can relate it afterwards, and which, therefore, is no dream of delirium, *always* has a meaning; why, it cannot be otherwise! For that which is in contradiction to itself can never be combined into a whole. The fact that time and space are often thoroughly shaken up, detracts not at all from the real content of the dream, because both are without any significance whatever for its essential content. We often do the same thing in waking life; think of fairy-tales, of so many bold and pregnant creations of fantasy, of which only a foolish person would say: 'That is nonsense! For it isn't possible.' "

"If only it were always possible to interpret dreams correctly, as you have just done with mine!" said the friend.

"That is certainly not an easy task, but with a little attention it must always be possible to the dreamer. You ask why it is generally impossible? In your case there seems to be something veiled in your dreams, something unchaste in a special and exalted fashion, a certain secrecy in your nature, which it is difficult to fathom; and that is why your dreams so often seem to be without meaning, or even nonsensical. But in the profoundest sense, this is by no means the case; indeed it cannot be, for a man is always the same person, whether he wakes or dreams."

teract with one another in dream-formation—which is the ruling factor and which the subordinate one—all this will be reserved as a subject for later investigation. In the meantime, we may state, as a second condition which the elements that find their way into the dream must satisfy, that *they must be withdrawn from the resistance of the censorship.* But henceforth, in the interpretation of dreams, we shall reckon with dream-displacement as an unquestionable fact.

C. *The Means of Representation in Dreams*

Besides the two factors of *condensation* and *displacement* in dreams, which we have found to be at work in the transformation of the latent dream-material into the manifest dream-content, we shall, in the course of this investigation, come upon two further conditions which exercise an unquestionable influence over the selection of the material that eventually appears in the dream. But first, even at the risk of seeming to interrupt our progress, I shall take a preliminary glance at the processes by which the interpretation of dreams is accomplished. I do not deny that the best way of explaining them, and of convincing the critic of their reliability, would be to take a single dream as an example, to detail its interpretation, as I did (in Chapter II) in the case of the dream of Irma's injection, but then to assemble the dream-thoughts which I had discovered, and from them to reconstruct the formation of the dream—that is to say, to supplement dream-analysis by dream-synthesis. I have done this with several specimens for my own instruction; but I cannot undertake to do it here, as I am prevented by a number of considerations (relating to the psychic material necessary for such a demonstration) such as any right-thinking person would approve. In the analysis of dreams these considerations present less difficulty, for an analysis may be incomplete and still retain its value, even if it leads only a little way into the structure of the dream. I do not see how a synthesis, to be convincing, could be anything short of complete. I could give a complete synthesis only of the dreams of such persons as are unknown to the reading public. Since, however, neurotic patients are the only persons who furnish me with the means of making such a synthesis, this part of the description of dreams must be postponed until I can carry the psychological explanation of the neuroses far enough to demonstrate their relation to our subject.[1] This will be done elsewhere.

From my attempts to construct dreams synthetically from their dream-thoughts, I know that the material which is yielded by interpretation varies in value. Part of it consists of the essential dream-thoughts, which would completely replace the dream and would in themselves be a sufficient substitute for it, were there no dream-censorship. To the other part, one is wont to ascribe slight importance, nor does one set any value on the assertion that all these thoughts have participated in the formation of the dream; on the contrary. they may include notions which are associated with experiences that have occurred subsequently to the dream, between the dream and the interpretation. This part comprises not only all the connecting-paths which have led from the manifest to the latent dream-content, but also the intermediate and approximating associations by means of which one has arrived at a knowledge of these connecting-paths during the work of interpretation.

At this point we are interested exclusively in the essential dream-thoughts. These commonly reveal themselves as a complex of thoughts and memories of the most intricate possible construction, with all the characteristics of the thought-processes known to us in waking life. Not infrequently they are trains of thought which proceed from more than one centre, but which are not without points of contact; and almost invariably we find, along with a train of thought, its contradictory counterpart, connected with it by the association of contrast.

The individual parts of this complicated structure naturally stand in the most manifold logical relations to one another. They constitute foreground and background, digressions, illustrations, conditions, lines of argument and objections. When the whole mass of these dream-thoughts is subjected to the pressure of the dream-work, during which the fragments are turned about, broken up and compacted, somewhat like drifting ice, the question arises: What becomes of the logical ties which had hitherto provided the framework of the structure? What representation do *if, because, as*

[1] I have since given the complete analysis and synthesis of two dreams in the *Bruchstück einer Hysterieanalyse*, (1905) (*Ges. Schriften*, Vol. VIII). "Fragment of an Analysis of a Case of Hysteria," translated by Strachey, *Collected Papers*, Vol. III, (Hogarth Press, London). O. Rank's analysis, *Ein Traum der sich selbst deutet*, deserves mention as the most complete interpretation of a comparatively long dream.

though, although, either—or and all the other conjunctions, without which we cannot understand a phrase or a sentence, receive in our dreams?

To begin with, we must answer that the dream has at its disposal no means of representing these logical relations between the dream-thoughts. In most cases it disregards all these conjunctions, and undertakes the elaboration only of the material content of the dream-thoughts. It is left to the interpretation of the dream to restore the coherence which the dream-work has destroyed.

If dreams lack the ability to express these relations, the psychic material of which they are wrought must be responsible for this defect. As a matter of fact, the representative arts—painting and sculpture—are similarly restricted, as compared with poetry, which is able to employ speech; and here again the reason for this limitation lies in the material by the elaboration of which the two plastic arts endeavour to express something. Before the art of painting arrived at an understanding of the laws of expression by which it is bound, it attempted to make up for this deficiency. In old paintings little labels hung out of the mouths of the persons represented, giving in writing the speech which the artist despaired of expressing in the picture.

Here, perhaps an objection will be raised, challenging the assertion that our dreams dispense with the representation of logical relations. There are dreams in which the most complicated intellectual operations take place; arguments for and against are adduced, jokes and comparisons are made, just as in our waking thoughts. But here again appearances are deceptive; if the interpretation of such dreams is continued it will be found that *all these things are dream-material, not the representation of intellectual activity in the dream.* The *content* of the dream-thoughts is reproduced by the apparent thinking in our dreams, but not *the relations of the dream-thoughts to one another,* in the determination of which relations thinking consists. I shall give some examples of this. But the fact which is most easily established is that all speeches which occur in dreams, and which are expressly designated as such, are unchanged or only slightly modified replicas of speeches which occur likewise among the memories in the dream-material. Often the speech is only an allusion to an event contained in the dream-thoughts; the meaning of the dream is quite different.

However, I shall not dispute the fact that even critical thought-activity, which does not simply repeat material from the dream-thoughts, plays a part in dream-formation. I shall have to explain the influence of this factor at the close of this discussion. It will then become clear that this thought activity is evoked not by the dream-thoughts, but by the dream itself, after it is, in a certain sense, already completed.

Provisionally, then, it is agreed that the logical relations between the dream-thoughts do not obtain any particular representation in the dream. For instance, where there is a contradiction in the dream, this is either a contradiction directed against the dream itself or a contradiction contained in one of the dream-thoughts; a contradiction in the dream corresponds with a contradiction *between* the dream-thoughts only in the most indirect and intermediate fashion.

But just as the art of painting finally succeeded in depicting, in the persons represented, at least the intentions behind their words—tenderness, menace, admonition, and the like—by other means than by floating labels, so also the dream has found it possible to render an account of certain of the logical relations between its dream-thoughts by an appropriate modification of the peculiar method of dream-representation. It will be found by experience that different dreams go to different lengths in this respect; while one dream will entirely disregard the logical structure of its material, another attempts to indicate it as completely as possible. In so doing, the dream departs more or less widely from the text which it has to elaborate; and its attitude is equally variable in respect to the temporal articulation of the dream-thoughts, if such has been established in the unconscious (as, for example, in the dream of Irma's injection).

But what are the means by which the dream-work is enabled to indicate those relations in the dream-material which are difficult to represent? I shall attempt to enumerate these, one by one.

In the first place, the dream renders an account of the connection which is undeniably present between all the portions of the dream-thoughts by combining this material into a unity as a situation or a proceeding. It reproduces *logical connections* in the form of *simultaneity;* in this case it behaves rather like the painter who groups together all the philosophers or poets in a picture of the School of Athens, or Parnassus. They never were assembled in any hall or on any mountain-top, although to the reflective mind they do constitute a community.

The dream carries out in detail this mode of representation. Whenever it shows two elements close together, it vouches for a particularly intimate connection between their corresponding representatives in the dream-thoughts. It is as in our method of writing: *to* signifies that the two letters are to be pronounced as one syllable; while *t* with *o* following a blank space indicates that *t* is the last letter of one word and *o* the first letter of another. Consequently, dream-combinations are not made up of arbitrary, completely incongruous elements of the dream-material, but of elements that are pretty intimately related in the dream-thoughts also.

For representing *causal relations* our dreams employ two methods, which are essentially reducible to one. The method of representation more frequently employed—in cases, for example, where the dream-thoughts are to the effect: "Because this was thus and thus, this and that must happen"—consists in making the subordinate clause a prefatory dream and joining the principal clause on to it in the form of the main dream. If my interpretation is correct, the sequence may likewise be reversed. The principal clause always corresponds to that part of the dream which is elaborated in the greatest detail.

An excellent example of such a representation of causality was once provided by a female patient, whose dream I shall subsequently give in full. The dream consisted of a short prologue, and of a very circumstantial and very definitely centred dream-composition. I might entitle it "Flowery language." The preliminary dream is as follows: *She goes to the two maids in the kitchen and scolds them for taking so long to prepare " a little bite of food." She also sees a very large number of heavy kitchen utensils in the kitchen turned upside down in order to drain, even heaped up in stacks. The two maids go to fetch water, and have, as it were, to climb into a river, which reaches up to the house or into the courtyard.*

Then follows the main dream, which begins as follows: *She is climbing down from a height over a curiously shaped trellis, and she is glad that her dress doesn't get caught anywhere, etc.* Now the preliminary dream refers to the house of the lady's parents. The words which are spoken in the kitchen are words which she has probably often heard spoken by her mother.

The piles of clumsy pots and pans are taken from an unpretentious hardware shop located in the same house. The second part of this dream contains an allusion to the dreamer's father, who was always pestering the maids, and who during a flood—for the house stood close to the bank of the river—contracted a fatal illness. The thought which is concealed behind the preliminary dream is something like this: "Because I was born in this house, in such sordid and unpleasant surroundings . . ." The main dream takes up the same thought, and presents it in a form that has been altered by a wish-fulfilment: "I am of exalted origin." Properly then: "Because I am of such humble origin, the course of my life has been so and so."

As far as I can see, the division of a dream into two unequal portions does not always signify a causal relation between the thoughts of the two portions. It often seems as though in the two dreams the same material were presented from different points of view; this is certainly the case when a series of dreams, dreamed the same night, end in a seminal emission, the somatic need enforcing a more and more definite expression. Or the two dreams have proceeded from two separate centres in the dream-material, and they overlap one another in the content, so that the subject which in one dream constitutes the centre co-operates in the other as an allusion, and vice versa. But in a certain number of dreams the division into short preliminary dreams and long subsequent dreams actually signifies a causal relation between the two portions. The other method of representing the causal relation is employed with less comprehensive material, and consists in the transformation of an image in the dream into another image, whether it be of a person or a thing. Only where this transformation is actually seen occurring in the dream shall we seriously insist on the causal relation; not where we simply note that one thing has taken the place of another. I said that both methods of representing the causal relation are really reducible to the same method; in both cases *causation* is represented by succession, sometimes by the succession of dreams, sometimes by the immediate transformation of one image into another. In the great majority of cases, of course, the causal relation is not represented at all, but is effaced amidst the succession of elements that is unavoidable even in the dream-process.

Dreams are quite incapable of expressing the alternative *either—or;* it is their custom to take both members of this alternative into the same context, as though they had an equal right to be there. A classic example of this is contained in the dream of Irma's injection. Its latent thoughts obviously mean: I am not responsible for the persistence of Irma's pains; the responsibility rests *either* with her resistance to accepting the solution *or* with the fact that she is living under unfavourable sexual conditions, which I am unable to change, *or* her pains are not hysterical at all, but organic. The dream, however, carries out all these possibilities, which are almost mutually exclusive, and is quite ready to add a fourth solution derived from the dream-wish. After interpreting the dream, I then inserted the *either—or* in its context in the dream-thoughts.

But when in narrating a dream the narrator is inclined to employ the alternative *either—or:* "It was either a garden or a living-room," etc., there is not really an alternative in the dream-thoughts, but an *and*—a simple addition. When we use *either—or* we are as a rule describing a quality of vagueness in some element of the dream, but a vagueness which may still be cleared up. The rule to be applied in this case is as follows: The individual members of the alternative are to be treated as equal and connected by an *and*. For instance, after waiting long and vainly for the address of a friend who is travelling in Italy, I dream that I receive a telegram which gives me the address. On the telegraph form I see printed in blue letters: the first word is blurred—perhaps *via*

or *villa;* the second is distinctly *Sezerno,* or even (*Casa*).

The second word, which reminds me of Italian names, and of our discussions on etymology, also expresses my annoyance in respect of the fact that my friend has kept his address a secret from me; but each of the possible first three words may be recognized on analysis as an independent and equally justifiable starting-point in the concatenation of ideas.

During the night before the funeral of my father I dreamed of a printed placard, a card or poster rather like the notices in the waiting-rooms of railway stations which announce that smoking is prohibited. The sign reads either:

You are requested to shut the eyes
or
You are requested to shut one eye

an alternative which I am in the habit of representing in the following form:

$$\text{You are requested to shut } \frac{the}{one} \text{ eye(s).}$$

Each of the two versions has its special meaning, and leads along particular paths in the dream-interpretation. I had made the simplest possible funeral arrangements, for I knew what the deceased thought about such matters. Other members of the family, however, did not approve of such puritanical simplicity; they thought we should feel ashamed in the presence of the other mourners. Hence one of the wordings of the dream asks for the *shutting of one eye*, that is to say, it asks that people should show consideration. The significance of the vagueness, which is here represented by an *either—or*, is plainly to be seen. The dream-work has not succeeded in concocting a coherent and yet ambiguous wording for the dream-thoughts. Thus the two principal trains of thought are separated from each other, even in the dream-content.

In some few cases the division of a dream into two equal parts expresses the alternative which the dream finds it so difficult to present.

The attitude of dreams to the category of *antithesis* and *contradiction* is very striking. This category is simply ignored; the word *No* does not seem to exist for a dream. Dreams are particularly fond of reducing antitheses to uniformity, or representing them as one and the same thing. Dreams likewise take the liberty of representing any element whatever by its desired opposite, so that it is at first impossible to tell, in respect of any element which is capable of having an opposite, whether it is contained in the dream-thoughts in the negative or the positive sense.[1] In one of the recently cited dreams, whose introductory portion we have already interpreted ("because my origin is so and so"), the dreamer climbs down over a trellis, and holds a blossoming bough in her hands. Since this picture suggests to her the angel in paintings of the Annunciation (her own name is Mary) bearing a lily-stem in his

hand, and the white-robed girls walking in procession on Corpus Christi Day, when the streets are decorated with green boughs, the blossoming bough in the dream is quite clearly an allusion to sexual innocence. But the bough is thickly studded with red blossoms, each of which resembles a camellia. At the end of her walk (so the dream continues) the blossoms are already beginning to fall; then follow unmistakable allusions to menstruation. But this very bough, which is carried like a lily-stem and as though by an innocent girl, is also an allusion to Camille, who, as we know, usually wore a white camellia, but a red one during menstruation. The same blossoming bough ("the flower of maidenhood" in Goethe's songs of the miller's daughter) represents at once sexual innocence and its opposite. Moreover, the same dream, which expresses the dreamer's joy at having succeeded in passing through life unsullied, hints in several places (as in the falling of the blossom) at the opposite train of thought, namely, that she had been guilty of various sins against sexual purity (that is, in her childhood). In the analysis of the dream we may clearly distinguish the two trains of thought, of which the comforting one seems to be superficial, and the reproachful one more profound. The two are diametrically opposed to each other, and their similar yet contrasting elements have been represented by identical dream-elements.

The mechanism of dream-formation is favourable in the highest degree to only one of the logical relations. This relation is that of similarity, agreement, contiguity, *just as;* a relation which may be represented in our dreams, as no other can be, by the most varied expedients. The *screening* which occurs in the dream-material, or the cases of *just as* are the chief points of support for dream-formation, and a not inconsiderable part of the dream-work consists in creating new *screenings* of this kind in cases where those that already exist are prevented by the resistance of the censorship from making their way into the dream. The effort towards condensation evinced by the dream-work facilitates the representation of a relation of similarity.

Similarity, agreement, community, are quite generally expressed in dreams by contraction into a *unity*, which is either already found in the dream-material or is newly created. The first case may be referred to as *identification*, the second as *composition*. Identification is used where the dream is concerned with persons,

---

[1] From a work of K. Abel's, *Der Gegensinn der Urworte*, (1884), (see my review of it in the Bleuler-Freud *Jahrbuch*, ii (1910) (*Ges. Schriften*, Vol. x). I learned the surprising fact, which is confirmed by other philologists, that the oldest languages behaved just as dreams do in this regard. They had originally only one word for both extremes in a series of qualities or activities (strong—weak, old—young, far—near, bind—separate), and formed separate designations for the two opposites only secondarily, by slight modifications of the common primitive word. Abel demonstrates a very large number of those relationships in ancient Egyptian, and points to distinct remnants of the same development in the Semitic and Indo-Germanic languages.

composition where things constitute the material to be unified; but compositions are also made of persons. Localities are often treated as persons.

Identification consists in giving representation in the dream-content to only one of two or more persons who are related by some common feature, while the second person or other persons appear to be suppressed as far as the dream is concerned. In the dream this one "screening" person enters into all the relations and situations which derive from the persons whom he screens. In cases of composition, however, when persons are combined, there are already present in the dream-image features which are characteristic of, but not common to, the persons in question, so that a new unity, a composite person, appears as the result of the union of these features. The combination itself may be effected in various ways. Either the dream-person bears the name of one of the persons to whom he refers—and in this case we simply know, in a manner that is quite analogous to knowledge in waking life, that this or that person is intended—while the visual features belong to another person; or the dream-image itself is compounded of visual features which in reality are derived from the two. Also, in place of the visual features, the part played by the second person may be represented by the attitudes and gestures which are usually ascribed to him by the words he speaks, or by the situations in which he is placed. In this latter method of characterization the sharp distinction between the identification and the combination of persons begins to disappear. But it may also happen that the formation of such a composite person is unsuccessful. The situations or actions of the dream are then attributed to one person, and the other—as a rule the more important—is introduced as an inactive spectator. Perhaps the dreamer will say: "My mother was there too" (Stekel). Such an element of the dream-content is then comparable to a determinative in hieroglyphic script which is not meant to be expressed, but is intended only to explain another sign.

The common feature which justifies the union of two persons—that is to say, which enables it to be made—may either be represented in the dream or it may be absent. As a rule identification or composition of persons actually serves to avoid the necessity of representing this common feature. Instead of repeating: "A is ill-disposed towards me, and so is B," I make, in my dream, a composite person of A and B; or I conceive A as doing something which is alien to his character, but which is characteristic of B. The dream-person obtained in this way appears in the dream in some new connection, and the fact that he signifies both A and B justifies my inserting that which is common to both persons—their hostility towards me—at the proper place in the dream-interpretation. In this manner I often achieve a quite extraordinary degree of condensation of the dream-content; I am able to dispense with the direct representation of the very complicated relations belonging to one person, if I can find a second person who has an equal claim to some of these relations. It will be readily understood how far this representation by means of identification may circumvent the censoring resistance which sets up such harsh conditions for the dream-work. The thing that offends the censorship may reside in those very ideas which are connected in the dream-material with the one person; I now find a second person, who likewise stands in some relation to the objectionable material, but only to a part of it. Contact at that one point which offends the censorship now justifies my formation of a composite person, who is characterized by the indifferent features of each. This person, the result of combination or identification, being free of the censorship, is now suitable for incorporation in the dream-content. Thus, by the application of dream-condensation, I have satisfied the demands of the dream-censorship.

When a common feature of two persons is represented in a dream, this is usually a hint to look for another concealed common feature, the representation of which is made impossible by the censorship. Here a displacement of the common feature has occurred, which in some degree facilitates representation. From the circumstance that the composite person is shown to me in the dream with an indifferent common feature, I must infer that another common feature which is by no means indifferent exists in the dream-thoughts.

Accordingly, the identification or combination of persons serves various purposes in our dreams; in the first place, that of representing a feature common to two persons; secondly, that of representing a *displaced* common feature; and, thirdly, that of expressly a community of features which is merely *wished for*. As the wish for a community of features in two persons often coincides with the *inter-*

changing of these persons, this relation also is expressed in dreams by identification. In the dream of Irma's injection I wish to exchange one patient for another—that is to say, I wish this other person to be my patient, as the former person has been; the dream deals with this wish by showing me a person who is called Irma, but who is examined in a position such as I have had occasion to see only the other person occupy. In the dream about my uncle this substitution is made the centre of the dream; I identify myself with the minister by judging and treating my colleagues as shabbily as he does.

It has been my experience—and to this I have found no exception—that every dream treats of oneself. Dreams are absolutely egoistic.[1] In cases where not my ego but only a strange person occurs in the dream-content, I may safely assume that by means of identification my ego is concealed behind that person. I am permitted to supplement my ego. On other occasions, when my ego appears in the dream, the situation in which it is placed tells me that another person is concealing himself, by means of identification, behind the ego. In this case I must be prepared to find that in the interpretation I should transfer something which is connected with this person—the hidden common feature—to myself. There are also dreams in which my ego appears together with other persons who, when the identification is resolved, once more show themselves to be my ego. Through these identifications I shall then have to connect with my ego certain ideas to which the censorship has objected. I may also give my ego multiple representation in my dream, either directly or by means of identification with other people. By means of several such identifications an extraordinary amount of thought material may be condensed.[2] That one's ego should appear in the same dream several times or in different forms is fundamentally no more surprising than that it should appear, in conscious thinking, many times and in different places or in different relations: as, for example, in the sentence: "When *I* think what a healthy child *I* was."

Still easier than in the case of persons is the resolution of identifications in the case of localities designated by their own names, as here the disturbing influence of the all-powerful ego is lacking. In one of my dreams of Rome (p. 218) the name of the place in which I find myself is *Rome;* I am surprised, however, by a large number of German placards at a street corner. This last is a wish-fulfilment, which immediately suggests *Prague;* the wish itself probably originated at a period of my youth when I was imbued with a German nationalistic spirit which today is quite subdued. At the time of my dream I was looking forward to meeting a friend in *Prague;* the identification of Rome with Prague is therefore explained by a desired common feature; I would rather meet my friend in Rome than in Prague; for the purpose of this meeting I should like to exchange Prague for Rome.

The possibility of creating composite formations is one of the chief causes of the fantastic character so common in dreams, in that it introduces into the dream-content elements which could never have been objects of perception. The psychic process which occurs in the creation of composite formations is obviously the same as that which we employ in conceiving or figuring a dragon or a centaur in our waking senses. The only difference is that, in the fantastic creations of waking life, the impression intended is itself the decisive factor, while the composite formation in the dream is determined by a factor—the common feature in the dream-thoughts—which is independent of its form. Composite formations in dreams may be achieved in a great many different ways. In the most artless of these methods, only the properties of the one thing are represented, and this representation is accompanied by a knowledge that they refer to another object also. A more careful technique combines features of the one object with those of the other in a new image, while it makes skillful use of any really existing resemblances between the two objects. The new creation may prove to be wholly absurd, or even successful as a phantasy, according as the material and the wit employed in constructing it may permit. If the objects to be condensed into a unity are too incongruous, the dream-work is content with creating a composite formation with a comparatively distinct nucleus, to which are attached more indefinite modifications. The unification into one image has here been to some extent unsuccessful; the two representations overlap one another, and give rise to something like a contest between the visual images. Similar representations might be obtained in a drawing if one were to attempt to give form to a uni-

---

[1] Cf. here the observations made on pp. 249-50.

[2] If I do not know behind which of the persons appearing in the dream I am to look for my ego, I observe the following rule: That person in the dream who is subject to an emotion which I am aware of while asleep is the one that conceals my ego.

fied abstraction of disparate perceptual images.

Dreams naturally abound in such composite formations; I have given several examples of these in the dreams already analysed, and will now cite more such examples. In the dream on p. 268, which describes the career of my patient in flowery language, the dream-ego carries a spray of blossoms in her hand which, as we have seen, signifies at once sexual innocence and sexual transgression. Moreover, from the manner in which the blossoms are set on, they recall *cherry*-blossom; the blossoms themselves, considered singly, are *camellias,* and finally the whole spray gives the dreamer the impression of an *exotic* plant. The common feature in the elements of this composite formation is revealed by the dream-thoughts. The blossoming spray is made up of allusions to presents by which she was induced or was to have been induced to behave in a manner agreeable to the giver. So it was with cherries in her childhood, and with a camellia-tree in her later years; the exotic character is an allusion to a much-travelled naturalist, who sought to win her favour by means of a drawing of a flower. Another female patient contrives a composite mean out of *bathing machines* at a seaside resort, country *privies,* and the *attics* of our city dwelling-houses. A reference to human nakedness and exposure is common to the first two elements; and we may infer from their connection with the third element that (in her childhood) the garret was likewise the scene of bodily exposure. A dreamer of the male sex makes a composite locality out of two places in which "treatment" is given—my office and the assembly rooms in which he first became acquainted with his wife. Another, a female patient, after her elder brother has promised to regale her with caviar, dreams that his legs are *covered all over with black beads of caviar.* The two elements, *taint* in a moral sense and the recollection of a cutaneous eruption in childhood which made her legs look as though studded over with *red* instead of black spots, have here combined with the beads of *caviar* to form a new idea—the idea of *what she gets from her brother.* In this dream parts of the human body are treated as objects, as is usually the case in dreams. In one of the dreams recorded by Ferenczi there occurs a composite formation made up of the person of a *physician* and a *horse,* and this composite being wears a *night-shirt.* The common feature in these three components was revealed in the analysis, after the nightshirt had been recognized as an allu-

sion to the father of the dreamer in a scene of childhood. In each of the three cases there was some object of her sexual curiosity. As a child she had often been taken by her nurse to the army stud, where she had the amplest opportunity to satisfy her curiosity, at that time still uninhibited.

I have already stated that the dream has no means of expressing the relation of contradiction, contrast, negation. I shall now contradict this assertion for the first time. A certain number of cases of what may be summed up under the word *contrast* obtain representation, as we have seen, simply by means of identification—that is, when an exchange, a substitution, can be bound up with the contrast. Of this we have cited repeated examples. Certain other of the contrasts in the dream-thoughts, which perhaps come under the category of *inverted, turned into the opposite,* are represented in dreams in the following remarkable manner, which may almost be described as witty. The *inversion* does not itself make its way into the dream-content, but manifests its presence in the material by the fact that a part of the already formed dream-content which is, for other reasons, closely connected in context is—as it were subsequently—*inverted.* It is easier to illustrate this process than to describe it. In the beautiful "Up and Down" dream (pp. 255-6) the dream-representation of ascending is an inversion of its prototype in the dream-thoughts: that is, of the introductory scene of Daudet's *Sappho;* in the dream, climbing is difficult at first and easy later on, whereas, in the novel, it is easy at first, and later becomes more and more difficult. Again, *above* and *below,* with reference to the dreamer's brother, are reversed in the dream. This points to a relation of inversion or contrast between two parts of the material in the dream-thoughts, which indeed we found in them, for in the childish phantasy of the dreamer he is carried by his nurse, while in the novel, on the contrary, the hero carries his beloved. My dream of *Goethe's* attack on Herr M (to be cited later) likewise contains an inversion of this sort, which must be set right before the dream can be interpreted. In this dream, Goethe attacks a young man, Herr M; the reality, as contained in the dream-thoughts, is that an eminent man, a friend of mine, has been attacked by an unknown young author. In the dream I reckon time from the date of Goethe's death; in reality the reckoning was made from the year in which the paralytic was born. The thought which influences the dream-material reveals itself as my opposition to the treatment of Goethe as though he were a lunatic. "It is the other way about," says the dream; "if you don't understand the book it is you who are feeble-minded, not the author." All these dreams of inversion, moreover, seem to me to imply an allusion to the contemptuous phrase, "to turn one's back upon a person" (German: *einem die Kehrseite zeigen*, lit. to show a person one's backside): cf. the inversion in respect of the dreamer's brother in the Sappho dream. It is further worth noting how frequently inversion is employed in precisely those dreams which are inspired by repressed homosexual impulses.

Moreover, inversion, or transformation into the opposite, is one of the most favoured and most versatile methods of representation which the dream-work has at its disposal. It serves, in the first place, to enable the wish-fulfilment to prevail against a definite element of the dream-thoughts. "If only it were the other way about!" is often the best expression for the reaction of the ego against a disagreeable recollection. But inversion becomes extraordinarily useful in the service of the censorship, for it effects, in the material to be represented, a degree of distortion which at first simply paralyses our understanding of the dream. It is therefore always permissible, if a dream stubbornly refuses to surrender its meaning, to venture on the experimental inversion of definite portions of its manifest content. Then, not infrequently, everything becomes clear.

Besides the inversion of content, the temporal inversion must not be overlooked. A frequent device of dream-distortion consists in presenting the final issue of the event or the conclusion of the train of thought at the beginning of the dream, and appending at the end of the dream the premises of the conclusion, or the causes of the event. Anyone who forgets this technical device of dream-distortion stands helpless before the problem of dream-interpretation.[1]

---

[1] The hysterical attack often employs the same device of temporal inversion in order to conceal its meaning from the observer. The attack of a hysterical girl, for example, consists in enacting a little romance, which she has imagined in the unconscious in connection with an encounter in a tram. A man, attracted by the beauty of her foot, addresses her while she is reading, whereupon she goes with him and a passionate love-scene ensues. Her attack begins with the representation of this scene by writhing movements of the body (accompanied by movements of the lips and folding of the arms to signify kisses and embraces), whereupon she hurries into the next room, sits down on a chair, lifts her skirt in order to show her foot,

In many cases, indeed, we discover the meaning of the dream only when we have subjected the dream-content to a multiple inversion, in accordance with the different relations. For example, in the dream of a young patient who is suffering from obsessional neurosis, the memory of the childish death-wish directed against a dreaded father concealed itself behind the following words: *His father scolds him because he comes home so late,* but the context of the psycho-analytic treatment and the impressions of the dreamer show that the sentence must be read as follows: *He is angry with his father,* and further, that his father always *came home too early* (i.e., too soon). He would have preferred that his father should not come home at all, which is identical with the wish (see p. 245) that his father would die. As a little boy, during the prolonged absence of his father, the dreamer was guilty of a sexual aggression against another child, and was punished by the threat: "Just you wait until your father comes home!"

If we should seek to trace the relations between the dream-content and the dream-thoughts a little farther, we shall do this best by making the dream itself our point of departure, and asking ourselves: What do certain formal characteristics of the dream-presentation signify in relation to the dream-thoughts? First and foremost among the formal characteristics which are bound to impress us in dreams are the differences in the sensory intensity of the single dream-images, and in the distinctness of various parts of the dream, or of whole dreams as compared with one another. The differences in the intensity of individual dream-images cover the whole gamut, from a sharpness of definition which one is inclined—although without warrant—to rate more highly than that of reality, to a provoking indistinctness which we declare to be characteristic of dreams, because it really is not wholly comparable to any of the degrees of indistinctness which we occasionally perceive in real objects. Moreover, we usually describe the impression which we receive of an indistinct object in a dream as *fleeting*, while we think of the more distinct dream-images as having been perceptible also for a longer period of time. We must now ask ourselves by what conditions in the

---

acts as though she were about to read a book, and speaks to me (answers me). Cf. the observation of Artemidorus: "In interpreting dream-stories, one must consider them the first time from the beginning to the end, and the second time from the end to the beginning."

dream-material these differences in the distinctness of the individual portions of the dream-content are brought about.

Before proceeding farther, it is necessary to deal with certain expectations which seem to be almost inevitable. Since actual sensations experienced during sleep may constitute part of the dream-material, it will probably be assumed that these sensations, or the dream-elements resulting from them, are emphasized by a special intensity, or conversely, that anything which is particularly vivid in the dream can probably be traced to such real sensations during sleep. My experience, however, has never confirmed this. It is not true that those elements of a dream which are derivatives of real impressions perceived in sleep (nerve stimuli) are distinguished by their special vividness from others which are based on memories. The factor of reality is inoperative in determining the intensity of dream-images.

Further, it might be expected that the sensory intensity (vividness) of single dream-images is in proportion to the psychic intensity of the elements corresponding to them in the dream-thoughts. In the latter, intensity is identical with psychic value; the most intense elements are in fact the most significant, and these constitute the central point of the dream-thoughts. We know, however, that it is precisely these elements which are usually not admitted to the dream-content, owing to the vigilance of the censorship. Still, it might be possible for their most immediate derivatives, which represent them in the dream, to reach a higher degree of intensity without, however, for that reason constituting the central point of the dream-representation. This assumption also vanishes as soon as we compare the dream and the dream-material. The intensity of the elements in the one has nothing to do with the intensity of the elements in the other; as a matter of fact, a complete *transvaluation of all psychic values* takes place between the dream-material and the dream. The very element of the dream which is transient and hazy, and screened by more vigorous images, is often discovered to be the one and only direct derivative of the topic that completely dominates the dream-thoughts.

The intensity of the dream-elements proves to be determined in a different manner: that is by two factors which are mutually independent. It will readily be understood that those elements by means of which the wish-fulfilment expresses itself are those which are intensely represented. But analysis tells us that from the most vivid elements of the dream the greatest number of trains of thought proceed, and that those which are most vivid are at the same time those which are best determined. No change of meaning is involved if we express this latter empirical proposition in the following formula: The greatest intensity is shown by those elements of the dream for whose formation the most extensive *condensation-work* was required. We may, therefore, expect that it will be possible to express this condition, as well as the other condition of the wish-fulfilment, in a single formula.

I must utter a warning that the problem which I have just been considering—the causes of the greater or lesser intensity or distinctness of single elements in dreams—is not to be confounded with the other problem—that of variations in the distinctness of whole dreams or sections of dreams. In the former case the opposite of distinctness is haziness; in the latter, confusion. It is, of course, undeniable that in both scales the two kinds of intensities rise and fall in unison. A portion of the dream which seems clear to us usually contains vivid elements; an obscure dream, on the contrary, is composed of less vivid elements. But the problem offered by the scale of definition, which ranges from the apparently clear to the indistinct or confused, is far more complicated than the problem of fluctuations in vividness of the dream-elements. For reasons which will be given later, the former cannot at this stage be further discussed. In isolated cases one observes, not without surprise, that the impression of distinctness or indistinctness produced by a dream has nothing to do with the dream-structure, but proceeds from the dream-material, as one of its ingredients. Thus, for example, I remember a dream which on waking seemed so particularly well-constructed, flawless and clear that I made up my mind, while I was still in a somnolent state, to admit a new category of dreams—those which had not been subject to the mechanism of condensation and distortion, and which might thus be described as *phantasies during sleep.* A closer examination, however, proved that this unusual dream suffered from the same structural flaws and breaches as exist in all other dreams; so I abandoned the idea of a category of dream-phantasies.[1] The content of the dream, reduced to its lowest terms, was that I was expounding to a friend a difficult

---

[1] I do not know today whether I was justified in doing so.

and long-sought theory of bisexuality, and the wish-fulfilling power of the dream was responsible for the fact that this theory (which, by the way, was not communicated in the dream) appeared to be so lucid and flawless. Thus, what I believed to be a judgment as regards the finished dream was a part, and indeed the most essential part, of the dream-content. Here the dream-work reached out, as it were, into my first waking thoughts, and presented to me, in the form of a *judgment* of the dream, that part of the dream-material which it had failed to represent with precision in the dream. I was once confronted with the exact counterpart of this case by a female patient who at first absolutely declined to relate a dream which was necessary for the analysis "because it was so hazy and confused," and who finally declared, after repeatedly protesting the inaccuracy of her description, that it seemed to her that several persons—herself, her husband, and her father—had occurred in the dream, and that she had not known whether her husband was her father, or who really was her father, or something of that sort. Comparison of this dream with the ideas which occurred to the dreamer in the course of the sitting showed beyond a doubt that it dealt with the rather commonplace story of a maidservant who has to confess that she is expecting a child, and hears doubts expressed as to "who the father really is."[1] The obscurity manifested by this dream, therefore, was once more a portion of the dream-exciting material. A fragment of this material was represented in the *form* of the dream. *The form of the dream or of dreaming is employed with astonishing frequency to represent the concealed content.*

Glosses on the dream, and seemingly harmless comments on it, often serve in the most subtle manner to conceal—although, of course, they really betray—a part of what is dreamed. As, for example, when the dreamer says: *Here the dream was wiped out,* and the analysis gives an infantile reminiscence of listening to someone cleaning himself after defecation. Or another example, which deserves to be recorded in detail: A young man has a very distinct dream, reminding him of phantasies of his boyhood which have remained conscious. He found himself in a hotel at a seasonal resort; it was night; he mistook the number of his room, and entered a room in which an elderly lady and her two

daughters were undressing to go to bed. He continues: "*Then there are some gaps in the dream;* something is missing; and at the end there was a man in the room, who wanted to throw me out, and with whom I had to struggle." He tries in vain to recall the content and intention of the boyish phantasy to which the dream obviously alluded. But we finally become aware that the required content had already been given in his remarks concerning the indistinct part of the dream. The *gaps* are the genital apertures of the women who are going to bed: *Here something is missing* describes the principal characteristic of the female genitals. In his young days he burned with curiosity to see the female genitals, and was still inclined to adhere to the infantile sexual theory which attributes a male organ to women.

A very similar form was assumed in an analogous reminiscence of another dreamer. He dreamed: *I go with Fräulein K into the restaurant of the Volksgarten . . . then comes a dark place, an interruption . . . then I find myself in the salon of a brothel, where I see two or three women, one in a chemise and drawers.*

Analysis. Fräulein K is the daughter of his former employer; as he himself admits, she was a sister-substitute. He rarely had the opportunity of talking to her, but they once had a conversation in which "one recognized one's sexuality, so to speak, as though one were to say: I am a man and you are a woman." He had been only once to the above-mentioned restaurant, when he was accompanied by the sister of his brother-in-law, a girl to whom he was quite indifferent. On another occasion he accompanied three ladies to the door of the restaurant. The ladies were his sister, his sister-in-law, and the girl already mentioned. He was perfectly indifferent to all three of them, but they all belonged to the *sister category.* He had visited a brothel but rarely, perhaps two or three times in his life.

The interpretation is based on the *dark place,* the *interruption* in the dream, and informs us that on occasion, but in fact only rarely, obsessed by his boyish curiosity, he had inspected the genitals of his sister, a few years his junior. A few days later the misdemeanor indicated in the dream recurred to his conscious memory.

All dreams of the same night belong, in respect of their content, to the same whole; their division into several parts, their grouping and number, are all full of meaning and may be regarded as pieces of information about the latent dream-thoughts. In the interpretation of dreams

---

[1] Accompanying hysterical symptoms; amenorrhoea and profound depression were the chief troubles of this patient.

consisting of several main sections, or of dreams belonging to the same night, we must not overlook the possibility that these different and successive dreams mean the same thing, expressing the same impulses in different material. That one of these homologous dreams which comes first in time is usually the most distorted and most bashful, while the next dream is bolder and more distinct.

Even Pharaoh's dream of the ears and the kine, which Joseph interpreted, was of this kind. It is given by Josephus in greater detail than in the Bible. After relating the first dream, the King said: "After I had seen this vision I awaked out of my sleep, and, being in disorder, and considering with myself what this appearance should be, I fell asleep again, and saw another dream much more wonderful than the foregoing, which still did more affright and disturb me." After listening to the relation of the dream, Joseph said: "This dream, O King, although seen under two forms, signifies one and the same event of things."[1]

Jung, in his *Beitrag zur Psychologie des Gerüchtes,* relates how a veiled erotic dream of a schoolgirl was understood by her friends without interpretation, and continued by them with variations, and he remarks, with reference to one of these narrated dreams, that "the concluding idea of a long series of dream-images had precisely the same content as the first image of the series had endeavoured to represent. The censorship thrust the complex out of the way as long as possible by a constant renewal of symbolic screenings, displacements, transformations into something harmless, etc." Scherner was well acquainted with this peculiarity of dream-representation, and describes it in his *Leben des Traumes* (p. 166) in terms of a special law in the Appendix to his doctrine of organic stimulation: "But finally, in all symbolic dream-formations emanating from definite nerve stimuli, the phantasy observes the general law that at the beginning of the dream it depicts the stimulating object only by the remotest and freest allusions, but towards the end, when the graphic impulse becomes exhausted, the stimulus itself is nakedly represented by its appropriate organ or its function; whereupon the dream, itself describing its organic motive, achieves its end. . . ."

A pretty confirmation of this law of Scherner's has been furnished by Otto Rank in his essay: *Ein Traum, der sich selbst deutet.* This dream, related to him by a girl, consisted of two dreams of the same night, separated by an interval of time, the second of which ended with an orgasm. It was possible to interpret this orgastic dream in detail in spite of the few ideas contributed by the dreamer, and the wealth of relations between the two dream-contents made it possible to recognize that the first dream expressed in modest language the same thing as the second, so that the latter—the orgastic dream—facilitated a full explanation of the former. From this example, Rank very justifiably argues the significance of orgastic dreams for the theory of dreams in general.

But, in my experience, it is only in rare cases that one is in a position to translate the lucidity or confusion of a dream, respectively, into a certainty or doubt in the dream-material. Later on I shall have to disclose a hitherto unmentioned factor in dream-formation, upon whose operation this qualitative scale in dreams is essentially dependent.

In many dreams in which a certain situation and environment are preserved for some time, there occur interruptions which may be described in the following words: "But then it seemed as though it were, at the same time, another place, and there such and such a thing happened." In these cases, what interrupts the main action of the dream, which after a while may be continued again, reveals itself in the dream-material as a subordinate clause, an interpolated thought. *Conditionality* in the dream-thoughts is represented by simultaneity in the dream-content (*wenn or wann=if* or *when, while*).

We may now ask: What is the meaning of the sensation of inhibited movement which so often occurs in dreams, and is so closely allied to anxiety? One wants to move, and is unable to stir from the spot; or wants to accomplish something, and encounters obstacle after obstacle. The train is about to start, and one cannot reach it; one's hand is raised to avenge an insult, and its strength fails, etc. We have already met with this sensation in exhibition-dreams, but have as yet made no serious attempt to interpret it. It is convenient, but inadequate, to answer that there is motor paralysis in sleep, which manifests itself by means of the sensation alluded to. We may ask: Why is it, then, that we do not dream continually of such inhibited movements? And we may permissibly suspect that this sensation, which may at any time occur during sleep, serves some

---

[1] Josephus; *Antiquities of the Jews,* book. II, chap. v, trans. by Wm. Whiston (David McKay, Philadelphia).

sort of purpose for representation, and is evoked only when the need of this representation is present in the dream-material.

Inability to do a thing does not always appear in the dream as a sensation; it may appear simply as part of the dream-content. I think one case of this kind is especially fitted to enlighten us as to the meaning of this peculiarity. I shall give an abridged version of a dream in which I seem to be accused of dishonesty. *The scene is a mixture made up of a private sanatorium and several other places. A manservant appears, to summon me to an inquiry. I know in the dream that something has been missed, and that the inquiry is taking place because I am suspected of having appropriated the lost article. Analysis shows that inquiry is to be taken in two senses; it includes the meaning of medical examination. Being conscious of my innocence, and my position as consultant in this sanatorium, I calmly follow the manservant. We are received at the door by another manservant, who says, pointing at me, "Have you brought him? Why, he is a respectable man." Thereupon, and unattended, I enter a great hall where there are many machines, which reminds me of an inferno with its hellish instruments of punishment. I see a colleague strapped to an appliance; he has every reason to be interested in my appearance, but he takes no notice of me. I understand that I may now go. Then I cannot find my hat, and cannot go after all.*

The wish that the dream fulfils is obviously the wish that my honesty shall be acknowledged, and that I may be permitted to go; there must therefore be all sorts of material in the dream-thoughts which comprise a contradiction of this wish. The fact that I may go is the sign of my absolution; if, then, the dream provides at its close an event which prevents me from going, we may readily conclude that the suppressed material of the contradiction is asserting itself in this feature. The fact that I cannot find my hat therefore means: "You are not after all an honest man." The inability to do something in the dream is *the expression of a contradiction, a No;* so that our earlier assertion, to the effect that the dream is not capable of expressing a negation, must be revised accordingly.[1]

In other dreams in which the inability to do something occurs, not merely as a situation, but also as a sensation, the same contradiction is more emphatically expressed by the sensation of inhibited movement, or a will to which a counter-will is opposed. Thus the sensation of inhibited movement represents a *conflict of will.* We shall see later on that this very motor paralysis during sleep is one of the fundamental conditions of the psychic process which functions during dreaming. Now an impulse which is conveyed to the motor system is none other than the will, and the fact that we are certain that the impulse will be inhibited in sleep makes the whole process extraordinarily well-adapted to the representation of a *will* towards something and of a *No* which opposes itself thereto. From my explanation of anxiety, it is easy to understand why the sensation of the inhibited will is so closely allied to anxiety, and why it is so often connected with it in dreams. Anxiety is a libidinal impulse which emanates from the unconscious and is inhibited by the preconscious.[2] Therefore, when a sensation of inhibition in the dream is accompanied by anxiety, the dream must be concerned with a volition which was at one time capable of arousing libido; there must be a sexual impulse.

As for the judgment which is often expressed during a dream: "Of course, it is only a dream," and the psychic force to which it may be ascribed, I shall discuss these questions later on. For the present I will merely say that they are intended to depreciate the importance of what is being dreamed. The interesting problem allied to this, as to what is meant if a certain content in the dream is characterized in the dream itself as having been dreamed—the riddle of a *dream within a dream*—has been solved in a similar sense by W. Stekel, by the analysis of some convincing examples. Here again the part of the dream dreamed is to be depreciated in value and robbed of its reality; that which the dreamer continues to dream after waking from the *dream within a dream* is what the dream-wish desires to put in place

---

[1] A reference to an experience of childhood emerges, in the complete analysis, through the following connecting-links: "The Moor has done his duty, the Moor can go." And then follows the waggish question: "How old is the Moor when he has done his duty?"—"A year, then he can go (walk)." (It is said that I came into the world with so much black curly hair that my young mother declared that I was a little Moor.) The fact that I cannot find my hat is an experience of the day which has been exploited in various senses. Our servant, who is a genius at stowing things away, had hidden the hat. A rejection of melancholy thoughts of death is concealed behind the conclusion of the dream: "I have not nearly done my duty yet; I cannot go yet." Birth and death together—as in the dream of Goethe and the paralytic, which was a little earlier in date.

[2] This theory is not in accordance with more recent views.

of the obliterated reality. It may therefore be assumed that the part dreamed contains the representation of the reality, the real memory, while, on the other hand, the continued dream contains the representation of what the dreamer merely wishes. The inclusion of a certain content in *a dream within a dream* is, therefore, equivalent to the wish that what has been characterized as a dream had never occurred. In other words: when a particular incident is represented by the dream-work in a dream, it signifies the strongest confirmation of the reality of this incident, the most emphatic *affirmation* of it. The dream-work utilizes the dream itself as a form of repudiation, and thereby confirms the theory that a dream is a wish-fulfilment.

D. *Regard for Representability*

We have hitherto been concerned with investigating the manner in which our dreams represent the relations between the dream-thoughts, but we have often extended our inquiry to the further question as to what alterations the dream-material itself undergoes for the purposes of dream-formation. We now know that the dream-material, after being stripped of a great many of its relations, is subjected to compression, while at the same time displacements of the intensity of its elements enforce a psychic transvaluation of this material. The displacements which we have considered were shown to be substitutions of one particular idea for another, in some way related to the original by its associations, and the displacements were made to facilitate the condensation, inasmuch as in this manner, instead of two elements, a common mean between them found its way into the dream. So far, no mention has been made of any other kind of displacement. But we learn from the analyses that displacement of another kind does occur, and that it manifests itself in *an exchange of the verbal expression* for the thought in question. In both cases we are dealing with a displacement along a chain of associations, but the same process takes place in different psychic spheres, and the result of this displacement in the one case is that one element is replaced by another, while in the other case an element exchanges its verbal shape for another.

This second kind of displacement occurring in dream-formation is not only of great theoretical interest, but also peculiarly well-fitted to explain the appearance of phantastic absurdity in which dreams disguise themselves. Displacement usually occurs in such a way that a colourless and abstract expression of the dream-thought is exchanged for one that is pictorial and concrete. The advantage, and along with it the purpose, of this substitution is obvious. Whatever is pictorial is *capable of representation* in dreams and can be fitted into a situation in which abstract expression would confront the dream-representation with difficulties not unlike those which would arise if a political leading article had to be represented in an illustrated journal. Not only the possibility of representation, but also the interests of condensation and of the censorship, may be furthered by this exchange. Once the abstractly expressed and unserviceable dream-thought is translated into pictorial language, those contacts and identities between this new expression and the rest of the dream-material which are required by the dream-work, and which it contrives whenever they are not available, are more readily provided, since in every language concrete terms, owing to their evolution, are richer in associations than are abstract terms. It may be imagined that a good part of the intermediate work in dream-formation, which seeks to reduce the separate dream-thoughts to the tersest and most unified expression in the dream, is effected in this manner, by fitting paraphrases of the various thoughts. The one thought whose mode of expression has perhaps been determined by other factors will therewith exert a distributive and selective influence on the expressions available for the others, and it may even do this from the very start, just as it would in the creative activity of a poet. When a poem is to be written in rhymed couplets, the second rhyming line is bound by two conditions: it must express the meaning allotted to it, and its expression must permit of a rhyme with the first line. The best poems are, of course, those in which one does not detect the effort to find a rhyme, and in which both thoughts have as a matter of course, by mutual induction, selected the verbal expression which, with a little subsequent adjustment, will permit of the rhyme.

In some cases the change of expression serves the purposes of dream-condensation more directly, in that it provides an arrangement of words which, being ambiguous, permits of the expression of more than one of the dream-thoughts. The whole range of verbal wit is thus made to serve the purpose of the dream-work. The part played by words in dream-formation ought not to surprise us. A word, as the point

of junction of a number of ideas, possesses, as
it were, a predestined ambiguity, and the neuroses (obsessions, phobias) take advantage of
the opportunities for condensation and disguise
afforded by words quite as eagerly as do
dreams.[1] That dream-distortion also profits by
this displacement of expression may be readily
demonstrated. It is indeed confusing if one ambiguous word is substituted for two with single
meanings, and the replacement of sober, everyday language by a plastic mode of expression
baffles our understanding, especially since a
dream never tells us whether the elements
presented by it are to be interpreted literally or
metaphorically, whether they refer to the
dream-material directly, or only by means of
interpolated expressions. Generally speaking,
in the interpretation of any element of a dream
it is doubtful whether it

(a) is to be accepted in the negative or the
    positive sense (contrast relation);
(b) is to be interpreted historically (as a
    memory);
(c) is symbolic; or whether
(d) its valuation is to be based upon its
    wording.

In spite of this versatility, we may say that the
representation effected by the dream-work,
*which was never even intended to be under-
stood*, does not impose upon the translator any
greater difficulties than those that the ancient
writers of hieroglyphics imposed upon their
readers.

I have already given several examples of
dream-representations which are held together
only by ambiguity of expression (*her mouth
opens without difficulty*, in the dream of Irma's
injection; *I cannot go yet after all*, in the last
dream related, etc.). I shall now cite a dream
in the analysis of which plastic representation
of the abstract thoughts plays a greater part.
The difference between such dream-interpretation and the interpretation by means of symbols
may nevertheless be clearly defined; in the
symbolic interpretation of dreams, the key to
the symbolism is selected arbitrarily by the
interpreter, while in our own cases of verbal disguise these keys are universally known and are
taken from established modes of speech. Provided one hits on the right idea on the right
occasion, one may solve dreams of this kind,
either completely or in part, independently of

any statements made by the dreamer.

A lady, a friend of mine, dreams: *She is at
the opera. It is a Wagnerian performance,
which has lasted until 7.45 in the morning. In
the stalls and pit there are tables, at which
people are eating and drinking. Her cousin and
his young wife, who have just returned from
their honeymoon, are sitting at one of these
tables; beside them is a member of the aristocracy. The young wife is said to have brought
him back with her from the honeymoon quite
openly, just as she might have brought back a
hat. In the middle of the stalls there is a high
tower, on the top of which there is a platform
surrounded by an iron railing. There, high overhead, stands the conductor, with the features of
Hans Richter, continually running round behind
the railing, perspiring terribly; and from this
position he is conducting the orchestra, which
is arranged round the base of the tower. She
herself is sitting in a box with a friend of her
own sex (known to me). Her younger sister
tries to hand her up, from the stalls, a large
lump of coal, alleging that she had not known
that it would be so long, and that she must by
this time be miserably cold. (As though the
boxes ought to have been heated during the
long performance.)*

Although in other respects the dream gives
a good picture of the situation, it is, of course,
nonsensical enough: the tower in the middle
of the stalls, from which the conductor leads
the orchestra, and above all the coal which her
sister hands up to her. I purposely asked for
no analysis of this dream. With some knowledge of the personal relations of the dreamer,
I was able to interpret parts of it independently of her. I knew that she had felt intense sympathy for a musician whose career had been
prematurely brought to an end by insanity. I
therefore decided to take the tower in the stalls
verbally. It then emerged that the man whom
she wished to see in the place of Hans Richter
towered above all the other members of the
orchestra. This tower must be described as a
composite formation by means of apposition;
by its substructure it represents the greatness
of the man, but by the railing at the top, behind which he runs round like a prisoner or an
animal in a cage (an allusion to the name of
the unfortunate man),[2] it represents his later
fate. *Lunatic-tower* is perhaps the expression
in which the two thoughts might have met.

Now that we have discovered the dream's
method of representation, we may try, with

[1] Compare *Wit and its Relation to the Unconscious.*

[2] Hugo Wolf.

the same key, to unlock the meaning of the second apparent absurdity, that of the coal which her sister hands up to the dreamer. *Coal* should mean *secret love.*

No fire, no coal so hotly glows
As the secret love of which no one knows.

She and her friend *remain seated*[1] while her younger sister, who still has a prospect of marrying, hands her up the coal because she did not know *that it would be so long.* What would be so long is not told in the dream. If it were an anecdote, we should say *the performance;* but in the dream we may consider the sentence as it is. declare it to be ambiguous, and add *before she married.* The interpretation *secret love* is then confirmed by the mention of the cousin who is sitting with his wife in the stalls, and by the *open love-affair* attributed to the latter. The contrasts between secret and open love, between the dreamer's fire and the coldness of the young wife, dominate the dream. Moreover, here once again there is a person *in a high position* as a middle term between the aristocrat and the musician who is justified in raising high hopes.

In the above analysis we have at last brought to light a third factor, whose part in the transformation of the dream-thoughts into the dream-content is by no means trivial: namely, consideration of the *suitability of the dream-thoughts for representation in the particular psychic material of which the dream makes use*—that is, for the most part in visual images. Among the various subordinate ideas associated with the essential dream-thoughts, those will be preferred which permit of visual representation, and the dream-work does not hesitate to recast the intractable thoughts into another verbal form, even though this is a more unusual form, provided it makes representation possible, and thus puts an end to the psychological distress caused by strangulated thinking. This pouring of the thought-content into another mould may at the same time serve the work of condensation, and may establish relations with another thought which otherwise would not have been established. It is even possible that this second thought may itself have previously changed its original expression for the purpose of meeting the first one halfway.

Herbert Silberer[2] has described a good meth-od of directly observing the transformation of thoughts into images which occurs in dream-formation, and has thus made it possible to study in isolation this one factor of the dream-work. If, while in a state of fatigue and somnolence, he imposed upon himself a mental effort, it frequently happened that the thought escaped him, and in its place there appeared a picture in which he could recognize the substitute for the thought. Not quite appropriately, Silberer described this substitution as *autosymbolic.* I shall cite here a few examples from Silberer's work, and on account of certain peculiarities of the phenomena observed I shall refer to the subject later on.

"*Example* 1. I remember that I have to correct a halting passage in an essay.

"*Symbol.* I see myself planing a piece of wood.

"*Example* 5. I endeavour to call to mind the aim of certain metaphysical studies which I am proposing to undertake.

"This aim, I reflect, consists in working one's way through, while seeking for the basis of existence, to ever higher forms of consciousness or levels of being.

"*Symbol.* I run a long knife under a cake as though to take a slice out of it.

"*Interpretation.* My movement with the knife signifies *working one's way through.* . . . The explanation of the basis of the symbolism is as follows: At table it devolves upon me now and again to cut and distribute a cake, a business which I perform with a long, flexible knife, and which necessitates a certain amount of care. In particular, the neat extraction of the cut slices of cake presents a certain amount of difficulty; the knife must be carefully pushed *under* the slices in question (the slow *working one's way through* in order to get to the bottom). But there is yet more symbolism in the picture. The cake of the symbol was really a *dobos-cake*—that is, a cake in which the knife has to cut through several *layers* (the levels of consciousness and thought).

"*Example* 9. I lost the thread in a train of thought. I make an effort to find it again, but I have to recognize that the point of departure has completely escaped me.

"*Symbol.* Part of a form of type, the last lines of which have fallen out."

In view of the part played by witticisms, puns, quotations, songs, and proverbs in the intellectual life of educated persons, it would be entirely in accordance with our expectations to

---

[1] The German *sitzen geblieben* is often applied to women who have not succeeded in getting married.—TR.

[2] Bleuler-Freud *Jahrbuch,* i (1909).

find disguises of this sort used with extreme frequency in the representation of the dream-thoughts. Only in the case of a few types of material has a generally valid dream-symbolism established itself on the basis of generally known allusions and verbal equivalents. A good part of this symbolism, however, is common to the psychoneuroses, legends, and popular usages as well as to dreams.

In fact, if we look more closely into the matter, we must recognize that in employing this kind of substitution the dream-work is doing nothing at all original. For the achievement of its purpose, which in this case is representation without interference from the censorship, it simply follows the paths which it finds already marked out in unconscious thinking, and gives the preference to those transformations of the repressed material which are permitted to become conscious also in the form of witticisms and allusions, and with which all the phantasies of neurotics are replete. Here we suddenly begin to understand the dream-interpretations of Scherner, whose essential correctness I have vindicated elsewhere. The preoccupation of the imagination with one's own body is by no means peculiar to or characteristic of the dream alone. My analyses have shown me that it is constantly found in the unconscious thinking of neurotics, and may be traced back to sexual curiosity, whose object, in the adolescent youth or maiden, is the genitals of the opposite sex, or even of the same sex. But, as Scherner and Volkelt very truly insist, the house does not constitute the only group of ideas which is employed for the symbolization of the body, either in dreams or in the unconscious phantasies of neurosis. To be sure, I know patients who have steadily adhered to an architectural symbolism for the body and the genitals (sexual interest, of course, extends far beyond the region of the external genital organs)—patients for whom posts and pillars signify legs (as in the Song of Songs), to whom every door suggests a bodily aperture (hole), and every water-pipe the urinary system, and so on. But the groups of ideas appertaining to plant-life, or to the kitchen, are just as often chosen to conceal sexual images;[1] in respect of the former everyday language, the sediment of imaginative comparisons dating from the remotest times, has abundantly paved the way (the vineyard of the Lord, the seed of Abra-

ham, the garden of the maiden in the Song of Songs). The ugliest as well as the most intimate details of sexual life may be thought or dreamed of in apparently innocent allusions to culinary operations, and the symptoms of hysteria will become absolutely unintelligible if we forget that sexual symbolism may conceal itself behind the most commonplace and inconspicuous matters as its safest hiding-place. That some neurotic children cannot look at blood and raw meat, that they vomit at the sight of eggs and macaroni, and that the dread of snakes, which is natural to mankind, is monstrously exaggerated in neurotics—all this has a definite sexual meaning. Wherever the neurosis employs a disguise of this sort, it treads the paths once trodden by the whole of humanity in the early stages of civilization—paths to whose thinly veiled existence our idiomatic expressions, proverbs, superstitions, and customs testify to this day.

I here insert the promised *flower-dream* of a female patient, in which I shall print in Roman type everything which is to be sexually interpreted. This beautiful dream lost all its charm for the dreamer once it had been interpreted.

(a) Preliminary dream: *She goes to the two maids in the kitchen and scolds them for taking so long to prepare a little bite of food. She also sees a very large number of heavy kitchen utensils in the kitchen, heaped into piles and turned upside down in order to drain.* Later addition: *The two maids go to fetch water, and have, as it were, to climb into a river which reaches up to the house or into the courtyard.*[2]

(b) Main dream:[3] *She is descending from a height*[4] *over curiously constructed railings, or a fence which is composed of large square trellis-work hurdles with small square apertures.*[5] *It is really not adapted for climbing; she is constantly afraid that she cannot find a place for her foot, and she is glad that her dress doesn't get caught anywhere, and that she is able to climb it so respectably.*[6] *As she climbs*

---

[1] A mass of corroborative material may be found in the three supplementary volumes of Edward Fuchs's *Illustrierte Sittengeschichte;* privately printed by A. Lange, Munich.

[2] For the interpretation of this preliminary dream, which is to be regarded as *causal, see* p. 266.

[3] Her career.

[4] Exalted origin, the wish-contrast to the preliminary dream.

[5] A composite formation, which unites two localities, the so-called garret (German: *Boden*="floor," "garret") of her father's house, in which she used to play with her brother, the object of her later phantasies, and the farm of a malicious uncle, who used to tease her.

[6] Wish-contrast to an actual memory of her uncle's farm, to the effect that she used to expose herself while she was asleep.

she is carrying a big branch in her hand,[1] *really like a tree, which is thickly studded with red flowers; a spreading branch, with many twigs.*[2] *With this is connected the idea of cherry-blossoms* (Blüten=flowers), *but they look like fully opened camellias, which of course do not grow on trees. As she is descending, she first has one, then suddenly two, and then again only one.*[3] *When she has reached the ground the lower* flowers *have already begun to fall. Now that she has reached the bottom she sees an "odd man" who is combing—as she would like to put it—just such a tree, that is, with a piece of wood he is scraping* thick bunches of hair *from it, which hang from it like moss. Other men have chopped off such branches in a garden, and have flung them into the road, where they are lying about, so that* a number of people *take some of them. But she asks whether this is right, whether she may take one, too.*[4] *In the garden there stands a young* man (*he is a foreigner, and known to her*) *toward whom she goes in order to ask him how it is possible to transplant such* branches in her own garden.[5] *He embraces her, whereupon she struggles and asks him what he is thinking of, whether it is permissible to embrace her in such a manner. He says there is nothing wrong in it, that it is permitted.*[6] *He then declares himself willing to go with her into the* other garden, *in order to show her how to put them in, and he says something to her which she does not quite understand: "Besides this I need three* metres (*later she says: square metres) or three fathoms of ground." It seems as though he were asking her for something in return for his willingness, as though he had the intention of* indemnifying (reimbursing) *himself in her garden, as though he wanted to* evade *some law or other, to derive some advantage from it without causing her an injury. She does not know whether or not he really shows her anything.*

The above dream, which has been given prominence on account of its symbolic elements, may be described as a *biographical*

[1] Just as the angel bears a lily-stem in the Annunciation.

[2] For the explanation of this composite formation, *see* p. 268; innocence, menstruation, *La Dame aux Camélias.*

[3] Referring to the plurality of the persons who serve her phantasies.

[4] Whether it is permissible to masturbate. [*Sich einen herunterreissen* means "to pull off" and colloquially "to masturbate."—Tr.]

[5] The branch (*Ast*) has long been used to represent the male organ, and, moreover, contains a very distinct allusion to the family name of the dreamer.

[6] Refers to matrimonial precautions, as does that which immediately follows.

dream. Such dreams occur frequently in psychoanalysis, but perhaps only rarely outside it.[7]

I have, of course, an abundance of such material, but to reproduce it here would lead us too far into the consideration of neurotic conditions. Everything points to the same conclusion, namely, that we need not assume that any special symbolizing activity of the psyche is operative in dream-formation; that, on the contrary, the dream makes use of such symbolizations as are to be found ready-made in unconscious thinking, since these, by reason of their ease of representation, and for the most part by reason of their being exempt from the censorship, satisfy more effectively the requirements of dream-formation.

E. *Representation in Dreams by Symbols: Some Further Typical Dreams*

The analysis of the last biographical dream shows that I recognized the symbolism in dreams from the very outset. But it was only little by little that I arrived at a full appreciation of its extent and significance, as the result of increasing experience, and under the influence of the works of W. Stekel, concerning which I may here fittingly say something.

This author, who has perhaps injured psychoanalysis as much as he has benefited it, produced a large number of novel symbolic translations, to which no credence was given at first, but most of which were later confirmed and had to be accepted. Stekel's services are in no way belittled by the remark that the sceptical reserve with which these symbols were received was not unjustified. For the examples upon which he based his interpretations were often unconvincing, and, moreover, he employed a method which must be rejected as scientifically unreliable. Stekel found his symbolic meanings by way of intuition, by virtue of his individual faculty of immediately understanding the symbols. But such an art cannot be generally assumed; its efficiency is immune from criticism, and its results have therefore no claim to credibility. It is as though one were to base one's diagnosis of infectious diseases on the olfactory impressions received beside the sick-bed, although of course there have been clinicians to whom the sense of smell—atrophied in most people—has been of greater service than to others, and who really have been able to diagnose a case of abdominal typhus by their sense of smell.

[7] An analogous *biographical* dream is recorded on p. 287, among the examples of dream symbolism.

The progressive experience of psycho-analysis has enabled us to discover patients who have displayed in a surprising degree this immediate understanding of dream-symbolism. Many of these patients suffered from dementia praecox, so that for a time there was an inclination to suspect that all dreamers with such an understanding of symbols were suffering from that disorder. But this did not prove to be the case; it is simply a question of a personal gift or idiosyncrasy without perceptible pathological significance.

When one has familiarized oneself with the extensive employment of symbolism for the representation of sexual material in dreams, one naturally asks oneself whether many of these symbols have not a permanently established meaning, like the signs in shorthand; and one even thinks of attempting to compile a new dream-book on the lines of the cipher method. In this connection it should be noted that symbolism does not appertain especially to dreams, but rather to the unconscious imagination, and particularly to that of the people, and it is to be found in a more developed condition in folklore, myths, legends, idiomatic phrases, proverbs, and the current witticisms of a people than in dreams. We should have, therefore, to go far beyond the province of dream-interpretation in order fully to investigate the meaning of symbolism, and to discuss the numerous problems—for the most part still unsolved—which are associated with the concept of the symbol.[1] We shall here confine ourselves to saying that representation by a symbol comes under the heading of the indirect representations, but that we are warned by all sorts of signs against indiscriminately classing symbolic representation with the other modes of indirect representation before we have clearly conceived its distinguishing characteristics. In a number of cases, the common quality shared by the symbol and the thing which it represents is obvious; in others, it is concealed; in these latter cases the choice of the symbol appears to be enigmatic. And these are the very cases that must be able to elucidate the ultimate meaning of the symbolic relation; they point to the fact that it is of a genetic nature. What is today

symbolically connected was probably united, in primitive times, by conceptual and linguistic identity.[2] The symbolic relationship seems to be a residue and reminder of a former identity. It may also be noted that in many cases the symbolic identity extends beyond the linguistic identity, as had already been asserted by Schubert (1814).[3]

Dreams employ this symbolism to give a disguised representation to their latent thoughts. Among the symbols thus employed there are, of course, many which constantly, or all but constantly, mean the same thing. But we must bear in mind the curious plasticity of psychic material. Often enough a symbol in the dream-content may have to be interpreted not symbolically but in accordance with its proper meaning; at other times the dreamer, having to deal with special memory-material, may take the law into his own hands and employ anything whatever as a sexual symbol, though it is not generally so employed. Wherever he has the choice of several symbols for the representation of a dream-content, he will decide in favour of that symbol which is in addition objectively related to his other thought-material; that is to say, he will employ an individual motivation besides the typically valid one.

Although since Scherner's time the more recent investigations of dream-problems have definitely established the existence of dream-symbolism—even Havelock Ellis acknowledges that our dreams are indubitably full of symbols—it must yet be admitted that the existence of symbols in dreams has not only facilitated dream-interpretation, but has also made it more difficult. The technique of interpretation in accordance with the dreamer's free associations more often than otherwise leaves us in the lurch as far as the symbolic elements of the dream-content are concerned. A return to the arbitrariness of dream-interpretation as it was

---

[1] Cf. the works of Bleuler and his Zürich disciples, Maeder, Abraham, and others, and of the non-medical authors (Kleinpaul and others) to whom they refer. But the most pertinent things that have been said on the subject will be found in the work of O. Rank and H. Sachs, *Die Bedeutung der Psychoanalyse für die Geisteswissenschaft*, (1913), chap. i; also E. Jones, *Die Theorie der Symbolik Intern. Zeitschr. für Psychoanalyse*, v. (1919).

[2] This conception would seem to find an extraordinary confirmation in a theory advanced by Hans Sperber (*"Uber den Einfluss sexueller momente auf Entstehung und Entwicklung der Sprache,"* in *Imago*, i. [1912]). Sperber believes that primitive words denoted sexual things exclusively, and subsequently lost their sexual significance and were applied to other things and activities, which were compared with the sexual.

[3] For example, a ship sailing on the sea may appear in the urinary dreams of Hungarian dreamers, despite the fact that the term of *to ship*, for *to urinate*, is foreign to this language (Ferenczi). In the dreams of the French and the other romance peoples *room* serves as a symbolic representation for *woman*, although these peoples have nothing analogous to the German *Frauenzimmer*. Many symbols are as old as language itself, while others are continually being coined (e.g., the aeroplane, the Zeppelin).

practised in antiquity, and is seemingly revived by Stekel's wild interpretations, is contrary to scientific method. Consequently, those elements in the dream-content which are to be symbolically regarded compel us to employ a combined technique, which on the one hand is based on the dreamer's associations, while on the other hand the missing portions have to be supplied by the interpreter's understanding of the symbols. Critical circumspection in the solution of the symbols must coincide with careful study of the symbols in especially transparent examples of dreams in order to silence the reproach of arbitrariness in dream-interpretation. The uncertainties which still adhere to our function as dream-interpreters are due partly to our imperfect knowledge (which, however, can be progressively increased) and partly to certain peculiarities of the dream-symbols themselves. These often possess many and varied meanings, so that, as in Chinese script, only the context can furnish the correct meaning. This multiple significance of the symbol is allied to the dream's faculty of admitting over-interpretations, of representing, in the same content, various wish-impulses and thought-formations, often of a widely divergent character.

After these limitations and reservations, I will proceed. The Emperor and the Empress (King and Queen)[1] in most cases really represent the dreamer's parents; the dreamer himself or herself is the prince or princess. But the high authority conceded to the Emperor is also conceded to great men, so that in some dreams, for example, Goethe appears as a father symbol (Hitschmann).—All elongated objects, sticks, tree-trunks, umbrellas (on account of the opening, which might be likened to an erection), all sharp and elongated weapons, knives, daggers, and pikes, represent the male member. A frequent, but not very intelligible symbol for the same is a nail-file (a reference to rubbing and scraping?).—Small boxes, chests, cupboards, and ovens correspond to the female organ; also cavities, ships, and all kinds of vessels.—A room in a dream generally represents a woman; the description of its various entrances and exits is scarcely calculated to make us doubt this interpretation.[2] The interest

as to whether the room is *open* or *locked* will be readily understood in this connection. (Cf. Dora's dream in *Fragment of an Analysis of Hysteria.*) There is no need to be explicit as to the sort of key that will unlock the room; the symbolism of *lock and key* has been gracefully if broadly employed by Uhland in his song of the *Graf Eberstein.*—The dream of walking through a suite of rooms signifies a brothel or a harem. But, as H. Sachs has shown by an admirable example, it is also employed to represent marriage (contrast). An interesting relation to the sexual investigations of childhood emerges when the dreamer dreams of two rooms which were previously one, or finds that a familiar room in a house of which he dreams has been divided into two, or the reverse. In childhood the female genitals and anus (the "behind")[3] are conceived of as a single opening according to the infantile cloaca theory, and only later is it discovered that this region of the body contains two separate cavities and openings. Steep inclines, ladders and stairs, and going up or down them, are symbolic representations of the sexual act.[4] Smooth walls over which one climbs, façades of houses, across which one lets oneself down—often with a sense of great anxiety—correspond to erect human bodies, and probably repeat in our dreams childish memories of climbing up parents or nurses. *Smooth* walls are men; in anxiety dreams one often holds firmly to *projections* on houses. Tables, whether bare or covered, and boards, are women, perhaps by virtue of contrast, since they have no protruding contours. *Wood* generally speaking, seems, in accordance with its linguistic relations, to represent feminine matter *(Materie).* The name of the island Madeira means wood in Portuguese. Since *bed and board (mensa et thorus)* constitute marriage, in dreams the latter is often substituted for the former, and as far as practicable the sexual representation-complex is transposed to the eating-complex.—Of ar-

---

fact, entered into relations with the girl in question, and has often had her in his bedroom. She feared, as may be imagined, that the landlady suspected her, and had proposed, on the day before the dream, that they should meet in one of the unoccupied rooms. In reality this room had the number 14, while in the dream the woman bore this number. A clearer proof of the identification of woman and room could hardly be imagined," (Ernest Jones, *Intern. Zeitschr. f. Psychoanalyse,* ii, [1914]). (Cf. Artemidorus, *The Symbolism of Dreams* [German version by F. S. Krauss, Vienna, 1881, p. 110]: "Thus, for example, the bedroom signifies the wife, supposing one to be in the house.")

[3] Cf. "the *cloaca* theory" in *Three Contributions to the Theory of Sex.*   [4] See p. 123-124 above.

---

[1] In the U.S.A. the father is represented in dreams as the President, and even more often as the Governor—a title which is frequently applied to the parent in everyday life.—TR.

[2] "A patient living in a boarding-house dreams that he meets one of the servants, and asks her what her number is; to his surprise she answers: 14. He has, in

ticles of dress, a woman's hat may very often be interpreted with certainty as the male genitals. In the dreams of men, one often finds the necktie as a symbol for the penis; this is not only because neckties hang down in front of the body, and are characteristic of men, but also because one can select them at pleasure, a freedom which nature prohibits as regards the original of the symbol. Persons who make use of this symbol in dreams are very extravagant in the matter of ties, and possess whole collections of them.[1] All complicated machines and appliances are very probably the genitals—as a rule the male genitals—in the description of which the symbolism of dreams is as indefatigable as human wit. It is quite unmistakable that all weapons and tools are used as symbols for the male organ: e.g., ploughshare, hammer, gun, revolver, dagger, sword, etc. Again, many of the landscapes seen in dreams, especially those that contain bridges or wooded mountains, may be readily recognized as descriptions of the genitals. Marcinowski collected a series of examples in which the dreamer explained his dream by means of drawings, in order to represent the landscapes and places appearing in it. These drawings clearly showed the distinction between the manifest and the latent meaning of the dream. Whereas, naïvely regarded, they seemed to represent plans, maps, and so forth, closer investigation showed that they were representations of the human body, of the genitals, etc., and only after conceiving them thus could the dream be understood.[2] Finally, where one finds incomprehensible neologisms one may suspect combinations of components having a sexual significance.—Children, too, often signify the genitals, since men and women are in the habit of fondly referring to their genital organs as *little man, little woman, little thing*. The *little brother* was correctly recognized by Stekel as the penis. To play with or to beat a little child is often the dream's representation of masturbation. The dream-work represents castration by baldness, hair-cutting, the loss of teeth, and beheading. As an insurance against castration, the dream uses one of the common

symbols of the penis in double or multiple form; and the appearance in a dream of a lizard—an animal whose tail, if pulled off, is regenerated by a new growth—has the same meaning. Most of those animals which are utilized as genital symbols in mythology and folklore play this part also in dreams: the fish, the snail, the cat, the mouse (on account of the hairiness of the genitals), but above all the snake, which is the most important symbol of the male member. Small animals and vermin are substitutes for little children, e.g., undesired sisters or brothers. To be infected with vermin is often the equivalent for pregnancy.—As a very recent symbol of the male organ I may mention the airship, whose employment is justified by its relation to flying, and also, occasionally, by its form.—Stekel has given a number of other symbols, not yet sufficiently verified, which he has illustrated by examples. The works of this author, and especially his book: *Die Sprache des Traumes,* contain the richest collection of interpretations of symbols, some of which were ingeniously guessed and were proved to be correct upon investigation, as, for example, in the section on the symbolism of death. The author's lack of critical reflection, and his tendency to generalize at all costs, make his interpretations doubtful or inapplicable, so that in making use of his works caution is urgently advised. I shall therefore restrict myself to mentioning a few examples.

Right and *left,* according to Stekel, are to be understood in dreams in an ethical sense. "The right-hand path always signifies the way to righteousness, the left-hand path the path to crime. Thus the left may signify homosexuality, incest, and perversion, while the right signifies marriage, relations with a prostitute, etc. The meaning is always determined by the individual moral standpoint of the dreamer" (loc. cit., p. 466). *Relatives* in dreams generally stand for the genitals (p. 473). Here I can confirm this meaning only for the son, the daughter, and the younger sister—that is, wherever *little thing* could be employed. On the other hand, verified examples allow us to recognize *sisters* as symbols of the breasts, and *brothers* as symbols of the larger hemispheres. To be unable to overtake a carriage is interpreted by Stekel as regret at being unable to catch up with a difference in age (p. 479). The *luggage* of a traveller is the burden of sin by which one is oppressed (*ibid.*) But a traveller's luggage often proves to be an unmistakable symbol

---

[1] Cf. in the *Zentralblatt für Psychoanalyse,* ii, 675, the drawing of a nineteen-year-old manic patient: a man with a snake as a neck-tie, which is turning towards a girl. Also the story *Der Schamhaftige (Anthropophyteia,* vi, 334): A woman entered a bathroom, and there came face to face with a man who hardly had time to put on his shirt. He was greatly embarrassed, but at once covered his throat with the front of his shirt, and said: "Please excuse me, I have no necktie."

[2] Cf. Pfister's works on cryptography and picture-puzzles.

of one's own genitals. To numbers, which frequently occur in dreams, Stekel has assigned a fixed symbolic meaning, but these interpretations seem neither sufficiently verified nor of universal validity, although in individual cases they can usually be recognized as plausible. We have, at all events, abundant confirmation that the figure three is a symbol of the male genitals. One of Stekel's generalizations refers to the double meaning of the genital symbols. "Where is there a symbol," he asks, "which (if in any way permitted by the imagination) may not be used simultaneously in the masculine and the feminine sense?" To be sure, the clause in parenthesis retracts much of the absolute character of this assertion, for this double meaning is not always permitted by the imagination. Still, I think it is not superfluous to state that in my experience this general statement of Stekel's requires elaboration. Besides those symbols which are just as frequently employed for the male as for the female genitals, there are others which preponderantly, or almost exclusively, designate one of the sexes, and there are yet others which, so far as we know, have only the male or only the female signification. To use long, stiff objects and weapons as symbols of the female genitals, or hollow objects (chests, boxes, etc.) as symbols of the male genitals, is certainly not permitted by the imagination.

It is true that the tendency of dreams, and of the unconscious phantasy, to employ the sexual symbols bisexually, reveals an archaic trait, for in childhood the difference in the genitals is unknown, and the same genitals are attributed to both sexes. One may also be misled as regards the significance of a bisexual symbol if one forgets the fact that in some dreams a general reversal of sexes takes place, so that the male organ is represented by the female, and vice versa. Such dreams express, for example, the wish of a woman to be a man.

The genitals may even be represented in dreams by other parts of the body: the male member by the hand or the foot, the female genital orifice by the mouth, the ear, or even the eye. The secretions of the human body—mucus, tears, urine, semen, etc.—may be used in dreams interchangeably. This statement of Stekel's, correct in the main, has suffered a justifiable critical restriction as the result of certain comments of R. Reitler's (*Internat. Zeitschr. für Psych.*, i, 1913). The gist of the matter is the replacement of an important secretion, such as the semen, by an indifferent one.

These very incomplete indications may suffice to stimulate others to make a more painstaking collection.[1] I have attempted a much more detailed account of dream-symbolism in my *General Introduction to Psycho-Analysis*.

I shall now append a few instances of the use of such symbols, which will show how impossible it is to arrive at the interpretation of a dream if one excludes dream-symbolism, but also how in many cases it is imperatively forced upon one. At the same time, I must expressly warn the investigator against overestimating the importance of symbols in the interpretation of dreams, restricting the work of dream-translation to the translation of symbols, and neglecting the technique of utilizing the associations of the dreamer. The two techniques of dream-interpretation must supplement one another; practically, however, as well as theoretically, precedence is retained by the latter process, which assigns the final significance to the utterances of the dreamer, while the symbol-translation which we undertake play an auxiliary part.

1. The hat as the symbol of a man (of the male genitals):[2] (A fragment from the dream of a young woman who suffered from agoraphobia as the result of her fear of temptation.)

I am walking in the street in summer; I am wearing a straw hat of peculiar shape, the middle piece of which is bent upwards, while the side pieces hang downwards (here the description hesitates), and in such a fashion that one hangs lower than the other. I am cheerful and in a confident mood, and as I pass a number of young officers I think to myself: You can't do anything to me.

As she could produce no associations to the hat, I said to her: "The hat is really a male genital organ, with its raised middle piece and the two downward-hanging side pieces." It is perhaps peculiar that her hat should be supposed to be a man, but after all one says: *Unter die Haube kommen* (to get under the cap) when we mean: *to get married.* I intentionally refrained from interpreting the details concerning the unequal dependence of the two side pieces, although the determination of just such details must point the way to the inter-

[1] In spite of all the differences between Scherner's conception of dream-symbolism and the one developed here, I must still insist that Scherner should be recognized as the true discoverer of symbolism in dreams, and that the experience of psycho-analysis has brought his book (published in 1861) into posthumous repute.
[2] From *"Nachträge zur Traumdeutung"* in *Zentralblatt für Psychoanalyse*, i, Nos. 5 and 6, (1911).

pretation. I went on to say that if, therefore, she had a husband with such splendid genitals she would not have to fear the officers; that is, she would have nothing to wish from them, for it was essentially her temptation-phantasies which prevented her from going about unprotected and unaccompanied. This last explanation of her anxiety I had already been able to give her repeatedly on the basis of other material.

It is quite remarkable how the dreamer behaved after this interpretation. She withdrew her description of the hat and would not admit that she had said that the two side pieces were hanging down. I was, however, too sure of what I had heard to allow myself to be misled, and so I insisted that she did say it. She was quiet for a while, and then found the courage to ask why it was that one of her husband's testicles was lower than the other, and whether it was the same with all men. With this the peculiar detail of the hat was explained, and the whole interpretation was accepted by her.

The hat symbol was familiar to me long before the patient related this dream. From other but less transparent cases I believed that I might assume the hat could also stand for the female genitals.[1]

2. The *little one* as the genital organ. Being run over as a symbol of sexual intercourse.

(Another dream of the same agoraphobic patient.)

Her mother sends away her little daughter so that she has to go alone. She then drives with her mother to the railway station, and sees her little one walking right along the track, so that she is bound to be run over. She hears the bones crack. (At this she experiences a feeling of discomfort but no real horror.) She then looks out through the carriage window, to see whether the parts cannot be seen behind. Then she reproaches her mother for allowing the little one to go out alone.

Analysis.—It is not an easy matter to give here a complete interpretation of the dream. It forms part of a cycle of dreams, and can be fully understood only in connection with the rest. For it is not easy to obtain the material necessary to demonstrate the symbolism in a sufficiently isolated condition. The patient at first finds that the railway journey is to be interpreted historically as an allusion to a de-

parture from a sanatorium for nervous diseases, with whose director she was, of course, in love. Her mother fetched her away, and before her departure the physician came to the railway station and gave her a bunch of flowers; she felt uncomfortable because her mother witnessed this attention. Here the mother, therefore, appears as the disturber of her tender feelings, a rôle actually played by this strict woman during her daughter's girlhood.—The next association referred to the sentence: *She then looks to see whether the parts cannot be seen behind.* In the dream-façade one would naturally be compelled to think of the pieces of the little daughter who had been run over and crushed. The association, however, turns in quite a different direction. She recalls that she once saw her father in the bath-room, naked, from behind; she then begins to talk about sex differences, and remarks that in the man the genitals can be seen from behind, but in the woman they cannot. In this connection she now herself offers the interpretation that *the little one* is the genital organ, and her little one (she has a four-year-old daughter) her own organ. She reproaches her mother for wanting her to live as though she had no genitals, and recognizes this reproach in the introductory sentence of the dream: the mother sends her little one away, so that she has to go alone. In her phantasy, going alone through the streets means having no man, no sexual relations *(coire* = to go together), and this she does not like. According to all her statements, she really suffered as a girl through her mother's jealousy, because her father showed a preference for her.

The deeper interpretation of this dream depends upon another dream of the same night, in which the dreamer identifies herself with her brother. She was a tomboy, and was always being told that she should have been born a boy. This identification with the brother shows with especial clearness that *the little one* signifies the genital organ. The mother threatened him (her) with castration, which could only be understood as a punishment for playing with the genital parts, and the identification, therefore, shows that she herself had masturbated as a child, though she had retained only a memory of her brother's having done so. An early knowledge of the male genitals, which she lost later, must, according to the assertions of this second dream, have been acquired at this time. Moreover, the second dream points to the infantile sexual theory that girls origi-

[1] Cf. Kirchgraber for a similar example (*Zentralblatt für Psychoanalyse*, iii, [1912], p. 95). Stekel reported a dream in which the hat with an obliquely-standing feather in the middle symbolized the (impotent) man.

nate from boys as a result of castration. After I had told her of this childish belief, she at once confirmed it by an anecdote in which the boy asks the girl: "Was it cut off?" to which the girl replies: "No, it's always been like that."

Consequently the sending away of *the little one,* of the genital organ, in the first dream refers also to the threatened castration. Finally, she blames her mother for not having borne her as a boy.

That *being run over* symbolizes sexual intercourse would not be evident from this dream if we had not learned it from many other sources.

3. Representation of the genitals by buildings, stairs, and shafts.

(Dream of a young man inhibited by a father complex.)

He is taking a walk with his father in a place which is certainly the Prater, for one can see the Rotunda, in front of which there is a small vestibule to which there is attached a captive balloon; the balloon, however, seems rather limp. His father asks him what this is all for; he is surprised at it, but he explains it to his father. They come into a courtyard in which lies a large sheet of tin. His father wants to pull off a big piece of this, but first looks round to see if anyone is watching. He tells his father that all he needs to do is to speak to the overseer, and then he can take as much as he wants to without any more ado. From this courtyard a flight of stairs leads down into a shaft, the walls of which are softly upholstered, rather like a leather arm-chair. At the end of this shaft there is a long platform, and then a new shaft begins...

Analysis. This dreamer belonged to a type of patient which is not at all promising from a therapeutic point of view; up to a certain point in the analysis such patients offer no resistance whatever, but from that point onwards they prove to be almost inaccessible. This dream he analysed almost independently. "The Rotunda," he said, "is my genitals, the captive balloon in front is my penis, about whose flaccidity I have been worried." We must, however, interpret it in greater detail: the Rotunda is the buttocks, constantly associated by the child with the genitals; the smaller structure in front is the scrotum. In the dream his father asks him what this is all for—that is, he asks him about the purpose and arrangement of the genitals. It is quite evident that this state of affairs should be reversed, and that

he ought to be the questioner. As such questioning on the part of the father never occurred in reality, we must conceive the dream-thought as a wish, or perhaps take it conditionally, as follows. "If I had asked my father for sexual enlightenment . . . " The continuation of this thought we shall presently find in another place.

The courtyard in which the sheet of tin is spread out is not to be conceived symbolically in the first instance, but originates from his father's place of business. For reasons of discretion I have inserted the tin for another material in which the father deals without, however, changing anything in the verbal expression of the dream. The dreamer had entered his father's business, and had taken a terrible dislike to the somewhat questionable practices upon which its profit mainly depended. Hence the continuation of the above dream-thought ("if I had asked him") would be: "He would have deceived me just as he does his customers." for the *pulling off,* which serves to represent commercial dishonesty, the dreamer himself gives a second explanation, namely, masturbation. This is not only quite familiar to us (see above, p. 281), but agrees very well with the fact that the secrecy of masturbation is expressed by its opposite (one can do it quite openly). Thus, it agrees entirely with our expectations that the autoerotic activity should be attributed to the father, just as was the questioning in the first scene of the dream. The shaft he at once interprets as the vagina, by referring to the soft upholstering of the walls. That the action of coition in the vagina is described as a going down instead of in the usual way as a going up agrees with what I have found in other instances.[1]

The details—that at the end of the first shaft there is a long platform, and then a new shaft—he himself explains biographically. He had for some time had sexual intercourse with women, but had given it up on account of inhibitions, and now hopes to be able to begin it again with the aid of treatment. The dream, however, becomes indistinct towards the end, and to the experienced interpreter it becomes evident that in the second scene of the dream the influence of another subject has already begun to assert itself; which is indicated by his father's business, his dishonest practices, and the vagina represented by the first shaft, so that one may assume a reference to his mother.

[1] Cf. comment in the *Zentralblatt für Psychoanalyse,* i; and *see* above, p. 281. note 4.

4. The male organ symbolized by persons and the female by a landscape.

(Dream of a woman of the lower class, whose husband is a policeman, reported by B. Dattner.)

. . . Then someone broke into the house and she anxiously called for a policeman. But he went peacefully with two tramps into a church,[1] to which a great many steps led up,[2] behind the church there was a mountain[3] on top of which there was a dense forest.[4] The policeman was provided with a helmet, a gorget, and a cloak.[5] The two vagrants, who went along with the policeman quite peaceably, had sack-like aprons tied round their loins.[6] A road led from the church to the mountain. This road was overgrown on each side with grass and brushwood, which became thicker and thicker as it reached the top of the mountain, where it spread out into quite a forest.

5. Castration dreams of children.

(a) *A boy aged three years and five months, for whom his father's return from military service is clearly inconvenient, wakes one morning in a disturbed and excited state, and constantly repeats the question: Why did Daddy carry his head on a plate? Last night Daddy carried his head on a plate.*

(b) *A student who is now suffering from a severe obsessional neurosis remembers that in his sixth year he repeatedly had the following dream: He goes to the barber to have his hair cut. Then a large woman with severe features comes up to him and cuts off his head. He recognizes the woman as his mother.*

6. A modified staircase dream.

To one of my patients, a sexual abstainer, who was very ill, whose phantasy was fixated upon his mother, and who repeatedly dreamed of climbing stairs while accompanied by his mother, I once remarked that moderate masturbation would probably have been less harmful to him than his enforced abstinence. The influence of this remark provoked the following dream:

His piano teacher reproaches him for neglecting his piano-playing, and for not practicing the Etudes *of Moscheles and Clementi's* Gradus ad Parnassum. With reference to this he remarked that the *Gradus,* too, is a stair-

---

[1] Or Chapel=vagina.
[2] Symbol of coitus.
[3] Mons Veneris.
[4] Crines pubis.
[5] Demons in cloaks and hoods are, according to the explanation of a specialist, of a phallic character.
[6] The two halves of the scrotum.

way, and that the piano itself is a stairway, as it has a scale.

It may be said that there is no class of ideas which cannot be enlisted in the representation of sexual facts and wishes.

7. The sensation of reality and the representation of repetition.

A man, now thirty-five, relates a clearly remembered dream which he claims to have had when he was four years of age: *The notary with whom his father's will was deposited—* he had lost his father at the age of three— *brought two large Emperor-pears, of which he was given one to eat. The other lay on the window-sill of the living-room.* He woke with the conviction of the reality of what he had dreamt, and obstinately asked his mother to give him the second pear; it was, he said, still lying on the window-sill. His mother laughed at this.

Analysis. The notary was a jovial old gentleman who, as he seems to remember, really sometimes brought pears with him. The window-sill was as he saw it in the dream. Nothing else occurs to him in this connection, except, perhaps, that his mother has recently told him a dream. She has two birds sitting on her head; she wonders when they will fly away, but they do not fly away, and one of them flies to her mouth and sucks at it.

The dreamer's inability to furnish associations justifies the attempt to interpret it by the substitution of symbols. The two pears— *pommes ou poires*—are the breasts of the mother who nursed him; the window-sill is the projection of the bosom, analogous to the balconies in the dream of houses. His sensation of reality after waking is justified, for his mother had actually suckled him for much longer than the customary term, and her breast was still available. The dream is to be translated: "Mother, give (show) me the breast again at which I once used to drink." The *once* is represented by the eating of the one pear, the *again* by the desire for the other. *The temporal repetition of an act is habitually represented in dreams by the numerical multiplication of an object.*

It is naturally a very striking phenomenon that symbolism should already play a part in the dream of a child of four, but this is the rule rather than the exception. One may say that the dreamer has command of symbolism from the very first.

The early age at which people make use of symbolic representation, even apart from the dream-life, may be shown by the following uninfluenced memory of a lady who is now twenty-seven: *She is in her fourth year. The nursemaid is driving her, with her brother, eleven months younger, and a cousin, who is between the two in age, to the lavatory, so that they can do their little business there before going for their walk. As the oldest, she sits on the seat and the other two on chambers. She asks her (female) cousin: Have you a purse, too? Walter has a little sausage, I have a purse. The cousin answers: Yes, I have a purse, too. The nursemaid listens, laughing, and relates the conversation to the mother, whose reaction is a sharp reprimand.*

Here a dream may be inserted whose excellent symbolism permitted of interpretation with little assistance from the dreamer:

8. The question of symbolism in the dreams of normal persons.[1]

An objection frequently raised by the opponents of psycho-analysis—and recently also by Havelock Ellis[2]—is that, although dream-symbolism may perhaps be a product of the neurotic psyche, it has no validity whatever in the case of normal persons. But while psycho-analysis recognizes no essential distinctions, but only quantitative differences, between the psychic life of the normal person and that of the neurotic, the analysis of those dreams in which, in sound and sick persons alike, the repressed complexes display the same activity, reveals the absolute identity of the mechanisms as well as of the symbolism. Indeed, the natural dreams of healthy persons often contain a much simpler, more transparent, and more characteristic symbolism than those of neurotics, which, owing to the greater strictness of the censorship and the more extensive dream-distortion resulting therefrom, are frequently troubled and obscured, and are therefore more difficult to translate. The following dream serves to illustrate this fact. This dream comes from a non-neurotic girl of a rather prudish and reserved type. In the course of conversation I found that she was engaged to be married, but that there were hinderances in the way of the marriage which threatened to postpone it. She related spontaneously the following dream:

I arrange the centre of a table with flowers for a birthday. On being questioned she states that in the dream she seemed to be at home

(she has no home at the time) and experienced a feeling of happiness.

The *popular* symbolism enables me to translate the dream for myself. It is the expression of her wish to be married: the table, with the flowers in the centre, is symbolic of herself and her genitals. She represents her future wishes as fulfilled, inasmuch as she is already occupied with the thoughts of the birth of a child; so the wedding has taken place long ago.

I call her attention to the fact that *the centre of a table* is an unusual expression, which she admits; but here, of course, I cannot question her more directly. I carefully refrain from suggesting to her the meaning of the symbols, and ask her only for the thoughts which occur to her mind in connection with the individual parts of the dream. In the course of the analysis her reserve gave way to a distinct interest in the interpretation, and a frankness which was made possible by the serious tone of the conversation. To my question as to what kind of flowers they had been, her first answer is: *expensive flowers; one has to pay for them;* then she adds that they were *lilies-of-the-valley, violets, and pinks or carnations.* I took the word *lily* in this dream in its popular sense, as a symbol of chastity; she confirmed this, as purity occurred to her in association with *lily. Valley* is a common feminine dream-symbol. The chance juxtaposition of the two symbols in the name of the flower is made into a piece of dream-symbolism, and serves to emphasize the preciousness of her virginity—*expensive flowers; one has to pay for them*—and expresses the expectation that her husband will know how to appreciate its value. The comment, *expensive flowers,* etc. has, as will be shown, a different meaning in every one of the three different flower-symbols.

I thought of what seemed to me a venture-some explanation of the hidden meaning of the apparently quite asexual word *violets* by an unconscious relation to the French *viol.* But to my surprise the dreamer's association was the English word *violate.* The accidental phonetic similarity of the two words *violet* and *violate* is utilized by the dream to express in *the language of flowers* the idea of the violence of defloration (another word which makes use of flower-symbolism), and perhaps also to give expression to a masochistic tendency on the part of the girl. An excellent example of the word bridges across which run the paths to the

---

[1] Alfred Robitsek in the *Zentralblatt für Psychoanalyse,* ii (1911), p. 340.
[2] *The World of Dreams,* London (1911), p. 168.

unconscious. *One has to pay for them* here means *life,* with which she has to pay for becoming a wife and a mother.

In association with *pinks,* which she then calls *carnations,* I think of *carnal.* But her association is *colour,* to which she adds that *carnations* are the flowers which her fiancé gives her frequently and in large quantities. At the end of the conversation she suddenly admits, spontaneously, that she has not told me the truth; the word that occurred to her was not *colour,* but *incarnation,* the very word I expected. Moreover, even the word *colour* is not a remote association; it was determined by the meaning of *carnation* (i.e., *flesh-colour*)—that is, by the complex. This lack of honesty shows that the resistance here is at its greatest because the symbolism is here most transparent, and the struggle between libido and repression is most intense in connection with this phallic theme. The remark that these flowers were often given her by her fiancé is, together with the double meaning of *carnation,* a still further indication of their phallic significance in the dream. The occasion of the present of flowers during the day is employed to express the thought of a sexual present and a return present. She gives her virginity and expects in return for it a rich love-life. But the words: *expensive flowers; one has to pay for them* may have a real, financial meaning. The flower-symbolism in the dream thus comprises the virginal female, the male symbol, and the reference to violent defloration. It is to be noted that sexual flower-symbolism, which, of course, is very widespread, symbolizes the human sexual organs by flowers, the sexual organs of plants; indeed, presents of flowers between lovers may have this unconscious significance.

The birthday for which she is making preparations in the dream probably signifies the birth of a child. She identifies herself with the bridegroom, and represents him preparing her for a birth (having coitus with her). It is as though the latent thought were to say: "If I were he, I would not wait, but I would deflower the bride without asking her; I would use violence." Indeed, the word *violate* points to this. Thus even the sadistic libidinal components find expression.

In a deeper stratum of the dream the sentence *I arrange,* etc., probabiy has an autoerotic, that is, an infantile significance.

She also has a knowledge—possibly only in the dream—of her physical need; she sees herself flat like a table, so that she emphasizes all the more her virginity, the costliness of the *centre* (another time she calls it a *centre-piece of flowers*). Even the horizontal element of the table may contribute something to the symbol. The concentration of the dream is worthy of remark; nothing is superfluous, every word is a symbol.

Later on she brings me a supplement to this dream: *I decorate the flowers with green crinkled paper.* She adds that it was *fancy paper* of the sort which is used to disguise ordinary flower-pots. She says also: "To hide untidy things, whatever was to be seen which was not pretty to the eye; there is a gap, a little space in the flowers. The paper looks like velvet or moss." With *decorate* she associates *decorum,* as I expected. The green colour is very prominent, and with this she associates *hope,* yet another reference to pregnancy. In this part of the dream the identification with the man is not the dominant feature, but thoughts of shame and frankness express themselves. She makes herself beautiful for him; she admits physical defects, of which she is ashamed and which she wishes to correct. The associations *velvet* and *moss* distinctly point to *crines pubis.*

The dream is an expression of thoughts hardly known to the waking state of the girl; thoughts which deal with the love of the senses and its organs; she is *prepared for a birth-day,* i.e., she has coitus; the fear of defloration and perhaps the pleasurably toned pain find expression; she admits her physical defects and overcompensates them by means of an over-estimation of the value of her virginity. Her shame excuses the emerging sensuality by the fact that the aim of it all is the child. Even material considerations, which are foreign to the lover, find expression here. The affect of the simple dream—the feeling of bliss—shows that here strong emotional complexes have found satisfaction.

I close with the

9. Dream of a chemist.

(A young man who has been trying to give up his habit of masturbation by substituting intercourse with a woman.)

Preliminary statement: On the day before the dream he had been instructing a student as to *Grignard's* reaction, in which magnesium is dissolved in absolutely pure ether under the catalytic influence of iodine. Two days earlier there had been an explosion in the course of the same reaction, in which someone had burned his hand.

Dream I. *He is going to make phenylmagne-siumbromide; he sees the apparatus with particular distinctness, but he has substituted himself for the magnesium. He is now in a curious, wavering attitude. He keeps on repeating to himself: "This is the right thing, it is working, my feet are beginning to dissolve, and my knees are getting soft." Then he reaches down and feels for his feet, and meanwhile (he does not know how) he takes his legs out of the carboy, and then again he says to himself: "That can't be . . . Yes, it has been done correctly." Then he partially wakes, and repeats the dream to himself, because he wants to tell it to me. He is positively afraid of the analysis of the dream. He is much excited during this state of semi-sleep, and repeats continually: "Phenyl, phenyl."*

II. *He is in . . . with his whole family. He is supposed to be at the Schottentor at half-past eleven in order to keep an appointment with the lady in question, but he does not wake until half-past eleven. He says to himself: "It is too late now; when you get there it will be half-past twelve." The next moment he sees the whole family gathered about the table—his mother and the parlourmaid with the souptureen with peculiar distinctness. Then he says to himself: "Well, if we are sitting down to eat already, I certainly can't get away."*

Analysis. He feels sure that even the first dream contains a reference to the lady whom he is to meet at the place of rendezvous (the dream was dreamed during the night before the expected meeting). The student whom he was instructing is a particularly unpleasant fellow; the chemist had said to him: "That isn't right, because the magnesium was still unaffected," and the student had answered, as though he were quite unconcerned: "Nor it is." He himself must be this student; he is as indifferent to his *analysis* as the student is to his *synthesis;* the *he* in the dream, however, who performs the operation, is myself. How unpleasant he must seem to me with his indifference to the result!

Again, he is the material with which the analysis (synthesis) is made. For the question is the success of the treatment. The legs in the dream recall an impression of the previous evening. He met a lady at a dancing class of whom he wished to make a conquest; he pressed her to him so closely that she once cried out. As he ceased to press her legs he felt her firm, responding pressure against his lower thighs as far as just above the knees, the spot men-

tioned in the dream. In this situation, then, the woman is the magnesium in the retort, which is at last working. He is feminine towards me, as he is virile towards the woman. If he succeeds with the woman, the treatment will also succeed. Feeling himself and becoming aware of his knees refers to masturbation, and corresponds to his fatigue of the previous day . . . The rendezvous had actually been made for half-past eleven. His wish to oversleep himself and to keep to his sexual object at home (that is, masturbation) corresponds to his resistance.

He says, in respect to the repetition of the name phenyl, that all these radicals ending in *yl* have always been pleasing to him; they are very convenient to use: benzyl, acetyl, etc. That, however, explained nothing. But when I proposed the root *Schlemihl* he laughed heartily, and told me that during the summer he had read a book by Prévost which contained a chapter: *"Les exclus de l'amour,"* and in this there was some mention of *Schlemiliés;* and in reading of these outcasts he said to himself: "That is my case." He would have played the *Schlemihl* if he had missed the appointment.

It seems that the sexual symbolism of dreams has already been directly confirmed by experiment. In 1912 Dr. K. Schrötter, at the instance of H. Swoboda, produced dreams in deeply hypnotized persons by suggestions which determined a large part of the dream-content. If the suggestion proposed that the subject should dream of normal or abnormal sexual relations, the dream carried out these orders by replacing sexual material by the symbols with which psycho-analytic dream-interpretation has made us familiar. Thus, following the suggestion that the dreamer should dream of homosexual relations with a lady friend, this friend appeared in the dream carrying a shabby travelling-bag, upon which there was a label with the printed words: "For ladies only." The dreamer was believed never to have heard of dream-symbolization or of dream-interpretation. Unfortunately, the value of this important investigation was diminished by the fact that Dr. Schrötter shortly afterwards committed suicide. Of his dream-experiments he gave us only a preliminary report in the *Zentralblatt für Psychoanalyse.*

Similar results were reported in 1923 by G. Roffenstein. Especially interesting were the experiments performed by Betlheim and Hartmann, because they eliminated hypnosis. These

authors told stories of a crude sexual content
to confused patients suffering from Korsakoff's
psychosis, and observed the distortions which
appeared when the material related was reproduced.[1] It was shown that the reproduced material contained symbols made familiar by the
interpretation of dreams (climbing stairs, stab-
bing and shooting as symbols of coitus, knives
and cigarettes as symbols of the penis). Special
value was attached to the appearance of the
symbol of climbing stairs, for, as the authors
justly observed, "a symbolization of this sort
could not be effected by a conscious wish to
distort."

Only when we have formed a due estimate
of the importance of symbolism in dreams can
we continue the study of the *typical dreams*
which was interrupted in an earlier chapter (p.
248). I feel justified in dividing these dreams
roughly into two classes; first, those which always really have the same meaning, and second, those which despite the same or a similar
content must nevertheless be given the most
varied interpretations. Of the typical dreams
belonging to the first class I have already dealt
fairly fully with the examination-dream.

On account of their similar affective character, the dreams of missing a train deserve to be
ranked with the examination-dreams; moreover, their interpretation justifies this approximation. They are consolation-dreams, directed
against another anxiety perceived in dreams—
the fear of death. *To depart* is one of the most
frequent and one of the most readily established of the death-symbols. The dream therefore says consolingly: "Reassure yourself, you
are not going to die (to depart)," just as the
examination-dream calms us by saying: "Don't
be afraid; this time, too, nothing will happen
to you." The difficulty is understanding both
kinds of dreams is due to the fact that the
anxiety is attached precisely to the expression
of consolation.

The meaning of the *dreams due to dental
stimulus* which I have often enough had to
analyse in my patients escaped me for a long
time because, much to my astonishment, they
habitually offered too great a resistance to interpretation. But finally an overwhelming mass
of evidence convinced me that in the case of
men nothing other than the masturbatory desires of puberty furnish the motive power of
these dreams. I shall analyse two such dreams,
one of which is also a *flying dream*. The two

[1] *"Über Fehlreaktionen bei der Korsakoffschen Psychose,"* Arch. f. Psychiatrie, Vol. LXXII (1924).

dreams were dreamed by the same person—a
young man of pronounced homosexuality which,
however, has been inhibited in life.

He is witnessing a performance of Fidelio
*from the stalls of the operahouse; he is sitting
next to L, whose personality is congenial to
him, and whose friendship he would like to
have. Suddenly he flies diagonally right across
the stalls; he then puts his hand in his mouth
and draws out two of his teeth.*

He himself describes the flight by saying
that it was as though he were thrown into the
air. As the opera performed was *Fidelio,* he
recalls the words:

He who a charming wife acquires . . . .

But the acquisition of even the most charming
wife is not among the wishes of the dreamer.
Two other lines would be more appropriate:

*He who succeeds in the lucky (big) throw
The friend of a friend to be. . . .*

The dream thus contains the *lucky (big) throw*
which is not, however, a wish-fulfilment only.
For it conceals also the painful reflection that
in his striving after friendship he has often
had the misfortune to be *thrown out,* and the
fear lest this fate may be repeated in the case
of the young man by whose side he has enjoyed the performance of *Fidelio.* This is now
followed by a confession, shameful to a man of
his refinement, to the effect that once, after
such a rejection on the part of a friend, his
profound sexual longing caused him to masturbate twice in succession.

The other dream is as follows: *Two university professors of his acquaintance are treating him in my place. One of them does something to his penis; he is afraid of an operation.
The other thrusts an iron bar against his mouth,
so that he loses one or two teeth. He is bound
with four silk handkerchiefs.*

The sexual significance of this dream can
hardly be doubted. The silk handkerchiefs allude to an identification with a homosexual of
his acquaintance. The dreamer, who has never
achieved coition (nor has he ever actually
sought sexual intercourse) with men, conceives
the sexual act on the lines of masturbation
with which he was familiar during puberty.

I believe that the frequent modifications of
the typical dream due to dental stimulus—that,
for example, in which another person draws the
tooth from the dreamer's mouth—will be made

intelligible by the same explanation.[1] It may, however, be difficult to understand how *dental stimulus* can have come to have this significance. But here I may draw attention to the frequent *displacement from below to above* which is at the service of sexual repression, and by means of which all kinds of sensations and intentions occurring in hysteria, which ought to be localized in the genitals, may at all events be realized in other, unobjectionable parts of the body. We have a case of such displacement when the genitals are replaced by the face in the symbolism of unconscious thought. This is corroborated by the fact that verbal usage relates the buttocks to the cheeks, and the *labia minora* to the lips which enclose the orifice of the mouth. The nose is compared to the penis in numerous allusions, and in each case the presence of hair completes the resemblance. Only one feature—the teeth—is beyond all possibility of being compared in this way; but it is just this coincidence of agreement and disagreement which makes the teeth suitable for purposes of representation under the pressure of sexual repression.

I will not assert that the interpretation of dreams due to dental stimulus as dreams of masturbation (the correctness of which I cannot doubt) has been freed of all obscurity.[2] I carry the explanation as far as I am able, and must leave the rest unsolved. But I must refer to yet another relation indicated by a colloquial expression. In Austria there is in use an indelicate designation for the act of masturbation, namely: "To pull one out," or "to pull one off."[3] I am unable to say whence these colloquialisms originate, or on what symbolisms they are based; but the teeth would very well fit in with the first of the two.

Dreams of pulling teeth, and of teeth falling out, are interpreted in popular belief to mean the death of a connection. Psycho-analysis can admit of such a meaning only at the most as a joking allusion to the sense already indicated.

To the second group of typical dreams belong those in which one is flying or hovering, falling, swimming, etc. What do these dreams signify? Here we cannot generalize. They mean, as we shall learn, something different in each case; only, the sensory material which they contain always comes from the same source.

We must conclude from the information obtained in psycho-analysis that these dreams also repeat impressions of our childhood—that is, that they refer to the games involving movement which have such an extraordinary attraction for children. Where is the uncle who has never made a child fly by running with it across the room, with outstretched arms, or has never played at falling with it by rocking it on his knee and then suddenly straightening his leg, or by lifting it above his head and suddenly pretending to withdraw his supporting hand? At such moments children shout with joy and insatiably demand a repetition of the performance, especially if a little fright and dizziness are involved in it. In after years they repeat their sensations in dreams, but in dreams they omit the hands that held them, so that now they are free to float or fall. We know that all small children have a fondness for such games as rocking and see-sawing; and when they see gymnastic performances at the circus their recollection of such games is refreshed. In some boys the hysterical attack consists simply in the reproduction of such performances, which they accomplish with great dexterity. Not infrequently sexual sensations are excited by these games of movement, innocent though they are in themselves. To express the matter in a few words: it is these romping games of childhood which are being repeated in dreams of flying, falling, vertigo, and the like, but the pleasurable sensations are now transformed into anxiety. But, as every mother knows, the romping of children often enough ends in quarrelling and tears.

I have therefore good reason for rejecting the explanation that it is the condition of our cutaneous sensations during sleep, the sensation of the movements of the lungs, etc., that evoke dreams of flying and falling. As I see it, these sensations have themselves been reproduced from the memory to which the dream refers—that they are therefore dream-content, and not dream-sources.[4]

This material, consisting of sensations of motion, similar in character, and originating from the same sources, is now used for the

---

[1] The extraction of a tooth by another is usually to be interpreted as castration (cf. hair-cutting; Stekel). One must distinguish between dreams due to dental stimulus and dreams referring to the dentist, such as have been recorded, for example, by Coriat (*Zentralblatt für Psychoanalyse*, iii, 440).

[2] According to C. G. Jung, dreams due to dental stimulus in the case of women have the significance of parturition dreams. E. Jones has given valuable confirmation of this. The common element of this interpretation with that represented above may be found in the fact that in both cases (castration-birth) there is a question of removing a part from the whole body.

[3] Cf. the *biographical* dream on pp. 280-1.

[4] This passage, dealing with dreams of motion, is repeated on account of the context. Cf. p. 250.

representation of the most manifold dream-thoughts. Dreams of flying or hovering, for the most part pleasurably toned, will call for the most widely differing interpretations—interpretations of a quite special nature in the case of some dreamers, and interpretations of a typical nature in that of others. One of my patients was in the habit of dreaming very frequently that she was hovering a little way above the street without touching the ground. She was very short of stature, and she shunned every sort of contamination involved by intercourse with human beings. Her dream of suspension—which raised her feet above the ground and allowed her head to tower into the air—fulfilled both of her wishes. In the case of other dreamers of the same sex, the dream of flying had the significance of the longing: "If only I were a little bird!" Similarly, others become angels at night, because no one has ever called them angels by day. The intimate connection between flying and the idea of a bird makes it comprehensible that the dream of flying, in the case of male dreamers, should usually have a coarsely sensual significance;[1] and we should not be surprised to hear that this or that dreamer is always very proud of his ability to fly.

Dr. Paul Federn (Vienna) has propounded the fascinating theory that a great many flying dreams are erection dreams, since the remarkable phenomenon of erection, which constantly occupies the human phantasy, cannot fail to be impressive as an apparent suspension of the laws of gravity (cf. the winged phalli of the ancients).

It is a noteworthy fact that a prudent experimenter like Mourly Vold, who is really averse to any kind of interpretation, nevertheless defends the erotic interpretation of the dreams of flying and hovering.[2] He describes the erotic element as "the most important motive factor of the hovering dream," and refers to the strong sense of bodily vibration which accompanies this type of dream, and the frequent connection of such dreams with erections and emissions.

Dreams of *falling* are more frequently characterized by anxiety. Their interpretation, when they occur in women, offers no difficulty, because they nearly always accept the symbolic meaning of falling, which is a circumlocution for giving way to an erotic temptation. We have not yet exhausted the infantile sources of the dream of falling; nearly all children have fallen occasionally, and then been picked up and fondled; if they fell out of bed at night, they were picked up by the nurse and taken into her bed.

People who dream often, and with great enjoyment, of *swimming*, cleaving the waves, etc., have usually been bed-wetters, and they now repeat in the dream a pleasure which they have long since learned to forego. We shall soon learn, from one example or another, to what representations dreams of swimming easily lend themselves.

The interpretation of dreams of *fire* justifies a prohibition of the nursery, which forbids children to play with fire so that they may not wet the bed at night. These dreams also are based on reminiscences of the *enuresis nocturna* of childhood. In my "Fragment of an Analysis of Hysteria"[3] I have given the complete analysis and synthesis of such a dream of fire in connection with the infantile history of the dreamer, and have shown for the representation of what maturer impulses this infantile material has been utilized.

It would be possible to cite quite a number of other *typical* dreams, if by such one understands dreams in which there is a frequent recurrence, in the dreams of different persons, of the same manifest dream-content. For example: dreams of passing through narrow alleys, or a whole suite of rooms; dreams of burglars, in respect of whom nervous people take measures of precaution before going to bed; dreams of being chased by wild animals (bulls, horses); or of being threatened with knives, daggers, and lances. The last two themes are characteristic of the manifest dream-content of persons suffering from anxiety, etc. A special investigation of this class of material would be well worth while. In lieu of this I shall offer two observations, which do not, however, apply exclusively to typical dreams.

The more one is occupied with the solution of dreams, the readier one becomes to acknowledge that the majority of the dreams of adults deal with sexual material and give expression to erotic wishes. Only those who really analyse dreams, that is, those who penetrate from their manifest content to the latent dream-thoughts, can form an opinion on this subject; but never those who are satisfied with registering merely the manifest content (as, for example, Näcke

---

[1] A reference to the German slang word *vögeln* (to copulate) from *Vogel* (a bird).—TR.
[2] *"Uber den Traum," Ges. Schriften,* Vol. III.
[3] *Collected Papers,* III.

in his writings on sexual dreams). Let us recognize at once that there is nothing astonishing in this fact, which is entirely consistent with the principles of dream-interpretation. No other instinct has had to undergo so much suppression, from the time of childhood onwards, as the sexual instinct in all its numerous components:[1] from no other instincts are so many and such intense unconscious wishes left over, which now, in the sleeping state, generate dreams. In dream-interpretation this importance of the sexual complexes must never be forgotten, though one must not, of course, exaggerate it to the exclusion of all other factors.

Of many dreams it may be ascertained, by careful interpretation, that they may even be understood bisexually, inasmuch as they yield an indisputable over-interpretation, in which they realize homosexual impulses—that is, impulses which are contrary to the normal sexual activity of the dreamer. But that all dreams are to be interpreted bisexually, as Stekel[2] maintains, and Adler,[3] seems to me to be a generalization as insusceptible of proof as it is improbable, and one which, therefore, I should be loth to defend; for I should, above all, be at a loss to know how to dispose of the obvious fact that there are many dreams which satisfy other than erotic needs (taking the word in the widest sense), as, for example, dreams of hunger, thirst, comfort, etc. And other similar assertions, to the effect that "behind every dream one finds a reference to death" (Stekel), or that every dream shows "an advance from the feminine to the masculine line" (Adler), seem to me to go far beyond the admissible in the interpretation of dreams. The assertion that *all dreams call for a sexual interpretation*, against which there is such an untiring polemic in the literature of the subject, is quite foreign to my *Interpretation of Dreams*. It will not be found in any of the eight editions of this book, and is in palpable contradiction to the rest of its contents.

We have stated elsewhere that dreams which are conspicuously *innocent* commonly embody crude erotic wishes, and this we might confirm by numerous further examples. But many dreams which appear indifferent, in which we should never suspect a tendency in any particular direction, may be traced, according to the analysis, to unmistakably sexual wish-impulses, often of an unsuspected nature. For example, who, before it had been interpreted, would have suspected a sexual wish in the following dream? The dreamer relates: *Between two stately palaces there stands, a little way back, a small house, whose doors are closed. My wife leads me along the little bit of road leading to the house and pushes the door open, and then I slip quickly and easily into the interior of a courtyard that slopes steeply upwards.*

Anyone who has had experience in the translating of dreams will, of course, at once be reminded that penetration into narrow spaces and the opening of locked doors are among the commonest of sexual symbols, and will readily see in this dream a representation of attempted coition from behind (between the two stately buttocks of the female body). The narrow, steep passage is, of course, the vagina; the assistance attributed to the wife of the dreamer requires the interpretation that in reality it is only consideration for the wife which is responsible for abstention from such an attempt. Moreover, inquiry shows that on the previous day a young girl had entered the household of the dreamer; she had pleased him, and had given him the impression that she would not be altogether averse to an approach of this sort. The little house between the two palaces is taken from a reminiscence of the Hradschin in Prague, and once more points to the girl, who is a native of that city.

If, in conversation with my patients, I emphasize the frequency of the Oedipus dream—the dream of having sexual intercourse with one's mother—I elicit the answer: "I cannot remember such a dream." Immediately afterwards, however, there arises the recollection of another, an unrecognizable, indifferent dream, which the patient has dreamed repeatedly, and which on analysis proves to be a dream with this very content—that is, yet another Oedipus dream. I can assure the reader that disguised dreams of sexual intercourse with the dreamer's mother are far more frequent than undisguised dreams to the same effect.[4]

---

[1] Cf. *Three Contributions to the Theory of Sex.*

[2] W. Stekel, *Die Sprache des Traumes* (1911).

[3] Alf. Adler, "*Der Psychische Hermaphroditismus im Leben und in der Neurose,*" in *Fortschritte der Medizin* (1910), No. 16, and later papers in the *Zentralblatt für Psychoanalyse,* i (1910-11).

[4] I have published a typical example of such a disguised Oedipus dream in No. 1 of the *Zentralblatt für Psychoanalyse* (see below); another, with a detailed analysis, was published in No. 4 of the same journal by Otto Rank. For other disguised Oedipus dreams in which the *eye* appears as a symbol, see Rank (*Int. Zeitschr. für Ps. A.,* i, [1913]). Papers upon eye dreams and eye symbolism by Eder, Ferenczi, and Reitler will be found in the same issue. The blinding in the Oedipus

There are dreams of landscapes and localities in which emphasis is always laid upon the assurance: "I have been here before." But this *Déjà vu* has a special significance in dreams. In this case the locality is always the genitals of the mother; of no other place can it be asserted with such certainty that one *has been here before*. I was once puzzled by the account of a dream given by a patient afflicted with obsessional neurosis. He dreamed that he called at a house where he had been *twice* before. But this very patient had long ago told me of an episode of his sixth year. At that time he shared his mother's bed, and had abused the occasion by inserting his finger into his mother's genitals while she was asleep.

A large number of dreams, which are frequently full of anxiety, and often have for content the traversing of narrow spaces, or

---

legend and elsewhere is a substitute for castration. The ancients, by the way, were not unfamiliar with the symbolic interpretation of the undisguised Oedipus dream (*see* O. Rank, *Jahrb.* ii, p. 534: "Thus, a dream of Julius Caesar's of sexual relations with his mother has been handed down to us, which the oneiroscopists interpreted as a favourable omen signifying his taking possession of the earth (Mother Earth). Equally well known is the oracle delivered to the Tarquinii, to the effect that that one of them would become the ruler of Rome who should be the first to kiss his mother (*osculum matri tulerit*), which Brutus conceived as referring to Mother Earth (*terram osculo contigit, scilicet quod ea communis mater omnium mortalium esset*, Livy, I, lvi). Cf. here the dream of Hippias in Herodotus vi, 107. These myths and interpretations point to a correct psychological insight. I have found that those persons who consider themselves preferred or favoured by their mothers manifest in life that confidence in themselves, and that unshakable optimism, which often seem heroic, and not infrequently compel actual success.

Typical example of a disguised Oedipus dream:

A man dreams: *He has a secret affair with a woman whom another man wishes to marry. He is concerned lest the other should discover this relation and abandon the marriage; he therefore behaves very affectionately to the man; he nestles up to him and kisses him.* The facts of the dreamer's life touch the dream-content only at one point. He has a secret affair with a married woman, and an equivocal expression of her husband, with whom he is on friendly terms, aroused in him the suspicion that he might have noticed something of this relationship. There is, however, in reality, yet another factor, the mention of which was avoided in the dream, and which alone gives the key to it. The life of the husband is threatened by an organic malady. His wife is prepared for the possibility of his sudden death, and our dreamer consciously harbours the intention of marrying the young widow after her husband's decease. It is through this objective situation that the dreamer finds himself transferred into the constellation of the Oedipus dream; his wish is to be enabled to kill the man, so that he may win the woman for his wife; his dream gives expression to the wish in a hypocritical distortion. Instead of representing her as already married to the other man, it represents the other man only as wishing to marry her, which indeed corresponds with his own secret intention, and the hostile wishes directed against the man are concealed under demonstrations of affection, which are reminiscences of his childish relations to his father.

---

staying long in the water, are based upon phantasies concerning the intra-uterine life, the sojourn in the mother's womb, and the act of birth. I here insert the dream of a young man who, in his phantasy, has even profited by the intra-uterine opportunity of spying upon an act of coition between his parents.

He is in a deep shaft, in which there is a window, as in the Semmering tunnel. Through this he sees at first an empty landscape, and then he composes a picture in it, which is there all at once and fills up the empty space. The picture represents a field which is being deeply tilled by an implement, and the wholesome air, the associated idea of hard work, and the bluish-black clods of earth make a pleasant impression on him. He then goes on and sees a work on education lying open . . . and is surprised that so much attention is devoted in it to the sexual feelings (of children), which makes him think of me.

Here is a pretty water-dream of a female patient, which was turned to special account in the course of treatment.

At her usual holiday resort on the . . . Lake, she flings herself into the dark water at a place where the pale moon is reflected in the water.

Dreams of this sort are parturition dreams; their interpretation is effected by reversing the fact recorded in the manifest dream-content; thus, instead of *flinging oneself into the water*, read *coming out of the water*—that is, *being born*.[1] The place from which one is born may be recognized if one thinks of the humorous sense of the French *la lune*. The pale moon thus becomes the white *bottom*, which the child soon guesses to be the place from which it came. Now what can be the meaning of the patient's wishing to be born at a holiday resort? I asked the dreamer this, and she replied without hesitation: "Hasn't the treatment made me as though I were *born again?*" Thus the dream becomes an invitation to continue the treatment at this summer resort—that is, to visit her there; perhaps it also contains a very bashful allusion to the wish to become a mother herself.[2]

---

[1] For the mythological meaning of water-birth, see Rank: *Der Mythus von der Geburt des Helden* (1909).

[2] It was not for a long time that I learned to appreciate the significance of the phantasies and unconscious thoughts relating to life in the womb. They contain the explanation of the curious dread, felt by so many people, of being buried alive, as well as the profoundest unconscious reason for the belief in a life after death, which represents only the projection into the future of this mysterious life before birth. *The act of birth, moreover, is the first experience attended by anxiety, and is thus, the source and model of the affect of anxiety.*

Another dream of parturition, with its interpretation, I take from a paper by E. Jones. *"She stood at the seashore watching a small boy, who seemed to be hers, wading into the water. This he did till the water covered him and she could only see his head bobbing up and down near the surface. The scene then changed to the crowded hall of an hotel. Her husband left her, and she 'entered into conversation with' a stranger.*

"The second half of the dream was discovered in the analysis to represent flight from her husband, and the entering into intimate relations with a third person, behind whom was plainly indicated Mr. X's brother, mentioned in a former dream. The first part of the dream was a fairly evident birth-phantasy. In dreams, as in mythology, the delivery of a child from the uterine waters is commonly represented, by way of distortion, as the entry of the child into water; among many other instances, the births of Adonis, Osiris, Moses, and Bacchus are well-known illustrations of this. The bobbing up and down of the head in the water at once recalled to the patient the sensation of quickening which she had experienced in her only pregnancy. Thinking of the boy going into the water induced a reverie in which she saw herself taking him out of the water, carrying him into the nursery, washing and dressing him, and installing him in her household.

"The second half of the dream, therefore, represents thoughts concerning the elopement, which belonged to the first half of the underlying latent content; the first half of the dream corresponded with the second half of the latent content, the birth phantasy. Besides this inversion in the order, further inversions took place in each half of the dream. In the first half the child entered the water, and then his head bobbed; in the underlying dream-thoughts the quickening occurred first, and then the child left the water (a double inversion). In the second half her husband left her; in the dream-thoughts she left her husband."

Another parturition dream is related by Abraham—the dream of a young woman expecting her first confinement: *From one point of the floor of the room a subterranean channel leads directly into the water (path of parturition—amniotic fluid). She lifts up a trap in the floor, and there immediately appears a creature dressed in brownish fur, which almost resembles a seal. This creature changes into the dreamer's younger brother, to whom her relation has always been maternal in character.*

Rank has shown from a number of dreams that parturition-dreams employ the same symbols as micturition-dreams. The erotic stimulus expresses itself in these dreams as an urethral stimulus. The stratification of meaning in these dreams corresponds with a change in the significance of the symbol since childhood.

We may here turn back to the interrupted theme (see p. 190) of the part played by organic, sleep-disturbing stimuli in dream-formation. Dreams which have come into existence under these influences not only reveal quite frankly the wishfulfilling tendency, and the character of convenience-dreams, but they very often display a quite transparent symbolism as well, since waking not infrequently follows a stimulus whose satisfaction in symbolic disguise has already been vainly attempted in the dream. This is true of emission dreams as well as those evoked by the need to urinate or defecate. The peculiar character of emission dreams permits us directly to unmask certain sexual symbols already recognized as typical, but nevertheless violently disputed, and it also convinces us that many an apparently innocent dream-situation is merely the symbolic prelude to a crudely sexual scene. This, however, finds *direct* representation, as a rule, only in the comparatively infrequent emission dreams, while it often enough turns into an anxiety-dream, which likewise leads to waking.

The symbolism of *dreams due to urethral stimulus* is especially obvious, and has always been divined. Hippocrates had already advanced the theory that a disturbance of the bladder was indicated if one dreamt of fountains and springs (Havelock Ellis). Scherner, who has studied the manifold symbolism of the urethral stimulus, agrees that "the powerful urethral stimulus always turns into the stimulation of the sexual sphere and its symbolic imagery.... The dream due to urethral stimulus is often at the same time the representative of the sexual dream."

O. Rank, whose conclusions (in his paper on *Die Symbolschichtung im Wecktraum*) I have here followed, argues very plausibly that a large number of "dreams due to urethral stimulus" are really caused by sexual stimuli, which at first seek to gratify themselves by way of regression to the infantile form of urethral erotism. Those cases are especially instructive in which the urethral stimulus thus produced leads to waking and the emptying of the bladder, whereupon, in spite of this relief, the dream is continued, and expresses its need in undisguisedly erotic images.[1]

In a quite analogous manner dreams due to *intestinal stimulus* disclose the pertinent symbolism, and thus confirm the relation, which is also amply verified by ethno-psychology, of *gold* and *feces*.[2] "Thus, for example, a woman, at a time when she is under the care of a physician on account of an *intestinal disorder*, dreams of a digger for hidden treasure who is burying a treasure in the vicinity of a little wooden shed which looks like a rural *privy*. A second part of the dream has as its content how she *wipes* the *posterior* of her child, a little girl, who has *soiled herself*."

Dreams of *rescue* are connected with parturition dreams. To rescue, especially to rescue from the water, is, when dreamed by a woman, equivalent to giving birth; this sense is, however, modified when the dreamer is a man.[3]

Robbers, burglars, and ghosts, of which we are afraid before going to bed, and which sometimes even disturb our sleep, originate in one and the same childish reminiscence. They are the nightly visitors who have waked the child in order to set it on the chamber, so that it may not wet the bed, or have lifted the coverlet in order to see clearly how the child is holding its hands while sleeping. I have been able to induce an exact recollection of the nocturnal visitor in the analysis of some of these anxiety dreams. The robbers were always the father, the ghosts more probably correspond to female persons in white night-gowns.

F. *Examples—Arithmetic and Speech in Dreams*

Before I proceed to assign to its proper place the fourth of the factors which control the

formation of dreams, I shall cite a few examples from my collection of dreams, partly for the purpose of illustrating the co-operation of the three factors with which we are already acquainted, and partly for the purpose of adducing evidence for certain unsupported assertions which have been made, or of bringing out what necessarily follows from them. It has, of course, been difficult in the foregoing account of the dream-work to demonstrate my conclusions by means of examples. Examples in support of isolated statements are convincing only when considered in the context of an interpretation of a dream as a whole; when they are wrested from their context, they lose their value; on the other hand, a dream-interpretation, even when it is by no means profound, soon becomes so extensive that it obscures the thread of the discussion which it is intended to illustrate. This technical consideration must be my excuse if I now proceed to mix together all sorts of things which have nothing in common except their reference to the text of the foregoing chapter.

We shall first consider a few examples of very peculiar or unusual methods of representation in dreams. A lady dreamed as follows: *A servant-girl is standing on a ladder as though to clean the windows, and has with her a chimpanzee and a gorilla cat* (later corrected, *angora cat*). *She throws the animals on to the dreamer; the chimpanzee nestles up to her, and this is very disgusting.* This dream has accomplished its purpose by a very simple means, namely, by taking a mere figure of speech literally, and representing it in accordance with the literal meaning of its words. *Monkey*, like the names of animals in general, is an opprobrious epithet, and the situation of the dream means merely *to hurl invectives*. This same collection will soon furnish us with further examples of the employment of this simple artifice in the dream-work.

Another dream proceeds in a very similar manner: *A woman with a child which has a conspicuously deformed cranium; the dreamer has heard that the child acquired this deformity owing to its position in its mother's womb. The doctor says that the cranium might be given a better shape by means of compression, but that this would injure the brain. She thinks that because it is a boy it won't suffer so much from deformity.* This dream contains a plastic representation of the abstract concept: *Childish impressions*, with which the dreamer has become familiar in the course of the treatment.

[1] "The same symbolic representations which in the infantile sense constitute the basis of the vesical dream appear in the recent sense in purely sexual significance: water=urine=semen=amniotic fluid; ship=to pump ship (urinate)=seed-capsule; getting wet=enuresis=coitus=pregnancy; swimming=full bladder=dwelling-place of the unborn; rain=urination=symbol of fertilization; traveling (journeying—alighting)=getting out of bed=having sexual intercourse (honeymoon journey); urinating=sexual ejaculation" (Rank, i, c).
[2] Freud, "Character and Anal Erotism," *Collected Papers*, ii; Rank, *Die Symbolschictung*, etc.; Dattner, *Intern. Zeitschr. f. Psych.* i (1913); Reik, *Intern. Zeitschr.*, iii (1915).
[3] For such a dream see Pfister, *"Ein Fall von psychoanalytischer Seelensorge und Seelenheilung,"* in *Evangelische Freiheit* (1909). Concerning the symbol of "rescuing," see my paper, "The Future Prospects of Psycho-Analytic Therapy" (p. 123 above). Also "Contribution to the Theory of Love, I: A Special Type of Object Choice in Men," in *Collected Papers*, iv. Also Rank, *"Beilege zur Rettungs-phantasie,"* in the *Zentralblatt für Psychoanalyse*, i (1910), p. 331; Reik; *"Zur Rettungssymbolic,"* ibid., p. 299.

In the following example the dream-work follows rather a different course. The dream contains a recollection of an excursion to the Hilmteich, near Graz: *There is a terrible storm outside; a miserable hotel—the water is dripping from the walls, and the beds are damp.* (The latter part of the content was less directly expressed than I give it.) The dream signifies *superfluous*. The abstract idea occurring in the dream-thoughts is first made equivocal by a certain abuse of language; it has perhaps been replaced by *overflowing*, or by *fluid* and *superfluid (-fluous)*, and has then been brought to representation by an accumulation of like impressions. Water within, water without, water in the beds in the form of dampness—everything fluid and *super* fluid. That for the purposes of dream-representation the spelling is much less considered than the sound of words ought not to surprise us when we remember that rhyme exercises a similar privilege.

The fact that language has at its disposal a great number of words which were originally used in a pictorial and concrete sense, but are at present used in a colourless and abstract fashion, has, in certain other cases, made it very easy for the dream to represent its thoughts. The dream has only to restore to these words their full significance, or to follow their change of meaning a little way back. For example, a man dreams that his friend, who is struggling to get out of a very tight place, calls upon him for help. The analysis shows that the tight place is a hole, and that the dreamer symbolically uses these very words to his friend: "Be careful, or you'll get yourself into a hole."[1] Another dreamer climbs a mountain from which he obtains an extraordinarily extensive view. He identifies himself with his brother, who is editing a *review* dealing with the Far East.

In a dream in *Der Grüne Heinrich*, a spirited horse is plunging about in a field of the finest oats, every grain of which is really "a sweet almond, a raisin and a new penny" wrapped in red silk and tied with a bit of pig's bristle." The poet (or the dreamer) immediately furnishes the meaning of this dream, for the horse felt himself pleasantly tickled, so that he exclaimed: "The oats are pricking me" ("I feel my oats").

In the old Norse sagas (according to Henzen) prolific use is made in dreams of colloquialisms and witty expressions; one scarcely finds a dream without a double meaning or a play upon words.

[1] English example.—TR.

It would be a special undertaking to collect such methods of representation and to arrange them in accordance with the principles upon which they are based. Some of the representations are almost witty. They give one the impression that one would have never guessed their meaning if the dreamer himself had not succeeded in explaining it.

1. A man dreams *that he is asked for a name, which, however, he cannot recall.* He himself explains that this means: "I shouldn't dream of it."

2. A female patient relates a dream in which *all the persons concerned were singularly large.* "That means," she adds, "that it must deal with an episode of my early childhood, for at that time all grown-up people naturally seemed to me immensely large." She herself did not appear in the dream.

The transposition into childhood is expressed differently in other dreams—by the translation of time into space. One sees persons and scenes as though at a great distance, at the end of a long road, or as though one were looking at them through the wrong end of a pair of opera-glasses.

3. A man who in waking life shows an inclination to employ abstract and indefinite expressions, but who otherwise has his wits about him, dreams, in a certain connection, *that he reaches a railway station just as a train is coming in. But then the platform moves towards the train, which stands still;* an absurd inversion of the real state of affairs. This detail, again, is nothing more than an indication to the effect that something else in the dream must be inverted. The analysis of the same dream leads to recollections of picture-books in which men were represented standing on their heads and walking on their hands.

4. The same dreamer, on another occasion, relates a short dream which almost recalls the technique of a rebus. *His uncle gives him a kiss in an automobile.* He immediately adds the interpretation, which would never have occurred to me: it means *auto-erotism.* In the waking state this might have been said in jest.

5. At a New Year's Eve dinner the host, the patriarch of the family, ushered in the New Year with a speech. One of his sons-in-law, a lawyer, was not inclined to take the old man seriously, especially when in the course of his speech he expressed himself as follows: "When I open the ledger for the Old Year and glance at its pages I see everything on the asset side and nothing, thank the Lord, on the side of lia-

bility; all you children have been a great *asset,*
none of you a *liability.*" On hearing this the
young lawyer thought of X, his wife's brother,
who was a cheat and a liar, and whom he had
recently extricated from the entanglements of
the law. That night, in a dream, he saw the New
Year's celebration once more, and heard the
speech, or rather saw it. Instead of speaking,
the old man actually opened the ledger, and on
the side marked *assets* he saw his name amongst
others, but on the other side, marked *liability,*
there was the name of his brother-in-law, X.
However, the word *liability* was changed into
Lie-Ability, which he regarded as X's main
characteristic.[1]

6. A dreamer *treats another person for a
broken bone.* The analysis shows that the frac-
ture represents a *broken marriage vow, etc.*

7. In the dream-content the time of day
often represents a certain period of the dreamer's childhood. Thus, for example, 5:15 a.m.
means to one dreamer the age of five years and
three months; when he was that age, a younger
brother was born.

8. Another representation of *age* in a
dream: *A woman is walking with two little
girls; there is a difference of fifteen months in
their ages.* The dreamer cannot think of any
family of her acquaintance in which this is the
case. She herself interprets it to mean that the
two children represent her own person, and that
the dream reminds her that the two traumatic
events of her childhood were separated by this
period of time (3½ and 4¾ years).

9. It is not astonishing that persons who are
undergoing psycho-analytic treatment frequently dream of it, and are compelled to give
expression in their dreams to all the thoughts
and expectations aroused by it. The image
chosen for the treatment is as a rule that of a
journey, usually in a motor-car, this being a
modern and complicated vehicle; in the reference to the speed of the car the patient's iron-
ical humour is given free play. If the *unconscious,* as an element of waking thought, is to
be represented in the dream, it is replaced, appropriately enough, by *subterranean* localities,
which at other times, when there is no reference to analytic treatment, have represented
the female body or the womb. *Below* in the
dream very often refers to the genitals, and
its opposite, *above,* to the face, mouth or breast.
By *wild beasts* the dream-work usually symbolizes passionate impulses; those of the dream-

[1] Reported by Brill in his *Fundamental Conceptions
of Psychoanalysis.*

er, and also those of other persons of whom the
dreamer is afraid; or thus, by means of a very
slight displacement, the persons who experience these passions. From this it is not very far
to the totemistic representation of the dreaded
father by means of vicious animals, dogs, wild
horses, etc. One might say that wild beasts serve
to represent the *libido,* feared by the ego, and
combated by repression. Even the neurosis
itself, the *sick person,* is often separated from
the dreamer and exhibited in the dream as an
independent person.

One may go so far as to say that the dream-
work makes use of all the means accessible
to it for the visual representation of the dream-
thoughts, whether these appear admissible or
inadmissible to waking criticism, and thus exposes itself to the doubt as well as the derision
of all those who have only hearsay knowledge
of dream-interpretation, but have never themselves practised it. Stekel's book, *Die Sprache
des Traumes,* is especially rich in such examples,
but I avoid citing illustrations from this work
as the author's lack of critical judgment and
his arbitrary technique would make even the
unprejudiced observer feel doubtful.

10. From an essay by V. Tausk (*"Kleider
und Farben im Dienste der Traumdarstellung,"
in Interna. Zeitschr. für Ps.A., ii* [1914]):

(a) A dreams that *he sees his former governess wearing a dress of black lustre, which
fits closely over her buttocks.* That means he
declares this woman to be *lustful.*

(b) C in a dream *sees a girl on the road to
X, bathed in a white light and wearing a white
blouse.*

The dreamer began an affair with a Miss
White on this road.

11. In an analysis which I carried out in the
French language I had to interpret a dream in
which I appeared as an elephant. I naturally
had to ask why I was thus represented: *"Vous
me trompez,"* answered the dreamer (*Trompe
= trunk*).

The dream-work often succeeds in representing very refractory material, such as proper
names, by means of the forced exploitation of
very remote relations. In one of my dreams
*old Brücke has set me a task. I make a prepa-
ration, and pick something out of it which looks
like crumpled tinfoil.* (I shall return to this
dream later.) The corresponding association,
which is not easy to find, is *stanniol,* and now
I know that I have in mind the name of the
author *Stannius,* which appeared on the title-
page of a treatise on the nervous system of

fishes, which in my youth I regarded with reverence. The first scientific problem which my teacher set me did actually relate to the nervous system of a fish—the *Ammocoetes*. Obviously, this name could not be utilized in the picture-puzzle.

Here I must not fail to include a dream with a curious content, which is worth noting also as the dream of a child, and which is readily explained by analysis. A lady tells me: "I can remember that when I was a child I repeatedly dreamed that *God wore a conical paper hat on His head*. They often used to make me wear such a hat at table, so that I shouldn't be able to look at the plates of the other children and see how much they had received of any particular dish. Since I had heard that God was omniscient, the dream signified that I knew everything in spite of the hat which I was made to wear."

What the dream-work consists in, and its unceremonious handling of its material, the dream-thoughts, may be shown in an instructive manner by the numbers and calculations which occur in dreams. Superstition, by the way, regards numbers as having a special significance in dreams. I shall therefore give a few examples of this kind from my collection.

1. From the dream of a lady, shortly before the end of her treatment:

She wants to pay for something or other; her daughter takes 3 florins 65 kreuzer from her purse; but the mother says: "What are you doing? It costs only 21 kreuzer." This fragment of the dream was intelligible without further explanation owing to my knowledge of the dreamer's circumstances. The lady was a foreigner, who had placed her daughter at school in Vienna, and was able to continue my treatment as long as her daughter remained in the city. In three weeks the daughter's scholastic year would end, and the treatment would then stop. On the day before the dream the principal of the school had asked her whether she could not decide to leave the child at school for another year. She had then obviously reflected that in this case she would be able to continue the treatment for another year. Now, this is what the dream refers to, for a year is equal to 365 days; the three weeks remaining before the end of the scholastic year, and of the treatment, are equivalent to 21 days (though not to so many hours of treatment). The numerals, which in the dream-thoughts refer to periods of time, are given money values in the dream, and simultaneously a deeper meaning finds expression—

for *time is money*. 365 kreuzer, of course, are 3 *florins 65 kreuzer*. The smallness of the sums which appear in the dream is a self-evident wish-fulfilment; the wish has reduced both the cost of the treatment and the year's school fees.

2. In another dream the numerals are involved in even more complex relations. A young lady, who has been married for some years, learns that an acquaintance of hers, of about the same age, Elise L, has just become engaged. Thereupon she dreams: *She is sitting in the theatre with her husband, and one side of the stalls is quite empty. Her husband tells her that Elise L and her fiancé had also wished to come to the theatre, but that they only could have obtained poor seats; three for 1 florin 50 kreuzer, and of course they could not take those. She thinks they didn't lose much, either.*

What is the origin of the 1 *florin 50 kreuzer*? A really indifferent incident of the previous day. The dreamer's sister-in-law had received 150 florins as a present from her husband, and hastened to get rid of them by buying some jewellery. Let us note that 150 florins is 100 *times* 1 florin 50 kreuzer. But whence the 3 in connection with the seats in the theatre? There is only one association for this, namely, that the fiancé is three months younger than herself. When we have ascertained the significance of the fact that one side of the stalls is empty we have the solution of the dream. This feature is an undisguised allusion to a little incident which had given her husband a good excuse for teasing her. She had decided to go to the theatre that week; she had been careful to obtain tickets a few days beforehand, and had had to pay the advance booking-fee. When they got to the theatre they found that one side of the house was almost empty; so that she certainly *need not have been in such a hurry*.

I shall now substitute the dream-thoughts for the dream: "It surely was nonsense to marry so early; there was *no need for* my being in such a hurry. From Elise L's example I see that I should have got a husband just the same— and one a *hundred times* better—If I had only waited (antithesis to the *haste* of her sister-in-law), I could have bought *three* such men for the money (the dowry)!"—Our attention is drawn to the fact that the numerals in this dream have changed their meanings and their relations to a much greater extent than in the one previously considered. The transforming and distorting activity of the dream has in this case been greater—a fact which we interpret as meaning that these dream-thoughts had to overcome an unusual degree of endo-psychic resistance before they attained to representation. And we must not overlook the fact that the dream contains an absurd element, namely, that *two* persons are expected to take *three seats*. It will throw some light on the question of the interpretation of absurdity in dreams if I remark that this absurd detail of the dream-content is intended to represent the most strongly emphasized of the dream-thoughts: "It was *nonsense* to marry so early." The figure 3, which occurs in a quite subordinate relation between the two persons compared (three months' difference in their ages), has thus been adroitly utilized to produce the idea of nonsense required by the dream. The reduction of the actual 150 florins to 1 florin 50 kreuzer corresponds to the dreamer's disparagement of her husband in her suppressed thoughts.

3. Another example displays the arithmetical powers of dreams, which have brought them into such disrepute. A man dreams: *He is sitting in the B's house* (the B's are a family with which he was formerly acquainted), *and he says: "It was nonsense that you didn't give me Amy for my wife." Thereupon, he asks the girl: "How old are you?" Answer: "I was born in 1882." "Ah, then you are 28 years old."*

Since the dream was dreamed in the year 1898, this is obviously bad arithmetic, and the inability of the dreamer to calculate may, if it cannot be otherwise explained, be likened to that of a general paralytic. My patient was one of those men who cannot help thinking about every woman they see. The patient who for some months came next after him in my consulting-room was a young lady; he met this lady after he had constantly asked about her, and he was very anxious to make a good impression on her. This was the lady whose age he estimated at 28. So much for explaining the result of his apparent calculation. But 1882 was the year in which he had married. He had been unable to refrain from entering into conversation with the two other women whom he met at my house—the two by no means youthful maids who alternately opened the door to him—and as he did not find them very responsive, he had told himself that they probably regarded him as elderly and *serious*.

Bearing in mind these examples, and others of a similar nature (to follow), we may say: The dream-work does not calculate at all, whether correctly or incorrectly; it only strings together, in the *form* of a sum, numerals which occur in the dream-thoughts, and which may serve as allusions to material which is insusceptible of representation. It thus deals with figures, as material for expressing its intentions, just as it deals with all other concepts, and with names and speeches which are only verbal images.

For the dream-work cannot compose a new speech. No matter how many speeches and answers, which may in themselves be sensible or absurd, may occur in dreams, analysis shows us that the dream has merely taken from the dream-thoughts fragments of speeches which have really been delivered or heard, and has dealt with them in the most arbitrary fashion. It has not only torn them from their context and mutilated them, accepting one fragment and rejecting another, but it has often fitted them together in a novel manner, so that the speech which seems coherent in a dream is dissolved by analysis into three or four components. In this new application of the words the dream has often ignored the meaning which they had in the dream-thoughts, and has drawn an entirely new meaning from them.[1] Upon closer inspection, the more distinct and compact ingredients of the dream-speech may be distinguished from others, which serve as connectives, and have probably been supplied, just as we supply omitted letters and syllables in reading. The dream-speech thus has the structure of *breccia*, in which the larger pieces of various material are held together by a solidified cohesive medium.

Strictly speaking, of course, this description is correct only for those dream-speeches which have something of the sensory character of a speech, and are described as *speeches*. The others, which have not, as it were, been perceived as heard or spoken (which have no accompanying acoustic or motor emphasis in the

---

[1] Analyses of other numerical dreams have been given by Jung, Marcinowski and others. Such dreams often involve very complicated arithmetical operations, which are none the less solved by the dreamer with astonishing confidence. Cf. also Ernest Jones, *"Über unbewusste Zahlenbehandlung," Zentralb. für Psychoanalyse*, 4, ii, [1912], p. 241).

Neurosis behaves in the same fashion. I know a patient who—involuntarily and unwillingly—hears (hallucinates) songs or fragments of songs without being able to understand their significance for her psychic life. She is certainly not a paranoiac. Analysis shows that by exercising a certain license she gave the text of these songs a false application. "Oh, thou blissful one! Oh, thou happy one!" This is the first line of Christmas carol, but by not continuing it to the word, Christmastide, she turns it into a bridal song, etc. The same mechanism of distortion may operate, without hallucination, merely in association.

dream) are simply thoughts, such as occur in our waking life, and find their way unchanged into many of our dreams. Our reading, too, seems to provide an abundant and not easily traceable source for the indifferent speech-material of dreams. But anything that is at all conspicuous as a speech in a dream can be referred to actual speeches which have been made or heard by the dreamer.

We have already found examples of the derivation of such dream-speeches in the analyses of dreams which have been cited for other purposes. Thus, in the *innocent market-dream* (p. 213) where the speech: *That is no longer to be had* serves to identify me with the butcher, while a fragment of the other speech: *I don't know that, I don't take that,* precisely fulfils the task of rendering the dream innocent. On the previous day, the dreamer, replying to some unreasonable demand on the part of her cook, had waved her aside with the words: *I don't know that, behave yourself properly,* and she afterwards took into the dream the first, indifferent-sounding part of the speech in order to allude to the latter part, which fitted well into the phantasy underlying the dream, but which might also have betrayed it.

Here is one of many examples which all lead to the same conclusion:

A large courtyard in which dead bodies are being burned. The dreamer says, "I'm going, I can't stand the sight of it." (Not a distinct speech.) *Then he meets two butcher boys and asks, "Well, did it taste good?" And one of them answers, "No, it wasn't good." As though it had been human flesh.*

The innocent occasion of this dream is as follows: After taking supper with his wife, the dreamer pays a visit to his worthy but by no means *appetizing neighbour.* The hospitable old lady is just sitting down to her own supper, and *presses* him (among men a composite, sexually significant word is used jocosely in the place of this word) to taste it. He declines, saying that he has no appetite. She replies: *"Go on with you, you can manage it all right,"* or something of the kind. The dreamer is thus forced to taste and praise what is offered him. "But that's good!" When he is alone again with his wife, he complains of his neighbour's importunity, and of the quality of the food which he has tasted. "I can't stand the sight of it," a phrase that in the dream, too, does not emerge as an actual speech, is a thought relating to the physical charms of the lady who invites him, which may be translated by the statement that he has no desire to look at her.

The analysis of another dream—which I will cite at this stage for the sake of a very distinct speech, which constitutes its nucleus, but which will be explained only when we come to evaluate the affects in dreams—is more instructive. I dream very vividly: *I have gone to Brücke's laboratory at night, and on hearing a gentle knocking at the door, I open it to (the deceased) Professor Fleischl, who enters in the company of several strangers, and after saying a few words sits down at his table.* Then follows a second dream: *My friend Fl has come to Vienna, unobtrusively, in July; I meet him in the street, in conversation with my (deceased) friend P, and I go with them somewhere, and they sit down facing each other as though at a small table, while I sit facing them at the narrow end of the table. Fl speaks of his sister, and says: "In three-quarters of an hour she was dead," and then something like "That is the threshold." As P does not understand him, Fl turns to me, and asks me how much I have told P of his affairs. At this, overcome by strange emotions, I try to tell Fl that P (cannot possibly know anything, of course, because he) is not alive. But noticing the mistake myself, I say: "Non vixit." Then I look searchingly at P, and under my gaze he becomes pale and blurred, and his eyes turn a sickly blue—and at last he dissolves. I rejoice greatly at this; I now understand that Ernst Fleischl, too, is only an apparition, a revenant, and I find that it is quite possible that such a person should exist only so long as one wishes him to, and that he can be made to disappear by the wish of another person.*

This very pretty dream unites so many of the enigmatical characteristics of the dream-content—the criticism made in the dream itself, inasmuch as I myself notice my mistake in saying *Non vixit* instead of *Non vivit,* the unconstrained intercourse with deceased persons, whom the dream itself declares to be dead, the absurdity of my conclusion, and the intense satisfaction which it gives me—that "I would give my life" to expound the complete solution of the problem. But in reality I am incapable of doing what I do in the dream, i.e., of sacrificing such intimate friends to my ambition. And if I attempted to disguise the facts, the true meaning of the dream, with which I am perfectly familiar, would be spoiled. I must therefore be content to select a few of the elements of the dream for interpretation, some here, and some at a later stage.

The scene in which I annihilate P with a glance forms the centre of the dream. His eyes become strange and weirdly blue, and then he dissolves. This scene is an unmistakable imitation of a scene that was actually experienced. I was a demonstrator at the Physiological Institute; I was on duty in the morning, and Brücke learned that on several occasions I had been unpunctual in my attendance at the students' laboratory. One morning, therefore, he arrived at the hour of opening, and waited for me. What he said to me was brief and to the point; but it was not what he said that mattered. What overwhelmed me was the terrible gaze of his blue eyes, before which I melted away— as P does in the dream, for P has exchanged rôles with me, much to my relief. Anyone who remembers the eyes of the great master, which were wonderfully beautiful even in his old age, and has ever seen him angered, will readily imagine the emotions of the young transgressor on that occasion.

But for a long while I was unable to account for the *Non vixit* with which I pass sentence in the dream. Finally, I remembered that the reason why these two words were so distinct in the dream was not because they were heard or spoken, but because they were *seen*. Then I knew at once where they came from. On the pedestal of the statue of the Emperor Joseph in the Vienna Hofburg are inscribed the following beautiful words:

*Saluti patriae v i x i t
n o n diu sed totus.*[1]

From this inscription I had taken what fitted one inimical train of thought in my dream-thoughts, and which was intended to mean: "That fellow has nothing to say in the matter, he is not really alive." And I now recalled that the dream was dreamed a few days after the unveiling of the memorial to Fleischl, in the cloisters of the University, upon which occasion I had once more seen the memorial to Brücke, and must have thought with regret (in the unconscious) how my gifted friend P, with all his devotion to science, had by his premature death forfeited his just claim to a memorial in these halls. So I set up this memorial to

him in the dream; Josef is my friend P's baptismal name.[2]

According to the rules of dream-interpretation, I should still not be justified in replacing *non vivit*, which I need, by *non vixit*, which is placed at my disposal by the recollection of the Kaiser Josef memorial. Some other element of the dream-thoughts must have contributed to make this possible. Something now calls my attention to the fact that in the dream scene two trains of thought relating to my friend P meet, one hostile, the other affectionate—the former on the surface, the latter covered up—and both are given representation in the same words: *non vixit*. As my friend P has deserved well of science, I erect a memorial to him; as he has been guilty of a malicious wish (expressed at the end of the dream), I annihilate him. I have here constructed a sentence with a special cadence, and in doing so I must have been influenced by some existing model. But where can I find a similar antithesis, a similar parallel between two opposite reactions to the same person, both of which can claim to be wholly justified, and which nevertheless do not attempt to affect one another? Only in one passage which, however, makes a profound impression upon the reader—Brutus's speech of justification in Shakespeare's *Julius Caesar:* "As Caesar loved me, I weep for him; as he was fortunate, I rejoice at it; as he was valiant, I honour him; but as he was ambitious, I slew him." Have we not here the same verbal structure, and the same antithesis of thought, as in the dream-thoughts? So I am playing Brutus in my dream. If only I could find in my dream-thoughts another collateral connection to confirm this! I think it might be the following: *My friend Fl comes to Vienna in July.* This detail is not the case in reality. To my knowledge, my friend has never been in Vienna in July. But the month of *July* is named after *Julius Caesar*, and might therefore very well furnish the required allusion to the intermediate thought—that I am playing the part of Brutus.[3]

Strangely enough, I once did actually play the part of Brutus. When I was a boy of fourteen, I presented the scene between Brutus and Caesar in Schiller's poem to an audience of children: with the assistance of my nephew, who was a year older than I, and who had come to us from England—and was thus a *revenant*—

---

[1] The inscription in fact reads:
    *Saluti p u b l i c a e vixit
    non diu sed totus.*
[He lived for the safety of the public, not for a long time, but always.]
The motive of the mistake: *patriae* [fatherland] for *publicae*, has probably been correctly divined by Wittels.

[2] As an example of over-determination: My excuse for coming late was that after working late into the night, in the morning I had to make the long journey from Kaiser-Josef-Strasse to Währinger Strasse.
[3] And also, *Caesar=Kaiser.*

for in him I recognized the playmate of my early childhood. Until the end of my third year we had been inseparable; we had loved each other and fought each other and, as I have already hinted, this childish relation has determined all my later feelings in my intercourse with persons of my own age. My nephew John has since then had many incarnations, which have revivified first one and then another aspect of a character that is ineradicably fixed in my unconscious memory. At times he must have treated me very badly, and I must have opposed my tyrant courageously, for in later years I was often told of a short speech in which I defended myself when my father—his grandfather—called me to account: "Why did you hit John?" *"I hit him because he hit me."* It must be this childish scene which causes *non vivit* to become *non vixit*, for in the language of later childhood striking is known as *wichsen* (German: *wichsen = to polish, to wax, i.e., to thrash*); and the dream-work does not disdain to take advantage of such associations. My hostility towards my friend P, which has so little foundation in reality—he was greatly my superior, and might therefore have been a new edition of my old playmate—may certainly be traced to my complicated relations with John during our childhood. I shall, as I have said, return to this dream later on.

G. *Absurd Dreams—Intellectual Performances in Dreams*

I

Hitherto, in our interpretation of dreams, we have come upon the element of *absurdity* in the dream-content so frequently that we must no longer postpone the investigation of its cause and its meaning. We remember, of course, that the absurdity of dreams has furnished the opponents of dream-interpretation with their chief argument for regarding the dream as merely the meaningless product of an attenuated and fragmentary activity of the psyche.

I will begin with a few examples in which the absurdity of the dream-content is apparent only, disappearing when the dream is more thoroughly examined. These are certain dreams which—accidently, one begins by thinking—are concerned with the dreamer's dead father.

1. Here is the dream of a patient who had lost his father six years before the date of the dream:

His father had been involved in a terrible accident. He was travelling by the night express when the train was derailed, the seats were telescoped, and his head was crushed from side to side. The dreamer sees him lying on his bed; from his left eyebrow a wound runs vertically upwards. The dreamer is surprised that his father should have met with an accident (since he is dead already, as the dreamer adds in relating his dream). *His father's eyes are so clear.*

According to the prevailing standards of dream-criticism, this dream-content would be explained as follows: At first, while the dreamer is picturing his father's accident, he has forgotten that his father has already been many years in his grave; in the course of the dream this *memory* awakens, so that he is surprised at his own dream even while he is dreaming it. Analysis, however, tells us that it is quite superfluous to seek for such explanations. The dreamer had commissioned a sculptor to make a *bust* of his father, and he had inspected the bust two days before the dream. It is this which seems to him to have come to grief (the German word means *gone wrong* or *met with an accident*). The sculptor has never seen his father, and has had to work from photographs. On the very day before the dream the son had sent an old family servant to the studio in order to see whether he, too, would pass the same judgment upon the marble bust—namely, that it was *too narrow between the temples.* And now follows the memory-material which has contributed to the formation of the dream: The dreamer's father had a habit, whenever he was harassed by business cares or domestic difficulties, of pressing his temples between his hands, as though his head was growing too large and he was trying to compress it. When the dreamer was four years old, he was present when a pistol was accidentally discharged, and his father's eyes were blackened (*his eyes are so clear*). When his father was thoughtful or depressed, he had a deep furrow in his forehead just where the dream shows his wound. The fact that in the dream this wrinkle is replaced by a wound points to the second occasion for the dream. The dreamer had taken a photograph of his little daughter; the plate had fallen from his hand, and when he picked it up it revealed a crack which ran like a vertical furrow across the child's forehead, extending as far as the eyebrow. He could not help feeling a superstitious foreboding, for on the day before his mother's death the negative of her portrait had been cracked.

Thus, the absurdity of this dream is simply the result of a carelessness of verbal expression, which does not distinguish between the bust or the photograph and the original. We are all accustomed to making remarks like: "Don't you think it's exactly your father?" The appearance of absurdity in this dream might, of course, have been easily avoided. If it were permissible to form an opinion on the strength of a single case, one might be tempted to say that this semblance of absurdity is admitted or even desired.

II

Here is another example of the same kind from my own dreams (I lost my father in the year 1896):

After his death, my father has played a part in the political life of the Magyars, and has united them into a political whole; and here I see, indistinctly, a little picture: *a number of men, as though in the Reichstag; a man is standing on one or two chairs; there are others round about him. I remember that on his death-bed he looked so like Garibaldi, and I am glad that this promise has really come true.*

Certainly this is absurd enough. It was dreamed at the time when the Hungarians were in a state of anarchy, owing to Parliamentary *obstruction,* and were passing through the crisis from which Koloman *Széll* subsequently delivered them. The trivial circumstance that the scenes beheld in dreams consist of such little pictures is not without significance for the elucidation of this element. The customary visual dream-representations of our thoughts present images that impress us as being life-size; my dream-picture, however, is the reproduction of a wood-cut inserted in the text of an illustrated history of Austria, representing Maria Theresa in the Reichstag of Pressburg —the famous scene of *Moriamur pro rege nostro.*[1] Like Maria Theresa, my father, in my dream, is surrounded by the multitude; but he is standing on one or two chairs *(Stühlen),* and is thus, like a *Stuhlrichter* (presiding judge). (He has *united* them; here the intermediary is the phrase: "We shall need no *judge.*") Those of us who stood about my father's death-bed did actually notice that he looked very like Garibaldi. He had a *post-mortem* rise of temperature; his cheeks shone redder and redder . . . involuntarily we continue: "And behind him, in unsub-

stantial (radiance), lay that which subdues us all—the common fate."

This uplifting of our thoughts prepares us for the fact that we shall have to deal with this *common fate.* The *post-mortem* rise in temperature corresponds to the words *after his death* in the dream-content. The most agonizing of his afflictions had been a complete paralysis of the intestines *(obstruction)* during the last few weeks of his life. All sorts of disrespectful thoughts associate themselves with this. One of my contemporaries, who lost his father while still at the *Gymnasium*—upon which occasion I was profoundly moved, and tendered him my friendship—once told me, derisively, of the distress of a relative whose father had died in the street, and had been brought home, when it appeared, upon undressing the corpse, that at the moment of death, or *post-mortem,* an evacuation of the bowels *(Stuhlentleerung)* had taken place. The daughter was deeply distressed by this circumstance, because this ugly detail would inevitably spoil her memory of her father. We have now penetrated to the wish that is embodied in this dream. To stand after one's death before one's children great and undefiled: who would not wish that? What now has become of the absurdity of this dream? The appearance of absurdity was due only to the fact that a perfectly permissible figure of speech, in which we are accustomed to ignore any absurdity that may exist as between its components, has been faithfully represented in the dream. Here again we can hardly deny that the appearance of absurdity is desired and has been purposely produced.

The frequency with which dead persons appear in our dreams as living and active and associating with us has evoked undue astonishment, and some curious explanations, which afford conspicuous proof of our misunderstanding of dreams. And yet the explanation of these dreams is close at hand. How often it happens that we say to ourselves: "If my father were still alive, what would he say to this?" The dream can express this *if* in no other way than by his presence in a definite situation. Thus, for instance, a young man whose grandfather has left him a great inheritance dreams that the old man is alive, and calls his grandson to account, reproaching him for his lavish expenditure. What we regard as an objection to the dream on account of our better knowledge that the man is already dead, is in reality the consoling thought that the dead man does not need to learn the truth, or satisfaction over the fact

[1] [We die for our king.] I have forgotten in what author I found a reference to a dream which was overrun with unusually small figures, the source of which proved to be one of the engravings of Jacques Callot, which the dreamer had examined during the day. These engravings contain an enormous number of very small figures; a whole series of them deals with the horrors of the Thirty Years War.

that he can no longer have a say in the matter.

Another form of absurdity found in dreams of deceased relatives does not express scorn and derision; it serves to express the extremest repudiation, the representation of a suppressed thought which one would like to believe the very last thing one would think of. Dreams of this kind appear to be capable of solution only if we remember that a dream makes no distinction between desire and reality. For example, a man who nursed his father during his last illness, and who felt his death very keenly, dreamed some time afterwards the following senseless dream: *His father was again living, and conversing with him as usual, but* (and this was the remarkable thing) *he had nevertheless died, though he did not know it.* This dream is intelligible if, after *he had nevertheless died*, we insert *in consequence of the dreamer's wish*, and if after *but he did not know it*, we add *that the dreamer had entertained this wish.* While nursing him, the son had often wished that his father was dead; that is, he had had the really compassionate thought that it would be a good thing if death would at last put an end to his sufferings. While he was mourning his father's death, even this compassionate wish became an unconscious reproach, as though it had really contributed to shorten the sick man's life. By the awakening of the earliest infantile feelings against his father, it became possible to express this reproach as a dream; and it was precisely because of the extreme antithesis between the dream-instigator and the day-thoughts that this dream had to assume so absurd a form.[1]

As a general thing, the dreams of a deceased person of whom the dreamer has been fond confront the interpreter with difficult problems, the solution of which is not always satisfying. The reason for this may be sought in the especially pronounced ambivalence of feeling which controls the relation of the dreamer to the dead person. In such dreams it is quite usual for the deceased person to be treated at first as living; then it suddenly appears that he is dead; and in the continuation of the dream he is once more living. This has a confusing effect. I at last divined that this alternation of death and life is intended to represent the *indifference* of the dreamer ("It is all one to me whether he is alive or dead"). This indifference, of course, is not real, but wished; its purpose is to help the dreamer to deny his very intense

[1] Cf. "Formulations regarding the Two Principles in Mental Functioning," *Collected Papers*, IV.

and often contradictory emotional attitudes, and so it becomes the dream-representation of his *ambivalence.* For other dreams in which one meets with deceased persons the following rule will often be a guide: If in the dream the dreamer is not reminded that the dead person is dead, he sets himself on a par with the dead; he dreams of his own death. The sudden realization or astonishment in the dream ("but he has long been dead!") is a protest against this identification, and rejects the meaning that the dreamer is dead. But I will admit that I feel that dream-interpretation is far from having elicited all the secrets of dreams having this content.

III

In the example which I shall now cite, I can detect the dream-work in the act of purposely manufacturing an absurdity for which there is no occasion whatever in the dream-material. It is taken from the dream which I had as a result of meeting Count Thun just before going away on a holiday. *I am driving in a cab, and I tell the driver to drive to a railway station. "Of course, I can't drive with you on the railway track itself," I say, after the driver had reproached me, as though I had worn him out; at the same time, it seems as though I had already made with him a journey that one usually makes by train.* Of this confused and senseless story analysis gives the following explanation: During the day I had hired a cab to take me to a remote street in Dornbach. The driver, however, did not know the way, and simply kept on driving, in the manner of such worthy people, until I became aware of the fact and showed him the way, indulging in a few derisive remarks. From this driver a train of thought led to the aristocratic personage whom I was to meet later on. For the present, I will only remark that one thing that strikes us middle-class plebeians about the aristocracy is that they like to put themselves in the driver's seat. Does not Count Thun guide the Austrian *car of State?* The next sentence in the dream, however, refers to my brother, whom I thus also identify with the cab-driver. I had refused to go to Italy with him this year *(Of course, I can't drive with you on the railway track itself)*, and this refusal was a sort of punishment for his accustomed complaint that I usually *wear him out* on this tour (this finds its way into the dream unchanged) by rushing him too quickly from place to place, and making him see too many beautiful things in a single day. That evening my brother had accompanied me to the railway station, but shortly before the carriage had reached the Western station of the Metropolitan Railway he had jumped out in order to take the train to Purkersdorf. I suggested to him that he might remain with me a little longer, as he did not travel to Purkersdorf by the Metropolitan but by the Western Railway. This is why, in my dream, I made in the cab a journey which one usually makes by train. In reality, however, it was the other way about: what I told my brother was: "The distance which you travel on the Metropolitan Railway you could travel in my company on the Western Railway." The whole confusion of the dream is therefore due to the fact that in my dream I replace "Metropolitan Railway" by *cab,* which, to be sure, does good service in bringing the driver and my brother into conjunction. I then elicit from the dream some nonsense which is hardly disentangled by elucidation, and which almost constitutes a contradiction of my earlier speech *(Of course, I cannot drive with you on the railway track itself).* But as I have no excuse whatever for confronting the Metropolitan Railway with the cab, I must intentionally have given the whole enigmatical story this peculiar form in my dream.

But with what intention? We shall now learn what the absurdity in the dream signifies, and the motives which admitted it or created it. In this case the solution of the mystery is as follows: In the dream I need an absurdity, and something incomprehensible, in connection with *driving (Fahren=* riding, driving) because in the dream-thoughts I have a certain opinion that demands representation. One evening, at the house of the witty and hospitable lady who appears, in another scene of the same dream, as the *housekeeper,* I heard two riddles which I could not solve. As they were known to the other members of the party, I presented a somewhat ludicrous figure in my unsuccessful attempts to find the solutions. They were two puns turning on the words *Nachkommen* (to obey orders—offspring) and *Vorfahren* (to drive—forefathers, ancestry). They ran, I believe, as follows:

> The coachman does it
> At the master's behests;
> Everyone has it;
> In the grave it rests.
> *(Vorfahren)*

A confusing detail was that the first halves of the two riddles were identical:

> The coachman does it
> At the master's behests;
> Not everyone has it,
> In the cradle it rests.
> *(Nachkommen)*

When I saw Count Thun drive up *(vorfahren)* in state, and fell into the Figaro-like mood, in which one finds that the sole merit of such aristocratic gentlemen is that they have taken the trouble to be born (to become *Nachkommen),* these two riddles became intermediary thoughts for the dream-work. As aristocrats may readily be replaced by coachmen, and since it was once the custom to call a coachman *Herr Schwäger* (brother-in-law), the work of condensation could involve my brother in the same representation. But the dream-thought at work in the background is as follows: It is nonsense to be proud of one's ancestors *(Vorfahren).* I would rather be an ancestor *(Vorfahr)* myself. On account of this opinion, *it is nonsense,* we have the nonsense in the dream. And now the last riddle in this obscure passage of the dream is solved—namely that I have driven before *(vorher gefahren, vorgefahren)* with this driver.

Thus, a dream is made absurd if there occurs in the dream-thoughts, as one of the elements of the contents, the opinion: "That is nonsense"; and, in general, if criticism and derision are the motives of one of the dreamer's unconscious trains of thought. Hence, absurdity is one of the means by which the dream-work represents contradiction; another means is the inversion of material relation between the dream-thoughts and the dream-content; another is the employment of the feeling of motor inhibition. But the absurdity of a dream is not to be translated by a simple *no;* it is intended to reproduce the tendency of the dream-thoughts to express laughter or derision simultaneously with the contradiction. Only with this intention does the dream-work produce anything ridiculous. Here again it transforms a part of the latent content into a manifest form.[1]

As a matter of fact, we have already cited

---

[1] Here the dream-work parodies the thought which it qualifies as ridiculous, in that it creates something ridiculous in relation to it. Heine does the same thing when he wishes to deride the bad rhymes of the King of Bavaria. He does it by using even worse rhymes:

> *Herr Ludwig ist ein grosser Poet*
> *Und singt er, so stürzt Apollo*
> *Vor ihm auf die Knie und bittet und fleht,*
> *Halt ein, ich werde sonst toll, oh!*

a convincing example of this significance of an absurd dream. The dream (interpreted without analysis) of the Wagnerian performance which lasted until 7.45 a.m., and in which the orchestra is conducted from a tower, etc. (see p. 278), is obviously saying: It is a crazy world and an insane society. He who deserves a thing doesn't get it, and he who doesn't care for it does get it. In this way the dreamer compares her fate with that of her cousin. The fact that dreams of a dead father were the first to furnish us with examples of absurdity in dreams is by no means accidental. The conditions for the creation of absurd dreams are here grouped together in a typical fashion. The authority proper to the father has at an early age evoked the criticism of the child, and the strict demands which he has made have caused the child, in self-defence, to pay particularly close attention to every weakness of his father's; but the piety with which the father's personality is surrounded in our thoughts, especially after his death, intensifies the censorship which prevents the expression of this criticism from becoming conscious.

IV

Here is another absurd dream of a deceased father:

I receive a communication from the town council of my native city concerning the cost of accommodation in the hospital in the year 1851. This was necessitated by a seizure from which I was suffering. I make fun of the matter for, in the first place, I was not yet born in 1851, and in the second place, my father, to whom the communication might refer, is already dead. I go to him in the adjoining room, where he is lying in bed, and tell him about it. To my surprise he remembers that in the year 1851 he was once drunk and had to be locked up or confined. It was when he was working for the firm of T. "Then you, too, used to drink?" I ask. "You married soon after?" I reckon that I was born in 1856, which seems to me to be immediately afterwards.

In the light of the foregoing exposition, we shall translate the insistence with which this dream exhibits its absurdities as a sure sign of a particularly embittered and passionate polemic in the dream-thoughts. All the greater, then, is our astonishment when we perceive that in this dream the polemic is waged openly, and that my father is denoted as the person who is made a laughing-stock. Such frankness seems to contradict our assumption of a censor-ship controlling the dream-work. The explanation is that here the father is only an interposed figure, while the quarrel is really with another person, who appears in the dream only in a single allusion. Whereas a dream usually treats of revolt against other persons, behind whom the father is concealed, here it is the other way about: the father serves as the man of straw to represent another, and hence the dream dares to concern itself openly with a person who is usually hallowed, because there is present the certain knowledge that he is not in reality intended. We learn of this condition of affairs by considering the occasion of the dream. It was dreamed after I had heard that an older colleague, whose judgment was considered infallible, had expressed disapproval and astonishment on hearing that one of my patients had already been undergoing psycho-analytic treatment at my hands for five years. The introductory sentences of the dream allude in a transparently disguised manner to the fact that this colleague had for a time taken over the duties which my father could no longer perform (statement of expenses, accommodation in the hospital); and when our friendly relations began to alter for the worse I was thrown into the same emotional conflict as that which arises in the case of a misunderstanding between father and son (by reason of the part played by the father, and his earlier functions). The dream-thoughts now bitterly resent the reproach that I am not making better progress, which extends itself from the treatment of this patient to other things. Does my colleague know anyone who can get on any faster? Does he not know that conditions of this sort are usually incurable and last for life? What are four or five years in comparison to a whole lifetime, especially when life has been made so much easier for the patient during the treatment?

The impression of absurdity in this dream is brought about largely by the fact that sentences from different divisions of the dream-thoughts are strung together without any reconciling transition. Thus, the sentence, *I go to him in the adjoining room*, etc., leaves the subject from which the preceding sentences are taken, and faithfully reproduces the circumstances under which I told my father that I was engaged to be married. Thus the dream is trying to remind me of the noble disinterestedness which the old man showed at that time, and to contrast this with the conduct of another newly-introduced person. I now perceive that the dream is allowed to make fun of my father because in the dream-thoughts, in the full recognition of his merits, he is held up as an example to others. It is in the nature of every censorship that one is permitted to tell untruths about forbidden things rather than the truth. The next sentence, to the effect that my father remembers that he was *once drunk*, and was *locked up* in consequence, contains nothing that really relates to my father any more. The person who is screened by him is here a no less important personage than the great Meynert, in whose footsteps I followed with such veneration, and whose attitude towards me, after a short period of favouritism, changed into one of undisguised hostility. The dream recalls to me his own statement that in his youth he had at one time formed the habit of *intoxicating himself with chloroform*, with the result that he had to *enter a sanatorium;* and also my second experience with him, shortly before his death. I had an embittered literary controversy with him in reference to masculine hysteria, the existence of which he denied, and when I visited him during his last illness, and asked him how he felt, he described his condition at some length, and concluded with the words: "You know, I have always been one of the prettiest cases of masculine hysteria." Thus, to my satisfaction, and to my astonishment, he admitted what he so long and so stubbornly denied. But the fact that in this scene of my dream I can use my father to screen Meynert is explained not by any discovered analogy between the two persons, but by the fact that it is the brief yet perfectly adequate representation of a conditional sentence in the dream-thoughts which, if fully expanded, would read as follows: "Of course, if I belonged to the second generation, if I were the son of a professor or a privy councillor, I should have progressed more rapidly." In my dream I make my father a professor and a privy councillor. The most obvious and most annoying absurdity of the dream lies in the treatment of the date 1851, which seems to me to be indistinguishable from 1856, *as though a difference of five years meant nothing whatever.* But it is just this one of the dream-thoughts that requires expression. Four or five years—that is precisely the length of time during which I enjoyed the support of the colleague mentioned at the outset; but it is also the duration of time I kept my fiancée waiting before I married her; and by a coincidence that is eagerly exploited by the dream-thoughts, it is also the time I have kept my oldest patient waiting for a complete cure. "What are five years?" ask the dream-thoughts. *"That is no time at all to me, that isn't worth consideration.* I have time enough ahead of me, and just as what you wouldn't believe came true at last, so I shall accomplish this also." Moreover, the number 51, when considered apart from the number of the century, is determined in yet another manner and in an opposite sense; for which reason it occurs several times over in the dream. It is the age at which man seems particularly exposed to danger; the age at which I have seen colleagues die suddenly, among them one who had been appointed a few days earlier to a professorship for which he had long been waiting.

V

Another absurd dream which plays with figures:

An acquaintance of mine, Herr M, has been attacked in an essay by no less a person than Goethe and, as we all think, with unjustifiable vehemence. Herr M is, of course, crushed by this attack. He complains of it bitterly at a dinner-party; but his veneration for Goethe has not suffered as a result of this personal experience. I try to elucidate the temporal relations a little, as they seem improbable to me. Goethe died in 1832; since his attack upon M must, of course, have taken place earlier, M was at the time quite a young man. It seems plausible to me that he was 18 years old. But I do not know exactly what the date of the present year is, and so the whole calculation lapses into obscurity. The attack, by the way, is contained in Goethe's well-known essay on "Nature."

We shall soon find the means of justifying the nonsense of this dream. Herr M, with whom I became acquainted *at a dinner-party*, had recently asked me to examine his brother, who showed signs of *general paralysis.* The conjecture was right; the painful thing about this visit was that the patient gave his brother away by alluding to his *youthful pranks*, though our conversation gave him no occasion to do so. I had asked the patient to tell me the year of his birth, and had repeatedly got him to make trifling calculations in order to show the weakness of his memory—which tests, by the way, he passed quite well. Now I can see that I behave like a paralytic in the dream (*I do not know exactly what the date of the present year is*). Other material of the dream is drawn from another recent source. The editor of a medical periodical, a friend of mine, had accepted for his paper a very unfavourable *crushing* review of the last book of my Berlin friend, Fl, the critic being a very *youthful reviewer,* who was not very competent to pass judgment. I thought I had a right to interfere, and called the editor to account; he greatly regretted his acceptance of the review, but he would not promise any redress. I thereupon broke off my relations with the periodical, and in my letter of resignation I expressed the hope that *our personal relations would not suffer* as a result of the incident. The third source of this dream is an account given by a female patient—it was fresh in my memory at the time—of the psychosis of her brother who had fallen into a frenzy crying "*Nature, Nature.*" The physicians in attendance thought that the cry was derived from a reading of Goethe's beautiful *essay,* and that it pointed to the patient's overwork in the study of natural philosophy. I thought, rather, of the sexual meaning in which even our less cultured people use the word *Nature,* and the fact that the unfortunate man afterwards mutilated his genitals seems to show that I was not far wrong. Eighteen years was the age of this patient at the time of this access of frenzy.

If I add, further, that the book of my so severely criticized friend ("One asks oneself whether the author or oneself is crazy" had been the opinion of another critic) treats of the *temporal conditions* of life, and refers the duration of Goethe's life to the multiple of a number significant from the biological point of view, it will readily be admitted that in my dream I am putting myself in my friend's place. (*I try to elucidate the temporal relations a little.*) But I behave like a paretic, and the dream revels in absurdity. This means that the dream-thoughts say, ironically: "Naturally, he is the fool, the lunatic, and you are the clever people who know better. Perhaps, however, it is the other way about?" Now, *the other way about* is abundantly represented in my dream, inasmuch as Goethe has attacked the young man, which is absurd, while it is perfectly possible even today for a young fellow to attack the immortal Goethe; and inasmuch as I reckon from the *year of Goethe's death,* while I made the paretic reckon from the *year of his birth.*

But I have further promised to show that no dream is inspired by other than egoistical motives. Accordingly, I must account for the fact that in this dream I make my friend's cause my own, and put myself in his place. My critical conviction in waking life would not justify

my doing so. Now, the story of the eighteen-year-old patient, and the divergent interpretations of his cry, "*Nature,*" allude to the fact that I have put myself into opposition to the majority of physicians by claiming a sexual aetiology for the psychoneuroses. I may say to myself: "You will meet with the same kind of criticism as your friend; indeed you have already done so to some extent"; so that I may now replace the *he* in the dream-thoughts by *we.* "Yes, you are right; we two are the fools." That *mea res agitur* is clearly shown by the mention of the short, incomparably beautiful essay of Goethe's, for it was a popular lecture on this essay which induced me to study the natural sciences when I left the Gymnasium, and was still undecided as to my future.

VI

I have to show that yet another dream in which my ego does not appear is none the less egoistic. On p. 249 I referred to a short dream in which Professor M says: "*My son, the myopic . . .*"; and I stated that this was only a preliminary dream, preceding another in which I play a part. Here is the main dream, previously omitted, which challenges us to explain its absurd and unintelligible word-formation.

On account of something or other that is happening in Rome, it is necessary for the children to flee, and this they do. The scene is then laid before a gate, a double gate in the ancient style (the Porta Romana in Siena, as I realize while I am dreaming). I am sitting on the edge of a well, and I am greatly depressed; I am almost weeping. A woman—a nurse, a nun —brings out the two boys and hands them over to their father, who is not myself. The elder is distinctly my eldest son, but I do not see the face of the other boy. The woman asks the eldest boy for a parting kiss. She is remarkable for a red nose. The boy refuses her the kiss, but says to her, extending her his hand in parting, "Auf Geseres," and to both of us (or to one of us) "Auf Ungeseres." I have the idea that this indicates a preference.

This dream is built upon a tangle of thoughts induced by a play I saw at the theatre, called *Das neue Ghetto (The New Ghetto).* The Jewish question, anxiety as to the future of my children, who cannot be given a fatherland, anxiety as to educating them so that they may enjoy the privileges of citizens—all these features may easily be recognized in the accompanying dream-thoughts.

"By the waters of Babylon we sat down and

wept." Siena, like Rome, is famous for its beautiful fountains. In the dream I have to find some sort of substitute for Rome (cf. p. 217) from among localities which are known to me. Near the Porta Romana of Siena we saw a large, brightly-lit building, which we learned was the *Manicomio*, the insane asylum. Shortly before the dream I had heard that a co-religionist had been forced to resign a position, which he had secured with great effort, in a State asylum.

Our interest is aroused by the speech: *"Auf Geseres,"* where one might expect, from the situation continued throughout the dream, *"Auf Wiedersehen"* *(Au revoir)*, and by its quite meaningless antithesis: *"Auf Ungeseres."* (*Un* is a prefix meaning "not.")

According to information received from Hebrew scholars, *Geseres* is a genuine Hebrew word, derived from the verb *goiser*, and may best be rendered by "ordained sufferings, fated disaster." From its employment in the Jewish jargon one would take it to mean "wailing and lamentation." *Ungeseres* is a coinage of my own, and is the first to attract my attention, but for the present it baffles me. The little observation at the end of the dream—that *Ungeseres* indicates an advantage over *Geseres* —opens the way to the associations, and therewith to understanding. This relation holds good in the case of caviar; the *unsalted kind* is more highly prized than the salted. "Caviar to the general"—"noble passions." Herein lies concealed a jesting allusion to a member of my household, of whom I hope—for she is younger than I—that she will watch over the future of my children; this, too, agrees with the fact that another member of my household, our worthy nurse, is clearly indicated by the nurse (or nun) of the dream. But a connecting-link is wanting between the pair, *salted—unsalted* and *Geseres—Ungeseres.* This is to be found in *gesauert* and *ungesauert (leavened* and *unleavened)*. In their flight or exodus from Egypt the children of Israel had not time to allow their dough to become leavened, and in commemoration of this event they eat unleavened bread at Passover to this day. Here, too, I can find room for the sudden association which occurred to me in this part of the analysis. I remembered how we, my friend from Berlin and myself, had strolled about the streets of Breslau, a city which was strange to us, during the last days of Easter. A little girl asked me the way to a certain street; I had to tell her that I did not know it; I then remarked to my

friend, "I hope that later on in life the child will show more perspicacity in selecting the persons whom she allows to direct her." Shortly afterwards a sign caught my eye: "Dr. *Herod*, consulting hours..." I said to myself: "I hope this colleague does not happen to be a children's specialist." Meanwhile, my friend had been developing his views on the biological significance of *bilateral symmetry*, and had begun a sentence with the words: "If we had only one eye in the middle of the forehead, like Cyclops . . ." This leads us to the speech of the professor in the preliminary dream: *"My son, the myopic."* And now I have been led to the chief source for *Geseres*. Many years ago, when this son of Professor M's, who is today an independent thinker, was still sitting on his school-bench, he contracted an affection of the eye which, according to the doctor, gave some cause for anxiety. He expressed the opinion that so long as it was confined *to one eye* it was of no great significance, but that if it should extend to the other eye it would be serious. The affection subsided in the one eye without leaving any ill effects; shortly afterwards, however, the same symptoms did actually appear in the other eye. The boy's terrified mother immediately summoned the physician to her distant home in the country. But the doctor was now of a different opinion (took *the other side*). *"What sort of 'Geseres' is this you are making?"* he asked the mother, impatiently. *"If one side got well, the other will, too."* And so it turned out.

And now as to the connection between this and myself and my family. The *school-bench* upon which Professor M's son learned his first lessons has become the property of my eldest son; it was given to him by the boy's mother, and it is into his mouth that I put the words of farewell in the dream. One of the wishes that may be connected with this tranference may now be readily guessed. This school-bench is intended by its construction to guard the child from becoming *shortsighted* and *one-sided*. Hence *myopia* (and behind it the Cyclops), and the discussion about *bilateralism.* The fear of one-sidedness has a twofold significance; it might mean not only physical one-sidedness, but intellectual one-sidedness also. Does it not seem as though the scene in the dream, with all its craziness, were contradicting precisely this anxiety? When *on the one hand* the boy has spoken his words of farewell, *on the other hand* he calls out the very opposite, as though to establish an equilibrium. He is acting, as it were, in obedience to bilateral symmetry!

Thus, a dream frequently has the profoundest meaning in the places where it seems most absurd. In all ages those who have had something to say and have been unable to say it without danger to themselves have gladly donned the cap and bells. He for whom the forbidden saying was intended was more likely to tolerate it if he was able to laugh at it, and to flatter himself with the comment that what he disliked was obviously absurd. Dreams behave in real life as does the prince in the play who is obliged to pretend to be a madman, and hence we may say of dreams what Hamlet said of himself, substituting an unintelligible jest for the actual truth: "I am but mad north-north-west; when the wind is southerly I know a hawk from a handsaw" (Act II, sc. ii).[1]

Thus, my solution of the problem of absurdity in dreams is that the dream-thoughts are never absurd—at least, not those of the dreams of sane persons—and that the dream-work produces absurd dreams, and dreams with individually absurd elements, when the dream-thoughts contain criticism, ridicule, and derision, which have to be given expression. My next concern is to show that the dream-work is exhausted by the co-operation of the three factors enumerated—and of a fourth which has still to be mentioned—that it does no more than translate the dream-thoughts, observing the four conditions prescribed, and that the question whether the mind goes to work in dreams with all its intellectual faculties, or with only part of them, is wrongly stated, and does not meet the actual state of affairs. But since there are plenty of dreams in which judgments are passed, criticisms made, and facts recognized in which astonishment at some individual element of the dream appears, and explanations are attempted, and arguments adduced, I must meet the objections deriving from these occurrences by the citation of selected examples.

My answer is as follows: *Everything in dreams which occurs as the apparent functioning of the critical faculty is to be regarded, not as the intellectual performance of the dream-work, but as belonging to the substance of the dream-thoughts, and it has found its way from these, as a completed structure, into the manifest dream-content.* I may go even farther than this! I may even say that the judgments which are passed upon the dream as it is remembered *after waking,* and the feelings which are aroused by the reproduction of the dream, belong largely to the latent dream-content, and must be fitted into place in the interpretation of the dream.

1. One striking example of this has already been given. A female patient does not wish to relate her dream *because it was too vague.* She saw a person in the dream, and does not know *whether it was her husband or her father.* Then follows a second dream-fragment, in which there occurs a *manure-pail,* with which the following reminiscence is associated. As a young housewife she once declared jestingly, in the presence of a young male relative who frequented the house, that her next business would be to procure a new manure-pail. Next morning one was sent to her, but it was filled with lilies of the valley. This part of the dream served to represent the phrase, "Not grown on my own manure." [2] If we complete the analysis, we find in the dream-thoughts the after-effect of a story heard in youth; namely, that a girl had given birth to a child, and that *it was not clear who was the father.* The dream-representation here overlaps into the waking thought, and allows one of the elements of the dream-thoughts to be represented by a judgment, formed in the waking state, of the whole dream.

2. A similar case: One of my patients has a dream which strikes him as being an interesting one, for he says to himself, immediately after waking: "*I must tell that to the doctor.*" The dream is analysed, and shows the most distinct allusion to an affair in which he had become involved during the treatment, and of which he had decided to *tell me nothing.*[3]

3. Here is a third example from my own experience:

I go to the hospital with P, through a neighbourhood in which there are houses and gardens. Thereupon I have an idea that I have

---

[1] This dream furnishes a good example in support of the universally valid doctrine that dreams of the same night, even though they are separated in the memory, spring from the same thought-material. The dream-situation in which I am rescuing my children from the city of Rome, moreover, is distorted by a reference back to an episode of my childhood. The meaning is that I envy certain relatives who years ago had occasion to transplant their children to the soil of another country.

[2] This German expression is equivalent to our saying: "I am not responsible for that," "That's not my funeral," or "That's not due to my own efforts."—TR.
[3] The injunction or resolve already contained in the dream: "*I must tell that to the doctor,*" when it occurs in dreams during psycho-analytic treatment, is constantly accompanied by a great resistance to confessing the dream, and is not infrequently followed by the forgetting of the dream.

already seen this locality several times in my dreams. I do not know my way very well; P shows me a way which leads round a corner to a restaurant (indoor); here I ask for Frau Doni, and I hear that she is living at the back of the house, in a small room, with three children. I go there, and on the way I meet an undefined person with my two little girls. After I have been with them for a while, I take them with me. A sort of reproach against my wife for having left them there.

On waking I am conscious of a great *satisfaction,* whose motive seems to be the fact that I shall now learn from the analysis what is meant by *I have already dreamed of this.*[1] But the analysis of the dream tells me nothing about this; it shows me only that the satisfaction belongs to the latent dream-content, and not to a judgment of the dream. It is *satisfaction concerning the fact that I have had children by my marriage.* P's path through life and my own ran parallel for a time; now he has outstripped me both socially and financially, but his marriage has remained childless. Of this the two occasions of the dream give proof on complete analysis. On the previous day I had read in the newspaper the obituary notice of a certain Frau *Dona A—y* (which I turn into Doni), who had died in childbirth; I was told by my wife that the dead woman had been nursed by the same midwife whom she herself had employed at the birth of our two youngest boys. The name *Dona* had caught my attention, for I had recently met with it for the first time in an English novel. The other occasion for the dream may be found in the date on which it was dreamed; this was the night before the birthday of my eldest boy, who, it seems, is poetically gifted.

4. The same satisfaction remained with me after waking from the absurd dream that my father, after his death, had played a political rôle among the Magyars. It is motivated by the persistence of the feeling which accompanied the last sentence of the dream: *I remember that on his deathbed he looked so like Garibaldi, and* I am glad *that it has really come true... (Followed by a forgotten continuation.)* I can now supply from the analysis what should fill this gap. It is the mention of my second boy, to whom I have given the baptismal name of an eminent historical personage who attracted me greatly during my boyhood, especially during my stay in England. I had to wait for a year before I could fulfil my intention of using this name if the next child should be a son, and with great *satisfaction* I greeted him by this name as soon as he was born. It is easy to see how the father's suppressed desire for greatness is, in his thoughts, transferred to his children; one is inclined to believe that this is one of the ways by which the suppression of this desire (which becomes necessary in the course of life) is effected. The little fellow won his right to inclusion in the text of this dream by virtue of the fact that the same accident—that of soiling his clothes (quite pardonable in either a child or in a dying person)—had occurred to him. Compare with this the allusion *Stuhlrichter* (presiding judge) and the wish of the dream: to stand before one's children *great* and *undefiled.*

5. If I should now have to look for examples of judgments or expressions of opinion which remain in the dream itself, and are not continued in, or transferred to, our waking thoughts, my task would be greatly facilitated were I to take my examples from dreams which have already been cited for other purposes. The dream of Goethe's attack on Herr M appears to contain quite a number of acts of judgment. *I try to elucidate the temporal relations a little, as they seem improbable to me.* Does not this look like a critical impulse directed against the nonsensical idea that Goethe should have made a literary attack upon a young man of my acquaintance? *It seems plausible to me that he was* 18 *years old.* That sounds quite like the result of a calculation, though a silly one; and the *I do not know exactly what is the date of the present year* would be an example of uncertainty or doubt in dreams.

But I know from analysis that these acts of judgment, which seem to have been performed in the dream for the first time, admit of a different construction, in the light of which they become indispensable for interpreting the dream, while at the same time all absurdity is avoided. With the sentence *I try to elucidate the temporal relations a little,* I put myself in the place of my friend, who is actually trying to elucidate the temporal relations of life. The sentence then loses its significance as a judgment which objects to the nonsense of the previous sentences. The interposition, *Which seems improbable to me,* belongs to the following: *It seems plausible to me.* With almost these identical words I replied to the lady who

---

[1] A subject which has been extensively discussed in recent volumes of the *Revue Philosophique* (paramnesia in dreams).

told me of her brother's illness: "It seems improbable to me" that the cry of "Nature, Nature," was in any way connected with Goethe; it seems much more plausible to me that it has the sexual significance which is known to you. In this case, it is true, a judgment was expressed, but in reality, not in a dream, and on an occasion which is remembered and utilized by the dream-thoughts. The dream-content appropriates this judgment like any other fragment of the dream-thoughts.

The number 18 with which the judgment in the dream is meaninglessly connected still retains a trace of the context from which the real judgment was taken. Lastly, the *I do not know exactly what is the date of the present year* is intended for no other purpose than that of my identification with the paralytic, in examining whom this particular fact was established.

In the solution of these apparent acts of judgment in dreams, it will be well to keep in mind the above-mentioned rule of interpretation, which tells us that we must disregard the coherence which is established in the dream between its constituent parts as an unessential phenomenon, and that every dream-element must be taken separately and traced back to its source. The dream is a compound, which for the purposes of investigation must be broken up into its elements. On the other hand, we become alive to the fact that there is a psychic force which expresses itself in our dreams and establishes this apparent coherence; that is, the material obtained by the dream-work undergoes a secondary elaboration. Here we have the manifestations of that psychic force which we shall presently take into consideration as the fourth of the factors which co-operate in dream-formation.

6. Let us now look for other examples of acts of judgment in the dreams which have already been cited. In the absurd dream about the communication from the town council, I ask the question, *"You married soon after?"* *I reckon that I was born in* 1856, *which seems to me to be directly afterwards.* This certainly takes the form of an *inference.* My father married shortly after his attack, in the year 1851. I am the eldest son, born in 1856; so this is correct. We know that this inference has in fact been falsified by the wish-fulfilment, and that the sentence which dominates the dream-thoughts is as follows: *Four or five years—that is no time at all—that need not be counted.* But every part of this chain of reasoning may

be seen to be otherwise determined from the dream-thoughts, as regards both its content and its form. It is the patient of whose patience my colleague complains who intends to marry immediately the treatment is ended. The manner in which I converse with my father in this dream reminds me of an *examination* or *cross-examination,* and thus of a university professor who was in the habit of compiling a complete docket of personal data when entering his pupils' names: You were born when?—1856.— *Patre?*—Then the applicant gave the Latin form of the baptismal name of the father and we students assumed that the Hofrat drew inferences from the father's name which the baptismal name of the candidate would not always have justified. Hence, the *drawing of inferences* in the dream would be merely the repetition of the *drawing of inferences* which appears as a scrap of material in the dream-thoughts. From this we learn something new. If an inference occurs in the dream-content, it assuredly comes from the dream-thoughts; but it may be contained in these as a fragment of remembered material, or it may serve as the logical connective of a series of dream-thoughts. In any case, an inference in the dream represents an inference taken from the dream-thoughts.[1]

It will be well to continue the analysis of this dream at this point. With the inquisition of the professor is associated the recollection of an index (in my time published in Latin) of the university students; and further, the recollection of my own course of study. The *five years* allowed for the study of medicine were, as usual, too little for me. I worked unconcernedly for some years longer; my acquaintances regarded me as a loafer, and doubted whether I should get through. Then, suddenly, I decided to take my examinations, and I got through *in spite of the postponement.* A fresh confirmation of the dream-thoughts with which I defiantly meet my critics: "Even though you won't believe it, because I am taking my time, I shall reach the *conclusion* (German, *Schluss* = end, conclusion, *inference*). It has often happened like that."

In its introductory portion, this dream contains several sentences which, we can hardly deny, are of the nature of an argument. And this argument is not at all absurd; it might

---

[1] These results correct at several points my earlier statements concerning the representation of logical relations (p. 265). These described the general procedure of the dream-work, but overlooked its most delicate and most careful operations.

just as well occur in my waking thoughts. *In my dream I make fun of the communication from the town council, for in the first place I was not yet born in 1851, and in the second place my father, to whom it might refer, is already dead.* Not only is each of these statements perfectly correct in itself, but they are the very arguments that I should employ if I received such a communication. We know from the foregoing analysis (p. 309) that this dream has sprung from the soil of deeply embittered and scornful dream-thoughts; and if we may also assume that the motive of the censorship is a very powerful one, we shall understand that the dream-thought has every occasion to create *a flawless refutation of an unreasonable demand*, in accordance with the pattern contained in the dream-thoughts. But the analysis shows that in this case the dream-work has not been required to make a free imitation, but that material taken from the dream-thoughts had to be employed for the purpose. It is as though in an algebraic equation there should occur, besides the figures, plus and minus signs, and symbols of powers and of roots, and as though someone, in copying this equation, without understanding it, should copy both the symbols and the figures, and mix them all up together. The two arguments may be traced to the following material: It is painful to me to think that many of the hypotheses upon which I base my psychological solution of the psychoneuroses will arouse scepticism and ridicule when they first become known. For instance, I shall have to assert that impressions of the second year of life, and even the first, leave an enduring trace upon the emotional life of subsequent neuropaths, and that these impressions —although greatly distorted and exaggerated by the memory—may furnish the earliest and profoundest basis of a hysterical symptom. Patients to whom I explain this at a suitable moment are wont to parody my explanation by offering to search for reminiscences of the period *when they were not yet born.* My disclosure of the unsuspected part played by the father in the earliest sexual impulses of female patients may well have a similar reception. (Cf. the discussion on p. 244). Nevertheless, it is my well-founded conviction that both doctrines are true. In confirmation of this I recall certain examples in which the death of the father occurred when the child was very young, and subsequent incidents, otherwise inexplicable, proved that the child had unconsciously preserved recollections of the person who had so early gone out of its life. I know that both my assertions are based upon *inferences* whose validity will be attacked. It is the doing of the wish-fulfilment that precisely the material of those inferences, which I fear will be contested, should be utilized by the dream-work for establishing *incontestable conclusions*.

7. In one dream, which I have hitherto only touched upon, astonishment at the subject emerging is distinctly expressed at the outset.

The elder Brücke must have set me some task or other; strangely enough, it relates to the preparation of the lower part of my own body, the pelvis and legs, which I see before me as though in the dissecting-room, but without feeling the absence of part of my body, and without a trace of horror. Louise N is standing beside me, and helps me in the work. The pelvis is eviscerated; now the upper, now the lower aspect is visible, and the two aspects are commingled. Large fleshy red tubercles are visible (which, even in the dream, make me think of haemorrhoids). Also something lying over them had to be carefully picked off; it looked like crumpled tinfoil.[1] Then I was once more in possession of my legs, and I made a journey through the city, but I took a cab (as I was tired). To my astonishment, the cab drove into the front door of a house, which opened and allowed it to pass into a corridor, which was broken off at the end, and eventually led on into the open.[2] Finally I wandered through changing landscapes, with an Alpine guide, who carried my things. He carried me for some distance, out of consideration for my tired legs. The ground was swampy; we went along the edge; people were sitting on the ground, like Red Indians or gypsies; among them a girl. Until then I had made my way along on the slippery ground, in constant astonishment that I was so well able to do so after making the preparation. At last we came to a small wooden house with an open window at one end. Here the guide set me down, and laid two planks, which stood in readiness, on the window-sill so as to bridge the chasm which had to be crossed from the window. Now I grew really alarmed about my legs. Instead of the expected crossing, I saw two grown-up men lying upon wooden benches which were fixed on the walls of the hut, and something like two

---

[1] Stanniol, allusion to *Stannius;* the nervous system of fishes; cf. p. 300.

[2] The place in the corridor of my apartment-house where the perambulators of the other tenants stand; it is also otherwise hyper-determined several times over.

sleeping children next to them; as though not the planks but the children were intended to make the crossing possible. I awoke with terrified thoughts.

Anyone who has been duly impressed by the extensive nature of dream-condensation will readily imagine what a number of pages the exhaustive analysis of this dream would fill. Fortunately for the context, I shall make this dream only the one example of astonishment in dreams, which makes its appearance in the parenthetical remark, *strangely enough*. Let us consider the occasion of the dream. It is a visit of this lady, Louise N, who helps me with my work in the dream. She says: "Lend me something to read." I offer her *She*, by Rider Haggard. A *strange* book, but full of hidden meaning," I try to explain; "the eternal feminine, the immortality of our emotions—" Here she interrupts me: "I know that book already. Haven't you something of your own?" "No, my own immortal works are still unwritten." "Well, when are you going to publish your so-called 'latest revelations,' which, you promised us, even we should be able to read?" she asks, rather sarcastically. I now perceive that she is a mouthpiece for someone else, and I am silent. I think of the effort it cost me to make public even my work on dreams, in which I had to surrender so much of my own intimate nature. ("The best that you know you can't tell the boys.") The preparation of *my own body* which I am ordered to make in my dream is thus the *self-analysis* involved in the communication of my dreams. The elder Brücke very properly finds a place here; in the first years of my scientific work it so happened that I neglected the publication of a certain discovery until his insistence forced me to publish it. But the further trains of thought, proceeding from my conversation with Louise N, go too deep to become conscious; they are sidetracked by way of the material which has been incidentally awakened in me by the mention of Rider Haggard's *She*. The comment *strangely enough* applies to this book, and to another by the same author, *The Heart of the World;* and numerous elements of the dream are taken from these two fantastic romances. The swampy ground over which the dreamer is carried, the chasm which has to be crossed by means of planks, come from *She;* the Red Indians, the girl, and the wooden house, from *The Heart of the World*. In both novels a woman is the leader, and both treat of perilous wanderings; *She* has to do with an adventurous

journey to an undiscovered country, a place almost untrodden by the foot of man. According to a note which I find in my record of the dream, the fatigue in my legs was a real sensation from those days. Probably a weary mood corresponded with this fatigue, and the doubting question: "How much farther will my legs carry me?" In *She*, the end of the adventure is that the heroine meets her death in the mysterious central fire, instead of winning immortality for herself and for others. Some related anxiety has mistakably arisen in the dream-thoughts. The *wooden house* is assuredly also a *coffin*—that is, the grave. But in representing this most unwished-for of all thoughts by means of a wish-fulfilment, the dream-work has achieved its masterpiece. I was once in a grave, but it was an empty Etruscan grave near Orvieto—a narrow chamber with two stone benches on the walls, upon which were lying the skeletons of two adults. The interior of the wooden house in the dream looks exactly like this grave, except that stone has been replaced by wood. The dream seems to say: "If you must already sojourn in your grave, let it be this Etruscan grave," and by means of this interpolation it transforms the most mournful expectation into one that is really to be desired. Unfortunately, as we shall learn, the dream is able to change into its opposite only the idea accompanying an affect, but not always the affect itself. Hence, I awake with *thoughts of terror*, even after the idea that perhaps my children will achieve what has been denied to their father has forced its way to representation: a fresh allusion to the strange romance in which the identity of a character is preserved through a series of generations covering two thousand years.

8. In the context of another dream there is a similar expression of astonishment at what is experienced in the dream. This, however, is connected with such a striking, far-fetched, and almost intellectual attempt at explanation that if only on this account I should have to subject the whole dream to analysis, even if it did not possess two other interesting features. On the night of the eighteenth of July I was travelling on the Southern Railway, and in my sleep I heard someone call out: "*Hollthurn, 10 minutes.*" *I immediately think of Holothuria—of a natural history museum—that here is a place where valiant men have vainly resisted the domination of their overlord.— Yes, the counter-reformation in Austria!—As though it were a place in Styria or the Tyrol.*

Now I see indistinctly a small museum, in which the relics or the acquisitions of these men are preserved. I should like to leave the train, but I hesitate to do so. There are women with fruit on the platform; they squat on the ground, and in that position invitingly hold up their baskets.—I hesitated, in doubt as to whether we have time, but here we are still stationary.—I am suddenly in another compartment, in which the leather and the seats are so narrow that one's spine directly touches the back.[1] I am surprised at this, but I may have changed carriages while asleep. Several people, among them an English brother and sister; a row of books plainly on a shelf on the wall.—I see The Wealth of Nations, *and* Matter and Motion *(by Maxwell), thick books bound in brown linen. The man asks his sister about a book of Schiller's, whether she has forgotten it. These books seem to belong now to me, now to them. At this point I wish to join in the conversation in order to confirm or support what is being said . . .* I wake sweating all over, because all the windows are shut. The train stops at *Marburg*.

While writing down the dream, a part of it occurs to me which my memory wished to pass over. *I tell the brother and sister (in English), referring to a certain book: "It is from . . ." but I correct myself: "It is by . . ." The man remarks to his sister: "He said it correctly."*

The dream begins with the name of a station, which seems to have almost waked me. For this name, which was *Marburg*, I substitute *Hollthurn*. The fact that I heard Marburg the first, or perhaps the second time it was called out, is proved by the mention of Schiller in the dream; he was born in Marburg, though not the Styrian Marburg.[2] Now on this occasion, although I was travelling first class, I was doing so under very disagreeable circumstances. The train was overcrowded; in my compartment I had come upon a lady and gentleman who seemed very fine people, and had not the good breeding, or did not think it worth while, to conceal their displeasure at my intrusion. My polite greeting was not returned, and al-

though they were sitting side by side (with their backs to the engine), the woman before my eyes hastened to pre-empt the seat opposite her, and next to the window, with her umbrella; the door was immediately closed, and pointed remarks about the opening of windows were exchanged. Probably I was quickly recognized as a person hungry for fresh air. It was a hot night, and the atmosphere of the compartment, closed on both sides, was almost suffocating. My experience as a traveller leads me to believe that such inconsiderate and overbearing conduct marks people who have paid for their tickets only partly, or not at all. When the conductor came round, and I presented my dearly bought ticket, the lady exclaimed haughtily and almost threateningly: "My husband has a pass." She was an imposing-looking person, with a discontented expression, in age not far removed from the autumn of feminine beauty; the man had no chance to say anything; he sat there motionless. I tried to sleep. In my dream I take a terrible revenge on my disagreeable travelling companions; no one would suspect what insults and humiliations are concealed behind the disjointed fragments of the first half of the dream. After this need has been satisfied, the second wish, to exchange my compartment for another, makes itself felt. The dream changes its scene so often, and without making the slightest objection to such changes, that it would not have seemed at all remarkable had I at once, from my memories, replaced my travelling companions by more agreeable persons. But here was a case where something or other opposes the change of scene, and finds it necessary to explain it. How did I suddenly get into another compartment? I could not postively remember having changed carriages. So there was only one explanation. *I must have left the carriage while asleep*—an unusual occurrence, examples of which, however, are known to neuropathologists. We know of persons who undertake railway journeys in a crepuscular state, without betraying their abnormal condition by any sign whatever, until at some stage of their journey they come to themselves, and are surprised by the gap in their memory. Thus, while I am still dreaming, I declare my own case to be such a case of *automatisme ambulatoire*.

Analysis permits of another solution. The attempt at explanation, which so surprises me if I am to attribute it to the dream-work, is not original, but is copied from the neurosis of one of my patients. I have already spoken

---

[1] This description is not intelligible even to myself, but I follow the principle of reproducing the dream in those words which occur to me while I am writing it down. The wording itself is a part of the dream-representation.

[2] Schiller was not born in one of the *Marburgs*, but in *Marbach*, as every German schoolboy knows, and as I myself knew. This again is one of those errors (cf. p. 218) which creep in as substitutes for an intentional falsification in another place and which I have endeavoured to explain in *The Psycho-pathology of Everyday Life*.

in another chapter of a highly cultured and kindly man who began, shortly after the death of his parents, to accuse himself of murderous tendencies, and who was distressed by the precautionary measures which he had to take to secure himself against these tendencies. His was a case of severe obsessional ideas with full insight. To begin with, it was painful to him to walk through the streets, as he was obsessed by the necessity of accounting for all the persons he met; he had to know whither they had disappeared; if one of them suddenly eluded his pursuing glance, he was left with a feeling of distress and the idea that he might possibly have made away with the man. Behind this obsessive idea was concealed, among other things, a Cain-phantasy, for "all men are brothers." Owing to the impossibility of accomplishing this task, he gave up going for walks, and spent his life imprisoned within his four walls. But reports of murders which had been committed in the world outside were constantly reaching his room by way of the newspapers, and his conscience tormented him with the doubt that he might be the murderer for whom the police were looking. The certainty that he had not left the house for weeks protected him for a time against these accusations, until one day there dawned upon him the possibility that *he might have left his house while in an unconscious state,* and might thus have committed murder without knowing anything about it. From that time onwards he locked his front door, and gave the key to his old housekeeper, strictly forbidding her to give it into his hands, even if he demanded it.

This, then, is the origin of the attempted explanation that I may have changed carriages while in an unconscious state; it has been taken into the dream ready-made, from the material of the dream-thoughts, and is evidently intended to identify me with the person of my patient. My memory of this patient was awakened by natural association. My last night journey had been made a few weeks earlier in his company. He was cured, and we were going into the country together to his relatives, who had sent for me; as we had a compartment to ourselves, we left all the windows open throughout the night, and for as long as I remained awake we had a most interesting conversation. I knew that hostile impulses towards his father in childhood, in a sexual connection, had been at the root of his illness. By identifying myself with him, I wanted to make an analogous confession to myself. The second scene of the

dream really resolves itself into a wanton phantasy to the effect that my two elderly travelling companions had acted so uncivilly towards me because my arrival on the scene had prevented them from exchanging kisses and embraces during the night, as they had intended. This phantasy, however, goes back to an early incident of my childhood when, probably impelled by sexual curiosity, I had intruded into my parents' bedroom, and was driven thence by my father's emphatic command.

I think it would be superfluous to multiply such examples. They would all confirm what we have learned from those already cited: namely, that an act of judgment in a dream is merely the repetition of an original act of judgment in the dream-thoughts. In most cases it is an unsuitable repetition, fitted into an inappropriate context; occasionally, however, as in our last example, it is so artfully applied that it may almost give one the impression of independent intellectual activity in the dream. At this point we might turn our attention to that psychic activity which, though it does not appear to co-operate constantly in the formation of dreams, yet endeavours to fuse the dream-elements of different origin into a flawless and significant whole. We consider it necessary, however, first of all to consider the expressions of affect which appear in dreams, and to compare these with the affects which analysis discovers in the dream-thoughts.

H. *The Affects in Dreams*

A shrewd remark of Stricker's called our attention to the fact that the expressions of affects in dreams cannot be disposed of in the contemptuous fashion in which we are wont to shake off the dream-content after we have waked. "If I am afraid of robbers in my dreams, the robbers, to be sure, are imaginary, but the fear of them is real"; and the same thing is true if I rejoice in my dream. According to the testimony of our feelings, an affect experienced in a dream is in no way inferior to one of like intensity experienced in waking life, and the dream presses its claim to be accepted as part of our real psychic experiences, by virtue of its affective rather than its ideational content. In the waking state, we do not put the one before the other, since we do not know how to evaluate an affect psychically except in connection with an ideational content. If an affect and an idea are ill-matched as regards their nature or their intensity, our waking judgment becomes confused.

The fact that in dreams the ideational content does not always produce the affective result which in our waking thoughts we should expect as its necessary consequence has always been a cause of astonishment. Strümpell declared that ideas in dreams are stripped of their psychic values. But there is no lack of instances in which the reverse is true; when an intensive manifestation of affect appears in a content which seems to offer no occasion for it. In my dream I may be in a horrible, dangerous, or disgusting situation, and yet I may feel no fear or aversion; on the other hand, I am sometimes terrified by harmless things, and sometimes delighted by childish things.

This enigma disappeared more suddenly and more completely than perhaps any other dream-problem if we pass from the manifest to the latent content. We shall then no longer have to explain it, for it will no longer exist. Analysis tells us that *the ideational contents have undergone displacements and substitutions, while the affects have remained unchanged*. No wonder, then, that the ideational content which has been altered by dream-distortion no longer fits the affect which has remained intact; and no cause for wonder when analysis has put the correct content into its original place.[1]

In a psychic complex which has been subjected to the influence of the resisting censorship, the affects are the unyielding constituent, which alone can guide us to the correct completion. This state of affairs is revealed in the psychoneuroses even more distinctly than in dreams. Here the affect is always in the right, at least as regards its quality; its intensity may, of course, be increased by displacement of the neurotic attention. When the hysterical patient wonders that he should be so afraid of a trifle, or when the sufferer from obsessions is astonished that he should reproach himself so bitterly for a mere nothing, they are both in error, inasmuch as they regard the conceptual content—the trifle, the mere nothing—as the essential thing, and they defend themselves in vain, because they make this conceptual content the starting-point of their thought-work. Psycho-analysis, however, puts them on the right path, inasmuch as it recognizes that, on the contrary, it is the affect that is justified, and looks for the concept which pertains to it, and which has been repressed by a substitution. All that we need assume is that the liberation of affect and the conceptual content do not constitute the indissoluble organic unity as which we are wont to regard them, but that the two parts may be welded together, so that analysis will separate them. Dream-interpretation shows that this is actually the case.

I will first of all give an example in which analysis explains the apparent absence of affect in a conceptual content which ought to compel a liberation of affect.

I

The dreamer sees three lions in a desert, one of which is laughing, but she is not afraid of them. Then, however, she must have fled from them, for she is trying to climb a tree. But she finds that her cousin, the French teacher, is already up in the tree, etc.

The analysis yields the following material: The indifferent occasion of the dream was a sentence in the dreamer's English exercise: "The *lion's* greatest adornment is his mane." Her father used to wear a beard which encircled his face like a *mane*. The name of her English teacher is Miss *Lyons*. An acquaintance of hers sent her the ballads of *Loewe* (*Loewe* = lion). These, then, are the three lions; why should she be afraid of them? She has read a story in which a negro who has incited his fellows to revolt is hunted with bloodhounds, and climbs a tree to save himself Then follow fragmentary recollections in the merriest mood, such as the following directions for catching lions (from *Die Fliegende Blätter*): "Take a desert and put it through a sieve; the lions will be left behind." Also a very amusing, but not very proper anecdote about an official who is asked why he does not take greater pains to win the favour of his chief, and who replies that he has been trying to creep into favour, but that his immediate superior was *already up there*. The whole matter becomes intelligible as soon as one learns that on the dream-day the lady had received a visit from her husband's superior. He was very polite to her, and

---

[1] If I am not greatly mistaken, the first dream which I was able to elicit from my grandson (aged 20 months) points to the fact that the dream-work had succeeded in transforming its material into a wish-fulfilment, while the affect which belonged to it remained unchanged even in the sleeping state. The night before its father was to return to the front the child cried out, sobbing violently: "Papa, Papa—Baby." That may mean: Let Papa and Baby still be together; while the weeping takes cognizance of the imminent departure. The child was at the time very well able to express the concept of separation. *Fort* (=*away*, replaced by a peculiarly accented, long-drawn-out *ooooh*) had been his first word, and for many months before this first dream he had played at *away* with all his toys; which went back to his early self-conquest in allowing his mother to go away.

kissed her hand, and *she was not at all afraid of him,* although he is a *big bug (Grosses Tier* = big animal) and plays the part of a *social lion* in the capital of her country. This lion is, therefore, like the lion in *A Midsummer Night's Dream,* who is unmasked as Snug the joiner; and of such stuff are all the dream-lions of which one is not afraid.

II

As my second example, I will cite the dream of the girl who saw her sister's little son lying as a corpse in his coffin, but who, it may be added, was conscious of no pain or sorrow. Why she was unmoved we know from the analysis. The dream only disguised her wish to see once more the man she loved; the affect had to be attuned to the wish, and not to its disguisement. There was thus no occasion for sorrow.

In a number of dreams the affect does at least remain connected with the conceptual content which has replaced the content really belonging to it. In others, the dissolution of the complex is carried farther. The affect is entirely separated from the idea belonging to it, and finds itself accommodated elsewhere in the dream, where it fits into the new arrangement of the dream-elements. We have seen that the same thing happens to acts of judgment in dreams. If an important inference occurs in the dream-thoughts, there is one in the dream also; but the inference in the dream may be displaced to entirely different material. Not infrequently this displacement is effected in accordance with the principle of antithesis.

I will illustrate the latter possibility by the following dream, which I have subjected to the most exhaustive analysis.

III

A castle by the sea; afterwards it lies not directly on the coast, but on a narrow canal leading to the sea. A certain Herr P is the governor of the castle. I stand with him in a large salon with three windows, in front of which rise the projections of a wall, like battlements of a fortress. I belong to the garrison, perhaps as a volunteer naval officer. We fear the arrival of enemy warships, for we are in a state of war. Herr P intends to leave the castle; he gives me instructions as to what must be done if what we fear should come to pass. His sick wife and his children are in the threatened castle. As soon as the bombardment begins, the large hall is to be cleared. He breathes heavily, and tries to get away; I detain him, and ask him how I am to send him news in *case of need. He says something further, and immediately afterwards he sinks to the floor dead. I have probably taxed him unnecessarily with my questions. After his death, which makes no further impression upon me, I consider whether the widow is to remain in the castle, whether I should give notice of the death to the higher command, whether I should take over the control of the castle as the next in command. I now stand at the window, and scrutinize the ships as they pass by; they are cargo steamers, and they rush by over the dark water; several with more than one funnel, others with bulging decks* (these are very like the railway stations in the preliminary dream, which has not been related). *Then my brother is standing beside me, and we both look out of the window on to the canal. At the sight of one ship we are alarmed, and call out: "Here comes the warship!"* It turns out, however, that they *are only the ships which I have already seen, returning. Now comes a small ship, comically truncated, so that it ends amidships; on the deck one sees curious things like cups or little boxes. We call out as with one voice: "That is the breakfast ship."*

The rapid motion of the ships, the deep blue of the water, the brown smoke of the funnels —all these together produce an intense and gloomy impression.

The localities in this dream are compiled from several journeys to the Adriatic (Miramare, Duino, Venice, Aquileia). A short but enjoyable Easter trip to Aquileia with my brother, a few weeks before the dream, was still fresh in my memory; also the *naval war* between America and Spain, and, associated with this my anxiety as to the fate of my relatives in America, play a part in the dream. Manifestations of affect appear at two places in this dream. In one place an affect that would be expected is lacking: it expressly emphasized that the death of the governor makes no impression upon me; at another point, when I see the warships, I am *frightened,* and experience all the sensations of fright in my sleep. The distribution of affects in this well-constructed dream has been effected in such a way that any obvious contradiction is avoided. For there is no reason why I should be frightened at the governor's death, and it is fitting that, as the commander of the castle, I should be alarmed by the sight of the warship. Now analysis shows that Herr P is nothing but a substitute for my own ego (in the dream I am his substitute).

I am the governor who suddenly dies. The dream-thoughts deal with the future of my family after my premature death. No other disagreeable thought is to be found among the dream-thoughts. The alarm which goes with the sight of the warship must be transferred from it to this disagreeable thought. Inversely, the analysis shows that the region of the dream-thoughts from which the warship comes is laden with most cheerful reminiscences. In Venice, a year before the dream, one magically beautiful day, we stood at the windows of our room on the Riva Schiavoni and looked out over the blue lagoon, on which there was more traffic to be seen than usual. Some English ships were expected; they were to be given a festive reception; and suddenly my wife cried, happy as a child: *"Here comes the English warship!"* In the dream I am frightened by the very same words; once more we see that speeches in dreams have their origin in speeches in real life. I shall presently show that even the element *English* in this speech has not been lost for the dream-work. Here, then, between the dream-thoughts and the dream-content, I turn joy into fright, and I need only point to the fact that by means of this transformation I give expression to part of the latent dream-content. The example shows, however, that the dream-work is at liberty to detach the occasion of an affect from its connections in the dream-thoughts, and to insert it at any other place it chooses in the dream-content.

I will take the opportunity which is here, incidentally offered of subjecting to a closer analysis the *breakfast ship,* whose appearance in the dream so absurdly concludes a situation that has been rationally adhered to. If I look more closely at this dream-object, I am impressed after the event by the fact that it was black, and that by reason of its truncation at its widest beam it achieved, at the truncated end, a considerable resemblance to an object which had aroused our interest in the museums of the Etruscan cities. This object was a rectangular cup of black clay, with two handles, upon which stood things like coffee-cups or tea-cups, very similar to our modern service for the *breakfast table.* Upon inquiry we learned that this was the toilet set of an Etruscan lady, with little boxes for rouge and powder; and we told one another jestingly that it would not be a bad idea to take a thing like that home to the lady of the house. The dream-object, therefore, signifies a *black toilet (toi-*

lette = dress), or mourning, and refers directly to a death. The other end of the dream-object reminds us of the *boat* (German, *Nachen,* from the Greek root, νεχυς, as a philological friend informs me), upon which corpses were laid in prehistoric times, and were left to be buried by the sea. This is associated with the return of the ships in the dream.

"Silently on his rescued boat the old man drifts into harbour."

It is the return voyage after the ship*wreck* (German: *Schiff-bruch* = ship-*breaking*); the breakfast ship looks as though it were *broken* off amidships. But whence comes the name *breakfast ship?* This is where *English* comes in, which we have left over from the warships. *Breakfast,* a *breaking of the fast. Breaking* again belongs to shipwreck *(Schiff-bruch),* and *fasting* is associated with the black (mourning).

But the only thing about this breakfast ship which has been newly created by the dream is its name. The thing existed in reality, and recalls to me one of the merriest moments of my last journey. As we distrusted the fare in Aquileia, we took some food with us from Goerz, and bought a bottle of the excellent Istrian wine in Aquileia; and while the little mailsteamer slowly travelled through the *canale delle Mee* and into the lonely expanse of lagoon in the direction of Grado, we had breakfast on deck in the highest spirits—we were the only passengers—and it tasted to us as few breakfasts have ever tasted. This, then, was the *breakfast ship,* and it is behind this very recollection of the gayest *joie de vivre* that the dream hides the saddest thoughts of an unknown and mysterious future.

The detachment of affects from the groups of ideas which have occasioned their liberation is the most striking thing that happens to them in dream-formation, but it is neither the only nor even the most essential change which they undergo on the way from the dream-thoughts to the manifest dream. If the affects in the dream-thoughts are compared with those in the dream, one thing at once becomes clear: Wherever there is an affect in the dream, it is to be found also in the dream-thoughts; the converse, however, is not true. In general, a dream is less rich in affects than the psychic material from which it is elaborated. When I have reconstructed the dream-thoughts, I see that the most intense psychic impulses are constantly striving in them for self-assertion, usually in conflict with others which are sharply opposed to them. Now, if I turn back to the dream, I often find it colourless and devoid of any very intensive affective tone. Not only the content, but also the affective tone of my thoughts is often reduced by the dream-work to the level of the indifferent. I might say that a *suppression of the affects* has been accomplished by the dream-work. Take, for example, the dream of the botanical monograph. It corresponds to a passionate plea for my freedom to act as I am acting, to arrange my life as seems right to me, and to me alone. The dream which results from this sounds indifferent; I have written a monograph; it is lying before me; it is provided with coloured plates, and dried plants are to be found in each copy. It is like the peace of a deserted battlefield; no trace is left of the tumult of battle.

But things may turn out quite differently; vivid expressions of affect may enter into the dream itself; but we will first of all consider the unquestioned fact that so many dreams appear indifferent, whereas it is never possible to go deeply into the dream-thoughts without deep emotion.

The complete theoretical explanation of this suppression of affects during the dream-work cannot be given here; it would require a most careful investigation of the theory of the affects and of the mechanism of repression. Here I can put forward only two suggestions. I am forced—for other reasons—to conceive the liberation of affects as a centrifugal process directed towards the interior of the body, analogous to the processes of motor and secretory innervation. Just as in the sleeping state the emission of motor impulses towards the outer world seems to be suspended, so the centrifugal awakening of affects by unconscious thinking during sleep may be rendered more difficult. The affective impulses which occur during the course of the dream-thoughts may thus in themselves be feeble, so that those that find their way into the dream are no stronger. According to this line of thought, the *suppression of the affects* would not be a consequence of the dream-work at all, but a consequence of the state of sleep. This may be so, but it cannot possibly be all the truth. We must remember that all the more complex dreams have revealed themselves as the result of a compromise between conflicting psychic forces. On the one hand, the wish-forming thoughts have to oppose the contradiction of a censorship; on the other hand, as we have often seen, even in unconscious thinking, every train of thought is harnessed to its contradictory counterpart. Since all these trains of thought are capable of arousing affects, we shall, broadly speaking, hardly go astray if we conceive the suppression of affects as the result of the inhibition which the contrasts impose upon one another, and the censorship upon the urges which it has suppressed. *The inhibition of affects would accordingly be the second consequence of the dream-censorship, just as dream-distortion was the first consequence.*

I will here insert an example of a dream in which the indifferent emotional tone of the dream-content may be explained by the antagonism of the dream-thoughts. I must relate the following short dream, which every reader will read with disgust.

IV

Rising ground, and on it something like an open-air latrine; a very long bench, at the end of which is a wide aperture. The whole of the back edge is thickly covered with little heaps of excrement of all sizes and degrees of freshness. A thicket behind the bench. I urinate upon the bench; a long stream of urine rinses everything clean, the patches of excrement come off easily and fall into the opening. Nevertheless, it seems as though something remained at the end.

Why did I experience no disgust in this dream?

Because, as the analysis shows, the most pleasant and gratifying thoughts have co-operated in the formation of this dream. Upon analysing it, I immediately think of the *Augean stables* which were cleansed by Hercules. I am this Hercules. The rising ground and the thicket belong to Aussee, where my children are now staying. I have discovered the infantile aetiology of the neuroses, and have thus guarded my own children from falling ill. The bench (omitting the aperture, of course) is the faithful copy of a piece of furniture of which an affectionate female patient has made me a present. This reminds me how my patients honour me. Even the museum of human excrement is susceptible of a gratifying interpretation. However much it disgusts me, it is a souvenir of the beautiful land of Italy, where in the small cities, as everyone knows, the privies are not equipped in any other way. The stream of urine that washes everything clean is an unmistakable allusion to greatness. It is in this manner that *Gulliver* extinguishes the great fire in Lilliput; to be sure, he thereby incurs the displeasure of the tiniest of queens. In this way, too, Gargantua, the superman of Master Rabelais, takes vengeance upon the Parisians, straddling Notre-Dame and training his stream of urine upon the city. Only yesterday I was turning over the leaves of Garnier's illustrations to Rabelais before I went to bed. And, strangely enough, here is another proof that I am the superman! The platform of Notre-Dame was my favourite nook in Paris; every free afternoon I used to go up into the towers of the cathedral and there clamber about between the monsters and gargoyles. The circumstance that all the excrement vanishes so rapidly before the stream of urine corresponds to the motto: *Afflavit et dissipati sunt,* which I shall some day make the title of a chapter on the therapeutics of hysteria.

And now as to the affective occasion of the dream. It had been a hot summer afternoon; in the evening, I had given my lecture on the connection between hysteria and the perversions, and everything which I had to say displeased me thoroughly, and seemed utterly valueless. I was tired; I took not the least pleasure in my difficult work, and longed to get away from this rummaging in human filth; first to see my children, and then to revisit the beauties of Italy. In this mood I went from the lecture-hall to a café to get some little refreshment in the open air, for my appetite had forsaken me. But a member of my audience went with me; he begged for permission to sit with me while I drank my coffee and gulped down my roll, and began to say flattering things to me. He told me how much he had learned from me, that he now saw everything through different eyes, that I had cleansed the *Augean stables* of error and prejudice, which encumbered the theory of the neuroses—in short, that I was a very great man. My mood was ill-suited to his hymn of praise; I struggled with my disgust, and went home earlier in order to get rid of him; and before I went to sleep I turned over the leaves of *Rabelais,* and read a short story by C. F. Meyer entitled *Die Leiden eines Knaben* (The Sorrows of a Boy).

The dream had originated from this material, and Meyer's novel had supplied the recollections of scenes of childhood.[1] The day's mood of annoyance and disgust is continued in the dream, inasmuch as it is permitted to furnish nearly all the material for the dream-con-

[1] Cf. the dream about Count Thun, last scene.

tent. But during the night the opposite mood of vigorous, even immoderate self-assertion awakened and dissipated the earlier mood. The dream had to assume such a form as would accommodate both the expressions of self-depreciation and exaggerated self-glorification in the same material. This compromise-formation resulted in an ambiguous dream-content, but, owing to the mutual inhibition of the opposites, in an indifferent emotional tone.

According to the theory of wish-fulfilment, this dream would not have been possible had not the opposed, and indeed suppressed, yet pleasure-emphasized megalomaniac train of thought been added to the thoughts of disgust. For nothing painful is intended to be represented in dreams; the painful elements of our daily thoughts are able to force their way into our dreams only if at the same time they are able to disguise a wish-fulfilment.

The dream-work is able to dispose of the affects of the dream-thoughts in yet another way than by admitting them or reducing them to zero. *It can transform them into their opposites.* We are acquainted with the rule that for the purposes of interpretation every element of the dream may represent its opposite, as well as itself. One can never tell beforehand which is to be posited; only the context can decide this point. A suspicion of this state of affairs has evidently found its way into the popular consciousness; the dream-books, in their interpretations, often proceed according to the principle of contraries. This transformation into the contrary is made possible by the intimate associative ties which in our thoughts connect the idea of a thing with that of its opposite. Like every other displacement, this serves the purposes of the censorship, but it is often the work of wish-fulfilment, for wish-fulfilment consists in nothing more than the substitution of an unwelcome thing by its opposite. Just as concrete images may be transformed into their contraries in our dreams, so also may the affects of the dream-thoughts, and it is probable that this inversion of affects is usually brought about by the dream-censorship. The *suppression and inversion of affects* is useful even in social life, as is shown by the familiar analogy of the dream-censorship and, above all, hypocrisy. If I am conversing with a person to whom I must show consideration while I should like to address him as an enemy, it is almost more important that I should conceal the expression of my affect from him than that I should modify the verbal expression of my thoughts. If I address him in courteous terms, but accompany them by looks or gestures of hatred and disdain, the effect which I produce upon him is not very different from what it would have been had I cast my unmitigated contempt into his face. Above all, then, the censorship bids me suppress my affects, and if I am a master of the art of dissimulation I can hypocritically display the opposite affect—smiling where I should like to be angry, and pretending affection where I should like to destroy.

We have already had an excellent example of such an inversion of affect in the service of the dream-censorship. In the dream *of my uncle's beard* I feel great affection for my friend R, while (and because) the dream-thoughts berate him as a simpleton. From this example of the inversion of affects we derived our first proof of the existence of the censorship. Even here it is not necessary to assume that the dream-work creates a counter-affect of this kind that is altogether new; it usually finds it lying ready in the material of the dream-thoughts, and merely intensifies it with the psychic force of the defence-motives until it is able to predominate in the dream-formation. In the dream of my uncle, the affectionate counter-affect probably has its origin in an infantile source (as the continuation of the dream would suggest), for owing to the peculiar nature of my earliest childhood experiences the relation of uncle and nephew has become the source of all my friendships and hatreds (cf. analysis on pp. 304-5 above).

An excellent example of such a reversal of affect is found in a dream recorded by Ferenczi.[1] "An elderly gentleman was awakened at night by his wife, who was frightened because he laughed so loudly and uncontrollably in his sleep. The man afterwards related that he had had the following dream: *I lay in my bed, a gentleman known to me came in, I wanted to turn on the light, but I could not; I attempted to do so repeatedly, but in vain. Thereupon my wife got out of bed, in order to help me, but she, too, was unable to manage it; being ashamed of her négligé in the presence of the gentleman, she finally gave it up and went back to her bed; all this was so comical that I had to laugh terribly. My wife said: 'What are you laughing at, what are you laughing at?' but I continued to laugh until I woke.* The following day the man was extremely depressed, and suffered from headache: 'From too much laugh-*

[1] *Internat. Zeitschr. f. Psychoanalyse*, IV (1916)

ter, which shook me up,' he thought.

"Analytically considered, the dream looks less comical. In the latent dream-thoughts the *gentleman known* to him who came into the room is the image of death as the 'great unknown,' which was awakened in his mind on the previous day. The old gentleman, who suffers from arteriosclerosis, had good reason to think of death on the day before the dream. The uncontrollable laughter takes the place of weeping and sobbing at the idea that he has to die. It is the light of life that he is no longer able to turn on. This mournful thought may have associated itself with a failure to effect sexual intercourse, which he had attempted shortly before this, and in which the assistance of his wife *en négligé* was of no avail; he realized that he was already on the decline. The dream-work knew how to transform the sad idea of impotence and death into a comic scene, and the sobbing into laughter."

There is one class of dreams which has a special claim to be called *hypocritical*, and which severely tests the theory of wish-fulfilment. My attention was called to them when Frau Dr. M. Hilferding proposed for discussion by the Psychoanalytic Society of Vienna a dream recorded by Rosegger, which is here reprinted:

In *Waldheimat*, vol. xi, Rosegger writes as follows in his story, *Fremd gemacht* (p. 303):

"I usually enjoy healthful sleep, yet I have gone without repose on many a night; in addition to my modest existence as a student and literary man, I have for long years dragged out the shadow of a veritable tailor's life—like a ghost from which I could not become divorced.

"It is not true that I have occupied myself very often or very intensely with thoughts of my past during the day. A stormer of heaven and earth who has escaped from the hide of the Philistine has other things to think about. And as a gay young fellow, I hardly gave a thought to my nocturnal dreams; only later, when I had formed the habit of thinking about everything, or when the Philistine within me began to assert itself a little, did it strike me that—when I dreamed at all—I was always a journeyman tailor, and that in that capacity I had already worked in my master's shop for a long time without any pay. As I sat there beside him, and sewed and pressed, I was perfectly well aware that I no longer belonged there, and that as a burgess of the town I had other things to attend to; but I was always on a holiday, or away in the country, and so I sat beside my master and helped him. I often felt far from comfortable about it, and regretted the waste of time which I might have employed for better and more useful purposes. If anything was not quite correct in measure and cut I had to put up with a scolding from my master. Of wages there was never a question. Often, as I sat with bent back in the dark workshop, I decided to give notice and make myself scarce. Once I actually did so, but the master took no notice of me, and next time I was sitting beside him again and sewing.

"How happy I was when I woke up after such weary hours! And I then resolved that, if this intrusive dream should ever occur again, I would energetically throw it off, and would cry aloud: 'It is only a delusion, I am lying in bed, and I want to sleep' . . . And the next night I would be sitting in the tailor's shop again.

"So it went on for years, with dismal regularity. Once when the master and I were working at Alpelhofer's, at the house of the peasant with whom I began my apprenticeship, it happened that my master was particularly dissatisfied with my work. 'I should like to know where in the world your thoughts are?' he cried, and looked at me sullenly. I thought the most sensible thing to do would be to get up and explain to the master that I was working with him only as a favour, and then take my leave. But I did not do this. I even submitted when the master engaged an apprentice, and ordered me to make room for him on the bench. I moved into the corner, and kept on sewing. On the same day another journeyman was engaged; a bigoted fellow; he was the Bohemian who had worked for us nineteen years earlier, and then had fallen into the lake on his way home from the public-house. When he tried to sit down there was no room for him. I looked at the master inquiringly, and he said to me: 'You have no talent for tailoring; *you may go; you're a stranger henceforth.*' My fright on that occasion was so overpowering that I woke.

"The grey of morning glimmered through the clear windows of my familiar home. *Objets d'art* surrounded me; in the tasteful bookcase stood the eternal Homer, the gigantic Dante, the incomparable Shakespeare, the glorious Goethe—all radiant and immortal. From the adjoining room resounded the clear little voices of the children, who were waking up and prattling to their mother. I felt as though I had rediscovered that idyllically sweet, peaceful, poetical and spiritualized life in which I have so often and so deeply been conscious of con-templative human happiness. And yet I was vexed that I had not given my master notice first, but had been dismissed by him.

"And how remarkable this seems to me: since that night, when my master 'made a stranger' of me, I have enjoyed restful sleep; I no longer dream of my tailoring days, which now lie in the remote past; which in their unpretentious simplicity were really so cheerful, but which, none the less, have cast a long shadow over the later years of my life."

In this series of dreams of a poet who, in his younger years, had been a journeyman tailor, it is hard to recognize the domination of the wish-fulfilment. All the delightful things occurred in his waking life, while the dream seemed to drag along with it the ghost-like shadow of an unhappy existence which had long been forgotten. Dreams of my own of a similar character enable me to give some explanation of such dreams. As a young doctor, I worked for a long time in the Chemical Institute without being able to accomplish anything in that exacting science, so that in the waking state I never think about this unfruitful and actually somewhat humiliating period of my student days. On the other hand, I have a recurring dream to the effect that I am working in the laboratory, making analyses, and experiments, and so forth; these dreams, like the examination-dreams, are disagreeable, and they are never very distinct. During the analysis of one of these dreams my attention was directed to the word *analysis*, which gave me the key to an understanding of them. Since then I have become an *analyst*. I make analyses which are greatly praised—psycho-analyses, of course. Now I understand: when I feel proud of these analyses in my waking life, and feel inclined to boast of my achievements, my dreams hold up to me at night those other, unsuccessful analyses, of which I have no reason to be proud; they are the punitive dreams of the upstart, like those of the journeyman tailor who became a celebrated poet. But how is it possible for a dream to place itself at the service of self-criticism in its conflict with parvenu pride, and to take as its content a rational warning instead of a prohibited wish-fulfilment? I have already hinted that the answer to this question presents many difficulties. We may conclude that the foundation of the dream consisted at first of an arrogant phantasy of ambition; but that in its stead only its suppression and abasement has reached the dream-content. One must remember that there are masochistic tendencies in mental life to which such an inversion might be attributed. I see no objection to regarding such dreams as *punishment-dreams,* as distinguished from wish-fulfilling dreams. I should not see in this any limitation of the theory of dreams hitherto as presented, but merely a verbal concession to the point of view to which the convergence of contraries seems strange. But a more thorough investigation of individual dreams of this class allows us to recognize yet another element. In an indistinct, subordinate portion of one of my laboratory dreams, I was just at the age which placed me in the most gloomy and most unsuccessful year of my professional career; I still had no position, and no idea how I was going to support myself, when I suddenly found that I had the choice of several women whom I might marry! I was, therefore, young again and, what is more, she was young again—the woman who has shared with me all these difficult years. In this way, one of the wishes which constantly gnaws at the heart of the ageing man was revealed as the unconscious dream-instigator. The conflict raging in other psychic strata between vanity and self-criticism had certainly determined the dream-content, but the more deeply-rooted wish for youth had alone made it possible as a dream. One often says to oneself even in the waking state: "To be sure, things are going well with you today, and once you found life very hard; but, after all, life was sweet in those days, when you were still so young."[1]

Another group of dreams, which I have often myself experienced, and which I have recognized to be hypocritical, have as their content a reconciliation with persons with whom one has long ceased to have friendly relations. The analysis constantly discovers an occasion which might well induce me to cast aside the last remnants of consideration for these former friends, and to treat them as strangers or enemies. But the dream chooses to depict the contrary relation.

In considering dreams recorded by a novelist or poet, we may often enough assume that he has excluded from the record those details which he felt to be disturbing and regarded as unessential. His dreams thus set us a problem which could be readily solved if we had an exact reproduction of the dream-content.

[1] Ever since psycho-analysis has dissected the personality into an ego and a super-ego (*Group Psychology and the Analysis of the Ego,* p. 664 below), it has been easy to recognize in these punishment-dreams wishfulfilments of the super-ego.

O. Rank has called my attention to the fact that in Grimm's fairy-tale of the valiant little tailor, or *Seven at One Stroke,* there is related a very similar dream of an upstart. The tailor, who has become a hero, and has married the king's daughter, dreams one night while lying beside the princess, his wife, about his trade; having become suspicious, on the following night she places armed guards where they can listen to what is said by the dreamer, and arrest him. But the little tailor is warned, and is able to correct his dream.

The complicated processes of removal, diminution, and inversion by which the affects of the dream-thoughts finally become the affects of the dream may be very well surveyed in suitable syntheses of completely analysed dreams. I shall here discuss a few examples of affective manifestations in dreams which will, I think, prove this conclusively in some of the cases cited.

V

In the dream about the odd task which the elder Brücke sets me—that of preparing my own pelvis—I am aware in the dream itself of not feeling *appropriate horror.* Now this is a wish-fulfilment in more senses than one. The preparation signifies the self-analyses which I perform, as it were, by publishing my book on dreams, which I actually found so painful that I postponed the printing of the completed manuscript for more than a year. The wish now arises that I may disregard this feeling of aversion, and for that reason I feel no horror (*Grauen,* which also means *to grow grey*) in the dream. I should much like to escape *Grauen* in the other sense too, for I am already growing quite grey, and the grey in my hair warns me to delay no longer. For we know that at the end of the dream this thought secures representation: "I shall have to leave my children to reach the goal of their difficult journey without my help."

In the two dreams that transfer the expression of satisfaction to the moments immediately after waking, this satisfaction is in the one case motivated by the expectation that I am now going to learn what is meant by *I have already dreamed of this,* and refers in reality to the birth of my first child, and in the other case it is motivated by the conviction that "that which has been announced by a premonitory sign" is now going to happen, and the satisfaction is that which I felt on the arrival of my second son. Here the same affects that dominated in the dream-thoughts have remained in the dream, but the process is probably not quite so simple as this in any dream. If the two analyses are examined a little more closely it will be seen that this satisfaction, which does not succumb to the censorship, receives reinforcement from a source which must fear the censorship, and whose affect would certainly have aroused opposition if it had not screened itself by a similar and readily admitted affect of satisfaction from the permitted source, and had, so to speak, sneaked in behind it. I am unfortunately unable to show this in the case of the actual dream, but an example from another situation will make my meaning intelligible. I will put the following case: Let there be a person near me whom I hate so strongly that I have a lively impulse to rejoice should anything happen to him. But the moral side of my nature does not give way to this impulse; I do not dare to express this sinister wish, and when something does happen to him which he does not deserve I suppress my satisfaction, and force myself to thoughts and expressions of regret. Everyone will at some time have found himself in such a position. But now let it happen that the hated person, through some transgression of his own, draws upon himself a well-deserved calamity; I shall now be allowed to give free rein to my satisfaction at his being visited by a just punishment, and I shall be expressing an opinion which coincides with that of other impartial persons. But I observe that my satisfaction proves to be more intense than that of others, for it has received reinforcement from another source—from my hatred, which was hitherto prevented by the inner censorship from furnishing the affect, but which, under the altered circumstances, is no longer prevented from doing so. This case generally occurs in social life when antipathetic persons or the adherents of an unpopular minority have been guilty of some offence. Their punishment is then usually commensurate not with their guilt, but with their guilt plus the ill-will against them that has hitherto not been put into effect. Those who punish them doubtless commit an injustice, but they are prevented from becoming aware of it by the satisfaction arising from the release within themselves of a suppression of long standing. In such cases the quality of the affect is justified, but not its degree; and the self-criticism that has been appeased in respect of the first point is only too ready to neglect to scrutinize the second point. Once you have opened the doors, more people enter than it was your original intention to admit.

A striking feature of the neurotic character, namely, that in it causes capable of evoking affect produce results which are qualitatively justified but quantitatively excessive, is to be explained on these lines, in so far as it admits of a psychological explanation at all. But the excess of affect proceeds from unconscious and hitherto suppressed affective sources which are able to establish an associative connection with the actual occasion, and for whose liberation of affect the unprotested and permitted source of affects opens up the desired path. Our attention is thus called to the fact that the relation of mutual inhibition must not be regarded as the only relation obtaining between the suppressed and the suppressing psychic institution. The cases in which the two institutions bring about a pathological result by co-operation and mutual reinforcement deserve just as much attention. These hints regarding the psychic mechanism will contribute to our understanding of the expressions of affects in dreams. A gratification which makes its appearance in a dream, and which, of course, may readily be found in its proper place in the dream-thoughts, may not always be fully explained by means of this reference. As a rule, it is necessary to search for a second source in the dream-thoughts, upon which the pressure of the censorship rests, and which, under this pressure, would have yielded not gratification but the contrary affect, had it not been enabled by the presence of the first dream-source to free its gratification-affect from repression, and reinforce the gratification springing from the other source. Hence affects which appear in dreams appear to be formed by the confluence of several tributaries, and are over-determined in respect of the material of the dream-thoughts. *Sources of affect which are able to furnish the same affect combine in the dream-work in order to produce it.*[1]

Some insight into these involved relations is gained from the analysis of the admirable dream in which *Non vixit* constitutes the central point (cf. p. 304). In this dream expressions of affect of different qualities are concentrated at two points in the manifest content. Hostile and painful impulses (in the dream itself we have the phrase *overcome by strange emotions*) overlap one another at the point where I destroy my antagonistic friend with a

[1] I have since explained the extraordinary effect of pleasure produced by tendency wit on analogous lines.

couple of words. At the end of the dream I am greatly pleased, and am quite ready to believe in a possibility which I recognize as absurd when I am awake, namely, that there are *revenants* who can be swept away by a mere wish.

I have not yet mentioned the occasion of this dream. It is an important one, and leads us far down into the meaning of the dream. From my friend in Berlin (whom I have designated as Fl) I had received the news that he was about to undergo an operation, and that relatives of his living in Vienna would inform me as to his condition. The first few messages after the operation were not very reassuring, and caused me great anxiety. I should have liked to go to him myself, but at that time I was afflicted with a painful complaint which made every movement a torment. I now learn from the dream-thoughts that I feared for this dear friend's life. I knew that his only sister, with whom I had never been acquainted, had died young, after a very brief illness. (*In the dream Fl tells me about his sister, and says: "In three-quarters of an hour she was dead."*) I must have imagined that his own constitution was not much stronger, and that I should soon be travelling, in spite of my health, in response to far worse news—and that I should arrive too late, for which I should eternally reproach myself.[1] This reproach, that I should arrive too late, has become the central point of the dream, but it has been represented in a scene in which the revered teacher of my student years—Brücke—reproaches me for the same thing with a terrible look from his blue eyes. What brought about this alteration of the scene will soon become apparent: the dream cannot reproduce the scene itself as I experienced it. To be sure, it leaves the blue eyes to the other man, but it gives me the part of the annihilator, an inversion which is obviously the work of the wish-fulfilment. My concern for the life of my friend, my self-reproach for not having gone to him, my shame (*he had come to me in Vienna unobtrusively*), my desire to consider myself excused on account of my illness—all this builds up an emotional tempest which is distinctly felt in my sleep, and which rages in that region of the dream-thoughts.

But there was another thing in the occasion of the dream which had quite the opposite ef-

fect. With the unfavourable news during the first days of the operation I received also an injunction to speak to no one about the whole affair, which hurt my feelings, for it betrayed an unnecessary distrust of my discretion. I knew, of course, that this request did not proceed from my friend, but that it was due to clumsiness or excessive timidity on the part of the messenger; yet the concealed reproach affected me very disagreeably, because it was not altogether unjustified. As we know, only reproaches which *have something in them* have the power to hurt. Years ago, when I was younger than I am now, I knew two men who were friends, and who honoured me with their friendship; and I quite superfluously told one of them what the other had said of him. This incident, of course, had nothing to do with the affairs of my friend Fl, but I have never forgotten the reproaches to which I had to listen on that occasion. One of the two friends between whom I made trouble was Professor Fleischl; the other one I will call by his baptismal name, Josef, a name which was borne also by my friend and antagonist P, who appears in this dream.

In the dream the element unobtrusively points to the reproach that I cannot keep anything to myself, and so does the question of Fl as to *how much of his affairs I have told P.* But it is the intervention of that old memory which transposes the reproach for arriving too late from the present to the time when I was working in Brücke's laboratory; and by replacing the second person in the annihilation scene of the dream by a Josef, I enable this scene to represent not only the first reproach—that I have arrived too late—but also that other reproach, more strongly affected by the repression, to the effect that I do not keep secrets. The work of condensation and displacement in this dream, as well as the motives for it, are now obvious.

My present trivial annoyance at the injunction not to divulge secrets draws reinforcement from springs that flow far beneath the surface, and so swells to a stream of hostile impulses towards persons who are in reality dear to me. The source which furnishes the reinforcement is to be found in my childhood. I have already said that my warm friendships as well as my enmities with persons of my own age go back to my childish relations to my nephew, who was a year older than I. In these he had the upper hand, and I early learned how to defend myself; we lived together, were inseparable,

---

[1] It is this fancy from the unconscious dream-thoughts which peremptorily demands *non vixit* instead of *non vivit*. "You have come too late, he is no longer alive." The fact that the manifest situation of the dream aims at the *non vivit* has been mentioned on page 305.

and loved one another, but at times, as the statements of older persons testify, we used to squabble and *accuse* one another. In a certain sense, all my friends are incarnations of this first figure; they are all *revenants*. My nephew himself returned when a young man, and then we were like Caesar and Brutus. An intimate friend and a hated enemy have always been indispensable to my emotional life; I have always been able to create them anew, and not infrequently my childish ideal has been so closely approached that friend and enemy have coincided in the same person; but not simultaneously, of course, nor in constant alternation, as was the case in my early childhood.

How, when such associations exist, a recent occasion of emotion may cast back to the infantile occasion and substitute this as a cause of affect, I shall not consider now. Such an investigation would properly belong to the psychology of unconscious thought, or a psychological explanation of the neuroses. Let us assume, for the purposes of dream-interpretation, that a childish recollection presents itself, or is created by the phantasy with, more or less, the following content: We two children quarrel on account of some object—just what we shall leave undecided, although the memory, or illusion of memory, has a very definite object in view—and each claims that *he got there first,* and therefore has the first right to it. We come to blows; Might comes before Right; and, according to the indications of the dream, I must have known that I was in the wrong (*noticing the error myself*); but this time I am the stronger, and take possession of the battlefield; the defeated combatant hurries to my father, his grandfather, and accuses me, and I defend myself with the words, which I have heard from my father: "*I hit him because he hit me.*" Thus, this recollection, or more probably phantasy, which forces itself upon my attention in the course of the analysis—without further evidence I myself do not know how—becomes a central item of the dream-thoughts, which collects the affective impulses prevailing in the dream-thoughts, as the bowl of a fountain collects the water that flows into it. From this point the dream-thoughts flow along the following channels: "It serves you right that you have had to make way for me; why did you try to push me off? I don't need you; I'll soon find someone else to play with," etc. Then the channels are opened through which these thoughts flow back again into the dream-representation.

For such an "*ôte-toi que je m'y mette,*"[1] I once had to reproach my deceased friend Josef. He was next to me in the line of promotion in Brücke's laboratory, but advancement there was very slow. Neither of the two assistants budged from his place, and youth became impatient. My friend, who knew that his days were numbered, and was bound by no intimate relation to his superior, sometimes gave free expression to his impatience. As this superior was a man seriously ill, the wish to see him removed by promotion was susceptible of an obnoxious secondary interpretation. Several years earlier, to be sure, I myself had cherished, even more intensely, the same wish—to obtain a post which had fallen vacant; wherever there are gradations of rank and promotion the way is opened for the suppression of covetous wishes. Shakespeare's Prince Hal cannot rid himself of the temptation to see how the crown fits, even at the bedside of his sick father. But, as may readily be understood, the dream inflicts this inconsiderate wish not upon me, but upon my friend.[2]

"As he was ambitious, I slew him." As he could not expect that the other man would make way for him, the man himself has been put out of the way. I harbour these thoughts immediately after attending the unveiling of the memorial to the other man at the University. Part of the satisfaction which I feel in the dream may therefore be interpreted: A just punishment; it serves you right.

At the funeral of this friend a young man made the following remark, which seemed rather out of place: "The preacher talked as though the world could no longer exist without this one human being." Here was a stirring of revolt in the heart of a sincere man, whose grief had been disturbed by exaggeration. But with this speech are connected the dream-thoughts: "No one is really irreplaceable; how many men have I already escorted to the grave! But I am still alive; I have survived them all; I claim the field." Such a thought, at the moment when I fear that if I make a journey to see him I shall find my friend no longer among the living, permits only of the further development that I am glad once more to have survived someone; that it is not *I* who have died but he; that I am master of the field, as

---

[1] Make room for me.—ED.

[2] It will have been obvious that the name *Josef* plays a great part in my dreams (see the dream about my uncle). It is particularly easy for me to hide my ego in my dreams behind persons of this name, since Joseph was the name of the dream-interpreter in the Bible.

once I was in the imagined scene of my childhood. This satisfaction, infantile in origin, at the fact that I am master of the field, covers the greater part of the affect which appears in the dream. I am glad that I am the survivor; I express this sentiment with the naïve egoism of the husband who says to his wife: "If one of us dies, I shall move to Paris." My expectation takes it as a matter of course that I am not the one to die.

It cannot be denied that great self-control is needed to interpret one's dreams and to report them. One has to reveal oneself as the sole villain among all the noble souls with whom one shares the breath of life. Thus, I find it quite comprehensible that *revenants* should exist only as long as one wants them, and that they can be obliterated by a wish. It was for this reason that my friend Josef was punished. But the *revenants* are the successive incarnations of the friend of my childhood; I am also gratified at having replaced this person for myself over and over again, and a substitute will doubtless soon be found even for the friend whom I am now on the point of losing. No one is irreplaceable.

But what has the dream-censorship been doing in the meantime? Why does it not raise the most emphatic objection to a train of thoughts characterized by such brutal selfishness, and transform the satisfaction inherent therein into extreme discomfort? I think it is because other unobjectionable trains of thought referring to the same persons result also in satisfaction, and with their affect cover that proceeding from the forbidden infantile sources. In another stratum of thought I said to myself, at the ceremony of unveiling the memorial: "I have lost so many dear friends, some through death, some through the dissolution of friendship; is it not good that substitutes have presented themselves, that I have gained a friend who means more to me than the others could, and whom I shall now always retain, at an age when it is not easy to form new friendships?" The gratification of having found this substitute for my lost friend can be taken over into the dream without interference, but behind it there sneaks in the hostile feeling of malicious gratification from the infantile source. Childish affection undoubtedly helps to reinforce the rational affection of today; but childish hatred also has found its way into the representation.

But besides this, there is in the dream a distinct reference to another train of thoughts which may result in gratification. Some time before this, after long waiting, a little daughter was born to my friend. I knew how he had grieved for the sister whom he had lost at an early age, and I wrote to him that I felt that he would transfer to this child the love he had felt for her, that this little girl would at last make him forget his irreparable loss.

Thus this train also connects up with the intermediary thoughts of the latent dream-content, from which paths radiate in the most contrary directions: "No one is irreplaceable. See, here are only *revenants;* all those whom one has lost return." And now the bonds of association between the contradictory components of the dream-thoughts are more tightly drawn by the accidental circumstance that my friend's little daughter bears the same name as the girl playmate of my own youth, who was just my own age, and the sister of my oldest friend and antagonist. I heard the name *Pauline* with *satisfaction,* and in order to allude to this coincidence I replaced one Josef in the dream by another Josef, and found it impossible to suppress the identical initials in the name Fleischl and Fl. From this point a train of thought runs to the naming of my own children. I insisted that the names should not be chosen according to the fashion of the day, but should be determined by regard for the memory of those dear to us. The children's names make them *revenants.* And, finally, is not the procreation of children for all men the only way of access to immortality?

I shall add only a few observations as to the affects of dreams considered from another point of view. In the psyche of the sleeper an affective tendency—what we call a mood—may be contained as its dominating element, and may induce a corresponding mood in the dream. This mood may be the result of the experiences and thoughts of the day, or it may be of somatic origin; in either case it will be accompanied by the corresponding trains of thought. That this ideational content of the dream-thoughts should at one time determine the affective tendency primarily, while at another time it is awakened in a secondary manner by the somatically determined emotional disposition, is indifferent for the purposes of dream-formation. This is always subject to the restriction that it can represent only a wish-fulfilment, and that it may lend its psychic energy to the wish alone. The mood actually present will receive the same treatment as the sensation which actually emerges during sleep (cf. p. 234), which is either neglected or reinterpreted in the sense of a wish-fulfilment. Painful moods during sleep become the motive force of the dream, inasmuch as they awake energetic wishes which the dream has to fulfil. The material in which they inhere is elaborated until it is serviceable for the expression of the wish-fulfilment. The more intense and the more dominating the element of the painful mood in the dream-thoughts, the more surely will the most strongly suppressed wish-impulses take advantage of the opportunity to secure representation; for thanks to the actual existence of discomfort, which otherwise they would have to create spontaneously, they find that the more difficult part of the work necessary to ensure representation has already been accomplished; and with these observations we touch once more upon the problem of anxiety-dreams, which will prove to be the boundary-case of dream-activity.

I. The Secondary Elaboration

We will at last turn our attention to the fourth of the factors participating in dream-formation.

If we continue our investigation of the dream-content on the lines already laid down— that is, by examining the origin in the dream-thoughts of conspicuous occurrences—we come upon elements that can be explained only by making an entirely new assumption. I have in mind cases where one manifests astonishment, anger, or resistance in a dream, and that, too, in respect of part of the dream-content itself. Most of these impulses of criticism in dreams are not directed against the dream-content, but prove to be part of the dream-material, taken over and fittingly applied, as I have already shown by suitable examples. There are, however, criticisms of this sort which are not so derived: their correlatives cannot be found in the dream-material. What, for instance, is meant by the criticism not infrequent in dreams: "After all, it's only a dream"? This is a genuine criticism of the dream, such as I might make if I were awake. Not infrequently it is only the prelude to waking; even oftener it is preceded by a painful feeling, which subsides when the actuality of the dream-state has been affirmed. The thought: "After all, it's only a dream" in the dream itself has the same intention as it has on the stage on the lips of Offenbach's *Belle Hélène;* it seeks to minimize what has just been experienced, and to secure indulgence for what is to follow. It serves to lull to sleep a certain mental agency which at the given moment has every occasion to rouse itself and forbid the continuation of the dream, or the scene. But it is more convenient to go on sleeping and to tolerate the dream, "because, after all, it's only a dream." I imagine that the disparaging criticism: "After all, it's only a dream," appears in the dream at the moment when the censorship, which is never quite asleep, feels that it has been surprised by the already admitted dream. It is too late to suppress the dream, and the agency therefore meets with this remark the anxiety or painful emotion which rises into the dream. It is an expression of the *esprit d'escalier* on the part of the psychic censorship.

In this example we have incontestable proof that everything which the dream contains does not come from the dream-thoughts, but that a psychic function, which cannot be differentiated from our waking thoughts, may make contributions to the dream-content. The question arises, does this occur only in exceptional cases, or does the psychic agency, which is otherwise active only as the censorship, play a constant part in dream-formation?

One must decide unhesitatingly for the latter view. It is indisputable that the censoring agency, whose influence we have so far recognized only in the restrictions of and omissions in the dream-content, is likewise responsible for interpolations in and amplifications of this content. Often these interpolations are readily recognized; they are introduced with hesitation, prefaced by an "as if"; they have no special vitality of their own, and are constantly inserted at points where they may serve to connect two portions of the dream-content or create a continuity between two sections of the dream. They manifest less ability to adhere in the memory than do the genuine products of the dream-material; if the dream is forgotten, they are forgotten first, and I strongly suspect that our frequent complaint that although we have dreamed so much we have forgotten most of the dream, and have remembered only fragments, is explained by the immediate falling away of just these cementing thoughts. In a complete analysis, these interpolations are often betrayed by the fact that no material is to be found for them in the dream-thoughts. But after careful examination I must describe this case as the less usual one; in most cases the interpolated thoughts can be traced to material in the dream-thoughts which can claim a place in the dream neither by its own merits nor by way of over-determination. Only in the most extreme cases does the psychic function in dream-formation which we are now considering rise to original creation; whenever possible it makes use of anything appropriate that it can find in the dream-material.

What distinguishes this part of the dream-work, and also betrays it, is its tendency. This function proceeds in a manner which the poet maliciously attributes to the philosopher: with its rags and tatters it stops up the breaches in the structure of the dream. The result of its efforts is that the dream loses the appearance of absurdity and incoherence, and approaches the pattern of an intelligible experience. But the effort is not always crowned with complete success. Thus, dreams occur which may, upon superficial examination, seem faultlessly logical and correct; they start from a possible situation, continue it by means of consistent changes, and bring it—although this is rare—to a not unnatural conclusion. These dreams have been subjected to the most searching elaboration by a psychic function similar to our waking thought; they seem to have a meaning, but this meaning is very far removed from the real meaning of the dream. If we analyse them, we are convinced that the secondary elaboration has handled the material with the greatest freedom, and has retained as little as possible of its proper relations. These are the dreams which have, so to speak, already been once interpreted before we subject them to waking interpretation. In other dreams this tendencious elaboration has succeeded only up to a point; up to this point consistency seems to prevail, but then the dream becomes nonsensical or confused; but perhaps before it concludes it may once more rise to a semblance of rationality. In yet other dreams the elaboration has failed completely; we find ourselves helpless, confronted with a senseless mass of fragmentary contents.

I do not wish to deny to this fourth dream-forming power, which will soon become familiar to us—it is in reality the only one of the four dream-creating factors which is familiar to us in other connections—I do not wish to deny to this fourth factor the faculty of creatively making new contributions to our dreams. But its influence is certainly exerted, like that of the other factors, mainly in the preference and selection of psychic material already formed in the dream-thoughts. Now there is a case where it is to a great extent spared the work of building, as it were, a façade to the dream by the fact that such a structure, only waiting to be used, already exists in the material of the dream-thoughts. I am accustomed to describe the element of the dream-thoughts which I have in mind as *phantasy;* I shall perhaps avoid misunderstanding if I at once point to the *day-dream* as an analogy in waking life.[1] The part played by this element in our psychic life has not yet been fully recognized and revealed by psychiatrists; though M. Benedikt has, it seems to me, made a highly promising beginning. Yet the significance of the day-dream has not escaped the unerring insight of the poets; we are all familiar with the description of the day-dreams of one of his subordinate characters which Alphonse Daudet has given us in his *Nabab.* The study of the psychoneuroses discloses the astonishing fact that these phantasies or day-dreams are the immediate predecessors of symptoms of hysteria—at least, of a great many of them; for hysterical symptoms are dependent not upon actual memories, but upon the phantasies built up on a basis of memories. The frequent occurrence of conscious day-phantasies brings these formations to our ken; but while some of these phantasies are conscious, there is a superabundance of unconscious phantasies, which must perforce remain unconscious on account of their content and their origin in repressed material. A more thorough examination of the character of these day-phantasies shows with what good reason the same name has been given to these formations as to the products of nocturnal thought—*dreams.* They have essential features in common with nocturnal dreams; indeed, the investigation of day-dreams might really have afforded the shortest and best approach to the understanding of nocturnal dreams.

Like dreams, they are wish-fulfilments; like dreams, they are largely based upon the impressions of childish experiences; like dreams, they obtain a certain indulgence from the censorship in respect of their creations. If we trace their formation, we become aware how the wish-motive which has been operative in their production has taken the material of which they are built, mixed it together, rearranged it, and fitted it together into a new whole. They bear very much the same relation to the childish memories to which they refer as many of the baroque palaces of Rome bear to the ancient ruins, whose hewn stones and columns have furnished the material for the structures built in the modern style.

[1] *Rêve, petit roman*=day-dream, story.

In the *secondary elaboration* of the dream-content which we have ascribed to our fourth dream-forming factor, we find once more the very same activity which is allowed to manifest itself, uninhibited by other influences, in the creation of day-dreams. We may say, without further preliminaries, that this fourth factor of ours seeks to construct *something like* a day-dream from the material which offers itself. But where such a day-dream has already been constructed in the context of the dream-thoughts, this factor of the dream-work will prefer to take possession of it, and contrive that it gets into the dream-content. There are dreams that consist merely of the repetition of a day-phantasy, which has perhaps remained unconscious—as, for instance, the boy's dream that he is riding in a war-chariot with the heroes of the Trojan war. In my *Autodidasker* dream the second part of the dream at least is the faithful repetition of a day-phantasy—harmless in itself—of my dealings with Professor N. The fact that the exciting phantasy forms only a part of the dream, or that only a part of it finds its way into the dream-content, is due to the complexity of the conditions which the dream must satisfy at its genesis. On the whole, the phantasy is treated like any other component of the latent material; but it is often still recognizable as a whole in the dream. In my dreams there are often parts which are brought into prominence by their producing a different impression from that produced by the other parts. They seem to me to be in a state of flux, to be more coherent and at the same time more transient than other portions of the same dream. I know that these are unconscious phantasies which find their way into the context of the dream, but I have never yet succeeded in registering such a phantasy. For the rest, these phantasies, like all the other component parts of the dream-thoughts, are jumbled together, condensed, superimposed, and so on; but we find all the transitional stages, from the case in which they may constitute the dream-content, or at least the dream-façade, unaltered, to the most contrary case, in which they are represented in the dream-content by only one of their elements, or by a remote allusion to such an element. The fate of the phantasies in the dream-thoughts is obviously determined by the advantages they can offer as against the claims of the censorship and the pressure of condensation.

In my choice of examples for dream-interpretation I have, as far as possible, avoided those dreams in which unconscious phantasies play a considerable part, because the introduction of this psychic element would have necessitated an extensive discussion of the psychology of unconscious thought. But even in this connection I cannot entirely avoid the *phantasy,* because it often finds its way into the dream complete, and still more often perceptibly glimmers through it. I might mention yet one more dream, which seems to be composed of two distinct and opposed phantasies, overlapping here and there, of which the first is superficial, while the second becomes, as it were, the interpretation of the first.[1]

The dream—it is the only one of which I possess no careful notes—is roughly to this effect: *The dreamer—a young unmarried man—is sitting in his favourite inn, which is seen correctly; several persons come to fetch him, among them someone who wants to arrest him. He says to his table companions, "I will pay later, I am coming back." But they cry, smiling scornfully: "We know all about that; that's what everybody says." One guest calls after him: "There goes another one." He is then led to a small place where he finds a woman with a child in her arms. One of his escorts says: "This is Herr Müller." A commissioner or some other official is running through a bundle of tickets or papers, repeating Müller, Müller, Müller. At last the commissioner asks him a question, which he answers with a "Yes." He then takes a look at the woman, and notices that she has grown a large beard.*

The two component parts are here easily separable. What is superficial is the *phantasy of being arrested;* this seems to be newly created by the dream-work. But behind it the *phantasy of marriage* is visible, and this material, on the other hand, has been slightly modified by the dream-work, and the features which may be common to the two phantasies appear with special distinctness, as in Galton's composite photographs. The promise of the young man, who is at present a bachelor, to

---

[1] I have analysed an excellent example of a dream of this kind, having its origin in the stratification of several phantasies, in the *Fragment of an Analysis of a Case of Hysteria* (*Collected Papers,* vol. III). I undervalued the significance of such phantasies for dream-formation as long as I was working principally on my own dreams, which were rarely based upon day-dreams but most frequently upon discussions and mental conflicts. With other persons it is often much easier to prove the *complete analogy between the nocturnal dream and the day-dream.* In hysterical patients an attack may often be replaced by a dream; it is then obvious that the day-dream phantasy is the first step for both these psychic formations.

return to his place at his accustomed table—the scepticism of his drinking companions, made wise by their many experiences—their calling after him: *"There goes* (marries) *another one"*—are all features easily susceptible of the other interpretation, as is the affirmative answer given to the official. Running through a bundle of papers and repeating the same name corresponds to a subordinate but easily recognized feature of the marriage ceremony—the reading aloud of the congratulatory telegrams which have arrived at irregular intervals, and which, of course, are all addressed to the same name. In the personal appearance of the bride in this dream the marriage phantasy has even got the better of the arrest phantasy which screens it. The fact that this bride finally wears a beard I can explain from information received—I had no opportunity of making an analysis. The dreamer had, on the previous day, been crossing the street with a friend who was just as hostile to marriage as himself, and had called his friend's attention to a beautiful brunette who was coming towards them. The friend had remarked: "Yes, if only these women wouldn't get beards as they grow older, like their fathers."

Of course, even in this dream there is no lack of elements with which the dream-distortion has done deep work. Thus, the speech, *"I will pay later,"* may have reference to the behaviour feared on the part of the father-in-law in the matter of a dowry. Obviously all sorts of misgivings are preventing the dreamer from surrendering himself with pleasure to the phantasy of marriage. One of these misgivings—that with marriage he might lose his freedom—has embodied itself in the transformation of a scene of arrest.

If we once more return to the thesis that the dream-work prefers to make use of a ready-made phantasy, instead of first creating one from the material of the dream-thoughts, we shall perhaps be able to solve one of the most interesting problems of the dream. I have related the dream of Maury, who is struck on the back of the neck by a small board, and wakes after a long dream—a complete romance of the period of the French Revolution. Since the dream is produced in a coherent form, and completely fits the explanation of the waking stimulus, of whose occurrence the sleeper could have had no forboding, only one assumption seems possible, namely, that the whole richly elaborated dream must have been composed and dreamed in the short interval of time between the falling of the board on Maury's cervical vertebrae and the waking induced by the blow. We should not venture to ascribe such rapidity to the mental operations of the waking state, so that we have to admit that the dream-work has the privilege of a remarkable acceleration of its issue.

To this conclusion, which rapidly became popular, more recent authors (Le Lorrain, Egger, and others) have opposed emphatic objections; some of them doubt the correctness of Maury's record of the dream, some seek to show that the rapidity of our mental operations in waking life is by no means inferior to that which we can, without reservation, ascribe to the mental operations in dreams. The discussion raises fundamental questions, which I do not think are at all near solution. But I must confess that Egger's objections, for example, to Maury's dream of the guillotine, do not impress me as convincing. I would suggest the following explanation of this dream: Is it so very improbable that Maury's dream may have represented a phantasy which had been preserved for years in his memory, in a completed state, and which was awakened—I should like to say, alluded to—at the moment when he became aware of the waking stimulus? The whole difficulty of composing so long a story, with all its details, in the exceedingly short space of time which is here at the dreamer's disposal then disappears; the story was already composed. If the board had struck Maury's neck when he was awake, there would perhaps have been time for the thought: "Why, that's just like being guillotined." But as he is struck by the board while asleep, the dream-work quickly utilizes the incoming stimulus for the construction of a wish-fulfilment, *as if* it thought (this is to be taken quite figuratively): "Here is a good opportunity to realize the wish-phantasy which I formed at such and such a time while I was reading." It seems to me undeniable that this dream-romance is just such a one as a young man is wont to construct under the influence of exciting impressions. Who has not been fascinated—above all, a Frenchman and a student of the history of civilization—by descriptions of the Reign of Terror, in which the aristocracy, men and women, the flower of the nation, showed that it was possible to die with a light heart, and preserved their ready wit and the refinement of their manners up to the moment of the last fateful summons? How tempting to fancy oneself in the midst of all this, as one of these young men who take leave of their ladies with a kiss of the hand, and fearlessly ascend the scaffold! Or perhaps ambition was the ruling motive of the phantasy—the ambition to put oneself in the place of one of those powerful personalities who, by their sheer force of intellect and their fiery eloquence, ruled the city in which the heart of mankind was then beating so convulsively; who were impelled by their convictions to send thousands of human beings to their death, and were paving the way for the transformation of Europe; who, in the meantime, were not sure of their own heads, and might one day lay them under the knife of the guillotine, perhaps in the rôle of a Girondist or the hero Danton? The detail preserved in the memory of the dream, *accompanied by an enormous crowd,* seems to show that Maury's phantasy was an ambitious one of just this character.

But the phantasy prepared so long ago need not be experienced again in sleep; it is enough that it should be, so to speak, "touched off." What I mean is this: If a few notes are struck, and someone says, as in *Don Juan:* "That is from *The Marriage of Figaro* by Mozart," memories suddenly surge up within me, none of which I can recall to consciousness a moment later. The phrase serves as a point of irruption from which a complete whole is simultaneously put into a condition of stimulation. It may well be the same in unconscious thinking. Through the waking stimulus the psychic station is excited which gives access to the whole guillotine phantasy. This phantasy, however, is not run through in sleep, but only in the memory of the awakened sleeper. Upon waking, the sleeper remembers in detail the phantasy which was transferred as a whole into the dream. At the same time, he has no means of assuring himself that he is really remembering something which was dreamed. The same explanation—namely, that one is dealing with finished phantasies which have been evoked as wholes by the waking stimulus— may be applied to other dreams which are adapted to the waking stimulus—for example, to Napoleon's dream of a battle before the explosion of a bomb. Among the dreams collected by Justine Tobowolska in her dissertation on the apparent duration of time in dreams,[1] I think the most corroborative is that related by Macario (1857) as having been dreamed by a playwright, Casimir Bonjour.

[1] Justine Tobowolska, *Étude sur les illusions de temps dans les rêves du sommeil normal* (1900), p.53.

Bonjour intended one evening to witness the first performance of one of his own plays, but he was so tired that he dozed off in his chair behind the scenes just as the curtain was rising. In his sleep he went through all the five acts of his play, and observed all the various signs of emotion which were manifested by the audience during each individual scene. At the close of the performance, to his great satisfaction, he heard his name called out amidst the most lively manifestations of applause. Suddenly he woke. He could hardly believe his eyes or his ears; the performance had not gone beyond the first lines of the first scene; he could not have been asleep for more than two minutes. As for the dream, the running through the five acts of the play and the observing the attitude of the public towards each individual scene need not, we may venture to assert, have been something new, produced while the dreamer was asleep; it may have been a repetition of an already completed work of the phantasy. Tobowolska and other authors have emphasized a common characteristic of dreams that show an accelerated flow of ideas: namely, that they seem to be especially coherent, and not at all like other dreams, and that the dreamer's memory of them is summary rather than detailed. But these are precisely the characteristics which would necessarily be exhibited by ready-made phantasies touched off by the dream-work—a conclusion which is not, of course, drawn by these authors. I do not mean to assert that all dreams due to a waking stimulus admit of this explanation, or that the problem of the accelerated flux of ideas in dreams is entirely disposed of in this manner.

And here we are forced to consider the relation of this secondary elaboration of the dream-content to the other factors of the dream-work. May not the procedure perhaps be as follows? The dream-forming factors, the efforts at condensation, the necessity of evading the censorship, and the regard for representability by the psychic means of the dream first of all create from the dream-material a provisional dream-content, which is subsequently modified until it satisfies as far as possible the exactions of a secondary agency. No, this is hardly probable. We must rather assume that the requirements of this agency constitute from the very first one of the conditions which the dream must satisfy, and that this condition, as well as the conditions of condensation, the opposing censorship, and representability, simultaneously influence, in an inductive and selective manner, the whole mass of material in the dream-thoughts. But of the four conditions necessary for dream-formation, the last recognized is that whose exactions appear to be least binding upon the dream. The following consideration makes it seem very probable that this psychic function, which undertakes the so-called secondary elaboration of the dream-content, is identical with the work of our waking thought: Our waking (preconscious) thought behaves towards any given perceptual material precisely as the function in question behaves towards the dream-content. It is natural to our waking thought to create order in such material, to construct relations, and to subject it to the requirements of an intelligible coherence. Indeed, we go rather too far in this respect; the tricks of conjurers befool us by taking advantage of this intellectual habit of ours. In the effort to combine in an intelligible manner the sensory impressions which present themselves we often commit the most curious mistakes, and even distort the truth of the material before us. The proofs of this fact are so familiar that we need not give them further consideration. We overlook errors which make nonsense of a printed page because we imagine the proper words. The editor of a widely read French journal is said to have made a bet that he could print the words *from in front* or *from behind* in every sentence of a long article without any of his readers noticing it. He won his bet. Years ago I came across a comical example of false association in a newspaper. After the session of the French Chamber in which Dupuy quelled the panic, caused by the explosion of a bomb thrown by an anarchist, with the courageous words, *"La séance continue,"*[1] the visitors in the gallery were asked to testify as to their impressions of the outrage. Among them were two provincials. One of these said that immediately after the end of a speech he had heard a detonation, but that he had thought that it was the parliamentary custom to fire a shot whenever a speaker had finished. The other, who had apparently already listened to several speakers, had got hold of the same idea, but with this variation, that he supposed the shooting to be a sign of appreciation following a specially successful speech.

Thus, the psychic agency which approaches the dream-content with the demand that it must be intelligible, which subjects it to a first interpretation, and in doing so leads to the complete misunderstanding of it, is none other than our normal thought. In our interpretation the rule will be, in every case, to disregard the apparent coherence of the dream as being of suspicious origin and, whether the elements are confused or clear, to follow the same regressive path to the dream-material.

At the same time, we note those factors upon which the above-mentioned (p. 272) scale of quality in dreams—from confusion to clearness—is essentially dependent. Those parts of the dream seem to us clear in which the secondary elaboration has been able to accomplish something; those seem confused where the powers of this performance have failed. Since the confused parts of the dream are often likewise those which are less vividly presented, we may conclude that the secondary dream-work is responsible also for a contribution to the plastic intensity of the individual dream-structures.

If I seek an object of comparison for the definitive formation of the dream, as it manifests itself with the assistance of normal thinking, I can think of none better than those mysterious inscriptions with which *Die Fliegende Blätter* has so long amused its readers. In a certain sentence which, for the sake of contrast, is in dialect, and whose significance is as scurrilous as possible, the reader is led to expect a Latin inscription. For this purpose the letters of the words are taken out of their syllabic groupings, and are rearranged. Here and there a genuine Latin word results; at other points, on the assumption that letters have been obliterated by weathering, or omitted, we allow ourselves to be deluded about the significance of certain isolated and meaningless letters. If we do not wish to be fooled we must give up looking for an inscription, must take the letters as they stand, and combine them, disregarding their arrangement, into words of our mother tongue.

The secondary elaboration is that factor of the dream-work which has been observed by most of the writers on dreams, and whose importance has been duly appreciated. Havelock Ellis gives an amusing allegorical description of its performances: "As a matter of fact, we might even imagine the sleeping consciousness as saying to itself: 'Here comes our master, Waking Consciousness, who attaches such mighty importance to reason and logic and so forth. Quick! gather things up, put them in

---

[1] The meeting will continue.—ED.

order—any order will do—before he enters to take possession.' " [1]

The identity of this mode of operation with that of waking thought is very clearly stated by Delacroix in his *Sur la structure logique du rêve* (p. 526): "*Cette fonction d'interprétation n'est pas particulière au rêve; c'est le même travail de coordination logique que nous faisons sur nos sensations pendant la veille.*"[2]

J. Sully is of the same opinion; and so is Tobowolska:"*Sur ces successions incohérentes d'hallucinations, l'esprit s'efforce de faire le même travail de coordination logique qu'il fait pendant le veille sur les sensations. Il relie entre elles par un lien imaginaire toutes ces images décousues et bouche les écarts trop grands qui se trouvaient entre elles*" [3] (p. 93).

Some authors maintain that this ordering and interpreting activity begins even in the dream and is continued in the waking state. Thus Paulhan (p. 547): "*Cependant j'ai souvent pensé qu'il pouvait y avoir une certain déformation, ou plutôt reformation du rêve dans le souvenir. . . . La tendence systématisante de l'imagination pourrait fort bien achever après le réveil ce qu'elle a ébauché pendant le sommeil. De la sorte, la rapidité réelle de la pensée serait augmentée en apparence par les perfectionnements dûs à l'imagination éveillée.*" [4]

Leroy and Tobowolska (p. 592): "*Dans le rêve, au contraire, l'interprétation et la co-ordination se font non seulement à l'aide des données du rêve, mais encore à l'aide de celles de la veille. . . .*" [5]

It was therefore inevitable that this one recognized factor of dream-formation should be over-estimated, so that the whole process of creating the dream was attributed to it. This creative work was supposed to be accomplished at the moment of waking, as was assumed by

Goblot, and with deeper conviction by Foucault, who attributed to waking thought the faculty of creating the dream out of the thoughts which emerged in sleep.

In respect to this conception, Leroy and Tobowolska express themselves as follows:"*On a cru pouvoir placer le rêve au moment du reveil et ils ont attribué à la pensée de la veille la fonction de construire le rêve avec les images présentes dans la pensée du sommeil.*" [6]

To this estimate of the secondary elaboration I will add the one fresh contribution to the dream-work which has been indicated by the sensitive observations of H. Silberer. Silberer has caught the transformation of thoughts into images *in flagranti*, by forcing himself to accomplish intellectual work while in a state of fatigue and somnolence. The elaborated thought vanished, and in its place there appeared a vision which proved to be a substitute for—usually abstract—thoughts. In these experiments it so happened that the emerging image, which may be regarded as a dream-element, represented something other than the thoughts which were waiting for elaboration: namely, the exhaustion itself, the difficulty or distress involved in this work; that is, the subjective state and the manner of functioning of the person exerting himself rather than the object of his exertions. Silberer called this case, which in him occurred quite often, the *functional phenomenon*, in contradistinction to the *material phenomenon* which he expected.

"For example: one afternoon I am lying, extremely sleepy, on my sofa, but I nevertheless force myself to consider a philosophical problem. I endeavour to compare the views of Kant and Schopenhauer concerning time. Owing to my somnolence I do not succeed in holding on to both trains of thought, which would have been necessary for the purposes of comparison. After several vain efforts, I once more exert all my will-power to formulate for myself the Kantian deduction in order to apply it to Schopenhauer's statement of the problem. Thereupon, I directed my attention to the latter, but when I tried to return to Kant, I found that he had again escaped me, and I tried in vain to fetch him back. And now this fruitless endeavour to rediscover the Kantian documents mislaid somewhere in my head suddenly presented itself, my eyes being closed, as in a

---

[1] *The World of Dreams*, pp. 10, 11 (London, 1911).

[2] This function of interpretation is not particular to the dream; it is the same work of logical coordination that we use on our sensations when awake.—ED.

[3] With these series of incoherent halucinations, the mind must do the same work of logical coordination that it does with the sensations when awake. With a bon of imagination, it reunites all the disconnected images, and fills in the gaps found which are too great.—ED.

[4] However, I have often thought that there might be a certain deformation, or rather reformation, of the dream when it is recalled. . . . The systematizing tendency of the imagination can well finish, after waking, the sketch begun in sleep. In that way, the real speed of thought will be augmented in appearance by improvements due to the wakened imagination.—ED.

[5] In the dream, on the contrary, the interpretation and coordination are made not only with the aid of what is given by the dream, but also with what is given by the wakened mind.—ED.

[6] It was thought that the dream could be placed at the moment of waking, and they attributed to the waking thoughts the function of constructing the dream from the images present in the sleeping thoughts.—ED.

dream-image, in the form of a visible, plastic symbol: *I demand information of a grumpy secretary, who, bent over a desk, does not allow my urgency to disturb him; half straightening himself, he gives me a look of angry refusal.*[1]

Other examples, which relate to the fluctuation between sleep and waking:

"Example No. 2. Conditions: Morning, while awaking. While to a certain extent asleep (crepuscular state), thinking over a previous dream, in a way repeating and finishing it, I feel myself drawing nearer to the waking state, yet I wish to remain in the crepuscular state.

. .*"Scene: I am stepping with one foot over a stream, but I at once pull it back again and resolve to remain on this side."*[2]

"Example No. 6. Conditions the same as in Example No. 4 (he wishes to remain in bed a little longer without oversleeping). I wish to indulge in a little longer sleep.

. .*"Scene: I am saying good-bye to somebody, and I agree to meet him (or her) again before long."*

I will now proceed to summarize this long disquisition on the dream-work. We were confronted by the question whether in dream-formation the psyche exerts all its faculties to their full extent, without inhibition, or only a fraction of them, which are restricted in their action. Our investigations lead us to reject such a statement of the problem as wholly inadequate in the circumstances. But if, in our answer, we are to remain on the ground upon which the question forces us, we must assent to two conceptions which are apparently opposed and mutually exclusive. The psychic activity in dream-formation resolves itself into two achievements: the production of the dream-thoughts and the transformation of these into the dream-content. The dream-thoughts are perfectly accurate, and are formed with all the psychic profusion of which we are capable; they belong to the thoughts which have not become conscious, from which our conscious thoughts also result by means of a certain transposition. There is doubtless much in them that is worth knowing, and also mysterious, but these problems have no particular relation to our dreams, and cannot claim to be treated under the head of dream-problems.[3] On the other hand, we have

the process which changes the unconscious thoughts into the dream-content, which is peculiar to the dream-life and characteristic of it. Now, this peculiar dream-work is much farther removed from the pattern of waking thought than has been supposed by even the most decided depreciators of the psychic activity in dream-formation. It is not so much that it is more negligent, more incorrect, more forgetful, more incomplete than waking thought; it is something altogether different, qualitatively, from waking thought, and cannot therefore be compared with it. It does not think, calculate, or judge at all, but limits itself to the work of transformation. It may be exhaustively described if we do not lose sight of the conditions which its product must satisfy. This product, the dream, has above all to be withdrawn from the censorship, and to this end the dream-work makes use of the *displacement of psychic intensities*, even to the transvaluation of all psychic values; thoughts must be exclusively or predominantly reproduced in the material of visual and acoustic memory-traces, and from this requirement there proceeds the *regard of the dream-work for representability*, which it satisfies by fresh displacements. Greater intensities have (probably) to be produced than are at the disposal of the night dream-thoughts, and this purpose is served by the extensive *condensation* to which the constituents of the dream-thoughts are subjected. Little attention is paid to the logical relations of the thought-material; they ultimately find a veiled representation in the *formal* peculiarities of the dream. The affects of the dream-thoughts undergo slighter alterations than their conceptual content. As a rule, they are suppressed; where they are preserved, they are freed from the concepts and combined in

---

[1] *Jahrb.*, i, p. 514.

[2] *Jahrb.*, iii, p. 625.

[3] Formerly I found it extraordinarily difficult to accustom my readers to the distinction between the manifest dream-content and the latent dream-thoughts. Over and over again arguments and objections were adduced from the uninterpreted dream as it was retained in the memory, and the necessity of interpreting the dream was ignored. But now, when the analysts have at least become reconciled to substituting for the manifest dream its meaning as found by interpretation, many of them are guilty of another mistake, to which they adhere just as stubbornly. They look for the essence of the dream in this latent content, and thereby overlook the distinction between latent dream-thoughts and the dream-work. The dream is fundamentally nothing more than a special *form* of our thinking, which is made possible by the conditions of the sleeping state. It is the dream-work which produces this form, and it alone is the essence of dreaming—the only explanation of its singularity. I say this in order to correct the reader's judgment of the notorious *prospective tendency* of dreams. That the dream should concern itself with efforts to perform the tasks with which our psychic life is confronted is no more remarkable than that our conscious waking life should so concern itself, and I will only add that this work may be done also in the preconscious, a fact already familiar to us.

accordance with their similarity. Only one part of the dream-work—the revision, variable in amount, which is effected by the partially wakened conscious thought—is at all consistent with the conception which the writers on the subject have endeavoured to extend to the whole performance of dream-formation.

VII. THE PSYCHOLOGY OF THE DREAM PROCESSES

AMONG the dreams which have been communicated to me by others, there is one which is at this point especially worthy of our attention. It was told me by a female patient who had heard it related in a lecture on dreams. Its original source is unknown to me. This dream evidently made a deep impression upon the lady, since she went so far as to imitate it, i.e., to repeat the elements of this dream in a dream of her own; in order, by this transference, to express her agreement with a certain point in the dream.

The preliminary conditions of this typical dream were as follows: A father had been watching day and night beside the sick-bed of his child. After the child died, he retired to rest in an adjoining room, but left the door ajar so that he could look from his room into the next, where the child's body lay surrounded by tall candles. An old man, who had been installed as a watcher, sat beside the body, murmuring prayers. After sleeping for a few hours the father dreamed that *the child was standing by his bed, clasping his arm and crying reproachfully: "Father, don't you see that I am burning?"* The father woke up and noticed a bright light coming from the adjoining room. Rushing in, he found that the old man had fallen asleep, and the sheets and one arm of the beloved body were burnt by a fallen candle.

The meaning of this affecting dream is simple enough, and the explanation given by the lecturer, as my patient reported it, was correct. The bright light shining through the open door on to the sleeper's eyes gave him the impression which he would have received had he been awake: namely, that a fire had been started near the corpse by a falling candle. It is quite possible that he had taken into his sleep his anxiety lest the aged watcher should not be equal to his task.

We can find nothing to change in this interpretation; we can only add that the content of the dream must be overdetermined, and that the speech of the child must have consisted of phrases which it had uttered while still alive, and which were associated with important events for the father. Perhaps the complaint, *"I am burning,"* was associated with the fever from which the child died, and *"Father, don't you see?"* to some other affective occurrence unknown to us.

Now, when we have come to recognize that the dream has meaning, and can be fitted into the context of psychic events, it may be surprising that a dream should have occurred in circumstances which called for such an immediate waking. We shall then note that even this dream is not lacking in a wish-fulfilment. The dead child behaves as though alive; he warns his father himself; he comes to his father's bed and clasps his arm, as he probably did in the recollection from which the dream obtained the first part of the child's speech. It was for the sake of this wish-fulfilment that the father slept a moment longer. The dream was given precedence over waking reflection because it was able to show the child still living. If the father had waked first, and had then drawn the conclusion which led him into the adjoining room, he would have shortened the child's life by this one moment.

There can be no doubt about the peculiar features in this brief dream which engage our particular interest. So far, we have endeavoured mainly to ascertain wherein the secret meaning of the dream consists, how it is to be discovered, and what means the dream-work uses to conceal it. In other words, our greatest interest has hitherto been centered on the problems of interpretation. Now, however, we encounter a dream which is easily explained, and the meaning of which is without disguise; we note that nevertheless this dream preserves the essential characteristics which conspicuously differentiate a dream from our waking thoughts, and this difference demands an explanation. It is only when we have disposed of all the problems of interpretation that we feel how incomplete is our psychology of dreams.

But before we turn our attention to this new path of investigation, let us stop and look back, and consider whether we have not overlooked something important on our way hither. For we must understand that the easy and comfortable part of our journey lies behind us. Hitherto, all the paths that we have followed have led, if I mistake not, to light, to explanation, and to full understanding; but from the moment when we seek to penetrate more deeply into the psychic processes in dreaming, all paths lead into darkness. It is quite impossible to *explain* the dream as a psychic process, for to explain means to trace back to the known, and as yet we have no psychological knowledge to which we can refer such explanatory fundamentals as may be inferred from the psychological investigation of dreams. On the contrary, we shall be compelled to advance a number of new assumptions, which do little more than conjecture the structure of the psychic apparatus and the play of the energies active in it; and we shall have to be careful not to go too far beyond the simplest logical construction, since otherwise its value will be doubtful. And even if we should be unerring in our inferences, and take cognizance of all the logical possibilities, we should still be in danger of arriving at a completely mistaken result, owing to the probable incompleteness of the preliminary statement of our elementary data. We shall not be able to arrive at any conclusions as to the structure and function of the psychic instrument from even the most careful investigation of dreams, or of any other *isolated* activity; or, at all events, we shall not be able to confirm our conclusions. To do this we shall have to collate such phenomena as the comparative study of a whole series of psychic activities proves to be reliably constant. So that the psychological assumptions which we base on the analysis of the dream-processes will have to mark time, as it were, until they can join up with the results of other investigations which, proceeding from another starting-point, will seek to penetrate to the heart of the same problem.

A. *The Forgetting of Dreams*

I propose, then, that we shall first of all turn our attention to a subject which brings us to a hitherto disregarded objection, which threatens to undermine the very foundation of our efforts at dream-interpretation. The objection has been made from more than one quarter that the dream which we wish to interpret is really unknown to us, or, to be more precise, that we have no guarantee that we know it as it really occurred.

What we recollect of the dream, and what we subject to our methods of interpretation, is, in the first place, mutilated by the unfaithfulness of our memory, which seems quite peculiarly incapable of retaining dreams, and which may have omitted precisely the most significant parts of their content. For when we try to consider our dreams attentively, we often have reason to complain that we have dreamed much more than we remember; that unfortunately we know nothing more than this one fragment, and that our recollection of even this fragment seems to us strangely uncertain. Moreover, everything goes to prove that our memory reproduces the dream not only incompletely but also untruthfully, in a falsifying manner. As, on the one hand, we may doubt whether what we dreamed was really as disconnected as it is in our recollections, so on the other hand we may doubt whether a dream was really as coherent as our account of it; whether in our attempted reproduction we have not filled in the gaps which really existed, or those which are due to forgetfulness, with new and arbitrarily chosen material; whether we have not embellished the dream, rounded it off and corrected it, so that any conclusion as to its real content becomes impossible. Indeed, one writer (Spitta)[1] surmises that all that is orderly and coherent is really first put into the dream during the attempt to recall it. Thus we are in danger of being deprived of the very object whose value we have undertaken to determine.

In all our dream-interpretations we have hitherto ignored these warnings. On the contrary, indeed, we have found that the smallest, most insignificant, and most uncertain components of the dream-content invited interpretations no less emphatically than those which were distinctly and certainly contained in the dream. In the dream of Irma's injection we read: "I *quickly* called in Dr. M.," and we assumed that even this small addendum would not have got into the dream if it had not been susceptible of a special derivation. In this way we arrived at the history of that unfortunate patient to whose bedside I *quickly* called my older colleague. In the seemingly absurd dream which treated the difference between fifty-one and fifty-six as a *quantité négligeable* the number fifty-one was mentioned repeatedly. Instead of regarding this as a matter of course, or a detail of indifferent value, we proceeded from this to a second train of thought in the latent dream-content, which led to the number fifty-one, and by following up this clue we arrived at the fears which proposed fifty-one years as the term of life in the sharpest opposition to a dominant train of thought which was boastfully lavish of the years. In the dream *Non*

[1] Similar views are expressed by Foucault and Tannery.

vixit I found, as an insignificant interpolation, that I had at first overlooked the sentence: *As P does not understand him, Fl asks me*, etc. The interpretation then coming to a standstill, I went back to these words, and I found through them the way to the infantile phantasy which appeared in the dream-thoughts as an intermediate point of junction. This came about by means of the poet's verses:

Selten habt ihr mich verstanden,
Selten auch verstand ich Euch,
Nur wenn wir im Kot *uns fanden*
So verstanden wir uns gleich! [1]

Every analysis will afford evidence of the fact that the most insignificant features of the dream are indispensable to interpretation, and will show how the completion of the task is delayed if we postpone our examination of them. We have given equal attention, in the interpretation of dreams, to every nuance of verbal expression found in them; indeed, whenever we are confronted by a senseless or insufficient wording, as though we had failed to translate the dream into the proper version, we have respected even these defects of expression. In brief, what other writers have regarded as arbitrary improvisations, concocted hastily to avoid confusion, we have treated like a sacred text. This contradiction calls for explanation.

It would appear, without doing any injustice to the writers in question, that the explanation is in our favour. From the standpoint of our newly-acquired insight into the origin of dreams, all contradictions are completely reconciled. It is true that we distort the dream in our attempt to reproduce it; we once more find therein what we have called the secondary and often misunderstanding elaboration of the dream by the agency of normal thinking. But this distortion is itself no more than a part of the elaboration to which the dream-thoughts are constantly subjected as a result of the dream-censorship. Other writers have here suspected or observed that part of the dream-distortion whose work is manifest; but for us this is of little consequence, as we know that a far more extensive work of distortion, not so easily apprehended, has already taken the dream for its object from among the hidden dream-thoughts. The only mistake of these writers consists in believing the modification

effected in the dream by its recollection and verbal expression to be arbitrary, incapable of further solution, and consequently liable to lead us astray in our cognition of the dream. They underestimate the determination of the dream in the psyche. Here there is nothing arbitrary. It can be shown that in all cases a second train of thought immediately takes over the determination of the elements which have been left undetermined by the first. For example, I wish quite arbitrarily to think of a number; but this is not possible; the number that occurs to me is definitely and necessarily determined by thoughts within me which may be quite foreign to my momentary purpose. [2] The modifications which the dream undergoes in its revision by the waking mind are just as little arbitrary. They preserve an associative connection with the content, whose place they take, and serve to show us the way to this content, which may itself be a substitute for yet another content.

In analysing the dreams of patients I impose the following test of this assertion, and never without success. If the first report of a dream seems not very comprehensible, I request the dreamer to repeat it. This he rarely does in the same words. But the passages in which the expression is modified are thereby made known to me as the weak points of the dream's disguise; they are what the embroidered emblem on Siegfried's raiment was to Hagen. These are the points from which the analysis may start. The narrator has been admonished by my announcement that I intend to take special pains to solve the dream, and immediately, obedient to the urge of resistance, he protects the weak points of the dream's disguise, replacing a treacherous expression by a less relevant one. He thus calls my attention to the expressions which he has discarded. From the efforts made to guard against the solution of the dream, I can also draw conclusions about the care with which the raiment of the dream has been woven.

The writers whom I have mentioned are, however, less justified when they attribute so much importance to the doubt with which our judgment approaches the relation of the dream. For this doubt is not intellectually warranted; our memory can give no guarantees, but nevertheless we are compelled to credit its statements far more frequently than is objectively justifiable. Doubt concerning the accurate reproduction of the dream, or of individual

---

[1] *Seldom have you understood me,*
Seldom have I understood you,
But when we found ourselves in the mire,
We at once understood each other!

[2] Cf. *The Psycho-pathology of Everyday Life.*

data of the dream, is only another offshoot of the dream-censorship, that is, of resistance to the emergence of the dream-thoughts into consciousness. This resistance has not yet exhausted itself by the displacements and substitutions which it has effected, so that it still clings, in the form of doubt, to what has been allowed to emerge. We can recognize this doubt all the more readily in that it is careful never to attack the intensive elements of the dream, but only the weak and indistinct ones. But we already know that a transvaluation of all the psychic values has taken place between the dream-thoughts and the dream. The distortion has been made possible only by devaluation; it constantly manifests itself in this way and sometimes contents itself therewith. If doubt is added to the indistinctness of an element of the dream-content, we may, following this indication, recognize in this element a direct offshoot of one of the outlawed dream-thoughts. The state of affairs is like that obtaining after a great revolution in one of the republics of antiquity or the Renaissance. The once powerful, ruling families of the nobility are now banished; all high posts are filled by upstarts; in the city itself only the poorer and most powerless citizens, or the remoter followers of the vanquished party, are tolerated. Even the latter do not enjoy the full rights of citizenship. They are watched with suspicion. In our case, instead of suspicion we have doubt. I must insist, therefore, that in the analysis of a dream one must emancipate oneself from the whole scale of standards of reliability; and if there is the slightest possibility that this or that may have occurred in the dream, it should be treated as an absolute certainty. Until one has decided to reject all respect for appearances in tracing the dream-elements, the analysis will remain at a standstill. Disregard of the element concerned has the psychic effect, in the person analysed, that nothing in connection with the unwished ideas behind this element will occur to him. This effect is really not self-evident; it would be quite reasonable to say, "Whether this or that was contained in the dream I do not know for certain; but the following ideas happen to occur to me." But no one ever does say so; it is precisely the disturbing effect of doubt in the analysis that permits it to be unmasked as an offshoot and instrument of the psychic resistance. Psycho-analysis is justifiably suspicious. One of its rules runs: Whatever disturbs the progress of the work is a resistance.[1]

The forgetting of dreams, too, remains inexplicable until we seek to explain it by the power of the psychic censorship. The feeling that one has dreamed a great deal during the night and has retained only a little of it may have yet another meaning in a number of cases: it may perhaps mean that the dream-work has continued in a perceptible manner throughout the night, but has left behind it only one brief dream. There is, however, no possible doubt that a dream is progressively forgotten on waking. One often forgets it in spite of a painful effort to recover it. I believe, however, that just as one generally overestimates the extent of this forgetting, so also one overestimates the lacunae in our knowledge of the dream due to the gaps occurring in it. All the dream-content that has been lost by forgetting can often be recovered by analysis; in a number of cases, at all events, it is possible to discover from a single remaining fragment, not the dream, of course—which, after all, is of no importance—but the whole of the dream-thoughts. It requires a greater expenditure of attention and self-suppression in the analysis; that is all; but it shows that the forgetting of the dream is not innocent of hostile intention.[2]

A convincing proof of the tendencious nature of dream-forgetting—of the fact that it serves the resistance—is obtained on analysis by investigating a preliminary stage of forgetting.[3] It often happens that, in the midst of an interpretation, an omitted fragment of the dream suddenly emerges which is described as having been previously forgotten. This part of the dream that has been wrested from forgetfulness is always the most important part. It lies on the shortest path to the solution of

[1] This peremptory statement: "Whatever disturbs the progress of the work is a resistance" might easily be misunderstood. It has, of course, the significance merely of a technical rule, a warning for the analyst. It is not denied that during an analysis events may occur which cannot be ascribed to the intention of the person analysed. The patient's father may die in other ways than by being murdered by the patient, or a war may break out and interrupt the analysis. But despite the obvious exaggeration of the above statement there is still something new and useful in it. Even if the disturbing event is real and independent of the patient, the extent of the disturbing influence does often depend only on him, and the resistance reveals itself unmistakably in the ready and immoderate exploitation of such an opportunity.

[2] As an example of the significance of doubt and uncertainty in a dream with a simultaneous shrinking of the dream-content to a single element, see my *General Introduction to Psycho-Analysis* the dream of the sceptical lady patient, p. 492 below, the analysis of which was successful, despite a short postponement.

[3] Concerning the intention of forgetting in general, see my *The Psycho-pathology of Everyday Life*.

the dream, and for that very reason it was most exposed to the resistance. Among the examples of dreams that I have included in the text of this treatise, it once happened that I had subsequently to interpolate a fragment of dream-content. The dream is a dream of travel, which revenges itself on two unamiable traveling companions; I have left it almost entirely uninterpreted, as part of its content is crudely obscene. The part omitted reads: *"I said, referring to a book of Schiller's: 'It is from . . .' but corrected myself, as I realized my mistake: 'It is by . . .' Whereupon the man remarked to his sister, 'Yes, he said it correctly'."*[1]

Self-correction in dreams, which to some writers seems so wonderful, does not really call for consideration. But I will draw from my own memory an instance typical of verbal errors in dreams. I was nineteen years of age when I visited England for the first time, and I spent a day on the shore of the Irish Sea. Naturally enough, I amused myself by picking up the marine animals left on the beach by the tide, and I was just examining a starfish (the dream begins with *Hollthurn—Holothurian*) when a pretty little girl came up to to me and asked me: *"Is it a starfish? Is it alive?"* I replied, *"Yes, he is alive,"* but then felt ashamed of my mistake, and repeated the sentence correctly. For the grammatical mistake which I then made, the dream substitutes another which is quite common among German people. *"Das Buch ist von Schiller"* is not to be translated by *"the book is from,"* but by *"the book is by."* That the dream-work accomplishes this substitution, because the word *from*, owing to its consonance with the German adjective *fromm* (pious, devout) makes a remarkable condensation possible, should no longer surprise us after all that we have heard of the intentions of the dream-work and its unscrupulous selection of means. But what relation has this harmless recollection of the seashore to my dream? It explains, by means of a very innocent example, that I have used the word—the word denoting gender, or *sex* or the *sexual* (*he*)—in the wrong place. This is surely one of the keys to the solution of the dream. Those who have heard of the derivation of the book-title *Matter and Motion* (Molière

in *Le Malade Imaginaire: La Matière est-elle laudable?—A Motion of the bowels*) will readily be able to supply the missing parts.

Moreover, I can prove conclusively, by a *demonstratio ad oculos*, that the forgetting of the dream is in a large measure the work of the resistance. A patient tells me that he has dreamed, but that the dream has vanished without leaving a trace, as if nothing had happened. We set to work, however; I come upon a resistance which I explain to the patient; encouraging and urging him, I help him to become reconciled to some disagreeable thought; and I have hardly succeeded in doing so when he exclaims: "Now I can recall what I dreamed!" The same resistance which that day disturbed him in the work of interpretation caused him also to forget the dream. By overcoming this resistance I have brought back the dream to his memory.

In the same way the patient, having reached a certain part of the work, may recall a dream which occurred three, four, or more days ago, and which has hitherto remained in oblivion.[2]

Psycho-analytical experience has furnished us with yet another proof of the fact that the forgetting of dreams depends far more on the resistance than on the mutually alien character of the waking and sleeping states, as some writers have believed it to depend. It often happens to me, as well as to other analysts, and to patients under treatment, that we are waked from sleep by a dream, as we say, and that immediately thereafter, while in full possession of our mental faculties, we begin to interpret the dream. Often in such cases I have not rested until I have achieved a full understanding of the dream, and yet it has happened that after waking I have forgotten the interpretation-work as completely as I have forgotten the dream-content itself, though I have been aware that I have dreamed and that I had interpreted the dream. The dream has far more frequently taken the result of the interpretation with it into forgetfulness than the intellectual faculty has succeeded in retaining the dream in the memory. But between this work of interpretation and the waking thoughts there is not that psychic abyss by which other writers have sought to explain the forgetting of dreams. When Morton Prince objects to my explanation of the forgetting of dreams on

---

[1] Such corrections in the use of foreign languages are not rare in dreams, but they are usually attributed to foreigners. Maury (p. 143), while he was studying English, once dreamed that he informed someone that he had called on him the day before in the following words: "I called for you yesterday." The other answered correctly: "You mean: I called on you yesterday."

[2] Ernest Jones describes an analogous case of frequent occurrence; during the analysis of one dream another dream of the same night is often recalled which until then was not merely forgotten, but was not even suspected.

the ground that it is only a special case of the amnesia of dissociated psychic states, and that the impossibility of applying my explanation of this special amnesia to other types of amnesia makes it valueless even for its immediate purpose, he reminds the reader that in all his descriptions of such dissociated states he has never attempted to discover the dynamic explanation underlying these phenomena. For had he done so, he would surely have discovered that repression (and the resistance produced thereby) is the cause not of these dissociations merely, but also of the amnesia of their psychic content.

That dreams are as little forgotten as other psychic acts, that even in their power of impressing themselves on the memory they may fairly be compared with the other psychic performances, was proved to me by an experiment which I was able to make while preparing the manuscript of this book. I had preserved in my notes a great many dreams of my own which, for one reason or another, I could not interpret, or, at the time of dreaming them, could interpret only very imperfectly. In order to obtain material to illustrate my assertion, I attempted to interpret some of them a year or two later. In this attempt I was invariably successful; indeed, I may say that the interpretation was effected more easily after all this time than when the dreams were of recent occurrence. As a possible explanation of this fact, I would suggest that I had overcome many of the internal resistances which had disturbed me at the time of dreaming. In such subsequent interpretations I have compared the old yield of dream-thoughts with the present result, which has usually been more abundant, and I have invariably found the old dream-thoughts unaltered among the present ones. However, I soon recovered from my surprise when I reflected that I had long been accustomed to interpret dreams of former years that had occasionally been related to me by my patients as though they had been dreams of the night before; by the same method, and with the same success. In the section on anxiety-dreams I shall include two examples of such delayed dream-interpretations. When I made this experiment for the first time I expected, not unreasonably, that dreams would behave in this connection merely like neurotic symptoms. For when I treat a psychoneurotic, for instance, an hysterical patient, by psychoanalysis, I am compelled to find explanations for the first symptoms of the malady, which

have long since disappeared, as well as for those still existing symptoms which have brought the patient to me; and I find the former problem easier to solve than the more exigent one of today. In the *Studies in Hysteria*,[1] published as early as 1895, I was able to give the explanation of a first hysterical attack which the patient, a woman over forty years of age, had experienced in her fifteenth year.[2]

I will now make a few rather unsystematic remarks relating to the interpretations of dreams, which will perhaps serve as a guide to the reader who wishes to test my assertions by the analysis of his own dreams.

He must not expect that it will be a simple and easy matter to interpret his own dreams. Even the observation of endoptic phenomena, and other sensations which are commonly immune from attention, calls for practice, although this group of observations is not opposed by any psychic motive. It is very much more difficult to get hold of the *unwished ideas*. He who seeks to do so must fulfil the requirements laid down in this treatise, and while following the rules here given, he must endeavour to restrain all criticism, all preconceptions, and all affective or intellectual bias in himself during the work of analysis. He must be ever mindful of the precept which Claude Bernard held up to the experimenter in the physiological laboratory: *"Travailler comme une bête"*—that is, he must be as enduring as an animal, and also as disinterested in the results of his work. He who will follow this advice will no longer find the task a difficult one. The interpretation of a dream cannot always be accomplished in one session; after following up a chain of associations you will often feel that your working capacity is exhausted; the dream will not tell you anything more that day; it is then best to break off, and to resume the work the following day. Another portion of the dream-content then solicits your attention, and you thus obtain access to a fresh stratum of the dream-thoughts. One might call this the *fractional* interpretation of dreams.

It is most difficult to induce the beginner in dream-interpretation to recognize the fact that his task is not finished when he is in possession

---

[1] *Studien über Hysterie,* Case II.
[2] Dreams which have occurred during the first years of childhood, and which have sometimes been retained in the memory for decades with perfect sensorial freshness, are almost always of great importance for the understanding of the development and the neurosis of the dreamer. The analysis of them protects the physician from errors and uncertainties which might confuse him even theoretically.

of a complete interpretation of the dream which is both ingenious and coherent, and which gives particulars of all the elements of the dream-content. Besides this, another interpretation, an over-interpretation of the same dream, one which has escaped him, may be possible. It is really not easy to form an idea of the wealth of trains of unconscious thought striving for expression in our minds, or to credit the adroitness displayed by the dream-work in killing—so to speak—seven flies at one stroke, like the journeyman tailor in the fairy-tale, by means of its ambiguous modes of expression. The reader will constantly be inclined to reproach the author for a superfluous display of ingenuity, but anyone who has had personal experience of dream-interpretation will know better than to do so.

On the other hand, I cannot accept the opinion, first expressed by H. Silberer, that every dream—or even that many dreams, and certain groups of dreams—calls for two different interpretations, between which there is even supposed to be a fixed relation. One of these, which Silberer calls the *psycho-analytic* interpretation, attributes to the dream any meaning you please, but in the main an infantile sexual one. The other, the more important interpretation, which he calls the *anagogic* intrepretation, reveals the more serious and often profound thoughts which the dream-work has used as its material. Silberer does not prove this assertion by citing a number of dreams which he has analysed in these two directions. I am obliged to object to this opinion on the ground that it is contrary to facts. The majority of dreams require no over-interpretation, and are especially insusceptible of an anagogic interpretation. The influence of a tendency which seeks to veil the fundamental conditions of dream-formation and divert our interest from its instinctual roots is as evident in Silberer's theory as in other theoretical efforts of the last few years. In a number of cases I can confirm Silberer's assertions; but in these the analysis shows me that the dream-work was confronted with the task of transforming a series of highly abstract thoughts, incapable of direct representation, from waking life into a dream. The dream-work attempted to accomplish this task by seizing upon another thought-material which stood in loose and often *allegorical* relation to the abstract thoughts, and thereby diminished the difficulty of representing them. The abstract interpretation of a dream originating in this manner will be given by the dreamer immediately, but the correct interpretation of the substituted material can be obtained only by means of the familiar technique.

The question whether every dream can be interpreted is to be answered in the negative. One should not forget that in the work of interpretation one is opposed by the psychic forces that are responsible for the distortion of the dream. Whether one can master the inner resistances by one's intellectual interest, one's capacity for self-control, one's psychological knowledge, and one's experience in dream-interpretation depends on the relative strength of the opposing forces. It is always possible to make some progress; one can at all events go far enough to become convinced that a dream has meaning, and generally far enough to gain some idea of its meaning. It very often happens that a second dream enables us to confirm and continue the interpretation assumed for the first. A whole series of dreams, continuing for weeks or months, may have a common basis, and should therefore be interpreted as a continuity. In dreams that follow one another, we often observe that one dream takes as its central point something that is only alluded to in the periphery of the next dream, and conversely, so that even in their interpretations the two supplement each other. That different dreams of the same night are always to be treated, in the work of interpretation, as a whole, I have already shown by examples.

In the best interpreted dreams we often have to leave one passage in obscurity because we observe during the interpretation that we have here a tangle of dream-thoughts which cannot be unravelled, and which furnishes no fresh contribution to the dream-content. This, then, is the keystone of the dream, the point at which it ascends into the unknown. For the dream-thoughts which we encounter during the interpretation commonly have no termination, but run in all directions into the net-like entanglement of our intellectual world. It is from some denser part of this fabric that the dream-wish then arises, like the mushroom from its mycelium.

Let us now return to the facts of dream-forgetting. So far, of course, we have failed to draw any important conclusion from them. When our waking life shows an unmistakable intention to forget the dream which has been formed during the night, either as a whole, immediately after waking, or little by little in the course of the day, and when we recognize as the chief factor in this process of forgetting the psychic resistance against the dream which has already done its best to oppose the dream at night, the question then arises: What actually has made the dream-formation possible against this resistance? Let us consider the most striking case, in which the waking life has thrust the dream aside as though it had never happened. If we take into consideration the play of the psychic forces, we are compelled to assert that the dream would never have come into existence had the resistance prevailed at night as it did by day. We conclude, then, that the resistance loses some part of its force during the night; we know that it has not been discontinued, as we have demonstrated its share in the formation of dreams—namely, the work of distortion. We have therefore to consider the possibility that at night the resistance is merely diminished, and that dream-formation becomes possible because of this slackening of the resistance; and we shall readily understand that as it regains its full power on waking it immediately thrusts aside what it was forced to admit while it was feeble. Descriptive psychology teaches us that the chief determinant of dream-formation is the dormant state of the psyche; and we may now add the following explanation: *The state of sleep makes dream-formation possible by reducing the endopsychic censorship.*

We are certainly tempted to look upon this as the only possible conclusion to be drawn from the facts of dream-forgetting, and to develop from this conclusion further deductions as to the comparative energy operative in the sleeping and waking states. But we shall stop here for the present. When we have penetrated a little farther into the psychology of dreams we shall find that the origin of dream-formation may be differently conceived. The resistance which tends to prevent the dream-thoughts from becoming conscious may perhaps be evaded without suffering reduction. It is also plausible that both the factors which favour dream-formation, the reduction as well as the evasion of the resistance, may be simultaneously made possible by the sleeping state. But we shall pause here, and resume the subject a little later.

We must now consider another series of objections against our procedure in dream-interpretation. For we proceed by dropping all the directing ideas which at other times control reflection, directing our attention to a single element of the dream, noting the involuntary thoughts that associate themselves with this element. We then take up the next component of the dream-content, and repeat the operation with this; and, regardless of the direction taken by the thoughts, we allow ourselves to be led onwards by them, rambling from one subject to another. At the same time, we harbour the confident hope that we may in the end, and without intervention on our part, come upon the dream-thoughts from which the dream originated. To this the critic may make the following objection: That we arrive somewhere if we start from a single element of the dream is not remarkable. Something can be associatively connected with every idea. The only thing that is remarkable is that one should succeed in hitting upon the dream-thoughts in this arbitrary and aimless excursion. It is probably a self-deception; the investigator follows the chain of associations from the one element which is taken up until he finds the chain breaking off, whereupon he takes up a second element; it is thus only natural that the originally unconfined associations should now become narrowed down. He has the former chain of associations still in mind, and will therefore in the analysis of the second dream-idea hit all the more readily upon single associations which have something in common with the associations of the first chain. He then imagines that he has found a thought which represents a point of junction between two of the dream-elements. As he allows himself all possible freedom of thought-connection, excepting only the transitions from one idea to another which occur in normal thinking, it is not difficult for him finally to concoct out of a series of *intermediary thoughts,* something which he calls the dream-thoughts; and without any guarantee, since they are otherwise unknown, he palms these off as the psychic equivalent of the dream. But all this is a purely arbitrary procedure, an ingenious-looking exploitation of chance, and anyone who will go to this useless trouble can in this way work out any desired interpretation for any dream whatever.

If such objections are really advanced against us, we may in defence refer to the impression produced by our dream-interpretations, the surprising connections with other dream-elements which appear while we are following up the individual ideas, and the improbability that anything which so perfectly covers and explains the dream as do our dream-interpretations could be achieved otherwise than by following previously established psychic connections. We might also point to the fact that the procedure in dream-interpretation is identical with the procedure followed in the resolution of hysterical symptoms, where the correctness of the method is attested by the emergence and disappearance of the symptoms —that is, where the interpretation of the text is confirmed by the interpolated illustrations. But we have no reason to avoid this problem— namely, how one can arrive at a pre-existent aim by following an arbitrarily and aimlessly maundering chain of thoughts—since we shall be able not to solve the problem, it is true, but to get rid of it entirely.

For it is demonstrably incorrect to state that we abandon ourselves to an aimless excursion of thought when, as in the interpretation of dreams, we renounce reflection and allow the involuntary ideas to come to the surface. It can be shown that we are able to reject only those directing ideas which are known to us, and that with the cessation of these the unknown—or, as we inexactly say, unconscious— directing ideas immediately exert their influence, and henceforth determine the flow of the involuntary ideas. Thinking without directing ideas cannot be ensured by any influence we ourselves exert on our own psychic life; neither do I know of any state of psychic derangement in which such a mode of thought establishes itself.[1] The psychiatrists have here far too

prematurely relinquished the idea of the solidity of the psychic structure. I know that an unregulated stream of thoughts, devoid of directing ideas, can occur as little in the realm of hysteria and paranoia as in the formation or solution of dreams. Perhaps it does not occur at all in the endogenous psychic affections, and, according to the ingenious hypothesis of Lauret, even the deliria observed in confused psychic states have meaning and are incomprehensible to us only because of omissions. I have had the same conviction whenever I have had an opportunity of observing such states. The deliria are the work of a censorship which no longer makes any effort to conceal its sway, which, instead of lending its support to a revision that is no longer obnoxious to it, cancels regardlessly anything to which it objects, thus causing the remnant to appear disconnected. This censorship proceeds like the Russian censorship on the frontier, which allows only those foreign journals which have had certain passages blacked out to fall into the hands of the readers to be protected.

The free play of ideas following any chain of associations may perhaps occur in cases of destructive organic affections of the brain. What, however, is taken to be such in the psychoneuroses may always be explained as the influence of the censorship on a series of thoughts which have been pushed into the foreground by the concealed directing ideas.[2] It has been considered an unmistakable sign of free association unencumbered by directing ideas if the emerging ideas (or images) appear to be connected by means of the so-called superficial associations—that is, by assonance, verbal ambiguity, and temporal coincidence, without inner relationship of meaning; in other words, if they are connected by all those asso-

---

[1] Only recently has my attention been called to the fact that Ed. von Hartmann took the same view with regard to this psychologically important point: Incidental to the discussion of the rôle of the unconscious in artistic creation (*Philos. d. Unbew.*, Vol. i, Sect. B., Chap. V) Eduard von Hartmann clearly enunciated the law of association of ideas which is directed by unconscious directing ideas, without however realizing the scope of this law. With him it was a question of demonstrating that "every combination of a sensuous idea when it is not left entirely to chance, but is directed to a definite end, is in need of help from the unconscious," and that the conscious interest in any particular thought-association is a stimulus for the unconscious to discover from among the numberless possible ideas the one which corresponds to the directing idea. "It is the unconscious that selects, and appropriately, in accordance with the aims of the interest: and this holds true *for the associations in abstract thinking (as sensible representations and artistic combinations as well as for flashes of wit)*." Hence, a limiting of the association of ideas to ideas that evoke and are evoked in the sense of pure association-psychology is untenable. Such a restriction "would be justified only if there were states in human life in which man was free not only from any conscious purpose, but also from the domination or cooperation of any unconscious interest, any passing mood. But such a state hardly ever comes to pass, *for even if one leaves one's train of thought seemingly altogether to chance, or if one surrenders oneself entirely to the involuntary dreams*

of phantasy, yet always other leading interests, dominant feelings and moods prevail at one time rather than another, and these will always exert an influence on the association of ideas." (*Philos. d. Unbew.*, 11e Aufl. i. 246). In semi-conscious dreams there always appear only such ideas as correspond to the (unconscious) momentary main interest. By rendering prominent the feelings and moods over the free thought-series, the methodical procedure of psycho-analysis is thoroughly justified even from the standpoint of Hartmann's Psychology (N. E. Pohorilles, *Internat. Zeitschrift. f. Ps.A.*, 1, [1913], p. 605). Du Prel concludes from the fact that a name which we vainly try to recall suddenly occurs to the mind that there is an unconscious but none the less purposeful thinking, whose result then appears in consciousness (*Philos. d. Mystik*, p. 107).

[2] Jung has brilliantly corroborated this statement by analyses of dementia praecox. (Cf. *The Psychology of Dementia Praecox*, translated by A. A. Brill. Monograph Series, [Journal of Nervous and Mental Diseases Publishing Co., New York].)

ciations which we allow ourselves to exploit in wit and in playing upon words. This distinguishing mark holds good with associations which lead us from the elements of the dream-content to the intermediary thoughts, and from these to the dream-thoughts proper; in many analyses of dreams we have found surprising examples of this. In these no connection was too loose and no witticism too objectionable to serve as a bridge from one thought to another. But the correct understanding of such surprising tolerance is not far to seek. *Whenever one psychic element is connected with another by an obnoxious and superficial association, there exists also a correct and more profound connection between the two, which succumbs to the resistance of the censorship.*

The correct explanation for the predominance of the superficial associations is the pressure of the censorship, and not the suppression of the directing ideas. Whenever the censorship renders the normal connective paths impassable, the superficial associations will replace the deeper ones in the representation. It is as though in a mountainous region a general interruption of traffic, for example an inundation, should render the broad highways impassable: traffic would then have to be maintained by steep and inconvenient tracks used at other times only by the hunter.

We can here distinguish two cases which, however, are essentially one. In the first case, the censorship is directed only against the connection of two thoughts which, being detached from one another, escape its opposition. The two thoughts then enter successively into consciousness; their connection remains concealed; but in its place there occurs to us a superficial connection between the two which would not otherwise have occurred to us, and which as a rule connects with another angle of the conceptual complex instead of that from which the suppressed but essential connection proceeds. Or, in the second case, both thoughts, owing to their content, succumb to the censorship; both then appear not in their correct form but in a modified, substituted form; and both substituted thoughts are so selected as to represent, by a superficial association, the essential relation which existed between those that they have replaced. *Under the pressure of the censorship, the displacement of a normal and vital association by one superficial and apparently absurd has thus occurred in both cases.*

Because we know of these displacements, we unhesitatingly rely upon even the superficial associations which occur in the course of dream-interpretation.[1]

The psycho-analysis of neurotics makes abundant use of the two principles: that with the abandonment of the conscious directing ideas the control over the flow of ideas is transferred to the concealed directing ideas; and that superficial associations are only a displacement-substitute for suppressed and more profound ones. Indeed, psycho-analysis makes these two principles the foundation-stones of its technique. When I request a patient to dismiss all reflection, and to report to me whatever comes into his mind, I firmly cling to the assumption that he will not be able to drop the directing idea of the treatment, and I feel justified in concluding that what he reports, even though it may seem to be quite ingenuous and arbitrary, has some connection with his morbid state. Another directing idea of which the patient has no suspicion is my own personality. The full appreciation, as well as the detailed proof of both these explanations, belongs to the description of the psycho-analytic technique as a therapeutic method. We have here reached one of the junctions, so to speak, at which we purposely drop the subject of dream-interpretation.[2]

Of all the objections raised, only one is justified and still remains to be met; namely, that we ought not to ascribe all the associations of the interpretation-work to the nocturnal dream-work. By interpretation in the waking state we are actually opening a path running back from the dream-elements to the dream-thoughts. The dream-work has followed the contrary direction, and it is not at all probable that these paths are equally passable in opposite directions. On the contrary, it appears that during the day, by means of new thought-connections, we sink shafts that strike the intermediary thoughts and the dream-thoughts now in this place, now in that. We can see how the recent thought-material of the day forces its way into the interpretation-series, and how the

---

[1] The same considerations naturally hold good of the case in which superficial associations are exposed in the dream-content, as, for example, in both the dreams reported by Maury (p. 50, *pélerinage—pelletier—pelle, kilometer—kilograms—gilolo, Lobelia—Lopez—Lotto*). I know from my work with neurotics what kind of reminiscence is prone to represent itself in this manner. It is the consultation of encyclopedias by which most people have satisfied their need of an explanation of the sexual mystery when obsessed by the curiosity of puberty.

[2] The above statements, which when written sounded very improbable, have since been corroborated and applied experimentally by Jung and his pupils in the *Diagnostiche Assoziationsstudien*.

additional resistance which has appeared since the night probably compels it to make new and further detours. But the number and form of the collaterals which we thus contrive during the day are, psychologically speaking, indifferent, so long as they point the way to the dream-thoughts which we are seeking.

B. *Regression*

Now that we have defended ourselves against the objections raised, or have at least indicated our weapons of defence, we must no longer delay entering upon the psychological investigations for which we have so long been preparing. Let us summarize the main results of our recent investigations: The dream is a psychic act full of import; its motive power is invariably a wish craving fulfilment; the fact that it is unrecognizable as a wish, and its many peculiarities and absurdities, are due to the influence of the psychic censorship to which it has been subjected during its formation. Besides the necessity of evading the censorship, the following factors have played a part in its formation: first, a need for condensing the psychic material; second, regard for representability in sensory images; and third (though not constantly), regard for a rational and intelligible exterior of the dream-structure. From each of these propositions a path leads onward to psychological postulates and assumptions. Thus, the reciprocal relation of the wish-motives, and the four conditions, as well as the mutual relations of these conditions, must now be investigated; the dream must be inserted in the context of the psychic life.

At the beginning of this section we cited a certain dream in order that it might remind us of the problems that are still unsolved. The interpretation of this dream (of the burning child) presented no difficulties, although in the analytical sense it was not given in full. We asked ourselves why, after all, it was necessary that the father should dream instead of waking, and we recognized the wish to represent the child as living as a motive of the dream. That there was yet another wish operative in the dream we shall be able to show after further discussion. For the present, however, we may say that for the sake of the wish-fulfilment the thought-process of sleep was transformed into a dream.

If the wish-fulfilment is cancelled out, only one characteristic remains which distinguishes the two kinds of psychic events. The dream-thought would have been: "I see a glimmer coming from the room in which the body is lying. Perhaps a candle has fallen over, and the child is burning!" The dream reproduces the result of this reflection unchanged, but represents it in a situation which exists in the present and is perceptible by the senses like an experience of the waking state. This, however, is the most common and the most striking psychological characteristic of the dream; a thought, usually the one wished for, is objectified in the dream, and represented as a scene, or—as we think—experienced.

But how are we now to explain this characteristic peculiarity of the dream-work, or—to put it more modestly—how are we to bring it into relation with the psychic processes?

On closer examination, it is plainly evident that the manifest form of the dream is marked by two characteristics which are almost independent of each other. One is its representation as a present situation with the omission of *perhaps;* the other is the translation of the thought into visual images and speech.

The transformation to which the dream-thoughts are subjected because the expectation is put into the present tense is, perhaps, in this particular dream not so very striking. This is probably due to the special and really subsidiary rôle of the wish-fulfilment in this dream. Let us take another dream, in which the dream-wish does not break away from the continuation of the waking thoughts in sleep; for example, the dream of Irma's injection. Here the dream-thought achieving representation is in the conditional: "If only Otto could be blamed for Irma's illness!" The dream suppresses the conditional, and replaces it by a simple present tense: "Yes, Otto is to blame for Irma's illness." This, then, is the first of the transformations which even the undistorted dream imposes on the dream-thoughts. But we will not linger over this first peculiarity of the dream. We dispose of it by a reference to the conscious phantasy, the day-dream, which behaves in a similar fashion with its conceptual content. When Daudet's M. Joyeuse wanders unemployed through the streets of Paris while his daughter is led to believe that he has a post and is sitting in his office, he dreams, in the present tense, of circumstances that might help him to obtain a recommendation and employment. The dream, then, employs the present tense in the same manner and with the same right as the day-dream. The present is the tense in which the wish is represented as fulfilled.

The second quality peculiar to the dream alone, as distinguished from the day-dream, is that the conceptual content is not thought, but is transformed into visual images, to which we give credence, and which we believe that we experience. Let us add, however, that not all dreams show this transformation of ideas into visual images. There are dreams which consist solely of thoughts, but we cannot on that account deny that they are substantially dreams. My dream *Autodidasker—the day-phantasy about Professor N* is of this character; it is almost as free of visual elements as though I had thought its content during the day. Moreover, every long dream contains elements which have not undergone this transformation into the visual, and which are simply thought or known as we are wont to think or know in our waking state. And we must here reflect that this transformation of ideas into visual images does not occur in dreams alone, but also in hallucinations and visions, which may appear spontaneously in health, or as symptoms in the psychoneuroses. In brief, the relation which we are here investigating is by no means an exclusive one; the fact remains, however, that this characteristic of the dream, whenever it occurs, seems to be its most noteworthy characteristic, so that we cannot think of the dream-life without it. To understand it, however, requires a very exhaustive discussion.

Among all the observations relating to the theory of dreams to be found in the literature of the subject, I should like to lay stress upon one as being particularly worthy of mention. The famous G. T. H. Fechner makes the conjecture,[1] in a discussion as to the nature of the dreams, *that the dream is staged elsewhere than in the waking ideation.* No other assumption enables us to comprehend the special peculiarities of the dream-life.

The idea which is thus put before us is one of *psychic locality.* We shall wholly ignore the fact that the psychic apparatus concerned is known to us also as an anatomical preparation, and we shall carefully avoid the temptation to determine the psychic locality in any anatomical sense. We shall remain on psychological ground, and we shall do no more than accept the invitation to think of the instrument which serves the psychic activities much as we think of a compound microscope, a photographic camera, or other apparatus. The psychic locality, then, corresponds to a place within such an apparatus in which one of the preliminary

[1] *Psychophysik,* Part. II, p. 520.

phases of the image comes into existence. As is well known, there are in the microscope and the telescope such ideal localities or planes, in which no tangible portion of the apparatus is located. I think it superfluous to apologize for the imperfections of this and all similar figures. These comparisons are designed only to assist us in our attempt to make intelligible the complication of the psychic performance by dissecting it and referring the individual performances to the individual components of the apparatus. So far as I am aware, no attempt has yet been made to divine the construction of the psychic instrument by means of such dissection. I see no harm in such an attempt; I think that we should give free rein to our conjectures, provided we keep our heads and do not mistake the scaffolding for the building. Since for the first approach to any unknown subject we need the help only of auxiliary ideas, we shall prefer the crudest and most tangible hypothesis to all others.

Accordingly, we conceive the psychic apparatus as a compound instrument, the component parts of which we shall call *instances,* or, for the sake of clearness, *systems.* We shall then anticipate that these systems may perhaps maintain a constant spatial orientation to one another, very much as do the different and successive systems of lenses of a telescope. Strictly speaking, there is no need to assume an actual spatial arrangement of the psychic system. It will be enough for our purpose if a definite sequence is established, so that in certain psychic events the system will be traversed by the excitation in a definite temporal order. This order may be different in the case of other processes; such a possibility is left open. For the sake of brevity, we shall henceforth speak of the component parts of the apparatus as ψ-systems.

The first thing that strikes us is the fact that the apparatus composed of ψ-systems has a direction. All our psychic activities proceed from (inner or outer) stimuli and terminate in innervations. We thus ascribe to the apparatus a sensory and a motor end; at the sensory end we find a system which receives the perceptions, and at the motor end another which opens the sluices of motility. The psychic process generally runs from the perceptive end to the motor end. The most general scheme of the psychic apparatus has therefore the following appearance as shown in Fig. 1 on page 352. But this is only in compliance with the requirement, long familiar to us, that the psychic apparatus must be constructed like a reflex apparatus. The reflex act remains the type of every psychic activity as well.

We now have reason to admit a first differentiation at the sensory end. The percepts that come to us leave in our psychic apparatus a trace, which we may call a *memory-trace*. The function related to this memory-trace we call *the memory*. If we hold seriously to our resolution to connect the psychic processes into systems, the memory-trace can consist only of lasting changes in the elements of the systems. But, as has already been shown elsewhere,

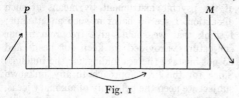

Fig. 1

obvious difficulties arise when one and the same system is faithfully to preserve changes in its elements and still to remain fresh and receptive in respect of new occasions of change. In accordance with the principle which is directing our attempt, we shall therefore ascribe these two functions to two different systems. We assume that an initial system of this apparatus receives the stimuli of perception but retains nothing of them — that is, it has no memory; and that behind this there lies a second system, which transforms the momentary excitation of the first into lasting traces. The following would then be the diagram of our psychic apparatus:

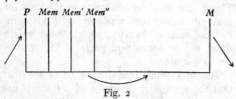

Fig. 2

We know that of the percepts which act upon the *P*-system, we retain permanently something else as well as the content itself. Our percepts prove also to be connected with one another in the memory, and this is especially so if they originally occurred simultaneously. We call this the fact of *association*. It is now clear that, if the *P*-system is entirely lacking in memory, it certainly cannot preserve traces for the associations; the individual *P*-elements would be intolerably hindered in their functioning if a residue of a former connection should make

its influence felt against a new perception. Hence we must rather assume that the memory-system is the basis of association. The fact of association, then, consists in this— that in consequence of a lessening of resistance and a smoothing of the ways from one of the *mem*-elements, the excitation transmits itself to a second rather than to a third *mem*-element.

On further investigation we find it necessary to assume not one but many such *mem*-systems, in which the same excitation transmitted by the *P*-elements undergoes a diversified fixation. The first of these *mem*-systems will in any case contain the fixation of the association through simultaneity, while in those lying farther away the same material of excitation will be arranged according to other forms of combination; so that relationships of similarity, etc., might perhaps be represented by these later systems. It would, of course, be idle to attempt to express in words the psychic significance of such a system. Its characteristic would lie in the intimacy of its relations to elements of raw material of memory—that is (if we wish to hint at a more comprehensive theory) in the gradations of the conductive resistance on the way to these elements.

An observation of a general nature, which may possibly point to something of importance, may here be interpolated. The *P*-system, which possesses no capacity for preserving changes, and hence no memory, furnishes to consciousness the complexity and variety of the sensory qualities. Our memories, on the other hand, are unconscious in themselves; those that are most deeply impressed form no exception. They can be made conscious, but there is no doubt that they unfold all their activities in the unconscious state. What we term our character is based, indeed, on the memory-traces of our impressions, and it is precisely those impressions that have affected us most strongly, those of our early youth, which hardly ever become conscious. But when memories become conscious again they show no sensory quality, or a very negligible one in comparison with the perceptions. If, now, it can be confirmed *that for consciousness memory and quality are mutually exclusive in the ψ-systems*, we have gained a most promising insight into the determinations of the neuron excitations.[1]

What we have so far assumed concerning the composition of the psychic apparatus at

[1] Since writing this, I have thought that consciousness occurs actually *in the locality* of the memory-trace. (Cf. "*Notiz über den Wünderblock*," 1925, *Ges. Schriften*, Vol. vi.)

the sensible end has been assumed regardless of dreams and of the psychological explanations which we have hitherto derived from them. Dreams, however, will serve as a source of evidence for our knowledge of another part of the apparatus. We have seen that it was impossible to explain dream-formation unless we ventured to assume two psychic *instances,* one of which subjected the activities of the other to criticism, the result of which was exclusion from consciousness.

We have concluded that the criticizing *instance* maintains closer relations with the consciousness than the *instance* criticized. It stands between the latter and the consciousness like a screen. Further, we have found that there is reason to identify the criticizing *instance* with that which directs our waking life and determines our voluntary conscious activities. If, in accordance with our assumptions, we now replace these *instances* by systems, the criticizing system will therefore be moved to the motor end. We now enter both systems in our diagram, expressing, by the names given them, their relation to consciousness.

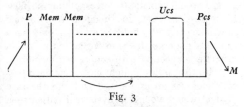

Fig. 3

The last of the systems at the motor end we call the *preconscious (Pcs.)* to denote that the exciting processes in this system can reach consciousness without any further detention, provided certain other conditions are fulfilled, e.g., the attainment of a definite degree of intensity, a certain apportionment of that function which we must call attention, etc. This is at the same time the system which holds the keys of voluntary motility. The system behind it we call the *unconscious (Ucs),* because it has no access to consciousness *except through the preconscious,* in the passage through which the excitation-process must submit to certain changes.[1]

In which of these systems, then, do we localize the impetus to dream-formation? For the sake of simplicity, let us say in the system *Ucs.* We shall find, it is true, in subsequent discussions, that this is not altogether correct;

that dream-formation is obliged to make connection with dream-thoughts which belong to the system of the preconscious. But we shall learn elsewhere, when we come to deal with the dream-wish, that the motive-power of the dream is furnished by the *Ucs,* and on account of this factor we shall assume the unconscious system as the starting-point for dream-formation. This dream-excitation, like all the other thought-structures, will now strive to continue itself in the *Pcs,* and thence to gain admission to the consciousness.

Experience teaches us that the path leading through the preconscious to consciousness is closed to the dream-thoughts during the day by the resisting censorship. At night they gain admission to consciousness; the question arises: In what way and because of what changes? If this admission were rendered possible to the dream-thoughts by the weakening, during the night, of the resistance watching on the boundary between the unconscious and the preconscious, we should then have dreams in the material of our ideas, which would not display the hallucinatory character that interests us at present.

The weakening of the censorship between the two systems, *Ucs* and *Pcs,* can explain to us only such dreams as the *Autodidasker* dream but not dreams like that of the burning child, which—as will be remembered—we stated as a problem at the outset in our present investigations.

What takes place in the hallucinatory dream we can describe in no other way than by saying that the excitation follows a retrogressive course. It communicates itself not to the motor end of the apparatus, but to the sensory end, and finally reaches the system of perception. If we call the direction which the psychic process follows from the unconscious into the waking state *progressive,* we may then speak of the dream as having a *regressive* character.[2]

This *regression* is therefore assuredly one of the most important psychological peculiarities of the dream-process; but we must not forget that it is not characteristic of the dream alone. Intentional recollection and other component

---

[1] The further elaboration of this linear diagram will have to reckon with the assumption that the system following the *Pcs* represents the one to which we must attribute consciousness *(Cs),* so that $P = Cs$.

[2] The first indication of the element of regression is already encountered in the writings of Albertus Magnus. According to him the *imaginatio* constructs the dream out of the tangible objects which it has retained. The process is the converse of that operating in the waking state. Hobbes states *(Leviathan,* ch. 2): "In sum our dreams are the reverse of our imagination, the motion, when we are awake, beginning at one end, and when we dream at another" (quoted by Havelock Ellis, *loc. cit.,* p. 112).

processes of our normal thinking likewise necessitate a retrogression in the psychic apparatus from some complex act of ideation to the raw material of the memory-traces which underlie it. But during the waking state this turning backwards does not reach beyond the memory-images; it is incapable of producing the hallucinatory revival of the perceptual images. Why is it otherwise in dreams? When we spoke of the condensation-work of the dream we could not avoid the assumption that by the dream-work the intensities adhering to the ideas are completely transferred from one to another. It is probably this modification of the usual psychic process which makes possible the cathexis[1] of the system of P to its full sensory vividness in the reverse direction to thinking.

I hope that we are not deluding ourselves as regards the importance of this present discussion. We have done nothing more than give a name to an inexplicable phenomenon. We call it *regression* if the idea in the dream is changed back into the visual image from which it once originated. But even this step requires justification. Why this definition if it does not teach us anything new? Well, I believe that the word *regression* is of service to us, inasmuch as it connects a fact familiar to us with the scheme of the psychic apparatus endowed with direction. At this point, and for the first time, we shall profit by the fact that we have constructed such a scheme. For with the help of this scheme we shall perceive, without further reflection, another peculiarity of dream-formation. If we look upon the dream as a process of regression within the hypothetical psychic apparatus, we have at once an explanation of the empirically proven fact that all thought-relations of the dream-thoughts are either lost in the dream-work or have difficulty in achieving expression. According to our scheme, these thought-relations are contained not in the first *mem*-systems, but in those lying farther to the front, and in the regression to the perceptual images they must forfeit expression. *In regression, the structure of the dream-thoughts breaks up into its raw material.*

But what change renders possible this regression which is impossible during the day? Let us here be content with an assumption. There must evidently be changes in the cathexis of the individual systems, causing the latter to become more accessible or inaccessible to the

discharge of the excitation; but in any such apparatus the same effect upon the course of the excitation might be produced by more than one kind of change. We naturally think of the sleeping state, and of the many cathectic changes which this evokes at the sensory end of the apparatus. During the day there is a continuous stream flowing from the ψ-system of the P toward the motility end; this current ceases at night, and can no longer block the flow of the current of excitation in the opposite direction. This would appear to be that *seclusion from the outer world* which, according to the theory of some writers, is supposed to explain the psychological character of the dream. In the explanation of the regression of the dream we shall, however, have to take into account those other regressions which occur during morbid waking states. In these other forms of regression the explanation just given plainly leaves us in the lurch. Regression occurs in spite of the uninterrupted sensory current in a progressive direction.

The hallucinations of hysteria and paranoia, as well as the visions of mentally normal persons, I would explain as corresponding, in fact, to regressions, i.e., to thoughts transformed into images; and would assert that only such thoughts undergo this transformation as are in intimate connection with suppressed memories, or with memories which have remained unconscious. As an example, I will cite the case of one of my youngest hysterical patients—a boy of twelve, who was prevented from falling asleep by "green faces with red eyes," which terrified him. The source of this manifestation was the suppressed, but once conscious memory of a boy whom he had often seen four years earlier, and who offered a warning example of many bad habits, including masturbation, for which he was now reproaching himself. At that time his mother had noticed that the complexion of this ill-mannered boy was *greenish* and that he had *red* (i.e., red-rimmed) *eyes.* Hence his terrifying vision, which merely determined his recollection of another saying of his mother's, to the effect that such boys become demented, are unable to learn anything at school, and are doomed to an early death. A part of this prediction came true in the case of my little patient; he could not get on at school, and, as appeared from his involuntary associations, he was in terrible dread of the remainder of the prophecy. However, after a brief period of successful treatment his sleep was restored, his anxiety removed, and he fin-

[1] From the Greek *Kathexo*, to occupy, used here in place of the author's term *Besetzung,* to signify a charge or investment of energy.—TR.

ished his scholastic year with an excellent record.

Here I may add the interpretation of a vision described to me by an hysterical woman of forty, as having occurred when she was in normal health. One morning she opened her eyes and saw her brother in the room, although she knew him to be confined in an insane asylum. Her little son was asleep by her side. Lest the child *should be frightened* on seeing his *uncle,* and *fall into convulsions,* she pulled the sheet over his face. This done, the phantom disappeared. This apparition was the revision of one of her childish memories, which, although conscious, was most intimately connected with all the unconscious material in her mind. Her nurserymaid had told her that her mother, who had died young (my patient was then only eighteen months old), had suffered from epileptic or hysterical convulsions, which dated back to a fright caused by her brother (the patient's *uncle*) who appeared to her disguised as a spectre with a *sheet* over his head. The vision contains the same elements as the reminiscence, viz., the appearance of the brother, the sheet, the fright, and its effect. These elements, however, are arranged in a fresh context, and are transferred to other persons. The obvious motive of the vision, and the thought which it replaced, was her solicitude lest her little son, who bore a striking resemblance to his uncle, should share the latter's fate.

Both examples here cited are not entirely unrelated to the state of sleep, and may for that reason be unfitted to afford the evidence for the sake of which I have cited them. I will, therefore, refer to my analysis of an hallucinatory paranoic woman patient[1] and to the results of my hitherto unpublished studies on the psychology of the psychoneuroses, in order to emphasize the fact that in these cases of regressive thought-transformation one must not overlook the influence of a suppressed memory, or one that has remained unconscious, this being usually of an infantile character. This memory draws into the regression, as it were, the thoughts with which it is connected, and which are kept from expression by the censorship—that is, into that form of representation in which the memory itself is psychically existent. And here I may add, as a result of my studies of hysteria, that if one succeeds in bringing to consciousness infantile scenes

(whether they are recollections or phantasies) they appear as hallucinations, and are divested of this character only when they are communicated. It is known also that even in persons whose memories are not otherwise visual, the earliest infantile memories remain vividly visual until late in life.

If, now, we bear in mind the part played in the dream-thoughts by the infantile experiences, or by the phantasies based upon them, and recollect how often fragments of these re-emerge in the dream-content, and how even the dream-wishes often proceed from them, we cannot deny the probability that in dreams, too, the transformation of thoughts into visual images may be the result of the *attraction* exercised by the visually represented memory, striving for resuscitation, upon the thoughts severed from the consciousness and struggling for expression. Pursuing this conception, we may further describe the dream as the *substitute for the infantile scene modified by transference to recent material.* The infantile scene cannot enforce its own revival, and must therefore be satisfied to return as a dream.

This reference to the significance of the infantile scenes (or of their phantastic repetitions) as in a certain degree furnishing the pattern for the dream-content renders superfluous the assumption made by Scherner and his pupils concerning inner sources of stimuli. Scherner assumes a state of *visual excitation,* of internal excitation in the organ of sight, when the dreams manifest a special vividness or an extraordinary abundance of visual elements. We need raise no objection to this assumption; we may perhaps content ourselves with assuming such a state of excitation only for the psychic perceptive system of the organ of vision; we shall, however, insist that this state of excitation is a reanimation by the memory of a former actual visual excitation. I cannot, from my own experience, give a good example showing such an influence of an infantile memory; my own dreams are altogether less rich in perceptual elements than I imagine those of others to be; but in my most beautiful and most vivid dream of late years I can easily trace the hallucinatory distinctness of the dream-contents to the visual qualities of recently received impressions. On p. 321 I mentioned a dream in which the dark blue of the water, the brown of the smoke issuing from the ship's funnels, and the sombre brown and red of the buildings which I saw made a profound and lasting impression upon my mind.

---

[1] *Selected Papers on Hysteria,* "Further Observations on the Defence-Neuro-Psychoses," p. 97 above.

This dream, if any, must be attributed to visual excitation, but what was it that had brought my organ of vision into this excitable state? It was a recent impression which had joined itself to a series of former impressions. The colours I beheld were in the first place those of the toy blocks with which my children had erected a magnificent building for my admiration, on the day preceding the dream. There was the sombre red on the large blocks, the blue and brown on the small ones. Joined to these were the colour impressions of my last journey in Italy: the beautiful blue of the Isonzo and the lagoons, the brown hue of the Alps. The beautiful colours seen in the dream were but a repetition of those seen in memory.

Let us summarize what we have learned about this peculiarity of dreams: their power of recasting their idea-content in visual images. We may not have explained this character of the dream-work by referring it to the known laws of psychology, but we have singled it out as pointing to unknown relations, and have given it the name of the *regressive* character. Wherever such regression has occurred, we have regarded it as an effect of the resistance which opposes the progress of thought on its normal way to consciousness, and of the simultaneous attraction exerted upon it by vivid memories.[1] The regression in dreams is perhaps facilitated by the cessation of the progressive stream flowing from the sense-organs during the day; for which auxiliary factor there must be some compensation, in the other forms of regression, by the strengthening of the other regressive motives. We must also bear in mind that in pathological cases of regression, just as in dreams, the process of energy-transference must be different from that occurring in the regressions of normal psychic life, since it renders possible a full hallucinatory cathexis of the perceptive system. What we have described in the analysis of the dream-work as *regard for representability* may be referred to the *selective attraction* of visually remembered scenes touched by the dream-thoughts.

As to the regression, we may further observe that it plays a no less important part in the theory of neurotic symptom-formation than in the theory of dreams. We may therefore dis-

tinguish a threefold species of regression: *(a)* a *topical* one, in the sense of the scheme of the ψ-systems here exponded; *(b)* a *temporal* one, in so far as it is a regression to older psychic formations; and *(c)* a *formal* one, when primitive modes of expression and representation take the place of the customary modes. These three forms of regression are, however, basically one, and in the majority of cases they coincide, for that which is older in point of time is at the same time formally primitive and, in the psychic topography, nearer to the perception-end.

We cannot leave the theme of regression in dreams without giving utterance to an impression which has already and repeatedly forced itself upon us, and which will return to us reinforced after a deeper study of the psychoneuroses: namely, that dreaming is on the whole an act of regression to the earliest relationships of the dreamer, a resuscitation of his childhood, of the impulses which were then dominant and the modes of expression which were then available. Behind this childhood of the individual we are then promised an insight into the phylogenetic childhood, into the evolution of the human race, of which the development of the individual is only an abridged repetition influenced by the fortuitous circumstances of life. We begin to suspect that Friedrich Nietzsche was right when he said that in a dream "there persists a primordial part of humanity which we can no longer reach by a direct path," and we are encouraged to expect, from the analysis of dreams, a knowledge of the archaic inheritance of man, a knowledge of psychical things in him that are innate. It would seem that dreams and neuroses have preserved for us more of the psychical antiquities than we suspected; so that psycho-analysis may claim a high rank among those sciences which endeavour to reconstruct the oldest and darkest phases of the beginnings of mankind.

It is quite possible that we shall not find this first part of our psychological evaluation of dreams particularly satisfying. We must, however, console ourselves with the thought that we are, after all, compelled to build out into the dark. If we have not gone altogether astray, we shall surely reach approximately the same place from another starting-point, and then, perhaps, we shall be better able to find our bearings.

C. *The Wish-Fulfilment*

The dream of the burning child (cited above) affords us a welcome opportunity for appreci-

[1] In a statement of the theory of repression it should be explained that a thought passes into repression owing to the co-operation of two of the factors which influence it. On the one side (the censorship of *Cs*) it is pushed, and from the other side (the *Ucs*) it is pulled, much as one is helped to the top of the Great Pyramid. (Compare the paper *Repression*, p. 422 below.)

ating the difficulties confronting the theory of wish-fulfilment. That a dream should be nothing but a wish-fulfilment must undoubtedly seem strange to us all—and not only because of the contradiction offered by the anxiety-dream. Once our first analyses had given us the enlightenment that meaning and psychic value are concealed behind our dreams, we could hardly have expected so unitary a determination of this meaning. According to the correct but summary definition of Aristotle, the dream is a continuation of thinking in sleep. Now if, during the day, our thoughts perform such a diversity of psychic acts—judgments, conclusions, the answering of objections, expectations, intentions, etc.—why should they be forced at night to confine themselves to the production of wishes only? Are there not, on the contrary, many dreams that present an altogether different psychic act in dream-form—for example, anxious care—and is not the father's unusually transparent dream of the burning child such a dream? From the gleam of light that falls upon his eyes while he is asleep the father draws the apprehensive conclusion that a candle has fallen over and may be burning the body; he transforms this conclusion into a dream by embodying it in an obvious situation enacted in the present tense. What part is played in this dream by the wish-fulfilment? And how can we possibly mistake the predominance of the thought continued from the waking state or evoked by the new sensory impression?

All these considerations are justified, and force us to look more closely into the rôle of the wish-fulfilment in dreams, and the significance of the waking thoughts continued in sleep.

It is precisely the wish-fulfilment that has already caused us to divide all dreams into two groups. We have found dreams which were plainly wish-fulfilments; and others in which the wish-fulfilment was unrecognizable and was often concealed by every available means. In this latter class of dreams we recognized the influence of the dream-censorship. The undisguised wish-dreams were found chiefly in children; *short,* frank wish-dreams *seemed* (I purposely emphasize this word) to occur also in adults.

We may now ask whence in each case does the wish that is realized in the dream originate? But to what opposition or to what diversity do we relate this *whence?* I think to the opposition between conscious daily life and an un-

conscious psychic activity which is able to make itself perceptible only at night. I thus, find a threefold possibility for the origin of a wish. Firstly, it may have been excited during the day, and owing to external circumstances may have remained unsatisfied; there is thus left for the night an acknowledged and unsatisfied wish. Secondly, it may have emerged during the day, only to be rejected; there is thus left for the night an unsatisfied but suppressed wish. Thirdly, it may have no relation to daily life, but may belong to those wishes which awake only at night out of the suppressed material in us. If we turn to our scheme of the psychic apparatus, we can localize a wish of the first order in the system *Pcs*. We may assume that a wish of the second order has been forced back from the *Pcs* system into the *Ucs* system, where alone, if anywhere, can it maintain itself; as for the wish-impulse of the third order, we believe that it is wholly incapable of leaving the *Ucs* system. Now, have the wishes arising from these different sources the same value for the dream, the same power to incite a dream?

On surveying the dreams at our disposal with a view to answering this question, we are at once moved to add as a fourth source of the dream-wish the actual wish-impetus which arises during the night (for example, the stimulus of thirst, and sexual desire). It then seems to us probable that the source of the dream-wish does not affect its capacity to incite a dream. I have in mind the dream of the child who continued the voyage that had been interrupted during the day, and the other children's dreams cited in the same chapter; they are explained by an unfulfilled but unsuppressed wish of the daytime. That wishes suppressed during the day assert themselves in dreams is shown by a great many examples. I will mention a very simple dream of this kind. A rather sarcastic lady, whose younger friend has become engaged to be married, is asked in the daytime by her acquaintances whether she knows her friend's fiancé, and what she thinks of him. She replies with unqualified praise, imposing silence on her own judgment, although she would have liked to tell the truth, namely, that he is a *commonplace fellow — one meets such by the dozen (Dutzendmensch).* The following night she dreams that the same question is put to her, and that she replies with the formula: *"In case of subsequent orders, it will suffice to mention the reference number."* Finally, as the result of numerous analyses, we learn that the wish in all dreams that have been subject to distortion has its origin in the uncon-scious, and could not become perceptible by day. At first sight, then, it seems that in re-spect of dream-formation all wishes are of equal value and equal power.

I cannot prove here that this is not really the true state of affairs, but I am strongly in-clined to assume a stricter determination of the dream-wish. Children's dreams leave us in no doubt that a wish unfulfilled during the day may instigate a dream. But we must not forget that this is, after all, the wish of a child; that it is a wish-impulse of the strength peculiar to childhood. I very much doubt whether a wish unfulfilled in the daytime would suffice to cre-ate a dream in an adult. It would rather seem that, as we learn to control our instinctual life by intellection, we more and more renounce as unprofitable the formation or retention of such intense wishes as are natural to child-hood. In this, indeed, there may be individual variations; some retain the infantile type of the psychic processes longer than others; just as we find such differences in the gradual de-cline of the originally vivid visual imagination. In general, however, I am of the opinion that unfulfiled wishes of the day are insufficient to produce a dream in adults. I will readily admit that the wish-impulses originating in conscious-ness contribute to the instigation of dreams, but they probably do no more. The dream would not occur if the preconscious wish were not re-inforced from another source.

That source is the unconscious. I believe that *the conscious wish becomes effective in ex-citing a dream only when it succeeds in arous-ing a similar unconscious wish which reinforces it.* From the indications obtained in the psycho-analysis of the neuroses, I believe that these unconscious wishes are always active and ready to express themselves whenever they find an opportunity of allying themselves with an im-pulse from consciousness, and transferring their own greater intensity to the lesser intensity of the latter.[1] It must, therefore, seem that the conscious wish alone has been realized in the dream; but a slight peculiarity in the form of the dream will put us on the track of the pow-erful ally from the unconscious. These ever-active and, as it were, immortal wishes of our unconscious recall the legendary Titans who, from time immemorial, have been buried un-der the mountains which were once hurled upon them by the victorious gods, and even now quiv-er from time to time at the convulsions of their mighty limbs. These wishes, existing in repres-sion, are themselves of infantile origin, as we learn from the psychological investigation of the neuroses. Let me, therefore, set aside the view previously expressed, that it matters lit-tle whence the dream-wish originates, and re-place it by another, namely: *the wish mani-fested in the dream must be an infantile wish.* In the adult it originates in the *Ucs,* while in the child, in whom no division and censorship exist as yet between the *Pcs* and *Ucs,* or in whom these are only in process of forma-tion, it is an unfulfilled and unrepressed wish from the waking state. I am aware that this conception cannot be generally demonstrated, but I maintain that it can often be demon-strated even where one would not have sus-pected it, and that it cannot be generally refuted.

In dream-formation, the wish-impulses which are left over from the conscious waking life are, therefore, to be relegated to the back-ground. I cannot admit that they play any part except that attributed to the material of actual sensations during sleep in relation to the dream-content. If I now take into account those other psychic instigations left over from the waking life of the day, which are not wish-es, I shall merely be adhering to the course mapped out for me by this line of thought. We may succeed in provisionally disposing of the energetic cathexis of our waking thoughts by deciding to go to sleep. He is a good sleeper who can do this; Napoleon I is reputed to have been a model of this kind. But we do not al-ways succeed in doing it, or in doing it com-pletely. Unsolved problems, harassing cares, overwhelming impressions, continue the activ-ity of our thought even during sleep, maintain-ing psychic processes in the system which we have termed the preconscious. The thought-im-pulses continued into sleep may be divided in-to the following groups:

1. Those which have not been completed during the day, owing to some accidental cause.

2. Those which have been left uncomplet-

[1] They share this character of indestructibility with all other psychic acts that are really unconscious—that is, with psychic acts belonging solely to the system *Ucs.* These paths are opened once and for all; they never fall into disuse; they conduct the excitation-process to discharge as often as they are charged again with unconscious excitation. To speak metaphorically, they suffer no other form of annihilation than did the shades of the lower regions in the *Odyssey,* who awoke to new life the moment they drank blood. The processes depending on the preconscious system are destructible in quite another sense. The psychotherapy of the neu-roses is based on this difference.

ed because our mental powers have failed us, i.e., unsolved problems.

3. Those which have been turned back and suppressed during the day. This is reinforced by a powerful fourth group:

4. Those which have been excited in our *Ucs* during the day by the workings of the *Pcs;* and finally we may add a fifth, consisting of:

5. The indifferent impressions of the day, which have therefore been left unsettled.

We need not underrate the psychic intensities introduced into sleep by these residues of the day's waking life, especially those emanating from the group of the unsolved issues. It is certain that these excitations continue to strive for expression during the night, and we may assume with equal certainty that the state of sleep renders impossible the usual continuance of the process of excitation in the preconscious and its termination in becoming conscious. In so far as we can become conscious of our mental processes in the ordinary way, even during the night, to that extent we are simply not asleep. I cannot say what change is produced in the *Pcs* system by the state of sleep,[1] but there is no doubt that the psychological characteristics of sleep are to be sought mainly in the cathectic changes occurring just in this system, which dominates, moreover, the approach to motility, paralysed during sleep. On the other hand, I have found nothing in the psychology of dreams to warrant the assumption that sleep produces any but secondary changes in the conditions of the *Ucs* system. Hence, for the nocturnal excitations in the *Pcs* there remains no other path than that taken by the wish-excitations from the *Ucs;* they must seek reinforcement from the *Ucs,* and follow the detours of the unconscious excitations. But what is the relation of the preconscious day-residues to the dream? There is no doubt that they penetrate abundantly into the dream; that they utilize the dream-content to obtrude themselves upon consciousness even during the night; indeed, they sometimes even dominate the dream-content, and impel it to continue the work of the day; it is also certain that the day-residues may just as well have any other character as that of wishes. But it is highly instructive, and for the theory of wish-fulfilment of quite decisive importance,

[1] I have endeavoured to penetrate farther into the relations of the sleeping state and the conditions of hallucination in my essay, "Metapsychological Supplement to the Theory of Dreams," *Collected Papers,* IV, p. 137.

to see what conditions they must comply with in order to be received into the dream.

Let us pick out one of the dreams cited above, e.g., the dream in which my friend Otto seems to show the symptoms of *Basedow's disease* (p. 249). Otto's appearance gave me some concern during the day, and this worry, like everything else relating to him, greatly affected me. I may assume that this concern followed me into sleep. I was probably bent on finding out what was the matter with him. During the night my concern found expression in the dream which I have recorded. Not only was its content senseless, but it failed to show any wish-fulfilment. But I began to search for the source of this incongruous expression of the solicitude felt during the day, and analysis revealed a connection. I identified my friend Otto with a certain Baron L and myself with a Professor R. There was only one explanation of my being impelled to select just this substitute for the day-thought. I must always have been ready in the *Ucs* to identify myself with Professor R, as this meant the realization of one of the immortal infantile wishes, viz., the wish to become great. Repulsive ideas respecting my friend, ideas that would certainly have been repudiated in a waking state, took advantage of the opportunity to creep into the dream; but the worry of the day had likewise found some sort of expression by means of a substitute in the dream-content. The day-thought, which was in itself not a wish, but on the contrary a worry, had in some way to find a connection with some infantile wish, now unconscious and suppressed, which then allowed it—duly dressed up—to *arise* for consciousness. The more domineering the worry the more forced could be the connection to be established; between the content of the wish and that of the worry there need be no connection, nor was there one in our example.

It would perhaps be appropriate, in dealing with this problem, to inquire how a dream behaves when material is offered to it in the dream-thoughts which flatly opposes a wish-fulfilment; such as justified worries, painful reflections and distressing realizations. The many possible results may be classified as follows: *(a)* The dream-work succeeds in replacing all painful ideas by contrary ideas, and suppressing the painful affect belonging to them. This, then, results in a pure and simple satisfaction-dream, a palpable *wish-fulfilment,* concerning which there is nothing more to be said. *(b)* The painful ideas find their way into the manifest dream-content, more or less modified, but nevertheless quite recognizable. This is the case which raises doubts about the wish-theory of dreams, and thus calls for further investigation. Such dreams with a painful content may either be indifferent in feeling, or they may convey the whole painful affect, which the ideas contained in them seem to justify, or they may even lead to the development of anxiety to the point of waking.

Analysis then shows that even these painful dreams are wish-fulfilments. An unconscious and repressed wish, whose fulfilment could only be felt as painful by the dreamer's ego, has seized the opportunity offered by the continued cathexis of painful day-residues, has lent them its support, and has thus made them capable of being dreamed. But whereas in case *(a)* the unconscious wish coincided with the conscious one, in case *(b)* the discord between the unconscious and the conscious—the repressed material and the ego—is revealed, and the situation in the fairy-tale, of the three wishes which the fairy offers to the married couple, is realized (see p. 534 below). The gratification in respect of the fulfilment of the repressed wish may prove to be so great that it balances the painful affects adhering to the day-residues; the dream is then indifferent in its affective tone, although it is on the one hand the fulfilment of a wish, and on the other the fulfilment of a fear. Or it may happen that the sleeper's ego plays an even more extensive part in the dream-formation, that it reacts with violent resentment to the accomplished satisfaction of the repressed wish, and even goes so far as to make an end of the dream by means of anxiety. It is thus not difficult to recognize that dreams of pain and anxiety are, in accordance with our theory, just as much wish-fulfilments as are the straightforward dreams of gratification.

Painful dreams may also be *punishment dreams*. It must be admitted that the recognition of these dreams adds something that is, in a certain sense, new to the theory of dreams. What is fulfilled by them is once more an unconscious wish—the wish for the punishment of the dreamer for a repressed, prohibited wish-impulse. To this extent, these dreams comply with the requirement here laid down: that the motive-power behind the dream-formation must be furnished by a wish belonging to the unconscious. But a finer psychological dissection allows us to recognize the difference between this and the other wish-dreams. In the

dreams of group *(b)* the unconscious dream-forming wish belonged to the repressed material. In the punishment-dreams it is likewise an unconscious wish, but one which we must attribute not to the repressed material but to the *ego*.

Punishment-dreams point, therefore, to the possibility of a still more extensive participation of the ego in dream-formation. The mechanism of dream-formation becomes indeed in every way more transparent if in place of the antithesis *conscious* and *unconscious*, we put the antithesis: *ego* and *repressed*. This, however, cannot be done without taking into account what happens in the psychoneuroses, and for this reason it has not been done in this book. Here I need only remark that the occurrence of punishment-dreams is not generally subject to the presence of painful day-residues. They originate, indeed, most readily if the contrary is true, if the thoughts which are day-residues are of a gratifying nature, but express illicit gratifications. Of these thoughts nothing, then, finds its way into the manifest dream except their contrary, just as was the case in the dreams of group *(a)*. Thus it would be the essential characteristic of punishment-dreams that in them it is not the unconscious wish from the repressed material (from the system *Ucs*) that is responsible for dream-formation, but the punitive wish reacting against it, a wish pertaining to the ego, even though it is unconscious (i.e., preconscious).[1]

I will elucidate some of the foregoing observations by means of a dream of my own, and above all I will try to show how the dream-work deals with a day-residue involving painful expectation:

Indistinct beginning. *I tell my wife I have some news for her, something very special. She becomes frightened, and does not wish to hear it. I assure her that on the contrary it is something which will please her greatly, and I begin to tell her that our son's Officers' Corps has sent a sum of money (5,000 k.?) ... something about honourable mention ... distribution ... at the same time I have gone with her into a small room, like a store-room, in order to fetch something from it. Suddenly I see my son appear; he is not in uniform but rather in a tight-fitting sports suit (like a seal?) with a small cap. He climbs on to a basket which stands to one side near a chest, in order to put something on this chest. I address him; no answer.*

[1] Here one may consider the idea of the super-ego which was later recognized by psycho-analysis.

It seems to me that his face or forehead is bandaged, he arranges something in his mouth, pushing something into it. Also his hair shows a glint of grey. I reflect: Can he be so exhausted? And has he false teeth? Before I can address him again I awake without anxiety, but with palpitations. My clock points to 2.30 a.m.

To give a full analysis is once more impossible. I shall therefore confine myself to emphasizing some decisive points. Painful expectations of the day had given occasion for this dream; once again there had been no news for over a week from my son, who was fighting at the Front. It is easy to see that in the dream-content the conviction that he has been killed or wounded finds expression. At the beginning of the dream one can observe an energetic effort to replace the painful thoughts by their contrary. I have to impart something very pleasing, something about sending money, honourable mention, and distribution. (The sum of money originates in a gratifying incident of my medical practice; it is therefore trying to lead the dream away altogether from its theme.) But this effort fails. The boy's mother has a presentiment of something terrible and does not wish to listen. The disguises are too thin; the reference to the material to be suppressed shows through everywhere. If my son is killed, then his comrades will send back his property; I shall have to distribute whatever he has left among his sisters, brothers and other people. Honourable mention is frequently awarded to an officer after he has died the "hero's death." The dream thus strives to give direct expression to what it at first wished to deny, whilst at the same time the wish-fulfilling tendency reveals itself by distortion. (The change of locality in the dream is no doubt to be understood as threshold symbolism, in line with Silberer's view.) We have indeed no idea what lends it the requisite motive-power. But my son does not appear as *falling* (on the field of battle) but *climbing.*—He was, in fact, a daring mountaineer.—He is not in uniform, but in a sports suit; that is, the place of the fatality now dreaded has been taken by an accident which happened to him at one time when he was ski-running, when he fell and fractured his thigh. But the nature of his costume, which makes him look like a seal, recalls immediately a younger person, our comical little grandson; the grey hair recalls his father, our son-in-law, who has had a bad time in the War. What does this signify? But let us leave this: the locality, a

pantry, the chest, from which he wants to take something (in the dream, to put something on it), are unmistakable allusions to an accident of my own, brought upon myself when I was between two and three years of age. I climbed on a foot-stool in the pantry, in order to get something nice which was on a chest or table. The footstool tumbled over and its edge struck me behind the lower jaw. I might very well have knocked all my teeth out. At this point, an admonition presents itself: it serves you right—like a hostile impulse against the valiant warrior. A profounder analysis enables me to detect the hidden impulse, which would be able to find satisfaction in the dreaded mishap to my son. It is the envy of youth which the elderly man believes that he has thoroughly stifled in actual life. There is no mistaking the fact that it was the very intensity of the painful apprehension lest such a misfortune should really happen that searched out for its alleviation such a repressed wish-fulfilment.

I can now clearly define what the unconscious wish means for the dream. I will admit that there is a whole class of dreams in which the *incitement* originates mainly or even exclusively from the residues of the day; and returning to the dream about my friend Otto, I believe that even my desire to become at last a *professor extraordinarius* would have allowed me to sleep in peace that night, had not the day's concern for my friend's health continued active. But this worry alone would not have produced a dream; the *motive-power* needed by the dream had to be contributed by a wish, and it was the business of my concern to find such a wish for itself, as the motive power of the dream. To put it figuratively, it is quite possible that a day-thought plays the part of the *entrepreneur* in the dream; but the *entrepreneur*, who, as we say, has the idea, and feels impelled to realize it, can do nothing without *capital;* he needs a *capitalist* who will defray the expense, and this capitalist, who contributes the psychic expenditure for the dream, is invariably and indisputably, whatever the nature of the waking thoughts, *a wish from the unconscious.*

In other cases the capitalist himself is the *entrepreneur;* this, indeed, seems to be the more usual case. An unconscious wish is excited by the day's work, and this now creates the dream. And the dream-processes provide a parallel for all the other possibilities of the economic relationship here used as an illustration. Thus the *entrepreneur* may himself contribute a little of the capital, or several *entrepreneurs* may seek the aid of the same capitalist, or several capitalists may jointly supply the capital required by the *entrepreneurs*. Thus there are dreams sustained by more than one dream-wish, and many similar variations, which may be readily imagined, and which are of no further interest to us. What is still lacking to our discussion of the dream-wish we shall only be able to complete later on.

The *tertium comparationis* in the analogies here employed, the quantitative element of which an allotted amount is placed at the free disposal of the dream, admits of a still closer application to the elucidation of the dream-structure. As shown on p. 263, we can recognize in most dreams a centre supplied with a special sensory intensity. This is, as a rule, the direct representation of the wish-fulfilment; for, if we reverse the displacements of the dream-work, we find that the psychic intensity of the elements in the dream-thoughts is replaced by the *sensory* intensity of the elements in the dream-content. The elements in the neighbourhood of the wish-fulfilment have often nothing to do with its meaning, but prove to be the offshoots of painful thoughts which are opposed to the wish. But owing to their connection with the central element, often artificially established, they secure so large a share of its intensity as to become capable of representation. Thus, the representative energy of the wish-fulfilment diffuses itself over a certain sphere of association, within which all elements are raised to representation, including even those that are in themselves without resources. In dreams containing several dynamic wishes we can easily separate and delimit the spheres of the individual wish-fulfilments, and we shall find that the gaps in the dream are often of the nature of boundary-zones.

Although the foregoing remarks have restricted the significance of the day-residues for the dream, they are none the less deserving of some further attention. For they must be a necessary ingredient in dream-formation, inasmuch as experience reveals the surprising fact that every dream shows in its content a connection with a recent waking impression, often of the most indifferent kind. So far we have failed to understand the necessity for this addition to the dream-mixture (p. 212). This necessity becomes apparent only when we bear in mind the part played by the unconscious wish, and seek further information in the psychology of the neuroses. We shall then learn that an unconscious idea, as such, is quite incapable of entering into the preconscious, and that it can exert an influence there only by establishing touch with a harmless idea already belonging to the preconscious, to which it transfers its intensity, and by which it allows itself to be screened. This is the fact of *transference,* which furnishes the explanation of so many surprising occurrences in the psychic life of neurotics. The transference may leave the idea from the preconscious unaltered, though the latter will thus acquire an unmerited intensity, or it may force upon this some modification derived from the content of the transferred idea. I trust the reader will pardon my fondness for comparisons with daily life, but I feel tempted to say that the situation for the repressed idea is like that of the American dentist in Austria, who may not carry on his practice unless he can get a duly installed doctor of medicine to serve him as a signboard and legal "cover." Further, just as it is not exactly the busiest physicians who form such alliances with dental practitioners, so in the psychic life the choice as regards covers for repressed ideas does not fall upon such preconscious or conscious ideas as have themselves attracted enough of the attention active in the preconscious. The unconscious prefers to entangle with its connections either those impressions and ideas of the preconscious which have remained unnoticed as being indifferent or those which have immediately had attention withdrawn from them again (by rejection). It is a well-known proposition of the theory of associations, confirmed by all experience, that ideas which have formed a very intimate connection in one direction assume a negative type of attitude towards whole groups of new connections. I have even attempted at one time to base a theory of hysterical paralysis on this principle.

If we assume that the same need of transference on the part of the repressed ideas, of which we have become aware through the analysis of the neurosis, makes itself felt in dreams also, we can at once explain two of the problems of the dream: namely, that every dream-analysis reveals an interweaving of a recent impression, and that this recent element is often of the most indifferent character. We may add what we have already learned elsewhere, that the reason why these recent and indifferent elements so frequently find their way into the dream-content as substitutes for the very oldest elements of the dream-thoughts is that they have the least to fear from the resisting censorship. But while this freedom from censorship explains only the preference shown to the trivial elements, the constant presence of recent elements points to the necessity for transference. Both groups of impressions satisfy the demand of the repressed ideas for material still free from associations, the indifferent ones because they have offered no occasion for extensive associations, and the recent ones because they have not had sufficient time to form such associations.

We thus see that the day-residues, among which we may now include the indifferent impressions, not only borrow something from the *Ucs* when they secure a share in dream-formation—namely, the motive-power at the disposal of the repressed wish—but they also offer to the unconscious something that is indispensable to it, namely, the points of attachment necessary for transference. If we wished to penetrate more deeply into the psychic processes, we should have to throw a clearer light on the play of excitations between the preconscious and the unconscious, and indeed the study of the psychoneuroses would impel us to do so; but dreams, as it happens, give us no help in this respect.

Just one further remark as to the day-residues. There is no doubt that it is really these that disturb our sleep, and not our dreams which, on the contrary, strive to guard our sleep. But we shall return to this point later.

So far we have discussed the dream-wish; we have traced it back to the sphere of the *Ucs*, and have analysed its relation to the day-residues, which, in their turn, may be either wishes, or psychic impulses of any other kind, or simply recent impressions. We have thus found room for the claims that can be made for the dream-forming significance of our waking mental activity in all its multifariousness. It might even prove possible to explain, on the basis of our train of thought, those extreme cases in which the dream, continuing the work of the day, brings to a happy issue an unsolved problem of waking life. We merely lack a suitable example to analyse, in order to uncover the infantile or repressed source of wishes, the tapping of which has so successfully reinforced the efforts of the preconscious activity. But we are not a step nearer to answering the question: Why is it that the unconscious can furnish in sleep nothing more than the motive-power for a wish-fulfilment? The answer to this question must elucidate the psychic nature of the state of wishing: and it will be given with the aid of the notion of the psychic apparatus.

We do not doubt that this apparatus, too, has only arrived at its present perfection by a long process of evolution. Let us attempt to restore it as it existed in an earlier stage of capacity. From postulates to be confirmed in other ways, we know that at first the apparatus strove to keep itself as free from stimulation as possible, and therefore, in its early structure, adopted the arrangement of a reflex apparatus, which enabled it promptly to discharge by the motor paths any sensory excitation reaching it from without. But this simple function was disturbed by the exigencies of life, to which the apparatus owes the impetus toward further development. The exigencies of life first confronted it in the form of the great physical needs. The excitation aroused by the inner need seeks an outlet in motility, which we may describe as *internal change* or *expression of the emotions*. The hungry child cries or struggles helplessly. But its situation remains unchanged; for the excitation proceeding from the inner need has not the character of a momentary impact, but of a continuing pressure. A change can occur only if, in some way (in the case of the child by external assistance), there is an *experience of satisfaction*, which puts an end to the internal excitation. An essential constituent of this experience is the appearance of a certain percept (of food in our example), the memory-image of which is henceforth associated with the memory-trace of the excitation arising from the need. Thanks to the established connection, there results, at the next occurrence of this need, a psychic impulse which seeks to revive the memory-image of the former percept, and to re-evoke the former percept itself; that is, it actually seeks to re-establish the situation of the first satisfaction. Such an impulse is what we call a wish; the reappearance of the perception constitutes the wish-fulfilment, and the full cathexis of the perception, by the excitation springing from the need, constitutes the shortest path to the wish-fulfilment. We may assume a primitive state of the psychic apparatus in which this path is actually followed, i.e., in which the wish ends in hallucination. This first psychic activity therefore aims at an identity of perception: that is, at a repetition of that perception which is connected with the satisfaction of the need.

This primitive mental activity must have

been modified by bitter practical experience into a secondary and more appropriate activity. The establishment of identity of perception by the short regressive path within the apparatus does not produce the same result in another respect as follows upon cathexis of the same perception coming from without. The satisfaction does not occur, and the need continues. In order to make the internal cathexis equivalent to the external one, the former would have to be continuously sustained, just as actually happens in the hallucinatory psychoses and in hunger-phantasies, which exhaust their performance in *maintaining their hold* on the object desired. In order to attain to more appropriate use of the psychic energy, it becomes necessary to suspend the full regression, so that it does not proceed beyond the memory-image, and thence can seek other paths, leading ultimately to the production of the desired identity from the side of the outer world.[1] This inhibition, as well as the subsequent deflection of the excitation, becomes the task of a second system, which controls voluntary motility, i.e., a system whose activity first leads on to the use of motility for purposes remembered in advance. But all this complicated mental activity, which works its way from the memory-image to the production of identity of perception via the outer world, merely represents *a roundabout way to wish-fulfilment* made necessary by experience.[2] Thinking is indeed nothing but a substitute for the hallucinatory wish; and if the dream is called a wish-fulfilment, this becomes something self-evident, since nothing but a wish can impel our psychic apparatus to activity. The dream, which fulfils its wishes by following the short regressive path, has thereby simply preserved for us a specimen of the *primary* method of operation of the psychic apparatus, which has been abandoned as inappropriate. What once prevailed in the waking state, when our psychic life was still young and inefficient, seems to have been banished into our nocturnal life; just as we still find in the nursery those discarded primitive weapons of adult humanity, the bow and arrow. *Dreaming is a fragment of the superseded psychic life of the child.* In the psychoses,

those modes of operation of the psychic apparatus which are normally suppressed in the waking state reassert themselves, and thereupon betray their inability to satisfy our demands in the outer world.[3]

The unconscious wish-impulses evidently strive to assert themselves even during the day, and the fact of transference, as well as the psychoses, tells us that they endeavour to force their way through the preconscious system to consciousness and the command of motility. Thus, in the censorship between *Ucs* and *Pcs*, which the dream forces us to assume, we must recognize and respect the guardian of our psychic health. But is it not carelessness on the part of this guardian to diminish his vigilance at night, and to allow the suppressed impulses of the *Ucs* to achieve expression, thus again making possible the process of hallucinatory regression? I think not, for when the critical guardian goes to rest—and we have proof that his slumber is not profound—he takes care to close the gate to motility. No matter what impulses from the usually inhibited *Ucs* may bustle about the stage, there is no need to interfere with them; they remain harmless, because they are not in a position to set in motion the motor apparatus which alone can operate to produce any change in the outer world. Sleep guarantees the security of the fortress which has to be guarded. The state of affairs is less harmless when a displacement of energies is produced, not by the decline at night in the energy put forth by the critical censorship, but by the pathological enfeeblement of the latter, or the pathological reinforcement of the unconscious excitations, and this while the preconscious is cathected and the gates of motility are open. The guardian is then overpowered; the unconscious excitations subdue the *Pcs*, and from the *Pcs* they dominate our speech and action, or they enforce hallucinatory regressions, thus directing an apparatus not designed for them by virtue of the attraction exerted by perceptions on the distribution of our psychic energy. We call this condition psychosis.

We now find ourselves in the most favourable position for continuing the construction of our psychological scaffolding, which we left after inserting the two systems, *Ucs* and *Pcs*.

---

[1] In other words: the introduction of a *test of reality* is recognized as necessary.

[2] Le Lorrain justly extols the wish-fulfilments of dreams: *"Sans fatigue sérieuse, sans être obligé de recourir à cette lutte opiniâtre et longue qui use et corrode les jouissances poursuivies."* [Without serious fatigue, without being obliged to have recourse to that long and stubborn struggle which exhausts and wears away pleasures sought.]

[3] I have further elaborated this train of thought elsewhere, where I have distinguished the two principles involved as the pleasure-principle and the reality-principle. *Formulations regarding the Two Principles in Mental Functioning*, in *Collected Papers*, Vol. iv, p. 13.

However, we still have reason to give further consideration to the wish as the sole psychic motive-power in the dream. We have accepted the explanation that the reason why the dream is in every case a wish-fulfilment is that it is a function of the system *Ucs*, which knows no other aim than wish-fulfilment, and which has at its disposal no forces other than the wish-impulses. Now if we want to continue for a single moment longer to maintain our right to develop such far-reaching psychological speculations from the facts of dream-interpretation, we are in duty bound to show that they insert the dream into a context which can also embrace other psychic structures. If there exists a system of the *Ucs*—or something sufficiently analogous for the purposes of our discussion—the dream cannot be its sole manifestation; every dream may be a wish-fulfilment, but there must be other forms of abnormal wish-fulfilment as well as dreams. And in fact the theory of all psychoneurotic symptoms culminates in the one proposition *that they, too, must be conceived as wish-fulfilments of the unconscious.*[1] Our explanation makes the dream only the first member of a series of the greatest importance for the psychiatrist, the understanding of which means the solution of the purely psychological part of the psychiatric problem.[2] But in other members of this group of wish-fulfilments—for example, in the hysterical symptoms—I know of one essential characteristic which I have so far failed to find in the dream. Thus, from the investigations often alluded to in this treatise, I know that the formation of an hysterical symptom needs a junction of both the currents of our psychic life. The symptom is not merely the expression of a realized unconscious wish; the latter must be joined by another wish from the preconscious, which is fulfilled by the same symptom; so that the symptom is at least doubly determined, once by each of the conflicting systems. Just as in dreams, there is no limit to further over-determination. The determination which does not derive from the *Ucs* is, as far as I can see, invariably a thought-stream of reaction against the unconscious wish; for example, a self-punishment. Hence I can say, quite generally, that *an hysterical symptom originates only where two contrary wish-fulfilments, having their source in different psychic systems, are able to meet in a single expression.*[3] Examples would help us but little here, as nothing but a complete unveiling of the complications in question can carry conviction. I will therefore content myself with the bare assertion, and will cite one example, not because it proves anything, but simply as an illustration. The hysterical vomiting of a female patient proved, on the one hand, to be the fulfilment of an unconscious phantasy from the years of puberty—namely, the wish that she might be continually pregnant, and have a multitude of children; and this was subsequently supplemented by the wish that she might have them by as many fathers as possible. Against this immoderate wish there arose a powerful defensive reaction. But as by the vomiting the patient might have spoilt her figure and her beauty, so that she would no longer find favour in any man's eyes, the symptom was also in keeping with the punitive trend of thought, and so, being admissible on both sides, it was allowed to become a reality. This is the same way of acceding to a wish-fulfilment as the queen of the Parthians was pleased to adopt in the case of the triumvir Crassus. Believing that he had undertaken his campaign out of greed for gold, she caused molten gold to be poured into the throat of the corpse. "Here thou hast what thou hast longed for!"

Of the dream we know as yet only that it expresses a wish-fulfilment of the unconscious; and apparently the dominant preconscious system permits this fulfilment when it has compelled the wish to undergo certain distortions. We are, moreover, not in fact in a position to demonstrate regularly the presence of a train of thought opposed to the dream-wish, which is realized in the dream as well as its antagonist. Only now and then have we found in dream-analyses signs of reaction-products as, for instance, my affection for my friend R in the *dream of my uncle* (p. 195). But the contribution from the preconscious which is missing here may be found in another place. The dream can provide expression for a wish from the *Ucs* by means of all sorts of distortions, once the dominant system has withdrawn itself into the *wish to sleep,* and has realized this wish by

---

[1] Expressed more exactly: One portion of the symptom corresponds to the unconscious wish-fulfilment, while the other corresponds to the reaction-formation opposed to it.

[2] Hughlings Jackson has expressed himself as follows: "Find out all about dreams, and you will have found out all about insanity."

[3] Cf. my latest formulation (in *Zeitschrift für Sexualwissenschaft*, Bd. I) of the origin of hysterical symptoms in the treatise on "Hysterical Phantasies and their Relation to Bisexuality," *Collected Papers*, II, p. 51. This forms chapter X of *Selected Papers on Hysteria*, p. 115 above.

producing the changes of cathexis within the psychic apparatus which are within its power; thereupon holding on to the wish in question for the whole duration of sleep.[1]

Now this persistent wish to sleep on the part of the preconscious has a quite general facilitating effect on the formation of dreams. Let us recall the dream of the father who, by the gleam of light from the death-chamber, was led to conclude that his child's body might have caught fire. We have shown that one of the psychic forces decisive in causing the father to draw this conclusion in the dream instead of allowing himself to be awakened by the gleam of light was the wish to prolong the life of the child seen in the dream by one moment. Other wishes originating in the repressed have probably escaped us, for we are unable to analyse this dream. But as a second source of motive-power in this dream we may add the father's desire to sleep, for, like the life of the child, the father's sleep is prolonged for a moment by the dream. The underlying motive is: "Let the dream go on, or I must wake up." As in this dream, so in all others, the wish to sleep lends its support to the unconscious wish. On page 189 we cited dreams which were manifestly dreams of convenience. But in truth all dreams may claim this designation. The efficacy of the wish to go on sleeping is most easily recognized in the awakening dreams, which so elaborate the external sensory stimulus that it becomes compatible with the continuance of sleep; they weave it into a dream in order to rob it of any claims it might make as a reminder of the outer world. But this wish to go on sleeping must also play its part in permitting all other dreams, which can only act as disturbers of the state of sleep from within. "Don't worry; sleep on; it's only a dream," is in many cases the suggestion of the *Pcs* to consciousness when the dream gets too bad; and this describes in a quite general way the attitude of our dominant psychic activity towards dreaming, even though the thought remains unuttered. I must draw the conclusion that *throughout the whole of our sleep we are just as certain that we are dreaming as we are certain that we are sleeping*. It is imperative to disregard the objection that our consciousness is never directed to the latter knowledge, and that it is directed to the former knowledge only on special occasions, when the censorship feels, as it were, taken by surprise. On the contrary, there are persons in whom the retention at night of the knowledge that they are sleeping and dreaming becomes quite manifest, and who are thus apparently endowed with the conscious faculty of guiding their dream-life. Such a dreamer, for example, is dissatisfied with the turn taken by a dream; he breaks it off without waking, and begins it afresh, in order to continue it along different lines, just like a popular author who, upon request, gives a happier ending to his play. Or on another occasion, when the dream places him in a sexually exciting situation, he thinks in his sleep: "I don't want to continue this dream and exhaust myself by an emission; I would rather save it for a real situation."

The Marquis Hervey (Vaschide) declared that he had gained such power over his dreams that he could accelerate their course at will, and turn them in any direction he wished. It seems that in him the wish to sleep had accorded a place to another, a preconscious wish, the wish to observe his dreams and to derive pleasure from them. Sleep is just as compatible with such a wish-resolve as it is with some proviso as a condition of waking up (wet-nurse's sleep). We know, too, that in all persons an interest in dreams greatly increases the number of dreams remembered after waking.

Concerning other observations as to the guidance of dreams, Ferenczi states: "The dream takes the thought that happens to occupy our psychic life at the moment, and elaborates it from all sides. It lets any given dream-picture drop when there is a danger that the wish-fulfilment will miscarry, and attempts a new kind of solution, until it finally succeeds in creating a wish-fulfilment that satisfies in one compromise both instances of the psychic life."

D. *Waking Caused by Dreams. The Function of Dreams. The Anxiety Dream*

Now that we know that throughout the night the preconscious is orientated to the wish to sleep, we can follow the dream-process with proper understanding. But let us first summarize what we already know about this process. We have seen that day-residues are left over from the waking activity of the mind, residues from which it has not been possible to withdraw all cathexis. Either one of the unconscious wishes has been aroused through the waking activity during the day or it so happens that the

---

[1] This idea has been borrowed from the theory of sleep of Liébault, who revived hypnotic research in modern times (*Du Sommeil provoqué*, etc., Paris [1889]).

two coincide; we have already discussed the multifarious possibilities. Either already during the day or only on the establishment of the state of sleep the unconscious wish has made its way to the day-residues, and has effected a transference to them. Thus there arises a wish transferred to recent material; or the suppressed recent wish is revived by a reinforcement from the unconscious. This wish now endeavours to make its way to consciousness along the normal path of the thought processes, through the preconscious, to which indeed it belongs by virtue of one of its constituent elements. It is, however, confronted by the censorship which still subsists, and to whose influence it soon succumbs. It now takes on the distortion for which the way has already been paved by the transference to recent material. So far it is on the way to becoming something resembling an obsession, a delusion, or the like, i.e., a thought reinforced by a transference, and distorted in expression owing to the censorship. But its further progress is now checked by the state of sleep of the preconscious; this system has presumably protected itself against invasion by diminishing its excitations. The dream-process, therefore, takes the regressive course, which is just opened up by the peculiarity of the sleeping state, and in so doing follows the attraction exerted on it by memory-groups, which are, in part only, themselves present as visual cathexis, not as translations into the symbols of the later systems. On its way to regression it acquires representability. The subject of compression will be discussed later. The dream-process has by this time covered the second part of its contorted course. The first part threads its way progressively from the unconscious scenes or phantasies to the preconscious, while the second part struggles back from the boundary of the censorship to the tract of the perceptions. But when the dream-process becomes a perception-content, it has, so to speak, eluded the obstacle set up in the *Pcs* by the censorship and the sleeping state. It succeeds in drawing attention to itself, and in being remarked by consciousness. For consciousness, which for us means a sense-organ for the apprehension of psychic qualities, can be excited in waking life from two sources: firstly, from the periphery of the whole apparatus, the perceptive system; and secondly, from the excitations of pleasure and pain which emerge as the sole psychic qualities yielded by the transpositions of energy in the interior of the apparatus. All other processes in

the ψ-systems, even those in the preconscious, are devoid of all psychic quality, and are therefore not objects of consciousness, inasmuch as they do not provide either pleasure or pain for its perception. We shall have to assume that *these releases of pleasure and pain automatically regulate the course of the cathectic processes.* But in order to make possible more delicate performances, it subsequently proved necessary to render the flow of ideas more independent of pain-signals. To accomplish this, the *Pcs* system needed qualities of its own which could attract consciousness, and most probably received them through the connection of the preconscious processes with the memory-system of speech-symbols, which was not devoid of quality. Through the qualities of this system, consciousness, hitherto only a sense-organ for perceptions, now becomes also a sense-organ for a part of our thought-processes. There are now, as it were, two sensory surfaces, one turned toward perception and the other toward the preconscious thought-processes.

I must assume that the sensory surface of consciousness which is turned to the preconscious is rendered far more unexcitable by sleep than the surface turned toward the *P*-system. The giving up of interest in the nocturnal thought-process is, of course, an appropriate procedure. Nothing is to happen in thought; the preconscious wants to sleep. But once the dream becomes perception, it is capable of exciting consciousness through the qualities now gained. The sensory excitation performs what is in fact its function; namely, it directs a part of the cathectic energy available in the *Pcs* to the exciting cause in the form of attention. We must therefore admit that the dream always has a *waking* effect—that is, it calls into activity part of the quiescent energy of the *Pcs*. Under the influence of this energy, it now undergoes the process which we have described as secondary elaboration with a view to coherence and comprehensibility. This means that the dream is treated by this energy like any other perception-content; it is subjected to the same anticipatory ideas as far, at least, as the material allows. As far as this third part of the dream-process has any direction, this is once more progressive.

To avoid misunderstanding, it will not be amiss to say a few words as to the temporal characteristics of these dream-processes. In a very interesting discussion, evidently suggested by Maury's puzzling guillotine dream, Goblot tries to demonstrate that a dream takes up no other time than the transition period between sleeping and waking. The process of waking up requires time; during this time the dream occurs. It is supposed that the final picture of the dream is so vivid that it forces the dreamer to wake; in reality it is so vivid only because when it appears the dreamer is already very near waking. *"Un rêve, c'est un réveil qui commence."* [1]

It has already been pointed out by Dugas that Goblot, in order to generalize his theory, was forced to ignore a great many facts. There are also dreams from which we do not awaken; for example, many dreams in which we dream that we dream. From our knowledge of the dream-work, we can by no means admit that it extends only over the period of waking. On the contrary, we must consider it probable that the first part of the dream-work is already begun during the day, when we are still under the domination of the preconscious. The second phase of the dream-work, viz., the alteration by the censorship, the attraction exercised by unconscious scenes, and the penetration to perception, continues probably all through the night, and accordingly we may always be correct when we report a feeling that we have been dreaming all night, even although we cannot say what we have dreamed. I do not, however, think that it is necessary to assume that up to the time of becoming conscious the dream-processes really follow the temporal sequence which we have described; viz., that there is first the transferred dream-wish, then the process of distortion due to the censorship, and then the change of direction to regression, etc. We were obliged to construct such a sequence for the sake of description; in reality, however, it is probably rather a question of simultaneously trying this path and that, and of the excitation fluctuating to and fro, until finally, because it has attained the most apposite concentration, one particular grouping remains in the field. Certain personal experiences even incline me to believe that the dream-work often requires more than one day and one night to produce its result, in which case the extraordinary art manifested in the construction of the dream is shorn of its miraculous character. In my opinion, even the regard for the comprehensibility of the dream as a perceptual event may exert its influence before the dream attracts consciousness to itself. From this point, however, the process is accelerated, since the dream is henceforth subjected to the same

[1] A dream is the beginning of wakening.—ED.

treatment as any other perception. It is like fire works, which require hours for their preparation and then flare up in a moment.

Through the dream-work, the dream-process now either gains sufficient intensity to attract consciousness to itself and to arouse the preconscious (quite independently of the time or profundity of sleep), or its intensity is insufficient, and it must wait in readiness until attion, becoming more alert immediately before waking, meets it half-way. Most dreams seem to operate with relatively slight psychic intensities, for they wait for the process of waking. This, then, explains the fact that as a rule we perceive something dreamed if we are suddenly roused from a deep sleep. Here, as well as in spontaneous waking, our first glance lights upon the perception-content created by the dream-work, while the next falls on that provided by the outer world.

But of greater theoretical interest are those dreams which are capable of waking us in the midst of our sleep. We may bear in mind the purposefulness which can be demonstrated in all other cases, and ask ourselves why the dream, that is, the unconscious wish, is granted the power to disturb our sleep, i.e., the fulfilment of the preconscious wish. The explanation is probably to be found in certain relations of energy which we do not yet understand. If we did so, we should probably find that the freedom given to the dream and the expenditure upon it of a certain detached attention represent a saving of energy as against the alternative case of the unconscious having to be held in check at night just as it is during the day. As experience shows, dreaming, even if it interrupts our sleep several times a night, still remains compatible with sleep. We wake up for a moment, and immediately fall asleep again. It is like driving off a fly in our sleep; we awake *ad hoc.* When we fall asleep again we have removed the cause of disturbance. The familiar examples of the sleep of wet-nurses, etc., show that the fulfilment of the wish to sleep is quite compatible with the maintenance of a certain amount of attention in a given direction.

But we must here take note of an objection which is based on a greater knowledge of the unconscious processes. We have ourselves described the unconscious wishes as always active, whilst nevertheless asserting that in the daytime they are not strong enough to make themselves perceptible. But when the state of sleep supervenes, and the unconscious wish has shown its power to form a dream, and with it to awaken the preconscious, why does this power lapse after cognizance has been taken of the dream? Would it not seem more probable that the dream should continually renew itself, like the disturbing fly which, when driven away, takes pleasure in returning again and again? What justification have we for our assertion that the dream removes the disturbance to sleep?

It is quite true that the unconscious wishes are always active. They represent paths which are always practicable, whenever a quantum of excitation makes use of them. It is indeed an outstanding peculiarity of the unconscious processes that they are indestructible. Nothing can be brought to an end in the unconscious; nothing is past or forgotten. This is impressed upon us emphatically in the study of the neuroses, and especially of hysteria. The unconscious path of thought which leads to the discharge through an attack is forthwith passable again when there is a sufficient accumulation of excitation. The mortification suffered thirty years ago operates, after having gained access to the unconscious sources of affect, during all these thirty years as though it were a recent experience. Whenever its memory is touched, it revives, and shows itself to be cathected with excitation which procures a motor discharge for itself in an attack. It is precisely here that psychotherapy must intervene, its task being to ensure that the unconscious processes are settled and forgotten. Indeed, the fading of memories and the weak affect of impressions which are no longer recent, which we are apt to take as self-evident, and to explain as a primary effect of time on our psychic memory-residues, are in reality secondary changes brought about by laborious work. It is the preconscious that accomplishes this work; *and the only course which psychotherapy can pursue is to bring the Ucs under the dominion of the Pcs.*

There are, therefore, two possible issues for any single unconscious excitation-process. Either it is left to itself, in which case it ultimately breaks through somewhere and secures, on this one occasion, a discharge for its excitation into motility, or it succumbs to the influence of the preconscious, and through this its excitation becomes *bound* instead of being *discharged. It is the latter case that occurs in the dream-process.* The cathexis from the *Pcs* which goes to meet the dream once this has attained to perception, because it has been drawn thither by the excitation of consciousness, binds the unconscious excitation of the dream and renders it harmless as a disturber of sleep. When the dreamer wakes up for a moment, he has really chased away the fly that threatened to disturb his sleep. We may now begin to suspect that it is really more expedient and economical to give way to the unconscious wish, to leave clear its path to regression so that it may form a dream, and then to bind and dispose of this dream by means of a small outlay of preconscious work, than to hold the unconscious in check throughout the whole period of sleep. It was, indeed, to be expected that the dream, even if originally it was not a purposeful process, would have seized upon some definite function in the play of forces of the psychic life. We now see what this function is. The dream has taken over the task of bringing the excitation of the *Ucs*, which had been left free, back under the domination of the preconscious; it thus discharges the excitation of the *Ucs*, acts as a safety-valve for the latter, and at the same time, by a slight outlay of waking activity, secures the sleep of the preconscious. Thus, like the other psychic formations of its group, the dream offers itself as a compromise, serving both systems simultaneously, by fulfilling the wishes of both, in so far as they are mutually compatible. A glance at Robert's "elimination theory" will show that we must agree with this author on his main point, namely, the determination of the function of dreams, though we differ from him in our general presuppositions and in our estimation of the dream-process.[1]

[1] Is this the only function which we can attribute to dreams? I know of no other. A. Maeder, to be sure, has endeavoured to claim for the dream yet other *secondary* functions. He started from the just observation that many dreams contain attempts to provide solutions of conflicts, which are afterwards actually carried through. They thus behave like preparatory practice for waking activities. He therefore drew a parallel between dreaming and the play of animals and children, which is to be conceived as a training of the inherited instincts, and a preparation for their later serious activity, thus setting up a *fonction ludique* for the dream. A little while before Maeder, Alfred Adler likewise emphasized the function of *thinking ahead* in the dream. (An analysis which I published in 1905 contained a dream which may be conceived as a resolution-dream, which was repeated night after night until it was realized.)

But an obvious reflection must show us that this *secondary* function of the dream has no claim to recognition within the framework of any dream-interpretation. Thinking ahead, making resolutions, sketching out attempted solutions which can then perhaps be realized in waking life—these and many more performances are functions of the unconscious and preconscious activities of the mind which continue as *day-residues* in the sleeping state, and can then combine with an unconscious wish to form a dream (p. 362 above).

The above qualification—*in so far as the two wishes are mutually compatible*—contains a suggestion that there may be cases in which the function of the dream fails. The dream-process is, to begin with, admitted as a wish-fulfilment of the unconscious, but if this attempted wish-fulfilment disturbs the preconscious so profoundly that the latter can no longer maintain its state of rest, the dream has broken the compromise, and has failed to perform the second part of its task. It is then at once broken off, and replaced by complete awakening. But even here it is not really the fault of the dream if, though at other times the guardian, it has now to appear as the disturber of sleep, nor need this prejudice us against its averred purposive character. This is not the only instance in the organism in which a contrivance that is usually to the purpose becomes inappropriate and disturbing so soon as something is altered in the conditions which engender it; the disturbance, then, at all events serves the new purpose of indicating the change, and of bringing into play against it the means of adjustment of the organism. Here, of course, I am thinking of the anxiety-dream, and lest it should seem that I try to evade this witness against the theory of wish-fulfilment whenever I encounter it, I will at least give some indications as to the explanation of the anxiety-dream.

That a psychic process which develops anxiety may still be a wish-fulfilment has long ceased to imply any contradiction for us. We may explain this occurrence by the fact that the wish belongs to one system (the *Ucs*), whereas the other system (the *Pcs*) has rejected and suppressed it.[1] The subjection of the *Ucs* by the *Pcs* is not thoroughgoing even in perfect psychic health; the extent of this suppression indicates the degree of our psychic normality. Neurotic symptoms indicate to us that the two systems are in mutual conflict; the symptoms are the result of a compromise in this conflict, and they temporarily put an end to it. On the one hand, they afford the *Ucs* a way out for the discharge of its excitation—they serve it as a kind of sally-gate—while, on the other hand, they give the *Pcs* the possi-

bility of dominating the *Ucs* in some degree. It is instructive to consider, for example, the significance of a hysterical phobia, or of agoraphobia. A neurotic is said to be incapable of crossing the street alone, and this we should rightly call a *symptom*. Let someone now remove this symptom by constraining him to this action which he deems himself incapable of performing. The result will be an attack of anxiety, just as an attack of anxiety in the street has often been the exciting cause of the establishment of an agoraphobia. We thus learn that the symptom has been constituted in order to prevent the anxiety from breaking out. The phobia is thrown up before the anxiety like a frontier fortress.

We cannot enlarge further on this subject unless we examine the rôle of the affects in these processes, which can only be done here imperfectly. We will therefore affirm the proposition that the principal reason why the suppression of the *Ucs* becomes necessary is that, if the movement of ideas in the *Ucs* were allowed to run its course, it would develop an affect which originally had the character of pleasure, but which, since the process of *repression*, bears the character of pain. The aim, as well as the result, of the suppression is to prevent the development of this pain. The suppression extends to the idea-content of the *Ucs*, because the liberation of pain might emanate from this idea-content. We here take as our basis a quite definite assumption as to the nature of the development of affect. This is regarded as a motor or secretory function, the key to the innervation of which is to be found in the ideas of the *Ucs*. Through the domination of the *Pcs* these ideas are as it were strangled, that is, inhibited from sending out the impulse that would develop the affect. The danger which arises, if cathexis by the *Pcs* ceases, thus consists in the fact that the unconscious excitations would liberate an affect that—in consequence of the repression that has previously occurred—could only be felt as pain or anxiety.

This danger is released if the dream-process is allowed to have its own way. The conditions for its realization are that repressions shall have occurred, and that the suppressed wish-impulses can become sufficiently strong. They, therefore, fall entirely outside the psychological framework of dream-formation. Were it not for the fact that our theme is connected by just one factor with the theme of the development of anxiety, namely, by the setting free of

---

The function of *thinking ahead* in the dream is thus rather a function of preconscious waking thought, the result of which may be disclosed to us by the analysis of dreams or other phenomena. After the dream has so long been fused with its manifest content, one must now guard against confusing it with the latent dream-thoughts.

[1] *General Introduction to Psycho-Analysis*, p. 534 below.

the *Ucs* during sleep, I could refrain from the discussion of the anxiety-dream altogether, and thus avoid all the obscurities involved in it.

The theory of the anxiety-dream belongs, as I have already repeatedly stated, to the psychology of the neuroses. I might further add that anxiety in dreams is an anxiety-problem and not a dream-problem. Having once exhibited the point of contact of the psychology of the neuroses with the theme of the dream-process, we have nothing further to do with it. There is only one thing left which I can do. Since I have asserted that neurotic anxiety has its origin in sexual sources, I can subject anxiety-dreams to analysis in order to demonstrate the sexual material in their dream-thoughts.

For good reasons, I refrain from citing any of the examples so abundantly placed at my disposal by neurotic patients, and prefer to give some anxiety-dreams of children.

Personally, I have had no real anxiety-dream for decades, but I do recall one from my seventh or eighth year which I subjected to interpretation some thirty years later. The dream was very vivid, and showed me *my beloved mother, with a peculiarly calm, sleeping countenance, carried into the room and laid on the bed by two (or three) persons with birds' beaks.* I awoke crying and screaming, and disturbed my parents' sleep. The peculiarly draped, excessively tall figures with beaks I had taken from the illustrations of Philippson's Bible; I believe they represented deities with the heads of sparrowhawks from an Egyptian tomb-relief. The analysis yielded, however, also the recollection of a house-porter's boy, who used to play with us children on a meadow in front of the house; I might add that his name was Philip. It seemed to me then that I first heard from this boy the vulgar word signifying sexual intercourse, which is replaced among educated persons by the Latin word *coitus*, but which the dream plainly enough indicates by the choice of the birds' heads. I must have guessed the sexual significance of the word from the look of my worldly-wise teacher. My mother's expression in the dream was copied from the countenance of my grandfather, whom I had seen a few days before his death snoring in a state of coma. The interpretation of the secondary elaboration in the dream must therefore have been that my *mother* was dying; the *tomb*-relief, too, agrees with this. I awoke with this anxiety, and could not calm myself until I had waked my parents. I remember that I suddenly became calm when I saw my mother; it

was as though I had needed the assurance: then she was not dead. But this secondary interpretation of the dream had only taken place when the influence of the developed anxiety was already at work. I was not in a state of anxiety because I had dreamt that my mother was dying; I interpreted the dream in this manner in the preconscious elaboration because I was already under the domination of the anxiety. The latter, however, could be traced back, through the repression to a dark, plainly sexual craving, which had found appropriate expression in the visual content of the dream.

A man twenty-seven years of age, who had been seriously ill for a year, had repeatedly dreamed, between the ages of eleven and thirteen, dreams attended with great anxiety, to the effect that *a man with a hatchet was running after him; he wanted to run away, but seemed to be paralysed, and could not move from the spot.* This may be taken as a good and typical example of a very common anxiety-dream, free from any suspicion of a sexual meaning. In the analysis, the dreamer first thought of a story told him by his uncle (chronologically later than the dream), viz., that he was attacked at night in the street by a suspicious-looking individual; and he concluded from this association that he might have heard of a similar episode at the time of the dream. In association with the hatchet, he recalled that during this period of his life he once hurt his hand with a *hatchet* while chopping wood. This immediately reminded him of his relations with his younger brother, whom he used to maltreat and knock down. He recalled, in particular, one occasion when he hit his brother's head with his boot and made it bleed, and his mother said: "I'm afraid he will kill him one day." While he seemed to be thus held by the theme of *violence*, a memory from his ninth year suddenly emerged. His parents had come home late and had gone to bed, whilst he was pretending to be asleep. He soon heard panting, and other sounds that seemed to him mysterious, and he could also guess the position of his parents in bed. His further thoughts showed that he had established an analogy between this relation between his parents and his own relation to his younger brother. He subsumed what was happening between his parents under the notion of "an act of violence and a fight." The fact that he had frequently noticed *blood in his mother's bed* corroborated this conception.

That the sexual intercourse of adults appears

strange and alarming to children who observe it, and arouses anxiety in them, is, I may say, a fact established by everyday experience. I have explained this anxiety on the ground that we have here a sexual excitation which is not mastered by the child's understanding, and which probably also encounters repulsion because their parents are involved, and is therefore transformed into anxiety. At a still earlier period of life the sexual impulse towards the parent of opposite sex does not yet suffer repression, but as we have seen (pp. 244-45) expresses itself freely.

For the night terrors with hallucinations (*pavor nocturnus*) so frequent in children I should without hesitation offer the same explanation. These, too, can only be due to misunderstood and rejected sexual impulses which, if recorded, would probably show a temporal periodicity, since an intensification of sexual *libido* may equally be produced by accidentally exciting impressions and by spontaneous periodic processes of development.

I have not the necessary observational material for the full demonstration of this explanation.[1] On the other hand, pediatrists seem to lack the point of view which alone makes intelligible the whole series of phenomena, both from the somatic and from the psychic side. To illustrate by a comical example how closely, if one is made blind by the blinkers of medical mythology, one may pass by the understanding of such cases, I will cite a case which I found in a thesis on *pavor nocturnus* (Debacker, 1881, p. 66).

A boy of thirteen, in delicate health, began to be anxious and dreamy; his sleep became uneasy, and once almost every week it was interrupted by an acute attack of anxiety with hallucinations. The memory of these dreams was always very distinct. Thus he was able to relate that the devil had shouted at him: "Now we have you, now we have you!" and then there was a smell of pitch and brimstone, and the fire burned his skin. From this dream he woke in terror; at first he could not cry out; then his voice came back to him, and he was distinctly heard to say: "No, no, not me; I haven't done anything," or: "Please, don't; I will never do it again!" At other times he said: "Albert has never done that!" Later he avoided undressing, "because the fire attacked him only when he was undressed." In the midst of these evil dreams, which were endangering his

health, he was sent into the country, where he recovered in the course of eighteen months. At the age of fifteen he confessed one day: "*Je n'osais pas l'avouer, mais j'éprouvais continuellement des picotements et des surexcitations aux* parties;[2] *à la fin, cela m'énervait tant que plusieurs fois j'ai pensé me jeter par la fenêtre du dortoir.*"[3]

It is, of course, not difficult to guess: 1. That the boy had practised masturbation in former years, that he had probably denied it, and was threatened with severe punishment for his bad habit (His confession: *Je ne le ferai plus;*[4] his denial: *Albert n'a jamais fait ça.*[5]) 2. That, under the advancing pressure of puberty, the temptation to masturbate was re-awakened through the titillation of the genitals. 3. That now, however, there arose within him a struggle for repression, which suppressed the libido and transformed it into anxiety, and that this anxiety now gathered up the punishments with which he was originally threatened.

Let us, on the other hand, see what conclusions were drawn by the author (p. 69):

"1. It is clear from this observation that the influence of puberty may produce in a boy of delicate health a condition of extreme weakness, and that this may lead to a *very marked cerebral anaemia.*[6]

"2. This cerebral anaemia produces an alteration of character, demono-maniacal hallucinations, and very violent nocturnal, and perhaps also diurnal, states of anxiety.

"3. The demonomania and the self-reproaches of the boy can be traced to the influences of a religious education which had acted upon him as a child.

"4. All manifestations disappeared as a result of a lengthy sojourn in the country, bodily exercise, and the return of physical strength after the termination of puberty.

"5. Possibly an influence predisposing to the development of the boy's cerebral state may be attributed to heredity and to the father's former syphilis."

Then finally come the concluding remarks: "*Nous avons fait entrer cette observation dans le cadre délires apyrétiques d'inanition, car*

---

[1] This material has since been provided in abundance by the literature of psycho-analysis.

[2] The emphasis is my own, though the meaning is plain enough without it.

[3] I did not dare admit it, but I continually felt tinglings and overexcitements of the *parts;* at the end, it wearied me so much that several times I thought to throw myself from the dormitory window.—ED.

[4] I will not do it again.—ED.

[5] Albert never did that.—ED.

[6] The italics are mine.

*'est à l'ischémie cérébrale que nous rattachons
:et état particulier."[1]*

E. *The Primary and Secondary Processes. Repression*

In attempting to penetrate more profoundly into the psychology of the dream-processes, I have undertaken a difficult task, to which, indeed, my powers of exposition are hardly adequate. To reproduce the simultaneity of so complicated a scheme in terms of a successive description, and at the same time to make each part appear free from all assumptions, goes fairly beyond my powers. I have now to atone for the fact that in my exposition of the psychology of dreams I have been unable to follow the historic development of my own insight. The lines of approach to the comprehension of the dream were laid down for me by previous investigations into the psychology of the neuroses, to which I should not refer here, although I am constantly obliged to do so; whereas I should like to work in the opposite direction, starting from the dream, and then proceeding to establish its junction with the psychology of the neuroses. I am conscious of all the difficulties which this involves for the reader, but I know of no way to avoid them.

Since I am dissatisfied with this state of affairs, I am glad to dwell upon another point of view, which would seem to enhance the value of my efforts. As was shown in the introductory section, I found myself confronted with a theme which had been marked by the sharpest contradictions on the part of those who had written on it. In the course of our treatment of the problems of the dream, room has been found for most of these contradictory views. We have been compelled to take decided exception to two only of the views expressed: namely, that the dream is a meaningless process, and that it is a somatic process. Apart from these, we have been able to find a place for the truth of all the contradictory opinions at one point or another of the complicated tissue of the facts, and we have been able to show that each expressed something genuine and correct. That our dreams continue the impulses and interests of waking life has been generally confirmed by the discovery of the hidden dream-thoughts. These concern themselves only with things that seem to us important and of great interest. Dreams never occupy

themselves with trifles. But we have accepted also the opposite view, namely, that the dream gathers up the indifferent residues of the day, and cannot seize upon any important interest of the day until it has in some measure withdrawn itself from waking activity. We have found that this holds true of the dream-content, which by means of distortion gives the dream-thought an altered expression. We have said that the dream-process, owing to the nature of the mechanism of association, finds it easier to obtain possession of recent or indifferent material, which has not yet been put under an embargo by our waking mental activity; and that, on account of the censorship, it transfers the psychic intensity of the significant but also objectionable material to the indifferent. The hypermnesia of the dream and its ability to dispose of infantile material have become the main foundations of our doctrine; in our theory of dreams we have assigned to a wish of infantile origin the part of the indispensable motive-power of dream-formation. It has not, of course, occurred to us to doubt the experimentally demonstrated significance of external sensory stimuli during sleep; but we have placed this material in the same relation to the dream-wish as the thought-residues left over from our waking activity. We need not dispute the fact that the dream interprets objective sensory stimuli after the manner of an illusion; but we have supplied the motive for this interpretation, which has been left indeterminate by other writers. The interpretation proceeds in such a way that the perceived object is rendered harmless as a source of disturbance of sleep, whilst it is made usable for the wish-fulfilment. Though we do not admit as a special source of dreams the subjective state of excitation of the sensory organs during sleep (which seems to have been demonstrated by Trumbull Ladd), we are, nevertheless, able to explain this state of excitation by the regressive revival of the memories active behind the dream. As to the internal organic sensations, which are wont to be taken as the cardinal point of the explanation of dreams, these, too, find a place in our conception, though indeed a more modest one. These sensations—the sensations of falling, of soaring, or of being inhibited—represent an ever-ready material, which the dream-work can employ to express the dream-thought as often as need arises.

That the dream-process is a rapid and momentary one is, we believe, true as regards the perception by consciousness of the pre-formed dream-content; but we have found that

---

[1] We put this case in the file of apyretic delirias of inanition, for it is to cerebral anaemia that we attach this particular state.—ED.

the preceding portions of the dream-process probably follow a slow, fluctuating course. As for the riddle of the superabundant dream-content compressed into the briefest moment of time, we have been able to contribute the explanation that the dream seizes upon ready-made formations of the psychic life. We have found that it is true that dreams are distorted and mutilated by the memory, but that this fact presents no difficulties, as it is only the last manifest portion of a process of distortion which has been going on from the very beginning of the dream-work. In the embittered controversy, which has seemed irreconcilable, whether the psychic life is asleep at night, or can make the same use of all its faculties as during the day, we have been able to conclude that both sides are right, but that neither is entirely so. In the dream-thoughts we found evidence of a highly complicated intellectual activity, operating with almost all the resources of the psychic apparatus; yet it cannot be denied that these dream-thoughts have originated during the day, and it is indispensable to assume that there is a sleeping state of the psychic life. Thus, even the doctrine of partial sleep received its due, but we have found the characteristic feature of the sleeping state not in the disintegration of the psychic system of connections, but in the special attitude adopted by the psychic system which is dominant during the day—the attitude of the wish to sleep. The deflection from the outer world retains its significance for our view, too; though not the only factor at work, it helps to make possible the regressive course of the dream-representation. The abandonment of voluntary guidance of the flow of ideas is incontestable; but psychic life does not thereby become aimless, for we have seen that upon relinquishment of the voluntary directing ideas, involuntary ones take charge. On the other hand, we have not only recognized the loose associative connection of the dream, but have brought a far greater area within the scope of this kind of connection than could have been suspected; we have, however, found it merely an enforced substitute for another, a correct and significant type of association. To be sure, we too have called the dream absurd, but examples have shown us how wise the dream is when it simulates absurdity. As regards the functions that have been attributed to the dream, we are able to accept them all. That the dream relieves the mind, like a safety-valve, and that, as Robert has put it, all kinds of harmful material are

rendered harmless by representation in the dream, not only coincides exactly with our own theory of the twofold wish-fulfilment in the dream, but in its very wording becomes more intelligible for us than it is for Robert himself. The free indulgence of the psyche in the play of its faculties is reproduced in our theory as the non-interference of the preconscious activity with the dream. The *return of the embryonal standpoint of psychic life in the dream,* and Havelock Ellis's remark that the dream is *"an archaic world of vast emotions and imperfect thoughts,"* appear to us as happy anticipations of our own exposition, which asserts that *primitive* modes of operations that are suppressed during the day play a part in the formation of dreams. We can fully identify ourselves with Sully's statement, that "our dreams bring back again our earlier and successively developed personalities, our old ways of regarding things, with impulses and modes of reaction which ruled us long ago"; and for us, as for Delage, the *suppressed* material becomes the mainspring of the dream.

We have fully accepted the rôle that Scherner ascribes to the dream-phantasy, and his own interpretations, but we have been obliged to transpose them, as it were, to another part of the problem. It is not the dream that creates the phantasy, but the activity of unconscious phantasy that plays the leading part in the formation of the dream-thoughts. We remain indebted to Scherner for directing us to the source of the dream-thoughts, but almost everything that he ascribes to the dream-work is attributable to the activity of the unconscious during the day, which instigates dreams no less than neurotic symptoms. The dream-work we had to separate from this activity as something quite different and far more closely controlled. Finally, we have by no means renounced the relation of the dream to psychic disturbances, but have given it, on new ground, a more solid foundation.

Held together by the new features in our theory as by a superior unity, we find the most varied and most contradictory conclusions of other writers fitting into our structure; many of them are given a different turn, but only a few of them are wholly rejected. But our own structure is still unfinished. For apart from the many obscure questions in which we have involved ourselves by our advance into the dark regions of psychology, we are now, it would seem, embarrassed by a new contradiction. On the one hand, we have made it appear that the dream-thoughts proceed from perfectly normal psychic activities, but on the other hand we have found among the dream-thoughts a number of entirely abnormal mental processes, which extend also to the dream-content, and which we reproduce in the interpretation of the dream. All that we have termed the *dream-work* seems to depart so completely from the psychic processes which we recognize as correct and appropriate that the severest judgments expressed by the writers mentioned as to the low level of psychic achievement of dreams must appear well founded.

Here, perhaps, only further investigations can provide an explanation and set us on the right path. Let me pick out for renewed attention one of the constellations which lead to dream-formation.

We have learned that the dream serves as a substitute for a number of thoughts derived from our daily life, and which fit together with perfect logic. We cannot, therefore, doubt that these thoughts have their own origin in our normal mental life. All the qualities which we value in our thought-processes, and which mark them out as complicated performances of a high order, we shall find repeated in the dream-thoughts. There is, however, no need to assume that this mental work is performed during sleep; such an assumption would badly confuse the conception of the psychic state of sleep to which we have hitherto adhered. On the contrary, these thoughts may very well have their origin in the daytime, and, unremarked by our consciousness, may have gone on from their first stimulus until, at the onset of sleep, they have reached completion. If we are to conclude anything from this state of affairs, it can only be that it proves *that the most complex mental operations are possible without the cooperation of consciousness*—a truth which we have had to learn anyhow from every psycho-analysis of a patient suffering from hysteria or obsessions. These dream-thoughts are certainly not in themselves incapable of consciousness; if we have not become conscious of them during the day, this may have been due to various reasons. The act of becoming conscious depends upon a definite psychic function—attention—being brought to bear. This seems to be available only in a determinate quantity, which may have been diverted from the train of thought in question by other aims. Another way in which such trains of thought may be withheld from consciousness is the following: From our conscious reflection we know that, when applying our attention, we follow a particular course. But if that course leads us to an idea which cannot withstand criticism, we break off and allow the cathexis of attention to drop. Now, it would seem that the train of thought thus started and abandoned may continue to develop without our attention returning to it, unless at some point it attains a specially high intensity which compels attention. An initial conscious rejection by our judgment, on the ground of incorrectness or uselessness for the immediate purpose of the act of thought, may, therefore, be the cause of a thought-process going on unnoticed by consciousness until the onset of sleep.

Let us now recapitulate: We call such a train of thought a *preconscious* train, and we believe it to be perfectly correct, and that it may equally well be a merely neglected train or one that has been interrupted and suppressed. Let us also state in plain terms how we visualize the movement of our thought. We believe that a certain quantity of excitation, which we call *cathectic energy*, is displaced from a purposive idea along the association paths selected by this directing idea. A *neglected* train of thought has received no such cathexis, and the cathexis has been withdrawn from one that was *suppressed* or *rejected;* both have thus been left to their own excitations. The train of thought cathected by some aim becomes able under certain conditions to attract the attention of consciousness, and by the mediation of consciousness it then receives *hyper-cathexis*. We shall be obliged presently to elucidate our assumptions as to the nature and function of consciousness.

A train of thought thus incited in the *Pcs* may either disappear spontaneously, or it may continue. The former eventuality we conceive as follows: it diffuses its energy through all the association paths emanating from it, and throws the entire chain of thoughts into a state of excitation, which continues for a while, and then subsides, through the excitation which had called for discharge being transformed into dormant cathexis. If this first eventuality occurs, the process has no further significance for dream-formation. But other directing ideas are lurking in our preconscious, which have their source in our unconscious and ever-active wishes. These may gain control of the excitation in the circle of thoughts thus left to itself, establish a connection between it and the unconscious wish, and *transfer* to it the energy inherent in the unconscious wish. Henceforth the neglected or suppressed train of thought is in a position to maintain itself, although this reinforcement gives it no claim to access to consciousness. We may say, then, that the hitherto preconscious train of thought *has been drawn into the unconscious.*

Other constellations leading to dream-formation might be as follows: The preconscious train of thought might have been connected from the beginning with the unconscious wish, and for that reason might have met with rejection by the dominating aim-cathexis. Or an unconscious wish might become active for other (possibly somatic) reasons, and of its own accord seek a transference to the psychic residues not cathected by the *Pcs.* All three cases have the same result: there is established in the preconscious a train of thought which, having been abandoned by the preconscious cathexis, has acquired cathexis from the unconscious wish.

From this point onward the train of thought is subjected to a series of transformations which we no longer recognize as normal psychic processes, and which give a result that we find strange, a psychopathological formation. Let us now emphasize and bring together these transformations:

1. The intensities of the individual ideas become capable of discharge in their entirety, and pass from one idea to another, so that individual ideas are formed which are endowed with great intensity. Through the repeated occurrence of this process, the intensity of an entire train of thought may ultimately be concentrated in a single conceptual unit. This is the fact of *compression* or *condensation* with which we become acquainted when investigating the dream-work. It is condensation that is mainly responsible for the strange impression produced by dreams, for we know of nothing analogous to it in the normal psychic life that is accessible to consciousness. We get here, too, ideas which are of great psychic significance as nodal points or as end-results of whole chains of thought, but this value is not expressed by any character *actually manifest* for our internal perception; what is represented in it is not in any way made more intensive. In the process of condensation the whole set of psychic connections becomes transformed into the *intensity* of the idea-content. The situation is the same as when, in the case of a book, I italicize or print in heavy type any word to which I attach outstanding value for the understanding of the text. In speech, I should

pronounce the same word loudly, and deliberately, and with emphasis. The first simile points immediately to one of the examples which were given of the dream-work (*trimethylamine* in the dream of Irma's injection). Historians of art call our attention to the fact that the most ancient sculptures known to history follow a similar principle, in expressing the rank of the persons represented by the size of the statues. The king is made two or three times as tall as his retinue or his vanquished enemies. But a work of art of the Roman period makes use of more subtle means to accomplish the same end. The figure of the Emperor is placed in the centre, erect and in his full height, and special care is bestowed on the modelling of this figure; his enemies are seen cowering at his feet; but he is no longer made to seem a giant among dwarfs. At the same time, in the bowing of the subordinate to his superior, even in our own day, we have an echo of this ancient principle of representation.

The direction followed by the condensations of the dream is prescribed on the one hand by the true preconscious relations of the dream-thoughts, and, on the other hand, by the attraction of the visual memories in the unconscious. The success of the condensation-work produces those intensities which are required for penetration to the perception-system.

2. By the free transference of intensities, and in the service of the condensation, *intermediary ideas*—compromises, as it were—are formed (cf. the numerous examples). This, also, is something unheard of in the normal movement of our ideas, where what is of most importance is the selection and the retention of the right conceptual material. On the other hand, composite and compromise formations occur with extraordinary frequency when we are trying to find verbal expression for preconscious thoughts; these are considered slips of the tongue.

3. The ideas which transfer their intensities to one another are *very loosely connected,* and are joined together by such forms of association as are disdained by our serious thinking, and left to be exploited solely by wit. In particular, assonances and punning associations are treated as equal in value to any other associations.

4. Contradictory thoughts do not try to eliminate one another, but continue side by side, and often combine to form condensation-products, *as though no contradiction existed;*

or they form compromises for which we should never forgive our thought, but which we frequently sanction in our action.

These are some of the most conspicuous abnormal processes to which the dream-thoughts which have previously been rationally formed are subjected in the course of the dream-work. As the main feature of these processes, we may see that the greatest importance is attached to rendering the cathecting energy mobile and *capable of discharge;* the content and the intrinsic significance of the psychic elements to which these cathexes adhere become matters of secondary importance. One might perhaps assume that condensation and compromise-formation are effected only in the service of regression, when the occasion arises for changing thoughts into images. But the analysis—and still more plainly the synthesis—of such dreams as show no regression towards images, e.g., the dream *Autodidasker: Conversation with Professor N,* reveals the same processes of displacement and condensation as do the rest.

We cannot, therefore, avoid the conclusion that two kinds of essentially different psychic processes participate in dream-formation; one forms perfectly correct and fitting dream-thoughts, equivalent to the results of normal thinking, while the other deals with these thoughts in a most astonishing and, as it seems, incorrect way. The latter process we have already set apart in chapter VI as the dream-work proper. What can we say now as to the derivation of this psychic process?

It would be impossible to answer this question here if we had not penetrated a considerable way into the psychology of the neuroses, and especially of hysteria. From this, however, we learn that the same "incorrect" psychic processes—as well as others not enumerated—control the production of hysterical symptoms. In hysteria, too, we find at first a series of perfectly correct and fitting thoughts, equivalent to our conscious ones, of whose existence in this form we can, however, learn nothing, i.e., which we can only subsequently reconstruct. If they have forced their way anywhere to perception, we discover from the analysis of the symptom formed that these normal thoughts have been subjected to abnormal treatment, and *that by means of condensation and compromise-formation, through superficial associations which cover up contradictions, and eventually along the path of regression, they have been conveyed into the symptom.* In view of the complete identity between the peculiarities of the dream-work and those of the psychic activity which issues in psychoneurotic symptoms, we shall feel justified in transferring to the dream the conclusions urged upon us by hysteria.

From the theory of hysteria we borrow the proposition that *such an abnormal psychic elaboration of a normal train of thought takes place only when the latter has been used for the transference of an unconscious wish which dates from the infantile life and is in a state of repression.* Complying with this proposition, we have built up the theory of the dream on the assumption that the actuating dream-wish invariably originates in the unconscious; which, as we have ourselves admitted, cannot be universally demonstrated, even though it cannot be refuted. But in order to enable us to say just what *repression* is, after employing this term so freely, we shall be obliged to make a further addition to our psychological scaffolding.

We had elaborated the fiction of a primitive psychic apparatus, the work of which is regulated by the effort to avoid accumulation of excitation, and as far as possible to maintain itself free from excitation. For this reason it was constructed after the plan of a reflex apparatus; motility, in the first place as the path to changes within the body, was the channel of discharge at its disposal. We then discussed the psychic results of experiences of gratification, and were able at this point to introduce a second assumption, namely, that the accumulation of excitation—by processes that do not concern us here—is felt as pain, and sets the apparatus in operation in order to bring about again a state of gratification, in which the diminution of excitation is perceived as pleasure. Such a current in the apparatus, issuing from pain and striving for pleasure, we call a *wish.* We have said that nothing but a wish is capable of setting the apparatus in motion and that the course of any excitation in the apparatus is regulated automatically by the perception of pleasure and pain. The first occurrence of wishing may well have taken the form of a hallucinatory cathexis of the memory of gratification. But this hallucination, unless it could be maintained to the point of exhaustion, proved incapable of bringing about a cessation of the need, and consequently of securing the pleasure connected with gratification.

Thus, there was required a second activity—in our terminology the activity of a second system—which would not allow the memory-cathexis to force its way to perception and thence to bind the psychic forces, but would lead the excitation emanating from the need-stimulus by a detour, which by means of voluntary motility would ultimately so change the outer world as to permit the real perception of the gratifying object. Thus far we have already elaborated the scheme of the psychic apparatus; these two systems are the germ of what we set up in the fully developed apparatus as the *Ucs* and *Pcs*.

To change the outer world appropriately by means of motility requires the accumulation of a large total of experiences in the memory-systems, as well as a manifold consolidation of the relations which are evoked in this memory-material by various directing ideas. We will now proceed further with our assumptions. The activity of the second system, groping in many directions, tentatively sending forth cathexes and retracting them, needs on the one hand full command over all memory-material, but on the other hand it would be a superfluous expenditure of energy were it to send along the individual thought-paths large quantities of cathexis, which would then flow away to no purpose and thus diminish the quantity needed for changing the outer world. Out of a regard for purposiveness, therefore, I postulate that the second system succeeds in maintaining the greater part of the energic cathexes in a state of rest, and in using only a small portion for its operations of displacement. The mechanics of these processes is entirely unknown to me; anyone who seriously wishes to follow up these ideas must address himself to the physical analogies, and find some way of getting a picture of the sequence of motions which ensues on the excitation of the neurones. Here I do no more than hold fast to the idea that the activity of the first ψ-system aims at *the free outflow of the quantities of excitation,* and that the second system, by means of the cathexes emanating from it, effects an *inhibition* of this outflow, a transformation into dormant cathexis, probably with a rise of potential. I therefore assume that the course taken by any excitation under the control of the second system is bound to quite different mechanical conditions from those which obtain under the control of the first system. After the second system has completed its work of experimental thought, it removes the inhibition and damming up of the excitations and allows them to flow off into motility.

An interesting train of thought now presents itself if we consider the relations of this inhibition of discharge by the second system to the process of regulation by the pain-principle. Let us now seek out the counterpart of the primary experience of gratification, namely, the *objective experience of fear*. Let a perception-stimulus act on the primitive apparatus and be the source of a pain-excitation. There will then ensue uncoordinated motor manifestations, which will go on until one of these withdraws the apparatus from perception, and at the same time from the pain. On the reappearance of the percept this manifestation will immediately be repeated (perhaps as a movement of flight), until the percept has again disappeared. But in this case no tendency will remain to recathect the perception of the source of pain by hallucination or otherwise. On the contrary, there will be a tendency in the primary apparatus to turn away again from this painful memory-image immediately if it is in any way awakened, since the overflow of its excitation into perception would, of course, evoke (or more precisely, begin to evoke) pain. This turning away from a recollection, which is merely a repetition of the former flight from perception, is also facilitated by the fact that, unlike the perception, the recollection has not enough quality to arouse consciousness, and thereby to attract fresh cathexis. This effortless and regular turning away of the psychic process from the memory of anything that had once been painful gives us the prototype and the first example of *psychic repression*. We all know how much of this turning away from the painful, the tactics of the ostrich, may still be shown as present even in the normal psychic life of adults.

In obedience to the pain-principle, therefore, the first ψ-system is quite incapable of introducing anything unpleasant into the thought-nexus. The system cannot do anything but wish. If this were to remain so, the activity of thought of the second system, which needs to have at its disposal all the memories stored up by experience, would be obstructed. But two paths are now open: either the work of the second system frees itself completely from the pain-principle, and continues its course, paying no heed to the pain attached to given memories, or it contrives to cathect the memory of the pain in such a manner as to preclude the liberation of pain. We can reject the first possibility, as the pain-principle also proves to act as a regulator of the cycle of excitation in the second system; we are therefore thrown back upon the second possibility, namely, that this system cathects a memory in such a manner as to inhibit any outflow of excitation from it, and hence, also, the outflow, comparable to a motor-innervation, needed for the development of pain. And thus, setting out from two different starting-points, i.e., from regard for the pain-principle, and from the principle of the least expenditure of innervation, we are led to the hypothesis that cathexis through the second system is at the same time an inhibition of the discharge of excitation. Let us, however, keep a close hold on the fact—for this is the key to the theory of repression—*that the second system can only cathect an idea when it is in a position to inhibit any pain emanating from this idea.* Anything that withdrew itself from this inhibition would also remain inaccessible for the second system, i.e., would immediately be given up by virtue of the pain-principle. The inhibition of pain, however, need not be complete; it must be permitted to begin, since this indicates to the second system the nature of the memory, and possibly its lack of fitness for the purpose sought by the process of thought.

The psychic process which is alone tolerated by the first system I shall now call the *primary process;* and that which results under the inhibiting action of the second system I shall call the *secondary process.* I can also show at another point for what purpose the second system is obliged to correct the primary process. The primary process strives for discharge of the excitation in order to establish with the quantity of excitation thus collected an *identity of perception;* the secondary process has abandoned this intention, and has adopted instead the aim of an *identity of thought.* All thinking is merely a detour from the memory of gratification (taken as a purposive idea) to the identical cathexis of the same memory, which is to be reached once more by the path of motor experiences. Thought must concern itself with the connecting-paths between ideas without allowing itself to be misled by their intensities. But it is obvious that condensations of ideas and intermediate or compromise-formations are obstacles to the attainment of the identity which is aimed at; by substituting one idea for another they swerve away from the path which would have led onward from the first idea. Such procedures are, therefore, carefully avoided in our secondary thinking. It will readily be seen, moreover, that the pain-principle, although at other times it provides the thought-process with its most important clues, may also put difficulties in its way in the pursuit of identity of thought. Hence, the ten-dency of the thinking process must always be to free itself more and more from exclusive regulation by the pain-principle, and to restrict the development of affect through the work of thought to the very minimum which remains effective as a signal. This refinement in functioning is to be achieved by a fresh hyper-cathexis, effected with the help of consciousness. But we are aware that this refinement is seldom successful, even in normal psychic life, and that our thinking always remains liable to falsification by the intervention of the pain-principle.

This, however, is not the breach in the functional efficiency of our psychic apparatus which makes it possible for thoughts representing the result of the secondary thought-work to fall into the power of the primary psychic process; by which formula we may now describe the operations resulting in dreams and the symptoms of hysteria. This inadequacy results from the converging of two factors in our development, one of which pertains solely to the psychic apparatus, and has exercised a determining influence on the relation of the two systems, while the other operates fluctuatingly, and introduces motive forces of organic origin into the psychic life. Both originate in the infantile life, and are a precipitate of the alteration which our psychic and somatic organism has undergone since our infantile years.

When I termed one of the psychic processes in the psychic apparatus the *primary* process, I did so not only in consideration of its status and function, but was also able to take account of the temporal relationship actually involved. So far as we know, a psychic apparatus possessing only the primary process does not exist, and is to that extent a theoretical fiction; but this at least is a fact: that the primary processes are present in the apparatus from the beginning, while the secondary processes only take shape gradually during the course of life, inhibiting and overlaying the primary, whilst gaining complete control over them perhaps only in the prime of life. Owing to this belated arrival of the secondary processes, the essence of our being, consisting of unconscious wish-impulses, remains something which cannot be grasped or inhibited by the preconscious; and its part is once and for all restricted to indicating the most appropriate paths for the wish-impulses originating in the unconscious. These unconscious wishes represent for all subsequent psychic strivings a compulsion to which they must submit themselves, although they may perhaps endeavour to divert them and to guide them to superior aims. In consequence of this retardation, an extensive region of the memory-material remains in fact inaccessible to preconscious cathexis.

Now among these wish-impulses originating in the infantile life, indestructible and incapable of inhibition, there are some the fulfilments of which have come to be in contradiction with the purposive ideas of our secondary thinking. The fulfilment of these wishes would no longer produce an affect of pleasure, but one of pain; *and it is just this conversion of affect that constitutes the essence of what we call* repression. In what manner and by what motive forces such a conversion can take place constitutes the problem of repression, which we need here only to touch upon in passing. It will suffice to note the fact that such a conversion of affect occurs in the course of development (one need only think of the emergence of disgust, originally absent in infantile life), and that it is connected with the activity of the secondary system. The memories from which the unconscious wish evokes a liberation of affect have never been accessible to the *Pcs*, and for that reason this liberation cannot be inhibited. It is precisely on account of this generation of affect that these ideas are not now accessible even by way of the preconscious thoughts to which they have transferred the energy of the wishes connected with them. On the contrary, the pain-principle comes into play, and causes the *Pcs* to turn away from these transference-thoughts. These latter are left to themselves, are *repressed*, and thus, the existence of a store of infantile memories, withdrawn from the beginning from the *Pcs*, becomes the preliminary condition of repression.

In the most favourable case, the generation of pain terminates so soon as the cathexis is withdrawn from the transference-thoughts in the *Pcs*, and this result shows that the intervention of the pain-principle is appropriate. It is otherwise, however, if the repressed unconscious wish receives an organic reinforcement which it can put at the service of its transference-thoughts, and by which it can enable them to attempt to break through with their excitation, even if the cathexis of the *Pcs* has been taken away from them. A defensive struggle then ensues, inasmuch as the *Pcs* reinforces the opposite to the repressed thoughts (counter-cathexis), and the eventual outcome is that the transference-thoughts (the carriers of the unconscious wish) break through in some form of compromise through symptom-formation. But from the moment that the repressed thoughts are powerfully cathected by the unconscious wish-impulse, but forsaken by the preconscious cathexis, they succumb to the primary psychic process, and aim only at motor discharge; or, if the way is clear, at hallucinatory revival of the desired identity of perception. We have already found, empirically, that the *incorrect* processes described are enacted only with thoughts which are in a state of repression. We are now in a position to grasp yet another part of the total scheme of the facts. These *incorrect* processes are the *primary* processes of the psychic apparatus; they occur wherever ideas abandoned by the preconscious cathexis are left to themselves and can become filled with the uninhibited energy which flows from the unconscious and strives for discharge. There are further facts which go to show that the processes described as incorrect are not really falsifications of our normal procedure, or defective thinking, but the modes of operation of the psychic apparatus when freed from inhibition. Thus we see that the process of the conveyance of the preconscious excitation to motility occurs in accordance with the same procedure, and that in the linkage of preconscious ideas with words we may easily find manifested the same displacements and confusions (which we ascribe to inattention). Finally, a proof of the increased work made necessary by the inhibition of these primary modes of procedure might be found in the fact that we achieve a *comical effect*, a surplus to be discharged through *laughter, if we allow these modes of thought to come to consciousness*.

The theory of the psychoneuroses asserts with absolute certainty that it can only be sexual wish-impulses from the infantile life, which have undergone repression (affect-conversion) during the developmental period of childhood, which are capable of renewal at later periods of development (whether as a result of our sexual constitution, which has, of course, grown out of an original bi-sexuality, or in consequence of unfavourable influences in our sexual life); and which therefore supply the motive-power for all psychoneurotic symptom-formation. It is only by the introduction of these sexual forces that the gaps still demonstrable in the theory of repression can be filled. Here, I will leave it undecided whether the postulate of the sexual and infantile holds good for the theory of dreams as well; I am not completing the latter, because in assuming that the dream-wish invariably originates in the unconscious I have already gone a step beyond the demonstrable.[1] Nor will I inquire further into the nature of the difference between the play of psychic forces in dream-formation and in the formation of hysterical symptoms, since there is missing here the needed fuller knowledge of one of the two things to be compared. But there is another point which I regard as important, and I will confess at once that it was only on account of this point that I entered upon all the discussions concerning the two psychic systems, their modes of operation, and the fact of repression. It does not greatly matter whether I have conceived the psychological relations at issue with approximate correctness, or, as is easily possible in such a difficult matter, wrongly and imperfectly. However our views may change about the interpretation of the psychic censorship or the correct and the abnormal elaboration of the dream-content, it remains certain that such processes are active in dream-formation, and that in their essentials they reveal the closest analogy with the processes observed in the formation of hysterical symptoms. Now the dream is not a pathological phenomenon; it does not presuppose any disturbance of our psychic equilibrium; and it does not leave behind it any weakening of our

efficiency or capacities. The objection that no conclusions can be drawn about the dreams of healthy persons from my own dreams and from those of my neurotic patients may be rejected without comment. If, then, from the nature of the given phenomena we infer the nature of their motive forces, we find that the psychic mechanism utilized by the neuroses is not newly-created by a morbid disturbance that lays hold of the psychic life, but lies in readiness in the normal structure of our psychic apparatus. The two psychic systems, the frontier-censorship between them, the inhibition and overlaying of the one activity by the other, the relations of both to consciousness—or whatever may take place of these concepts on a juster interpretation of the actual relations—all these belong to the normal structure of our psychic instrument, and the dream shows us one of the paths which lead to a knowledge of this structure. If we wish to be content with a minimum of perfectly assured additions to our knowledge, we shall say that the dream affords proof that *the suppressed material continues to exist even in the normal person and remains capable of psychic activity*. Dreams are one of the manifestations of this suppressed material; theoretically, this is true in all cases; and in tangible experience, it has been found true in at least a great number of cases, which happen to display most plainly the more striking features of the dream-life. The suppressed psychic material, which in the waking state has been prevented from expression and cut off from internal perception *by the mutual neutralization of contradictory attitudes*, finds ways and means, under the sway of compromise-formations, of obtruding itself on consciousness during the night.

Flectere si nequeo superos, Acheronta movebo.[2]

At any rate, *the interpretation of dreams is the* via regia *to a knowledge of the unconscious element in our psychic life*.

By the analysis of dreams we obtain some insight into the composition of this most marvellous and most mysterious of instruments; it is true that this only takes us a little way, but it gives us a start which enables us, setting out from the angle of other (properly pathological) formations, to penetrate further in our disjoining of the instrument. For disease—at all events that which is rightly called functional—does not necessarily presuppose the destruction of this apparatus, or the establish-

[1] Here, as elsewhere, there are gaps in the treatment of the subject, which I have deliberately left, because to fill them up would, on the one hand, require excessive labour, and, on the other hand, I should have to depend on material which is foreign to the dream. Thus, for example, I have avoided stating whether I give the word *suppressed* a different meaning from that of the word *repressed*. No doubt, however, it will have become clear that the latter emphasizes more than the former the relation to the unconscious. I have not gone into the problem, which obviously arises, of why the dream-thoughts undergo distortion by the censorship even when they abandon the progressive path to consciousness, and choose the path of regression. And so with other similar omissions. I have, above all, sought to give some idea of the problems to which the further dissection of the dream-work leads, and to indicate the other themes with which these are connected. It was, however, not always easy to decide just where the pursuit should be discontinued. That I have not treated exhaustively the part which the psycho-sexual life plays in the dream, and have avoided the interpretation of dreams of an obviously sexual content, is due to a special reason—which may not perhaps be that which the reader would expect. It is absolutely alien to my views and my neuropathological doctrines to regard the sexual life as a *pudendum* with which neither the physician nor the scientific investigator should concern himself. To me, the moral indignation which prompted the translator of Artemidorus of Daldis to keep from the reader's knowledge the chapter on sexual dreams contained in the *Symbolism of Dreams* is merely ludicrous. For my own part, what decided my procedure was solely the knowledge that in the explanation of sexual dreams I should be bound to get deeply involved in the still unexplained problems of perversion and bisexuality; it was for this reason that I reserved this material for treatment elsewhere.

[2] If I cannot influence the gods, I will stir up Acheron.—ED.

ment of new cleavages in its interior; it can be explained *dynamically* by the strengthening and weakening of the components of the play of forces, so many of the activities of which are covered up in normal functioning. It might be shown elsewhere how the fact that the apparatus is a combination of two instances also permits of a refinement of its normal functioning which would have been impossible to a single system.[1]

F. *The Unconscious and Consciousness. Reality*

If we look more closely, we may observe that the psychological considerations examined in the foregoing chapter require us to assume, not the existence of two systems near the motor end of the psychic apparatus, but *two kinds of processes or courses taken by excitation*. But this does not disturb us; for we must always be ready to drop our auxiliary ideas, when we think we are in a position to replace them by something which comes closer to the unknown reality. Let us now try to correct certain views which may have taken a misconceived form as long as we regarded the two systems, in the crudest and most obvious sense, as two localities within the psychic apparatus—views which have left a precipitate in the terms *repression* and *penetration*. Thus, when we say that an unconscious thought strives for translation into the preconscious in order subsequently to penetrate through to consciousness, we do not mean that a second idea has to be formed, in a new locality, like a paraphrase, as it were, whilst the original persists by its side; and similarly, when we speak of penetration into consciousness, we wish carefully to detach from this notion any idea of a change of locality. When we say that a preconscious idea is repressed and subsequently absorbed by the unconscious, we might be tempted by these images, borrowed from the idea of a struggle for a particular territory, to assume that an arrangement is really broken up in the one psychic locality and replaced by a new one in the other locality. For these comparisons we will substitute a description which would seem to correspond more closely to the real state of affairs; we will say that an energic cathexis is shifted to or withdrawn from a certain arrangement, so that the psychic formation falls under the domination of a given instance or is withdrawn from it. Here again we replace a topographical mode of representation by a dynamic one; it is not the psychic formation that appears to us as the mobile element, but its innervation.[2]

Nevertheless, I think it expedient and justifiable to continue to use the illustrative idea of the two systems. We shall avoid any abuse of this mode of representation if we remember that ideas, thoughts, and psychic formations in general must not in any case be localized in organic elements of the nervous system but, so to speak, *between them*, where resistances and association-tracks form the correlate corresponding to them. Everything that can become an object of internal perception is *virtual*, like the image in the telescope produced by the crossing of light-rays. But we are justified in thinking of the systems—which have nothing psychic in themselves, and which never become accessible to our psychic perception—as something similar to the lenses of the telescope, which project the image. If we continue this comparison, we might say that the censorship between the two systems corresponds to the refraction of rays on passing into a new medium.

Thus far, we have developed our psychology on our own responsibility; it is now time to turn and look at the doctrines prevailing in modern psychology, and to examine the relation of these to our theories. The problem of the unconscious in psychology is, according to the forcible statement of Lipps,[3] less *a* psychological problem than *the* problem of psychology. As long as psychology disposed of this problem by the verbal explanation that the *psychic* is the *conscious*, and that *unconscious psychic occurrences* are an obvious contradiction, there was no possibility of a physician's observations of abnormal mental states being turned to any psychological account. The physician and the philosopher can meet only when both acknowledge that *unconscious psychic processes* is the *appropriate and justified expression for an established fact*. The physician cannot but reject, with a shrug of his shoulders, the assertion that

---

[1] The dream is not the only phenomenon that permits us to base our psycho-pathology on psychology. In a short unfinished series of articles in the *Monatsschrift für Psychiatrie und Neurologie* ("*über den psychischen Mechanismus der Vergesslichkeit*," 1898, and "*über Deckerinnerungen*," 1899) I attempted to interpret a number of psychic manifestations from everyday life in support of the same conception. (These and other articles on "Forgetting," "Lapses of Speech," etc., have now been published in the *Psycho-pathology of Everyday Life*.)

[2] This conception underwent elaboration and modification when it was recognized that the essential character of a preconscious idea was its connection with the residues of verbal ideas. See *The Unconscious*, p. 428 below.

[3] *Der Begriff des Unbewussten in der Psychologie*. Lecture delivered at the Third International Psychological Congress at Munich, 1897.

consciousness is the indispensable quality of the psychic; if his respect for the utterances of the philosophers is still great enough, he may perhaps assume that he and they do not deal with the same thing and do not pursue the same science. For a single intelligent observation of the psychic life of a neurotic, a single analysis of a dream, must force upon him the unshakable conviction that the most complicated and the most accurate operations of thought, to which the name of psychic occurrences can surely not be refused, may take place without arousing consciousness.[1] The physician, it is true, does not learn of these unconscious processes until they have produced an effect on consciousness which admits of communication or observation. But this effect on consciousness may show a psychic character which differs completely from the unconscious process, so that internal perception cannot possibly recognize in the first a substitute for the second. The physician must reserve himself the right to penetrate, by a *process of deduction,* from the effect on consciousness to the unconscious psychic process; he learns in this way that the effect on consciousness is only a remote psychic product of the unconscious process, and that the latter has not become conscious as such, and has, moreover, existed and operated without in any way betraying itself to consciousness.

A return from the over-estimation of the property of consciousness is the indispensable preliminary to any genuine insight into the course of psychic events. As Lipps has said, the unconscious must be accepted as the general basis of the psychic life. The unconscious is the larger circle which includes the smaller circle of the conscious; everything conscious has a preliminary unconscious stage, whereas the unconscious can stop at this stage, and yet claim to be considered a full psychic function. The unconscious is the true psychic reality; *in its inner nature it is just as much unknown to us as the reality of the external world, and it is just as*

imperfectly communicated to us by the data of consciousness as is the external world by the reports of our sense-organs.

We get rid of a series of dream-problems which have claimed much attention from earlier writers on the subject when the old antithesis between conscious life and dream-life is discarded, and the unconscious psychic assigned to its proper place. Thus, many of the achievements which are a matter for wonder in a dream are now no longer to be attributed to dreaming, but to unconscious thinking, which is active also during the day. If the dream seems to make play with a symbolical representation of the body, as Scherner has said, we know that this is the work of certain unconscious phantasies, which are probably under the sway of sexual impulses and find expression not only in dreams, but also in hysterical phobias and other symptoms. If the dream continues and completes mental work begun during the day, and even brings valuable new ideas to light, we have only to strip off the dream-disguise from this, as the contribution of the dream-work, and a mark of the assistance of dark powers in the depths of the psyche (cf. the devil in Tartini's sonata-dream). The intellectual achievement as such belongs to the same psychic forces as are responsible for all such achievements during the day. We are probably much too inclined to over-estimate the conscious character even of intellectual and artistic production. From the reports of certain writers who have been highly productive, such as Goethe and Helmholtz, we learn, rather, that the most essential and original part of their creations came to them in the form of inspirations, and offered itself to their awareness in an almost completed state. In other cases, where there is a concerted effort of all the psychic forces, there is nothing strange in the fact that conscious activity, too, lends its aid. But it is the much-abused privilege of conscious activity to hide from us all other activities wherever it participates.

It hardly seems worth while to take up the historical significance of dreams as a separate theme. Where, for instance, a leader has been impelled by a dream to engage in a bold undertaking, the success of which has had the effect of changing history, a new problem arises only so long as the dream is regarded as a mysterious power and contrasted with other more familiar psychic forces. The problem disappears as soon as we regard the dream as *a form of expression* for impulses to which a resistance was attached during the day, whilst at night

---

[1] I am happy to be able to point to an author who has drawn from the study of dreams the same conclusion as regards the relation between consciousness and the unconscious.

Du Prel says: "The problem: what is the psyche, manifestly requires a preliminary examination as to whether consciousness and psyche are identical. But it is just this preliminary question which is answered in the negative by the dream, which shows that the concept of the psyche extends beyond that of consciousness, much as the gravitational force of a star extends beyond its sphere of luminosity" (*Philos. d. Mystik,* p. 47).

"It is a truth which cannot be sufficiently emphasized that the concepts of consciousness and of the psyche are not co-extensive" (p. 306).

they were able to draw reinforcement from deep-lying sources of excitation.[1] But the great respect with which the ancient peoples regarded dreams is based on a just piece of psychological divination. It is a homage paid to the unsubdued and indestructible element in the human soul, to the *demonic* power which furnishes the dream-wish, and which we have found again *in our unconscious.*

It is not without purpose that I use the expression *in our unconscious,* for what we so call does not coincide with the unconscious of the philosophers, nor with the unconscious of Lipps. As they use the term, it merely means the opposite of the conscious. That there exist not only conscious but also unconscious psychic processes is the opinion at issue, which is so hotly contested and so energetically defended. Lipps enunciates the more comprehensive doctrine that everything psychic exists as unconscious, but that some of it may exist also as conscious. But it is not to prove *this* doctrine that we have adduced the phenomena of dreams and hysterical symptom-formation; the observation of normal life alone suffices to establish its correctness beyond a doubt. The novel fact that we have learned from the analysis of psycho-pathological formations, and indeed from the first member of the group, from dreams, is that the unconscious—and hence all that is psychic—occurs as a function of two separate systems, and that as such it occurs even in normal psychic life. There are consequently *two kinds of unconscious,* which have not as yet been distinguished by psychologists. Both are unconscious in the psychological sense; but in our sense the first, which we call *Ucs,* is likewise *incapable of consciousness;* whereas the second we call *Pcs* because its excitations, after the observance of certain rules, are capable of reaching consciousness; perhaps not before they have again undergone censorship, but nevertheless regardless of the *Ucs* system. The fact that in order to attain consciousness the excitations must pass through an unalterable series, a succession of instances, as is betrayed by the changes produced in them by the censorship, has enabled us to describe them by analogy in spatial terms. We described the relations of the two systems to each other and to consciousness by saying that the system *Pcs* is like a screen between the system *Ucs* and consciousness. The system *Pcs* not only bars access to consciousness, but also controls the

access to voluntary motility, and has control of the emission of a mobile cathectic energy, a portion of which is familiar to us as attention.[2]

We must also steer clear of the distinction between the *super-conscious* and the *subconscious,* which has found such favour in the more recent literature on the psychoneuroses, for just such a distinction seems to emphasize the equivalence of what is psychic and what is conscious.

What rôle is now left, in our representation of things, to the phenomenon of consciousness, once so all-powerful and over-shadowing all else? None other than *that of a sense-organ for the perception of psychic qualities.* According to the fundamental idea of our schematic attempt we can regard conscious perception only as the function proper to a special system for which the abbreviated designation *Cs* commends itself. This system we conceive to be similar in its mechanical characteristics to the perception-system *P,* and hence excitable by qualities, and incapable of retaining the trace of changes: i.e., devoid of memory. The psychic apparatus which, with the sense-organ of the *P*-systems, is turned to the outer world, is itself the outer world for the sense-organ of *Cs,* whose teleological justification depends on this relationship. We are here once more confronted with the principle of the succession of instances which seems to dominate the structure of the apparatus. The material of excitation flows to the sense-organ *Cs* from two sides: first from the *P*-system, whose excitation, qualitatively conditioned, probably undergoes a new elaboration until it attains conscious perception; and, secondly, from the interior of the apparatus itself, whose quantitative processes are perceived as a qualitative series of pleasures and pains once they have reached consciousness after undergoing certain changes.

The philosophers, who became aware that accurate and highly complicated thought-structures are possible even without the co-operation of consciousness, thus found it difficult to ascribe any function to consciousness; it appeared to them a superfluous mirroring of the completed psychic process. The analogy of our *Cs* system with the perception-systems relieves us of this embarrassment. We see that perception through our sense-organs results in directing an attention-cathexis to the paths along which the incoming sensory excitation diffuses itself;

---

[1] Cf (p. 179 above) the dream (Σά-Τύρος) of Alexander the Great at the siege of Tyre.

[2] Cf. here my remarks in the *Proceedings of the Society for Psychical Research,* vol. xxvi, in which the descriptive, dynamic and systematic meanings of the ambiguous word *Unconscious* are distinguished from one another.

the qualitative excitation of the P-system serves the mobile quantity in the psychic apparatus as a regulator of its discharge. We may claim the same function for the overlying sense-organ of the Cs system. By perceiving new qualities, it furnishes a new contribution for the guidance and suitable distribution of the mobile cathexis-quantities. By means of perceptions of pleasure and pain, it influences the course of the cathexes within the psychic apparatus, which otherwise operates unconsciously and by the displacement of quantities. It is probable that the pain-principle first of all regulates the displacements of cathexis automatically, but it is quite possible that consciousness contributes a second and more subtle regulation of these qualities, which may even oppose the first, and perfect the functional capacity of the apparatus, by placing it in a position contrary to its original design, subjecting even that which induces pain to cathexis and to elaboration. We learn from neuro-psychology that an important part in the functional activity of the apparatus is ascribed to these regulations by the qualitative excitations of the sense-organs. The automatic rule of the primary pain-principle, together with the limitation of functional capacity bound up with it, is broken by the sensory regulations, which are themselves again automatisms. We find that repression, which, though originally expedient, nevertheless finally brings about a harmful lack of inhibition and of psychic control, overtakes memories much more easily than it does perceptions, because in the former there is no additional cathexis from the excitation of the psychic sense-organs. Whilst an idea which is to be warded off may fail to become conscious because it has succumbed to repression, it may on other occasions come to be repressed simply because it has been withdrawn from conscious perception on other grounds. These are clues which we make use of in therapy in order to undo accomplished repressions.

The value of the hyper-cathexis which is produced by the regulating influence of the Cs sense-organs on the mobile quantity is demonstrated in a teleological context by nothing more clearly than by the creation of a new series of qualities, and consequently a new regulation, which constitutes the prerogative of man over animals. For the mental processes are in themselves unqualitative except for the excitations of pleasure and pain which accompany them: which, as we know, must be kept within limits as possible disturbers of thought.

In order to endow them with quality, they are associated in man with verbal memories, the qualitative residues of which suffice to draw upon them the attention of consciousness, which in turn endows thought with a new mobile cathexis.

It is only on a dissection of hysterical mental processes that the manifold nature of the problems of consciousness becomes apparent. One then receives the impression that the transition from the preconscious to the conscious cathexis is associated with a censorship similar to that between Ucs and Pcs. This censorship, too, begins to act only when a certain quantitative limit is reached, so that thought-formations which are not very intense escape it. All possible cases of detention from consciousness and of penetration into consciousness under certain restrictions are included within the range of psychoneurotic phenomena; all point to the intimate and twofold connection between the censorship and consciousness. I shall conclude these psychological considerations with the record of two such occurrences.

On the occasion of a consultation a few years ago, the patient was an intelligent-looking girl with a simple, unaffected manner. She was strangely attired; for whereas a woman's dress is usually carefully thought out to the last pleat, one of her stockings was hanging down and two of the buttons of her blouse were undone. She complained of pains in one of her legs, and exposed her calf without being asked to do so. Her chief complaint, however, was as follows: She had a feeling in her body *as though something were sticking into it which moved to and fro and shook her through and through.* This sometimes seemed to make her whole body *stiff.* On hearing this, my colleague in consultation looked at me; the trouble was quite obvious to him. To both of us it seemed peculiar that this suggested nothing to the patient's mother, though she herself must repeatedly have been in the situation described by her child. As for the girl, she had no idea of the import of her words, or she would never have allowed them to pass her lips. Here the censorship had been hoodwinked so successfully that under the mask of an innocent complaint a phantasy was admitted to consciousness which otherwise would have remained in the preconscious.

Another example: I began the psycho-analytic treatment of a boy fourteen who was suffering from *tic convulsif,* hysterical vomiting, headache, etc., by assuring him that after closing his eyes he would see pictures or that ideas would occur to him, which he was to communicate to me. He replied by describing pictures. The last impression he had received before coming to me was revived visually in his memory. He had been playing a game of checkers with his uncle, and now he saw the checkerboard before him. He commented on various positions that were favourable or unfavourable, on moves that were not safe to make. He then saw a dagger lying on the checker-board—an object belonging to his father, but which his phantasy laid on the checker-board. Then a sickle was lying on the board; a scythe was added; and finally, he saw the image of an old peasant mowing the grass in front of his father's house far away. A few days later I discovered the meaning of this series of pictures. Disagreeable family circumstances had made the boy excited and nervous. Here was a case of a harsh, irascible father, who had lived unhappily with the boy's mother, and whose educational methods consisted of threats; he had divorced his gentle and delicate wife, and remarried; one day he brought home a young woman as the boy's new mother. The illness of the fourteen-year-old boy developed a few days later. It was the suppressed rage against his father that had combined these images into intelligible allusions. The material was furnished by a mythological reminiscence. The sickle was that with which Zeus castrated his father; the scythe and the image of the peasant represented Kronos, the violent old man who devours his children, and upon whom Zeus wreaks his vengeance in so unfilial a manner. The father's marriage gave the boy an opportunity of returning the reproaches and threats which the child had once heard his father utter because he *played* with his genitals (the draught-board; the prohibited moves; the dagger with which one could kill). We have here long-impressed memories and their unconscious derivatives which, *under the guise of meaningless pictures,* have slipped into consciousness by the devious paths opened to them.

If I were asked what is the theoretical value of the study of dreams, I should reply that it lies in the additions to psychological knowledge and the beginnings of an understanding of the neuroses which we thereby obtain. Who can foresee the importance a thorough knowledge of the structure and functions of the psychic apparatus may attain, when even our present state of knowledge permits of successful therapeutic intervention in the curable forms of psy-

choneuroses? But, it may be asked, what of the practical value of this study in regard to a knowledge of the psyche and discovery of the hidden peculiarities of individual character? Have not the unconscious impulses revealed by dreams the value of real forces in the psychic life? Is the ethical significance of the suppressed wishes to be lightly disregarded, since, just as they now create dreams, they may some day create other things?

I do not feel justified in answering these questions. I have not followed up this aspect of the problem of dreams. In any case, however, I believe that the Roman Emperor was in the wrong in ordering one of his subjects to be executed because the latter had dreamt that he had killed the Emperor. He should first of all have endeavoured to discover the significance of the man's dreams; most probably it was not what it seemed to be. And even if a dream of a different content had actually had this treasonable meaning, it would still have been well to recall the words of Plato—that the virtuous man contents himself with dreaming of that which the wicked man does in actual life. I am therefore of the opinion that dreams should be acquitted of evil. Whether any *reality* is to be attributed to the unconscious wishes, I cannot say. Reality must, of course, be denied to all transitory and intermediate thoughts. If we had before us the unconscious wishes, brought to their final and truest expression, we should still do well to remember that *psychic reality* is a special form of existence which must not be confounded with *material reality*. It seems, therefore, unnecessary that people should refuse to accept the responsibility for the immorality of their dreams. With an appreciation of the mode of functioning of the psychic apparatus, and an insight into the relations between conscious and unconscious, all that is ethically offensive in our dream-life and the life of phantasy for the most part disappears.

"What a dream has told us of our relations to the present (reality) we will then seek also in our consciousness, and we must not be surprised if we discover that the monster we saw under the magnifying-glass of the analysis is a tiny little infusorian" (H. Sachs).

For all practical purposes in judging human character, a man's actions and conscious expressions of thought are in most cases sufficient. Actions, above all, deserve to be placed in the front rank; for many impulses which penetrate into consciousness are neutralized by real forces in the psychic life before they find issue in action; indeed, the reason why they frequently do not encounter any psychic obstacle on their path is because the unconscious is certain of their meeting with resistances later. In any case, it is highly instructive to learn something of the intensively tilled soil from which our virtues proudly emerge. For the complexity of human character, dynamically moved in all directions, very rarely accommodates itself to the arbitrament of a simple alternative, as our antiquated moral philosophy would have it.

And what of the value of dreams in regard to our knowledge of the future? That, of course, is quite out of the question. One would like to substitute the words: *in regard to our knowledge of the past.* For in every sense a dream has its origin in the past. The ancient belief that dreams reveal the future is not indeed entirely devoid of the truth. By representing a wish as fulfilled the dream certainly leads us into the future; but this future, which the dreamer accepts as his present, has been shaped in the likeness of the past by the indestructible wish.

Bibliography

(A) Before the Publication of the First German Edition of this Book (1900)

Achmetis, F. Serim, *Oneirocriticae,* ed. Nik. Rigaltius, Paris, 1603.

Alberti, Michael, *Diss. de insomniorum influxi in sanitatem et morbos,* Resp. Titius Halae M., 1744.

Alix, "Les Rêves," *Rev. Scientif.,* 3e série, Vol. VI (32e de la coll.), 3e année, 2e sem., Nov., 1883, pp. 554-561.

— *Etude du rêve,* Mém. de l'acad. de sc., etc., de Toulouse, 9e série, Vol. I, pp. 283-326, Toulouse, 1889.

Almoli, Salomo, *Pithrôn Chalômôth, Solkiew,* 1848.

Aristoteles, *Über Träume und Traumdeutungen,* trans. Bender *(On Dreams).*

— *Von der Weissagung im Traume (On Prophecying by Dreams).*

Artemidoros of Daldis, *Symbolik der Träume,* trans. Friedr. S. Krauss, Vienna, 1881.

— "Erotische Träume und ihre Symbolik," *Anthropophyteia,* Vol. IX, pp. 316-328.

Artigues, *Essai sur la valeur séméiologique du rêve,* Thèse de Paris, 1884.

Bacci Domenico, *Sui sogni e sul sonnombulismo, pensieri fisiologico-metafisici,* Venice, 1857.

Ball, *La Morphinomanie, les rêves prolongés,* Paris, 1885.

Benezé, Emil, *Das Traummotiv in der mittelhochdeutschen Dichtung bis 1250 und in allen deutschen Volksliedern,* Halle, 1897. (Benezé, *Sagengesch, und lit.-hist., Unters.* 1, *Das Traummotiv.)*

Benini, V., "La Memoria e la durata dei sogni," *Rivista italiana di filosofia,* March, April, 1898.

— "Nel moneto dei sogni," *Il Pensiero nuovo,* April, 1898.

Binz, C., *Über den Traum,* Bonn, 1878.

Birkmaier, Hieron, *Licht im Finsternüss der nächtlichen Gesichte und Träume,* Nürnberg, 1715.

Bisland, E., "Dreams and their Mysteries," *N. Ann. Rev.,* 1896, 152, pp. 716-726.

Börner, J. *Das Alpdrücken, seine Bergründung und Verhütung,* Würzburg, 1855.

Bradley, J. H., "On the Failure of Movement in Dream," *Mind,* July, 1894.

Brander, R., *Der Schlaf und das Traumleben,* Leipzig, 1884.

Bouché-Leclercq, *Historie de la divination dans l'antiquité,* Vol. I, Paris, 1879.

Bremer, L., "Traum und Krankheiten," *New York Med. Monthly,* 1893, V, pp. 281-286.

Büchsenschütz, B., *Traum und Traumdeutung im Altertum,* Berlin, 1868.

Burdach, *Die Physiologie als Erfahrungswissenschaft,* Vol. III, 1830.

Bussola, Serafino, *De somniis.* Diss. Ticini Reg., 1834.

Caëtani-Lovatelli, "I Sogni e l'ipnotismo nel mondo antico," *Nuova Antol.,* 1, December, 1889.

Calkins, Mary Whiton, "Statistics of Dreams," *Amer. J. of Psychology,* V, 1893.

Cane, Francis E., "The Physiology of Dreams," *The Lancet,* December, 1889.

Cardanus, Hieron, *Synesiorum somniorum, omni generis insomnit, explicantes libri IV,* Basileae, 1562. (2nd edition in *Opera Omnia Cardani,* Vol. V, pp. 593-727, Lugduni, 1603.)

Cariero, Alessandro, *De somniis deque divinatione per somnia,* Patavii, 1575.

Carpenter, "Dreaming" in *Cyclop. of Anat. and Phys.,* IV, p. 687.

Chabaneix, *Le Subconscient chez les artistes, les savants et les écrivains,* Paris, 1897.

Chaslin, Ph., *Du Rôle du rêve dans l'évolution du délire,* Thèse de Paris, 1887.

Clavière, "La Rapidité de la pensée dans le rêve," *Revue philosophique,* XLIII, 1897.

Coutts, G. A., "Night-terrors," *Americ. J. of Med. Sc.,* 1896.

D. L., "A propos de l'appréciation du temps dans le rêve," *Rev. philos.,* Vol. 40, 1895, pp. 69-72.

Dagonet, "Du Rêve et du délire alcoolique," *Ann. méd.-psychol.,* 1889, série 7, Vol. X, p. 193.

Dandolo, G., *La coscienza nel sonno,* Padua, 1889.

Davidson, Wolf, *Versuch über den Schlaf,* 2nd edition, Berlin, 1799.

Debacker, *Terreurs nocturnes des enfants,* Thèse de Paris, 1881.

Dechambre, "Cauchemar," *Dict. encycl. de sc. méd.*

Delage, Yves, "Une Théorie du rêve," *Revue scientifique,* II, July, 1891.

Delbœuf, J., *Le Sommeil et les rêves,* Paris, 1885.

Dietrich, Joh. Dav., *An ea, quae hominibus in somno et somnio accidunt iisdem possint imputari?* resp. Gava Vitembergae, 1726.

Dochmasa, A. M., *Dreams and their Significance as Forebodings of Disease,* Kazan, 1890.

Dreher, E., "Sinneswahrnehmung und Traumbild," *Reichs-med. Anzeiger,* Leipzig, 1890, XV.

Ducosté, M., *Les Songes d'attaques epileptiques,* 1889.

Dugas, "Le Souvenir du rêve," *Revue philosophique,* XLIV, 1897.

— "Le Sommeil et la cérébration inconsciente durant le sommeil," *Revue philosophique,* XLIII, 1897.

DU PREL, CARL, "Oneirokritikon; der Traum vom Standpunkte des transcend. Idealismus," *Deutsche Vierteljahrschrift*, Vol. II, Stuttgart, 1869.

Psychologie der Lyrik, Leipzig, 1880.

Die Philosophie der Mystik, Leipzig, 1887.

"Künstliche Träume," *Sphinx*, July, 1889.

EGGER, V., "Le Sommeil et la certitude, le sommeil et la mémoire," *La Critique philos.*, May, 1888, I, pp. 341-350.

"La Durée apparente des rêves," *Revue philosophique*, July, 1895.

"Le Souvenir dans le rêve," *Revue philosophique*, XLVI, 1898.

ELLIS, HAVELOCK, "On Dreaming of the Dead," *The Psychological Revue*, II, No. 5, September, 1895.

"The Stuff that Dreams are Made of," *Appleton's Popular Science Monthly*, April, 1899.

"A Note on Hypnagogic Paramnesia," *Mind*, April, 1897.

ERDMANN, J. E., *Psychologische Briefe*, 6th edition, Leipzig, 1848.

Ernste Spiele (XII: *Das Träumen*), 3rd edition, Berlin, 1875.

ERK, VINZ V., *Über den Unterschied von Traum und Wachen*, Prague, 1874.

ESCANDE DE MESSIÈRES, *Les rêves chez les hystériques*, Th. méd., Bordeaux, 1895.

FAURE, "Etude sur les rêves morbides, Rêves persistants," *Arch. génér., de méd.*, 1876, Vol. I, p. 558.

FECHNER, G. TH., *Elemente der Psychophysik*, 2nd edition, 1889.

FENIZIA, "L'azione suggestiva delle cause esterne nei sogni," *Arch. per l'Anthrop.*, XXVI.

FÉRÉ, CH., "A Contribution to the Pathology of Dreams and of Hysterical Paralysis," *Brain*, January, 1887.

"Les Rêves d'accès chez les épileptiques," *La Med. mod.*, 8. Dec., 1897.

FICHTE, J. H., *Psychologie, Die Lehre vom bewussten Geiste des Menschen*, Vol. I, Leipzig, 1864.

FISCHER, JOH., *Ad artis veterum onirocriticae historiam symbola*, Diss. Jenae, 1899.

FLORENTIN, V., "Das Traumleben, Plauderei," *Die alte und die neue Welt*, 1899, 33. J., p. 725.

FORNASCHON, H., "Geschichte eines Traumes als Beitrag der transcendentalen Psychologie," *Psychische Studien*, 1897, pp. 274-281.

FREILIGRATH, *Traumbuch* (*Biographie von Buchner*).

FRENSBERG, *Schlaf und Traum. Samml. gemeinverst. wiss. Vortr. Virchow Holtzendorf*, Ser. XX, H. 466, Berlin, 1885.

FRERICHS, JOH. H., *Der Mensch: Traum, Herz, Verstand*, 2nd edition, Norden, 1878.

GALENUS, *Von der Weissagung im Traume*.

GIESSLER, C. M., *Beitrag zur Phänomenologie des Traumlebens*, Halle, 1888.

Aus den Tiefen des Traumlebens, Halle, 1890.

Die physiologischen Beziehungen der Traumvorgänge, Halle, 1896.

GIRGENSOHN, L., *Der Traum, psychol.-physiol. Versuch.*, S. A. 1845.

GLEICHEN-RUSSWURM, A. v., "Traum in der Dichtung," *Nat.-Ztg.*, 1899, Nos. 553-559.

GLEY, E., "Appréciation du temps pendant le sommeil," *L'Intermédiare des Biologistes*, 20 March, 1898, No. 10, p. 228.

GOBLOT, "Sur le Souvenir des rêves," *Revue philosophique*, XLII, 1896.

GOMPERZ, TH., *Traumdeutung und Zauberei*, *Vortrag.*, Vienna, 1866.

GORTON, D. A., "Psychology of the Unconscious," *N. Y. Med. Times*, 1896, XXIV, 33, 37.

GOULD, Dreams—Sleep—Consciousness, Open Court, 1899.

GRABENER, GOTTL. CHR., *Ex antiquitate iudaica de menûdim bachalôm sive excommunicatis per insomnia exerc. resp. Klebius*, Vitembergae, 1710.

GRAFFUNDER, *Traum und Traumdeutung*, 1894.

GREENWOOD, *Imaginations in Dreams and Their Study*, London, 1899.

GRIESINGER, *Pathologie und Therapie der psychischen Krankheiten*, 3rd edition, 1871.

GROT NICOLAUS, *Die Träume, ein Gegenstand wissenschaftl. Analyse* (russ.). Kiev, 1878.

GUARDIA, J. M., "La Personnalité dans les rêves," *Rev. philos.*, Paris 1892, XXXIV, pp. 225-258.

GUTFELDT, J., "Ein Traum," *Psych. Studien*, 1899, pp. 491-494.

HAFFNER, P., *Schlafen und Träumen*, 1884. *Frankfurter zeitgemässe Broschüren*, Vol. V, No. 10.

HALLAM, FL., and SARAH WEED, "A Study of the Dream Consciousness," *Amer. J. of Psychology*, VII, No. 3, April, 1896.

HAMPE, TH., "Über Hans Sachsens Traumgedichte," *Zeitschrift für den deutschen Unterricht*, 10 Jahrg., 1896, p. 616 f.

HEERWAGEN, "Statist. Untersuch, über Träume u. Schlaf.," *Philos. Stud.*, V, 1888, p. 88.

HENNINGS, JUSTUS CHR., *Von Träumen und Nachtwandlern*, Weimar, 1802.

HENZEN, WILH., *Über die Träume in der altnord. Sagaliteratur*, Diss. Leipzig, 1890.

D'HERVEY, *Les Rêves et les moyens de les diriger*, Paris, 1867 (anonym.).

HILDEBRANDT, F. W., *Der Traum und seine Verwertung fürs Leben*, Leipzig, 1875.

HILLER, G., "Traum. Ein Kapitel zu den zwölf Nächten," *Leipz. Tagbl. und Anz.*, 1899, No. 657, 1. Teil.

HIPPOKRATES, *Buch über die Träume*, in *Sämtliche Werke*, translated by Dr. Robert Fuchs, Munich, 1895-1900, Vol. I, pp. 361-369.

HITSCHMANN, F., "Uber das Traumleben der Blinden," *Zeitschr. f. Psychol.*, VII, 5-6, 1894.

IDELER, "Die Entstehung des Wahnsinns aus den Träumen," *Charité Annalen*, 1862, Vol. III.

JASTROW, "The Dreams of the Blind," *New Princetown Rev.*, New York, January, 1888.

JEAN PAUL, *Blicke in die Traumwelt*. In *Werke*, ed. by Hempel, Vol. 44, pp. 128-152.

Über Wahl- und Halbträume, ibid., p. 142 f.
Wahrheit aus seinem Leben, Vol. 2, pp. 106-126.

JENSEN, JULIUS, *Traum und Denken*, Berlin, 1871. (*Samml. gemeinverst. wiss. Vortr. Virchow-Holtzendorf*, Ser. VI, No. 134).

JESSEN, *Versuch einer wissenschaftlichen Begründung der Psychologie*, Berlin, 1856.

JODL, *Lehrbuch der Psychologie*, Stuttgart, 1896. (3rd edition, 1908).

KANT, J., *Anthropologie in pragmatischer Hinsicht*, ed. Kirchmann, Leipzig, 1880.

KINGSFORD, A. B., *Dreams and Dream-stories*, ed. Maitland, 2nd edition, London, 1888.

KLOEPFELL, F., "Träumerei und Traum. Allerlei aus unserem Traumleben," *Universum*, 1899, 15. J., pp. 2469-2484, 2607-2622.

KRAMÁŘ, OLDŘICH, *O spánku a snu*, Prager Akad. Gymn., 1882.

KRASNICKI, E. v., "Karls IV. Wahrtraum," *Psych. Stud.*, 1897, p. 697.

KRAUSS, A., "Der Sinn im Wahnsinn," *Allgemeine Zeitschrift für Psychologie*, XV and XVI. 1858-1859.

KUČERA, ED., *Aus dem Traumleben*, Mähr-Weisskirchen Gymn. 1895.

LADD, "Contribution to the Psychology of Visual Dreams," *Mind*, April, 1892.

LAISTNER, LUDW., *Das Rätsel der Sphinx*, 2 Vols., Berlin, 1889.

LANDAU, M., "Aus dem Traumleben," *Münchner Neueste Nachrichten*, 9. January, 1892.

LASÈGUE, "Le Délire alcoolique n'est pas un délire, mais un rêve," *Arch. gén de méd.*, 1881. (Reprinted in *Etudes méd.* Vol. II, pp. 203-227, Paris, 7e série, Vol. VI, pp. 513-536, 1884.)

LAUPTS, "Le Fonctionnement cérébral pendant le rêve et pendant le sommeil hypnotique," *Annales méd.-psychol.*, 1895.

LEIDESDORF, M., *Das Traumleben*, Vienna, 1880.

LE LORRAIN, "La Durée du temps dans les rêves," *Rev. philos.*, Vol. 38, 1894, pp. 275-279.

"Le Rêve," *Revue philosophique*, July, 1895.

LÉLUT, "Mémoire sur le sommeil, les songes et le somnambulisme," *Ann. méd.-psych.*, 1852, Vol. IV.

LEMOINE, *Du Sommeil au point de vue physiologique et psychologique*, Paris, 1855.

LERCH, MATH., FR., "Das Traumleben und seine Bedeutung," *Gymn. Progr. Komotau*, 1883-1884.

LIBERALI, FRANCESCO, *Dei Sogni*, Diss. Padova, 1834.

LIÉBEAULT, A., *Le sommeil provoqué et les états analogues*, Paris, 1889.

"A travers les états passifs, le sommeil et les rêves," *Rev. de l'hypoth.*, etc. Paris, 1893, 4, VIII, 41, 65, 106.

LIPPS, TH., *Grundtatsachen des Seelenlebens*, Bonn, 1883.

LUKSCH, L., *Wunderbare Traumerfüllung als Inhalt des wirklichen Lebens*, Leipzig, 1894.

MACARIO, "Du Sommeil, des rêves et du somnambulisme dans l'état de santé et dans l'état de maladie," *Ann. méd.-psychol.*, 1858, Vol. IV, V.

"Des rêves considérés sous le rapport physiologique et pathologique," *Ibid.*, 1846, Vol. VIII.

"Des rêves morbides," *Gaz. méd. de Paris*, No. 8, 1889.

MACFARLANE, A. W., "Dreaming," *The Edinb. Med. J.*, 1890, Vol. 36.

MAINE DE BIRAN, *Nouvelles considérations sur le sommeil, les songes et le somnambulisme*, ed. Cousin, 1792.

Sleep; Its Physiology, Pathology and Psychology, London, 1897.

MANACEINE, MARIE DE, *Le sommeil, tiers de notre vie*, Paris, 1896.

Sleep: Its Physiology, Pathology and Psychology, London, 1897.

MAUDSLEY, *The Pathology of Mind*, 1879.

MAURY, A., "Analogies des phénomènes du rêve et de l'aliénation mentale," *Annales méd. psych.*, 1853, V, VI.

"De certains faits observés dans les rêves," *Ann. méd.-psychol.*, 1857, Vol. III.

Le sommeil et les rêves, Paris, 1878.

MEISEL (PSEUD.), *Natürlich-gottliche und teuflische Träume*, Sieghartstein, 1783.

MELINAUD, "Dream and Reality," *Pop. Sc. Mo.*, Vol. LIV, pp. 96-103.

MELZENTIN, C., Über wissenschaftliche Traumdeutung," *Die Gegenwart*, No. 50, 1899.

MENTZ, RICH., *Die Träume in den altfranzösischen Karls- und Artus-Epen.*, Marburg, 1888.

MONROE, W. S., "A Study of Taste-Dreams," *Am. J. of Psychol.*, January, 1899.

MOREAU DE LA SARTHE, "Rêve," *Dict. des. sc. méd.* Vol. 48. Paris, 1820.

MOREAU, J., "De l'Identité de l'état de rêve et de folie," *Annales méd.-psych.*, 1855, p. 261.

MORSELLI, A., "Dei sogni nei Genii," *La Cultura*, 1899.

MOTET, "Cauchemar," *Dict. de méd. et de chir. pratiques*.

MURRY, J. C., "Do we ever Dream of Tasting?" *Proc. of the Americ. Psychol.*, 1894, 20.

NAGELE, ANTON, "Der Traum in der epischen Dichtung," *Programm der Realschule*, Marburg, 1889.

NELSON, J., "A Study of Dreams," *Amer. J. of Psychology*, I, 1888.

392 SIGMUND FREUD

NEWBOLD, W. R., "Sub-conscious Reasoning," *Proc. Soc. Ps. Res.,* 1896, XII, 11-20.
"Über Traumleistungen," *Psychol. Rev.,* March, 1896, p. 132.

PASSAVANTI, JAC., *Libro dei sogni.* Bibl. diamante, Rome, 1891.

PAULHAN, *L'activité mentale et les éléments de l'esprit,* Paris, 1889.
"A Propos de l'activité de l'esprit dans le rêve," *Rev. philos.,* Vol. 38, 1894, pp. 546-548.

PFAFF, E. R., *Das Traumleben und seine Deutung nach den Prinzipien der Araber, Perser, Griechen, Indier und Ägypter,* Leipzig, 1868.

PICHON, *Contribution à l'étude des délires oniriques ou délires de rêve,* Thèse de Bordeaux, 1896.

PICK, A., "Über pathologische Träumerei und ihre Beziehungen zur Hysterie," *Jahrbuch für Psychiatrie,* 1896.

PILCZ, "Über eine gewisse Gesetzmässigkeit in den Träumen," *Monatsschrift für Psychologie und Neurologie,* March, 1899.

PRÉVOST, "Quelques observations psychologiques sur le sommeil." *Bibl. univ. des sc., belles-lettres et arts,* 1834, Vol. I, *Littérature,* pp. 225-248.

PURKINJE, "Wachen, Schlaf, Traum und verwandte Zustände" in Wagners *Handwörterbuch der Physiologie,* 1846.

RADESTOCK, P., *Schlaf und Traum,* Leipzig, 1878.

RAMM, KONRAD, *Diss, pertractans somnia,* Vienna, 1889.

RÉGIS, "Les Rêves," *La Gironde (Variétés),* Bordeaux, May 31, 1890.
"Des Hallucinations oniriques des dégénérés mystiques," *C. R. du Congrès des méd. aliénistes,* etc., 5th sess., 1894, Paris, 1895, p. 260.
"Rêves et l'hypnotisme," *Le Monde,* August 25, 1890.

RICHARD, JÉRÔME, *La théorie des songes,* Paris, 1766.

RICHARDSON, B. W., "The Psychology of Dreams," *The Asclep.,* London, 1892, IX, 129, 160.

ROBERT, W., *Der Traum als Naturnotwendigkeit erklärt,* Hamburg, 1886.

RICHIER, *Onéirologie ou dissertation sur les songes considérés dans l'état de maladie,* Thèse de Paris, 1816.

ROBINSON, L., "What Dreams are made of," *N. Americ. Rev. New York,* 1893, CI, VII, 687-697.

ROUSSET, *Contribution à l'étude du cauchemar,* Thèse de Paris, 1876.

ROUX, J., "Les Rêves et les délires oniriques," *Province méd.,* 1898, p. 212.

RYFF, WALTHER HERM., *Traumbüchlein,* Strassburg, 1554.

SANTE DE SANCTIS, *Emozione e sogni,* 1896.
"I Sogni nei delinquenti," *Arch. di psichiatr. e antrop. criminale,* Turin, 1896, XVII, 488-498.
I Sogni e il sonno nell' isterismo e nella epilessia, Rome, 1896.

Les Maladies mentales at les rêves, 1897, (Extract from *Annales de la Société de médecine de Gand*).
"Sui Rapporti d' identità, di somiglianza, di analogia e di equivilenza fra sogno e pazzia," *Rivista quindicinale di Psicologia, Psichiatria, Neuro-patologia,* 15. Nov., 1897.
"I sogni dei neuropatici e dei pazzi," *Arch. di psichiatr. e. antrop. crim.,* 1898, 4 Vols.
"Psychoses et rêves," *Rapport au Congrès de neurol. et d'hypnologie de Bruxelles,* 1898. Comptes rendus. H, p. 137.
I Sogni, Torino, 1899 (German trans. by O. Schmidt, Halle, 1901).

SANTEL, ANTON, "Poskus raz kladbe nekterih pomentjivih prikazni spanja in sanj.," *Progr. Gym. Görz,* 1874.

SARLO, F. DE, "I Sogni," *Saggio psicologico,* Naples, 1887.

SCH., FR., "Etwas über Träume," *Psych. Studien,* 1897, pp. 686-694.

SCHERNER, R. A., *Das Leben des Traumes,* Berlin, 1861.

SCHLEICH, K. L., "Traum und Schlaf," *Die Zukunft,* 1899, Vol. 29, pp. 14-27, 54-65.

SCHLEIERMACHER, FR., *Psychologie,* edited by L. George, Berlin, 1862.

SCHOLZ, FR., *Schlaf und Traum,* Leipzig, 1887.

SCHOPENHAUER, "Versuch über das Geistersehen und was damit zusammenhängt," in *Parerga und Paralipomena,* Berlin, 1857.

SCHUBERT, GOTTHILF HEINRICH, *Die Symbolik des Traumes,* Bamberg, 1844.

SCHWARTZKOPFF, P., *Das Leben im Traum, Eine Studie,* Leipzig, 1887.

"Science of Dreams," *The Lyceum.* Dublin, October, 1890, p. 28.

SIEBECK, A., *Das Traumleben der Seele,* 1877, Sammlung Virchow-Holtzendorf, No. 279.

SIMON, M., *Le monde des rêves,* Paris, 1888, *Bibliothèque scientifique contemporaine.*

SPITTA, W., *Die Schlaf- und Traumzustände der menschlichen Seele,* 2nd. edition, Freiburg i. B., 1892.

STEVENSON, R. L., "A Chapter on Dreams," in *Across the Plains,* 1892.

STRICKER, *Studien über das Bewusstsein,* Vienna, 1879.
Studien über die Assoziation der Vorstellungen, Vienna, 1883.

STRÜMPELL, L. *Die Natur und Entstehung der Träume,* Leipzig, 1877.

STRYK, M. v., "Der Traum und die Wirklichkeit," (nach C. Melinaud) *Baltische Monatsschrift,* Riga, 1899, pp. 189-210.

STUMPF, E. J. G., *Der Traum und seine Deutung,* Leipzig, 1899.

SULLY, J., "Etude sur les rêves," *Rev. scientif.,* 1882, p. 385.
Les illusions des sens et de l'esprit. Bibl. scientif. internat., vol. 62. Paris.

Human mind, London, 1892.

"Dreams as a Revelation," *Fortnightly Rev.* March, 1893.

"Laws of Dream-Fancy," *Cornhill Mag.*, Vol. L, p. 540.

"Dreams," in *Encyclop. Brit.*, 9th edition.

Summers, T. O., "The Physiology of Dreaming," *Saint-Louis Clin.*, 1895, VIII, 401-406.

Surbled, *Le Rêve*, 2nd edition, 1898.

"Origine des rêves," *Rev. de quest. scient.*, 1895.

Synesius, *Oneiromantik* (German trans. by Krauss), Vienna, 1888.

Tannery, M. P., "Sur l'Activité de l'esprit dans le rêve," *Rev. philos.*, XXXVIII, pp. 630-634, 1894.

"Sur les Rêves des mathématiciens," *Rev. philos.*, 1898, I, p. 639.

"Sur la Paramnésie dans les rêves," *Rev. philos.*, 1898.

"Sur la Mémoire dans le rêve," *Revue philosophique*, XLV, 1898.

Thiéry, A., "Aristote et Psychologie physiologique du rêve," *Rev. nev. scol.*, 1896, III, 260-271.

Thomayer, S., "Sur la Signification de quelques rêves," *Rev. neurol.*, No. 4, 1897.

"Beitr. zur Pathologie der Träume," *Poliklinik der tschechischen Universität*, Prag, 1897.

Tissié, Ph., "Les Rêves; rêves pathogènes et thérapeutiques; rêves photographiés," *Journ. de méd. de Bordeaux*, 1896, XXVI.

Les rêves, physiologie et pathologie, 1898. Bibliothèque de philosophie contemporaine.

Titchener, "Taste Dreams," *Amer. J. of Psychology*, VI, 1893.

Tonnini, "Suggestione e sogni," *Arch. di psichiatr. antrop. crim.*, III, 1887.

Tonsor, J. Heinrich, *Disp. de vigilia, somno et somniis, prop. Lucas*, Marpurgi, 1627.

"Traum," *Allgemeinen Enzyklopädie der Wissenschaft und Künste*, von Ersch und Gruber.

Traumbuch. Apomasaris (German trans. from the Latin trans. from the Greek by Lewenklaw). Wittemberg.

Tuke Hack, "Dreaming," *Dict. of Psycholog. Med.*, 1892.

Ullrich, M. W., *Der Schlaf und das Traumleben, Geisteskraft und Geistesschwäche*, 3rd edition, Berlin, 1897.

Unger, F., *Die Magie des Traumes als Unsterblichkeitsbeweis*. Nebst Vorw.: *Okkultismus und Sozialismus* von C. du Prel, 2nd edition, Münster, 1898.

Utility of Dreams. Edit. *J. Comp. Neurol.* Granville, 1893, III, 17-34.

Vaschide, "Recherches experim. sur les rêves," *Comptes rendus de l'acad. des sciences*, 17 July, 1899.

Vespa, B., "I sogni nei neuro-psicopatici," *Bull. Soc. Lancisiana*, Rome, 1897.

Vignoli, "Von den Träumen, Illusionen und Halluzinationen. *Internationale wissenschaftliche Bibliothek*, Vol. 47.

Vischer, F. Th., "Studien über den Traum," *Beilage z. Allg. Ztg.*, 1876, Nos. 105-107.

Vold, J. Mourly, "Einige Experimente über Gesichtsbilder im Traume," *Dritter internationaler Kongress für Psychologie in München*, 1897; *Zeitschr. für Psychologie und Physiologie der Sinnesorgane*, XIII, 66-74.

Expériences sur les rêves et en particulier sur ceux d'origine musculaire et optique, Christiana, 1896; reprinted in *Revue philosophique*, XLII. 1896.

Vykoukal, F. V., *Über Träume und Traumdeutungen (tschechisch)*, Prague, 1898.

Wedel, R., "Untersuchungen ausländischer Gelehrter über gew. Traumphänomene," *Beiträge zur Grenzwissenschaft*, 1899, pp. 24-77.

Weed, Hallam, and Phinney, "A Study of the Dream-Consciousness," *Americ. J. of Psychol.*, Vol. VII, 1895, pp. 405-411.

Wehr, Hans, "Das Unbewusste im menschlichen Denken," *Programm der Oberrealschule zu Klagenfurt*, 1887.

Weil, Alex, *La philosophie du rêve*, Paris.

Wendt, K., *Kriemhilds Traum*, Diss. Rostock, 1858.

Weygandt, W., *Entstehung der Träume*, Leipzig, 1893.

Wilks, S., "On the Nature of Dreams," *Med. Mag. London*, 1893-1894, II, 597-606.

Williams, H. S. "The Dream State and its Psychic Correlatives," *Americ. J. of Insanity*, 1891-1892, Vol. 17, 445-457.

Woodworth, "Note on the Rapidity of Dreams," *Psychol. Review*, IV, 1897, No. 5.

Wundt, *Grundzüge der physiologischen Psychologie*, 2 Vols., 2nd edition, 1880.

X, "Ce qu'on peut rêver en cinq secondes," *Rev. sc.*, 3ᵉ série, I, XII, 30 October, 1886.

Zucarelli, "Pollutions nocturnes et épilepsie," *Bull. de la Soc. le méd. ment. de Belgique*, March, 1895.

(B) Since 1900

Abraham, Karl, *Traum und Mythos, Eine Studie zur Völkerpsychologie*. Schriften zur angew. Seelenkunde, No. 4, Vienna and Leipzig, 1900.

"Über hysterische Traumzustände," *Jahrbuch f. psychoanalyt. und psychopathol. Forschungen.* Vol. II, 1910.

"Sollen wir die Pat ihre Träume aufschreiben lassen?" *Intern. Zeitschr. für ärztl. Ps.-A.*, I, 1913, p. 194.

"Zur narzisstischen Bewertung der Exkretionsvorgänge im Traum und Neurose," *Internat. Zeitschr. f. Ps.-A.*, VI, 64.

Adler, Alfred, "Zwei Träume einer Prostituierten," *Zeitschrift f. Sexualwissenschaft*, 1908, No. 2.

"Ein erlogener Traum." *Zentralbl. f. Psychoanalyse*," 1910, No. 3.

"Traum und Traumdeutung," *Ibid.*, III, 1912-1913, p. 174.

AMRAM, NATHAN, *Sepher pithrôn chalômôth*, Jerusalem, 1901.

BANCHIERI, F., "I Sogni dei bambini di cinque anni," *Riv. di psicol.*, 8, 325-330.

BETLHEIM u. HARTMANN, "Über Fehlreaktionen bei der Korsakoffschen Psychose," *Arch. f. Psychiatrie*, Vol. 72, 1924.

BLEULER, E., "Die Psychoanalyse Freuds," *Jahrb. f. psychoanalyt. u. psychopatholog. Forschungen*, Vol. II, 1910.

"Träume mit auf der Hand liegender Deutung," *Münch. Med. Woch.* 60. Jahrg. No. 47, 11 November, 1913.

BLOCH, ERNST, "Beitrag zu den Träumen nach Coitus interruptus," *Zentralbl. für Ps.-A.*, II, 1911-1912, p. 276.

BREWSTER, E. T., "Dreams and Forgetting, New discoveries in dream psychology," *McClure's Magazine*, October, 1912.

BRILL, A. A., "Dreams and their Relation to the Neuroses," *New York Medical Journ.*, 23 April, 1910.

Psychoanalysis, Its theory and practical application, Philadelphia and New York, 1912.

"Hysterical Dreamy States," *New York Medical Journ.*, 25 May, 1912.

"Artificial Dreams and Lying," *Journ. of Abn. Psych.*, Vol. IX, p. 321.

"Fairy-tales as a Determinant of Dreams and Neurotic Symptoms," *New York Medical Journ.*, 21 March, 1914.

BROWN, W., "Freud's Theory of Dreams," *The Lancet*, 19 and 26, April, 1913.

BRUCE, A. H., "The Marvels of Dream-Analysis," *McClure's Magazine*, November, 1912.

BURCKHARD, MAX, "Ein modernes Traumbuch," *Die Zeit*, 1900, Nos. 275, 276.

BUSEMANN, A., "Traumleben der Schulkinder," *Ztschr. f. päd. Psychol.*, 10, J. 1909, 294-301.

"Psychol. d. kindl. Traumerlebnisse," *Zeitschr. f. päd. Psychol.*, 1910, XI, p. 320.

CLAPARÉDE, E., "Esquisse d'une théorie biologique du sommeil," *Arch. de Psychol.*, Vol. IV, Nos. 15-16, February-March, 1905.

"Rêve utile," *Arch. de Psychol.*, 9, 1910, 148.

CORIAT, I., "Zwei sexual-symbolische Beispiele von Zahnarzt-Träumen," *Zentralbl. f. Ps.-A.*, III, 1912-1913, p. 440.

"Träume vom Kahlwerden," *Int. Zeitschr. f. Ps.-A.*, II, p. 460.

The Meaning of Dreams, Mind and Health series. London, Heinemann.

DELACROIX, "Sur la structure logique du rêve," *Rev. metaphys.*, November, 1904.

"Note sur la cohérence des rêves," *Rapp. et C. R. du 2. Congrès intern. de Philos.*, 556-560.

DELAGE, "La Nature des images hypnagogiques et le rôle des lueurs entoptiques dans le rêve," *Bull. de l'Instit. général psychol.*, 1903, pp. 235-247.

DOGLIA, S., and BIANCHIERI, F., "I sogni dei bambini di tre anni, L'inizio dell' attivita onirica," *Contributi psicol.*, 1, 9.

EDER, M. D., "Freud's Theory of Dreams," *Transactions of the Psycho-Medic. Soc.*, London, Vol. III, Part 3, 1912.

"Augenträume," *Internat. Ztschr. f. ärztl. Ps.-A*, I, 1913, p. 157.

EEDEN, FREDERIK VAN, "A Study of Dreams," *Proceedings of the Society for Psych. Research*, Part LXVII, Vol. XXVI.

ELLIS, HAVELOCK, "The Logic of Dreams," *Contemp. Rev.*, 98, 1910, pp. 353-359.

"The Symbolism of Dreams," *The Popular Science Monthly*, July, 1910.

"Symbolismen in den Träumen," *Zeitschr. f. Psychotherapie*, III, 1911, pp. 29-46.

The World of Dreams, London, 1911.

"The Relation of Erotic Dreams to Vesical Dreams," *Journ. of Abn. Psychol.*, VIII, 3, August-September, 1913.

FEDERN, PAUL, "Ein Fall von pavor nocturnus mit subjektiven Lichterscheinungen," *Internat. Zeitschr. f. ärztl. Ps.-A.*, I, 1913, H. 6.

"Über zwei typische Traumsensationen," *Jahrb. f. Ps.-A.*, VI, p. 89.

"Zur Frage des Hemmungstraumes," *Internat. Zeitschr. f. Ps.-A.*, VI, p. 73.

FERENCZI, S., "Die psychologische Analyse der Träume," *Psychiatrisch-Neurologische Wochenschrift*, XII. Nos. 11-13, June, 1910. (English translation: "The Psychological Analysis of Dreams," *The American Journal of Psychology*, April, 1910.)

"Symbolische Darstellung des Lust- und Realitätsprinzips im Ödipus-Mythos," *Imago*, I, 1912, p. 276.

"Über lenkbare Träume," *Zentralbl. f. Ps.-A.*, II, 1911-1912, p. 31.

"Vergessen eines Symptoms und seine Aufklärung im Traume," *Internat. Zeitschr. f. Ps.-A.*, II, p. 384.

"Affektvertauschung im Traum," *Internat. Zeitschr. f. Ps.-A.*, IV, p. 112.

"Träume von Ahnungslosen," *Internat. Zeitschr. f. Ps.-A.*, IV, p. 208.

"Pollution ohne orgastischen Traum und Orgasmus im Traum ohne Pollution," *Internat. Zeitschr. f. Ps.-A.*, IV, p. 187.

FLOURNOY, "Quelques Rêves au sujet de la signification symbolique de l'eau et du feu," *Internat. Zeitschr. f. Ps.-A.*, VI, p. 328.

FÖRSTER, M., "Das lat.-altengl. Traumbuch," *Arch. f. d. Stud. d. n. Spr. u. Lit.*, Vol. 120, p. 43ff; Vol. 125, pp. 39-70; Vol. 127, p. 1ff.

"Mittelenglische Traumbücher," *Herrings Archiv*, 1911.

FOUCAULT, MARCEL, *Le Rêve, Etudes et observations*, Bibl. de Philosophie contemporaine. Paris, 1906.

Friedjung, J. K., "Traum eines sechsjährigen Mädchens," *Internat. Ztschr. f. ärztl. Ps.-A.*, I, 913, p. 71.

Frink, H. W., "Dreams and their Analysis in Reference to Psychotherapy," *Med. Record*, 27 May, 1911.
"On Freud's Theory of Dreams," *Americ. Med.*, Burlington, New York, VI, pp. 652-661.
"Dream and Neurosis," *Interstate Med. Journ.*, 1915.

Gincburg, Mira, "Mitteilung von Kindheitsträumen mit spezieller Bedeutung," *Int. Ztschr. f. ärztl. Ps.-A.*, I, 913, p. 79.

Gottschalk, "Le Rêve D'après les idées du prof. Freud," *Archives de Neurol.*, 1912, No. 4.

Gregory, J. C., "Dreams as a By-product of Waking Activity," *Westm. Rev.*, London, 1911, Vol. 175, pp. 561-567.

Harnik, J., "Gelungene Auslegung eines Traumes," *Zentralbl. f. Ps.-A.*, II, 1911-1912, p. 417.

Hitschmann, Ed., *Freuds Neurosenlehre, Nach ihrem gegenwärtigen Stande zusammenfassend dargestellt*, Wien und Leipzig, 1911, 2nd edition, 1913 (chapter 5 *"Der Traum"*) (English translation by C. R. Payne, New York, 1912).
"Ein Fall von Symbolik für Ungläubige," *Zentralbl. f. Ps.-A.*, I, 1910-1911, p. 235.
"Beiträge zur Sexualsymbolik des Traumes," *Ibid.*, p. 561.
"Weitere Mitt. von Kindheitsträumen mit spez. Bedeutung," *Intern. Ztschr. für ärztl. Ps.-A.*, I, 1913, p. 476.
"Goethe als Vatersymbol in Träumen," *Ibid.*, No. 6.
"Über Träume Gottfried Kellers," *Internat. Zeitschr. f. Ps.-A.*, II, p. 41.
"Weitere Mitteilung von Kindheitsträumen mit spezieller Bedeutung," *Internat. Zeitschr. f. Ps.-A.*, II, p. 31.
"Über eine im Traum angekündigte Reminiszenz an ein sexuelles Jugenderlebnis," *Internat. Zeitschr. f. Ps.-A.*, V, p. 205.

Hug-Hellmuth, H. v., "Analyse eines Traumes eines 5½ jährigen Knaben," *Zentralbl. f. Ps.-A.*, II, 1911-1912, pp. 122-127.
"Kinderträume," *Internat. Zeitschr. f. ärztl. Ps.-A.*, I, 1913, p. 470.
Aus dem Seelenleben des Kindes. Schr. z. angew. Seelenk., ed. Freud, No. 15, Vienna and Leipzig, 1913.
"Ein Traum, der sich selber deutet," *Internat. Zeitschr. f. Ps.-A.*, III, p. 33.

Jones, Ernest, "On the Nightmare," *American Journ. of Insanity*, January, 1910.
"The Oedipus-Complex as an Explanation of Hamlet's Mystery: A Study in Motive," *American Journ. of Psychology*, January, 1910, pp. 72-113.
"Freud's Theory of Dreams," *American Journ. of Psychology*, April, 1910.

"Remarks on Dr. M. Prince's Article: 'The Mechanism and Interpr. of Dreams'," *Journ. of Abn. Psychol.*, 1910-1911, pp. 328-336.
"Some Instances of the Influence of Dreams on Waking Life," *Journ. of Abn. Psychol.*, April-May, 1911.
"The Relationship between Dreams and Psychoneurotic Symptoms," *American Journ. of Insanity*, Vol. 68, No. 1, July, 1911.
"A Forgotten Dream," *Journ. of Abn. Psychol.*, April-May, 1912.
Papers on Psycho-Analysis, London, 1912.
Der Alptraum in seiner Beziehung zu gewissen Formen des mittelalterl. Aberglaubens. Schriften zur angew. Seelenk., ed. Freud, No. 14, Leipzig and Vienna, 1912.
"Die Theorie der Symbolik," *Internat, Zeitschr. f. Ps.-A.*, V, p. 244.

Jung, C. G., "L'analyse des rêves," *L'année Psychologique*, Vol. XV.
Assoziation, Traum und hysterisches Symptom. Diagnostische Assoziationsstudien. Beiträge zur experimentellen Psychopathologie, ed. C. G. Jung, vol. II, Leipzig, 1910 (No. VIII, pp. 31-66).
"Ein Beitrag zur Psychologie des Gerüchtes," *Zentralbl. für Psychoanalyse.*, I, 1910, No. 3.

Jung, C. G., "Ein Beitrag zur Kenntnis des Zahlentraumes," *ibid.* 1910-1911, pp. 567-572.
"Morton Prince's: 'The Mechanism and Interpretation of Dreams,' Eine kritische Besprechung," *Jahrb. f. Ps.-A. u. psychopathol. Forsch.*, III, 1911.

Iwaya, S., "Traumdeutung in Japan," *Ostasien*, 1902, p. 302.

Karpinska, L., "Ein Beitrag zur Analyse sinnloser Worte im Traume," *Internat. Zeitschr. f. Ps.-A.*, III, p. 164.

Kazodowsky, A., "Zusammenhang von Träumen und Wahnvorstellungen," *Neurolog. Cbl.*, 1901, pp. 440-447, 508-514.

Kostyleff, "Freud et le probléme des rêves," *Rev. philos.*, Vol. 72, July-December, 1911, pp. 491-522.

Kraepelin, E., "Über Sprachstörungen im Traume," *Psychol. Arbeiten*, 5, Leipzig, 1907.

Lauer, Ch., "Das Wesen des Traumes in der Beurteilung der talmudischen und rabbinischen Literatur," *Intern. Ztschr. f. ärztl. Ps.-A.*, I, 1913, No. 5.

Lehmann, *Aberglaube und Zauberei von den ältesten Zeiten bis in die Gegenwart. Deutsch von Petersen.* (2nd enlarged edition.) Stuttgart, 1908.

Leroy, B., "A propos de quelques rêves symboliques," *Journ. de psychol. Norm. et pathol.*, 5, 1908, pp. 358-365.
And Tobowolska, J., "Mécanisme intellectuel du rêve," *Rev. philos.*, 1901, I, Vol. 51, pp. 570-593.

LÖWINGER, *Der Traum in der jüdischen Literatur,* Leipzig, 1908. *Mitteilungen zur jüd. Volkskunde,* 10. Jahrg., Nos. 1 and 2.

MAEDER, ALPHONSE, "Essai d'interprétation de quelques rêves," *Archives de Psychol.,* Vol. VI, No. 24, April, 1907.

"Die Symbolik in den Legenden, Märchen, Gebräuchen und Träumen," *Psychiatrisch-Neurolog. Wochenschr.,* X. Jahrg., 1908.

"Zur Entstehung der Symbolik im Traum, in der Dementia praecox, etc." *Zentralblatt f. Ps.-A.,* I, 1910-1911, pp. 383-389.

"Über die Funktion des Traumes," *Jahrb. f. psychoanalyt. Forsch.,* IV, 1912.

"Über das Traumproblem," *Ibid.,* V, 1913, p. 647.

"Zur Frage der teleologischen Traumfunktion," *Ibid.,* p. 453.

MARCINOWSKI, J., "Gezeichnete Träume," *Zentralbl. f. Ps.-A.,* II, 1911-1912, pp. 490-518.

"Drei Romane in Zahlen," *Ibid.,* pp. 619-638.

MITCHELL, A., *About Dreaming, Laughing and Blushing,* London, 1905.

MIURA, K., "Japanische Traumdeuterei," *Mitt. d. deutsch. Ges. f. Natur- u, Völkerk Ostasiens,* X, pp. 291-306.

NÄCKE, P., "Über sexuelle Träume," *H. Gross' Archiv.,* 1903, p. 307.

"Der Traum als feinstes Reagens f. d. Akt d. sexuellen Empfindens," *Monatsschrift f. Krim.-Psychol.,* 1905.

"Kontrastträume und spez. sexuelle Kontrastträume," *H. Gross' Archiv,* Vol. 24, 1907, pp. 1-19.

"Beiträge zu den sexuellen Träumen," *H. Gross' Archiv.,* 29, pp. 363 ff.

"Die diagnostische und prognostische Brauchbarkeit der sex. Träume," *Arztl. Sachv.-Ztg.,* 1911, No. 2.

NEGELEIN, J. v., *Der Traumschlüssel des Yaggaddeva,* Giessen, 1912. (*Relig. Gesch. Vers.,* XI, 4.)

PACHANTONI, D., "Der Traum als Ursprung von Wahnideen bei Alkoholdeliranten," *Zentralbl. f. Nervenheilk.,* 32. Jahrg., 1909, p. 796.

PEAR, T. H., "The Analysis of Some Personal Dreams, with Special Reference to Freud's Interpretation; Meeting at the British Assoc. for the advancement of science, Birmingham, 16-17 September, 1913," *British Journ. of. Psychol.,* VI, 3-4, February, 1914.

PÖTZL, OTTO, "Experimentell erregte Traumbilder in ihren Beziehungen zum indirekten Sehen," *Zeitschr. f. d. ges. Neurol. u. Psych.,* Vol. 37, 1917.

PFISTER, OSKAR, "Wahnvorstellung und Schülerselbstmord. Auf Grund einer Traumanalyse beleuchtet," *Schweiz. Blätter für Schulgesundheitspflege,* 1909, No. 1.

"Kryptolalie, Kryptographie und unbewusstes Vexierbild bei Normalen," *Jahrb. f. Ps.-A. Forschg.,* V, 1, 1913.

PRINCE, MORTON, "The Mechanism and Interpretation of Dreams," *Journ. of Abn. Psychol.,* October-November, 1910.

"The Mechanism and Interpretation of Dreams; a reply to Dr. Jones," *Journ. of Abn. Psychol.,* 1910-1911, pp. 337-353.

PUTNAM, J. J., "Aus der Analyse zweier Treppen-Träume," *Zentralbl. f. Ps.-A.,* II, 1911-1912, p. 264.

"Ein charakteristischer Kindertraum," *Ibid.,* p. 328.

"Dream-interpretation and the theory of Psycho-analysis," *Journ. of Abn. Psychol.,* IX, No. 1, p. 36.

RAALTE, F. van, "Kinderdroomen," *Het Kind,* 1912. January.

RANK, OTTO, *Der Mythus von der Geburt des Helden.* Schr. z. angew. Seelenkunde, No. 5, Vienna and Leipzig, 1909.

"Beispiel eines verkappten Ödipus-Traumes," *Zentralblatt für Psychoanalyse,* I, 1910.

"Zum Thema der Zahnreizträume," *Ibid.*

"Das Verlieren als Symptomhandlung, zugleich ein Beitrag zum Verständnis der Beziehungen des Traumlebens zu den Fehlleistungen des Alltagslebens," *Ibid.*

"Ein Traum, der sich selbst deutet," *Jahrbuch für psychoanalyt. und psychopathol. Forschungen,* Vol. II, 1910.

"Ein Beitrag zum Narzissmus," *Ibid.,* Vol. III, 1911.

"Fehlleistung und Traum," *Zentralbl. f. Ps.-A.,* II, 1911-1912, p. 266.

"Aktuelle Sexualregungen als Traumanlässe," *Ibid.,* pp. 596-602.

"Die Symbolschichtung im Wecktraum und ihre Wiederkehr im mythischen Denken," *Jahrb. f. Ps.-A.,* IV, 1912.

Das Inzestmotiv in Dichtung und Sage, Grundzüge einer Psychologie des dichterischen Schaffens, Vienna and Leipzig, 1912.

"Die Nacktheit in Sage und Dichtung. Eine Ps.-A. Studie," *Imago,* II, 1912.

"Eine noch nicht beschriebene Form des Ödipus-Traumes," *Intern. Zeitschr. f. ärztl. Ps.-A.,* I, 1913, p. 151.

"Fehlhandlung und Traum," *Internat. Zeitschr. f. Ps.-A.,* III, p. 158.

"Die Geburtsrettungsphantasie in Traum und Dichtung," *Internat. Zeitschr. f. Ps.-A.,* II, p. 43.

"Ein gedichteter Traum," *Internat. Zeitschr. f. Ps.-A.,* III, p. 231.

RANK, O., and SACHS, H., "Die Bedeutung der Psychoanalyse für die Geisteswissenschaften." *Grenzfr. d. Nerven- u. Seelenlebens,* ed. Löwenfeld, No. 93, Wiesbaden, 1913.

REIK, TH., "Zwei Träume Flauberts," *Zentralbl. f. Ps.-A.,* III, 1912-1913, p. 223.

"Kriemhilds Traum," *Ibid.*, II, p. 416.

"Beruf und Traumsymbolik," *Ibid.*, p. 531.

"Der Nacktheitstraum eines Forschungsreisenden," *Internat. Zeitschr. f. Ps.-A.*, II, p. 463.

"Gotthilf Schuberts 'Symbolik des Traumes'," *Internat. Zeitschr. f. Ps.-A.*, III, p. 295.

"Völkerpsychologische Parallelen zum Traumsymbol des Mantels," *Internat. Zeitschr. f. Ps.-A.*, VI, p. 310.

"Zum Thema: Traum und Traumwandeln," *Internat, Zeitschr. f. Ps.-A.*, VI, p. 311.

ROBITSEK, ALFRED, "Die Analyse von Egmonts Traum," *Jahrb für psychoanalyt. und psychopathol. Forschungen*, Vol. II, 1910.

"Die Stiege, Leiter, als sexuelles Symbol in der Antike," *Zentralbl. f. Ps.-A.*, I, 1910-1911, p. 586.

"Zur Frage der Symbolik in den Träumen Gesunder," *Ibid.*, II, p. 340.

RÓHEIM, G., "Die Urszene im Traume," *Internat. Zeitschr. f. Ps.-A.*, VI, p. 337.

SACHS, HANNS, "Zur Darstellungstechnik des Träumes," *Zentralbl. f. Ps.-A.* I, 1910-1911.

"Ein Fall intensiver Traumentstellung," *Ibid.*, p. 588.

"Traumdeutung und Menschenkenntnis," *Jahrb. f. Ps.-A.*, III, 1911, p. 568.

"Ein Traum Bismarcks," *Intern. Ztschr. f. ärztl. Ps.-A.*, I, 1913, H. 1.

"Traumdarstellungen analer Weckreize," *Ibid.*, p. 489.

"Das Zimmer als Traumdarstellung des Weibes," *Internat. Zeitschr. f. Ps.-A.*, II, p. 35.

"Ein absurder Traum," *Internat. Zeitschr. f. Ps.-A.*, III, p. 35.

SADGER, J., "Über dass Unbewusste und die Träume bei Hebbel," *Imago*, June, 1913.

SCHRÖTTER, KARL, "Experimentelle Träume," *Zentralbl. f. Ps.-A.*, II, 1912, p. 638.

SCHWARZ, F., "Traum u. Traumdeutung nach 'Abdalgani an Nābulusi'," *Zeitschr. d. deutsch. morgenl. Ges.*, Vol. 67, 1913, No. 3, pp. 473-493.

SECKER, F., "Chines. Ansichten über den Traum," *Neue metaph. Rdschr.*, Vol. 17, 1909-1910, p. 101.

SILBERER, HERBERT, "Bericht über eine Methode, gewisse symbolische Halluzinations-erscheinungen hervorzurufen und zu beobachten," *Jahrb.* Vol. I, 1909.

"Phantasie und Mythos," *Ibid.* Vol. II, 1910.

"Symbolik des Erwachens und Schwellensymbolik überh." *Ibid.*, III, 1911.

"Über die Symbolbildung," *Ibid.*

"Zur Symbolbildung," *Ibid.*, IV, 1912.

"Spermatozoenträume," *Ibid.*

"Zur Frage der Spermatozoenträume," *Ibid.*

SPIELREIN, S., "Traum vom 'Pater Freudenreich'," *Intern. Ztschr. f. ärztl. Ps.-A.*, I, 1913, p. 484.

SPITTELER, KARL, "Meine frühesten Erlebnisse. I. Hilflos und sprachlos. Die Träume des Kindes," *Südd. Monatsh.*, October, 1913.

STÄRCKE, AUGUST, "Ein Traum, der das Gegenteil einer Wunscherfüllung zu verwirklichen schien, zugleich ein Beispiel eines Traumes, der von einem anderen Traum gedeutet wird," *Zentralbl. f. Ps.-A.*, II, 1911-1912, p. 86.

"Traumbeispiele," *Internat. Zeitschr. f. Ps.-A.*, II, p. 381.

STÄRCKE, JOHANN, "Neue Traumexperimente in Zusammenhang mit älteren und neueren Traumtheorien," *Jahrb. f. Ps.-A.*, V, 1913, p. 233.

STEGMANN, MARG., "Darstellung epileptischer Anfälle im Traume," *Intern. Zeitschr. f. ärztl. Ps.-A.*, I, 1913.

"Ein Vexiertraum," *Ibid.*, p. 486.

STEKEL, WILHELM, "Beiträge zur Traumdeutung," *Jahrbuch für psycho-analytische und psychopatholog. Forschungen*, Vol. 1. 1909.

Nervöse Angstzustände und ihre Behandlung, Vienna-Berlin, 1908, 2nd edition, 1912.

Die Sprache des Traumes. Eine Darstellung der Symbolik und Deutung des Traumes in ihren Beziehungen zur kranken und gesunden Seele für Ärzte und Psychologen, Wiesbaden, 1911.

Die Träume der Dichter, Wiesbaden, 1912.

"Ein prophetischer Nummerntraum," *Zentralbl. f. Ps.-A.*, II, 1911-1912, pp. 128-130.

"Fortschritte der Traumdeutung," *Zentralbl. f. Ps.-A.*, III, 1912-1913, pp. 154, 426.

"Darstellung der Neurose im Traum," *Ibid.*, p. 26.

SWOBODA, HERMANN, *Die Perioden des menschlichen Organismus*, Vienna and Leipzig, 1904.

TAUSK, V., "Zur Psychologie der Kindersexualität," *Intern. Zeitschr. f. ärztl. Ps.-A.*, I, 1913, p. 444.

"Zwei homosexuelle Träume," *Internat. Zeitschr. f. Ps.-A.*, II, p. 36.

"Ein Zahlentraum," *Internat. Zeitschr. f. Ps.-A.*, II, p. 39.

TFINKDJI, JOSEPH, ABBÉ, "Essai sur les songes et l'art de les interpréter (onirocritie) en Mésopotamie," *Anthropos*, VIII, 2s. 3d., March-June, 1913.

TOBOWOLSKA, JUSTINE, *Etude sur les illusions de temps dans les rêves du sommeil normal*," Thèse de Paris, 1900.

VASCHIDE, N. *Le Sommeil et les rêves*, Paris, 1911, *Bibl. de Philos. scient.* (66) (Contains bibliography of other titles by the same author on dreams and sleep).

AND PIÉRON. *La psychol. du rêve au point de vue médical*, Paris. 1902.

VOLD, J. MOURLY, *Über den Traum, Experimentell-psychologische Untersuchungen*, ed. O. Klemm, Vol. I, Leipzig, 1910; Vol. II, 1912.

WEISS, EDOARDO, "Totemmaterial im Traume," *Internat. Zeitschr. f. Ps.-A.* II, p. 159.

WEISS, KARL, "Ein Pollutionstraum," *Internat. Zeitschr. f. Ps.-A.,* VI, p. 343.

WEYGANDT, W., "Beitr. z. Psychologie des Traumes," *Philos. Studien,* Vol. 20, 1902, pp. 456-486.

WIGGAM, A., "A Contribution to the Data of Dream Psychology," *Pedagogical Seminary,* June, 1909.

WINTERSTEIN, ALFR. v., "Zum Thema: 'Lenkbare Träume'," *Zentralbl. f. Ps.-A.,* II, 1911-1912, p. 290.

WULFF, M., "Ein interessanter Zusammenhang von Traum, Symbolhandlung und Krankheitssymptom," *Internat. Ztschr. f. ärztl. Ps.-A.,* I, 1913, No. 6.

On Narcissism: an Introduction[1]

I

The word *narcissism* is taken from clinical terminology and was chosen by P. Näcke[2] in 1899 to denote the attitude of a person who treats his own body in the same way as otherwise the body of a sexual object is treated; that is to say, he experiences sexual pleasure in gazing at, caressing and fondling his body, till complete gratification ensues upon these activities. Developed to this degree, narcissism has the significance of a perversion, which has absorbed the whole sexual life of the subject; consequently, in dealing with it we may expect to meet with phenomena similar to those for which we look in the study of all perversions.

Now those engaged in psycho-analytic observation were struck by the fact that isolated features of the narcissistic attitude are found in many people who are characterized by other aberrations—for instance, as Sadger states, in homosexuals—and at last it seemed that a disposition of the libido which must be described as narcissistic might have to be reckoned with in a much wider field, and that it might claim a place in the regular sexual development of human beings.[3] Difficulties in psycho-analytic work upon neurotics led to the same supposition, for it seemed as though this kind of narcissistic attitude in them was one of the factors limiting their susceptibility to influence. Narcissism in this sense would not be a perversion, but the libidinal complement to the egoism of the instinct of self-preservation, a measure of which may justifiably be attributed to every living creature.

A pressing motive for occupying ourselves with the conception of a primary and normal narcissism arose when the attempt was made to bring our knowledge of dementia praecox (Kraepelin), or schizophrenia (Bleuler), into line with the hypothesis upon which the libido-theory is based. Such patients, whom I propose to term *paraphrenics*, display two fundamental characteristics: they suffer from megalomania and they have withdrawn their interest from the external world (people and things). In consequence of this latter change in them, they are inaccessible to the influence of psycho-analysis and cannot be cured by our endeavours. But this turning away of the paraphrenic from the outer world needs to be more precisely characterized. A patient suffering from hysteria or obsessional neurosis has also, as far as the influence of his illness goes, abandoned his relation to reality. But analysis shows that he has by no means broken off his erotic relations to persons and things. He still retains them in phantasy; i.e., he has, on the one hand, substituted for actual objects imaginary objects founded on memories, or has blended the two; while, on the other hand, he has ceased to direct his motor activities to the attainment of his aims in connection with real objects. It is only to this condition of the libido that we may legitimately apply the term *introversion* of the libido which is used by Jung indiscriminately. It is otherwise with the paraphrenic. He seems really to have withdrawn his libido from persons and things in the outer world, without replacing them by others in his phantasy. When this does happen, the process seems to be a secondary one, part of an effort towards recovery, designed to lead the libido back towards an object.[4]

The question arises: What is the fate of the libido when withdrawn from external objects in schizophrenia? The megalomania characteristic of these conditions affords a clue here. It has doubtless come into being at the expense of the object-libido. The libido withdrawn from the outer world has been directed on to the ego, giving rise to a state which we may call *narcissism*. But the megalomania itself is no new phenomenon; on the contrary, it is, as we know, an exaggeration and plainer manifestation of a condition which had already existed previously. This leads us to the conclusion that the narcissism which arises when libidinal cathexes are called in away from external objects must be conceived of as a secondary form,

[1] First published in *Jahrbuch*, Vol. VI, 1914; reprinted in *Sammlung*, 4th Series.
[2] [In a later paper Professor Freud has corrected this slip and added the name of Havelock Ellis.—Ed.]
[3] Otto Rank, *Ein Beitrag zum Narzissmus*.

[4] Compare with these propositions my discussion of the *end of the world* in the analysis of Senatspräsident Schreber, *Collected Papers*, III, "Psycho-Analytic Notes upon an Autobiographical Account of a Case of Paranoia (Dementia Paranoides)." Also Abraham, *Die psychosexuellen Differenzen der Hysterie und der Dementia Praecox*.

superimposed upon a primary one that is obscured by manifold influences.

Let me expressly state that I am not attempting here to explain or penetrate further into the problem of schizophrenia, but am merely putting together what has been said elsewhere, in order that I may justify this introduction of the concept of narcissism.

This development of the libido-theory—in my opinion, a legitimate development—receives reinforcement from a third quarter, namely, from the observations we make and the conceptions we form of the mental life of primitive peoples and of children. In the former, we find characteristics which, if they occurred singly, might be put down to megalomania: an over-estimation of the power of wishes and mental processes, the *omnipotence of thoughts,* a belief in the magical virtue of words, and a method of dealing with the outer world—the art of *magic*—which appears to be a logical application of these grandiose premises.[1] In the child of our own day, whose development is much more obscure to us, we expect a perfectly analogous attitude towards the external world.[2] Thus we form a conception of an original libidinal cathexis of the ego, part of which cathexis is later yielded up to objects, but which fundamentally persists and is related to the object-cathexes much as the body of a protoplasmic animalcule is related to the pseudopodia which it puts out. In our researches, taking, as they did, neurotic symptoms for their starting point, this part of the disposition of the libido necessarily remained hidden from us at the outset. We were struck only by the emanations from this libido—the object-cathexes, which can be put forth and drawn back again. We perceive also, broadly speaking, a certain reciprocity between ego-libido and object-libido. The more that is absorbed by the one, the more impoverished does the other become. The highest form of development of which object-libido is capable is seen in the state of being in love, when the subject seems to yield up his whole personality in favor of object-cathexis; while we have the opposite condition in the paranoiac's phantasy (or self-perception) of the *end of the world.*[3] Finally, with reference to the differentiation of the energies operating in the

mind, we infer that at first in the narcissistic state they exist side by side and that our analysis is not a fine enough instrument to distinguish them; only where there is object-cathexis is it possible to discriminate a sexual energy—the libido—from an energy pertaining to the ego-instincts.

Before going any further, I must touch on two questions which lead us to the heart of the difficulties of our subject. In the first place: what is the relation of the narcissism of which we are now speaking to auto-erotism, which we have described as an early state of the libido? And secondly: if we concede to the ego a primary cathexis of libido, why is there any necessity for further distinguishing a sexual libido from a non-sexual energy pertaining to the ego-instincts? Would not the assumption of a uniform mental energy save us all the difficulties of differentiating the energy of the ego-instincts from ego-libido, and ego-libido from object-libido? On the first point I would comment as follows: it is impossible to suppose that a unity comparable to the ego can exist in the individual from the very start; the ego has to develop. But the auto-erotic instincts are primordial; so there must be something added to auto-erotism—some new operation in the mind—in order that narcissism may come into being.

To be required to give a definite answer to the second question must occasion perceptible uneasiness in every psycho-analyst. One dislikes the thought of abandoning observation for barren theoretical discussions, but all the same we must not shirk an attempt at explanation. Conceptions such as that of an ego-libido, an energy pertaining to the ego-instincts, and so on, are certainly neither very easy to grasp nor is their content sufficiently rich; a speculative theory of these relations of which we are speaking would, in the first place, require as its basis a sharply defined concept. But I am of the opinion that that is just the difference between a speculative theory and a science founded upon constructions arrived at empirically. The latter will not begrudge to speculation its privilege of a smooth, logically unassailable structure, but will itself be gladly content with nebulous, scarcely imaginable conceptions, which it hopes to apprehend more clearly in the course of its development, or which it is even prepared to replace by others. For these ideas are not the basis of the science upon which everything rests: that, on the contrary, is observation alone. They are not the foundation-stone, but

[1] Cf. the corresponding sections on this subject in my *Totem and Taboo,* (1913.)

[2] Cf. Ferenczi, *Stages in the Development of the Sense of Reality.*

[3] There are two mechanisms in this *end of the world* idea: in one case, the whole libidinal cathexis is drained off to the loved object, while, in the other, it all flows back to the ego.

the coping of the whole structure, and they can be replaced and discarded without damaging it. The same thing is happening in our day in the science of physics, the fundamental notions of which as regards matter, centres of force, attraction, etc., are scarcely less debatable than the corresponding ideas in psycho-analysis.

The value of the concepts *ego-libido* and *object-libido* is that they are derived from the study of the essential characteristics of neurotic and psychotic processes. The differentiation of the libido into that which is proper to the ego and that which attaches itself to objects is a necessary extension of an original hypothesis which discriminated between ego-instincts and sexual instincts. At any rate, analysis of the pure transference neuroses (hysteria and the obsessional neurosis) compelled me so to discriminate, and I only know that all attempts to account for these phenomena by other means have been completely unsuccessful.

In the complete absence of any theory of the instincts which would help us to find our bearings, we may be permitted, or rather, it is incumbent upon us, in the first place to work out any hypothesis to its logical conclusion, until it either fails or becomes confirmed. There are various points in favour of the hypothesis of a primordial differentiation between sexual instincts and other instincts, ego-instincts, besides the usefulness of such an assumption in the analysis of the transference neuroses. I admit that this latter consideration alone would not be decisive, for it might be a question of an indifferent energy operating in the mind which was converted into libido only by the act of object-cathexis. But, in the first place, this differentiation of concepts corresponds to the distinction between hunger and love, so widely current. And, in the second place, there are biological considerations in its favour. The individual does actually carry on a double existence: one designed to serve his own purposes and another as a link in a chain, in which he serves against, or at any rate without, any volition of his own. The individual himself regards sexuality as one of his own ends; while from another point of view he is only an appendage to his germ-plasm, to which he lends his energies, taking in return his toll of pleasure —the mortal vehicle of a (possibly) immortal substance—like the inheritor of an entailed property who is only the temporary holder of an estate which survives him. The differentiation of the sexual instincts from the ego-instincts would simply reflect this double func-

tion of the individual. Thirdly, we must recollect that all our provisional ideas in psychology will some day be based on an organic substructure. This makes it probable that special substances and special chemical processes control the operation of sexuality and provide for the continuation of the individual life in that of the species. We take this probability into account when we substitute special forces in the mind for special chemical substances.

Just because I try in general to keep apart from psychology everything that is not strictly within its scope, even biological thought, I wish at this point expressly to admit that the hypothesis of separate ego-instincts and sexual instincts (that is to say, the libido-theory) rests scarcely at all upon a psychological basis, but is essentially supported upon the facts of biology. So I shall also be consistent enough to drop this hypothesis if psycho-analytic work itself should suggest as more valuable another hypothesis about the instincts. So far, this has not happened. It may then be that—when we penetrate deepest and furthest—sexual energy, the libido, will be found to be only the product of a differentiation in the energy at work generally in the mind. But such a statement is of no importance. It has reference to matters so remote from the problems of our observation and so empty of available knowledge, that to dispute it is as idle as to affirm it; it is possible that this primordial identity has as little to do with our analytical interests as the primordial kinship of all human races has to do with the proof of kinship with a testator required by the Probate Court. All these speculations lead nowhere; since we cannot wait for another science to present us with a theory of the instincts ready-made, it is far more to the purpose that we should try to see what light may be thrown upon this basic problem of biology by a synthesis of psychological phenomena. Let us be fully aware of the possibility of error; but do not let us be deterred from carrying to its logical conclusion the hypothesis we first adopted of an antithesis between ego-instincts and sexual instincts (an hypothesis to which we were impelled by analysis of the transference neuroses), and so from seeing whether it turns out to be consistent and fruitful, and whether it may be applied to other affections also, e.g., to schizophrenia.

Of course, it would be a very different matter if it were proved that the libido-theory had already come to grief in the attempt to explain the last-named disease. That this is so has been maintained by C. G. Jung,[1] and so I have been obliged to enter upon this last disquisition, which I would gladly have been spared. I should have preferred, without any discussion of the premises, to follow out the course embarked upon in the analysis of the Schreber case. But Jung's assertion is, to say the least of it, premature. The grounds he gives for it are scanty. At the outset, he quotes me as saying that I myself have been obliged, owing to the difficulties of the Schreber analysis, to extend the conception of the libido, i.e., to give up its sexual content and to identify libido with psychic *interest* in general. Ferenczi, in an exhaustive criticism of Jung's work, has already said all that is necessary in correction of this erroneous interpretation.[2] I can only corroborate this critic and repeat that I have never thus retracted the libido-theory. Another argument of Jung's, namely, that we must not assume that the loss of the normal function of appreciating reality can be brought about only by the withdrawal of the libido, is no argument but a dictum. It begs the question, it anticipates the decision, and waives discussion; for whether and how this is possible is just what has to be investigated. In his next large work,[3] Jung just misses the solution which I had long since indicated: "At the same time there is this to be taken into consideration, a point to which Freud refers in his work on the Schreber case, that the introversion of the *libido sexualis* leads to a cathexis of the *ego* and that possibly it is this that produces the effect of a loss of reality. It is indeed a tempting possibility to explain the psychology of the loss of reality in this fashion." But Jung discusses this possibility very little further. A few pages later, he dismisses it with the remark that from this conditioning factor "would result, not dementia praecox, but the psychology of an ascetic anchorite." How little this inept comparison can help us to a conclusion may be learnt from the reflection that an anchorite who "tries to erase every trace of sexual interest" (but only in the popular sense of the word *sexual*) does not even necessarily display any pathogenic disposition of the libido. He may have turned away his interest from human beings entirely, and yet may have sublimated it to a heightened interest in the divine, in nature, or in the animal kingdom, without his libido having undergone introversion to his phantasies or retrogression to his ego. This comparison would seem to rule out in advance the possibility of differentiating between interest emanating from erotic or that from other sources. Further, when we remember that the researches of the Swiss school, however meritorious, have elucidated only two features in the picture of dementia praecox—the existence of complexes common to healthy and neurotic persons alike, and the similarity of the phantasy-formations of that disease to popular myths—but have not been able to throw any further light on the pathogenic mechanism, we may repudiate Jung's assertion that the libido-theory has broken down in the attempt to understand dementia praecox, and is therefore rendered invalid for the other neuroses also.

II

It seems to me that certain peculiar difficulties lie in the way of a direct study of narcissism. Our chief means of access to an understanding of this condition will probably remain the analysis of paraphrenics. As the transference neuroses have enabled us to trace the libidinal instinctual impulses, so dementia praecox and paranoia will give us insight into the psychology of the ego. Once more, in order to arrive at what is normal and apparently so simple, we shall have to study the pathological with its distortions and exaggerations. At the same time, there are other sources from which we may derive a knowledge of narcissism, which I will now mention in their order—namely, the study of organic disease, of hypochondria, and of love between the sexes.

In estimating the influence of organic disease upon the distribution of the libido, I follow a suggestion of S. Ferenczi's, which he made to me in conversation. It is universally known, and seems to us a matter of course, that a person suffering organic pain and discomfort relinquishes his interest in the things of the outside world, in so far as they do not concern his suffering. Closer observation teaches us that at the same time he withdraws libidinal interest from his love-objects: so long as he suffers, he ceases to love. The banality of this fact is no reason why we should be deterred from translating it into terms of the libido-theory. We should then say: the sick man withdraws his libidinal cathexes back upon his own ego, and sends them forth again when he recovers. "Concentrated is his soul," says W. Busch, of the poet suffering from toothache, "in

[1] *Wandlungen und Symbole der Libido.*
[2] *Zeitschrift*, Vol. I, 1913.
[3] *Versuch einer Darstellung der psychoanalytischen Theorie.*

his jaw-tooth's aching hole." Here libido and ego-interest share the same fate and have once more become indistinguishable from each other. The familiar egoism of the sick person covers them both. We find it so natural because we are certain that in the same situation we should behave in just the same way. The way in which the readiness to love, however great, is banished by bodily ailments, and suddenly replaced by complete indifference, is a theme which has been sufficiently exploited by comic writers.

The condition of *sleep*, like illness, implies a narcissistic withdrawal of the libido away from its attachments back to the subject's own person, or more precisely, to the single desire for sleep. The egoism of dreams fits in very well in this connection. In both states we have, if nothing else, examples of changes in the distribution of the libido which are consequent upon a change in the ego.

Hypochondria, like organic disease, manifests itself in distressing and painful bodily sensations and also concurs with organic disease in its effect upon the distribution of the libido. The hypochondriac withdraws both interest and libido—the latter specially markedly—from the objects of the outer world and concentrates both upon the organ which engages his attention. A difference between hypochondria and organic disease now becomes evident: in the latter, the distressing sensations are based upon demonstrable organic changes; in the former, this is not so. But it would be entirely in keeping with our general conception of the processes of neurosis if we decided to say that hypochondria must be right; organic changes cannot be absent in it either. Now in what could such changes consist?

Here we may fall back upon our experience, which shows that bodily sensations of a painful nature, comparable to those of hypochondria, are not lacking in the other neuroses. I have said once before that I am inclined to class hypochondria with neurasthenia and anxiety-neurosis as a third *actual neurosis*. Probably it would not be going too far to put it in this way: that in the other neuroses too there is regularly present some small admixture of hypochondria. Perhaps we have the best example of this in the anxiety-neurosis and in the hysteria superimposed upon it. Now the familiar prototype of an organ sensitive to pain, in some way changed and yet not diseased in the ordinary sense, is that of the genital organ in a state of excitation. It becomes congested with blood, swollen, moist, and is the seat of manifold sensations. If we apply to that activity of a given bodily area which consists in conveying sexually exciting stimuli to the mind the term *erotogenicity,* and if we reflect that the conclusions of our theory of sexuality have long accustomed us to the notion that certain other areas of the body—the *erotogenic* zones —may act as substitutes for the genitals and behave analogously to them, we then have only one step further to venture here. We can make up our minds to regard erotogenicity as a property common to all organs and are then justified in speaking of an increase or decrease in the degree of it in any given part of the body. It is possible that for every such change in the erotogenicity of the organs there is a parallel change in the libidinal cathexis in the ego. In such factors may lie the explanation of what is at the bottom of hypochondria and what it is that can have upon the distribution of the libido the same effect as actual organic disease.

We see that, if we follow out this line of thought, we encounter the problem not only of hypochondria, but of the other *actual neuroses*—neurasthenia and anxiety-neurosis. Let us therefore stop at this point. It is not within the scope of a purely psychological inquiry to penetrate so far behind the frontiers of physiological research. Let us only mention that from this point of view we may surmise that the relation of hypochondria to paraphrenia is similar to that of the other actual neuroses to hysteria and the obsessional neurosis: which is as much as to say that it is dependent on the ego-libido as the others are on the object-libido, and that hypochondriacal anxiety, emanating from the ego-libido, is the counterpart to neurotic anxiety. Further: since we are already familiar with the idea that the mechanism of disease and symptom-formation in the transference neuroses, the passage from introversion to regression, is to be connected with a damming-up of the object-libido,[1] we may come to closer quarters with the conception of a damming-up of the ego-libido also and may bring this conception into relation with the phenomena of hypochondria and paraphrenia.

Of course, curiosity will here suggest the question why such a damming-up of libido in the ego should be experienced as "painful." There I shall content myself with the answer that *pain* is in general the expression of in-

[1] Cf. Types of Neurotic Nosogenesis, *Collected Papers,* Vol. II.

creased tension, and thus a *quantity* of the material event is, here as elsewhere, transformed into the *quality* of "pain" in the mind; nevertheless, it may be not the absolute amount of the physical process which is decisive for the development of pain, but rather a certain function of this absolute amount. At this point we may even venture to touch on the question: whence does that necessity arise that urges our mental life to pass on beyond the limits of narcissism and to attach the libido to objects? The answer which would follow from our line of thought would once more be that we are so impelled when the cathexis of the ego with libido exceeds a certain degree. A strong egoism is a protection against disease, but, in the last resort, we must begin to love in order that we may not fall ill, and must fall ill if, in consequence of frustration, we cannot love. Somewhat after this fashion does Heine conceive of the psychogenesis of the Creation:

> *Krankheit ist wohl der letzte Grund*
> *Des ganzen Schöpferdrangs gewesen;*
> *Erschaffend konnte ich genesen,*
> *Erschaffend wurde ich gesund.*[1]

We have recognized our mental apparatus above all as a device for mastering excitations which would otherwise be felt as unpleasant or would have pathogenic effects. The "working-over" of stimuli in the mind accomplishes wonders for the internal discharge of excitations which are incapable of direct discharge outwards, or for which such a discharge is, for the moment, undesirable. Now it is in the first instance a matter of indifference whether the objects of this internal process of "working-over" are real or imaginary. The difference does not appear till later, when the turning of the libido towards unreal objects (introversion) has led to a damming-up. The megalomania of paraphrenics permits a similar internal working-over of the libido which has returned to the ego to be made; perhaps it is only when this process fails that the damming-up of the libido in the ego becomes pathogenic and starts the process of recovery which impresses us as being the disease itself.

I shall try here to penetrate a little further into the mechanism of paraphrenia and to put together those conceptions which today seem to me worthy of consideration. The difference

[1] *Disease at bottom brought about*
Creative urgence—for, creating,
I soon could feel the pain abating,
Creating, I could work it out.

between paraphrenic affections and the transference neuroses appears to me to lie in the circumstance that, in the former, the libido that is liberated by frustration does not remain attached to objects in phantasy, but returns to the ego; the megalomania then represents the mastery of this volume of libido, and thus corresponds with the introversion on to the phantasy-creations that is found in the transference neuroses; the hypochondria of paraphrenia, which is homologous to the anxiety of the transference neuroses, arises from a failure of this effort in the mental apparatus. We know that the anxiety of the neuroses can be relieved by further mental "working-over," e.g., by conversion, reaction-formation or defence-formation (phobia). The corresponding process in paraphrenics is the effort towards recovery, to which the striking phenomena of the disease are due. Since frequently, if not usually, an only partial detachment of the libido from objects accompanies paraphrenia, we can distinguish in the clinical picture three groups of phenomena: (1) those representing such remains as there may be of a normal state or of neurosis (phenomena of a residual nature); (2) those representing the morbid process (the detachment of the libido from its objects and, further, megalomania, hypochondria, affective disturbance, and every kind of regression); (3) those representing an attempt at recovery. In (3) the libido is once more attached to objects, after the manner of an hysteria (in dementia praecox or paraphrenia proper), or of an obsessional neurosis (in paranoia). This fresh libidinal cathexis takes place from another level and under other conditions than the primary one. The difference between the transference neurosis arising in this way and the corresponding formations where the ego is normal would afford us the deepest insight into the structure of our mental apparatus.

A third way in which we may study narcissism is by observing the behaviour of human beings in love, with its manifold differentiations in man and woman. In much the same way as the object-libido at first concealed from us the ego-libido, so in considering the object-choice of the child (and the adolescent) we first noticed that the sources from which he takes his sexual objects are his experiences of gratification. The first auto-erotic sexual gratifications are experienced in connection with vital functions in the service of self-preservation. The sexual instincts are at the outset supported upon the ego-instincts; only later do they become independent of these, and even then we have an indication of that original dependence in the fact that those persons who have to do with the feeding, care, and protection of the child become his earliest sexual objects: that is to say, in the first instance the mother or her substitute. Side by side with this type and source of object-choice, which may be called the *anaclitic* type, a second type, the existence of which we had not suspected, has been revealed by psycho-analytic investigation. We have found, especially in persons whose libidinal development has suffered some disturbance, as in perverts and homosexuals, that in the choice of their love-object they have taken as their model not the mother but their own selves. They are plainly seeking themselves as a love-object and their type of object-choice may be termed *narcissistic*. This observation provides us with our strongest motive for regarding the hypothesis of narcissism as a necessary one.

Now this does not mean that human beings are to be divided into two sharply differentiated groups, according as their object-choice conforms to the anaclitic or to the narcissistic type; we rather assume that both kinds of object-choice are open to each individual, though he may show a preference for one or the other. We say that the human being has originally two sexual objects: himself and the woman who tends him, and thereby we postulate a primary narcissism in everyone, which may in the long run manifest itself as dominating his object-choice.

Further, the comparison of man and woman shows that there are fundamental differences between the two in respect of the type of object-choice, although these differences are, of course, not universal. Complete object-love of the anaclitic type is, properly speaking, characteristic of the man. It displays the marked sexual over-estimation which is doubtless derived from the original narcissism of the child, now transferred to the sexual object. This sexual over-estimation is the origin of the peculiar state of being in love, a state suggestive of a neurotic compulsion, which is thus traceable to an impoverishment of the ego in respect of libido in favour of the love-object. A different course is followed in the type most frequently met with in women, which is probably the purest and truest feminine type. With the development of puberty, the maturing of the female sexual organs, which up till then have been in a condition of latency, seems to bring about an intensification of the original narcissism, and this is unfavourable to the development of a true object-love with its accompanying sexual over-estimation; there arises in the woman a certain self-sufficiency (especially when there is a ripening into beauty) which compensates her for the social restrictions upon her object-choice. Strictly speaking, such women love only themselves with an intensity comparable to that of the man's love for them. Nor does their need lie in the direction of loving, but of being loved; and that man finds favour with them who fulfils this condition. The importance of this type of woman for the erotic life of mankind must be recognized as very great. Such women have the greatest fascination for men, not only for aesthetic reasons, since as a rule they are the most beautiful, but also because of certain interesting psychological constellations. It seems very evident that one person's narcissism has a great attraction for those others who have renounced part of their own narcissism and are seeking after object-love; the charm of a child lies to a great extent in his narcissism, his self-sufficiency and inaccessibility, just as does the charm of certain animals which seem not to concern themselves about us, such as cats and the large beasts of prey. In literature, indeed, even the great criminal and the humorist compel our interest by the narcissistic self-importance with which they manage to keep at arm's length everything which would diminish the importance of their ego. It is as if we envied them their power of retaining a blissful state of mind—an unassailable libido-position which we ourselves have since abandoned. The great charm of the narcissistic woman has, however, its reverse side; a large part of the dissatisfaction of the lover, of his doubts of the woman's love, of his complaints of her enigmatic nature, have their root in this incongruity between the types of object-choice.

Perhaps it is not superfluous to give an assurance that, in this description of the feminine form of erotic life, no tendency to depreciate woman has any part. Apart from the fact that tendentiousness is alien to me, I also know that these different lines of development correspond to the differentiation of functions in a highly complicated biological connection; further, I am ready to admit that there are countless women who love according to the masculine type and who develop the over-estimation of the sexual object so characteristic of that type.

Even for women whose attitude towards the man remains cool and narcissistic, there is a way which leads to complete object-love. In the child to whom they give birth, a part of their own body comes to them as an object other than themselves, upon which they can lavish out of their narcissism complete object-love. Other women again do not need to wait for a child in order to take the step in development from (secondary) narcissism to object-love. Before puberty, they have had feelings of a likeness to men and have developed to some extent on masculine lines; after this tendency has been cut short when feminine maturity is reached, they still retain the capacity of longing for a masculine ideal which is really a survival of the boyish nature that they themselves once owned.

We may conclude these suggestions with a short survey of the paths leading to object-choice.

A person may love:

(1) According to the narcissistic type:
    (*a*) What he is himself (actually himself),
    (*b*) What he once was,
    (*c*) What he would like to be,
    (*d*) Someone who was once part of himself;

(2) According to the anaclitic type:
    (*a*) The woman who tends,
    (*b*) The man who protects;

and those substitutes which succeed them one after another. The justification for inserting case (*c*) of the first type has yet to be demonstrated later on in our discussion.

The significance of narcissistic object-choice for homosexuality in men must be appraised in another connection.

The primary narcissism of the child assumed by us, which forms one of the hypotheses in our theories of the libido, is less easy to grasp by direct observation than to confirm by deduction from another consideration. If we look at the attitude of fond parents towards their children, we cannot but perceive it as a revival and reproduction of their own, long since abandoned narcissism. Their feeling, as is well known, is characterized by over-estimation, that sure indication of a narcissistic feature in object-choice which we have already appreciated. Thus they are impelled to ascribe to the child all manner of perfections which sober observation would not confirm, to gloss over and forget all his shortcomings—a tendency with which, indeed, the denial of childish sex-

uality is connected. Moreover, they are inclined to suspend in the child's favour the operation of all those cultural acquirements which their own narcissism has been forced to respect, and to renew in his person the claims for privileges which were long ago given up by themselves. The child shall have things better than his parents; he shall not be subject to the necessities which they have recognized as dominating life. Illness, death, renunciation of enjoyment, restrictions on his own will, are not to touch him; the laws of nature, like those of society, are to be abrogated in his favour; he is really to be the centre and heart of creation, "His Majesty the Baby," as once we fancied ourselves to be. He is to fulfil those dreams and wishes of his parents which they never carried out, to become a great man and a hero in his father's stead, or to marry a prince as a tardy compensation for the mother. At the weakest point of all in the narcissistic position, the immortality of the ego, which is so relentlessly assailed by reality, security is achieved by fleeing to the child. Parental love, which is so touching and at bottom so childish, is nothing but parental narcissism born again and, transformed though it be into object-love, it reveals its former character infallibly.

III

The disturbances to which the original narcissism of the child is exposed, the reactions with which he seeks to protect himself from them, the paths into which he is thereby forced —these are themes which I shall leave on one side, as an important field for work which still awaits exploration; the most important of these matters, however, can be isolated from the rest and, as the *castration complex* (in the boy, anxiety concerning the penis; in the girl, envy of the penis), be treated in connection with the effect of early sexual intimidation. Elsewhere, psycho-analytic research leads us to vicissitudes undergone by the libidinal instincts in which they are isolated from, and in opposition to, the ego-instincts; but, where the castration complex is in question, our researches permit us to infer the existence of an epoch and a mental state in which the two groups of instincts are acting in harmony with each other, inseparably blent, as narcissistic interests. It is from this state of things that A. Adler has derived his conception of the *masculine protest,* which he has exalted almost to the position of the sole motive power concerned in the formation of neurosis and also of character, and which he conceives of as having its origin, not in a narcissistic, and therefore still libidinal, trend, but in a social valuation. Psycho-analytic research has, from the very beginning, recognized the existence and significance of the masculine protest, but has always regarded it, in opposition to Adler, as narcissistic in nature and derived from the castration complex. It appertains to the formation of character, into the genesis of which it enters along with many other factors, and it is completely inadequate to explain the problems of the neuroses, in which Adler will take account of nothing but the manner in which they serve the interests of the ego. I find it quite impossible to base the genesis of neurosis upon so narrow a foundation as the castration complex, however pre-eminent a part this may play in men amongst the resistances to the cure of a neurosis. Lastly, I know also of cases of neurosis in which the masculine protest, or in our sense the castration complex, plays no pathogenic part, or does not appear at all.

Observation of normal adults shows that their former megalomania has been subdued and that the mental characteristics from which we inferred their infantile narcissism have vanished. What has become of their ego-libido? Are we to assume that the whole of it has passed over into object-cathexes? Such a possibility is plainly contrary to the whole trend of our argument; but in the psychology of repression we may find a clue to another answer to the question.

We have learnt that libidinal impulses are fated to undergo pathogenic repression if they come into conflict with the subject's cultural and ethical ideas. By this we do not ever mean: if the individual in question has a merely intellectual knowledge of the existence of these ideas; we always mean: if he recognizes them as constituting a standard for himself and acknowledges the claims they make on him. Repression, as we have said, proceeds from the ego; we might say with greater precision: from the self-respect of the ego. The very impressions, experiences, impulses, and desires that one man indulges or at least consciously elaborates in his mind will be rejected with the utmost indignation by another, or stifled at once even before they enter consciousness. The difference between the two, however—and here we have the conditioning factor in repression—can easily be expressed in terms of the libido-theory. We may say that the one man

has set up an *ideal* in himself by which he measures his actual ego, while the other is without this formation of an ideal. From the point of view of the ego, this formation of an ideal would be the condition of repression.

To this ideal ego is now directed the self-love which the real ego enjoyed in childhood. The narcissism seems to be now displaced on to this new ideal ego, which, like the infantile ego, deems itself the possessor of all perfections. As always where the libido is concerned, here again man has shown himself incapable of giving up a gratification he has once enjoyed. He is not willing to forgo his narcissistic perfection in his childhood; and if, as he develops, he is disturbed by the admonitions of others and his own critical judgment is awakened, he seeks to recover the early perfection, thus wrested from him, in the new form of an ego-ideal. That which he projects ahead of him as his ideal is merely his substitute for the lost narcissism of his childhood—the time when he was his own ideal.

This suggests that we should examine the relation between this forming of ideals and sublimation. Sublimation is a process that concerns the object-libido and consists in the instinct's directing itself towards an aim other than, and remote from, that of sexual gratification; in this process the accent falls upon the deflection from the sexual aim. Idealization is a process that concerns the *object;* by it that object, without any alteration in its nature, is aggrandized and exalted in the mind. Idealization is possible in the sphere of the ego-libido as well as in that of the object-libido. For example, the sexual over-estimation of an object is an idealization of it. In so far as sublimation is a process that concerns the instinct and idealization one that concerns the object, the two concepts are to be distinguished one from the other.

The formation of the ego-ideal is often confounded with sublimation, to the detriment of clear comprehension. A man who has exchanged his narcissism for the worship of a high ego-ideal has not necessarily on that account succeeded in sublimating his libidinal instincts. It is true that the ego-ideal requires such sublimation, but it cannot enforce it; sublimation remains a special process which may be prompted by the ideal but the execution of which is entirely independent of any such incitement. It is just in neurotics that we find the highest degrees of tension between the development of their ego-ideal and the measure

of their sublimation of primitive libidinal instincts, and in general it is far harder to
convince the idealist of the inexpediency of the
hiding-place found by his libido than the plain
man whose demands in this respect are only
moderate. Further, the formation of an ego-
ideal and sublimation are quite differently
related to the causation of neurosis. As we have
learnt, the formation of the ideal increases the
demands of the ego and is the most powerful
factor favouring repression; sublimation is a
way out, a way by which the claims of the ego
can be met without involving repression.

It would not surprise us if we were to find a
special institution in the mind which performs
the task of seeing that narcissistic gratification
is secured from the ego-ideal and that, with
this end in view, it constantly watches the real
ego and measures it by that ideal. If such an
institution does exist, it cannot possibly be
something which we have not yet discovered;
we only need to recognize it, and we may say
that what we call our *conscience* has the required characteristics. Recognition of this
institution enables us to understand the so-
called *delusions of observation* or, more correctly, of *being watched*, which are such striking
symptoms in the paranoid diseases and may
perhaps also occur as an isolated form of illness,
or intercalated in a transference neurosis.
Patients of this sort complain that all their
thoughts are known and their actions watched
and overlooked; they are informed of the
functioning of this mental institution by voices
which characteristically speak to them in the
third person ("Now she is thinking of that
again" . . . "now he is going out"). This complaint is justified—it describes the truth; a
power of this kind, watching, discovering and
criticizing all our intentions, does really exist;
indeed, it exists with every one of us in normal
life. The delusion of being watched presents it
in a regressive form, thereby revealing the
genesis of this function and the reason why the
patient is in revolt against it.

For that which prompted the person to form
an ego-ideal, over which his conscience keeps
guard, was the influence of parental criticism
(conveyed to him by the medium of the voice),
reinforced, as time went on, by those who
trained and taught the child and by all the
other persons of his environment—an indefinite
host, too numerous to reckon (fellow-men,
public opinion).

Large quantities of libido which is essentially
homosexual are in this way drawn into the
formation of the narcissistic ego-ideal and find
outlet and gratification in maintaining it. The
institution of conscience was at bottom an
embodiment, first of parental criticism, and
subsequently of that of society; a similar process takes place when a tendency towards
repression develops out of a command or
prohibition imposed in the first instance from
without. The voices, as well as the indefinite
number of speakers, are brought into the foreground again by the disease, and so the evolution of conscience is regressively reproduced.
But the revolt against this *censorial institution*
springs from the person's desire (in accordance
with the fundamental character of his illness)
to liberate himself from all these influences,
beginning with that of his parents, and from
his withdrawal of homosexual libido from those
influences. His conscience then encounters him
in a regressive form as a hostile influence from
without.

The lament of the paranoiac shows also that
at bottom the self-criticism of conscience is
identical with, and based upon, self-observation.
That activity of the mind which took over the
function of conscience has also enlisted itself
in the service of introspection, which furnishes
philosophy with the material for its intellectual
operations. This must have something to do
with the characteristic tendency of paranoiacs
to form speculative systems.[1]

It will certainly be of importance to us if we
can see in other fields evidence of the activity
of this critically watching faculty, which becomes heightened into conscience and philosophic introspection. I would refer here to what
Herbert Silberer has called the "functional
phenomenon," one of the few indisputably
valuable additions to the theory of dreams.
Silberer, as is well known, has shown that in
the states between sleeping and waking we can
directly observe the translation of thoughts into visual images, but that in these circumstances we frequently have a presentation, not
of a thought-content, but of the actual state
of the mind (readiness, fatigue, etc.) of the
person who is struggling with sleep. Similarly,
Silberer has shown that often the end of a
dream or some section of the dream-content
signifies merely the dreamer's own perception
of his sleeping and waking. He has thus demon-

---

[1] I should like to add, merely by way of suggestion,
that the process of development and strengthening
of this watching institution might contain within it the
genesis later on of (subjective) memory and of the
time-factor, the latter of which has no application to
unconscious processes.

strated that self-observation—in the sense of the paranoiac's delusion of being watched—plays a part in dream-formation. This part is not invariable; probably I overlooked it because it does not appear in my own dreams to any great extent; in persons who are gifted philosophically, and therefore accustomed to introspection, it may become very clear.

We may here recall our discovery that dream-formation takes place under the sway of a censorship which compels distortion of the dream-thoughts. We did not picture this censorship as a special force, an entity, but we chose the term to designate a particular aspect of the repressive tendencies which control the ego; namely, their attitude towards the dream-thoughts. Penetrating further into the structure of the ego, we may recognize the *dream-censor* again in the ego-ideal and in the dynamic utterances of conscience. If this censor is to some extent on the alert even during sleep, we can understand that the necessary condition of its activity—self-observation and self-criticism—should contribute to the dream-content some such thoughts as these: "Now he is too sleepy to think . . .now he is waking up."[1]

At this point we may enter upon a discussion of the self-regarding attitude in normal persons and in neurotics.

First of all, the feeling of self-regard appears to us a measure of the ego; what various components go to make up that measure is irrelevant. Everything we possess or achieve, every remnant of the primitive feeling of omnipotence that experience has corroborated, helps to exalt the self-regard.

Applying our distinction between sexual and ego-instincts, we must recognize that the self-regard has a very intimate connection with the narcissistic libido. Here we are supported by two fundamental facts: that in paraphrenics the self-regard is exalted, while in the transference neuroses it is abased; and that where the erotic life is concerned not being loved lowers the self-regarding feelings, while being loved raises them. We have stated that to be loved is the aim and the satisfaction in a narcissistic object-choice.

Further, it is easy to observe that libidinal object-cathexis does not raise the self-regard. The effect of the dependence upon the loved object is to lower that feeling: the lover is

humble. He who loves has, so to speak, forfeited a part of his narcissism, which can only be replaced by his being loved. In all these respects the self-regarding feelings seem to remain in a relation to the narcissistic element in the erotic life.

The realization of impotence, of one's own inability to love in consequence of mental or physical disorder, has an exceedingly lowering effect upon the self-regard. Here, as I judge, we shall find one of the sources of the feelings of inferiority of which patients suffering from the transference neuroses so readily complain to us. The main source of these feelings is, however, the impoverishment of the ego, due to the withdrawal from it of extraordinarily large libidinal cathexes—due, that is to say, to the injury sustained by the ego through the sexual trends which are no longer subject to control.

A. Adler is right in maintaining that a person's realization of organic inferiorities in himself acts as a spur upon an active mental life, and produces by way of over-compensation a higher degree of ability. But it would be altogether an exaggeration if, following this lead of Adler's, we tried to prove that every fine achievement was conditioned by an original organic inferiority. Not all artists are handicapped with bad eyesight, nor did all orators originally stammer. And there are plenty of instances of excellent achievements springing from superior organic endowment. In the aetiology of neurosis, organic inferiority and imperfect development play an insignificant part, much the same as that played by actual perceptual material in the formation of dreams. The neurosis makes use of such inferiorities as a pretext, just as it does of all other suitable factors. So surely as we credit the assertion of one neurotic patient that it was inevitable that she should fall ill, since she is ugly, deformed, or lacking in charm and so no one could love her, the very next neurotic will convince us of our error; for she remains the victim of her neurosis and her aversion to sexuality, although she seems to be desirable, and indeed more desired than the average woman. The majority of hysterical women are among the attractive and even beautiful representatives of their sex, while, on the other hand, the frequency of ugliness, organic infirmities, and defects in the lower classes of society does not increase the incidence of neurotic illness amongst them.

The relations existing between self-regard and erotism (libidinal object-cathexes) may be

[1] I cannot here determine whether the differentiation of the censorial function from the rest of the ego is capable of forming the basis of the philosophic distinction between consciousness and self-consciousness.

expressed in the following formula: two cases must be distinguished—in the first, the erotic cathexes are *ego-syntonic, in accordance with the ego-tendencies;* in the second, on the contrary, those cathexes have suffered repression. In the former case (where the path taken by the libido is acceptable to the ego), love takes its place among all the other activities of the ego. Love in itself, in the form of longing and deprivation, lowers the self-regard; whereas to be loved, to have love returned, and to possess the beloved object, exalts it again. When the libido is repressed, the erotic cathexis is felt as a severe depletion of the ego, the satisfaction of love is impossible, and the re-enrichment of the ego can be effected only by a withdrawal of the libido from its objects. The return of the libido from the object to the ego and its transformation into narcissism represents, as it were, the restoration of a happy love, and, conversely, an actual happy love corresponds to the primal condition in which object-libido and ego-libido cannot be distinguished.

Perhaps the importance of the subject, and the difficulty in surveying it, may be my excuse for adding a few remarks that are rather loosely strung together.

The development of the ego consists in a departure from the primary narcissism and results in a vigorous attempt to recover it. This departure is brought about by means of the displacement of libido to an ego-ideal imposed from without, while gratification is derived from the attainment of this ideal.

At the same time, the ego has put forth its libidinal object-cathexes. It becomes impoverished in consequence both of these cathexes and of the formation of the ego-ideal, and it enriches itself again both by gratification of its object-love and by fulfilling its ideal.

Part of the self-regard is primary—the residue of childish narcissism; another part arises out of such omnipotence as experience corroborates (the fulfilment of the ego-ideal); whilst a third part proceeds from gratification of object-libido.

The ego-ideal has imposed severe conditions upon the gratification of libido through objects, for, by means of its censorship, it rejects some of them as incompatible with itself. Where no such ideal has been formed, the sexual trend in question makes its appearance unchanged in the personality in the form of a perversion. As in childhood, to be his own ideal once more, where sexual tendencies are concerned, is the happiness that man strives to attain.

The state of being in love consists in a flowing over of ego-libido to the object. This state has the power to remove repressions and to restore perversions. It exalts the sexual object to the position of sexual ideal. Since, in cases where the love is of the anaclitic or object type, this state results from the fulfilment of infantile conditions of love, we may say that whatever fulfils this condition of love becomes idealized.

The sexual ideal may enter into an interesting auxiliary relation to the ego-ideal. Where narcissistic gratification encounters actual hindrances, the sexual ideal may be used as a substitutive gratification. In such a case a person loves (in conformity with the narcissistic type of object-choice) someone whom he once was and no longer is, or else someone who possesses excellences which he never had at all (cf. above, (c)). The parallel formula to that given above runs thus: whoever possesses an excellence which the ego lacks for the attainment of its ideal, becomes loved. This expedient is of special importance for the neurotic, whose ego is depleted by his excessive object-cathexes and who on that acount is unable to attain to his ego-ideal. He then seeks a way back to narcissism from his prodigal expenditure of libido upon objects, by choosing a sexual ideal after the narcissistic type which shall possess the excellences to which he cannot attain. This is the cure by love, which he generally prefers to cure by analysis. Indeed, he cannot believe in any other curative mechanism; he usually brings expectations of this sort with him to the treatment and then directs them towards the person of the physician. The patient's incapacity for love, an incapacity resulting from his extensive repressions, naturally stands in the way of such a method of cure. When, by means of the treatment, he has been partially freed from his repressions, we are frequently met by the unintended result that he withdraws from further treatment in order to choose a love-object, hoping that life with the beloved person will complete his recovery. We might be satisfied with this result, if it did not bring with it all the dangers of an overwhelming dependence upon this helper in his need.

The ego-ideal is of great importance for the understanding of group psychology. Besides its individual side, this ideal has a social side; it is also the common ideal of a family, a class, or a nation. It not only binds the narcissistic libido, but also a considerable amount of the person's homosexual libido, which in this way becomes turned back into the ego. The dissatisfaction due to the non-fulfilment of this ideal liberates homosexual libido, which is transformed into sense of guilt (dread of the community). Originally this was a fear of punishment by the parents, or more correctly, the dread of losing their love; later the parents are replaced by an indefinite number of fellowmen. This helps us to understand why it is that paranoia is frequently caused by a wounding of the ego, by a frustration of the gratification desired within the sphere of the ego-ideal, and also to understand the coincidence of ideal-formation and sublimation in the ego-ideal, as well as the demolition of sublimations and possible transformation of ideals in paraphrenic disorders.

Instincts and Their Vicissitudes[1]

The view is often defended that sciences should be built up on clear and sharply defined basal concepts. In actual fact no science, not even the most exact, begins with such definitions. The true beginning of scientific activity consists rather in describing phenomena and then in proceeding to group, classify, and correlate them. Even at the stage of description, it is not possible to avoid applying certain abstract ideas to the material in hand, ideas derived from various sources and certainly not the fruit of the new experience only. Still more indispensable are such ideas—which will later become the basal concepts of the science—as the material is further elaborated. They must at first necessarily possess some measure of uncertainty; there can be no question of any clear delimitation of their content. So long as they remain in this condition, we come to an understanding about their meaning by repeated references to the material of observation, from which we seem to have deduced our abstract ideas, but which is, in point of fact, subject to them. Thus, strictly speaking, they are in the nature of conventions; although everything depends on their being chosen in no arbitrary manner, but determined by the important relations they have to the empirical material—relations that we seem to divine before we can clearly recognize and demonstrate them. It is only after more searching investigation of the field in question that we are able to formulate with increased clarity the scientific concepts underlying it, and progressively so to modify these concepts that they become widely applicable and at the same time consistent logically. Then, indeed, it may be time to immure them in definitions. The progress of science, however, demands a certain elasticity even in these definitions. The science of physics furnishes an excellent illustration of the way in which even those basal concepts that are firmly established in the form of definitions are constantly being altered in their content.

A conventional but still rather obscure basal concept of this kind, which is nevertheless indispensable to us in psychology, is that of *instinct*. Let us try to ascertain what is comprised in this conception by approaching it from different angles.

First, from the side of physiology. This has given us the concept of *stimuli* and the scheme of the reflex arc, according to which a stimulus applied *from the outer world* to living tissue (nervous substance) is discharged by action *towards the outer world*. The action answers the purpose of withdrawing the substance affected from the operation of the stimulus, removing it out of range of the simulus.

Now what is the relation between *instinct* and *stimulus?* There is nothing to prevent our including the concept of *instinct* under that of *stimulus* and saying that an instinct is a stimulus to the mind. But we are immediately set on our guard against treating instinct and mental stimulus as one and the same thing. Obviously, besides those of instinctual origin, there are other stimuli to the mind which behave far more like physiological stimuli. For example, a strong light striking upon the eye is not a stimulus of instinctual origin; it is one, however, when the mucous membrane of the oesophagus becomes parched or when a gnawing makes itself felt in the stomach.[2]

We have now obtained material necessary for discriminating between stimuli of instinctual origin and the other (physiological) stimuli which operate on our minds. First, a stimulus of instinctual origin does not arise in the outside world but from within the organism itself. For this reason, it has a different mental effect and different actions are necessary in order to remove it. Further, all that is essential in an external stimulus is contained in the assumption that it acts as a single impact, so that it can be discharged by a single appropriate action—a typical instance being that of motor flight from the source of stimulation. Of course, these impacts may be repeated and their force may be cumulative, but that makes no difference to our notion of the process and to the conditions necessary in order that the stimulus may be dispelled. An instinct, on the other hand, never acts as a momentary impact but always as a constant force. As it makes its

---

[1] *Collected Papers*, IV; first published in *Zeitschrift*, Vol. III (1915); reprinted in *Sammlung*, 4th Series.

[2] Assuming, of course, that these internal processes constitute the organic basis of the needs described as *thirst* and *hunger*.

attack not from without but from within the organism, it follows that no flight can avail against it. A better term for a stimulus of instinctual origin is a *need;* that which does away with this need is *satisfaction*. This can be attained only by a suitable (adequate) alteration of the inner source of stimulation.

Let us imagine ourselves in the position of an almost entirely helpless living organism, as yet unorientated in the world and with stimuli impinging on its nervous tissue. This organism will soon become capable of making a first discrimination and a first orientation. On the one hand, it will detect certain stimuli which can be avoided by an action of the muscles (flight)—these it ascribes to an outside world; on the other hand, it will also be aware of stimuli against which such action is of no avail and whose urgency is in no way diminished by it—these stimuli are the tokens of an inner world, the proof of instinctual needs. The apperceptive substance of the living organism will thus have found in the efficacy of its muscular activity a means for discriminating between *outer* and *inner*.

We thus find our first conception of the essential nature of an instinct by considering its main characteristics, its origin in sources of stimulation within the organism and its appearance as a constant force, and thence we deduce one of its further distinguishing features, namely, that no actions of flight avail against it. Now, in making these remarks, we cannot fail to be struck by a fact which compels us to a further admission. We do not merely accept as basal concepts certain conventions which we apply to the material we have acquired empirically, but we also make use of various complicated postulates to guide us in dealing with psychological phenomena. We have already cited the most important of these postulates; it remains for us expressly to lay stress upon it. It is of a biological nature, and makes use of the concept of *purpose* (one might say, of adaptation of the means to the end) and runs as follows: the nervous system is an apparatus having the function of abolishing stimuli which reach it, or of reducing excitation to the lowest possible level: an apparatus which would even, if this were feasible, maintain itself in an altogether unstimulated condition. Let us for the present not take exception to the indefiniteness of this idea and let us grant that the task of the nervous system is—broadly speaking—*to master stimuli*. We see then how greatly the simple physiological reflex scheme

is complicated by the introduction of instincts. External stimuli impose upon the organism the single task of withdrawing itself from their action: this is accomplished by muscular movements, one of which reaches the goal aimed at and, being the most appropriate to the end in view, is thenceforward transmitted as an hereditary disposition. Those instinctual stimuli which emanate from within the organism cannot be dealt with by this mechanism. Consequently, they make far higher demands upon the nervous system and compel it to complicated and inter-dependent activities, which effect such changes in the outer world as enable it to offer satisfaction to the internal source of stimulation; above all, instinctual stimuli oblige the nervous system to renounce its ideal intention of warding off stimuli, for they maintain an incessant and unavoidable afflux of stimulation. So we may probably conclude that instincts and not external stimuli are the true motive forces in the progress that has raised the nervous system, with all its incomparable efficiency, to its present high level of development. Of course there is nothing to prevent our assuming that the instincts themselves are, at least in part, the precipitates of different forms of external stimulation, which in the course of phylogenesis have effected modifications in the organism.

Then when we find further that the activity of even the most highly developed mental apparatus is subject to the pleasure-principle, i.e., is automatically regulated by feelings belonging to the pleasure-"pain" series, we can hardly reject the further postulate that these feelings reflect the manner in which the process of mastering stimuli takes place. This is certainly so in the sense that "painful" feelings are connected with an increase and pleasurable feelings with a decrease in stimulation. Let us, however, be careful to preserve this assumption in its present highly indefinite form, until we succeed, if that is possible, in discovering what sort of relation exists between pleasure and "pain," on the one hand, and fluctuations in the quantities of stimuli affecting mental life, on the other. It is certain that many kinds of these relations are possible, some of them by no means simple.

If now we apply ourselves to considering mental life from a biological point of view, an *instinct* appears to us as a borderland concept between the mental and the physical, being both the mental representative of the stimuli emanating from within the organism and penetrating to the mind, and at the same time **a** measure of the demand made upon the energy of the latter in consequence of its connection with the body.

We are now in a position to discuss certain terms used in reference to the concept of an instinct, for example, its impetus, its aim, its object and its source.

By the *impetus* of an instinct we understand its motor element, the amount of force or the measure of the demand upon energy which it represents. The characteristic of impulsion is common to all instincts, is, in fact, the very essence of them. Every instinct is a form of activity; if we speak loosely of passive instincts, we can only mean those whose aim is passive.

The *aim* of an instinct is in every instance satisfaction, which can only be obtained by abolishing the condition of stimulation in the source of the instinct. But although this remains invariably the final goal of every instinct, there may yet be different ways leading to the same goal, so that an instinct may be found to have various nearer or intermediate aims, capable of combination or interchange. Experience permits us also to speak of instincts which are *inhibited in respect of their aim,* in cases where a certain advance has been permitted in the direction of satisfaction and then an inhibition or deflection has occurred. We may suppose that even in such cases a partial satisfaction is achieved.

The *object* of an instinct is that in or through which it can achieve its aim. It is the most variable thing about an instinct and is not originally connected with it, but becomes attached to it only in consequence of being peculiarly fitted to provide satisfaction. The object is not necessarily an extraneous one: it may be part of the subject's own body. It may be changed any number of times in the course of the vicissitudes the instinct undergoes during life; a highly important part is played by this capacity for displacement in the instinct. It may happen that the same object may serve for the satisfaction of several instincts simultaneously, a phenomenon which Adler calls a *confluence* of instincts. A particularly close attachment of the instinct to its object is distinguished by the term *fixation:* this frequently occurs in very early stages of the instinct's development and so puts an end to its mobility, through the vigorous resistance it sets up against detachment.

By the *source* of an instinct is meant that somatic process in an organ or part of the body from which there results a stimulus represented in mental life by an instinct. We do not know whether this process is regularly of a chemical nature or whether it may also correspond with the release of other, e.g., mechanical, forces. The study of the sources of instinct is outside the scope of psychology; although its source in the body is what gives the instinct its distinct and essential character, yet in mental life we know it merely by its aims. A more exact knowledge of the sources of instincts is not strictly necessary for purposes of psychological investigation; often the source may be with certainty inferred from the aims.

Are we to suppose that the different instincts which operate upon the mind, but of which the origin is somatic, are also distinguished by different qualities and act in the mental life in a manner qualitatively different? This supposition does not seem to be justified; we are much more likely to find the simpler assumption sufficient—namely, that the instincts are all qualitatively alike and owe the effect they produce only to the quantities of excitation accompanying them, or perhaps further to certain functions of this quantity. The difference in the mental effects produced by the different instincts may be traced to the difference in their sources. In any event, it is only in a later connection that we shall be able to make plain what the problem of the quality of instincts signifies.

Now what instincts and how many should be postulated? There is obviously a great opportunity here for arbitrary choice. No objection can be made to anyone's employing the concept of an instinct of play or of destruction, or that of a social instinct, when the subject demands it and the limitations of psychological analysis allow of it. Nevertheless, we should not neglect to ask whether such instinctual motives, which are in one direction so highly specialized, do not admit of further analysis in respect of their sources, so that only those primal instincts which are not to be resolved further could really lay claim to the name.

I have proposed that two groups of such primal instincts should be distinguished: the *self-preservative* or *ego*-instincts and the *sexual* instincts. But this proposition has not the weight of a necessary postulate, such as, for instance, our assumption about the biological *purpose* in the mental apparatus (see above); it is merely an auxiliary construction, to be retained only so long as it proves useful, and it will make little difference to the results of our work of description and classification if we replace it by another. The occasion for it arose in the course of the evolution of psycho-analysis, which was first employed upon the psychoneuroses, actually upon the group designated *transference neuroses* (hysteria and obsessional neurosis); through them it became plain that at the root of all such affections there lies a conflict between the claims of sexuality and those of the ego. It is always possible that an exhaustive study of the other neurotic affections (especially of the narcissistic psychoneuroses, the schizophrenias) may oblige us to alter this formula and therewith to make a different classification of the primal instincts. But for the present we do not know what this new formula may be, nor have we met with any argument which seems likely to be prejudicial to the contrast between sexual and ego-instincts.

I am altogether doubtful whether work upon psychological material will afford any decisive indication for the distinction and classification of instincts. Rather it would seem necessary to apply to this material certain definite assumptions in order to work upon it, and we could wish that these assumptions might be taken from some other branch oi knowledge and transferred to psychology. The contribution of biology on this point certainly does not run counter to the distinction between sexual and ego-instincts. Biology teaches that sexuality is not on a level with the other functions of the individual, for its *purposes* go beyond the individual, their content being the production of new individuals and the preservation of the species. It shows, further, that the relation existing between the ego and sexuality may be conceived of in two ways, apparently equally well justified: in the one, the individual is regarded as of prime importance, sexuality as one of his activities and sexual satisfaction as one of his needs; while in the other, the individual organism is looked upon as a transitory and perishable appendage to the quasi-immortal germ-plasm bequeathed to him by the race. The assumption that the sexual function differs from other bodily processes in virtue of special chemical processes is, I understand, also a postulate of the Ehrlich school of biological research.

Since a study of the instincts from the side of consciousness presents almost insuperable difficulties, psycho-analytic investigation of mental disturbances remains the principal source of our knowledge. The development of this line of investigation, however, has necessarily produced hitherto information of a more or less definite nature only in regard to the sexual instincts, for it is this group in particular which can be observed in isolation, as it were, in the psychoneuroses. With the extension of psycho-analysis to other neurotic affections we may be sure that we shall find a basis for our knowledge of the ego-instincts also, though it would be optimistic to expect equally favourable conditions for observation in this further field of research.

An attempt to formulate the general characteristics of the sexual instincts would run as follows: they are numerous, emanate from manifold organic sources, act in the first instance independently of one another and only at a late stage achieve a more or less complete synthesis. The aim which each strives to attain is *organ-pleasure;* only when the synthesis is complete do they enter the service of the function of reproduction, becoming thereby generally recognizable as sexual instincts. At their first appearance, they support themselves upon the instincts of self-preservation, from which they only gradually detach themselves; in their choice of object, also, they follow paths indicated by the ego-instincts. Some of them remain throughout life associated with these latter and furnish them with libidinal components, which with normal functioning easily escape notice and are clearly recognizable only when disease is present. They have this distinctive characteristic—that they have in a high degree the capacity to act vicariously for one another and that they can readily change their objects. In consequence of the last-mentioned properties they are capable of activities widely removed from their original modes of attaining their aims (sublimation).

Our inquiry into the various vicissitudes which instincts undergo in the process of development and in the course of life must be confined to the sexual instincts, for these are the more familiar to us. Observation shows us that an instinct may undergo the following vicissitudes:

Reversal into its opposite,
Turning round upon the subject,
Repression,
Sublimation.

Since I do not intend to treat of sublimation here, and since repression requires a special chapter to itself, it only remains for us to describe and discuss the two first points. Bearing in mind that there are tendencies which are opposed to the instincts pursuing a straight-forward course, we may regard these vicissitudes as modes of defence against the instincts.

The *reversal* of an instinct *into its opposite* may on closer scrutiny be resolved into two different processes: a change from active to passive, and a reversal of the content. The two processes, being essentially distinct, must be treated separately.

Examples of the first process are met with in the two pairs of opposites: sadism-masochism and scoptophilia-exhibitionism. The reversal here concerns only the aims of the instincts. The passive aim (to be tortured, or looked at) has been substituted for the active aim (to torture, to look at). Reversal of content is found in the single instance of the change of love into hate.

The *turning round* of an instinct *upon the subject* is suggested to us by the reflection that masochism is actually sadism turned round upon the subject's own ego, and that exhibitionism includes the love of gazing at the subject's own body. Further, analytic observation leaves us in no doubt that the masochist also enjoys the *act* of torturing when this is being applied to himself, and the exhibitionist the exposing of someone in being exposed himself. So the essence of the process is the change of the object, while the aim remains unchanged.

We cannot fail to note, however, that in these examples turning round upon the subject's self and transformation from active to passive coincide or occur in one process. To elucidate the relation between the two processes, a more thorough investigation must be undertaken.

With the pair of opposites sadism-masochism, the process may be represented as follows:

(*a*) Sadism consists in the exercise of violence or power upon some other person as its object.

(*b*) This object is abandoned and replaced by the subject's self. Together with the turning round upon the self, the change from an active to a passive aim in the instinct is also brought about.

(*c*) Again another person is sought as object; this person, in consequence of the alteration which has taken place in the aim of the instinct, has to take over the original rôle of the subject.

Case (*c*) is the condition commonly termed *masochism*. Satisfaction follows in this case also by way of the original sadism, the passive ego placing itself in phantasy back in its former situation, which, however, has now been given up to another subject outside the self. Whether there is, besides this, a more direct masochistic satisfaction is highly doubtful. A primary masochism not derived in the manner I have described from sadism, does not appear to be met with.[1] That it is not superfluous to make the assumption of stage (*b*) is quite clear when we observe the behaviour of the sadistic impulse in cases of obsessional neurosis. In these we have the turning upon the subject's self, without the attitude of passivity towards another: the reversal has only reached the second stage. Self-torment and self-punishment have arisen from the desire to torture, but not masochism. The active voice is changed, not into the passive, but into the reflexive middle voice.

The conception of sadism is made more complicated by the circumstance that this instinct, side by side with its general aim (or perhaps rather, within it), seems to press towards a quite special aim: the infliction of pain, in addition to subjection and mastery of the object. Now psycho-analysis would seem to show that the infliction of pain plays no part in the original aims sought by the instinct: the sadistic child takes no notice of whether or not it inflicts pain, nor is it part of its purpose to do so. But when once the transformation into masochism has taken place, the experience of pain is very well adapted to serve as a passive masochistic aim, for we have every reason to believe that sensations of pain, like other unpleasant sensations, extend into sexual excitation and produce a condition which is pleasurable, for the sake of which the subject will even willingly experience the unpleasantness of pain. Where once the suffering of pain has been experienced as a masochistic aim, it can be carried back into the sadistic situation and result in a sadistic aim of *inflicting pain*, which will then be masochistically enjoyed by the subject while inflicting pain upon others, through his identification of himself with the suffering object. Of course, in either case it is not the pain itself which is enjoyed, but the accompanying sexual excitement, and this is especially easy for the sadist. The enjoyment of pain would thus be a primary masochistic aim, which, however, can then also become the aim of the originally sadistic instinct.

In order to complete my exposition, I would add that pity cannot be described as a result

[1] *Additional Note*, 1924. In later works (cf. "The Economic Problem of Masochism," 1924, *Collected Papers*, II) relating to problems of instinctual life, I have expressed the opposite view.

of the reversal of the sadistic instinct, but necessitates the conception of a *reaction-formation* against that instinct (for the difference, see below).

Rather different and simpler results are afforded by the investigation of another pair of opposites, namely, those instincts whose aim is sexual gazing (scoptophilia) and self-display (the *voyeur* and *exhibitionist* tendencies, as they are called in the language of the perversions). Here again we may postulate the same stages as in the previous instance: (*a*) scoptophilia as an activity directed towards an extraneous object; (*b*) abandonment of the object and a turning of the scoptophilic instinct towards a part of the subject's own person; therewith a transformation to passivity and the setting up of a new aim—that of being looked at; (*c*) the institution of a new subject to whom one displays oneself in order to be looked at. Here too, it is hardly possible to doubt that the active aim appears before the passive, that scoptophilia precedes exhibitionism. But there is an important divergence from what happens in the case of sadism, in that we can recognize in the scoptophilic instinct a yet earlier stage than that described as (*a*). That is to say, that at the beginning of its activity the scoptophilic instinct is auto-erotic: it has indeed an object, but that object is the subject's own body. It is only later that the instinct comes (by way of comparison) to exchange this object for the analogous one of the body of another (stage (*a*)). Now this preliminary stage is interesting because it is the source of both the situations represented in the resulting pair of opposites, according to which element in the original situation is reversed. The following might serve as a scheme for the scoptophilic instinct:

α Subject's looking at his own sexual organ = Subject's own sexual organ being looked at by himself

β Subject's looking at an extraneous object (active scoptophilia) | γ Subject's own sexual organ being looked at by another person (exhibitionism)

A preliminary stage of this kind is absent in sadism, which from the outset is directed upon an extraneous object, although it might not be altogether unreasonable to regard as such a stage the child's efforts to gain control of his limbs.[1]

With regard to both these instincts just ex-

[1] Cf. preceding footnote.

amined as examples, it must be said that transformation of them by a reversal from active to passive, and by a turning round upon the subject, never in fact concerns the whole amount of impelling force pertaining to the instinct. To some extent its earlier active direction always persists side by side with the later passive direction, even when the transformation is very extensive. The only correct description of the scoptophilic instinct would be that all phases of its development, the auto-erotic, preliminary phase as well as it final active or passive form, co-exist alongside one another; and the truth of this statement becomes manifest if we base our opinion, not upon the actions which are prompted by the instinct, but upon the mechanism of its satisfaction. Perhaps yet another way of conceiving and representing the matter may be justified. We may split up the life of each instinct into a series of *thrusts*, distinct from one another in the time of their occurrence but each homogeneous within its own period, whose relation to one another is comparable to that of successive eruptions of lava. We can then perhaps picture to ourselves that the earliest and most primitive instinct-eruption persists in an unchanged form and undergoes no development at all. The next *thrust* would then from the outset have undergone a change of form, being turned, for instance, from active to passive, and it would then, with this new characteristic, be superimposed upon the earlier layer, and so on. So that, if we take a survey of the instinctual tendency from its beginning up to any given stopping-point, the succession of thrusts which we have described would present the picture of a definite development of the instinct.

The fact that, at that later period of development, the instinct in its primary form may be observed side by side with its (passive) opposite deserves to be distinguished by the highly appropriate name introduced by Bleuler: *ambivalence*.

These considerations regarding the developmental history of an instinct and the permanent character of the intermediate stages in it should make instinct-development more comprehensible to us. Experience shows that the degree of demonstrable ambivalence varies greatly in individuals, groups, and races. Marked ambivalence of an instinct in a human being at the present day may be regarded as an archaic inheritance, for we have reason to suppose that the part played in the life of the instincts by the active impulses in their original form was greater in primitive times than it is on an average today.

We have become accustomed to call the early phase of the development of the ego, during which its sexual instincts find auto-erotic satisfaction, *narcissism*, without having so far entered into any discussion of the relation between auto-erotism and narcissism. It follows that, in considering the preliminary phase of the scoptophilic instinct, when the subject's own body is the object of the scoptophilia, we must place it under the heading of narcissism; it is a narcissistic formation. From this phase the active scoptophilic instinct, which has left narcissism behind, is developed, while the passive scoptophilic instinct, on the contrary, holds fast to the narcissistic object. Similarly, the transformation from sadism to masochism betokens a reversion to the narcissistic object, while in both cases the narcissistic (active) subject is exchanged by identification for another, extraneous ego. Taking into consideration the preliminary narcissistic stage of sadism constructed by us, we approach the more general view that those vicissitudes which consist in the instinct being turned round upon the subject's own ego and undergoing reversal from activity to passivity are dependent upon the narcissistic organization of the ego and bear the stamp of that phase. Perhaps they represent attempts at defence which at higher stages of the development of the ego are effected by other means.

At this point we may remember that so far we have discussed only two pairs of instincts and their opposites: sadism-masochism and scoptophilia-exhibitionism. These are the best-known sexual instincts which appear in ambivalent forms. The other components of the later sexual function are at present too inaccessible to analysis for us to be able to discuss them in a similar way. In general we can assert of them that their activities are auto-erotic, i.e., their object becomes negligible in comparison with the organ which is their source, and as a rule the two coincide. The object of the scoptophilic instinct, although it also in the first instance is a part of the subject's own body, nevertheless is not the eye itself; and with sadism the organic source, probably the musculature with its capacity for action, directly presupposes an object other than itself, even though that object be part of the subject's own body. In the auto-erotic instincts, the part played by the organic source is so decisive that, according to a plausible supposition of P. Fed-

ern and L. Jekels,[1] the form and function of the organ determine the activity or passivity of the instinct's aim.

The transformation of the *content* of an instinct into its opposite is observed in a single instance only—the changing of *love into hate*. It is particularly common to find both these directed simultaneously towards the same object, and this phenomenon of their co-existence furnishes the most important example of ambivalence of feeling.

The case of love and hate acquires a special interest from the circumstance that it resists classification in our scheme of the instincts. It is impossible to doubt the existence of a most intimate relation between these two contrary feelings and sexual life, but one is naturally unwilling to conceive of love as being a kind of special component-instinct of sexuality in the same way as are the others just discussed. One would prefer to regard loving rather as the expression of the whole sexual current of feeling, but this idea does not clear up our difficulties and we are at a loss how to conceive of an essential opposite to this striving.

Loving admits of not merely one, but of three antitheses. First there is the antithesis of loving—hating; secondly, there is loving—being loved; and, in addition to these, loving and hating together are the opposite of the condition of neutrality or indifference. The second of these two antitheses, loving—being loved, corresponds exactly to the transformation from active to passive and may be traced to a primal situation in the same way as the scoptophilic instinct. This situation is that of *loving oneself*, which for us is the characteristic of narcissism. Then, according to whether the self as object or subject is exchanged for an extraneous one, there results the active aim of loving or the passive one of being loved, the latter remaining nearly related to narcissism.

Perhaps we shall come to a better understanding of the manifold opposites of loving if we reflect that our mental life as a whole is governed by *three polarities*, namely, the following antitheses:

> Subject (ego)—Object (external world),
> Pleasure—Pain,
> Active—Passive.

The antithesis of ego—non-ego (outer), i.e., subject—object, is, as we have already said, thrust upon the individual being at an early stage, by the experience that it can abolish ex-

[1] *Zeitschrift*, Vol. I, (1913).

ternal stimuli by means of muscular action but is defenceless against those stimuli that originate in instinct. This antithesis remains sovereign above all in our intellectual activity and provides research with a fundamental situation which no amount of effort can alter. The polarity of pleasure—pain depends upon a feeling-series, the significance of which in determining our actions (will) is paramount and has already been emphasized. The antithesis of active and passive must not be confounded with that of ego-subject—external object. The relation of the ego to the outer world is passive in so far as it receives stimuli from it, active when it reacts to these. Its instincts compel it to a quite special degree of activity towards the outside world, so that, if we wished to emphasize the essence of the matter, we might say that the ego-subject is passive in respect of external stimuli, active in virtue of its own instincts. The antithesis of active—passive coalesces later with that of masculine—feminine, which, until this has taken place, has no psychological significance. The fusion of activity with masculinity and passivity with femininity confronts us, indeed, as a biological fact, but it is by no means so invariably complete and exclusive as we are inclined to assume.

The three polarities within the mind are connected with one another in various highly significant ways. There is a certain primal psychic situation in which two of them coincide. Originally, at the very beginning of mental life, the ego's instincts are directed to itself and it is to some extent capable of deriving satisfaction for them on itself. This condition is known as *narcissism*, and this potentiality for satisfaction is termed *auto-erotic*.[1] The outside world is at this time, generally speaking, not cathected with any interest and is indifferent for purposes of satisfaction. At this period, therefore, the ego-subject coincides with what is pleasurable and the outside world with what is indifferent (or even painful, as being a source of stimulation). Let us for the moment define *loving* as the re-

lation of the ego to its sources of pleasure: then the situation in which the ego loves itself only and is indifferent to the outside world illustrates the first of the polarities in which *loving* appeared.

In so far as it is auto-erotic, the ego has no need of the outside world, but, in consequence of experiences undergone by the instincts of self-preservation, it tends to find objects there and doubtless it cannot but for a time perceive inner instinctual stimuli as painful. Under the sway of the pleasure-principle, there now takes place a further development. The objects presenting themselves, in so far as they are sources of pleasure, are absorbed by the ego into itself, *introjected* (according to an expression coined by Ferenczi); while, on the other hand, the ego thrusts forth upon the external world whatever within itself gives rise to pain (see below: the mechanism of projection).

Thus the original *reality-ego*, which distinguished outer and inner by means of a sound objective criterion, changes into a purified *pleasure-ego*, which prizes above all else the quality of pleasure. For this pleasure-ego, the outside world is divided into a part that is pleasurable, which it has incorporated into itself, and a remainder that is alien to it. A part of itself it has separated off, and this it projects into the external world and regards as hostile. According to this new arrangement the congruence of the two polarities,

ego-subject with pleasure,

outside world with pain (or earlier with neutrality), is once more established.

When the stage of primary narcissism is invaded by the object, the second contrary attitude to that of love, namely, hate, attains to development.

As we have heard, the ego's objects are presented to it from the outside world in the first instance by the instincts of self-preservation, and it is undeniable also that hate originally betokens the relation of the ego to the alien external world with its afflux of stimuli. Neutrality may be classified as a special case of hate or rejection, after having made its appearance first as the forerunner of hate. Thus at the very beginning, the external world, objects and that which was hated were one and the same thing. When later on an object manifests itself as a source of pleasure, it becomes loved, but also incorporated into the ego, so that for the purified pleasure-ego the object once again coincides with what is extraneous and hated.

Now, however, we note that just as the an-

---

[1] Some of the sexual instincts are, as we know, capable of this auto-erotic satisfaction and so are adapted to be the channel for that development under the sway of the pleasure-principle which we shall describe later. The sexual instincts, which from the outset require an object, and the needs of the ego-instincts, which are never capable of auto-erotic satisfaction, interfere, of course, with this condition and prepare the way for progress. More, the primal narcissistic condition would not have been able to attain such a development were it not that every individual goes through a period of helplessness and dependence on fostering care, during which his urgent needs are satisfied by agencies outside himself and thereby withheld from developing along their own line.

tithesis love—indifference reflects the polarity
ego—external world, so the second antithesis,
love—hate, reproduces the polarity pleasure—
pain, which is bound up with the former. When
the purely narcissistic stage gives place to the
object-stage, pleasure and pain denote the relations of the ego to the object. When the object becomes a source of pleasurable feelings, a
motor tendency is set up which strives to bring
the object near to and incorporate it into the
ego; we then speak of the *attraction* exercised
by the pleasure-giving object, and say that we
love that object. Conversely, when the object
is the source of painful feelings, there is a tendency which endeavours to increase the distance
between object and ego and to repeat in relation to the former the primordial attempt at
flight from the external world with its flow of
stimuli. We feel a *repulsion* from the object,
and hate it; this hate can then be intensified
to the point of an aggressive tendency towards
the object, with the intention of destroying it.

We might at a pinch say of an instinct that
it loves the objects after which it strives for
purposes of satisfaction, but to say that it
hates an object strikes us as odd; so we become
aware that the attitudes of love and hate cannot be said to characterize the relations of instincts to their objects, but are reserved for
the relations of the ego as a whole to objects.
But, if we consider a colloquial usage which is
certainly full of meaning, we see that there is
yet another limitation to the significance of
love and hate. We do not say of those objects
which serve the interests of self-preservation
that we love them; rather we emphasize the
fact that we need them, and perhaps add an
element of a different kind in our relation to
them by words which denote a much lesser degree of love—for example, *to be fond of, to
like, to find agreeable.*

So the word *love* becomes shifted ever
further into the sphere of the pure pleasure-
relation existing between the ego and its object
and finally attaches itself to sexual objects in
the narrower sense and to those which satisfy
the needs of sublimated sexual instincts. The
discrimination of the ego-instincts from the
sexual, a discrimination which we have imposed
upon our psychology, is seen, therefore, to be
in conformity with the spirit of our speech.
Since we do not customarily say that the single
sexual component-instinct loves its object, but
see the most appropriate case in which to apply
the word *love* in the relation of the ego to its
sexual object, we learn from this fact that the

applicability of the word in this relation begins
only with the synthesis of all the component-
instincts under the primacy of the genitals and
in the service of the function of reproduction.

It is noteworthy that in the use of the word
hate no such intimate relation to sexual pleasure and the sexual function appears: on the
contrary, the painful character of the relation
seems to be the sole decisive feature. The ego
hates, abhors, and pursues with intent to destroy all objects which are for it a source of
painful feelings, without taking into account
whether they mean to it frustration of sexual
satisfaction or of gratification of the needs of
self-preservation. Indeed, it may be asserted
that the true prototypes of the hate-relation
are derived not from sexual life, but from the
struggle of the ego for self-preservation and
self-maintenance.

So we see that love and hate, which present
themselves to us as essentially antithetical,
stand in no simple relation to each other. They
did not originate in a cleavage of any common
primal element, but sprang from different
sources and underwent each its own development before the influence of the pleasure-pain
relation constituted them antitheses to each
other. At this point we are confronted with the
task of putting together what we know of the
genesis of love and hate.

Love originates in the capacity of the ego to
satisfy some of its instincts auto-erotically
through the obtaining of *organ-pleasure*. It is
primarily narcissistic, is then transferred to
those objects which have been incorporated in
the ego, now much extended, and expresses the
motor striving of the ego after these objects as
sources of pleasure. It is intimately connected
with the activity of the later sexual instincts
and, when these have been completely synthe-
tized, coincides with the sexual trend as a whole.
The preliminary stages of love reveal themselves as temporary sexual aims, while the sexual
instincts are passing through their complicated
development. First amongst these we recognize
the phase of incorporating or devouring, a type
of love which is compatible with abolition of
any separate existence on the part of the
object, and which may therefore be designated
ambivalent. At the higher stage of the pre-
genital sadistic-anal organization, the striving
after the object appears in the form of an impulsion to mastery, in which injury or annihilation of the object is a matter of indifference.
This form and preliminary stage of love is
hardly to be distinguished from hate in its be-

haviour towards the object. Only when the genital organization is established does love become the antithesis of hate.

The relation of hate to objects is older than that of love. It is derived from the primal repudiation by the narcissistic ego of the external world whence flows the stream of stimuli. As an expression of the pain-reaction induced by objects, it remains in constant intimate relation with the instincts of self-preservation, so that sexual and ego-instincts readily develop an antithesis which repeats that of love and hate. When the sexual function is governed by the ego-instincts, as at the stage of the sadistic-anal organization, they impart the qualities of hate to the instinct's aim as well.

The history of the origin and relations of love makes us understand how it is that love so constantly manifests itself as ambivalent, i.e., accompanied by feelings of hate against the same object. This admixture of hate in love is to be traced in part to those preliminary stages of love which have not been wholly outgrown, and in part is based upon reactions of aversion and repudiation on the part of the ego-instincts which, in the frequent conflicts between the interests of the ego and those of love, can claim to be supported by real and actual motives. In both cases, therefore, the admix-ture of hate may be traced to the source of self-preservative instincts. When a love-relationship with a given object is broken off, it is not infrequently succeeded by hate, so that we receive the impression of a transformation of love into hate. This descriptive characterization is amplified by the view that, when this happens, the hate which is motivated by considerations of reality is reinforced by a regression of the love to the sadistic preliminary stage, so that the hate acquires an erotic character and the continuity of a love-relation is ensured.

The third antithesis of love, the transformation of loving into being loved, represents the operation of the polarity of active and passive, and is to be judged in the same way as in scoptophilia and sadism. We may sum up by saying that the essential feature in the vicissitudes undergone by instincts is *their subjection to the influences of the three great polarities that govern mental life.* Of these three polarities we might describe that of activity—passivity as the *biological,* that of ego—external world as the *real,* and finally that of pleasure—pain as the *economic* respectively.

That possible vicissitude undergone by an instinct which we call *repression* will form the subject of a further inquiry.

Repression[1]

One of the vicissitudes an instinctual impulse may undergo is to meet with resistances the aim of which is to make the impulse inoperative. Under certain conditions, which we shall presently investigate more closely, the impulse then passes into the state of *repression*. If it were a question of the operation of an external stimulus, obviously flight would be the appropriate remedy; with an instinct, flight is of no avail, for the ego cannot escape from itself. Later on, rejection based on judgment (*condemnation*) will be found to be a good weapon against the impulse. Repression is a preliminary phase of condemnation, something between flight and condemnation; it is a concept which could not have been formulated before the time of psycho-analytic research.

It is not easy in theory to deduce the possibility of such a thing as repression. Why should an instinctual impulse suffer such a fate? For this to happen, obviously a necessary condition must be that attainment of its aim by the instinct should produce "pain" instead of pleasure. But we cannot well imagine such a contingency. There are no such instincts; satisfaction of an instinct is always pleasurable. We should have to assume certain peculiar circumstances, some sort of process which changes the pleasure of satisfaction into "pain".

In order the better to define repression we may discuss some other situations in which instincts are concerned. It may happen that an external stimulus becomes internal, for example, by eating into and destroying a bodily organ, so that a new source of constant excitation and increase of tension is formed. The stimulus thereby acquires a far-reaching similarity to an instinct. We know that a case of this sort is experienced by us as *physical pain*. The aim of this pseudo-instinct, however, is simply the cessation of the change in the organ and of the pain accompanying it. There is no other direct pleasure to be attained by cessation of the pain. Further, pain is imperative; the only things which can subdue it are the effect of some toxic agent in removing it and the influence of some mental distraction.

The case of physical pain is too obscure to

help us much in our purpose. Let us suppose that an instinctual stimulus such as hunger remains unsatisfied. It then becomes imperative and can be allayed by nothing but the appropriate action for satisfying it; it keeps up a constant tension of need. Anything like a repression seems in this case to be utterly out of the question.

So repression is certainly not an essential result of the tension produced by lack of satisfaction of an impulse being raised to an unbearable degree. The weapons of defence of which the organism avails itself to guard against that situation must be discussed in another connection.

Let us instead confine ourselves to the clinical experience we meet with in the practice of psycho-analysis. We then see that the satisfaction of an instinct under repression is quite possible; further, that in every instance such a satisfaction is pleasurable in itself, but is irreconcilable with other claims and purposes; it therefore causes pleasure in one part of the mind and "pain" in another. We see then that it is a condition of repression that the element of avoiding "pain" shall have acquired more strength than the pleasure of gratification. Psycho-analytic experience of the transference neuroses, moreover, forces us to the conclusion that repression is not a defence-mechanism present from the very beginning, and that it cannot occur until a sharp distinction has been established between what is conscious and what is unconscious: that *the essence of repression lies simply in the function of rejecting and keeping something out of consciousness*. This conception of repression would be supplemented by assuming that, before the mental organization reaches this phase, the other vicissitudes which may befall instincts, e.g., reversal into the opposite or turning round upon the subject, deal with the task of mastering the instinctual impulses.

It seems to us now that, in view of the very great extent to which repression and the unconscious are correlated, we must defer probing more deeply into the nature of repression until we have learnt more about the structure of the various institutions in the mind—and about what differentiates consciousness from the un-

[1] *Collected Papers*, IV; first published in *Zeitschrift*, Vol. III (1915); reprinted in *Sammlung*, 4th Series.

conscious. Till we have done this, all we can do is to put together in purely descriptive fashion some characteristics of repression noted in clinical practice, even though we run the risk of having to repeat unchanged much that has been said elsewhere.

Now we have reason for assuming *a primal repression*, a first phase of repression, which consists in a denial of entry into consciousness to the mental (ideational) presentation of the instinct. This is accompanied by a *fixation;* the ideational presentation in question persists unaltered from then onwards, and the instinct remains attached to it. This is due to certain properties of unconscious processes of which we shall speak later.

The second phase of repression, *repression proper,* concerns mental derivatives of the repressed instinct-presentation, or such trains of thought as, originating elsewhere, have come into associative connection with it. On account of this association, these ideas experience the same fate as that which underwent primal repression. Repression proper, therefore, is actually an after-expulsion. Moreover, it is a mistake to emphasize only the rejection which operates from the side of consciousness upon what is to be repressed. We have to consider just as much the attraction exercised by what was originally repressed upon everything with which it can establish a connection. Probably the tendency to repression would fail of its purpose if these forces did not co-operate, if there were not something previously repressed ready to assimilate that which is rejected from consciousness.

Under the influence of study of the psychoneuroses, which brings before us the important effects of repression, we are inclined to overestimate their psychological content and to forget too readily that repression does not hinder the instinct-presentation from continuing to exist in the unconscious and from organizing itself further, putting forth derivatives and instituting connections. Really, repression interferes only with the relation of the instinct-presentation to one system of the mind, namely, to consciousness.

Psycho-analysis is able to show us something else which is important for understanding the effects of repression in the psychoneuroses. It shows us, for instance, that the instinct-presentation develops in a more unchecked and luxuriant fashion if it is withdrawn by repression from conscious influence. It ramifies like a fungus, so to speak, in the dark, and takes on extreme forms of expression, which when translated and revealed to the neurotic are bound not merely to seem alien to him, but to terrify him by the way in which they reflect an extraordinary and dangerous strength of instinct. This illusory strength of instinct is the result of an uninhibited development of it in phantasy and of the damming-up consequent on lack of real satisfaction. The fact that this last result is bound up with repression points the direction in which we have to look for the true significance of the latter.

In reverting to the contrary aspect, however, let us state definitely that it is not even correct to suppose that repression withholds from consciousness all the derivatives of what was primally repressed. If these derivatives are sufficiently far removed from the repressed instinct-presentation, whether owing to the process of distortion or by reason of the number of intermediate associations, they have free access to consciousness. It is as though the resistance of consciousness against them was in inverse proportion to their remoteness from what was originally repressed. During 'he practice of the psycho-analytic method, we continually require the patient to produce such derivatives of what has been repressed as, in consequence either of their remoteness or of distortion, can pass the censorship of consciousness. Indeed, the associations which we require him to give, while refraining from any consciously directed train of thought or any criticism, and from which we reconstruct a conscious interpretation of the repressed instinct-presentation, are precisely derivatives of this kind. We then observe that the patient can go on spinning a whole chain of such associations, till he is brought up in the midst of them against some thought-formation, the relation of which to what is repressed acts so intensely that he is compelled to repeat his attempt at repression. Neurotic symptoms, too, must have fulfilled the condition referred to, for they are derivatives of the repressed, which has finally by means of these formations wrested from consciousness the right of way previously denied it.

We can lay down no general rule concerning the degree of distortion and remoteness necessary before the resistance of consciousness is abrogated. In this matter a delicate balancing takes place, the play of which is hidden from us; its mode of operation, however, leads us to infer that it is a question of a definite degree of intensity in the cathexis of the unconscious—

beyond which it would break through for satisfaction. Repression acts, therefore, in a *highly specific* manner in each instance; every single derivative of the repressed may have its peculiar fate—a little more or a little less distortion alters the whole issue. In this connection, it becomes comprehensible that those objects to which men give their preference, that is, their ideals, originate in the same perceptions and experiences as those objects of which they have most abhorrence, and that the two originally differed from one another only by slight modifications. Indeed, as we found in the origin of the fetish, it is possible for the original instinct-presentation to be split into two, one part undergoing repression, while the remainder, just on account of its intimate association with the other, undergoes idealization.

The same result as ensues from an increase or a decrease in the degree of distortion may also be achieved at the other end of the apparatus, so to speak, by a modification in the conditions producing pleasure and "pain." Special devices have been evolved, with the object of bringing about such changes in the play of mental forces that what usually gives rise to "pain" may on this occasion result in pleasure, and whenever such a device comes into operation the repression of an instinct-presentation that is ordinarily repudiated is abrogated. The only one of these devices which has till now been studied in any detail is that of joking. Generally the lifting of the repression is only transitory; the repression is immediately re-established.

Observations of this sort, however, suffice to draw our attention to some further characteristics of repression. Not only is it, as we have just explained, *variable* and *specific,* but it is also exceedingly *mobile.* The process of repression is not to be regarded as something which takes place once for all, the results of which are permanent, as when some living thing has been killed and from that time onward is dead; on the contrary, repression demands a constant expenditure of energy, and if this were discontinued the success of the repression would be jeopardized, so that a fresh act of repression would be necessary. We may imagine that what is repressed exercises a continuous straining in the direction of consciousness, so that the balance has to be kept by means of a steady counter-pressure. A constant expenditure of energy, therefore, is entailed in maintaining a repression, and economically its abrogation denotes a saving. The mobility of

the repression, incidentally, finds expression also in the mental characteristics of the condition of sleep, which alone renders dream-formation possible. With a return to waking life, the repressive cathexes which have been called in are once more put forth.

Finally, we must not forget that after all we have said very little about an instinctual impulse when we state it to be repressed. Without prejudice to the repression, such an impulse may find itself in widely different conditions; it may be inactive, i.e., cathected with only a low degree of mental energy, or its degree of cathexis (and consequently its capacity for activity) may vary. True, its activity will not result in a direct abrogation of the repression, but it will certainly set in motion all the processes which terminate in a breaking through into consciousness by circuitous routes. With unrepressed derivatives of the unconscious, the fate of a particular idea is often decided by the degree of its activity or cathexis. It is an everyday occurrence that such a derivative can remain unrepressed so long as it represents only a small amount of energy, although its content is of such a nature as to give rise to a conflict with conscious control. But the quantitative factor is manifestly decisive for this conflict; as soon as an idea which is fundamentally offensive exceeds a certain degree of strength, the conflict takes on actuality, and it is precisely activation of the idea that leads to its repression. So that, where repression is concerned, an increase in energic cathexis operates in the same way as an approach to the unconscious, while a decrease in that energy operates like distance from the unconscious or like distortion. We understand that the repressing tendencies can find a substitute for repression in a weakening or lessening of whatever is distasteful to them.

In our discussion hitherto we have dealt with the repression of an instinct-presentation, and by that we understood an idea or group of ideas which is cathected with a definite amount of the mental energy (libido, interest) pertaining to an instinct. Now clinical observation forces us further to dissect something that hitherto we have conceived of as a single entity, for it shows us that beside the idea there is something else, another presentation of the instinct to be considered, and that this other element undergoes a repression which may be quite different from that of the idea. We have adopted the term *charge of affect* for this other element in the mental presentation; it represents that part of the instinct which has become detached from the idea, and finds proportionate expression, according to its quantity, in processes which become observable to perception as affects. From this point on, in describing a case of repression, we must follow up the fate of the idea which undergoes repression separately from that of the instinctual energy attached to the idea.

We should be glad enough to be able to give some general account of the outcome of both of these, and when we have taken our bearings a little we shall actually be able to do so. In general, repression of the ideational presentation of an instinct can surely only have the effect of causing it to vanish from consciousness, if it had previously been in consciousness, or of holding it back, if it is about to enter it. The difference, after all, is not important; it amounts to much the same thing as the difference between ordering an undesirable guest out of my drawing-room or out of my front hall, and refusing to let him cross my threshold once I have recognized him.[1] The fate of the quantitative factor in the instinct-presentation may be one of three, as we see by a cursory survey of the observations made through psycho-analysis: either the instinct is altogether suppressed, so that no trace of it is found, or it appears in the guise of an affect of a particular qualitative tone, or it is transformed into anxiety. With the two last possibilities we are obliged to focus our attention upon the *transformation* into *affects*, and especially into *anxiety*, of the mental energy belonging to the *instincts*, this being a new possible vicissitude undergone by an instinct.

We recall the fact that the motive and purpose of repression was simply the avoidance of "pain." It follows that the fate of the charge of affect belonging to the presentation is far more important than that of the ideational content of it and is decisive for the opinion we form of the process of repression. If a repression does not succeed in preventing feelings of "pain" or anxiety from arising, we may say that it has failed, even though it may have achieved its aim as far as the ideational element is concerned. Naturally, the case of unsuccessful repression will have more claim on our interest than that of repression which is even-

tually successful; the latter will, for the most part, elude our study.

We now wish to gain some insight into the mechanism of the process of repression, and especially we want to know whether it has a single mechanism only, or more than one, and whether perhaps each of the psychoneuroses may be distinguished by a characteristic repression-mechanism peculiar to itself. At the outset of this inquiry, however, we encounter complications. The mechanism of a repression becomes accessible to us only when we deduce it from its final results. If we confine our observations to the results of its effect on the ideational part of the instinct-presentation, we discover that as a rule repression creates a *substitute-formation*. What, then, is the mechanism of such a substitute-formation, or must we distinguish several mechanisms here also? Further, we know that repression leaves *symptoms* in its train. May we then regard substitute-formation and symptom-formation as coincident processes, and, if this is on the whole possible, does the mechanism of substitute-formation coincide with that of repression? So far as we know at present, it seems probable that the two are widely divergent, that it is not the repression itself which produces substitute-formations and symptoms, but that these latter constitute indications of a *return of the repressed* and owe their existence to quite other processes. It would also seem advisable to examine the mechanisms of substitute- and symptom-formation before those of repression.

Obviously there is no ground here for speculation to explore: on the contrary, the solution of the problem must be found by careful analysis of the results of repression observable in the individual neuroses. I must, however, suggest that we should postpone this task, too, until we have formed reliable conceptions of the relation of consciousness to the unconscious. Only, in order that the present discussion may not be quite unfruitful, I will anticipate by saying: (1) that the mechanism of repression does not in fact coincide with the mechanism or mechanisms of substitute-formation, (2) that there are many different mechanisms of substitute-formation, and (3) that the different mechanisms of repression have at least this one thing in common: *a withdrawal of energic cathexis* (or of *libido,* if it is a question of sexual instincts).

Further, confining myself to the three best-known forms of psychoneurosis, I will show

---

[1] This metaphor, applicable to the process of repression, may also be extended to include one of the characteristics of repression mentioned earlier. I need only add that I have to place a sentinel to keep constant guard over the door which I have forbidden this guest to pass, lest he should burst it open (see above).

by means of some examples how the conceptions here introduced find application to the study of repression. From *anxiety-hysteria,* I will choose an instance which has been subjected to thorough analysis—that of an animal-phobia. The instinctual impulse subjected to repression here is a libidinal attitude towards the father, coupled with dread of him. After repression, this impulse vanishes out of consciousness: the father does not appear in consciousness as an object for the libido. As a substitute for him we find in a corresponding situation some animal which is more or less suited to be an object of dread. The substitute-formation of the ideational element has established itself by way of a displacement along the line of a series of associated ideas which is determined in some particular way. The quantitative element has not vanished, but has been transformed into anxiety. The result is a fear of a wolf, instead of a claim for love from the father. Of course the categories here employed are not enough to supply a complete explanation even of the simplest case of psychoneurosis: there are always other points of view to be taken into account.

Such a repression as that which takes place in an animal-phobia must be described as radically unsuccessful. All that it has done is to remove the idea and set another in its place; it has not succeeded at all in its aim of avoiding "pain." On this account, too, the work of the neurosis, far from ceasing, proceeds into a *second movement,* so to speak, which is designed to attain its immediate and more important aim. There follows an attempt at flight, the formation of the *phobia proper*—a number of things have to be *avoided* in order to prevent an outbreak of anxiety. A more particular investigation would enable us to understand the mechanism by which the phobia achieves its aim.

We are led to quite another view of the process of repression when we consider the picture of a true *conversion-hysteria.* Here the salient point is that it is possible to bring about a total disappearance of the charge of affect. The patient then displays towards his symptoms what Charcot called *"la belle indifférence des hystériques."* At other times, this suppression is not so completely successful: a part of the sensation of distress attaches to the symptoms themselves, or it has proved impossible entirely to prevent outbreaks of anxiety, and this in its turn sets the mechanism of phobia-formation working. The ideational content of the instinct-presentation is completely withdrawn from consciousness; as a substitute-formation—and concurrently, as a symptom—we have an excessive innervation (in typical cases, a somatic innervation), sometimes of a sensory, sometimes of a motor character, either as an excitation or as an inhibition. The area of over-innervation proves on closer observation to belong to the repressed instinct-presentation itself, and, as if by a process of *condensation,* to have absorbed the whole cathexis. Of course, these remarks do not cover the whole mechanism of a conversion-hysteria; the element of *regression* especially, which will be appraised in another connection, has to be taken into account.

In so far as it is rendered possible only by means of extensive substitute-formations, the repression which takes place in hysteria may be pronounced entirely unsuccessful; with reference to mastering the charge of affect however, which is the real task of repression, it generally betokens a complete success. Again, in conversion-hysteria the process of repression terminates with the formation of the symptom and does not, as in anxiety-hysteria, need to proceed to a *second-movement*—or, strictly speaking, an unlimited number of *movements.*

A totally different aspect of repression is shown in the third affection to which we are referring for purposes of this comparison: in the *obsessional neurosis.* Here we are at first in doubt what it is that we have to regard as the repressed instinct-presentation—a libidinal or a hostile trend. This uncertainty arises because the obsessional neurosis rests on the premise of a regression by means of which a sadistic trend has been substituted for a tender one. It is this hostile impulse against a loved person which has undergone repression. The effect at an early phase of the work of repression is quite different from that produced later. At first the repression is completely successful, the ideational content is rejected, and the affect made to disappear. As a substitute-formation, there arises an alteration in the ego, an increased sensitiveness of conscience, which can hardly be called a symptom. Substitute- and symptom-formation do not coincide here. Here, too, we learn something about the mechanism of repression. Repression, as it invariably does, has brought about a withdrawal of libido, but for this purpose it has made use of a *reaction-formation,* by intensifying an antithesis. So here the substitute-formation has the same mechanism as the repression and at bottom coincides with it, while yet chronologically, as well as in its content, it is distinct from the symptom-formation. It is very probable that the whole process is made possible by the ambivalent relation into which the sadistic impulse destined for repression has been introduced.

But the repression, at first successful, does not hold; in the further course of things its failure becomes increasingly obvious. The ambivalence which has allowed repression to come into being by means of reaction-formation also constitutes the point at which the repressed succeeds in breaking through again. The vanished affect is transformed, without any diminution, into dread of the community, pangs of conscience, or self-reproaches; the rejected idea is replaced by a *displacement-substitute,* often by displacement on to something utterly trivial or indifferent. For the most part, there is an unmistakable tendency to complete re-establishment of the repressed idea. Failure of repression of the quantitative factor brings into play, by means of various taboos and prohibitions, the same mechanism of flight as we have seen at work in the formation of hysterical phobias. The rejection of the idea from consciousness is, however, obstinately maintained, because it ensures abstention from action, preclusion of the motor expression of an impulse. So the final form of the work of repression in the obsessional neurosis is a sterile and never-ending struggle.

The short series of comparisons which have been presented here may easily convince us that more comprehensive investigations are necessary before we can hope to understand thoroughly the processes connected with repression and the formation of neurotic symptoms. The extraordinary intricacy of all the factors to be taken into consideration leaves us only one way open by which to present them. We must select first one and then another point of view, and follow it up through the material at our disposal, as long as application of it seems to prove fruitful. Each separate point so treated will be incomplete in itself and there cannot fail to be obscurities where we touch upon material not previously dealt with; but we may hope that the final synthesis of them all will lead to a good understanding of the subject.

The Unconscious[1]

PSYCHO-ANALYSIS has taught us that the essence of the process of repression lies, not in abrogating or annihilating the ideational presentation of an instinct, but in withholding it from becoming conscious. We then say of the idea that it is in a state of *unconsciousness,* of being not apprehended by the conscious mind, and we can produce convincing proofs to show that unconsciously it can also produce effects, even of a kind that finally penetrate to consciousness. Everything that is repressed must remain unconscious, but at the very outset let us state that the repressed does not comprise the whole unconscious. The unconscious has the greater compass: the repressed is a part of the unconscious.

How are we to arrive at a knowledge of the unconscious? It is, of course, only as something conscious that we know anything of it, after it has undergone transformation or translation into something conscious. The possibility of such translation is a matter of everyday experience in psycho-analytic work. In order to achieve this, it is necessary that the person analysed should overcome certain resistances, the very same as those which at some earlier time placed the material in question under repression by rejecting it from consciousness.

I. *Justification for the Conception of the Unconscious*

In many quarters our justification is disputed for assuming the existence of an unconscious system in the mind and for employing such an assumption for purposes of scientific work. To this we can reply that our assumption of the existence of the unconscious is *necessary* and *legitimate,* and that we possess manifold *proofs* of the existence of the unconscious. It is necessary because the data of consciousness are exceedingly defective; both in healthy and in sick persons, mental acts are often in process which can be explained only by presupposing other acts, of which consciousness yields no evidence. These include not only the parapraxes[2] and dreams of healthy persons, and

everything designated a *mental symptom* or an *obsession* in the sick; our most intimate daily experience introduces us to sudden ideas of the source of which we are ignorant, and to results of mentation arrived at we know not how. All these conscious acts remain disconnected and unintelligible if we are determined to hold fast to the claim that every single mental act performed within us must be consciously experienced; on the other hand, they fall into a demonstrable connection if we interpolate the unconscious acts that we infer. A gain in meaning and connection, however, is a perfectly justifiable motive, one which may well carry us beyond the limitations of direct experience. When, after this, it appears that the assumption of the unconscious helps us to construct a highly successful practical method, by which we are enabled to exert a useful influence upon the course of conscious processes, this success will have won us an incontrovertible proof of the existence of that which we assumed. We become obliged, then, to take up the position that it is both untenable and presumptuous to claim that whatever goes on in the mind must be known to consciousness.

We can go further and in support of an unconscious mental state allege that only a small content is embraced by consciousness at any given moment, so that the greater part of what we call *conscious knowledge* must in any case exist for very considerable periods of time in a condition of latency, that is to say, of unconsciousness, of not being apprehended by the mind. When all our latent memories are taken into consideration, it becomes totally incomprehensible how the existence of the unconscious can be gainsaid. We then encounter the objection that these latent recollections can no longer be described as *mental processes,* but that they correspond to residues of somatic processes from which something mental can once more proceed. The obvious answer to this should be that a latent memory is, on the contrary, indubitably a residuum of a mental process. But it is more important to make clear to our own minds that this objection is based on the identification—not, it is true, explicitly stated, but regarded as axiomatic—of conscious and mental. This identification is either a *petitio*

[1] *Collected Papers,* IV; first published in *Zeitschrift,* Vol. III (1915); reprinted in *Sammlung,* 4th Series.
[2] E.g., slips of the tongue, mislaying of objects, etc. —TR.

principii and begs the question whether all that is mental is also necessarily conscious, or else it is a matter of convention, of nomenclature. In this latter case, it is, of course, no more open to refutation than any other convention. The only question that remains is whether it proves so useful that we must needs adopt it. To this we may reply that the conventional identification of the mental with the conscious is thoroughly unpractical. It breaks up all mental continuity, plunges us into the insoluble difficulties of psychophysical parallelism, is open to the reproach that without any manifest grounds it overestimates the part played by consciousness, and finally it forces us prematurely to retire from the territory of psychological research without being able to offer us any compensation elsewhere.

At any rate, it is clear that the question—whether the latent states of mental life, whose existence is undeniable, are to be conceived of as unconscious mental states or as physical ones—threatens to resolve itself into a war of words. We shall, therefore, be better advised to give prominence to what we know with certainty of the nature of these debatable states. Now, as far as their physical characteristics are concerned, they are totally inaccessible to us: no physiological conception nor chemical process can give us any notion of their nature. On the other hand, we know for certain that they have abundant points of contact with conscious mental processes; on being submitted to a certain method of operation they may be transformed into or replaced by conscious processes, and all the categories which we employ to describe conscious mental acts, such as ideas, purposes, resolutions, and so forth, can be applied to them. Indeed, of many of these latent states we have to assert that the only point in which they differ from states which are conscious is just in the lack of consciousness of them. So we shall not hesitate to treat them as objects of psychological research, and that in the most intimate connection with conscious mental acts.

The stubborn denial of a mental quality to latent mental processes may be accounted for by the circumstance that most of the phenomena in question have not been objects of study outside psycho-analysis. Anyone who is ignorant of the facts of pathology, who regards the blunders of normal persons as accidental, and who is content with the old saw that dreams are froth need only ignore a few more problems of the psychology of consciousness in order to dispense with the assumption of an unconscious mental activity. As it happens, hypnotic experiments, and especially post-hypnotic suggestion, had demonstrated tangibly, even before the time of psycho-analysis, the existence and mode of operation of the unconscious in the mind.

The assumption of an unconscious is, moreover, in a further respect a perfectly *legitimate* one, inasmuch as in postulating it we do not depart a single step from our customary and accepted mode of thinking. By the medium of consciousness, each one of us becomes aware only of his own states of mind; that another man possesses consciousness is a conclusion drawn by analogy from the utterances and actions we perceive him to make, and it is drawn in order that this behaviour of his may become intelligible to us. (It would probably be psychologically more correct to put it thus: that without any special reflection we impute to everyone else our own constitution and therefore also our consciousness, and that this identification is a necessary condition of understanding in us.) This conclusion—or identification—was formerly extended by the ego to other human beings, to animals, plants, inanimate matter, and to the world at large, and proved useful as long as the correspondence with the individual ego was overwhelmingly great; but it became more untrustworthy in proportion as the gulf between the ego and the non-ego widened. Today, our judgment is already in doubt on the question of consciousness in animals; we refuse to admit it in plants and we relegate to mysticism the assumption of its existence in inanimate matter. But even where the original tendency to identification has withstood criticism—that is, when the non-ego is our fellow-man—the assumption of a consciousness in him rests upon an inference and cannot share the direct certainty we have of our own consciousness.

Now psycho-analysis demands nothing more than that we should apply this method of inference to ourselves also—a proceeding to which, it is true, we are not constitutionally disposed. If we do this, we must say that all the acts and manifestations which I notice in myself and do not know how to link up with the rest of my mental life must be judged as if they belonged to someone else and are to be explained by the mental life ascribed to that person. Further, experience shows that we understand very well how to interpret in others (i.e., how to fit into their mental context) those same acts which we refuse to acknowledge as mentally conditioned in ourselves. Some special hindrance evidently deflects our investigations from ourselves and interferes with our obtaining true knowledge of ourselves.

Now this method of inference, applied to oneself in spite of inner opposition, does not lead to the discovery of an unconscious, but leads logically to the assumption of another, second consciousness which is united in myself with the consciousness I know. But at this point criticism may fairly make certain comments. In the first place, a consciousness of which its own possessor knows nothing is something very different from that of another person, and it is questionable whether such a consciousness, lacking, as it does, its most important characteristic, is worthy of any further discussion at all. Those who have contested the assumption of an unconscious system in the mind will not be content to accept in its place an unconscious consciousness. Secondly, analysis shows that the individual latent mental processes inferred by us enjoy a high degree of independence, as though each had no connection with another, and knew nothing about any other. We must be prepared, it would appear, to assume the existence not only of a second consciousness in us, but of a third and fourth also, perhaps of an infinite series of states of consciousness, each and all unknown to us and to one another. In the third place—and this is the most weighty argument of all—we have to take into account that analytic investigation reveals some of these latent processes as having characteristics and peculiarities which seem alien to us, or even incredible, and running directly counter to the well-known attributes of consciousness. This justifies us in modifying our inference about ourselves and saying that what is proved is not a second consciousness in us, but the existence of certain mental operations lacking in the quality of consciousness. We shall also, moreover, be right in rejecting the term *subconsciousness* as incorrect and misleading. The known cases of *double conscience* (splitting of consciousness) prove nothing against our view. They may most accurately be described as cases of a splitting of the mental activities into two groups, whereby a single consciousness takes up its position alternately with either the one or the other of these groups.

In psycho-analysis there is no choice for us but to declare mental processes to be in themselves unconscious, and to compare the perception of them by consciousness with the perception of the outside world through the sense-organs; we even hope to extract some fresh knowledge from the comparison. The psycho-analytic assumption of unconscious mental activity appears to us, on the one hand, a further development of that primitive animism which caused our own consciousness to be reflected in all around us; and, on the other hand, it seems to be an extension of the corrections begun by Kant in regard to our views on external perception. Just as Kant warned us not to overlook the fact that our perception is subjectively conditioned and must not be regarded as identical with the phenomena perceived but never really discerned, so psycho-analysis bids us not to set conscious perception in the place of the unconscious mental process which is its object. The mental, like the physical, is not necessarily in reality just what it appears to us to be. It is, however, satisfactory to find that the correction of inner perception does not present difficulties so great as that of outer perception—that the inner object is less hard to discern truly than is the outside world.

II. Different Significance of the Term Unconscious; the Topographical Aspect

Before going any further, let us note the important, though inconvenient, fact that unconsciousness is only one attribute of the mental and by no means suffices to describe its character. There are mental acts of very varying values which yet have in common the characteristic of being unconscious. The unconscious comprises, on the one hand, processes which are merely latent, temporarily unconscious, but which differ in no other respect from conscious ones and, on the other hand, processes such as those which have undergone repression, which if they came into consciousness must stand out in the crudest contrast to the rest of the conscious mind. It would put an end to all misunderstandings if, from now on, in describing the various kinds of mental acts we were to pay no attention to whether they were conscious or unconscious, but, when classifying and correlating them, inquired only to which instincts and aims they were related, how they were composed and to which of the systems in the mind that are superimposed one upon another they belonged. This, however, is for various reasons impracticable, and it follows that we cannot escape the imputation of ambiguity in that we use the words *conscious* and *unconscious* sometimes in a descriptive and sometimes in a systematic sense, in which latter they signify inclusion in some particular system and possession of certain characteristics. We might still attempt to avoid confusion by employing for the recognized mental systems certain arbitrarily chosen names which have no reference to consciousness. Only we should first have to justify the principles on which we distinguish the systems, and we should not be able to ignore the question of consciousness, seeing that it forms the point of departure for all our investigations. Perhaps we may look for some assistance from the proposal to employ, at any rate in writing, the abbreviation *Cs* for consciousness and the *Ucs* for the unconscious when we are using the two words in the systematic sense.

To deal with the positive aspects, we now assert on the findings of psycho-analysis that a mental act commonly goes through two phases, between which is interposed a kind of testing process (censorship). In the first phase, the mental act is unconscious and belongs to the system *Ucs;* if upon the scrutiny of the censorship it is rejected, it is not allowed to pass into the second phase; it is then said to be *repressed* and must remain unconscious. If, however, it passes this scrutiny, it enters upon the second phase and thenceforth belongs to the second system, which we will call the *Cs.* But the fact that it so belongs does not unequivocally determine its relation to consciousness. It is not yet conscious, but it is certainly *capable of entering consciousness*, according to J. Breuer's expression; that is, it can now, without any special resistance and given certain conditions, become the object of consciousness. In consideration of this capacity to become conscious, we also call the system *Cs* the *preconscious*. If it should turn out that a certain censorship also determines whether the preconscious becomes conscious, we shall discriminate more sharply between the systems *Pcs* and *Cs.* For the present let it suffice us to bear in mind that the system *Pcs* shares the characteristics of the *Cs,* and that the rigorous censorship exercises its office at the point of transition from the *Ucs* to the *Pcs* (or *Cs*).

By accepting the existence of these (two or three) mental systems, psycho-analysis has departed a step further from the descriptive psychology of consciousness and has taken to itself a new problem and a new content. Up till now, it differed from academic (descriptive) psychology mainly by reason of its dynamic conception of mental processes; now we have to add that it professes to consider mental topography also, and to indicate in respect of any given mental operation within what system or between what systems it runs its course. This attempt, too, has won it the name of *depth-psychology*. We shall hear that it may be further amplified by yet another aspect of the subject.

If we wish to treat seriously the notion of a topography of mental acts, we must direct our interest to a doubt which arises at this point. When a mental act (let us confine ourselves here to an act of ideation) is transferred from the system *Ucs* into the system *Cs* (or *Pcs*), are we to suppose that this transposition involves a fresh registration comparable to a second record of the idea in question, situated, moreover, in a fresh locality in the mind and side by side with which the original unconscious record continues to exist? Or are we rather to believe that the transformation consists in a change in the state of the idea, involving the same material and occurring in the same locality? This question may appear abstruse, but it must be put if we wish to form a more definite conception of mental topography, of the depth-dimension in the mind. It is a difficult one because it goes beyond pure psychology and touches on the relations of the mental apparatus to anatomy. We know that a rough correlation of this sort exists. Research has afforded irrefutable proof that mental activity is bound up with the function of the brain as with that of no other organ. The discovery of the unequal importance of the different parts of the brain and their individual relations to particular parts of the body and to intellectual activities takes us a step further—we do not know how big a step. But every attempt to deduce from these facts a localization of mental processes, every endeavour to think of ideas as stored up in nerve-cells and of excitations as passing along nerve-fibres, has completely miscarried. The same fate would await any doctrine which attempted to recognize, let us say, the anatomical position of the system *Cs*—conscious mental activity—in the cortex and to localize the unconscious processes in the subcortical parts of the brain. Here there is an hiatus which at present cannot be filled, nor is it one of the tasks of psychology to fill it. Our mental topography has for the present nothing to do with anatomy; it is concerned not with anatomical locations, but with regions in the mental apparatus, irrespective of their possible situation in the body.

In this respect, then, our work is untrammelled and may proceed according to its own requirements. It will, moreover, be useful for us to remind ourselves that our hypotheses can in the first instance lay claim only to the value of illustrations. The former of the two possibilities which we considered—namely, that the conscious phase of an idea implies a fresh record of it, which must be localized elsewhere—is doubtless the cruder but also the more convenient. The second assumption—that of a merely functional change of state—is *a priori* more probable, but it is less plastic, less easy to handle. With the first, or topographical, assumption is bound up that of a topographical separation of the systems *Cs* and *Ucs* and also the possibility that an idea may exist simultaneously in two parts of the mental apparatus—indeed, that if it is not inhibited by the censorship, it regularly advances from the one position to the other, possibly without its first location or record being abandoned. This may seem odd, but it can be supported by observations from psycho-analytic practise.

If we communicate to a patient some idea which he has at one time repressed but which we have discovered in him, our telling him makes at first no change in his mental condition. Above all, it does not remove the repression nor undo its effects, as might perhaps be expected from the fact that the previously unconscious idea has now become conscious. On the contrary, all that we shall achieve at first will be a fresh rejection of the repressed idea. At this point, however, the patient has in actual fact the same idea in two forms in two separate localities in his mental apparatus: first, he has the conscious memory of the auditory impression of the idea conveyed in what we told him, and, secondly and side by side with this, he has—as we know for certain—the unconscious memory of his actual experience existing in him in its earlier form. Now in reality there is no lifting of the repression until the conscious idea, after overcoming the resistances, has united with the unconscious memory-trace. Only through bringing the latter itself into consciousness is the effect achieved. On superficial consideration this would seem to show that conscious and unconscious ideas are different and topographically separated records of the same content. But a moment's reflection shows that the identity of the information given to the patient with his own repressed memory is only apparent. To have listened to something and to have experienced something **are** psychologically two different things, even though the content of each be the same.

So, for the moment, we are not able to decide between the two possibilities that we have discussed. Perhaps later on we shall come upon certain factors which may turn the balance in favour of one or the other. Perhaps we shall discover that our question, as we formulated it, was not sufficiently comprehensive and that the difference between a conscious and an unconscience idea has to be defined quite otherwise.

III. *Unconscious Emotions*

We limited the foregoing discussion to ideas and may now raise a new question, the answer to which must contribute to the elucidation of our theoretical position. We said that there were conscious and unconscious ideas; but are there also unconscious instinctual impulses, emotions, and feelings, or are such constructions in this instance devoid of any meaning?

I am indeed of opinion that the antithesis of conscious and unconscious does not hold for instincts. An instinct can never be an object of consciousness—only the idea that represents the instinct. Even in the unconscious, moreover, it can only be represented by the idea. If the instinct did not attach itself to an idea or manifest itself as an affective state, we could know nothing about it. Though we do speak of an unconscious or a repressed instinctual impulse, this is a looseness of phraseology which is quite harmless. We can only mean an instinctual impulse the ideational presentation of which is unconscious, for nothing else comes into consideration.

We should expect the answer to the question about unconscious feelings, emotions, and affects to be just as easily given. It is surely of the essence of an emotion that we should feel it, i.e., that it should enter consciousness. So for emotions, feelings, and affects to be unconscious would be quite out of the question. But in psycho-analytic practise we are accustomed to speak of unconscious love, hate, anger, etc., and find it impossible to avoid even the strange conjunction, *unconscious consciousness of guilt,* or a paradoxical *unconscious anxiety.* Is there more meaning in the use of these terms than there is in speaking of *unconscious instincts?*

The two cases are really not on all fours. To begin with, it may happen that an affect or an emotion is perceived, but misconstrued. By the repression of its proper presentation, it is forced to become connected with another idea, and is now interpreted by consciousness as the expression of this other idea. If we restore the true connection, we call the original affect *unconscious,* although the affect was never unconscious, but its ideational presentation had undergone repression. In any event, the use of such terms as *unconscious affect and emotion* has reference to the fate undergone, in consequence of repression, by the quantitative factor in the instinctual impulse.[1] We know that an affect may be subjected to three different vicissitudes: either it remains, wholly or in part, as it is; or it is transformed into a qualitatively different charge of affect, above all into anxiety; or it is suppressed, i.e., its development is hindered altogether. (These possibilities may perhaps be studied even more easily in the technique of the dream-work than in the neuroses.) We know, too, that to suppress the development of affect is the true aim of repression and that its work does not terminate if this aim is not achieved. In every instance where repression has succeeded in inhibiting the development of an affect we apply the term *unconscious* to those affects that are restored when we undo the work of repression. So it cannot be denied that the use of the terms in question is logical; but a comparison of the unconscious affect with the unconscious idea reveals the significant difference that the unconscious idea continues, after repression, as an actual formation in the system *Ucs,* whilst to the unconscious affect there corresponds in the same system only a potential disposition which is prevented from developing further. So that, strictly speaking, although no fault be found with the mode of expression in question, there are no unconscious affects in the sense in which there are unconscious ideas. But there may very well be in the system *Ucs* affect-formations which, like others, come into consciousness. The whole difference arises from the fact that ideas are cathexes—ultimately of memory-traces—whilst affects and emotions correspond with processes of discharge, the final expression of which is perceived as feeling. In the present state of our knowledge of affects and emotions, we cannot express this difference more clearly.

It is of especial interest to us to have established the fact that repression can succeed in inhibiting the transformation of an instinctual impulse into affective expression. This shows us that the system *Cs* normally controls affectivity as well as access to motility; and this enhances the importance of repression, since it shows us that the latter is responsible, not

merely when something is withheld from consciousness, but also when affective development and the inauguration of muscular activity is prevented. Conversely, too, we may say that as long as the system *Cs* controls activity and motility, the mental condition of the person in question may be called *normal.* Nevertheless, there is an unmistakable difference in the relation of the controlling system to the two allied processes of discharge.[2] Whereas the control of the system *Cs* over voluntary motility is firmly rooted, regularly withstands the onslaught of neurosis, and only breaks down in psychosis, the control of the *Cs* over affective development is less firmly established. Even in normal life we can recognize that a constant struggle for primacy over affectivity goes on between the two systems *Cs* and *Pcs,* that certain spheres of influence are marked off one from another, and that the forces at work tend to mingle.

The importance of the system *Cs (Pcs)* for the avenues of affective and motor discharge enables us to understand also the rôle which falls to substitutive ideas in determining the form of a disease. It is possible for affective development to proceed directly from the system *Ucs;* in this case it always has the character of anxiety, the substitute for all repressed affects. Often, however, the instinctual impulse has to wait until it has found a substitutive idea in the system *Cs.* Affective development can then proceed from this conscious substitute, the nature of which determines the qualitative character of the affect. We have asserted that, under repression, a severance takes place between the affect and the idea to which it belongs, and that each then fulfils its separate destiny. For purposes of description this is incontrovertible; in actuality, however, the affect does not as a rule arise until it has succeeded in penetrating into the *Cs* in attachment to some new substitutive idea.

IV. *Topography and Dynamics of Repression*

So far we have gathered from our discussion that repression is essentially a process affecting ideas, on the border between the systems *Ucs* and *Pcs (Cs),* and we can now make a fresh attempt to describe this process more minutely. It must be a matter of withdrawal of cathexis; but the question is: in what system

[1] Cf. the preceding paper on *Repression,* p. 422.

[2] Affectivity manifests itself essentially in motor (i.e., secretory and circulatory) discharge resulting in an (internal) alteration of the subject's own body without reference to the outer world; motility, in actions designed to effect changes in the outer world.

does the withdrawal take place and to which system does the cathexis withdrawn belong?

In the *Ucs* the repressed idea remains capable of action and must therefore have retained its cathexis. So it must be something else which has been withdrawn. Let us take the case of repression proper *(after-expulsion)*, as it affects an idea which is preconscious or even has already entered consciousness. Repression can consist here only in the withdrawal from the idea of the (pre)conscious cathexis which belongs to the system *Pcs*. The idea then remains without cathexis, or receives cathexis from the *Ucs*, or retains the unconscious cathexis which it previously had. We have, therefore, withdrawal of the preconscious, retention of the unconscious, or substitution of an unconscious for a preconscious, cathexis. We notice, moreover, that we have unintentionally, as it were, based these reflections upon the assumption that the transition from the system *Ucs* to the system nearest to it is not effected through the making of a new record but through a change in its state, an alteration in its cathexis. The functional hypothesis has here easily routed the topographical.

But this process of withdrawal of libido does not suffice to make comprehensible to us another characteristic of repression. It is not clear why the idea which has retained its cathexis, or has received cathexis from the *Ucs,* should not, in virtue of its cathexis, renew the attempt to penetrate into the system *Pcs*. The withdrawal of libido would then have to be repeated, and the same performance would recur interminably, but the result would not be repression. In the same way the mechanism just discussed of withdrawal of preconscious cathexis would fail to explain the process of primal repression; for here we have to consider an unconscious idea which as yet has received no cathexis from the *Pcs* and therefore cannot be deprived of it.

What we are looking for, therefore, is another process which maintains the repression in the first case and, in the second, ensures its being established and continued; and this other process we can only find in the assumption of an *anti-cathexis*, by means of which the system *Pcs* guards itself against the intrusion of the unconscious idea. We shall see from clinical examples how such an anti-cathexis established in the system *Pcs* manifests itself. This it is which represents the continuous effort demanded by a primal repression but also guarantees its persistence. The anti-cathexis is the sole mechanism of primal repression; in the case of

repression proper *(after-expulsion)* there is in addition withdrawal of the preconscious cathexis. It is quite possible that the cathexis withdrawn from the idea is the very one used for anti-cathexis.

We see how we have gradually been led to introduce a third point of view into the scheme of mental phenomena—beside the dynamic and the topographical, we take the *economic* standpoint, one from which we try to follow out the fate of given volumes of excitation and to achieve, at least relatively, some assessment of it. It will be only right to give a special name to the way of regarding things which is the final result of psycho-analytic research. I propose that, when we succeed in describing a mental process in all its aspects, dynamic, topographic, and economic, we shall call this a *metapsychological* presentation. We must say beforehand that in the present state of our knowledge we shall succeed in this only at isolated points.

Let us make a tentative effort to give a metapsychological description of the process of repression in the three transference neuroses, which are familiar to us. Here we may substitute for the term *cathexis* that of *libido*, because, as we know, in this case it is the fates of sexual impulses with which we are dealing.

In anxiety-hysteria a preliminary phase of the process is frequently overlooked, perhaps indeed is really omitted; on careful observation, however, it can be clearly discerned. It consists in anxiety appearing without the subject knowing what he is afraid of. We must suppose that there was present in the *Ucs* some love-impulse which demanded to be translated into the system *Pcs;* the preconscious cathexis, however, recoiled from it in the manner of an attempt at flight, and the unconscious libidinal cathexis of the rejected idea was discharged in the form of anxiety. Then, at some repetition of this process, a first step was taken in the direction of mastering this distressing development of anxiety. The fugitive cathexis attached itself to a substitutive idea which, on the one hand, was connected by association with the rejected idea, and, on the other, escaped repression by reason of its remoteness from that idea (displacement-substitute), and which permitted of a rationalization of the still uncontrollable outbreak of anxiety. The substitutive idea now plays the part of an anti-cathexis for the system *Cs (Pcs)* by securing that system against an emergence into consciousness of the repressed idea; on the other hand, it is, or acts as if it were, the point at which the anxiety-affect, which is now all the more uncontrollable, may break out and be discharged. Clinical observation shows, for instance, that when a child suffers from an animal-phobia he experiences anxiety under two kinds of conditions: in the first place, when the repressed love-impulse becomes intensified, and, in the second, when the child perceives the animal it is afraid of. The substitutive idea acts in the one instance as a conductor from the system *Ucs* to the system *Cs;* in the other instance, as an independent source for the release of anxiety. The extending control on the part of the system *Cs* usually manifests itself by a tendency for the substitutive idea to be aroused more easily as time goes on in the second rather than the first way. Perhaps the child ends by behaving as though he had no liking at all for his father but had become quite free from him, and as though the fear of the animal were the real fear. Only that this fear of the animal, fed as such a fear is from the springs of unconscious instinct, proves obdurate and extravagant in the face of all influences brought to bear from the system *Cs*, and thereby betrays its origin in the system *Ucs*.

In the second phase of anxiety-hysteria, therefore, the anti-cathexis from the system *Cs* has led to substitute-formation. Soon the same mechanism is applied in a fresh direction. The process of repression, as we know, is not yet terminated, and finds a further aim in the task of inhibiting the outbreak of anxiety started by the substitute. This happens in the following manner: all the associations in the neighbourhood of the substitutive idea become endowed with a peculiar intensity of cathexis, so that they may display a high degree of sensibility to excitation. Excitation at any point of this protective structure must, on account of its connection with the substitutive idea, give rise to a slight degree of development of anxiety, which is then used as a signal to inhibit, by means of a fresh flight on the part of the cathexis, any further development of anxiety. The further the sensitive and vigilant anti-cathexis becomes extended round the substitute which is feared, the more exactly can the mechanism function which is designed to isolate the substitutive idea and to protect it from fresh excitation. Naturally these precautions guard only against excitations approaching the substitutive idea from without through perception, never against instinctual excitation which encounters the substitutive idea from the direction of its connection with the repressed idea.

So they begin to operate only when the substitute has successfully taken over representation of what has been repressed, and they can never operate with complete security. With each increase of instinctual excitation, the protecting rampart round the substitutive idea must be shifted a little further outwards. The whole construction, which is produced in analogous fashion in the other neuroses, is termed a *phobia*. The avoidances, renunciations, and prohibitions by which we recognize anxiety-hysteria are the manifestations of flight from conscious cathexis of the substitutive idea. Surveying the whole process, we may say that the third phase has repeated and amplified the work of the second. The system *Cs* now protects itself by an anti-cathexis of its surrounding associations against the activation of the substitutive idea, just as previously that system secured itself by cathexis of the substitutive idea against the emergence of the repressed idea. Substitute-formation by the way of displacement has thus proceeded in its course. We must also add that the system *Cs* had formerly only one little point at which the repressed instinctual impulse could break through, namely, the substitutive idea; but that ultimately the whole protective structure of the phobia corresponds to a salient of unconscious influence of this kind. Further, we may lay stress on the interesting point of view that, by the whole defence-mechanism thus set in action, a projection outwards of the menace from the instinct has been achieved. The ego behaves as if the danger of an outbreak of anxiety threatened it not from the direction of an instinct but from the direction of perception: this enables the ego to react against this external danger with the attempts at flight consisting of the avoidances characteristic of a phobia. In this process, repression succeeds in one particular: the discharge of anxiety may be to some extent dammed up, but only at a heavy sacrifice of personal freedom. Attempts at flight from the claims of instinct are, however, in general useless, and the result of the flight by means of a phobia remains still unsatisfactory.

A great deal of what we have recognized as true of anxiety-hysteria holds good for the two other neuroses also, so that we can confine our discussion to the points of difference and the part played by the anti-cathexis. In conversion-hysteria the instinctual cathexis of the repressed idea is transformed into the innervation necessary for the symptom. How far and in what circumstances the unconscious idea discharges its cathexis through this outlet towards inner-vation, so that it can relinquish its pressure towards the system *Cs*—these and similar questions had better be reserved for a special investigation of hysteria. In conversion-hysteria, the part played by the anti-cathexis proceeding from the system *Cs (Pcs)* is clear and becomes manifest in the symptom-formation. It is the anti-cathexis that decides upon what part of the instinct-presentation the whole cathexis may be concentrated. The part thus selected to form a symptom fulfils the condition of expressing the aim of the instinctual impulse no less than the defensive or punishing endeavour of the system *Cs;* so it achieves hyper-cathexis and is maintained from both directions like the substitutive idea in anxiety-hysteria. From this circumstance we may conclude without much more ado that the degree of expenditure in repression put forth by the system *Cs* need not be commensurate with the energic cathexis of the symptom; for the strength of the repression is measured by the anti-cathexis put forth, and the symptom is supported not only by this anti-cathexis, but also by the instinctual cathexis from the system *Ucs* which is interwoven with it.

With reference to the obsessional neurosis, we need only add to the observations brought forward in the preceding paper[1] that here the anti-cathexis of the system *Cs* comes most noticeably into the foreground. It is this that brings about the first repression, in the shape of a reaction-formation, and later it is the point at which the repressed idea breaks through. We may find room for the supposition that, if the work of repression seems far less successful in anxiety-hysteria and in the obsessional neurosis than in conversion-hysteria, it is because the anti-cathexis is so prominent, and all outlet is lacking.

V. *Special Characteristics of the System* Ucs

The differentiation we have drawn between the two systems within the mind receives fresh significance when we observe that processes in the one system, *Ucs,* show characteristics which are not again met with in the system immediately above it.

The kernel of the system *Ucs* consists of instinct-presentations whose aim is to discharge their cathexis; that is to say, they are wish-impulses. These instinctual impulses are co-ordinate with one another, exist independently side by side, and are exempt from mutual con-

tradiction. When two wishes whose aims must appear to us incompatible become simultaneously active, the two impulses do not detract one from the other or cancel each other, but combine to form an intermediate aim, a compromise.

There is in this system no negation, no dubiety, no varying degree of certainty: all this is only imported by the work of the censorship which exists between the *Ucs* and the *Pcs.* Negation is, at a higher level, a substitute for repression. In the *Ucs* there are only contents more or less strongly cathected.

Intensity of cathexis is mobile in a far greater degree in this than in the other systems. By the process of displacement, one idea may surrender to another the whole volume of its cathexis; by that of condensation it may appropriate the whole cathexis of several other ideas. I have proposed to regard these two processes as distinguishing marks of the so-called *primary process* in the mind. In the system *Pcs* the *secondary process*[2] holds sway; where a primary process is allowed to take its course in connection with elements belonging to the system *Pcs*, it appears comic and excites laughter.

The processes of the system *Ucs* are timeless; i.e., they are not ordered temporally, are not altered by the passage of time, in fact bear no relation to time at all. The time-relation also is bound up with the work of the system *Cs.*

The processes of the *Ucs* are just as little related to reality. They are subject to the pleasure-principle; their fate depends only upon the degree of their strength and upon their conformity to regulation by pleasure and pain.

Let us sum up: *exemption from mutual contradiction, primary process* (motility of cathexis), *timelessness,* and *substitution of psychic for external reality*—these are the characteristics which we may expect to find in processes belonging to the system *Ucs.*[3]

Unconscious processes can only be observed by us under the conditions of dreaming and of neurosis; that is to say, when the processes of the higher system *Pcs* revert to an earlier level by a certain process of degradation (regression). Independently they are unrecognizable, indeed cannot exist, for the system *Ucs* is at a very early stage overlaid by the system *Pcs* which has captured the means of access to con-

---

[1] P. 426.

[2] Cf. Section VII of *The Interpretation of Dreams,* which is based upon ideas developed by J. Breuer in *Studien über Hysterie.*

[3] We are reserving for a different context the mention of another notable privilege of the system *Ucs.*

sciousness and to motility. The means of discharge for the system *Ucs* is by means of physical innervation leading to development of affect, but even this outlet is, as we have seen, contested by the system *Pcs*. Left to itself, the system *Ucs* would not in normal conditions be able to bring about any purposive muscular acts, with the exception of those already organized as reflexes.

In order to grasp the full significance of the characteristics of the system *Ucs* described above, we should have to contrast and compare them with those of the system *Pcs*. But this would take us so far afield that I propose that we should once more call a halt and not undertake the comparison of the two till we can do so in connection with our discussion of the higher system: only the most pressing points of all shall be mentioned at this stage.

The processes of the system *Pcs* display, no matter whether they are already conscious or only capable of becoming conscious, an inhibition of the tendency of cathected ideas towards discharge. When a process moves over from one idea to another, the first retains a part of its cathexis, and only a small part undergoes displacement. Displacement and condensation after the mode of the primary process are excluded or very much restricted. This circumstance caused Breuer to assume the existence of two different stages of cathectic energy in mental life: one in which that energy is tonically *bound*, and the other in which it moves freely and presses towards discharge. I think that this discrimination represents the deepest insight we have gained up to the present into the nature of nervous energy, and I do not see how we are to evade such a conclusion. A metapsychological presentation most urgently calls for further discussion at this point, though perhaps that would still be too daring an undertaking.

Further, it devolves upon the system *Pcs* to make communication possible between the different ideational contents so that they can influence one another, to give them a relation to time, to set up the censorship or censorships, and to establish the institution of *testing reality* and the reality-principle. Conscious memory, too, seems to depend wholly on the *Pcs* and should be clearly distinguished from the memory-traces in which the experiences of the *Ucs* become fixed; it probably corresponds with the making of a special record—a conception which we tried to employ as explaining the relation of conscious to unconscious ideas, but

which we have already discarded. In this connection, also, we shall find the means to put an end to our uncertainty regarding the name of the higher system which at present we vaguely call sometimes the *Pcs* and sometimes the *Cs*.

Here, too, it will be as well to utter a warning against over-hasty generalizations about what we have brought to light in regard to apportioning the various mental activities to one or other of the two systems. We are describing the state of affairs as it appears in the adult human being, in whom the system *Ucs* in the strict sense functions only as a stage preliminary to the higher organization. The content and connections of this system as the individual develops, the significance it possesses in the case of animals—these are points on which no conclusion can be deduced from our description: they must be investigated independently. Moreover, in the human being we must be prepared to find possible pathological conditions under which the two systems alter, or even exchange, both their content and their characteristics.

VI. *Communication between the Two Systems*

It would certainly be wrong to imagine that the *Ucs* remains at rest while the whole work of the mind is performed by the *Pcs*, that the *Ucs* is something finished with, a vestigial organ, a residuum from the process of evolution; wrong also to assume that communication between the two systems is confined to the act of repression, the *Pcs* casting everything which disturbs it into the abyss of the *Ucs*. On the contrary, the *Ucs* is living and capable of development and maintains a number of other relations to the *Pcs*, amongst them that of co-operation. To sum up, we must say that the *Ucs* is continued into its so-called *derivatives*, is accessible to the influence of life, perpetually acts upon the *Pcs*, and even is, on its part, capable of influence by the latter system.

Study of the derivatives of the *Ucs* will altogether disappoint our expectations of a schematically clear division of the one mental system from the other. This circumstance will certainly give rise to dissatisfaction with our results and will probably be used to cast doubts upon the value of our way of distinguishing the two groups of mental processes. Our answer is, however, that we have no other aim but that of translating into theory the results of observation, and we shall deny that there is any obligation on us to achieve, at our very first attempt, a theory that commends itself by its simplicity, in which all is plain sailing. We defend its complexities so long as we find that they fit in with the results of observation, and we do not abandon our expectation of being guided in the end by those very complexities to recognition of a state of affairs that is at once simple in itself and at the same time answers to all the complications of reality.

Amongst the derivatives of the unconscious instinctual impulses, the character of which we have just described, there are some which unite in themselves opposite features. On the one hand, they are highly organized, exempt from self-contradictoriness, have made use of every acquisition of the system *Cs,* and would hardly be distinguished by our ordinary judgment from the formations of that system. On the other hand, they are unconscious and are incapable of becoming conscious. Thus they belong according to their qualities to the system *Pcs,* but in actual fact to the *Ucs.* Their origin remains decisive for the fate they will undergo. We may compare them with those human half-breeds who, taken all round, resemble white men, but betray their coloured descent by some striking feature or other, on account of which they are excluded from society and enjoy none of the privileges of white people. Of such a nature are the *phantasy-formations* of normal persons as well as of neurotics, which we have recognized as preliminary phases in the formation both of dreams and of symptoms, and which, in spite of their high degree of organization, remain repressed and therefore cannot become conscious. They draw near to consciousness and remain undisturbed so long as they do not become strongly cathected, but as soon as a certain degree of this is exceeded, they are thrust back. Substitute-formations are similar, more highly organized derivatives of the *Ucs;* but these succeed in breaking through into consciousness, thanks to some favourable relation, as, for example, when they coincide with a preconscious anti-cathexis.

When, on another occasion, we examine more closely the way in which entry into consciousness is conditioned, we shall be able to find a solution for some of the difficulties arising here. At this point, it seems a good plan to contrast with the foregoing points of view, which take their rise in consideration of the *Ucs,* one which presents itself from the direction of consciousness. Consciousness regards the whole sum of mental processes as belonging to the realm of the preconscious. A very great part of this preconscious material originates in the unconscious, has the characteristics of derivatives of the unconscious, and is subject to a censorship before it can pass into consciousness. Another part of the *Pcs* can become conscious without any censorship. Here we light upon a contradiction of an earlier assumption: from the point of view of repression, we were obliged to place the censorship which is decisive for consciousness between the systems *Ucs* and *Pcs.* Now it becomes probable to us that there is a censorship between the *Pcs* and the *Cs.* But we shall do well not to regard this complication as a difficulty, but to assume that to every transition from one system to that immediately above it (that is, every advance to a higher stage of mental organization) there corresponds a new censorship. As a corollary, we shall have, it is true, to discard the assumption of a continuous laying down of new records.

The reason for all these difficulties is that consciousness, the only characteristic of mental processes directly available to us, is in no wise suited to serve as a criterion for the erection of systems. Apart from the circumstance that what belongs to consciousness is not always in consciousness but can also be temporarily latent, observation has shown that much which shares the attributes of the system *Pcs* does not become conscious; and, further, we shall find that the entry into consciousness is circumscribed by certain dispositions of attention. Hence consciousness stands in no simple relation either to the different systems or to the process of repression. The truth is that it is not only what is repressed that remains alien to consciousness, but also some of the impulses which dominate our ego and which therefore form the strongest functional antithesis to what is repressed. In proportion as we try to win our way to a metapsychological view of mental life, we must learn to emancipate ourselves from our sense of the importance of that symptom which consists in *being conscious.*

So long as we still cling to this, we see our generalizations regularly invaded by exceptions. We see that derivatives of the *Pcs* enter consciousness as substitute-formations and as symptoms, generally after undergoing great distortion in contrast to the *Ucs,* although often many characteristics inviting repression have been retained. We find that many preconscious formations remain unconscious, though, to judge by their nature, we should suppose that they might very well become conscious. Probably in their case the stronger attraction of the *Ucs* asserts itself. We are led to look for the more important difference, not between the conscious and the preconscious, but between the preconscious and the unconscious. On the border of the *Pcs*, the censorship thrusts back the *Ucs*, but its derivatives can circumvent this censorship, achieve a high degree of organization, and in the *Pcs* reach a certain intensity of cathexis; when, however, this is exceeded, and they try to force themselves into consciousness, they are recognized as derivatives of the *Ucs*, and are repressed afresh at the new frontier by the censorship between the *Cs* and the *Pcs*. Thus the former censorship is exercised against the *Ucs* itself, and the latter against its preconscious derivatives. We might suppose that in the course of individual development the censorship had been advanced a step.

In psycho-analytic treatment the existence of the second censorship, located between the systems *Pcs* and *Cs*, is proved beyond question. We require the patient to produce freely derivatives of the *Ucs*, we pledge him to overcome the objections of the censorship against these preconscious formations becoming conscious, and, by overthrowing this censorship, we open up the way to abrogating the repression accomplished by the earlier one. To this let us add that the existence of the censorship between the *Pcs* and the *Cs* teaches us that becoming conscious is no mere act of perception, but is probably also a *hyper-cathexis,* a further advance in the mental organization.

Let us turn our attention to the communications existing between the unconscious and the other systems, not so much with a view to establishing any fresh fact as in order to avoid omitting the most prominent features. At the roots of instinctual activity, the systems communicate with one another in the freest possible way: some of the processes here set in motion pass through the *Ucs*, as through a preparatory stage, and reach the highest mental development in the *Cs*, whilst some are retained as the *Ucs*. But the *Ucs* is also affected by experiences originating in outer perception. Normally all the paths from perception to the *Ucs* remain open; only those leading out from the *Ucs* are barred by repression.

It is very remarkable that the *Ucs* of one human being can react upon that of another, without the *Cs* being implicated at all. This deserves closer investigation, especially with a view to finding out whether preconscious activity can be excluded as a factor in bringing this about; but for purposes of description the fact is incontestable.

The content of the system *Pcs* (or *Cs*) is derived partly from the instinctual life (through the medium of the *Ucs*), and partly from perception. It is doubtful how far the processes of this system can exert a direct influence on the *Ucs*; examination of pathological cases often reveals an almost incredible independence and lack of susceptibility to influence on the part of the *Ucs*. A complete divergence of their tendencies, a total dissociation of the two systems, is a general characteristic of disease. Yet psychoanalytic treatment is based upon influence by the *Cs* on the *Ucs*, and shows at any rate that, though laborious, this is not impossible. The derivatives of the *Ucs* which act as intermediaries between the two systems open the way, as we have already said, towards accomplishing this. But we may well suppose that a spontaneously effected alteration in the *Ucs* from the side of the *Cs* is a difficult and slow process.

Co-operation between a preconscious and an unconscious impulse, even when the latter is subject to very strong repression, may be established, if the situation permits of the unconscious impulse operating in harmony with one of the controlling tendencies. The repression is removed for the occasion, the repressed activity being admitted as a reinforcement of the one intended by the ego. In respect of this single constellation, the unconscious becomes ego-syntonic, falls into line with the ego, without any change taking place in the repression otherwise. The effect of the *Ucs* in this co-operation is unmistakable; the reinforced tendencies reveal themselves as, in spite of all, different from the normal—they make possible achievements of special perfection, and they manifest a resistance in the face of opposition similar to that of obsessional symptoms.

The content of the *Ucs* may be compared with a primitive population in the mental kingdom. If inherited mental formations exist in the human being—something analogous to instinct in animals—these constitute the nucleus of the *Ucs*. Later there is added all that is discarded as useless during childhood development, and this need not differ in its nature from what is inherited. A sharp and final division between the content of the two systems, as a rule, takes place only at puberty.

VII. *Recognition of the Unconscious*

So long as we derive our ideas of the *Ucs* only from our knowledge of dream-life and the transference neuroses, all that we can predicate of that system is probably represented in the foregoing remarks. It is certainly not much, and at some points it gives an impression of obscurity and confusion; especially do we look in vain for the possibility of bringing the *Ucs* into any connection, or classifying it under any heading, with which we are already familiar. Analysis of one of those affections called *narcissistic psychoneuroses* alone promises to furnish us with conceptions through which the enigmatic *Ucs* will be brought within our reach in a tangible fashion.

Since the publication of a work by Abraham (1908)—attributed by its conscientious author to my instigation—we have been trying to define Kraepelin's dementia praecox (Bleuler's schizophrenia) on the basis of its relation to that pair of opposites consisting of the ego and its object. In the transference neuroses (anxiety- and conversion-hysteria and the obsessional neurosis) there was nothing to give special prominence to these opposites. We knew, indeed, that frustration from the side of the object occasioned the outbreak of neurosis and that neurosis involved abandonment of the real object; also that the libido withdrawn from the real object reverted first to an object in phantasy and then to one that had been repressed (introversion). But object-cathexis in general is in such cases retained with great energy, and more minute examination of the processes of repression has forced us to assume that object-cathexis persists in the system *Ucs* in spite of—or rather in consequence of—the repression. Indeed the capacity for transference, of which we make use for therapeutic purposes in these affections, presupposes unimpaired object-cathexis.

In schizophrenia, on the other hand, we have been obliged to assume that after the process of repression the withdrawn libido does not seek a new object, but retreats into the ego; that is to say, that here the object-cathexes are given up, and a primitive objectless condition of narcissism is re-established. The incapacity of these patients for transference—so far as the process of disease extends—their consequent inaccessibility to therapeutic efforts, the repudiation of the outer world characteristic of them, the manifestations of hyper-cathexis of their ego, the final outcome in complete apathy—all these clinical features seem to accord excellently with the assumption that object-cathexes are relinquished. As regards the relation of the two psychical systems to each other, all observers have been struck by the fact that in schizophrenia a great deal is consciously expressed which in the transference neuroses can be demonstrated to exist in the *Ucs* only by means of psycho-analysis. But at the beginning we were not able to establish any intelligible connection between the ego-object relation and the relationships of consciousness.

In the following unexpected way, we seem to arrive at what we are seeking. In schizophrenics we observe—especially in the earlier stages which are so instructive—a number of changes in *speech*, some of which deserve to be regarded from a particular point of view. The patient often devotes peculiar care to his way of expressing himself, which becomes "precious" and "elaborate." The construction of the sentences undergoes a peculiar disorganization, making them so incomprehensible to us that the patient's remarks seem nonsensical. Often some relation to bodily organs or innervations is prominent in the content of these utterances. This may be correlated with another observation, namely, that, in such symptoms of schizophrenia as are comparable with the substitute-formations of hysteria or the obsessional neurosis, the relation between the substitute and the repressed material nevertheless displays peculiarities which would surprise us in these two forms of neurosis.

Dr. Viktor Tausk of Vienna has placed at my disposal some observations that he has made in the initial stages of schizophrenia, which are particularly valuable in that the patient herself was anxious to explain her utterances further. I will take two of his examples to illustrate the thesis I wish to defend, and I have no doubt that every observer could easily produce plenty of such material.

One of Tausk's patients, a girl who was brought to the clinic after a quarrel with her lover, complained that *her eyes were not right, they were twisted*. This she herself explained by uttering in properly constructed sentences a series of reproaches against her lover. "She could not understand him at all, he looked different every time; he was a shammer, an eye-twister,[1] he had twisted her eyes; now they were not her eyes any more; now she saw the world with different eyes."

The patient's remarks about her first incomprehensible utterance have the value of an analysis, for they contain the equivalent of the original words expressed in a generally com-

---

[1] *Augenverdreher,* used in German to mean a deceiver.—TR.

prehensible form; at the same time, they explain the meaning and the genesis of speech-formation in schizophrenia. In agreement with Tausk, I would here lay stress on the point that the relation to the bodily organ (the eye) has usurped the place of the whole content of the thought. The schizophrenic speech displays a hypochondriac trait: it has become *organ-speech*.

A second remark of the same patient's runs: "She was standing in church, suddenly she felt a jerk, she had to *change her position*, as though somebody put her into a position, as though she were *placed in a certain position*."

There follows the analysis by means of a fresh series of reproaches against her lover: "he was common, he had made her common, too, though she was naturally refined; he had made her like himself by leading her to think that he was superior to her; now she had become like him, because she thought she would be better if she were like him; he had *given a false impression of his own position;*[1] now she was just like him (identification!), he had *changed her position*."[2]

The movement by which she *changed her position*, Tausk remarks, stood for the idea of *misrepresenting her position* and for the identification with the lover. Again I would call attention to the manner in which the whole train of thought is dominated by that element which has for its content a bodily innervation (or, rather, the sensation of it). An hysteric would, in the first case, have convulsively rolled her eyes, and, in the second, have given actual jerks, instead of having the impulse to jerk or the sensation of being jerked; and in neither case would this have been accompanied by any conscious thoughts, nor would she afterwards have been able to express any such thoughts.

So far these two observations illustrate what we have called hypochrondriac language or *organ-speech*. But they also point to something which seems to us more important, namely, to another state of things of which we have innumerable instances (for example, in the cases quoted in Bleuler's monograph) and which may be reduced to a definite formula. In schizophrenia, *words* are subject to the same process as that which makes dream-images out of dream-thoughts, the one we have called the primary mental process. They undergo conden-

sation, and, by means of displacement, transfer their cathexes to one another without remainder; the process may extend so far that a single word, which on account of its manifold relations is especially suitable, can come to represent a whole train of thought. The works of Bleuler, Jung, and their pupils have yielded abundant material precisely in support of this very proposition.[3]

Before we draw any conclusion from impressions such as these, let us consider further the distinctions between the substitutive idea in schizophrenia and in hysteria and the obsessional neurosis—nice distinctions, it is true, yet producing a very strange effect. A patient whom I have at present under observation has let himself withdraw from all the interests of life on account of the unhealthy condition of the skin of his face. He declares that he has blackheads and that there are deep holes in his face which everyone notices. Analysis shows that he is working out his castration complex upon his skin. At first he busied himself with these blackheads without any misgivings; and it gave him great pleasure to squeeze them out, because, as he said, something spurted out when he did so. Then he began to think that there was a deep cavity wherever he had got rid of a blackhead and he reproached himself most vehemently with having ruined his skin forever by "constantly fiddling at it with his hand." Pressing out the content of the blackheads is clearly to him a substitute for onanism. The cavity which then appears in consequence of his guilty act is the female genital, i.e., stands for the fulfilment of the threat of castration (or the phantasy representing it) called forth by onanism. This substitute-formation has, in spite of its hypochondriacal character, considerable resemblance to an hysterical conversion; and yet we have the feeling that there must be something different in it, that we cannot believe such a substitute-formation possible in a case of hysteria, even before we can say in what the difference consists. A tiny little hole such as a pore of the skin will hardly be used by an hysteric as a symbol for the vagina, which otherwise he will compare with every imaginable object capable of enclosing a space. Besides, we should think that the multiplicity of these little cavities would prevent him from using them as a substitute for the female genital. The same applies to the case of a young patient re-

---

[1] *Sich verstellen*=to feign, disguise oneself.—TR.
[2] *Verstellen*=to change the place of. As with *Augen-verdreher*, there is again a play on words, the concrete meaning of the word replacing its metaphorical sense.—TR.

[3] The dream-work, too, occasionally treats words like things, and then creates very similar *schizophrenic* utterances or neologisms.

ported by Tausk some years ago to the Vienna Psycho-Analytical Society. This patient behaved in other respects exactly as though suffering from an obsessional neurosis; he took hours to dress, and so on. The striking feature of the case, however, was that he was able to tell the meaning of his inhibitions without any resistance. For example, in pulling on his stockings he was disturbed by the idea that he must draw apart the knitted stitches, i.e., the holes, and every hole was for him a symbol of the female genital aperture. This again is a thing with which we cannot credit a patient suffering from obsessional neurosis; a patient of this kind observed by R. Reitler (one who suffered from the same lingering over putting on his stockings), after overcoming the resistances, found the explanation that his foot symbolised the penis, putting on the stocking stood for an onanistic act, and that he had constantly to pull the stocking off and on, partly in order to complete the representation of onanism, and partly in order to undo the act.

If we ask ourselves what it is that gives the character of strangeness to the substitute-formation and the symptom in schizophrenia, we come at last to understand that it is the predominance of the word-relation over that of the thing. There is only a very slight similarity between the squeezing out of a blackhead and an ejaculation from the penis, still less similarity between the countless little pores of the skin and the vagina; but in the former case there *is,* in both instances, a spurting out, while in the latter the cynical saying, "a hole is a hole," is *literally* true. The identity of the two when expressed in *words,* not the resemblance of the objects designated, has dictated the substitution. Where the two—word and thing—do not coincide, the substitute-formation in schizophrenia deviates from that in the transference neuroses.

Let us bring these considerations into connection with the conclusion that in schizophrenia the object-cathexes are relinquished. We must then modify this assumption and say: The cathexis of the ideas of the words corresponding to the objects is retained. What we could permissibly call the *conscious idea* of the object can now be split up into the *idea of the word* (verbal idea) and the *idea of the thing* (concrete idea); the latter consists in the cathexis, if not of the direct memory-images of the thing, at least of remoter memory-traces derived from these. It strikes us all at once that now we know what is the difference between a conscious and an unconscious idea. The two are not, as we supposed, different records of the same content situated in different parts of the mind, nor yet different functional states of cathexis in the same part; but the conscious idea comprises the concrete idea plus the verbal idea corresponding to it, whilst the unconscious idea is that of the thing alone. The system *Ucs* contains the thing-cathexes of the objects, the first and true object-cathexes; the system *Pcs* originates in a hyper-cathexis of this concrete idea by a linking up of it with the verbal ideas of the words corresponding to it. It is such hyper-cathexes, we may suppose, that bring about higher organization in the mind and make it possible for the primary process to be succeeded by the secondary process which dominates *Pcs.* Now, too, we are in a position to state precisely what it is that repression denies to the rejected idea in the transference neuroses—namely, translation of the idea into words which are to remain attached to the object. The idea which is not put into words, or the mental act which has not received hyper-cathexis, then remains in the unconscious in a state of repression.

I may call attention to the fact that already very early we possessed the insight which today enables us to understand one of the most striking characteristics of schizophrenia. The last pages of *The Interpretation of Dreams,* published in 1900, expound the thesis that thought-processes, i.e., those cathected mental acts which are more remote from perception, are in themselves devoid of quality and are unconscious, deriving their capacity to enter consciousness only from association with the residues of word-perceptions. The verbal ideas, for their part, are derived from sense-perceptions in the same way as concrete ideas are; so that the question might be raised why ideas of objects cannot become conscious through the agency of their own residues of perceptions. But possibly thought proceeds in systems that are so far remote from the original residues of perception that they have no longer retained anything of the qualities of these residues, so that in order to become conscious the content of the thought-systems needs to be reinforced by new qualities. Besides, linking them up with words may impart quality even to cathexes to which, representing as they do only relations between the ideas of objects, no quality could accrue from the perceptions themselves. Such relations, comprehensible only through words, form one of the most important parts of our thought-processes. We understand that linking them up with verbal ideas is still not identical with actually becoming conscious, but only with the potentiality of this; it is therefore characteristic of the system *Pcs* and of that only. Now, however, we note that with these discussions we have departed from our real theme and find ourselves in the midst of problems concerning the preconscious and the conscious, which for good reasons we are reserving for separate treatment.

In considering schizophrenia, which, to be sure, we only touch on here so far as seems indispensable for general knowledge of the *Ucs*, the doubt must occur to us whether the process here termed *repression* has anything at all in common with the repression which takes place in the transference neuroses. The formula that repression is a process which occurs between the systems *Ucs* and *Pcs* (or *Cs*), and results in withholding the repressed material from consciousness, must in any event be modified, in order to embrace the case of dementia praecox and other narcissistic affections. But the ego's attempt at flight, expressing itself in withdrawal of conscious cathexis, nevertheless remains a common factor. The most superficial reflection shows us how much more radically and thoroughly this attempt at flight, this flight of the ego, is carried out in the narcissistic neuroses.

If, in schizophrenia, this flight consists in withdrawal of instinctual cathexis from those points which represent the unconscious idea of the object, it may seem strange that that part of the same idea which belongs to the system *Pcs*—the verbal ideas corresponding to it— should, on the contrary, undergo a more intense cathexis. We might rather expect that the verbal idea, being the preconscious part, would have to sustain the first impact of the repression, and that it would be wholly insusceptible of cathexis after the repression had proceeded as far as the unconscious concrete ideas. This is certainly difficult to understand. The solution suggests itself that the cathexis of the verbal idea is not part of the act of repression, but represents the first of the attempts at recovery or cure which so conspicuously dominate the clinical picture of schizophrenia. These endeavours are directed towards regaining the lost objects, and it may well be that to achieve this purpose their path to the object must be by way of the word belonging to it; they then have, however, to content themselves with words in the place of things. Our mental activity moves, generally speaking, in one of two opposite directions: either it starts from the instincts and passes through the system *Ucs* to conscious mentation, or, on excitation from without, it passes through the systems *Cs* and *Pcs* till it reaches the unconscious cathexes of the ego and of its objects. This second way must, in spite of the repression which has taken place, have remained clear, and for some distance there is nothing to block the endeavours of the neurosis to regain its objects. When we think in abstractions, there is a danger that we may neglect the relations of words to unconscious concrete ideas, and it must be confessed that the expression and content of our philosophizing begins to acquire an unwelcome resemblance to the schizophrenic's way of thinking. We may, on the other hand, attempt a characterization of the schizophrenic's mode of thought by saying that he treats concrete things as though they were abstract.

If we have really recognized the nature of the *Ucs* and have correctly defined the difference between an unconscious and a preconscious idea, then researches starting from many other points may be expected to bring us back to the same conclusions.

A General Introduction to
Psycho-Analysis

Contents: A General Introduction to Psycho-Analysis

A General Introduction to Psycho-Analysis

PART I

FIRST LECTURE

INTRODUCTION

I DO not know what knowledge any of you may already have of psycho-analysis, either from reading or from hearsay. But having regard to the title of my lectures—*Introductory Lectures on Psycho-Analysis*—I am bound to proceed as though you knew nothing of the subject and needed instruction, even in its first elements.

One thing, at least, I may pre-suppose that you know—namely, that psycho-analysis is a method of medical treatment for those suffering from nervous disorders; and I can give you at once an illustration of the way in which psycho-analytic procedure differs from, and often reverses, what is customary in other branches of medicine. Usually, when we introduce a patient to a new form of treatment we minimize its difficulties and give him confident assurances of its success. This is, in my opinion, perfectly justifiable, for we thereby increase the probability of success. But when we undertake to treat a neurotic psycho-analytically we proceed otherwise. We explain to him the difficulties of the method, its long duration, the trials and sacrifices which will be required of him; and, as to the result, we tell him that we can make no definite promises, that success depends upon his endeavours, upon his understanding, his adaptability and his perseverance. We have, of course, good reasons, into which you will perhaps gain some insight later on, for adopting this apparently perverse attitude.

Now forgive me if I begin by treating you in the same way as I do my neurotic patients, for I shall positively advise you against coming to hear me a second time. And with this intention I shall explain to you how of necessity you can

NOTE: A series of lectures delivered at the Vienna Psychiatrical Clinic, the first fifteen in 1915-16, the next thirteen in 1916-17, first published in German in 1917; edition here used translated by Joan Riviere for the 2nd English edition published in London in 1922. (First English edition had appeared in 1920.)

obtain from me only an incomplete knowledge of psycho-analysis and also what difficulties stand in the way of your forming an independent judgment on the subject. For I shall show you how the whole trend of your training and your accustomed modes of thought must inevitably have made you hostile to psycho-analysis, and also how much you would have to overcome in your own minds in order to master this instinctive opposition. I naturally, cannot foretell what degree of understanding of psycho-analysis you may gain from my lectures, but I can at least assure you that by attending them you will not have learnt how to conduct a psycho-analytic investigation, nor how to carry out a psycho-analytic treatment. And further, if any one of you should feel dissatisfied with a merely cursory acquaintance with psycho-analysis and should wish to form a permanent connection with it, I shall not merely discourage him, but I shall actually warn him against it. For, as things are at the present time, not only would the choice of such a career put an end to all chances of academic success, but, upon taking up work as a practitioner, such a man would find himself in a community which misunderstood his aims and intentions, regarded him with suspicion and hostility, and let loose upon him all the latent evil impulses harboured within it. Perhaps you can infer from the accompaniments of the war now raging in Europe what a countless host that is to reckon with.

However, there are always some people to whom the possibility of a new addition to knowledge will prove an attraction strong enough to survive all such inconveniences. If there are any such among you who will appear at my second lecture in spite of my words of warning they will be welcome. But all of you have a right to know what these inherent difficulties of psycho-analysis are to which I have alluded.

First of all, there is the problem of the teaching and exposition of the subject. In your medical studies you have been accustomed to use your eyes. You see the anatomical specimen, the precipitate of the chemical reaction, the contraction of the muscle as the result of the stimulation of its nerves. Later, you come into contact with the patients; you learn the symptoms of disease by the evidence of your senses; the results of pathological processes can be demonstrated to you, and in many cases even the exciting cause of them in an isolated form. On the surgical side, you are witnesses of the measures by which the patient is helped, and are permitted to attempt them yourselves. Even in psychiatry, demonstration of patients, of their altered expression, speech and behaviour, yields a series of observations which leave a deep impression on your minds. Thus a teacher of medicine acts for the most part as an exponent and guide, leading you as it were through a museum, while you gain in this way a direct relationship to what is displayed to you and believe yourselves to have been convinced by your own experience of the existence of the new facts.

But in psycho-analysis, unfortunately, all this is different. In psycho-analytic treatment nothing happens but an exchange of words between the patient and the physician. The patient talks, tells of his past experiences and present impressions, complains, and expresses his wishes and his emotions. The physician listens, attempts to direct the patient's thought-processes, reminds him, forces his attention in certain directions, gives him explanations and observes the reactions of understanding or denial thus evoked. The patient's unenlightened relatives—people of a kind to be impressed only by something visible and tangible, preferably by the sort of *action* that may be seen at a cinema—never omit to express their doubts of how "mere talk can possibly cure anybody." Their reasoning is of course as illogical as it is inconsistent. For they are the same people who are always convinced that the sufferings of neurotics are purely "in their own imagination." Words and magic were in the beginning one and the same thing, and even today words retain much of their magical power. By words one of us can give to another the greatest happiness or bring about utter despair; by words the teacher imparts his knowledge to the student; by words the orator sweeps his audience with him and determines its judgments and decisions. Words call forth emotions and are universally the means by which we influence our fellow-creatures. Therefore let us not despise the use of

words in psycho-therapy and let us be content if we may overhear the words which pass between the analyst and the patient.

But even that is impossible. The dialogue which constitutes the analysis will admit of no audience; the process cannot be demonstrated. One could, of course, exhibit a neurasthenic or hysterical patient to students at a psychiatric lecture. He would relate his case and his symptoms, but nothing more. He will make the communications necessary to the analysis only under the conditions of a special affective relationship to the physician; in the presence of a single person to whom he was indifferent he would become mute. For these communications relate to all his most private thoughts and feelings, all that which as a socially independent person he must hide from others, all that which, being foreign to his own conception of himself, he tries to conceal even from himself.

It is impossible, therefore, for you to be actually present during a psycho-analytic treatment; you can only be told about it, and can learn psycho-analysis, in the strictest sense of the word, only by hearsay. This tuition at second hand, so to say, puts you in a very unusual and difficult position as regards forming your own judgment on the subject, which will therefore largely depend on the reliance you can place on your informant.

Now imagine for a moment that you were present at a lecture in history instead of in psychiatry, and that the lecturer was dealing with the life and conquests of Alexander the Great. What reason would you have to believe what he told you? The situation would appear at first sight even more unsatisfactory than in the case of psycho-analysis, for the professor of history had no more part in Alexander's campaigns than you yourselves; the psycho-analyst at least informs you of matters in which he himself has played a part. But then we come to the question of what evidence there is to support the historian. He can refer you to the accounts of early writers who were either contemporaries or who lived not long after the events in question, such as Diodorus, Plutarch, Arrian, and others; he can lay before you reproductions of the preserved coins and statues of the king, and pass round a photograph of the mosaic at Pompeii representing the battle at Issus. Yet, strictly speaking, all these documents only prove that the existence of Alexander and the reality of his deeds were already believed in by former generations of men, and your criticism might begin anew at this point.

And then you would find that not everything reported of Alexander is worthy of belief or sufficiently authenticated in detail, but I can hardly suppose that you would leave the lecture room in doubt altogether as to the reality of Alexander the Great. Your conclusions would be principally determined by two considerations: first, that the lecturer could have no conceivable motive for attempting to persuade you of something which he did not himself believe to be true, and secondly, that all the available authorities agree more or less in their accounts of the facts. In questioning the accuracy of the early writers you would apply these tests again, the possible motives of the authors and the agreement to be found between them. The result of such tests would certainly be convincing in the case of Alexander, probably less so in regard to figures like Moses and Nimrod. Later on you will perceive clearly enough what doubts can be raised against the credibility of an exponent of psycho-analysis.

Now you will have a right to ask the question: "If no objective evidence for psycho-analysis exists and no possibility of demonstrating the process, how is it possible to study it at all or to convince oneself of its truth?" The study of it is indeed not an easy matter, nor are there many people who have thoroughly learned it; still, there is, of course, some way of learning it. Psycho-analysis is learnt first of all on oneself, through the study of one's own personality. This is not exactly what is meant by *introspection*, but it may be so described for want of a better word. There is a whole series of very common and well-known mental phenomena which can be taken as material for self-analysis when one has acquired some knowledge of the method. In this way one may obtain the required conviction of the reality of the processes which psycho-analysis describes, and of the truth of its conceptions, although progress on these lines is not without its limitations. One gets much further by submitting oneself to analysis by a skilled analyst, undergoing the working of the analysis in one's own person and using the opportunity to observe the finer details of the technique which the analyst employs. This, eminently the best way, is of course only practicable for individuals and cannot be used in a class of students.

The second difficulty you will find in connection with psycho-analysis is not, on the other hand, inherent in it, but is one for which I must hold you yourselves responsible, at least in so far as your medical studies have influenced you. Your training will have induced in you an attitude of mind very far removed from the psycho-analytical one. You have been trained to establish the functions and disturbances of the organism on an anatomical basis, to explain them in terms of chemistry and physics, and to regard them from a biological point of view; but no part of your interest has ever been directed to the mental aspects of life, in which, after all, the development of the marvellously complicated organism culminates. For this reason a psychological attitude of mind is still foreign to you, and you are accustomed to regard it with suspicion, to deny it a scientific status, and to leave it to the general public, poets, mystics, and philosophers. Now this limitation in you is undoubtedly detrimental to your medical efficiency; for on meeting a patient it is the mental aspects with which one first comes into contact, as in most human relationships, and I am afraid you will pay the penalty of having to yield a part of the curative influence at which you aim to the quacks, mystics, and faith-healers whom you despise.

I quite acknowledge that there is an excuse for this defect in your previous training. There is no auxiliary philosophical science that might be of service to you in your profession. Neither speculative philosophy nor descriptive psychology, nor even the so-called experimental psychology which is studied in connection with the physiology of the sense-organs, as they are taught in the schools, can tell you anything useful of the relations existing between mind and body, or can give you a key to comprehension of a possible disorder of the mental functions. It is true that the psychiatric branch of medicine occupies itself with describing the different forms of recognizable mental disturbances and grouping them in clinical pictures, but in their best moments psychiatrists themselves are doubtful whether their purely descriptive formulations deserve to be called science. The origin, mechanism, and interrelation of the symptoms which make up these clinical pictures are undiscovered: either they cannot be correlated with any demonstrable changes in the brain, or only with such changes as in no way explain them. These mental disturbances are open to therapeutic influence only when they can be identified as secondary effects of some organic disease.

This is the lacuna which psycho-analysis is striving to fill. It hopes to provide psychiatry with the missing psychological foundation, to discover the common ground on which a correlation of bodily and mental disorder becomes comprehensible. To this end it must dissociate itself from every foreign preconception, whether anatomical, chemical, or physiological, and must work throughout with conceptions of a purely psychological order, and for this very reason I fear that it will appear strange to you at first.

For the next difficulty I shall not hold you, your training or your mental attitude, responsible. There are two tenets of psycho-analysis which offend the whole world and excite its resentment; the one conflicts with intellectual, the other with moral and aesthetic prejudices. Let us not underestimate these prejudices; they are powerful things, residues of valuable, even necessary, stages in human evolution. They are maintained by emotional forces, and the fight against them is a hard one.

The first of these displeasing propositions of psycho-analysis is this: that mental processes are essentially unconscious, and that those which are conscious are merely isolated acts and parts of the whole psychic entity. Now I must ask you to remember that, on the contrary, we are accustomed to identify the mental with the conscious. Consciousness appears to us as positively the characteristic that defines mental life, and we regard psychology as the study of the content of consciousness. This even appears so evident that any contradiction of it seems obvious nonsense to us, and yet it is impossible for psycho-analysis to avoid this contradiction, or to accept the identity between the conscious and the psychic. The psycho-analytical definition of the mind is that it comprises processes of the nature of feeling, thinking, and wishing, and it maintains that there are such things as unconscious thinking and unconscious wishing. But in doing so psycho-analysis has forfeited at the outset the sympathy of the sober and scientifically minded, and incurred the suspicion of being a phantastic cult occupied with dark and unfathomable mysteries. You yourselves must find it difficult to understand why I should stigmatize an abstract proposition, such as "The psychic is the conscious," as a prejudice; nor can you guess yet what evolutionary process could have led to the denial of the unconscious, if it does indeed exist, nor what advantage could have been achieved by this denial. It seems like an empty wrangle over words to argue whether mental life is to be regarded as co-extensive with consciousness or whether it may be said to stretch beyond this limit, and yet I can assure you that

the acceptance of unconscious mental processes represents a decisive step towards a new orientation in the world and in science.

As little can you suspect how close is the connection between this first bold step on the part of psycho-analysis and the second to which I am now coming. For this next proposition, which we put forward as one of the discoveries of psycho-analysis, consists in the assertion that impulses, which can only be described as sexual in both the narrower and the wider sense, play a peculiarly large part, never before sufficiently appreciated, in the causation of nervous and mental disorders. Nay, more, that these sexual impulses have contributed invaluably to the highest cultural, artistic, and social achievements of the human mind.

In my opinion, it is the aversion from this conclusion of psycho-analytic investigation that is the most significant source of the opposition it has encountered. Are you curious to know how we ourselves account for this? We believe that civilization has been built up, under the pressure of the struggle for existence, by sacrifices in gratification of the primitive impulses, and that it is to a great extent forever being re-created, as each individual, successively joining the community, repeats the sacrifice of his instinctive pleasures for the common good. The sexual are amongst the most important of the instinctive forces thus utilized: they are in this way sublimated, that is to say, their energy is turned aside from its sexual goal and diverted towards other ends, no longer sexual and socially more valuable. But the structure thus built up is insecure, for the sexual impulses are with difficulty controlled; in each individual who takes up his part in the work of civilization there is a danger that a rebellion of the sexual impulses may occur, against this diversion of their energy. Society can conceive of no more powerful menace to its culture than would arise from the liberation of the sexual impulses and a return of them to their original goal. Therefore society dislikes this sensitive place in its development being touched upon; that the power of the sexual instinct should be recognized, and the significance of the individual's sexual life revealed, is very far from its interests; with a view to discipline, it has rather taken the course of diverting attention away from this whole field. For this reason, the revelations of psycho-analysis are not tolerated by it, and it would greatly prefer to brand them as aesthetically offensive, morally reprehensible, or dangerous. But since such objections are not valid arguments against conclusions which claim to represent the objective results of scientific investigation, the opposition must be translated into intellectual terms before it can be expressed. It is a characteristic of human nature to be inclined to regard anything which is disagreeable as untrue, and then without much difficulty to find arguments against it. So society pronounces the unacceptable to be untrue, disputes the results of psycho-analysis with logical and concrete arguments, arising, however, in affective sources, and clings to them with all the strength of prejudice against every attempt at refutation.

But we, on the other hand, claim to have yielded to no tendency in propounding this objectionable theory. Our intention has been solely to give recognition to the facts as we found them in the course of painstaking researches. And we now claim the right to reject unconditionally any such introduction of practical considerations into the field of scientific investigation, even before we have determined whether the apprehension which attempts to force these considerations upon us is justified or not.

These, now, are some of the difficulties which confront you at the outset when you begin to take an interest in psycho-analysis. It is probably more than enough for a beginning. If you can overcome their discouraging effect, we will proceed further.

SECOND LECTURE

THE PSYCHOLOGY OF ERRORS

WE SHALL now begin, not with postulates, but with an investigation. For this purpose we shall select certain phenomena which are very frequent, very familiar and much overlooked, and which have nothing to do with illness, since they may be observed in every healthy person. I refer to the errors that everyone commits: as when anyone wishes to say a certain thing but uses the wrong word (slip of the tongue); or when the same sort of mistake is made in writing (slip of the pen), in which case one may or may not notice it; or when anyone reads in print or writing something other than what is actually before him (misreading); or when anyone mis-hears what is said to him, naturally when there is no question of any disease of the auditory sense-organ. Another series of such phenomena are those based on forgetting something temporarily, though not permanently; as, for instance, when anyone cannot think of a name which he knows quite well and is always able to recognize whenever he sees it; or when anyone forgets to carry out some intention, which he afterwards remembers, and has therefore forgotten only for a certain time. This element of transitoriness is lacking in a third class, of which mislaying things so that they cannot be found is an example. This is a kind of forgetfulness which we regard differently from the usual kind; one is amazed or annoyed at it, instead of finding it comprehensible. Allied to this are certain *mistakes,* in which the temporary element is again noticeable, as when one believes something for a time which both before and afterwards one knows to be untrue, and a number of similar manifestations which we know under various names.

Some inner relation between all these kinds of occurrences is indicated in German, by the use of the prefix *ver* which is common to all the words designating them. These words almost all refer to acts of an unimportant kind, generally temporary and without much significance in life. It is only rarely that anything of the kind, such as the loss of some object, attains any practical importance. For this reason little attention is paid to such happenings and they arouse little feeling.

I am now going to ask you to consider these phenomena. But you will object, with annoyance: "There are so many tremendous puzzles both in the wide world and in the narrower life of the soul, so many mysteries in the field of mental disorder which demand and deserve explanation, that it really seems frivolous to waste labour and interest on these trifles. If you could explain to us how it is possible for anyone with sound sight and hearing, in broad daylight, to see and hear things which do not exist, or how anyone can suddenly believe that his nearest and dearest are persecuting him, or can justify with the most ingenious arguments a delusion which would seem nonsensical to any child, then we might be willing to take psychoanalysis seriously. But if psycho-analysis cannot occupy us with anything more interesting than the question why a speaker uses a wrong word or why a *Hausfrau* mislays her keys and similar trivialities, then we shall find something better to do with our time and our interest."

My reply is: Patience! Your criticism is not on the right track. It is true that psycho-analysis cannot boast that it has never occupied itself with trifles. On the contrary, the material of its observations is usually those commonplace occurrences which have been cast aside as all too insignificant by other sciences, the refuse, so to speak, of the phenomenal world. But in your criticism are you not confounding the magnitude of a problem with the conspicuous nature of its manifestations? Is it not possible, under certain conditions and at certain times, for very important things to betray themselves in very slight indications? I could easily cite many instances of this. What slight signs, for instance, convey to the young men in my audience that they have gained a lady's favour? Do they expect an explicit declaration, a passionate embrace, or are they not content with a glance which is almost imperceptible to others, a fleeting gesture, a handshake prolonged by a second? Or suppose you are a detective engaged in the investigation of a murder, do you actually expect to find that the murderer will leave his photograph with name and address on the scene of the crime? Are you not perforce content with slighter and less certain traces of the person you seek? So let us not under-value small signs: perhaps from them it may be possible to come upon the tracks of greater things. Besides, I think as you do that the larger problems of the world and of science have the first claim on our interest. But on the whole it avails little to take a definite resolution to devote oneself to the investigation of this or that great problem. One is then often at a loss how to set about the next step. In scientific work it is more profitable to take up whatever lies before one whenever a path towards its exploration presents itself. And then, if one carries it through thoroughly, without prejudice or pre-conceptions, one may, with good fortune and by virtue of the interrelationship linking each thing to every other (hence, also, the small to the great), find, even in the course of such humble labour, a road to the study of the great problems.

It is from this point of view that I hope to enlist your interest in considering the apparently trivial errors made by normal people. I propose now that we question someone who has no knowledge of psycho-analysis as to how he explains these occurrences.

His first answer is sure to be: "Oh, they are not worth any explanation; they are little accidents." What does the man mean by this? Does he mean to maintain that there are any occurrences so small that they fail to come within the causal sequence of things, that they might as well be other than they are? Anyone thus breaking away from the determination of natural phenomena, at any single point, has thrown

over the whole scientific outlook on the world *(Weltanschauung)*. One may point out to him how much more consistent is the religious outlook on the world, which emphatically assures us that "not one sparrow shall fall to the ground" except God wills it. I think our friend would not be willing to follow his first answer to its logical conclusion; he would give way and say that if he were to study these things he would soon find some explanation of them. It must be a matter of slight functional disturbances, of inaccuracies of mental performance, the conditions of which could be discovered. A man who otherwise speaks correctly may make a slip of the tongue, (1) when he is tired or unwell, (2) when he is excited, or (3) when his attention is concentrated on something else. It is easy to confirm this. Slips of the tongue do indeed occur most frequently when one is tired, or has a headache, or feels an attack of migraine coming on. Forgetting proper names very often occurs in these circumstances; many people are habitually warned of the onset of an attack of migraine by the inability to recall proper names. In excitement, too, one mixes up words or even things, one performs actions erroneously; and the forgetting of intentions, as well as a number of other undesigned acts, comes to the fore when one is distracted, in other words, when the attention is concentrated on other things. A familiar instance of such distraction is the professor in *Fliegende Blätter* who forgets his umbrella and takes the wrong hat, because he is thinking of the problems which are to be the subject of his next book. We all know from our own experience how one can forget to carry out intentions or promises when something has happened in the interval that absorbs one very deeply.

This seems so entirely comprehensible and also irrefutable. It is perhaps not very interesting or not so much so as we expected. Let us look at this explanation of errors more closely. The various conditions which have been cited as necessary for the occurrence of these phenomena are not all similar in kind. Illness and disorders of the circulation afford a physiological basis for an affection of the normal functions; excitement, tiredness, and distraction are conditions of a different kind which could be described as psycho-physiological. These last could easily be converted into a theory. Fatigue, as well as distraction, and perhaps also general excitement, cause a dissipation of the attention from which it may follow that the act in question has insufficient attention devoted to it. It can then very easily be disturbed and inexactly performed. Slight illness or a change in the distribution of blood in the central organ of the nervous system can have the same effect, by these conditions affecting the determining factor, the distribution of attention, in a similar way. In all cases it would be a question of the effects of a disturbance of the attention from organic or psychical causes.

But all this doesn't seem to promise much of interest for a psycho-analytic investigation. We might feel tempted to give up the topic. To be sure, a closer inspection of the facts shows that they are not all in accord with the *attention* theory of errors of this sort, or at least that not everything can be directly deduced from it. We find that such errors and such forgetfulness also take place when people are not fatigued or excited, but are in every way in their normal condition; unless, just because of the errors, we were subsequently to attribute to them a condition of excitement which they themselves did not acknowledge. Nor can the matter be quite so simple as that the successful performance of an act will be ensured by an intensification of attention, or endangered by a diminution of it. For a great number of actions may be carried out in a purely automatic way with very little attention and yet quite successfully. In walking, a man may perhaps scarcely know where he is going but keep to the right road and stop at his destination without having gone astray. At least, this is what usually happens. A practised pianist strikes the right notes without thinking of them. He may of course also make an occasional mistake, but if automatic playing increased the danger of errors the virtuoso, whose constant practice has made his playing entirely automatic, would be the most exposed to this danger. Yet we see, on the contrary, that many acts are most successfully carried out when they are not the objects of particularly concentrated attention, and that mistakes may occur just on occasions when one is most eager to be accurate, that is, when a distraction of the necessary attention is most certainly not present. One could then say that this is the effect of the *excitement*, but we do not understand why the excitement does not rather intensify the concentration on the end so much desired. So that if in an important speech anyone says the opposite of what he intends, it can hardly be explained according to the psycho-physiological or the attention theory.

There are also many other minor features in connection with these errors which we do not understand and which are not rendered more comprehensible by these explanations. For instance, when one has temporarily forgotten a name one is annoyed, one is determined to recall it and cannot desist from the attempt. Why is it that despite this annoyance the person so often cannot succeed, as he wishes, in directing his attention to the word which, as he says, is "on the tip of his tongue," and which he instantly recognizes when it is supplied to him? Or, to take another example, there are cases in which the errors multiply, link themselves together or act as substitutes for one another. The first time, one forgets an appointment; the next time, after having made a special resolution not to forget it, one discovers that one has made a mistake in the day or hour. Or one tries by devious ways to remember a forgotten word, and in the course of so doing loses track of a second name which would have been of use in finding the first. If one then pursues the second name, a third gets lost, and so on. It is notorious that the same thing happens with misprints, which are of course errors on the part of the compositor. A stubborn error of this sort is said once to have crept into a Social-Democratic newspaper, where, in the account of a festivity, the following words were printed: "Amongst those present was His Highness, the Clown Prince." The next day a correction was attempted. The paper apologized and said: "The sentence should of course have read, 'the Crow-Prince.'" Again, in a war-correspondent's account of meeting a famous general whose infirmities were pretty well known, a reference to the general was printed as "this battle-scared veteran." Next day an apology appeared which read "the words of course should have been 'the bottle-scarred veteran!'"[1] We like to attribute these occurrences to a devil in the typesetting machine or to some malevolent goblin —figurative expressions which at least imply something more than a psycho-physiological theory of the misprint.

I do not know if you are aware of the fact that slips of the tongue can be provoked, called forth by suggestion, as it were. An anecdote will serve to illustrate this. Once when a novice on the stage was entrusted with the important part in *The Maid of Orleans* of announcing to the King: "The Constable sends back his sword," the principal player, during the rehearsal, played the joke of several times repeating to the timid beginner, instead of the

[1] English example.—TR.

text, the following: "The *Komfortabel* sends back his steed."[1] At the performance the unfortunate actor actually made his début with this perverse announcement, though he had been amply warned against so doing, or perhaps just because he had been.

All these little characteristics of errors are not much illuminated by the theory of diverted attention. But that does not necessarily prove the theory wrong. There may be something missing, a link, by the addition of which the theory might be made completely satisfactory. But many of the errors themselves can be considered from another aspect.

Let us select slips of the tongue, as the type of error best suited to our purpose. We might equally well choose slips of the pen or of reading. Now we must first remind ourselves that, so far, we have only enquired when and under what conditions the wrong word is said, and have received an answer on that point only. Interest may be directed elsewhere, though, and the question raised why just this particular slip is made and no other: one can consider the nature of the mistake. You will see that so long as this question remains unanswered, and the *effect* of the mistake is not explained, the phenomenon remains a pure accident on the psychological side, even if a physiological explanation has been found for it. When it happens that I make a mistake in a word I could obviously do this in an infinite number of ways, in place of the right word substitute any one of a thousand others, or make innumerable distortions of the right word. Now, is there anything which forces upon me in a specific instance just this one special slip, out of all those which are possible, or does that remain accidental and arbitrary, and can nothing rational be found in answer to this question?

Two authors, Meringer and Mayer (a philologist and a psychiatrist) did indeed in 1895 make an attempt to approach the problem of slips of the tongue from this side. They collected examples and first treated them from a purely descriptive standpoint. This of course does not yet furnish any explanation, but it may lead the way to one. They differentiated the distortions which the intended phrase suffered through the slip into: interchanges (in the positions of words, syllables or letters), anticipations, perseverations, compoundings (contaminations), and substitutions. I will give

you examples of these authors' main categories. As an instance of an interchange (in the position of words) someone might say "The Milo of Venus" instead of "The Venus of Milo." The well-known slip of the hotel-boy who, knocking at the bishop's door, nervously replied to the question "Who is it?" "The Lord, my boy!" is another example of such an interchange in the position of words.[2] In the typical Spoonerism, the position of certain letters is interchanged, as when the preacher said: "How often do we feel a half-warmed fish within us!"[2] It is a case of anticipation if any one says: "The thought lies heartily . . ." instead of: "The thought lies heavily on my heart." A perseveration is illustrated by the well-known ill-fated toast, "Gentlemen, I call upon (*auf*) you to

> hiccough (= *auf*zustossen)
>
> (*auf*)   to the health of
>   our Chief."
>
> (drink) (= *an*zustossen)

And when a member of the House of Commons referred to another as the "honourable member for Central *Hell*," instead of "Hull," it was a case of perseveration; as also when a soldier said to a friend "I wish there were a thousand of our men *mortified* on that hill, Bill," instead of "fortified." In one case the *ell* sound has perseverated from the previous words "member for Centra*l*," and in the other the *m* sound in "*m*en" has perseverated to form "*m*ortified."[2] These three types of slip are not very common. You will find those cases much more frequent in which the slip happens by a compounding or contraction, as for example when a gentleman asks a lady if he may *insort* her on her way (*begleit-digen*); this contraction is made up of *begleiten* = to escort, and *beleidigen* = to insult. (And by the way, a young man addressing a lady in this way will not have much success with her.) A substitution takes place when a poor woman says she has an "incurable *infernal* disease,"[2] or in Mrs. Malaprop's mind when she says, for instance, "few gentlemen know how to value the *ineffectual* qualities in a woman." [2]

The explanation which the two authors attempt to formulate as the basis of their collection of examples is peculiarly inadequate. They hold that the sounds and syllables of a word have different values and that the innervation of the sounds of higher value can interfere with those of lower value. They obviously base this conclusion on the cases of

---

[1] *Komfortabel* is a slang Viennese expression for a one-horse cab.—TR.

[2] English examples —TR.

anticipation and perseveration which are not at all frequent; in other forms of slips of the tongue the question of such sound priorities, even if they exist, does not enter at all; for the most frequent type of slip is that in which instead of a certain word one says another which resembles it, and this resemblance is considered by many people sufficient explanation of it. For instance, a professor may say in his opening lecture, "I am not inclined (*geneigt* instead of *geeignet*=fitted) to estimate the merits of my predecessor." Or another professor says, "In the case of the female genital, in spite of the *tempting* . . . I mean, the *attempted* . . ." (*Versuchungen* instead of *Versuche*).

The commonest and also the most noticeable form of slip of the tongue, however, is that of saying the exact opposite of what one meant to say. These cases are quite outside the effect of any relations between sounds or confusion due to similarity, and in default one may therefore turn to the fact that opposites have a strong conceptual connection with one another and are psychologically very closely associated. There are well-known examples of this sort. For instance, the President of our Parliament once opened the session with the words "Gentlemen, I declare a quorum present and herewith declare the session *closed*."

Any other common association may work in a way as insidious as the association of opposites and may on occasion lead to results as inopportune. So there is a story to the effect that, at a festivity in honour of the marriage of a child of H. Helmholtz with a child of the well-known inventor and captain of industry, W. Siemens, the famous physiologist Dubois-Reymond was asked to speak. He concluded his doubtless brilliant speech with the toast "Success to the new partnership, Siemens and *Halske!*" which was of course the name of the old firm. The association of the two names must have been as familiar to a resident in Berlin as "Cross & Blackwell" to a Londoner.

So the effect of word-associations must be taken into account, as well as that of sound-values and similarities between words. But even that is not enough. In one type of case, before we can arrive at an adequate explanation of the slip we must consider some phrase which had been said, or perhaps only thought, previously. Again, that is, a case of perseveration, as Meringer insists, but arising in a more distant source.—I must confess that altogether I have the impression that we are further than ever from comprehension of slips of the tongue.

However, I hope I am not mistaken in thinking that in the course of our examination of the above examples an impression has formed itself in us which may be of a kind to repay further attention. We were considering the general conditions under which slips of the tongue occur and then the influences which determine the kind of distortion effected in the slip, but so far we have not examined at all the result of the slip itself, as an object of interest without regard to its origin. If we bring ourselves to do this we shall in the end have to assert courageously that in some of the examples the slip itself makes sense. Now what does it mean when we say "it makes sense"? Well, it means that the result of the slip may perhaps have a right to be regarded in itself as a valid mental process following out its own purpose, and as an expression having content and meaning. Hitherto we have only spoken of errors, but now it appears as if the error could sometimes be quite a proper act, except that it has intruded itself in the place of one more expected or intended.

In certain cases the sense belonging to the slip itself appears obvious and unmistakable. When the President in his opening speech closes the session of Parliament, a knowledge of the circumstances under which the slip was made inclines us to see a meaning in it. He expects no good result from the session and would be glad to be able to disperse forthwith; there is no difficulty in discovering the meaning, or interpreting the sense, of this slip. Or when a lady, appearing to compliment another, says "I am sure *you* must have *thrown* this delightful hat together" instead of "sewn it together" (*aufgepatzt* instead of *aufgeputzt*), no scientific theories in the world can prevent us from seeing in her slip the thought that the hat is an amateur production. Or when a lady who is well known for her determined character says: "My husband asked his doctor what sort of diet ought to be provided for him. But the doctor said he needed no special diet, he could eat and drink whatever *I* choose," the slip appears clearly as the unmistakable expression of a consistent scheme.

Now supposing it should turn out that not only a few cases of slips of the tongue and errors in general, but the great majority of them, have a meaning, then the meaning of the error, to which we have hitherto paid no attention, would become the point of greatest interest to us and would justifiably drive all other points of view into the background. All

physiological and psycho-physiological conditions could then be ignored and attention
could be devoted to the purely psychological
investigation of the *sense*, that is, the meaning,
the intention, in the errors. With this in view,
therefore, we shall soon consider further material.

Before undertaking this, however, I should
like to invite you to follow up another clue
with me. It often happens that a poet makes
use of a slip of the tongue or some other error
as a means of artistic expression. This fact in
itself proves that he thinks the error, for instance, a slip of the tongue, has a meaning; for
he constructs it intentionally. It could hardly
happen that a poet accidentally made a slip of
the pen and then allowed his slip of the pen
to stand as a slip of the tongue of the character.
He wishes to reveal something by means of
the slip and we may well enquire what that
may be—whether perhaps he wishes to indicate
that the person in question is distracted or overtired, or is expecting a headache. Of course we
should not exaggerate the importance of it if
poets do make use of slips to express their
meaning. Slips might be in reality without
meaning, accidents in the mental world, or only
occasionally have a meaning, and poets would
still be entitled to refine them by infusing
sense into them for their own purposes. However, it would not be surprising if more were
to be learned from poets about slips of the
tongue than from philologists and psychiatrists.

There is an example of a slip of this kind in
Schiller's *Wallenstein* (Piccolomini, Act I,
Scene 5). In the foregoing scene, young Max
Piccolomini had taken up Duke Wallenstein's
cause ardently, and had been passionately describing the blessings of peace, which he had
become aware of in the course of a journey
accompanying Wallenstein's beautiful daughter
to the camp. As he leaves the stage, his father
(Octavio) and the courtier Questenberg are
plunged in consternation. The fifth scene continues:

QUESTENBERG. Alas! and stands it so?
Friend, do we let him go
In this delusion? let him go from us?
Not call him back at once, not
Open his eyes here and now?
OCTAVIO (*recovering himself out of deep thought*).
He has now opened *mine*
And I see more than pleases me.
QUESTENBERG. What is it?
OCTAVIO. A curse upon this journey!
QUESTENBERG. But why so? What is it?
OCTAVIO. Come, come, friend! I must up

And follow the ill-omened clue at once
And see with mine own eyes—come with me
now!
QUESTENBERG. What now? Where go you then?
OCTAVIO (*hastily*). *To her, herself!*
QUESTENBERG. *To . . .*
OCTAVIO (*corrects himself*). To the Duke! Come,
let us go.

Octavio meant to say: "To him, to the Duke,"
but his tongue slips and he betrays (to us, at
least) by the words *"to her"* that he has clearly
recognized the influence at work behind the
famous young warrior's rhapsodies in favour
of peace.

A still more impressive example was found
by O. Rank in Shakespeare. It occurs in the
Merchant of Venice, in the famous scene in
which the fortunate suitor makes his choice
among the three caskets; and I can perhaps
not do better than read to you now Rank's
short account of it.

"A slip of the tongue which occurs in Shakespeare's *Merchant of Venice* (Act III, Sc. 2)
is exceedingly fine in the poetic feeling it shows
and in the brilliant way in which it is applied
technically. Like the slip in Wallenstein quoted
by Freud in his *Psycho-pathology of Everyday
Life,* it shows that the poets well understand
the mechanism and meaning of such slips and
assume that the audience will also understand
them. Portia, who by her father's wish has
been bound to the choice of a husband by lot,
has so far escaped all the unwelcome suitors
by the luck of fortune. Having at last found in
Bassanio the suitor to whom she is inclined,
she fears that he too will choose the wrong
casket. She would like to tell him that even
so he may rest assured of her love, but she is
prevented by her oath. In this inner conflict
the poet makes her say to her chosen suitor:

I pray you tarry; pause a day or two,
Before you hazard: for, in choosing wrong,
I lose your company; therefore, forbear awhile:
There's something tells me (but it is not love)
I would not lose you . . .
                    . . . I could teach you
How to choose right, but then I am forsworn;
So will I never be; so may you miss me;
But if you do you'll make me wish a sin,
That I had been forsworn. Beshrew your eyes,
They have o'erlooked me, and divided me;
*One half of me is yours, the other half yours,—
Mine own, I would say;* but if mine, then yours,
And so all yours.

Just that which she only meant to indicate
subtly to him because she should really have

concealed it from him altogether, namely, that even before the lot she was his and loved him, this the poet with exquisite fineness of psychological feeling causes to come to expression in her slip; and is able, by this artistic device, to relieve the unbearable uncertainty of the lover as well as the suspense of the audience as to the issue of the choice."

And notice, at the end, how subtly Portia reconciles the two declarations which are contained in the slip, how she resolves the contradiction between them, and finally even justifies the slip.

> ... but if mine, then yours,
> And so all yours.

It has happened that other thinkers outside the field of medicine have disclosed by an observation the meaning of some error and so anticipated our efforts in this direction. You all know the witty satirist Lichtenberg (1742-1799) of whom Goethe said: "Where he makes a joke, a problem lies concealed." And occasionally the solution of the problem is revealed in the joke. Lichtenberg writes in his witty and satirical *Notes*, "He always read *Agamemnon* for *angenommen* (verb meaning *to take for granted*), so deeply versed was he in Homer." This really contains the whole theory of slips in reading.

At the next lecture we will see whether we can agree with the poets in their conception of the meaning of psychological errors.

THIRD LECTURE
THE PSYCHOLOGY OF ERRORS (*Continued*)

AT THE last lecture it occurred to us to consider the error by itself alone, apart from its relation to the intended act with which it had interfered, and we perceived that in certain cases it seemed to betray a meaning of its own. We said to ourselves that if this conclusion, that the error has its own meaning, could be established on a larger scale, that meaning would soon prove more interesting to us than the investigation of the conditions under which errors arise.

Let us once more agree upon what we understand by the *meaning* of a mental process. This is nothing else but the intention which it serves and its place in a mental sequence. In most of the cases we examined we could substitute for the word *meaning* the words *intention* and *tendency*. Now was it only a deceptive appearance, or a poetic glorification of the error, that led us to believe that we could see an intention in it?

Let us still keep to the examples of slips of the tongue and review a larger number of such manifestations. We then find whole categories of cases in which the intention, the meaning, of the slip is quite obvious, particularly so in those instances in which the opposite of what was intended is said. The President says in his opening speech: "I declare the session *closed*." That is surely not ambiguous. The meaning and intention of this slip is that he wants to close the session. One might well say, "he said so himself"; we only take him at his word. Please do not interrupt me with the objection that this is impossible, that we know quite well that he wished to open the session, not to close it, and that he himself whom we have just recognized as the best judge of his intention will affirm that he meant to open it. In doing so you forget that we agreed to consider the error by itself; its relation to the intention which it disturbs will be discussed later. *You* would be guilty of an error in logic, by which you would conveniently dispose of the problem under discussion, which in English is called begging the question.

In other cases, where the form of the slip is not exactly the opposite of what is intended, a contradictory sense may still often come to expression. "I am not *inclined* (*geneigt*) to appreciate my predecessor's merits." *Inclined* is not the opposite of *in a position to* (*geeignet*), but it is an open confession of a thought in sharpest contradiction to the speaker's duty to meet the situation gracefully.

In still other cases, the slip simply adds a second meaning to the intended. The sentence then sounds like a contraction, an abbreviation, a condensation of several sentences into one. Thus the determined lady who said: "He may eat and drink whatever *I* choose." That is as if she had said: "He can eat and drink what he chooses, but what does it matter what he chooses? It is for me to do the choosing!" Slips of the tongue often give this impression of abbreviation; for instance, when a professor of anatomy at the end of his lecture on the nasal cavities asks whether his class has thoroughly understood it and, after a general reply in the affirmative, goes on to say: "I can hardly believe that that is so, since persons who can thoroughly understand the nasal cavities can be counted, even in a city of millions, on *one finger* ... I mean, on the fingers of one hand." The abbreviated sentence has its own meaning; it says that there is only one person who understands the subject.

In contrast to these types in which the slip

plainly discloses its meaning are others in which the slip of the tongue conveys nothing intelligible, and therefore directly controverts our expectations. The mis-pronunciation by mistake of proper names, or the enunciation of meaningless sounds, is such a frequent occurrence that this alone would appear to dispose at once of the question whether all errors have a meaning. Yet closer inspection of such examples discloses the fact that it is easily possible to understand such distortions; indeed, that the difference between these unintelligible cases and the previous more comprehensible ones is not so very great.

The owner of a horse, on being asked how it was, replied: "O, it may *stad*—it may *take* another month." Asked what he really meant to say, he answered that he was thinking it was a *sad* business, and the words *sad* and *take* together gave rise to *stad*. (Meringer and Mayer.)

Another man was relating some objectionable incidents and went on: "and then certain facts were *refilled*." He explained that he meant to say these facts were *filthy*. *Revealed* and *filthy* together combine to form *refilled*. (Meringer and Mayer.)

You will recall the case of the young man who offered to "insort" an unknown lady. We took the liberty of resolving this word into *insult* and *escort*, and were quite convinced of this interpretation without requiring proof of it. From these examples you can see that even these more obscure cases can be explained as the concurrence, or *interference*, of two different intentions of speech with one another; the differences arise only in that in the first type of slip the one intention has entirely excluded the other, as when the opposite is said; while in the second type the one intention only succeeds in distorting or modifying the other, from which arise combinations of a more or less senseless appearance.

We believe that we have now discovered the secret of a large number of slips of the tongue. If we keep this clear in mind we shall be able to comprehend still further groups hitherto entirely mysterious. Although, for instance, in a case of distortion of a name we cannot suppose that it is always a matter of a contest between two similar but different names, yet the second intention is easily perceived. Distortions of names are common enough apart from slips of the tongue; they are attempts to liken the name to something derogatory or degrading, a common form of abuse, which educated persons soon learn to avoid but nevertheless do not

willingly give up. It may be dressed up as a joke, although one of a very low order. To quote one gross and ugly example of such a distortion of a name, the name of the President of the French Republic, *Poincaré*, has lately been transformed into *Schweinskarré*. It is not going much further to assume that some such abusive intention may also be behind distortions of names produced by a slip of the tongue. In pursuing our idea, similar explanations suggest themselves for cases of slips where the effect is comic or absurd. In the case of the member of parliament who referred to the "honourable member for Central Hell," the sober atmosphere of the House is unexpectedly disturbed by the intrusion of a word that calls up a ludicrous and unflattering image; we are bound to conclude from the analogy with certain offensive and abusive expressions that an impulse has interposed here, to this effect: "You needn't be taken in. I don't mean a word of this. To hell with the fellow!" The same applies to slips of the tongue which transform quite harmless words into obscene and indecent ones.[1]

We are familiar with this tendency in certain people intentionally to convert harmless words into indecent ones for the sake of the amusement obtained; it passes for wit, and in fact when one hears of a case one at once asks whether it was intended as a joke or occurred unintentionally as a slip of the tongue.

Well, we seem to have solved the riddle of errors with comparatively little trouble! They are not accidents; they are serious mental acts; they have their meaning; they arise through the concurrence—perhaps better, the mutual interference—of two different intentions. But now I can well understand that you want to overwhelm me with a flood of questions and doubts, which must be answered and resolved before we can enjoy this first result of our efforts. I certainly do not want to press any hasty conclusions upon you. Let us coolly consider everything in turn.

What would you like to say? Whether I think that this explanation accounts for all cases of slips of the tongue or only for a certain number? Whether this conception can be extended to the many other types of errors, to misreading, slips of the pen, forgetting, wrongly performed actions, mislaying things and so on? What part the factors of fatigue, excitement

[1] Two untranslatable examples are given in the text, *apopos* for *a propos* and *Eischeissweibchen* for *Eiweisscheibchen*. (Meringer and Mayer.)—TR.

absent-mindedness and distraction of attention play in regard to the mental nature of errors? Besides this, it is clearly seen that of the two competing meanings in the slip one is always manifest, but not always the other. How is one to arrive at the latter? And if one believes that one has guessed it, how is one to find proof that this is not merely a probability but the only true meaning? Is there anything else you wish to ask? If not, then I myself will continue. I will remind you that we are not really greatly concerned with errors in themselves, but that we wished to learn from a study of them something of value from the point of view of psycho-analysis. Therefore I will put this question: "What sort of purposes or tendencies are these which thus interfere with other intentions, and what is the relation between the interfering tendency and the other?" Thus, as soon as we have found the answer to the riddle, our efforts begin again.

Very well then; is this the explanation of all cases of slips of the tongue? I am very much inclined to think so, and for this reason, because whenever one examines an instance of it this type of solution may be found. Still, one cannot prove that a slip of the tongue cannot come to pass without the agency of this mechanism. It may be so: for our purposes it is a matter of indifference, theoretically; for the conclusions which we wish to draw by way of an introduction to psycho-analysis remain valid, even if only a small proportion of the total incidence of slips of the tongue comes under our explanation, and this is certainly not so. The next question, whether this explanation extends to other forms of errors, may be answered by way of anticipation in the affirmative. You can convince yourselves of it when we turn to consider examples of slips of the pen, of wrongly performed acts, and so on. I propose, however, for technical reasons that we should postpone doing this until we have investigated the slip of the tongue itself more thoroughly.

The question what significance those factors, which some writers have placed in the foreground, can now have for us—such factors as disturbances of the circulation, fatigue, excitement, distraction, disturbances of attention— demands a more exhaustive reply if we assume the mental mechanism of slips described above. You will notice that we do not deny these factors. Indeed, in general it doesn't often happen that psycho-analysis contests anything which is maintained in other quarters; as a rule, psy-cho-analysis only adds something new to what has been said; and it does certainly happen on occasion that what has hitherto been overlooked, and is now supplied by psycho-analysis, is the most essential part of the matter. The influence of such physiological predispositions as arise in slight illness, circulatory disturbances and conditions of fatigue, upon the occurrence of slips of the tongue is to be admitted without more ado; everyday personal experience may convince you of it. But how little is explained by this admission! Above all, these are not necessary conditions of errors. Slips of the tongue may just as well occur in perfect health and normal conditions. These bodily factors, therefore, are merely contributory; they only favour and facilitate the peculiar mental mechanism which produces slips of the tongue. I once used an illustration for this state of things which I will repeat here, as I know of no better. Just suppose that on some dark night I am walking in a lonely neighbourhood and am assaulted by a rogue who seizes my watch and money, whereupon since I could not see the robber's face clearly, I make my complaint at the police-station in these words: "Loneliness and darkness have just robbed me of my valuables." The police officer might reply to me: "You seem to carry your support of the extreme mechanistic point of view too far for the facts. Suppose we put the case thus: Under cover of darkness and encouraged by the loneliness of the spot, some unknown thief has made away with your valuables. It appears to me that the essential thing to be done is to look about for the thief. Perhaps we shall then be able to take the plunder from him again."

Psycho-physiological factors such as excitement, absent-mindedness, distraction of attention, obviously provide very little in the way of explanation. They are mere phrases; they are screens, and we should not be deterred from looking behind them. The question is rather what has here called forth the excitement or the particular diversion of attention. The influence of sound-values, resemblances between words, and common associations connecting certain words, must also be recognized as important. They facilitate the slip by pointing out a path for it to take. But if there is a path before me, does it necessarily follow that I must go along it? I also require a motive to determine my choice and, further, some force to propel me forward. These sound-values and word associations are, therefore, just like the bodily conditions, the facilitating causes of slips of the tongue, and cannot provide the real explanation of them. Consider for a moment the enormous majority of cases in which the words I am using in my speech are not deranged on account of sound-resemblance to other words, intimate associations with opposite meanings, or with expressions in common use. It yet remains to suppose, with the philosopher Wundt, that a slip of the tongue arises when the tendency to associations gains an ascendance over the original intention owing to bodily fatigue. This would be quite plausible if experience did not controvert it by the fact that in a number of cases the bodily, and in another large group the associative, predisposing causes are absent.

Particularly interesting to me, however, is your next question, namely, by what means the two mutually disturbing tendencies may be ascertained. You probably do not suspect how portentous this question is. You will agree that one of these tendencies, the one which is interfered with, is always unmistakable; the person who commits the slip knows it and acknowledges it. Doubt and hesitation only arise in regard to the other, what we have called the interfering tendency. Now we have already heard, and you will certainly not have forgotten, that in a certain number of cases this other tendency is equally plain. It is evident in the result of the slip if only we have the courage to let the slip speak for itself. The President who said the opposite of what he meant—it is clear that he wishes to open the session, but equally clear that he would also like to close it. That is so plain that it needs no interpreting. But in the other cases, in which the interfering tendency merely distorts the original without itself coming to full expression, how can the interfering tendency be detected in the distortion?

In one group of cases by a very safe and simple method, by the same method, that is, by which we establish the tendency that is interfered with. We enquire of the speaker, who tells us then and there; after making the slip he restores the word he originally intended. "O, it may *stad*—no, it may *take* another month." Well, the interfering tendency may be likewise supplied by him. We say, "Now why did you first say *stad?*" He replies, "I meant to say it was a sad business"; and in the other case in which "refilled" was said, the speaker informs you that he first meant to say it was a filthy business, but controlled himself and substituted another expression. The discovery

of the disturbing tendency is here as definitely established as that of the disturbed tendency. It is not without intention that I have selected as examples cases which owe neither their origin nor their explanation to me or to any supporter of mine. Still, in both these cases, a certain intervention was necessary in order to produce the explanation. One had to ask the speaker why he made the slip, what explanation he could give. Without that he might have passed it by without seeking to explain it. Being asked, however, he gave as his answer the first idea that occurred to him. And see now, this little intervention and the result of it constitute already a psycho-analysis, a prototype of every psycho-analytic investigation that we may undertake further.

Now, should I be too suspicious if I were to surmise that, at the very moment at which psycho-analysis begins to dawn upon you, a resistance to it instantly raises itself within your mind? Are you not eager to object that information supplied by the person enquired of, who committed the slip, is not completely reliable evidence. He naturally wishes, you think, to meet your request to explain his slip, and so he says the first thing that he can think of, if it will do at all. There is no proof that that is actually how the slip arose. It may have been so, but it may just as well have been otherwise. Something else also might have occurred to him that would have met the case as well or even better.

It is remarkable how little respect you have, in your hearts, for a mental fact! Imagine that someone had undertaken a chemical analysis of a certain substance and had ascertained that one ingredient of it is of a certain weight, so and so many milligrams. From this weight, thus arrived at, certain conclusions may be drawn. Do you think now it would ever occur to a chemist to discredit these conclusions on the ground that the isolated substance might as well have had some other weight? Everyone recognizes the fact that it actually had this weight and no other, and builds further conclusions confidently on that fact. But when it is a question of mental fact, that it *was* such an idea and no other that occurred to the person when questioned, you will not accept that as valid, but say that something else might as well have occurred to him! The truth is that you have an illusion of a psychic freedom within you which you do not want to give up. I regret to say that on this point I find myself in sharpest opposition to your views.

Now you will break off here only to take up your resistance at another point. You will continue: "We understand that it lies in the peculiar technique of psycho-analysis to bring the person analysed to give the solution of its problems. Let us take another example, that in which the after-dinner speaker calls upon the company to *hiccough* to the health of their guest. The interfering tendency is, you say, in this case to ridicule; this it is which opposes the intention to do honour. But this is a mere interpretation on your part, based on observations made independently of the slip. If in this case you were to question the perpetrator of the slip he would not confirm your view that he intended an insult; on the contrary, he would vehemently deny it. Why do you not abandon your undemonstrable interpretation in the face of this flat denial?"

Yes, this time you have lighted upon something formidable. I can picture to myself that unknown speaker; he is probably an assistant of the guest of honour, perhaps already a junior lecturer himself, a young man with the brightest prospects. I will press him and ask whether he is sure he did not perceive some feeling in himself antagonistic to the demand that he should pay honour to his chief. A nice fuss there is! He becomes impatient and suddenly bursts out at me: "Look here, enough of this cross-examination, or I'll make myself disagreeable! You will ruin my career with your suspicions. I simply said *aufstossen* instead of *anstossen,* because I'd already said *auf* twice before it. It's the thing that Meringer calls a perseveration, and there's nothing else to be read into it. Do you understand me? That's enough." H'm, this is a startling reaction, a truly energetic repudiation. I see that there is nothing more to be done with the young man, but I think to myself that he betrays a strong personal interest in making out that his slip has no meaning. You will perhaps agree too that he has no right to become so uncivil over a purely theoretical investigation, but after all, you will think, he must know what he wanted to say and what not.

O, so he must? That is perhaps still open to question.

Now you think you have me in a trap. "So that is your technique," I hear you say. "When the person who commits a slip gives an explanation which fits your views then you declare him to be the final authority on the subject. He says so himself! But if what he says does not suit your book, then you suddenly assert that what he says does not count, one need not believe it."

Certainly that is so. But I can give you another instance of a similarly monstrous procedure. When an accused man confesses to a deed the judge believes him, but when he denies it the judge does not believe him. Were it otherwise the law could not be administered, and in spite of occasional miscarriages you will admit that the system, on the whole, works well.

"Well, but are you a judge, and is the person who commits a slip to be accused before you? Is a slip of the tongue a crime?"

Perhaps we need not reject even this comparison. But see now to what deep-seated differences our attempt to investigate the apparently harmless problems of errors has brought us, differences which at this stage we do not know in the least how to reconcile. I suggest that we should make a temporary compromise on the basis of the analogy with the judge and the prisoner. You shall grant me that the meaning of an error admits of no doubt when the subject of the analysis acknowledges it himself. I, in turn, will admit that a direct proof for the suspected meaning cannot be obtained if the subject refuses us the information, and, of course, this applies also when the subject is not present to give us the information. As also in legal proceedings, we are then thrown back upon indications in order to form a decision, the truth of which is sometimes more and sometimes less probable. At law, for practical reasons, guilt has to be declared also on circumstantial evidence. There is no such necessity here; but neither are we bound to refrain from considering such evidence. It is a mistake to believe that a science consists in nothing but conclusively proved propositions, and it is unjust to demand that it should. It is a demand only made by those who feel a craving for authority in some form and a need to replace the religious catechism by something else, even if it be a scientific one. Science in its catechism has but few apodictic precepts; it consists mainly of statements which it has developed to varying degrees of probability. The capacity to be content with these approximations to certainty and the ability to carry on constructive work despite the lack of final confirmation are actually a mark of the scientific habit of mind.

But where shall we find a starting-point for our interpretations, and the indications for our proof, in cases where the subject under analysis says nothing to explain the meaning of the error? From various sources. First, by analogy with similar phenomena not produced by error, as when we maintain that the distortion of a name by mistake has the same intention to ridicule behind it as intentional distortion of names. And then, from the mental situation in which the error arose, from our knowledge of the character of the person who commits it, and of the feelings active in him before the error, to which it may be a response. As a rule, what happens is that we find the meaning of the error according to general principles; and this, to begin with, is only a conjecture, a tentative solution, proof being discovered later by an examination of the mental situation. Sometimes it is necessary to await further developments, which have been so to speak, foreshadowed by the error, before we can find confirmation of our conjecture.

I cannot easily give you evidence of this if I have to limit myself to the field of slips of the tongue, although even here I have a few good examples. The young man who offered to "insort" the lady is in fact very shy; the lady whose husband may eat and drink what *she* likes I know to be one of those managing women who rule the household with a rod of iron. Or take the following case: At a general meeting of a club a young member made a violent attack in a speech, in the course of which he spoke of the officers of the society as *"Lenders* of the Committee," which appears to be a substitute for *Members* of the Committee.[1] We should conjecture that against his attack some interfering tendency was active which was itself in some way connected with the idea of *lending*. As a matter of fact, an informant tells us that the speaker is in constant money difficulties and was actually attempting to raise money at the time. So the interfering tendency really is to be translated into the thought: "Be more moderate in your opposition: these are the people whom you want to lend you money."

If I diverge into the field of other kinds of errors I can give you a wide selection of examples of such circumstantial evidence.

If anyone forgets an otherwise familiar proper name and has difficulty in retaining it in his memory—even with an effort—it is not hard to guess that he has something against the owner of the name and does not like to think of him; consider in the light of this the following notes on the mental situation in which an error of this kind was made.

A Mr. Y fell in love with a lady, who did not return the feeling and shortly after married a Mr. X. Although Mr. Y had already known Mr. X for some time, and even had business relations with him, he forgets his name over and over again, so that he frequently has to ask someone the man's name when it is necessary to write to him.[2] Obviously Mr. Y wants to obliterate all knowledge of his fortunate rival. "Never thought of shall he be."

Another example: a lady inquires of a doctor about a common acquaintance, calling her by her maiden name. She has forgotten the married name. She admits that she strongly objected to the marriage and dislikes the husband intensely.[3]

Later we shall have much to say in other connections in regard to the forgetting of names; at the moment we are chiefly interested in the *mental situation* in which the lapse of memory occurs.

The forgetting of resolutions can in general be referred to an opposing current of feeling which is against carrying out the intention. It is not only we psycho-analysts who hold this view, however; it is the ordinary attitude of everyone in their daily affairs, which they only deny in theory. The protégé whose patron apologizes for having forgotten his request is not pacified by such an apology. He thinks immediately: "It's evidently nothing to him; he promised, but he doesn't mean to do it." Forgetting is therefore criticized even in life, in certain connections, and the difference between the popular and the psycho-analytic conception of these errors seems to be dispelled. Imagine a hostess receiving a guest with the words: "What, is it today you were coming? I quite forgot that I had asked you for to-day"; or a young man confessing to his beloved that he had forgotten all about the appointment they had arranged on the last occasion. He will never admit it; he will rather invent on the spur of the moment the most wildly improbable hindrances which prevented his coming and made it impossible for him to communicate with her from that day to this. We all know that in military service the excuse of having forgotten is worthless and saves no one from punishment; the system is recognized as justifiable. Here everyone is suddenly agreed that a certain mistake has a meaning and what that meaning is. Why are they not consistent enough to extend their insight to other errors and then

[1] Vor*schussmitglieder* instead of Aus*schussmitglieder*.

[2] From C. G. Jung.
[3] From A. A. Brill.

openly acknowledge it? There is naturally also an answer to this.

If the meaning of forgetting resolutions is so little open to doubt in the minds of people in general you will be the less surprised to find that writers employ such mistakes in a similar sense. Those of you who have seen or read Shaw's *Cæsar and Cleopatra* will recall that Cæsar, when departing in the last scene, is pursued by the feeling that there was something else he intended to do which he had now forgotten. At last it turns out what it is: to say farewell to Cleopatra. By this small device the author attempts to ascribe to the great Cæsar a feeling of superiority which he did not possess and to which he did not at all aspire. You can learn from historical sources that Cæsar arranged for Cleopatra to follow him to Rome and that she was living there with her little Cæsarion when Cæsar was murdered, whereupon she fled the city.

The cases of forgetting resolutions are as a rule so clear that they are of little use for our purpose, which is to discover in the mental situation indications of the meaning of the error. Let us turn, therefore, to a particularly ambiguous and obscure form of error, that of losing and mislaying objects. It will certainly seem incredible to you that the person himself could have any purpose in losing things, which is often such a painful accident. But there are innumerable instances of this kind: A young man loses a pencil to which he was much attached. A few days before he had had a letter from his brother-in-law which concluded with these words: "I have neither time nor inclination at present to encourage you in your frivolity and idleness."[1] Now the pencil was a present from this brother-in-law. Had it not been for this coincidence we could not of course have maintained that the loss involved any intention to get rid of the gift. Similar cases are very numerous. One loses objects when one has quarrelled with the giver and no longer wants to be reminded of him, or again, when one has tired of them and wants an excuse to provide oneself with something different and better. Dropping, breaking, and destroying things of course serve a similar purpose in regard to the object. Can it be considered accidental when, just before his birthday, a child loses and damages his possessions, for instance, his watch and his schoolbag?

Anyone who has experienced often enough the annoyance of not being able to find some-

thing which he has himself put away will certainly be unwilling to believe that he could have had any intention in so doing. And yet cases are not at all rare in which the circumstances attendant on the act of mislaying point to a tendency to put the object aside temporarily or permanently. Perhaps the best example of this kind is the following.

A young man told me this story: "A few years ago there were misunderstandings between me and my wife; I thought her too cold, and, though I willingly acknowledged her excellent qualities, we lived together without affection. One day, on coming in from a walk, she brought me a book which she had bought me because she thought it would interest me. I thanked her for her little attention, promised to read the book, put it among my things and never could find it again. Months passed by and occasionally I thought of this derelict book and tried in vain to find it. About six months later my dear mother, who lived some distance away, fell ill. My wife left our house to go and nurse her mother-in-law, who became seriously ill, giving my wife an opportunity of showing her best qualities. One evening I came home full of enthusiasm and gratitude towards my wife. I walked up to my writing desk and opened a certain drawer in it, without a definite intention but with a kind of somnambulistic sureness, and there before me lay the lost book which I had so often looked for."

With the disappearance of the motive the inability to find the mislaid object also came to an end.

I could multiply this collection of examples indefinitely; but I will not do so now. In my *Psycho-pathology of Everyday Life* (first published in 1901) you will find plenty of examples for the study of errors.[2] All these examples demonstrate the same thing over and over again; they make it probable to you that mistakes have a meaning and they show you how the meaning can be guessed or confirmed from the attendant circumstances. I restrict myself rather to-day, because our intention here was limited to studying these phenomena with a view to obtaining an introduction to psycho-analysis. There are only two groups of occurrences into which I must still go, the accumulated and combined errors, and confirmation of our interpretations by subsequent events.

Accumulated and combined errors are cer-

[1] From B. Dattner.

[2] Also in the writings of A. Maeder (*French*), A. A. Brill and Ernest Jones (*English*), and J. Stärcke (*Dutch*) and others.

tainly the finest flowers of the species. If we were only concerned to prove that errors had a meaning, we should have limited ourselves to them at the outset, for the meaning in them is unmistakable, even to the dullest intelligence, and strong enough to impress the most critical judgment. The repetition of the occurrences betrays a persistence which is hardly ever an attribute of chance, but which fits well with the idea of design. Further, the exchanging of one kind of mistake for another shows us what is the most important and essential element in the error; and that is, not its form, or the means of which it makes use, but the *tendency* which makes use of it and can achieve its end in the most various ways. Thus I will give you a case of repeated forgetting: Ernest Jones relates that he once allowed a letter to lie on his writing desk for several days for some unknown reason. At last he decided to post it, but received it back from the dead-letter office, for he had forgotten to address it. After he had addressed it he took it to post but this time without a stamp. At this point he finally had to admit to himself his objection to sending the letter at all.

In another case, taking up a thing by mistake is combined with mislaying it. A lady travelled to Rome with her brother-in-law, a famous artist. The visitor was much fêted by the Germans living in Rome and received, among other things, a present of an antique gold medal. The lady was vexed because her brother-in-law did not appreciate the fine specimen highly enough. After her sister had arrived she returned home and discovered, upon unpacking, that she had brought the medal with her—how, she did not know. She wrote at once to her brother-in-law telling him that she would send the stolen property back to him the next day. But the next day the medal was so cleverly mislaid that it could not be discovered and could not be returned, and then it began to dawn upon the lady what her *absent-mindedness* had meant, namely, that she wanted to keep the work of art for herself.[1]

I have already given you an example of a combination of forgetfulness with an error, in the case in which someone forgets an appointment, and a second time, with the firm intention of not forgetting it again, appears at an hour which is not the appointed one. A quite analogous case was told me from his own experience by a friend who pursues literary as well as scientific interests. He said: "Some years

[1] From R. Reitler.

ago I accepted election to the Council of a certain literary society because I hoped that the society might at some time be useful to me in getting a play of mine produced; and, although not much interested, I attended the meetings regularly every Friday. A few months ago I received an assurance that my play would be produced at a theatre in F and since then it has invariably happened that I *forget* to attend the meetings of the society. When I read your writings on this subject, I reproached myself with my meanness in staying away now that these people can no longer be of use to me and determined on no account to forget on the following Friday. I kept reminding myself of my resolution until I carried it out and stood at the door of the meeting-room. To my amazement it was closed and the meeting was already over! I had made a mistake in the day of the week and it was then Saturday!"

It would be tempting to collect more of these examples, but I will pass on and, instead, let you glance at those cases in which interpretation has to wait for confirmation in the future.

The main condition in these cases is, as we might expect, that the mental situation at the time is unknown or cannot be ascertained. At the moment, therefore, our interpretation is no more than a supposition to which we ourselves would not ascribe too much weight. Later, however, something happens which shows us how well justified our previous interpretation was. I was once the guest of a young married couple and heard the young wife laughingly describe her latest experience, how the day after the return from the honeymoon she had called for her sister and gone shopping with her as in former times, while her husband went to his business. Suddenly she noticed a man on the other side of the street and, nudging her sister, said, "Look, there goes Mr. K." She had forgotten that this man had been her husband for some weeks. A shudder went over me as I heard the story, but I dared not draw the inference. Several years later the little incident came back to my mind after this marriage had come to a most unhappy end.

Maeder tells a story of a lady who had forgotten to try on her wedding-dress the day before the wedding, to the despair of the dressmaker, and remembered it only late in the evening. He connects it with the fact that soon after the marriage she was divorced by her husband. I know a woman now divorced from her husband who, in managing her money-affairs, frequently signed documents with her maiden name, many years before she really resumed it. I know of other women who lost their wedding-rings on the honeymoon and I know, too, that the course of the marriage lent meaning to this accident. And now one striking example more, with a better ending. It is told of a famous German chemist that his marriage never took place because he forgot the hour of the ceremony and went to the laboratory instead of to the church. He was wise enough to let the matter rest with one attempt, and died unmarried at a ripe age.

Perhaps the idea has also come to you that in these examples mistakes seem to have replaced the omens or portents of the ancients. And indeed, certain kinds of portents were nothing but errors, for instance, when anyone stumbled or fell down. It is true that another group of omens bore the character of objective events rather than of subjective acts. But you would not believe how difficult it is sometimes to decide whether a specific instance belongs to the first category or to the second. The act knows so often how to disguise itself as a passive experience.

Every one of us who can look back over a fairly long experience of life would probably say that he might have spared himself many disappointments and painful surprises, if he had had the courage and resolution to interpret as omens the little mistakes which he noticed in his intercourse with others, and to regard them as signs of tendencies still in the background. For the most part one does not dare to do this; one has an impression that one would become superstitious again by a circuitous scientific path. And then, not all omens come true, and our theories will show you how it is that they need not all come true.

FOURTH LECTURE

THE PSYCHOLOGY OF ERRORS (*Conclusion*)

THAT errors have a meaning we may certainly set down as established by our efforts up to this point, and may take this conclusion as a basis for our further investigations. Let me once more emphasize the fact that we do not maintain—and for our purposes do not need to maintain—that every single mistake which occurs has a meaning, although I think that probable. It is enough for us to prove that such a meaning is relatively frequent in the various forms of errors. In this respect, by the way, the various forms show certain differences. Some cases of slips of the tongue, slips of the pen,

and so on, may be the effect of a purely physiological cause, though I cannot believe this possible of those errors which depend upon forgetfulness (forgetting of names or intentions, mislaying, and so on); losing possessions is in all probability to be recognized as unintentional in some cases; altogether our conceptions are only to a certain extent applicable to the mistakes which occur in daily life. These limitations should be borne in mind by you when we proceed on the assumption that errors are mental acts arising from the mutual interference of two intentions.

This is the first result of our psycho-analysis. Hitherto psychology has known nothing of such interferences or of the possibility that they could occasion manifestations of this kind. We have widened the domain of mental phenomena to a very considerable extent and have won for psychology phenomena which were never before accredited to it.

Let us dwell for a moment on the proposition that errors are *mental acts*. Does this mean any more than our former statement, that they have a meaning? I do not think so; on the contrary, it is a more indefinite statement and one more open to misunderstanding. Everything that can be observed in mental life will be designated at one time or another as a mental phenomenon. It depends, however, whether the particular mental phenomenon is directly due to bodily, organic or material agencies, in which case it does not fall to psychology for investigation; or whether it arose directly from other mental processes, behind which at some point the succession of organic agencies then begins. We have in mind the latter state of things when we describe a phenomenon as a mental process, and it is therefore more expedient to put our statement in this form: The phenomenon has meaning; and by meaning we understand significance, intention, tendency and a position in a sequence of mental concatenations.

There is another group of occurrences which is very closely related to errors but for which this name is not suitable. We call them *accidental* and *symptomatic acts*. They also appear to be unmotivated, insignificant and unimportant but, in addition to this, they have very clearly the feature of superfluity. They are, on the one hand, distinguishable from errors by the absence of any second intention to which they are opposed and which they disturb; on the other hand, they merge without any definite line of demarcation into the gestures and movements which we regard as expressions of the

emotions. To this class of accidental performances belong all those apparently purposeless
acts which we carry out, as though in play,
with clothing, parts of the body, objects within reach; also the omission of such acts; and
again the tunes which we hum to ourselves. I
maintain that all such performances have meaning and are explicable in the same way as are
errors, that they are slight indications of other
more important mental processes, and are genuine mental acts. I propose, however, not to
linger over this further extension of the field
of mental phenomena, but to return to the errors; for by a consideration of them problems
of importance in the enquiry into psycho-analysis can be worked out much more clearly.

Undoubtedly, the most interesting questions
which we formulated while considering errors,
and have not yet answered, are the following:
We said that errors result from the mutual interference of two different intentions, of which
one may be called the intention interfered with,
and the other the interfering tendency. The intentions interfered with give rise to no further
questions, but concerning the others we wish to
know, first, what kind of intentions these are
that arise as disturbers of others, and secondly,
what are the relations between the interfering
tendencies and those which suffer the interference?

Allow me to take slips of the tongue again
as representative of the whole series, and to
answer the second question before the first.

The interfering tendency in the slip of the
tongue may be connected in meaning with the
intention interfered with, in which case the former contains a contradiction of the latter, or
corrects, or supplements it. Or, in other more
obscure and more interesting cases, the interfering tendency may have no connection whatever in meaning with the intention interfered
with.

Evidence for the first of these two relationships can be found without difficulty in the examples already studied and in others similar to
them. In almost all cases of slips of the tongue
where the opposite of what is meant is said the
interfering tendency expresses the opposite
meaning to that of the intention interfered
with, and the slip is the expression of the conflict between two incompatible impulses. "I
declare the meeting open, but would prefer to
have closed it" is the meaning of the President's
slip. A political paper which had been accused
of corruption defends itself in an article meant
to culminate with the words: "Our readers will

testify that we have always laboured for the
public benefit in the most *disinterested* manner." But the editor entrusted with the composition of the defence wrote "in the most *interested* manner." That is to say, he thinks, "I
have to write this stuff, but I know better." A
representative of the people, urging that the
Kaiser should be told the truth *rückhaltslos*
(unreservedly) hears an inner voice terrified
at his boldness, and by a slip of the tongue
transforms *rückhaltslos* into *rückgratslos* (without backbone, ineffectually).

In the examples already given, which produce
an impression of contraction and abbreviation,
the process represents a correction, addition,
or continuation, in which a second tendency
manifests itself alongside the first. "Things
were then revealed, but better say it straight
out, they were filthy, therefore—things were
then *refilled*." "The people who understand
this subject may be counted on the fingers
of one hand, but no, there is really only one
person who understands it, very well then—can
be counted on *one finger*." Or, "my husband
can eat and drink what he likes, but you know,
I don't permit him to like this and that; so
then—he may eat and drink what *I* like." In
all these cases the slip arises from the content
of the intention interfered with, or is directly
connected with it.

The other kind of relationship between the
two interfering tendencies seems strange. If the
interfering tendency has nothing to do with
the content of the one interfered with, whence
comes it then, and how does it happen to make
itself manifest just at that point? Observation,
which alone can supply the answer to this,
shows that the interfering tendency proceeds
from a train of thought which has occupied
the person shortly before and then reveals itself in this way as an after-effect, irrespective
of whether or not it has already been expressed
in speech. It is really therefore to be described
as a perseveration, though not necessarily a
perseveration of spoken words. An associative connection between the interfering tendency and that interfered with is not lacking here
either, though it is not found in the content
but is artificially established, sometimes with
considerable *forcing* of the connections.

Here is a simple example of this which I
observed myself. Once in the beautiful Dolo-
mites I met two Viennese ladies who were starting for a walking-tour. I accompanied them
part of the way and we discussed the pleasures,
but also the trials, of this way of life. One of

the ladies admitted that spending the day like this entailed much discomfort. "It certainly is very unpleasant to tramp all day in the sun till one's blouse . . . and things are soaked through." In this sentence she had to overcome a slight hesitation at one point. Then she continued: "But then, when one gets *nach Hose* and can change . . ." (*Hose* means *drawers:* the lady meant to say *nach Hause* which means *home*). We did not analyse this slip, but I am sure you will easily understand it. The lady's intention had been to enumerate a more complete list of her clothes, "blouse, chemise and drawers." From motives of propriety, mention of the drawers (*Hose*) was omitted; but in the next sentence, the content of which is quite independent, the unuttered word came to light as a distortion of the word it resembled in sound, *home* (*Hause*).

Now we can turn at last to the main question which has been so long postponed, namely, what kind of tendencies these are which bring themselves to expression in this unusual way by interfering with other intentions. They are evidently very various, yet our aim is to find some element common to them all. If we examine a series of examples for this purpose we shall soon find that they fall into three groups. To the *first* group belong the cases in which the interfering tendency is known to the speaker and, moreover, was felt by him before the slip. Thus, in the case of the slip "refilled," the speaker not only admitted that he had criticized the events in question as "filthy," but further, that he had had the intention, which he subsequently reversed, of expressing this opinion in words. A *second* group is formed by other cases in which the interfering tendency is likewise recognized by the speaker as his own, but he is not aware that it was active in him before the slip. He therefore accepts our interpretation, but remains to some extent surprised by it. Examples of this attitude are probably more easily found in other errors than in slips of the tongue. In the *third* group the interpretation of the interfering tendency is energetically repudiated by the speaker; not only does he dispute that it was active in him before the slip, but he will maintain that it is altogether entirely alien to him. Recall the case about hiccoughing and the positively discourteous rebuff which I brought upon myself by detecting the interfering tendency. You know that in our attitude towards these cases you and I are still far from an agreement. I should make nothing of the after-dinner speaker's de-nial and hold fast to my interpretation unwaveringly, while you, I imagine, are still impressed by his vehemence and are wondering whether one should not forego the interpretation of such errors and let them pass for purely physiological acts, as in the days before analysis. I can imagine what it is that alarms you. My interpretation includes the assumption that tendencies of which a speaker knows nothing can express themselves through him and that I can deduce them from various indications. You hesitate before a conclusion so novel and so pregnant with consequences. I understand that, and admit that up to a point you are justified. But let one thing be clear: if you intend to carry to its logical conclusion the conception of errors which has been confirmed by so many examples, you must decide to make this startling assumption. If you cannot do this, you will have to abandon again the understanding of errors which you had only just begun to obtain.

Let us pause a moment on that which unites the three groups and is common to the three mechanisms of a slip of the tongue. Fortunately this common element is unmistakable. In the first two groups the interfering tendency is admitted by the speaker; in the first, there is the additional fact that it showed itself immediately before the slip. But in both cases *it has been forced back. The speaker had determined not to convert the idea into speech and then it happens that he makes a slip of the tongue; that is to say, the tendency which is debarred from expression asserts itself against his will and gains utterance, either by altering the expression of the intention permitted by him, or by mingling with it, or actually by setting itself in place of it*. This then is the mechanism of a slip of the tongue.

For my own part I can bring the process in the third group also into perfect harmony with the mechanism here described. I need only assume that these three groups are differentiated by the varying degrees to which the forcing back of an intention is effective. In the first group, the intention is present and makes itself perceptible before the words are spoken; not until then does it suffer the rejection for which it indemnifies itself in the slip. In the second group the rejection reaches further back; the intention is no longer perceptible even before the speech. It is remarkable that this does not hinder it in the least from being the active cause of the slip. But this state of things simplifies the explanation of the process in the third group. I shall be bold enough to assume that a tendency can still express itself by an error though it has been debarred from expression for a long time, perhaps for a very long time, has not made itself perceptible at all, and can therefore be directly repudiated by the speaker. But leaving aside the problem of the third group, you must conclude from the other cases that a *suppression (Unterdrückung) of a previous intention to say something is the indispensable condition for the occurrence of a slip of the tongue.*

We may now claim to have made further progress in the understanding of errors. We not only know them to be mental phenomena in which meaning and purpose are recognizable, not only know that they arise from the mutual interference of two different intentions, but in addition we know that, for one of these intentions to be able to express itself by interfering with another, it must itself have been subject to some hindrance against its operation. It must first be itself interfered with, before it can interfere with others. Naturally this does not give us a complete explanation of the phenomena which we call errors. We see at once further questions arising, and in general we suspect that as we progress towards comprehension the more numerous will be the occasions for new questions. We might ask, for instance, why the matter does not proceed much more simply. If the intention to restrain a certain tendency instead of carrying it into effect is present in the mind, then this restraint ought to succeed, so that nothing whatever of the tendency gains expression, or else it might fail so that the restrained tendency achieves full expression. But errors are *compromise*-formations; they express part-success and part-failure for each of the two intentions; the threatened intention is neither entirely suppressed nor, apart from some instances, does it force itself through intact. We can imagine that special conditions must be present for the occurrence of such interference (or compromise)-formations, but we cannot even conjecture of what kind they may be. Nor do I think that we could discover these unknown circumstances by penetrating further into the study of errors. It will be necessary first to examine thoroughly yet other obscure fields of mental life: only the analogies to be met with there can give us courage to form those assumptions which are requisite for a more searching elucidation of errors. And one other point! To work from slight indications, as we constantly do in this field, is not without its dangers. There is a mental disorder called *combinatory paranoia* in which the practice of utilizing such small indications is carried beyond all limits, and I naturally do not contend that the conclusions which are built up on such a basis are throughout correct. Only by the breadth of our observations, by the accumulation of similar impressions from the most varied forms of mental life, can we guard against this danger.

So now we will leave the analysis of errors. But there is one thing more which I might impress upon you: to keep in mind, as a model, the method by which we have studied these phenomena. You can perceive from these examples what the aim of our psychology is. Our purpose is not merely to describe and classify the phenomena, but to conceive them as brought about by the play of forces in the mind, as expressions of tendencies striving towards a goal, which work together or against one another. We are endeavouring to attain a *dynamic conception* of mental phenomena. In this conception, the trends we merely infer are more prominent than the phenomena we perceive.

So we will probe no further into errors; but we may still take a fleeting glimpse over the breadth of this whole field, in the course of which we shall both meet with things already known and come upon the tracks of others that are new. In so doing, we will keep to the division into three groups made at the beginning of our study: slips of the tongue, with the coordinate forms of slips of the pen, misreading, mis-hearing; of forgetting with its subdivisions according to the object forgotten (proper names, foreign words, resolutions, impressions); and of mislaying, mistaking, and losing objects. Mistakes, in so far as they concern us, are to be grouped partly under the head of forgetting, partly under acts erroneously performed (picking up the wrong objects, etc.).

We have already treated slips of the tongue in great detail yet there is still something to add. There are certain small affective manifestations related to slips of the tongue which are not entirely without interest. No one likes to think he has made a slip of the tongue; one often fails to hear it when made by oneself, but never when made by someone else. Slips of the tongue are in a certain sense infectious; it is not at all easy to speak of them without making them oneself. It is not hard to detect the motivation of even the most trifling forms of them, although these do not throw any particular light on hidden mental processes. If, for instance, anyone pronounces a long vowel as a short one, in consequence of a disturbance over the word, no matter how motivated, he will as a result soon after lengthen a short vowel and commit a new slip in compensation for the first. The same thing occurs if anyone pronounces a diphthong indistinctly and carelessly, for instance, "ew" or "oy" as "i"; he tries to correct it by changing a subsequent "i" into "ew" or "oy." Some consideration relating to the hearer seems to be behind this behaviour, as though he were not to be allowed to think that the speaker is indifferent how he treats his mother-tongue. The second, compensating distortion actually has the purpose of drawing the hearer's attention to the first and assuring him that it has not escaped the speaker either. The most frequent, insignificant, and simple forms of slips consist in contractions and anticipations in inconspicuous parts of the speech. In a long sentence, for instance, slips of the tongue would be of the kind in which the last word intended influences the sound of an earlier word. This gives an impression of a certain impatience to be done with the sentence, and in general it points to a certain resistance against the communication of this sentence, or the speech altogether. From this we come to border-line cases, in which the differences between the psycho-analytical and the ordinary physiological conception of slips of the tongue become merged. We assume that in these cases a disturbing tendency is opposing the intended speech; but it can only betray its presence and not what its own purpose is. The interference which it causes follows some sound-influence or associative connection and may be regarded as a distraction of attention away from the intended speech. But neither in this distraction of attention, nor in the associative tendency which has been activated, lies the essence of the occurrence; the essence lies rather in the hint the occurrence gives of the presence of some other intention interfering with the intended speech, the nature of which cannot in this case be discovered from its effects, as is possible in all the more pronounced cases of slips of the tongue.

Slips of the pen, to which I now turn, are so like slips of the tongue in their mechanism that no new points of view are to be expected from them. Perhaps a small addition to our knowledge from this group will content us. Those very common little slips of the pen, contractions, anticipations of later words, particularly of the last words, point to a general distaste for writing and to an impatience to be done;

more pronounced effects in slips of the pen allow the nature and intention of the interference to be recognized. In general, if one finds a slip of the pen in a letter one knows that the writer's mind was not working smoothly at the moment; what was the matter one cannot always establish. Slips of the pen are frequently as little noticed by those who make them as slips of the tongue. The following observation is striking in this connection. There are, of course, some persons who have the habit of always re-reading every letter they write before sending it. Others do not do this; but, if the latter make an exception and re-read a letter, they then always have an opportunity of finding and correcting a striking slip of the pen. How is this to be explained? It almost looks as if such people knew that they had made a slip in writing the letter. Are we really to believe that this is so?

There is an interesting problem connected with the practical significance of slips of the pen. You may recall the case of the murderer H who managed, by asserting himself to be a bacteriologist, to obtain cultures of highly dangerous disease-germs from scientific institutions, but used them for the purpose of doing away in this most modern fashion with people connected with him. This man once complained to the authorities of one of these institutions about the ineffectiveness of the cultures sent him, but committed a slip of the pen and, instead of the words "in my experiments on mice and guinea-pigs *(Mäusen und Meerschweinchen),*" the words "in my experiments on people *(Menschen)*" were plainly legible. This slip even attracted the attention of the doctors at the institute but, so far as I know, they drew no conclusion from it. Now, what do you think? Would it not have been better if the doctors had taken the slip of the pen as a confession and started an investigation so that the murderer's proceedings might have been arrested in time? In this case, does not ignorance of our conception of errors result in neglect which, in actuality, may be very important? Well, I know that such a slip of the pen would certainly rouse great suspicion in me; but there is an important objection against regarding it as a confession. The matter is not so simple. The slip of the pen is certainly an indication but, alone, it would not have justified an enquiry. It does indeed betray that the man is occupied with the thought of infecting human beings; but it does not show with certainty whether this thought is a definite plan to do harm or a mere phantasy of no practical importance. It is even possible that a person making such a slip will deny, with the soundest subjective justification, the existence of such a phantasy in himself, and will reject the idea as a thing utterly alien to him. Later, when we come to consider the difference between psychical reality and material reality you will be better able to appreciate these possibilities. But this again is a case in which an error was found subsequently to have unsuspected significance.

Misreading brings us to a mental situation which is clearly different from that of slips of the tongue or the pen. One of the two conflicting tendencies is here replaced by a sensory excitation and is perhaps therefore less tenacious. What one is reading is not a product of one's own mind, as is that which one is going to write. In the large majority of cases, therefore, misreading consists in complete substitution. A different word is substituted for the word to be read, without there necessarily being any connection in the content between the text and the effect of the mistake, and usually by means of a resemblance between the words. Lichtenberg's example of this, *Agamemnon* instead of *angenommen*, is the best of this group. To discover the interfering tendency which causes the mistake one may put aside the original text altogether; the analytic investigation may begin with two questions: What is the first idea occurring in free association to the effect of the misreading (the substitute), and in what circumstances did the misreading occur? Occasionally a knowledge of the latter is sufficient in itself to explain the misreading, as, for instance, when someone wandering about a strange town, driven by urgent needs, reads the word *Closethaus* on a large sign on the first storey. He has just time to wonder that the board has been fixed at that height when he discovers that the word on it is actually *Corsethaus*. In other cases where there is a lack of connection in content between the text and the slip a thorough analysis is necessary, which cannot be accomplished without practice in psycho-analytic technique and confidence in it. But it is not usually so difficult to come by the explanation of a case of misreading. In the example *Agamemnon*, the substituted word betrays without further difficulty the line of thought from which the disturbance arose. In this time of war, for instance, it is very common for one to read everywhere names of towns, generals, and military expressions, which are continually in one's ears, wherever

one sees a word at all resembling them. Whatever interests and occupies the mind takes the place of what is alien and as yet uninteresting. The shadows of thoughts in the mind dim the new perceptions.

Another kind of misreading is possible, in which the text itself arouses the disturbing tendency, whereupon it is usually changed into its opposite. Someone is required to read something which he dislikes, and analysis convinces him that a strong wish to reject what is read is responsible for the alteration.

In the first-mentioned, more frequent cases of misreading two factors to which we ascribed great importance in the mechanism of errors are inconspicuous; these are the conflict between two tendencies and the forcing back of one of them which compensates itself by producing the error. Not that anything contradictory of this occurs in misreading, but nevertheless the importunity of the train of thought tending to the mistake is far more conspicuous than the restraint which it may have previously undergone. Just these two factors are most clearly observable in the different situations in which errors occur through forgetfulness.

The forgetting of resolutions has positively but one meaning; the interpretation of it, as we have heard, is not denied even by the layman. The tendency interfering with the resolution is always an opposing one, an unwillingness, concerning which it only remains to enquire why it does not come to expression in a different and less disguised form; for the existence of this opposing tendency is beyond doubt. Sometimes it is possible, too, to infer something of the motives which necessitate the concealment of this antipathy; one sees that it would certainly have been condemned if it declared its opposition openly, whereas by craft, in the error, it always achieves its end. When an important change in the mental situation occurs between the formation of the resolution and its execution, in consequence of which the execution would no longer be required, then if it were forgotten the occurrence could no longer come within the category of errors. There would be nothing to wonder at in the error, for one recognizes that it would have been superfluous to remember the resolution; it had been either permanently or temporarily cancelled. Forgetting to carry out a resolution can only be called an error when there is no reason to believe that any such cancellation has occurred.

Cases of forgetting to carry out resolutions are usually so uniform and transparent, that they are of no interest for our researches. There are two points, nevertheless, at which something new can be learnt by studying this type of error. We have said that forgetting and not executing a resolution indicate an antagonistic tendency in opposition to it. This is certainly true, but our own investigations show that this *counter-will* may be of two kinds, either immediate or mediate. What is meant by the latter is best explained by one or two examples. When the patron forgets to say a good word for his protégé to some third person, it may happen because he is actually not much interested in the protégé and therefore has no great inclination to do it. This, in any case, will be the protégé's view of the patron's omission. But the matter may be more complicated. The antipathy against executing the resolution may come from some other source in the patron and be directed to some other point. It need have nothing at all to do with the protégé, but is perhaps directed against the third person to whom the recommendation was to be made. Here again, you see, what objections there are against applying our interpretations practically. In spite of having correctly interpreted the error, the protégé is in danger of becoming too suspicious and of doing his patron a grave injustice. Again, if someone forgets an appointment which he had promised and was resolved to attend, the commonest cause is certainly a direct disinclination to meet the other person. But analysis might produce evidence that the interfering tendency was concerned, not with the person, but with the place of meeting, which was avoided on account of some painful memory associated with it. Or if one forgets to post a letter the opposing tendency may be concerned with the contents of the letter; but this does not exclude the possibility that the letter in itself is harmless and becomes the subject of a counter-tendency only because something in it reminds the writer of another letter, written previously, which did in fact afford a direct basis for antipathy. It may then be said that the antipathy has been *transferred* from the earlier letter, where it was justified, to the present one where it actually has no object. So you see that restraint and caution must be exercised in applying our quite well-founded interpretations; that which is psychologically equivalent may in actuality have many meanings.

That such things should be must seem very strange to you. Perhaps you will be inclined to assume that the *indirect* counter-will is enough to characterize the incident as pathological. But I can assure you that it is also found within the boundaries of health and normality. And further, do not misunderstand me; this is in no sense a confession on my part that our analytic interpretations are not to be relied on. I have said that forgetting to execute a plan may bear many meanings, but this is so only in those cases where no analysis is undertaken and which we have to interpret according to our general principles. If an analysis of the person in the case is carried out it can always be established with sufficient certainty whether the antipathy is a direct one, or what its source is otherwise.

The following is a second point: when we find proof in a large majority of cases that the forgetting of an intention proceeds from a counter-will, we gain courage to extend this solution to another group of cases in which the person analysed does not confirm, but denies, the presence of the counter-will inferred by us. Take as an example of this such exceedingly frequent occurrences as forgetting to return borrowed books or to pay bills or debts. We will be so bold as to suggest, to the person in question, that there is an intention in his mind of keeping the books and not paying the debts, whereupon he will deny this intention but will not be able to give us any other explanation of his conduct. We then insist that he has this intention but is not aware of it; it is enough for us, though, that it betrays itself by the effect of the forgetting. He may then repeat that he had merely forgotten about it. You will recognize the situation as one in which we have already been placed once before. If we intend to carry through, to their logical conclusions. the interpretations of errors which have been proved justified in so many cases, we shall be unavoidably impelled to the assumption that tendencies exist in human beings which can effect results without their knowing of them. With this, however, we place ourselves in opposition to all views prevailing in life and in psychology.

Forgetting proper names, and foreign names and words, can be traced in the same way to a counter-tendency aiming either directly or indirectly against the name in question. I have already given you several examples of such direct antipathy. Indirect causation is particularly frequent here and careful analysis is generally required to elucidate it. Thus, for instance, in the present time of war which forces us to forego so many of our former pleasures, our ability to recall proper names suffers severely by connections of the most far-fetched kind. It happened to me lately to be unable to remember the name of the harmless Moravian town of Bisenz; and analysis showed that I was guilty of no direct antagonism in the matter, but that the resemblance to the name of the Palazzo Bisenzi in Orvieto, where I had spent many happy times in the past, was responsible. As a motive of the tendency opposing the recollection of this name, we here for the first time encounter a principle which will later on reveal itself to be of quite prodigious importance in the causation of neurotic symptoms: namely, the aversion on the part of memory against recalling anything connected with painful feelings that would revive the pain if it were recalled. In this tendency towards *avoidance of pain* from recollection or other mental processes, this flight of the mind from that which is unpleasant, we may perceive the ultimate purpose at work behind not merely the forgetting of names, but also many other errors, omissions, and mistakes.

The forgetting of names seems, however, to be especially facilitated psycho-physiologically, and therefore does occur on occasions where the intervention of an unpleasantness-motive cannot be established. When anyone has a tendency to forget names, it can be confirmed by analytic investigation that names escape, not merely because he does not like them or because they remind him of something disagreeable, but also because the particular name belongs to some other chain of associations of a more intimate nature. The name is anchored there, as it were, and is refused to the other associations activated at the moment. If you recall the devices of memory systems you will realize with some surprise that the same associations which are there artificially introduced, in order to save names from being forgotten, are also responsible for their being forgotten. The most conspicuous example of this is afforded by proper names of persons, which naturally possess quite different values for different people. For instance, take a first name, such as Theodore. For some of you it will have no particular significance; for others it will be the name of father, brother, friend, or your own name. Analytic experience will show you that the former among you will be in no danger of forgetting that some stranger bears this name; whereas the latter will be continually inclined to grudge to strangers a name which to them seems reserved for an intimate relationship. Now let us assume that this inhibition due to

associations may coincide with the operation of the "pain"-principle, and in addition with an indirect mechanism; you will then be able to form a commensurate idea of the complexity, in causation, of such temporary forgetting of names. An adequate analysis that does justice to the facts will, however, completely disclose all these complications.

The forgetting of impressions and experiences shows the working of the tendency to ward off from memory that which is unpleasant much more clearly and invariably than the forgetting of names. It does not of course belong in its entirety to the category of errors, but only in so far as it appears to us remarkable and unjustified, judged by the standard of general experience; as, for instance, where recent or important impressions are forgotten, or where one memory is forgotten out of an otherwise well-remembered sequence. How and why we have the capacity of forgetting in general, particularly how we are able to forget experiences which have certainly left the deepest impression on us, such as the events of our childhood, is quite a different problem, in which the defence against painful associations plays a certain part but is far from explaining everything. That unwelcome impressions are easily forgotten is an indubitable fact. Various psychologists have remarked it; and the great Darwin was so well aware of it that he made a golden rule for himself of writing down with particular care observations which seemed unfavourable to his theory, having become convinced that just these would be inclined to slip out of recollection.

Those who hear for the first time of this principle of defence against unpleasant memory by forgetfulness seldom fail to raise the objection that, on the contrary, in their experience it is just that which is painful which it is hard to forget, since it always comes back to mind to torture the person against his will— as, for example, the recollection of grievances or humiliations. This fact is quite correct, but the objection is not sound. It is important to begin early to reckon with the fact that the mind is an arena, a sort of tumbling-ground, for the struggles of antagonistic impulses; or, to express it in non-dynamic terms, that the mind is made up of contradictions and pairs of opposites. Evidence of one particular tendency does not in the least preclude its opposite; there is room for both of them. The material questions are: How do these opposites stand to one another and what effects proceed from one of them and what from the other?

Losing and mislaying objects is of especial interest on account of the numerous meanings it may have, and the multiplicity of the tendencies in the service of which these errors may be employed. What is common to all the cases is the wish to lose something; what varies in them is the reason for the wish and the aim of it. One loses something if it has become damaged; if one has an impulse to replace it with a better; if one has ceased to care for it; if it came from someone with whom unpleasantness has arisen; or if it was acquired in circumstances that one no longer wishes to think of. Letting things fall, spoiling, or breaking things, serves the same tendency. In social life it is said that unwelcome and illegitimate children are found to be far more often weakly than those conceived in happier circumstances. This result does not imply that the crude methods of the so-called baby-farmers have been employed; some degree of carelessness in the supervision of the child should be quite enough. The preservation, or otherwise, of objects may well follow the same lines as that of children.

Then too it may happen that a thing will become destined to be lost without its having shed any of its value—that is, when there is an impulse to sacrifice something to fate in order to avert some other dreaded loss. According to the findings of analysis, such conjurings of fate are still very common among us, so that our losses are often voluntary sacrifices. Losing may equally well serve the impulses of spite or of self-punishment; in short, the more remote forms of motivation behind the impulse to do away with something by losing cannot easily be exhausted.

Mistaking of objects, or erroneous performance of actions, like other errors, is often made use of to fulfil a wish which should be denied; the intention masquerades as a lucky chance. Thus, as once happened to a friend, one has to take a train, most unwillingly, in order to pay a visit in the suburbs and then, in changing trains at a connection, gets by mistake into one which is returning to town; or, on a journey someone might greatly like to make a halt at some stopping-place, which cannot be done owing to fixed engagements elsewhere, whereupon he mistakes or misses the connection, so that the desired delay is forced upon him. Or, as happened to one of my patients whom I had forbidden to telephone to the lady he was in love with, he *by mistake* and *thoughtlessly* gave the wrong number when he meant to telephone to me, so that he was suddenly connected with her. The following account by an engineer is a pretty example of the conditions under which damage to material objects may be done, and also demonstrates the practical significance of directly faulty actions.

"Some time ago I worked with several colleagues in the laboratory of a High School on a series of complicated experiments in elasticity, a piece of work we had undertaken voluntarily; it was beginning to take up more time, however, than we had anticipated. One day, as I went into the laboratory with my friend F, he remarked how annoying it was to him to lose so much time today as he had so much to do at home; I could not help agreeing with him and said half-jokingly, referring to an occasion the week before: 'Let us hope the machine will break down again so that we can stop work and go home early.' In arranging the work it happened that F was given the regulation of the valve of the press; that is to say, he was, by cautiously opening the valve, to let the liquid pressure out of the accumulator slowly into the cylinder of the hydraulic press. The man who was conducting the experiment stood by the pressure gauge, and, when the right pressure was reached, called out loudly, 'Stop.' At this command F seized the valve and turned with all his might—to the left! (All valves without exception close to the right.) Thereby the whole pressure in the accumulator suddenly came into the press, a strain for which the connecting-pipes are not designed, so that one of them instantly burst—quite a harmless accident, but one which forced us, nevertheless, to cease work for the day and go home. It is characteristic, by the way, that not long after, when we were discussing the affair, my friend F had no recollection whatever of my remark, which I recalled with certainty."

So with this in mind you may begin to suspect that it is not always a mere chance which makes the hands of your servants such dangerous enemies to your household effects. And you may also raise the question whether it is always an accident when one injures oneself or exposes oneself to danger—ideas which you may put to the test by analysis when you have an opportunity.

This is far from being all that could be said about errors. There is still much to be enquired into and discussed. But I shall be satisfied if you have been shaken somewhat in your previous beliefs by our investigations, so far as they have gone, and if you have gained a certain readiness to accept new ones. For the rest, I must be content to leave you with certain problems still unsolved. We cannot prove all our principles by the study of errors, nor are we indeed by any means solely dependent on this material. The great value of errors for our purpose lies in this, that they are such common occurrences, may easily be observed in oneself, and are not at all contingent upon illness. I should like to mention one more of your unanswered questions before concluding: "If, as we see from so many examples, people come so close to understanding errors and so often act as if they perceived their meaning, how is it possible that they should so generally consider them accidental, senseless, and meaningless, and so energetically oppose the psycho-analytic explanation of them?"

You are right: this is indeed striking and requires an explanation. But I will not give it to you; I will rather guide you slowly towards the connections by which the explanation will be forced upon you without any aid from me.

PART II. DREAMS

FIFTH LECTURE

DIFFICULTIES AND PRELIMINARY APPROACH TO THE SUBJECT

ONE day the discovery was made that the symptoms of disease in certain nervous patients have meaning.[1] It was upon this discovery that the psycho-analytic method of treatment was based. In this treatment it happened that patients in speaking of their symptoms also mentioned their dreams, whereupon the suspicion arose that these dreams too had meaning.

However, we will not pursue this historical path, but will strike off in the opposite direction. Our aim is to demonstrate the meaning of dreams, in preparation for the study of the neuroses. There are good grounds for this reversal of procedure, since the study of dreams is not merely the best preparation for that of the neuroses, but a dream is itself a neurotic symptom and, moreover, one which possesses for us the incalculable advantage of occurring in all healthy people. Indeed, if all human beings were healthy and would only dream, we could gather almost all the knowledge from their dreams which we have gained from studying the neuroses.

So dreams become the object of psychoanalytic research—another of these ordinary, under-rated occurrences, apparently of no practical value, like *errors*, and sharing with them the characteristic of occurring in healthy persons. But in other respects the conditions of work are rather less favourable. Errors had only been neglected by science, people had not troubled their heads much about them, but at least it was no disgrace to occupy oneself with them. True, people said, there are things more important but still something may possibly come of it. To occupy oneself with dreams, however, is not merely unpractical and superfluous, but positively scandalous: it carries with it the taint of the unscientific and arouses the suspicion of personal leanings towards mysticism. The idea of a medical student troubling himself about dreams when there is so much in neuropathology and psychiatry itself that is more serious—tumours as large as apples compressing the organ of the mind, hæmorrhages, chronic inflammatory conditions in which the alterations in the tissues can be demonstrated under the microscope! No, dreams are far too unworthy and trivial to be objects of scientific research.

There is yet another factor involved which, in itself, sets at defiance all the requirements of exact investigation. In investigating dreams even the object of research, the dream itself, is indefinite. A delusion, for example, presents clear and definite outlines. "I am the Emperor of China," says your patient plainly. But a dream? For the most part it cannot be related at all. When a man tells a dream, has he any guarantee that he has told it correctly, and not perhaps altered it in the telling or been forced to invent part of it on account of the vagueness of his recollection? Most dreams cannot be remembered at all and are forgotten except for

[1] By Joseph Breuer, in the years 1880-1882. Cf. my lectures on Psycho-Analysis, delivered in the United States in 1909 [*The Origin and Development of Psycho-Analysis,* see p. 1 above].

some tiny fragments. And is a scientific psychology or a method of treatment for the sick to be founded upon material such as this?

A certain element of exaggeration in a criticism may arouse our suspicions. The arguments brought against the dream as an object of scientific research are clearly extreme. We have met with the objection of triviality already in "errors," and have told ourselves that great things may be revealed even by small indications. As to the indistinctness of dreams, that is a characteristic like any other—we cannot dictate to things their characteristics; besides, there are also dreams which are clear and well-defined. Further, there are other objects of psychiatric investigation which suffer in the same way from the quality of indefiniteness, e.g. the obsessive ideas of many cases, with which nevertheless many psychiatrists of repute and standing have occupied themselves. I will recall the last case of the kind which came before me in medical practice. The patient, a woman, presented her case in these words: "I have a certain feeling, as if I had injured, or had meant to injure, some living creature—perhaps a child—no, no, a dog rather, as if perhaps I had pushed it off a bridge—or done something else." Any disadvantage resulting from the uncertain recollection of dreams may be remedied by deciding that exactly what the dreamer tells is to count as the dream, and by ignoring all that he may have forgotten or altered in the process of recollection. Finally, one cannot maintain in so sweeping a fashion that dreams are unimportant things. We know from our own experience that the mood in which we awake from a dream may last throughout the day, and cases have been observed by medical men in which mental disorder began with a dream, the delusion which had its source in this dream persisting; further, it is told of historical persons that impulses to momentous deeds sprang from their dreams. We may therefore ask: What is the real cause of the disdain in which dreams are held in scientific circles? In my opinion it is the reaction from the over-estimation of them in earlier times. It is well known that it is no easy matter to reconstruct the past, but we may assume with certainty (you will forgive my jest) that as early as three thousand years ago and more our ancestors dreamt in the same way as we do. So far as we know, all ancient peoples attached great significance to dreams and regarded them as of practical value; they obtained from them auguries of the future and

looked for portents in them. For the Greeks and other Orientals, it was at times as unthinkable to undertake a campaign without a dream-interpreter as it would be today without air-scouts for intelligence. When Alexander the Great set out on his campaign of conquest the most famous interpreters of dreams were in his following. The city of Tyre, still at that time on an island, offered so stout a resistance to the king that he entertained the idea of abandoning the siege; then one night he dreamed of a satyr dancing in triumph, and when he related this dream to his interpreters they informed him that it foretold his victory over the city; he gave the order to attack and took Tyre by storm. Among the Etruscans and Romans other methods of foretelling the future were employed, but during the whole of the Græco-Roman period the interpretation of dreams was practiced and held in high esteem. Of the literature on this subject the principal work at any rate has come down to us, namely, the book of Artemidorus of Daldis, who is said to have lived at the time of the Emperor Hadrian. How it happened that the art of dream-interpretation declined later and dreams fell into disrepute, I cannot tell you. The progress of learning cannot have had very much to do with it, for in the darkness of the middle ages things far more absurd than the ancient practice of the interpretation of dreams were faithfully retained. The fact remains that the interest in dreams gradually sank to the level of superstition and could hold its own only amongst the uneducated. In our day, there survive, as a final degradation of the art of dream-interpretation, the attempts to find out from dreams numbers destined to draw prizes in games of chance. On the other hand, exact science of the present day has repeatedly concerned itself with the dream, but always with the sole object of illustrating *physiological* theories. By medical men, naturally, a dream was never regarded as a mental process but as the mental expression of physical stimuli. Binz in 1876 pronounced the dream to be "a physical process, always useless and in many cases actually morbid, a process above which the conception of the world-soul and of immortality stands as high as does the blue sky above the most low-lying, weed-grown stretch of sand." Maury compares dreams with the spasmodic jerkings of St. Vitus' dance, contrasted with the co-ordinated movements of the normal human being; in an old comparison a parallel is drawn between the content of a dream and the sounds which would be produced if "someone ignorant of music let his ten fingers wander over the keys of an instrument."

Interpretation means discovering a hidden meaning, but there can be no question of attempting this while such an attitude is maintained towards the dream-performance. Look up the description of dreams given in the writings of Wundt, Jodl and other recent philosophers: they are content with the bare enumeration of the divergences of the dream-life from waking thought with a view to depreciating the dreams: they emphasize the lack of connection in the associations, the suspended exercise of the critical faculty, the elimination of all knowledge, and other indications of diminished functioning. The single valuable contribution to our knowledge about dreams for which we are indebted to exact science relates to the influence upon the dream-content of physical stimuli operating during sleep. We have the work of a Norwegian author who died recently—J. Mourly Vold—two large volumes on experimental investigation of dreams (translated into German in 1910 and 1912), which are concerned almost entirely with the results obtained by change in the position of the limbs. These investigations have been held up to us as models of exact research in the subject of dreams. Now can you imagine what would be the comment of exact science on learning that we intend to try to find out the *meaning* of dreams? The comment that has perhaps been made already! However, we will not allow ourselves to be appalled at the thought. If it was possible for errors to have an underlying meaning, it is possible that dreams have one too; and errors have, in very many cases, a meaning which has eluded the researches of exact science. Let us adopt the assumption of the ancients and of simple folk, and follow in the footsteps of the dream-interpreters of old.

First of all, we must take our bearings in this enterprise and make a survey of the field of dreams. What exactly is a dream? It is difficult to define it in a single phrase. Yet we need not seek after a definition, when all we need is to refer to something familiar to everyone. Still we ought to pick out the essential features in dreams. How are we to discover these features? The boundaries of the region we are entering comprise such vast differences, differences whichever way we turn. That which we can show to be common to all dreams is probably what is essential.

Well then—the first common characteristic of all dreams would be that we are asleep at the time. Obviously, the dream is the life of the mind during sleep, a life bearing certain resemblances to our waking life and, at the same time, differing from it widely. That, indeed, was Aristotle's definition. Perhaps dream and sleep stand in yet closer relationship to each other. We can be waked by a dream; we often have a dream when we wake spontaneously or when we are forcibly roused from sleep. Dreams seem thus to be an intermediate condition between sleeping and waking. Hence, our attention is directed to sleep itself: what then is sleep?

That is a physiological or biological problem concerning which much is still in dispute. We can come to no decisive answer, but I think we may attempt to define one psychological characteristic of sleep. Sleep is a condition in which I refuse to have anything to do with the outer world and have withdrawn my interest from it. I go to sleep by retreating from the outside world and warding off the stimuli proceeding from it. Again, when I am tired by that world I go to sleep. I say to it as I fall asleep: "Leave me in peace, for I want to sleep." The child says just the opposite: "I won't go to sleep yet; I'm not tired, I want more things to happen to me!" Thus the biological object of sleep seems to be recuperation, its psychological characteristic the suspension of interest in the outer world. Our relationship with the world which we entered so unwillingly seems to be endurable only with intermission; hence we withdraw again periodically into the condition prior to our entrance into the world: that is to say, into intra-uterine existence. At any rate, we try to bring about quite similar conditions—warmth, darkness and absence of stimulus—characteristic of that state. Some of us still roll ourselves tightly up into a ball resembling the intra-uterine position. It looks as if we grown-ups do not belong wholly to the world, but only by two-thirds; one-third of us has never yet been born at all. Every time we wake in the morning it is as if we were newly born. We do, in fact, speak of the condition of waking from sleep in these very words: we feel "as if we were newly born,"—and in this we are probably quite mistaken in our idea of the general sensations of the new-born infant; it may be assumed on the contrary that it feels extremely uncomfortable. Again, in speaking of birth we speak of "seeing the light of day."

If this is the nature of sleep, then dreams do not come into its scheme at all, but seem rather to be an unwelcome supplement to it; and we do indeed believe that dreamless sleep is the best, the only proper sleep. There should be no mental activity during sleep; if any such activity bestirs itself, then in so far have we failed to reach the true pre-natal condition of peace; we have not been able to avoid altogether some remnants of mental activity, and the act of dreaming would represent these remnants. In that event it really does seem that dreams do not need to have meaning. With errors it was different, for they were at least activities manifested in waking life; but if I sleep and have altogether suspended mental activity, with the exception of certain remnants which I have not been able to suppress, there is no necessity whatever that they should have any meaning. In fact, I cannot even make use of any such meaning, seeing that the rest of my mind is asleep. It can really then be a matter of spasmodic reactions only, of such mental phenomena only as have their origin in physical stimulation. Hence, dreams must be remnants of the mental activity of waking life disturbing sleep, and we might as well make up our minds forthwith to abandon a theme so unsuited to the purposes of psycho-analysis.

Superfluous as dreams may be, however, they do exist nevertheless, and we can try to account for their existence to ourselves. Why does not mental life go off to sleep? Probably because there is something that will not leave the mind in peace; stimuli are acting upon it and to these it is bound to react. Dreams therefore are the mode of reaction of the mind to stimuli acting upon it during sleep. We note here a possibility of access to comprehension of dreams. We can now endeavour to find out, in various dreams, what are the stimuli seeking to disturb sleep, the reaction to which takes the form of dreams. By doing this we should have worked out the first characteristic common to all dreams.

Is there any other common characteristic? Yes, there is another, unmistakable, and yet much harder to lay hold of and describe. The character of mental processes during sleep is quite different from that of waking processes. In dreams we go through many experiences, which we fully believe in, whereas in reality we are perhaps only experiencing the single disturbing stimulus. For the most part our experiences take the form of visual images; there may be feeling as well, thoughts, too, mixed up with them, and the other senses may be drawn in; but for the most part dreams consist of visual images. Part of the difficulty of reciting a dream comes from the fact that we have to translate these images into words. "I could draw it," the dreamer often says to us, "but I do not know how to put it into words." Now this is not exactly a diminution in the mental capacity, as seen in a contrast between a feeble-minded person and a man of genius. The difference is rather a qualitative one, but it is difficult to say precisely wherein it lies. G. T. Fechner once suggested that the stage whereon the drama of the dream (within the mind) is played out is other than that of the life of waking ideas. That is a saying which we really do not understand, nor do we know what it is meant to convey to us, but it does actually reproduce the impression of strangeness which most dreams make upon us. Again, the comparison of the act of dreaming with the performances of an unskilled hand in music breaks down here, for the piano will certainly respond with the same notes, though not with melodies, to a chance touch on its keys. We will keep this second common characteristic of dreams carefully in view, even though we may not understand it.

Are there any other qualities common to all dreams? I can think of none, but can see differences only, whichever way I look, differences too in every respect—in apparent duration, definiteness, the part played by affects, persistence in the mind, and so forth. This is really not what we should naturally expect in the case of a compulsive attempt, at once meagre and spasmodic, to ward off a stimulus. As regards the length of dreams, some are very short, containing only one image, or very few, or a single thought, possibly even a single word; others are peculiarly rich in content, enact entire romances and seem to last a very long time. There are dreams as distinct as actual experiences, so distinct that for some time after waking we do not realize that they were dreams at all; others, which are ineffably faint, shadowy and blurred; in one and the same dream, even, there may be some parts of extraordinary vividness alternating with others so indistinct as to be almost wholly elusive. Again, dreams may be quite consistent or at any rate coherent, or even witty or fantastically beautiful; others again are confused, apparently imbecile, absurd or often absolutely mad. There are dreams which leave us quite cold, others in which every affect makes itself felt—pain to the point of tears, terror so intense as to wake us, amazement, delight, and so on. Most dreams are forgotten soon after waking; or they persist throughout the day, the recollection becoming fainter and more imperfect as the day goes on; others remain so vivid (as, for example, the dreams of childhood) that thirty years later we remember them as clearly as though they were part of a recent experience. Dreams, like people, may make their appearance once and never come back; or the same person may dream the same thing repeatedly, either in the same form or with slight alterations. In short, these scraps of mental activity at night-time have at command an immense repertory, can in fact create everything that by day the mind is capable of—only, it is never the same.

One might attempt to account for these diversities in dream by assuming that they correspond to different intermediate states between sleeping and waking, different levels of imperfect sleep. Very well; but then in proportion as the mind approached the waking state there should be not merely an increase in the value, content, and distinctness of the dream-performance, but also a growing perception that it *is* a dream; and it ought not to happen that side by side with a clear and sensible element in the dream there is one which is nonsensical or indistinct, followed again by a good piece of work. It is certain that the mind could not vary its depth of sleep so rapidly as that. This explanation therefore does not help; there is in fact no short cut to an answer.

For the present we will leave the *meaning* of the dream out of question, and try instead, by starting from the common element in dreams, to clear a path to a better understanding of their nature. From the relationship of dreams to sleep we have drawn the conclusion that dreams are the reaction to a stimulus disturbing sleep. As we have heard, this is also the single point at which exact experimental psychology can come to our aid; it affords proof of the fact that stimuli brought to bear during sleep make their appearance in dreams. Many investigations have been made on these lines, culminating in those of Mourly Vold whom I mentioned earlier; we have all, too, been in a position to confirm their results by occasional observations of our own. I will choose some of the earlier experiments to tell you. Maury had tests of this kind carried out on himself. Whilst dreaming, he was made to smell some eau de Cologne, whereupon he dreamt he was in Cairo, in the shop of Johann Maria Farina, and this was followed by some

crazy adventures. Again, someone gave his neck a gentle pinch, and he dreamt of the application of a blister and of a doctor who had treated him when he was a child. Again, they let a drop of water fall on his forehead and he was immediately in Italy, perspiring freely and drinking the white wine of Orvieto.

The striking feature about these dreams produced under experimental conditions will perhaps become still clearer to us in another series of *stimulus* dreams. These are three dreams of which we have an account by a clever observer, Hildebrandt, and all three are reactions to the sound of an alarm-clock:

"I am going for a walk on a spring morning, and I saunter through fields just beginning to grow green, till I come to a neighbouring village, where I see the inhabitants in holiday attire making their way in large numbers to the church, their hymn-books in their hands. Of course! it is Sunday and the morning service is just about to begin. I decide to take part in it, but first as I am rather overheated I think I will cool down in the churchyard which surrounds the church. Whilst reading some of the epitaphs there I hear the bell-ringer go up into the tower, where I now notice, high up, the little village bell which will give the signal for the beginning of the service. For some time yet it remains motionless, then it begins to swing, and suddenly the strokes ring out, clear and piercing—so clear and piercing that they put an end to my sleep. But the sound of the bell comes from the alarm-clock."

Here is another combination of images. "It is a bright winter day, and the roads are deep in snow. I have promised to take part in a sleighing expedition, but I have to wait a long time before I am told that the sleigh is at the door. Now follow the preparations for getting in, the fur rug is spread out and the foot-muff fetched and finally I am in my place. But there is still a delay while the horses wait for the signal to start. Then the reins are jerked and the little bells, shaken violently, begin their familiar janizary music, so loudly that in a moment the web of the dream is rent. Again it is nothing but the shrill of the alarm-clock."

Now for the third example! "I see a kitchen-maid with dozens of piled-up plates going along the passage to the dining-room. It seems to me that the pyramid of china in her arms is in danger of overbalancing. I call out a warning: 'Take care, your whole load will fall to the ground.' Of course I receive the usual answer: that they are accustomed to carrying china in that way, and so on; meanwhile I follow her as she goes with anxious looks. I thought so—the next thing is a stumble on the threshold, the crockery falls, crashing and clattering in a hundred pieces on the ground. But—I soon become aware that that interminably prolonged sound is no real crash, but a regular ringing—and this ringing is due merely to the alarm-clock, as I realize at last on awakening."

These dreams are very pretty, perfectly sensible, and by no means so incoherent as dreams usually are. We have no quarrel with them on those grounds. The thing common to them all is that in each case the situation arises from a noise, which the dreamer on waking recognizes as that of the alarm-clock. Hence we see here how a dream is produced, but we find out something more. In the dream there is no recognition of the clock, which does not even appear in it, but for the noise of the clock another noise is substituted; the stimulus which disturbs sleep is interpreted, but interpreted differently in each instance. Now why is this? There is no answer; it appears to be mere caprice. But to understand the dream we should be able to account for its choice of just this noise and no other to interpret the stimulus given by the alarm-clock. In analogous fashion we must object to Maury's experiments that, although it is clear that the stimulus brought to bear on the sleeper does appear in the dream, yet his experiments don't explain why it appears exactly in that form, which is one that does not seem explicable by the nature of the stimulus disturbing sleep. And further, in Maury's experiments there was mostly a mass of other dream-material attached to the direct result of the stimulus, for example, the crazy adventures in the eau de Cologne dream, for which we are at a loss to account.

Now will you reflect that the class of dreams which wake one up affords the best opportunity for establishing the influence of external disturbing stimuli. In most other cases it will be more difficult. We do not wake up out of all dreams, and if in the morning we remember a dream of the night before, how are we to assign it to a disturbing stimulus operating perhaps during the night? I once succeeded in subsequently establishing the occurrence of a sound-stimulus of this sort, but only, of course, because of peculiar circumstances. I woke up one morning at a place in the Tyrolese mountains knowing that I had dreamt that the Pope was dead. I could not explain the dream to myself, but later my wife asked me: "Did you hear quite early this morning the dreadful noise of bells breaking out in all the churches and chapels?" No, I had heard nothing, my sleep is too sound, but thanks to her telling me this I understood my dream. How often may such causes of stimulus as this induce dreams in the sleeper without his ever hearing of them afterwards? Possibly very often: and possibly not. If we can get no information of any stimulus we cannot be convinced on the point. And apart from this we have given up trying to arrive at an estimation of the sleep-disturbing external stimuli, since we know that they only explain a fragment of the dream and not the whole dream-reaction.

We need not on that account give up this theory altogether; there is still another possible way of following it out. Obviously it is a matter of indifference what disturbs sleep and causes the mind to dream. If it cannot always be something external acting as a stimulus to one of the senses, it is possible that, instead, a stimulus operates from the internal organs—a so-called somatic stimulus. This supposition lies very close, and moreover it corresponds to the view popularly held with regard to the origin of dreams, for it is a common saying that they come from the stomach. Unfortunately, here again we must suppose that in very many cases information respecting a somatic stimulus operating during the night would no longer be forthcoming after waking, so that it would be incapable of proof. But we will not overlook the fact that many trustworthy experiences support the idea that dreams may be derived from somatic stimuli; on the whole it is indubitable that the condition of the internal organs can influence dreams. The relation of the content of many dreams to distention of the bladder or to a condition of excitation of the sex-organs is so plain that it cannot be mistaken. From these obvious cases we pass to others, in which, to judge by the content of the dream, we are at least justified in suspecting that some such somatic stimuli have been at work, since there is something in this content which can be regarded as elaboration, representation, or interpretation of these stimuli. Scherner, the investigator of dreams (1861), emphatically supported the view which traces the origin of dreams to organic stimuli, and contributed some excellent examples towards it. For instance, he sees in a dream "two rows of beautiful boys, with fair hair and delicate complexions, confronting each other pugnaciously, joining in combat, seizing hold of one another, and again letting go their hold, only to take up the former position and go through the whole process again"; his interpretation of the two rows of boys as the teeth is in itself plausible and seems to receive full confirmation when after this scene the dreamer "pulls a long tooth from his jaw." Again, the interpretation of "long, narrow, winding passages" as being suggested by a stimulus originating in the intestine seems sound and corroborates Scherner's assertion that dreams primarily endeavour to represent, by like objects, the organ from which the stimulus proceeds.

We must therefore be prepared to admit that internal stimuli can play the same rôle in dreams as external ones. Unfortunately, evaluation of this factor is open to the same objections. In a great number of instances the attribution of dreams to somatic stimuli must remain uncertain or incapable of proof; not all dreams, but only a certain number of them, rouse the suspicion that stimuli from internal organs have something to do with their origin; and lastly, the internal somatic stimulus will suffice no more than the external sensory stimulus to explain any other part of the dream than the direct reaction to it. The origin of all the rest of the dream remains obscure.

Now, however, let us direct our attention to a certain peculiarity of the dream-life which appears when we study the operation of these stimuli. The dream does not merely reproduce the stimulus, but elaborates it, plays upon it, fits it into a context, or replaces it by something else. This is a side of the dream-work which is bound to be of interest to us because possibly it may lead us nearer to the true nature of dreams. The scope of a man's production is not necessarily limited to the circumstance which immediately gives rise to it. For instance, Shakespeare's *Macbeth* was written as an occasional drama on the accession of the king who first united in his person the crowns of the three kingdoms. But does this historical occasion cover the whole content of the drama, or explain its grandeur and its mystery? Perhaps in the same way the external and internal stimuli operating upon the sleeper are merely the occasion of the dream and afford us no insight into its true nature.

The other element common to all dreams, their peculiarity in mental life, is on the one hand very difficult to grasp and on the other seems to afford no clue for further inquiry.

Our experiences in dreams for the most part take the form of visual images. Can these be explained by the stimuli? Is it really the stimulus that we experience? If so, why is the experience visual, when it can only be in the very rarest instance that any stimulus has operated upon our eyesight? Or, can it be shown that when we dream of speech any conversation or sounds resembling conversation reached our ears during sleep? I venture to discard such a possibility without any hesitation whatever.

If we cannot get any further with the common characteristics of dreams as a starting-point, let us try beginning with their differences. Dreams are often meaningless, confused, and absurd, yet there are some which are sensible, sober, and reasonable. Let us see whether these latter sensible dreams can help to elucidate those which are meaningless. I will tell you the latest reasonable dream which was told to me, the dream of a young man: "I went for a walk in the Kärntnerstrasse and there I met Mr. X; after accompanying him for a short time I went into a restaurant. Two ladies and a gentleman came and sat down at my table. At first I was annoyed and refused to look at them, but presently I glanced across at them and found that they were quite nice." The dreamer's comment on this was that the evening before he had actually been walking in the Kärntnerstrasse, which is the way he usually goes, and that he had met Mr. X there. The other part of the dream was not a direct reminiscence, but only bore a certain resemblance to an occurrence of some time previously. Or here we have another prosaic dream, that of a lady. Her husband says to her: "Don't you think we ought to have the piano tuned?" and she replies: "It is not worth it, for the hammers need fresh leather anyhow." This dream repeats a conversation which took place in almost the same words between herself and her husband the day before the dream. What then do we learn from these two prosaic dreams? Merely that there occur in them recollections of daily life or of matters connected with it. Even that would be something if it could be asserted of all dreams without exception. But that is out of the question; this characteristic too belongs only to a minority of dreams. In most dreams we find no connection with the day before, and no light is thrown from this quarter upon meaningless and absurd dreams. All we know is that we have met with a new problem. Not only do we want to know what a dream is saying, but, if, as in our examples, that is quite plain, we want to know further from what cause and to what end we repeat in dreams this which is known to us and has recently happened to us.

I think you would be as tired as I of continuing the kind of attempts we have made up to this point. It only shows that all the interest in the world will not help us with a problem unless we have also an idea of some path to adopt in order to arrive at a solution. Till now we have not found this path. Experimental psychology has contributed nothing but some (certainly very valuable) information about the significance of stimuli in the production of dreams. Of philosophy we have nothing to expect, unless it be a lofty repetition of the reproach that our object is intellectually contemptible; while from the occult sciences we surely do not choose to borrow. History and the verdict of the people tell us that dreams are full of meaning and importance, and of prophetic significance; but that is hard to accept and certainly does not lend itself to proof. So then our first endeavours are completely baffled.

But unexpectedly there comes a hint from a direction in which we have not hitherto looked. Colloquial speech, which is certainly no matter of chance but the deposit, as it were, of ancient knowledge—a thing which must not indeed be made too much of—our speech, I say, recognizes the existence of something to which, strangely enough, it gives the name of *day-dreams*. Day-dreams are phantasies (products of phantasy); they are very common phenomena, are observable in healthy as well as in sick persons, and they also can easily be studied by the subject himself. The most striking thing about these "phantastic" creations is that they have received the name of *day-dreams*, for they have nothing in common with the two universal characteristics of dreams. Their name contradicts any relationship to the condition of sleep and, as regards the second universal characteristic, no experience or hallucination takes place in them, we simply imagine something; we recognize that they are the work of phantasy, that we are not seeing but thinking. These day-dreams appear before puberty, often indeed in late childhood, and persist until maturity is reached when they are either given up or retained as long as life lasts. The content of these phantasies is dictated by a very transparent motivation. They are scenes and events which gratify either the egoistic cravings of ambition or thirst for power, or the erotic desires of

the subject. In young men, ambitious phantasies predominate; in women, whose ambition centres on success in love, erotic phantasies; but the erotic requirement can often enough in men too be detected in the background, all their heroic deeds and successes are really only intended to win the admiration and favour of women. In other respects these day-dreams show great diversity and their fate varies. All of them are either given up after a short time and replaced by a new one, or retained, spun out into long stories, and adapted to changing circumstances in life. They march with the times; and they receive as it were "date-stamps" upon them which show the influence of new situations. They form the raw material of poetic production; for the writer by transforming, disguising, or curtailing them creates out of his day-dreams the situations which he embodies in his stories, novels, and dramas. The hero of a day-dream is, however, always the subject himself, either directly imagined in the part or transparently identified with someone else.

Perhaps day-dreams are so called on account of their similar relation to reality, as an indication that their content is no more to be accepted as real than is that of dreams. But it is possible that they share the name of dreams because of some mental characteristic of the dream which we do not yet know but after which we are seeking. On the other hand, it is possible that we are altogether wrong in regarding this similarity of name as significant. That is a question which can only be answered later.

SIXTH LECTURE

PRELIMINARY HYPOTHESES AND TECHNIQUE OF INTERPRETATION

WE THUS realize our need of a new way of approach, a definite method, if we are to make any advance in our researches into dreams. I will now offer an obvious suggestion: let us accept as the basis of the whole of our further enquiry the following hypothesis—that dreams are not a somatic, but a mental, phenomenon. You know what this means; but what is our justification in making this assumption? We have none, but on the other hand there is nothing to prevent us. The position is this: if the dream is a somatic phenomenon, it does not concern us; it can only be of interest to us on the hypothesis that it is a mental phenomenon. So we will assume that this hypothesis is true, in order to see what happens if we do so. The results of our work will determine whether we may adhere to the assumption, and uphold it in its turn as an inference fairly drawn. Now what exactly is the object of this enquiry of ours, or to what are we directing our efforts? Our object is that of all scientific endeavour—namely, to achieve an understanding of the phenomena, to establish a connection between them, and, in the last resort, wherever it is possible to increase our power over them.

So we continue our work on the assumption that dreams are a mental phenomenon. In that event, they are a performance and an utterance on the part of the dreamer, but of a kind that conveys nothing to us, and which we do not understand. Now supposing that I give utterance to something that you do not understand, what do you do? You ask me to explain, do you not? Why may not we do the same—*ask the dreamer the meaning of the dream?*

Remember, we have already found ourselves in a similar position. It was when we were enquiring into certain errors, and the instance we took was a slip of the tongue. Someone had said: "Then certain things were *re-filled*," and thereupon we asked—no, fortunately it was not *we* who asked, but other people who had nothing to do with psycho-analysis—*they* asked what he meant by this enigmatic expression. He answered at once that what he had intended to say was: "That was a filthy business," but had checked himself and substituted the milder words: "Things were revealed there." I explained to you then that this enquiry was the model for every psycho-analytic investigation, and you understand now that psycho-analytic technique endeavours as far as possible to let the persons being analysed give the answer to their own problems. The dreamer himself then should interpret his dream for us.

That is not so simple with dreams, however, as we all know. Where errors were concerned, this method proved possible in many cases; there were others where the person questioned refused to say anything and even indignantly repudiated the answer suggested to him. With dreams, instances of the first type are entirely lacking; the dreamer always says he knows nothing about it. He cannot very well repudiate our interpretation, since we have none to offer him. Shall we have to give up our attempt then? Since *he* knows nothing, and *we* know nothing, and a third person can surely know nothing either, there cannot be any prospect of finding the answer. Well, if you like, give up the attempt. But if you are not so minded, you can

accompany me. For I assure you that it is not only quite possible, but highly probable, that the dreamer really does know the meaning of his dream; *only he does not know that he knows, and therefore thinks that he does not.*

At this point you will probably call my attention to the fact that I am again introducing an assumption, the second in quite a short context, and that by so doing I greatly detract from the force of my claim to a trustworthy method of procedure. Given the hypothesis that dreams are a mental phenomenon, and given further the hypothesis that there are in the minds of men certain things which they know without knowing that they know them—and so forth! You have only to keep in view the intrinsic improbability of both these hypotheses, and you may with an easy mind abandon all interest in the conclusions to be drawn from them.

Well, I have not brought you here either to delude you or to conceal anything from you. True, I announced that I would give a course of lectures entitled "Introductory Lectures on Psycho-analysis"; but it was no part of my purpose to play the oracle, professing to show you an easy sequence of facts, whilst carefully concealing all difficulties, filling up gaps, and glossing over doubtful points, so that you might comfortably enjoy the belief that you have learnt something new. No, it is the very fact that you are beginners that makes me anxious to show you our science as it is, with all its excrescences and crudities, the claims that it makes and the criticism to which it may give rise. I know, indeed, that it is the same in every science and that, especially in the beginnings, it cannot be otherwise. I know too that, in teaching other sciences, an effort is made at first to hide these difficulties and imperfections from the learner. But that cannot be done in psycho-analysis. So I really have set up two hypotheses, the one within the other; and anyone who finds it all too laborious, or too uncertain, or who is used to higher degrees of certainty, or to more refined deductions, need go no further with me. Only I should advise him to leave psychological problems altogether alone, for it is to be feared that this is a field in which he will find no access to such exact and sure paths as he is prepared to tread. And further, it is quite superfluous for any science which can offer a real contribution to knowledge to strive to make itself heard and to win adherents. Its reception must depend upon its results, and it can afford to wait until these have compelled attention.

But I may warn those of you who are not to be deterred in this way that my two assumptions are not of equal importance. The first, that dreams are a mental phenomenon, is the hypothesis which we hope to prove by the results of our work. The second has already been proved in a different field, and I am merely taking the liberty of transferring it thence to our problems.

Where, and in what connection, is it supposed to have been proved that a man can possess knowledge without knowing that he does so, which is the assumption we are making of the dreamer? Surely that would be a remarkable and surprising fact, which would change our conception of mental life and would have no need of concealment. Incidentally, it would be a fact belied in the very statement of it, which yet intends to be literally true—a contradiction in terms. There is not, however, any attempt at concealment. We cannot blame the fact for people's ignorance of it, or lack of interest in it, any more than we ourselves are to blame because all these psychological problems have been passed in judgment by persons who have held aloof from all the observations and experiments which alone can be conclusive.

The proof to which I refer was found in the sphere of hypnotic phenomena. In the year 1889 I was present at the remarkably impressive demonstrations by Liébault and Bernheim, in Nancy, and there I witnessed the following experiment. A man was placed in a condition of somnambulism, and then made to go through all sorts of hallucinatory experiences. On being wakened, he seemed at first to know nothing at all of what had taken place during his hypnotic sleep. Bernheim then asked him in so many words to tell him what had happened while he was under hypnosis. The man declared that he could not remember anything. Bernheim, however, insisted upon it, pressed him, and assured him that he did know and that he must remember, and lo and behold! the man wavered, began to reflect, and remembered in a shadowy fashion first one of the occurrences which has been suggested to him, then something else, his recollection growing increasingly clear and complete until finally it was brought to light without a single gap. Now, since in the end he had the knowledge without having learnt anything from any other quarter in the meantime, we are justified in concluding that these recollections were in his mind from the outset.

They were merely inaccessible to him; he did not know that he knew them but believed that he did not know. In fact, his case was exactly similar to what we assume the dreamer's to be.

I hope you are duly surprised that this fact is already established and that you will ask me: "Why did you not refer to this proof before, when we were considering errors and came to the point of ascribing to a man who had made a slip of the tongue intentions behind his speech, of which he knew nothing, and which he denied? If it is possible for a man to believe that he knows nothing of experiences of which nevertheless he does possess the recollection, it seems no longer improbable that there should be other mental processes going on within him about which also he knows nothing. We should certainly have been impressed by this argument and should have been in a better position to understand about errors." Certainly, I might have brought forward this proof then, but I reserved it for a later occasion when there would be more need for it. Some of the errors explained themselves, others suggested to us that, in order to understand the connection between the phenomena, it would be advisable to postulate the existence of mental processes of which the person is entirely ignorant. With dreams we are compelled to seek our explanations elsewhere, and besides, I am counting on your being more ready to accept in this connection a proof from the field of hypnosis. The condition in which we perform errors must seem to you normal and, as such, to bear no similarity to that of hypnosis. On the other hand, there exists a clear relationship between the hypnotic state and sleep, the essential condition of dreaming. Hypnosis is actually called *artificial sleep;* we say to the people whom we hypnotize: "Sleep," and the suggestions made to them are comparable to the dreams of natural sleep. The mental situation is really analogous in the two cases. In natural sleep we withdraw our interest from the whole outer world; so also in hypnotic sleep, with the exception of the one person who has hypnotized us and with whom we remain in rapport. Again, the so-called "nurse's sleep" in which the nurse remains in rapport with the child and can be awakened only by him is a normal counterpart of hypnotic sleep. So it does not seem so very audacious to carry over to natural sleep something which is a condition in hypnosis. The assumption that some knowledge about his dream exists in the dreamer and that this knowledge is merely inaccessible to him, so that he himself does not believe he has it, is not a wild invention. Incidentally, we observe here that a third way of approaching the study of dreams is thus opened out for us; we may approach it by the avenue of sleep-disturbing stimuli, by that of day-dreams, and now by that of the dreams suggested during hypnosis.

Now perhaps we shall return to our task with greater confidence. We see it is very probable that the dreamer knows something about his dream; the problem is how to make it possible for him to get at his knowledge and impart it to us. We do not expect him immediately to tell us what his dream means, but we do think he will be able to discover its source, from what circle of thoughts and interests it is derived. With errors, you will remember the man was asked how the slip of the tongue "re-filled" had come about, and his first association gave us the explanation. The technique we employ in the case of dreams is very simple and is modelled on this example. Here again we shall ask the dreamer how he came to have the dream, and his next words must be regarded as giving the explanation in this case also. It makes no difference to us, therefore, whether he thinks that he does or does not know anything about it, and we treat both cases alike.

This technique is certainly very simple, nevertheless I am afraid it will provoke most strenuous opposition in you. You will say: "Another assumption, the third! And the most improbable of all! When I ask the dreamer what ideas come to him about the dream, do you mean to say that his very first association will give the desired explanation? But surely he might have no association at all, or heaven only knows what the association might be. We cannot imagine upon what grounds such an expectation is based. It really implies too much trust in Providence, and this at a point where rather more exercise of the critical faculty would better meet the case. Besides, a dream is not like a single slip of the tongue but is made up of many elements. That being so, upon which association is one to rely?"

You are right in all the unessentials. It is true that a dream differs from a slip of the tongue in the matter of its many elements as well as in other points. We must take account of that in our technique. So I suggest to you that we divide the dream up into its various elements, and examine each element separately; then we shall have re-established the analogy with a slip of the tongue. Again, you are right

in saying that the dreamer, when questioned on the single elements of the dream, may reply that he has no ideas about them. There are cases in which we accept this answer, and later I will tell you which these are; curiously enough, they are cases about which we ourselves may have certain definite ideas. But in general, when the dreamer declares that he has no ideas, we shall contradict him, press him to answer, assure him that he must have some idea and—shall find we are right. He will produce an association, any one, it does not matter to us what it is. He will be especially ready with information which we may term historical. He will say: "That is something which happened yesterday" (as in the instance of the two *prosaic* dreams quoted above) or: "That reminds me of something which happened recently," and in this way we shall come to notice that dreams are much more often connected with impressions of the day before than we thought at first. Finally, with the dream as his starting-point, he will recall events which happened less recently, and at last even some which lie very far back in the past.

In regard to the main issue, however, you are wrong. When you think it arbitrary to assume that the first association of the dreamer must give us just what we are looking for, or at any rate lead to it, and further, that the association is much more likely to be quite capricious and to have no connection with what we are looking for, and that it only shows my blind trust in Providence if I expect anything else—then you make a very great mistake. I have already taken the liberty of pointing out to you that there is within you a deeply rooted belief in psychic freedom and choice, that this belief is quite unscientific, and that it must give ground before the claims of a determinism which governs even mental life. I ask you to have some respect for the *fact* that that one association, and nothing else, occurs to the dreamer when he is questioned. Nor am I setting up one belief against another. It can be proved that the association thus given is not a matter of choice, nor indeterminate, and that it is not unconnected with what we are looking for. Indeed, I have recently learnt—not that I attach too much importance to the fact—that experimental psychology itself has brought forward similar proofs.

Because of the importance of the matter I ask you to pay special attention to this. When I ask a man to say what comes to his mind about any given element in a dream, I require

him to give himself up to the process of FREE
ASSOCIATION *which follows when he keeps in
mind the original idea.* This necessitates a peculiar attitude of the attention, something quite
different from reflection, indeed, precluding it.
Many people adopt this attitude without any
difficulty, but others when they attempt to do
so display an incredible inaptitude. There is a
still higher degree of freedom in association
which appears when I dispense with any particular stimulus-idea and perhaps only describe
the kind and species of association that I want;
for example, ask someone to let a proper name
or a number occur to him. An association of
this sort should, one would say, be even more
subject to choice and unaccountable than the
kind used in our technique. Nevertheless, it can
be shown that in every instance it will be
strictly determined by important inner attitudes of mind, which are unknown to us at the
moment when they operate, just as much unknown as are the disturbing tendencies which
cause errors, and those tendencies which bring
about so-called "chance" actions.

I myself and many after me have repeatedly made an examination of names and numbers
called up without any particular idea as a starting-point; some of these experiments have been
published. The method is this: a train of associations is stirred up by the name which occurred, and these associations, as you see, are
no longer quite free, but are attached just so
far as the associations to the different elements
of the dream are attached; this train of associations is then kept up until the thoughts arising from the impulse have been exhausted. By
that time, however, you will have explained
the motivation and significance of the free
association with a name. The experiments yield
the same result again and again; the information they give us often includes a wealth of material and necessitates going far afield into its
ramifications. The associations to numbers that
arise spontaneously are perhaps the most de-
monstrative; they follow upon one another so
swiftly and make for a hidden goal with such
astounding certainty that one is really quite
taken aback. I will give you just one example
of a name-analysis of this sort, because it happens to be one which does not involve the handling of a great mass of material.

Once, when I was treating a young man, I
happened to say something on this subject and
to assert that, in spite of our apparent freedom
of choice in such matters, we cannot, in point
of fact, think of any name which cannot be
shown to be narrowly determined by the immediate circumstances, the idiosyncrasies, of
the person experimented with and his situation
at the moment. As he was inclined to be
sceptical, I proposed that he should make the
experiment himself then and there. I knew that
he had usually numerous relationships of all
sorts with women and girls, so I told him that
I thought he would have an exceptionally large
number to choose from if he were to let the
name of a woman occur to him. He agreed. To
my surprise, or rather perhaps to his own, he
did not overwhelm me with an avalanche of
women's names, but remained silent for a time,
and then confessed that the only name which
came into his mind at all was "Albine." "How
curious! What do you connect with this name?
How many Albines do you know?" Strangely
enough, he knew no one of the name of Albine,
and he found no associations to the name. One
might infer that the analysis had failed; but no,
it was already complete, and no further association was required. The man himself was unusually fair in colouring, and whilst talking to
him in analysis I had often jokingly called him
an *albino;* moreover, we were just in the midst
of tracing the *feminine* element in his nature.
So it was he himself who was this female albino, the *woman* who interested him most at
the moment.

In the same way, the tunes which suddenly
come into a man's head can be shown to be
conditioned by some train of thought to which
they belong, and which for some reason is occupying his mind without his knowing anything about it. It is easy to show that the connection with the tune is to be sought either in
the words which belong to it or in the source
from which it comes: I must, however, make
this reservation, that I do not maintain this
in the case of really musical people of whom
I happen to have had no experience; in them
the musical value of the tune may account for
its suddenly emerging into consciousness. The
first case is certainly much more common; I
know of a young man who for some time was
absolutely haunted by the tune (a charming
one, I admit) of the song of Paris in *Helen of
Troy,* until his attention was drawn in analysis
to the fact that at that time an "Ida" and a
"Helen" were rivals in his interest.

If, then, the associations which arise quite
freely are determined in this way and belong to
some definite context, we are surely justified
in concluding that associations attached to one
single stimulus-idea must be equally narrow-

ly conditioned. Examination shows as a fact that they are not only attached in the first place to the stimulus-idea which we have provided for them, but that they are also dependent, in the second place, on circles of thoughts and interests of strong affective value (*complexes,* as we call them) of whose influence at the time nothing is known, that is to say, on unconscious activities.

Associations attached in this way have been made the subject of very instructive experiments, which have played a notable part in the history of psycho-analysis. Wundt's school originated the so-called *association-experiment,* in which the subject of the experiment is bidden to reply to a given *stimulus-word* as quickly as possible with whatever *reaction-word* occurs to him. The following points may then be noted: the interval which elapses between the utterance of the stimulus-word and of the re-action-word, the nature of the latter, and possibly any mistake which comes in when the same experiment is repeated later, and so on. The Zurich School, under the leadership of Bleuler and Jung, arrived at the explanation of the reactions to the association-experiment by asking the person experimented upon to throw light upon any associations which seemed at all remarkable, by means of subsequent associations. In this way it became clear that these unusual reactions were most strictly determined by the complexes of the person concerned. By this discovery Bleuler and Jung built the first bridge between experimental psychology and psycho-analysis.

Having heard this you may possibly say: "We admit now that free associations are subject to determination and not a matter of choice, as we thought at first, and we admit this also in the case of associations to the elements of dreams. But it is not this that we are bothering about. You maintain that the association to each element in the dream is determined by some mental background to this particular element, a background of which we know nothing. We cannot see that there is any proof of this: Naturally we expect that the association to the dream-element will be shown to be conditioned by one of the complexes of the dreamer, but what good is that to us? That does not help us to understand the dream; it merely leads to some knowledge of these so-called 'complexes,' as did the association-experiment; but what have these to do with the dream?"

You are right, but you are overlooking an important point, the very thing which deterred me from choosing the association-experiment as a starting-point for this discussion. In this experiment, the stimulus-word, the single thing which determines the reaction, is chosen by us at will, and the reaction stands as intermediary between this stimulus-word and the complex aroused in the person experimented upon. In the dream, the stimulus-word is replaced by something derived from the mental life of the dreamer, from sources unknown to him, and hence may very probably be itself a *derivative of a complex.* It is not, therefore, altogether fantastic to suppose that the further associations connected with elements of the dream are determined by no other complex than that which has produced the particular element itself, and that they will lead to the discovery of that complex.

Let me give you another instance which may serve to show that, in the case of dreams, the facts bear out our expectations. The forgetting of proper names is really an excellent prototype of what happens in dream-analysis, only that in the former case one person alone is concerned, while in the interpretation of dreams there are two. When I forget a name temporarily, I am still certain that I know it, and by way of a détour through Bernheim's experiment, we are now in a position to achieve a similar certainty in the case of the dreamer. Now this name which I have forgotten, and yet really know, eludes me. Experience soon teaches me that no amount of thinking about it, even with effort, is any use. I can, however, always think of another or of several other names instead of the forgotten one. When such a substitute name occurs to me spontaneously, only then is the similarity between this situation and that of dream-analysis evident. The dream-element also is not what I am really looking for; it is only a substitute for something else, for the real thing which I do not know and am trying to discover by means of dream-analysis. Again the difference is that when I forget a name I know perfectly well that the substitute is not the right one, whereas we only arrived at this conception of the dream-element by a laborious process of investigation. Now there also is a way in which, when we forget a name, we can by starting from the substitute, arrive at the real thing eluding our consciousness at the moment, i.e., the forgotten name. If I turn my attention to these substitute names and let further associations to them come into my mind, I arrive after a short or a long way around at the name I have forgotten, and in so doing I discover that the substitutes I have spontaneously produced had a definite connection with, and were determined by, the forgotten name.

I will give you an instance of an analysis of this sort: One day I found that I could not call to mind the name of the small country on the Riviera, of which Monte Carlo is the capital. It was most annoying, but so it was. I delved into all my knowledge about the country; I thought of Prince Albert of the House of Lusignan, of his marriages, of his passion for deep-sea exploration—in fact of everything I could summon up, but all to no purpose. So I gave up trying to think and, instead of the name I had lost, let substitute names come into my mind. They came quickly: Monte Carlo itself, then Piedmont, Albania, Montevideo, Colico. Albania was the first to attract my attention; it was immediately replaced by Montenegro, probably because of the contrast between black and white. Then I noticed that four of the substitute names have the same syllable "mon," and immediately I recalled the forgotten word and cried out "Monaco." You see the substitutes really originated in the forgotten name; the four first came from the first syllable and the last gave the sequence of the syllables and the whole of the final syllable. Incidentally, I could quite easily find out what had made me forget the name for the time being. Monaco is the Italian name for Munich, and it was some thoughts connected with this town which had acted as an inhibition.

Now that is a very pretty example, but it is too simple. In other cases you might have to take a longer succession of associations to the substitute name, and then the analogy to dream-analysis would be clearer. I have had experiences of that sort, too. A stranger once invited me to drink some Italian wine with him, and in the inn he found he had forgotten the name of the wine which he had meant to order on account of his very pleasant recollections of it. A number of dissimilar substitute names occurred to him, and from these I was able to infer that the thought of someone called Hedwig had made him forget the name of the wine. Sure enough, not only did he tell me that there had been a Hedwig with him on the occasion when he first tasted the wine, but this discovery brought back to him the name he wanted. He was now happily married, and Hedwig belonged to earlier days which he did not care to recall.

What is possible in the case of forgotten names must be also possible in the interpretation of dreams: starting from the substitute, we must be able to arrive at the real object of our search by means of a train of associations; and further, arguing from what happens with forgotten names, we may assume that the associations to the dream-element will have been determined not only by that element but also by the real thought which is not in consciousness. If we could do this, we should have gone some way towards justifying our technique.

SEVENTH LECTURE

MANIFEST CONTENT AND LATENT THOUGHTS

YOU see that our study of errors has not been fruitless. Thanks to our exertions in that direction, we have—reasoning from the hypotheses with which you are familiar—secured two results: a conception of the nature of the dream-element and a technique of dream-interpretation. The conception of the dream-element is as follows: it is not in itself a primary and essential thing, a *thought proper*, but a substitute for something else unknown to the person concerned, just as is the underlying intention of the error, a substitute for something the knowledge of which is indeed possessed by the dreamer but is inaccessible to him. We hope to be able to carry over the same conception on to the dream as a whole, which consists of a number of such elements. Our method is to allow other substitute-ideas, from which we are able to divine that which lies hidden, to emerge into consciousness by means of free association to the said elements.

I am now going to propose that we introduce an alteration in our nomenclature in order to make our terminology more flexible. Instead of using the words *hidden, inaccessible* or *proper,* let us give a more precise description and say *inaccessible to the consciousness of the dreamer* or *unconscious.* By that we mean nothing more than was implied in the case of the forgotten word, or the underlying intention responsible for the error; that is to say, *unconscious at the moment.* It follows that in contradistinction we may call the dream-elements themselves, and those substitute-ideas arrived at by the process of association, *conscious.* No theoretical implication is so far contained in these terms; no exception can be taken to the use of the word *unconscious* as a description at once applicable and easy to understand.

Now, transferring our conception from the single element to the dream as a whole, it follows that the latter is the distorted substitute for something else, something unconscious, and that the task of dream-interpretation is to discover these unconscious thoughts. Hence are derived three important rules which should be observed in the work of dream-interpretation:

1. We are not to trouble about the surface meaning of the dream, whether it be reasonable or absurd, clear or confused; in no case does it constitute the unconscious thoughts we are seeking. (An obvious limitation of this rule will force itself upon us later.)

2. We are to confine our work to calling up substitute-ideas for every element and not to ponder over them and try to see whether they contain something which fits in, nor to trouble ourselves about how far they are taking us from the dream-element.

3. We must wait until the hidden unconscious thoughts which we are seeking appear of their own accord, just as in the case of the missing word "Monaco" in the experiment which I described.

Now we understand also how entirely indifferent it is whether we remember much or little of our dreams, above all whether we remember them accurately or not. The dream as remembered is not the real thing at all, but *a distorted substitute* which, by calling up other substitute-ideas, provides us with a means of approaching the thought proper, of bringing into consciousness the unconscious thoughts underlying the dream. If our recollection was at fault, all that has happened is that a further distortion of the substitute has taken place, and this distortion itself cannot be without motivation.

We can interpret our own dreams as well as those of others; indeed, we learn more from our own and the process carries more conviction. Now if we experiment in this direction, we notice that something is working against us. Associations come, it is true, but we do not admit them all; we are moved to criticize and to select. We say to ourselves of one association: "No, that does not fit in—it is irrelevant," and of another: "That is too absurd," and of a third: "That is quite beside the point"; and then we can observe further that in making such objections we stifle, and in the end actually banish, the associations before they have become quite clear. So on the one hand we tend to hold too closely to the initial idea, that is, the dream-element itself, and on the other,

by allowing ourselves to select, we vitiate the results of the process of free association. If we are not attempting the interpretation by ourselves, but are allowing someone else to interpret, we shall clearly perceive another motive impelling us to this selection, forbidden as we know it to be. We find ourselves thinking at times: "No, this association is too unpleasant; I cannot, or will not, tell it to him."

Clearly these objections threaten to spoil the success of our work. We must guard against them when we are interpreting our own dreams by resolving firmly not to yield to them, and, in interpreting those of someone else, by laying down the hard and fast rule that he must not withhold any association, even if one of the four objections I have named rises up against it, namely, that it is too unimportant, too absurd, too irrelevant or too unpleasant to speak of. He promises to keep this rule, and we may well feel annoyed when we find how badly he fulfils his promise later on. At first we account for this by imagining that, in spite of our authoritative assurance, he is not convinced that the process of free association will be justified by its results; and perhaps our next idea will be to win him over first to our theory, by giving him books to read or sending him to lectures so that he may be converted to our views on the subject. But we shall be saved from any such false steps by observing that the same critical objections against certain associations arise even in ourselves, whom we surely cannot suspect of doubt, and can only subsequently, on second thoughts as it were, be overcome.

Instead of being annoyed at the dreamer's disobedience, we can turn this experience to good account as a means of learning something new, something which is the more important the more unprepared we were for it. We realize that the work of dream-interpretation is encountering opposition by a *resistance* which expresses itself in this very form of critical objections. This resistance is independent of the theoretical conviction of the dreamer. We learn even more than this. Experience shows that a critical objection of this nature is never justified. On the contrary, the associations which people wish to suppress in this way prove *without exception* to be the most important, to be decisive for the discovery of the unconscious thought. When an association is accompanied by an objection of this sort it positively calls for special notice.

This resistance is something entirely new; a phenomenon which we have found by following out our hypotheses, although it was not included in them. We are not altogether agreeably surprised by this new factor which we have to reckon with, for we suspect already that it will not make our work any easier: it might almost tempt us to give up the effort with dreams altogether. To take such a trivial subject and then to have so much trouble, instead of spinning along smoothly with our technique! But we might, on the other hand, find these difficulties fascinating and be led to suspect that the work will be worth the trouble. Resistances invariably confront us when we try to penetrate to the hidden unconscious thought from the substitute offered by the dream-element. We may suppose, therefore, that something very significant must be concealed behind the substitute; for, if not, why should we meet with such difficulties, the purpose of which is to keep up the concealment? When a child will not open his clenched fist to show what is in it, we may be quite certain that it is something which he ought not to have.

As soon as we introduce into our subject the dynamic conception of resistance, we must bear in mind that this factor is something quantitatively variable. There are greater and lesser resistances, and we are prepared to find these differences showing themselves in the course of our work. Perhaps we can connect with this another experience also met with in the process of dream-interpretation. I mean that sometimes only a few associations—perhaps not more than one—suffice to lead us from the dream-element to the unconscious thought behind it, whilst on other occasions long chains of associations are necessary and many critical objections have to be overcome. We shall probably think that the number of associations necessary varies with the varying strength of the resistances, and very likely we shall be right. If there is only a slight resistance, the substitute is not far removed from the unconscious thought; a strong resistance on the other hand causes great distortions of the latter, and thereby entails a long journey back from the substitute to the unconscious thought itself.

Perhaps this would be a good moment to select a dream and try our technique upon it, to see whether the expectations we have entertained are realized. Very well, but what dream shall we choose? You do not know how difficult it is for me to decide, nor can I make it clear to you yet what the difficulties are. Obviously

there must be dreams in which on the whole there is very little distortion, and one would think it would be best to begin with these. But which are the least distorted dreams? Those which make good sense and are not confused, of which I have already given you two examples? In assuming this, we should make a great mistake, for examination shows that these dreams have undergone an exceptionally high degree of distortion. Supposing, then, that I make no special condition but take any dream at random, you would probably be very much disappointed. We might have to observe and record such a vast number of associations to the single dream-elements that it would be quite impossible to gain any clear view of the work as a whole. If we write the dream down and compare with it all the associations which it produces, we are likely to find that they have multiplied the length of the text of the dream many times. So the most practical method would seem to be that of selecting for analysis several short dreams, each of which can at least convey some idea to us or confirm some supposition. This will be the course we shall decide to take, unless experience gives us a hint where we ought really to look for slightly distorted dreams.

But I can suggest another means of simplifying matters, one which lies right before us. Instead of attempting the interpretation of whole dreams, let us confine ourselves to single dream-elements and find out by taking a series of examples how the application of our technique explains them:

(a) A lady related that as a child she very often dreamt that *God had a pointed paper cap on his head.* How are you going to understand that without the help of the dreamer? It sounds quite nonsensical; but the absurdity disappears when the lady says that as a little girl she used to have a cap like that put on her head at table, because she wouldn't give up looking at the plates of her brothers and sisters to see whether any of them had been given more than she. Evidently the cap was meant to serve the purpose of blinkers; this piece of historical information was given, by the way, without any difficulty. The interpretation of this element and, with it, of the whole short dream becomes easy enough with the help of a further association of the dreamer's: "As I had been told that God knew everything and saw everything, the dream could only mean that I knew and saw everything as God did, even when they tried to prevent me." This example is perhaps too simple.

(b) A sceptical patient had a longer dream, in which certain people were telling her about my book on *Wit* and praising it very highly. Then something else came in about a *canal; it might have been another book in which the word* canal *occurred, or something else to do with a canal . . . she did not know . . . it was quite vague.*

Now you will certainly be inclined to suppose that the *canal* in the dream will defy interpretation on account of its vagueness. You are right in expecting difficulty, but the difficulty is not caused by the vagueness; on the contrary, the difficulty in interpretation is caused by something else, by the same thing that makes the element vague. The dreamer had no association to the word *canal;* naturally I did not know what to say either. Shortly afterwards, to be accurate, on the next day, she told me that an association had occurred to her which *perhaps* had something to do with it. It was in fact a witty remark which some one had told her. On board ship between Dover and Calais a well-known author was talking to an Englishman who in some particular context quoted the words: *"Du sublime au ridicule il n'y a qu'un pas."* The author answered: *"Oui, le Pas-de-Calais,"* meaning that he regarded France as sublime and England as ridiculous. Of course, the Pas-de-Calais is a *canal*—that is to say, the Canal la Manche—the English Channel. Now, you ask, do I think that this association had anything to do with the dream? Certainly I think so: it gives the true meaning of the puzzling dream-element. Or are you inclined to doubt that the joke already existed before the dream and was the unconscious thought behind the element *canal,* and to maintain that it was a subsequent invention? The association reveals the scepticism disguised under the obtrusive admiration, and resistance was no doubt the cause both of the association being so long in occurring to her, and of the corresponding dream-element being so vague. Observe here the relation between the dream-element and the unconscious thought underlying it: it is, as it were, a fragment of the thought, an allusion to it; by being isolated in that way it became quite incomprehensible.

(c) A patient had a fairly long dream, part of which was as follows: *Several members of his family were seated at a table of a particular shape . . .* etc. This table reminded the dreamer that he had seen one of the same sort when he was visiting a certain family. From that his thoughts ran on thus: in this family the relation between father and son was a peculiar one, and the patient presently added that his own relations with his father were, as a matter of fact, of the same nature. So the table was introduced into the dream to indicate this parallelism.

It happened that this dreamer had long been familiar with the demands of dream-interpretation; otherwise he might have taken exception to the idea of investigating so trivial a detail as the shape of a table. We do literally deny that anything in the dream is a matter of chance or of indifference, and it is precisely by enquiring into such trivial and (apparently) unmotivated details that we expect to arrive at our conclusion. You may perhaps still be surprised that the dream-work should happen to choose the table, in order to express the thought "Our relationship is just like theirs." But even this is explicable when you learn that the family in question was named *Tischler.* (*Tisch* = table.) In making his relations sit at this table the dreamer's meaning was that they too were *Tischler.* And notice another thing: that in relating dream-interpretations of this sort one is forced into indiscretion. There you have one of the difficulties I alluded to in the matter of choosing examples. I could easily have given you another example instead of this one, but probably I should have avoided this indiscretion only to commit another in its place.

This seems to me a good point at which to introduce two new terms which we might have used already. Let us call the dream as related *the manifest dream-content,* and the hidden meaning, which we should come by in following out the associations, *the latent dream-thoughts.* Then we must consider the relation between the manifest content and the latent thoughts, as shown in the above examples. There are many varieties of these relations. In examples *(a)* and *(b)* the manifest dream-element is also an integral part of the latent thoughts, but only a fragment of them. A small piece of a great, composite, mental structure in the unconscious dream-thoughts has made its way into the manifest dream also, in the form of a fragment or in other cases as an allusion, like a catch-word or an abbreviation in a telegraphic code. The interpretation has to complete the whole to which this scrap or allusion belongs, which it did most successfully in example *(b).* One method of the distorting process in which the dream-work consists is, therefore, that of substituting for something else a fragment or an allusion. In example *(c)* we notice, moreover, another possible relation between manifest content and latent thought, a relation which is even more plainly and distinctly expressed in the following examples:

(d) The dreamer was pulling a certain lady of his acquaintance out of a ditch. He himself found the meaning of this dream-element by means of the first association. It meant: he picked her out, preferred her.[1]

(e) Another man dreamt *that his brother was digging up his garden all over again.* The first association was to deep-trenching for vegetables, the second gave the meaning. The brother was *retrenching.* (Retrenching his expenses).[2]

(f) The dreamer was climbing a mountain from which he had a remarkably wide view. This sounds most reasonable; perhaps no interpretation is called for and we have only to find out what recollection is referred to in the dream, and what had aroused it. No, you are mistaken; it comes out that this dream needed interpretation just as much as any other, more confused. For the dreamer remembers nothing about mountain-climbing himself; instead, it occurs to him that an acquaintance is publishing a *Rundschau* (Review), on the subject of our relations with the most distant parts of the earth: hence, the latent thought is one in which the dreamer identifies himself with the *reviewer* (lit. one who takes a survey).

Here you come across a new type of relation between the manifest and the latent element in dreams. The former is not so much a distortion of the latter as a representation—a plastic, concrete piece of imagery, originating in the sound of a word. It is true that this amounts in effect to a distortion, for we have long forgotten from what concrete image the word sprang, and hence fail to recognize it when that image is substituted for it. When you consider that the manifest dream consists of visual images in by far the greatest number of cases, and less frequently of thoughts and words, you will easily realize that this kind of relation between the manifest and the latent has a special significance in the structure of dreams. You see too that in this way it becomes possible for a long series of abstract thoughts to create substitute-images in the manifest dream which do indeed serve the purpose of concealment. This

[1] This example has been altered in translation to bring in the play upon words in English.—TR.
[2] See note on preceding example.—T.

is how our picture-puzzles are made up. The source of the semblance of wit which goes with this type of representation is a special question which we need not touch on here.

There is a fourth kind of relation between the manifest and the latent elements which I will say nothing about until the time comes for it in my account of our technique. Even then I shall not have given you a full list of these possible relations, but we shall have sufficient for our purpose.

Now do you think you can summon up courage to venture on the interpretation of a whole dream? Let us see whether we are adequately equipped for the task. I shall not, of course, choose one of the most obscure, but all the same it shall be one which shows the characteristics of dreams in a well-marked form.

A young woman who had already been married for a number of years dreamt as follows: *She was at the theatre with her husband, and one side of the stalls was quite empty. Her husband told her that Elise L and her fiancé also wanted to come, but could only get bad seats, three for a florin and a half, and of course they could not take those. She replied that in her opinion they did not lose much by that.*

The first thing stated by the dreamer is that the occasion giving rise to the dream is alluded to in the manifest content: her husband had really told her that Elise L, an acquaintance of about her own age, had become engaged, and the dream is the reaction to this piece of news. We know already that in many dreams it is easy to point to some such occasion occurring on the day before, and that this is often traced by the dreamer without any difficulty. This dreamer supplies us with further information of the same sort about other elements in the manifest dream. To what did she trace the detail of one side of the stalls being empty? It was an allusion to a real occurrence of the week before, when she had meant to go to a certain play and had therefore booked seats *early*, so early that she had to pay extra for the tickets. On entering the theatre it was evident that her anxiety had been quite superfluous, for one side of the stalls was almost empty. It would have been time enough if she had bought the tickets on the actual day of the performance and her husband did not fail to tease her about having been in *too great a hurry*. Next, what about the one florin and a half (1 fl. 50)? This was traced to quite another context which had nothing to do with the former, but it again refers to some news received on the previous day. Her sister-in-law had had a present of 150 florins from her husband and had rushed off *in a hurry,* like a silly goose, to jeweller's shop and spent it all on a piece of jewellery. What about the number three? She knew nothing about that unless this idea could be counted an association, that the engaged girl, Elise L, was only three months younger than she herself who had been married ten years. And the absurdity of taking three tickets for two people? She had nothing to say to this and refused to give any more associations or information whatever.

Nevertheless, her few associations have provided us with so much material that it is possible to discover the latent dream-thoughts. We are struck by the fact that in her statements references to time are noticeable at several points, which form a common basis for the different parts of this material. She had got the theatre tickets *too soon,* taken them in *too great a hurry,* so that she had to pay extra for them; in the same way her sister-in-law had *hurried* off to the jeweller's with her money to buy an ornament with it, as though she might *miss something.* If the strongly emphasized points: *too early, too great a hurry,* are connected with the occasion for the dream (namely, the news that her friend, only three months *younger* than herself, had now found a good husband after all) and with the criticism expressed in her asperity about her sister-in-law, that it was *folly* to be so precipitate, there occurs to us almost spontaneously the following construction of the latent dream-thoughts, for which the manifest dream is a highly distorted substitute:

"It was really *foolish* of me to be in such a hurry to marry! Elise's example shows me that I too could have found a husband later on." (The over-haste is represented by her own conduct in buying the tickets and that of her sister-in-law in buying the jewellery. Going to the theatre is substituted for getting married.) This would be the main thought; perhaps we may go on, though with less certainty because the analysis in these passages ought not to be unsupported by statements of the dreamer: "And I might have had one a hundred times better for the money!" (150 florins is 100 times more than one florin and a half.) If we may substitute the dowry for the money, it would mean that the husband is bought with the dowry: both the jewellery and the bad seats would stand for the husband. It would be still

more desirable if we could see some connection between the element *three tickets* and a husband; but our knowledge does not as yet extend to this. We have only found out that the dream expresses *depreciation* of her own husband and regret at having *married so early.*

In my opinion we shall be more surprised and confused by the result of this our first attempt at dream-interpretation than satisfied with it. Too many ideas force themselves upon us at once, more than as yet we can master. We see already that we shall not come to the end of what the interpretation of this dream can teach us. Let us immediately single out those points in which we can definitely see some new knowledge.

In the first place: we note that in the latent thoughts the chief emphasis falls upon the element of hurry; in the manifest dream that is exactly a feature about which we find nothing. Without analysis we could have had no suspicion that this thought entered in at all. It seems possible, therefore, that precisely the main point round which the unconscious thoughts centre does not appear in the manifest dream at all. This fact must radically change the impression made upon us by the whole dream. In the second place: in the dream there is a nonsensical combination of ideas (three for one florin and a half); in the dream-thoughts we detect the opinion: "It was folly (to marry so early)." Can one reject the conclusion that this thought, "It was *folly,*" is represented by the introduction into the manifest dream of an *absurd* element? In the third place: comparison shows us that the relation between manifest and latent elements is no simple one, certainly not of such a kind that a manifest always replaces a latent element. The relation between the two is of the nature of a relation between two different groups, so that a manifest element can represent several latent thoughts or a latent thought be replaced by several manifest elements.

As regards the meaning of the dream and the dreamer's attitude towards it, here again we might find many surprising things to say. The lady certainly admitted the interpretation, but she wondered at it; she had not been aware that she had such disparaging thoughts of her husband; she did not even know why she should so disparage him. So there is still much that is incomprehensible about it. I really think that as yet we are not properly equipped for interpreting a dream and that we need further instruction and preparation first.

EIGHTH LECTURE
CHILDREN'S DREAMS

WE HAD the impression that we had advanced too rapidly; let us therefore retrace our steps a little. Before we made our last experiment in which we tried to overcome the difficulty of dream-distortion by means of our technique, we said that it would be best to circumvent it by confining our attention to dreams in which distortion is absent or occurs only to a very slight extent, if there are any such dreams. In doing this, we are again departing from the actual course of development of our knowledge; for in reality it was only after consistently applying our method of interpretation, and after exhaustive analysis of dreams in which distortion occurred, that we became aware of the existence of those in which it is lacking.

The dreams we are looking for are met with in children: short, clear, coherent, and easy to understand, they are free from ambiguity and yet are unmistakable dreams. You must not think, however, that all dreams in children are of this type. Distortion in dreams begins to appear very early in childhood, and there are on record dreams of children between five and eight years old which already show all the characteristics of the dreams of later life. But, if you confine yourselves to those occurring in the period between the dawn of recognizable mental activity and the fourth or fifth year of life, you will discover a series which we should characterize as infantile, and, in the later years of childhood, you may find single dreams of the same type; indeed, even in grown-up people under certain conditions dreams appear which in no way differ from the typically infantile.

Now from these children's dreams it is possible to obtain without any difficulty trustworthy information about the essential nature of dreams, which we hope will prove to be decisive and universally valid.

1. In order to understand these dreams there is no need for any analysis nor for the employment of any technique. It is not necessary to question the child who relates his dream. But we must know something about his life; in every instance there is some experience from the previous day which explains the dream. The dream is the mind's reaction in sleep to the experience of the previous day.

Let us consider some examples in order to base our further conclusions upon them:

(a) A boy of a year and ten months old had to present someone with a basket of cherries as a birthday gift. He plainly did it very unwillingly, although he had been promised some of them for himself. The next morning he told his dream: "Hermann eaten all the cherries."

(b) A little girl of three and a quarter years went for the first time for a trip on the lake. When they came to land, she did not wish to leave the boat and cried bitterly; the time on the water had evidently gone too quickly for her. Next morning she said: "Last night I was sailing on the lake." We may probably infer that this trip lasted longer.

(c) A boy five and a quarter years old was taken on an excursion to the Escherntal near Hallstatt. He had heard that Hallstatt lay at the foot of the Dachstein and had shown great interest in that mountain. From the lodgings in Aussee there was a fine view of the Dachstein, and with a telescope it was possible to make out the Simony Hut on top. The child had repeatedly endeavoured to see the hut through the telescope, but nobody knew whether he had succeeded. The excursion began in a mood of joyful expectation. Whenever a new mountain came into sight, the little boy asked: "Is that the Dachstein?" Every time his question was answered in the negative he grew more out of spirits and presently became silent and refused to climb a little way up to the waterfall with the others. He was thought to be overtired, but the next morning he said quite happily: "Last night I dreamt that we were in the Simony Hut." So it was with this expectation that he had taken part in the excursion. The only detail he gave was one he had heard before: "You have to climb up steps for six hours."

These three dreams will be enough to give us all the information we need at this point.

2. We see that these childhood dreams are not meaningless; they are complete, comprehensible mental acts. Remember the medical verdict about dreams, which I told you, and the comparison with unskilled fingers wandering over the keys of the piano. You cannot fail to notice how sharply this conception is contradicted by the children's dreams I have quoted. Now it would surely be most extraordinary if a child were able to achieve the performance of complete mental acts during sleep, and the grown-up person in the same situation contented himself with spasmodic reactions. Besides, we have every reason for attributing better and deeper sleep to a child.

3. In these dreams there is no distortion and therefore they need no interpretation: the

manifest and the latent content is here identical. From this we conclude that *distortion is not essential to the nature of the dream.* I expect that this statement will take a weight off your minds. Nevertheless, closer consideration forces us to admit that even in these dreams distortion is present, though in a very slight degree, that there is a certain difference between the manifest content and the latent dream-thought.

4. The child's dream is a reaction to an experience of the previous day, which has left behind a regret, a longing, or an unsatisfied wish. *In the dream we have the direct, undisguised fulfilment of this wish.* Now consider our discussion as to the part played by the external or internal somatic stimuli as disturbers of sleep and begetters of dreams. We learnt certain quite definite facts on this point, but this explanation only held good in a small number of dreams. In these children's dreams there is nothing to indicate the influence of such somatic stimuli; we can make no mistake about it, for the dreams are perfectly comprehensible and each can easily be grasped as a whole. But we need not on that account give up our notion of the stimulus as causing the dream. We can only ask why we forget from the outset that there are *mental* as well as bodily sleep-disturbing stimuli; surely we know that it is these which are mainly responsible for disturbing the sleep of the grown-up person, in that they hinder him from bringing about in himself the mental condition essential for sleep, i.e., the withdrawal of interest from the outside world. He wishes not to have any interruption in his life; he would prefer to continue working at whatever occupies him, and that is the reason why he does not sleep. The mental stimulus which disturbs sleep is therefore for a child the unsatisfied wish, and his reaction to this is a dream.

5. This takes us by a very short step to a conclusion about the function of dreams. If dreams are the reaction to a mental stimulus their value must lie in effecting a discharge of the excitation so that the stimulus is removed and sleep can continue. We do not yet know how this discharge through the dream is effected dynamically, but we notice already that dreams are not disturbers of sleep (the accusation commonly brought against them), but are guardians and deliverers of it from disturbing influences. True, we are apt to think we should have slept better if we had not dreamed, but there we are wrong: the truth is that without

the help of the dream we should not have slept at all, and we owe it to the dream that we slept as well as we did. It could not help disturbing us a little, just as a policeman often cannot avoid making a noise when driving off disturbers of the peace who would wake us.

6. That dreams are brought about by a wish and that the content of the dream expresses this wish is one main characteristic of dreams. The other equally constant feature is that the dream does not merely give expression to a thought, but represents this wish as fulfilled, in the form of an hallucinatory experience. "I should like to sail on the lake," runs the wish which gives rise to the dream; the content of the dream itself is: "I am sailing on the lake." So that even in these simple dreams belonging to childhood there is still a difference between the latent and the manifest dream, and still a distortion of the latent dream-thought, *in the translation of the thought into an experience.* In interpreting a dream, we must first of all undo this process of alteration. If this is to be regarded as one of the most universal characteristics of all dreams, we then know how to translate the dream-fragment I quoted before: "I see my brother digging" does not mean "my brother *is* retrenching," but "I wish my brother would retrench, he *is to* retrench." Of the two universal characteristics here mentioned the second is obviously more likely to be acknowledged without opposition than the first.

It is only by extensive investigations that we can make sure that what produces the dream must always be a *wish* and cannot sometimes be a preoccupation, a purpose, or reproach; but the other characteristic remains unaffected, namely, that the dream does not merely reproduce this stimulus, but, by a kind of living it through, removes it, sets it aside, relieves it.

7. In connection with these characteristics of dreams we may take up again our comparison between dreams and errors. In the latter we distinguished between a disturbing tendency and one which is disturbed, the error being a compromise between the two. Dreams fall into the same category; the disturbed tendency can only, of course, be the tendency to sleep, while the disturbing tendency resolves itself into the mental stimulus which we may call the *wish* (clamouring for gratification), since at present we know of no other mental stimulus disturbing sleep. Here again the dream is the result of a compromise; we sleep, and yet we experience the satisfaction of a wish; we gratify a wish and at the same time continue to

sleep. Each achieves part-success and part-failure.

8. You will remember that at one point we hoped to find a path to an understanding of the problems presented by dreams in the fact that certain very transparent phantasy-formations are called *day-dreams*. Now these day-dreams are literally wish-fulfilments, fulfilments of ambitious or erotic wishes, which we recognize as such; they are, however, carried out in thought, and, however vividly imagined, they never take the form of hallucinatory experiences. Here, therefore, the less certain of the two main characteristics of the dream is retained, whereas the other, to which the condition of sleep is essential and which cannot be realized in waking life, is entirely lacking. So in language we find a hint that a wish-fulfilment is a main characteristic of dreams. And further, if the experience we have in dreams is only another form of imaginative representation, a form which becomes possible under the peculiar conditions of the sleeping state—*a nocturnal day-dream*, as we might call it—we understand at once how it is that the process of dream-formation can abrogate the stimulus operating at night and can bring gratification; for day-dreaming also is a mode of activity closely linked up with gratification, which is in fact the only reason why people practise it.

Again, there are other linguistic expressions, besides this, which imply the same thing. We are familiar with the proverbs: "The pig dreams of acorns and the goose of maize." "What do chickens dream of? Of millet." The proverb, you see, goes even lower in the scale than we do, beyond the child to the animal, and asserts that the content of dreams is the satisfaction of a want. And there are many phrases which seem to point to the same thing: we say "as beautiful as a dream." "I should never have dreamt of such a thing." "I never imagined that in my wildest dreams." Here colloquial speech is clearly partial in its judgment. Of course there are also anxiety-dreams and dreams the content of which is painful or indifferent, but these have not given rise to any special phrases. We do indeed speak of *bad* dreams, but by a *dream* pure and simple common usage always understands some sort of exquisite wish-fulfilment. Nor is there any proverb which attempts to assert that pigs or geese dream of being slaughtered!

It is, of course, inconceivable that this wish-fulfilling character of dreams should have escaped the notice of writers on the subject. On the contrary, they have very often remarked upon it; but it has not occurred to any of them to recognize this characteristic as universal, and to take it as the key to the explanation of dreams. We can easily imagine what may have deterred them, and later we will discuss the question.

Now see how much information we have gained, and that with hardly any trouble, from our study of children's dreams! We have learnt that the function of dreams is to protect sleep; that they arise out of two conflicting tendencies, of which the one, the desire for sleep, remains constant, whilst the other endeavours to satisfy some mental stimulus; that dreams are proved to be mental acts, rich in meaning; that they have two main characteristics, i.e., they are wish-fulfilments and hallucinatory experiences. And meanwhile we could almost have forgotten that we were studying psycho-analysis. Apart from the connection we have made between dreams and errors our work has not borne any specific stamp. Any psychologist knowing nothing of the assumptions of psycho-analysis could have given this explanation of children's dreams. Why has no one done so?

If only all dreams were of the infantile type the problem would be solved and our task already achieved, and that without questioning the dreamer, referring to the unconscious or having recourse to the process of free association. Clearly it is in this direction that we must continue our work. We have already repeatedly found that characteristics alleged to be universally valid have afterwards proved to hold good only for a certain kind and a limited number of dreams. So the question we now have to decide is whether the common characteristics revealed by children's dreams are any more stable than these, and whether they hold also for those dreams whose meaning is not obvious and in whose manifest content we can recognize no reference to a wish remaining from the day before. Our idea is that these other dreams have undergone a good deal of distortion and on that account we must refrain from immediate judgment. We suspect too that to unravel this distortion we shall need the help of psycho-analytic technique, which we could dispense with while learning, as we have just now done, the meaning of children's dreams.

There is yet one other class of dreams at least in which no distortion is present and which, like children's dreams, we easily recognize to be wish-fulfilments. These are dreams which are occasioned all through life by im-

perative physical needs—hunger, thirst, sexual
desire—and are wish-fulfilments in the sense of
being reactions to internal somatic stimuli.
Thus I have on record the dream of a little girl,
one year and seven months old, which consisted of a kind of menu, together with her
name (Anna F . . . , strawberries, bilberries,
egg, pap), the dream being a reaction to a day
of fasting, enforced on account of indigestion
due to eating the fruit which appeared twice in
the dream. At the same time her grandmother
—their combined ages totalled seventy—was
obliged, owing to a floating kidney, to go without food for a day and dreamt that night that
she had been invited out and had had the most
tempting delicacies set before her. Observations
on prisoners who are left to go hungry, and on
people who suffer privations whilst traveling or
on expeditions, show that in these circumstances they regularly dream about the satisfaction of their wants. Thus Otto Nordenskjöld in
his book on the Antarctic (1904) tells us of
the band of men in whose company he spent
the winter (Vol. I, p. 336): "Our dreams
showed very clearly the direction our thoughts
were taking. Never had we dreamt so frequently and so vividly as at that time. Even
those of our comrades who usually dreamt but
rarely had now long stories to tell in the morn-
ings when we exchanged our latest experiences
in this realm of phantasy. All the dreams were
about that outside world now so far away, but
often they included a reference to our condition at the time . . . eating and drinking were,
incidentally, the pivot on which our dreams
most often turned. One of us, who was particularly good at going out to large dinners in his
sleep, was delighted when he could tell us in
the morning that he had had a three-course
dinner. Another dreamt of tobacco, whole
mountains of tobacco; another of a ship which
came full sail over the water, at last clear of
ice. Yet another dream deserves mention: the
postman came with the letters and gave a long
explanation of why they were so late; he said
he had made a mistake in delivering them, and
had had great trouble in getting them back
again. Of course, things even more impossible
occupied our minds in sleep, but the lack of
imagination in almost all the dreams which I
dreamt myself or heard the others tell was
quite striking. It would certainly be of great
psychological interest if we had a record of all
these dreams. You can imagine how we longed
for sleep, when it offered each one of us all
that he most eagerly desired." Another quota-

tion, this time from Du Prel: "Mungo Park,
when nearly dying of thirst on a journey in
Africa, dreamt continually of the well-watered
hills and valleys of his home. So Trenck, tormented with hunger in the redoubt at Magde-
bourg, saw himself in his dream surrounded by
sumptuous meals; and George Back, who took
part in Franklin's first expedition, when on the
point of dying of hunger owing to their terrible
privations, dreamt regularly of abundant food
to eat."

Anyone who has made himself thirsty at
night by eating highly seasoned dishes at supper
is likely to dream of drinking. Of course it is
not possible to relieve acute hunger or thirst
by dreaming; in that case we awake thirsty and
are obliged to drink real water. The service of
the dream is here of little practical account,
but it is none the less clear that it was called
up for the purpose of protecting sleep from the
stimulus impelling us to wake up and act.
Where the intensity of the desire is less, *satisfaction*-dreams do often answer the purpose.

In the same way, when the stimulus is that
of sexual desire, the dream provides satisfaction, but of a kind which shows peculiarities
worthy of mention. Since it is a characteristic
of the sexual impulse that it is a degree less dependent on its object than are hunger and
thirst, the satisfaction in a pollution-dream can
be real; and, in consequence of certain difficulties in the relation to the object (which will
be discussed later), it particularly often happens that the real satisfaction is yet connected
with a vague or distorted dream-content. This
peculiarity of pollution-dreams makes them,
as O. Rank has observed, suitable objects for
the study of dream-distortion. Moreover, with
adults, dreams of desire usually contain besides
the satisfaction something else, springing from
a purely mental source and requiring interpretation if it is to be understood.

We do not maintain, by the way, that wish-
fulfilment dreams of the infantile type occur
in adults solely as reactions to the imperative
desires I have mentioned. We are equally
familiar with short clear dreams of this type,
occasioned by certain dominating situations
and unquestionably produced by mental stimuli.
For example, there are *impatience*-dreams in
which someone making preparations for a journey, for a theatrical performance in which he
is specially interested, or for a lecture or a
visit, has his expectations prematurely realized
in a dream, and finds himself the night before
the actual experience already at his journey's

end, at the theatre, or talking to the friend he is going to visit. Or again, there is the *comfort*-dream, rightly so-called, in which someone who wants to go on sleeping dreams that he has already got up, that he is washing, or is at school, while all the time he is really continuing his sleep, meaning that he would rather dream of getting up than do so in reality. In these dreams the desire for sleep, which we have recognized as regularly participating in dream-formation, expresses itself plainly and appears as their actual originator. The need for sleep ranks itself quite rightly with the other great physical needs.

I would refer you at this point to ... a picture by Schwind in the Schack Gallery at Munich and would ask you to notice how correctly the artist has realized the way in which a dream arises out of a dominating situation. The picture is called *The Prisoner's Dream*, and the subject of the dream must undoubtedly be his escape. It is a happy thought that the prisoner is to escape by the window, for it is through the window that the ray of light has entered and roused him from sleep. The gnomes standing one above the other no doubt represent the successive positions he would have to assume in climbing up to the window; and, if I am not mistaken and do not attribute too much intentional design to the artist, the features of the gnome at the top, who is filing the grating through (the very thing the prisoner himself would like to do), resemble the man's own.

I have said that in all dreams, other than those of children and such as conform to the infantile type, we encounter the obstacle of distortion. We cannot immediately say whether they too are wish-fulfilments, as we are inclined to suppose, nor can we guess from their manifest content in what mental stimulus they originate, or prove that they, like the others, endeavour to remove or relieve the stimulus. They must, in fact, be interpreted, i.e., translated; the process of distortion must be reversed, and the manifest content replaced by the latent thought, before we can make any definite pronouncement whether what we have found out about infantile dreams may claim to hold good for all dreams alike.

NINTH LECTURE
THE DREAM-CENSORSHIP

Our study of children's dreams has taught us how dreams originate, what their essential character is, and what their function. Dreams are the means of removing, by hallucinatory satisfaction, mental stimuli that disturb sleep. It is true that with the dreams of adults we have been able to explain one group only, those which we termed dreams of the infantile type. We do not yet know how it may be with others, neither do we understand them. The result we have arrived at already is one, however, of which the significance is not to be under-estimated. Every time that we fully understand a dream it proves to be a wish-fulfilment; and this coincidence cannot be accidental or unimportant.

Dreams of another type are assumed by us to be distorted substitutes for an unknown content, which first of all has to be traced; we have various grounds for this assumption, amongst others the analogy to our conception of errors. Our next task is to investigate and understand this *dream-distortion*.

It is dream-distortion which makes dreams seem strange and incomprehensible. There are several things we want to know about it: first, whence it comes (its dynamics), secondly, what it does, and finally, how it does it. Further, we can say that distortion is the production of the *dream-work*. Let us describe the dream-work and trace out the forces in it.

Now let me tell you a dream recorded by a lady well-known in psycho-analytical circles,[1] who said that the dreamer was an elderly woman, highly cultivated and held in great esteem. The dream was not analysed and our informant observed that for psycho-analysts it needed no interpreting. Nor did the dreamer herself interpret it, but she criticized it and condemned it in such a way as though she knew what it meant. "Imagine," she said, "such abominable nonsense being dreamt by a woman of fifty, whose only thought day and night is concern for her child."

I will now tell you the dream, which is about "love service in war-time."[2] "She went to the First Military Hospital and said to the sentinel at the gate that she must speak to the physician-in-chief (giving a name which she did not know), as she wished to offer herself for service in the hospital. In saying this, she emphasized the word service in such a way that the sergeant at once perceived that she was speaking of 'love service.' As she was an old lady, he let her pass after some hesitation,

[1] Frau Dr. von Hug-Hellmuth.
[2] *Liebesdienst* = "love service," a popular expression adapted from "military service." —TR.

but instead of finding the chief physician, she came to a large gloomy room, where a number of officers and army doctors were standing or sitting around a long table. She turned to a staff doctor and told him her proposal; he soon understood her meaning. The words she said in her dream were: 'I and countless other women and girls of Vienna are ready for the soldiers, officers or men, to . . .' This ended in a murmur. She saw, however, by the half-embarrassed, half-malicious expressions of the officers that all of them grasped her meaning. The lady continued: 'I know our decision sounds odd, but we are in bitter earnest. The soldier on the battlefield is not asked whether he wishes to die or not.' There followed a minute of painful silence; then the staff doctor put his arm round her waist and said: 'Madam, supposing it really came to this, that . . . (murmur).' She withdrew herself from his arm, thinking: 'They are all alike,' and replied: 'Good heavens, I am an old woman and perhaps it won't happen to me. And one condition must be observed: age must be taken into account, so that an old woman and a young lad may not . . . (murmur); that would be horrible.' The staff doctor said: 'I quite understand'; but some of the officers, amongst them one who as a young man had made love to her, laughed loudly, and the lady asked to be taken to the physician-in-chief, whom she knew, so that everything might be put straight. It then struck her, to her great consternation, that she did not know his name. The staff doctor, however, with the utmost respect and courtesy, showed her the way to the second floor, up a very narrow iron spiral staircase leading direct from the room where they were to the upper storeys. As she went up, she heard an officer say: 'That is a tremendous decision, no matter whether she is young or old; all honour to her!' With the feeling that she was simply doing her duty, she went up an endless staircase."

This dream was repeated twice within a few weeks, with alterations here and there which, as the lady remarked, were quite unimportant and entirely meaningless.

The way in which this dream progresses corresponds to the course of a day-dream; there are only a few places where an interruption occurs, and many individual points in its content might have been cleared up by enquiry: this, however, as you know, was not undertaken. But the most striking and to us the most interesting thing about it is the occurrence of many gaps, not in the recollection, but in the content. In three places the latter is, as it were, blotted out; where these gaps occur the speeches are interrupted by a *murmur*. As we did not analyse the dream, we have, strictly speaking, no right to say anything about its meaning; but there are certain indications from which we may draw conclusions, e.g., the words *love service*; and, above all, the broken speeches immediately preceding the murmurs require completion of a kind which admits of only one construction. If we do so complete them a phantasy results, in which the content is that the dreamer is ready at the call of duty to offer herself to gratify the sexual needs of the troops, irrespective of rank. This is certainly shocking, a model of a shamelessly libidinous phantasy, but—the dream says nothing about this. Just where the context demands this confession, there is in the manifest dream an indistinct murmur: something has been lost or suppressed.

I hope you recognize how obvious is the inference that it is just the shocking nature of these passages which has led to their suppression. Now where will you find a parallel to what has taken place here? In these times you have not far to seek. Take up any political paper and you will find that here and there in the text something is omitted and in its place the blank white of the paper meets your eye: you know that this is the work of the press censor. Where these blank spaces occur, there originally stood something of which the official censors disapproved and which has been deleted on that account. You probably think it a pity, for that must have been the most interesting part, the *cream* of the news.

On other occasions the official censor has not dealt with the sentence in its completed form; for the writer, foreseeing which passages were likely to be objected to by the censor, has forestalled him by softening them down, making some slight modification or contenting himself with hints and allusions to what he really wants to write. In this case there are no blanks, but from the roundabout and obscure mode of expression you can detect the fact that, at the time of writing, the author had the censorship in mind.

Now keeping to this parallel we say that those speeches in the dream which were omitted or disguised by a murmur have also been sacrificed to some form of censorship. We actually use the term DREAM-CENSORSHIP, and ascribe part of the distortion to its agency. Wherever there are gaps in the manifest dream we know that the censorship is responsible; and indeed we should go further and recognize that wherever, amongst other more clearly defined elements, one appears which is fainter, more indefinite or more dubious in recollection, it is evidence of the work of the censorship. It is, however, seldom that it takes a form so undisguised, so naïve, as we might say, as it does in the case of the dream about *love service;* far more often the censorship makes itself felt in the second way I mentioned: by effecting modifications, hints, and allusions in place of the true meaning.

There is a third way in which the dream-censorship works, to which the ordinances of the press censorship supply no parallel; but it happens that I can demonstrate to you this particular mode of activity on the part of the dream-censorship in the only dream hitherto analysed by us. You will remember the dream of the "three bad theatre-tickets, costing one florin and a half." In the latent thoughts underlying this dream, the element *too great a hurry, too early* was in the foreground; the meaning was: "It was folly to marry so *early,* it was foolish also to take the tickets so *early,* it was ridiculous of the sister-in-law to spend her money so *hurriedly* on a piece of jewellery." Nothing of this central element of the dream-thoughts appeared in the manifest content, where everything was focussed on going to the theatre and taking tickets. By this displacement of the accent and regrouping of the dream-elements, the manifest content was made so unlike the latent thoughts that nobody would suspect the presence of the latter behind the former. This *displacement of accent* is one of the principal means employed in distortion, and it is this which gives the dream that character of strangeness which makes the dreamer himself reluctant to recognize it as the product of his own mind.

Omission, modification, regrouping of material—these then are the modes of the dream-censorship's activity and the means employed in distortion. The censorship itself is the originator, or one of the originators, of distortion, the subject of our present enquiry. Modification and alteration in arrangement are commonly included under the term *displacement.*

After these remarks on the activities of the dream-censorship, let us turn our attention to its dynamics. I hope you are not taking the expression *censorship* in too anthropomorphic a sense, picturing to yourselves the censor as a stern little manikin or a spirit, who lives in a little chamber of the brain and there discharges the duties of his office; and neither must you localize it too exactly, so that you imagine a *brain-centre* whence there emanates a censorial influence, liable to cease with the injury or disappearance of that centre. For the present we may regard it merely as a useful term by which to express a dynamic relationship. This need not hinder us from asking what sort of tendencies exercise this influence and is it exercised upon; and further, we must not be surprised to discover that we have already come across the censorship, perhaps without recognizing it.

Indeed this has actually happened. Remember a surprising experience we had when we began to apply our method of free association: we discovered that our efforts to penetrate from the dream-element to the unconscious thought proper for which the former is a substitute encountered a certain *resistance.* The strength of this resistance, we said, varies, being sometimes enormous and at other times very slight. In the latter case we need only a few connecting-links for the work of interpretation; but where there is great resistance we are compelled to go through long chains of associations, which carry us far from the initial idea, and on the way we have to overcome all the difficulties of professedly critical objections to associations arising. That which we encountered as resistance in the work of interpretation we now meet again as the censorship in the dream-work: the resistance is simply the censorship objectified; it proves to us that the power of the censorship is not exhausted in effecting distortion, being thereby extinguished, but that the censorship remains as a permanent institution, the object of which is to maintain the distortion when once it has been achieved. Moreover, just as the strength of the resistance encountered during interpretation varies with each element, so too the degree of distortion effected by the censorship is different for each element of a whole dream. A comparison of the manifest and the latent dream shows that certain latent elements are completely eliminated, others more or less modified, and others again appear in the manifest dream-content unaltered or perhaps even intensified.

Our purpose, however, was to find out which are the tendencies exercising the censorship and upon which tendencies it is exercised. Now this question, which is fundamental for the understanding of dreams and perhaps of human life altogether, is easy to answer when we survey the series of dreams which we have succeeded in interpreting. The tendencies which exercise the censorship are those which are acknowledged by the waking judgment of the dreamer and with which he feels himself to be at one. You may be sure that when you repudiate any correctly found interpretation of a dream of your own, you do so from the same motives as cause the censorship to be exercised and distortion effected, and make interpretation necessary. Consider the dream of our lady of fifty: her dream, although it had not been interpreted, struck her as shocking and she would have been even more outraged if Dr. von Hug-Hellmuth had told her something of its unmistakable meaning; it was just this attitude of condemnation which caused the offensive passages in the dream to be replaced by a murmur.

Those tendencies against which the dream-censorship is directed must next be described from the point of view of this inner critical standard. When we do this, we can only say that they are invariably of an objectionable nature, offensive from the ethical, aesthetic or social point of view, things about which we do not dare to think at all, or think of only with abhorrence. Above all are these censored wishes, which in dreams are expressed in a distorted fashion, manifestations of a boundless and ruthless egoism; for the dreamer's own ego makes its appearance in every dream, and plays the principal part, even if it knows how to disguise itself completely as far as the manifest content is concerned. This *sacro egoismo* of dreams is certainly not unconnected with the attitude of mind essential to sleep: the withdrawal of interest from the whole outside world.

The ego which has discarded all ethical bonds feels itself at one with all the demands of the sexual impulse, those which have long been condemned by our aesthetic training and those which are contrary to all the restraints imposed by morality. The striving for pleasure —the libido, as we say—chooses its objects unchecked by any inhibition, preferring indeed those which are forbidden: not merely the wife of another man, but, above all, the incestuous objects of choice which by common consent humanity holds sacred—the mother and the sister of men, the father and the brother of women. (Even the dream of our fifty-year-old lady is an incestuous one, the libido being unmistakably directed towards the son.) Desires which we believe alien to human nature show themselves powerful enough to give rise to dreams. Hate, too, rages unrestrainedly; wishes

for revenge, and death-wishes, against those who in life are nearest and dearest—parents, brothers and sisters, husband or wife, the dreamer's own children—are by no means uncommon. These censored wishes seem to rise up from a veritable hell; when we know their meaning, it seems to us in our waking moments as if no censorship of them could be severe enough. Dreams themselves, however, are not to blame for this evil content; you surely have not forgotten that their harmless, nay, useful, function is to protect sleep from disturbance. Depravity does not lie in the nature of dreams; in fact, you know that there are dreams which can be recognized as gratifying justifiable desires and urgent bodily needs. It is true that there is no distortion in these dreams, but then there is no need for it, they can perform their function without offending the ethical and aesthetic tendencies of the ego. Remember, too, that the degree of distortion is proportionate to two factors: on the one hand, the more shocking the wish that must be censored, the greater will be the distortion; but it is also great in proportion as the demands of the censorship are severe. Hence in a strictly brought up and prudish young girl, a rigid censorship will distort dream-excitations which we medical men would have recognized as permissible and harmless libidinous desires, and which the dreamer herself would judge in the same way ten years later.

Besides, we are still not nearly far enough advanced to allow ourselves to be outraged at the result of our work of interpretation. I think we still do not understand it properly; but first of all it is incumbent upon us to secure it against certain possible attacks. It is not at all difficult to detect weak points in it. Our interpretations were based on hypotheses which we adopted earlier: that there really is some meaning in dreams; that the idea of mental processes being unconscious for a time, which was first arrived at through hypnotic sleep, may be applied also to normal sleep; and that all associations are subject to determination. Now if, reasoning from these hypotheses, we had obtained plausible results in our dream-interpretation we should have been justified in concluding that these hypotheses were correct. But what if these discoveries are of the kind I have described? In that case, surely it seems natural to say: "These results are impossible, absurd, at the very least highly improbable, so there must have been something wrong about the hypotheses. Either the dream is, after all, not a mental phenomenon, or there is nothing which is unconscious in our normal condition, or there is a flaw somewhere in our technique. Is it not simpler and more satisfactory to assume this than to accept all the abominable conclusions which we profess to have deduced from our hypotheses?"

Both! It is both simpler and more satisfactory, but not on that account necessarily more correct. Let us give ourselves time: the matter is not yet ripe for judgment. First of all, we can make the case against our interpretations even stronger. The fact that our results are so unpleasant and repellent would not perhaps weigh so very heavily with us; a stronger argument is the emphatic and well-grounded repudiation by dreamers of the wish-tendencies which we try to foist upon them after interpreting their dreams. "What," says one, "you want to prove to me from my dream that I grudge the money I have spent on my sister's dowry and my brother's education? But it is out of the question; I spend my whole time working for my brothers and sisters and my only interest in life is to do my duty by them, as, being the eldest, I promised our dead mother I would." Or a woman says: "I am supposed to wish that my husband were dead? Really that is outrageous nonsense! Not only is our married life very happy, though perhaps you won't believe that, but if he died I should lose everything I possess in the world." Or someone else will reply: "Do you mean to suggest that I entertain sexual desires towards my sister? The thing is ludicrous; she is nothing to me; we get on badly with one another, and for years I have not exchanged a word with her." We still might not be much impressed if these dreamers neither admitted nor denied the tendencies attributed to them; we might say that these are just the things of which they are quite unconscious. But when they detect in their own minds the exact opposite of such a wish as is interpreted to them, and when they can prove to us by their whole conduct in life that the contrary desire predominates, surely we must be nonplussed. Is it not about time now for us to discard our whole work of dream-interpretation as something which has led to a *reductio ad absurdum*?

No, not even now. Even this stronger argument falls to pieces when subjected to a critical attack. Assuming that unconscious tendencies do exist in mental life, the fact that the opposite tendencies predominate in conscious life goes to prove nothing. Perhaps there is room in the mind for opposite tendencies, for contradictions, existing side by side; indeed, possibly the very predominance of the one tendency conditions the unconscious nature of the opposite. So the first objections raised only amount to the statement that the results of dream-interpretation are not simple and are very disagreeable. To the first charge we may reply that, however much enamoured of simplicity you may be, you cannot thereby solve one of the problems of dreams; you have to make up your mind at the outset to accept the fact of complicated relations. And, as regards the second point, you are manifestly wrong in taking the fact that something pleases or repels yourself as the motive for a scientific judgment. What does it matter if you do find the results of dream-interpretation unpleasant, or even mortifying and repulsive? *Ça n'empêche pas d'exister*[1]—as I, when a young doctor, heard my chief, Charcot, say in a similar case. We must be humble and put sympathies and antipathies honourably in the background if we would learn to know reality in this world. If a physicist could prove to you that organic life on the earth was bound to become extinct before long, would you venture to say to him also: "That cannot be so; I dislike the prospect too much." I think you would say nothing until another physicist came along and convicted the first of a mistake in his premises or his calculations. If you repudiate whatever is distasteful to you, you are repeating the mechanism of a dream structure rather than understanding and mastering it.

Perhaps, then, you will undertake to overlook the offensive nature of the censored dream-wishes and will fall back upon the argument that it is surely very improbable that we ought to concede so large a part in the human constitution to what is evil. But do your own experiences justify you in this statement? I will say nothing of how you may appear in your own eyes, but have you met with so much goodwill in your superiors and rivals, so much chivalry in your enemies and so little envy amongst your acquaintances, that you feel it incumbent on you to protest against the idea of the part played by egoistic baseness in human nature? Do you not know how uncontrolled and unreliable the average human being is in all that concerns sexual life? Or are you ignorant of the fact that all the excesses and aberrations of which we dream at night are crimes actually committed every day by men who are wide

[1] It won't kill you.—ED.

awake? What does psycho-analysis do in this connection but confirm the old saying of Plato that the good are those who content themselves with dreaming of what others, the wicked, actually do?

And now look away from individuals to the great war still devastating Europe: think of the colossal brutality, cruelty and mendacity which is now allowed to spread itself over the civilized world. Do you really believe that a handful of unprincipled place-hunters and corrupters of men would have succeeded in letting loose all this latent evil, if the millions of their followers were not also guilty? Will you venture, even in these circumstances, to break a lance for the exclusion of evil from the mental constitution of humanity?

You will accuse me of taking a one-sided view of war, and tell me that it has also called out all that is finest and most noble in mankind, heroism, self-sacrifice, and public spirit. That is true; but do not now commit the injustice, from which psycho-analysis has so often suffered, of reproaching it that it denies one thing because it affirms another. It is no part of our intention to deny the nobility in human nature, nor have we ever done anything to disparage its value. On the contrary, I show you not only the evil wishes which are censored but also the censorship which suppresses them and makes them unrecognizable. We dwell upon the evil in human beings with the greater emphasis only because others deny it, thereby making the mental life of mankind not indeed better, but incomprehensible. If we give up the one-sided ethical valuation then, we are sure to find the truer formula for the relation of evil to good in human nature.

Here the matter rests. We need not give up the results of our work of dream-interpretation, even though we cannot fail to find them strange. Perhaps later we shall be able to come nearer to understanding them by another path. For the present let us hold fast to this: dream-distortion is due to the censorship exercised, by certain recognized tendencies of the ego, over desires of an offensive character which stir in us at night during sleep. Obviously, when we ask ourselves why it is just at night that they appear and what is the origin of these reprehensible wishes, we find that there is still much to investigate and many questions to answer.

It would, however, be wrong if we neglected to give due prominence at this point to another result of these investigations. The dream-wishes which would disturb our sleep are unknown to us; we first learn about them by dream-interpretation; they are therefore to be designated *unconscious at the moment* in the sense in which we have used the term. But we must recognize that they are also more than unconscious at the moment; for the dreamer denies them, as we have so frequently found, even after he has learnt of them through the interpretation of his dream. Here we have a repetition of the case which we first met with when interpreting the slip of the tongue "hiccough," where the after-dinner speaker indignantly assured us that neither then nor at any time had he been conscious of any feeling of disrespect towards his chief. We ventured even then to doubt the value of this assertion and assumed instead that the speaker was permanently ignorant of the existence of this feeling within him. We meet with the same situation every time we interpret a dream in which there is a high degree of distortion, and this lends an added significance to our conception. We are now prepared to assume that there are processes and tendencies in mental life, of which we know nothing; have known nothing; have, for a very long time, perhaps even never, known anything about at all. This gives the term *unconscious* a fresh meaning for us: the qualification *at the moment* or *temporary* is seen to be no essential attribute, the term may also mean *permanently unconscious*, not merely *latent at the moment*. You see that later on we shall have to discuss this point further.

TENTH LECTURE
SYMBOLISM IN DREAMS

WE HAVE found out that the distortion in dreams which hinders our understanding of them is due to the activities of a censorship, directed against the unacceptable, unconscious wish-impulses. But of course we have not asserted that the censorship is the only factor responsible for the distortion, and as a matter of fact a further study of dreams leads to the discovery that there are yet other causes contributing to this effect; that is as much as to say, if the censorship were eliminated we should nevertheless be unable to understand dreams, nor would the manifest dream be identical with the latent dream-thoughts.

This other cause of the obscurity of dreams, this additional contribution to distortion, is revealed by our becoming aware of a gap in our technique. I have already admitted to you that there are occasions when persons being analysed really have no associations to single elements in their dreams. To be sure, this does not happen so often as they declare that it does; in very many instances the association may yet be elicited by perseverance; but still there remain a certain number of cases where association fails altogether or, if something is finally extorted, it is not what we need. If this happens during psycho-analytic treatment, it has a certain significance which does not concern us here; but it also occurs in the course of interpretation of dreams in normal people, or when we are interpreting our own. When we are convinced, in such circumstances, that no amount of pressing is of any use, we finally discover that this unwelcome contingency regularly presents itself where special dream-elements are in question; and we begin to recognize the operation of some new principle, whereas at first we thought we had only come across an exceptional case in which our technique had failed.

In this way it comes about that we try to interpret these *silent* elements, and attempt to translate them by drawing upon our own resources. It cannot fail to strike us that we arrive at a satisfactory meaning in every instance in which we venture on this substitution, whereas the dream remains meaningless and disconnected as long as we do not resolve to use this method. The accumulation of many exactly similar instances then affords us the required certainty, our experiment having been tried at first with considerable diffidence.

I am presenting all this somewhat in outline, but that is surely allowable for purposes of instruction, nor is it falsified by so doing, but merely made simpler.

We arrive in this way at constant translations for a series of dream-elements, just as in popular books on dreams we find such translations for everything that occurs in dreams. You will not have forgotten that, when we employ the method of free association, such constant substitutions for dream-elements never make their appearance.

Now you will at once say that this mode of interpretation seems to you far more uncertain and open to criticism than even the former method of free association. But there is still something more to be said: when we have collected from actual experience a sufficient number of such constant translations, we eventually realize that we could actually have filled in these portions of the interpretation from our own knowledge, and that they really could have been understood without using the dreamer's associations. How it is that we are bound to know their meaning is a matter which will be dealt with in the second half of our discussion.

We call a constant relation of this kind between a dream-element and its translation a *symbolic* one, and the dream-element itself a *symbol* of the unconscious dream-thought. You will remember that some time ago, when we were examining the different relations which may exist between dream-elements and the thoughts proper underlying them, I distinguished three relations: substitution of the part for the whole, allusion, and imagery. I told you then that there was a fourth possible relation, but I did not tell you what it was. This fourth relation is the symbolic, which I am now introducing; there are connected with it certain very interesting points for discussion, to which we will turn attention before setting forth our special observations on this subject. Symbolism is perhaps the most remarkable part of our theory of dreams.

First of all: since the relation between a symbol and the idea symbolized is an invariable one, the latter being as it were a translation of the former, symbolism does in some measure realize the ideal of both ancient and popular dream-interpretation, one from which we have moved very far in our technique. Symbols make it possible for us in certain circumstances to interpret a dream without questioning the dreamer, who indeed in any case can tell us nothing about the symbols. If the symbols commonly appearing in dreams are known, and also the personality of the dreamer, the conditions under which he lives, and the impressions in his mind after which his dream occurred, we are often in a position to interpret it straightaway; to translate it at sight, as it were. Such a feat flatters the vanity of the interpreter and impresses the dreamer; it is in pleasing contrast to the laborious method of questioning the latter. But do not let this lead you away: it is no part of our task to perform tricks nor is that method of interpretation which is based on a knowledge of symbolism one which can replace, or even compare with, that of free association. It is complementary to this latter, and the results it yields are only useful when applied in connection with the latter. As regards our knowledge of the dreamer's mental situation, moreover, you must reflect that you have not only to interpret dreams of people whom you know well; that, as a rule, you know nothing of the events of the previous day which stimulated the dream; and that the associations of the person analysed are the very source from which we obtain our knowledge of what we call the mental situation.

Further, it is especially remarkable, particularly with reference to certain considerations upon which we shall touch later, that the most strenuous opposition has manifested itself again here, over this question of the existence of a symbolic relation between the dream and the unconscious. Even persons of judgment and standing, who in other respects have gone a long way with psycho-analysis, have renounced their adherence at this point. This behaviour is the more remarkable when we remember two things: first, that symbolism is not peculiar to dreams, nor exclusively characteristic of them; and, in the second place, that the use of symbolism in dreams was not one of the discoveries of psycho-analysis, although this science has certainly not been wanting in surprising discoveries. If we must ascribe priority in this field to anyone in modern times, the discoverer must be recognized in the philosopher K. A. Scherner (1861); psycho-analysis has confirmed his discovery, although modifying it in certain important respects.

Now you will wish to hear something about the nature of dream-symbolism and will want some examples. I will gladly tell you what I know, but I confess that our knowledge is less full than we could wish.

The symbolic relation is essentially that of a comparison, but not any kind of comparison. We must suspect that this comparison is subject to particular conditions, although we cannot say what these conditions are. Not everything with which an object or an occurrence can be compared appears in dreams as symbolic of it, and, on the other hand, dreams do not employ symbolism for anything and everything, but only for particular elements of latent dream-thoughts; there are thus limitations in both directions. We must admit also that we cannot at present assign quite definite limits to our conception of a symbol; for it tends to merge into substitution, representation, etc., and even approaches closely to allusion. In one set of symbols the underlying comparison may be easily apparent, but there are others in which we have to look about for the common factor, the *tertium comparationis* contained in the supposed comparison. Further reflection may then reveal it to us, or on the other hand it may remain definitely hidden from us. Again,

if the symbol is really a comparison, it is remarkable that this comparison is not exposed by the process of free association, and also that the dreamer knows nothing about it, but makes use of it unawares; nay, more, that he is actually unwilling to recognize it when it is brought to his notice. So you see that the symbolic relation is a comparison of a quite peculiar kind, the nature of which is as yet not fully clear to us. Perhaps some indication will be found later which will throw some light upon this unknown quantity.

The number of things which are represented symbolically in dreams is not great. The human body as a whole, parents, children, brothers and sisters, birth, death, nakedness—and one thing more. The only typical, that is to say, regularly occurring, representation of the human form as a whole is that of a *house*, as was recognized by Scherner, who even wanted to attribute to this symbol an overwhelming significance which is not really due to it. People have dreams of climbing down the front of a house, with feelings sometimes of pleasure and sometimes of dread. When the walls are quite smooth, the house means a man; when there are ledges and balconies which can be caught hold of, a woman. Parents appear in dreams as *emperor* and *empress, king* and *queen* or other exalted personages; in this respect the dream attitude is highly dutiful. Children and brothers and sisters are less tenderly treated, being symbolized by *little animals* or *vermin*. Birth is almost invariably represented by some reference to *water*: either we are falling into water or clambering out of it, saving someone from it or being saved by them, i.e., the relation between mother and child is symbolized. For dying we have setting out upon a *journey* or *travelling* by train, while the state of death is indicated by various obscure and, as it were, timid allusions; *clothes* and *uniforms* stand for nakedness. You see that here the dividing line between the symbolic and the allusive kinds of representation tends to disappear.

In comparison with the poverty of this enumeration, it cannot fail to strike us that objects and matters belonging to another range of ideas are represented by a remarkably rich symbolism. I am speaking of what pertains to the sexual life—the genitals, sexual processes and intercourse. An overwhelming majority of symbols in dreams are sexual symbols. A curious disproportion arises thus, for the matters dealt with are few in number, whereas the symbols for them are extraordinarily numerous, so that each of these few things can be expressed by many symbols practically equivalent. When they are interpreted, therefore, the result of this peculiarity gives universal offense, for, in contrast to the multifarious forms of its representation in dreams, the interpretation of the symbols is very monotonous. This is displeasing to everyone who comes to know of it: but how can we help it?

As this is the first time in the course of these lectures that I have touched upon the sexual life, I owe you some explanation of the manner in which I propose to treat this subject. Psycho-analysis sees no occasion for concealments or indirect allusions, and does not think it necessary to be ashamed of concerning itself with material so important; it is of the opinion that it is right and proper to call everything by its true name, hoping in this way the more easily to avoid disturbing suggestions. The fact that I am speaking to a mixed audience can make no difference in this. No science can be treated *in usum delphini*, or in a manner adapted to school-girls; the women present, by appearing in this lecture-room, have tacitly expressed their desire to be regarded on the same footing as the men.

The male genital organ is symbolically represented in dreams in many different ways, with most of which the common idea underlying the comparison is easily apparent. In the first place, the sacred number *three* is symbolic of the whole male genitalia. Its more conspicuous and, to both sexes, more interesting part, the penis, is symbolized primarily by objects which resemble it in form, being long and up-standing, such as *sticks, umbrellas, poles, trees* and the like; also by objects which, like the thing symbolized, have the property of penetrating, and consequently of injuring, the body, —that is to say, pointed weapons of all sorts: *knives, daggers, lances, sabres;* fire-arms are similarly used: *guns, pistols and revolvers,* these last being a very appropriate symbol on account of their shape. In the anxiety-dreams of young girls, pursuit by a man armed with a knife or rifle plays a great part. This is perhaps the most frequently occurring dream-symbol: you can now easily translate it for yourselves. The substitution of the male organ by objects from which water flows is again easily comprehensible: *taps, watering-cans,* or *springs;* and by other objects which are capable of elongation, such as *pulley lamps, pencils which slide in and out of a sheath,* and so on. *Pencils, penholders, nail-files, hammers* and

other *implements* are undoubtedly male sexual symbols, based on an idea of the male organ which is equally easily perceived.

The peculiar property of this member of being able to raise itself upright in defiance of the law of gravity, part of the phenomenon of erection, leads to symbolic representation by means of *balloons, aeroplanes,* and, just recently, *Zeppelins.* But dreams have another, much more impressive, way of symbolizing erection; they make the organ of sex into the essential part of the whole person, so that the *dreamer himself flies.* Do not be upset by hearing that dreams of flying, which we all know and which are often so beautiful, must be interpreted as dreams of general sexual excitement, dreams of erection. One psycho-analytic investigator, P. Federn, has established the truth of this interpretation beyond doubt; but, besides this, Mourly Vold, a man highly praised for his sober judgment, who carried out the experiments with artificial postures of the arms and legs, and whose theories were really widely removed from those of psycho-analysis (indeed he may have known nothing about it), was led by his own investigations to the same conclusion. Nor must you think to object to this on the ground that women can also have dreams of flying; you should rather remind yourselves that the purpose of dreams is wish-fulfilment, and that the wish to be a man is frequently met with in women, whether they are conscious of it or not. Further, no one familiar with anatomy will be misled by supposing that it is impossible for a woman to realize this wish by sensations similar to those of a man, for the woman's sexual organs include a small one which resembles the penis, and this little organ, the clitoris, does actually play during childhood and in the years before sexual intercourse the same part as the large male organ.

Male sexual symbols less easy to understand are certain *reptiles and fishes:* above all, the famous symbol of the *serpent.* Why *hats and cloaks* are used in the same way is certainly difficult to divine, but their symbolic meaning is quite unquestionable. Finally, it may be asked whether the representation of the male organ by some other member, such as the *hand* or the *foot,* may be termed symbolic. I think the context in which this is wont to occur, and the female counterparts with which we meet, force this conclusion upon us.

The female genitalia are symbolically represented by all such objects as share with them the property of enclosing a space or are capable of acting as receptacles: such as *pits, hollows and caves,* and also *jars and bottles,* and *boxes* of all sorts and sizes, *chests, coffers, pockets,* and so forth. *Ships* too come into this category. Many symbols refer rather to the uterus than to the other genital organs: thus *cupboards, stoves* and, above all, *rooms.* Room symbolism here links up with that of houses, whilst *doors and gates* represent the genital opening. Moreover, material of different kinds is a symbol of woman—*wood, paper,* and objects made of these, such as *tables* and *books.* From the animal world, *snails and mussels* at any rate must be cited as unmistakable female symbols; of the parts of the body, the *mouth* as a representation of the genital opening, and, amongst buildings, *churches and chapels* are symbols of a woman. You see that all these symbols are not equally easy to understand.

The breasts must be included amongst the organs of sex; these, as well as the larger hemispheres of the female body, are represented by *apples, peaches and fruit* in general. The pubic hair in both sexes is indicated in dreams by *woods and thickets.* The complicated topography of the female sexual organs accounts for their often being represented by a *landscape* with rocks, woods and water, whilst the imposing mechanism of the male sexual apparatus lends it to symbolization by all kinds of complicated and indescribable *machinery.*

Yet another noteworthy symbol of the female genital organ is a *jewel case,* whilst *jewel* and *treasure* are used also in dreams to represent the beloved person,[1] and *sweetmeats* frequently stand for sexual pleasures. Gratification derived from a person's own genitals is indicated by any kind of *play,* including playing the piano. The symbolic representation of onanism by *sliding or gliding* and also by *pulling off a branch* is very typical. A particularly remarkable dream-symbol is the *falling out* or *extraction of teeth;* the primary significance of this is certainly castration as a punishment for onanism. Special representations of sexual intercourse are less frequent in dreams than we should expect after all this, but we may mention in this connection rhythmical activities such as *dancing, riding* and *climbing,* and also *experiencing some violence,* e.g., being run over. To these may be added certain manual occupations, and of course being threatened with weapons.

You must not imagine that these symbols are either employed or translated quite simply: on

[1] Cf. sweetheart, sweetest.—TR.

all sides we meet with what we do not expect. For instance, it seems hardly credible that there is often no sharp discrimination of the different sexes in these symbolic representations. Many symbols stand for sexual organs in general, whether male or female: for instance, a *little* child, or a *little* son or daughter. At another time a symbol which is generally a male one may be used to denote the female sexual organ, or vice versa. This is incomprehensible until we have acquired some knowledge of the development of conceptions about sexuality amongst human beings. In many cases this ambiguity of the symbols may be apparent rather than real; and moreover, the most striking amongst them, such as weapons, pockets and chests, are never used bisexually in this way.

I will now give a brief account, beginning with the symbols themselves instead of with the objects symbolized, to show you from what spheres the sexual symbols have for the most part been derived, and I will add a few remarks relating particularly to those in which the attribute in common with the thing symbolized is hard to detect. An instance of an obscure symbol of this kind is the *hat,* or perhaps head-coverings in general; this usually has a masculine significance, though occasionally a feminine one. In the same way a *cloak* betokens a man, though perhaps sometimes without special reference to the organs of sex. It is open to you to ask why this should be so. A *tie,* being an object which hangs down and is not worn by women is clearly a male symbol, whilst *underlinen* and *linen* in general stands for the female. *Clothes and uniforms,* as we have heard, represent nakedness or the human form; *shoes and slippers* symbolize the female genital organs. *Tables and wood* we have mentioned as being puzzling, but nevertheless certain, female symbols; the *act of mounting* ladders, steep places or stairs is indubitably symbolic of sexual intercourse. On closer reflection we shall notice that the rhythmic character of this climbing is the point in common between the two, and perhaps also the accompanying increase in excitation—the shortening of the breath as the climber ascends.

We have already recognized that *landscapes* represent the female sexual organs; mountains and rocks are symbols of the male organ; *gardens,* a frequently occurring symbol of the female genitalia. *Fruit* stands for the breasts, not for a child. *Wild animals* denote human beings whose senses are excited, and, hence, evil impulses or passions. *Blossoms and flowers* represent the female sexual organs, more particularly, in virginity. In this connection you will recollect that the blossoms are really the sexual organs of plants.

We already know how rooms are used symbolically. This representation may be extended, so that *windows and doors* (entrances and exits from rooms) come to mean the openings of the body; the fact of rooms being *open or closed* also accords with this symbolism: the *key*, which opens them, is certainly a male symbol.

This is some material for a study of dream-symbolism. It is not complete, and could be both extended and made deeper. However, I think it will seem to you more than enough; perhaps you may dislike it. You will ask: "Do I then really live in the midst of sexual symbols? Are all the objects round me, all the clothes I wear, all the things I handle, always sexual symbols and nothing else?" There really is good reason for surprised questions, and the first of these would be: How do we profess to arrive at the meaning of these dream-symbols, about which the dreamer himself can give us little or no information.

My answer is that we derive our knowledge from widely different sources: from fairy tales and myths, jokes and witticisms, from folklore, i.e., from what we know of the manners and customs, sayings and songs, of different peoples, and from poetic and colloquial usage of language. Everywhere in these various fields the same symbolism occurs, and in many of them we can understand it without being taught anything about it. If we consider these various sources individually, we shall find so many parallels to dream-symbolism that we are bound to be convinced of the correctness of our interpretations.

The human body is, we said, according to Scherner frequently symbolized in dreams by a house; by an extension of this symbolism, windows, doors and gates stand for the entrances to cavities in the body, and the façades may either be smooth or may have balconies and ledges to hold on to. The same symbolism is met with in colloquialisms; for instance, we speak of *a thatch of hair*, or a *tile hat*, or say of someone that he is not right *in the upper storey*. In anatomy, too, we speak of the openings of the body as its *portals*.

We may at first find it surprising that parents appear in our dreams as kings and emperors and their consorts, but we have a parallel to this in fairy tales. Does it not begin to dawn upon us that the many fairy tales which begin with the words "Once upon a time there were a king and queen" simply mean: "Once upon a time there were a father and mother"? In family life the children are sometimes spoken of jestingly as *princes*, and the eldest son as the *crown prince*. The king himself is called the *father* of his people. Again, in some parts, little children are often playfully spoken of as *little animals*, e.g., in Cornwall, as *little toad*, or in Germany as *little worm*, and, in sympathizing with a child, Germans say *poor little worm*.

Now let us return to the house symbolism. When in our dreams we make use of the projections of houses as supports, does that not suggest a well-known, popular German saying, with reference to a woman with a markedly developed bust: "She has something for one to hold on to" *(Die hat etwas zum Anhalten)*, whilst another colloquialism in the same connection is: "She has plenty of wood in front of her house" *(Die hat vied Holz vor dem Hause)*, as though our interpretation were to be borne out by this when we say that wood is a female maternal symbol.

There is still something to be said on the subject of wood. It is not easy to see why wood should have come to represent a woman or mother, but here a comparison of different languages may be useful to us. The German word *Holz* (wood) is said to be derived from the same root as the Greek ὕλη, which means *stuff*, raw material. This would be an instance of a process which is by no means rare, in that a general name for material has come finally to be applied to a particular material only. Now, in the Atlantic Ocean, there is an island named Madeira, and this name was given to it by the Portuguese when they discovered it, because at that time it was covered with dense forests; for in Portuguese the word for wood is *madeira*. But you cannot fail to notice that this *madeira* is merely a modified form of the Latin *materia*, which again signifies material in general. Now *materia* is derived from *mater* = mother, and the material out of which anything is made may be conceived of as giving birth to it. So, in the symbolic use of wood to represent woman or mother, we have a survival of this old idea.

Birth is regularly expressed by some connection with water: we are plunging into or emerging from water, that is to say, we give birth or are being born. Now let us not forget that this symbol has a twofold reference to the actual facts of evolution. Not only are all land mammals, from which the human race itself has sprung, descended from creatures inhabiting the water—this is the more remote of the two considerations—but also every single mammal, every human being, has passed the first phase of existence in water—that is to say, as an embryo in the amniotic fluid of the mother's womb—and thus, at birth, emerged from water. I do not maintain that the dreamer knows this; on the other hand, I contend that there is no need for him to know it. He probably knows something else from having been told it as a child, but even this, I will maintain, has contributed nothing to symbol-formation. The child is told in the nursery that the stork brings the babies, but then where does it get them? Out of a pond or a well—again, out of the water. One of my patients who had been told this as a child (a little count, as he was then) afterwards disappeared for a whole afternoon, and was at last found lying at the edge of the castle lake, with his little face bent over the clear water, eagerly gazing to see whether he could catch sight of the babies at the bottom of the water.

In the myths of the births of heroes, a comparative study of which has been made by O. Rank—the earliest is that of King Sargon of Akkad, about 2800 B.C.—exposure in water and rescue from it play a major part. Rank perceived that this symbolizes birth in a manner analogous to that employed in dreams. When anyone in his dream rescues somebody from the water, he makes that person into his mother, or at any rate *a* mother; and in mythology, whoever rescues a child from water confesses herself to be its real mother. There is a well-known joke in which an intelligent Jewish boy, when asked who was the mother of Moses, answers immediately: "The Princess." He is told: "No, she only took him out of the water." "That's what *she* said," he replies, showing that he had hit upon the right interpretation of the myth.

Going away on a journey stands in dreams for dying; similarly, it is the custom in the nursery, when a child asks questions as to the whereabouts of someone who has died and whom he misses, to tell him that that person has "gone away." Here again, I deprecate the idea that the dream-symbol has its origin in this evasive reply to the child. The poet uses the same symbol when he speaks of the other side as "the undiscovered country from whose bourne *no traveller* returns." Again, in everyday speech it is quite usual to speak of the "last journey," and everyone who is acquainted with ancient rites knows how seriously the idea of a journey into the land of the dead was taken, for instance, in ancient Egyptian belief. In many cases the *Book of the Dead* survives, which was given to the mummy, like a Baedeker, to take with him on the last journey. Since burial-grounds have been placed at a distance from the houses of the living, the last journey of the dead has indeed become a reality.

Nor does sexual symbolism belong only to dreams. You will all know the expression *a baggage* as applied contemptuously to a woman, but perhaps people do not know that they are using a genital symbol. In the New Testament we read: "The woman is the weaker *vessel.*" The sacred writings of the Jews, the style of which so closely approaches that of poetry, are full of expressions symbolic of sex, which have not always been correctly interpreted and the exegesis of which, e.g., in the Song of Solomon, has led to many misunderstandings.[1] In later Hebrew literature the woman is very frequently represented by a house, the door standing for the genital opening; thus a man complains, when he finds a woman no longer a virgin, that "he has found the door open." The symbol *table* for a woman also occurs in this literature; the woman says of her husband "I spread the table for him, but he overturned it." Lame children are said to owe their infirmity to the fact that the man "overturned the table." I quote here from a treatise by L. Levy in Brünn: *Sexual Symbolism in the Bible and the Talmud.*

That ships in dreams signify women is a belief in which we are supported by the etymologists, who assert that *ship (Schiff)* was originally the name of an earthen vessel and is the same word as *Schaff* (a tub or wooden vessel). That an oven stands for a woman or the mother's womb is an interpretation confirmed by the Greek story of Periander of Corinth and his wife Melissa. According to the version of Herodotus, the tyrant adjured the shade of his wife, whom he had loved passionately but had murdered out of jealousy, to tell him something about herself, whereupon the dead woman identified herself by reminding him that he, Periander, "had put his bread into a cold oven," thus expressing in a disguised form a circumstance of which everyone else was ignorant. In the *Anthropophyteia*, edited by F. S. Kraus, a work which is an indispensable textbook on

[1] e. g., Song of Sol. 8. 10.

everything concerning the sexual life of different peoples, we read that in a certain part of Germany people say of a woman who is delivered of a child that "her oven has fallen to pieces." The kindling of fire and everything connected with this is permeated through and through with sexual symbolism, the flame always standing for the male organ, and the fireplace or the hearth for the womb of the woman.

If you have chanced to wonder at the frequency with which landscapes are used in dreams to symbolize the female sexual organs, you may learn from mythologists how large a part has been played in the ideas and cults of ancient times by *Mother Earth* and how the whole conception of agriculture was determined by this symbolism. The fact that in dreams a room represents a woman you may be inclined to trace to the German colloquialism by which *Frauenzimmer* (*lit.* woman's room) is used for *Frau*, that is to say, the human person is represented by the place assigned for her occupation. Similarly we speak of the Porte, meaning thereby the Sultan and his government, and the name of the ancient Egyptian ruler, Pharaoh, merely means *great court*. (In the ancient Orient the courts between the double gates of the city were places of assembly, like the marketplace in classical times.) But I think this derivation is too superficial, and it strikes me as more probable that the room came to symbolize woman on account of its property of enclosing within it the human being. We have already met with the house in this sense; from mythology and poetry we may take towns, citadels, castles and fortresses to be further symbols for women. It would be easy to decide the point by reference to the dreams of people who neither speak nor understand German. Of late years I have mainly treated foreign patients, and I think I recollect that in their dreams rooms stand in the same way for women, even though there is no word analogous to our *Frauenzimmer* in their language. There are other indications that symbolism may transcend the boundaries of language, a fact already maintained by the old dream-investigator, Schubert, in 1862. Nevertheless, none of my patients were wholly ignorant of German, so that I must leave this question to be decided by those analysts who can collect instances in other countries from persons who speak only one language.[1]

Amongst the symbols for the male sexual organ, there is scarcely one which does not appear in jests, or in vulgar or poetic phrases,

[1] This is certainly so with English patients.—TR.

especially in the old classical poets. Here, however, we meet not only with such symbols as occur in dreams but also with new ones, e.g., the *implements* employed in various kinds of work, first and foremost, the *plough*. Moreover, when we come to male symbols, we tread on very extensive and much-contested ground which, in order not to waste time, we will avoid. I should just like to devote a few remarks to the one symbol which stands, as it were, by itself; I refer to the number *three*. Whether this number does not in all probability owe its sacred character to its symbolic significance is a question which we must leave undecided, but it seems certain that many tripartite natural objects, e.g., the clover-leaf, are used in coats-of-arms and as emblems on account of their symbolism. The so-called "French" lily with its three parts and, again, the *trisceles*, that curious coat-of-arms of two such widely separated islands as Sicily and the Isle of Man (a figure consisting of three bent legs projecting from a central point), are supposed to be merely disguised forms of the male sexual organ, images of which were believed in ancient times to be the most powerful means of warding off evil influences *(apotropaea)*; connected with this is the fact that the lucky *charms* of our own time may all be easily recognized as genital or sexual symbols. Let us consider a collection of such charms in the form of tiny silver pendants: a four-leaved clover, a pig, a mushroom, a horseshoe, a ladder and a chimney-sweep. The four-leaved clover has taken the place of that with three leaves, which was really more appropriate for the purpose of symbolism; the pig is an ancient symbol of fruitfulness; the mushroom undoubtedly symbolizes the penis, there are mushrooms which derive their name from their unmistakable resemblance to that organ *(Phallus impudicus)*; the horseshoe reproduces the contour of the female genital opening; while the chimney-sweep with his ladder belongs to this company because his occupation is one which is vulgarly compared with sexual intercourse. (Cf. *Anthropophyteia.*) We have learnt to recognize his ladder in dreams as a sexual symbol: expressions in language show what a completely sexual significance the word *steigen* (to mount) has, as in the phrases: *Den Frauen nachsteigen* (to run after women) and *ein alter Steiger* (an old roué). So, in French, where the word for *step* is *la marche*, we find the quite analogous expression for an old rake: *un vieux marcheur*. Probably the fact that with many of the larger animals sexual intercourse necessitates a mounting or *climbing upon* the female has something to do with this association of ideas.

Pulling off a branch to symbolize onanism is not only in agreement with vulgar descriptions of that act, but also has far-reaching parallels in mythology. But especially remarkable is the representation of onanism, or rather of castration as the punishment for onanism, by the falling-out or extraction of teeth; for we find in folk-lore a counterpart to this which could only be known to very few dreamers. I think that there can be no doubt that circumcision, a practice common to so many peoples, is an equivalent and replacement of castration. And recently we have learnt that certain aboriginal tribes in Australia practice circumcision as a rite to mark the attaining of puberty (at the celebration of the boy's coming of age), whilst other tribes living quite near have substituted for this practice that of knocking out a tooth.

I will end my account with these examples. They are only examples; we know more about this subject and you can imagine how much richer and more interesting a collection of this sort might be made, not by dilettanti like ourselves, but by real experts in mythology, anthropology, philology and folk-lore. We are forced to certain conclusions, which cannot be exhaustive, but nevertheless will give us plenty to think about.

In the first place, we are confronted with the fact that the dreamer has at his command a symbolic mode of expression of which he knows nothing, and does not even recognize, in his waking life. This is as amazing as if you made the discovery that your housemaid understood Sanscrit, though you know that she was born in a Bohemian village and had never learnt that language. It is not easy to bring this fact into line with our views on psychology. We can only say that the dreamer's knowledge of symbolism is unconscious and belongs to his unconscious mental life, but even this assumption does not help us much. Up till now we have only had to assume the existence of unconscious tendencies which are temporarily or permanently unknown to us; but now the question is a bigger one and we have actually to believe in unconscious knowledge, thought-relations, and comparisons between different objects, in virtue of which one idea can constantly be substituted for another. These comparisons are not instituted afresh every time, but are ready to hand, perfect for all time; this we infer from their

identity in different persons, even probably in spite of linguistic differences.

Whence is our knowledge of this symbolism derived? The usages of speech cover only a small part of it, whilst the manifold parallels in other fields are for the most part unknown to the dreamer; we ourselves had to collate them laboriously in the first instance.

In the second place, these symbolic relations are not peculiar to the dreamer or to the dream-work by which they are expressed, for we have discovered that the same symbolism is employed in myths and fairy tales, in popular sayings and songs, in colloquial speech and poetic phantasy. The province of symbolism is extraordinarily wide: dream-symbolism is only a small part of it; it would not even be expedient to attack the whole problem from the side of dreams. Many of the symbols commonly occurring elsewhere either do not appear in dreams at all or appear very seldom; on the other hand, many of the dream-symbols are not met with in every other department, but, as you have seen, only here and there. We get the impression that here we have to do with an ancient but obsolete mode of expression, of which different fragments have survived in different fields, one here only, another there only, a third in various spheres perhaps in slightly different forms. At this point I am reminded of the phantasy of a very interesting insane patient, who had imagined a *primordial language (Grundsprache)* of which all these symbols were survivals.

In the third place, it must strike you that the symbolism occurring in the other fields I have named is by no means confined to sexual themes, whereas in dreams the symbols are almost exclusively used to represent sexual objects and relations. This again is hard to account for. Are we to suppose that symbols originally of sexual significance were later employed differently and that perhaps the decline from symbolic to other modes of representation is connected with this? It is obviously impossible to answer these questions by dealing only with dream-symbolism; all we can do is to hold fast to the supposition that there is a specially close relation between true symbols and sexuality.

An important clue in this connection has recently been given to us in the view expressed by a philologist (H. Sperber, of Upsala, who works independently of psycho-analysis), that sexual needs have had the largest share in the origin and development of language. He says that the first sounds uttered were a means of communication, and of summoning the sexual partner, and that, in the later development, the elements of speech were used as an accompaniment to the different kinds of work carried on by primitive man. This work was performed by associated efforts, to the sound of rhythmically repeated utterances, the effect of which was to transfer a sexual interest to the work. Primitive man thus made his work agreeable, so to speak, by treating it as the equivalent of and substitute for sexual activities. The word uttered during the communal work had therefore two meanings, the one referring to the sexual act, the other to the labour which had come to be equivalent to it. In time the word was dissociated from its sexual significance and its application confined to the work. Generations later the same thing happened to a new word with a sexual signification, which was then applied to a new form of work. In this way a number of root-words arose which were all of sexual origin but had all lost their sexual meaning. If the statement here outlined be correct, a possibility at least of understanding dream-symbolism opens out before us. We should comprehend why it is that in dreams, which retain something of these primitive conditions, there is such an extraordinarily large number of sexual symbols; and why weapons and tools in general stand for the male, and materials and things worked on for the female. The symbolic relations would then be the survival of the old identity in words; things which once had the same name as the genitalia could now appear in dreams as symbolizing them.

Further, our parallels to dream-symbolism may assist you to appreciate what it is in psycho-analysis which makes it a subject of general interest, in a way that was not possible to either psychology or psychiatry; psycho-analytic work is so closely intertwined with so many other branches of science, the investigation of which gives promise of the most valuable conclusions: with mythology, philology, folk-lore, folk psychology and the study of religion. You will not be surprised to hear that a publication has sprung from psycho-analytic soil, of which the exclusive object is to foster these relations. I refer to *Imago*, first published in 1912 and edited by Hans Sachs and Otto Rank. In its relation to all these other subjects, psycho-analysis has in the first instance given rather than received. True, analysis reaps the advantage of receiving confirmation of its own results, seemingly so strange,

again in other fields; but on the whole it is psycho-analysis which supplies the technical methods and the points of view, the application of which is to prove fruitful in these other provinces. The mental life of the human individual yields, under psycho-analytic investigation, explanations which solve many a riddle in the life of the masses of mankind or at any rate can show these problems in their true light.

I have still given you no idea of the circumstances in which we may arrive at the deepest insight into that hypothetical *primordial language,* or of the province in which it is for the most part retained. As long as you do not know this you cannot appreciate the true significance of the whole subject. I refer to the province of neurosis; the material is found in the symptoms and other modes of expression of nervous patients, for the explanation and treatment of which psycho-analysis was indeed devised.

My fourth point of view takes us back to the place from which we started and leads into the track we have already marked out. We said that even if there were no dream-censorship we should still find it difficult to interpret dreams, for we should then be confronted with the task of translating the symbolic language of dreams into the language of waking life. SYMBOLISM, then, is a second and independent factor in dream-distortion, existing side by side with the censorship. But the conclusion is obvious that it suits the censorship to make use of symbolism, in that both serve the same purpose: that of making the dream strange and incomprehensible.

Whether a further study of the dream will not introduce us to yet another contributing factor in the distortion, we shall soon see. But I must not leave the subject of dream-symbolism without once more touching on the puzzling fact that it has succeeded in rousing such strenuous opposition amongst educated persons, although the prevalence of symbolism in myth, religion, art and language is beyond all doubt. Is it not probable that, here again, the reason is to be found in its relation to sexuality?

ELEVENTH LECTURE
THE DREAM WORK

When you have successfully grasped the dream-censorship and symbolic representation, you will not, it is true, have mastered dream-distortion in its entirety, but you will nevertheless be in a position to understand most dreams.

To do so, you will make use of the two complementary methods: you will call up the dreamer's associations till you have penetrated from the substitute to the thought proper for which it stands, and you will supply the meaning of the symbols from your own knowledge of the subject. We will speak later of certain doubtful points which may arise in the process.

We can now return to a task which we attempted earlier with inadequate equipment, when we were studying the relations between dream-elements and the thoughts proper underlying them. We then determined the existence of four such main relations: substitution of the part for the whole, hints or allusions, symbolic connection, and plastic word-representation (images). We will now try to deal with this subject on a larger scale, by a comparison of the *manifest* dream-content as a whole with the *latent* dream as laid bare by our interpretation.

I hope you will never again confuse these two things. If you succeed in distinguishing between them, you will have advanced further towards an understanding of dreams than in all probability most of the readers of my *Interpretation of Dreams* have done. Let me again remind you that *the process by which the latent dream is transformed into the manifest dream is called* THE DREAM-WORK; while the reverse process, which seeks to progress from the manifest to the latent thoughts, is our work of interpretation; the work of interpretation therefore aims at demolishing the dream-work. In dreams of the infantile type in which the obvious wish-fulfilments are easily recognized, the process of dream-work has nevertheless been operative to some extent, for the wish has been transformed into a reality and, usually, the thoughts also into visual images. Here no interpretation is necessary; we only have to retrace both these transformations. The further operations of the dream-work, as seen in the other types of dreams, we call *dream-distortion,* and here the original ideas have to be restored by our interpretative work.

Having had the opportunity of comparing many dream-interpretations, I am in a position to give you a comprehensive account of the manner in which the dream-work deals with the material of the latent dream-thoughts. But please do not expect to understand too much: it is a piece of description which should be listened to quietly and attentively.

The first achievement of the dream-work is CONDENSATION; by this term we mean to con-

vey the fact that the content of the manifest dream is less rich than that of the latent thoughts, is, as it were, a kind of abbreviated translation of the latter. Now and again condensation may be lacking, but it is present as a rule and is often carried to a very high degree. It never works in the opposite manner, i.e., it never happens that the manifest dream is wider in range or richer in content than is the latent dream. Condensation is accomplished in the following ways: (1) certain latent elements are altogether omitted; (2) of many complexes in the latent dream only a fragment passes over into the manifest content; (3) latent elements sharing some common characteristic are in the manifest dream put together, blended into a single whole.

If you prefer to do so, you can reserve the term "condensation" for this last process, the effects of which are particularly easy to demonstrate. Taking your own dreams, you will be able without any trouble to recall instances of the condensation of different persons into a single figure. Such a composite figure resembles A in appearance, but is dressed like B, pursues some occupation which recalls C, and yet all the time you know that it is really D. The composite picture serves, of course, to lay special emphasis upon some characteristic common to the four people. And it is possible also for a composite picture to be formed with objects or places, as with persons, provided only that the single objects or places have some common attribute upon which the latent dream lays stress. It is as though a new and fugitive concept were formed, of which the common attribute is the kernel. From the superimposing of the separate parts which undergo condensation there usually results a blurred and indistinct picture, as if several photographs had been taken on the same plate.

The formation of such composite figures must be of great importance in the dream-work, for we can prove that the common properties necessary to their formation are purposely manufactured where at first sight they would seem to be lacking, as, for example, by the choice of some particular verbal expression for a thought. We have already met with instances of condensation and composite-formation of this sort; they played an important part in originating many slips of the tongue. You will remember the case of the young man who wished to "insort" a lady (*beleidigen* = "insult," *begleiten* = "escort," composite word *begleitdigen*). Besides, there are jokes in which the technique is traceable to condensation of this sort. Apart from this, however, we may venture to assert that this process is something quite unusual and strange. It is true that in many a creation of phantasy we meet with counterparts to the formation of the composite persons of our dreams, component parts which do not belong to one another in reality being readily united into a single whole by phantasy, as, for instance, in the centaurs and fabulous animals of ancient mythology or of Boecklin's pictures. *Creative* phantasy can, in fact, invent nothing new, but can only regroup elements from different sources. But the peculiar thing about the way in which the dream-work proceeds is this: its material consists of thoughts, some of which may be objectionable and disagreeable, but which nevertheless are correctly formed and expressed. The dream-work transmutes these thoughts into another form, and it is curious and incomprehensible that in this process of translation—of rendering them, as it were, into another script or language—the means of blending and combining are employed. The translator's endeavour in other cases must surely be to respect the distinctions observed in the text, and especially to differentiate between things which are similar but not the same; the dream-work, on the contrary, strives to condense two different thoughts by selecting, after the manner of wit, an ambiguous word which can suggest both thoughts. We must not expect to understand this characteristic straightaway, but it may assume great significance for our conception of the dream-work.

Although condensation renders the dream obscure, yet it does not give the impression of being an effect of the dream-censorship. Rather we should be inclined to trace it to mechanical or economic factors; nevertheless the censorship's interests are served by it.

What condensation can achieve is sometimes quite extraordinary: by this device it is at times possible for two completely different latent trains of thought to be united in a single manifest dream, so that we arrive at an apparently adequate interpretation of a dream and yet overlook a second possible meaning.

Moreover, one of the effects of condensation upon the relationship between the manifest and the latent dream is that the connection between the elements of the one and of the other nowhere remains a simple one; for by a kind of interlacing a manifest element represents simultaneously several latent ones and, conversely, a latent thought may enter into several manifest elements. Again, when we come to interpret dreams, we see that the associations to a single manifest element do not commonly make their appearance in orderly succession; we often have to wait until we have the interpretation of the whole dream.

The dream-work, then, follows a very unusual mode of transcription for the dream-thoughts; not a translation, word for word, or sign for sign; nor yet a process of selection according to some definite rule, for instance, as though the consonants only of the words were reproduced and the vowels omitted; nor again what one might call a process of representation, one element being always picked out to represent several others. It works by a different and much more complicated method.

The second achievement of the dream-work is DISPLACEMENT. Fortunately here we are not breaking perfectly fresh ground; indeed, we know that it is entirely the work of the dream-censorship. Displacement takes two forms; first, a latent element may be *replaced*, not by a part of itself, but by something more remote, something of the nature of an allusion; and, secondly, the *accent* may be transferred from an important element to another which is unimportant, so that the centre of the dream is shifted as it were, giving the dream a foreign appearance.

Substitution by allusion is familiar to us in our waking thoughts also, but with a difference; for it is essential in the latter that the allusion should be easily comprehensible, and that the content of the substitute should be associated to that of the thought proper. Allusion is also frequently employed in wit, where the condition of association in content is dispensed with and replaced by unfamiliar external associations, such as similarity of sound, ambiguity of meaning, etc. The condition of comprehensibility, however, is observed: the joke would lose all its point if we could not recognize without any effort what is the actual thing to which the allusion is made. But in dreams allusion by displacement is unrestricted by either limitation. It is connected most superficially and most remotely with the element for which it stands, and for that reason is not readily comprehensible; and, when the connection is traced, the interpretation gives the impression of an unsuccessful joke or of a *forced*, far-fetched and *dragged in* explanation. The object of the dream-censorship is only obtained when it has succeeded in making it impossible to trace the thought proper back from the allusion.

Displacement of accent is not a legitimate device, if our object be the expression of thought; though we do sometimes admit it in waking life in order to produce a comic effect. I can to some extent convey to you the impression of confusion which then results, by reminding you of an anecdote, according to which there was in a certain village a smith who had committed a capital offence. The court decided that the smith was guilty; but, since he was the only one of his trade in the village and therefore indispensable, whereas there were three tailors living there, one of these three was hanged in his place!

The third achievement of the dream-work is the most interesting from the psychological point of view. It consists in the transformation of thoughts into *visual images*. Let us be quite clear that not everything in the dream-thoughts is thus transformed; much keeps its original form and appears also in the manifest dream as thought or knowledge, on the part of the dreamer; again, translation of them into visual images is not the only possible transformation of thoughts. But it is nevertheless the essential feature in the formation of dreams, and, as we know, this part of the dream-work is, if we except one other case, the least subject to variation; for single dream-elements, moreover, *plastic word-representation* is a process already familiar to us.

Obviously this achievement is by no means an easy one. In order to get some idea of its difficulty, imagine that you had undertaken to replace a political leading article in a newspaper by a series of illustrations; you would have to abandon alphabetic characters in favour of hieroglyphics. The people and concrete objects mentioned in the article could be easily represented, perhaps even more satisfactorily, in pictorial form; but you would expect to meet with difficulties when you came to the portrayal of all the abstract words and all those parts of speech which indicate relations between the various thoughts, e.g., particles, conjunctions, and so forth. With the abstract words you would employ all manner of devices: for instance, you would try to render the text of the article into other words, more unfamiliar perhaps, but made up of parts more concrete and therefore more capable of such representation. This will remind you of the fact that most abstract words were originally concrete, their original significance having faded; and therefore you will fall back on the original concrete meaning of these words wherever possible. So

you will be glad that you can represent the *possessing* of an object as a literal, physical *sitting upon* it (possess = *potis+sedeo*). This is just how the dream-work proceeds. In such circumstances you can hardly demand great accuracy of representation, neither will you quarrel with the dream-work for replacing an element which is difficult to reduce to pictorial form, such as the idea of breaking marriage vows, by some other kind of breaking, e.g., that of an arm or leg.[1] In this way you will to some extent succeed in overcoming the awkwardness of rendering alphabetic characters into hieroglyphs.

When you come to represent those parts of speech which indicate thought-relations, e.g., *because, therefore, but,* and so on, you have no such means as those described to assist you; so that these parts of the text must be lost, so far as your translation into pictorial form is concerned. Similarly, the content of the dream-

[1] Whilst correcting these pages, my eye happened to fall upon a newspaper paragraph which I reproduce here as affording unexpected confirmation of the above words.

DIVINE RETRIBUTION

A BROKEN ARM FOR A BROKEN MARRIAGE-VOW

Frau Anna M, the wife of a soldier in the reserve, accused Frau Clementine K of unfaithfulness to her husband. In her accusation she stated that Frau K had had an illicit relationship with Karl M during her husband's absence at the front, while he was sending her as much as 70 crowns a month. Besides this, she had already received a large sum of money from her (Frau M's) husband, while his wife and children had to live in hunger and misery. Some of her husband's comrades had informed her that he and Frau K had visited public-houses together and remained there drinking late into the night. The accused woman had once actually asked the husband of the accuser, in the presence of several soldiers, whether he would not soon leave his "old woman" and come to her, and the caretaker of the house where Frau K lived had repeatedly seen the plaintiff's husband in Frau K's room, in a state of complete undress.

Yesterday, before a magistrate in the Leopoldstadt, Frau K denied knowing M at all: any intimate relations between them were out of the question, she said.

Albertine M, a witness, however, gave evidence of having surprised Frau K in the act of kissing the accuser's husband.

M, who had been called as a witness in some earlier proceedings, had then denied any intimate relations with the accused. Yesterday, a letter was handed to the magistrate, in which the witness retracted his former denial and confessed that up to the previous June he had carried on illicit relations with Frau K. In the earlier proceedings he had denied his relations with the accused only because she had come to him before the action came into court and begged him on her knees to save her and say nothing. "To-day," wrote the witness, "I feel compelled to lay a full confession before the court, for I have broken my left arm and regard this as God's punishment for my offence."

The judge decided that the penal offence had been committed too long ago for the action to stand, whereupon the accuser withdrew her accusation and the accused was discharged.

thoughts is resolved by the dream-work into its "raw material," consisting of objects and activities. You may be satisfied if there is any possibility of indicating somehow, by a more minute elaboration of the images, certain relations which cannot be represented in themselves. In a precisely similar manner, the dream-work succeeds in expressing much of the content of the latent thoughts by means of peculiarities in the *form* of the manifest dream, by its distinctness or obscurity, its division into various parts, etc. The number of parts into which a dream is divided corresponds as a rule with the number of its main themes, the successive trains of thought in the latent dream; a short preliminary dream often stands in an introductory or casual relation to the subsequent detailed main dream; whilst a subordinate dream-thought is represented by the interpolation into the manifest dream of a change of scene, and so on. The form of dreams, then, is by no means unimportant in itself, and itself demands interpretation. Several dreams in the same night often have the same meaning, and indicate an endeavour to control more and more completely a stimulus of increasing urgency. In a single dream, a specially difficult element may be represented by *doubling* it, i.e., by more than one symbol.

If we continue the comparison of dream-thoughts with the manifest dreams representing them, we discover in all directions things we should never have expected, e.g., that even nonsense and absurdity in dreams have their meaning; in fact, at this point the contrast between the medical and the psycho-analytic view of dreams becomes more marked than ever before. According to the medical view, the dream is absurd because while dreaming our mental activity has renounced its functions; according to our view, on the other hand, the dream becomes absurd when it has to represent a criticism implicit in the latent thoughts—the opinion: "It is absurd." The dream I told you, about the visit to the theatre ("three tickets for one florin and a half") is a good example of this: the opinion thus expressed was as follows: "It was *absurd* to marry so early."

Similarly, we find out when we interpret dreams what is the real meaning of the doubts and uncertainties, so frequently mentioned by dreamers, whether a certain element did actually appear in the dream, whether it was really this and not rather something else. As a rule, there is nothing in the latent thoughts corresponding with these doubts and uncertainties; they originate wholly through the operation of the censorship and are comparable to a not entirely successful attempt at erasure.

One of our most surprising discoveries is the manner in which *opposites* in the latent dream are dealt with by the dream-work. We know already that points of agreement in the latent material are replaced by condensation in the manifest dream. Now contraries are treated in just the same way as similarities, with a marked preference for expression by means of the *same* manifest element. An element in the manifest dream which admits of an opposite may stand simply for itself, or for its opposite, or for both together; only the sense can decide which translation is to be chosen. It accords with this that there is no representation of a *No* in dreams, or at least none which is not ambiguous.

A welcome analogy to this strange behaviour of the dream-work is furnished in the development of language. Many philologists have maintained that in the oldest languages opposites such as: strong—weak, light—dark, large —small, were expressed by the same root word (*antithetical sense of primal words*). Thus, in old Egyptian *ken* stood originally for both "strong" and "weak." In speaking, misunderstanding was guarded against in the use of such ambivalent words by the intonation and accompanying gestures; in writing, by the addition of a so-called "determinative," that is to say, of a picture which was not meant to be expressed orally. Thus, *ken* = "strong" was written in such a way that after the letters there was a picture of a little man standing upright; when *ken* meant "weak," there was added the picture of a man in a slack, crouching attitude. Only at a later period did the two opposite meanings of the same primal word come to be designated in two different ways by slight modifications of the original. Thus, from *ken* meaning "strong—weak" were derived two words: *ken* = "strong" and *kan* = "weak." Nor is it only the oldest languages, in the last stages of their development, which have retained many survivals of these early words capable of meaning either of two opposites, but the same is true of much younger languages, even those which are today still living. I will quote some illustrations of this taken from the work of C. Abel (1884):

In Latin, such ambivalent words are:

altus = high or deep. *sacer* = sacred or accursed.

As examples of modifications of the original root, I quote:

clamare = to shout. *clam* = quietly, silently, secretly.

     siccus=dry. *succus*=juice.

and, in German: *Stimme* = voice. *stumm* = dumb.

A comparison of kindred languages yields a large number of examples:

English: lock=to shut. German: *Loch*=hole. *Lücke* = gap.
English: cleave.[1] German: *kleben*=to stick, adhere.

The English word "without," originally carrying with it both a positive and a negative connotation, is today used in the negative sense only, but it is clear that "with" has the signification, not merely of "adding to," but of "depriving of," from the compounds "withdraw," "withhold" (cf. the German *wieder*).

Yet another peculiarity of the dream-work has its counterpart in the development of language. In ancient Egyptian, as well as in other later languages, the sequence of sounds was transposed so as to result in different words for the same fundamental idea. Examples of this kind of parallels between English and German words may be quoted:

Topf (pot)—pot. Boat—tub. Hurry—*Ruhe* (rest).
Balken (beam)—*Kloben* (club). wait—*täuwen* (to wait).

Parallels between Latin and German:

capere—packen (to seize). *ren—Niere* (kidney).

Such transpositions as have taken place here in the case of single words are made by the dream-work in a variety of ways. The inversion of the meaning, i.e., substitution by the opposite, is a device with which we are already familiar; but, besides this, we find in dreams inversion of situations or of the relations existing between two persons, as though the scene were laid in a "topsy-turvy" world. In dreams often enough the hare chases the hunter. Again, inversion is met with in the sequence of events, so that in dreams cause follows effect, which reminds us of what sometimes happens in a third-rate theatrical performance, when first the hero falls and then the shot which kills him is fired from the wings. Or there are dreams in which the whole arrangement of the elements is inverted, so that in interpreting them the

last must be taken first, and the first last, in order to make sense at all. You remember that we also found this in our study of dream-symbolism, in which the act of plunging or falling into water has the same meaning as that of emerging from water, namely, giving birth or being born and going up steps or a ladder means the same as coming down them. We cannot fail to recognize the advantage reaped for dream-distortion by this freedom from restrictions in representing the dream-thoughts.

These features of the dream-work may be termed *archaic*. They cling to the primitive modes of expression of languages or scripts, and yield the same difficulties, which we shall touch upon later in the course of some critical observations on this topic.

Now let us consider some other aspects of the subject. Clearly what has to be accomplished by the dream-work is the transformation of the latent thoughts, as expressed in words, into perceptual forms, most commonly into visual images. Now our thoughts originated in such perceptual forms; their earliest material and the first stages in their development consisted of sense-impressions, or, more accurately, of memory-pictures of these. It was later that words were attached to these pictures and then connected so as to form thoughts. So that the dream-work subjects our thoughts to a *regressive* process and retraces the steps in their development; in the course of this regression all new acquisitions won during this development of memory-pictures into thoughts must necessarily fall away.

This then is what we mean by the dream-work. Besides what we have learnt of its processes our interest in the manifest dream is bound to recede far into the background; I will, however, devote still a few more remarks to the manifest dream, for, after all, that is the only part of the dream with which we have any direct acquaintance.

It is natural that the manifest dream should lose some of its importance in our eyes. It must strike us as a matter of indifference whether it is carefully composed or split up into a succession of disconnected pictures. Even when the outward form of the dream is apparently full of meaning, we know that this appearance has been arrived at by the process of dream-distortion, and can have as little organic connection with the inner content of the dream as exists between the *façade* of an Italian church and its general structure and ground-plan. At times, however, this *façade* of the dream has a

---

[1] Both senses of cleave are still alive in English: to cleave (= separate) and to cleave to (= adhere).—TR.

meaning too, reproducing an important part of the latent thoughts with little or no distortion. But we cannot know this until we have interpreted the dream and thus arrived at an opinion with regard to the degree of distortion present. A similar doubt obtains where two elements seem to be closely connected; such connection may contain a valuable hint that the corresponding elements in the latent dream are similarly related, but at other times we can convince ourselves that what is connected in thought has become widely separated in the dream.

In general we must refrain from attempting to explain one part of the manifest dream by another part, as though the dream were a coherent conception and a pragmatic representation. It is in most cases comparable rather to a piece of Breccia stone, composed of fragments of different kinds of stone cemented together in such a way that the markings upon it are not those of the original pieces contained in it. There is, as a matter of fact, one mechanism in the dream-work. known as secondary elaboration, the object of which is to combine the immediate results of the work into a single and fairly coherent whole; during this process the material is often so arranged as to give rise to total misunderstanding, and for this purpose any necessary interpolations are made.

On the other hand, we should not overrate the dream-work or attribute to it more than is its due. Its activity is limited to the achievements here enumerated; condensation, displacement, plastic representation and secondary elaboration of the whole dream; these are all that it can effect. Such manifestations of judgment, criticism, surprise, or deductive reasoning, as are met with in dreams are not brought about by the dream-work and are only very rarely the expression of subsequent reflection about the dream; but are for the most part fragments of the latent thoughts introduced into the manifest dream with more or less modification and in a form suited to the context. Again, the dream-work cannot create conversation in dreams; save in a few exceptional cases, it is imitated from, and made up of, things heard or even said by the dreamer himself on the previous day, which have entered into the latent thoughts as the material or incitement of his dream. Neither do mathematical calculations come into the province of the dream-work; anything of the sort appearing in the manifest dream is generally a mere combination of numbers, a pseudo-calculation, quite absurd as such, and again only a copy of some calculation comprised in the latent thoughts. In these circumstances it is not surprising that the interest which was felt in the dream-work soon becomes directed instead towards the latent thoughts which disclose themselves in a more or less distorted form through the manifest dream. We are not justified, however, in a theoretical consideration of the subject, in letting our interest stray so far that we altogether substitute the latent thoughts for the dream as a whole, and make some pronouncement on the latter which is only true of the former. It is strange that the findings of psycho-analysis could be so misused as to result in confusion between the two. The term *dream* can only be applied to the *results of the dream-work*, i.e., to the *form* into which the latent thoughts have been rendered by the dream-work.

This work is a process of a quite peculiar type; nothing like it has hitherto been known in mental life. This kind of condensation, displacement, and regressive translation of thoughts into images, is a novelty, the recognition of which in itself richly rewards our efforts in the field of psycho-analysis. You will again perceive, from the parallels to dream-work, the connections revealed between psycho-analytic and other research, especially in the fields of the development of speech and thought. You will only realize the further significance of the insight so acquired when you learn that the mechanism of the dream-work is a kind of model for the formation of neurotic symptoms.

I know, too, that it is not possible for us yet to grasp the full extent of the fresh gain accruing to psychology from these labours. We will only hint at the new proofs thereby afforded of the existence of unconscious mental activities —for this indeed is the nature of the latent dream-thoughts—and at the promise dream-interpretation gives of an approach, wider than we ever guessed at, to the knowledge of the unconscious life of the mind.

Now, however, I think the time has come to give you individual examples of various short dreams, which will illustrate the points for which I have already prepared you.

TWELFTH LECTURE

EXAMPLES OF DREAMS AND ANALYSIS OF THEM

YOU must not be disappointed if I present you once more with fragments of dream-interpretations, instead of inviting you to participate in the interpretation of one fine long dream. You will say that after so much preparation you surely have a right to expect that; and you will express your conviction that, after successful interpretations of so many thousands of dreams, it should long ago have been possible to collect a number of striking examples by which the truth of all our assertions about the dream-work and dream-thoughts could be demonstrated. Yes, but there are too many difficulties in the way of fulfilling this wish of yours.

In the first place, I must confess that there is nobody who makes the interpretation of dreams his main business. In what circumstances then, do we come to interpret them? At times we may occupy ourselves, for no particular purpose, with the dreams of a friend, or we may work out our own dreams over a period of time in order to train ourselves for psycho-analytic work; but chiefly we have to do with the dreams of nervous patients who are undergoing psycho-analytic treatment. These last dreams provide splendid material and are in no respect inferior to those of healthy persons, but the technique of the treatment obliges us to subordinate dream-interpretation to therapeutic purposes and to desist from the attempt to interpret a large number of the dreams as soon as we have extracted from them something of use for the treatment. Again, many dreams which occur during the treatment elude full interpretation altogether; since they have their origin in the whole mass of material in the mind which is as yet unknown to us, it is not possible to understand them until the completion of the cure. To relate such dreams would necessarily involve revealing all the secrets of a neurosis; this will not do for us, since we have taken up the problem of dreams in preparation for the study of the neuroses.

Now I expect you would willingly dispense with this material and would prefer to listen to the explanation of dreams of healthy persons or perhaps of your own. But the content of these dreams makes that impossible. One cannot expose oneself, nor anyone whose confidence has been placed in one, so ruthlessly as a thorough interpretation of a dream would necessitate; for, as you already know, they touch upon all that is most intimate in the personality. Apart from the difficulty arising out of the nature of the material, there is another difficulty as regards relating the dreams. You are aware that the dream seems foreign and strange to the dreamer himself;

how much more so to an outsider to whom his personality is unknown. The literature of psycho-analysis shows no lack of good and detailed dream-analyses; I myself have published some which formed part of the history of certain pathological cases. Perhaps the best example of a dream-interpretation is that published by O. Rank, consisting of the analysis of two mutually related dreams of a young girl. These cover about two pages of print, while the analysis of them runs into 76 pages. It would need almost a whole term's lectures in order to take you through a work of this magnitude. If we selected some fairly long and considerably distorted dream we should have to enter into so many explanations, to adduce so much material in the shape of associations and recollections, and to go down so many sidetracks, that a single lecture would be quite inadequate and would give no clear idea of it as a whole. So I must ask you to be content if I pursue a less difficult course, and relate some fragments from dreams of neurotic patients, in which this or that isolated feature may be recognized. Symbols are the easiest features to demonstrate and, after them, certain peculiarities of the regressive character of dream-representation. I will tell you why I regard each of the following dreams as worth relating.

1. A dream consisting only of two short pictures: *The dreamer's uncle was smoking a cigarette, although it was Saturday. A woman was fondling and caressing the dreamer as though he were her child.*

With reference to the first picture, the dreamer (a Jew) remarked that his uncle was a very pious man who never had done, and never would do, anything so sinful as smoking on the Sabbath. The only association to the woman in the second picture was that of the dreamer's mother. These two pictures or thoughts must obviously be related to one another; but in what way? Since he expressly denied that his uncle would in reality perform the action of the dream, the insertion of the conditional *if* will at once suggest itself. "If my uncle, that deeply religious man, were to smoke a cigarette on the Sabbath, then I myself might be allowed to let my mother fondle me." Clearly, that is as much as to say that being fondled by the mother was something as strictly forbidden as smoking on the Sabbath is to the pious Jew. You will remember my telling you that in the dream-work all relations among the dream-thoughts disappear; the thoughts are broken up into their raw material, and our task in interpreting is to reinsert these connections which have been omitted.

2. My writings on the subject of dreams have placed me to some extent in the position of public consultant on the question, and for many years now I have received letters from the most diverse quarters communicating dreams to me or asking for my opinion. Naturally I am grateful to all those who have given me sufficient material with their dreams to make an interpretation possible, or have themselves volunteered one. The following dream of a medical student in Munich dating from 1910, belongs to this category; and I quote it because it may prove to you how hard it is, generally speaking, to understand a dream until the dreamer has given us what information he can about it. For I have a suspicion that in the bottom of your hearts you think that the translating of the symbols is the ideal method of interpretation and that you would like to discard that of free association; I want, therefore, to clear your minds of so pernicious an error.

"July 13th, 1910. Towards morning I had the following dream: *I was bicycling down a street in Tübingen, when a brown dachshund came rushing after me and caught hold of one of my heels. I rode a little further and then dismounted, sat down on a step and began to beat the creature off, for it had set its teeth fast in my heel.* (The dog's biting me and the whole scene roused no unpleasant sensations.) *Two elderly ladies were sitting opposite, watching me with grinning faces. Then I woke up and, as has frequently happened before, with the transition to waking consciousness the whole dream was clear to me.*"

In this instance symbolism cannot help us much, but the dreamer goes on to tell us: "I recently fell in love with a girl, just from seeing her in the street; but I had no means of introduction to her. I should have liked best to make her acquaintance through her dachshund, for I am a great animal-lover myself and was attracted by seeing she was one too." He adds that several times he had separated fighting dogs very skilfully, often to the amazement of the onlookers. Now we learn that the girl who had taken his fancy was always seen walking with this particular dog. She, however, has been eliminated from the manifest dream; only the dog associated with her has remained. Possibly the elderly ladies who grinned at him represented her, but the rest of what he tells us does not clear up this point. The fact that he was riding a bicycle in the dream was a direct repetition of the situation as he remembered it, for he had not met the girl with the dog except when he was bicycling.

3. When a man has lost someone dear to him, for a considerable period afterwards he produces a special type of dream, in which the most remarkable compromises are effected between his knowledge that that person is dead and his desire to call him back to life. Sometimes the deceased is dreamt of as being dead, and yet still alive because he does not know that he is dead, as if he would only really die if he did know it; at other times he is half dead and half alive, and each of these conditions has its distinguishing marks. We must not call these dreams merely nonsensical, for to come to life again is no more inadmissible in dreams than in fairy-tales, in which it is quite a common fate. As far as I have been able to analyse such dreams, it appeared that they were capable of a reasonable explanation, but that the pious wish to recall the departed is apt to manifest itself in the strangest ways. I will submit a dream of this sort to you, which certainly sounds strange and absurd enough, and the analysis of which will demonstrate many points already indicated in our theoretical discussions. The dreamer was a man who had lost his father some years previously:

My father was dead but had been exhumed and looked ill. He went on living, and I did all I could to prevent his noticing it. Then the dream goes on to other matters, apparently very remote.

That the father was dead we know to be a fact; but the exhumation had not taken place in reality; indeed, the question of real fact has nothing to do with anything that follows. But the dreamer went on to say that after he returned from his father's funeral one of his teeth began to ache. He wanted to treat it according to the Jewish precept: "If thy tooth offend thee, pluck it out," and, accordingly, went to the dentist. The latter, however, said that that was not the way to treat a tooth; one must have patience with it. "I will put something in it," he said, "to kill the nerve, and you must come back in three days' time, when I will take it out again." "This 'taking out,'" said the dreamer suddenly, "is the exhuming."

Now was he right? True, the parallel is not exact, for it was not the tooth which was taken out, but only a dead part of it. As a result of experience, however, we can well credit the dream-work with inaccuracies of this sort. We must suppose that the dreamer had, by a process of condensation, combined the dead father with the tooth, which was dead and which he yet retained. No wonder then that an absurdity was the result in the manifest dream, for obviously not all that was said about the tooth could apply to the father. What then are we to regard as the *tertium comparationis* between the father and the tooth, what common factor makes the comparison possible?

Such a factor must have existed, for the dreamer went on to observe that he knew the saying that if one dreams of losing a tooth it means that one is about to lose a member of his family.

We know that this popular interpretation is incorrect or at least correct only in a very distorted sense. We shall therefore be the more surprised actually to discover the subject thus touched upon behind the other elements of the dream-content.

Without being pressed further, the dreamer then began to talk of his father's illness and death, and of the relations which had existed between father and son. The illness had been a long one, and the care and treatment of the invalid had cost the son a large sum of money. Yet it never seemed too much to him, nor did his patience ever fail or the wish occur to him that the end should come. He prided himself on his true Jewish filial piety and on his strict observance of the Jewish law. Does not a certain contradiction strike us here in the thoughts relating to the dream? He had identified the tooth with the father. He wanted to treat the former according to the Jewish law which commanded that a tooth which causes pain and annoyance should be plucked out. His father he also wanted to treat according to the precepts of the law, but here the command was that he must pay no heed to expense and annoyance, must take the whole burden upon himself, and not allow any hostile intention to arise against the cause of the trouble. Would not the agreement between the two situations be much more convincing if he had really gradually come to have the same feelings towards his sick father as he had towards his diseased tooth, that is to say, if he had wished for death to put a speedy end to his father's superfluous, painful and costly existence?

I have no doubt that this was, in reality, his attitude towards his father during the protracted illness and that his ostentatious assertions of filial piety were designed to divert his mind from any recollections of the sort. Under conditions such as these it is no uncommon thing for the death-wish against the father to be roused, and to mask itself with some ostensibly compassionate reflection, such as: "It would be a blessed release for him." But I want you particularly to notice that here in the latent thoughts themselves a barrier has been broken down. The first part of the thoughts was, we may be sure, only temporarily unconscious, that is, during the actual process of the dream-work; the hostile feelings towards the father, on the other hand, had probably been permanently so, possibly dating from childhood and having at times, during the father's illness, crept as it were timidly and in a disguised form into consciousness. We can maintain this with even greater certainty of other latent thoughts which have unmistakably contributed to the content of the dream. There are, it is true, no indications in it of hostile feelings towards the father; but when we enquire into the origin of such hostility in the life of the child we remember that fear of the father arises from the fact that in the earliest years of life it is he who opposes the sexual activity of the boy, as he is usually compelled to do again, after puberty, from motives of social expediency. This was the relation in which our dreamer stood to his father; his affection for him had been tinged with a good deal of respect and dread, the source of which was early sexual intimidation.

We can now explain the further phrases in the dream from the onanism complex. *"He looked ill"* was an allusion to another remark of the dentist's—that it did not look well for a tooth to be missing just there—but it also refers at the same time to the *"looking ill"* by which the young man, during the period of puberty, betrays, or fears lest he might betray, his excessive sexual activity. It was with a lightening of his own heart that in the manifest dream the dreamer transferred the look of illness from himself to his father, an inversion with which you are familiar as a device of the dream-work. *"He went on living"* accords both with the wish to recall the father to life and the promise of the dentist to save the tooth. The phrase *"I did everything I could to prevent his noticing"* is extremely subtly designed to lead us to complete it with the words "that he was dead." The only completion of them that really makes sense, however, is again to be traced to the onanism complex, where it is a matter of course that the young man should do all he can to conceal his sexual life from his father. Finally, I would remind you that the so-called "tooth-ache dreams" always refer to onanism, and the punishment for it that is feared.

You see how this incomprehensible dream is built up by a piece of remarkable and misleading condensation, by omitting from it all the thoughts that belong to the core of the latent train of thought, and by the creation of ambiguous substitute-formations to represent those thoughts which were deepest and most remote in time.

4. We have already tried repeatedly to get to the bottom of those prosaic and banal dreams which have nothing absurd or strange in them, but which suggest the question: Why should we dream about such trivialities at all? I will therefore quote a fresh example of this sort in the shape of three dreams connected with one another and dreamt by a young lady in the course of a single night.

(a) *She was going through the hall in her house and struck her head on a low-hanging chandelier with such force as to draw blood.* This episode did not remind her of anything that had actually happened; her remarks led in quite another direction: "You know how terribly my hair is coming out. Well, yesterday my mother said to me: 'My dear child, if it goes on like this, your head will soon be as bald as your buttocks.'" We see here that the head stands for the other end of the body. No further assistance is required to understand the symbolism of the chandelier: all objects capable of elongation are symbols of the male organ. The real subject of the dream then is a bleeding at the lower end of the body, caused by contact with the penis. This might still have other meanings; the dreamer's further associations show that the dream has to do with the belief that menstruation results from sexual intercourse with a man, a notion about sexual matters which is by no means uncommon amongst immature girls.

(b) *The dreamer saw in a vineyard a deep hole which she knew had been caused by the uprooting of a tree.* Her remark on this point was that "the tree was *missing*," meaning that she did not see the tree in the dream; but the same phrase serves to express another thought, which leaves us in no doubt as to the symbolic interpretation. The dream refers to another infantile notion on the subject of sex, to the belief that girls originally had the same genital organ as boys and that the later conformation of this organ has been brought about by castration (uprooting the tree).

(c) *The dreamer was standing in front of her writing-table drawer which she knows so well that, if anyone touched it, she would immediately be aware of it.* The writing-table drawer, like all drawers, chests and boxes, is a symbol of the female genital. She knew that when sexual intercourse (or, as she thought, any contact at all) has taken place the genital shows certain indications of the fact, and she had long had a fear of being convicted of this. I think that in all three dreams the main emphasis lies on the idea of *knowing*. She had in mind the time of childish investigations into sexual matters, of the results of which she had been very proud at the time.

5. Here is another example of symbolism. But this time I must preface it with a short account of the mental situation in which the dream occurred. A man and a woman who were in love had spent a night together; he described her nature as maternal, she was one of those women whose desire to have a child comes out irresistibly during caresses. The conditions of their meeting, however, made it necessary to take precautions to prevent the semen from entering the womb. On waking the next morning, the woman related the following dream:

An officer with a red cap was pursuing her in the street. She fled from him and ran up the staircase, with him after her. Breathless, she reached her rooms and slammed and locked the door behind her. The man remained outside and, peeping through the keyhole in the door, she saw him sitting on a bench outside, weeping.

In the pursuit by the officer with the red cap and the breathless climbing of the stairs you will recognize the representation of the sexual act. That the dreamer shuts her pursuer out may serve as an example of the device of inversion so frequently employed in dreams, for in reality it was the man who withdrew before the completion of the sexual act. In the same way, she has projected her own feeling of grief on to her partner, for it is he who weeps in the dream, his tears at the same time alluding to the seminal fluid.

You will certainly have heard it said at some time or other that psycho-analysis maintains that all dreams have a sexual meaning. You are now in a position yourselves to form an opinion as to the falseness of this reproach. You have learnt of wish-fulfilment dreams, dealing with the gratification of the most obvious needs—hunger, thirst, and the longing for liberty—comfort-dreams, and impatient-dreams, as well as those which are frankly avaricious and egoistical. You may, however, certainly bear it in mind that, according to the results of psycho-analysis, dreams in which a marked degree of distortion is present *mainly* (but here again not exclusively) give expression to sexual desires.

6. I have a special motive in giving many instances of the use of symbols in dreams. In our first lecture I complained of the difficulty of demonstrating my statements in such a way as to carry conviction with regard to the findings of psycho-analysis, and since then you have doubtless agreed with me. Now the separate propositions of psycho-analysis are nevertheless so intimately related that conviction on a single point easily leads to acceptance of the greater part of the whole theory. It might be said of psycho-analysis that if you give it your little finger it will soon have your whole hand. If you accept the explanation of errors as satisfactory, you cannot logically stop short of belief in all the rest. Now dream-symbolism provides another, equally good, approach to such acceptance. I will recount to you a dream, which has already been published, of a woman of the poorer classes, whose husband was a watchman and of whom we may be sure that she had never heard of dream-symbolism and psycho-analysis. You can then judge for yourselves whether the interpretation arrived at with the help of sexual symbols can justly be called arbitrary or forced.

"... Then someone broke into the house and in terror she cried for a watchman. But the watchman, accompanied by two tramps, had gone into a church, which had several steps leading up to it. Behind the church there was a mountain and, up above, a thick wood. The watchman wore a helmet, gorget and cloak, and had a full brown beard. The two tramps, who had gone along peaceably with him, had aprons twisted round their hips like sacks. A path led from the church to the mountain and was overgrown on both sides with grass and bushes which grew denser and denser, and at the top of the mountain there was a regular wood."

You will recognize without any trouble the symbols here employed: the male organ is represented by the trinity of *three* persons appearing, whilst the female sexual organs are symbolized by a landscape with a chapel, a mountain and a wood, and once more you have the act of going up steps as symbolic of the sexual act. The part of the body called in the dream *a mountain* is similarly termed in anatomy the *mons veneris*.

7. I will tell you another dream which is to be explained in the light of symbolism, a dream, moreover, which is noteworthy and convincing from the fact that the dreamer himself translated all the symbols, though he brought no previous theoretical knowledge to the interpretation. This is a very unusual circumstance and we have no accurate idea of the conditions which give rise to it.

He was walking with his father in a place which must have been the Prater, for they saw the Rotunda with a little building in front of it, to which was made fast a captive balloon which looked rather slack. His father asked him what it was all for; the son wondered at his asking, but explained it nevertheless. Then they came to a court-yard, where a large sheet of metal lay spread out. His father wanted to break off a big piece, but looked round first in case anyone should notice him. He said to his son that all the same he need only tell the overseer and then he could take it straightaway. Some steps led down from this court to a shaft, the sides of which were upholstered with some soft stuff, something like a leather armchair. At the bottom of this shaft was a rather long platform and, beyond it, another shaft.

The following is the dreamer's own interpretation: "The Rotunda stands for my genitals and the captive balloon in front of it for the penis, which I have had to complain of for being limp." A more detailed translation would then run thus: the rotunda stands for the buttocks (regularly included by children amongst the genitals), the smaller structure in front is the scrotum. In the dream, his father asks him what all this is, i.e., what are the purpose and function of the genitals. To invert this situation so that the son asks the questions is an obvious idea, and, since these questions were never asked in reality, we must construe the dream-thoughts as a wish or take them in a conditional sense: "If I had asked my father to explain ...." The sequel to this thought we shall find presently.

The court-yard where the sheet-metal lay is not in the first place to be explained symbolically, but is a reference to the father's place of business. From motives of discretion I have substituted *sheet-metal* for the actual material dealt with by him, but otherwise I have made no alteration in the words of the dream. The dreamer had entered his father's business and had been much scandalized by the extremely questionable practices upon which the high profits largely depended. Hence the sequel to the dream-thought mentioned above would run: "(If I had asked him), he would have deceived me as he deceives his customers." The dreamer himself gives a second explanation for the pulling off the piece of metal which serves to represent commercial dishonesty: it means, he says, the practice of masturbation. Not only is this an explanation with which we have long been familiar, but it is well in accordance with this interpretation that the secret practice of masturbation should be expressed by the opposite idea *("We may do it openly")*. So the fact that this practice is imputed to the father, as was the questioning in the first scene of the dream, is exactly what we should expect. The dreamer immediately interpreted the shaft, on account of the soft upholstering of the walls, as the vagina, and I, on my own account, offer the remark that going-down as well as going-up stands for sexual intercourse.

The details of the long platform at the bottom of the first shaft, and beyond that the second shaft, were explained by the dreamer himself from his own history. He had practised intercourse for some time and then given it up on account of inhibitions, but hoped to be able to resume it by the help of the treatment.

8. I quote the two following dreams, dreamt by a foreigner with marked polygamous tendencies, because they may serve to illustrate the statement that the dreamer's own person is present in every dream, even when it is disguised in the manifest content. The trunks in the dreams are female symbols.

(a) The dreamer was going on a journey and his luggage was being taken to the station on a carriage. There were a number of trunks piled one on the top of the other, and amongst them two large black boxes like those of a commercial traveller. He said consolingly to someone: "You see those are only going as far as the station."

He does, as a matter of fact, travel with a great deal of luggage, and he also brings many stories about women to the treatment. The two black trunks stand for two dark women who at the moment are playing the principal part in his life. One of them wanted to follow him to Vienna, but on my advice he had telegraphed to put her off.

(b) A scene at a customs house: A fellow-traveller opened his trunk and said nonchalantly, smoking a cigarette: "There is nothing to declare in that." The customs official seemed to believe him, but felt in the trunk again and found a strictly prohibited article. The traveller then said in a resigned way: "Well it can't be helped." The dreamer himself is the traveller and I am the official. He is generally very straightforward with me, but had made up his mind to conceal from me a relation which he had recently formed with a lady, for he assumed quite correctly that I knew her. He displaces on to a stranger the embarrassing situation of being detected, so that he himself does not seem to come into the dream at all.

9. Here we have an example of a symbol which I have not yet mentioned:

The dreamer met his sister with two friends who were themselves sisters. He shook hands with these two, but not with his sister.

There was no real episode connected with this in his mind. Instead, his thoughts went back to a time when his observations led him to wonder why a girl's breasts are so late in developing. The two sisters, therefore, stand for the breasts; he would have liked to grasp them with his hand, if only it had not been his sister.

10. Here is an example of death symbolism in dreams: *The dreamer was crossing a very high, steep, iron bridge, with two people whose names he knew but forgot on waking. Suddenly both of them had vanished and he saw a ghostly man in a cap and an overall. He asked him whether he were the telegraph messenger . . . "No." Or the coachman? . . . "No." He then went on,* and in the dream, had a feeling of great dread; on waking, he followed it up with the phantasy that the iron bridge suddenly broke and that he fell into the abyss.

When stress is laid upon the fact that people in a dream are unknown to the dreamer, or that he has forgotten their names, they are, as a rule, persons with whom he is intimately connected. The dreamer was one of a family of three children; if he had ever wished for the death of the other two, it would be only just that he should be visited with the fear of death. With reference to the telegraph messenger, he remarked that they always bring bad news. From his uniform, the man in the dream might have been a lamplighter, who also puts out the lights, as the spirit of death extinguishes the torch of life. With the coachman he associated Uhland's poem of the voyage of King Karl, and recalled a dangerous sail on a lake with two companions, when he played the part of the king in the poem. The iron bridge suggested to him a recent accident, also the stupid saying: "Life is a suspension bridge."

11. The following may be regarded as another example of a death-dream:

An unknown gentleman was leaving a black-edged visiting card on the dreamer.

12. I give another dream which will interest you from several points of view; it is to be traced partly, however, to a neurotic condition in the dreamer:

He was in a train which stopped in the open country. He thought there was going to be an accident and that he must make his escape, so he went through all the compartments, killing everyone he met—driver, guard, and so on.

This dream recalls a story told him by a friend. On a certain Italian line, an insane man was being conveyed in a small compartment, but by some mistake a passenger was allowed to get in with him. The madman murdered the other traveller. Thus, the dreamer identified himself with this insane man, his reason being that he was at times tormented by an obsession that he must make away with "everyone who shared his knowledge." Then he himself found a better motivation for the dream. The day before, he had seen at the theatre a girl he had meant to marry but had given up because she gave him cause for jealousy. Knowing the intensity which jealousy could assume in him, he would really have been mad to want to marry her. That is to say, he thought her so unreliable that his jealousy would have led him to murder everyone who got in his way. The going through a number of rooms, or, as here, compartments, we have already learnt to know as a symbol of marriage (the expression of monogamy according to the rule of opposites).

With reference to the train's stopping in the open country and the fear of an accident, he told the following story:

Once when such a sudden halt occurred on the line outside a station, a young lady who was in the carriage said that perhaps there was going to be a collision, and that the best thing to do was to raise the legs high. This phrase "raise the legs" had associations with many walks and excursions into the country, which he had shared with the girl mentioned above in the happy early days of their love. Here was a new argument for the contention that he would be mad to marry her now; nevertheless, my knowledge of the situation led me to regard it as certain that there existed in him all the same the desire to fall a victim to this form of madness.

THIRTEENTH LECTURE
ARCHAIC AND INFANTILE FEATURES IN DREAMS

LET us start afresh from our conclusion that, under the influence of the censorship, the dream-work translates the latent dream-thoughts into another form. These thoughts are of the same nature as the familiar, conscious thoughts of waking life; the new form in which they are expressed is, owing to many peculiar characteristics, incomprehensible to us. We have said that it goes back to phases in our intellectual development which we have long outgrown—to hieroglyphic writing, to symbolic-connections, possibly to conditions which existed before the language of thought was evolved. On this account we called the form of expression employed by the dream-work *archaic* or *regressive*.

From this you may draw the inference that a more profound study of the dream-work must lead to valuable conclusions about the initial stages of our intellectual development, of which at present little is known. I hope it will be so, but so far this task has not been attempted. The era to which the dream-work takes us back is *primitive* in a two-fold sense: in the first place, it means the early days of the *individual*—his childhood—and, secondly, in so far as each individual repeats in some abbreviated fashion during childhood the whole course of the development of the human race, the reference is *phylogenetic*. I believe it not impossible that we may be able to discriminate between that part of the latent mental processes which belongs to the early days of the individual and that which has its roots in the infancy of the race. It seems to me, for instance, that symbolism, a mode of expression which has never been individually acquired, may claim to be regarded as a racial heritage.

This, however, is not the only archaic feature in dreams. You are all familiar from actual experience with the peculiar *amnesia of childhood* to which we are subject. I mean that the first years of life, up to the age of five, six, or eight, have not left the same traces in memory as our later experiences. True, we come across individuals who can boast of continuous recollection from early infancy to the present time, but it is incomparably more common for the opposite, a blank in memory, to be found. In my opinion, this has not aroused sufficient surprise. At two years old the child can speak well and soon shows his capacity for adapting himself to complicated mental situations, and, moreover, says things which he himself has forgotten when they are repeated to him years later. And yet memory is more efficient in early years, being less overburdened than it is later. Again, there is no reason to regard the function of memory as an especially high or difficult form of mental activity; on the contrary, excellent memory may be found in people who are yet on a very low plane intellectually.

But I must draw your attention to a second peculiarity based upon the first—namely, that from the oblivion in which the first years of childhood are shrouded certain clearly retained recollections emerge, mostly in the form of plastic images, for the retention of which there seems no adequate ground. Memory deals with the mass of impressions received in later life by a process of selection, retaining what is important and omitting what is not; but with the recollections retained from childhood this is not so. They do not necessarily reflect important experiences in childhood, not even such as must have seemed important from the child's standpoint, but are often so banal and meaningless in themselves that we can only ask ourselves in amazement why just this particular detail has escaped oblivion. I have tried, with the help of analysis, to attack the problem of childhood amnesia and of the fragments of recollection which break through it, and have come to the conclusion that, whatever may appear to the contrary, the child no less than the adult only retains in memory what is important; but that what is important is represented (by the processes of condensation and, more especially of displacement, already familiar to you) in the memory by something apparently trivial. For this reason I have called these childhood recollections *screen-memories;* a thorough analysis can evolve from them all that has been forgotten.

It is a regular task in psycho-analytic treatment to fill in the blank in infantile memories, and, in so far as the treatment is successful to any extent at all (very frequently, therefore) we are enabled to bring to light the content of those early years long buried in oblivion. These impressions have never really been forgotten, but were only inaccessible and latent, having become part of the unconscious. But sometimes it happens that they emerge spontaneously from the unconscious, and it is in connection with dreams that this happens. It is clear that the dream-life knows the way back to these latent, infantile experiences. Many good illustrations of this are to be found in psychoanalytical literature, and I myself have been able to furnish a contribution of the sort. I once dreamt in a particular connection of someone who had evidently done me a service and whom I saw plainly. He was a one-eyed man, short, fat and high-shouldered; from the context I gathered that he was a doctor. Fortunately I was able to ask my mother, who was still living, what was the personal appearance of the doctor who attended us at the place where I was born and which I left at the age of three; she told me that he had only one eye and was short, fat and high-shouldered; I learnt also of the accident which was the occasion of this doctor's being called in and which I had forgotten. This command of the forgotten material of the earliest years of childhood is thus a further *archaic* feature of dreams.

This knowledge has a bearing on another of the problems which up to the present have proved insoluble. You will remember the astonishment caused by our discovery that dreams have their origin in actively evil or in excessive sexual desires, which have made both the dream-censorship and dream-distortion necessary. Supposing now that we have interpreted a dream of this sort, and the circumstances are specially favourable in that the dreamer does not quarrel with the interpretation itself, he does nevertheless invariably ask how any such wish could come into his mind, since it seems quite foreign to him and he is conscious of desiring the exact opposite. We need have no hesitation in pointing out to him the origin of the wish he repudiates: these evil impulses may be traced to the past, often indeed to a past which is not so very far away. It may be demonstrated that he once knew and was conscious of them, even if this is no longer so. A woman who had a dream meaning that she wished to see her only daughter (then seventeen years old) lying dead found, with our help, that at one time she actually had cherished this death-wish. The child was the offspring of an unhappy marriage, which ended in the speedy separation of husband and wife. Once when the child was as yet unborn the mother, in an access of rage after a violent scene with her husband, beat her body with her clenched fists in order to kill the baby in her womb. How many mothers who today love their children tenderly, perhaps with excessive tenderness, yet conceived them unwillingly and wished that the life within them might not develop further; and have indeed turned this wish into various actions, fortunately of a harmless kind. The later death-wish against beloved persons, which appears so puzzling, thus dates from the early days of the relationship to them.

A father, whose dream when interpreted shows that he wished for the death of his eldest and favourite child, is in the same way obliged to recall that there was a time when this wish was not unknown to him. The man, whose marriage had proved a disappointment, often thought when the child was still an infant that if the little creature who meant nothing to him were to die he would again be free and would make better use of his freedom. A large number of similar impulses of hate are to be traced to a similar source; they are recollections of something belonging to the past, something which was once in consciousness and played its part in mental life. From this you will be inclined to draw the conclusion that such dreams and such wishes would not occur in cases where there have been no changes of this sort in the relations between two persons, that is to say, where the relation has been of the same character from the beginning. I am prepared to grant you this conclusion, only I must warn you that you have to consider, not the literal meaning of the dream, but what it signifies on interpretation. It may be that the manifest dream of the death of some beloved person was only using this as a terrible mask, whilst really meaning something totally different, or it is possible that the beloved person is an illusory substitute for someone else.

This situation will, however, raise in you another and much more serious question. You will say: "Even though this death-wish did at one time actually exist and this is confirmed by recollection, that is still no true explanation; for the desire has long since been overcome and surely at the present time can exist in the unconscious merely as a recollection, of no affective value, and not as a powerful exciting agent. For this later assumption we have no evidence. Why is the wish recollected at all in dreams?" This is a question which you are really justified in asking; the attempt to answer it would take us far afield and would oblige us to define our position with regard to

one of the most important points in the theory of dreams. But I must keep within the limits of our discussion and must forbear to follow up this question; so you must be reconciled to leaving it for the present. Let us content ourselves with the actual evidence that this wish, long since subdued, can be proved to have given rise to the dream, and let us continue our enquiry whether other evil wishes also can be traced in the same way to the past.

Let us keep to the death-wishes, which we shall certainly find mostly derived from the unbounded egoism of the dreamer. Wishes of this sort are very often found to be the underlying agents of dreams. Whenever anyone gets in our way in life—and how often must this happen when our relations to one another are so complicated!—a dream is immediately prepared to make away with that person, even if it be father, mother, brother or sister, husband or wife. It appeared to us amazing that such wickedness should be innate in humanity, and certainly we were not inclined to admit without further evidence that this result of our interpretation of dreams was correct. But, when once we had seen that the origin of wishes of this sort must be looked for in the past, we had little difficulty in finding the period in the past of the individual in which there is nothing strange in such egoism and such wishes, even when directed against the nearest and dearest. A child in his earliest years (which later are veiled in oblivion) is just the person who frequently displays such egoism in boldest relief; invariably, unmistakable tendencies of this kind, or, more accurately, surviving traces of them, are plainly visible in him. For a child loves himself first and only later learns to love others and to sacrifice something of his own ego to them. Even the people whom he seems to love from the outset are loved in the first instance because he needs them and cannot do without them—again therefore, from motives of egoism. Only later does the impulse of love detach itself from egoism: it is a literal fact that the child learns how to love through his own egoism.

In this connection it will be instructive to compare a child's attitude towards his brothers and sisters with his attitude towards his parents. The little child does not necessarily love his brothers and sisters, and often he is quite frank about it. It is unquestionable that in them he sees and hates his rivals, and it is well known how commonly this attitude persists without interruption for many years, till the child reaches maturity and even later. Of course it often gives place to a more tender feeling, or perhaps we should say it is overlaid by this, but the hostile attitude seems very generally to be the earlier. We can most easily observe it in children of two and a half to four years old when a new baby arrives, which generally meets with a very unfriendly reception; remarks such as "I don't like it. The stork is to take it away again" are very common. Subsequently every opportunity is seized to disparage the new-comer; attempts are even made to injure it and actual attacks upon it are by no means unheard-of. If the difference in age is less, by the time the child's mental activity is more fully developed the rival is already in existence and he adapts himself to the situation; if on the other hand there is a greater difference between their ages, the new baby may rouse certain kindly feelings from the first, as an object of interest, a sort of living doll; and when there is as much as eight years or more between them, especially if the elder child is a girl, protective, motherly impulses may at once come into play. But, speaking honestly, when we find a wish for the death of a brother or a sister latent in a dream we need seldom be puzzled, for we find its origin in early childhood without much trouble, or indeed, quite often in the later years when they still lived together.

There is probably no nursery without violent conflicts between the inhabitants, actuated by rivalry for the love of the parents, competition for possessions shared by them all, even for the actual space in the room they occupy. Such hostility is directed against older as well as younger brothers and sisters. I think it was Bernard Shaw who said: "If there is anyone whom a young English lady hates more than her mother it is her elder sister." Now there is something in this dictum which jars upon us; it is hard enough to bring ourselves to understand hatred and rivalry between brothers and sisters, but how can feelings of hate force themselves into the relation between mother and daughter, parents and children?

This relationship is no doubt a more favourable one, also from the children's point of view; and this too is what our expectations require: we find it far more offensive for love to be lacking between parents and children than between brothers and sisters. We have, so to speak, sanctified the former love while allowing the latter to remain profane. Yet everyday observation may show us how frequently the sentiments entertained towards each other by parents and grown-up children fall short of the ideal set up by society, and how much hostility lies smouldering, ready to burst into flame if it were not stifled by considerations of filial or parental duty and by other, tender impulses. The motives for this hostility are well known, and we recognize a tendency for those of the same sex to become alienated, daughter from mother and father from son. The daughter sees in her mother the authority which imposes limits to her will, whose task it is to bring her to that renunciation of sexual freedom which society demands; in certain cases, too, the mother is still a rival, who objects to being set aside. The same thing is repeated still more blatantly between father and son. To the son the father is the embodiment of the social compulsion to which he so unwillingly submits, the person who stands in the way of his following his own will, of his early sexual pleasures and, when there is family property, of his enjoyment of it. When a throne is involved, this impatience for the death of the father may approach tragic intensity. The relation between father and daughter or mother and son would seem less liable to disaster; the latter relation furnishes the purest examples of unchanging tenderness, undisturbed by any egoistic consideration.

Why, you ask, do I speak of things so banal and so well-known to everybody? Because there exists an unmistakable tendency in people's minds to deny the significance of these things in real life and to pretend that the social ideal is much more frequently realized than it actually is. But it is better that psychology should tell the truth than that it should be left to cynics to do so. This general denial is only applied to real life, it is true; for fiction and drama are free to make use of the motives laid bare when these ideals are rudely disturbed.

There is nothing to wonder at therefore if the dreams of a great number of people bring to light the wish for the removal of their parents, especially of the parent whose sex is the same as the dreamer's. We may assume that the wish exists in waking life as well, sometimes even in consciousness if it can disguise itself behind another motive, as the dreamer in our third example disguised his real thought by pity for his father's useless suffering. It is but rarely that hostility reigns alone—far more often it yields to more tender feelings which finally suppress it, when it has to wait in abeyance till a dream shows it, as it were, in isolation. That which the dream shows in a form magnified by this very isolation resumes its true proportions when our interpretation has assigned to it its proper place in relation to the rest of the dreamer's life. (H. Sachs.) But we also find this death-wish where there is no basis for it in real life and where the adult would never have to confess to entertaining it in his waking life. The reason for this is that the deepest and most common motive for estrangement, especially between parent and child of the same sex, came into play in the earliest years of childhood. I refer to that rivalry of affections in which sexual elements are plainly emphasized. The son, when quite a little child, already begins to develop a peculiar tenderness towards his mother, whom he looks upon as his own property, regarding his father in the light of a rival who disputes this sole possession of his; similarly the little daughter sees in her mother someone who disturbs her tender relation to her father and occupies a place which she feels she herself could very well fill. Observation shows us how far back these sentiments date, sentiments which we describe by the term *Oedipus complex,* because in the Oedipus myth the two extreme forms of the wishes arising from the situation of the son—the wish to kill the father and to marry the mother—are realized in an only slightly modified form. I do not assert that the Oedipus complex exhausts all the possible relations which may exist between parents and children; these relations may well be a great deal more complicated. Again, this complex may be more or less strongly developed, or it may even become inverted, but it is a regular and very important factor in the mental life of the child; we are more in danger of underestimating than of overestimating its influence and that of the developments which may follow from it. Moreover, the parents themselves frequently stimulate the children to react with an Oedipus complex, for parents are often guided in their preferences by the difference in sex of their children, so that the father favours the daughter and the mother the son; or else, where conjugal love has grown cold, the child may be taken as a substitute for the love-object which has ceased to attract.

It cannot be said that the world has shown great gratitude to psycho-analytic research for the discovery of the Oedipus complex; on the contrary, the idea has excited the most violent opposition in grown-up people; and those who omitted to join in denying the existence of sentiments so universally reprehended and tabooed have later made up for this by proffering interpretations so wide of the mark as to rob the complex of its value. My own unchanged conviction is that there is nothing in it to deny or to gloss over. We ought to reconcile ourselves to facts in which the Greek myth itself saw the hand of inexorable destiny. Again, it is interesting to find that the Oedipus complex, repudiated in actual life and relegated to fiction, has there come to its own. O. Rank in a careful study of this theme has shown how this very complex has supplied dramatic poetry with an abundance of motives in countless variations, modifications and disguises, in short, subject to just the distortion familiar to us in the work of the dream-censorship. So we may look for the Oedipus complex even in those dreamers who have been fortunate enough to escape conflicts with their parents in later life; and closely connected with this we shall find what is termed the *castration complex,* the reaction to that intimidation in the field of sex or to that restraint of early infantile sexual activity which is ascribed to the father.

What we have already ascertained has guided us to the study of the child's mental life, and we may now hope to find in a similar way an explanation of the source of the other kind of prohibited wishes in dreams, i.e., the excessive sexual desires. We are impelled therefore to study the development of the sexual life of the child, and here from various sources we learn the following facts. In the first place, it is an untenable fallacy to suppose that the child has no sexual life and to assume that sexuality first makes its appearance at puberty, when the genital organs come to maturity. On the contrary he has from the very beginning a sexual life rich in content, though it differs in many points from that which later is regarded as normal. What in adult life are termed *perversions* depart from the normal in the following respects: (1) in a disregard for the barriers of species (the gulf between man and beast), (2) in the insensibility to barriers imposed by disgust, (3) in the transgression of the incest-barrier (the prohibition against seeking sexual gratification with close blood-relations), (4) in homosexuality and, (5) in the transferring of the part played by the genital organs to other organs and different areas of the body. All these barriers are not in existence from the outset, but are only gradually built up in the course of development and education. The little child is free from them: he does not perceive any immense gulf between man and beast, the arrogance with which man separates himself from the other animals only dawns in him at a later period. He shows at the beginning of life no disgust for excrement, but only learns this feeling slowly under the influence of education; he attaches no particular importance to the difference between the sexes, in fact he thinks that both have the same formation of the genital organs; he directs his earliest sexual desires and his curiosity to those nearest to him or to those who for other reasons are specially beloved—his parents, brothers and sisters or nurses; and finally we see in him a characteristic which manifests itself again later at the height of some love-relationship—namely, he does not look for gratification in the sexual organs only, but discovers that many other parts of the body possess the same sort of sensibility and can yield analogous pleasurable sensations, playing thereby the part of genital organs. The child may be said then to be *polymorphously perverse,* and even if mere traces of all these impulses are found in him, this is due on the one hand to their lesser intensity as compared with that which they assume in later life and, on the other hand, to the fact that education immediately and energetically suppresses all sexual manifestations in the child. This suppression may be said to be embodied in a theory; for grown-up people endeavour to overlook some of these manifestations, and, by misinterpretation, to rob others of their sexual nature, until in the end the whole thing can be altogether denied. It is often the same people who first inveigh against the sexual *naughtiness* of children in the nursery and then sit down to their writing-tables to defend the sexual purity of the same children. When they are left to themselves or when they are seduced, children often display perverse sexual activity to a really remarkable extent. Of course grown-up people are right in not taking this too seriously and in regarding it, as they say, as *childish tricks* and *play,* for the child cannot be judged either by a moral or legal code as if he were mature and fully responsible; nevertheless these things do exist, and they have their significance both as evidence of innate constitutional tendencies and inasmuch as they cause and foster later devel-

opments: they give us an insight into the child's sexual life and so into that of humanity as a whole. If, then, we find all these perverse wishes behind the distortions of our dreams, it only means that dreams in *this respect also* have regressed completely to the infantile condition.

Amongst these forbidden wishes special prominence must still be given to the incestuous desires, i.e., those directed towards sexual intercourse with parents or brothers and sisters. You know in what abhorrence human society holds, or at least professes to hold, such intercourse, and what emphasis is laid upon the prohibitions of it. The most preposterous attempts have been made to account for this horror of incest: some people have assumed that it is a provision of nature for the preservation of the species, manifesting itself in the mind by these prohibitions because inbreeding would result in racial degeneration; others have asserted that propinquity from early childhood has deflected sexual desire from the persons concerned. In both these cases, however, the avoidance of incest would have been automatically secured and we should be at a loss to understand the necessity for stern prohibitions, which would seem rather to point to a strong desire. Psycho-analytic investigations have shown beyond the possibility of doubt that *an incestuous love-choice* is in fact the first and the regular one, and that it is only later that any opposition is manifested towards it, the causes of which are not to be sought in the psychology of the individual.

Let us sum up the results which our excursions into child-psychology have brought to the understanding of dreams. We have learnt not only that the material of the forgotten childish experiences is accessible to the dream, but also that the child's mental life, with all its peculiarities, its egoism, its incestuous object-choice, persists in it and therefore in the unconscious, and that our dreams take us back every night to this infantile stage. This corroborates the belief that *the Unconscious is the infantile mental life,* and, with this, the objectionable impression that so much evil lurks in human nature grows somewhat less. For this terrible evil is simply what is original, primitive and infantile in mental life, what we find in operation in the child, but in part overlook in him because it is on so small a scale, and in part do not take greatly to heart because we do not demand a high ethical standard in a child. By regressing to this infantile stage our dreams appear to have brought the evil in us to light, but the appearance is deceptive, though we have let ourselves be dismayed by it; we are not so evil as the interpretation of our dreams would lead us to suppose.

If the evil impulses of our dreams are merely infantile, a reversion to the beginnings of our ethical development, the dream simply making us children again in thought and feeling, it is surely not reasonable to be ashamed of these evil dreams. But the reasoning faculty is only part of our mental life; there is much in it besides which is not reasonable, and so it happens that, although it is unreasonable, we nevertheless are ashamed of such dreams. We subject them to the dream-censorship and are ashamed and indignant when one of these wishes by way of exception penetrates our consciousness in a form so undisguised that we cannot fail to recognize it; yes, we even at times feel just as much ashamed of a distorted dream as if we really understood it. Just think of the outraged comment of the respectable elderly lady upon her dream about *love service,* although it was not interpreted to her. So the problem is not yet solved, and it is still possible that if we pursue this question of the evil in dreams we may arrive at another conclusion and another estimate of human nature.

Our whole enquiry has led to two results which, however, merely indicate the beginning of new problems and new doubts. In the first place: the regression in dreams is one not only of form but of substance. Not only does it translate our thoughts into a primitive form of expression, but it also re-awakens the peculiarities of our primitive mental life—the old supremacy of the ego, the initial impulses of our sexual life, even restores to us our old intellectual possession if we may conceive of symbolism in this way. And secondly: all these old infantile characteristics, which were once dominant and solely dominant, must today be accounted to the unconscious and must alter and extend our views about it. *Unconscious* is no longer a term for what is temporarily latent: the unconscious is a special realm, with its own desires and modes of expression and peculiar mental mechanisms not elsewhere operative. Yet the latent dream-thoughts disclosed by our interpretation do not belong to this realm; rather they correspond to the kind of thoughts we have in waking life also. And yet they are unconscious: how is the paradox to be resolved? We begin to realize that here we must discriminate. Something which has its origin in our

conscious life and shares its characteristics— we call it the *residue* from the previous day— meets together with something from the realm of the unconscious in the formation of a dream, and it is between these two regions that the dream-work is accomplished. The influence of the unconscious impinging upon this residue probably constitutes the condition for regression. This is the deepest insight into the nature of dreams possible to us until we have explored further fields in the mind; but soon it will be time to give another name to the unconscious character of the latent dream-thoughts, in order to distinguish it from that unconscious material which has its origin in the province of the infantile.

We can of course also ask: What is it that forces our mental activity during sleep to such regression? Why cannot the mental stimuli that disturb sleep be dealt with without it? And if on account of the dream-censorship the mental activity has to disguise itself in the old, and now incomprehensible, form of expression, what is the object of re-animating the old impulses, desires and characteristics, now surmounted; what, in short, is the use of *regression in substance* as well as in *form?* The only satisfactory answer would be that this is the one possible way in which dreams can be formed, that, dynamically considered, the relief from the stimulus giving rise to the dream cannot otherwise be accomplished. But this is an answer for which, at present, we have no justification.

FOURTEENTH LECTURE

WISH-FULFILMENT

SHALL I remind you once more of the steps by which we have arrived at our present position? When in applying our technique we came upon the distortion in dreams, we made up our minds to avoid it for the moment and turned to the study of infantile dreams for some definite information about the nature of dreams in general. Next, equipped with the results of this investigation, we attacked the question of dream-distortion directly, and I hope that bit by bit we have also mastered that. Now, however, we are bound to admit that our findings in these two directions do not exactly tally, and it behooves us to combine and correlate our results.

Both enquiries have made it plain that the essential feature in the dream-work is the transformation of thoughts into hallucinatory experience. It is puzzling enough to see how this process is accomplished, but this is a problem for general psychology, and we have not to deal with it here. We have learnt from children's dreams that the object of the dream-work is to remove, by means of the fulfilment of some wish, a mental stimulus which is disturbing sleep. We could make no similar pronouncement with regard to distorted dreams until we understood how to interpret them, but from the outset we expected to be able to bring our ideas about them into line with our views on infantile dreams. This expectation was for the first time fulfilled when we recognized that all dreams are really children's dreams; that they make use of infantile material and are characterized by impulses and mechanisms which belong to the childish mind. When we feel we have mastered the distortion in dreams we must go on to find out whether the notion that dreams are WISH-FULFILMENTS holds good of distorted dreams also.

We have just subjected a series of dreams to interpretation, but without taking the question of wish-fulfilment into consideration at all. I feel certain that, while we were talking about them, the question repeatedly forced itself upon you: "What has become of the wish-fulfilment which is supposed to be the object of the dream-work?" Now this question is important, for it is the one which our lay critics are constantly asking. As you know, mankind has an instinctive antipathy to intellectual novelties; one of the ways in which this shows itself is that any such novelty is immediately reduced to its very smallest compass, and if possible embodied in some catch-word. *Wish-fulfilment* has become the catch-word for the new theory of dreams. Directly they hear that dreams are said to be wish-fulfilments, the laity asks: "Where does the wish-fulfilment come in?" and their asking the question amounts to a repudiation of the idea. They can immediately think of countless dreams of their own which were accompanied by feeling so unpleasant as sometimes to reach the point of agonizing dread; and so this statement of the psycho-analytical theory of dreams appears to them highly improbable. It is easy to reply that in distorted dreams the wish-fulfilment is not openly expressed, but has to be looked for, so that it cannot be shown until the dreams have been interpreted. We know too that the wishes underlying these distorted dreams are those which are prohibited and rejected by the censorship, and that it is just their existence which is the

cause of distortion and the motive for the intervention of the censorship. But it is difficult to make the lay critic understand that we must not ask about the wish-fulfilment in a dream before it has been interpreted; he always forgets this. His reluctance to accept the theory of wish-fulfilment is really nothing but the effect of the dream-censorship, causing him to replace the real thought by a substitute, and following from his repudiation of these censored dream-wishes.

Of course we ourselves must feel the need to explain why so many dreams are painful in content; and in particular we shall want to know how we come to have *anxiety-dreams*. Here for the first time we are confronted with the problem of the affects in dreams; a problem which deserves special study, but one which we cannot concern ourselves with just now, unfortunately. If the dream is a wish-fulfilment, it should be impossible for any painful emotions to come into it: on this point the lay critics seem to be right. But the matter is complicated by three considerations which they have overlooked.

First, it may happen that the dream-work is not wholly successful in creating a wish-fulfilment, so that part of the painful feeling in the latent thoughts is carried over into the manifest dream. Analysis would then have to show that these thoughts were a great deal more painful than the dream which is formed from them; this much can be proved in every instance. We admit then that the dream-work has failed in its purpose, just as a dream of drinking excited by the stimulus of thirst fails to quench that thirst. One is still thirsty after it and has to wake up and drink. Nevertheless, it is a proper dream: it has renounced nothing of its essential nature. We must say: *"Ut desint vires, tamen est laudanda voluntas.*[1] The clearly recognizable intention remains a praiseworthy one, at any rate. Such instances of failure in the work are by no means rare, and one reason is that it is so much more difficult for the dream-work to produce the required change in the nature of the affect than to modify the content; affects are often very intractable. So it happens that in the process of the dream-work the painful *content* of the dream-thoughts is transformed into a wish-fulfilment while the painful *affect* persists unchanged. When this occurs, the affect is quite out of harmony with the content, which gives our critics the oppor-

---

[1] The will is commendable, though the ability may be wanting.

tunity of remarking that the dream is so far
from being a wish-fulfilment that even a harmless content may be accompanied in it by painful feelings. Our answer to this rather unintelli-
gent comment will be that it is just in dreams
of this sort that the wish-fulfilling tendency of
the dream-work is most apparent, because it is
there seen in isolation. The mistake in this
criticism arises because people who are not
familiar with the neuroses imagine a more intimate connection between content and affect
than actually exists, and so cannot understand
that there may be an alteration in the content
while the accompanying affect remains unchanged.

A second consideration, much more important
and far-reaching but equally overlooked by the
laity, is the following. A wish-fulfilment must
certainly bring some pleasure; but we go on to
ask: "To whom?" Of course, to the person
who has the wish. But we know that the attitude of the dreamer towards his wishes is a
peculiar one: he rejects them, censors them, in
short, he will have none of them. Their fulfilment then can afford him no pleasure, rather
the opposite, and here experience shows that
this *opposite*, which has still to be explained,
takes the form of *anxiety*. The dreamer, where
his wishes are concerned, is like two separate
people closely linked together by some important thing in common. Instead of enlarging
upon this I will remind you of a well-known
fairy-tale in which you will see these relationships repeated. A good fairy promised a poor
man and his wife to fulfil their first three
wishes. They were delighted and made up their
minds to choose the wishes carefully. But the
woman was tempted by the smell of some sausages being cooked in the next cottage and
wished for two like them. Lo! and behold, there
they were—and the first wish was fulfilled.
With that, the man lost his temper and in his
resentment wished that the sausages might hang
on the tip of his wife's nose. This also came to
pass, and the sausages could not be removed
from their position; so the second wish was
fulfilled, but it was the man's wish and its fulfilment was most unpleasant for the woman.
You know the rest of the story: as they were
after all man and wife, the third wish had to
be that the sausages should come off the end
of the woman's nose. We might make use of
this fairy-tale many times over in other con-
texts, but here it need only serve to illustrate
the fact that it is possible for the fulfilment of
one person's wish to be very disagreeable to

someone else, unless the two people are entirely at one.

It will not be difficult now to arrive at a still
better understanding of anxiety-dreams. There
is just one more observation to be made use of
and then we may adopt an hypothesis which
is supported by several considerations. The
observation is that anxiety-dreams often have
a content in which there is no distortion; it
has, so to speak, escaped the censorship. This
type of dream is frequently an undisguised
wish-fulfilment, the wish being of course not
one which the dreamer would accept but one
which he has rejected; anxiety has developed
in place of the working of the censorship.
Whereas the infantile dream is an open fulfilment of a wish admitted by the dreamer, and
the ordinary distorted dream is the disguised fulfilment of a repressed wish, the formula for the
anxiety-dream is that it is the open fulfilment
of a repressed wish. Anxiety is an indication
that the repressed wish has proved too strong
for the censorship and has accomplished or was
about to accomplish its fulfilment in spite of
it. We can understand that fulfilment of a repressed wish can only be, for us who are on
the side of the censorship, an occasion for
painful emotions and for setting up a defence.
The anxiety then manifested in our dreams is,
if you like to put it so, anxiety experienced because of the strength of wishes which at other
times we manage to stifle. The study of dreams
alone does not reveal to us why this defence
takes the form of anxiety; obviously we must
consider the latter in other connections.

The hypothesis which holds good for anxiety-
dreams without any distortion may be adopted
also for those which have undergone some degree of distortion, and for other kinds of unpleasant dreams in which the accompanying
unpleasant feelings probably approximate to
anxiety. Anxiety-dreams generally wake us; we
usually break off our sleep before the repressed
wish behind the dream overcomes the censorship and reaches complete fulfilment. In such
a case the dream has failed to achieve its purpose, but its essential character is not thereby
altered. We have compared the dream with a
night-watchman, a guardian of sleep, whose
purpose it is to protect sleep from interruption.
Now night-watchmen also, just like dreams,
have to rouse sleepers when they are not strong
enough to ward off the cause of disturbance or
danger alone. Nevertheless we do sometimes
succeed in continuing to sleep even when our
dreams begin to give us some uneasiness and

to turn to anxiety. We say to ourselves in sleep: "It is only a dream after all," and go on sleeping.

You may ask *when* it happens that the dream-wish is able to overcome the censorship. This may depend either on the wish or on the censorship: it may be that for unknown reasons the strength of the wish at times becomes excessive; but our impression is that it is more often the attitude of the censorship which is responsible for this shifting in the balance of power. We have already heard that the censorship works with varying intensity in each individual instance, treating the different elements with different degrees of strictness; now we may add that it is very variable in its general behaviour and does not show itself always equally severe towards the same element. If then it chances that the censorship feels itself for once powerless against some dream-wish which threatens to overflow it, it then, instead of making use of distortion, employs the last weapon left to it and destroys sleep by bringing about an access of anxiety.

At this point it strikes us that we still have no idea why these evil, rejected wishes rise up just at night-time, so as to disturb us when we sleep. The answer can hardly be found except in another hypothesis which goes back to the nature of sleep itself. During the day the heavy pressure of a censorship is exercised upon these wishes and, as a rule, it is impossible for them to make themselves felt at all. But in the night it is probable that this censorship, like all the other interests of mental life, is suspended, or at least very much weakened, in favour of the single desire for sleep. So it is due to this partial abrogation of the censorship at night that the forbidden wishes can again become active. There are nervous people suffering from insomnia who confess that their sleeplessness was voluntary in the first instance; for they did not dare to go to sleep because they were afraid of their dreams—that is to say, they feared the consequences of the diminished vigilance of the censorship. You will have no difficulty in understanding that this curtailment of the censorship does not argue any flagrant carelessness: sleep impairs our motor functions; even if our evil intentions do begin to stir within us the utmost they can do is to produce a dream, which is for all practical purposes harmless; and it is this comforting circumstance which gives rise to the sleeper's remark, made, it is true, in the night but yet not part of his dream-life: "It is only a dream."

So we let it have its way and continue to sleep.

Thirdly, if you call to mind our idea that the dreamer striving against his own wishes is like a combination of two persons, separate and yet somehow intimately united, you will be able to understand another possible way in which something that is highly unpleasant may be brought about through wish-fulfilment: I am speaking of punishment. Here again the fairy-tale of the three wishes may help to make things clear. The sausages on the plate were the direct fulfilment of the first person's (the woman's) wish; the sausages on the tip of her nose were the fulfilment of the second person's (the husband's) wish, but at the same time they were the punishment for the foolish wish of the wife. In the neuroses we shall meet with wishes corresponding in motivation to the third wish of the fairy-tale, the only one left. There are many such punishment tendencies in the mental life of man; they are very strong and we may well regard them as responsible for some of our painful dreams. Now you will probably think that with all this there is very little of the famous wish-fulfilment left; but on closer consideration you will admit that you are wrong. In comparison with the manifold possibilities (to be discussed later) of what dreams might be—according to some writers, what they actually are—the solution: wish-fulfilment, anxiety-fulfilment, punishment-fulfilment, is surely quite a narrow one. Add to this, that anxiety is the direct opposite of a wish and that opposites lie very near one another in association and, as we have learned, actually coincide in the unconscious. Moreover, punishment itself is the fulfilment of a wish, namely, the wish of the other, censoring person.

On the whole then, I have made no concession to your objections to the wish-fulfilment theory; we are bound, however, to demonstrate its presence in any and every distorted dream, and we have certainly no desire to shirk this task. Let us go back to the dream we have already interpreted, about the three bad theatre tickets for one florin and a half, from which we have already learnt a good deal. I hope you still remember it: A lady, whose husband told her one day about the engagement of her friend Elise who was only three months younger than herself, dreamt on the following night that she and her husband were at the theatre and that one side of the stalls was almost empty. Her husband told her that Elise and her fiancé had wanted to go to the theatre too; but could not, because they could only get such bad seats, three tickets for a florin and a half. His wife said that they had not lost much by it. We discovered that the dream-thoughts had to do with her vexation at having been in such a hurry to marry and her dissatisfaction with her husband. We may well be curious how these gloomy thoughts can have been transformed into a wish-fulfilment, and what trace of it can be found in the manifest content. Now we know already that the element *too soon, too great a hurry*, was eliminated by the censorship; the empty stalls are an allusion to this element. The puzzling phrase *"three for one florin and a half"* is now more comprehensible to us than at first, through the knowledge of symbolism that we have acquired since then.[1] The number *three* really stands for a man and we can easily translate the manifest element to mean: *to buy a man* (husband) *with the dowry.* ("I could have bought one ten times better for my dowry.") *Going to the theatre* obviously stands for marriage. *Getting the tickets too soon* is in fact a direct substitute for *marrying too soon.* Now this substitution is the work of the wish-fulfilment. The dreamer had not always felt so dissatisfied with her premature marriage as she was on the day when she heard of her friend's engagement. She had been proud of her marriage at the time and considered herself more highly favoured than her friend. One hears that naïve girls, on becoming engaged, frequently express their delight at the idea that they will now soon be able to go to all plays and see everything hitherto forbidden them.

The indication of curiosity and a desire to "look on" evinced here comes, without doubt, originally from the sexual *gazing impulse,* especially regarding the parents, and this became a strong motive impelling the girl to marry early; in this manner going to the theatre became an obvious allusive substitute for getting married. In her vexation at the present time on account of her premature marriage she therefore reverted to the time when this same marriage fulfilled a wish, by gratifying her *skoptophilia;* and so, guided by this old wish-impulse, she replaced the idea of marriage by that of going to the theatre.

We may say that the example we have chosen to demonstrate a hidden wish-fulfilment is not the most convenient one, but in all other distorted dreams we should have to proceed in a manner analogous to that employed above. It is not possible for me to do this here and now, so I will merely express my conviction that such procedure will invariably meet with success. But I wish to dwell longer upon this point in our theory: experience has taught me that it is one of the most perilous of the whole theory of dreams, exposed to many contradictions and misunderstandings. Besides, you are perhaps still under the impression that I have already retracted part of my statement by saying that the dream may be either a wish-fulfilment, or its opposite, an anxiety or a punishment, brought to actuality; and you may think this a good opportunity to force me to make further reservations. Also I have been reproached with presenting facts that seem obvious to myself in a manner too condensed to carry conviction.

When anyone has gone as far as this in dream-interpretation and has accepted all our conclusions up to this point, it often happens that he comes to a standstill at this question of wish-fulfilment and asks: "Admitting that every dream means something and that this meaning may be discovered by employing the technique of psycho-analysis, why must it always, in face of all the evidence to the contrary, be forced into the formula of wish-fulfilment? Why must our thoughts at night be any less many-sided than our thoughts by day; so that at one time a dream might be a fulfilment of some wish, at another time, as you say yourself, the opposite, the actualization of a dread; or, again, the expression of a resolution, a warning, a weighing of some problem with its pros and cons, or a reproof, some prick of conscience, or an attempt to prepare oneself for something which has to be done—and so forth? Why this perpetual insistence upon a wish or, at the most, its opposite?"

It might be supposed that a difference of opinion on this point is a matter of no great moment, if there is agreement on all others. Cannot we be satisfied with having discovered the meaning of dreams and the ways by which we can find out the meaning? We surely go back on the advance we have made if we try to limit this meaning too strictly. But this is not so. A misunderstanding on this head touches what is essential to our knowledge of dreams and imperils its value for the understanding of neuroses. Moreover, that readiness to *oblige the other party* which has its value in business life is not only out of place but actually harmful in scientific matters.

My first answer to the question why dreams

---

[1] Another interpretation of the number *three,* occurring in the dream of this childless woman, lies very close; but I will not mention it here, because this analysis did not furnish any material illustrating it.

should not be many-sided in their meaning is the usual one in such a case: I do not know why they should not be so, and should have no objection if they were. As far as I am concerned, they can be so! But there is just one trifling obstacle in the way of this wider and more convenient conception of dreams—that as a matter of fact they are not so. My second answer would emphasize the point that to assume that dreams represent manifold modes of thought and intellectual operations is by no means a novel idea to myself: once, in the history of a pathological case, I recorded a dream which occurred three nights running and never again; and gave it as my explanation that this dream corresponded to a resolution, the repetition of which became unnecessary as soon as that resolution was carried out. Later on, I published a dream which represented a confession. How is it possible for me then to contradict myself and assert that dreams are always and only wish-fulfilments?

I do it rather than permit a stupid misunderstanding which might cost us the fruit of all our labours on the subject of dreams; a misunderstanding that *confounds the dream with the latent dream-thoughts*, and makes statements with regard to the former which are applicable to the *latter and to the latter only*. For it is perfectly true that dreams can represent, and be themselves replaced by, all the modes of thought just enumerated: resolutions, warnings, reflections, preparations or attempts to solve some problem in regard to conduct, and so on. But when you look closely, you will recognize that all this is true only of the latent thoughts which have been transformed into the dream. You learn from interpretations of dreams that the unconscious thought-processes of mankind are occupied with such resolutions, preparations and reflections, out of which dreams are formed by means of the dream-work. If your interest at any given moment is not so much in the dream-work, but centres on the unconscious thought-processes in people, you will then eliminate the dream-formation and say of dreams themselves, what is for all practical purposes correct, that they represent a warning, a resolve, and so on. This is what is often done in psycho-analytic work: generally we endeavour simply to demolish the manifest form of dreams and to substitute for it the corresponding latent thoughts in which the dream originated.

Thus it is that we learn quite incidentally from our attempt to assess the latent dream-thoughts that all the highly complicated mental acts we have enumerated can be performed unconsciously—a conclusion surely as tremendous as it is bewildering.

But to go back a little: you are quite right in speaking of dreams as representing these various modes of thought, provided that you are quite clear in your own minds that you are using an abbreviated form of expression and do not imagine that the manifold variety of which you speak is in itself part of the essential nature of *dreams*. When you speak of *a dream* you must mean either the manifest dream, i.e., the product of the dream-work, or at most that work itself, i.e., the mental process which forms the latent dream-thoughts into the manifest dream. To use the word in any other sense is a confusion of ideas which is bound to be mischievous. If what you say is meant to apply to the latent thoughts behind the dream, then say so plainly, and do not add to the obscurity of the problem by your loose way of expressing yourselves. The latent dream-thoughts are the material which is transformed by the dream-work into the manifest dream. What makes you constantly confound the material with the process which deals with it? If you do that, in what way are you superior to those who know of the final product only, without being able to explain where it comes from or how it is constructed?

The only thing essential to the dream itself is the dream-work which has operated upon the thought-material; and when we come to theory we have no right to disregard this, even if in certain practical situations it may be neglected. Further, analytic observation shows that the dream-work never consists merely in translating the latent thoughts into the archaic or regressive forms of expression described. On the contrary, something is invariably added which does not belong to the latent thoughts of the day-time, but which is the actual motive force in dream-formation; this indispensable component being the equally unconscious *wish*, to fulfil which the content of the dream is transformed. In so far, then, as you are considering only the thoughts represented in it, the dream may be any conceivable thing—a warning, a resolve, a preparation, and so on; but besides this, it itself is always the fulfilment of an unconscious wish, and, when you regard it as the result of the dream-work, it is this alone. A dream, then, is never simply the expression of a resolve or warning, and nothing more: in it the resolve, or whatever it may be, is trans-

lated into the archaic form with the assistance
of an unconscious wish, and metamorphosed in
such a way as to be a fulfilment of that wish.
This single characteristic, that of fulfilling a
wish, is the constant one: the other component
varies; it may indeed itself be a wish; in which
event the dream represents the fulfilment of
a latent wish from our waking hours brought
about by the aid of an unconscious wish.

Now all this is quite clear to myself, but I
do not know whether I have succeeded in making it equally clear to you; and it is difficult to
prove it to you; for, on the one hand, proof
requires the evidence afforded by a careful
analysis of many dreams and, on the other
hand, this, the crucial and most important
point in our conception of dreams, cannot be
presented convincingly without reference to
considerations upon which we have not yet
touched. Seeing how closely linked up all phenomena are, you can hardly imagine that we
can penetrate very far into the nature of any
one of them without troubling ourselves about
others of a similar nature. Since as yet we
know nothing about those phenomena which
are so nearly akin to dreams—neurotic symptoms—we must once more content ourselves
with what we actually have achieved. I will
merely give you the explanation of one more
example and adduce a new consideration.

Let us take once more that dream to which
we have already reverted several times, the one
about the three theatre tickets for one florin
and a half. I can assure you that I had no
ulterior motive in selecting it in the first instance for an illustration. You know what the
latent thoughts were: the vexation, after hearing that her friend had only just become engaged, that she herself should have married so
hastily; depreciation of her husband and the
idea that she could have found a better one if
only she had waited. We also know already
that the wish which made a dream out of these
thoughts was the desire to *look on,* to be able to
go to the theatre—very probably an offshoot
of an old curiosity to find out at last what
really does happen after marriage. It is well
known that in children this curiosity is regularly directed towards the sexual life of the
parents; that is to say, it is an infantile impulse and, wherever it persists later in life, it
has its roots in the infantile period. But the
news received on the day previous to the dream
gave no occasion for the awakening of this
skoptophilia; it only roused vexation and re-

gret. This wish-impulse (of skoptophilia) was
not at first connected with the latent thoughts,
and the results of the dream-interpretation
could have been used by the analysis without
taking it into consideration at all. But again,
the vexation was not in itself capable of producing a dream: no dream could be formed out
of the thought: "It was folly to be in such a
hurry to marry" until that thought had stirred
up the early wish to see at last what happened
after marriage. Then this wish formed the
dream-content, substituting for marriage the
going to the theatre; and the form was that of
the fulfilment of the earlier wish: "Now I
may go to the theatre and look at all that we
have never been allowed to see; and you may
not. I am married and you have got to wait."
In this way the actual situation was transformed into its opposite and an old triumph
substituted for the recent discomfiture; and
incidentally, satisfaction both of a *gazing* impulse and of one of egoistic rivalry was brought
about. It is this latter satisfaction which determines the manifest content of the dream; for
in it she is actually sitting in the theatre, while
her friend cannot get in. Those portions of the
dream-content behind which the latent thoughts
still conceal themselves are to be found in the
form of inappropriate and incomprehensible
modifications of the gratifying situation. The
business of *interpretation* is to put aside those
features in the whole which merely represent a
wish-fulfilment and to reconstruct the painful
latent dream-thoughts from these indications.

The consideration which I said I wished to
call to your notice is intended to direct your
attention to these latent dream-thoughts now
brought into prominence. I must beg you not
to forget that, first, the dreamer is unconscious
of them; secondly, that they are quite reasonable and coherent, so that we can understand
them as comprehensible reactions to whatever
stimulus has given rise to the dream; and,
thirdly, that they may have the value of any
mental impulse or intellectual operation. I will
designate these thoughts more strictly now than
hitherto as *the residue from the previous day;*
the dreamer may acknowledge them or not. I
then distinguish between this *residue* and *latent
dream-thoughts* so that, as we have been accustomed to do all along, I will call everything
which we learn from the interpretation of the
dream *the latent dream-thoughts,* while *the
residue from the previous day* is only a part of
the latent dream-thoughts. Then our conception of what happens is this: something has

been added to the residue from the previous day, something which also belongs to the unconscious, a strong but repressed wish-impulse, and it is this alone which makes the formation of a dream possible. The wish-impulse, acting upon the *residue*, creates the other part of the latent dream-thoughts, that part which no longer need appear rational or comprehensible from the point of view of our waking life.

To illustrate the relation between the residue and the unconscious wish I have elsewhere made use of a comparison which I cannot do better than repeat here. Every business undertaking requires a capitalist to defray the expenses and an entrepreneur who has the idea and understands how to carry it out. Now the part of the capitalist in dream-formation is always and only played by the unconscious wish; it supplies the necessary fund of mental energy for it: the entrepreneur is the residue from the previous day, determining the manner of the expenditure. It is, of course, quite possible for the capitalist himself to have the idea and the special knowledge needed, or for the entrepreneur himself to have capital. This simplifies the practical situation but makes the theory of it more difficult. In economics we discriminate between the man in his function of capitalist and the same man in his capacity as entrepreneur; and this distinction restores the fundamental situation upon which our comparison is based. The same variations are to be found in the formation of dreams: I leave you to follow them out for yourselves.

We cannot go any further at this point; for I think it likely that a disturbing thought has long since occurred to you and it deserves a hearing. You may ask: "Is the so-called *residue* really unconscious in the sense in which the wish necessary for the formation of the dream is unconscious?" Your suspicion is justified: this is the salient point in the whole matter. They are not both unconscious in the same sense. The dream-wish belongs to a different type of UNCONSCIOUS, which, as we have seen, has its roots in the infantile period and is furnished with special mechanisms. It is very expedient to distinguish the two types of *unconscious* from one another by speaking of them in different terms. But, all the same, we will rather wait until we have familiarized ourselves with the phenomena of the neuroses. If our conception of the existence of any kind of unconscious be already regarded as fantastic, what will people say if we admit that to reach our solution we have had to assume two kinds?

Let us break off at this point. Once more you have heard only an incomplete statement; but is it not a hopeful thought that this knowledge will be carried further, either by ourselves or by those who come after us? And have not we ourselves learnt enough that is new and startling?

FIFTEENTH LECTURE
DOUBTFUL POINTS AND CRITICAL OBSERVATIONS

WE will not leave the subject of dreams without dealing with the most common doubts and uncertainties arising in connection with the novel ideas and conceptions we have been discussing: those of you who have followed these lectures attentively will have collected some material of the kind.

1. You may have received an impression that even with strict adherence to technique our work of dream-interpretation leaves so much room for uncertainty that reliable translation of manifest dreams into their latent dream-thoughts will be thereby frustrated. You will urge first that one never knows whether any particular element in a dream is to be understood literally or symbolically, since things employed as symbols do not thereby cease to be themselves. Where there is no objective evidence to decide the question the interpretation on that particular point will be left to be arbitrarily determined by the interpreter. Further, since in the dream-work opposites coincide, it is in every instance uncertain whether a specific dream-element is to be understood in a positive or a negative sense, as itself or as its opposite—another opportunity for the interpreter to exercise a choice. Thirdly, on account of the frequency with which inversion of every kind is employed in dreams, it is open to him to assume whenever he chooses that such an inversion has taken place. Finally you will point to having heard that one is seldom certain that the interpretation arrived at is the only possible one, and that there is danger of overlooking another perfectly admissible interpretation of the same dream. In these circumstances, you will conclude, the discretion of the interpreter has a latitude that seems incompatible with any objective certainty in the result. Or you may also assume that the fault does not lie in dreams themselves, but that something erroneous in our conceptions and premises produces the unsatisfactory character of our interpretations.

All that you say is undeniable and yet I do not think it justifies either of your conclusions: that dream-interpretation as practised by us is at the mercy of the interpreter's arbitrary decisions or that the inadequacy of the results calls in question the correctness of our procedure. If for the *arbitrary decision* of the interpreter you will substitute his skill, his experience and his understanding, then I am with you. This kind of personal factor is of course indispensable, especially when interpretation is difficult; it is just the same in other scientific work, however; it can't be helped that one man will use any given technique less well, or apply it better, than another. The impression of arbitrariness made, for example, by the interpretation of symbols is corrected by the reflection that as a rule the connection of the dream-thoughts with one another, and of the dream with the life of the dreamer and the whole mental situation at the time of the dream, points directly to one of all the possible interpretations and renders all the rest useless. The conclusion that the imperfect character of the interpretations proceeds from fallacious hypotheses loses its force when consideration shows that, on the contrary, the ambiguity or indefiniteness of dreams is a quality which we should necessarily expect in them.

Let us call to mind our statement that the dream-work undertakes a translation of the dream-thoughts into a primitive mode of expression, analogous to hieroglyphics. Now all such primitive systems of expression are necessarily acompanied by ambiguity and indefiniteness; but we should not on that account be justified in doubting their practicability. You know that the coincidence of opposites in the dream-work is analogous to what is called the antithetical sense of primal words in the oldest languages. The philologist, R. Abel, to whom we owe this information, writing in 1884, begs us not on any account to imagine that there was any ambiguity in what one person said to another by means of ambivalent words of this sort. On the contrary, intonation, gestures and the whole context can have left no doubt whatever which of the two opposites the speaker had in mind to convey. In writing where gestures are absent the addition of little pictorial signs, not meant to receive separate oral expression, replaced them: e.g., a drawing of a little man, either crouching or standing upright, according as the ambiguous *ken* of the hieroglyphic meant *weak* or *strong*. So that mis-

understanding was avoided in spite of the ambiguity of sounds and signs.

In ancient systems of expression, for instance, in the scripts of the oldest languages, indefiniteness of various kinds is found with a frequency which we should not tolerate in our writings today. Thus in many Semitic writings only the consonants of the words appear: the omitted vowels have to be supplied by the reader from his knowledge and from the context. Hieroglyphic writing follows a similar principle, although not exactly the same; and this is the reason why nothing is known of the pronunciation of ancient Egyptian. There are besides other kinds of indefiniteness in the sacred writings of the Egyptians: for example, it is left to the writer's choice to inscribe the pictures from right to left or from left to right. To be able to read them, we have to remember that we must be guided by the direction of the faces of the figures, birds, and so forth. But it was also open to the writer to set the pictures in vertical columns and, in the case of inscriptions on smaller objects, he was led by considerations of what was pleasing to the eye, and of the space at his disposal, to introduce still further alterations in the arrangement of the signs. The most confusing feature in hieroglyphic script is that there is no spacing between the words. The pictures are all placed at equal intervals on the page, and it is generally impossible to know whether any given sign goes with the preceding one or forms the beginning of a new word. In Persian cuneiform writing, on the other hand, a slanting sign is used to separate the words.

The Chinese language, both spoken and written, is exceedingly ancient but is still used today by four hundred million people. Don't suppose that I understand it at all; I only obtained some information about it because I hoped to find in it analogies to the kinds of indefiniteness occurring in dreams; nor was I disappointed in my expectation, for Chinese is so full of uncertainties as positively to terrify one. As is well known, it consists of a number of syllabic sounds which are pronounced singly or doubled in combination. One of the chief dialects has about four hundred of these sounds, and since the vocabulary of this dialect is estimated at somewhere about four thousand words it is evident that every sound has an average of ten different meanings—some fewer, but some all the more. For this reason there are a whole series of devices to escape ambiguity, for the context alone will not show which of the ten possible meanings of the syllable the speaker wishes to convey to the hearer. Amongst these devices is the combining of two sounds into a single word and the use of four different "tones" in which these syllables may be spoken. For purposes of our comparison a still more interesting fact is that this language is practically without grammar: it is impossible to say of any of the one-syllable words whether it is a noun, a verb or an adjective; and, further there are no inflections to show gender, number, case, tense or mood. The language consists, as we may say, of the raw material only; just as our thought-language is resolved into its raw material by the dream-work omitting to express the relations in it. Wherever there is any uncertainty in Chinese the decision is left to the intelligence of the listener, who is guided by the context. I made a note of a Chinese saying, which literally translated runs thus: "Little what see, much what wonderful." This is simple enough to understand. It may mean: "The less a man has seen, the more he finds to wonder at," or "There is much to wonder at for the man who has seen little." Naturally there is no occasion to choose between these two translations which differ only in grammatical construction. We are assured that in spite of these uncertainties the Chinese language is a quite exceptionally good medium of expression; so it is clear that indefiniteness does not necessarily lead to ambiguity.

Now we must certainly admit that the position of affairs is far less favourable in regard to the mode of expression in dreams than it is with these ancient tongues and scripts; for these latter were originally designed as a means of communication; that is, they were intended to be understood, no matter what ways or means they had to employ. But just this character is lacking to dreams: their object is not to tell anyone anything; they are not a means of communication; on the contrary, it is important to them not to be understood. So we ought not to be surprised or misled if the result is that a number of the ambiguities and uncertainties in dreams cannot be determined. The only certain piece of knowledge gained from our comparison is that this indefiniteness (which people would like to make use of as an argument against the accuracy of our dream-interpretations) is rather to be recognized as a regular characteristic of all primitive systems of expression.

Practice and experience alone can determine the extent to which dreams can in actual fact be understood. My own opinion is that this is possible to a very great extent; and a comparison of the results obtained by properly trained analysts confirms my view. It is well known that the lay public, even in scientific circles, delights to make a parade of superior scepticism in the face of the difficulties and uncertainties which beset a scientific achievement; I think they are wrong in so doing. You may possibly not all know that the same thing happened at the time when the Babylonian and Assyrian inscriptions were being deciphered. There was a point at which public opinion was active in declaring that the men deciphering the cuneiform writing were victims of a chimera and that the whole business of investigation was a fraud. But in the year 1857 the Royal Asiatic Society made a conclusive test. They challenged four of the most distinguished men engaged in this branch of research—Rawlinson, Hincks, Fox Talbot and Oppert—to send to the Society in sealed envelopes independent translations of a newly discovered inscription, and, after comparing the four versions, they were able to announce that there was sufficient agreement between the four to justify belief in what had been achieved and confidence in further progress. The mockery of the learned laity then gradually came to an end, and certainty in the reading of cuneiform documents has advanced enormously since then.

2. A second series of objections is closely connected with an impression which you also have probably not escaped; namely, that a number of the solutions achieved by our method of dream-interpretation seem strained, specious, *dragged in*—in other words, forced, or even comical or joking. These criticisms are so frequent that I will take at random the last that has come to my ears. Now listen: a head-master in Switzerland—that free country—was recently asked to resign his post on account of his interest in psycho-analysis. He protested and a Berne paper published the decision of the school authorities on his case. I shall quote from the article a few sentences which refer to psycho-analysis: "Further, we are amazed at the far-fetched and factitious character of many of the examples given in the said book by Dr. Pfister of Zurich. . . . It is indeed a matter for surprise that the head-master of a Training College should accept so credulously all these assertions and such specious evidence." These sentences purport to be the final opinion

of "One who judges calmly." I am much more inclined to think this "calm" factitious. Let us examine these remarks more closely in the expectation that a certain amount of reflection and knowledge of the subject will do no harm, even to a "calm judgment."

It is really quite refreshing to see how swiftly and unerringly anyone relying merely on his first impressions can arrive at an opinion on some critical question of psychology in its more abstruse aspects. The interpretations seem to him far-fetched and strained, and do not commend themselves to him; consequently, they are wrong and the whole business is rubbish. Such critics never give even a passing thought to the possibility that there may be good reasons why the interpretations are bound to convey this very impression—a thought which would lead to the further question what these good reasons are.

The circumstance which calls forth this criticism is essentially related to the effect of displacement, which you have learnt to know as the most powerful instrument in the service of the dream-censorship. With its aid the substitute-formations which we call allusions are created; but these allusions are of a kind not easy to recognize as such; nor is it easy to discover the thought proper by working back from them, for they are connected with it by the most extraordinary and unusual extrinsic associations. But the whole matter throughout concerns things which are meant to be hidden, intended to be concealed: that is exactly the object of the dream-censorship. We must not expect, though, to find something that has been hidden by looking in the very place where it ordinarily belongs. The frontier surveillance authorities nowadays are a good deal more cunning in this respect than the Swiss school authorities; for they are not content with examining portfolios and letter-cases when hunting for documents and plans; but consider the possibility that spies and smugglers may conceal anything compromising about their persons, in places where it is most difficult to detect and where such things certainly do not belong, for example, between the double soles of their boots. If the concealed articles are found there, it is certainly true that they have been *dragged* to light, but they are none the less a very good *find*.

In admitting the possibility that the connection between a latent dream-element and its manifest substitute may appear most remote and extraordinary, sometimes even comical or joking, we are guided by our wide experience of instances in which we did not as a rule find the meaning ourselves. It is often impossible to arrive at such interpretations by our own efforts: no sane person could guess the bridge connecting the two. The dreamer either solves the riddle straightaway by a direct association (*he* can do it because it is in his mind that the substitute-formation originated); or else he provides so much material that there is no longer any need for special penetration in order to solve it—the solution thrusts itself upon us as inevitable. If the dreamer does not help us in either of these two ways the manifest element in question will remain for ever incomprehensible. Let me give you one more instance of this kind which happened recently. A patient of mine lost her father during the course of the treatment, after which she seized every opportunity to bring him back to life in her dreams. In one of these her father appeared in a certain connection otherwise not applicable and said: *"It is quarter past eleven, it is half past eleven, it is quarter to twelve."* For the interpretation of this curious detail she could only provide the association that her father was pleased when his older children were punctual at the midday meal. This certainly fitted in with the dream-element, but it threw no light on its origin. The situation which had just been reached in the treatment gave good grounds for the suspicion that a carefully suppressed critical antagonism to her much loved and honoured father had played a part in this dream. Following out her further associations, apparently quite remote from the dream, she told how she had heard a long discussion of psychological questions on the day before and a relative had said: "Primitive man (*Urmensch*) survives in all of us." Now a light dawns on us. Here was again a splendid opportunity for her to imagine that her dead father survived, and so in the dream she made him a "clock-man" (*Uhrmensch*), telling the quarters up to the time of the midday meal.

The likeness to a pun in this cannot be ignored, and as a matter of fact it has often happened that a dreamer's pun has been ascribed to the interpreter; there are yet other examples in which it is not at all easy to decide whether we are dealing with a joke or a dream. But you will remember that the same sort of doubt arose with some slips of the tongue. A man related as a dream that he and his uncle were sitting in the latter's *auto* (automobile) and his uncle kissed him. The dreamer himself instantly volunteered the interpretation: it meant *auto-erotism* (a term used in our theory of the libido, signifying gratification obtained without any external love-object). Now was this man allowing himself a joke at our expense and pretending that a pun which occurred to him was part of a dream? I do not think so: he really did dream it. But where does this bewildering resemblance between dreams and jokes come from? At one time this question took me somewhat out of my way, for it necessitated my making a thorough investigation into the question of wit itself. This led to the conclusion that wit originates as follows: a preconscious train of thought is for a moment left to a process of unconscious elaboration, from which it emerges in the form of a witticism. While under the influence of the unconscious it is subject to the mechanisms there operative—to condensation and displacement; that is to say, to the same processes as we found at work in the dream-work; and the similarity sometimes found between dreams and wit is to be ascribed to this character common to both. But the unintentional *dream-joke* does not amuse us as does an ordinary witticism; a deeper study of wit may show you why this is so. The *dream-joke* strikes us as a poor form of wit; it does not make us laugh, it leaves us cold.

Now in this we are following the path of the ancient method of dream-interpretation, which has given us, besides much that is useless, many a valuable example of interpretation upon which we ourselves could not improve. I will tell you a dream of historic importance which is related in slightly different versions by Plutarch and Artemidorus of Daldis, the dreamer being Alexander the Great. When he was laying siege to the city of Tyre, which was putting up an obstinate resistance (B.C. 322), he dreamt one night that he saw a dancing satyr. The dream-interpreter Aristandros, who accompanied the army on its campaigns, interpreted this dream by dividing the word *satyros* into Σὰ Τύρος (Tyre is thine), and prophesied from this the king's victory over the city. This interpretation decided Alexander to continue the siege and eventually the city fell. The interpretation, factitious as it seems, was undoubtedly the right one.

3. I can well imagine that you will be especially impressed on being told that even people who have long studied the interpretation of dreams in the course of their work as psycho-analysts have raised objections to our conception of dreams. It would indeed have been exceptional if so excellent an opportunity for new mistakes had been let slip; and so assertions have been made, due to confusion of ideas and based on unjustifiable generalizations, which are hardly less incorrect than the medical conception of dreams. One of these statements you know already: that dreams deal with attempts at adaptation to the situation at the moment and with the solution of future problems; in other words, that they pursue a "prospective tendency" or aim (A. Maeder). We have already demonstrated that this statement rests upon a confusion between dreams and the latent dream-thoughts and ignores the process of dream-work. If those who speak of this "prospective tendency" mean thereby to characterize the unconscious mental activity to which the latent thoughts belong, then, on the one hand, they tell us nothing new and, on the other hand, the description is not exhaustive; for the unconscious mental activity occupies itself with many other things besides preparation for the future. There seems to be a much worse confusion behind the assurance that the *death clause* may be found underlying every dream; I am not quite clear what this formula is intended to mean, but I suspect that behind it the dream is confounded with the whole personality of the dreamer.

An unjustifiable generalization, based on a few striking examples, is contained in the statement that every dream admits of two kinds of interpretation: one of the kind we have described, the so-called *psycho-analytic* interpretation, and the other the so-called *anagogic,* which disregards the instinctual tendencies and aims at a representation of the higher mental functions (H. Silberer); there are dreams of this kind, but you will seek in vain to extend this conception to include even a majority of dreams. After all you have heard, the statement that all dreams are to be interpreted bisexually, as a combination of two tendencies which may be called male and female (A. Adler), will seem to you quite incomprehensible. Here again, single dreams of this sort do of course occur and later on you may learn that their structure is similar to that of certain hysterical symptoms. I mention all these discoveries of new general characteristics of dreams in order to warn you against them, or at least to leave you in no doubt about my own opinion of them.

4. At one time the objective value of research

into dreams seemed to be discredited by the fact that patients treated analytically appeared to suit the content of their dreams to the favourite theories of their doctors, one class dreaming mainly of sexual impulses, and another of impulses for mastery, others again even of rebirth (W. Stekel). The force of this observation is weakened by the reflection that people dreamed dreams before there was any such thing as psycho-analytic treatment to influence their dreams and that the patients undergoing treatment nowadays also used to dream before they began it. The actual fact in this supposedly new observation is soon shown to be self-evident and of no consequence for the theory of dreams. The residue from the previous day which gives rise to dreams is a residue from the great interests of waking life. If the physician's words and the stimuli which he gives have become of importance to the patient they then enter into whatever constitutes the residue and can act as mental stimuli for dream-formation, just like other interests of affective value roused on the preceding day which have not subsided; they operate in the same way as bodily stimuli which affect the sleeper during sleep. Like these other factors inciting dreams, the trains of thought roused by the physician can appear in the manifest dream-content or be revealed in the latent thoughts. We know indeed that dreams can be experimentally produced, or, to speak more accurately, a part of the dream-material can be thus introduced into the dream. In influencing his patients thus the analyst plays a part no different from that of an experimenter, like Mourly Vold, who placed in certain positions the limbs of the person upon whom he experimented.

We can often influence what a man shall dream *about*, but never *what* he will dream; for the mechanism of the dream-work and the unconscious dream-wish are inaccessible to external influence of any sort. We realized, when we were considering dreams arising out of bodily stimuli, that in the reaction to the bodily or mental stimuli brought to bear upon the dreamer the peculiarity and independence of dream-life is clearly seen. The criticism I have just discussed which tends to cast a doubt upon the objectivity of dream investigation is again an assertion based upon confounding, this time confounding dreams with—their material.

I wanted to tell you as much as this about the problems of dreams. You will guess that I have passed over a great deal and will have discovered for yourselves that my treatment of nearly every point has necessarily been incomplete; but this is due to the phenomena of dreams being so closely connected with those of the neuroses. Our plan was to study dreams as an introduction to the study of the neuroses and it was certainly a better one than beginning the other way about; but since dreams prepare us for comprehension of the neuroses, so also can a correctly formed estimate of dreams be acquired only after some knowledge of neurotic manifestations has been gained.

I do not know how you may think about it, but I can assure you that I do not regret having taken up so much of your interest and of the time at our disposal in the consideration of problems connected with dreams. I know no other way by which one can so speedily arrive at conviction of the correctness of those statements by which psycho-analysis stands or falls. It requires strenuous work for many months, and even years, to demonstrate that the symptoms in a case of neurotic illness have a meaning, serve a purpose, and arise from the patient's experiences in life. On the other hand, a few hours' effort may be enough to show these things in some dream which at first seemed utterly confused and incomprehensible, and in this way to confirm all the premises upon which psycho-analysis rests—the existence of unconscious mental processes, the special mechanisms which they obey, and the instinctive propelling forces which are expressed by them. And when we remember how far-reaching is the analogy in the structure of dreams to that of neurotic symptoms and, with that, reflect how rapid is the transformation of a dreamer into a wide-awake, reasonable human being, we acquire an assurance that the neuroses too depend only upon an alteration in the balance of the forces at work in mental life.

PART III. GENERAL THEORY OF NEUROSES

SIXTEENTH LECTURE

PSYCHO-ANALYSIS AND PSYCHIATRY

IT pleases me greatly to see you here again to continue our discussions after a year has passed. Last year the subject of my lectures was the application of psycho-analysis to errors and to dreams; I hope this year to lead you to some comprehension of neurotic phenomena which, as you will soon discover, have much in common with both our former subjects. I must tell you before I begin, however, that I cannot concede you the same attitude towards me now as I did last year. Then I endeavoured to make no step without being in agreement with your judgment; I debated a great deal with you, submitted to your objections, in fact, recognized you and your *healthy common sense* as the deciding factor. That is no longer possible and for a very simple reason. Errors and dreams are phenomena which were familiar to you; one might say you had as much experience of them as I, or could easily have obtained it. The manifestations of neurosis, however, are an unknown region to you; those of you who are not yourselves medical men have no access there except through the accounts I give you; and of what use is the most excellent judgment where there is no knowledge of the subject under debate?

However, do not receive this announcement as though I were going to give these lectures *ex cathedra* or to demand unconditional acceptance from you. Any such misconception would do me a gross injustice. I do not aim at producing conviction—my aim is to stimulate enquiry and to destroy prejudices. If, owing to ignorance of the subject, you are not in a position to adjudicate, then you should neither believe nor reject. You should only listen and allow what I tell you to make its own effect upon you. Convictions are not so easily acquired, or, when they are achieved without much trouble, they soon prove worthless and unstable. No one has a right to conviction on these matters who has not worked at this subject for many years, as I have, and has not himself experienced the same new and astonishing discoveries. Then why these sudden convictions in intellectual matters, lightning conversions, and instantaneous repudiations? Do you not see that the *coup de foudre*, love

at first sight, proceeds from a very different mental sphere, from the affective one? We do not require even our patients to bring with them any conviction in favour of psychoanalysis or any devotion to it. It would make us suspicious of them. Benevolent scepticism is the attitude in them which we like best. Therefore will you also try to let psycho-analytical conceptions develop quietly in your minds alongside the popular or the psychiatric view, until opportunities arise for them to influence each other and be united into a decisive opinion.

On the other hand, you are not for a moment to suppose that the psycho-analytic point of view which I shall lay before you is a speculative system of ideas. On the contrary, it is the result of experience, being founded either on direct observations or on conclusions drawn from observation. Whether these have been drawn in an adequate or a justifiable manner future advances in science will show; after nearly two and a half decades and now that I am fairly well advanced in years I may say, without boasting, that it was particularly difficult, intense, and all-absorbing work that yielded these observations. I have often had the impression that our opponents were unwilling to consider this source of our statements, as if they looked upon them as ideas derived subjectively which anyone could dispute at his own sweet will. This attitude on the part of my opponents is not quite comprehensible to me. Perhaps it comes from the circumstance that physicians pay so little attention to neurotics and listen so carelessly to what they say that it has become impossible for them to perceive anything in the patients' communications or to make detailed observations from them. I will take this opportunity of assuring you that in these lectures I shall make few controversial references, least of all to individuals. I have never been able to convince myself of the truth of the saying that "strife is the father of all things." I think the source of it was the philosophy of the Greek sophists and that it errs, as does the latter, through the overestimation of dialectics. It seems to me, on the contrary, that scientific controversy, so-called, is on the whole quite unfruitful, apart from the fact that it is almost always conducted in a highly personal manner. Until a few years ago I could boast that I had only once been engaged in a regular scientific dispute, and that with one single investigator, Löwenfeld of Munich. The end of it was that we became friends and have remained so to this day. But I did not repeat the experiment for a very long time because I was not certain that the outcome would be the same.

Now you will surely judge that a refusal of this kind to discuss matters publicly points to a high degree of inaccessibility to criticism, to obstinacy, or, in the polite colloquialism of the scientific world, to *pig-headedness*. My reply to you would be that, should you have arrived at a conviction by means of such hard work, you would also thereby derive a certain right to maintain it with some tenacity. Further, on my own behalf, I can say that in the course of my work I have modified my views on important points, changed them or replaced them by others, and have of course in each case published the fact. What has been the result of this frankness? Some people have ignored my corrections of myself altogether and still today criticize me in respect of views which no longer mean the same to me. Others positively reproach me for these changes and declare me to be unreliable on that account. No one who changes his views once or twice deserves to be believed, for it is only too likely that he will be mistaken again in his latest assertions; but anyone who sticks to anything he has once said, or refuses to give way upon it easily enough, is obstinate or pig-headed; is it not so? What is to be done in the face of these self-contradictory criticisms except to remain as one is and behave as seems best to one? This is what I decided to do; and I am not deterred from remodelling and improving my theories in accordance with later experience. I have so far found nothing to alter in my fundamental standpoint and I hope this will never be necessary.

So now I have to lay before you the psycho-analytic theory of neurotic manifestations. For this purpose it will be simplest, on account of both the analogy and the contrast, to take an example which links up with the phenomena we have already considered. I will take a *symptomatic act* which I see many people commit in my own consulting-room. The analyst has little to offer to the people who come to a physician's consulting-room for half-an-hour to recount the lifelong misery of their fate. His deeper comprehension makes it difficult for him to give, as another might, the opinion that there is nothing wrong with them and that they had better take a light course of hydro therapy. One of our colleagues once replied, with a shrug, when asked how he dealt with consultation patients, that he "fined them so many crowns for 'wasting the time of the court.'" You will, therefore, not be surprised to hear that even the busiest psycho-analysts are not much sought after for consultations. I have had the ordinary door between the waiting-room and my consulting-room supplemented by another door and covered with felt. The reason for this is obvious. Now it constantly happens when I admit people from the waiting-room that they omit to close these doors, leaving even both doors open behind them. When I see this happen, I at once, with some stiffness, request him or her to go back and make good the omission, no matter how fine a gentleman he may be or how many hours she has spent on her toilet. My action gives the impression of being uncalled-for and pedantic; occasionally too I have found myself in the wrong, when the person turned out to be one of those who cannot themselves grasp a door-handle and are glad when those with them avoid it. But in the majority of cases I was right, for anyone who behaves in this way and leaves the door of a physician's consulting-room open into the waiting-room belongs to the rabble and deserves to be received with coldness. Now don't allow yourselves to be biased before you have heard the rest. This omission on the part of a patient occurs only when he has been waiting alone in the outer room and thus leaves an empty room behind him, never when others, strangers to him, have also been waiting there. In the latter case he knows very well that it is to his own interest not to be overheard while he talks to the physician and he never neglects to close both doors carefully.

Occuring in this way, the patient's omission is neither accidental nor meaningless, and not even unimportant, for it betrays the visitor's attitude to the physician. He belongs to that large class who seek those in high places, and wish to be dazzled and intimidated. Perhaps he had made enquiries by telephone at what time he would be most likely to gain admittance and had been expecting to find a crowd of applicants in a queue, as if at the grocer's in war-time. Then he is shown into an empty room which, moreover, is most modestly furnished, and he is dumbfounded. He must somehow make the physician atone for the superfluous respect he had been prepared to show him;

and so he omits to close the doors between the waiting- and the consulting-rooms. He intends this to mean: "Pooh! there is no one here and I daresay there won't be, however long I stay!" He would behave during the interview in an uncivil and supercilious manner, too, if his presumption were not curbed at the outset by a sharp reminder.

In the analysis of this little symptomatic act you find nothing that is not already known to you; namely, the conclusion that it is no accident but has in it motive, meaning, and intention; that it belongs to a mental context which can be specified; and that it provides a small indication of a more important mental process. But above all it implies that the process thus indicated is not known to the consciousness of the person who carries it out; for not one of the patients who left the two doors open would have admitted that he wished to show any depreciation of me by his neglect. Many of them could probably recall a sense of disappointment on entering the empty waiting-room, but the connection between this impression and the succeeding symptomatic act certainly remained outside their consciousness.

Now let us place this little analysis of a symptomatic act by the side of an observation made on a patient. I will choose one which is fresh in my memory, and also because it can be described in comparatively few words. A certain amount of detail is indispensable for any such account.

A young officer, home on short leave of absence, asked me to treat his mother-in-law, who was living in the happiest surroundings and yet was embittering her own and her family's lives by a nonsensical idea. I found her a well-preserved lady, fifty-three years of age, of a friendly, simple disposition, who gave without hesitation the following account of herself. She is most happily married, and lives in the country with her husband who manages a large factory. She cannot say enough of her husband's kindness and consideration; theirs had been a love-marriage thirty years ago, since when they had never had a cloud, a quarrel, or a moment's jealousy. Her two children have both married well, but her husband's sense of duty keeps him still at work. A year before, an incredible and, to her, incomprehensible thing happened. She received an anonymous letter telling her that her excellent husband was carrying on an intrigue with a young girl, and believed it on the spot—since then her happiness has been destroyed. The details were more or less as follows: she had a housemaid with whom she discussed confidential matters, perhaps rather too freely. This young woman cherished a positively venomous hatred for another girl who had succeeded better in life than herself, although of no better origin. Instead of going into service, the other young woman had had a commercial training, been taken into the factory and, owing to vacancies caused by the absence of staff on service in the field, had been promoted to a good position. She lived in the factory, knew all the gentlemen, and was even addressed as "Miss." The other one who had been left behind in life was only too ready to accuse her former schoolmate of all possible evil. One day our patient and her housemaid were discussing an elderly gentleman who had visited the house and of whom it was said that he did not live with his wife but kept a mistress. Why, she did not know, but she suddenly said: "I cannot imagine anything more awful than to hear that my husband had a mistress." The next day she received by post an anonymous letter in disguised handwriting which informed her of the very thing she had just imagined. She concluded—probably correctly—that the letter was the handiwork of her malicious housemaid, for the woman who was named as the mistress of her husband was the very girl who was the object of this housemaid's hatred. Although she at once saw through the plot and had seen enough of such cowardly accusations in her own surroundings to place little credence in them, our patient was nevertheless prostrated by this letter. She became terribly excited and at once sent for her husband to overwhelm him with reproaches. The husband laughingly denied the accusation and did the best thing he could. He sent for the family physician (who also attended the factory), and he did his best to calm the unhappy lady. The next thing they did was also most reasonable. The housemaid was dismissed, but not the supposed mistress. From that time on the patient claims to have repeatedly brought herself to a calm view of the matter, so that she no longer believes the contents of the letter; but it has never gone very deep nor lasted very long. It was enough to hear the young woman's name mentioned, or to meet her in the street, for a new attack of suspicion, agony, and reproaches to break out.

This is the clinical picture of this excellent woman's case. It did not require much experience of psychiatry to perceive that, in contrast to other neurotics, she described her symptoms too mildly—as we say, dissimulated them—and that she had never really overcome her belief in the anonymous letter.

Now what attitude does a psychiatrist take up to such a case? We know already what he would say to the symptomatic act of a patient who does not close the waiting-room doors. He explains it as an accident, without interest psychologically, and no concern of his. But he cannot continue to take up this attitude in regard to the case of the jealous lady. The symptomatic action appears to be unimportant; the symptom calls for notice as a grave matter. Subjectively it involves intense suffering, and objectively it threatens to break up a family; its claim to psychiatric interest is therefore indisputable. First the psychiatrist tries to characterize the symptom by some essential attribute. The idea with which this lady torments herself cannot be called nonsensical in itself; it does happen that elderly husbands contract relationships with young women. But there is something else about it that is nonsensical and incomprehensible. The patient has absolutely no grounds, except the anonymous letter, for supposing that her loving and faithful husband belongs to this category of men, otherwise not so uncommon. She knows that this communication carries no proof, she can explain its origin satisfactorily; she ought therefore to be able to say to herself that she has no grounds for her jealousy and she does even say so, but she suffers just as much as if she regarded her jealousy as well-founded. Ideas of this kind that are inaccessible to logic and the arguments of reality are unanimously described as *delusions*. The good lady suffers therefore, from a *delusion of jealousy*. That is evidently the essential characteristic of the case.

Having established this first point, our psychiatric interest increases. When a delusion cannot be dissipated by the facts of reality, it probably does not spring from reality. Where else then does it spring from? Delusions can have the most various contents; why is the content of it in this case jealousy? What kind of people have delusions, and particularly delusions of jealousy? Now we should like to listen to the psychiatrist, but he leaves us in the lurch here. He considers only one of our questions. He will examine the family history of this woman and will *perhaps* bring us the answer that the kind of people who suffer from delusions are those in whose families similar or different disorders have occurred repeatedly.

In other words, this lady has developed a delusion because she had an hereditary predisposition to do so. That is certainly something; but is it all that we want to know? Is it the sole cause of her disease? Does it satisfy us to assume that it is unimportant, arbitrary, or inexplicable that one kind of delusion should have been developed instead of another? And are we to understand the proposition—that the hereditary predisposition is decisive—also in a negative sense; that is, that no matter what experiences and emotions life had brought her she was destined some time or other to produce a delusion? You will want to know why scientific psychiatry gives no further explanation. And I reply: "Only a rogue gives more than he has." The psychiatrist knows of no path leading to any further explanation in such a case. He has to content himself with a diagnosis and, in spite of wide experience, with a very uncertain prognosis of its future course.

Now can psycho-analysis do better than this? Yes, certainly I hope to show you that even in such an obscure case as this it is possible to discover something which makes closer comprehension possible. First, I shall ask you to notice this incomprehensible detail; that the anonymous letter on which her delusion is founded was positively provoked by the patient herself, by her saying to the scheming housemaid the day before that nothing could be more awful than to hear that her husband had an intrigue with a young woman. She first put the idea of sending the letter into the servant's mind by this. So the delusion acquires a certain independence of the letter; it existed beforehand as a fear—or, as a wish?—in her mind. Besides this, the further small indications revealed in the bare two hours of analysis are noteworthy. The patient responded very coldly, it is true, to the request to tell me her further thoughts, ideas, and recollections, after she had finished her story. She declared that nothing came to her mind, she had told me everything; and after two hours the attempt had to be given up, because she announced that she felt quite well already and was certain that the morbid idea would not return. Her saying this was naturally due to resistance and to the fear of further analysis. In these two hours she had let fall some remarks, nevertheless, which made a certain interpretation not only possible but inevitable, and this interpretation threw a sharp light on the origin of the delusion of jealousy. There actually existed in her an infatuation for a young man, for the very son-in-law who had urged her to seek my assistance. Of this infatuation she herself knew nothing or only perhaps very little; in the circumstances of their relationship it was easily possible for it to disguise itself as harmless tenderness on her part. After what we have already learnt it is not difficult to see into the mind of this good woman and excellent mother. Such an infatuation, such a monstrous, impossible thing, could not come into her conscious mind; it persisted, nevertheless, and unconsciously exerted a heavy pressure. Something had to happen, some sort of relief had to be found; and the simplest alleviation lay in that mechanism of displacement which so regularly plays its part in the formation of delusional jealousy. If not merely she, old woman that she was, were in love with a young man, but if only her old husband too were in love with a young mistress, then her torturing conscience would be absolved from the infidelity. The phantasy of her husband's infidelity was thus a cooling balm on her burning wound. Of her own love she never became conscious; but its reflection in the delusion, which brought such advantages, thus became compulsive, delusional and conscious. All arguments against it could naturally avail nothing; for they were directed only against the reflection, and not against the original to which its strength was due and which lay buried out of reach in the unconscious.

Let us now piece together the results of this short, obstructed psycho-analytic attempt to understand this case. It is assumed, of course, that the information acquired was correct, a point which I cannot submit to your judgment here. First of all, the delusion is no longer senseless and incomprehensible; it is sensible, logically motivated, and has its place in connection with an affective experience of the patient's. Secondly, it has arisen as a necessary reaction to another mental process which has itself been revealed by other indications; and it owes its delusional character, its quality of resisting real and logical objections, to this relation with this other mental process. It is something desired in itself, a kind of consolation. Thirdly, the fact that the delusion is one of jealousy and no other is unmistakably determined by the experience underlying the disease. You will also recognize the two important analogies with the symptomatic act we analysed; namely, the discovery of the sense or intention behind the symptom and the relation of it to something in the given situation which is unconscious.

This does not, of course, answer all the questions arising out of this case. On the contrary, it bristles with further problems, some of which have not yet proved soluble at all, while others cannot be solved owing to the unfavourable circumstances met with in this case. For instance, why does this happily married lady fall in love with her son-in-law, and why does relief come to her in the form of this kind of reflection, this projection of her own state of mind on to her husband, when other forms of relief were also possible? Do not think that it is idle and uncalled for to propound these questions. We have already a good deal of material at hand to provide possible answers. The patient had come to that critical time of life which brings a sudden and unwelcome increase of sexual desire to a woman; that may have been sufficient in itself. Or there may have been an additional reason, in that the sexual capacity of her excellent and faithful husband may have been for some years insufficient for the still vigorous woman's needs. Observation has taught us that it is just such men, whose fidelity is thus a matter of course, who treat their wives with particular tenderness and are unusually considerate of their nervous ailments. Neither is it unimportant, moreover, that the object of this abnormal infatuation should be her daughter's young husband. A strong erotic attachment to the daughter, with its roots in the individual sexual constitution of the mother, often manages to maintain itself in such a transformation. I may perhaps remind you in this connection that the relation between mother-in-law and son-in-law has from time immemorial been regarded by mankind as a particularly sensitive one, which among primitive races has given rise to very powerful taboos and precautions.[1] On the positive as well as on the negative side it frequently exceeds the limits regarded as desirable in civilized society. Of these three possible factors, whether one of them has been at work in the case before us, or two of them, or whether all three together have taken part, I cannot tell you; though only because the analysis of the case could not be continued beyond the second hour.

I perceive now that I have been speaking entirely of things which you were not yet prepared to understand. I did so in order to carry out the comparison between psychiatry and psychoanalysis. But I may ask you one thing at this point: Have you observed anything in the nature of a contradiction between the two? Psy-

[1] Cf. *Totem and Taboo*.

chiatry does not employ the technical methods of psycho-analysis, neglects any consideration of the content of the delusion, and in pointing to heredity gives us but a general and remote aetiology instead of first disclosing the more scientific and immediate one. But is any contradiction or opposition contained in this? Is not the one rather a supplement to the other? Is the hereditary factor inconsistent with the importance of experience and would they not both work together most effectively? You will admit that there is nothing essential in the work of psychiatry which could oppose psycho-analytic researches. It is therefore the psychiatrists who oppose it, and not psychiatry itself. Psycho-analysis stands to psychiatry more or less as histology does to anatomy; in one, the outer forms of organs are studied, in the other, the construction of these out of the tissues and constituent elements. It is not easy to conceive of any contradiction between these two fields of study, in which the work of the one is continued in the other. You know that nowadays anatomy is the basis of the scientific study of medicine; but time was when dissecting human corpses in order to discover the internal structure of the body was as much a matter for severe prohibition as practising psycho-analysis in order to discover the internal workings of the human mind seems today to be a matter for condemnation. And, presumably at a not too distant date, we shall have perceived that there can be no psychiatry which is scientifically radical without a thorough knowledge of the deep-seated unconscious processes in mental life.

There may be some of you who perhaps are friendly enough towards psycho-analysis, often attacked as it is, to wish that it would justify itself in another direction also, that is, therapeutically. You know that psychiatric therapy has hitherto been unable to influence delusions. Can psycho-analysis do so perhaps, by reason of its insight into the mechanism of these symptoms? No, I have to tell you that it cannot; for the present, at any rate, it is just as powerless as any other therapy to heal these sufferers. It is true that we can understand what has happened to the patient; but we have no means by which we can make him understand it himself. You have heard that I could not continue the analysis of this delusion beyond the first preliminaries. Would you then maintain that analysis of such cases is undesirable because it remains fruitless? I do not think so. It is our right, yes, and our duty, to pursue

our researches without respect to the immediate gain effected. The day will come, where and when we know not, when every little piece of knowledge will be converted into power, and into therapeutic power. Even if psycho-analysis showed itself as unsuccessful with all other forms of nervous and mental diseases as with delusions, it would still remain justified as an irreplaceable instrument of scientific research. It is true that we should not be in a position to practise it; the human material on which we learn lives, and has its own will, and must have its own motives in order to participate in the work; and it would then refuse to do so. I will therefore close my lecture for today by telling you that there are large groups of nervous disturbances for which this conversion of our own advance in knowledge into therapeutic power has actually been carried out; and that with these diseases, otherwise so refractory, our measures yield under certain conditions, results which give place to none in the domain of medical therapy.

SEVENTEENTH LECTURE
THE MEANING OF SYMPTOMS

IN THE last lecture I explained to you that clinical psychiatry troubles itself little about the actual form of the individual symptom or the content of it; but that psycho-analysis has made this its starting-point, and has ascertained that the symptom itself has a meaning and is connected with experiences in the life of the patient. The meaning of neurotic symptoms was first discovered by J. Breuer in the study and successful cure of a case of hysteria (1880-82), which has since then become famous. It is true that P. Janet independently reached the same result; in fact, priority in publication must be granted to the French investigator, for Breuer did not publish his observations until more than a decade later (1893-95), during the period of our work together. Incidentally, it is of no great importance to us who made the discovery, for you know that every discovery is made more than once, and none is made all at once, nor is success meted out according to deserts. America is not called after Columbus. Before Breuer and Janet, the great psychiatrist Leuret expressed the opinion that even the delusions of the insane would prove to have some meaning, if only we knew how to translate them. I confess that for a long time I was willing to accord Janet very high recognition for his explanation of neurotic symptoms, because he regarded them as expressions of *"idées inconscientes"* possessing the patient's mind. Since then, however, Janet has taken up an attitude of undue reserve, as if he meant to imply that the unconscious had been nothing more to him than a manner of speaking, a makeshift, *une façon de parler,* and that he had nothing "real" in mind. Since then I have not understood Janet's views, but I believe that he has gratuitously deprived himself of great credit.

Neurotic symptoms then, just like errors and dreams, have their meaning and, like these, are related to the life of the person in whom they appear. This is an important matter which I should like to demonstrate to you by some examples. I can merely assert, I cannot prove, that it is so in every case; anyone observing for himself will be convinced of it. For certain reasons though, I shall not take these examples from cases of hysteria, but from another very remarkable form of neurosis, closely allied in origin to the latter, about which I must say a few preliminary words. This, which we call *the obsessional neurosis,* is not so popular as the widely known *hysteria;* it is, if I may so express myself, not so noisily ostentatious, behaves more as if it were a private affair of the patient's, dispenses almost entirely with bodily manifestations and creates all its symptoms in the mental sphere. The obsessional neurosis and hysteria are the two forms of neurotic disease upon the study of which psycho-analysis was first built up, and in the treatment of which also our therapy celebrates its triumphs. In the obsessional neurosis, however, that mysterious leap from the mental to the physical is absent, and it has really become more intimately comprehensible and transparent to us through psycho-analytic research than hysteria; we have come to understand that it displays far more markedly certain extreme features of the neurotic constitution.

The obsessional neurosis[1] takes this form: the patient's mind is occupied with thoughts that do not really interest him, he feels impulses which seem alien to him, and he is impelled to perform actions which not only afford him no pleasure but from which he is powerless to desist. The thoughts (obsessions) may be meaningless in themselves or only of no interest to the patient; they are often absolutely silly; in every case they are the starting-point of a strained concentration of thought which

[1] Sometimes called in English *compulsion-neurosis.* —Tr.

exhausts the patient and to which he yields most unwillingly. Against his will he has to worry and speculate as if it were a matter of life or death to him. The impulses which he perceives within him may seem to be of an equally childish and meaningless character; mostly, however, they consist of something terrifying, such as temptations to commit serious crimes, so that the patient not only repudiates them as alien, but flees from them in horror, and guards himself by prohibitions, precautions, and restrictions against the possibility of carrying them out. As a matter of fact he never, literally not even once, carries these impulses into effect; flight and precautions invariably win. What he does really commit are very harmless, certainly trivial acts—what are termed the obsessive actions—which are mostly repetitions and ceremonial elaborations of ordinary every-day performances, making these common necessary actions—going to bed, washing, dressing, going for walks, etc.—into highly laborious tasks of almost insuperable difficulty. The morbid ideas, impulses, and actions are not by any means combined in the same proportions in individual types and cases of the obsessional neurosis; on the contrary, the rule is that one or another of these manifestations dominates the picture and gives the disease its name; but what is common to all forms of it is unmistakable enough.

This is a mad disease, surely. I don't think the wildest psychiatric phantasy could have invented anything like it, and if we did not see it every day with our own eyes we could hardly bring ourselves to believe in it. Now do not imagine that you can do anything for such a patient by advising him to distract himself, to pay no attention to these silly ideas, and do something sensible instead of his nonsensical practises. This is what he would like himself; for he is perfectly aware of his condition, he shares your opinion about his obsessional symptoms, he even volunteers it quite readily. Only he simply cannot help himself; the actions performed in an obsessional condition are supported by a kind of energy which probably has no counterpart in normal mental life. Only one thing is open to him—he can displace and he can exchange; instead of one silly idea he can adopt another of a slightly milder character, from one precaution or prohibition he can proceed to another, instead of one ceremonial rite he can perform another. He can displace his sense of compulsion, but he cannot dispel it. This capacity for displacing all the symptoms, involving radical alteration of their original forms, is a main characteristic of the disease; it is, moreover, striking that in this condition the *opposite values (polarities)* pervading mental life appear to be exceptionally sharply differentiated. In addition to compulsions of both positive and negative character, doubt appears in the intellectual sphere, gradually spreading until it gnaws even at what is usually held to be certain. All these things combine to bring about an ever-increasing indecisiveness, loss of energy, and curtailment of freedom; and that although the obsessional neurotic is originally always a person of a very energetic disposition, often highly opinionated, and as a rule intellectually gifted above the average. He has usually attained to an agreeably high standard of ethical development, is over-conscientious, and more than usually correct. You may imagine that it is a sufficiently arduous task to find one's bearings in this maze of contradictory character-traits and morbid manifestations. At the moment our aim is merely to interpret some symptoms of this disease.

Perhaps in view of our previous discussions you would like to know what present-day psychiatry has to offer concerning the obsessional neurosis; it is but a miserable contribution, however. Psychiatry has given names to the various compulsions, and has nothing more to say about them. It asserts instead that persons exhibiting these symptoms are *degenerate*. That is not much satisfaction to us; it is no more than an estimate of their value, a condemnation instead of an explanation. We are intended, I suppose, to conclude that deterioration from type would naturally produce all kinds of oddities in people. Now, we do believe that people who develop such symptoms must be somewhat different in type from other human beings; but we should like to know whether they are more *degenerate* than other nervous patients, than hysterical or insane people. The characterization is clearly again much too general. One may even doubt whether it is justified at all when one learns that such symptoms occur in men and women of exceptional ability who have left their mark on their generation. Thanks to their own discretion and the untruthfulness of biographers we usually learn very little of an intimate nature about our exemplary great men; but it does happen occasionally that one of them is a fanatic about truth like Emile Zola,[1] and then we hear of the

many extraordinary obsessive habits from which he suffered throughout life.

Psychiatry has got out of this difficulty by dubbing these people *"dégénerés superieurs."* Very well; but psycho-analysis has shown that these extraordinary obsessional symptoms can be removed permanently, like the symptoms of other diseases, and as in other people who are not degenerate. I myself have frequently succeeded in doing so.

I shall only give you two examples of analysis of obsessional symptoms; one is an old one. but I have never found a better; and one is a recent one. I shall limit myself to these two because an account of this kind must be very explicit and go into great detail.

A lady of nearly thirty years of age suffered from very severe obsessional symptoms. I might perhaps have been able to help her if my work had not been destroyed by the caprice of fate—perhaps I shall tell you about it later. In the course of a day she would perform the following peculiar obsessive act, among others, several times over. She would run out of her room into the adjoining one, there take up a certain position at the table in the center of the room, ring for her maid, give her a trivial order or send her away without, and then run back again. There was certainly nothing very dreadful about this, but it might well arouse curiosity. The explanation presented itself in the simplest and most unexceptionable manner, without any assistance on the part of the analyst. I cannot imagine how I could even have suspected the meaning of this obsession or could possibly have suggested an interpretation for it. Every time I had asked the patient, "Why do you do this? What is the meaning of it?" she had answered, "I don't know." But one day, after I had succeeded in overcoming a great hesitation on her part, involving a matter of principle, she suddenly did know, for she related the history of the obsessive act. More than ten years previously she had married a man very much older than herself, who had proved impotent on the wedding-night. Innumerable times on that night he had run out of his room into hers in order to make the attempt, but had failed every time. In the morning he had said angrily: "It's enough to disgrace one in the eyes of the maid who does the beds," and seizing a bottle of red ink which happened to be at hand he poured it on the sheet, but not exactly in the place where such a mark might have been. At first I did not understand what this recollec-

[1] E. Toulouse, *Émile Zola: Enquête medico-psychologique* (Paris, 1896).

tion could have to do with the obsessive act in question; for I could see no similarity between the two situations, except in the running from one room into the other, and perhaps also in the appearance of the servant on the scene. The patient then led me to the table in the adjoining room, where I found a great mark on the table-cover. She explained further that she stood by the table in such a way that when the maid came in she could not miss seeing this mark. After this, there could no longer be any doubt about the connection between the current obsessive act and the scene of the wedding-night, though there was still a great deal to learn about it.

It was clear, first of all, that the patient identified herself with her husband; in imitating his running from one room into another she acted his part. To keep up the similarity we must assume that she has substituted the table and table-cover for the bed and sheet. This might seem too arbitrary; but then we have not studied dream-symbolism in vain. In dreams a table is very often found to represent a bed. *Bed and board* together mean marriage, so that the one easily stands for the other.

All this would be proof enough that the obsessive act is full of meaning; it *seems* to be a representation, a repetition of that all-important scene. But we are not bound to stop at this semblance; if we investigate more closely the relation between the two situations we shall probably find out something more, the purpose of the obsessive act. The kernel of it evidently lies in the calling of the maid, to whom she displays the mark, in contrast to her husband's words: "It's enough to disgrace one before the servant." In this way he, whose part she is playing, is *not* ashamed before the servant, the stain is where it ought to be. We see therefore that she has not simply repeated the scene, she has continued it and corrected it, transformed it into what it ought to have been. This implies something else, too, a correction of the circumstance which made that night so distressing, and which made the red ink necessary: namely, the husband's impotence. The obsessive act thus says: "No, it is not true, he was not disgraced before the servant, he was not impotent." As in a dream she represents this wish as fulfilled, in a current obsessive act, which serves the purpose of restoring her husband's credit after that unfortunate incident.

Everything else which I could tell you about this lady fits in with this, or, more correctly stated, everything else that we know about her

points to this interpretation of the obsessive act, in itself so incomprehensible. She had been separated from her husband for years and was trying to make up her mind to divorce him legally. But there would have been no prospect of being free from him in her mind; she forced herself to be true to him. She withdrew from the world and from everyone so that she might not be tempted, and in her phantasies she excused and idealized him. The deepest secret of her illness was that it enabled her to shield him from malicious gossip, to justify her separation from him, and to make a comfortable existence apart from her possible for him. The analysis of a harmless obsessive act thus leads straight to the inmost core of the patient's disease, and at the same time betrays a great deal of the secret of the obsessional neurosis in general. I am quite willing that you should spend some time over this example, for it unites conditions which cannot reasonably be expected in all cases. The interpretation of the symptom was discovered by the patient herself in a flash, without guidance or interference from the analyst, and it had arisen in connection with an event which did not belong, as it commonly does, to a forgotten period in childhood, but which had occurred in the patient's adult life and was clear in her memory. All those objections which critics habitually raise against our interpretations of symptoms are quite out of place here. To be sure, we cannot always be so fortunate.

And one thing more! Has it not struck you that this innocent obsessive act leads directly to this lady's most private affairs? A woman can hardly have anything more intimate to relate than the story of her wedding-night; and is it by chance and without special significance that we are led straight to the innermost secrets of her sexual life? It might certainly be due to the choice I made of this example. Let us not decide this point too quickly; but let us turn to the second example, which is of a totally different nature, and belongs to a very common type, that of rituals preparatory to sleep.

A well-grown clever girl of 19, the only child of her parents, superior to them in education and intellectual activity, was a wild, high-spirited child, but of late years had become very nervous without any apparent cause. She was very irritable, particularly with her mother, was discontented and depressed, inclined to indecision and doubt, finally confessing that she could no longer walk alone through squares and wide streets. We will not go very closely into her complicated condition, which requires at least two diagnoses: agoraphobia and obsessional neurosis; but will turn our attention to the ritual elaborated by this young girl preparatory to going to bed, as a result of which she caused her parents great distress. In a certain sense, every normal person may be said to carry out a ritual before going to sleep, or at least, he requires certain conditions without which he is hindered in going to sleep; the transition from waking life to sleep has been made into a regular formula which is repeated every night in the same manner. But everything that a healthy person requires as a condition of sleep can be rationally explained, and if the external circumstances make any alteration necessary he adapts himself easily to it without waste of time. The morbid ritual on the other hand is inexorable, it will be maintained at the greatest sacrifices; it is disguised, too, under rational motives and appears superficially to differ from the normal only in a certain exaggerated carefulness of execution. On a closer examination, however, it is clear that the disguise is insufficient, that the ritual includes observances which go far beyond what reason can justify and even some which directly contravene this. As the motive of her nightly precautions, our patient declares that she must have silence at night and must exclude all possibility of noise. She does two things for this purpose; she stops the large clock in her room and removes all other clocks out of the room, including even the tiny wrist-watch on her bedtable. Flower-pots and vases are placed carefully together on the writing-table, so that they cannot fall down in the night and break, and so disturb her sleep. She knows that these precautions have only an illusory justification in the demand for quiet; the ticking of the little watch could not be heard, even if it lay on the table by the bed; and we all know that the regular ticking of a pendulum-clock never disturbs sleep, but is more likely to induce it. She also admits that her fear that the flower-pots and vases, if left in their places at night, might fall down of themselves and break is utterly improbable. For some other practices in her ritual this insistence upon silence as a motive is dropped; indeed, by ordaining that the door between her bedroom and that of her parents shall remain half-open (a condition which she ensures by placing various objects in the doorway) she seems, on the contrary, to open the way to sources of noise. The most important observances are concerned with the bed itself, however. The bolster at the head of the bed

must not touch the back of the wooden bedstead. The pillow must lie across the bolster exactly in a diagonal position and in no other; she then places her head exactly in the middle of this diamond, lengthways. The eiderdown must be shaken before she puts it over her, so that all the feathers sink to the foot-end; she never fails, however, to press this out and redistribute them all over it again.

I will pass over other trivial details of her ritual; they would teach us nothing new and lead us too far from our purpose. Do not suppose, though, that all this is carried out with perfect smoothness. Everything is accompanied by the anxiety that it has not all been done properly; it must be tested and repeated; her doubts fix first upon one, then another, of the precautions; and the result is that one or two hours elapse before the girl herself can sleep, or lets the intimidated parents sleep.

The analysis of these torments did not proceed so simply as that of the former patient's obsessive act. I had to offer hints and suggestions of its interpretation which were invariably received by her with a positive denial or with scornful doubt. After this first reaction of rejection, however, there followed a period in which she herself took up the possibilities suggested to her, noted the associations they aroused, produced memories, and established connections until she herself had accepted all the interpretations in working them out for herself. In proportion as she did this she began to relax the performance of her obsessive precautions and before the end of the treatment she had given up the whole ritual. I must also tell you that analytic work, as we conduct it nowadays, definitely excludes any uninterrupted concentration on a single symptom until its meaning becomes fully clear. It is necessary, on the contrary, to abandon a given theme again and again, in the assurance that one will come upon it anew in another context. The interpretation of the symptom, which I am now going to tell you, is therefore a synthesis of the results which, amid the interruptions of work on other points, took weeks and months to procure.

The patient gradually learnt to understand that she banished clocks and watches from her room at night because they were symbols of the female genitals. Clocks, which we know may have other symbolic meanings beside this, acquire this significance of a genital organ by their relation to periodical processes and regular intervals. A woman may be heard to boast that menstruation occurs in her as regularly as clockwork. Now this patient's special fear was that the ticking of the clocks would disturb her during sleep. The ticking of a clock is comparable to the throbbing of the clitoris in sexual excitation. This sensation, which was distressing to her, had actually on several occasions wakened her from sleep; and now her fear of an erection of the clitoris expressed itself by the imposition of a rule to remove all going clocks and watches far away from her during the night. Flower-pots and vases are, like all receptacles, also symbols of the female genitals. Precautions to prevent them from falling and breaking during the night are therefore not lacking in meaning. We know the very widespread custom of breaking a vessel or a plate on the occasion of a betrothal; everyone present possesses himself of a fragment in symbolic acceptance of the fact that he may no longer put forward any claim to the bride, presumably a custom which arose with monogamy. The patient also contributed a recollection and several associations to this part of her ritual. Once as a child she had fallen while carrying a glass or porcelain vessel, and had cut her finger which had bled badly. As she grew up and learnt the facts about sexual intercourse, she developed the apprehension that on her wedding-night she would not bleed and so would prove not to be a virgin. Her precautions against the vases breaking signified a rejection of the whole complex concerned with virginity and with the question of bleeding during the first act of intercourse; a rejection of the anxiety both that she would bleed and that she would not bleed. These precautions were in fact only remotely connected with the prevention of noise.

One day she divined the central idea of her ritual when she suddenly understood her rule not to let the bolster touch the back of the bed. The bolster had always seemed a woman to her, she said, and the upright back of the bedstead a man. She wished therefore, by a magic ceremony, as it were, to keep man and woman apart; that is to say, to separate the parents and prevent intercourse from occurring. Years before the institution of her ritual, she had attempted to achieve this end by a more direct method. She had simulated fear, or had exploited a tendency to fear, so that the door between her bedroom and that of her parents should not be closed. This regulation was still actually included in her present ritual; in this way she managed to make it possible to overhear her parents; a proceeding which at one time had caused her months of sleeplessness. Not content with disturbing her parents in this way, she at that time even succeeded occasionally in sleeping between the father and mother in their bed. *Bolster* and *bedstead* were then really prevented from coming together. As she finally grew too big to be comfortable in the same bed with the parents, she achieved the same thing by consciously simulating fear and getting her mother to change places with her and to give up to her, her place by the father. This incident was undoubtedly the starting-point of phantasies, the effect of which was evident in the ritual.

If the bolster was a woman, then the shaking of the eiderdown till all the feathers were at the bottom, making a protuberance there, also had a meaning. It meant impregnating a woman; she did not neglect, though, to obliterate the pregnancy again, for she had for years been terrified that intercourse between her parents might result in another child and present her with a rival. On the other hand, if the larger bolster meant the mother then the small pillow could only represent the daughter. Why had this pillow to be placed diamond-wise upon the bolster and her head be laid exactly in its middle lengthways? She was easily reminded that a diamond is repeatedly used in drawings on walls to signify the open female genitals. The part of the man (the father) she thus played herself and replaced the male organ by her own head. (Cf. Symbolism of beheading for castration.)

Horrible thoughts, you will say, to run in the mind of a virgin girl. I admit that; but do not forget that I have not invented these ideas, only exposed them. A ritual of this kind before sleep is also peculiar enough, and you cannot deny the correspondence, revealed by the interpretation, between the ceremonies and the phantasies. It is more important to me, however, that you should notice that the ritual was the outcome, not of one single phantasy, but of several together which of course must have had a nodal point somewhere. Note, too, that the details of the ritual reflect the sexual wishes both positively and negatively, and serve in part as expressions of them, in part as defences against them.

It would be possible to obtain much more out of the analysis of this ritual by bringing it into its place in connection with the patient's other symptoms. But that is not our purpose at the moment. You must be content with a reference to an erotic attachment to the father, originating very early in childhood, which had enslaved this girl. It was perhaps for this reason that she was so unfriendly towards her mother. Also we cannot overlook the fact that the analysis of this symptom has again led to the patient's sexual life. The more insight we gain into the meaning and purpose of neurotic symptoms, the less surprising will this seem.

From two selected examples I have now shown you that neurotic symptoms have meaning, like errors and like dreams, and that they are closely connected with the events of the patient's life. Can I expect you to believe this exceptionally significant statement on the strength of two examples? No. But can you expect me to go on quoting examples to you until you declare yourselves convinced? Again, no; for in view of the exhaustive treatment given to each individual case I should have to devote five hours a week for a whole term to the consideration of this one point in the theory of the neuroses. I will content myself therefore with the samples given, as evidence of my statement; and will refer you for more to the literature on the subject, to the classical interpretation of symptoms in Breuer's first case (hysteria), to the striking elucidations of very obscure symptoms in dementia praecox, so-called, made by C. G. Jung at a time when this investigator was a mere psycho-analyst and did not yet aspire to be a prophet, and to all the subsequent contributions with which our periodicals have been filled since then. Precisely this type of investigation is plentiful. Analysis, interpretation, and translation of neurotic symptoms has proved so attractive to psycho-analysts that in comparison they have temporarily neglected the other problems of the neuroses.

Any one of you who makes the necessary effort to look up this question will certainly be strongly impressed by the wealth of evidential material. But he will also meet with a difficulty. The meaning of a symptom lies, as we have seen, in its connection with the life of the patient. The more individually the symptom has been formed, the more clearly may we expect to establish this connection. Then the task resolves itself specifically into a discovery, for every nonsensical idea and every useless action, of the past situation in which the idea was justified and the action served a useful purpose. The obsessive act of the patient who ran to the table and rang for the maid is a perfect model of this kind of symptom. But symptoms of quite a different type are very frequently seen. They are what we call *typical* symptoms of a

disease, in each case they are practically identical, the individual differences in them vanish or at least fade away, so that it is difficult to connect them with the patient's life or to relate them to special situations in his past. Let us consider the obsessional neurosis again. The second patient's ceremonies preparatory to sleep are in many ways quite typical, although showing enough individual features as well to make an "historical" interpretation, so to speak, possible. But all obsessional patients are given to repetitions, to isolating certain of their actions and to rhythmic performances. Most of them wash too much. Those patients who suffer from agoraphobia (topophobia, fear of space), no longer reckoned as an obsessional neurosis but now classified as anxiety-hysteria, reproduce the same features of the pathological picture often with fatiguing monotony. They fear enclosed spaces, wide, open squares, long stretches of road, and avenues; they feel protected if accompanied, or if a vehicle drives behind them, and so on. Nevertheless, on this groundwork of similarity the various patients construct individual conditions of their own, moods, one might call them, which directly contrast with other cases. One fears narrow streets only, another wide streets only, one can walk only when few people are about, others only when surrounded with people. Similarly in hysteria, beside the wealth of individual features there are always plenty of common typical symptoms which appear to resist an easy interpretation on historical lines. Do not let us forget that it is these typical symptoms which enable us to take our bearings in forming a diagnosis. Supposing we do trace back a typical symptom in a case of hysteria to an experience or to a chain of similar experiences (for instance, an hysterical vomiting to a series of impressions of a disgusting nature), it will be confusing to discover in another case of vomiting an entirely dissimilar series of apparently causative experiences. It almost looks as though hysterical patients must vomit, for some unknown reason, and as though the historical factors revealed by analysis were but pretexts, seized upon by an inner necessity, when opportunity offered, to serve its purpose.

This brings us to the discouraging conclusion that, although individual forms of neurotic symptoms can certainly be satisfactorily explained by their relation to the patient's experiences, yet our science fails us for the far more frequent typical symptoms in the same cases. In addition to this, I have not nearly explained to you all the difficulties that arise during a resolute pursuit of the historical meaning of a symptom. Nor shall I do so; for although my intention is to conceal nothing from you and to gloss over nothing, I do not need to confuse you and stupefy you at the outset of our studies together. It is true that our understanding of symptom-interpretation has only just begun, but we will hold fast to the knowledge gained and proceed to overcome step by step the difficulties of the unknown. I will try to cheer you with the thought that it is hardly possible to presume a fundamental difference between the one kind of symptom and the other. If the individual form of symptom is so unmistakably connected with the patient's experiences, it is possible that the typical symptom relates to an experience which is itself typical and common to all humanity. Other regularly recurring features of a neurosis, such as the repetition and doubt of the obsessional neurosis, may be universal reactions which the patient is compelled to exaggerate by the nature of the morbid change. In short, there is no reason to give up hastily in despair; let us see what more we can find out.

There is a very similar difficulty met with in the theory of dreams, one which I could not deal with in the course of our previous discussions of dreams. The manifest content of dreams is multifarious and highly differentiated individually, and we have shown exhaustively what can be obtained by analysis from this content. But there are also dreams which may in the same way be called *typical* and occur in everybody, dreams with an identical content, which present the same difficulties to analysis. These are the dreams of falling, flying, floating, swimming, of being hindered, of being naked, and certain other anxiety-dreams; which yield first this, then that, interpretation, according to the person concerned, without any explanation of their monotonous and typical recurrence. But we notice that in these dreams also the common groundwork is embroidered with additions of an individually varying character. Most probably they too will prove to fit in with other knowledge about the dream-life, gained from a study of other kinds of dreams—not by any forcible twist, but by a gradual widening of our comprehension of these things.

EIGHTEENTH LECTURE

FIXATION UPON TRAUMAS: THE UNCONSCIOUS

I SAID last time that we would take, as a starting-point for further work, the knowledge we

have gained already, and not the doubts which it has roused in us. We have not yet even begun to discuss two of the most interesting conclusions arising from the analysis of the two examples.

First: both the patients give the impression that they are *fixed* to a particular point in their past, that they do not know how to release themselves from it, and are consequently alienated from both present and future. They are marooned in their illness, as it were; just as in former times people used to withdraw to the cloister to live out their unhappy fate there. In the case of the first patient, it was the marriage to the husband, which in reality had long ago come to an end, that had settled this doom upon her. Her symptoms enabled her to continue her relationship with him; we could perceive in them the voices which pleaded for him, excused him, exalted him, lamented his loss. Although she is young and could attract other men, she has seized upon every possible real and imaginary (magical) precaution that will preserve her fidelity to him. She will not meet strangers, she neglects her appearance; moreover, she cannot readily rise from any chair which she sits upon, and she refuses to sign her name and can give no presents, because no one must have anything which is hers.

With the second patient, the young girl, it is the erotic attachment to the father established in the years before puberty that plays this part in her life. She also has herself perceived that she cannot marry as long as she is so ill. We may suspect that she became so ill in order to be unable to marry and so to remain with her father.

We cannot avoid asking the question how, by what means and impelled by what motives, anyone can take up such an extraordinary and unprofitable attitude towards life. Provided, that is, that this attitude is a universal character of neurosis and is not a special peculiarity of these two patients. As a matter of fact, this is so; it is a universal trait common to every neurosis, and one of great practical significance. Breuer's first hysterical patient was *fixated*, in the same way, to the time when her father was seriously ill and she nursed him. In spite of her recovery, she has remained to some extent cut off from life since that time; for although she has remained healthy and active, she did not take up the normal career of a woman. In every one of our patients we learn through analysis that the symptoms and their effects have set the sufferer back into some past period of his life. In the majority of cases it is actually a very early phase of the life history which has been thus selected, a period in childhood, even, absurd as it may sound, the period of existence as a suckling infant.

The closest analogy to this behaviour in our nervous patients is provided by the forms of illness recently made so common by the war— the so-called *traumatic neuroses.* Of course similar cases have occurred before the war, after railway accidents and other terrifying experiences involving danger to life. The traumatic neuroses are not fundamentally the same as those which occur spontaneously, which we investigate analytically and are accustomed to treat; neither have we been successful so far in correlating them with our views on other subjects; later on I hope to show you where this limitation lies. Yet there is a complete agreement between them on one point which may be emphasized. The traumatic neuroses demonstrate very clearly that a fixation to the moment of the traumatic occurrence lies at their root. These patients regularly produce the traumatic situation in their dreams; in cases showing attacks of an hysterical type in which analysis is possible, it appears that the attack constitutes a complete reproduction of this situation. It is as though these persons had not yet been able to deal adequately with the situation, as if this task were still actually before them unaccomplished. We take this attitude of theirs in all seriousness; it points the way to what we may call an *economic* conception of the mental processes. The term *traumatic* has actually no other meaning but this *economic* one. An experience which we call traumatic is one which within a very short space of time subjects the mind to such a very high increase of stimulation that assimilation or elaboration of it can no longer be effected by normal means, so that lasting disturbances must result in the distribution of the available energy in the mind.

This analogy tempts us also to classify as traumatic those experiences to which our nervous patients seem to be fixated. In this way we should be provided with a simple condition for a neurotic illness; it would be incomparable to a traumatic illness and would result from an incapacity to deal with an overpowering affective experience. Indeed, the first formula in which Breuer and I, in 1893-95, reduced our new observations to a theory was expressed very similarly. A case like that of the first

patient described, the young woman separated from her husband, fits very well into this description; she had not been able to get over the impracticability of her marriage and was still attached to her trauma. But the second case of the young girl who was tied to her father shows us at once that the formula is not comprehensive enough. On the one hand, an infantile adoration of her father by a little girl is such a common experience and so frequently grown out of that the term *traumatic* would lose all its meaning if applied to it; on the other hand, the history of the case shows that this first erotic fixation was gone through by the patient quite harmlessly at the time, to all appearances, and only several years later came to expression in the obsessional neurosis. So we see that there are complications ahead, a considerable variety and number of determining factors in neurosis; but we divine that the traumatic view will not necessarily be abandoned as false, and that it will fit in and have to be coordinated properly elsewhere.

Here again we must leave the path we have been following. At the moment it will take us no further, and we have much more to learn before we can find a satisfactory continuation of it. But before leaving the subject of fixation to traumas it should be noted that it is a phenomenon manifested extensively outside the neuroses; every neurosis contains such a fixation, but not every fixation leads to a neurosis, or is necessarily combined with a neurosis, or arises in the course of a neurosis. Grief is a prototype and perfect example of an affective fixation upon something that is past, and, like the neuroses, it also involves a state of complete alienation from the present and the future. But even the lay public distinguishes clearly between grief and neurosis. On the other hand, there are neuroses which may be described as morbid forms of grief.

It does also happen that persons may be brought to a complete standstill in life by a traumatic experience which has shaken the whole structure of their lives to the foundations, so that they give up all interest in the present and the future, and live permanently absorbed in their retrospections; but these unhappy persons do not necessarily become neurotic. Therefore this single feature must not be overestimated as a characteristic of neurosis, however invariable and significant it may be otherwise.

Now let us turn to the second conclusion to be drawn from our analyses; it is one upon which we shall not need to impose any subsequent limitation. With the first patient we have heard of the senseless obsessive act she performed and of the intimate memories she recalled in connection with it; we also considered the relation between the two, and deduced the purpose of the obsessive act from its connection with the memory. But there is one factor which we have entirely neglected, and yet it is one which deserves our fullest attention. As long as the patient continued this performance she did not know that it was in any way connected with the previous experience; the connection between the two things was hidden; she could quite truly answer that she did not know what impulse led her to do it. Then it happened suddenly that, under the influence of the treatment, she found this connection and was able to tell it. But even then she knew nothing of the purpose she had in performing the action, the purpose that was to correct a painful event of the past and to raise the husband she loved in her own estimation. It took a long time and much effort for her to grasp, and admit to me, that such a motive as this alone could have been the driving force behind the obsessive act.

The connection with the scene on the morning after the unhappy bridal-night, and the patient's own tender feeling for her husband, together, make up what we have called the *meaning* of the obsessive act. But both sides of this meaning were hidden from her, she understood neither the *whence* nor the *whither* of her act, as long as she carried it on. Mental processes had been at work in her, therefore, of which the obsessive act was the effect; she was aware in a normal manner of their effect; but nothing of the mental antecedents of this effect had come to the knowledge of her consciousness. She was behaving exactly like a subject under hypnotism whom Bernheim had ordered to open an umbrella in the ward five minutes after he awoke, but who had no idea why he was doing it. This is the kind of occurrence we have in mind when we speak of the existence of *unconscious mental processes;* we may challenge anyone in the world to give a more correctly scientific explanation of this matter, and will then gladly withdraw our inference that unconscious mental processes exist. Until they do, however, we will adhere to this inference and, when anyone objects that in a scientific sense the unconscious has no reality, that it is a mere makeshift, *une façon de parler*, we must resign ourselves with a shrug to rejecting his statement as incomprehensible. Something unreal, which can nevertheless produce something so real and palpable as an obsessive action!

In the second patient fundamentally the same thing is found. She has instituted a rule that the bolster must not touch the back of the bedstead, and she had to carry out this rule, but she does not know whence it comes, what it means, or to what it owes its strength. Whether she regards it indifferently, or struggles against it, or rages against it, or determines to overcome it, matters not; it will be followed. It must be followed; in vain she asks herself why. It is undeniable that these symptoms of the obsessional neurosis, these ideas and these impulses which arise no man knows where and which oppose such a powerful resistance against all the influences to which an otherwise normal mental life is susceptible, give the impression, even to the patients themselves, of being all-powerful visitants from another world, immortal beings mingling in the whirlpool of mortal things. In these symptoms lies the clearest indication of a special sphere of mental activity cut off from all the rest. They show the way unmistakably to conviction on the question of the unconscious in the mind; and for that very reason clinical psychiatry, which only recognizes a psychology of consciousness, can do nothing with these symptoms except to stigmatize them as signs of a special kind of degeneration. Naturally, the obsessive idea and impulses are not themselves unconscious, any more that is the performance of the obsessive acts. They would not have become symptoms if they had not penetrated into consciousness. But the mental antecedents of them disclosed by analysis, the connections into which they fit after interpretation, are unconscious, at least until the time when we make the patient conscious of them by the work of the analysis.

Consider now, in addition, that the facts established in these two cases are confirmed in every symptom of every neurotic disease; that always and everywhere the meaning of the symptoms is unknown to the sufferer; that analysis invariably shows that these symptoms are derived from unconscious mental processes which can, however, under various favourable conditions, become conscious. You will then understand that we cannot dispense with the unconscious part of the mind in psycho-analysis, and that we are accustomed to deal with it as with something actual and tangible. Perhaps you will also be able to realize how unfitted all those who only know the unconscious as a phrase, who have never analysed, never interpreted dreams, or translated neurotic symptoms into their meaning and intention, are to form an opinion on this matter. I will repeat the substance of it again in order to impress it upon you: The fact that it is possible to find meaning in neurotic symptoms by means of analytic interpretation is an irrefutable proof of the existence—or, if you prefer it, of the necessity for assuming the existence—of unconscious mental processes.

But that is not all. Thanks to a second discovery of Breuer's, for which he alone deserves credit and which seems to me even more far-reaching in its significance than the first, more still has been learnt about the relation between the unconscious and the symptoms of neurotics. Not merely is the meaning of the symptom invariably unconscious; there exists also a connection of a substitutive nature between the two; the existence of the symptom is only possible by reason of this unconscious activity. You will soon understand what I mean. With Breuer, I maintain the following: Every time we meet with a symptom we may conclude that definite unconscious activities which contain the meaning of the symptom are present in the patient's mind. Conversely, this meaning must be unconscious before a symptom can arise from it. Symptoms are not produced by conscious processes; as soon as the unconscious processes involved are made conscious the symptom must vanish. You will perceive at once that here is an opening for therapy, a way by which symptoms can be made to disappear. It was by this means that Breuer actually achieved the recovery of his patient, that is, freed her from her symptoms; he found a method of bringing into her consciousness the unconscious processes which contained the meaning of her symptoms and the symptoms vanished.

This discovery of Breuer's was not the result of any speculation but of a fortunate observation made possible by the co-operation of the patient. Now you must not rack your brains to try and understand this by seeking to compare it with something similar that is already familiar to you; but you must recognize in it a fundamentally new fact, by means of which much else becomes explicable. Allow me therefore to express it again to you in other words.

The symptom is formed as a substitute for something else which remains submerged. Certain mental processes would, under normal conditions, develop until the person became aware of them consciously. This has not happened; and, instead, the symptom has arisen out of these processes which have been interrupted and interfered with in some way and have had to remain unconscious. Thus something in the nature of an exchange has occurred; if we can succeed in reversing this process by our therapy, we shall have performed our task of dispersing the symptom.

Breuer's discovery still remains the foundation of psycho-analytic therapy. The proposition that symptoms vanish when their unconscious antecedents have been made conscious has been borne out by all subsequent research; although the most extraordinary and unexpected complications are met with in attempting to carry this proposition out in practice. Our therapy does its work by transforming something unconscious into something conscious, and only succeeds in its work in so far as it is able to effect this transformation.

Now for a rapid digression, lest you should run the risk of imagining that this therapeutic effect is achieved too easily. According to the conclusions we have reached so far, neurosis would be the result of a kind of ignorance, a not-knowing of mental processes which should be known. This would approach very closely to the well-known Socratic doctrine according to which even vice is the result of ignorance. Now it happens in analysis that an experienced practitioner can usually surmise very easily what those feelings are which have remained unconscious in each individual patient. It should not therefore be a matter of great difficulty to cure the patient by imparting his knowledge to him and so relieving his ignorance. At least, one side of the unconscious meaning of the symptom would be easily dealt with in this way, although it is true that the other side of it, the connection between the symptom and the previous experiences in the patient's life, can hardly be divined thus; for the analyst does not know what the experiences have been, he has to wait till the patient remembers them and tells him. But one might find a substitute even for this in many cases. One might ask for information about his past life from the friends and relations; they are often in a position to know what events have been of a traumatic nature, perhaps they can even relate some of which the patient is ignorant because they took place at some very early period of childhood. By a combination of these two means it would seem that the pathogenic ignorance of the patients might be overcome in a short time without much trouble.

If only it were so! But we have made discoveries that we were quite unprepared for at first. There is knowing and knowing; they are not always the same thing. There are various kinds of knowing, which psychologically are not by any means of equal value. *Il y a fagots et fagots*,[1] as Molière says. Knowing on the part of the physician is not the same thing as knowing on the part of the patient and does not have the same effect. When the physician conveys his knowledge to the patient by telling him what he knows, it has effect. No, it would be incorrect to say that. It does not have the effect of dispersing the symptoms; but it has a different one, it sets the analysis in motion, and the first result of this is often an energetic denial. The patient has learned something that he did not know before—the meaning of his symptom—and yet he knows it as little as ever. Thus we discover that there is more than one kind of ignorance. It requires a considerable degree of insight and understanding of psychological matters in order to see in what the difference consists. But the proposition that symptoms vanish with the acquisition of knowledge of their meaning remains true, nevertheless. The necessary condition is that the knowledge must be founded upon an inner change in the patient which can only come about by a mental operation directed to that end. We are here confronted by problems which to us will soon develop into the *dynamics* of symptom-formation.

Now I must really stop and ask you whether all that I have been saying is not too obscure and complicated? Am I confusing you by so often qualifying and restricting, spinning out trains of thought and then letting them drop? I should be sorry if it were so. But I have a strong dislike of simplification at the expense of truth, I am not averse from giving you a full impression of the many-sidedness and intricacy · of the subject, and also I believe that it does no harm to tell you more about each point than you can assimilate at the moment. I know that every listener and every reader arranges what is offered him as suits him in his own mind, shortens it, simplifies it, and extracts from it what he will retain. Within certain limits it is true that the more we begin with the more we shall have at the end. So let me hope that, in spite of the elaboration, you will have grasped the essential substance of my remarks concern-

[1] There are men and men.—ED.

ing the meaning of symptoms, the unconscious, and the connection between the two. You have probably understood also that our further efforts will proceed in two directions; first, towards discovering how people become ill, how they come to take up the characteristic neurotic attitude towards life, which is a clinical problem; and secondly, how they develop the morbid symptoms out of the conditions of a neurosis, which remains a problem of mental dynamics. The two problems must somewhere have a point of contact.

I shall not go further into this today; but as our time is not yet up I propose to draw your attention to another characteristic of our two analyses; namely, *the memory gaps or amnesias*, again a point which only later will appear in its full significance. You have heard that the task of the psycho-analytic treatment can be summed up in this formula: "Everything pathogenic in the unconscious must be transferred into consciousness." Now you will perhaps be astonished to hear that another formula may be substituted for that one: "All gaps in the patient's memory must be filled in, his amnesias removed." It amounts to the same thing; which means that an important connection is to be recognized between the development of the symptoms and the amnesias. If you consider the case of the first patient analysed you will, however, not find this view of amnesia justified; the patient had not forgotten the scene from which the obsessive act is derived; on the contrary, it was vivid in her memory, nor is there any other forgotten factor involved in the formation of her symptom. The situation is quite analogous, although less clear, in the second case, the girl with the obsessional ceremonies. She, too, had not really forgotten her behaviour in former years, the fact that she had insisted upon the open door between her parents' bedroom and her own, and that she had turned her mother out of her place in the parents' bed; she remembered it quite clearly, although with hesitation and unwillingness. What is remarkable about it is that the first patient, although she had carried out her obsessive act such a countless number of times, had not *once* been reminded of its similarity to the scene after the wedding-night, nor did this recollection ever occur to her when she was directly asked to search for the origin of her obsessive act. The same thing is true in the case of the girl, where not merely the ritual, but the situation which gave rise to it, was repeated identically every evening. In neither case was there really an amnesia, a lapse of memory; but a connection, which should have existed intact and have led to the reproduction, the recollection, of the memory, had been broken. This kind of disturbance of memory suffices for the obsessional neurosis; in hysteria it is different. This latter neurosis is usually characterized by amnesias on a grand scale. As a rule the analysis of each single hysterical symptom leads to a whole chain of former impressions, which upon their return may be literally described as having been hitherto forgotten. This chain reaches, on the one hand, back to the earliest years of childhood, so that the hysterical amnesia is seen to be a direct continuation of the infantile amnesia which hides the earliest impressions of our mental life from all of us. On the other hand, we are astonished to find that the most recent experiences of the patient are liable to be forgotten also, and that in particular the provocations which induced the outbreak of the disease or aggravated it are at least partially obliterated, if not entirely wiped out, by amnesia. From the complete picture of any such recent recollection, important details have invariably disappeared or been replaced by falsifications. It happens again and again, almost invariably, that not until shortly before the completion of an analysis do certain recollections of recent experiences come to the surface, which had managed to be withheld throughout it and had left noticeable gaps in the context.

These derangements in the capacity to recall memories are, as I have said, characteristic of hysteria, in which disease it also happens even that states occur as symptoms (the hysterical attacks) without necessarily leaving a trace of recollection behind them. Since it is otherwise in the obsessional neurosis, you may infer that these amnesias are part of the psychological character of the hysterical change and are not a universal trait of neurosis in general. The importance of this difference will be diminished by the following consideration. Two things are combined to constitute the meaning of a symptom; its *whence* and its *whither* or *why;* that is, the impressions and experiences from which it sprang, and the purpose which it serves. The *whence* of a symptom is resolved into impressions which have been received from without, which were necessarily at one time conscious, and which may have become unconscious by being forgotten since that time. The *why* of the symptom, its tendency, is however always an endo-psychic process, which may

possibly have been conscious at first, but just as possibly may never have been conscious and may have remained in the unconscious from its inception. Therefore, it is not very important whether the amnesia has also infringed upon the *whence,* the impressions upon which the symptom is supported, as happens in hysteria; the *whither,* the tendency of the symptom, which may have been unconscious from the beginning, is what maintains the symptom's dependence upon the unconscious, in the obsessional neurosis no less strictly than in hysteria.

By thus emphasizing the unconscious in mental life we have called forth all the malevolence in humanity in opposition to psychoanalysis. Do not be astonished at this and do not suppose that this opposition relates to the obvious difficulty of conceiving the unconscious or to the relative inaccessibility of the evidence which supports its existence. I believe it has a deeper source. Humanity has in the course of time had to endure from the hands of science two great outrages upon its naïve self-love. The first was when it realized that our earth was not the centre of the universe, but only a tiny speck in a world-system of a magnitude hardly conceivable; this is associated in our minds with the name of Copernicus, although Alexandrian doctrines taught something very similar. The second was when biological research robbed man of his peculiar privilege of having been specially created, and relegated him to a descent from the animal world, implying an ineradicable animal nature in him: this transvaluation has been accomplished in our own time upon the instigation of Charles Darwin, Wallace, and their predecessors, and not without the most violent opposition from their contemporaries. But man's craving for grandiosity is now suffering the third and most bitter blow from present-day psychological research which is endeavouring to prove to the *ego* of each one of us that he is not even master in his own house, but that he must remain content with the veriest scraps of information about what is going on unconsciously in his own mind. We psycho-analysts were neither the first nor the only ones to propose to mankind that they should look inward; but it appears to be our lot to advocate it most insistently and to support it by empirical evidence which touches every man closely. This is the kernel of the universal revolt against our science, of the total disregard of academic courtesy in dispute, and the liberation of opposition from all the constraints of impartial logic. And besides this, we have been compelled to disturb the peace of the world in yet another way, as you will soon hear.

NINETEENTH LECTURE
RESISTANCE AND REPRESSION

WE now need more data before we can advance further in our understanding of the neuroses; two observations lie to hand for us. Both are very remarkable and at first were very surprising. You are of course prepared for both of them by the work we did last year.

First: when we undertake to cure a patient of his symptoms, he opposes against us a vigorous and tenacious *resistance* throughout the entire course of the treatment. This is such an extraordinary thing that we cannot expect much belief in it. It is best to say nothing about it to the patient's relations, for they invariably regard it as a pretext set up by us to excuse the length or the failure of the treatment. The patient, too, exhibits all the manifestations of this resistance without recognizing it as such, and it is a great step forward when we have brought him to realize this fact and to reckon with it. To think that the patient, whose symptoms cause him and those about him such suffering, who is willing to make such sacrifices in time, money, effort, and self-conquest in order to be freed from them—that he should, in the interests of his illness, resist the help offered him. How improbable this statement must sound! And yet it is so, and if the improbability is made a reproach against us we need only reply that it is not without its analogies; for a man who has rushed off to a dentist with a frightful toothache may very well fend him off when he takes his forceps to the decayed tooth.

The resistance shown by patients is highly varied and exceedingly subtle, often hard to recognize and protean in the manifold forms it takes; the analyst needs to be continually suspicious and on his guard against it. In psycho-analytic therapy we employ the technique which is already familiar to you through dream-interpretation: we require the patient to put himself into a condition of calm self-observation, without trying to think of anything, and then to communicate everything which he becomes inwardly aware of, feelings, thoughts, remembrances, in the order in which they arise in his mind. We expressly warn him against giving way to any kind of motive which would cause him to select from or to exclude any of the ideas (associations), whether because they are too "disagreeable," or too "indiscreet" to be mentioned, or too "unimportant" or "irrelevant" or "nonsensical" to be worth saying. We impress upon him that he has only to attend to what is on the surface consciously in his mind, and to abandon all objections to whatever he finds, no matter what form they take; and we inform him that the success of the treatment, and, above all, its duration, will depend upon his conscientious adherence to this fundamental technical rule. We know from the technique of dream-interpretation that it is precisely those associations against which innumerable doubts and objections are raised that invariably contain the material leading to the discovery of the unconscious.

The first thing that happens as a result of instituting this technical rule is that it becomes the first point of attack for the resistance. The patient attempts to escape from it by every possible means. First he says nothing comes into his head, then that so much comes into his head that he can't grasp any of it. Then we observe with displeasure and astonishment that he is giving in to his critical objections, first to this, then to that; he betrays it by the long pauses which occur in his talk. At last he admits that he really cannot say something, he is ashamed to, and he lets this feeling get the better of his promise. Or else, he has thought of something but it concerns someone else and not himself, and is therefore to be made an exception to the rule. Or else, what he has just thought of is really too unimportant, too stupid and too absurd, I could never have meant that he should take account of such thoughts. So it goes on, with untold variations, to which one continually replies that telling everything really means telling everything.

One hardly ever meets with a patient who does not attempt to make a reservation in some department of his thoughts, in order to guard them against intrusion by the analysis. One patient, who in the ordinary way was remarkably intelligent, concealed a most intimate love-affair from me for weeks in this way; when accused of this violation of the sacred rule he defended himself with the argument that he considered this particular story his private affair. Naturally analytic treatment cannot countenance a right of sanctuary like this; one might as well try to allow an exception to be made in certain parts of a town like Vienna, and forbid that any arrests should be made in the market-place or in the square by St. Stephen's church, and then attempt to take up a wanted man. Of course he would never be found anywhere but in those safe places. Once I decided to permit a man to make an exception of such a point; for a great deal depended on his recovering his capacity for work and he was bound by his oath as a civil servant not to communicate certain matters to any other person. He was content with the result, it is true, but I was not: I made up my mind never again to repeat the attempt under such conditions.

Obsessional patients are exceedingly clever at making the technical rule almost useless by bringing their over-conscientiousness and doubt to bear upon it. Patients with anxiety-hysteria sometimes succeed in reducing it to absurdity by only producing associations which are so far removed from what is wanted that they yield nothing for analysis. However, I do not intend to introduce you to these technical difficulties of the treatment. It is enough to know that finally, with resolution and perseverance, we do succeed in extracting from the patient a certain amount of obedience for the rules of the technique; and then the resistance takes another line altogether. It appears as intellectual opposition, employs arguments as weapons, and turns to its own use all the difficulties and improbabilities which normal but uninstructed reasoning finds in analytical doctrines. We then have to hear from the mouth of the individual patient all the criticisms and objections which thunder about us in chorus in scientific literature. What the critics outside shout at us is nothing new, therefore. It is indeed a storm in a teacup. Still, the patient can be argued with; he is very glad to get us to instruct him, teach him, defeat him, point out the literature to him so that he can learn more; he is perfectly ready to become a supporter of psycho-analysis on the condition that analysis shall spare him personally. We recognize resistance in this desire for knowledge, however; it is a digression from the particular task in hand and we refuse to allow it. In the obsessional neurosis the resistance makes use of special tactics which we are prepared for. It permits the analysis to proceed uninterruptedly along its course, so that more and more light is thrown upon the problems of the case, until we begin to wonder at last why these explanations have no practical effect and entail no corresponding improvement in the symptoms. Then we discover that the resistance has fallen back upon the doubt characteristic of the obsessional neurosis and is holding us successfully at bay from this vantage-point. The patient has said to himself something of this kind: "This is all very pretty and very interesting. I should like to go on with it. I am sure it would do me a lot of good if it were true. But I don't believe it in the least, and as long as I don't believe it, it doesn't affect my illness." So it goes on for a long time, until at last this reservation itself is reached and then the decisive battle begins.

The intellectual resistances are not the worst; one can always get the better of them. But the patient knows how to set up resistances within the boundaries of analysis proper, and the defeat of these is one of the most difficult tasks of the technique. Instead of remembering certain of the feelings and states of mind of his previous life, he reproduces them, lives through again such of them as, by means of what is called the *transference,* may be made effective in opposition against the physician and the treatment. If the patient is a man, he usually takes this material from his relationship with his father, in whose place he has now put the physician; and in so doing he erects resistance out of his struggles to attain to personal independence and independence of judgment, out of his ambition, the earliest aim of which was to equal or to excel the father, out of his disinclination to take the burden of gratitude upon himself for the second time in his life. There are periods in which one feels that the patient's desire to put the analyst in the wrong, to make him feel his impotence, to triumph over him, has completely ousted the worthier desire to bring the illness to an end. Women have a genius for exploiting in the interests of resistance a tender erotically tinged transference to the analyst; when this attraction reaches a certain intensity all interest in the actual situation of treatment fades away, together with every obligation incurred upon undertaking it. The inevitable jealousy and the embitterment consequent upon the unavoidable rejection, however considerately it is handled, is bound to injure the personal relationship with the physician, and so to put out of action one of the most powerful propelling forces in the analysis.

Resistances of this kind must not be narrowly condemned. They contain so much of the most important material from the patient's past life and bring it back in so convincing a fashion that they come to be of the greatest assistance to the analysis, if a skilful technique is employed correctly to turn them to the best use. What is noteworthy is that this material always serves at first as a resistance and comes forward in a guise which is inimical to the treatment. Again it may be said that they are character-traits, individual attitudes of the ego, which are thus mobilized to oppose the attempted alterations. One learns then how these character-traits have been developed in connection with the conditions of the neurosis and in reaction against its demands, and observes features in this character which would not otherwise have appeared, at least, not so clearly: that is, which may be designated latent. Also you must not carry away the impression that we look upon the appearance of these resistances as an unforeseen danger threatening our analytic influence. No, we know that these resistances are bound to appear; we are dissatisfied only if we cannot rouse them definitely enough and make the patient perceive them as such. Indeed, we understand at last that the overcoming of these resistances is the essential work of the analysis, that part of the work which alone assures us that we have achieved something for the patient.

Besides this, you must take into account that all accidental occurrences arising during the treatment are made use of by the patient to interfere with it, anything which could distract him or deter him from it, every hostile expression of opinion from anyone in his circle whom he can regard as an authority, any chance organic illness or one complicating the neurosis; indeed, he even converts every improvement in his condition into a motive for slackening his efforts. Then you will have obtained an approximate, though still incomplete, picture of the forms and the measures taken by the resistances which must be met and overcome in the course of every analysis. I have given such a detailed consideration to this point because I am about to inform you that our dynamic conception of the neuroses is founded upon this experience of ours of the resistances that neurotic patients set up against the cure of their symptoms. Breuer and I both originally practiced psycho-therapy by the hypnotic method. Breuer's first patient was treated throughout in a state of hypnotic suggestibility; at first I followed his example. I admit that at that time my work went forward more easily and agreeably and also took much less time: but the results were capricious and not permanent; therefore I finally gave up hypnotism.

And then I understood that no comprehension of the dynamics of these affections was possible as long as hypnosis was employed. In this condition the very existence of resistances is concealed from the physician's observation. Hypnosis drives back the resistances and frees a certain field for the work of the analysis, but dams them up at the boundaries of this field so that they are insurmountable; it is similar in effect to the doubt of the obsessional neurosis. Therefore I may say that true psycho-analysis only began when the help of hypnosis was discarded.

If it is a matter of such importance to establish these resistances then surely it would be wise to allow caution and doubt full play, in case we have been too ready with our assumption that they exist. Perhaps cases of neurosis may be found in which the associations really fail for other reasons, perhaps the arguments against our theories really deserve serious attention, and we may be wrong in so conveniently disposing of the patient's intellectual objections by stigmatizing them as resistance. Well, I can only assure you that our judgment in this matter has not been formed hastily; we have had opportunity to observe these critical patients both before the resistance comes to the surface and after it disappears. In the course of the treatment the resistance varies in intensity continually; it always increases as a new topic is approached, it is at its height during the work upon it, and dies down again when this theme has been dealt with. Unless certain technical errors have been committed, we never have to meet the full measure of resistance, of which any patient is capable, at once. Thus we could definitely ascertain that the same man would take up and then abandon his critical objections over and over again in the course of the analysis. Whenever we are on the point of bringing to his consciousness some piece of unconscious material which is particularly painful to him, then he is critical in the extreme; even though he may have previously understood and accepted a great deal, yet now all these gains seem to be obliterated; in his struggles to oppose at all costs he can behave just as though he were mentally deficient, a form of *emotional stupidity*. If he can be successfully helped to overcome this new resistance he regains his insight and comprehension. His critical faculty is not functioning independently, and therefore is not to be respected as if it were; it is merely a maid-of-all-work for his affective attitudes and is directed by his resistance. When he dislikes anything he can defend himself against it most ingeniously; but when anything suits his book he can be credulous enough. We are perhaps all much the same; a person being analysed shows this dependence of the intellect upon the affective life so clearly because in the analysis he is so hard-pressed.

In what way can we now account for this fact observed, that the patient struggles so energetically against the relief of his symptoms and the restoration of his mental processes to normal functioning? We say that we have come upon the traces of powerful forces at work here opposing any change in the condition; they must be the same forces that originally induced the condition. In the formation of symptoms some process must have been gone through, which our experience in dispersing them makes us able to reconstruct. As we already know from Breuer's observations, it follows from the existence of a symptom that some mental process has not been carried through to an end in a normal manner so that it could become conscious; the symptom is a substitute for that which has not come through. Now we know where to place the forces which we suspect to be at work. A vehement effort must have been exercised to prevent the mental process in question from penetrating into consciousness and as a result it has remained unconscious; being unconscious it had the power to construct a symptom. The same vehement effort is again at work during analytic treatment, opposing the attempt to bring the unconscious into consciousness. This we perceive in the form of resistances. The pathogenic process which is demonstrated by the resistances we call REPRESSION.

It will now be necessary to make our conception of this process of *repression* more precise. It is the essential preliminary condition for the development of symptoms, but it is also something else, a thing to which we have no parallel. Let us take as a model an impulse, a mental process seeking to convert itself into action: we know that it can suffer rejection, by virtue of what we call *repudiation* or *condemnation;* whereupon the energy at its disposal is withdrawn, it becomes powerless, but it can continue to exist as a memory. The whole process of decision on the point takes place with the full cognizance of the ego. It is very different when we imagine the same impulse subject to *repression:* it would then retain its energy and no memory of it would be left behind; the process of repression, too, would

be accomplished without the cognizance of the ego. This comparison therefore brings us no nearer to the nature of repression.

I will expound to you those theoretical conceptions which alone have proved useful in giving greater definiteness to the term *repression.* For this purpose it is first necessary that we should proceed from the purely descriptive meaning of the word *unconscious* to its systematic meaning; that is, we resolve to think of the consciousness or unconsciousness of a mental process as merely one of its qualities and not necessarily definitive. Suppose that a process of this kind has remained unconscious, its being withheld from consciousness may be merely a sign of the fate it has undergone, not necessarily the fate itself. Let us suppose, in order to gain a more concrete notion of this fate, that every mental process—there is one exception, which I will go into later—first exists in an unconscious state or phase, and only develops out of this into a conscious phase, much as a photograph is first a negative and then becomes a picture through the printing of the positive. But not every negative is made into a positive, and it is just as little necessary that every unconscious mental process should convert itself into a conscious one. It may be best expressed as follows: Each single process belongs in the first place to the unconscious psychical system; from this system it can under certain conditions proceed further into the conscious system.

The crudest conception of these systems is the one we shall find most convenient, a spatial one. The unconscious system may therefore be compared to a large ante-room, in which the various mental excitations are crowding upon one another, like individual beings. Adjoining this is a second, smaller apartment, a sort of reception-room, in which consciousness resides. But on the threshold between the two there stands a personage with the office of door-keeper, who examines the various mental excitations, censors them, and denies them admittance to the reception-room when he disapproves of them. You will see at once that it does not make much difference whether the door-keeper turns any one impulse back at the threshold, or drives it out again once it has entered the reception-room; that is merely a matter of the degree of his vigilance and promptness in recognition. Now this metaphor may be employed to widen our terminology. The excitations in the unconscious, in the ante-chamber, are not visible to consciousness, which is of course in the other room, so to begin with they remain unconscious. When they have pressed forward to the threshold and been turned back by the door-keeper, they are *incapable of becoming conscious;* we call them then *repressed.* But even those excitations which are allowed over the threshold do not necessarily become conscious; they can only become so if they succeed in attracting the eye of consciousness. This second chamber therefore may be suitably called *the preconscious system.* In this way the process of becoming conscious retains its purely descriptive sense. Being repressed, when applied to any single impulse, means being unable to pass out of the unconscious system because of the door-keeper's refusal of admittance into the preconscious. The door-keeper is what we have learnt to know as resistance in our attempts in analytic treatment to loosen the repressions.

Now I know very well that you will say that these conceptions are as crude as they are fantastic and not at all permissible in a scientific presentation. I know they are crude; further indeed, we even know that they are incorrect, and unless I am mistaken, we have something better ready as a substitute for them; whether you will then continue to think them so fantastic, I do not know. At the moment they are useful aids to understanding, like *Ampére's* manikin swimming in the electric current, and, in so far as they do assist comprehension, are not to be despised. Still, I should like to assure you that these crude hypotheses, the two chambers, the door-keeper on the threshold between the two, and consciousness as a spectator at the end of the second room, must indicate an extensive approximation to the actual reality. I should also like to hear you admit that our designations, unconscious, preconscious, and conscious, are less prejudicial and more easily defensible than some others which have been suggested or have come into use, e.g., sub-conscious, inter-conscious, co-conscious, etc.

If so, I should think it more significant if you then went on to point out that any such constitution of the mental apparatus as I have assumed in order to account for neurotic symptoms can only be of universal validity and must throw light on normal functioning. In this, of course, you are perfectly right. We cannot follow up this conclusion at the moment; but our interest in the psychology of symptom-development would certainly be enormously increased if we could see any prospect of obtaining, by the study of pathological conditions, an insight into normal mental functioning, hitherto such a mystery.

Do you not recognize, moreover, what it is that supports these conceptions of the two systems and the relationship between them and consciousness? The door-keeper between the unconscious and the preconscious is nothing else than the *censorship* to which we found the form of the manifest dream subjected. The residue of the day's experiences which we found to be the stimuli exciting the dream, was preconscious material which at night during sleep had been influenced by unconscious and repressed wishes and excitations; and had thus by association with them been able to form the latent dream, by means of their energy. Under the dominion of the unconscious system this material had been elaborated (worked over)— by condensation and displacement—in a way which in normal mental life, i.e., in the preconscious system, is unknown or admissible very rarely. This difference in their manner of functioning is what distinguishes the two systems for us; the relationship to consciousness, which is a permanent feature of the preconscious, indicates to which of the two systems any given process belongs. Neither is dreaming a pathological phenomenon; every healthy person may dream while asleep. Every inference concerning the constitution of the mental apparatus which comprises an understanding of both dreams and neurotic symptoms has an irrefutable claim to be regarded as applying also to normal mental life.

This is as much as we will say about repression for the present. Moreover, it is but a necessary preliminary condition, a prerequisite, of symptom-formation. We know that the symptom is a substitute for some other process which was held back by repression; but even given repression we have still a long way to go before we can obtain comprehension of this substitute-formation. There are other sides to the problem of repression itself which present questions to be answered: What kind of mental excitations suffer repression? What forces effect it? and from what motives? On one point only, so far, have we gained any knowledge relevant to these questions. While investigating the problem of resistance we learned that the forces behind it proceed from the ego, from character-traits, recognizable or latent: it is these forces therefore which have also effected the repression, or at least they have taken a part in it. We know nothing more than this at present.

The second observation for which I prepared you will help us now. By means of analysis we can always discover the purpose behind the neurotic symptom. This is of course nothing new to you: I have already pointed it out in two cases of neurosis. But, to be sure, what do two cases signify? You have a right to demand two hundred cases, innumerable cases, in demonstration of it. But then, I cannot comply with that. So you must fall back on personal experience, or upon belief, which in this matter can rely upon the unanimous testimony of all psycho-analysts.

You will remember that in the two cases in which we submitted the symptoms to detailed investigation analysis led to the innermost secrets of the patient's sexual life. In the first case, moreover, the purpose or tendency of the symptom under examination was particularly evident; in the second case, it was perhaps to some extent veiled by another factor to be mentioned later. Well now, what we found in these two examples we should find in every case we submitted to analysis. Every time we should be led by analysis to the sexual experiences and desires of the patient, and every time we should have to affirm that the symptom served the same purpose. This purpose shows itself to be the gratification of sexual wishes; the symptoms serve the purpose of sexual gratification for the patient; they are a substitute for satisfactions which he does not obtain in reality.

Think of the obsessive act of our first patient. This woman has to do without the husband she loved so intensely; on account of his deficiencies and short-comings she could not share his life. She had to be faithful to him; she could not put anyone else in his place. Her obsessional symptom gives her what she so much desires; it exalts her husband, denies and corrects his deficiencies, above all, his impotence. This symptom is fundamentally a wish-fulfilment, in that respect exactly like a dream; it is, moreover, what a dream is not always, an erotic wish-fulfilment. In the case of the second patient you could see that her ritual aims at preventing intercourse between the parents or at hindering the procreation of another child; you have probably also divined that fundamentally it seeks to set her in her mother's place. It again, therefore, constitutes a removal of hindrances to sexual satisfaction and the fulfilment of the subject's own sexual

wishes. Of the complications referred to in the second case I shall speak shortly.

I wish to avoid making reservations later on about the universal applicability of these statements, and therefore I will ask you to notice that all I have just been saying about repression, symptom-formation and symptom-interpretation has been obtained from the study of three types of neurosis, and for the present is only applicable to these three types—namely, *anxiety-hysteria, conversion-hysteria,* and *the obsessional neurosis*. These three disorders, which we are accustomed to combine together in a group as the TRANSFERENCE NEUROSES, constitute the field open to psycho-analytic therapy. The other neuroses have been far less closely studied psycho-analytically; in one group of them the impossibility of therapeutic influence has no doubt been one reason for this neglect. You must not forget that psycho-analysis is still a very young science, that much time and trouble are required for the study of it, and that not so very long ago there was only one man practising it: yet we are approaching from all directions to a nearer comprehension of these other conditions which are not transference neuroses. I hope I shall still be able to tell you of the developments that our hypotheses and conclusions have undergone in the course of adaptation to this new material, and to show you that these further studies have not yielded contradictions but have led to a higher degree of unification in our knowledge. Everything that has been said, then, applies only to the three transference neuroses and I will now add another piece of information which throws further light upon the significance of the symptoms. A comparative examination of the situation out of which the disease arose yields the following result, which may be reduced to a formula—namely, that these persons have fallen ill from the privation (frustration) which they suffer when reality withholds from them gratification of their sexual wishes. You will perceive how beautifully these two conclusions supplement one another. The symptoms are now explicable as substitute-gratifications for desires which are unsatisfied in life.

It is certainly possible to make all kinds of objections to the proposition that neurotic symptoms are substitutes for sexual gratifications. I will discuss two of them today. If any one of you has himself undertaken the analysis of a large number of neurotics, he will perhaps shake his head and say: "In certain cases this is not at all applicable, in them the symptoms seem rather to contain the opposite purpose, of excluding or of discontinuing sexual gratification." I shall not dispute your interpretation. In psycho-analysis things are often a good deal more complicated than we could wish: if they had been simpler psycho-analysis would perhaps not have been required to bring them to light. Certain features of the ritual of our second patient are distinctly recognizable as being of this ascetic character, inimical to sexual satisfaction; e.g., her removing the clocks for the magic purpose of preventing erections at night, or her trying to prevent the falling and breaking of vessels, which amounts to a protection of her virginity. In other cases of ceremonials on going to bed which I have analysed this negative character was far more marked; the whole ritual could consist of defensive regulations against sexual recollections and temptations. But we have long ago learnt from psycho-analysis that opposites do not constitute a contradiction. We might extend our proposition and say that the purpose of the symptom is either a sexual gratification or a defence against it; in hysteria the positive, wish-fulfilling character predominates on the whole, and in the obsessional neurosis the negative ascetic character. The symptoms can serve the purpose both of sexual gratification and of its opposite so well because this double-sidedness, or *polarity*, has a most suitable foundation in one element of their mechanism which we have not yet had an opportunity to mention. They are in fact, as we shall see, the effects of *compromises* between two opposed tendencies, acting on one another; they represent both that which is repressed, and also that which has effected the repression and has co-operated in bringing them about. The representation of either one or another of these two factors may predominate in the symptom, but it happens very rarely that one of them is absent altogether. In hysteria a collaboration of the two tendencies in one symptom is usually achieved. In the obsessional neurosis the two parts are often distinct: the symptom is then a double one and consists of two successive actions which cancel each other.

It will not be so easy to dispose of a second difficulty. When you consider a whole series of symptom-interpretations your first opinion would probably be that the conception of a sexual substitute-gratification has to be stretched to its widest limits in order to include them. You will not neglect to point out that these symptoms offer nothing real in the way of gratification, that often enough they are confined to re-animating a sensation, or to enacting a phantasy arising from some sexual complex. Further, that the ostensible sexual gratification is very often of an infantile and unworthy character, perhaps approximating to a masturbatory act, or is reminiscent of dirty habits which long ago in childhood had been forbidden and abandoned. And further still, you will express your astonishment that anyone should reckon among sexual gratifications those which can only be described as gratifications of cruel or horrible appetites, or which may be termed unnatural. Indeed, we shall come to no agreement on these latter points until we have submitted human sexuality to a thorough investigation and have thus established what we are justified in calling sexual.

TWENTIETH LECTURE

THE SEXUAL LIFE OF MAN

ONE would certainly think that there could be no doubt about what is to be understood by the term *sexual*. First and foremost, of course, it means the *improper*, that which must not be mentioned. I have been told a story about some pupils of a famous psychiatrist, who once endeavoured to convince their master that the symptoms of an hysteric are frequently representations of sexual things. With this object, they took him to the bedside of an hysterical woman whose attacks were unmistakable imitations of childbirth. He objected, however: "Well, there is nothing sexual about childbirth." To be sure, childbirth is not necessarily always improper.

I perceive that you don't approve of my joking about such serious matters. It is not altogether a joke, however. Seriously, it is not so easy to define what the term *sexual* includes. Everything connected with the difference between the two sexes is perhaps the only way of hitting the mark; but you will find that too general and indefinite. If you take the sexual act itself as the central point, you will perhaps declare *sexual* to mean everything which is concerned with obtaining pleasurable gratification from the body (and particularly the sexual organs) of the opposite sex; in the narrowest sense, everything which is directed to the union of the genital organs and the performance of the sexual act. In doing so, however, you come very near to reckoning the sexual and the improper as identical, and childbirth would really have nothing to do with sex. If then you make the function of reproduction the kernel of sexuality you run the risk of excluding from it a whole host of things like masturbation, or even kissing, which are not directed towards reproduction, but which are nevertheless undoubtedly sexual. However, we have already found that attempts at definition always lead to difficulties; let us give up trying to do any better in this particular case. We may suspect that in the development of the concept *sexual* something has happened which has resulted in what H. Silberer has aptly called a *covering error*. On the whole, indeed, we know pretty well what is meant by sexual.

In the popular view, which is sufficient for all practical purposes in ordinary life, sexual is something which combines references to the difference between the sexes, to pleasurable excitement and gratification, to the reproductive function, and to the idea of impropriety and the necessity for concealment. But this is no longer sufficient for science. For painstaking researches (only possible, of course, in a spirit of self-command maintained by self-sacrifice) have revealed that classes of human beings exist whose sexual life deviates from the usual one in the most striking manner. One group among these *perverts* has, as it were, expunged the difference between the sexes from its scheme of life. In these people, only the same sex as their own can rouse sexual desire; the other sex (especially the genital organ of the other sex) has absolutely no sexual attraction for them, can even in extreme cases be an object of abhorrence to them. They have thus, of course, foregone all participation in the process of reproduction. Such persons are called *homosexuals* or *inverts*. Often, though not always, they are men and women who otherwise have reached an irreproachably high standard of mental growth and development, intellectually and ethically, and are only afflicted with this one fateful peculiarity. Through the mouths of their scientific spokesmen they lay claim to be a special variety of the human race, a *third sex*, as they call it, standing with equal rights alongside the other two. We may perhaps have an opportunity of critically examining these claims. They are not, of course, as they would gladly maintain, the *elect* of mankind; they contain in their ranks at least as many inferior and worthless individuals as are to be found among those differently constituted sexually.

These perverts do at least seek to achieve very much the same ends with the objects of their desires as normal people do with theirs. But after them comes a long series of abnormal types, in whom the sexual activities become increasingly further removed from anything which appears attractive to a reasonable being. In their manifold variety and their strangeness these types may be compared to the grotesque monstrosities painted by P. Breughel to represent the temptation of St. Anthony, or to the long procession of effete gods and worshippers which G. Flaubert shows us passing before his pious penitent, and to nothing else. The chaotic assembly calls out for classification if it is not to bewilder us completely. We divide them into those in whom the *sexual object* has been altered, as with the homosexuals, and those in whom, first and foremost, the *sexual aim* has been altered. In the first group belong those who have dispensed with the mutual union of the genital organs and who have substituted for the genitals, in one of the partners in the act, another organ or part of the body (mouth or anus, in place of the vagina) making light of both the anatomical difficulties and the suppression of disgust involved. There follow others who, it is true, still retain the genital organs as object; not, however, by virtue of their sexual function, but on account of other functions in which they take part anatomically or by reason of their proximity. These people demonstrate that the excretory functions, which in the course of the child's upbringing are relegated to a limbo as indecent, remain capable of attracting the entire sexual interest. There are others who have given up altogether the genital organs as object; and, instead, have exalted some other part of the body to serve as the object of desire, a woman's breast, foot, or plait of hair. There are others yet to whom even a part of the body is meaningless, while a particle of clothing, a shoe or a piece of underclothing, will gratify all their desires; these are the fetichists. Farther on in the scale come those who indeed demand the object as a whole: but whose requirements in regard to it take specific forms, of an extraordinary or horrible nature—even to the point of seeking it as a defenceless corpse and, urged on by their criminal obsessions, of making it one in order so to enjoy it. But enough of these horrors!

Foremost in the second group are those perverts whose sexual desires aim at the performance of an act which normally is but an introductory or preparatory one. They are those who seek gratification in looking and touching, or in watching the other person's most intimate doings; or those who expose parts of their own bodies which should be concealed, in the vague expectation of being rewarded by a similar action on the part of the other. Then come the incomprehensible sadists, in whom all affectionate feeling strains towards the one goal of causing their object pain and torture, ranging in degree from mere indications of a tendency to humiliate the other up to the infliction of severe bodily injuries. Then, as though complementary to these, come the masochists whose only longing is to suffer, in real or in symbolic form, humiliations and tortures at the hands of the loved object. There are others yet, in whom several abnormal characteristics of this kind are combined and interwoven with one another. Finally, we learn that the persons belonging to each of these groups may be divided again: into those who seek their particular form of sexual satisfaction in reality and those who are satisfied merely to imagine it in their own minds, needing no real object at all but being able to substitute for it a creation of phantasy.

There is not the slightest possible doubt that these mad, extraordinary and horrible things do actually constitute the sexual activities of these people. Not merely do they themselves so regard them, recognizing their substitutive character; but we also have to acknowledge that they play the same part in their lives as normal sexual satisfaction plays in ours, exacting the same, often excessive, sacrifices. It is possible to trace out, both broadly and in great detail, where these abnormalities merge into the normal and where they diverge from it. Nor will it escape you that that quality of impropriety which adheres inevitably to a sexual activity is not absent from these forms of it: in most of them it is intensified to the point of odium.

Well, now, what attitude are we to take up to these unusual forms of sexual satisfaction? Indignation and expressions of our personal disgust, together with assurances that we do not share these appetites, will obviously not carry us very far. That is not the point at issue. After all, this is a field of phenomena like any other; attempts to turn away and flee from it, on the pretext that these are but rarities and curiosities, could easily be rebutted. On the contrary, the phenomena are common enough and widely distributed. But if it is objected that our views on the sexual life of mankind require no revision on this account, since these things are one and all aberrations and divagations of the sexual instinct, a serious reply will be necessary. If we do not understand these morbid forms of sexuality and cannot relate them to what is normal in sexual life, then neither can we understand normal sexuality. It remains, in short, our undeniable duty to account satisfactorily in theory for the existence of all the perversions described and to explain their relation to normal sexuality, so-called.

In this task we can be helped by a point of view, and by two new evidential observations. The first we owe to Ivan Bloch; according to him, the view that all the perversions are "signs of degeneration" is incorrect; because of the evidence existing that such aberrations from the sexual aim, such erratic relationships to the sexual object, have been manifested since the beginning of time through every age of which we have knowledge, in every race from the most primitive to the most highly civilized, and at times have succeeded in attaining to toleration and general prevalence. The two evidential observations have been made in the course of psycho-analytic investigations of neurotic patients; they must undoubtedly influence our conception of sexual perversions in a decisive manner.

We have said that neurotic symptoms are substitutes for sexual satisfactions and I have already indicated that many difficulties will be met with in proving this statement from the analysis of symptoms. It is, indeed, only accurate if the *perverse* sexual needs, so-called, are included under sexual satisfactions; for an interpretation of the symptoms on this basis is forced upon us with astonishing frequency. The claim made by homosexuals or inverts, that they constitute a select class of mankind, falls at once to the ground when we discover that, in every single neurotic, evidence of homosexual tendencies is forthcoming and that a large proportion of the symptoms are expressions of this latent inversion. Those who openly call themselves homosexuals are merely those in whom the inversion is conscious and manifest; their number is negligible compared with those in whom it is latent. We are bound, in fact, to regard the choice of an object of the same sex as a regular type of offshoot of the capacity to love, and are learning every day more and more to recognize it as especially important. The differences between manifest homosexuality and the normal attitude are certainly not thereby abrogated; they have their practical importance, which remains, but theoretically their value is very considerably diminished. In fact, we have even come to the conclusion that one particular mental disorder, paranoia, no longer to be reckoned among the transference neuroses, invariably arises from an attempt to subdue unduly powerful homosexual tendencies. Perhaps you will remember that one of our patients,[1] in her obsessive act, played the part of a man—of her own husband, that is, whom she had left; such symptoms, representing the impersonation of a man, are very commonly produced by neurotic women. If this is not actually attributable to homosexuality, it is certainly very closely connected with its origins.

As you probably know, the neurosis of hysteria can create its symptoms in all systems of the body (circulatory, respiratory, etc.) and may thus disturb all the functions. Analysis shows that all those impulses, described as *perverse*, which aim at replacing the genital organ by another come to expression in these symptoms. These organs thus behave as substitutes for the genital organs: it is precisely from the study of hysterical symptoms that we have arrived at the view that, besides their functional rôle, a sexual—*erotogenic*—significance must be ascribed to the bodily organs; and that the needs of the former will be interfered with if the demands of the latter upon them are too great. Countless sensations and innervations, which we meet as hysterical symptoms, in organs apparently not concerned with sexuality, are thus discovered to be essentially fulfilments of perverse sexual desires, by the other organs having usurped the function of the genitalia. In this way also the very great extent to which the organs of nutrition and of excretion, in particular, may serve in yielding sexual excitement is brought home to us. It is indeed the same as is manifested in the perversions; except that in the latter it is unmistakable and recognizable without any difficulty, whereas in hysteria we have to make the detour of interpreting the symptom, and then do not impute the perverse sexual impulse in question to the person's consciousness, but account it to the unconscious part of his personality.

Of the many types of symptoms characteristic of the obsessional neurosis, the most important are found to be brought about by the undue strength of one group of sexual tendencies with a perverted aim, i.e., the sadistic group. These symptoms, in accordance with the structure of the obsessional neurosis, serve mainly as a de-

fence against these wishes or else they express the conflict between satisfaction and rejection. Satisfaction does not find short shrift, however; it knows how to get its own way by a roundabout route in the patient's behaviour, by preference turning against him in self-inflicted torment. Other forms of this neurosis are seen in excessive *worry* and brooding; these are the expressions of an exaggerated sexualization of acts which are normally only preparatory to sexual satisfaction: the desire to see, to touch and to investigate. In this lies the explanation of the very great importance dread of contact and obsessive washing attains to in this disease. An unsuspectedly large proportion of obsessive actions are found to be disguised repetitions and modifications of masturbation, admittedly the only uniform act which accompanies all the varied flights of sexual phantasy.

It would not be difficult to show you the connections between perversion and neurosis in a much more detailed manner, but I believe that I have said enough for our purposes. We must beware, however, of overestimating the frequency and intensity of the perverse tendencies in mankind, after these revelations of their importance in the interpretation of symptoms. You have heard that frustration of normal sexual satisfactions may lead to the development of neurosis. In consequence of this frustration in reality the need is forced into the abnormal paths of sexual excitation. Later you will be able to understand how this happens. You will at any rate understand that a *collateral* damming-up of this kind must swell the force of the perverse impulses, so that they become more powerful than they would have been had no hindrance to normal sexual satisfaction been present in reality. Incidentally, a similar factor may be recognized also in the manifest perversions. In many cases they are provoked or activated by the unduly great difficulties in the way of normal satisfaction of the sexual instinct which are produced either by temporary conditions or by permanent social institutions. In other cases, certainly, perverse tendencies are quite independent of such conditions; they are, as it were, the natural kind of sexual life for the individual concerned.

Perhaps you are momentarily under the impression that all this tends to confuse rather than to explain the relations between normal and perverted sexuality. But keep in mind this consideration. If it is correct that real obstacles to sexual satisfaction or frustration in regard to it bring to the surface perverse tendencies in people who would otherwise have shown none, we must conclude that something in these people is ready to embrace the perversions; or, if you prefer it, the tendencies must have been present in them in a latent form. Thus we come to the second of the new evidential observations of which I spoke. Psycho-analytic investigation has found it necessary also to concern itself with the sexual life of children, for the reason that in the analysis of symptoms the forthcoming reminiscences and associations invariably lead back to the earliest years of childhood. That which we discovered in this way has since been corroborated point by point by the direct observation of children. In this way it has been found that all the perverse tendencies have their roots in childhood, that children are disposed towards them all and practise them all to a degree conforming with their immaturity; in short, *perverted sexuality* is nothing else but infantile sexuality, magnified and separated into its component parts.

Now you will see the perversions in an altogether different light and no longer ignore their connection with the sexual life of mankind; but what distressing emotions these astonishing and grotesque revelations will provoke in you! At first you will certainly be tempted to deny everything—the fact that there is anything in children which can be termed sexual life, the accuracy of our observations, and the justification of our claim to see in the behaviour of children any connection with that which in later years is condemned as perverted. Permit me first to explain to you the motives of your antagonism and then to put before you a summary of our observations. That children should have no sexual life—sexual excitement, needs, and gratification of a sort—but that they suddenly acquire these things in the years between twelve and fourteen would be, apart from any observations at all, biologically just as improbable, indeed, nonsensical, as to suppose that they are born without genital organs which first begin to sprout at the age of puberty. What does actually awake in them at this period is the reproductive function, which then makes use for its own purposes of material lying to hand in body and mind. You are making the mistake of confounding sexuality and reproduction with each other and thus you obstruct your own way to the comprehension of sexuality, the perversions, and the neuroses. This mistake, moreover, has a meaning in it. Strange to say, its origin lies in the fact that you yourselves have

all been children and as children were subject to the influence of education. For it is indeed one of the most important social tasks of education to restrain, confine, and subject to an individual control (itself identical with the demands of society) the sexual instinct when it breaks forth in the form of the reproductive function. In its own interests, accordingly, society would postpone the child's full development until it has attained a certain stage of intellectual maturity, since educability practically ceases with the full onset of the sexual instinct. Without this the instinct would break all bounds, and the laboriously erected structure of civilization would be swept away. Nor is the task of restraining it ever an easy one: success in this direction is often poor and, sometimes, only too great. At bottom society's motive is economic; since it has not means enough to support life for its members without work on their part, it must see to it that the number of these members is restricted and their energies directed away from sexual activities on to their work—the eternal primordial struggle for existence, therefore, persisting to the present day.

Experience must have taught educators that the task of moulding the sexual will of the next generation can only be carried out by beginning to impose their influence very early, and intervening in the sexual life of children before puberty, instead of waiting till the storm bursts. Consequently almost all infantile sexual activities are forbidden or made disagreeable to the child; the ideal has been to make the child's life asexual, and in course of time it has come to this that it is really believed to be asexual, and is given out as such, even at the hands of science. In order, then, to avoid any contradiction with established beliefs and aims, the sexual activity of children is overlooked—no small achievement by the way—while science contents itself with otherwise explaining it away. The little child is supposed to be pure and innocent; he who says otherwise shall be condemned as a hardened blasphemer against humanity's tenderest and most sacred feelings.

The children alone take no part in this convention; they assert their animal nature naïvely enough and demonstrate persistently that they have yet to learn their *purity*. Strange to say, those who deny sexuality in children are the last to relax educative measures against it; they follow up with the greatest severity every manifestation of the *childish tricks* the existence of which they deny. Moreover, it is theoretically of great interest that the time of life which most flagrantly contradicts the prejudice about asexual childhood, the years of infancy up to five or six, is precisely the period which is veiled by oblivion in most people's memories; an oblivion which can only be dispelled completely by analysis but which even before this was sufficiently penetrable to allow some of the dreams of childhood to be retained.

I will now tell you the most clearly recognizable of the child's sexual activities. It will be expedient if I first introduce you to the term libido. In every way analogous to *hunger,* libido is the force by means of which the instinct, in this case the sexual instinct, as, with hunger, the nutritional instinct, achieves expression. Other terms, such as *sexual excitation* and *satisfaction,* require no definition. Interpretation finds most to do in regard to the sexual activities of the infant, as you will easily perceive; and no doubt you will find a reason for objections. This interpretation is formed on the basis of analytic investigation, working backwards from a given symptom. The infant's first sexual excitations appear in connection with the other functions important for life. Its chief interest, as you know, is concerned with taking nourishment; as it sinks asleep at the breast, utterly satisfied, it bears a look of perfect content which will come back again later in life after the experience of the sexual orgasm. This would not be enough to found a conclusion upon. However, we perceive that infants wish to repeat, without really getting any nourishment, the action necessary to taking nourishment; they are therefore not impelled to this by hunger. We call this action *pleasure-sucking* (German: *lutschen,* signifying the enjoyment of sucking for its own sake—as with a rubber comforter); and as when it does this the infant again falls asleep with a blissful expression we see that the action of sucking is sufficient in itself to give it satisfaction. Admittedly, it very soon contrives not to go to sleep without having sucked in this way. An old physician for children in Budapest, Dr. Lindner, was the first to maintain the sexual nature of this procedure. Nurses and people who look after children appear to take the same view of this pleasure-sucking, though without taking up any theoretic attitude about it. They have no doubt that its only purpose is in the pleasure derived; they account it one of the child's *naughty tricks;* and take severe measures to force it to give it up, if it will not do so of its own accord. And so we learn that an infant performs actions with no other object but that of obtaining pleasure. We believe that this pleasure is first of all experienced while nourishment is being taken, but that the infant learns rapidly to enjoy it apart from this condition. The gratification obtained can only relate to the region of the mouth and lips; we therefore call these areas of the body *erotogenic zones* and describe the pleasure derived from this sucking as a *sexual* one. To be sure, we have yet to discuss the justification for the use of this term.

If the infant could express itself, it would undoubtedly acknowledge that the act of sucking at its mother's breast is far and away the most important thing in life. It would not be wrong in this, for by this act it gratifies at the same moment the two greatest needs in life. Then we learn from psycho-analysis, not without astonishment, how much of the mental significance of this act is retained throughout life. Sucking for nourishment becomes the point of departure from which the whole sexual life develops, the unattainable prototype of every later sexual satisfaction, to which in times of need phantasy often enough reverts. The desire to suck includes within it the desire for the mother's breast, which is therefore the first *object* of sexual desire; I cannot convey to you any adequate idea of the importance of this first object in determining every later object adopted, of the profound influence it exerts, through transformation and substitution, upon the most distant fields of mental life. First of all, however, as the infant takes to sucking for pleasure this object is given up and is replaced by a part of its own body; it sucks its thumb or its own tongue. For purposes of obtaining pleasure it thus makes itself independent of the concurrence of the outer world and, in addition, it extends the region of excitation to a second area of the body, thus intensifying it. The erotogenic zones are not all equally capable of yielding enjoyment; it is therefore an important experience when, as Dr. Lindner says, the infant in feeling about on its own body discovers the particularly excitable region of its genitalia, and so finds the way from pleasure-sucking to onanism.

This assessment of the nature of pleasure-sucking has now brought to our notice two of the decisive characteristics of infantile sexuality. It appears in connection with the satisfaction of the great organic needs, and it behaves *auto-erotically,* that is to say, it seeks and finds its objects in its own person. What is most clearly discernible in regard to the taking of nourishment is to some extent repeated with the process of excretion. We conclude that infants experience pleasure in the evacuation of urine and the contents of the bowels, and that they very soon endeavour to contrive these actions so that the accompanying excitation of the membranes in these erotogenic zones may secure them the maximum possible gratification. As Lou Andreas has pointed out, with fine intuition, the outer world first steps in as a hindrance at this point, a hostile force opposed to the child's desire for pleasure—the first hint he receives of external and internal conflicts to be experienced later on. He is not to pass his excretions whenever he likes but at times appointed by other people. To induce him to give up these sources of pleasure he is told that everything connected with these functions is *improper,* and must be kept concealed. In this way he is first required to exchange pleasure for value in the eyes of others. His own attitude to the excretions is at the outset very different. His own fæces produce no disgust in him; he values them as part of his own body and is unwilling to part with them, he uses them as the first present by which he can mark out those people whom he values especially. Even after education has succeeded in alienating him from these tendencies, he continues to feel the same high regard for his presents and his money; while his achievements in the way of urination appear to be the subject of particular pride.

I know that for some time you have been longing to interrupt me with cries of: "Enough of these monstrosities! The motions of the bowels a source of pleasurable sexual satisfaction exploited even by infants! Fæces a substance of great value and the anus a kind of genital organ! We do not believe it; but we understand why children's physicians and educationists have emphatically rejected psychoanalysis and its conclusions!" Not at all; you have merely forgotten for the moment that I have been endeavouring to show you the connection between the actual facts of infantile sexual life and the actual facts of the sexual perversions. Why should you not know that in many adults, both homosexual and heterosexual, the anus actually takes over the part played by the vagina in sexual intercourse? And that there are many persons who retain the pleasurable sensations accompanying evacuations of the bowels throughout life and describe them as far from insignificant? You may

hear from children themselves, when they are a little older and able to talk about these things, what an interest they take in the act of defæcation and what pleasure they find in watching others in the act. Of course if you have previously systematically intimidated these children they will understand very well that they are not to speak of such things. And for all else that you refuse to believe I refer you to the evidence brought out in analysis and to the direct observation of children and I tell you that it will require the exercise of considerable ingenuity to avoid seeing all this or to see it in a different light. Nor am I at all averse from your thinking the relationship between childish sexual activities and the sexual perversions positively striking. It is a matter of course that there should be this relationship; for if a child has a sexual life at all it must be of a perverted order, since, apart from a few obscure indications, he is lacking in all that transforms sexuality into the reproductive function. Moreover, it is a characteristic common to all the perversions that in them reproduction as an aim is put aside. This is actually the criterion by which we judge whether a sexual activity is perverse—if it departs from reproduction in its aims and pursues the attainment of gratification independently. You will understand therefore that the gulf and turning-point in the development of the sexual life lies at the point of its subordination to the purposes of reproduction. Everything that occurs before this conversion takes place, and everything which refuses to conform to it and serves the pursuit of gratification alone, is called by the unhonoured title of *perversion* and as such is despised.

So let me continue my brief account of infantile sexuality. I could supplement what I have told you concerning two of the bodily systems by extending the same scrutiny to the others. The sexual life of the child consists entirely in the activities of a series of component-instincts which seek for gratification independently of one another, some in his own body and others already in an external object. Among the organs of these bodily systems the genitalia rapidly take the first place; there are people in whom pleasurable gratification in their own genital organ, without the aid of any other genital organ or object, is continued without interruption from the onanism habitual in the suckling period of infancy to the onanism of necessity occurring in the years of puberty, and then maintained indefinitely beyond that. Incidentally, the subject of onanism is not so easily exhausted; it contains material for consideration from various angles.

In spite of my wish to limit the extent of this discussion I must still say something about sexual curiosity in children. It is too characteristic of childish sexuality and too important for the symptom-formation of the neuroses to be omitted. Infantile sexual curiosity begins very early, sometimes before the third year. It is not connected with the difference between the sexes, which is nothing to children, since they—boys, at least—ascribe the same male genital organ to both sexes. If, then, a boy discovers the vagina in a little sister or playmate, he at once tries to deny the evidence of his senses, for he cannot conceive of a human being like himself without his most important attribute. Later, he is horrified at the possibilities it reveals to him; the influence of previous threats occasioned by too great a preoccupation with his own little member now begins to be felt. He comes under the dominion of the castration complex, which will play such a large part in the formation of his character if he remains healthy, and of his neurosis if he falls ill, and of his resistances if he comes under analytic treatment. Of little girls we know that they feel themselves heavily handicapped by the absence of a large visible penis and envy the boy's possession of it; from this source primarily springs the wish to be a man which is resumed again later in the neurosis, owing to some mal-adjustment to a female development The clitoris in the girl, moreover, is in every way equivalent during childhood to the penis; it is a region of especial excitability in which auto-erotic satisfaction is achieved. In the transition to womanhood very much depends upon the early and complete relegation of this sensitivity from the clitoris over to the vaginal orifice. In those women who are sexually anaesthetic, as it is called, the clitoris has stubbornly retained this sensitivity.

The sexual interest of children is primarily directed to the problem of birth—the same problem that lies behind the riddle of the Theban Sphinx. This curiosity is for the most part aroused by egoistic dread of the arrival of another child. The answer which the nursery has ready for the child. that the stork brings the babies, meets with incredulity even in little children much more often than we imagine. The feeling of having been deceived by grown-up people, and put off with lies, contributes greatly to a sense of isolation and to the de-

velopment of independence. But the child is not able to solve this problem on his own account. His undeveloped sexual constitution sets definite limits to his capacity to understand it. He first supposes that children are made by mixing some special thing with the food taken; nor does he know that only women can have children. Later, he learns of this limitation and gives up the idea of children being made by food, though it is retained in fairy-tales. A little later he soon sees that the father must have something to do with making babies, but he cannot discover what it is. If by chance he is witness of the sexual act he conceives it as an attempt to overpower the woman, as a combat, the sadistic misconception of coitus; at first, however, he does not connect this act with the creation of children; if he discovers blood on the mother's bed or under-linen he takes it as evidence of injury inflicted by the father. In still later years of childhood he probably guesses that the male organ of the man plays an essential part in the procreation of children, but cannot ascribe to this part of the body any function but that of urination.

Children are all united from the outset in the belief that the birth of a child takes place by the bowel; that is to say, that the baby is produced like a piece of fæces. Not until all interest has been weaned from the anal region is this theory abandoned and replaced by the supposition that the navel opens, or that the area between the two nipples is the birthplace of the child. In some such manner as this the enquiring child approaches some knowledge of the facts of sex, unless, misled by his ignorance, he overlooks them until he receives an imperfect and discrediting account of them, usually in the period before puberty, which not infrequently affects him traumatically.

Now you will probably have heard that the term *sexual* has suffered an unwarrantable expansion of meaning at the hands of psychoanalysis, in order that its assertions regarding the sexual origin of the neuroses and the sexual significance of the symptoms may be maintained. You can now judge for yourselves whether this amplification is justified or not. We have extended the meaning of the concept *sexuality* only so far as to include the sexual life of perverted persons and also of children; that is to say, we have restored to it its true breadth of meaning. What is called *sexuality* outside psycho-analysis applies only to the restricted sexual life that is subordinated to the reproductive function and is called *normal*.

TWENTY-FIRST LECTURE

DEVELOPMENT OF THE LIBIDO AND SEXUAL ORGANIZATIONS

It is my impression that I have not succeeded in bringing home to you with complete conviction the importance of the perversions for our conception of sexuality. I wish therefore, as far as I am able, to review and improve upon what I have already said on this subject.

Now I do not wish you to think that it was the perversions alone that required us to make the alteration in the meaning of the term sexuality which has aroused such vehement opposition. The study of infantile sexuality has contributed even more to it, and the unanimity between the two was decisive. But, however unmistakably they may be in the later years of childhood, the manifestations of infantile sexuality in its earliest forms do seem to fade away indefinitely. Those who do not wish to pay attention to evolution and to the connections brought out by analysis will dispute the sexual nature of them, and will ascribe in consequence some other, undifferentiated character to them. You must not forget that as yet we have no generally acknowledged criterion for the sexual nature of a phenomenon, unless it is some connection with the reproductive function—a definition which we have had to reject as too narrow. The biological criteria, such as the periodicities of twenty-three and twenty-eight days, suggested by W. Fliess, are exceedingly debatable; the peculiar chemical features which we may perhaps assume for sexual purposes are yet to be discovered. The sexual perversions in adults, on the other hand, are something definite and unambiguous. As their generally accepted description implies, they are unquestionably of a sexual nature; whether you call them marks of degeneration or anything else, no one has yet been so bold as to rank them anywhere but among the phenomena of sexual life. In view of them alone we are justified in maintaining that sexuality and the reproductive function are not identical, for they one and all abjure the aim of reproduction.

I notice a not uninteresting parallel here. Whereas, for most people, the word *mental* means *conscious,* we found ourselves obliged to widen the application of the term *mental* to include a part of the mind that is not conscious. In a precisely similar way, most people declare *sexual* identical with *pertaining to reproduction* —or, if you like it expressed more concisely, with *genital;* whereas we cannot avoid admitting things as *sexual* that are not *genital* and have nothing to do with reproduction. It is only a formal analogy, but it is not without deeper significance.

However, if the existence of sexual perversions is such a forcible argument on this point, why has it not long ago done its work and settled the question? I really am unable to say. It seems to me that the sexual perversions have come under a very special ban, which insinuates itself into the theory, and interferes even with scientific judgment on the subject. It seems as if no one could forget, not merely that they are detestable, but that they are also something monstrous and terrifying; as if they exerted a seductive influence; as if at bottom a secret envy of those who enjoy them had to be strangled—the same sort of feeling that is confessed by the count who sits in judgment in the famous parody of *Tannhäuser:*

So in the Mount of Venus conscience, duty, are forgot!
—Remarkable that such a thing has never been my lot!

In reality, perverts are more likely to be poor devils who have to pay most bitterly for the satisfaction they manage to procure with such difficulty.

That which makes perverse activities so unmistakably sexual, in spite of all that seems unnatural in their objects or their aims, is the fact that in perverse satisfaction the act still terminates usually in a complete orgasm with evacuation of the genital product. This is of course only the consequence of adult development in the persons concerned; in children, orgasm and genital excretion are not very well possible; as substitutes they have approximations to them which are again not recognized definitely as sexual.

I must still add something more in order to complete our assessment of the sexual perversions. Abominated as they are, sharply distinguished from normal sexual activity as they may be, simple observation will show that very rarely is one feature or another of them absent from the sexual life of a normal person. The kiss, to begin with, has some claim to be called a perverse act, for it consists of the union of the two erotogenic mouth zones instead of the two genital organs. But no one condemns it as perverse; on the contrary, in the theatre it is permitted as a refined indication of the sexual act. Nevertheless, kissing is a thing that can easily become an absolute perversion—namely, when it occurs in such intensity that orgasm and emission directly accompany it, which happens not at all uncommonly. Further, it will be found that gazing at and handling the object are in one person an indispensable condition of sexual enjoyment, while another at the height of sexual excitement pinches or bites; that in another lover not always the genital region, but some other bodily region in the object, provokes the greatest excitement, and so on in endless variety. It would be absurd to exclude people with single idiosyncrasies of this kind from the ranks of the normal and place them among perverts; rather, it becomes more and more clear that what is essential to the perversions lies, not in the overstepping of the sexual aim, not in the replacement of the genitalia, not always even in the variations in the object, but solely in the *exclusiveness* with which these deviations are maintained, so that the sexual act which serves the reproductive process is rejected altogether. In so far as perverse performances are included in order to intensify or to lead up to the performance of the normal sexual act, they are no longer actually perverse. Facts of the kind just described naturally tend to diminish the gulf between normal and perverse sexuality very considerably. The obvious inference is that normal sexuality has arisen, out of something existing prior to it, by a process of discarding some components of this material as useless, and by combining the others so as to subordinate them to a new aim, that of reproduction.

The point of view thus gained in regard to the perversions can now be employed by us in penetrating more deeply, with a clear perspective, into the problem of infantile sexuality; but before doing this I must draw your attention to an important difference between the two. Perverse sexuality is as a rule exceedingly concentrated, its whole activity is directed to one —and mostly to only one—aim; one particular component-impulse is supreme; it is either the only one discernible or it has subjected the others to its own purposes. In this respect there is no difference between perverse and normal sexuality, except that the dominating component-impulse, and therefore the sexual aim, is a different one. Both of them constitute a well-organized tyranny; only that in one case one ruling family has usurped all the power, and in the other, another. This concentration and organization, on the other hand, is in the main absent from infantile sexuality; its component-

impulses are equally valid, each of them strives independently after its own pleasure. Both the lack of this concentration (in childhood) and the presence of it (in the adult) correspond well with the fact that both normal and perverse sexuality are derived from the same source, namely, infantile sexuality. There are indeed also cases of perversion which correspond even more closely to infantile sexuality in that numerous component-instincts, independently of one another, with their aims, are developed or, better, perpetuated in them. With these cases it is more correct to speak of infantilism than of perversion of the sexual life.

Thus prepared we may now go on to consider a suggestion which we shall certainly not be spared. It will be said: "Why are you so set upon declaring as already belonging to sexuality those indefinite manifestations of childhood out of which what is sexual later develops, and which you yourself admit to be indefinite? Why are you not content rather to describe them physiologically and simply to say that activities, such as sucking for its own sake and the retaining of excreta, may be observed already in young infants, showing that they seek *pleasure in their organs?* In that way you would have avoided the conception of a sexual life even in babies which is so repugnant to all our feelings." Well, I can only answer that I have nothing against pleasure derived from the organs of the body; I know indeed that the supreme pleasure of the sexual union is also only a bodily pleasure, derived from the activity of the genital organ. But can you tell me when this originally indifferent bodily pleasure acquires the sexual character that it undoubtedly possesses in later phases of development? Do we know any more about this *organ-pleasure* than we know about sexuality? You will answer that the sexual character is added to it when the genitalia begin to play their part; sexuality simply means genital. You will even evade the obstacle of the perversions by pointing out that after all with most of them a genital orgasm occurs, although brought about by other means than the union of the genitalia. If you were to eliminate the relation to reproduction from the essential characteristics of sexuality since this view is untenable in consequence of the existence of the perversions, and were to emphasize instead activity of the genital organs, you would actually take up a much better position. But then we should no longer differ very widely; it would be a case of the genital organs *versus* the other organs. What do you now make of the abundant evidence that the genital organs may be replaced by other organs for the purpose of gratification, as in the normal kiss, or the perverse practices of loose living, or in the symptomatology of hysteria? In this neurosis it is quite usual for stimulation phenomena, sensations, innervations, and even the processes of erection, which properly belong to the genitalia to be displaced on to other distant areas of the body (e.g., the displacement from below upwards to the head and face). Thus you will find that nothing is left of all that you cling to as essentially characteristic of sexuality; and you will have to make up your minds to follow my example and extend the designation *sexual* to include those activities of early infancy which aim at *organ-pleasure*.

And now will you permit me to bring forward two further considerations in support of my view. As you know, we call the doubtful and indefinable activities of earliest infancy towards pleasure *sexual,* because in the course of analysing symptoms we reach them by way of material that is undeniably sexual. They would not thereby necessarily be sexual themselves, let us grant; but let us take an analogous case. Suppose that there were no way to observe the development from seed of two dicotyledonous plants—the apple-tree and the bean; but imagine that in both it was possible to follow back its development from the fully developed plant to the first seedling with two cotyledons. The two cotyledons are indistinguishable in each; they look exactly alike in both plants. Shall I conclude from this that they actually are exactly alike and that the specific differences between apple-tree and bean-plant arise *later* in the plant's development? Or is it not more correct biologically to believe that this difference exists *already* in the seedlings, although I cannot see any in the cotyledons? This is what we do when we call infantile pleasurable activities sexual. Whether each and every organ-pleasure may be called sexual or whether there exists, besides the sexual, another kind of pleasure that does not deserve this name is a matter I cannot discuss here. I know too little about organ-pleasure and its conditions; and I am not at all surprised that, in consequence of the retrogressive character of analysis, I arrive finally at factors which at the present time do not permit of definite classification.

One thing more. You have on the whole gained very little for what you are so eager to maintain, the sexual purity of children, even if you can convince me that the infant's activities had better not be regarded as sexual. For from the third year onwards there is no longer any doubt about sexual life in the child; at this period the genital organs begin already to show signs of excitation; there is perhaps a regular period of infantile masturbation, that is, of gratification in the genital organs. The mental and social sides of sexual life need no longer be overlooked: choice of object, distinguishing of particular persons with affection, even decision in favour of one sex or the other, and jealousy, were conclusively established independently by impartial observation before the time of psycho-analysis; they may be confirmed by any observer who will use his eyes. You will object that you never doubted the early awakening of affection but only that this affection was of a *sexual* quality. Children between the ages of three and eight have certainly learnt to conceal this element in it; but nevertheless if you look attentively you will collect enough evidence of the *sensual* nature of this affection, and whatever still escapes your notice will be amply and readily supplied by analytic investigation. The sexual aims in this period of life are in closest connection with the sexual curiosity arising at the same time, of which I have given you some description. The perverse character of some of these aims is a natural result of the immature constitution of the child who has not yet discovered the aim of the act of intercourse.

From about the sixth or eighth year onwards a standstill or retrogression is observed in the sexual development, which in those cases reaching a high cultural standard deserves to be called a *latency period*. This latency period, however, may be absent; nor does it necessarily entail an interruption of sexual activities and sexual interests over the whole field. Most of the mental experiences and excitations occurring before the latency period then succumb to the infantile amnesia, already discussed, which veils our earliest childhood from us and estranges us from it. It is the task of every psycho-analysis to bring this forgotten period of life back into recollection; one cannot resist the supposition that the beginnings of sexual life belonging to this period are the motive for this forgetting, that is, that this oblivion is an effect of repression.

From the third year onwards, the sexual life of children shows much in common with that of adults; it is differentiated from the latter, as we already know, by the absence of a stable organization under the primacy of the genital organs, by inevitable traits of a perverse order, and of course also by far less intensity in the whole impulse. But those phases of the sexual development, or as we will call it, of the *libido-development,* which are of greatest interest theoretically lie before this period. This development is gone through so rapidly that direct observation alone would perhaps never have succeeded in determining its fleeting forms. Only by the help of psycho-analytic investigation of the neuroses has it become possible to penetrate so far back and to discover these still earlier phases of libido-development. These phases are certainly only theoretic constructions, but in the practice of psycho-analysis you will find them necessary and valuable constructions. You will soon understand how it happens that a pathological condition enables us to discover phenomena which we should certainly overlook in normal conditions.

Thus we can now define the forms taken by the sexual life of the child before the primacy of the genital zone is reached; this primacy is prepared for in the early infantile period, before the latent period, and is premanently organized from puberty onwards. In this early period a loose sort of organization exists which we shall call *pre-genital;* for during this phase it is not the genital component-instincts, but the *sadistic* and *anal,* which are most prominent. The contrast between *masculine* and *feminine* plays no part as yet; instead of it there is the contrast between *active* and *passive,* which may be described as the forerunner of the sexual polarity with which it also links up later. That which in this period seems masculine to us, regarded from the stand-point of the genital phase, proves to be the expression of an impulse to mastery, which easily passes over into cruelty. Impulses with a passive aim are connected with the erotogenic zone of the rectal orifice, at this period very important; the impulses of skoptophilia (gazing) and curiosity are powerfully active; the function of excreting urine is the only part actually taken by the genital organ in the sexual life. Objects are not wanting to the component-instincts in this period, but these objects are not necessarily all comprised in one object. The sadistic-anal organization is the stage immediately preceding the phase of primacy of the genital zone. Closer study reveals how much of it is retained intact in the later final structure, and what are the paths by which these component-instincts are forced into the service of the new *genital organization.* Behind the sadistic-anal phase of the libido-development we obtain a glimpse of an even more primitive stage of development, in which the erotogenic mouth zone plays the chief part. You can guess that the sexual activity of sucking (for its own sake) belongs to this stage; and you may admire the understanding of the ancient Egyptians in whose art a child, even the divine Horus, was represented with a finger in the mouth. Abraham has quite recently published work showing that traces of this primitive *oral* phase of development survive in the sexual life of later years.

I can indeed imagine that you will have found this last information about the sexual organizations less of an enlightenment than an infliction. Perhaps I have again gone too much into detail; but have patience! what you have just heard will be of more use when we employ it later. Keep in view at the moment the idea that the sexual life—the *libido-function,* as we call it—does not first spring up in its final form, does not even expand along the lines of its earliest forms, but goes through a series of successive phases unlike one another; in short, that many changes occur in it, like those in the development of the caterpillar into the butterfly. The turning-point of this development is the *subordination of all the sexual component-instincts under the primacy of the genital zone* and, together with this, the enrolment of sexuality in the service of the reproductive function. Before this happens the sexual life is, so to say, disparate—independent activities of single component-impulses each seeking *organ-pleasure* (pleasure in a bodily organ). This anarchy is modified by attempts at *pre-genital organizations,* of which the chief is the sadistic-anal phase, behind which is the oral, perhaps the most primitive. In addition there are the various processes, about which little is known as yet, which effect the transition from one stage of organization to the next above it. Of what significance this long journey over so many stages in the development of the libido is for comprehension of the neuroses we shall learn later on.

Today we will follow up another aspect of this development—namely, the relation of the sexual component-impulses to an *object;* or, rather, we will take a fleeting glimpse over this development so that we may spend more time upon a comparatively late result of it. Certain of the component-impulses of the sexual instinct have an object from the very beginning and hold fast to it: such are the impulses to mastery (sadism), to gazing (skoptophilia) and curiosity. Others, more plainly connected with particular erotogenic areas in the body, only have an object in the beginning, so long as they are still dependent upon the non-sexual functions, and give it up when they become detached from these later. Thus the first object of the oral component of the sexual instinct is the mother's breast which satisfies the infant's need for nutrition. In the act of sucking for its own sake the erotic component, also gratified in sucking for nutrition, makes itself independent, gives up the object in an external person, and replaces it by a part of the child's own person. The oral impulse becomes *auto-erotic,* as the anal and other erotogenic impulses are from the beginning. Further development has, to put it as concisely as possible, two aims: first, to renounce auto-erotism, to give up again the object found in the child's own body in exchange again for an external one; and secondly, to combine the various objects of the separate impulses and replace them by one single one. This naturally can only be done if the single object is again itself complete, with a body like that of the subject; nor can it be accomplished without some part of the auto-erotic impulse-excitations being abandoned as useless.

The processes by which an object is found are rather involved, and have not so far received comprehensive exposition. For our purposes it may be emphasized that, when the process has reached a certain point in the years of childhood before the latency period, the object adopted proves almost identical with the first object of the oral pleasure impulse, adopted by reason of the child's dependent relationship to it; it is, namely, the mother, although not the mother's breast. We call the mother the first *love*-object. We speak of *love* when we lay the accent upon the mental side of the sexual impulses and disregard, or wish to forget for a moment, the demands of the fundamental physical or *sensual* side of the impulses. At about the time when the mother becomes the love-object, the mental operation of repression has already begun in the child and has withdrawn from him the knowledge of some part of his sexual aims. Now with this choice of the mother as love-object is connected all that which, under the name of *the Oedipus complex,* has become of such great importance in the psycho-analytic explanation of the neuroses, and which has had a perhaps equally important

share in causing the opposition against psycho-analysis.

Here is a little incident which occurred during the present war. One of the staunch adherents of psycho-analysis was stationed in his medical capacity on the German front in Poland; he attracted the attention of his colleagues by the fact that he occasionally effected an unexpected influence upon a patient. On being questioned, he admitted that he worked with psycho-analytic methods and with readiness agreed to impart his knowledge to his colleagues. So every evening the medical men of the corps, his colleagues and superiors, met to be initiated into the mysteries of psychoanalysis. For a time all went well; but when he had introduced his audience to the Oedipus complex a superior officer rose and announced that he did not believe this, it was the behaviour of a cad for the lecturer to relate such things to brave men, fathers of families, who were fighting for their country, and he forbade the continuation of the lectures. This was the end; the analyst got himself transferred to another part of the front. In my opinion, however, it is a bad outlook if a victory for German arms depends upon an organization of science such as this, and German science will not prosper under any such organization.

Now you will be impatiently waiting to hear what this terrible Oedipus complex comprises. The name tells you: you all know the Greek myth of King Oedipus, whose destiny it was to slay his father and to wed his mother, who did all in his power to avoid the fate prophesied by the oracle, and who in self-punishment blinded himself when he discovered that in ignorance he had committed both these crimes. I trust that many of you have yourselves experienced the profound effect of the tragic drama fashioned by Sophocles from this story. The Attic poet's work portrays the gradual discovery of the deed of Oedipus, long since accomplished, and brings it slowly to light by skilfully prolonged enquiry, constantly fed by new evidence; it has thus a certain resemblance to the course of a psycho-analysis. In the dialogue, the deluded mother-wife, Jocasta, resists the continuation of the enquiry; she points out that many people in their dreams have mated with their mothers, but that dreams are of no account. To us dreams are of much account, especially typical dreams which occur in many people; we have no doubt that the dream Jocasta speaks of is intimately related to the shocking and terrible story of the myth.

It is surprising that Sophocles' tragedy does not call forth indignant remonstrance in its audience; this reaction would be much better justified in them than it was in the blunt army doctor. For at bottom it is an immoral play; it sets aside the individual's responsibility to social law, and displays divine forces ordaining the crime and rendering powerless the moral instincts of the human being which would guard him against the crime. It would be easy to believe that an accusation against destiny and the gods was intended in the story of the myth; in the hands of the critical Euripides, at variance with the gods, it would probably have become such an accusation. But with the reverent Sophocles there is no question of such an intention; the pious subtlety which declares it the highest morality to bow to the will of the gods, even when they ordain a crime, helps him out of the difficulty. I do not believe that this moral is one of the virtues of the drama, but neither does it detract from its effect; it leaves the hearer indifferent; he does not react to this, but to the secret meaning and content of the myth itself. He reacts as though by self-analysis he had detected the Oedipus complex in himself, and had recognized the will of the gods and the oracle as glorified disguises of his own unconscious; as though he remembered in himself the wish to do away with his father and in his place to wed his mother, and must abhor the thought. The poet's words seem to him to mean: "In vain do you deny that you are accountable, in vain do you proclaim how you have striven against these evil designs. You are guilty, nevertheless; for you could not stifle them; they still survive unconsciously in you." And psychological truth is contained in this; even though man has repressed his evil desires into his Unconscious and would then gladly say to himself that he is no longer answerable for them, he is yet compelled to feel his responsibility in the form of a sense of guilt for which he can discern no foundation.

There is no possible doubt that one of the most important sources of the sense of guilt which so often torments neurotic people is to be found in the Oedipus complex. More than this: in 1913, under the title of *Totem and Taboo,* I published a study of the earliest forms of religion and morality in which I expressed a suspicion that perhaps the sense of guilt of mankind as a whole, which is the ultimate source of religion and morality, was acquired in the beginnings of history through the Oedipus complex. I should much like to tell you

more of this, but I had better not; it is difficult to leave this subject when once one begins upon it, and we must return to individual psychology.

Now what does direct observation of children, at the period of object-choice before the latency period, show us in regard to the Oedipus complex? Well, it is easy to see that the little man wants his mother all to himself, finds his father in the way, becomes restive when the latter takes upon himself to caress her, and shows his satisfaction when the father goes away or is absent. He often expresses his feelings directly in words and promises his mother to marry her; this may not seem much in comparison with the deeds of Oedipus, but it is enough in fact; the kernel of each is the same. Observation is often rendered puzzling by the circumstance that the same child on other occasions at this period will display great affection for the father; but such contrasting—or, better, *ambivalent*—states of feeling, which in adults would lead to conflicts, can be tolerated alongside one another in the child for a long time, just as later on they dwell together permanently in the unconscious. One might try to object that the little boy's behaviour is due to egoistic motives and does not justify the conception of an erotic complex; the mother looks after all the child's needs and consequently it is to the child's interest that she should trouble herself about no one else. This too is quite correct; but it is soon clear that in this, as in similar dependent situations, egoistic interests only provide the occasion on which the erotic impulses seize. When the little boy shows the most open sexual curiosity about his mother, wants to sleep with her at night, insists on being in the room while she is dressing, or even attempts physical acts of seduction, as the mother so often observes and laughingly relates, the erotic nature of this attachment to her is established without a doubt. Moreover, it should not be forgotten that a mother looks after a little daughter's needs in the same way without producing this effect; and that often enough a father eagerly vies with her in trouble for the boy without succeeding in winning the same importance in his eyes as the mother. In short, the factor of sex preference is not to be eliminated from the situation by any criticisms. From the point of view of the boy's egoistic interests, it would merely be foolish if he did not tolerate two people in his service rather than only one of them.

As you see, I have only described the relationship of a boy to his father and mother; things proceed in just the same way, with the necessary reversal, in little girls. The loving devotion to the father, the need to do away with the superfluous mother and to take her place, the early display of coquetry and the arts of later womanhood, make up a particularly charming picture in a little girl, and may cause us to forget its seriousness and the grave consequences which may later result from this situation. Let us not fail to add that frequently the parents themselves exert a decisive influence upon the awakening of the Oedipus complex in a child, by themselves following the sex attraction where there is more than one child; the father in an unmistakable manner prefers his little daughter with marks of tenderness, and the mother, the son: but even this factor does not seriously impugn the spontaneous nature of the infantile Oedipus complex. When other children appear, the Oedipus complex expands and becomes a family complex. Reinforced anew by the injury resulting to the egoistic interests, it actuates a feeling of aversion towards these new arrivals and an unhesitating wish to get rid of them again. These feelings of hatred are as a rule much more often openly expressed than those connected with the parental complex. If such a wish is fulfilled and after a short time death removes the unwanted addition to the family, later analysis can show what a significant event this death is for the child, although it does not necessarily remain in memory. Forced into the second place by the birth of another child and for the first time almost entirely parted from the mother, the child finds it very hard to forgive her for this exclusion of him; feelings which in adults we should describe as profound embitterment are roused in him, and often become the groundwork of a lasting estrangement. That sexual curiosity and all its consequences is usually connected with these experiences has already been mentioned. As these new brothers and sisters grow up the child's attitude to them undergoes the most important transformations. A boy may take his sister as love-object in place of his faithless mother; where there are several brothers to win the favour of a little sister hostile rivalry, of great importance in after life, shows itself already in the nursery. A little girl takes an older brother as a substitute for the father who no longer treats her with the same tenderness as in her earliest years; or she takes a little sister as a substitute for the child that she vainly wished for from her father.

So much and a great deal more of a similar kind is shown by direct observation of children, and by consideration of clear memories of childhood, uninfluenced by any analysis. Among other things you will infer from this that a child's position in the sequence of brothers and sisters is of very great significance for the course of his later life, a factor to be considered in every biography. What is even more important, however, is that in the face of these enlightening considerations, so easily to be obtained, you will hardly recall without smiling the scientific theories accounting for the prohibition of incest. What has not been invented for this purpose! We are told that sexual attraction is diverted from the members of the opposite sex in one family owing to their living together from early childhood; or that a biological tendency against in-breeding has a mental equivalent in the horror of incest! Whereby it is entirely overlooked that no such rigorous prohibitions in law and custom would be required if any trustworthy natural barriers against the temptation to incest existed. The opposite is the truth. The first choice of object in mankind is regularly an incestuous one, directed to the mother and sister of men, and the most stringent prohibitions are required to prevent this sustained infantile tendency from being carried into effect. In the savage and primitive peoples surviving today the incest prohibitions are a great deal stricter than with us; Theodor Reik has recently shown in a brilliant work that the meaning of the savage rites of puberty, which represent re-birth, is the loosening of the boy's incestuous attachment to the mother and his reconciliation with the father.

Mythology will show you that incest, ostensibly so much abhorred by men, is permitted to their gods without a thought; and from ancient history you may learn that incestuous marriage with a sister was prescribed as a sacred duty for kings (the Pharaohs of Egypt and the Incas of Peru); it was therefore in the nature of a privilege denied to the common herd.

Incest with the mother is one of the crimes of Oedipus and parricide the other. Incidentally, these are the two great offences condemned by totemism, the first social-religious institution of mankind. Now let us turn from the direct observation of children to the analytic investigation of adults who have become neurotic; what does analysis yield in further knowledge of the Oedipus complex? Well, this is soon told. The complex is revealed just as the myth relates it; it will be seen that every one of these neurotics was himself an Oedipus or, what amounts to the same thing, has become a Hamlet in his reaction to the complex. To be sure, the analytic picture of the Oedipus complex is an enlarged and accentuated edition of the infantile sketch; the hatred of the father and the death-wishes against him are no longer vague hints, the affection for the mother declares itself with the aim of possessing her as a woman. Are we really to accredit such grossness and intensity of the feelings to the tender age of childhood; or does the analysis deceive us by introducing another factor? It is not difficult to find one. Every time anyone describes anything past, even if he be a historian, we have to take into account all that he unintentionally imports into that past period from present and intermediate times, thereby falsifying it. With the neurotic it is even doubtful whether this retroversion is altogether unintentional; we shall hear later on that there are motives for it and we must explore the whole subject of the *retrogressive phantasy-making* which goes back to the remote past. We soon discover, too, that the hatred against the father has been strengthened by a number of motives arising in later periods and other relationships in life, and that the sexual desires towards the mother have been moulded into forms which would have been as yet foreign to the child. But it would be a vain attempt if we endeavoured to explain the whole of the Oedipus complex by *retrogressive phantasy-making,* and by motives originating in later periods of life. The infantile nucleus with more or less of the accretions to it, remains intact, as is confirmed by direct observation of children.

The clinical fact which confronts us behind the form of the Oedipus complex as established by analysis now becomes of the greatest practical importance. We learn that at the time of puberty, when the sexual instinct first asserts its demand in full strength, the older familiar incestuous objects are taken up again, and again invested by the libido. The infantile objectchoice was but a feeble venture in play, as it were, but it laid down the direction for the object-choice of puberty. At this time a very intense flow of feeling towards the Oedipus complex or in reaction to it comes into force; since their mental antecedents have become intolerable, however, these feelings must remain for the most part outside consciousness. From the time of puberty onward the human

individual must devote himself to the great task of *freeing himself from the parents;* and only after this detachment is accomplished can he cease to be a child and so become a member of the social community. For a son, the task consists in releasing his libidinal desires from his mother, in order to employ them in the quest of an external love-object in reality; and in reconciling himself with his father if he has remained antagonistic to him, or in freeing himself from his domination if, in the reaction to the infantile revolt, he has lapsed into subservience to him. These tasks are laid down for every man; it is noteworthy how seldom they are carried through ideally, that is, how seldom they are solved in a manner psychologically as well as socially satisfactory. In neurotics, however, this detachment from the parents is not accomplished at all; the son remains all his life in subjection to his father, and incapable of transferring his libido to a new sexual object. In the reversed relationship the daughter's fate may be the same. In this sense the Oedipus complex is justifiably regarded as the kernel of the neuroses.

You will imagine how incompletely I am sketching a large number of the connections bound up with the Oedipus complex which practically and theoretically are of great importance. I shall not go into the variations and possible inversions of it at all. Of its less immediate effects I should like to allude to one only, which proves it to have influenced literary production in a far-reaching manner. Otto Rank has shown in a very valuable work that dramatists throughout the ages have drawn their material principally from the Oedipus and incest complex and its variations and masked forms. It should also be remarked that long before the time of psycho-analysis the two criminal offences of Oedipus were recognized as the true expressions of unbridled instinct. Among the works of the Encyclopaedist Diderot you will find the famous dialogue, *Le neveu de Rameau,* which was translated into German by no less a person than Goethe. There you may read these remarkable words: *Si le petit sauvage était abandonné à lui-même, qu'il conserva toute son imbecillité et qu'il réunit au peu de raison de l'enfant au berceau la violence des passions de l'homme de trente ans, il tordrait le cou à son père et coucherait avec sa mère.*[1]

---

[1] If the young savage were left to himself, so that he could keep all his foolishness and could unite to the slight reason of the baby in the crib the violent emotions of a man of thirty, he would wring the neck of his father and go to bed with his mother —ED.

There is yet one thing more which I cannot pass over. The mother-wife of Oedipus must not remind us of dreams in vain. Do you still remember the results of our dream-analyses, how so often the dream-forming wishes proved perverse and incestuous in their nature, or betrayed an unsuspected enmity to near and beloved relatives? We then left the source of these evil strivings of feeling unexplained. Now you can answer this question yourselves. They are dispositions of the libido, and investments of objects by libido, belonging to early infancy and long since given up in conscious life, but which at night prove to be still present and in a certain sense capable of activity. But, since all men and not only neurotic persons have perverse, incestuous, and murderous dreams of this kind, we may infer that those who are normal today have also made the passage through the perversions and the object-investments of the Oedipus complex; and that this is the path of normal development; only that neurotics show in a magnified and exaggerated form what we also find revealed in the dream-analyses of normal people. And this is one of the reasons why we chose the study of dreams to lead up to that of neurotic symptoms.

TWENTY-SECOND LECTURE

ASPECTS OF DEVELOPMENT AND REGRESSION. AETIOLOGY

As we have heard, the libido-function goes through an extensive development before it can enter the service of reproduction in the way that is called normal. Now I wish to show you the significance of this fact for the causation of the neuroses.

I think that it will be in agreement with the doctrines of general pathology to assume that such a development involves two dangers; first, that of *inhibition*, and secondly, that of *regression*. That is to say, owing to the general tendency to variation in biological processes it must necessarily happen that not all these preparatory phases will be passed through and completely out-grown with the same degree of success; some parts of the function will be permanently arrested at these early stages, with the result that with the general development there goes a certain amount of inhibited development.

Let us seek analogies to these processes in other fields. When a whole people leaves its dwellings in order to seek a new country, as often happened in earlier periods of human history, their entire number certainly did not reach the new destination. Apart from losses due to other causes, it must invariably have happened that small groups or bands of the migrating people halted on the way, and settled down in these stopping-places, while the main body went further. Or, to take a nearer comparison, you know that in the higher mammals the seminal glands, which are originally located deep in the abdominal cavity, begin a movement at a certain period of intra-uterine development which brings them almost under the skin of the pelvic extremity. In a number of males it is found that one of this pair of organs has remained in the pelvic cavity, or else that it has taken up a permanent position in the inguinal canal which both of them had to pass through on the journey, or at least that this canal has not closed as it normally should after the passage of the seminal glands through it. When as a young student I was doing my first piece of scientific research under von Brücke, I was working on the origin of the dorsal nerve-roots in the spinal cord of a small fish, still very archaic in form. I found that the nerve-fibres of these roots grew out of large cells in the posterior horn of the grey matter, a condition which is no longer found in other vertebrates. But soon after I discovered that similar nerve-cells were to be found outside the grey matter along the whole length to the so-called spinal ganglion of the posterior roots, from which I concluded that the cells of this ganglion had moved out of the spinal cord along the nerve-roots. Evolutionary development shows this too; in this little fish, however, the whole route of this passage was marked by cells arrested on the way. Closer consideration will soon show you the weak points of these comparisons. Therefore let me simply say that we consider it possible that single portions of every separate sexual impulse may remain in an early stage of development, although at the same time other portions of it may have reached their final goal. You will see from this that we conceive each such impulse as a current continuously flowing from the beginning of life, and that we have divided its flow to some extent artificially into separate successive forward movements. Your impression that these conceptions require further elucidation is correct, but the attempt would lead us too far afield. We will, however, decide at this point to call this *arrest* in a component impulse at an early stage a FIXATION (of the impulse).

The second danger in a development by stages such as this we call REGRESSION; it also happens that those portions which have proceeded further may easily revert in a backward direction to these earlier stages. The impulse will find occasion to *regress* in this way when the exercise of its function in a later and more developed form meets with powerful external obstacles, which thus prevent it from attaining the goal of satisfaction. It is a short step to assume that fixation and regression are not independent of each other; the stronger the fixations in the path of development the more easily will the function yield before the external obstacles, by regressing on to those fixations; that is, the less capable of resistance against the external difficulties in its path will the developed function be. If you think of a migrating people who have left large numbers at the stopping-places on their way, you will see that the foremost will naturally fall back upon these positions when they are defeated or when they meet with an enemy too strong for them. And again, the more of their number they leave behind in their progress, the sooner will they be in danger of defeat.

It is important for comprehension of the neuroses that you should keep in mind this relation between fixation and regression. You will thus acquire a secure foothold from which to investigate the causation of the neuroses— their aetiology—which we shall soon consider.

For the present we will keep to the question of regression. After what you have heard about the development of the libido you may anticipate two kinds of regression; a return to the first objects invested with libido, which we know to be incestuous in character, and a return of the whole sexual organization to earlier stages. Both kinds occur in the transference neuroses and play a great part in their mechanism. In particular, the return to the first incestuous objects of the libido is a feature found with quite fatiguing regularity in neurotics. There is much more to be said about the regressions of libido if another group of neuroses, called the narcissistic, is taken into account; but this is not our intention at the moment. These affections yield conclusions about other developmental processes of the libido-function, not yet mentioned, and also show us new types of regression corresponding with them. I think, however, that I had better warn you now above all not to confound

regression with *repression* and that I must assist you to clear your minds about the relation between the two processes. *Repression,* as you will remember, is the process by which a mental act capable of becoming conscious (that is, one which belongs to the preconscious system) is made unconscious and forced back into the unconscious system. And we also call it *repression* when the unconscious mental act is not permitted to enter the adjacent preconscious system at all, but is turned back upon the threshold by the censorship. There is, therefore, no connection with sexuality in the concept *repression;* please mark this very carefully. It denotes a purely psychological process; and would be even better described as *topographical,* by which we mean that it has to do with the spatial relationships we assume within the mind, or, if we again abandon these crude aids to the formulation of theory, with the structure of the mental apparatus out of separate psychical systems.

The comparisons just now instituted showed us that hitherto we have not been using the word *regression* in its general sense but in a quite specific one. If you give it its general sense, that of a reversion from a higher to a lower stage of development in general, then repression also ranges itself under regression; for repression can also be described as reversion to an earlier and lower stage in the development of a mental act. Only, in repression this retrogressive direction is not a point of any moment to us; for we also call it repression in a dynamic sense when a mental process is arrested before it leaves the lower stage of the unconscious. Repression is thus a topographic-dynamic conception, while regression is a purely descriptive one. But what we have hitherto called *regression* and considered in its relation to fixation signified exclusively the return of *the libido* to its former halting-places in development, that is, something which is essentially quite different from repression and quite independent of it. Nor can we call regression of the libido a purely psychical process; neither do we know where to localize it in the mental apparatus; for though it may exert the most powerful influence upon mental life, the organic factor in it is nevertheless the most prominent.

Discussions of this sort tend to be rather dry; therefore let us turn to clinical illustrations of them in order to get a more vivid impression of them. You know that the group of the transference neuroses consists principally of hysteria and the obsessional neurosis. Now in hysteria, a regression of the libido to the primary incestuous sexual objects is without doubt quite regular, but there is little or no regression to an earlier stage of sexual organization. Consequently the principal part in the mechanism of hysteria is played by repression. If I may be allowed to supplement by a construction the certain knowledge of this neurosis acquired up to the present, I might describe the situation as follows: The fusion of the component-impulses under the primacy of the genital zone has been accomplished; but the results of this union meet with resistance from the direction of the preconscious system with which consciousness is connected. The genital organization therefore holds good for the unconscious, but not also for the preconscious, and this rejection on the part of the preconscious results in a picture which has a certain likeness to the state prior to the primacy of the genital zone. It is nevertheless actually quite different. Of the two kinds of regression of the libido, that on to an earlier phase of sexual organization is much the more striking. Since it is absent in hysteria and our whole conception of the neuroses is still far too much dominated by the study of hysteria which came first in point of time, the significance of libido-regression was recognized much later than that of repression. We may be sure that our points of view will undergo still further extensions and alterations when we include consideration of still other neuroses (the narcissistic) in addition to hysteria and the obsessional neurosis.

In the obsessional neurosis, on the other hand, regression of the libido to the antecedent stage of the sadistic-anal organization is the most conspicuous factor and determines the form taken by the symptoms. The impulse to love must then mask itself under the sadistic impulse. The obsessive thought, "I should like to murder you," means (when it has been detached from certain superimposed elements that are not, however, accidental but indispensable to it) nothing else but "I should like to enjoy love of you." When you consider in addition that regression to the primary objects has also set in at the same time, so that this impulse concerns only the nearest and most beloved persons, you can gain some idea of the horror roused in the patient by these obsessive ideas and at the same time how unaccountable they appear to his conscious perception. But repression also has its share, a great one, in the

mechanism of this neurosis, and one which is not easy to expound in a rapid survey such as this. Regression of libido without repression would never give rise to a neurosis, but would result in a perversion. You will see from this that repression is the process which distinguishes the neuroses particularly and by which they are best characterized. Perhaps, however, I may have an opportunity at some time of expounding to you what we know of the mechanism of the perversions, and you will then see that there again nothing proceeds so simply as we should like to imagine in our constructions.

I think that you will be soonest reconciled to this exposition of fixation and regression of the libido if you will regard it as preparatory to a study of the *aetiology* of the neuroses. So far I have only given you one piece of information on this subject, namely, that people fall ill of a neurosis when the possibility of satisfaction for the libido is removed from them—they fall ill in consequence of a *frustration,* as I called it, therefore—and that their symptoms are actually substitutes for the missing satisfaction. This of course does not mean that every frustration in regard to libidinal satisfaction makes everyone who meets with it neurotic, but merely that in all cases of neurosis investigated the factor of frustration was demonstrable. The statement, therefore, cannot be reversed. You will no doubt have understood that this statement was not intended to reveal the whole secret of the aetiology of the neuroses, but that it merely emphasized an important and indispensable condition.

Now in order to consider this proposition further we do not know whether to begin upon the nature of the frustration or the particular character of the person affected by it. The frustration is very rarely a comprehensive and absolute one; in order to have a pathogenic effect it would probably have to strike at the only form of satisfaction which that person desires, the only form of which he is capable. In general, there are very many ways by which it is possible to endure lack of libidinal satisfaction without falling ill. Above all we know of people who are able to take such abstinence upon themselves without injury; they are then not happy, they suffer from unsatisfied longing, but they do not become ill. We therefore have to conclude that the sexual impulse-excitations are exceptionally plastic, if I may use the word. One of them can step in in place of another; if satisfaction of one is denied in reality, satisfaction of another can offer full recompense. They are related to one another like a network of communicating canals filled with fluid, and this in spite of their subordination to the genital primacy, a condition which is not at all easily reduced to an image. Further, the component-instincts of sexuality, as well as the united sexual impulse which comprises them, show a great capacity to change their object, to exchange it for another—i.e., for one more easily attainable; this capacity for displacement and readiness to accept surrogates must produce a powerful counter-effect to the effect of a frustration. One amongst these processes serving as protection against illness arising from want has reached a particular significance in the development of culture. It consists in the abandonment, on the part of the sexual impulse, of an aim previously found either in the gratification of a component-impulse or in the gratification incidental to reproduction, and the adoption of a new aim—which new aim, though genetically related to the first, can no longer be regarded as sexual, but must be called social in character. We call this process SUBLIMATION, by which we subscribe to the general standard which estimates social aims above sexual (ultimately selfish) aims. Incidentally, sublimation is merely a special case of the connections existing between sexual impulses and other, asexual ones. We shall have occasion to discuss this again in another context.

Your impression now will be that we have reduced want of satisfaction to a factor of negligible proportions by the recognition of so many means of enduring it. But no; this is not so: it retains its pathogenic power. The means of dealing with it are not always sufficient. The measure of unsatisfied libido that the average human being can take upon himself is limited. The plasticity and free mobility of the libido is not by any means retained to the full in all of us; and sublimation can never discharge more than a certain proportion of libido, apart from the fact that many people possess the capacity for sublimation only in a slight degree. The most important of these limitations is clearly that referring to the mobility of the libido, since it confines the individual to the attaining of aims and objects which are very few in number. Just remember that incomplete development of the libido leaves behind it very extensive (and sometimes also numerous) libido-fixations upon earlier phases of organization and types of object-choice, mostly incapable of satisfaction in reality; you will then recognize fixation of libido as the second powerful factor working together with frustration in the causation of illness. We may condense this schematically and say that libido-fixation represents the internal, predisposing factor, while frustration represents the external, accidental factor, in the aetiology of the neuroses.

I will take this opportunity to warn you against taking sides in a quite superfluous dispute. It is a popular habit in scientific matters to seize upon one side of the truth and set it up as the whole truth, and then in favour of that element of truth to dispute all the rest which is equally true. More than one faction has already split off in this way from the psycho-analytic movement; one of them recognizes only the egoistic impulses and denies the sexual; another perceives only the influence of real tasks in life but overlooks that of the individual's past life, and so on. Now here is occasion for another of these antitheses and moot-points: Are the neuroses exogenous or endogenous diseases—the inevitable result of a certain type of constitution or the product of certain injurious (traumatic) events in the person's life? In particular, are they brought about by the fixation of libido and the rest of the sexual constitution, or by the pressure of frustration? This dilemma seems to me about as sensible as another I could point to: Is the child created by the father's act of generation or by the conception in the mother? You will properly reply: Both conditions are alike indispensable. The conditions underlying the neuroses are very similar, if not exactly the same. From the point of view of causation, cases of neurotic illness fall into a *series*, within which the two factors—sexual constitution and events experienced, or, if you wish, fixation of libido and frustration—are represented in such a way that where one of them predominates the other is proportionally less pronounced. At one end of the series stand those extreme cases of whom one can say: "These people would have fallen ill whatever happened, whatever they experienced, however merciful life has been to them, because of their anomalous libido development." At the other end stand cases which call forth the opposite verdict—they would undoubtedly have escaped illness if life had not put such and such burdens upon them. In the intermediate cases in the series, more or less of the disposing factor (the sexual constitution) is combined with less or more of the injurious impositions of life. Their sexual constitution would not have brought about their neurosis if they had not gone through such and such experiences, and life's vicissitudes would not have worked traumatically upon them if the libido had been otherwise constituted. In this series I can perhaps admit a certain preponderance in the effect of the predisposing factor, but this admission again depends upon where you draw the line in marking the boundaries of nervousness.

I shall now suggest to you that we should call series such as these *complemental series,* and will inform you beforehand that we shall find occasion to establish others of this kind.

The tenacity with which the libido holds to particular channels and particular objects, the *adhesiveness* of the libido, so to say, seems to be an independent factor, varying in individuals, the determining conditions of which are completely unknown to us, but the importance of which in the aetiology of the neuroses we shall certainly no longer underestimate. At the same time we should not overestimate the close relation between the two things. A similar adhesiveness of the libido occurs—from unknown causes—in normal people under numerous conditions, and is found as a decisive factor in those persons who in a certain sense are the extreme opposite of neurotics—namely, perverted persons. It was known before the time of psycho-analysis that in the anamnesis of such persons a very early impression, relating to an abnormal instinct-tendency or object-choice, is frequently discovered, to which the libido of that person henceforth remains attached for life (Binet). It is often hard to say what has enabled this impression to exert such an intense power of attraction upon the libido. I will describe a case of this kind observed by myself. A man to whom the genitals and all the other attractions in a woman now mean nothing can be aroused to irresistible sexual excitation only by a shoe-clad foot of a certain shape; he can remember an event in his sixth year which determined this fixation of libido. He was sitting upon a stool by the side of his governess who was to give him an English lesson. She was a plain, elderly, shrivelled old maid, with watery blue eyes and a snub nose, and on this day she had hurt her foot and had it therefore stretched out on a cushion in a velvet slipper, with the leg itself most decorously concealed. Later on, after a timid attempt at normal sexual activity during puberty,

a thin sinewy foot like that of the governess became his only sexual object; and if still other features in the person reminded him of the type of woman represented by the English governess, the man was helplessly attracted. This fixation of the libido, however, rendered him not neurotic but perverse; he became, as we say, a foot-fetichist. So you see that although an excessive and, in addition, premature fixation of libido is an indispensable condition in the causation of neuroses, the extent of its influence far exceeds the boundaries of the neuroses. This condition by itself is also as little decisive as the frustration mentioned previously.

So the problem of the causation of the neuroses seems to become more complicated. In fact, psycho-analytic investigation acquaints us with yet a new factor, not considered in our aetiological series, and best observed in someone whose previous good health is suddenly disturbed by falling ill of a neurosis. In these people, signs of contradictory and opposed wishes, or, as we say, of *mental conflict,* are regularly found. One side of the personality stands for certain wishes, while another part struggles against them and fends them off. There is no neurosis without such a CONFLICT. There might seem to be nothing very special in this; you know that mental life in all of us is perpetually engaged with conflicts that have to be decided. Therefore it would seem that special conditions must be fulfilled before such a conflict can become pathogenic; we may ask what these conditions are, what forces in the mind take part in these pathogenic conflicts, and what relation conflict bears to the other causative factors.

I hope to be able to give you answers to these questions which will be satisfactory although perhaps schematically condensed. Conflict is produced by frustration, in that the libido which lacks satisfaction is urged to seek other paths and other objects. A condition of it then is that these other paths and objects arouse disfavour in one side of the personality, so that a veto ensues, which at first makes the new way of satisfaction impossible. This is the point of departure for the formation of symptoms, which we shall follow up later. The rejected libidinal longings manage to pursue their course by circuitous paths, though not indeed without paying toll to the prohibition in the form of certain disguises and modifications. The circuitous paths are the ways of symptom-formation; the symptoms are the new and substitutive satisfactions necessitated by the fact of the frustration.

The significance of the mental conflict can be defined in another way, thus: in order to become pathogenic *external* frustration must be supplemented by *internal* frustration. When this is so, the external and the internal frustration relate of course to different paths and different objects; external frustration removes one possibility of satisfaction, internal frustration tries to exclude another possibility, and it is this second possibility which becomes the debatable ground of the conflict. I choose this form of presentation because it contains a certain implication; it implies that the internal impediment arose originally, in primitive phases of human development, out of real external obstacles.

But what are these forces out of which the prohibition against the libidinal longings proceeds, the other parties in the pathogenic conflict? Speaking very broadly, we may say that they are the non-sexual instincts. We include them all under the name *ego-instincts;* analysis of the transference neuroses offers no adequate opportunity for further investigation of them; at most we learn something of them from the resistances opposed to the analysis. The pathogenic conflict is, therefore, one between the ego-instincts and the sexual instincts. In a whole series of cases it looks as though there might also be conflict between various purely sexual impulses; at bottom, however, this is the same thing, because of the two sexual impulses engaged in a conflict one will always be found *consistent with the ego* (ego-syntonic) while the other calls forth a protest from the ego. It remains, therefore, a conflict between ego and sexuality.

Over and over again when psycho-analysis has regarded something happening in the mind as an expression of the sexual instincts, indignant protests have been raised to the effect that other instincts and other interests exist in mental life besides the sexual, that one should not derive everything from sexuality, and so on. Well, it is a real pleasure for once to be in agreement with one's opponents. Psycho-analysis has never forgotten that non-sexual instincts also exist; it has been built upon a sharp distinction between sexual instincts and ego-instincts; and in the face of all opposition it has insisted, *not* that they arise from sexuality, but that the neuroses owe their origin to a *conflict* between ego and sexuality. It has no conceiv-able motive in denying the existence or the significance of the ego-instincts while it investigates the part played by sexual instincts in disease and in life generally. Only, psycho-analysis has been destined to concern itself first and foremost with the sexual instincts, because in the transference neuroses these are the most accessible to investigation, and because it was obliged to study what others had neglected.

It is not any more accurate to say that psycho-analysis has not occupied itself at all with the non-sexual side of the personality. The very distinction between the ego and sexuality has shown us with particular clearness that the ego-instincts also undergo an important development which is neither entirely independent of the development of the libido nor without influence upon the latter. We certainly understand the development of the ego much less well than the development of the libido, because it is only by the study of the narcissistic neuroses that we have just reached some hope of insight into the structure of the ego. Nevertheless, we have already a notable attempt on the part of Ferenczi[1] to reconstruct theoretically the developmental stages of the ego; and there are at least two points at which we have a secure foothold from which to examine this development further. We are not at all disposed to think that the libidinal interests of a human being are from the outset in opposition to the interests of self-preservation; the ego is rather impelled at every stage to attempt to remain in harmony with the corresponding stage of sexual organization and to accommodate itself to that. The succession of the separate phases in the development of the libido probably follows a prescribed course; it is undeniable, however, that this course may be influenced from the direction of the ego. A certain parallelism, a definite correspondence between the phases in the two developments (of the ego and of the libido) may also be assumed; indeed, a disturbance in this correspondence may become a pathogenic factor. More important to us is the question of how the ego behaves when the libido has undergone a powerful fixation at an earlier point in its development. The ego may countenance the fixation and will then be perverse to that extent, or, what is the same thing, infantile; it

[1] Ferenczi, *Contributions to Psycho-Analysis.* English translation by Ernest Jones (1916) chap. viii, p. 181.

may, however, hold itself averse from this attachment of libido, the result of which is that where the libido undergoes a *fixation* there the ego institutes an act of *repression*.

In this way we arrive at the conclusion that the third factor in the aetiology of the neuroses, the susceptibility to conflict, is as much connected with the development of the ego as with the development of the libido; our insight into the causation of the neuroses is thus enlarged. First, there is the most general condition of privation, then the fixation of libido (forcing it into particular channels), and thirdly, the *susceptibility to conflict* produced by the development of the ego having repudiated libidinal excitations of that particular kind. The thing is, therefore, not so very obscure and intricate as you probably thought it during the course of my exposition. To be sure, though, after all, we have not done with it yet; there is still something new to add and something we already know to dissect further.

In order to demonstrate the effect of the development of the ego upon the tendency to conflict and therewith upon the causation of the neurosis, I will quote an example which, although entirely imaginary, is not at all improbable in any respect. I will give it the title of Nestroy's farce: *On the Ground-Floor and in the Mansion.* Suppose that a caretaker is living on the ground-floor of a house, while the owner, a rich and well-connected man, lives above. They both have children, and we will assume that the owner's little girl is permitted to play freely without supervision with the child of lower social standing. It may then very easily happen that their games become "naughty," that is, take on a sexual character: that they play "father and mother," watch each other in the performance of intimate acts, and stimulate each other's genital parts. The caretaker's daughter may have played the temptress in this, since in spite of her five or six years she has been able to learn a great deal about sexual matters. These occurrences, even though they are only kept up for a short period. will be enough to rouse certain sexual excitations in both children which will come to expression in the practice of masturbation for a few years, after the games have been discontinued. There is common ground so far, but the final result will be very different in the two children. The caretaker's daughter will continue masturbation, perhaps up to the onset of menstruation, and then give it up without difficulty; a few

years later will find a lover, perhaps bear a child; choose this or that path in life, perhaps become a popular actress and end as an aristocrat. Probably her career will turn out less brilliantly, but in any case she will be unharmed by the premature sexual activity, free from neurosis, and able to live her life. Very different is the result in the other child. She will very soon, while yet a child, acquire a sense of having done wrong; after a fairly short time she will give up the masturbatory satisfaction, though perhaps only with a tremendous struggle, but will nevertheless retain an inner feeling of subdued depression. When later on as a young girl she comes to learn something of sexual intercourse, she will turn from it with inexplicable horror and wish to remain ignorant. Probably she will then again suffer a fresh irresistible impulse to masturbation about which she will not dare to unburden herself to anyone. When the time comes for a man to choose her as a wife the neurosis will break out and cheat her out of marriage and the joy of life. If analysis makes it possible to obtain an insight into this neurosis, it will be found that this well-brought-up, intelligent and idealistic girl has completely repressed her sexual desires; but that they are, unconsciously, attached to the few little experiences she had with the childish play-mate.

The differences which ensue in these two destinies in spite of the common experiences undergone, arise because in one girl the ego has sustained a development absent in the other. To the caretaker's daughter sexual activity seemed as natural and harmless in later years as in childhood. The gentleman's daughter had been "well-brought-up" and had adopted the standards of her education. Thus stimulated, her ego had formed ideals of womanly purity and absence of desire that were incompatible with sexual acts; her intellectual training had caused her to depreciate the feminine rôle for which she is intended. This higher moral and intellectual development in her ego has brought her into conflict with the claims of her sexuality.

I will explore one more aspect of the development of the libido today, both because it leads out upon certain wide prospects, and also because it is well-suited to justify the sharp, and not immediately obvious, line of demarcation we are wont to draw between go-instincts and sexual instincts. In considering the two developments undergone by the ego and by the libido we must emphasize an aspect which hitherto has received little attention. Both of them are at bottom inheritances, abbreviated repetitions of the evolution undergone by the whole human race through long-drawn out periods and from prehistoric ages. In the development of the libido this phylogenetic origin is readily apparent, I should suppose. Think how in one class of animals the genital apparatus is in closest relation with the mouth, in another it is indistinguishable from the excretory mechanism, in another it is part of the organs of motility; you will find a delightful description of these facts in W. Bölsche's valuable book. One sees in animals all the various perversions, ingrained, so to speak, in the form taken by their sexual organizations. Now the phylogenetic aspect is to some extent obscured in man by the circumstances that what is fundamentally inherited is nevertheless individually acquired anew, probably because the same conditions that originally induced its acquisition still prevail and exert their influence upon each individual. I would say, where they originally created a new response they now stimulate a predisposition. Apart from this, it is unquestionable that the course of the prescribed development in each individual can be disturbed and altered by current impressions from without. But the power which has enforced this development upon mankind, and still today maintains its pressure in the same course, is known to us; it is, again, the frustration exacted by reality; or, if we give it its great real name, it is *necessity*, the struggle for life, ἀνάγκη. Necessity has been a severe taskmistress, and she has taught us a great deal. Neurotics are those of her children upon whom this severity has had evil effects, but that risk is inevitable in any education. Incidentally, this view of the struggle for existence as the motive force in evolution need not detract from the significance of *inner evolutionary tendencies,* if such are found to exist.

Now it is very noteworthy that sexual instincts and self-preservative instincts do not behave alike when confronted with the necessity of real life. The self-preservative instincts and all that hangs together with them are more easily moulded; they learn early to conform to necessity and to adapt their development according to the mandates of reality. This is comprehensible, for they cannot obtain the objects they require by any other means, and without these objects the individual must perish. The sexual instincts are less easily moulded; for in the beginning they do not know any lack of objects. Since they are connected parasitically, as it were, with the other physical functions and at the same time can be auto-erotically gratified on their own body, they are at first isolated from the educative influence of real necessity; and in most people they retain throughout life, in some respect or other, this character of obstinacy and inaccessibility to influence which we call *unreasonableness.* Moreover, the educability of a young person as a rule comes to an end when sexual desire breaks out in its final strength. Educators know this and act accordingly; but perhaps they will yet allow themselves to be influenced by the results of psycho-analysis so that they will transfer the main emphasis in education to the earliest years of childhood, from the suckling period onward. The little human being is frequently a finished product in his fourth or fifth year, and only gradually reveals in later years what lies buried in him.

To appreciate the full significance of this difference between the two groups of instincts we must digress some distance, and include one of those aspects which deserve to be called *economic;* we enter here upon one of the most important, but unfortunately one of the most obscure, territories of psycho-analysis. We may put the question whether a main purpose is discernible in the operation of the mental apparatus; and our first approach to an answer is that this purpose is directed to the attainment of pleasure. It seems that our entire psychical activity is bent upon *procuring pleasure* and *avoiding pain,* that it is automatically regulated by the PLEASURE-PRINCIPLE. Now of all things in the world we should like to know what are the conditions giving rise to pleasure and pain, but that is just where we fall short. We may only venture to say that pleasure is *in some way* connected with lessening, lowering, or extinguishing the amount of stimulation present in the mental apparatus; and that pain involves a heightening of the latter. Consideration of the most intense pleasure of which man is capable, the pleasure in the performance of the sexual act, leaves little doubt upon this point. Since pleasurable processes of this kind are bound up with the distribution of quantities of mental excitation and energy, we term considerations of this kind *economic* ones. It appears that we can describe the tasks and performances of the mental apparatus in another way and more generally than by emphasizing the attainment of pleasure. We can say that the mental apparatus serves the purpose of mastering and discharging the masses of supervening stimuli, the quantities of energy. It is quite plain that the sexual instincts pursue the aim of gratification from the beginning to the end of their development; throughout they keep up this primary function without alteration. At first the other group, the ego-instincts, do the same; but under the influence of necessity, their mistress, they soon learn to replace the pleasure-principle by a modification of it. The task of avoiding pain becomes for them almost equal in importance to that of gaining pleasure; the ego learns that it must inevitably go without immediate satisfaction, postpone gratification, learn to endure a degree of pain, and altogether renounce certain sources of pleasure. Thus trained, the ego becomes "reasonable," is no longer controlled by the pleasure-principle, but follows the REALITY-PRINCIPLE, which at bottom also seeks pleasure—although a delayed and diminished pleasure, one which is assured by its realization of fact, its relation to reality.

The transition from the pleasure-principle to the reality principle is one of the most important advances in the development of the ego. We already know that the sexual instincts follow late and unwillingly through this stage; presently we shall learn what the consequences are to man that his sexuality is satisfied with such a slight hold upon external reality. And now in conclusion one more observation relevant in this connection. If the ego in mankind has its evolution like libido, you will not be surprised to hear that there exist *ego-regressions* too, and will wish to know the part this reversion of the ego to earlier stages in development can play in neurotic disease.

TWENTY-THIRD LECTURE
THE PATHS OF SYMPTOM-FORMATION

IN the eyes of the general public, the symptoms are the essence of a disease, and to them a cure means the removal of the symptoms. In medicine, however, we find it important to differentiate between symptoms and disease, and state that the disappearance of the symptoms is by no means the same as the cure of the disease. The only tangible element of the disease that remains after the removal of the symptoms, however, is the capacity to form new

symptoms. Therefore for the moment let us adopt the lay point of view and regard a knowledge of the foundation of the symptoms as equivalent to understanding the disease.

The symptoms—of course we are here dealing with mental (or psychogenic) symptoms, and mental disease—are activities which are detrimental, or at least useless, to life as a whole; the person concerned frequently complains of them as obnoxious to him or they involve distress and suffering for him. The principal injury they inflict lies in the expense of mental energy they entail and, besides this, in the energy needed to combat them. Where the symptoms are extensively developed, these two kinds of effort may exact such a price that the person suffers a very serious impoverishment in available mental energy, which consequently disables him for all the important tasks of life. This result depends principally upon the amount of energy taken up in this way, therefore you will see that *illness* is essentially a practical conception. But if you look at the matter from a theoretical point of view and ignore this question of degree you can very well say that we are all ill, i.e., neurotic; for the conditions required for symptom-formation are demonstrable also in normal persons.

Of neurotic symptoms we already know that they are the result of a conflict arising when a new form of satisfaction of libido is sought. The two powers which have entered into opposition meet together again in the symptom and become reconciled by means of the *compromise* contained in symptom-formation. That is why the symptom is capable of such resistance; it is sustained from both sides. We also know that one of the two partners to the conflict is the unsatisfied libido, frustrated by reality and now forced to seek other paths to satisfaction. If reality remains inexorable, even when the libido is prepared to take another object in place of that denied, the libido will then finally be compelled to resort to regression, and to seek satisfaction in one of the organizations it had already surmounted or in one of the objects it had relinquished earlier. The libido is drawn into the path of regression by the fixations it has left behind it at these places in its development.

Now the path of perversion branches off sharply from that of neurosis. If these regressions do not call forth a prohibition on the part of the ego, no neurosis results; the libido succeeds in obtaining a real, although not a normal satisfaction. But if the ego, which controls not merely consciousness but also the approaches to motor innervation and hence the realization in actuality of mental impulses, is not in agreement with these regressions, conflict ensues. The libido is blocked, as it were, and must seek an escape by which it can find an outlet for its cathexis (charge of energy) in conformity with the demands of the pleasure-principle: it must elude, eschew the ego. The fixations upon the path of development now regressively traversed—fixations against which the ego had previously guarded itself by repressions—offer just such an escape. In streaming backward and re-*cathecting* these repressed positions, the libido withdraws itself from the ego and its laws; but it also abandons all the training acquired under the influence of the ego. It was docile as long as satisfaction was in sight; under the double pressure of external and internal frustration it becomes intractable and harks back to former happier days. That is its essential unchangeable character. The ideas to which the libido now transfers its cathexis belong to the unconscious system and are subject to the special processes characteristic of that system—namely, condensation and displacement. Conditions are thus set up which correspond exactly with those of dream-formation. Just as the latent dream, first formed in the unconscious out of the thoughts proper, and constituting the fulfilment of an unconscious wish-phantasy, meets with some (pre)conscious activity which exerts a censorship upon it and permits, according to its verdict, the formation of a compromise in the manifest dream, so the ideas to which the libido is attached (libido-representatives) in the unconscious have still to contend with the power of the preconscious ego. The opposition against it in the ego follows it as an anti-cathexis (counter-charge) and forces it to adopt a form of expression by which the opposing forces can at the same time express themselves. In this way the symptom then comes into being, as a derivative, distorted in manifold ways, of the unconscious libidinal wish-fulfilment, as a cleverly chosen ambiguity with two completely contradictory significations. In this last point alone is there a difference between dream-formation and symptom-formation; for the preconscious purpose in dream-formation is merely to preserve sleep and to allow nothing that would disturb it to penetrate consciousness; it does not insist upon confronting the unconscious wish-impulse with a sharp prohibiting "No, on the contrary." It

can be more tolerant because a sleeping person is in a less dangerous position; the condition of sleep is enough in itself to prevent the wish from being realized in actuality.

You see that this escape of the libido under the conditions of conflict is rendered possible by the existence of fixations. The regressive cathexis (with libido) of these fixations leads to a circumventing of the repressions and to a discharge—or a satisfaction—of the libido, in which the conditions of a compromise have nevertheless to be maintained. By this detour through the unconscious and the old fixations the libido finally succeeds in attaining to a real satisfaction, though the satisfaction is certainly of an exceedingly restricted kind and hardly recognizable as such. Let me add two remarks on this outcome. First, will you notice how closely connected the libido and the unconscious, on the one hand, and the ego, consciousness, and reality, on the other, show themselves to be, although there were no such connections between them originally; and secondly, let me tell you that all I have said and have still to say on this point concerns the neurosis of hysteria only.

Where does the libido find the fixations it needs in order to break through the repressions? In the activities and experiences of infantile sexuality, in the component-tendencies and the objects of childhood which have been relinquished and abandoned. It is to them, therefore, that the libido turns back. The significance of childhood is a double one; on the one hand the congenitally determined instinct-dispositions are first shown at that time, and secondly, other instincts are then first awakened and activated by external influences and accidental events experienced. In my opinion we are quite justified in laying down this dichotomy. That the innate predisposition comes to expression will certainly not be disputed; but analytic observation even requires us to assume that purely accidental experiences in childhood are capable of inducing fixations of libido. Nor do I see any theoretical difficulty in this. Constitutional predispositions are undoubtedly the after-effects of the experiences of an earlier ancestry; they also have been at one time acquired; without such acquired characters there would be no heredity. And is it conceivable that the acquisition of characters which will be transmitted further should suddenly cease in the generation which is being observed today? The importance of the infantile experiences should not, however, be entirely overlooked, as so often happens, in favour of ancestral experiences or of experiences in adult life; but on the contrary they should be particularly appreciated. They are all the more pregnant with consequences because they occur at a time of uncompleted development, and for this very reason are likely to have a traumatic effect. The work done by Roux and others on the mechanism of development has shown that a needle pricked into an embryonic cell-mass undergoing division results in serious disturbances of the development; the same injury to a larva or a full-grown animal would be innocuous.

The libido-fixation of an adult, which we have referred to as representing the constitutional factor in the aetiology of the neuroses, may therefore now be divided into two further elements: the inherited predisposition and the predisposition acquired in early childhood. Since a schematic mode of presentation is always acceptable to a student, let us formulate these relations as follows:

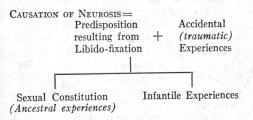

CAUSATION OF NEUROSIS=

| Predisposition resulting from Libido-fixation | + | Accidental *(traumatic)* Experiences |

Sexual Constitution   Infantile Experiences
(Ancestral experiences)

The hereditary sexual constitution provides a great variety of predispositions, according as this or that component-impulse, alone or in combination with others, is specially strongly accentuated. Together with the infantile experiences the sexual constitution forms another *complemental series*, quite similar to that already described as being formed out of the predisposition and accidental experiences of an adult. In each series similar extreme cases are met with, and also similar degrees and relationships between the factors concerned. It would be appropriate at this point to consider whether the more striking of the two kinds of libido-regression (that which reverts to earlier stages of sexual organization) is not predominantly conditioned by the hereditary constitutional factor; but the answer to this question is best postponed until a wider range of forms of neurotic disease can be considered.

Now let us devote attention to the fact that analytic investigation shows the libido of neu-

rotics to be attached to their infantile sexual experiences. In this light these experiences seem to be of enormous importance in the lives and illnesses of mankind. This importance remains undiminished in so far as the therapeutic work of analysis is concerned; but regarded from another point of view it is easy to see that there is a danger of a misunderstanding here, one which might delude us into regarding life too exclusively from the angle of the situation in neurotics. The importance of the infantile experiences is after all diminished by the reflection that the libido reverts regressively to them *after* it has been driven from its later positions. This would lead us towards the opposite conclusion, that the libido-experiences had no importance at the time of their occurrence, but only acquired it later by regression. You will remember that we discussed a similar alternative before, in dealing with the Oedipus complex.

To decide this point is again not difficult. The statement is undoubtedly correct that regression greatly augments the cathexis of the infantile experiences with libido—and with that their pathogenic significance; but it would be misleading to allow this alone to become decisive. Other considerations must be taken into account as well. To begin with, observation shows in a manner excluding all doubt that infantile experiences have their own importance which is demonstrated already during childhood. There are, indeed, neuroses in children too; in their neuroses the factor of displacement backwards in time is necessarily much diminished, or quite absent, the outbreak of illness following immediately upon a traumatic experience. The study of infantile neuroses guards us from many risks of misunderstanding the neuroses of adults, just as children's dreams gave us the key to comprehension of the dreams of adults. Neurosis in children is very common, far more common than is usually supposed. It is often overlooked, regarded as a manifestation of bad behaviour or naughtiness, and often subdued by the authorities in the nursery; but in retrospect it is always easily recognizable. It appears most often in the form of anxiety-hysteria; we shall learn what that means on another occasion. When a neurosis breaks out in later life analysis invariably reveals it to be a direct continuation of that infantile neurosis, which had perhaps been expressed in a veiled and incipient form only; as has been said, however, there are cases in which the childish nervousness is carried on into lifelong illness without a break. In a few instances we have been able to analyse a child actually in a condition of neurosis; far more often we have had to be satisfied with the retrospective insight into a childhood-neurosis that can be gained through someone who has fallen ill in mature years, a situation in which due corrections and precautions must not be neglected.

In the second place, it would certainly be inexplicable that the libido should regress so regularly to the time of childhood if there had been nothing there which could exert an attraction upon it. The fixation upon certain stages of development, which we assume, only has meaning if we regard it as attaching to itself a definite amount of libidinal energy. Finally, I may point out that a complemental relationship exists here between the intensity and pathogenic importance of the *infantile* and of the *later* experiences, again a similar relationship to that found in the other two series we have already studied. There are cases in which the whole accent of causation falls on the sexual experiences in childhood; cases in which these impressions undoubtedly had a traumatic effect, nothing more than the average sexual constitution and its immaturity being required to supplement them. Then there are others in which all the accent lies on the later conflicts, and the analytic emphasis upon the childhood-impressions seems to be the effect of regression alone. There exist, therefore, the two extremes—*inhibited development* and *regression*—and between them every degree of combination of the two factors.

This state of things has a certain interest for those looking to pedagogy for the prevention of neuroses by early intervention in the matter of the child's sexual development. As long as attention is directed mainly to the infantile sexual experiences one would think everything in the way of prophylaxis of later neurosis could be done by ensuring that this development should be retarded and the child secured against this kind of experience. But we know that the conditions causing neurosis are more complicated than this and that they cannot be influenced in a general way by attending to one factor only. Strict supervision in childhood loses value because it is helpless against the constitutional factor; more than this, it is less easy to carry out than specialists in education imagine; and it entails two new risks, which are not to be lightly disregarded. It may accomplish too much; in that it favours an exag-

gerated degree of sexual repression which is harmful in its effects, and it sends the child into life without power to resist the urgent demands of his sexuality that must be expected at puberty. It therefore remains most doubtful how far prophylaxis in childhood can go with advantage, and whether a changed attitude to actuality would not constitute a better point of departure for attempts to forestall the neuroses.

Let us return to consideration of the symptoms. They yield a satisfaction in place of one lacking in reality; they achieve this by means of a regression of the libido to a previous time of life, with which regression is indissolubly connected, a reversion to earlier phases in the object-choice or in the organization. We learned some time ago that the neurotic is in some way *tied* to a period in his past life; we know now that this period in the past is one in which his libido could attain satisfaction, one in which he was happy. He looks back on his life-story, seeking some such period, and goes on seeking it, even if he must go back to the time when he was a suckling infant to find it according to his recollection or his imagination of it under later influences. In some way the symptom reproduces that early infantile way of satisfaction, disguised though it is by censorship implicit in the conflict, converted as it usually is into a sensation of suffering, and mingled with elements drawn from the experiences leading up to the outbreak of the illness. The kind of satisfaction which the symptom brings has much about it which estranges us, quite apart from the fact that the person concerned is unaware of the satisfaction and perceives this that we call satisfaction much more as suffering, and complains of it. This transformation belongs to the mental conflict, by the pressure of which the symptom had to be formed; what was at one time a satisfaction must today arouse resistance or horror in him. We are familiar with a simple but instructive instance of such a change of feeling: the same child that sucked milk with voracity from its mother's breast often shows, some years later, a strong dislike of milk which can with difficulty be overcome by training; this dislike is intensified to the point of horror if the milk or any other kind of liquid containing it has a skin formed upon it. It is possible that the skin calls up reverberations of a memory of the mother's breast, once so ardently desired; it is true that the traumatic experience of weaning has intervened meanwhile.

There is still something else which makes the

symptoms seem remarkable and inexplicable as a means of libidinal satisfaction. They so entirely fail to remind us of all that we are accustomed normally to connect with satisfaction. They are mostly quite independent of an object and thus have given up a relation to external reality. We understand this as a consequence of the rejection of the reality-principle and the return to the pleasure-principle; it is also, however, a return to a kind of amplified auto-erotism, the kind which offered the sexual instinct its first gratifications. In the place of effecting a change in the outer world they set up a change in the body itself; that is, an internal action instead of an external one, an adaptation instead of an activity—from a phylogenetic point of view again a very significant regression. We shall understand this better when we consider it in connection with a new factor yet to be learnt from among those which analytic research has yielded in regard to symptom-formation. Further, we remember that in symptom-formation the same unconscious processes are at work as in dream-formation, namely, condensation and displacement. Like the dream, the symptom represents something as fulfilled, a satisfaction infantile in character; but by the utmost condensation this satisfaction can be compressed into a single sensation or innervation, or by farthest displacement can be whittled away to a tiny detail out of the entire libidinal complex. It is no wonder that we often find it difficult to recognize in the symptom the libidinal satisfaction which we suspect and can always verify in it.

I have indicated that we have still to learn of a new element; it is really something most surprising and bewildering. You know that from analysis of symptoms we arrive at a knowledge of the infantile experiences to which the libido is fixated and out of which the symptoms are made up. Now the astonishing thing is that these scenes of infancy are not always true. Indeed, in the majority of cases they are untrue, and in some cases they are in direct opposition to historical truth. You will see that this discovery is more likely than any other to discredit either the analysis which leads to such results, or the patient, upon whose testimony the analysis and comprehension of the neuroses as a whole is built up. There is besides this still something utterly bewildering about it. If the infantile experiences brought to light by the analysis were in every case real we should have the feeling that we were on firm ground; if they were invariably falsified and found to be inventions and phantasies of the patient's we should have to forsake this insecure foothold and save ourselves some other way. But it is neither one thing nor the other; for what we find is that the childhood-experiences reconstructed or recollected in analysis are on some occasions undeniably false, while others are just as certainly quite true, and that in most cases truth and falsehood are mixed up. So the symptoms are thus at one minute reproductions of experiences which actually took place and which one can credit with an influence on the fixation of the libido; and at the next a reproduction of phantasies of the patient's to which, of course, it is difficult to ascribe any aetiological significance. It is hard to find one's way here. We may perhaps find our first clue in a discovery of a similar kind, namely, that the meagre childish recollections which people have always, long before analysis, consciously preserved can be falsified in the same way, or at least can contain a generous admixture of truth and falsehood; evidence of error in them is nearly always plainly visible, and so we have at least the reassurance that not the analysis but the patient in some way, must bear the responsibility for this unexpected disappointment.

After a little reflection we can easily understand what it is that is so bewildering in this matter. It is the depreciation of reality, the neglect of the difference between reality and phantasy; we are tempted to be offended with the patient for taking up our time with invented stories. According to our way of thinking heaven and earth are not farther apart than fiction from reality, and we value the two quite differently. The patient himself, incidentally, takes the same attitude when he is thinking normally. When he brings forward the material that leads us to the wished-for situations (which underlie the symptoms and are formed upon the childhood experiences), we are certainly in doubt at first whether we have to deal with reality or with phantasies. Decision on this point becomes possible later by means of certain indications, and we are then confronted with the task of making this result known to the patient. This is never accomplished without difficulty. If we tell him at the outset that he is now about to bring to light the phantasies in which he has shrouded the history of his childhood, just as every race weaves myths about its forgotten early history, we observe to our dissatisfaction that his interest in pursuing the subject further suddenly declines—he also wishes to find out facts and despises what is called *imagination*. But if we leave him to believe until this part of the work has been carried through that we are investigating the real events of his early years, we run the risk of being charged with the mistake later and of being laughed at for our apparent gullibility. It takes him a long time to understand the proposal that phantasy and reality are to be treated alike and that it is to begin with of no account whether the childhood-experiences under consideration belong to the one class or to the other. And yet this is obviously the only correct attitude towards these products of his mind. They have indeed also a kind of reality; it is a fact that the patient has created these phantasies, and for the neurosis this fact is hardly less important than the other—if he had really experienced what they contain. In contrast to *material* reality these phantasies possess *psychical* reality, and we gradually come to understand that *in the world of neurosis* PSYCHICAL REALITY *is the determining factor*.

Among the occurrences which continually recur in the story of a neurotic's childhood, and seem hardly ever absent, are some of particular significance which I therefore consider worthy of special attention. As models of this type I will enumerate: observation of parental intercourse, seduction by an adult, and the threat of castration. It would be a great mistake to suppose that they never occur in reality; on the contrary, they are often confirmed beyond doubt by the testimony of older relatives. Thus, for example, it is not at all uncommon for a little boy, who is beginning to play with his penis and has not yet learnt that he must conceal such activities, to be threatened by parents or nurses that his member or his offending hand will be cut off. Parents will often admit the fact on being questioned, since they imagine that such intimidation was the right course to take; many people have a clear conscious recollection of this threat, especially if it took place in later childhood. If the mother or some other woman makes the threat she usually shifts the execution of it to someone else, indicating that the father or the doctor will perform the deed. In the famous *Struwelpeter* by the Frankfort physician for children, Hoffmann, which owes its popularity precisely to his undertanding of the sexual and other complexes of children, you will find the castration idea modified and replaced by cutting off the thumbs as a punishment for stubborn sucking of them. It is, however, highly improbable that the threat of castration has been delivered as

often as would appear from the analysis of a neurotic. We are content to understand that the child concocts a threat of this kind out of its knowledge that auto-erotic satisfactions are forbidden, on the basis of hints and allusions, and influenced by the impression received on discovering the female genital organ. Similarly, it is not at all impossible that a small child, credited as he is with no understanding and no memory, may be witness of the sexual act on the part of his parents or other adults in other families besides those of the proletariat; and there is reason to think that the child can *subsequently* understand the impression received and react to it. But when this act of intercourse is described with minute details which can hardly have been observed, or when it appears, as it most frequently does, to have been performed from behind, *more ferarum*,[1] there can be little doubt that this phantasy has grown out of the observation of copulating animals (dogs) and that its motive force lies in the unsatisfied skoptophilia (gazing-impulse) of the child during puberty. The greatest feat achieved by this kind of phantasy is that of observing parental intercourse while still unborn in the mother's womb.

The phantasy of seduction has special interest, because only too often it is no phantasy but a real remembrance; fortunately, however, it is still not as often real as it seemed at first from the results of analysis. Seduction by children of the same age or older is more frequent than by adults; and when girls who bring forward this event in the story of their childhood fairly regularly introduce the father as the seducer, neither the phantastic character of this accusation nor the motive actuating it can be doubted. When no seduction has occurred, the phantasy is usually employed to cover the childhood period of auto-erotic sexual activity; the child evades feelings of shame about onanism by retrospectively attributing in phantasy a desired object to the earliest period. Do not suppose, however, that sexual misuse of children by the nearest male relatives is entirely derived from the world of phantasy; most analysts will have treated cases in which such occurrences actually took place and could be established beyond doubt; only even then they belonged to later years of childhood and had been transposed to an earlier time.

All this seems to lead to but one impression, that childhood experiences of this kind are in some way necessarily required by the neurosis,

[1] In the manner of animals.—ED.

that they belong to its unvarying inventory. If they can be found in real events, well and good; but if reality has not supplied them they will be evolved out of hints and elaborated by phantasy. The effect is the same, and even today we have not succeeded in tracing any variation in the results according as phantasy or reality plays the greater part in these experiences. Here again is one of those complemental series so often referred to already; it is certainly the strangest of all those we have encountered. Whence comes the necessity for these phantasies, and the material for them? There can be no doubt about the instinctual sources; but how is it to be explained that the same phantasies are always formed with the same content? I have an answer to this which I know will seem to you very daring. I believe that these *primal phantasies* (as I should like to name these, and certainly some others also) are a phylogenetic possession. In them the individual, wherever his own experience has become insufficient, stretches out beyond it to the experience of past ages. It seems to me quite possible that all that today is narrated in analysis in the form of phantasy, seduction in childhood, stimulation of sexual excitement upon observation of parental coitus, the threat of castration—or rather, castration itself—was in prehistoric periods of the human family a reality; and that the child in its phantasy simply fills out the gaps in its true individual experiences with true prehistoric experiences. We have again and again been led to suspect that more knowledge of the primordial forms of human development is stored up for us in the psychology of the neuroses than in any other field we may explore.

Now these things that we have been discussing require us to consider more closely the origin and meaning of that mental activity called *phantasy-making*. In general, as you know, it enjoys high esteem, although its place in mental life has not been clearly understood. I can tell you as much as this about it. You know that the ego in man is gradually trained by the influence of external necessity to appreciate reality and to pursue the reality-principle, and that in so doing it must renounce temporarily or permanently various of the objects and aims—not only sexual—of its desire for pleasure. But renunciation of pleasure has always been very hard to man; he cannot accomplish it without some kind of compensation. Accordingly he has evolved for himself a mental activity in which all these relinquished sources of pleasure and abandoned paths of gratification are permitted to continue their existence, a form of existence in which they are free from the demands of reality and from what we call the exercise of *testing reality*. Every longing is soon transformed into the idea of its fulfilment; there is no doubt that dwelling upon a wish-fulfilment in phantasy brings satisfaction, although the knowledge that it is not reality remains thereby unobscured. In phantasy, therefore, man can continue to enjoy a freedom from the grip of the external world, one which he has long relinquished in actuality. He has contrived to be alternately a pleasure-seeking animal and a reasonable being; for the meagre satisfaction that he can extract from reality leaves him starving. "There is no doing without accessory constructions," said Fontane. The creation of the mental domain of phantasy has a complete counterpart in the establishment of *reservations* and *nature-parks* in places where the inroads of agriculture, traffic, or industry threaten to change the original face of the earth rapidly into something unrecognizable. The *reservation* is to maintain the old condition of things which has been regretfully sacrificed to necessity everywhere else; there everything may grow and spread as it pleases, including what is useless and even what is harmful. The mental realm of phantasy is also such a reservation reclaimed from the encroaches of the reality-principle.

The best-known productions of phantasy have already been met by us; they are called *day-dreams*, and are imaginary gratifications of ambitious, grandiose, erotic wishes, dilating the more extravagantly the more reality admonishes humility and patience. In them is shown unmistakably the essence of imaginary happiness, the return of gratification to a condition in which it is independent of reality's sanction. We know that these day-dreams are the kernels and models of night-dreams; fundamentally the night-dream is nothing but a day-dream distorted by the nocturnal form of mental activity and made possible by the nocturnal freedom of instinctual excitations. We are already familiar with the idea that a day-dream is not necessarily conscious, that unconscious day-dreams also exist; such unconscious day-dreams are therefore just as much the source of night-dreams as of neurotic symptoms.

The significance of phantasy for symptom-formation will become clear to you in what follows. We said that, under frustration, the libido regressively invests the positions it had left but to which nevertheless some portions of its energy had remained attached. We shall not retract or correct this statement, but we shall have to interpolate a connecting-link in it. How does the libido find its way back to these fixation-points? Now the objects and channels which have been forsaken by the libido have not been forsaken in every sense; they, or their derivatives, are still retained to some degree of intensity in the conceptions of phantasy. The libido has only to withdraw on to the phantasies in order to find the way open to it back to all the repressed fixations. These phantasies had enjoyed a certain sort of toleration; no conflict between them and the ego had developed, however sharp an opposition there was between them, as long as a certain condition was preserved—a condition of a *quantitative* nature, now disturbed by the return of the libido-stream on to the phantasies. By this accession, the cathexis of the phantasies with energy becomes so much augmented that they become assertive and begin to press towards realization; then, however, conflict between them and the ego becomes unavoidable. Although previously they were preconscious or conscious, now they are subject to repression from the side of the ego and are exposed to the attraction exerted from the side of the unconscious. The libido travels from the phantasies, now unconscious, to their sources in the unconscious —back to its own fixation-points again.

The return of the libido on to phantasy is an intermediate step on the way to symptom-formation which well deserves a special designation. C. G. Jung has coined for it the very appropriate name of INTROVERSION, but inappropriately he uses it also to describe other things. We will adhere to the position that *introversion* describes the deflection of the libido away from the possibilities of real satisfaction and its excessive accumulation upon phantasies previously tolerated as harmless. An introverted person is not yet neurotic, but he is in an unstable condition; the next disturbance of the shifting forces will cause symptoms to develop, unless he can yet find other outlets for his pent-up libido. The unreal character of neurotic satisfaction and the disregard of the difference between phantasy and reality are already determined by the arrest at this stage of introversion.

You will doubtless have noticed that in these last remarks I have introduced a new factor into the concatenation of the aetiological chain —namely, the *quantity,* the magnitude of the energies concerned; we must always take this factor into account as well. A purely qualitative analysis of the aetiological conditions does not suffice; or, to put it in another way, a purely *dynamic* conception of these processes is insufficient, the *economic* aspect is also required. We have to realize that the conflict between the two forces in opposition does not break out until a certain intensity in the degree of investment is reached, even though the substantive conditions have long been in existence. In the same way, the pathogenic significance of the constitutional factor is determined by the preponderance of one of the component-instincts in *excess* over another in the disposition; it is even possible to conceive disposition as qualitatively the same in all men and only differentiated by this quantitative factor. No less important is this quantitative factor for the capacity to withstand neurotic illness; it depends upon the *amount* of undischarged libido that a person can hold freely suspended, and upon *how large* a portion of it he can deflect from the sexual to a nonsexual goal in sublimation. The final aim of mental activity, which can be qualitatively described as a striving towards pleasure and avoidance of pain, is represented economically in the task of mastering the distribution of the quantities of excitation (stimulus-masses) present in the mental apparatus, and in preventing the accumulation of them which gives rise to pain.

I set out to tell you as much as this about symptom-formation in the neuroses. Yes, but I must not neglect to mention once more that everything said today relates only to symptom-formation in hysteria. Even the obsessional neurosis shows great differences, although the essentials are the same. The *counter-charges* from the ego against the demands made by instincts for satisfaction, mentioned already in connection with hysteria, are more strongly marked in the obsessional neurosis and govern the clinical picture in the form of what we call *reaction-formations*. Similar and more extensive deviations still are found in the other neuroses, in which field researches into the mechanisms of symptom-formation are not yet complete in any direction.

Before you leave today I should like to direct your attention for a moment to a side of phantasy-life of very general interest. There is, in fact, a path from phantasy back again to reality, and that is—art. The artist has also an introverted disposition and has not far to go to become neurotic. He is one who is urged on by instinctual needs which are too clamorous; he longs to attain to honour, power, riches, fame, and the love of women; but he lacks the means of achieving these gratifications. So, like any other with an unsatisfied longing, he turns away from reality and transfers all his interest, and all his libido too, on to the creation of his wishes in the life of phantasy, from which the way might readily lead to neurosis. There must be many factors in combination to prevent this becoming the whole outcome of his development; it is well known how often artists in particular suffer from partial inhibition of their capacities through neurosis. Probably their constitution is endowed with a powerful capacity for sublimation and with a certain flexibility in the repressions determining the conflict. But the way back to reality is found by the artist thus: He is not the only one who has a life of phantasy; the intermediate world of phantasy is sanctioned by general human consent, and every hungry soul looks to it for comfort and consolation. But to those who are not artists the gratification that can be drawn from the springs of phantasy is very limited; their inexorable repressions prevent the enjoyment of all but the meagre day-dreams which can become conscious. A true artist has more at his disposal. First of all he understands how to elaborate his day-dreams, so that they lose that personal note which grates upon strange ears and become enjoyable to others; he knows too how to modify them sufficiently so that their origin in prohibited sources is not easily detected. Further, he possesses the mysterious ability to mould his particular material until it expresses the ideas of his phantasy faithfully; and then he knows how to attach to this reflection of his phantasy-life so strong a stream of pleasure that, for a time at least, the repressions are out-balanced and dispelled by it. When he can do all this, he opens out to others the way back to the comfort and consolation of their own unconscious sources of pleasure, and so reaps their gratitude and admiration; then he has won—through his phantasy—what before he could only win in phantasy: honour, power, and the love of women.

TWENTY-FOURTH LECTURE
ORDINARY NERVOUSNESS

AFTER such a difficult piece of work as we got through in our last lecture I shall leave the subject for a time and turn to my audience.

For I know that you are dissatisfied. You imagined that *A General Introduction to Psycho-Analysis* would be something quite different. You expected illustrations from life instead of theories; you will tell me that the story of the two children, on the ground-floor and in the mansion, revealed something of the causation of neurosis to you, except that it ought to have been an actual fact instead of an invention of my own. Or you will say that, when at the beginning I described two symptoms to you (not also imaginary, let us hope), and unfolded the solution of them and their connection with the lives of the patients, it threw some light on the meaning of symptoms, and you had hoped I would continue in the same way. Instead of doing so I gave you long-drawn-out and very obscure theories which were never complete, and to which I was constantly adding something; I dealt with conceptions which I had not yet introduced to you; I let go of descriptive explanation and took up the dynamic aspect and dropped this again for a so-called economic one; made it difficult for you to understand how many of these technical terms mean the same thing and are only exchanged for one another on account of euphony; I let vast conceptions, such as those of the pleasure and reality principles, and the inherited residue of phylogenetic development, appear, and then instead of explaining anything to you I let them drift away before your eyes out of sight.

Why did I not begin the introduction to the study of the neuroses with what you all know of nervousness, a thing that has long roused your interest, or with the peculiar nature of nervous persons, their incomprehensible reactions to human intercourse and external influences, their excitability, their unreliability, and their inability to do well in anything? Why not lead you step by step from an explanation of the simple every-day forms of nervousness to the problems of the enigmatic extreme manifestations?

Indeed, I cannot deny any of this or say that you are wrong. I am not so much in love with my powers of presentation as to imagine that every blemish in it is a peculiar charm. I think myself that I might with advantage to you have proceeded differently, and, indeed, such was my intention. But one cannot always carry through a reasoned scheme; something in the material itself often intervenes and takes possession of one and turns one from one's first intentions. Even such an ordinary task as the arrangement of familiar material is not entirely subject to the author's will; it comes out in its own way and one can but wonder afterwards why it happened so and not otherwise.

One of the reasons probably is that my theme, an introduction to psycho-analysis, no longer covers this section dealing with the subject of the neuroses. The introduction to psycho-analysis lies in the study of errors and of dreams; the theory of neurosis is psycho-analysis itself. I do not think that in such a short time I could have given you any knowledge of the material contained in the theory of the neuroses except in this very concentrated form. It was a matter of presenting to you in their proper context the sense and meaning of symptoms, together with the external and internal conditions and mechanisms of symptom-formation. This I attempted to do; it is more or less the core of what psycho-analysis is able to offer today. In conjunction with it there was much to be said about the libido and its development, and something about that of the ego. You were already prepared by the preliminary lectures for the main principles of our method and for the broad aspects involved in the conceptions of the unconscious and of repression (resistance). In one of the following lectures you will learn at what point the work of psycho-analysis finds its organic continuation. So far I have not concealed from you that all our results proceed from the study of one single group only of nervous disorders—namely, the transference neuroses; and even so I have traced out the mechanism of symptom-formation only in the hysterical neurosis. Though you will probably have gained no very thorough knowledge and have not retained every detail, yet I hope that you have acquired a general idea of the means with which psycho-analysis works, the problems it has to deal with, and the results it has to offer.

I have ascribed to you a wish that I had begun the subject of the neuroses with a description of the neurotic's behaviour, and of the ways in which he suffers from his disorder, protects himself against it and adapts himself to it. This is certainly a very interesting subject, well worth studying, and not difficult to treat: nevertheless there are reasons against beginning with this aspect. The danger is that the unconscious will be overlooked, the great importance of the libido ignored, and that everything will be judged as it appears to the patient's own ego. Now it is obvious that his ego is not a reliable and impartial authority. The ego is, after all, the force which denies the existence of the

unconscious and has subjected it to repressions; how then can we trust its good faith where the unconscious is concerned? That which has been repressed consists first and foremost of the repudiated claims of the sexuality; it is perfectly self-evident that we shall never learn their extent and their significance from the ego's view of the matter. As soon as the nature of repression begins to dawn upon us we are advised not to allow one of the two contending parties, and certainly not the victorious one, to be judged in the dispute. We are forewarned against being misled by what the ego tells us. According to its evidence it would appear to have been the active force throughout, so that the symptoms arise by its will and agency; we know that to a large extent it has played a passive part, a fact which it then endeavours to conceal and to gloss over. It is true that it cannot always keep up this pretence—in the symptoms of the obsessional neurosis it has to confess to being confronted by something alien which it must strenuously resist.

It is certainly plain sailing enough for anyone who does not heed these warnings against taking the falsifications of the ego at their face-value; he will escape all the opposition which psycho-analysis has to encounter in accentuating the unconscious, sexuality, and the passivity of the ego. He can agree with Alfred Adler that the *nervous character* is the cause of the neurosis, instead of the result; but he will not be in a position to account for a single detail of symptom-formation or a single dream.

You will ask: "May it not be possible to do justice to the part played by the ego in nervousness and in symptom-formation without absolutely glaring neglect of the other factors discovered by psycho-analysis?" I reply: Certainly it must be possible, and some time or other it will be done; but the work which lies at hand for psycho-analysis is not suited for a beginning at this end. One can, no doubt, predict the point at which this task also will be included. There are neuroses, called by us the *narcissistic* neuroses, in which the ego is far more deeply involved than in those we have studied; analytic investigation of these disorders will enable us to estimate impartially and reliably the share taken by the ego in neurotic disease.

One of the relations the ego bears to its neurosis is, however, so conspicuous that it was quite appreciable from the beginning. It never seems to be absent; but it is most clearly discernible in a form of disorder which we are far from understanding, the traumatic neurosis. You must know that in the causation and mechanism of all the various different forms of neurosis the same factors are found at work over and over again, only that in one type this factor and in another type that factor is of greatest significance in symptom-formation. It is just the same as with the personnel of a theatrical company, where every member plays a special type of part—hero, confidant, villain, etc.; each of them will choose a different piece for his own benefit-performance. Hence, the phantasies which are transformed into the symptoms are nowhere so manifest as in hysteria; the *counter-charges* (anti-cathexes) or re-action-formations of the ego dominate the picture in the obsessional neurosis; the mechanism which in dreams we called *secondary elaboration* is the prominent feature in the delusions of paranoia, and so on.

In the *traumatic neuroses*, especially in those arising from the terrors of war, we are particularly impressed by a self-seeking, egoistic motive, a straining towards protection and self-interest; this alone perhaps could not produce the disease, but it gives its support to the latter and maintains it once it has been formed. This tendency aims at protecting the ego from the dangers which led by their imminence to the outbreak of illness; nor does it permit of recovery until a repetition of the dangers appear to be no longer possible, or until some gain in compensation for the danger undergone has been received.

The ego takes a similar interest in the origin and maintenance of all the other forms of neurosis; we have said already that the symptom is supported by the ego because one side of it offers a satisfaction to the repressing ego-tendency. More than this, a solution of the conflict by a symptom-formation is the most convenient one, most in accordance with the pleasure-principle; for it undoubtedly spares the ego a severe and painful piece of internal labour. There are indeed cases in which the physician himself must admit that the solution of a conflict by a neurosis is the one most harmless and most tolerable socially. Do not be astonished to hear then that the physician himself occasionally takes sides with the illness which he is attacking. It is not for him to confine himself in all situations in life to the part of fanatic about health; he knows that there is *other* misery in the world besides neurotic misery—real unavoidable suffering—that necessity may even demand of a man that he

sacrifice his health to it, and he learns that such suffering in one individual may often avert incalculable hardship for many others. Therefore, although it may be said of every neurotic that he has taken *flight into illness,* it must be admitted that in many cases this flight is fully justified, and the physician who has perceived this state of things will silently and considerately retire.

But let us continue our discussion without regard to these exceptional cases. In the ordinary way it is apparent that by flight into neurosis the ego gains a certain internal *advantage through illness,* as we call it; under certain conditions a tangible external advantage, more or less valuable in reality, may be combined with this. To take the commonest case of this kind: a woman who is brutally treated and mercilessly exploited by her husband fairly regularly takes refuge in a neurosis, if her disposition admits of it. This will happen if she is too cowardly or too conventional to console herself secretly with another man, if she is not strong enough to defy all external reasons against it and separate from her husband, if she has no prospect of being able to maintain herself or of finding a better husband, and last of all, if she is still strongly attached sexually to this brutal man. Her illness becomes her weapon in the struggle against him, one that she can use for her protection, or misuse for purposes of revenge. She can complain of her illness, though she probably dare not complain of her marriage; her doctor is her ally; the husband who is otherwise so ruthless is required to spare her, to spend money on her, to grant her absence from home and thus some freedom from marital oppression. Whenever this external or *accidental* advantage through illness is at all pronounced, and no substitute for it can be found in reality, you need not look forward very hopefully to influencing the neurosis by your therapy.

You will now say that what I have just told you about the *advantage through illness* is all in favour of the view I have rejected, namely, that the ego itself desires the neurosis and creates it. But just a moment! Perhaps it means merely this: that the ego is pleased to accept the neurosis which it is in any case unable to prevent, and that if there is anything at all to be made out of it it makes the best of it. This is only one side of the matter. In so far as there is advantage in it the ego is quite happy to be on good terms with a neurosis, but there are also disadvantages to be considered. As a rule it is soon apparent that by accepting a neurosis the ego has made a bad bargain. It has paid too heavily for the solution of the conflict; the sufferings entailed by the symptoms are perhaps as bad as those of the conflict they replace, and they may quite probably be very much worse. The ego wishes to be rid of the pain of the symptoms, but not give up its advantage through illness; and that is just what it cannot succeed in doing. It appears, therefore, that the ego was not quite so actively concerned in the matter throughout as it had thought, and we will keep this well in mind.

If, as physicians, you have much to do with neurotics, you will soon cease to expect that those who complain most bitterly of their illness will be most ready to accept your help and make least difficulty—quite the contrary. You will at all events easily understand that everything which contributes to the advantage through illness reinforces the resistance arising from the repressions, and increases the therapeutic difficulties. And there is yet another kind of advantage through illness, one which supervenes later than that born with the symptom, so to speak. When such a mental organization as the disease has persisted for a considerable time it seems finally to acquire the character of an independent entity; it displays something like a self-preservative instinct; it forms a kind of pact, a *modus vivendi*, with the other forces in mental life, even with those fundamentally hostile to it, and opportunities can hardly fail to arise in which it once more manifests itself as useful and expedient, thus acquiring a *secondary function* which again strengthens its position. Instead of taking an example from pathology let us consider a striking illustration in everyday life. A capable working-man earning his living is crippled by an accident in the course of his employment; he can work no more, but he gets a small periodical dole in compensation and learns how to exploit his mutilation as a beggar. His new life, although so inferior, nevertheless is supported by the very thing which destroyed his old life; if you were to remove his disability you would deprive him for a time of his means of subsistence, for the question would arise whether he would still be capable of resuming his former work. When a secondary exploitation of the illness such as this is formed in a neurosis we can range it alongside the first and call it a *secondary advantage through illness*.

I should like to advise you in a general way not to underestimate the practical importance of the advantage through illness, and yet not to be too much impressed by its theoretical significance. Apart from the exceptions previously recognized, this factor always reminds one of the illustrations of "Intelligence in Animals" by Oberländer in *Fliegende Blätter*. An Arab is riding a camel along a narrow path cut in the side of a steep mountain. At a turn in the path he suddenly finds himself confronted by a lion ready to spring at him. There is no escape; on one side the abyss, on the other the sheer wall; retreat and flight are impossible; he gives himself up for lost. Not so the camel. He takes one leap with his rider into the abyss— and the lion is left a spectator. The remedies provided by neurosis avail the patient no better as a rule; perhaps because the solution of the conflict by a symptom-formation is after all an automatic process which may show itself inadequate to meet the demands of life, and involves man in a renunciation of his best and highest powers. The more honourable choice, if there be a choice, is to go down in fair fight with destiny.

I still owe you a further explanation of my motive in not taking ordinary nervousness as my starting-point. Perhaps you think I avoided doing so because it would have been more difficult to bring in evidence of the sexual origin of the neuroses in that way; but in this you would be mistaken. In the transference neuroses the symptoms have to be submitted to interpretation before we arrive at this; but in the ordinary forms of what are called the ACTUAL NEUROSES the aetiological significance of the sexual life is a crudely obvious fact which courts notice. I became aware of it more than twenty years ago, as one day I began to wonder why, when we examine nervous patients, we so invariably exclude from consideration all matters concerning their sexual life. Investigations on this point led to the sacrifice of my popularity with my patients, but in a very short time my efforts had brought me to this conclusion: that no neurosis—actual neurosis, I meant—is present where sexual life is normal. It is true that this statement ignores the individual differences in people rather too much, and it also suffers from the indefinite connotation inseparable from the word *normal;* but as a broad outline it has retained its value to this day. At that time I got so far as to be able to establish particular connections between certain forms of nervousness and certain injurious sexual conditions; I do not doubt that I could repeat these observations today if I still had similar material for investigation. I noticed often enough that a man who contented himself with some kind of incomplete sexual satisfaction, e.g., with manual masturbation, would suffer from a definite type of actual neurosis, and that this neurosis would promptly give way to another form if he adopted some other equally unsatisfactory form of sexual life. I was then in a position to infer the change in his mode of sexual life from the alteration in the patient's condition; and I learnt to abide stubbornly by my conclusions until I had overcome the prevarications of my patients and had compelled them to give me confirmation. It is true that they then thought it advisable to seek other physicians who would not take so much interest in their sexual life.

It did not escape me at that time either that sexuality was not always indicated as the cause of a neurosis; one person certainly would fall ill because of some injurious sexual condition, but another because he had lost his fortune or recently sustained a severe organic illness. The explanation of these variations was revealed later, when insight was obtained into the interrelationships suspected between the ego and the libido; and the further this subject was explored the more satisfactory became our insight into it. A person only falls ill of a neurosis when the ego loses its capacity to deal in some way or other with the libido. The stronger the ego the more easily can it accomplish this task; every weakening of the ego, from whatever cause, must have the same effect as an increase in the demands of the libido; that is, make a neurosis possible. There are yet other and more intimate relations between the ego and the libido, which I shall not go into now as we have not yet come to them in the course of our discussions. The most essential and most instructive point for us is that the fund of energy supporting the symptoms of a neurosis, in every case and regardless of the circumstances inducing their outbreak, is provided by the libido, which is thus put to an abnormal use.

Now I must point out to you the decisive difference between the symptoms of the *actual neuroses* and those of the *psychoneuroses*, with the first group of which (the transference neuroses) we have hitherto been so much occupied. In both the actual neuroses and the psychoneuroses the symptoms proceed from the libido; that is, they are abnormal ways of using it, substitutes for satisfaction of it. But the symptoms of an actual neurosis—headache, sensation of pain, an irritable condition of some

organ, the weakening or inhibition of some function—have no *meaning*, no signification in the mind. Not merely are they manifested principally in the body, as also happens, for instance with hysterical symptoms, but they are in themselves purely and simply physical processes; they arise without any of the complicated mental mechanisms we have been learning about. They really are, therefore, what psychoneurotic symptoms were for so long held to be. But then, how can they be expressions of the libido which we have come to know as a force at work in the mind? Now, really, the answer to that is very simple. Let me resurrect one of the very first objections ever made against psycho-analysis. It was said that the theories were an attempt to account for neurotic symptoms by psychology alone and that the outlook was consequently hopeless, since no illness could ever be accounted for by psychological theories. These critics were pleased to forget that the sexual function is not a purely mental thing, any more than it is merely a physical thing. It affects bodily life as well as mental life. Having learnt that the symptoms of the psychoneuroses express the mental consequences of some disturbance in this function, we shall not be surprised to find that the actual neuroses represent the direct somatic consequences of sexual disturbances.

Clinical medicine gives us a useful hint (recognized by many different investigators) towards comprehension of the actual neuroses. In the details of their symptomatology, and also in the peculiarity by which all the bodily systems and functions are affected together, they exhibit an unmistakable similarity with pathological conditions resulting from the chronic effect or the sudden removal of foreign toxins— i.e., with states of intoxication or of abstinence. The two groups of affections are brought still closer together by comparison with conditions like Basedow's disease[1] that have also been found to result from poisoning, not, however, from poisons derived externally, but from such as arise in the internal metabolism. In my opinion, these analogies necessitate our regarding the neuroses as the effects of disturbances in the sexual metabolism, due either to more of these sexual toxins being produced than the person can dispose of, or else to internal and even mental conditions which interfere with the proper disposal of these substances. Assumptions of this kind about the nature of sexual desire have found acceptance in the mind of

[1] *i.e.*, Grave's disease, exophthalmic goitre.—TR.

the people since the beginning of time; love is called an *intoxication,* it can be induced by "potions"—in these ideas the agency at work is to some extent projected on to the outer world. We find occasion at this point to remember the erotogenic zones, and to reflect upon the proposition that sexual excitation may arise in the most various organs. Beyond this the subject of *sexual metabolism* or the *chemistry of sexuality* is an empty chapter: we know nothing about it, and cannot even determine whether to assume two kinds of sexual substances, to be called *male* and *female,* or to content ourselves with *one* sexual toxin as the agent of the stimuli effected by the libido. The edifice of psycho-analytic doctrine which we have erected is in reality but a superstructure, which will have to be set on its organic foundation at some time or other; but this foundation is still unknown to us.

As a science, psycho-analysis is characterized by the methods with which it works, not by the subject-matter with which it deals. These methods can be applied without violating their essential nature to the history of civilization, to the science of religion, and to mythology as well as to the study of the neuroses. Psycho-analysis aims at and achieves nothing more than the discovery of the unconscious in mental life. The problems of the actual neuroses, in which the symptoms probably arise through direct toxic injury, offer no point of attack for psycho-analysis; it can supply little towards elucidation of them and must leave this task to biological and medical research. Now perhaps you understand better why I chose this arrangement of my material. If I had intended an *Introduction to the Study of the Neuroses* it would undoubtedly have been correct to begin with the simple forms of (actual) neuroses and proceed from them to the more complicated psychical disorders resulting from disturbances of the libido. I should have had to collect from various quarters what we know or think we know about the former, and about the latter psycho-analysis would have been introduced as the most important technical means of obtaining insight into these conditions. An *Introduction to Psycho-Analysis* was what I had undertaken and announced, however; I thought it more important to give you an idea of psycho-analysis than to teach you something about the neuroses; and therefore the actual neuroses which yield nothing towards the study of psycho-analysis could not suitably be put in the foreground. I think, too,

that my choice was the wiser for you, since the radical axioms and far-reaching connections of psycho-analysis make it worthy of every educated person's interest; the theory of the neuroses, however, is a chapter of medicine like any other.

However, you are justified in expecting that we should take some interest in the actual neuroses; their close clinical connection with the psycho-neuroses even necessitates this. I will tell you then that we distinguish three pure forms of actual neurosis: *neurasthenia, anxiety-neurosis* and *hypochondria.* Even this classification has been disputed; the terms are certainly all in use, but their connotation is vague and unsettled. There are some medical men who are opposed to all discrimination in the confusing world of neurotic manifestations, who object to any distinguishing of clinical entities or types of disease, and do not even recognize the difference between actual neuroses and psychoneuroses; in my opinion they go too far, and the direction they have chosen does not lead to progress. The three kinds of neurosis named above are occasionally found in a pure form; more frequently, it is true, they are combined with one another and with a psychoneurotic affection. This fact need not make us abandon the distinctions between them. Think of the difference between the science of minerals and that of ores in mineralogy: the minerals are classified individually, in part no doubt because they are frequently found as crystals, sharply differentiated from their surroundings; the ores consist of mixtures of minerals which have indeed coalesced, not accidentally, but according to the conditions at their formation. In the theory of the neuroses we still understand too little of the process of their development to formulate anything similar to our knowledge of ores; but we are certainly working in the right direction in first isolating from the mass the recognizable clinical elements, which are comparable to the individual minerals.

A noteworthy connection between the symptoms of the actual neuroses and the psychoneuroses adds a valuable contribution to our knowledge of symptom-formation in the latter; the symptom of the actual neurosis is frequently the nucleus and incipient stage of the psychoneurotic symptom. A connection of this kind is most clearly observable between neurasthenia and the transference neurosis known as conversion-hysteria, between the anxiety-neurosis and anxiety-hysteria, but also between hypochondria and forms of a neurosis which we shall deal with later on, namely, paraphrenia (dementia praecox and paranoia). As an example, let us take an hysterical headache or backache. Analysis shows that, by means of condensation and displacement, it has become a substitutive satisfaction for a whole series of libidinal phantasies or memories; at one time, however, this pain was real, a direct symptom of a sexual toxin, the bodily expression of a sexual excitation. We do not by any means maintain that all hysterical symptoms have a nucleus of this kind, but it remains true that this very often is so, and that all effects (whether normal or pathological) of the libidinal excitation upon the body are especially adapted to serve the purposes of hysterical symptom-formation. They play the part of the grain of sand which the oyster envelops in mother-of-pearl. The temporary signs of sexual excitation accompanying the sexual act serve the psychoneurosis in the same way, as the most suitable and convenient material for symptom-formation.

There is a similar process of special diagnostic and therapeutic interest. In persons who are disposed to be neurotic without having yet developed a neurosis on a grand scale, some morbid organic condition—perhaps an inflammation, or an injury—very commonly sets the work of symptom-formation in motion; so that the latter process swiftly seizes upon the symptom supplied by reality, and uses it to represent those unconscious phantasies that have only been lying in wait for some means of expression. In such a case, the physician will try first one therapy and then the other; will either endeavour to abolish the organic foundation on which the symptom rests, without troubling about the clamorous neurotic elaboration of it; or will attack the neurosis which this opportunity has brought to birth, while leaving on one side the organic stimulus which incited it. Sometimes one and sometimes the other procedure will be found justified by success; no general rules can be prescribed for mixed cases of this kind.

TWENTY-FIFTH LECTURE
ANXIETY

You will certainly have judged the information that I gave you in the last lecture about ordinary nervousness as the most fragmentary and most inadequate of all my accounts. I know that it was; and I expect that nothing

surprised you more than that I made no mention of the *anxiety* which most nervous people complain of and themselves describe as their most terrible burden. Anxiety or dread can really develop tremendous intensity and in consequence be the cause of the maddest precautions. But in this matter at least I wished not to cut you short; on the contrary, I had determined to put the problem of nervous anxiety to you as clearly as possible and to discuss it at some length.

Anxiety (or *dread*) itself needs no description; everyone has personally experienced this sensation, or to speak more correctly this affective condition at some time or other. But in my opinion not enough serious consideration has been given to the question why nervous persons in particular suffer from anxiety so much more intensely, and so much more altogether, than others. Perhaps it has been taken for granted that they should; indeed, the words *nervous* and *anxious* are used interchangeably, as if they meant the same thing. This is not justifiable, however; there are anxious people who are otherwise not in any way nervous and there are, besides, neurotics with numerous symptoms who exhibit no tendency to dread.

However this may be, one thing is certain, that the problem of anxiety is a nodal point, linking up all kinds of most important questions; a riddle, of which the solution must cast a flood of light upon our whole mental life. I do not claim that I can give you a complete solution; but you will certainly expect psychoanalysis to have attacked this problem too in a different manner from that adopted by academic medicine. Interest there centres upon the anatomical processes by which the anxiety condition comes about. We learn that the medulla oblongata is stimulated, and the patient is told that he is suffering from a neurosis in the vagal nerve. The medulla oblongata is a wondrous and beauteous object; I well remember how much time and labour I devoted to the study of it years ago. But today I must say I know of nothing less important for the psychological comprehension of anxiety than a knowledge of the nerve-paths by which the excitations travel.

One may consider anxiety for a long time without giving a thought to nervousness. You will understand me at once when I describe this form of anxiety as OBJECTIVE ANXIETY, in contrast to neurotic anxiety. Now *real* anxiety or dread appears to us a very natural and rational thing; we should call it a reaction to the perception of an external danger, of an injury which is expected and foreseen; it is bound up with the reflex of flight, and may be regarded as an expression of the instinct of self-preservation. The occasions of it, i.e., the objects and situations about which anxiety is felt, will obviously depend to a great extent upon the state of the person's knowledge and feeling of power regarding the outer world. It seems to us quite natural that a savage should be afraid of a cannon or of an eclipse of the sun, while a white man who can handle the weapon and foretell the phenomenon remains unafraid in the same situation. At other times, it is knowledge itself which inspires fear, because it reveals the danger sooner; thus a savage will recoil with terror at the sight of a track in the jungle which conveys nothing to an ignorant white man, but means that some wild beast is near at hand; and an experienced sailor will perceive with dread a little cloud on the horizon because it means an approaching hurricane, while to a passenger it looks quite insignificant.

The view that objective anxiety is rational and expedient, however, will on deeper consideration be admitted to need thorough revision. In face of imminent danger the only expedient behaviour, actually, would be first a cool appraisement of the forces at disposal as compared with the magnitude of the danger at hand, and then a decision whether flight or defence, or possibly attack, offered the best prospect of a successful outcome. Dread, however, has no place in this scheme; everything to be done will be accomplished as well and probably better if dread does not develop. You will see, too, that when dread is excessive it becomes in the highest degree inexpedient; it paralyses every action, even that of flight. The reaction to danger usually consists in a combination of the two things, the fear-affect and the defensive action; the frightened animal is afraid *and* flees, but the expedient element in this is the *flight,* not the *being afraid.*

One is tempted therefore to assert that the development of anxiety is never expedient; perhaps a closer dissection of the situation in dread will give us a better insight into it. The first thing about it is the *readiness* for danger, which expresses itself in heightened sensorial perception and in motor tension. This expectant readiness is obviously advantageous; indeed, absence of it may be responsible for grave results. It is then followed on the one hand by a motor action, taking the form pri-

marily of flight and, on a higher level, of defensive action; and on the other hand by the condition we call a sensation of *anxiety* or dread. The more the development of dread is limited to a flash, to a mere signal, the less does it hinder the transition from the state of anxious readiness to that of action, and the more expediently does the whole course of events proceed. The *anxious readiness* therefore seems to me to be the expedient element, and the *development* of anxiety the inexpedient element, in what we call anxiety or dread.

I shall not enter upon a discussion whether the words *anxiety, fear, fright,* mean the same or different things in common usage. In my opinion, *anxiety* relates to the condition and ignores the object, whereas in the word *fear* attention is directed to the object; *fright* does actually seem to possess a special meaning—namely, it relates specifically to the condition induced when danger is unexpectedly encountered without previous anxious readiness. It might be said, then, that anxiety is a protection again fright.

It will not have escaped you that a certain ambiguity and indefiniteness exists in the use of the word *anxiety.* It is generally understood to mean the subjective condition arising upon the perception of what we have called *developed* anxiety; such a condition is called an *affect.* Now what is an affect, in a dynamic sense? It is certainly something very complex. An affect comprises first of all certain motor innervations or discharges; and, secondly, certain sensations, which moreover are of two kinds—namely, the perceptions of the motor actions which have been performed, and the directly pleasurable or painful sensations which give the affect what we call its dominant note. But I do not think that this description penetrates to the essence of an affect. With certain affects one seems to be able to see deeper, and to recognize that the core of it, binding the whole complex structure together, is of the nature of a *repetition* of some particular very significant previous experience. This experience could only have been an exceedingly early impression of a universal type, to be found in the previous history of the species rather than of the individual. In order to be better understood I might say that an affective state is constructed like an hysterical attack, i.e., is the precipitate of a reminiscence. An hysterical attack is, therefore, comparable to a newly formed individual affect, and the normal affect to a universal hysteria which has become a heritage.

Do not imagine that what I am telling you now about affects is the common property of normal psychology. On the contrary, these conceptions have grown on the soil of psycho-analysis and are only indigenous there. What psychology has to say about affects—the James-Lange theory, for instance—is utterly incomprehensible to us psycho-analysts and imposable for us to discuss. We do not however regard what we know of affects as at all final; it is a first attempt to take our bearings in this obscure region. To continue, then: we believe we know what this early impression is which is reproduced as a repetition in the anxiety affect. We think it is the experience of *birth*—an experience which involves just such a concatenation of painful feelings, of discharges of excitation, and of bodily sensations, as to have become a prototype for all occasions on which life is endangered, ever after to be reproduced again in us as the dread or *anxiety* condition. The enormous increase in stimulation effected by the interruption of the renewal of blood (the internal respiration) was the cause of the anxiety experience at birth—the first anxiety was therefore toxically induced. The name *Angst* (anxiety)—*angustiæ, Enge,* a narrow place, a strait—accentuates the characteristic tightening in the breathing which was then the consequence of a real situation and is subsequently repeated almost invariably with an affect. It is very suggestive, too, that the first anxiety state arose on the occasion of the separation from the mother. We naturally believe that the disposition to reproduce this first anxiety condition has become so deeply ingrained in the organism, through countless generations, that no single individual can escape the anxiety affect; even though, like the legendary Macduff, he "was from his mother's womb untimely ripped" and so did not himself experience the act of birth. What the prototype of the anxiety condition may be for other animals than mammals we cannot say; neither do we know what the complex of sensations in them is which is equivalent to fear in us.

It may perhaps interest you to know how it was possible to arrive at such an idea as this—that birth is the source and prototype of the anxiety affect. Speculation had least of all to do with it; on the contrary, I borrowed a thought from the naïve intuitive mind of the people. Many years ago a number of young house-physicians, including myself, were sitting round a dinner-table, and one of the assistants at the obstetrical clinic was telling us all the funny stories of the last midwives' examination. One of the candidates was asked what it meant when the meconium (child's excreta) was present in the waters at birth, and promptly replied: "That the child is frightened." She was ridiculed and failed. But I silently took her part and began to suspect that the poor unsophisticated woman's unerring perception had revealed a very important connection.

Now let us turn to neurotic anxiety; what are the special manifestations and conditions found in the anxiety of nervous persons? There is a great deal to be described here. First of all, we find a general apprehensiveness in them, a *free-floating* anxiety, as we call it, ready to attach itself to any thought which is at all appropriate, affecting judgments, inducing expectations, lying in wait for any opportunity to find a justification for itself. We call this condition *expectant dread* or *anxious expectation*. People who are tormented with this kind of anxiety always anticipate the worst of all possible outcomes, interpret every chance happening as an evil omen, and exploit every uncertainty to mean the worst. The tendency to this kind of expectation of evil is found as a character-trait in many people who cannot be described as ill in any other way, and we call them *over-anxious* or pessimistic; but a marked degree of expectant dread is an invariable accompaniment of the nervous disorder which I have called anxiety-neurosis and include among the actual neuroses.

In contrast to this type of anxiety, a second form of it is found to be much more circumscribed in the mind, and attached to definite objects and situations. This is the anxiety of the extraordinarily various and often very peculiar phobias. Stanley Hall, the distinguished American psychologist, has recently taken the trouble to designate a whole series of these phobias by gorgeous Greek titles; they sound like the ten plagues of Egypt, except that there are far more than ten of them. Just listen to the things that can become the object or content of a phobia: darkness, open air, open spaces, cats, spiders, caterpillars, snakes, mice, thunder, sharp points, blood, enclosed places, crowds, loneliness, crossing bridges, travelling by land or sea, and so on. As a first attempt to take one's bearings in this chaos we may divide them into three groups. Many of the objects and situations feared are rather sinister, even to us normal people they have some connection with danger; and these phobias are not entirely incomprehensible to us, although their intensity seems very much exaggerated. Most of us, for instance, have a feeling of repulsion upon encountering a snake. It may be said that the snake-phobia is universal in mankind. Charles Darwin has described most vividly how he could not control his dread of a snake that darted at him, although he knew that he was protected from it by a thick plate of glass. The second group consists of situations that still have some relation to danger, but to one that is usually belittled or not emphasized by us; most situation-phobias belong to this group. We know that there is more chance of meeting with a disaster in a railway train than at home —namely, a collision; we also know that a ship may sink, whereupon it is usual to be drowned; but we do not brood upon these dangers and we travel without anxiety by train and boat. Nor can it be denied that, if a bridge were to break at the moment we are crossing it, we should be hurled into the torrent, but that only happens so very occasionally that it is not a danger worth considering. Solitude too has its dangers, which in certain circumstances we avoid, but there is no question of never being able to endure it for a moment under any conditions. The same thing applies to crowds, enclosed spaces, thunderstorms, and so on. What is foreign to us in these phobias is not so much their content as their intensity. The anxiety accompanying a phobia is positively indescribable! And we sometimes get the impression that neurotics are not really at all fearful of those things which can, under certain conditions, arouse anxiety in us and which they call by the same names.

There remains a third group which is entirely unintelligible to us. When a strong full-grown man is afraid to cross a street or square in his own so familiar town, or when a healthy well-developed woman becomes almost senseless with fear because a cat has brushed against her dress or a mouse has scurried through the room, how can we see the connection with danger which is obviously present to these people? With this kind of animal-phobia it is no question of an increased intensity of common human antipathies; to prove the contrary, there are numbers of people who, for instance, cannot pass a cat without attracting and petting it. A mouse is a thing that so many women are afraid of, and yet it is at the same time a very favourite pet name; many a girl who is delighted to be called so by her lover will scream with terror at the sight of the dainty little creature itself. The behaviour of the man who is afraid to cross streets and squares only suggests one thing to us—that he behaves like a little child. A child is directly taught that such situations are dangerous, and the man's anxiety, too, is allayed when he is led by someone across the open space.

The two forms of anxiety described, the *free-floating* expectant dread and that attached to phobias, are independent of each other. The one is not the other at a further stage; they are only rarely combined, and then as if fortuitously. The most intense general apprehensiveness does not necessarily lead to a phobia; people who have been hampered all their lives by agoraphobia may be quite free from pessimistic expectant dread. Many phobias, e.g., fear of open spaces, of railway travelling, are demonstrably acquired first in later life; others, such as fear of darkness, thunder, animals, seem to have existed from the beginning. The former signify serious illness, the latter are more of the nature of idiosyncrasies, peculiarities; anyone exhibiting one of these latter may be suspected of harbouring others similar to it. I must add that we group all these phobias under *anxiety-hysteria,* that is, we regard them as closely allied to the well-known disorder called conversion-hysteria.

The third form taken by neurotic anxiety brings us to an enigma; there is no visible connection at all between the anxiety and the danger dreaded. This anxiety occurs in hysteria, for instance, accompanying the hysterical symptoms; or under various conditions of excitement in which, it is true, we should expect some affect to be displayed, but least of all an anxiety-affect; or without reference to any conditions, incomprehensible both to us and to the patient, an unrelated anxiety-attack. We may look far and wide without discovering a danger or an occasion which could even be exaggerated to account for it. These spontaneous attacks show, therefore, that the complex condition which we describe as anxiety can be split up into components. The whole attack can be represented (as a substitute) by a single intensively developed symptom—shuddering, faintness, palpitation of the heart, inability to breathe—and the general feeling which we recognize as anxiety may be absent or may have become unnoticeable. And yet these states which are termed *anxiety equivalents* have the same clinical and aetiological validity as anxiety itself.

Two questions arise now: Is it possible to

bring neurotic anxiety, in which such a small part or none at all is played by danger, into relation with *objective anxiety*, which is essentially a reaction to danger? And, how is neurotic anxiety to be understood? We will at present hold fast to the expectation that where there is anxiety there must be something of which one is afraid.

Clinical observation yields various clues to the comprehension of neurotic anxiety, and I will now discuss their significance with you.

(a) It is not difficult to see that expectant dread or general apprehensiveness stands in intimate relation to certain processes in the sexual life—let us say, to certain modes of libido-utilization. The simplest and most instructive case of this kind arises in people who expose themselves to what is called frustrated excitation, i.e., when a powerful sexual excitation experiences insufficient discharge and is not carried on to a satisfying termination. This occurs, for instance, in men during the time of an engagement to marry, and in women whose husbands are not sufficiently potent, or who perform the sexual act too rapidly or incompletely with a view to preventing conception. Under these conditions the libidinal excitation disappears and anxiety appears in place of it, both in the form of expectant dread and in that of attacks and anxiety-equivalents. The precautionary measure of *coitus interruptus*, when practised as a customary sexual régime, is so regularly the cause of anxiety-neurosis in men, and even more so in women, that medical practitioners would be wise to enquire first of all into the possibility of such an aetiology in all such cases. Innumerable examples show that the anxiety-neurosis vanishes when the sexual malpractice is given up.

So far as I know, the fact that a connection exists between sexual restraint and anxiety conditions is no longer disputed, even by physicians who hold aloof from psycho-analysis. Nevertheless I can well imagine that they do not neglect to invert the connection, and to put forward the view that such persons are predisposed to apprehensiveness and consequently practice caution in sexual matters. Against this, however, decisive evidence is found in the reactions in women, in whom the sexual function is essentially passive, so that its course is determined by the treatment accorded by the man. The more *temperament*, i.e., the more inclination for sexual intercourse and capacity for satisfaction, a woman has, the more certainly will she react with anxiety manifesta-

tions to the man's impotence or to *coitus interruptus;* whereas such abuse entails far less serious results with anaesthetic women or those in whom the sexual hunger is less strong.

Sexual abstinence, which is nowadays so warmly recommended by physicians, of course only has the same significance for anxiety conditions when the libido which is denied a satisfactory outlet is correspondingly insistent, and is not being utilized to a large extent in sublimation. Whether or not illness will ensue is indeed always a matter of the quantitative factor. Even apart from illness, it is easy to see in the sphere of character-formation that sexual restraint goes hand in hand with a certain anxiousness and cautiousness, whereas fearlessness and a boldly adventurous spirit bring with them a free tolerance of sexual needs. However these relations may be altered and complicated by the manifold influences of civilization, it remains incontestable that, for the average human being, anxiety is closely connected with sexual restriction.

I have by no means told you all the observations which point to this genetic connection between libido and anxiety. There is, for instance, the effect upon anxiety states of certain periods of life, such as puberty and the menopause, in which the production of libido is considerably augmented. In many states of excitement, too, the mingling of sexual excitation with anxiety may be directly observed as well as the final replacement of the libidinal excitation by anxiety. The impression received from all this is a double one; first, that it is a matter of an accumulation of libido, debarred from its normal utilization; and secondly, that the question is one of somatic processes only. How anxiety develops out of sexual desire is at present obscure; we can only ascertain that desire is lacking and anxiety is found in its place.

(b) A second clue is obtained from analysis of the psychoneuroses, in particular, of hysteria. We have heard that anxiety frequently accompanies the symptoms in this disease, and that unattached anxiety may also be chronically present or come to expression in attacks. The patients cannot say what it is they fear; they link it up by unmistakable secondary elaboration to the most convenient phobias: of dying, of going mad, of having a stroke, etc. When we subject to analysis the situation in which the anxiety, or the symptom accompanied by anxiety, arose, we can as a rule discover what normal mental process has been checked in its

course and replaced by a manifestation of anxiety. To express it differently: we construe the unconscious process as though it had not undergone repression and had gone through unhindered into consciousness. This process would have been accompanied by a particular affect and now we discover, to our astonishment, that this affect, which would normally accompany the mental process through into consciousness, is in every case replaced by anxiety, no matter what particular type it had previously been. So that when we have a hysterical anxiety condition before us, its unconscious correlative may be an excitation of a similar character, such as apprehension, shame, embarrassment; or quite as possibly a *positive* libidinal excitation; or an antagonistic, aggressive one, such as rage or anger. Anxiety is thus general current coin for which all the affects are exchanged or can be exchanged, when the corresponding ideational content is under repression.

(c) A third observation is provided by patients whose symptoms take the form of obsessive acts, and who seem to be remarkably immune from anxiety. When we restrain them from carrying out their obsessive performances, their washing, their ceremonies, etc., or when they themselves venture an attempt to abandon one of their compulsions, they are forced by an appalling dread to yield to the compulsion and to carry out the act. We perceive that the anxiety was concealed under the obsessive act and that this is only performed to escape the feeling of dread. In the obsessional neurosis, therefore, the anxiety which would otherwise ensue is replaced by the symptom-formation; and when we turn to hysteria we find a similar relation existing—as a consequence of the process of repression either a pure developed anxiety, or anxiety with symptom-formation, or symptom-formation without anxiety. In an abstract sense, therefore, it seems correct to say that symptoms altogether are formed purely for the purpose of escaping the otherwise inevitable development of anxiety. Thus anxiety comes to the fore-front of our interest in the problems of the neuroses.

We concluded from our observations on the anxiety-neurosis that the diversion of the libido away from its normal form of utilization, a diversion which releases anxiety, took place on the basis of somatic processes. The analyses of hysterical and obsessional neuroses furnish the additional conclusion that a similar diversion with a similar result can follow from opposition on the part of institutions in the mind. We

know as much as this, therefore, about the origin of neurotic anxiety; it still sounds rather indefinite. But for the moment I know of no path which will take us further. The second task we undertook, that of establishing a connection between neurotic anxiety (abnormally utilized libido) and *objective anxiety* (which corresponds with the reaction to danger), seems even more difficult to accomplish. One would think there could be no comparison between the two things, and yet there are no means by which the sensations of neurotic anxiety can be distinguished from those of real anxiety.

The desired connection may be found with the help of the antithesis, so often put forward, between the ego and the libido. As we know, the development of anxiety is the reaction of the ego to danger and the signal preparatory to flight; it is, then, not a great step to imagine that in neurotic anxiety also the ego is attempting a flight, from the demands of its libido, and is treating this internal danger as if it were an external one. Then our expectation, that where anxiety is present there must be something of which one is afraid, would be fulfilled. The analogy goes further than this, however. Just as the tension prompting the attempt to flee from external danger is resolved into holding one's ground and taking appropriate defensive measures, so the development of neurotic anxiety yields to a symptom-formation, which enables the anxiety to be "bound."

Our difficulty in comprehension now lies elsewhere. The anxiety which signifies the flight of the ego from its libido is nevertheless supposed to have had its source in that libido. This is obscure, and we are warned not to forget that the libido of a given person is fundamentally part of that person and cannot be contrasted with him as if it were something external. It is the question of the topographical dynamics of anxiety-development that is still obscure to us —what kind of mental energies are being expended and to what systems do they belong? I cannot promise you to answer this question also; but we will not neglect to follow up two other clues, and in so doing will again summon direct observation and analytic investigation to aid our speculation. We will turn to the sources of anxiety in children, and to the origin of the neurotic anxiety which is attached to phobias.

Apprehensiveness is very common among children, and it is difficult enough to decide whether it is objective or neurotic anxiety. Indeed the very value of this distinction is called in question by the attitude of children themselves. For on the one hand we are not surprised that children are afraid of strangers, of strange objects and situations, and we account for this reaction to ourselves very easily by reflecting on their weakness and ignorance. Thus we ascribe to the child a strong tendency to objective anxiety and should regard it as only practical if this apprehensiveness had been transmitted by inheritance. The child would only be repeating the behaviour of prehistoric man and of primitive man today who, in consequence of his ignorance and helplessness, experiences a dread of anything new and strange, and of much that is familiar to him, none of which any longer inspires fear in us. It would also correspond to our expectations if the phobias of children were, at least in part, such as might be attributed to those primeval periods of human development.

On the other hand, it cannot be overlooked that children are not all equally apprehensive, and that the very children who are more than usually timid in the face of all kinds of objects and situations are just those who later become neurotic. The neurotic disposition is, therefore, betrayed, amongst other signs, by a marked tendency to objective anxiety; apprehensiveness rather than nervousness appears to be primary; and we arrive at the conclusion that the child, and later the adult, experiences a dread of the strength of his libido simply because he is afraid of everything. The derivation of anxiety from the libido itself would then be discarded; and investigation of the conditions of real anxiety would logically lead to the view that consciousness of personal weakness and helplessness—inferiority, as A. Adler calls it— when it is able to maintain itself into later life is the final cause of neurosis.

This sounds so simple and plausible that it has a claim on our attention. It is true that it would involve shifting the point of view from which we regard the problem of nervousness. That such feelings of inferiority do persist into later life—together with a disposition to anxiety and symptom-formation—seems so well established that much more explanation is required when, in an exceptional case, what we call *health* is the outcome. But what can be learnt from the close observation of apprehensiveness in children? The small child is first of all afraid of strange people; situations become important only on account of the people concerned in them, and objects always much later. But the child is not afraid of these strange people because he attributes evil intentions to

them, comparing their strength with his weakness and thus recognizing in them a danger to his existence, his safety, and his freedom from pain. Such a conception of a child, so suspicious and terrified of an overpowering aggressivity in the world, is a very poor sort of theoretical construction. On the contrary, the child starts back in fright from a strange figure because is used to—and therefore expects— a beloved and familiar figure, primarily his mother. It is his disappointment and longing which are transformed into dread—his libido, unable to be expended, and at that time not to be held suspended, is discharged through being converted into dread. It can hardly be a coincidence, too, that in this situation, which is the prototype of childish anxiety, the condition of the primary anxiety state during birth, a separation from the mother, is again reproduced.

The first phobias of situations in children concern darkness and loneliness; the former is often retained throughout life; common to both is the desire for the absent attendant, for the mother, therefore. I once heard a child who was afraid of the darkness call out: "Auntie, talk to me, I'm frightened." "But what good will that do? You can't see me"; to which the child replied: "If someone talks, it gets lighter." The longing felt *in* the darkness is thus transformed into fear of the darkness. Far from finding that neurotic anxiety is only secondary and a special case of objective anxiety, we see on the contrary that there is something in the small child which behaves like real anxiety and has an essential feature in common with neurotic anxiety—namely, origin in undischarged libido. Of genuine *objective anxiety* the child seems to bring very little into the world. In all those situations which can become the conditions of phobias later, on heights, on narrow bridges over water, in trains and boats, the small child shows no fear—the less it knows the less it fears. It is much to be wished that it inherited more of these life-preserving instincts; the task of looking after it and preventing it from exposing itself to one danger after another would have been very much lightened. Actually, you see, a child overestimates his powers, to begin with, and behaves without fear because he does not recognize dangers. He will run along the edge of the water, climb upon the window-sill, play with sharp things and with fire, in short, do anything that injures him and alarms his attendants. Since he cannot be allowed to learn it himself through bitter experience, it is entirely due to training that real anxiety does eventually awake in him.

Now if some children embrace this training in apprehensiveness very readily, and then find for themselves dangers which they have not been warned against, it is explicable on the ground that these children have inherently a greater amount of libidinal need in their constitution than others, or else that they have been spoiled early with libidinal gratifications. It is no wonder if those who later become nervous also belong to this type as children; we know that the most favourable circumstance for the development of a neurosis lies in the inability to tolerate a considerable degree of pent-up libido for any length of time. You will observe now that here the constitutional factor, which we have never denied, comes into its own. We protest only when others emphasize it to the exclusion of all other claims, and when they introduce the constitutional factor even where according to the unanimous findings both of observation and of analysis, it does not belong, or only plays a minor part.

Let us sum up the conclusions drawn from the observation of apprehensiveness in children: Infantile dread has very little to do with objective anxiety (dread of real danger), but is, on the other hand, closely allied to the neurotic anxiety of adults. It is derived, like the latter, from undischarged libido, and it substitutes some other external object or some situation for the love-object which it misses.

Now you will be glad to hear that the analysis of phobias has little more to teach us than we have learnt already. The same thing happens in them as in the anxiety of children; libido that cannot be discharged is continuously being converted into an apparently *objective* anxiety, and so an insignificant external danger is taken as a representative of what the libido desires. The agreement between the two forms of anxiety is not surprising; for infantile phobias are not merely prototypes of those which appear later in anxiety-hysteria, but they are a direct preliminary condition and prelude of them. Every hysterical phobia can be traced back to a childish dread, of which it is a continuation, even if it has a different content and must be called by a different name. The difference between the two conditions lies in their mechanism. In order that the libido should be converted into anxiety in the adult, it is no longer sufficient that the libido should be momentarily unable to be utilized. The adult has long since learned to maintain such libido suspended, or to apply it in different ways. But, when the libido is attached to a mental excitation which has undergone repression, conditions similar to those in the child, in whom there is not yet any distinction between conscious and unconscious, are re-established; and, by a regression to the infantile phobia, a bridge, so to speak, is provided by which the conversion of libido into anxiety can be conveniently effected. As you will remember, we have treated repression at some length, but in so doing we have been concerned exclusively with the fate of the *idea* to be repressed; naturally, because this was easier to recognize and to present. But we have so far ignored the question of what happened to the *affect* attached to this idea, and now we learn for the first time that it is the immediate fate of the affect to be converted into anxiety, no matter what quality of affect it would otherwise have been had it run a normal course. This transformation of affect is, moreover, by far the more important effect of the process of repression. It is not so easy to present to you; for we cannot maintain the existence of unconscious affects in the same sense as that of unconscious ideas. An idea remains up to a point the same whether it is conscious or unconscious; we can indicate something that corresponds to an unconscious idea. But an affect is a process involving a discharge of energy, and it is to be regarded quite differently from an idea; without searching examination and clarification of our hypotheses concerning mental processes, we cannot tell what corresponds with it in the unconscious— and that cannot be undertaken here. However, we will preserve the impression we have gained, that the development of anxiety is closely connected with the unconscious system.

I said that conversion into anxiety, or better, discharge in the form of anxiety, was the immediate fate of libido which encounters repression; I must add that it is not the only or the final fate of it. In the neuroses, processes take place which are intended to prevent the development of anxiety, and which succeed in so doing by various means. In the phobias, for instance, two stages in the neurotic process are clearly discernible. The first effects the repressions and conversion of the libido into anxiety which is then attached to some external danger. The second consists in building up all those precautions and safeguards by which all contact with this externalized danger shall be avoided. Repression is an attempt at flight on the part of the ego from the libido, which it feels to be dangerous; the phobia may be compared to a fortification against the outer danger, which now stands for the dreaded libido. The weakness of this defensive system in the phobias is, of course, that the fortress which is so well guarded from without remains exposed to danger from within; projection externally of danger from libido can never be a very successful measure. In the other neuroses, therefore, other defensive systems are employed against the possibility of the development of anxiety; this is a very interesting part of the psychology of the neuroses. Unfortunately it would take us too far afield and also it would require a thorough grounding in special knowledge of the subject. I will merely add this. I have already spoken of the *counter-charges* that are instituted by the ego upon repression, which must be maintained so that the repression can persist. It is the task of this counter-charge to carry out the various forms of defence against the development of anxiety after repression.

To return to the phobias: I may now hope that you realize how inadequate it is to attempt merely to explain their content, and to take no interest in them apart from their derivation—this or that object or situation which has been made into a phobia. The content of the phobia has an importance comparable to that of the manifest dream—it is a façade. With all due modifications, it is to be admitted that among the contents of the various phobias many are found which, as Stanley Hall points out, are specially suited by phylogenetic inheritance to become objects of dread. It is even in agreement with this that many of these dreaded things have no connection with danger, except through a *symbolic* relation to it.

Thus we are convinced of the quite central position which the problem of anxiety fills in the psychology of the neuroses. We have received a strong impression of how the development of anxiety is bound up with the fate of the libido and with the unconscious system. There is only one unconnected thread, only one gap in our structure, the fact, which after all can hardly be disputed, that *objective anxiety* must be regarded as an expression of the ego's instinct for self-preservation.

TWENTY-SIXTH LECTURE
THE THEORY OF THE LIBIDO: NARCISSISM

WE have repeatedly, and again quite recently, referred to the distinction between the sexual and the ego-instincts. First of all, repression showed how they can oppose each other, how the sexual instincts are then apparently brought to submission, and required to procure their satisfaction by circuitous regressive paths, where in their impregnability they obtain compensation for their defeat. Then it appeared that from the outset they each have a different relation to the task-mistress Necessity, so that their developments are different and they acquire different attitudes to the reality-principle. Finally we believe we can observe that the sexual instincts are connected by much closer ties with the affective state of anxiety than are the ego-instincts—a conclusion which in one important point only still seems incomplete. In support of it we may bring forward the further remarkable fact that want of satisfaction of hunger or thirst, the two most elemental of the self-preservative instincts, never results in conversion of them into anxiety, whereas the conversion of unsatisfied libido into anxiety is, as we have heard, a very well-known and frequently observed phenomenon.

Our justification for distinguishing between sexual and ego-instincts can surely not be contested; it is indeed assumed by the existence of the sexual instinct as a special activity in the individual. The only question is what significance is to be attached to this distinction, how radical and decisive we intend to consider it. The answer to this depends upon what we can ascertain about the extent to which the sexual instincts, both in their bodily and their mental manifestations, conduct themselves differently from the other instincts which we set against them; and how important the results arising from these differences are found to be. We have, of course, no motive for maintaining any difference in the fundamental nature of the two groups of instincts, and, by the way, it would be difficult to apprehend any. They both present themselves to us merely as descriptions of the sources of energy in the individual, and the discussion whether fundamentally they are one, or essentially different, and if one, when they became separated from each other, cannot be carried through on the basis of these concepts alone, but must be grounded on the biological facts underlying them. At present we know too little about this, and even if we knew more it would not be relevant to the task of psycho-analysis.

We should clearly, also, profit very little by emphasizing the primordial unity of all the instincts, as Jung has done, and describing all the energies which flow from them as *libido*.

We should then be compelled to speak of sexual and asexual libido, since the sexual function is not to be eliminated from the field of mental life by any such device. The name *libido*, however, remains properly reserved for the instinctual forces of the sexual life, as we have hitherto employed it.

In my opinion, therefore, the question how far the quite justifiable distinction between sexual and self-preservative instincts is to be carried has not much importance for psycho-analysis, nor is psycho-analysis competent to deal with it. From the biological point of view, there are certainly various indications that the distinction is important. For the sexual function is the only function of a living organism which extends beyond the individual and secures its connection with its species. It is undeniable that the exercise of this function does not always bring advantage to the individual, as do his other activities, but that, for the sake of an exceptionally high degree of pleasure, he is involved by this function in dangers which jeopardize his life and often enough exact it. Quite peculiar metabolic processes, different from all others, are probably required in order to preserve a portion of the individual's life as a disposition for posterity. And finally, the individual organism that regards itself as first in importance and its sexuality as a means like any other to its own satisfaction is, from a biological point of view, only an episode in a series of generations, a short-lived appendage to a germ-plasm which is endowed with virtual immortality, comparable to the temporary holder of an entail that will survive his death.

We are not concerned with such far-reaching considerations, however, in the psycho-analytic elucidation of the neuroses. By means of following up the distinction between the sexual and the ego-instincts we have gained the key to comprehension of the group of transference neuroses. We were able to trace back their origin to a fundamental situation in which the sexual instincts had come into conflict with the self-preservative instincts, or—to express it biologically, though at the same time less exactly —in which the ego in its capacity of independent individual organism had entered into opposition with itself in its other capacity as a member of a series of generations. Such a dissociation perhaps only exists in man, so that, taken all in all, his superiority over the other animals may come down to his capacity for neurosis. The excessive development of his libido and the rich elaboration of his mental

life (perhaps directly made possible by it) seem to constitute the conditions which give rise to a conflict of this kind. It is at any rate clear that these are the conditions under which man has progressed so greatly beyond what he has in common with the animals, so that his capacity for neurosis would merely be the obverse of his capacity for cultural development. However, these again are but speculations which distract us from the task in hand.

Our work so far has been conducted on the assumption that the manifestations of the sexual and the ego-instincts can be distinguished from one another. In the transference neuroses this is possible without any difficulty. We called the investments of energy directed by the ego towards the object of its sexual desires *libido*, and all the other investments proceeding from the self-preservative instincts its *interest;* and by following up the investments with libido, their transformations, and their final fates, we were able to acquire our first insight into the workings of the forces in mental life. The transference neuroses offered the best material for this exploration. The ego, however—its composition out of various organizations with their structure and mode of functioning—remained undiscovered; we were led to believe that analysis of other neurotic disturbances would be required before light could be gained on these matters.

The extension of psycho-analytic conceptions on to these other affections was begun in early days. Already in 1908, K. Abraham expressed the view after a discussion with me that the main characteristic of dementia praecox (reckoned as one of the psychoses) is that in this disease *the investments of objects with libido is lacking. (The Psycho-Sexual Differences between Hysteria and Dementia Praecox)*. But then the question arose: what happens to the libido of dementia patients when it is diverted from its objects? Abraham did not hesitate to answer that it is turned back upon the ego, and that *this reflex reversion of it is the source of the delusions of grandeur in dementia praecox*. The delusion of grandeur is in every way comparable to the well-known overestimation of the object in a love-relationship. Thus we come for the first time to understand a feature of a psychotic affection by bringing it into relation to the normal mode of loving in life.

I will tell you at once that these early views of Abraham's have been retained in psycho-analysis and have become the basis of our position regarding the psychoses. We became slowly accustomed to the conception that the libido, which we find attached to certain objects and which is the expression of a desire to gain some satisfaction in these objects, can also abandon these objects and set the ego itself in their place; and gradually this view developed itself more and more consistently. The name for this utilization of the libido—NARCISSISM—we borrowed from a perversion described by P. Näcke, in which an adult individual lavishes upon his own body all the caresses usually expended only upon a sexual object other than himself.

Reflection, then, at once disclosed that, if a fixation of this kind to the subject's own body and his own person can occur, it cannot be an entirely exceptional or meaningless phenomenon. On the contrary, it is probable that this *narcissism* is the universal original condition, out of which *object-love* develops later without thereby necessarily effecting a disappearance of the narcissism. One also had to remember the evolution of object-libido, in which to begin with many of the sexual impulses are gratified on the child's own body—as we say, auto-erotically—and that this capacity for auto-erotism accounts for the backwardness of sexuality in learning to conform to the reality-principle. Thus it appeared that auto-erotism was the sexual activity of the narcissistic phase of direction of the libido.

To put it briefly, we formed an idea of the relation between the ego-libido and the object-libido which I can illustrate to you by a comparison taken from zoology. Think of the simplest forms of life consisting of a little mass of only slightly differentiated protoplasmic substances. They extend protrusions which are called *pseudopodia* into which the protoplasm overflows. They can, however, again withdraw these extensions of themselves and re-form themselves into a mass. We compare this extending of protrusions to the radiation of libido on to the objects, while the greatest volume of libido may yet remain within the ego; we infer that under normal conditions ego-libido can transform itself into object-libido without difficulty and that this can again subsequently be absorbed into the ego.

With the help of these conceptions it is now possible to explain a whole series of mental states, or, to express it more modestly, to describe in terms of the libido-theory conditions that belong to normal life; for instance, the mental attitude pertaining to the conditions of "being in love," of organic illness, and of sleep. Of the condition of sleep we assumed that it is

founded upon a withdrawal from the outer world and a concentration upon the wish to sleep. We found that the nocturnal mental activity which is expressed in dreams served the purpose of the wish to sleep, and, moreover, that it was governed exclusively by egoistic motives. In the light of the libido-theory we may carry this further and say that sleep is a condition in which all investments of objects, the libidinal as well as the egoistic are abandoned and withdrawn again into the ego. Does not this shed a new light upon the recuperation afforded by sleep and upon the nature of fatigue in general? The likeness we see in the condition which the sleeper conjures up again every night to the blissful isolation of the intra-uterine existence is thus confirmed and amplified in its mental aspects. In the sleeper the primal state of the libido-distribution is again reproduced, that of absolute narcissism, in which libido and ego-interests dwell together still, united and indistinguishable in the self-sufficient self.

Two observations are in place here. First, how is the concept *narcissism* distinguished from *egoism?* In my opinion, narcissism is the libidinal complement of egoism. When one speaks of egoism one is thinking only of the *interests* of the person concerned, narcissism relates also to the satisfaction of his libidinal needs. It is possible to follow up the two separately for a considerable distance as practical motives in life. A man may be absolutely egoistic and yet have strong libidinal attachments to objects, in so far as libidinal satisfaction in an object is a need of his ego: his egoism will then see to it that his desires towards the object involve no injury to his ego. A man may be egoistic and at the same time strongly narcissistic (i.e., feel very little need for objects), and this again either in the form taken by the need for direct sexual satisfaction, or in those higher forms of feeling derived from the sexual needs which are commonly called *love,* and as such are contrasted with *sensuality.* In all these situations egoism is the self-evident, the constant element, and narcissism the variable one. The antithesis of egoism, *altruism,* is not an alternative term for the investment of an object with libido; it is distinct from the latter in its lack of the desire for sexual satisfaction in the object. But when the condition of love is developed to its fullest intensity, altruism coincides with the investment of an object with libido. As a rule, the sexual object draws to itself a portion of the ego's narcissism, which becomes apparent in what is called the *sexual overestimation* of the object. If to this is added an altruism directed towards the object and derived from the egoism of the lover, the sexual object becomes supreme; it has entirely swallowed up the ego.

I think you will find it a relief if, after these scientific phantasies, which are after all very dry, I submit to you a poetic description of the *economic* contrast between the condition of narcissism and that of love in full intensity. I take it from a dialogue between Zuleika and her lover in Goethe's *Westöstliche Divan:*

Zuleika
The slave, the lord of victories,
The crowd, with single voice, confess
In sense of personal being lies
A child of earth's true happiness.
There's not a life he need refuse
If his true self he does not miss:
There's not a thing he cannot lose
If he remains the man he is.

Hâtem
So it is held! so well may be!
But down a different track I come
Of all the bliss earth holds for me
I in Zuleika find the sum.
Does she expend her being on me,
Myself grows to myself of cost;
Turns she away, then instantly
I to my very self am lost.
And then with Hâtem all were over;
Though yet I should but change my state
Swift, should she grace some happy lover,
In him I were incorporate.[1]

The second observation is an amplification of the theory of dreams. The way in which a dream originates is not explicable unless we assume that what is repressed in the unconscious has acquired a certain independence of the ego, so that it does not subordinate itself to the wish for sleep and maintains its investments, although all the object-investments proceeding from the ego have been withdrawn for the purpose of sleep. Only this makes it possible to understand how it is that this unconscious material can make use of the abrogation or diminution in the activities of the censorship which takes place at night, and that it knows how to mould the day's residue so as to form a forbidden dream-wish from the ma-

terial to hand in that residue. On the other hand, some of the resistance against the wish to sleep, and the withdrawal of libido thereby induced, may have its origin in an association already in existence between this residue and the repressed unconscious material. This important dynamic factor must, therefore, now be incorporated into the conception of dream-formation which we formed in our earlier discussions.

Certain conditions—organic illness, painful accesses of stimulation, an inflammatory condition of an organ—have clearly the effect of loosening the libido from its attachment to its objects. The libido, which has thus been withdrawn, attaches itself again to the ego in the form of a stronger investment of the diseased region of the body. Indeed, one may venture the assertion that in such conditions the withdrawal of the libido from its objects is more striking than the withdrawal of the egoistic interests from their concerns in the outer world. This seems to lead to a possibility of understanding hypochondria, in which some organ, without being perceptibly diseased, becomes in a very similar way the subject of solicitude on the part of the ego. I shall, however, resist the temptation to follow this up, or to discuss other situations which become explicable or capable of exposition on this assumption of a return of the object-libido into the ego; for I feel bound to meet two objections which I know have all your attention at the moment. First of all, you want to know why when I discuss sleep, illness, and similar conditions, I insist upon distinguishing between libido and interests, sexual instincts and ego-instincts, while the observations are satisfactorily explained by assuming a single uniform energy which is freely mobile, can invest either object or ego, and can serve the purposes of the one as well as of the other. Secondly, you will want to know how I can be so bold as to treat the detachment of the libido from its objects as the origin of a pathological condition, if such a transformation of object-libido into ego-libido —or into ego-energy in general—is a normal mental process repeated every day and every night.

The answer is: Your first objection sounds a good one. Examination of the conditions of sleep, illness, and falling in love would probably never have led to a distinction between ego-libido and object-libido, or between libido and interests. But in this you omit to take into account the investigations with which we start-

[1] Taken, with very slight modifications, from Edward Dowden's translation.—TR.

ed, in the light of which we now regard the mental situations under discussion. The necessity of distinguishing between libido and interests, between sexual and self-preservative instincts, has been forced upon us by our insight into the conflict from which the transference neuroses arise. We have to reckon with this distinction henceforth. The assumption that object-libido can transform itself into ego-libido, in other words, that we shall also have to reckon with an ego-libido, appears to be the only one capable of solving the riddle of what are called the narcissistic neuroses, e.g., dementia praecox, or of giving any satisfactory explanation of their likeness to hysteria and obsessions and differences from them. We then apply what we have found undeniably proved in these cases to illness, sleep, and the condition of intense love. We are at liberty to apply them in any direction and see where they will take us. The single conclusion which is not directly based on analytical experience is that libido is libido and remains so, whether it is attached to objects or to the ego itself, and is never transformed into egoistic interests, and vice versa. This statement, however, is another way of expressing the distinction between sexual instincts and ego-instincts which we have already critically examined, and which we shall hold to from heuristic motives until such time as it may prove valueless.

Your second objection, too, raises a justifiable question, but it is directed to a false issue. The withdrawal of object-libido into the ego is certainly not pathogenic; it is true that it occurs every night before sleep can ensue, and that the process is reversed upon awakening. The protoplasmic animalcule draws in its protrusions and sends them out again at the next opportunity. But it is quite a different matter when a definite, very forcible process compels the withdrawal of the libido from its objects. The libido that has then become narcissistic can no longer find its way back to its objects, and this obstruction in the way of the free movement of the libido certainly does prove pathogenic. It seems that an accumulation of narcissistic libido over and above a certain level becomes intolerable. We might well imagine that it was this that first led to the investment of objects, that the ego was obliged to send forth its libido in order not to fall ill of an excessive accumulation of it. If it were part of our scheme to go more particularly into the disorder of dementia praecox I would show you that the process which detaches the libido

from its objects and blocks the way back to them again is closely allied to the process of repression, and is to be regarded as a counterpart of it. In any case you would recognize familiar ground under your feet when you found that the preliminary conditions giving rise to these processes are almost identical, so far as we know at present, with those of repression. The conflict seems to be the same and to be conducted between the same forces. Since the outcome is so different from that of hysteria, for instance, the reason can only lie in some difference in the disposition. The weak point in the libido-development in these patients is found at a different phase of the development; the decisive fixation which, as you will remember, enables the process of symptom-formation to break out is at another point, probably at the stage of primary narcissism, to which dementia praecox finally returns. It is most remarkable that for all the narcissistic neuroses we have to assume fixation-points of the libido at very much earlier phases of development than those found in hysteria or the obsessional neurosis. You have heard, however, that the concepts we have elicited from the study of the transference neuroses also suffice to show us our bearings in the narcissistic neuroses, which are in practice so much more severe. There is a very wide community between them; fundamentally they are phenomena of a single class. You may imagine how hopeless a task it is for anyone to attempt to explain these disorders (which properly belong to psychiatry) without being first equipped with the analytic knowledge of the transference neuroses.

The picture formed by the symptoms of dementia praecox, incidentally a very variable one, is not determined exclusively by the symptoms arising from the forcing of the libido back from the objects and the accumulation of it as narcissism in the ego. Other phenomena occupy a large part of the field, and may be traced to the efforts made by the libido to reach its objects again, which correspond therefore to attempts at restitution and recovery. These are in fact the conspicuous, clamorous symptoms; they exhibit a marked similarity to those of hysteria, or more rarely of the obsessional neurosis; they are nevertheless different in every respect. It seems that in dementia praecox the efforts of the libido to get back to its objects, that is, to the mental idea of its objects, do really succeed in conjuring up something of them, something that at the same time is only the shadow of them—namely, the verbal images, the words, attached to them. This is not the place to discuss this matter further, but in my opinion this reversed procedure on the part of the libido gives us an insight into what constitutes the real difference between a conscious and an unconscious idea.

This has now brought us into the field where the next advances in analytic work are to be expected. Since the time when we resolved upon our formulation of the conception of ego-libido, the narcissistic neuroses have become accessible to us; the task before us was to find the dynamic factors in these disorders, and at the same time to amplify our knowledge of mental life by a comprehension of the ego. The psychology of the ego, at which we are aiming, cannot be founded upon data provided by our own self-perceptions; it must be based, as is that of the libido, upon analysis of the disturbances and disintegrations of the ego. We shall probably think very little of our present knowledge of the fate of the libido, gained from the study of the transference neuroses, when that further, greater work has been achieved. But as yet we have not got very far towards it. The narcissistic neuroses can hardly be approached at all by the method which has availed for the transference neuroses; you shall soon hear why this is. With these patients it always happens that, after one has penetrated a little way, one comes up against a stone wall which cannot be surmounted. You know that in the transference neuroses, too, barriers of resistance of this kind are met with, but that it is possible bit by bit to pull them down. In the narcissistic neuroses the resistance is insuperable; at the most we can satisfy our curiosity by craning our necks for a glimpse or two at what is going on over the wall. Our technique will, therefore, have to be replaced by other methods; at present we do not know whether we shall succeed in finding a substitute. There is no lack of material with these patients; they bring forward a great deal, although not in answer to our questions; at present all we can do is to interpret what they say in the light of the understanding gained from the study of the transference neuroses. The agreement between the two forms of disease goes far enough to ensure us a satisfactory start with them. How much we shall be able to achieve by this method remains to be seen.

There are other difficulties, besides this, in the way of our progress. The narcissistic disorders and the psychoses related to them can only be unriddled by observers trained in the analytic study of the transference neuroses. But our psychiatrists do not study psycho-analysis and we psycho-analysts see too little of psychiatric cases. We shall have to develop a breed of psychiatrists who have gone through the training of psycho-analysis as a preparatory science. A beginning in this direction is being made in America, where several of the leading psychiatrists lecture on psycho-analytic doctrines to their students, and where medical superintendents of institutions and asylums endeavour to observe their patients in the light of this theory. But all the same it has sometimes been possible for us here to take a peep over the wall of narcissism, so I will now proceed to tell you what we think we have discovered in this way.

The disease of paranoia, a chronic form of systematic insanity, has a very uncertain position in the attempts at classification made by present-day psychiatry. There is no doubt, however, that it is closely related to dementia praecox; I have in fact proposed that they should both be included under the common designation of *paraphrenia*. The forms taken by paranoia are described according to the content of the delusion, e.g., delusions of grandeur, of persecution, of jealousy, of being loved (erotomania), etc. We do not expect attempts at explanation from psychiatry; as an example, an antiquated and not very fair example, I grant, I will tell you the attempt which was made to derive one of these symptoms from another, by means of a piece of intellectual rationalization: The patient who has a primary tendency to believe himself persecuted draws from this the conclusion that he must necessarily be a very important person and therefore develops a delusion of grandeur. According to our analytic conception, the delusion of grandeur is the direct consequence of the inflation of the ego by the libido withdrawn from the investment of objects, a secondary narcissism ensuing as a return of the original early infantile form. In the case of delusions of persecution, however, we observed things which led us to follow up a certain clue. In the first place we noticed that in the great majority of cases the persecuting person was of the same sex as the persecuted one; this was capable of a harmless explanation, it is true, but in certain cases which were closely studied it appeared that the person of the same sex who had been most beloved while the patient was normal became the persecutor after the disease broke out. A further development of this becomes possible through the well-known paths of association by which a loved person may be replaced by someone else, e.g., the father by masters or persons in authority. From these observations, which were continually corroborated, we drew the conclusion that persecutory paranoia is the means by which a person defends himself against a homosexual impulse which has become too powerful. The conversion of the affectionate feeling into the hate which, as is well-known, can seriously endanger the life of the loved and hated object then corresponds to the conversion of libidinal impulses into anxiety, which is a regular result of the process of repression. As an illustration I will quote the last case I had of this type. A young doctor had to be sent away from the place where he lived because he had threatened the life of the son of a university professor there who had previously been his greatest friend. He imputed superhuman power and the most devilish intentions to this friend; he was to blame for all the misfortunes which had occurred in recent years to the family of the patient and for all his ill-luck in public and in private. This was not enough, however; the wicked friend and his father, the professor, had caused the war and brought the Russians over the border; he had ruined his life in a thousand ways; our patient was convinced that the death of this criminal would be the end of all evil in the world. And yet his old love for him was still so strong that it had paralysed his hand when he had an opportunity of shooting his enemy at sight. In the short conversation which I had with the patient it came to light that this intimate friendship between the two men went right back to their school-days; on at least one occasion it had passed beyond the boundaries of friendship, a night spent together had been the occasion of complete sexual intercourse. The patient had never developed any of the feeling towards women that would have been natural at his age with his attractive personality. He had been engaged to a handsome, well-connected girl, but she had broken off the engagement because her lover was so cold. Years after, his disease broke out at the very moment when he had for the first time succeeded in giving full sexual gratification to a woman; as she encircled him in her arms in gratitude and devotion he suddenly felt a mysterious stab of pain running like a sharp knife round the crown of his head. Afterwards he described the sensation as being like that of the incision made at a post-mortem to bare the brain; and as his friend was a pathological anatomist he slowly came to the conclusion that he alone could have sent him this woman as a temptation. Then his eyes began to be opened about the other persecutions of which he had been the victim by the machinations of his former friend.

But how about those cases in which the persecutor is of a different sex from that of the persecuted one, and which appear therefore to contradict our explanation of this disease as a defence against homosexual libido? Some time ago I had an opportunity of examining a case of the kind, and behind the apparent contradiction I was able to elicit a confirmation. A young girl imagined herself persecuted by a man with whom she had twice had intimate relations; actually she had first of all cherished the delusions against a woman who could be recognized to be a mother-substitute. Not until after the second meeting with him did she make the advance of transferring the delusional idea from the woman to the man; so that in this case also the condition that the sex of the persecutor is the same as that of the victim originally held good also. In her complaint to the lawyer and the doctor the patient had not mentioned the previous phase of her delusion and this gave rise to an apparent contradiction of our theory of paranoia.

The homosexual choice of object is originally more closely related to narcissism than the heterosexual; hence, when a strong unwelcome homosexual excitation suffers repudiation, the way back to narcissism is especially easy to find. I have so far had very little opportunity in these lectures of speaking about the fundamental plan on which the course of the love-impulse during life is based, so far as we know it; nor can I supplement it now. I will only select this to tell you: that the choice of object, the step forward in the development of the libido which comes after the narcissistic stage, can proceed according to two types. These are: either *the narcissistic type,* according to which, in place of the ego itself, someone as nearly as possible resembling it is adopted as an object; or *the anaclitic type (Anlehnungstypus)*[1] in which those persons who became prized on account of the satisfactions they rendered to the primal needs in life are chosen as objects by the libido also. A strong libido-fixation on the

[1] This name refers to the *dependence* of the sexual instincts on the self-preservative instincts for their first object, i.e., the suckling mother —TR.

narcissistic type of object-choice is also found as a trait in the disposition of manifest homosexuals.

You will remember that in the first lecture given this session I described to you a case of delusional jealousy in a woman. Now that we have so nearly reached the end you will certainly want to know how we account for a delusion psycho-analytically. I have less to say about it than you would expect, however. The inaccessibility of delusions to logical arguments and to actual experience is to be explained, as it is with obsessions, by the connection they bear to the unconscious material which is both expressed by, and held in check by, the delusion or the obsession. The differences between the two are based on the topographical and dynamic differences in the two affections.

As with paranoia, so also with melancholia (under which, by the way, very different clinical types are classified), it has been possible to obtain a glimpse into the inner structure of the disorder. We have perceived that the self-reproaches with which these sufferers torment themselves so mercilessly actually relate to another person, to the sexual object they have lost or whom they have ceased to value on account of some fault. From this we concluded that the melancholic has indeed withdrawn his libido from the object, but that by a process which we must call *narcissistic identification* he has set up the object within the ego itself, projected it on to the ego. I can only give you a descriptive representation of this process, and not one expressed in terms of topography and dynamics. The ego itself is then treated as though it were the abandoned object; it suffers all the revengeful and aggressive treatment which is designed for the object. The suicidal impulses of melancholics also become more intelligible on the supposition that the bitterness felt by the diseased mind concerns the ego itself at the same time as, and equally with, the loved and hated objects. In melancholia, as in the other narcissistic disorders, a feature of the emotional life which, after Bleuler, we are accustomed to call *ambivalence* comes markedly to the fore; by this we mean a directing of antithetical feelings (affectionate and hostile) towards the same person. It is unfortunate that I have not been able to say more about ambivalence in these lectures.

There is also, besides the narcissistic, an hysterical form of identification which has long been known to us. I wish it were possible to make the differences between them clear to you in a few definite statements. I can tell you something of the periodic and cyclic forms of melancholia which will interest you. It is possible in favourable circumstances—I have twice achieved it—to prevent the recurrence of the condition, or of its antithesis, by analytic treatment during the lucid intervals between the attacks. One learns from this that in melancholia and mania as well as other conditions a special kind of solution of a conflict is going on, which in all its pre-requisites agrees with those of the other neuroses. You may imagine how much there remains for psycho-analysis to do in this field.

I also told you that, by analysis of the narcissistic disorders, we hoped to gain some knowledge of the composition of the ego and of its structure out of various faculties and elements. We have made a beginning towards this at one point. From analysis of the delusion of observation we have come to the conclusion that in the ego there exists a faculty that incessantly watches, criticizes, and compares, and in this way is set against the other part of the ego. In our opinion, therefore, the patient reveals a truth which has not been appreciated as such when he complains that at every step he is spied upon and observed, that his very thought is known and examined. He has erred only in attributing this disagreeable power to something outside himself and foreign to him; he perceives within his ego the rule of a faculty which measures his actual ego and all his activities by an *ego-ideal*, which he has created for himself in the course of his development. We also infer that he created this ideal for the purpose of recovering thereby the self-satisfaction bound up with the primary infantile narcissism, which since those days has suffered so many shocks and mortification. We recognize in this self-criticizing faculty the ego-censorship, the *conscience;* it is the same censorship as that exercised at night upon dreams, from which the repressions against inadmissible wish-excitations proceed. When this faculty disintegrates in the delusion of being observed, we are able to detect its origin and that it arose out of the influence of parents and those who trained the child, together with his social surroundings, by a process of identification with certain of these persons who were taken as a model.

These are some of the results yielded by the application of psycho-analysis to the narcissistic disorders. They are still not very numerous, and many of them still lack that sharpness of outline which cannot be achieved in a new field until some degree of familiarity has been attained. All of them have been made possible by employing the conception of ego-libido, or narcissistic libido, by means of which we can extend the conclusions established for the transference neuroses on to the narcissistic neuroses. But now you will put the question whether it is possible for us to bring all the disorders of the narcissistic neuroses and of the psychoses into the range of the libido-theory, for us to find the libidinal factor in mental life always and everywhere responsible for the development of disease, and for us never to have to attribute any part in the causation to the same alteration in the functions of the self-preservative instincts. Well now, it seems to me that decision on this point is not very urgent, and above all that the time is not yet ripe for us to make it; we may leave it calmly to be decided by advance in the work of science. I should not be astonished if it should prove that the capacity to induce a pathogenic effect were actually a prerogative of the libidinal impulses, so that the theory of the libido would triumph all along the line from the actual neuroses to the severest psychotic form of individual derangement. For we know it to be characteristic of the libido that it refuses to subordinate itself to reality in life, to necessity. But I consider it extremely probable that the ego-instincts are involved secondarily and that disturbances in their functions may be necessitated by the pathogenic affections of the libido. Nor can I see that the direction taken by our investigations will be invalidated if we should have to recognize that in severe psychosis the ego-instincts themselves are primarily deranged; the future will decide —for you, at least.

Let me return for a moment to anxiety, in order to throw light upon the one obscure point we left there. We said that the relation between anxiety and libido, otherwise so well defined, is with difficulty harmonized with the almost indisputable assumption that objective anxiety in the face of danger is the expression of the self-preservative instincts. But how if the anxiety-affect is provided, not by self-interest on the part of the ego-instincts, but by the ego-libido? The condition of anxiety is after all invariably detrimental; its disadvantage becomes conspicuous when it reaches an intense degree. It then interferes with the

action that alone would be expedient and would serve the purposes of self-preservation, whether it be flight or self-defence. Therefore if we ascribe the affective component of objective anxiety to the ego-libido, and the action undertaken to the ego-preservative instincts, every theoretical difficulty will be overcome. You will hardly maintain seriously that we run away *because* we perceive fear? No, we perceive fear *and* we take to flight, out of the common impulse that is roused by the perception of danger. Men who have survived experiences of imminent danger to life tell us that they did not perceive any fear, that they simply acted— for instance, pointed their gun at the oncoming beast—which was undoubtedly the best thing they could do.

TWENTY-SEVENTH LECTURE
TRANSFERENCE

Now that we are coming to the end of our discussions you will feel a certain expectation which must not be allowed to mislead you. You are probably thinking that I surely have not led you through all these complicated mazes of psycho-analysis only to dismiss you at the end without a word about the therapy, upon which after all the possibility of undertaking psycho-analytic work depends. As a matter of fact I could not possibly leave out this aspect of it; for some of the phenomena belonging to it will teach you a new fact, without knowledge of which you would be quite unable to assimilate properly your understanding of the diseases we have been studying.

I know you do not expect directions in the technique of practising analysis for therapeutic purposes; you only want to know in a general way by what means the psycho-analytic therapy works and to gain a general idea of what it accomplishes. And you have an undeniable right to learn this; nevertheless I am not going to tell you—I am going to insist upon your finding out for yourselves.

Think for a moment! You have already learnt everything essential, from the conditions by which illness is provoked to all the factors which take effect within the diseased mind. Where is the opening in all this for therapeutic influence? First of all there is the hereditary disposition—we do not often mention it because it is so strongly emphasized in other quarters and we have nothing new to say about it. But do not suppose that we underestimate it; as practitioners, we are well aware of its power. In any event we can do nothing to change it; for us also it is a fixed datum in the problem, which sets a limit to our efforts. Next, there is the influence of the experiences of childhood, which we are accustomed in analysis to rank as very important; they belong to the past, we cannot undo them. Then there is all that unhappiness in life which we have included under *frustration in reality,* from which all the absence of love in life proceeds—namely, poverty, family strife, mistaken choice in marriage, unfavourable social conditions, and the severity of the demands by which moral convention oppresses the individual. There is indeed a wide opening for a very effective treatment in all this; but it would have to follow the course of the dispensations of Kaiser Joseph in the Viennese legend—the benevolent despotism of a potentate before whose will men bow and difficulties disappear! But who are we that we can exert such beneficence as a therapeutic measure? Poor as we are and without influence socially, with our living to earn by our medical practice, we are not even in a position to extend our efforts to penniless folk, as other physicians with other methods can do; our treatment takes too much time and labour for that. But perhaps you are still clinging on to one of the factors put forward and believe you see an opening for our influence there. If the conventional restrictions imposed by society have had a part in the privations forced upon the patient, the treatment could give him the courage and even directly advise him to defy these obstacles, and to seize satisfactions and health for himself at the cost of failing to achieve an ideal which, though highly esteemed, is after all often set at naught by the world. Health is to be won by "free living," then. There would be this blot upon analysis, to be sure, that it would not be serving general morality; what it gave to the individual it would take from the rest of the world.

But now, who has given you such a false impression of analysis? It is out of the question that part of the analytic treatment should consist of advice to "live freely"—if for no other reason because we ourselves tell you that a stubborn conflict is going on in the patient between libidinal desires and sexual repression, between sensual and ascetic tendencies. This conflict is not resolved by helping one side to win a victory over the other. It is true we see that in neurotics asceticism has gained the day; the result of which is that the suppressed sexual impulses have found a vent for themselves in the symptoms. If we were to make victory possible to the sensual side instead, the disregarded forces repressing sexuality would have to indemnify themselves by symptoms. Neither of these measures will succeed in ending the inner conflict; one side in either event will remain unsatisfied. There are but few cases in which the conflict is so unstable that a factor like medical advice can have any effect upon it, and these cases do not really require analytic treatment. People who can be so easily influenced by physicians would have found their own way to that solution without this influence. After all, you know that a young man living in abstinence who makes up his mind to illicit sexual intercourse, or an unsatisfied wife who seeks compensation with a lover, does not as a rule wait for the permission of a physician, still less of an analyst, to do so.

In considering this question, people usually overlook the essential point of the whole difficulty—namely, that the pathogenic conflict in a neurotic must not be confounded with a normal struggle between conflicting impulses all of which are in the same mental field. It is a battle between two forces of which one has succeeded in coming to the level of the preconscious and conscious part of the mind, while the other has been confined on the unconscious level. That is why the conflict can never have a final outcome one way or the other; the antagonists meet each other as little as the whale and the polar bear in the well-known story. An effective decision can be reached only when they confront each other on the same ground. And, in my opinion, to accomplish this is the sole task of the treatment.

Besides this, I can assure you that you are quite misinformed if you imagine that advice and guidance concerning conduct in life forms an integral part of the analytic method. On the contrary, so far as possible we refrain from playing the part of mentor; we want nothing better than that the patient should find his own solutions for himself. To this end we expect him to postpone all vital decisions affecting his life, such as choice of career, business enterprises, marriage or divorce, during treatment and to execute them only after it has been completed. Now confess that you had imagined something very different. Only with certain very young or quite helpless and defenceless persons is it impossible to keep within such strict limitations as we should wish. With them we have to combine the positions of physician and educator; we are then well aware of our responsibility and act with the necessary caution.

You must not be led away by my eagerness to defend myself against the accusation that in analytic treatment neurotics are encouraged to "live a free life" and conclude from it that we influence them in favour of conventional morality. That is at least as far removed from our purpose as the other. We are not reformers, it is true; we are merely observers; but we cannot avoid observing with critical eyes, and we have found it impossible to give our support to conventional sexual morality or to approve highly of the means by which society attempts to arrange the practical problems of sexuality in life. We can demonstrate with ease that what the world calls its code of morals demands more sacrifices than it is worth, and that its behaviour is neither dictated by honesty nor instituted with wisdom. We do not absolve our patients from listening to these criticisms; we accustom them to an unprejudiced consideration of sexual matters like all other matters; and if after they have become independent by the effect of the treatment they choose some intermediate course between unrestrained sexual licence and unconditional asceticism, our conscience is not burdened whatever the outcome. We say to ourselves that anyone who has successfully undergone the training of learning and recognizing the truth about himself is henceforth strengthened against the dangers of immorality, even if his standard of morality should in some respect deviate from the common one. Incidentally, we must beware of overestimating the importance of abstinence in affecting neurosis; only a minority of pathogenic situations due to frustration and the subsequent accumulation of libido thereby induced can be relieved by the kind of sexual intercourse that is procurable without any difficulty.

So you cannot explain the therapeutic effect of psycho-analysis by supposing that it permits patients free sexual indulgence; you must look round for something else. I think that one of the remarks I made while I was disposing of this conjecture on your part will have put you on the right track. Probably it is the substitution of something conscious for something unconscious, the transformation of the unconscious thoughts into conscious thoughts, that makes our work effective. You are right; that is exactly what it is. By extending the unconscious into consciousness the repressions are raised, the conditions of symptom-formation are abolished, and the pathogenic conflict ex-

changed for a normal one which must be decided one way or the other. We do nothing for our patients but enable this one mental change to take place in them; the extent to which it is achieved is the extent of the benefit we do them. Where there is no repression or mental process analogous to it to be undone there is nothing for our therapy to do.

The aim of our efforts may be expressed in various formulas—making conscious the unconscious, removing the repressions, filling in the gaps in memory; they all amount to the same thing. But perhaps you are dissatisfied with this declaration; you imagined the recovery of a nervous person rather differently, that after he had been subjected to the laborious process of psycho-analysis he would emerge a different person altogether, and then you hear that the whole thing only amounts to his having a little less that is unconscious and a little more that is conscious in him than before. Well, you probably do not appreciate the importance of an inner change of this kind. A neurotic who has been cured has really become a different person, although at bottom of course he remains the same—that is, he has become his best self, what he would have been under the most favourable conditions. That, however, is a great deal. Then when you hear of all that has to be done, of the tremendous exertion required to carry out this apparently trifling change in his mental life, the significance attached to these differences between the various mental levels will appear more comprehensible to you.

I will digress a moment to enquire whether you know what *a causal therapy* means? This name is given to a procedure which puts aside the manifestations of a disease and looks for a point of attack in order to eradicate the cause of the illness. Now is psycho-analysis a causal therapy or not? The answer is not a simple one, but it may give us an opportunity to convince ourselves of the futility of such questions. In so far as psycho-analytic therapy does not aim immediately at removing the symptoms it is conducted like a causal therapy. In other respects you may say it is not, for we have followed the causal chain back far beyond the repressions to the instinctive predispositions, their relative intensity in the constitution, and the aberrations in the course of their development. Now suppose that it were possible by some chemical means to affect this mental machinery, to increase or decrease the amount of libido available at any given moment, or to reinforce the strength of one impulse at the expense of another—that would be a causal therapy in the literal sense, and our analysis would be the indispensable preliminary work of reconnoitring the ground. As you know, there is at present no question of any such influence upon the processes of the libido; our mental therapy makes its attack at another point in the concatenation, not quite at the place where we perceive the manifestations to be rooted, but yet comparatively far behind the symptoms themselves, at a place which becomes accessible to us in very remarkable circumstances.

What then have we to do in order to bring what is unconscious in the patient into consciousness? At one time we thought that would be very simple; all we need do would be to identify this unconscious matter and then tell the patient what it was. However, we know already that that was a short-sighted mistake. Our knowledge of what is unconscious in him is not equivalent to his knowledge of it; when we tell him what we know, he does not assimilate it *in place of* his own unconscious thoughts, but *alongside* of them, and very little has been changed. We have rather to regard this unconscious material topographically; we have to look for it in his memory at the actual spot where the repression of it originally ensued. This repression must be removed, and then the substitution of conscious thought for unconscious thought can be effected straightway. How is a repression such as this to be removed? Our work enters upon a second phase here; first, the discovery of the repression, and then the removal of the resistance which maintains this repression.

How can this resistance be got rid of? In the same way: by finding it out and telling the patient about it. The resistance, too, arises in a repression, either from the very one which we are endeavouring to dispel, or in one that occurred earlier. It is set up by the counter-charge which rose up to repress the repellent impulse. So that we now do just the same as we were trying to do before; we interpret, identify, and inform the patient; but this time we are doing it at the right spot. The counter-charge or the resistance is not part of the unconscious, but of the ego which co-operates with us, and this is so, even if it is not actually conscious. We know that a difficulty arises here in the ambiguity of the word *unconscious,* on the one hand, as a phenomenon, on the other hand, as a system. That sounds very obscure

and difficult; but after all it is only a repetition of what we have said before, is it not? We have come to this point already long ago. Well then, we expect that this resistance will be abandoned, and the counter-charge withdrawn, when we have made the recognition of them possible by our work of interpretation. What are the instinctive propelling forces at our disposal to make this possible? First, the patient's desire for recovery, which impelled him to submit himself to the work in co-operation with us, and secondly, the aid of his intelligence which we reinforce by our interpretation. There is no doubt that it is easier for the patient to recognize the resistance with his intelligence, and to identify the idea in his unconscious which corresponds to it, if we have first given him an idea which rouses his expectations in regard to it. If I say to you: "Look up at the sky and you will see a balloon," you will find it much more quickly than if I merely tell you to look up and see whether you can see anything; a student who looks through a microscope for the first time is told by the instructor what he is to see; otherwise he sees nothing, although it is there and quite visible.

And now for the fact! In quite a number of the various forms of nervous illness, in the hysterias, anxiety-conditions, obsessional neuroses, our hypothesis proves sound. By seeking out the repression in this way, discovering the resistances, indicating the repressed, it is actually possible to accomplish the task, to overcome the resistances, to break down the repression, and to change something unconscious into something conscious. As we do this we get a vivid impression of how, as each individual resistance is being mastered, a violent battle goes on in the soul of the patient—a normal mental struggle between two tendencies on the same ground, between the motives striving to maintain the counter-charge and those which are ready to abolish it. The first of these are the old motives which originally erected the repression; among the second are found new ones more recently acquired which it is hoped will decide the conflict in our favour. We have succeeded in revivifying the old battle of the repression again, in bringing the issue, so long ago decided, up for revision again. The new contribution we make to it lies, first of all, in demonstrating that the original solution led to illness and in promising that a different one would pave the way to health, and secondly, in pointing out that the circumstances have all changed immensely since the time of that original repudiation of these impulses. Then the ego was weak, infantile, and perhaps had reason to shrink with horror from the claims of the libido as being dangerous to it. Today it is strong and experienced and moreover has a helper at hand in the physician. So we may expect to lead the revived conflict through a better outcome than repression; and, as has been said, in hysteria, anxiety-neurosis, and the obsessional neurosis success in the main justifies our claims.

There are other forms of illness, however, with which our therapeutic treatment never is successful, in spite of the similarity of the conditions. In them also there was originally a conflict between ego and libido, leading to repression—although this conflict may be characterized by topographical differences from the conflict of the transference neuroses; in them too it is possible to trace out the point in the patient's life at which the repressions occurred; we apply the same method, are ready to make the same assurances, offer the same assistance by telling the patient what to look out for; and here also the interval in time between the present and the point at which the repressions were established is all in favour of a better outcome of the conflict. And yet we cannot succeed in overcoming one resistance or in removing one of the repressions. These patients, paranoiacs, melancholics, and those suffering from dementia praecox, remain on the whole unaffected, proof against psycho-analytic treatment. What can be the cause of this? It is not due to lack of intelligence; a certain degree of intellectual capacity must naturally be stipulated for analysis, but there is no deficiency in this respect in, for instance, the very quick-witted deductive paranoiac. Nor are any of the other propelling forces regularly absent: melancholics, for instance, in contrast to paranoiacs, experience a very high degree of realization that they are ill and that their sufferings are due to this; but they are not on that account any more accessible to influence. In this we are confronted with a fact that we do not understand, and are therefore called upon to doubt whether we have really understood all the conditions of the success possible with the other neuroses.

When we keep to consideration of hysterical and obsessional neurotics we are very soon confronted with a second fact, for which we were quite unprepared. After the treatment has proceeded for a while we notice that these patients behave in a quite peculiar manner towards ourselves. We thought indeed that we had taken into account all the motive forces affecting the treatment and had reasoned out the situation between ourselves and the patient fully, so that it balanced like a sum in arithmetic; and then, after all, something seems to slip in which was quite left out of our calculation. This new and unexpected feature is in itself many-sided and complex; I will first of all describe some of its more frequent and simpler forms to you.

We observe then that the patient, who ought to be thinking of nothing but the solution of his own distressing conflicts, begins to develop a particular interest in the person of the physician. Everything connected with this person seems to him more important than his own affairs and to distract him from his illness. Relations with the patient then become for a time very agreeable; he is particularly docile, endeavours to show his gratitude wherever he can, exhibits a fineness of character and other good qualities which we had perhaps not anticipated in him. The analyst thus forms a very good opinion of the patient and values his luck in being able to render assistance to such an admirable personality. If the physician has occasion to see the patient's relatives he hears with satisfaction that this esteem is mutual. The patient at home is never tired of praising the analyst and attributing new virtues to him. "He has quite lost his head over you; he puts implicit trust in you; everything you say is like a revelation to him," say the relatives. Here and there, one among this chorus having sharper eyes will say: "It is positively boring the way he never speaks of anything but you: he quotes you all the time."

We will hope that the physician is modest enough to ascribe the patient's estimate of his value to the hopes of recovery which he has been able to offer to him, and to the widening in the patient's intellectual horizon consequent upon the surprising revelations entailed by the treatment and their liberating influence. The analysis too makes splendid progress under these conditions, the patient understands the suggestions offered to him, concentrates upon the tasks appointed by the treatment, the material needed—his recollections and associations —is abundantly available; he astonishes the analyst by the sureness and accuracy of his interpretations, and the latter has only to observe with satisfaction how readily and willingly a sick man will accept all the new psychological ideas that are so hotly contested by the healthy in the world outside. A general improvement in the patient's condition, objectively confirmed on all sides, also accompanies this harmonious relationship in the analysis.

But such fair weather cannot last for ever. There comes a day when it clouds over. There begin to be difficulties in the analysis; the patient says he cannot think of anything more to say. One has an unmistakable impression that he is no longer interested in the work, and that he is casually ignoring the injunction given him to say everything that comes into his mind and to yield to none of the critical objections that occur to him. His behaviour is not dictated by the situation of the treatment; it is as if he had not made an agreement to that effect with the physician; he is obviously preoccupied with something which at the same time he wishes to reserve to himself. This is a situation in which the treatment is in danger. Plainly a very powerful resistance has risen up. What can have happened?

If it is possible to clear up this state of things, the cause of the disturbance is found to consist in certain intense feelings of affection which the patient has transferred on to the physician, not accounted for by the latter's behaviour nor by the relationship involved by the treatment. The form in which this affectionate feeling is expressed and the goal it seeks naturally depend upon the circumstances of the situation between the two persons. If one of them is a young girl and the other still a fairly young man, the impression received is that of normal love; it seems natural that a girl should fall in love with a man with whom she is much alone and can speak of very intimate things, and who is in the position of an adviser with authority—we shall probably overlook the fact that in a neurotic girl some disturbance of the capacity for love is rather to be expected. The farther removed the situation between the two persons is from this supposed example, the more unaccountable it is to find that nevertheless the same kind of feeling comes to light in other cases. It may be still comprehensible when a young woman who is unhappily married seems to be overwhelmed by a serious passion for her physician, if he is still unattached, and that she should be ready to seek a divorce and give herself to him, or, where circumstances would prevent this, to enter into a secret love-affair with him. That sort of thing, indeed, is known to occur outside psycho-analysis. But in this situation girls and women make the most astonishing confessions which reveal a quite peculiar attitude on their part to the therapeutic problem: they had

always known that nothing but love would cure them, and from the beginning of the treatment they had expected that this relationship would at last yield them what life had so far denied them. It was only with this hope that they had taken such pains over the analysis and had conquered all their difficulties in disclosing their thoughts. We ourselves can add: "and had understood so easily all that is usually so hard to accept." But a confession of this kind astounds us; all our calculations are blown to the winds. Could it be that we have omitted the most important element in the whole problem?

And actually it is so; the more experience we gain the less possible does it become for us to contest this new factor, which alters the whole problem and puts our scientific calculations to shame. The first few times one might think that the analytic treatment had stumbled upon an obstruction in the shape of an accidental occurrence, extraneous to its purpose and unconnected with it in origin. But when it happens that this kind of attachment to the physician regularly evinces itself in every fresh case, under the most unfavourable conditions, and always appears, even in circumstances of a positively grotesque incongruity—in elderly women, in relation to grey-bearded men, even on occasions when our judgment assures us that no temptations exist—then we are compelled to give up the idea of a disturbing accident and to admit that we have to deal with a phenomenon in itself essentially bound up with the nature of the disease.

The new fact which we are thus unwillingly compelled to recognize, we call *transference*. By this we mean a transference of feelings on to the person of the physician, because we do not believe that the situation in the treatment can account for the origin of such feelings. We are much more disposed to suspect that the whole of this readiness to develop feeling originates in another source; that it was previously formed in the patient, and has seized the opportunity provided by the treatment to transfer itself on to the person of the physician. The transference can express itself as a passionate petitioning for love, or it can take less extreme forms; where a young girl and an elderly man are concerned, instead of the wish to be wife or mistress, a wish to be adopted as a favourite daughter may come to light, the libidinous desire can modify itself and propose itself as a wish for an everlasting, but ideally platonic friendship. Many women understand how to sublimate the transference and to mould it until it acquires a sort of justification for its existence; others have to express it in its crude, original, almost impossible form. But at bottom it is always the same, and its origin in the same source can never be mistaken.

Before we enquire where we are to range this new fact, we will amplify the description of it a little. How is it with our male patients? There at least we might hope to be spared the troublesome element of sex difference and sex attraction. Well, the answer is very much the same as with women. The same attachment to the physician, the same overestimation of his qualities, the same adoption of his interests, the same jealousy against all those connected with him. The sublimated kinds of transference are the forms more frequently met with between man and man, and the directly sexual declaration more rarely, in the same degree to which the manifest homosexuality of the patient is subordinated to the other ways by which this component-instinct can express itself. Also, it is in male patients that the analyst more frequently observes a manifestation of the transference which at the first glance seems to controvert the description of it just given—that is, the hostile or *negative* transference.

First of all, let us realize at once that the transference exists in the patient from the beginning of the treatment, and is for a time the strongest impetus in the work. Nothing is seen of it and one does not need to trouble about it as long as its effect is favourable to the work in which the two persons are co-operating. When it becomes transformed into a resistance, attention must be paid to it; and then it appears that the two different and contrasting states of mind have supervened in it and have altered its attitude to the treatment: first, when the affectionate attraction has become so strong and betrays signs of its origin in sexual desire so clearly that it was bound to arouse an inner opposition against itself; and secondly, when it consists in antagonistic instead of affectionate feeling. The hostile feelings as a rule appear later than the affectionate and under cover of them; when both occur simultaneously they provide a very good exemplification of that ambivalence in feeling which governs most of our intimate relationships with other human beings. The hostile feelings therefore indicate an attachment of feeling quite similar to the affectionate, just as defiance indicates a similar dependence upon the other person to that belonging to obedience, though with a reversed

prefix. There can be no doubt that the hostile feelings against the analyst deserve the name of *transference,* for the situation in the treatment certainly gives no adequate occasion for them; the necessity for regarding the negative transference in this light is a confirmation of our previous similar view of the positive or affectionate variety.

Where the transference springs from, what difficulties it provides for us, how we can overcome them, and what advantage we can finally derive from it, are questions which can only be adequately dealt with in a technical exposition of the analytic method; I can merely touch upon them here. It is out of the question that we should yield to the demands made by the patient under the influence of his transference; it would be nonsensical to reject them unkindly, and still more so, indignantly. The transference is overcome by showing the patient that his feelings do not originate in the current situation, and do not really concern the person of the physician, but that he is reproducing something that had happened to him long ago. In this way we require him to transform his *repetition* into *recollection.* Then the transference which, whether affectionate or hostile, every time seemed the greatest menace to the cure becomes its best instrument, so that with its help we can unlock the closed doors in the soul. I should like, however, to say a few words to dispel the unpleasant effects of the shock that this unexpected phenomenon must have been to you. After all, we must not forget that this illness of the patient's which we undertake to analyse is not a finally accomplished and, as it were, consolidated thing; but that it is growing and continuing its development all the time like a living thing. The beginning of the treatment puts no stop to this development; but, as soon as the treatment has taken a hold upon the patient, it appears that the entire productivity of the illness henceforward becomes concentrated in one direction—namely, upon the relationship to the physician. The transference then becomes comparable to the cambium layer between the wood and the bark of a tree, from which proceeds the formation of new tissue and the growth of the trunk in diameter. As soon as the transference has taken on this significance the work upon the patient's recollections recedes far into the background. It is then not incorrect to say that we no longer have to do with the previous illness, but with a newly created and transformed neurosis which has replaced the earlier one. This new edition of the old disease has been followed from its inception, one sees it come to light and grow, and is particularly familiar with it since one is oneself its central object. All the patient's symptoms have abandoned their original significance and have adapted themselves to a new meaning, which is contained in their relationship to the transference; or else only those symptoms remain which were capable of being adapted in this way. The conquest of this new artificially acquired neurosis coincides with the removal of the illness which existed prior to the treatment, that is, with accomplishing the therapeutic task. The person who has become normal and free from the influence of repressed instinctive tendencies in his relationship to the physician remains so in his own life when the physician has again been removed from it.

The transference has this all-important, absolutely central significance for the cure in hysteria, anxiety-hysteria, and the obsessional neurosis, which are in consequence rightly grouped together as the *transference neuroses*. Anyone who has grasped from analytic experience a true impression of the fact of transference can never again doubt the nature of the suppressed impulses which have manufactured an outlet for themselves in the symptoms; and he will require no stronger proof of their libidinal character. We may say that our conviction of the significance of the symptoms as a substitutive gratification of the libido was only finally and definitely established by evaluating the phenomenon of transference.

Now, however, we are called upon to correct our former dynamic conception of the process of cure and to bring it into agreement with the new discovery. When the patient has to fight out the normal conflict with the resistances which we have discovered in him by analysis, he requires a powerful propelling force to influence him towards the decision we aim at, leading to recovery. Otherwise it might happen that he would decide for a repetition of the previous outcome, and allow that which had been raised into consciousness to slip back again under repression. The outcome in this struggle is not decided by his intellectual insight—it is neither strong enough nor free enough to accomplish such a thing—but solely by his relationship to the physician. In so far as his transference bears the positive sign, it clothes the physician with authority, transforms itself into faith in his findings and in his views. Without this kind of transference or with a

negative one, the physician and his arguments would never even be listened to. Faith repeats the history of its own origin; it is a derivative of love and at first it needed no arguments. Not until later does it admit them so far as to take them into critical consideration, if they have been offered by someone who is loved. Without this support, arguments have no weight with the patient, never do have any with most people in life. A human being is therefore on the whole only accessible to influence, even on the intellectual side, in so far as he is capable of investing objects with libido; and we have good cause to recognize, and to fear, in the measure of his narcissism a barrier to his susceptibility to influence, even by the best analytic technique.

The capacity for the radiation of libido towards other persons in object-investment must, of course, be ascribed to all normal people; the tendency to transference in neurotics, so called, is only an exceptional intensification of a universal characteristic. Now it would be very remarkable if a human character-trait of this importance and universality had never been observed and made use of. And this has really been done. Bernheim with unerring perspicacity, based the theory of hypnotic manifestations upon the proposition that all human beings are more or less open to suggestion, are *suggestible*. What he called *suggestibility* is nothing else but the tendency to transference, rather too narrowly circumscribed so that the negative transference did not come within its scope. But Bernheim could never say what suggestion actually was nor how it arises; it was an axiomatic fact to him and he could give no explanation of its origin. He did not recognize the dependence of *suggestibility* on sexuality, on the functioning of the libido. And we have to admit that we have only abandoned hypnosis in our methods in order to discover suggestion again in the shape of transference.

But now I will pause and let you take up the thread. I observe that an objection is invading your thoughts with such violence that it would deprive you of all power of attention if it were not given expression. "So now at last you have confessed that you too work with the aid of suggestion like the hypnotists. We have been thinking so all along. But then, what is the use of all these round-about routes by way of past experiences, discovering the unconscious material, interpreting and retranslating the distortions, and the enormous expenditure of time, trouble, and money, when, after all, the only effective agent is suggestion? Why do you not suggest directly against the symptoms, as others do who are honest hypnotists? And besides, if you are going to make out that by these round-about routes you have made numerous important psychological discoveries, which are concealed in direct suggestion, who is to vouch for their validity? Are not they too the result of suggestion, of unintentional suggestion, that is? Cannot you impress upon the patient what you please and whatever seems good to you in this direction also?"

What you charge me with in this way is exceedingly interesting and must be answered. But I cannot do that today; our time is up. Till next time, then. You will see that I shall be answerable to you. Today I must finish what I began. I promised to explain to you, through the factor of transference, why it is that our therapeutic efforts have no success in the narcissistic neuroses.

I can do it in a few words, and you will see how simply the riddle is solved, and how well everything fits together. Experience shows that persons suffering from the narcissistic neuroses have no capacity for transference, or only insufficient remnants of it. They turn from the physician, not in hostility, but in indifference. Therefore they are not to be influenced by him; what he says leaves them cold, makes no impression on them, and therefore the process of cure which can be carried through with others, the revivification of the pathogenic conflict and the overcoming of the resistance due to the repressions, cannot be effected with them. They remain as they are. They have often enough undertaken attempts at recovery on their own account which have led to pathological results; we can do nothing to alter this.

On the basis of our clinical observations of these patients, we stated that they must have abandoned the investment of objects with libido and transformed object-libido into ego-libido. By this we differentiated them from the first group of neurotics (hysteria, anxiety, and obsessional neurosis). Their behaviour during the attempt to cure them confirms this suspicion. They produce no transference, and are, therefore, inaccessible to our efforts, not to be cured by us.

TWENTY-EIGHTH LECTURE

The Analytic Therapy

You know what we are going to discuss today. When I admitted that the influence of the psycho-analytic therapy is essentially founded upon transference, i.e., upon suggestion, you asked me why we do not make use of direct suggestion, and you linked this up with a doubt whether, in view of the fact that suggestion plays such a large part, we can still vouch for the objectivity of our psychological discoveries. I promised to give you a comprehensive answer.

Direct suggestion is suggestion delivered directly against the forms taken by the symptoms, a struggle between your authority and the motives underlying the disease. In this struggle you do not trouble yourself about these motives, you only require the patient to suppress the manifestation of them in the form of symptoms. In the main it makes no difference whether you place the patient under hypnosis or not. Bernheim, with his characteristic acuteness, repeatedly stated that suggestion was the essence of the manifestations of hypnotism, and that hypnosis itself was already a result of suggestion, a suggested condition; he preferred to use suggestion in the waking state, which can achieve the same results in hypnosis.

Now which shall I take first, the results of experience or theoretical considerations?

Let us begin with experience. I sought out Bernheim in Nancy in 1889 and became a pupil of his; I translated his book on suggestion into German. For years I made use of hypnotic treatment, first with prohibitory suggestions and later combined with Breuer's system of the fullest inquiry into the patient's life; I can therefore speak from wide experience about the results of the hypnotic or suggestive therapy. According to an old medical saying, an ideal therapy should be rapid, reliable and not disagreeable to the patient; Bernheim's method certainly fulfilled two of these requirements. It was much more rapid, that is, incomparably more rapid in its course than the analytic, and it involved the patient in no trouble or discomfort. For the physician, it eventually became monotonous; it meant treating every case in the same way, always employing the same ritual to prohibit the existence of the most diverse symptoms, without being able to grasp anything of their meaning or significance. It was a sort of mechanical drudgery—hodman's work—not scientific work; it was reminiscent of magic, conjuring, and hocus-pocus, yet in the patient's interests one had to ignore that. In the third desideratum, however, it failed; it was not reliable in any respect. It could be employed in certain cases only and not in others; with some much could be achieved by it, and with others very little, one never knew why. But worse than its capricious nature was the lack of permanence in the results; after a time, if one heard from the patient again, the old malady had reappeared or had been replaced by another. Then one could begin to hypnotize again. In the background there was the warning of experienced men against robbing the patient of his independence by frequent repetitions of hypnosis, and against accustoming him to this treatment as though it were a narcotic. It is true, on the other hand, that at times everything fell out just as one could wish; one obtained complete and lasting success with little difficulty; but the conditions of this satisfactory outcome remained hidden. In one case, when I had completely removed a severe condition by a short hypnotic treatment, it recurred unchanged after the patient (a woman) had developed ill feeling against me without just cause; then after a reconciliation I was able to effect its disappearance again and this time far more thoroughly; but it reappeared again when she had a second time become hostile to me. Another time I had the following experience: during the treatment of an especially obstinate attack in a patient whom I had several times relieved of nervous symptoms, she suddenly threw her arms round my neck. Whether one wished to do so or not, this kind of thing finally made it imperative to enquire into the problem of the nature and source of one's suggestive authority.

So much for experience; it shows that in abandoning direct suggestion we have given up nothing irreplaceable. Now let us link on to the facts a few comments. The exercise of the hypnotic method makes as little demand for effort on the part of the patient as it does on the physician. The method is in complete harmony with the view of the neuroses generally accepted by the majority of medical men. The practitioner says to the nervous person: "There is nothing the matter with you; it is merely nervousness, therefore a few words from me will scatter all your troubles to the winds in five minutes." But it is contrary to all our beliefs about energy in general that a minimal exertion should be able to remove a heavy load by approaching it directly without the assistance of any suitably devised appliance. In so far as the circumstances are at all comparable, experience shows that this trick cannot be performed successfully with the neuroses. I

know, however, that this argument is not unassailable; there are such things as explosions.

In the light of the knowledge we have obtained through psycho-analysis, the difference between hypnotic and psycho-analytic suggestion may be described as follows: The hypnotic therapy endeavours to cover up and as it were to whitewash something going on in the mind, the analytic to lay bare and to remove something. The first works cosmetically, the second surgically. The first employs suggestion to interdict the symptoms; it reinforces the repressions, but otherwise it leaves unchanged all the processes that have led to symptom-formation. Analytic therapy takes hold deeper down nearer the roots of the disease, among the conflicts from which the symptoms proceed; it employs suggestion to change the outcome of these conflicts. Hypnotic therapy allows the patient to remain inactive and unchanged, consequently also helpless in the face of every new incitement to illness. Analytic treatment makes as great demands for efforts on the part of the patient as on the physician, efforts to abolish the inner resistances. The patient's mental life is permanently changed by overcoming these resistances, is lifted to a higher level of development, and remains proof against fresh possibilities of illness. The labour of overcoming the resistances is the essential achievement of the analytic treatment; the patient has to accomplish it and the physician makes it possible for him to do this by suggestions which are in the nature of an *education*. It has been truly said therefore, that psycho-analytic treatment is a kind of *re-education*.

I hope I have now made clear to you the difference between our method of employing suggestion therapeutically and the method which is the only possible one in hypnotic therapy. Since we have traced the influence of suggestion back to the transference, you also understand the striking capriciousness of the effect in hypnotic therapy, and why analytic therapy is, within its limits, dependable. In employing hypnosis, we are entirely dependent upon the condition of the patient's transference and yet we are unable to exercise any influence upon this condition itself. The transference of a patient being hypnotized may be negative, or, as most commonly, ambivalent, or he may have guarded himself against his transference by adopting special attitudes; we gather nothing about all this. In psycho-analysis we work upon the transference itself, dissipate whatever stands in the way of it, and manipulate the instrument which is to do the work. Thus it becomes possible for us to derive entirely new benefits from the power of suggestion; we are able to control it; the patient alone no longer manages his suggestibility according to his own liking, but in so far as he is amenable to its influence at all, we guide his suggestibility.

Now you will say that, regardless of whether the driving force behind the analysis is called *transference* or *suggestion,* the danger still remains that our influence upon the patient may bring the objective certainty of our discoveries into doubt; and that what is an advantage in therapy is harmful in research. This is the objection that has most frequently been raised against psycho-analysis; and it must be admitted that, even though it is unjustified, it cannot be ignored as unreasonable. If it were justified, psycho-analysis, after all, would be nothing else but a specially well-disguised and particularly effective kind of suggestive treatment; and all its conclusions about the experiences of the patient's past life, mental dynamics, the unconscious, and so on, could be taken very lightly. So our opponents think; the significance of sexual experiences in particular, if not the experiences themselves, we are supposed to have "put into the patient's mind," after having first concocted these conglomerations in our own corrupt minds. These accusations are more satisfactorily refuted by the evidence of experience than by the aid of theory. Anyone who has himself conducted psychoanalyses has been able to convince himself numberless times that it is impossible to suggest things to a patient in this way. There is no difficulty, of course, in making him a disciple of a particular theory, and thus making it possible for him to share some mistaken belief possibly harboured by the physician. He behaves like anyone else in this, like a pupil; but by this one has only influenced his intellect, not his illness. The solving of his conflicts and the overcoming of his resistances succeeds only when what he is told to look for in himself corresponds with what actually does exist in him. Anything that has been inferred wrongly by the physician will disappear in the course of the analysis; it must be withdrawn and replaced by something more correct. One's aim is, by a very careful technique, to prevent temporary successes arising through suggestion; but if they do arise no great harm is done, for we are not content with the first result. We do not consider the analysis completed unless all obscurities in the case are explained, the gaps in memory filled out, and the original occasions of the repressions discovered. When results appear prematurely, one regards them as obstacles rather than as furtherances of the analytic work, and one destroys them again by continually exposing the transference on which they are founded. Fundamentally, it is this last feature which distinguishes analytic treatment from that of pure suggestion, and which clears the results of analysis from the suspicion of being the results of suggestion. In every other suggestive treatment, the transference is carefully preserved and left intact; in analysis, it is itself the object of the treatment and is continually being dissected in all its various forms. At the conclusion of the analysis the transference itself must be dissolved; if success then supervenes and is maintained it is not founded on suggestion, but on the overcoming of the inner resistances effected by the help of suggestion, on the inner change achieved within the patient.

That which probably prevents single effects of suggestion from arising during the treatment is the struggle that is incessantly being waged against the resistances, which know how to transform themselves into a negative (hostile) transference. Nor will we neglect to point to the evidence that a great many of the detailed findings of analysis, which would otherwise be suspected of being produced by suggestion, are confirmed from other, irreproachable sources. We have unimpeachable witnesses on these points, namely, dements and paranoiacs, who are of course quite above any suspicion of being influenced by suggestion. All that these patients relate in the way of phantasies and translations of symbols, which have penetrated through into their consciousness, corresponds faithfully with the results of our investigations into the unconscious of transference neurotics, thus confirming the objective truth of the interpretations made by us which are so often doubted. I do not think you will find yourselves mistaken if you choose to trust analysis in these respects.

We now need to complete our description of the process of recovery by expressing it in terms of the libido theory. The neurotic is incapable of enjoyment or of achievement—the first because his libido is attached to no real object, the last because so much of the energy which would otherwise be at his disposal is expended in maintaining the libido under repression, and in warding off its attempts to assert itself. He would be well, if the conflict between his ego and his libido came to an end, and if his ego again had the libido at its disposal. The task of the treatment, therefore, consists in the task of loosening the libido from its previous attachments, which are beyond the reach of the ego, and in making it again serviceable to the ego. Now where is the libido of a neurotic? Easily found: it is attached to the symptoms, which offer it the substitutive satisfaction that is all it can obtain as things are. We must master the symptoms then, dissolve them—just what the patient asks of us. In order to dissolve the symptoms it is necessary to go back to the point at which they originated, to review the conflict from which they proceeded, and with the help of propelling forces which at that time were not available to guide it towards a new solution. This revision of the process of repression can only partially be effected by means of the memory-traces of the processes which led up to repression. The decisive part of the work is carried through by creating—in the relationship to the physician, in the *transference*—new editions of those early conflicts, in which the patient strives to behave as he originally behaved, while one calls upon all the available forces in his soul to bring him to another decision. The transference is thus the battlefield where all the contending forces must meet.

All the libido and the full strength of the opposition against it are concentrated upon the one thing, upon the relationship to the physician; thus it becomes inevitable that the symptoms should be deprived of their libido; in place of the patient's original illness appears the artificially acquired transference, the transference-disorder; in place of a variety of unreal objects of his libido appears the one object, also *phantastic,* of the person of the physician. This new struggle which arises concerning this object is by means of the analyst's suggestions lifted to the surface, to the higher mental levels, and there worked out as a normal mental conflict. Since a new repression is thus avoided, the opposition between the ego and the libido comes to an end; unity is restored within the patient's mind. When the libido has been detached from its temporary object in the person of the physician, it cannot return to its earlier objects, but is now at the disposal of the ego. The forces opposing us in this struggle during the therapeutic treatment are, on the one hand, the ego's aversion against certain tendencies on the part of the libido, which had expressed itself in repressing tendencies; and, on

the other hand, the tenacity or *adhesiveness* of the libido, which does not readily detach itself from objects it has once invested.

The therapeutic work thus falls into two phases: in the first, all the libido is forced away from the symptoms into the transference and there concentrated; in the second, the battle rages round this new object and the libido is made free from it. The change that is decisive for a successful outcome of this renewed conflict lies in the preclusion of repression, so that the libido cannot again withdraw itself from the ego by a flight into the unconscious. It is made possible by changes in the ego ensuing as a consequence of the analyst's suggestions. At the expense of the unconscious, the ego becomes wider by the work of interpretation which brings the unconscious material into consciousness; through education it becomes reconciled to the libido and is made willing to grant it a certain degree of satisfaction; and its horror of the claims of its libido is lessened by the new capacity it acquires to expend a certain amount of the libido in sublimation. The more nearly the course of the treatment corresponds with this ideal description the greater will be the success of the psycho-analytic therapy. Its barriers are found in the lack of mobility in the libido, which resists being released from its objects, and in the rigidity of the patient's narcissism, which will not allow more than a certain degree of object-transference to develop. Perhaps the dynamics of the process of recovery will become still clearer if we describe it by saying that, in attracting a part of it to ourselves through transference, we gather in the whole amount of the libido which has been withdrawn from the ego's control.

It is as well here to make clear that the distributions of the libido which ensue during and by means of the analysis afford no direct inference of the nature of its disposition during the previous illness. Given that a case can be successfully cured by establishing and then resolving a powerful father-transference to the person of the physician, it would not follow that the patient had previously suffered in this way from an unconscious attachment of the libido to his father. The father-transference is only the battlefield on which we conquer and take the libido prisoner; the patient's libido has been drawn hither away from other positions. The battlefield does not necessarily constitute one of the enemy's most important strongholds; the defence of the enemy's capital city need not be conducted immediately before its gates.

Not until after the transference has been again resolved can one begin to reconstruct in imagination the dispositions of the libido that were represented by the illness.

In the light of the libido theory there is a final word to be said about dreams. The dreams of a neurotic, like his *errors* and his free associations, enable us to find the meaning of the symptoms and to discover the dispositions of the libido. The forms taken by the wish-fulfilment in them show us what are the wish-impulses that have undergone repression, and what are the objects to which the libido has attached itself after withdrawal from the ego. The interpretation of dreams therefore plays a great part in psycho-analytic treatment, and in many cases it is for lengthy periods the most important instrument at work. We already know that the condition of sleep in itself produces a certain relaxation of the repressions. By this diminution in the heavy pressure upon it, the repressed desire is able to create for itself a far clearer expression in a dream than can be permitted to it by day in the symptoms. Hence the study of dreams becomes the easiest approach to a knowledge of the repressed unconscious, which is where the libido which has withdrawn from the ego belongs.

The dreams of neurotics, however, differ in no essential from those of normal people; they are indeed perhaps not in any way distinguishable from them. It would be illogical to account for the dreams of neurotics in a way that would not also hold good of the dreams of normal people. We have to conclude, therefore, that the difference between neurosis and health prevails only by day; it is not sustained in dream-life. It thus becomes necessary to transfer to healthy persons a number of conclusions arrived at as a result of the connections between the dreams and the symptoms of neurotics. We have to recognize that the healthy man as well possesses those factors in mental life which alone can bring about the formation of a dream or of a symptom, and we must conclude further that the healthy also have instituted repressions and have to expend a certain amount of energy to maintain them; that their unconscious minds, too, harbour repressed impulses which are still suffused with energy, and that *a part of the libido is in them also withdrawn from the disposal of the ego*. The healthy man, too, is therefore virtually a neurotic, but the only symptom that he *seems* capable of developing is a dream. To be sure, when you subject his waking life also to a critical investigation, you discover something that contradicts this specious conclusion; for this apparently healthy life is pervaded by innumerable trivial and practically unimportant symptom-formations.

The difference between nervous health and nervous illness (neurosis) is narrowed down therefore to a practical distinction, and is determined by the practical result—how far the person concerned remains capable of a sufficient degree of capacity for enjoyment and active achievement in life. The difference can probably be traced back to the proportion of the energy which has remained free relative to that of the energy which has been bound by repression, i.e., it is a quantitative and not a qualitative difference. I do not need to remind you that this view provides a theoretical basis for our conviction that the neuroses are essentially amenable to cure, in spite of their being based on a constitutional disposition.

So much, therefore, in the way of knowledge of the characteristics of health may be inferred from the identity of the dreams dreamt by neurotic and by healthy persons. Of dreams themselves, however, a further inference must be drawn—namely, that it is not possible to detach them from their connection with neurotic symptoms; that we are not at liberty to believe that their essential nature is exhausted by compressing them into the formula of *a translation of thoughts into archaic forms of expression;* and that we are bound to conclude that they disclose dispositions of the libido and objects of desire which are actually in operation and valid at the moment.

We have now come very nearly to the end. Perhaps you are disappointed that, under the heading of psycho-analytic therapy, I have limited myself to theory and have told you nothing of the conditions under which the cure is undertaken, or of the results it achieves. I omit both, however: the first, because in fact I never intended to give you a practical training in the exercise of the analytic method; and the last, because I have several motives against it. At the beginning of these discussions I said emphatically that under favourable conditions we achieve cures that are in no way inferior to the most brilliant in other fields of medical therapy; I may perhaps add that these results could be achieved by no other method. If I said more I should be suspected of wishing to drown the depreciatory voices of our opponents by self-advertisement. Medical "colleagues" have, even at public congresses, repeatedly held out a threat to psycho-analysts that by publishing a collection of the failures and harmful effects of analysis they will open the eyes of the injured public to the worthlessness of this method of treatment. Apart from the malicious, denunciatory character of such a measure, however, a collection of that kind would not even be valid evidence upon which a correct estimate of the therapeutic results of analysis might be formed. Analytic therapy, as you know, is still young; it needed many years to elaborate the technique, which could only be done in the course of the work under the influence of increasing experience. On account of the difficulties of imparting instruction in the methods, the beginner is thrown much more upon his own resources for development of his capacity than any other kind of specialist, and the results of his early years can never be taken as indicating the full possible achievements of analytic therapy.

Many attempts at treatment made in the beginning of psycho-analysis were failures because they were undertaken with cases altogether unsuited to the procedure, which nowadays we should exclude by following certain indications. These indications, however, could only be discovered by trying. In the beginning we did not know that paranoia and dementia præcox, when fully developed, are not amenable to analysis; we were still justified in trying the method on all kinds of disorders. Most of the failures of those early years, however, were not due to the fault of the physician, or to the unsuitability in the choice of subject, but to unpropitious external conditions. I have spoken only of the inner resistances, those on the part of the patient, which are inevitable and can be overcome. The external resistances which the patient's circumstances and surroundings set up against analysis have little theoretic interest but the greatest practical importance. Psychoanalytic treatment is comparable to a surgical operation and, like that, for its success it has the right to expect to be carried out under the most favourable conditions. You know the preliminary arrangements a surgeon is accustomed to make—a suitable room, a good light, expert assistance, exclusion of the relatives, and so on. Now ask yourselves how many surgical operations would be successful if they had to be conducted in the presence of the patient's entire family poking their noses into the scene of the operation and shrieking aloud at every cut. In psycho-analytic treatment, the intervention of the relatives is a positive danger

and, moreover, one which we do not know how to deal with. We are armed against the inner resistances of the patient, which we recognize as necessary, but how can we protect ourselves against these outer resistances? It is impossible to get round the relatives by any sort of explanation, nor can one induce them to hold aloof from the whole affair; one can never take them into one's confidence, because then we run the danger of losing the patient's trust in us, for he —quite rightly, of course—demands that the man he confides in should take his part. Anyone who knows anything of the dissensions commonly splitting up family life will not be astonished in his capacity of analyst to find that those nearest to the patient frequently show less interest in his recovery than in keeping him as he is. When, as so often occurs, the neurosis is connected with conflicts between different members of a family, the healthy person does not make much of putting his own interest before the patient's recovery. After all, it is not surprising that the husband does not favour a treatment in which, as he correctly supposes, his sins will all come to light; nor do we wonder at this, but then we cannot blame ourselves when our efforts remain fruitless and are prematurely broken off because the husband's resistance is added to that of the sick wife. We had simply undertaken something which, under the existing conditions, it was impossible to carry out.

Instead of describing many cases to you I will tell you of one only, in which I had to suffer for the sake of professional conscientiousness. I took a young girl—many years ago— for analytic treatment; for a considerable time previously she had been unable to go out of doors on account of a dread, nor could she stay at home alone. After much hesitation the patient confessed that her thoughts had been a good deal occupied by some signs of affection that she had noticed by chance between her mother and a well-to-do friend of the family. Very tactlessly—or else very cleverly—she then gave the mother a hint of what had been discussed during the analysis; she did this by altering her behaviour to her mother, by insisting that no one but her mother could protect her against the dread of being alone, and by holding the door against her when she attempted to leave the house. The mother herself had formerly been very nervous, but had been cured years before by a visit to a hydropathic establishment—or, putting it otherwise, we may say she had there made the acquaintance of the man with whom she had established a relationship that had proved satisfying in more than one respect. Made suspicious by her daughter's passionate demands, the mother suddenly *understood* what the girl's dread signified. She had become ill in order to make her mother a prisoner and rob her of the freedom necessary for her to maintain her relations with her lover. The mother's decision was instantly taken; she put an end to the harmful treatment. The girl was sent to a home for nervous patients, and for many years was there pointed out as an "unhappy victim of psycho-analysis"; for just as long I was pursued by damaging rumours about the unfortunate results of the treatment. I maintained silence because I supposed myself bound by the rules of professional secrecy. Years later I learned from a colleague who had visited the home and there seen the girl with agoraphobia that the intimacy between the mother and the wealthy man was common knowledge, and that in all probability it was connived at by the husband and father. To this *secret* the girl's cure had been sacrificed.

In the years before the war, when the influx of patients from many countries made me independent of the goodwill or disfavour of my native city, I made it a rule never to take for treatment anyone who was not *sui juris*, independent of others in all the essential relations of life. Every psycho-analyst cannot make these stipulations. Perhaps you will conclude from my warnings about relatives that one should take the patient out of his family circle in the interests of analysis, and restrict this therapy to those living in private institutions. I could not support this suggestion, however; it is far more advantageous for the patients—those who are not in a condition of severe prostration, at least—to remain during the treatment in those circumstances in which they have to struggle with the demands that their ordinary life makes on them. But the relatives ought not to counteract this advantage by their behaviour, and above all should not oppose their hostility to one's professional efforts. But how are you going to induce people who are inaccessible to you to take up this attitude? You will naturally also conclude that the social atmosphere and degree of cultivation of the patient's immediate surroundings have considerable influence upon the prospects of the treatment.

This is a gloomy outlook for the efficacy of psycho-analysis as a therapy, even if we may explain the overwhelming majority of our failures by taking into account these disturbing external factors! Friends of analysis have advised us to counter-balance a collection of failures by drawing up a statistical enumeration of our successes. I have not taken up this suggestion either. I brought forward the argument that statistics would be valueless if the units collated were not alike, and the cases which had been treated were in fact not equivalent in many respects. Further, the period of time that could be reviewed was too short for one to be able to judge of the permanence of the cures; and of many cases it would be impossible to give any account. They were persons who had kept both their illness and their treatment secret, and whose recovery in consequence had similarly to be kept secret. The strongest reason against it, however, lay in the recognition of the fact that, in matters of therapy, humanity is in the highest degree irrational, so that there is no prospect of influencing it by reasonable arguments. A novelty in therapeutics is either taken up with frenzied enthusiasm, as for instance when Koch first published his results with tuberculin; or else it is regarded with abysmal distrust, as happened for instance with Jenner's vaccination, actually a heaven-sent blessing, but one which still has its implacable opponents. A very evident prejudice against psycho-analysis made itself apparent. When one had cured a very difficult case one would hear: "That is no proof of anything; he would have got well of himself after all this time." And when a patient who had already gone through four cycles of depression and mania came to me in an interval after the melancholia and three weeks later again began to develop an attack of mania, all the members of the family, and also all the high medical authorities who were called in, were convinced that the fresh attack could be nothing but a consequence of the attempted analysis. Against prejudice one can do nothing, as you can now see once more in the prejudices that each group of the nations at war has developed against the other. The most sensible thing to do is to wait and allow them to wear off with the passage of time. A day comes when the same people regard the same things in quite a different light from what they did before; why they thought differently before remains a dark secret.

It is possible that the prejudice against the analytic therapy has already begun to relax. The continual spread of analytic doctrine and the numbers of medical men taking up analytic treatment in many countries seem to point in that direction. As a young man I was caught in just such a storm of indignation roused in the medical profession by the hypnotic suggestion-treatment, which nowadays is held up in opposition to psycho-analysis by the "soberminded." As a therapeutic instrument, however, hypnotism did not bear out the hopes placed in it; we psycho-analysts may claim to be its rightful heirs and should not forget how much encouragement and theoretic enlightenment we owe to it. The harmful effects reported of psycho-analysis are essentially confined to transitory manifestations of an exacerbation of the conflict, which may occur when the analysis is clumsily handled, or when it is broken off suddenly. You have heard an account of what we do with our patients, and you can form your own judgment whether our efforts are likely to lead to lasting injury. Misuse of analysis is possible in various ways: the transference especially, in the hands of an unscrupulous physician,

is a dangerous instrument. But no medical remedy is proof against misuse; if a knife will not cut, neither will it serve a surgeon.

I have now reached the end. It is more than a conventional formality when I say that I myself am heavily oppressed by the many defects of the lectures I have delivered before you. I regret most of all that I have so often promised to return again in another place to a subject that I had just touched upon shortly, and that then the context in which I could keep my word did not offer itself. I undertook to give you an account of a thing that is still unfinished, still developing, and now my short summary itself has become an incomplete one. In many places I laid everything ready for drawing a conclusion, and then I did not draw it. But I could not aim at making you experts in psycho-analysis; I only wished to put you in the way of some understanding of it, and to arouse your interest in it.

Beyond the Pleasure Principle[1]

I

IN the psycho-analytical theory of the mind, we take it for granted that the course of mental processes is automatically regulated by *the pleasure-principle*: that is to say, we believe that any given process originates in an unpleasant state of tension and thereupon determines for itself such a path that its ultimate issue coincides with a relaxation of this tension, i.e., with avoidance of "pain"[2] or with production of pleasure. When we consider the psychic processes under observation in reference to such a sequence we are introducing into our work the *economic* point of view. In our opinion, a presentation which seeks to estimate, not only the *topographical* and *dynamic*, but also the economic element, is the most complete that we can at present imagine, and deserves to be distinguished by the term *metapsychological*.

We are not interested in examining how far in our assertion of the pleasure-principle we have approached to or adopted any given philosophical system historically established. Our approach to such speculative hypotheses is by way of our endeavour to describe and account for the facts falling within our daily sphere of observation. Priority and originality are not among the aims which psycho-analysis sets itself, and the impressions on which the statement of this principle is founded are of so unmistakable a kind that it is scarcely possible to overlook them. On the other hand, we should willingly acknowledge our indebtedness to any philosophical or psychological theory that could tell us the meaning of these feelings of pleasure and "pain" which affect us so powerfully. Unfortunately, no theory of any value is forthcoming. It is the obscurest and least penetrable region of psychic life, and, while it is impossible for us to avoid touching on it, the most elastic hypothesis will be, to my mind, the best. We have decided to consider pleasure and "pain" in relation to the quantity of excitation present in the psychic life—and not confined in any way—along such lines that "pain" corresponds with an increase and pleasure with a decrease in this quantity. We do not thereby commit

ourselves to a simple relationship between the strength of the feelings and the changes corresponding with them, least of all, judging from psycho-physiological experiences, to any view of a direct proportion existing between them; probably the amount of diminution or increase in a given time is the decisive factor for feeling. Possibly there is room here for experimental work, but it is inadvisable for us analysts to go further into these problems until we can be guided by quite definite observations.

We cannot, however, profess the like indifference when we find that an investigator of such penetration as G. Th. Fechner has advocated a conception of pleasure and "pain," which in essentials coincides with that forced upon us by psycho-analytic work. Fechner's pronouncement is to be found in his short work, *Einige Ideen zur Schöpfungs- und Entwicklungsgeschichte der Organismen*, 1873 (Section XI, note p. 94), and reads as follows: "In so far as conscious impulses always bear a relation to pleasure or 'pain,' pleasure or 'pain' may be thought of in psycho-physical relationship to conditions of stability and instability, and upon this may be based the hypothesis I intend to develop elsewhere: viz., that every psycho-physical movement rising above the threshold of consciousness is charged with pleasure in proportion as it approximates—beyond a certain limit—to complete equilibrium, and with 'pain' in proportion as it departs from it beyond a certain limit; while between the two limits which may be described as the qualitative thresholds of 'pain' or pleasure, there is a certain area of aesthetic indifference."

The facts that have led us to believe in the supremacy of the pleasure-principle in psychic life also find expression in the hypothesis that there is an attempt on the part of the psychic apparatus to keep the quantity of excitation present as low as possible, or, at least, constant. This is the same supposition only put into another form, for, if the psychic apparatus operates in the direction of keeping down the quantity of excitation, all that tends to increase it must be felt to be contrary to function, that is to say, painful. The pleasure-principle is deduced from the principle of constancy; in reality, the principle of constancy was inferred

[1] Translated from the second German edition.—ED.
[2] The word *Unlust*, as in the phrase "pleasure-pain principle," has been translated as "pain"; pain without quotation marks signifies *Schmerz* in the original.—TR.

from the facts that necessitated our assumption of the pleasure-principle. On more detailed discussion we shall find further that this tendency on the part of the psychic apparatus postulated by us may be classified as a special case of Fechner's principle of the *tendency towards stability* to which he has related the pleasure-pain feelings.

In that event, however, it must be affirmed that it is not strictly correct to speak of a supremacy of the pleasure-principle over the course of psychic processes. If such existed, then the vast majority of our psychic processes would necessarily be accompanied by pleasure or would conduce to it, while the most ordinary experience emphatically contradicts any such conclusion. One can only say that a strong tendency towards the pleasure-principle exists in the psyche, to which, however, certain other forces or conditions are opposed, so that the ultimate issue cannot always be in accordance with the pleasure-tendency. Compare the comment of Fechner in a similar connection. "Therewithal it is to be noted that the tendency towards the goal does not imply the attainment of it and that in general the goal is only approximately attainable . . ." [1] If we now address ourselves to the question of what circumstances have the power to frustrate the successful carrying out of the pleasure-principle, we shall be treading on safer and better-known ground, and we can draw in abundant measure on our analytical experiences for the answer.

The first case of such a check on the pleasure-principle is perfectly familiar to us in the regularity of its occurrence. We know that the pleasure-principle is adjusted to a primary mode of operation on the part of the psychic apparatus, and that for the preservation of the organism amid the difficulties of the external world it is *ab initio* useless and indeed extremely dangerous. Under the influence of the instinct of the ego for self-preservation, it is replaced by the *reality-principle,* which, without giving up the intention of ultimately attaining pleasure, yet demands and enforces the postponement of satisfaction, the renunciation of manifold possibilities of it, and the temporary endurance of "pain" on the long and circuitous road to pleasure. The pleasure-principle, however, remains for a long time the method of operation of the sex impulses, which are not so easily educable, and it happens over and over again that, whether acting through these impulses or operating in the ego itself, it prevails

[1] *Op. cit.,* p. 90.

over the reality-principle to the detriment of the whole organism.

It is at the same time indubitable that the replacement of the pleasure-principle by the reality-principle can account only for a small part, and that not the most intense, of painful experiences. Another and no less regular source of "pain" proceeds from the conflicts and dissociations in the psychic apparatus during the development of the ego towards a more highly co-ordinated organization. Nearly all the energy with which the apparatus is charged,[2] comes from the inborn instincts, but not all of these are allowed to develop to the same stage. On the way, it over and again happens that particular instincts, or portions of them, prove irreconcilable in their aims or demands with others which can be welded into the comprehensive unity of the ego. They are, thereupon, split off from this unity by the process of repression, retained on lower stages of psychic development, and for the time being cut off from all possibility of gratification. If they then succeed, as so easily happens with the repressed sex-impulses, in fighting their way through—along circuitous routes—to a direct or a substitutive gratification, this success, which might otherwise have brought pleasure, is experienced by the ego as "pain." In consequence of the old conflict which ended in repression, the pleasure-principle has been violated anew, just at the moment when certain impulses were at work on the achievement of fresh pleasure in pursuance of the principle. The details of the process by which repression changes a possibility of pleasure into a source of "pain" are not yet fully understood, or are not yet capable of clear presentation, but it is certain that all neurotic "pain" is of this kind, is pleasure which cannot be experienced as such.

The two sources of "pain" here indicated still do not nearly cover the majority of our painful experiences, but as to the rest one may say with a fair show of reason that their presence does not impugn the supremacy of the pleasure-principle. Most of the "pain" we experience is of a perceptual order, perception either of the urge of unsatisfied instincts or of something in the external world which may be painful in itself or may arouse painful anticipations in the psychic apparatus and is recognized by it as *danger.* The reaction to these

[2] The word *Besetzung* (literally: "state of being occupied"), as in the expressions *Besetzungsenergie* and *Energiebesetzung,* has been rendered by the words "investment" and "charge," the latter being taken from the analogy of electricity.—TR.

claims of impulse and these threats of danger, a reaction in which the real activity of the psychic apparatus is manifested, may be guided correctly by the pleasure-principle or by the reality-principle which modifies this. It seems thus unnecessary to recognize a still more far-reaching limitation of the pleasure-principle, and, nevertheless, it is precisely the investigation of the psychic reaction to external danger that may supply new material and new questions in regard to the problem here treated.

II

AFTER severe shock of a mechanical nature, railway collision, or other accident in which danger to life is involved, a condition may arise which has long been recognized and to which the name *traumatic neurosis* is attached. The terrible war that is just over has been responsible for an immense number of such maladies and, at least, has put an end to the inclination to explain them on the basis of organic injury to the nervous system due to the operation of mechanical force.[1] The clinical picture of traumatic neurosis approaches that of hysteria in its wealth of similar motor symptoms, but usually surpasses it in its strongly marked signs of subjective suffering—in this, resembling rather hypochondria or melancholia —and in the evidences of a far more comprehensive general weakening and shattering of the mental functions. Neither the war neuroses nor the traumatic neuroses of peace are as yet fully understood. With the war neuroses some light was contributed, but, also, on the other hand, a certain confusion introduced, by the fact that the same type of malady could occasionally occur without the interposition of gross mechanical force. In the traumatic neuroses, there are two outstanding features which might serve as clues for further reflection: first, that the chief causal factor seemed to lie in the element of surprise, in the fright; and secondly, that an injury or wound sustained at the same time generally tended to prevent the occurrence of the neurosis. *Fright, fear, apprehension* are incorrectly used as synonymous expressions: in their relation to danger they admit of quite clear distinction. Apprehension (*Angst*) denotes a certain condition as of expectation of danger and preparation for it, even though it be an unknown one; fear (*Furcht*) requires a definite object of which one is afraid; fright

(*Schreck*) is the name of the condition to which one is reduced if one encounters a danger without being prepared for it; it lays stress on the element of surprise. In my opinion, apprehension cannot produce a traumatic neurosis; in apprehension there is something which protects against fright and therefore against the fright-neurosis. We shall return later to this dictum.

The study of dreams may be regarded as the most trustworthy approach to the exploration of the deeper psychic processes. Now in the traumatic neuroses the dream life has this peculiarity: it continually takes the patient back to the situation of his disaster, from which he awakens in renewed terror. This fact has caused less surprise than it merits. The obtrusion on the patient over and again, even in sleep, of the impression made by the traumatic experience is taken as being merely a proof of its strength. The patient has, so to speak, undergone a psychical fixation as to the trauma. Fixations of this kind on the experience which has brought about the malady have long been known to us in connection with hysteria. Breuer and I stated in 1893 that hysterics suffer for the most part from reminiscences. In the war neuroses, observers, such as Ferenczi and Simmel, have been able to explain a number of motor symptoms as fixation on the factor of the trauma.

But I am not aware that the patients suffering from traumatic neuroses are much occupied in waking life with the recollection of what happened to them. They, perhaps, strive rather not to think of it. To regard it as self-evident that the dream at night takes them back to the situation which has caused the trouble is to misunderstand the nature of dreams. It would be more in correspondence with that nature if the patient were presented (in sleep) with images from the time of his normal health or of his hoped-for recovery. If we are not to go thoroughly astray as to the wish-fulfilment tendency of the dream in consequence of these dreams of the shock neuroses, perhaps the expedient is left us of supposing that in this condition the dream function suffers dislocation along with the others and is diverted from its usual ends, or else we should have to think of the enigmatic masochistic tendencies of the ego.

I propose now to leave the obscure and gloomy theme of the traumatic neuroses and to study the way in which the psychic apparatus works in one of its earliest normal activities. I refer to the play of children.

The different theories of child-play have

[1] Ferenczi, Abraham, Simmel, and Ernest Jones, *Psycho-Analysis and the War Neuroses*, No. 2 of the International Psycho-Analytical Library, 1921.

recently been collated by S. Pfeifer in *Imago*[1] and their analytical value estimated; I may here refer the reader to this work. These theories endeavour to conjecture the motives of children's play, though without placing any special stress on the *economic* point of view, i.e., consideration of the attainment of pleasure. Without the intention of making a comprehensive study of these phenomena I availed myself of an opportunity which offered of elucidating the first game invented by himself of a boy eighteen months old. It was more than a casual observation, for I lived for some weeks under the same roof as the child and his parents, and it was a considerable time before the meaning of his puzzling and continually repeated performance became clear to me.

The child was in no respect forward in his intellectual development; at eighteen months he spoke only a few intelligible words, making, besides, sundry significant sounds which were understood by those about him. But he made himself understood by his parents and the maidservant, and had a good reputation for behaving "properly." He did not disturb his parents at night; he scrupulously obeyed orders about not touching various objects and not going into certain rooms; and above all he never cried when his mother went out and left him for hours together, although the tie to his mother was a very close one: she had not only nourished him herself, but had cared for him and brought him up without any outside help. Occasionally, however, this well-behaved child evinced the troublesome habit of flinging into the corner of the room or under the bed all the little things he could lay his hands on, so that to gather up his toys was often no light task. He accompanied this by an expression of interest and gratification, emitting a loud longdrawn-out "o-o-o-oh" which, in the judgment of the mother (one that coincided with my own), was not an interjection but meant "go away" *(fort)*. I saw at last that this was a game, and that the child used all his toys only to play "being gone" *(fortsein)* with them. One day, I made an observation that confirmed my view. The child had a wooden reel with a piece of string wound round it. It never occurred to him, for example, to drag this after him on the floor and so play horse and cart with it, but he kept throwing it with considerable skill, held by the string, over the side of his little draped cot, so that the reel disappeared into it, then

[1] Vol. V, 243, 1919.

said his significant "o-o-o-oh" and drew the reel by the string out of the cot again, greeting its reappearance with a joyful *"Da"* (there). This was, therefore, the complete game, disappearance and return, the first act being the only one generally observed by the onlookers, and the one untiringly repeated by the child as a game for its own sake, although the greater pleasure unquestionably attached to the second act.[2]

The meaning of the game was then not far to seek. It was connected with the child's remarkable cultural achievement—the foregoing of the satisfaction of an instinct—as the result of which he could let his mother go away without making any fuss. He made it right with himself, so to speak, by dramatizing the same disappearance and return with the objects he had at hand. It is, of course, of no importance for the affective value of this game whether the child invented it himself or adopted it from a suggestion from outside. Our interest will attach itself to another point. The departure of the mother cannot possibly have been pleasant for the child, nor merely a matter of indifference. How then does it accord with the pleasure-principle that he repeats this painful experience as a game? The answer will perhaps be forthcoming that the departure must be played as the necessary prelude to the joyful return, and that in this latter lay the true purpose of the game. As against this, however, there is the observation that the first act, the going away, was played by itself as a game and far more frequently than the whole drama with its joyful conclusion.

The analysis of a single case of this kind yields no sure conclusion: on impartial consideration one gains the impression that it is from another motive that the child has turned the experience into a game. He was in the first place passive, was overtaken by the experience, but now brings himself in as playing an active part, by repeating the experience as a game in spite of its unpleasing nature. This effort might be ascribed to the impulse to obtain the mastery of a situation (the *power* instinct), which remains independent of any question of whether

[2] This interpretation was fully established by a further observation. One day, when the mother had been out for some hours she was greeted on her return by the information "Baby o-o-o-o" which at first remained unintelligible. It soon proved that during his long, lonely hours he had found a method of bringing about his own disappearance. He had discovered his reflection in the long mirror which nearly reached to the ground and had then crouched down in front of it, so that the reflection was *fort.*

the recollection was a pleasant one or not. But another interpretation may be attempted. The flinging away of the object so that it is gone might be the gratification of an impulse of revenge suppressed in real life but directed against the mother for going away, and would then have the defiant meaning: "Yes, you can go, I don't want you, I am sending you away myself." The same child, a year later than my observations, used to throw on the floor a toy which displeased him, and to say "Go to the war!" He had been told that his absent father was at the war, and he did not miss him at all, giving the clearest indications that he did not wish to be disturbed in the sole possession of his mother.[1] It is known of other children also that they can give vent to similar hostile feelings by throwing objects away in place of people.[2] Thus, one is left in doubt whether the compulsion to work over in psychic life what has made a deep impression, to make oneself fully master of it, can express itself primarily and independently of the pleasure-principle. In the case discussed here, however, the child might have repeated a disagreeable impression in play only because with the repetition was bound up a pleasure gain of a different kind but more direct.

Nor does the further pursuit of the question of play resolve our hesitations between two conceptions. We see that children repeat in their play everything that has made a great impression on them in actual life, that they thereby ab-react the strength of the impression and so to speak make themselves masters of the situation. But on the other hand, it is clear enough that all their play is influenced by the dominant wish of their time of life: viz., to be grown-up and to be able to do what grown-up people do. It is also observable that the unpleasing character of the experience does not always prevent its being utilized as a game. If a doctor examines a child's throat, or performs a small operation on him, the alarming experience will quite certainly be made the subject of the next game, but in this the pleasure gain from another source is not to be overlooked. In passing from the passivity of experience to the activity of play the child applies to his playfellow the unpleasant occurrence

that befell himself and so avenges himself on the person of this proxy.

From this discussion, it is at all events evident that it is unnecessary to assume a particular imitation impulse as the motive of play. We may add the reminder that the dramatic and imitative art of adults, which differs from the behaviour of children in being directed towards the spectator, does not, however, spare the latter the most painful impressions, e.g., in tragedy, and yet can be felt by him as highly enjoyable. This convinces us that even under the domination of the pleasure-principle there are ways and means enough of making what is in itself disagreeable the object of memory and of psychic preoccupation. A theory of aesthetics with an economic point of view should deal with these cases and situations ending in final pleasure gain: for our purposes, they are of no help, since they presuppose the existence and supremacy of the pleasure-principle and bear no witness to the operation of tendencies beyond the pleasure-principle, that is to say, tendencies which might be of earlier origin and independent of this.

III

FIVE-AND-TWENTY years of intensive work have brought about a complete change in the more immediate aims of psycho-analytic technique. At first the endeavours of the analytic physician were confined to divining the unconscious of which his patient was unaware, effecting a synthesis of its various components, and communicating it at the right time. Psycho-analysis was above all an art of interpretation. Since the therapeutic task was not thereby accomplished, the next aim was to compel the patient to confirm the reconstruction through his own memory. In this endeavour, the chief emphasis was on the resistances of the patient; the art now lay in unveiling these as soon as possible, in calling the patient's attention to them, and by human influence—here came in suggestion acting as *transference*—teaching him to abandon the resistances.

It then became increasingly clear however, that the aim in view, the bringing into consciousness of the unconscious, was not fully attainable by this method either. The patient cannot recall all of what lies repressed, perhaps not even the essential part of it, and so gains no conviction that the conclusion presented to him is correct. He is obliged rather to *repeat* as a current experience what is repressed, instead of, as the physician would prefer to see

---

[1] When the child was five and three-quarter years old his mother died. Now, when she was really *gone* (o-o-o), the boy showed no grief for her. A second child had, it is true, been born in the meantime and had aroused his strongest jealousy.

[2] See "A Childhood-Memory from *Dichtung und Wahrheit*," in *Collected Papers*, IV.

him do, *recollecting* it as a fragment of the past.[1] This reproduction appearing with unwelcome fidelity always contains a fragment of the infantile sex-life, therefore of the Oedipus complex and its off-shoots, and is played regularly in the sphere of transference, i.e., the relationship to the physician. When this point in the treatment is reached, it may be said that the earlier neurosis is now replaced by a fresh one, viz., the transference-neurosis. The physician makes it his concern to limit the scope of this transference-neurosis as much as he can, to force into memory as much as possible, and to leave as little as possible to repetition. The relation established between memory and reproduction is different for every case. As a rule, the physician cannot spare the patient this phase of the cure; he must let him live through a certain fragment of his forgotten life, and has to see to it that some measure of ascendency remains, in the light of which the apparent reality is always recognized as a reflection of a forgotten past. If this is successfully accomplished, then conviction on the part of the patient is attained, and with it the therapeutic result that depends on it.

In order to render more comprehensible this *repetition-compulsion* which appears in the psycho-analytic treatment of neurotics, we must above all get entirely rid of the erroneous idea that in this struggle with resistances we are concerned with any resistance on the part of the unconscious. The unconscious, i.e., the *repressed* material, offers no resistance whatever to the curative efforts; indeed it has no other aim than to force its way through the pressure weighing on it, either to consciousness or to discharge by means of some real action. The resistance in the treatment proceeds from the same higher levels and systems in the psychic life that in their time brought about the repression. But since the motives of the resistances, and indeed the resistances themselves, are found in the process of the treatment to be unconscious, we are well advised to amend an inadequacy in our mode of expression. We escape ambiguity if we contrast not the conscious and the unconscious, but the coherent ego and the repressed. Much in the ego is certainly unconscious itself, just what may be called the kernel of the ego; only a part of it comes under the category of *preconscious*. After thus replacing a purely descriptive method of expression

by a systematic or dynamic one, we may say that the resistance on the part of the analysed person proceeds from his ego, and then we at once see that the *repetition-compulsion* must be ascribed to the repressed element in the unconscious. It probably could not find expression till the work of the treatment coming to meet it had loosened the repression.

There is no doubt that the resistance of the conscious and preconscious ego subserves the pleasure-principle; it is trying to avoid the "pain" that would be aroused by the release of the repressed material, and our efforts are directed to effecting an entry for such painful feeling by an appeal to the reality-principle. In what relation to the pleasure-principle, then, does the repetition-compulsion stand, that which expresses the force of what is repressed? It is plain that most of what is revived by the repetition-compulsion cannot but bring discomfort to the ego, for it promotes the bringing to light of the activities of repressed impulses; but that is a discomfort we have already taken into account and without subversion of the pleasure-principle, since it is "pain" in respect of one system and at the same time satisfaction for the other. The new and remarkable fact, however, that we have now to describe is that the repetition-compulsion also revives experiences of the past that contain no potentiality of pleasure, and which could at no time have been satisfactions, even of impulses since repressed.

The efflorescense of infantile sex-life was, by reason of the irreconcilability of its wishes with reality and the inadequacy of the childhood stage of development reached, destined to pass away. It perished in most painful circumstances and with feelings of a deeply distressing nature. Loss and failure in the sphere of the affections left behind on the ego-feeling marks of injury comparable to a narcissistic scar, which, according to my experience and the exposition given by Marcinowski,[2] yields the most important contribution to the *inferiority complex* common among neurotics. The sex-quest to which the physical development of the child set limits could be brought to no satisfying conclusion; hence the plaint in later life: "I can't do anything, I am never successful." The bonds of tenderness linking the child more especially to the parent of the opposite sex succumbed to disappointment, to the vain expectation of sat-

---

[1] See "Further Recommendations in the Technique of Psycho-Analysis, II: Recollection, Repetition, and Working-Through," *Collected Papers*, II.

[2] Marcinowski, *"Die erotischen Quellen der Minderwertigkeitsgefühle," Zeitschrift für Sexualwissenschaft,* 1918, IV.

isfaction, and to the jealousy aroused by the birth of a new child, unmistakable proof as it is of the faithlessness of the loved parent; the child's attempt, undertaken with tragic seriousness, to produce another such child himself met with humiliating failure; while the partial withdrawal of the tenderness lavished on the little one, the more exacting demands of discipline and education, severe words and an occasional punishment finally revealed to him the whole extent of the disdain which is his portion. Some few regularly recurring types are to be found, according to the way in which the typical love of this period was brought to an end.

All these undesired happenings and painful affective situations are repeated by neurotics in the *transference* stage and re-animated with much ingenuity. They struggle to break off the unfinished treatment, they know how to re-create the feeling of being disdained, how to force the physician to adopt brusque speech and a chilling manner towards them, they find suitable objects for their jealousy, they substitute for the ardently desired child of early days the promise of some great gift which becomes as little real as that was. Nothing of all this could ever have afforded any pleasure; one would suppose it ought to bring somewhat less "pain" if revealed as memory rather than if lived through as a new experience. It is a question naturally of the action of impulses that should lead to satisfaction, but the experience that instead of this they even then brought "pain" has borne no result. The act is repeated in spite of everything; a powerful compulsion insists on it.

That which psycho-analysis reveals in the transference phenomena with neurotics can also be observed in the life of normal persons. It here gives the impression of a pursuing fate, a demonic trait in their destiny, and psycho-analysis has from the outset regarded such a life history as in a large measure self-imposed and determined by infantile influences. The compulsion which thereby finds expression is in no way different from the repetition-compulsion of neurotics, even though such persons have never shown signs of a neurotic conflict resulting in symptoms. Thus one knows people with whom every human relationship ends in the same way: benefactors whose protégés, however different they may otherwise have been, invariably after a time desert them in ill-will, so that they are apparently condemned to drain to the dregs all the bitterness of ingratitude; men with whom every friendship ends in the friend's treachery; others who indefinitely often in their lives invest some other person with authority either in their own eyes or generally, and themselves overthrow such authority after a given time, only to replace it by a new one; lovers whose tender relationships with women each and all run through the same phases and come to the same end, and so on. We are less astonished at this "endless repetition of the same" if there is involved a question of active behaviour on the part of the person concerned, and if we detect in his character an unalterable trait which must always manifest itself in the repetition of identical experiences. Far more striking are those cases where the person seems to be experiencing something passively, without exerting any influence of his own, and yet always meets with the same fate over and over again. One may recall, for example, the story of the woman who married three men in succession, each of whom fell ill after a short time and whom she had to nurse till their death.[1] Tasso gives a singularly affecting poetical portrayal of such a trend of fate in the romantic epic, *Gerusalemme Liberta*. The hero, Tancred, has unwittingly slain Clorinda, the maiden he loved, who fought with him disguised in the armour of an enemy knight. After her burial he penetrates into the mysterious enchanted wood, the bane of the army of the crusaders. Here he hews down a tall tree with his sword, but from the gash in the trunk blood streams forth and the voice of Clorinda, whose soul is imprisoned in the trees, cries out to him in reproach that he has once more wrought a baleful deed on his beloved.

In the light of such observations as these, drawn from the behaviour during transference and from the fate of human beings, we may venture to make the assumption that there really exists in psychic life a repetition-compulsion, which goes beyond the pleasure-principle. We shall now also feel disposed to relate to this compelling force the dreams of shock-patients and the play-impulse in children. We must, of course, remind ourselves that only in rare cases can we recognize the workings of this repetition-compulsion in a pure form, without the co-operation of other motives. As regards children's play, we have already pointed out what other interpretations its origin permits. The repetition-compulsion and direct

[1] See the pertinent observations of C. G. Jung in his article, *"Die Bedeutung des Vaters für das Schicksal des Einzelnen,"* *Jahrbuch für psychoanal. u. psychopath. Forschungen,* 1901, Vol. I.

pleasurable satisfaction of impulse seem there to be inextricably intertwined. The transference phenomena obviously subserve the purpose of the resistance made by the ego persisting in its repression: the repetition-compulsion is, as it were, called to the aid of the ego, which is resolved to hold fast to the pleasure-principle. In what one might call the destiny-compulsion much appears capable of rational explanation, so that no need is felt to establish a new and mysterious impulse. The least suspicious case is perhaps that of the shock-dream, but on closer examination it must be admitted that in the other examples, too, the state of affairs is not completely explained by the operation of the motives known to us. There remains enough over to justify the assumption of a repetition-compulsion, and this seems to us more primitive, more elementary, more instinctive than the pleasure-principle which is displaced by it. But if there is such a repetition-compulsion in psychic life, we should naturally like to know with what function it corresponds, under what conditions it may appear, and in what relation it stands to the pleasure-principle, to which we have heretofore ascribed the domination over the course of the processes of excitation in the psychic life.

IV

WHAT follows now is speculation, speculation often far-fetched, which each will, according to his particular attitude, acknowledge or neglect. Or one may call it the exploitation of an idea out of curiosity to see whither it will lead.

Psycho-analytic speculation starts from the impression gained on investigating unconscious processes that consciousness cannot be the most general characteristic of psychic processes, but merely a special function of them. Metapsychologically expressed, it asserts that consciousness is the functioning of a particular system which may be called *Bw.* Since consciousness essentially yields perceptions of excitations coming from without and feeling *(Empfindungen)* of pleasure and "pain" which can only be derived from within the psychic apparatus, we may allot the system W-Bw^1 (= perceptual consciousness) a position in space. It must lie on the boundary between outer and inner, must face towards the outer world, and must envelop the other psychic systems. We then note that in this assumption we have ventured nothing new, but are in agreement with the localizing

tendencies of cerebral anatomy, which places the *seat* of consciousness in the cortical layer, the outermost enveloping layer of the central organ. Cerebral anatomy does not need to wonder why—anatomically speaking—consciousness should be accommodated on the surface of the brain, instead of being safely lodged somewhere in the deepest recesses of it. Perhaps we may carry matters a little further than this in our deduction of such a position for our system W-$Bw.$

Consciousness is not the only peculiar feature that we ascribe to the processes in this system. Our impressions gained by psychoanalytic experience lead us to the supposition that all excitation processes in the other systems leave in them permanent traces forming the foundations of memory-records which have nothing to do with the question of becoming conscious. They are often strongest and most enduring when the process that left them behind never reached consciousness at all. But we find it difficult to believe that such lasting traces of excitation are formed also in the system W-Bw itself. If they remained permanently in consciousness, they would very soon limit the fitness of the system for registration of new excitations;[2] on the other hand, if they became unconscious, we should be confronted with the task of explaining the existence of unconscious processes in a system whose functioning is otherwise accompanied by the phenomenon of consciousness. We should, so to speak, have gained nothing and altered nothing by our supposition which relegates to a special system the process of becoming conscious. Though this may not be an absolutely binding consideration, it may, at any rate, lead us to conjecture that becoming conscious and leaving behind a memory-trace are processes incompatible with each other in the same system. We should thus be able to say: in the system *Bw,* the process of excitation becomes conscious, but it leaves behind no lasting trace; all the traces of it on which memory relies would come about in the next systems inwards from the propagation of the excitation on to them. It is on these lines that the scheme is sketched which I inserted into the speculative section of my *Interpretation of Dreams* in 1900. If one reflects how little we know from other sources about the origin of consciousness, the pronouncement that *consciousness arises in*

---

[1] Thus named after the German words *Wahrnehmung* (=perception) and *Bewusstsein* (=consciousness).—TR.

[2] Here I follow throughout J. Breuer's exposition in the theoretical section of the *Studien über Hysterie,* 1895.

the place of the memory-trace must be conceded at least the importance of a statement which is to some extent definite.

The system *Bw* would thus be characterized by the peculiarity that the excitation process does not leave in it, as it does in all other psychic systems, a permanent alteration of its elements, but is, as it were, discharged in the phenomenon of becoming conscious and vanishes. Such a departure from the general rule requires an explanation on the ground of a factor which comes into account in this one system only: this factor which is absent from all other systems might well be the exposed situation of the *Bw* system—its immediate contact with the outer world.

Let us imagine the living organism in the simplest possible form as an undifferentiated vesicle of sensitive substance: then its surface, exposed as it is to the outer world, is by its very position differentiated and serves as an organ for receiving stimuli. Embryology, repeating as it does the history of evolution, does, in fact, show that the central nervous system arises from the ectoderm; the grey cortex of the brain remains a derivative of the primitive superficial layer and may have inherited essential properties from this. It would then be easily conceivable that, owing to the constant impact of external stimuli on the superficies of the vesicle, its substance would undergo lasting alteration to a certain depth, so that its excitation process takes a different course from that taken in the deeper layers. Thus, a rind would be formed which would finally have been so burned through by the effects of stimulation that it presents the most favourable conditions for the reception of stimuli and is incapable of any further modification. Applying this idea to the system *Bw*, this would mean that its elements are not susceptible of any further lasting alteration from the passage of the excitation, because they are already modified to the uttermost in that respect. But they are then capable of giving rise to consciousness. In what exactly these modifications of the substance and of the excitation process in it consist many views may be held which as yet cannot be tested. It may be assumed that the excitation has, in its transmission from one element to another, to overcome a resistance, and that this diminution of the resistance itself lays down the permanent trace of the excitation (a path): in system *Bw*, there would no longer exist any such resistance to transmission from one element to another. We

may associate with this conception Breuer's distinction between quiescent (bound) and free-moving *investment-energy* in the elements of the psychic systems;[1] the elements of the system *Bw* would then convey no *bound* energy, only free energy capable of discharge. In my opinion, however, it is better for the present to express oneself as to these conditions in the least committal way. At any rate, by these speculations we should have brought the origin of consciousness into a certain connection with the position of the system *Bw* and with the peculiarities of the excitation process to be ascribed to this.

We have more to say about the living vesicle with its receptive outer layer. This morsel of living substance floats about in an outer world which is charged with the most potent energies, and it would be destroyed by the operation of the stimuli proceeding from this world if it were not furnished with a protection against stimulation (*Reizschutz*). It acquires this through its outermost layer—which gives the structure that belongs to living matter—becoming in a measure inorganic, and this now operates as a special integument or membrane that keeps off the stimuli, i.e., makes it impossible for the energies of the outer world to act with more than a fragment of their intensity on the layers immediately below which have preserved their vitality. These are now able under cover of the protecting layer to devote themselves to the reception of those stimulus masses that have been let through. But the outer layer has by its own death secured all the deeper layers from a like fate—at least, so long as no stimuli present themselves of such a strength as to break through the protective barrier. For the living organism, protection against stimuli is almost a more important task than reception of stimuli; the protective barrier is equipped with its own store of energy and must above all endeavour to protect the special forms of energy-transformations going on within itself from the equalising and, therefore, destructive influence of the enormous energies at work in the outer world. The reception of stimuli serves above all the purpose of collecting information about the direction and nature of the external stimuli, and for that it must suffice to take little samples of the outer world, to taste it, so to speak, in small quantities. In highly developed organisms the receptive external layer of what was once a vesicle has long been withdrawn into the depths of the

[1] J. Breuer and S. Freud, *Studien über Hysterie.*

body, but portions of it have been left on the surface immediately beneath the common protective barrier. These portions form the sense organs, which essentially comprise arrangements for the reception of specific stimuli, but also possess special arrangements adapted for a fresh protection against an overwhelming amount of stimulus, and for warding off unsuitable kinds of stimuli. It is characteristic of them that they assimilate only very small quantities of the outer stimulus, and take in only samples of the outer world; one might compare them to antennae which touch at the outer world and then constantly withdraw from it again.

At this point, I shall permit myself to touch cursorily upon a theme which would deserve the most thorough treatment. The Kantian proposition that time and space are necessary modes of thought may be submitted to discussion today in the light of certain knowledge reached through psycho-analysis. We have found by experience that unconscious mental processes are in themselves *timeless*. That is to say, to begin with: they are not arranged chronologically, time alters nothing in them, nor can the idea of time be applied to them. These are negative characteristics, which can be made plain only by instituting a comparison with conscious psychic processes. Our abstract conception of time seems rather to be derived wholly from the mode of functioning of the system *W-Bw*, and to correspond with a self-perception of it. In this mode of functioning of the system, another form of protection against stimulation probably comes into play. I know that these statements sound very obscure, but I must confine myself to these few hints.

So far we have got to the point that the living vesicle is equipped with a protection against stimuli from the outer world. Before that, we had decided that the cortical layer next to it must be differentiated as the organ for reception of external stimuli. But this sensitive layer (what is later the system *Bw*) also receives excitations from within: the position of the system between outer and inner and the difference in the conditions under which this receptivity operates on the two sides become deciding factors for the functioning of the system and of the whole psychic apparatus. Towards the outer world there is a barrier against stimuli, and the mass of excitations coming up against it will take effect only on a reduced scale; towards what is within, no protection against stimuli is possible; the excitations of the deeper layers

pursue their way direct and in undiminished mass into the system, while certain characteristics of their course produce the series of pleasure-pain feelings. Naturally, the excitations coming from within will, in conformity with their intensity and other qualitative characteristics (or possibly their amplitude), be more proportionate to the mode of operation of the system than the stimuli streaming in from the outer world. Two things are, however, decisively determined by these conditions: first, the preponderance over all outer stimuli of the pleasure and "pain" feelings, which are an index for processes within the mechanism; and, secondly, a shaping of behaviour towards such inner excitations as bring with them an overplus of "pain." There will be a tendency to treat them as though they were acting not from within but from without, in order for it to be possible to apply against them the defensive measures of the barrier against stimuli (*Reizschutz*). This is the origin of projection, for which so important a part is reserved in the production of pathological states.

I have the impression that by these last considerations we have approached nearer to a comprehension of the supremacy of the pleasure-principle, but we have not attained to an explanation of those cases which are opposed to it. Let us, therefore, go a step further. Such external excitations as are strong enough to break through the barrier against stimuli we call *traumatic*. In my opinion, the concept of trauma involves such a relationship to an otherwise efficacious barrier. An occurrence such as an external trauma will undoubtedly provoke a very extensive disturbance in the workings of the energy of the organism, and will set in motion every kind of protective measure. But the pleasure-principle is, to begin with, put out of action here. The flooding of the psychic apparatus with large masses of stimuli can no longer be prevented: on the contrary, another task presents itself—to bring the stimulus under control, to *bind* in the psyche the stimulus mass that has broken its way in, so as to bring about a discharge of it.

Probably, the specific discomfort of bodily pain is the result of some local breaking through of the barrier against stimuli. From this point in the periphery there stream to the central psychic apparatus continual excitations such as would otherwise come only from within.[1] What are we to expect as the reaction of the

[1] See the paper *Instincts and their Vicissitudes*, p. 412 above.

psychic life to this invasion? From all sides the *charging energy* is called on in order to create all round the breach correspondingly high *charges* of energy. An immense *counter-charge* is set up, in favour of which all the other psychic systems are impoverished, so that a wide-spread paralysis or diminution of other psychic activity follows. We endeavour to learn from examples such as these to base our meta-psychological conjectures on such prototypes. Thus, from this behaviour we draw the conclusion that even a highly charged system is able to receive new energy streaming in, to convert it into a *quiescent charge*, thus to *bind* it psychically. The more intense is the intrinsic quiescent charge, the greater is its binding force: and, conversely, the lower the charge of the system, the less capable is it of receiving the energy that streams in, and so the more violent are the consequences when the barrier against stimuli is broken through. It is not a valid objection to this view that the intensifying of the charges round the place of irruption could be much more simply explained as the direct action of the oncoming mass of excitation. If that were so, the psychic apparatus would merely undergo an increase of its energy charges, and the paralyzing character of pain, with the impoverishment of all the other systems, would remain without explanation. Nor do the very violent discharge effects of pain invalidate our explanation, for they happen in a reflex manner, that is to say, they follow without the interposition of the psychic apparatus. The indefinite nature of all the discussions that we term *metapsychological* naturally comes from the fact that we know nothing about the nature of the excitation process in the elements of the psychic systems and do not feel justified in making any assumption about it. Thus we are all the time operating with a large X, which we carry over into every new formula. That this process is accomplished with energies which differ quantitatively is an easily admissible postulate; that it also has more than one quality (e.g., in the direction of amplitude) may be regarded as probable: the new consideration we have brought in is Breuer's proposition that we have to do with two ways in which a system may be filled with energy, so that a distinction has to be made between a *charging* of the psychic systems (or its elements) that is free-flowing and striving to be discharged and one that is quiescent. Perhaps we may admit the conjecture that the binding of the energy streaming into the psychic ap-paratus consists in a translating of it from the free-flowing to the quiescent state.

I think one may venture (tentatively) to regard the ordinary traumatic neurosis as the result of an extensive rupture of the barrier against stimuli. In this way the old naïve doctrine of *shock* would come into its own again, apparently in opposition to a later and psychologically more pretentious view which ascribes aetiological significance not to the effect of the mechanical force, but to the fright and the menace to life. But these opposing views are not irreconcilable, and the psycho-analytic conception of the traumatic neurosis is far from being identical with the crudest form of the *shock* theory. While the latter takes the essential nature of the shock as residing in the direct injury to the molecular structure, or even to the histological structure, of the nervous elements, we seek to understand the effect of the shock by considering the breaking through of the barrier with which the psychic organ is provided against stimuli, and from the tasks with which this is thereby faced. Fright retains its meaning for us too. What conditions it is the failure of the mechanism of apprehension to make the proper preparation, including the over-charging of the systems first receiving the stimulus. In consequence of this lower degree of charging, these systems are hardly in a position to bind the oncoming masses of excitation, and the consequences of the breaking through of the protective barrier appear all the more easily. We thus find that the apprehensive preparation, together with the over-charging of the receptive systems, represents the last line of defence against stimuli. For a great number of traumata, the difference between the unprepared systems and those prepared by over-charging may turn the scale as to the outcome: with a trauma beyond a certain strength, such a difference may no longer be of any importance. When the dreams of patients suffering from traumatic neuroses so regularly take them back to the situation of the disaster, they do not thereby, it is true, serve the purpose of wish-fulfilment, the hallucinatory conjuring up of which has, under the domination of the pleasure-principle, become the function of dreams. But we may assume that they thereby subserve another purpose, which must be fulfilled before the pleasure-principle can begin its sway. These dreams are attempts at restoring control of the stimuli by developing apprehension, the pretermission of which caused the traumatic neurosis. They thus afford us an insight into a function of the psychic apparatus, which without contradicting the pleasure-principle is nevertheless independent of it, and appears to be of earlier origin than the aim of attaining pleasure and avoiding "pain."

This is, therefore, the moment to concede for the first time an exception to the principle that the dream is a wish-fulfilment. Anxiety dreams are no such exception, as I have repeatedly and in detail shown; nor are the *punishment dreams,* for they merely put in the place of the interdicted wish-fulfilment the punishment appropriate to it, and are thus the wish-fulfilment of the sense of guilt reacting on the contemned impulse. But the dreams mentioned above of patients suffering from traumatic neuroses do not permit of classification under the category of wish-fulfilment, nor do the dreams occurring during psycho-analysis that bring back the recollection of the psychic traumata of childhood. They obey rather the repetition-compulsion, which in analysis, it is true, is supported by the (not unconscious) wish to conjure up again what has been forgotten and repressed. Thus, the function of the dream, viz., to do away with the motives leading to interruption of sleep by presenting wish-fulfilments of the disturbing excitations, would not be its original one; the dream could secure control of this function only after the whole psychic life had accepted the domination of the pleasure-principle. If there is a *beyond the pleasure-principle,* it is logical to admit a prehistoric past also for the wish-fulfilling tendency of the dream, though to do so is no contradiction of its later function. Now, when this tendency is once broken through, there arises the further question: are such dreams, which in the interests of the psychical binding of traumatic impressions follow the repetition-compulsion, not possible apart from analysis? The answer is certainly in the affirmative.

With regard to the war neuroses, so far as the term has any significance apart from a reference to the occasion of the appearance of the illness, I have explained elsewhere that they might very well be traumatic neuroses which have arisen the more easily on account of an ego-conflict.[1] The fact mentioned on page 641, viz., that a severe injury inflicted at the same time by the trauma lessens the chance of a neurosis arising, is no longer difficult to understand if two circumstances emphasised by psy-

cho-analytic research are borne in mind. First, that mechanical concussion must be recognized as one of the sources of sexual excitation;[2] and, secondly, that a painful and feverish illness exerts for the time it lasts a powerful influence on the distribution of the libido. Thus, the mechanical force of the trauma would set free the quota of sexual excitation which, in consequence of the lacking preparation by apprehension, has a traumatic effect: but, on the other hand, the contemporaneous bodily injury would bind the surplus excitation by the putting in of a claim to a narcissistic over-charging of the injured part.[3] It is also known, though the idea has not been sufficiently made use of in the Libido theory, that disturbances in the distribution of the libido so severe as those of melancholia may be removed for a time by an intercurrent organic disease; in fact even the condition of a fully developed *dementia praecox* is capable of a transitory improvement in these circumstances.

V

THE fact that the sensitive cortical layer has no protective barrier against excitations emanating from within will have one inevitable consequence: viz., that these transmissions of stimuli acquire increased economic significance and frequently give rise to economic disturbances comparable to the traumatic neuroses. The most prolific sources of such inner excitations are the so-called *instincts* of the organism, the representatives of all forces arising within the body and transmitted to the psychic apparatus—the most important and most obscure element in psychological research.

Perhaps we shall not find it too rash an assumption that the excitations proceeding from the instincts do not conform to the type of the *bound* but of the free-moving nerve processes that are striving for discharge. The most trustworthy knowledge we have of these processes comes from the study of dreams. There we found that the processes in the unconscious systems are fundamentally different from those in the (pre)conscious; that in the unconscious *charges* may easily be completely transferred, displaced or condensed, while if this happened with preconscious material only defective results would be obtained. This is the reason for the well-known peculiarities of the manifest dream, after the preconscious residues of the

[1] *Psycho-Analysis and the War Neuroses,* Introduction, International Psycho-Analytical Library, No. 2. 1921.

[2] See the remarks: "The effects of swinging and railway travelling," in *Three Contributions to the Theory of Sex.*
[3] See *On Narcissism: an Introduction,* p. 399 above.

day before have undergone elaboration according to the laws of the unconscious. I termed this kind of process in the unconscious the psychic *primary process* in contradistinction to the secondary process valid in our normal waking life. Since the excitations of instincts all affect the unconscious systems, it is scarcely an innovation to say that they follow the lines of the primary process, and little more so to identify the psychic primary process with the freely mobile charge, the secondary process with changes in Breuer's bound or tonic charge.[1] It would then be the task of the higher layers of the psychic apparatus to bind the instinct-excitation that reaches the primary process. The failure to effect this binding would evoke a disturbance analogous to the traumatic neuroses; it is only after the binding had been successfully accomplished that the pleasure-principle (and its modification the reality-principle) would have an opportunity to assert its sway without hindrance. Till then, the other task of the psychic apparatus would take precedence, viz., to obtain control of or to bind the excitation, not in opposition to the pleasure-principle but independently of it and, in part, without regard to it.

The expressions of a repetition-compulsion which we have described, both in the early activities of infantile psychic life and in the experiences of psycho-analytic treatment, show in a high degree an instinctive character, and, where they come into contrast with the pleasure-principle, a demonic character. In the play of children, we seem to arrive at the conclusion that the child repeats even the unpleasant experiences because through his own activity he gains a far more thorough mastery of the strong impression than was possible by mere passive experience. Every fresh repetition seems to strengthen this mastery for which the child strives; even with pleasurable experiences the child cannot do enough in the way of repetition and will inexorably insist on the identity of the impression. This characteristic is destined later to disappear. A witticism heard for the second time will almost fail of effect; a theatrical performance will never make the same impression the second time that it did on the first occasion; indeed, it is hard to persuade the adult to read again at all soon a book he has enjoyed. Novelty is always the necessary condition of enjoyment. The child, however, never gets tired of demanding from a grown-up the repetition of a game he has played with him before or has

shown him, till at last the grown-up refuses, utterly worn out; similarly, if he has been told a pretty story, he wants always to hear the same story instead of a new one, insists inexorably on exact repetition and corrects each deviation which the narrator lets slip by mistake, which, perhaps, he even thought to gain new merit by inserting. Here, there is no contradiction of the pleasure-principle: it is evident that the repetition, the rediscovery of the identity, is itself a source of pleasure. In the case of a patient in analysis, on the other hand, it is plain that the compulsion to repeat in the transference the occurrences of his infantile life disregards *in every way* the pleasure-principle. The patient behaves in this respect completely like a child, and thus makes it clear to us that the repressed memory-traces of his primitive experience are not present in a *bound* form, are indeed, in a sense, not capable of the secondary process. To this fact of their not being bound they owe their power to weave a wish-phantasy that will be represented in a dream, by adhering to the residues from waking experiences. We frequently encounter the same repetition-compulsion as a therapeutic obstacle, when at the end of the treatment we wish to bring about complete detachment from the physician; and it may be supposed that the vague dread with which those who are unfamiliar with it view analysis, as though they feared to wake what they think is better left to sleep, is at root a fear of the appearance of this demonic compulsion.

In what way is the instinctive connected with the compulsion to repetition? At this point, the idea is forced upon us that we have stumbled on the trace of a general and hitherto not clearly recognized—or at least not expressly emphasized—characteristic of instinct, perhaps of all organic life. According to this, *an instinct would be a tendency innate in living organic matter impelling it towards the reinstatement of an earlier condition*, one which it had to abandon under the influence of external disturbing forces—a kind of organic elasticity, or, to put it another way, the manifestation of inertia in organic life.[2]

This conception of instinct strikes us as strange, since we are accustomed to see in instinct the factor urging towards change and development, and now we find ourselves required to recognize in it the very opposite, viz., the

---

[1] See "Psychology of the Dream-Processes," Section VII, in my *Interpretation of Dreams* (p. 340 above).

[2] I have little doubt that similar conjectures about the nature of instinct have been already repeatedly put forward.

expression of the conservative nature of living beings. On the other hand, we soon think of those examples in animal life which appear to confirm the idea of instinct having been historically conditioned. When certain fish undertake arduous journeys at spawning-time, in order to deposit the spawn in certain definite waters far removed from their usual habitats, according to the interpretation of many biologists they are only seeking the earlier homes of their kind, which in course of time they have exchanged for others. The same is said to be true of the migratory flights of birds of passage, but the search for further examples becomes superfluous when we remember that in the phenomena of heredity and in the facts of embryology we have the most imposing proofs of the organic compulsion to repetition. We see that the germ cell of a living animal is obliged to repeat in its development—although in a fleeting and curtailed fashion—the structures of all the forms from which the animal is descended, instead of hastening along the shortest path to its own final shape. A mechanical explanation of this except in some trifling particulars is impossible, and the historical explanation cannot be disregarded. In the same way, we find extending far upwards in the animal kingdom a power of reproduction whereby a lost organ is replaced by the growth of a new one exactly like it.

The obvious objection, that it may well be that besides the conservative instincts compelling repetition there are others which press towards new formation and progress, should certainly not be left unnoticed; it will be considered at a later stage of our discussion. But we may first be tempted to follow to its final consequences the hypothesis that all instincts have as their aim the reinstatement of an earlier condition. If what results gives an appearance of *profundity* or bears a resemblance to mysticism, still we know ourselves to be clear of the reproach of having striven after anything of the sort. We are in search of sober results of investigation or of reflections based upon it, and the only character we wish for in these results is that of certainty.

If, then, all organic instincts are conservative, historically acquired, and are directed towards regression, towards reinstatement of something earlier, we are obliged to place all the results of organic development to the credit of external, disturbing, and distracting influences. The rudimentary creature would from its very beginning not have wanted to change, would, if circumstances had remained the same, have always merely repeated the same course of existence. But in the last resort it must have been the evolution of our earth, and its relation to the sun, that has left its imprint on the development of organisms. The conservative organic instincts have absorbed every one of these enforced alterations in the course of life and have stored them for repetition; they thus present the delusive appearance of forces striving after change and progress, while they are merely endeavouring to reach an old goal by ways both old and new. This final goal of all organic striving can be stated too. It would be counter to the conservative nature of instinct if the goal of life were a state never hitherto reached. It must rather be an ancient starting point, which the living being left long ago, and to which it harks back again by all the circuitous paths of development. If we may assume as an experience admitting of no exception that everything living dies from causes within itself, and returns to the inorganic, we can only say *"The goal of all life is death,"* and, casting back, *"The inanimate was there before the animate."*

At one time or another, by some operation of force which still completely baffles conjecture, the properties of life were awakened in lifeless matter. Perhaps the process was a prototype resembling that other one which later in a certain stratum of living matter gave rise to consciousness. The tension then aroused in the previously inanimate matter strove to attain an equilibrium; the first instinct was present, that to return to lifelessness. The living substance at that time had death within easy reach; there was probably only a short course of life to run, the direction of which was determined by the chemical structure of the young organism. So through a long period of time the living substance may have been constantly created anew, and easily extinguished, until decisive external influences altered in such a way as to compel the still surviving substance to ever greater deviations from the original path of life, and to ever more complicated and circuitous routes to the attainment of the goal of death. These circuitous ways to death, faithfully retained by the conservative instincts, would be neither more nor less than the phenomena of life as we now know it. If the exclusively conservative nature of the instincts is accepted as true, it is impossible to arrive at any other suppositions with regard to the origin and goal of life.

If these conclusions sound strangely in our ears, equally so will those we are led to make concerning the great groups of instincts which we regard as lying behind the vital phenomena of organisms. The postulate of the self-preservative instincts we ascribe to every living being stands in remarkable contrast to the supposition that the whole life of instinct serves the one end of bringing about death. The theoretic significance of the instincts of self-preservation, power, and self-assertion, shrinks to nothing, seen in this light; they are part-instincts designed to secure the path to death peculiar to the organism and to ward off possibilities of return to the inorganic other than the immanent ones, but the enigmatic struggle of the organism to maintain itself in spite of all the world, a struggle that cannot be brought into connection with anything else, disappears. It remains to be added that the organism is resolved to die only in its own way; even these watchmen of life were originally the myrmidons of death. Hence, the paradox comes about that the living organism resists with all its energy influences (dangers) which could help it to reach its life-goal by a short way (a short circuit, so to speak); but this is just the behaviour that characterizes a pure instinct as contrasted with an intelligent striving.

But we must bethink ourselves: this cannot be the whole truth. The sexual instincts, for which the theory of the neuroses claims a position apart, lead us to quite another point of view. Not all organisms have yielded to the external compulsion driving them to an ever further development. Many have succeeded in maintaining themselves on their low level up to the present time: there are in existence to-day, if not all, at all events many forms of life that must resemble the primitive stages of the higher animals and plants. And, similarly, not all the elementary organisms that make up the complicated body of a higher form of life take part in the whole path of evolution to the natural end, i.e., death. Some among them, the reproductive cells, probably retain the original structure of the living substance and, after a given time, detach themselves from the parent organism, charged as they are with all the inherited and newly acquired instinctive dispositions. Possibly it is just those two features that make their independent existence possible. If brought under favourable conditions they begin to develop, that is, to repeat the same cycle to which they owe their origin, the end being that again one portion of the substance carries through its development to a finish, while another part, as a new germinal core, again harks back to the beginning of the development. Thus, these reproductive cells operate against the death of the living substance and are able to win for it what must seem to us to be potential immortality, although perhaps it only means a lengthening of the path to death. Of the highest significance is the fact that the reproductive cell is fortified for this function, or only becomes capable of it, by the mingling with another like it and yet different from it.

There is a group of instincts that care for the destinies of these elementary organisms which survive the individual being, that concern themselves with the safe sheltering of these organisms as long as they are defenceless against the stimuli of the outer world, and finally bring about their conjunction with other reproductive cells. These are collectively the sexual instincts. They are conservative in the same sense as the others are, in that they reproduce earlier conditions of the living substance; but they are so in a higher degree, in that they show themselves specially resistant to external influences; and they are more conservative in a wider sense still, since they preserve life itself for a longer time. They are the actual life-instincts; the fact that they run counter to the trend of the other instincts which lead towards death indicates a contradiction between them and the rest, one which the theory of neuroses has recognized as full of significance. There is, as it were, an oscillating rhythm in the life of organisms; the one group of instincts presses forward to reach the final goal of life as quickly as possible, the other flies back at a certain point on the way only to traverse the same stretch once more from a given spot and thus to prolong the duration of the journey. Although sexuality and the distinction of the sexes certainly did not exist at the dawn of life, nevertheless, it remains possible that the instincts which are later described as sexual were active from the very beginning and took up the part of opposition to the rôle of the *ego-instincts* then, and not only at some later time.

Let us now retrace our steps for the first time, to ask whether all these speculations are not, after all, without foundation. Are there really, *apart from the sexual instincts,* no other instincts than those which have as their object the reinstatement of an earlier condition, none that strive towards a condition never yet attained? I am not aware of any satisfactory example in the organic world running counter to

the characteristic I have suggested. The existence of a general impulse towards higher development in the plant and animal world can
certainly not be established, though some such
line of development is as a fact unquestionable.
But, on the one hand, it is often merely a question of our own valuation when we pronounce
one stage of development to be higher than another, and, on the other hand, biology makes
clear to us that a higher development in one
particular is often purchased with, or balanced
by, retrogression in another. Then there are
plenty of animal forms the youthful stages
of which teach us that their development has
taken a retrograde character rather than otherwise. Higher development and retrogression
alike might well be the results of external forces
impelling towards adaptation, and the part
played by the instincts might be confined in
both cases to retaining the enforced changes as
sources of pleasure.[1]

Many of us will also find it hard to abandon
our belief that in man himself there dwells an
impulse towards perfection, which has brought
him to his present heights of intellectual prow-
ess and ethical sublimation, and from which it
might be expected that his development into
superman will be ensured. But I do not believe
in the existence of such an inner impulse, and
I see no way of preserving this pleasing illusion. The development of man up to now does
not seem to me to need any explanation differing from that of animal development, and the
restless striving towards further perfection
which may be observed in a minority of human beings is easily explicable as the result of
that repression of instinct upon which what is
most valuable in human culture is built. The
repressed instinct never ceases to strive after
its complete satisfaction, which would consist
in the repetition of a primary experience of
satisfaction: all substitution- or reaction-formations and sublimations avail nothing towards
relaxing the continual tension; and out of the
excess of the satisfaction demanded over that
found is born the driving momentum which allows of no abiding in any situation presented
to it, but in the poet's words "urges ever for-

ward, ever unsubdued."[2] The path in the other
direction, back to complete satisfaction, is as a
rule barred by the resistances that maintain the
repressions, and thus there remains nothing for
it but to proceed in the other, still unobstructed
direction, that of development, without, however, any prospect of being able to bring the
process to a conclusion or to attain the goal.
What occurs in the development of a neurotic
phobia, which is really nothing but an attempt
at flight from the satisfaction of an instinct,
gives us the prototype for the origin of this
ostensible "impulse towards perfection," which,
however, we cannot possibly ascribe to all
human beings. The dynamic conditions are,
it is true, quite generally present, but the
economic relations seem only in rare cases to
favour the phenomenon.

VI

OUR discussion so far results in the establishing
of a sharp antithesis between the *ego-instincts*
and the sexual instincts, the former impelling
towards death and the latter towards the preservation of life, a result which we ourselves
must surely find in many respects far from
adequate. Further, only for the former can we
properly claim the conservative—or, better,
regressive—character corresponding to a repetition-compulsion. For, according to our hypothesis, the ego-instincts spring from the
vitalizing of inanimate matter, and have as
their aim the reinstatement of lifelessness. As
to the sexual instincts, on the other hand: it is
obvious that they reproduce primitive states
of the living being, but the aim they strive for
by every means is the union of two germ cells
which are specifically differentiated. If this
union does not take place, then the germ cell
dies like all other elements of the multicellular
organism. Only on this condition can the sexual
function prolong life and lend it the semblance
of immortality. Of what important happening,
then, in the process of development of the
living substance is sexual reproduction, or its
forerunner, the copulation of two individual
protozoa, the repetition? That question we do
not know how to answer, and therefore we
should feel relieved if the whole structure of
our arguments were to prove erroneous. The
opposition of ego- (or death-) instincts and
sexual (life-) instincts would then disappear,
and the repetition-compulsion would thereupon

---

[1] By a different route, Ferenczi has arrived at the
possibility of this conception. ("Stages of Development in the Sense of Reality," Ch. VIII of his *Contributions to Psycho-Analysis*, 1916.) He writes: "By
following through this process of thought logically, one
is obliged to gain familiarity with the idea of a tendency to persistence or regression governing organic
life also, while the tendency to progress in development, adaptation, etc., is manifested only as against
external stimuli."

[2] Mephistopheles in *Faust;* Part I, "Faust's Study."

also lose the significance we have attributed to it.

Let us turn back, therefore, to one of the assumptions we interpolated, in the expectation that it will permit of exact refutation. We built up further conclusions on the basis of the assumption that all life must die from internal causes. We made this assumption so light-heartedly because it does not seem to us to be one. We are accustomed so to think, and every poet encourages us in the idea. Perhaps we have resolved so to think because there lies a certain consolation in this belief. If man must himself die, after first losing his most beloved ones by death, he would prefer that his life be forfeit to an inexorable law of nature, the sublime Ἀνάγκη, than to a mere accident which perhaps could have been in some way avoided. But perhaps this belief in the incidence of death as the necessary consequence of an inner law of being is also only one of those illusions that we have fashioned for ourselves "so as to endure the burden of existence." It is certainly not a primordial belief: the idea of a *natural death* is alien to primitive races; they ascribe every death occurring among themselves to the influence of an enemy or an evil spirit. So let us not neglect to turn to biological science to test the belief.

If we do so, we may be astonished to find how little agreement exists among biologists on the question of natural death, that indeed the very conception of death altogether eludes them. The fact of a certain average length of life, at least among the higher animals, is of course an argument for death from inner causes, but the circumstance that certain large animals and giant trees reach a very great age, one not to be computed up to now, once more removes this impression. According to the grandiose conception of W. Fliess, all the vital phenomena—and certainly also death—are linked with the accomplishment of certain periods of time, among which there finds expression of the dependence of two living substances, one male and one female, upon the solar year. But observations of how easily and extensively the influences of external forces can alter vital manifestations, especially in the plant world, as to their occurrence in time, can hasten or retard them, militate against the rigidity of the formulae laid down by Fliess and leaves at least doubtful the universality of the laws he sought to establish.

The treatment of these themes, death and the duration of life among organisms, in the works of A. Weismann[1] possesses the greatest interest for us. This investigator originated the distinction of living substance into a mortal and an immortal half; the mortal is the body in the narrower sense, the soma, which alone is subject to natural death; while the germ cells are potentially immortal, in so far as they are capable under certain favourable conditions of developing into a new individual, or, expressed otherwise, of surrounding themselves with a new soma.[2]

What here arrests our attention is the unexpected analogy with our conception developed along so different a line of thought. Weismann, who is considering living substance morphologically, recognizes in it a constituent which is the prey of death, the soma, the body viewed apart from sex or heredity elements, and, on the other hand, an immortal part, the germ-plasm, which serves the purpose of preservation of the species, of propagation. We have fixed our attention not on the living matter, but on the forces active in it, and have been led to distinguish two kinds of instincts: those the purpose of which is to guide life towards death, and the others, the sexual instincts, which perpetually strive for, and bring about, the renewal of life. This sounds like a dynamic corollary to Weismann's morphological theory.

This appearance of an important correspondence vanishes as soon as we examine Weismann's pronouncement on the problem of death. For Weismann admits the differentiation between the mortal soma and the immortal germ-plasm only in relation to multicellular organisms; with the unicellular beings, the individual and the reproductive cell are still one and the same.[3] The unicellular he thus affirms to be potentially immortal; death appears only among the metazoa, the multicellular. This death of the higher organisms is, it is true, a natural one, a death from inner causes, but it does not depend on an inherent quality of the living substance,[4] is not to be conceived as an absolute necessity based on the nature of life.[5] Death is rather a purposive contrivance, a phenomenon of adaptation to the external conditions of life, because after the differentiation of the corporeal cells into soma and germ-plasm the indefinite prolongation of the life of the

[1] *Über die Dauer des Lebens*, 1882; *Über Leben und Tod*, 2nd ed., 1892; *Das Keimplasma*, 1892, etc.
[2] *Über Leben und Tod*, 2nd ed., p. 20.
[3] *Über die Dauer des Lebens*, p. 38.
[4] *Über Leben und Tod*, 2nd ed., p. 67.
[5] *Über die Dauer des Lebens*, p. 33.

individual would have become a quite inexpedient luxury. With the appearance of this differentiation among multicellular organisms, death became possible and expedient. Since then, the soma of the higher organisms dies after a certain time from internal causes; the protozoa, however, remain immortal. Propagation, on the other hand, was not first introduced with death; it is, on the contrary, a primordial property of living matter like growth, in which it originated, and life has gone on uninterruptedly from its inception on the earth.[1]

It is easy to see that to concede natural death to the higher organisms does not greatly help our case. If death is a late acquisition of life, then death-instincts traceable to the beginning of life on this planet no longer come into question. Multicellular organisms may continue to die from internal causes, whether defect of differentiation or imperfections of their metabolism; it possesses no interest for the inquiry on which we are engaged. Such a conception and derivation of death certainly more nearly approaches the ordinary human view of it than the unwonted assumption of *death-instincts*.

The discussion which has centred round Weismann's assertions has, in my opinion, had no decisive result in any direction.[2] Many writers have reverted to the standpoint of Goethe (1883), who saw in death the direct consequence of propagation. Hartmann does not regard as the characteristic of death the appearance of a *corpse,* a piece of living substance which has *died off,* but defines it as the "definitive end of individual development." In this sense, protozoa are also subject to death; with them death invariably coincides with propagation, but it is, so to speak, disguised by the latter, for the whole substance of the parent organism may be absorbed directly into the new individuals.[3]

The interest of the inquiry was soon directed towards testing experimentally the asserted immortality of living substance in unicellular beings. An American, named Woodruff, instituted a culture of a ciliated infusorium, a *slipper-animalcule,* which reproduces itself by division into two individuals; each time, he isolated one of the products and put it into fresh water. He traced the propagation to the 3,029th generation, when he discontinued the experiment. The last descendant of the first slipper-animalcule was just as lively as its original ancestor, without any sign of age or degeneration: if such numbers are convincing, the immortality of protozoa seemed thus experimentally demonstrable.[4]

Other investigators have arrived at other results. Maupas, Calkins, etc., found, in contradiction to Woodruff, that even these infusoria, after a certain number of divisions, become weaker, decrease in size, lose a portion of their organization, and finally die, if they do not encounter certain invigorating influences. According to this, protozoa die after a phase of senile decay just like higher animals, in direct contravention of what is maintained by Weismann, who recognizes in death a late acquisition of living organisms.

Taking the net result of these researches together, we note two facts which seem to afford us a firm foothold. First: if the animalculae, at a time when they as yet show no signs of age, have the opportunity of mingling with each other, of *conjugating*—afterwards again separating—then they remain exempt from age, they have been *rejuvenated*. This conjugation is doubtless the prototype of sexual propagation of higher organisms: as yet, it has nothing to do with multiplication, it is confined to the mingling of the substances of both individuals (Weismann's *Amphimixis*). The invigorating influence of conjugation can also be replaced, however, by certain modes of stimulation, changes in the composition of the nutrient fluid, raising of temperature, or shaking. The famous experiment of J. Loeb will be recalled, who, by the application of certain chemical stimuli to the ova of sea-urchins, brought about processes of division which usually take place only after fertilization.

Secondly: it is, after all, probable that the infusoria are brought to a natural death through their own vital process, for the contradiction between Woodruff's findings and those of others arises from Woodruff having placed each generation in fresh nutrient fluid. When he refrained from doing so, he observed, as did the other investigators, that the generations showed signs of age. He concluded that the animalculae were injured by the products of metabolism which they gave off into the surrounding fluid, and was then able to prove convincingly that only the products of *its own* metabolism

---

[1] *Über Leben und Tod*, Conclusion.

[2] See Max Hartmann, *Tod und Fortpflanzung*, 1906; Alex. Lipschütz, "Warum wir sterben," *Kosmosbücher*, 1914; Franz Doflein, *Das Problem des Todes und der Unsterblichkeit bei den Pflanzen und Tieren*, 1919.

[3] *Hartmann, op. cit.*, p. 29.

[4] For this, and what follows, see Lipschütz. *op. cit.*, pp. 26 and 52 ff.

had this effect in bringing about the death of the generation. For in a solution over-saturated with waste products of a distantly related species, the very same animalculae throve excellently which when allowed to accumulate in their own nutrient fluid inevitably perished. Thus, left to itself, the infusorium dies a natural death from the imperfect disposal of its own metabolic products: perhaps all higher animals die ultimately from the same inability.

At this point, the doubt may then occur to us whether any good purpose has been served in looking for the answer to the question as to natural death in the study of the protozoa. The primitive organization of these forms of life may conceal from us important conditions which are present in them too, but can be recognized only among the higher animals where they have achieved for themselves a morphological expression. If we abandon the morphological point of view for the dynamic, it may be a matter of entire indifference to us whether the natural death of the protozoa can be proved or not. With them the substance later recognized as immortal has not yet separated itself in any way from the part subject to death. The instinctive forces which endeavour to conduct life to death might be active in them, too, from the beginning and yet their effect might be so obscured by that of the forces tending to preserve life that any direct evidence of their existence becomes hard to establish. We have heard, it is true, that the observations of biologists allow us to assume such death-ward tending inner processes also among the protozoa. But even if the protozoa prove to be immortal in Weismann's sense, his assertion that death is a late acquisition holds good only of the outward manifestations of death, and does not invalidate any hypothesis as to such processes as impel towards death. Our expectation that biology would entirely put out of court any recognition of the death-instincts has not been fulfilled. It is open to us to occupy ourselves further with this possibility, if we have other reasons for doing so. The striking resemblance between Weismann's separation of soma and germ-plasm and our distinction between the death and the life-instincts remains unshaken, moreover, and retains its value.

Let us dwell for a moment on this exquisitely dualistic conception of the instinctive life. According to E. Hering's theory of the processes in living matter, there course through it uninterruptedly two kinds of processes of opposite direction, one anabolic, assimilatory, the other katabolic, disintegrating. Shall we venture to recognize in these two directions of the vital processes the activity of our two instinctive tendencies, the life-instincts and the death-instincts? And we cannot disguise another fact from ourselves, that we have steered unawares into the haven of Schopenhauer's philosophy for whom death is the "real result" of life,[1] and, therefore, in so far its aim, while the sexual instinct is the incarnation of the will to live.

Let us boldly try to go a step further. According to general opinion, the union of numerous cells into one vital connection, the multicellularity of organisms, has become a means to the prolongation of their span of life. One cell helps to preserve the life of the others, and the cell-community can go on living even if single cells have to perish. We have already heard that also conjugation, the temporary mingling of two unicellular entities, has a preservative and rejuvenating effect on both. The attempt might consequently be made to transfer the libido theory yielded by psycho-analysis to the relationship of the cells to one another and to imagine that it is the vital or sexual instincts active in every cell that take the other cells for their *object*, partially neutralize their death-instincts, i.e., the processes stimulated by these, and so preserve those cells in life, while other cells do the same for them, and still others sacrifice themselves in the exercise of this libidinous function. The germ cells themselves would behave in a completely *narcissistic* fashion, as we are accustomed to describe it in the theory of the neuroses when an individual concentrates his libido on the ego, and gives out none of it for the charging of objects. The germ cells need their libido— the activity of their vital instincts—for themselves as a provision for their later enormous constructive activity. Perhaps the cells of the malignant growths that destroy the organism can also be considered to be narcissistic in the same sense. Pathology is indeed prepared to regard the kernels of them as congenital in origin and to ascribe embryonal attributes to them. Thus the libido of our sexual instincts would coincide with the Eros of poets and philosophers, which holds together all things living.

At this point, opportunity offers of reviewing the gradual development of our libido theory. The analysis of the transference-neuroses

[1] *Über die anscheinende Absichtlichkeit im Schicksale des Einzelnen* (edited by Grand Duke Wilhelm Ernst) Vol. IV. p. 268.

forced on our notice in the first place the opposition between *sexual instincts,* which are directed towards an object, and other instincts which we only imperfectly discerned and provisionally described as *ego-instincts.* Among the latter, those which subserve the self-preservation of the individual had the first claim for recognition. What other distinctions were to be made, it was impossible to say. No knowledge would have been so important for the establishment of a sound psychology as some approximate understanding of the common nature and possible differences of the instincts. But in no department of psychology did one grope more in the dark. Everyone posited as many instincts or *fundamental instincts* as he pleased, and contrived with them just as the ancient Greek philosophers did with their four elements: earth, air, fire, and water. Psychoanalysis, which could not dispense with some kind of hypothesis as to the instincts, adhered, to begin with, to the popular distinction, typically represented by the phrase *hunger and love.* It was at least no new arbitrary creation. With this, one adequately covered a considerable distance in the analysis of the psychoneuroses. The conception of *sexuality*—and therewith that of a sexual instinct—certainly had to be extended, till it included much that did not come into the category of the function of propagation, and this led to outcry enough in a severe and superior or merely hypocritical world.

The next step followed when psycho-analysis was able to feel its way a little nearer to the psychological ego, which was at first known to us only as a repressing, censoring agency, capable of constituting defences and reaction-formations. Critical and other far-seeing minds had indeed for a long time raised objections to the narrowing of the libido concept down to the energy of the sexual instinct as directed to the object. But they omitted to say whence they obtained this fuller comprehension, and failed to deduce anything from it of value for psycho-analysis. In the course of more deliberate advance, it came under psycho-analytic observation how regularly libido is withdrawn from the object and directed towards the ego (introversion), and through the study of the libido-development of the child in its earliest phases it became clear that the ego is the true and original reservoir of the libido, which is extended to the object only from this. The ego took its place as one of the sexual objects and was immediately recognized as the choicest

among them. Where the libido thus remained attached to the ego, it was termed *narcissistic.*[1] This narcissistic libido was naturally also the expression of the energy of sexual instincts in the analytical sense which now had to be identified with the *instincts of self-preservation,* the existence of which was admitted from the first. Whereupon, the original antithesis between the ego-instincts and the sexual instincts became inadequate. A part of the ego-instincts was recognized as libidinous: in the ego, sexual instincts were found to be active—probably in addition to others; nevertheless, one is justified in saying that the old formula, viz., that a psychoneurosis arises out of a conflict between the ego-instincts and the sexual instincts, contained nothing that we should have to reject today. Only, the difference of the two kinds of instincts which was supposed originally to be in some kind of way qualitative has now to be defined otherwise, namely on a topographical basis. In particular, the transference-neurosis, the real object of psycho-analytic study, is still seen to be the result of a conflict between the ego and libidinous investment of an object.

We are the more compelled now to accentuate the libidinous character of the self-preservative instincts, since we are venturing on the further step of recognizing the sexual instinct as the Eros, the all-sustaining, and of deriving the narcissistic libido of the ego from the sum of the libido quantities that bring about the mutual adherence of the somatic cells. But we now find ourselves suddenly confronted with this question: If the self-preservative instincts are also of a libidinous kind, then perhaps we have no other instincts at all than libidinous ones. There are at least no others apparent. In that event, we must admit the critics to be in the right who from the first have suspected that psycho-analysis makes sexuality the explanation of everything, or the innovators, like Jung, who, quickly making up their minds, have used *libido* as a synonym for *instinctive force* in general. Is that not so?

This result was at all events one not intended by us. On the contrary, we took as our starting point a sharp distinction between the ego-instincts (=death-instincts) and the sexual instincts (=life-instincts). We were prepared, indeed, to reckon even the alleged self-preservative instincts of the ego among death-instincts, a position which we have since corrected and withdrawn from. Our standpoint was a dualistic one from the beginning, and is so today more

[1] See *On Narcissism: an Introduction,* p. 399 above.

sharply than before, since we no longer call the contrasting tendencies *egoistic* and *sexual* instincts, but *life-instincts* and *death-instincts*. Jung's libido theory, on the other hand, is a monistic one; that he has applied the term *libido* to his only instinctive energy was bound to create confusion, but should not have any further effect on us. We suspect that there are in the ego other instincts than those of self-preservation; only we ought to be in a position to demonstrate them. Unfortunately, so little progress has been made in the analysis of the ego that this proof becomes extraordinarily difficult of attainment. The libidinous instincts of the ego may indeed be conjoined in a special way with other ego-instincts of which we as yet know nothing. Before ever we had clearly recognized narcissism, the conjecture was already present in the minds of psycho-analysts that the *ego-instincts* had drawn libidinous components to themselves. But these are merely vague possibilities which our opponents will hardly take into account. It remains an awkward fact that analysis up to now has only put us in the position of demonstrating libidinous impulses. The conclusion that therefore there are no others is one to which we do not assent.

In the obscurity that at present shrouds the theory of instinct, we shall certainly not do well to reject any idea that promises to throw light. We have made the antithesis between the life and death instincts our point of departure. Object-love itself displays a second such polarity, that of love (tenderness) and hate (aggression). What if we could succeed in bringing these two polarities into relation with each other, in tracing the one to the other! We have long recognized a sadistic component of the sexual instinct:[1] it can, as we know, attain independence, and as a perversion, dominate the whole sexual trend of a person. In one of the organizations which I have termed *pregenital* it appears as a dominating part-instinct. But how is one to derive the sadistic impulse, which aims at the injury of the object, from the life-sustaining Eros! Does not the assumption suggest itself that this sadism is properly a death-instinct which is driven apart from the ego by the influence of the narcissistic libido, so that it becomes manifest only in reference to the object? It then enters the service of the sexual function; at the oral stage of organization of the libido, amorous possession is still one and the same as annihilation of the object;

[1] *Three Contributions to the Theory of Sex.*

later, the sadistic impulse separates itself, and, at last, at the stage of the genital primacy, it takes over, with the aim of propagation, the function of so far overpowering the sex-object as the carrying out of the sexual act demands. One might even say that the sadism expelled from the ego has acted as guide to the libidinous components of the sexual instinct; these later press on towards the object. Where the original sadism experiences no abatement or fusion, the well-known hate-love ambivalence of the love-life is set up.

If the above assumption is justifiable, then we have met the challenge of demonstrating an example of a death-instinct—though a displaced one. This conception, however, is far from being evident, and creates a frankly mystical impression. We incur the suspicion of having attempted at all costs to find a way out of an *impasse*. We may appeal against this verdict by saying that the assumption is no new one, that we have once before made it when there was no question of an *impasse*. Clinical observations forced upon us the view that the part-instinct of masochism, the one complementary to sadism, is to be understood as a recoil of the sadism on to the ego itself.[2] A turning of the instinct from the object to the ego is, however, essentially the same as a turning from the ego to the object, which is just now the new idea in question. Masochism, the turning of the instinct against the self, would then be in reality a return to an earlier phase of this, a regression. The exposition I then gave of masochism needs correction in one respect as being too exclusive: masochism may also be what I was there concerned to deny, primary.[3]

Let us return, however, to the life-sustaining sexual instincts. We have already learned from the investigation of the protozoa that the mingling of two individuals without consequent

[2] See *Three Contributions to the Theory of Sex* and *Instincts and their Vicissitudes*, p. 412 above.

[3] A considerable part of this speculation has been anticipated in a work which is full of valuable matter and ideas but is unfortunately not entirely clear to me: Sabina Spielrein, "Die Destruktion als Ursache des Werdens," *Jahrbuch für Psychoanalyse*, IV, 1912. She designates the sadistic component as *destructive*. In still another way. A. Stärcke (*Inleiding* by de vertaling von S. Freud, De sexuele beschavingsmoral, etc., 1914), has attempted to identify the libido concept itself with the biological concept of an impulsion towards death which is to be assumed on theoretical grounds. (See also Rank, *Der Künstler.*) All these attempts, as the one in the text, indicate how much the need is felt for a clarification, in the theory of instinct, which we do not yet possess.

partition, just as copulation between two individuals which soon after separate, has a strengthening and rejuvenating effect (see above, Lipschütz). There is no sign of degeneration in their descendants, and they also seem to have gained the capacity for withstanding for a longer time the injurious results of their own metabolism. I think that this one observation may be taken as a prototype of the effect of sexual intercourse also. But in what way does the blending of two slightly different cells bring about such a renewal of life? The experiment which substitutes for conjugation among protozoa the effect of chemical or even of mechanical stimuli[1] admits of our giving a reply with certainty: it comes about by the introduction of new stimulus-masses. This is in close agreement with the hypothesis that the life-process of an individual leads, from internal causes, to the equalizing of chemical tensions: i.e., to death, while union with an individually different living substance increases these tensions—so to speak, introduces new vital differentia, which then have to be again lived out. For this difference between the two there must naturally be one or more optima. Our recognition that the ruling tendency of psychic life, perhaps of nerve life altogether, is the struggle for reduction, keeping at a constant level, or removal of the inner stimulus tension (the Nirvana-principle, as Barbara Low terms it) —a struggle which comes to expression in the pleasure-principle—is indeed one of our strongest motives for believing in the existence of death-instincts.

But the course of our argument is still disturbed by an uneasy feeling that just in the case of the sexual instinct we are unable to demonstrate that character of a repetition-compulsion which first put us on the track of the death-instincts. It is true that the realm of embryonic developmental processes offers an abundance of such repetition phenomena—the two germ cells of sexual propagation and their life-history are themselves only repetitions of the beginning of organic life: but the essential feature in the processes designed by the sexual instinct is, nevertheless, the mingling of two cells. Only by this is the immortality of the living substance among the higher forms of life assured.

To put it in other words: we have to make enquiry into the origin of sexual propagation and the source of the sexual instincts in general, a task before which the lay mind quails and

[1] *Loc. cit.*

which even specialists have not yet been able to solve. Let us, therefore, make a condensed selection from all the conflicting accounts and opinions of whatever can be brought into relation with our train of thought.

One view deprives the problem of propagation of its mysterious attraction by representing it as part of the phenomenon of growth (multiplication by division, germination, budding). The arising of propagation by means of germ-cells sexually differentiated might be conceived, in accordance with the sober Darwinian mode of thought, as a way of maintaining and utilizing for further development the advantage of the amphimixis which resulted in the first instance from the fortuitous conjugation of two protozoa.[2] *Sex* would not thus be of very ancient origin and the extraordinarily powerful instincts which aim at bringing about sexual union would thereby repeat something which once chanced to happen and since became established as being advantageous.

The same question now recurs as arose in respect of death—namely, whether the protozoa can be credited with anything beyond what they exhibit, and whether we may assume that forces and processes which become perceptible only in the case of the higher animals did first arise in the more primitive. For our purpose the view of sexuality mentioned above helps very little. The objection may be raised against it that it presupposes the existence of life-instincts as already operative in the simplest forms of life, for otherwise conjugation, which works against the expiration of life and makes the task of dying harder, would not have been retained and elaborated, but would have been avoided. If, then, we are not to abandon the hypothesis of death-instincts maintained, we must associate them with life-instincts from the beginning. But we must admit that we are working here at an equation with two unknown quantities. Anything else that science can tell us of the origin of sexuality amounts to so little that this problem may be likened to an obscurity into which not even the ray of an hypothesis has penetrated. In quite another quarter, however, we encounter such an hypothesis, but it is of so fantastic a kind—assuredly a myth rather than a scientific explanation—

[2] Although Weismann (*Das Keimplasma,* 1892) denies even this advantage: "Fertilization in no way signifies a rejuvenation or renewing of life—it is in no way necessary for the prolongation of life; it is nothing but a device for making possible the blending of two different inheritance tendencies." Still, he considers an increase of variability in living organisms to be the result of such blending.

that I should not venture to bring it forward if it did not exactly fulfil the one condition for the fulfilment of which we are labouring. That is to say, it derives an instinct from the *necessity for the reinstatement of an earlier situation.*

I refer, of course, to the theory that Plato in his *Symposium* puts into the mouth of Aristophanes and which deals not only with the origin of the sexual instinct but also with its most important variations in relation to the object. "Human nature was once quite other than now. Originally there were three sexes, three and not as today two: besides the male and the female there existed a third sex which had an equal share in the two first. . . . In these beings everything was double: thus, they had four hands and four feet, two faces, two genital parts, and so on. Then Zeus allowed himself to be persuaded to cut these beings in two, as one divides pears to stew them. . . . When all nature was divided in this way, to each human being came the longing for his own other half, and the two halves embraced and entwined their bodies *and desired to grow together again.*"[1]

Are we to follow the clue of the poet-philosopher and make the daring assumption that living substance was at the time of its animation

[1] I am indebted to Prof. Heinrich Gomperz of Vienna for the following indications as to the origin of the Platonic myth, which I repeat partly in his own words: I should like to call attention to the fact that essentially the same theory is also to be found in the Upanishads. The Brihad-Aranyaka Upanishad 1, 4, 3 (Deussen, 60 Upanishads des Veda, p. 393), where the creation of the world from the Âtman (the self or ego) is described, has the following passage: "Nor did he [the Âtman, the self or ego] experience any joy, and for that reason no one has joy when he is alone. So he longed for a partner. He was as big as a woman and a man together when they embrace. He divided himself into two parts, which made a husband and a wife. This body is, therefore, one half of the self, according to Yajnavalkya. And for the same reason this empty space here becomes filled by the woman."

The Brihad-Aranyaka Upanishad is the oldest of all the Upanishads, and no expert authority would date it later than 800 B.C. In opposition to the prevailing opinion, I should not like definitely to deny the possibility of Plato having been dependent, even though very indirectly, on these Indian thoughts, for this possibility cannot be absolutely put aside even for the doctrine of re-incarnation. A dependence of this sort, first conveyed through Pythagoras, would scarcely detract from the significance of the coincidence in thought, for Plato would not have adopted any such story conveyed in some way from Oriental traditions, let alone have given it such an important place, had he not himself felt the truth contained in it to be illuminating.

In an article by K. Ziegler ("*Menschen- und Weltwerden,*" *Neue Jahrbücher für das klassische Altertum,* Vol. xxxi, 1913), which contains a systematic investigation of the thought in question, it is traced back to Babylonian ideas.

rent into small particles, which since that time strive for reunion by means of the sexual instincts? That these instincts—in which the chemical affinity of inanimate matter is continued—passing through the realm of the protozoa gradually overcome all hindrances set to their striving by an environment charged with stimuli dangerous to life, and are impelled by it to form a protecting covering layer? And that these dispersed fragments of living substance thus achieve a multicellular organization, and finally transfer to the germ-cells in a highly concentrated form the instinct for reunion? I think this is the point at which to break off.

But not without a few words of critical reflection in conclusion. I might be asked whether I am myself convinced of the views here set forward, and if so how far. My answer would be that I am neither convinced myself, nor am I seeking to arouse conviction in others. More accurately: I do not know how far I believe in them. It seems to me that the affective feature *conviction* need not come into consideration at all here. One may surely give oneself up to a line of thought, and follow it up as far as it leads, simply out of scientific curiosity, or—if you prefer—as *advocatus diaboli,* without, however, making a pact with the devil about it. I am perfectly aware that the third step in the theory of instinct which I am taking here cannot claim the same certainty as the two former ones, viz., the extending of the conception of sexuality and the establishing of narcissism. These innovations were direct translations of observation into theory, subject to no greater sources of error than is inevitable in anything of the kind. The assertion of the regressive character of instinct rests also, it is true, on observed material, namely, on the facts of the repetition-compulsion. But perhaps I have overestimated their significance. At all events there is no way of working out this idea except by combining facts with pure imagination many times in succession, and thereby departing far from observation. We know that the final result becomes the more untrustworthy the oftener one does this in the course of building up a theory, but the precise degree of uncertainty is not ascertainable. One may thereby have made a brilliant discovery or one may have gone ignominiously astray. In such work I trust little to so-called *intuition:* what I have seen of it seems to me to be the result of a certain impartiality of the intellect—only that people, unfortunately, are seldom impartial where they are concerned with the ultimate things, the great problems of science and of life. My belief is that there everyone is under the sway of preferences deeply rooted within, into the hands of which he unwittingly plays as he pursues his speculation. Where there are such good grounds for distrust, only a tepid feeling of indulgence is possible towards the results of one's own mental labours. But I hasten to add that such self-criticism does not render obligatory any special tolerance of divergent opinions. One may inexorably reject theories that are contradicted by the very first steps in the analysis of observation and yet at the same time be aware that those one holds oneself have only a tentative validity. Were we to appraise our speculations upon the life- and death-instincts it would disturb us but little that so many processes go on which are surprising and hard to picture, such as one instinct being expelled by others, or turning from the ego to an object, and so on. This comes only from our being obliged to operate with scientific terms, i.e., with the metaphor- ical expressions peculiar to psychology (or more correctly: psychology of the deeper layers). Otherwise, we should not be able to describe the corresponding processes at all, nor, in fact, even to have remarked them. The shortcomings of our description would probably disappear if for the psychological terms we could substitute physiological or chemical ones. These, too, only constitute a metaphorical language, but one familiar to us for a much longer time and perhaps also simpler.

On the other hand, we wish to make it quite clear that the uncertainty of our speculation is enhanced in a high degree by the necessity of borrowing from biological science. Biology is truly a realm of limitless possibilities; we have the most surprising revelations to expect from it, and cannot conjecture what answers it will offer in some decades to the questions we have put to it. Perhaps, they may be such as to over- throw the whole artificial structure of hypoth- eses. If that is so, someone may ask why does one undertake such work as the one set out in this article, and why should it be communicated to the world? Well, I cannot deny that some of the analogies, relations and connections therein traced appeared to me worthy of consideration.[1]

[1] I would here subjoin a few words to clarify our nomenclature, one which has undergone a certain development in the course of our discussion. What *sexual instincts* are, we knew through their relation to the sexes and to the function of propagation. We then retained this term when the findings of psycho-

VII

IF this attempt to reinstate an earlier con- dition really is so universal a characteristic of the instincts, we should not find it surprising that so many processes in the psychic life are performed independently of the pleasure-prin- ciple. This characteristic would communicate itself to every part-instinct and would in that case concern a harking back to a definite point on the path of development. But all that the pleasure-principle has not yet acquired power over is not therefore necessarily in opposition to it, and we have not yet solved the problem of determining the relation of the instinctive repetition processes to the domination of the pleasure-principle.

We have recognized that one of the earliest and most important functions of the psychic apparatus is to *bind* the instreaming instinctive excitations, to substitute the *secondary process* for the *primary process* dominating them, and to transform their freely mobile energy-charge into a predominantly quiescent (tonic) charge. During this transformation, no attention can be paid to the development of the "pain," but the pleasure-principle is not thereby annulled. On the contrary, the transformation takes place in the service of the pleasure-principle; the binding is an act of preparation, which intro- duces and secures its sovereignty.

analysis compelled us to regard its relation to propa- gation as less close. With the discovery of narcissistic libido, and the extension of the libido-concept to the individual cells, the sexual instinct became for us transformed into the Eros that endeavours to impel the separate parts of living matter to one another and to hold them together; what is commonly called the *sexual instinct* appears as that part of the Eros that is turned towards the object. Our speculation then supposes that this Eros is at work from the beginnings of life, manifesting itself as the *life-instinct* in con- tradistinction to the *death-instinct* which developed through the animation of the inorganic. It endeavours to solve the riddle of life by the hypothesis of these two instincts striving with each other from the very beginning. The transformation which the concept of the *ego-instincts* has undergone is perhaps harder to review. Originally, we applied this term to all those instinct-directions—now better known to us—which can be distinguished from the sexual instincts that have the object as their aim, thus contrasting the ego- instincts with the sexual ones, the expression of which is the libido. Later on, we approached the analysis of the ego and saw that a part also of the ego-instincts is of a libidinous nature, having taken its own self as an object. These narcissistic instincts of self-preser- vation, therefore, had now to be reckoned to the libi- dinous sexual instincts. The contrast between egoistic and sexual instincts was now converted into one be- tween egoistic and object-instincts, both libidinous in nature. In its place, however, arose a new contrast between libidinous (ego and object) instincts and others whose existence can be determined in the ego and can perhaps be detected in the destruction-in- stincts. Speculation transforms this contrast into that of life-instincts (Eros) and death-instincts.

Let us distinguish function and tendency more sharply than we have hitherto done. The pleasure-principle is, then, a tendency which subserves a certain function—namely, that of rendering the psychic apparatus as a whole free from any excitation, or to keep the amount of excitation constant or as low as possible. We cannot yet decide with certainty for either of these conceptions, but we note that the function so defined would partake of the most universal tendency of all living matter—to return to the peace of the inorganic world. We all know by experience that the greatest pleasure it is possible for us to attain, that of the sexual act, is bound up with the temporary quenching of a greatly heightened state of excitation. The *binding* of instinct-excitation, however, would be a preparatory function, which would direct the excitation towards its ultimate adjustment in the pleasure of discharge.

In the same connection, the question arises whether the sensations of pleasure and "pain" can emanate as well from the bound as from the *unbound* excitation-processes. It appears quite beyond doubt that the *unbound*, the primary, processes give rise to much more intense sensations in both directions than the bound ones, those of the *secondary processes*. The primary processes are also the earlier in point of time; at the beginning of mental life there are no others, and we may conclude that if the pleasure-principle were not already in action in respect to them, it would not establish itself in regard to the later processes. We thus arrive at the result which at bottom is not a simple one, that the search for pleasure manifests itself with far greater intensity at the beginning of psychic life than later on, but less unrestrictedly: it has to put up with repeated breaches. At a maturer age the dominance of the pleasure-principle is very much more assured, though this principle as little escapes limitations as all the other instincts. In any case, whatever it is in the process of excitation that engenders the sensations of pleasure and "pain" must be equally in existence when the secondary process is at work as with the primary process.

This would seem to be the place to institute further studies. Our consciousness conveys to us from within not only the sensations of pleasure and "pain," but also those of a peculiar tension, which again may be either pleasurable or painful in itself. Now, is it the *bound* and *unbound* energy processes that we have to distinguish from each other by the help of these sensations, or is the sensation of tension to be related to the absolute quantity, perhaps to the level of the charge, while the pleasure-pain series refers to the changes in the quantity of charge in the unit of time? We must also be struck with the fact that the life-instincts have much more to do with our inner perception, since they make their appearance as disturbers of the peace, and continually bring along with them states of tension the resolution of which is experienced as pleasure; while the death-instincts, on the other hand, seem to fulfil their function unostentatiously. The pleasure-principle seems directly to subserve the death-instincts; it keeps guard, of course, also over the external stimuli, which are regarded as dangers by both kinds of instincts, but in particular over the inner increases in stimulation which have for their aim the complication of the task of living. At this point, innumerable other questions arise to which no answer can yet be given. We must be patient and wait for other means and opportunities for investigation. We must hold ourselves, too, in readiness to abandon the path we have followed for a time, if it should seem to lead to no good result. Only such "true believers" as expect from science a substitute for the creed they have relinquished will take it amiss if the investigator develops his views further or even transforms them.

For the rest we may find consolation in the words of a poet for the slow rate of progress in scientific knowledge:

Whither we cannot fly, we must go limping.
The Scripture saith that limping is no sin.[1]

[1] Rückert in the *Makamen des Hariri*.

Group Psychology and the
Analysis of the Ego

I. INTRODUCTION

THE contrast between individual psychology and social or group[1] psychology, which at a first glance may seem to be full of significance, loses a great deal of its sharpness when it is examined more closely. It is true that individual psychology is concerned with the individual man and explores the paths by which he seeks to find satisfaction for his instincts; but only rarely and under certain exceptional conditions is individual psychology in a position to disregard the relations of this individual to others. In the individual's mental life someone else is invariably involved, as a model, as an object, as a helper, as an opponent, and so from the very first individual psychology is at the same time social psychology as well—in this extended but entirely justifiable sense of the words.

The relations of an individual to his parents and to his brothers and sisters, to the object of his love, and to his physician—in fact all the relations which have hitherto been the chief subject of psycho-analytic research—may claim to be considered as social phenomena; and in this respect they may be contrasted with certain other processes, described by us as *narcissistic*, in which the satisfaction of the instincts is partially or totally withdrawn from the influence of other people. The contrast between social and narcissistic—Bleuler would perhaps call them *autistic*—mental acts therefore falls wholly within the domain of individual psychology, and is not well calculated to differentiate it from a social or group psychology.

The individual in the relations which have already been mentioned—to his parents and to his brothers and sisters, to the person he is in love with, to his friend, and to his physician—comes under the influence of only a single person, or of a very small number of persons, each one of whom has become enormously important to him. Now in speaking of social or group psychology it has become usual to leave these relations on one side and to isolate as the subject of inquiry the influencing of an individual by a large number of people simultaneously, people with whom he is connected by something, though otherwise they may in many respects be strangers to him. Group psychology is therefore concerned with the individual man as a member of a race, of a nation, of a caste, of a profession, of an institution, or as a component part of a crowd of people who have been organized into a group at some particular time for some definite purpose. When once natural continuity has been severed in this way, it is easy to regard the phenomena that appear under these special conditions as being expressions of a special instinct that is not further reducible, the social instinct (herd instinct, group mind), which does not come to light in any other situations, But we may perhaps venture to object that it seems difficult to attribute to the factor of number a significance so great as to make it capable by itself of arousing in our mental life a new instinct that is otherwise not brought into play. Our expectation is therefore directed towards two other possibilities: that the social instinct may not be a primitive one and insusceptible of dissection, and that it may be possible to discover the beginnings of its development in a narrower circle, such as that of the family.

Although group psychology is only in its infancy, it embraces an immense number of separate issues and offers to investigators countless problems which have hitherto not even been properly distinguished from one another. The mere classification of the different forms of group formation and the description of the mental phenomena produced by them require a great expenditure of observation and exposition, and have already given rise to a copious literature. Anyone who compares the narrow dimensions of this little book with the extent of group psychology will at once be able to guess that only a few points chosen from the whole material are to be dealt with here.

[1] "Group" is used throughout this translation as equivalent to the rather more comprehensive German *Masse*. The author uses this latter word to render both McDougall's *group*, and also Le Bon's *foule*, which would more naturally be translated *crowd* in English. For the sake of uniformity, however, *group* has been preferred in this case as well, and has been substituted for *crowd* even in the extracts from the English translation of Le Bon.—TR.

And they will in fact only be a few questions with which the depth-psychology of psycho-analysis is specially concerned.

II. LE BON'S DESCRIPTION OF THE GROUP MIND

INSTEAD of starting from a definition, it seems more useful to begin with some indication of the range of the phenomena under review, and to select from among them a few specially striking and characteristic facts to which our inquiry can be attached. We can achieve both of these aims by means of quotation from Le Bon's deservedly famous work, *Psychologie des Foules*.[1]

Let us make the matter clear once again. If a psychology, concerned with exploring the predispositions, the instincts, the motives, and the aims of an individual man down to his actions and his relations with those who are nearest to him, had completely achieved its task, and had cleared up the whole of these matters with their inter-connections, it would then suddenly find itself confronted by a new task which would lie before it unachieved. It would be obliged to explain the surprising fact that under a certain condition this individual whom it had come to understand thought, felt, and acted in quite a different way from what would have been expected. And this condition is his insertion into a collection of people which has acquired the characteristic of a *psychological group*. What, then, is a *group*? How does it acquire the capacity for exercising such a decisive influence over the mental life of the individual? And what is the nature of the mental change which it forces upon the individual?

It is the task of a theoretical group psychology to answer these three questions. The best way of approaching them is evidently to start with the third. Observation of the changes in the individual's reactions is what provides group psychology with its material; for every attempt at an explanation must be preceded by a description of the thing that is to be explained.

I will now let Le Bon speak for himself. He says: "The most striking peculiarity presented by a psychological group[2] is the following. Whoever be the individuals that compose it, however like or unlike be their mode of life, their occupations, their character, or their intelligence, the fact that they have been transformed into a group puts them in possession of a sort of collective mind which makes them feel, think, and act in a manner quite different from that in which each individual of them would feel, think, and act were he in a state of isolation. There are certain ideas and feelings which do not come into being, or do not transform themselves into acts except in the case of individuals forming a group. The psychological group is a provisional being formed of heterogeneous elements, which for a moment are combined, exactly as the cells which constitute a living body form by their re-union a new being which displays characteristics very different from those possessed by each of the cells singly" (p. 29).[3]

We shall take the liberty of interrupting Le Bon's exposition with glosses of our own, and shall accordingly insert an observation at this point. If the individuals in the group are combined into a unity, there must surely be something to unite them, and this bond might be precisely the thing that is characteristic of a group. But Le Bon does not answer this question; he goes on to consider the alteration which the individual undergoes when in a group and describes it in terms which harmonize well with the fundamental postulates of our own depth-psychology.

"It is easy to prove how much the individual forming part of a group differs from the isolated individual, but it is less easy to discover the causes of this difference.

"To obtain at any rate a glimpse of them, it is necessary in the first place to call to mind the truth established by modern psychology, that unconscious phenomena play an altogether preponderating part not only in organic life, but also in the operations of the intelligence. The conscious life of the mind is of small importance in comparison with its unconscious life. The most subtle analyst, the most acute observer, is scarcely successful in discovering more than a very small number of the conscious motives that determine his conduct. Our conscious acts are the outcome of an unconscious substratum created in the mind in the main by hereditary influences. This substratum consists of the innumerable common characteristics handed down from generation to generation, which constitute the genius of a race. Behind the avowed causes of our acts there undoubtedly lie secret causes that we do not avow, but behind these secret causes there are many others more secret still, of which we ourselves are ignorant. The greater part of our

[1] *The Crowd: a Study of the Popular Mind* (Fisher Unwin, 12th Impression, 1920).
[2] See footnote page 664.—TR.

[3] References are to the English translation.—TR.

daily actions are the result of hidden motives which escape our observation" (p. 30).

Le Bon thinks that the particular acquirements of individuals become obliterated in a group, and that in this way their distinctiveness vanishes. The racial unconscious emerges; what is heterogeneous is submerged in what is homogeneous. We may say that the mental superstructure, the development of which in individuals shows such dissimilarities, is removed, and that the unconscious foundations, which are similar in everyone, stand exposed to view.

In this way individuals in a group would come to show an average character. But Le Bon believes that they also display new characteristics which they have not previously possessed, and he seeks the reason for this in three different factors.

"The first is that the individual forming part of a group acquires, solely from numerical considerations, a sentiment of invincible power which allows him to yield to instincts which, had he been alone, he would perforce have kept under restraint. He will be the less disposed to check himself from the consideration that, a group being anonymous, and in consequence irresponsible, the sentiment of responsibility which always controls individuals disappears entirely" (p. 33).

From our point of view we need not attribute so much importance to the appearance of new characteristics. For us it would be enough to say that in a group the individual is brought under conditions which allow him to throw off the repressions of his unconscious instincts. The apparently new characteristics which he then displays are in fact the manifestations of this unconscious, in which all that is evil in the human mind is contained as a predisposition. We can find no difficulty in understanding the disappearance of conscience or of a sense of responsibility in these circumstances. It has long been our contention that "dread of society"*(soziale Angst)* is the essence of what is called *conscience.*[1]

"The second cause, which is contagion, also intervenes to determine the manifestation in

groups of their special characteristics, and at the same time the trend they are to take. Contagion is a phenomenon of which it is easy to establish the presence, but that it is not easy to explain. It must be classed among those phenomena of a hypnotic order, which we shall shortly study. In a group every sentiment and act is contagious, and contagious to such a degree that an individual readily sacrifices his personal interest to the collective interest. This is an aptitude very contrary to his nature, and of which a man is scarcely capable, except when he makes part of a group" (p. 33).

We shall later on base an important conjecture upon this last statement.

"A third cause, and by far the most important, determines in the individuals of a group special characteristics which are quite contrary at times to those presented by the isolated individual. I allude to that suggestibility of which, moreover, the contagion mentioned above is only an effect.

"To understand this phenomenon it is necessary to bear in mind certain recent physiological discoveries. We know today that by various processes an individual may be brought into such a condition that, having entirely lost his conscious personality, he obeys all the suggestions of the operator who has deprived him of it, and commits acts in utter contradiction with his character and habits. The most careful investigations seem to prove that an individual immersed for some length of time in a group in action soon finds himself—either in consequence of the magnetic influence given out by the group, or from some other cause of which we are ignorant—in a special state, which much resembles the state of fascination in which the hypnotized individual finds himself in the hands of the hypnotizer. . . . The conscious personality has entirely vanished; will and discernment are lost. All feelings and thoughts are bent in the direction determined by the hypnotizer.

"Such also is approximately the state of the individual forming part of a psychological group. He is no longer conscious of his acts. In his case, as in the case of the hypnotized subject, at the same time that certain faculties are destroyed, others may be brought to a high degree of exaltation. Under the influence of a suggestion, he will undertake the accomplishment of certain acts with irresistible impetuosity. This impetuosity is the more irresistible in the case of groups than in that of the hypnotized subject. from the fact that, the suggestion

---

[1] There is some difference between Le Bon's view and ours, owing to his concept of the unconscious not quite coinciding with the one adopted by psycho-analysis. Le Bon's unconscious more especially contains the most deeply buried features of the racial mind, which, as a matter of fact, lies outside the scope of psychoanalysis. We do not fail to recognize, indeed, that the ego's nucleus, which comprises the "archaic inheritance" of the human mind, is unconscious; but in addition to this we distinguish the *unconscious repressed,* which arose from a portion of that inheritance. This concept of the repressed is not to be found in Le Bon.

being the same for all the individuals of the group, it gains in strength by reciprocity" (p. 34).

"We see, then, that the disappearance of the conscious personality, the predominance of the unconscious personality, the turning by means of suggestion and contagion of feelings and ideas in an identical direction, the tendency immediately to transform the suggested ideas into acts; these, we see, are the principal characteristics of the individual forming part of a group. He is no longer himself, but has become an automaton who has ceased to be guided by his will" (p. 35).

I have quoted this passage so fully in order to make it quite clear that Le Bon explains the condition of an individual in a group as being actually hypnotic, and does not merely make a comparison between the two states. We have no intention of raising any objection at this point, but wish only to emphasize the fact that the two last causes of an individual becoming altered in a group (the contagion and the heightened suggestibility) are evidently not on a par, since the contagion seems actually to be a manifestation of the suggestibility. Moreover the effects of the two factors do not seem to be sharply differentiated in the text of Le Bon's remarks. We may perhaps best interpret his statement if we connect the contagion with the effects of the individual members of the group upon one another, while we point to another source for those manifestations of suggestion in the group which are put on a level with the phenomena of hypnotic influence. But to what source? We cannot avoid being struck with a sense of deficiency when we notice that one of the chief elements of the comparison, namely the person who is to replace the hypnotist in the case of the group, is not mentioned in Le Bon's exposition. But he nevertheless distinguishes between this influence of fascination which remains plunged in obscurity and the contagious effect which the individuals exercise upon one another and by which the original suggestion is strengthened.

Here is yet another important consideration for helping us to understand the individual in a group: "Moreover, by the mere fact that he forms part of an organized group, a man descends several rungs in the ladder of civilization. Isolated, he may be a cultivated individual; in a crowd he is a barbarian—that is, a creature acting by instinct. He possesses the spontaneity, the violence, the ferocity, and also the enthusiasm and heroism of primitive be-ings" (p. 36). He then dwells especially upon the lowering in intellectual ability which an individual experiences when he becomes merged in a group.[1]

Let us now leave the individual, and turn to the group mind, as it has been outlined by Le Bon. It shows not a single feature which a psycho-analyst would find any difficulty in placing or in deriving from its source. Le Bon himself shows us the way by pointing to its similarity with the mental life of primitive people and of children (p. 40).

A group is impulsive, changeable, and irritable. It is led almost exclusively by the unconscious.[2] The impulses which a group obeys may according to circumstances be generous or cruel, heroic or cowardly, but they are always so imperious that no personal interest, not even that of self-preservation, can make itself felt (p. 41). Nothing about it is premeditated. Though it may desire things passionately, yet this is never so for long, for it is incapable of perseverance. It cannot tolerate any delay between its desire and the fulfilment of what it desires. It has a sense of omnipotence; the notion of impossibility disappears for the individual in a group.[3]

A group is extraordinarily credulous and open to influence, it has no critical faculty, and the improbable does not exist for it. It thinks in images, which call one another up by association (just as they arise with individuals in states of free imagination), and whose agreement with reality is never checked by any reasonable function *(Instanz)*. The feelings of a group are always very simple and very exaggerated. So that a group knows neither doubt nor uncertainty.[4]

---

[1] Compare Schiller's couplet:
"Jeder, sieht man ihn einzeln, ist leidlich klug und verständig;
Sind sie in corpore, *gleich wird euch ein Dummkopf daraus."*
[*Everyone, seen by himself, is passably shrewd and discerning;*
When they're in corpore, *then straightway you'll find he's an ass.*]—TR.

[2] *Unconscious* is used here correctly by Le Bon in the descriptive sense, where it does not only mean the *repressed.*

[3] Compare *Totem and Taboo,* III, *"Animism, Magic, and the Omnipotence of Thought."*

[4] In the interpretation of dreams, to which, indeed, we owe our best knowledge of unconscious mental life, we follow a technical rule of disregarding doubt and uncertainty in the narrative of the dream, and of treating every element of the manifest dream as being quite certain. We attribute doubt and uncertainty to the influence of the censorship to which the dream-work is subjected, and we assume that the primary dream-thoughts are not acquainted with doubt and uncertainty as critical processes. They may naturally

It goes directly to extremes; if a suspicion is expressed, it is instantly changed into an incontrovertible certainty; a trace of antipathy is turned into furious hatred (p. 56).[1]

Inclined as it itself is to all extremes, a group can only be excited by an excessive stimulus. Anyone who wishes to produce an effect upon it needs no logical adjustment in his arguments; he must paint in the most forcible colours, he must exaggerate, and he must repeat the same thing again and again.

Since a group is in no doubt as to what constitutes truth or error, and is conscious, moreover, of its own great strength, it is as intolerant as it is obedient to authority. It respects force and can only be slightly influenced by kindness, which it regards merely as a form of weakness. What it demands of its heroes is strength, or even violence. It wants to be ruled and oppressed and to fear its masters. Fundamentally it is entirely conservative, and it has a deep aversion from all innovations and advances and an unbounded respect for tradition (p. 62).

In order to make a correct judgment upon the morals of groups, one must take into consideration the fact that when individuals come together in a group all their individual inhibitions fall away and all the cruel, brutal, and destructive instincts, which lie dormant in individuals as relics of a primitive epoch, are stirred up to find free gratification. But under the influence of suggestion, groups are also capable of high achievements in the shape of abnegation, unselfishness, and devotion to an ideal. While with isolated individuals personal interest is almost the only motive force, with groups it is very rarely prominent. It is possible to speak of an individual having his moral standards raised by a group (p. 65). Whereas the intellectual capacity of a group is always far below that of an individual, its ethical conduct may rise as high above his as it may sink deep below it.

Some other features in Le Bon's description show in a clear light how well justified is the identification of the group mind with the mind of primitive people. In groups the most contradictory ideas can exist side by side and tolerate each other, without any conflict arising from the logical contradiction between them. But this is also the case in the unconscious mental life of individuals, of children, and of neurotics, as psycho-analysis has long pointed out.[2]

A group, further, is subject to the truly magical power of words; they can evoke the most formidable tempests in the group mind, and are also capable of stilling them (p. 117). "Reason and arguments are incapable of combating certain words and formulas. They are uttered with solemnity in the presence of groups, and as soon as they have been pronounced an expression of respect is visible on every countenance, and all heads are bowed. By many they are considered as natural forces, as supernatural powers" (p. 117). It is only necessary in this connection to remember the taboo upon names among primitive people and the magical powers which they ascribe to names and words.[3]

And, finally, groups have never thirsted after truth. They demand illusions, and cannot do without them. They constantly give what is

---

be present, like everything else, as part of the content of the day's residue which leads to the dream. See *The Interpretation of Dreams*, p. 343 above.

[1] The same extreme and unmeasured intensification of every emotion is also a feature of the affective life of children, and it is present as well in dream life. Thanks to the isolation of the single emotions in the unconscious, a slight annoyance during the day will express itself in a dream as a wish for the offending person's death, or a breath of temptation may give the impetus to the portrayal in the dream of a criminal action. Hanns Sachs has made an appropriate remark on this point: "If we try to discover in consciousness all that the dream has made known to us of its bearing upon the present (upon reality), we need not be surprised that what we saw as a monster under the microscope of analysis now reappears as an infusorium." *The Interpretation of Dreams,* p. 386 above.

[2] In young children, for instance, ambivalent emotional attitudes towards those who are nearest to them exist side by side for a long time, without either of them interfering with the expression of the other and contrary one. If eventually a conflict breaks out between the two, it is often settled by the child making a change of object and displacing one of the ambivalent emotions on to a substitute. The history of the development of a neurosis in an adult will also show that a suppressed emotion may frequently persist for a long time in unconscious or even in conscious phantasies, the content of which naturally runs directly counter to some predominant tendency, and yet that this antagonism does not result in any proceedings on the part of the ego against what it has repudiated. The phantasy is tolerated for quite a long time, until suddenly one day, usually as a result of an increase in the affective cathexis of the phantasy, a conflict breaks out between it and the ego with all the usual consequences. In the process of a child's development into a mature adult, there is a more and more extensive integration of its personality, a co-ordination of the separate instinctive feelings and desires which have grown up in him independently of one another. The analogous process in the domain of sexual life has long been known to us as the co-ordination of all the sexual instincts into a definitive genital organization. (*Three Contributions to the Sexual Theory*, Nervous and Mental Disease Monograph Series, No. 7, 1910.) Moreover, that the unification of the ego is liable to the same interferences as that of the libido is shown by numerous familiar instances, such as that of men of science who have preserved their faith in the Bible, and the like.

[3] See *Totem and Taboo*.

unreal precedence over what is real; they are almost as strongly influenced by what is untrue as by what is true. They have an evident tendency not to distinguish between the two (p. 77).

We have pointed out that this predominance of the life of phantasy and of the illusion born of an unfulfilled wish is the ruling factor in the psychology of neuroses. We have found that what neurotics are guided by is not ordinary objective reality but psychological reality. A hysterical symptom is based upon phantasy instead of upon the repetition of real experience, and the sense of guilt in an obsessional neurosis is based upon the fact of an evil intention which was never carried out. Indeed, just as in dreams and in hypnosis, in the mental operations of a group the function for testing the reality of things falls into the background in comparison with the strength of wishes with their affective cathexis.

What Le Bon says on the subject of leaders of groups is less exhaustive, and does not enable us to make out an underlying principle so clearly. He thinks that as soon as living beings are gathered together in certain numbers, no matter whether they are a herd of animals or a collection of human beings, they place themselves instinctively under the authority of a chief (p. 134). A group is an obedient herd, which could never live without a master. It has such a thirst for obedience that it submits instinctively to anyone who appoints himself its master.

Although in this way the needs of a group carry it half-way to meet the leader, yet he too must fit in with it in his personal qualities. He must himself be held in fascination by a strong faith (in an idea) in order to awaken the group's faith; he must possess a strong and imposing will, which the group, which has no will of its own, can accept from him. Le Bon then discusses the different kinds of leaders, and the means by which they work upon the group. On the whole, he believes that the leaders make themselves felt by means of the ideas in which they themselves are fanatical believers.

Moreover, he ascribes both to the ideas and to the leaders a mysterious and irresistible power, which he calls *prestige*. Prestige is a sort of domination exercised over us by an individual, a work or an idea. It entirely paralyzes our critical faculty, and fills us with astonishment and respect. It would seem to arouse a feeling like that of fascination in hypnosis (p. 148).

He distinguishes between acquired or artificial and personal prestige. The former is attached to persons in virtue of their name, fortune, and reputation, and to opinions, works of art, etc., in virtue of tradition. Since in every case it harks back to the past, it cannot be of much help to us in understanding this puzzling influence. Personal prestige is attached to a few people, who become leaders by means of it, and it has the effect of making everything obey them as though by the operation of some magnetic magic. All prestige, however, is also dependent upon success, and is lost in the event of failure (p. 159).

We cannot feel that Le Bon has brought the function of the leader and the importance of prestige completely into harmony with his brilliantly executed picture of the group mind.

III. OTHER ACCOUNTS OF COLLECTIVE MENTAL LIFE

WE have made use of Le Bon's description by way of introduction, because it fits in so well with our own psychology in the emphasis which it lays upon unconscious mental life. But we must now add that as a matter of fact none of that author's statements bring forward anything new. Everything that he says to the detriment and depreciation of the manifestations of the group mind had already been said by others before him with equal distinctness and equal hostility, and has been repeated in unison by thinkers, statesmen, and writers since the earliest periods of literature.[1] The two theses which comprise the most important of Le Bon's opinions, those touching upon the collective inhibition of intellectual functioning and the heightening of affectivity in groups, had been formulated shortly before by Sighele.[2] At bottom, all that is left over as being peculiar to Le Bon are the two notions of the unconscious and of the comparison with the mental life of primitive people, and even these had naturally often been alluded to before him.

But, what is more, the description and estimate of the group mind as they have been given by Le Bon and the rest have not by any means been left undisputed. There is no doubt that all the phenomena of the group mind which have just been mentioned have been correctly ob-

[1] B. Krásković jun.: *Die Psychologie der Kollektivitäten,* translated (into German) from the Croatian by Siegmund von Posavec, Vukovar, 1915. See the body of the work as well as the bibliography.

[2] See Walter Moede *"Die Massen- und Sozialpsychologie im kritischen Überblick,"* Meumann and Scheibner's *Zeitschrift für pädagogische Psychologie und experimentelle Pädagogik,* 1915, XVI.

served, but it is also possible to distinguish other manifestations of the group formation, which operate in a precisely opposite sense, and from which a much higher opinion of the group mind must necessarily follow.

Le Bon himself was prepared to admit that in certain circumstances the morals of a group can be higher than those of the individuals that compose it, and that only collectivities are capable of a high degree of unselfishness and devotion. "While with isolated individuals personal interest is almost the only motive force, with groups it is very rarely prominent" (p. 65). Other writers adduce the fact that it is only society which prescribes any ethical standards at all for the individual, while he as a rule fails in one way or another to come up to its high demands. Or they point out that in exceptional circumstances there may arise in communities the phenomenon of enthusiasm, which has made the most splendid group achievements possible.

As regards intellectual work, it remains a fact, indeed, that great decisions in the realm of thought and momentous discoveries and solutions of problems are only possible to an individual, working in solitude. But even the group mind is capable of genius in intellectual creation, as is shown above all by language itself, as well as by folk-song, folk-lore and the like. It remains an open question, moreover, how much the individual thinker or writer owes to the stimulation of the group in which he lives, or whether he does more than perfect a mental work in which the others have had a simultaneous share.

In face of these completely contradictory accounts, it looks as though the work of group psychology were bound to come to an ineffectual end. But it is easy to find a more hopeful escape from the dilemma. A number of very different formations have probably been merged under the term *group* and may require to be distinguished. The assertions of Sighele, Le Bon and the rest relate to groups of a short-lived character, which some passing interest has hastily agglomerated out of various sorts of individuals. The characteristics of revolutionary groups, and especially those of the great French Revolution, have unmistakably influenced their descriptions. The opposite opinions owe their origin to the consideration of those stable groups or associations in which mankind pass their lives, and which are embodied in the institutions of society. Groups of the first kind stand in the same sort of relation to those of the second as a high but choppy sea to a ground swell.

McDougall, in his book on *The Group Mind*,[1] starts out from the same contradiction that has just been mentioned, and finds a solution for it in the factor of organization. In the simplest case, he says, the *group* possesses no organization at all, or one scarcely deserving the name. He describes a group of this kind as a *crowd*. But he admits that a crowd of human beings can hardly come together without possessing at all events the rudiments of an organization, and that precisely in these simple groups many of the fundamental facts of collective psychology can be observed with special ease (p. 22). Before the members of a random crowd of people can constitute something in the nature of a group in the psychological sense of the word, a condition has to be fulfilled; these individuals must have something in common with one another, a common interest in an object, a similar emotional bias in some situation or other, and ("consequently," I should like to interpolate) "some degree of reciprocal influence" (p. 23). The higher the degree of "this mental homogeneity," the more readily do the individuals form a psychological group, and the more striking are the manifestations of a group mind.

The most remarkable and also the most important result of the formation of a group is the "exaltation or intensification of emotion" produced in every member of it (p. 24). In McDougall's opinion, men's emotions are stirred in a group to a pitch that they seldom or never attain under other conditions; and it is a pleasurable experience for those who are concerned to surrender themselves so unreservedly to their passions and thus to become merged in the group and to lose the sense of the limits of their individuality. The manner in which individuals are thus carried away by a common impulse is explained by McDougall by means of what he calls the "principle of direct induction of emotion by way of the primitive sympathetic response" (p. 25), that is, by means of the emotional contagion with which we are already familiar. The fact is that the perception of the signs of an emotional state is calculated automatically to arouse the same emotion in the person who perceives them. The greater the number of people in whom the same emotion can be simultaneously observed, the stronger does this automatic compulsion grow. The individual loses his power of criticism and lets himself slip into the same emotion. But in so

[1] Cambridge University Press, 1920.

doing he increases the excitement of the other people, who had produced this effect upon him, and thus the emotional charge of the individuals becomes intensified by mutual interaction. Something is unmistakably at work in the nature of a compulsion to do the same as the others, to remain in harmony with the many. The coarser and simpler emotions are the more apt to spread through a group in this way (p. 39).

This mechanism for the intensification of emotion is favoured by some other influences which emanate from groups. A group impresses the individual with a sense of unlimited power and of insurmountable peril. For the moment, it replaces the whole of human society, which is the wielder of authority, whose punishments the individual fears, and for whose sake he has submitted to so many inhibitions. It is clearly perilous for him to put himself in opposition to it, and it will be safer to follow the example of those around him and perhaps even "hunt with the pack." In obedience to the new authority he may put his former conscience out of action, and so surrender to the attraction of the increased pleasure that is certainly obtained from the removal of inhibitions. On the whole, therefore, it is not so remarkable that we should see an individual in a group doing or approving things which he would have avoided in the normal conditions of life; and in this way we may even hope to clear up a little of the mystery which is so often covered by the enigmatic word *suggestion*.

McDougall does not dispute the thesis as to the collective inhibition of intelligence in groups (p. 41). He says that the minds of lower intelligence bring down those of a higher order to their own level. The latter are obstructed in their activity, because in general an intensification of emotion creates unfavourable conditions for sound intellectual work, and, further, because the individuals are intimidated by the group and their mental activity is not free, and because there is a lowering in each individual of his sense of responsibility for his own performances.

The judgment with which McDougall sums up the psychological behaviour of a simple "unorganized" group is no more friendly than that of Le Bon. Such a group "is excessively emotional, impulsive, violent, fickle, inconsistent, irresolute, and extreme in action, displaying only the coarser emotions and the less refined sentiments; extremely suggestible, careless in deliberation, hasty in judgment, incapable of

any but the simpler and imperfect forms of reasoning; easily swayed and led, lacking in self-consciousness, devoid of self-respect and of sense of responsibility, and apt to be carried away by the consciousness of its own force, so that it tends to produce all the manifestations we have learnt to expect of any irresponsible and absolute power. Hence its behaviour is like that of an unruly child or an untutored passionate savage in a strange situation, rather than like that of its average member; and in the worst cases it is like that of a wild beast, rather than like that of human beings" (p. 45).

Since McDougall contrasts the behaviour of a highly organized group with what has just been described, we shall be particularly interested to learn in what this organization consists, and by what factors it is produced. The author enumerates five "principal conditions" for raising collective mental life to a higher level.

The first and fundamental condition is that there should be some degree of continuity of existence in the group. This may be either material or formal: the former, if the same individuals persist in the group for some time; and the latter, if there is developed within the group a system of fixed positions which are occupied by a succession of individuals.

The second condition is that in the individual member of the group some definite idea should be formed of the nature, composition, functions, and capacities of the group, so that from this he may develop an emotional relation to the group as a whole.

The third is that the group should be brought into interaction (perhaps in the form of rivalry) with other groups similar to it but differing from it in many respects.

The fourth is that the group should possess traditions, customs, and habits, and especially such as determine the relations of its members to one another.

The fifth is that the group should have a definite structure, expressed in the specialization and differentiation of the functions of its constituents.

According to McDougall, if these conditions are fulfilled, the psychological disadvantages of the group formation are removed. The collective lowering of intellectual ability is avoided by withdrawing the performance of intellectual tasks from the group and reserving them for individual members of it.

It seems to us that the condition which McDougall designates as the "organization" of a group can with more justification be described in another way. The problem consists in how to procure for the group precisely those features which were characteristic of the individual and which are extinguished in him by the formation of the group. For the individual, outside the primitive group, possessed his own continuity, his self-consciousness, his traditions and customs, his own particular functions and position, and kept apart from his rivals. Owing to his entry into an "unorganized" group, he had lost this distinctiveness for a time. If we thus recognize that the aim is to equip the group with the attributes of the individual, we shall be reminded of a valuable remark of Trotter's,[1] to the effect that the tendency towards the formation of groups is biologically a continuation of the multicellular character of all the higher organisms.

IV. SUGGESTION AND LIBIDO

WE started from the fundamental fact that an individual in a group is subjected through its influence to what is often a profound alteration in his mental activity. His emotions become extraordinarily intensified, while his intellectual ability becomes markedly reduced, both processes being evidently in the direction of an approximation to the other individuals in the group; and this result can only be reached by the removal of those inhibitions upon his instincts which are peculiar to each individual, and by his resigning those expressions of his inclinations which are especially his own. We have heard that these often unwelcome consequences are to some extent at least prevented by a higher "organization" of the group; but this does not contradict the fundamental fact of group psychology—the two theses as to the intensification of the emotions and the inhibition of the intellect in primitive groups. Our interest is now directed to discovering the psychological explanation of this mental change which is experienced by the individual in a group.

It is clear that rational factors (such as the intimidation of the individual which has already been mentioned, that is, the action of his instinct of self-preservation) do not cover the observable phenomena. Beyond this, what we are offered as an explanation by authorities upon sociology and group psychology is always the same, even though it is given various names, and that is—the magic word *suggestion*. Tarde

calls it "imitation"; but we cannot help agreeing with a writer who protests that imitation comes under the concept of suggestion, and is in fact one of its results.[2] Le Bon traces back all the puzzling features of social phenomena to two factors: the mutual suggestion of individuals and the prestige of leaders. But prestige, again, is only recognizable by its capacity for evoking suggestion. McDougall for a moment gives us an impression that his principle of "primitive induction of emotion" might enable us to do without the assumption of suggestion. But on further consideration we are forced to perceive that this principle says no more than the familiar assertions about "imitation" or "contagion," except for a decided stress upon the emotional factor. There is no doubt that something exists in us which, when we become aware of signs of an emotion in someone else, tends to make us fall into the same emotion; but how often do we not successfully oppose it, resist the emotion, and react in quite an opposite way? Why, therefore, do we invariably give way to this contagion when we are in a group? Once more we should have to say that what compels us to obey this tendency is imitation, and what induces the emotion in us is the group's suggestive influence. Moreover, quite apart from this, McDougall does not enable us to evade suggestion; we hear from him as well as from other writers that groups are distinguished by their special suggestibility.

We shall therefore be prepared for the statement that suggestion (or more correctly suggestibility) is actually an irreducible, primitive phenomenon, a fundamental fact in the mental life of man. Such, too, was the opinion of Bernheim, of whose astonishing arts I was a witness in the year 1889. But I can remember even then feeling a muffled hostility to this tyranny of suggestion. When a patient who showed himself unamenable was met with the shout: "What are you doing? *Vous vous contresuggestionnez!*" I said to myself that this was an evident injustice and an act of violence. For the man certainly had a right to counter-suggestions if they were trying to subdue him with suggestions. Later on, my resistance took the direction of protesting against the view that suggestion, which explained everything, was itself to be preserved from explanation. Thinking of it, I repeated the old conundrum:[3]

[1] *Instincts of the Herd in Peace and War*, Fisher Unwin, 1916.

[2] Brugeilles, *"L'Essence du phénomène social: la suggestion," Revue philosophique*, 1913, xxv.
[3] Konrad Richter, *"Der deutsche S. Christoph,"* Berlin, 1896, *Acta Germanica*, v, 1.

Christoph trug Christum,
Christus trug die ganze Welt,
Sag' wo hat Christoph
Damals hin den Fuss gestellt?[1]
Christophorus Christum, sed Christus sustulit
   orbem:
   Constiterit pedibus dic ubi Christophorus?

Now that I once more approach the riddle of suggestion after having kept away from it for some thirty years, I find there is no change in the situation. To this statement I can discover only a single exception, which I need not mention, since it is one which bears witness to the influence of psycho-analysis. I notice that particular efforts are being made to formulate the concept of suggestion correctly, that is, to fix the conventional use of the name.[2] And this is by no means superfluous, for the word is acquiring a more and more extended use and a looser and looser meaning, and will soon come to designate any sort of influence whatever, just as in English, where "to suggest" and "suggestion" correspond to our *nahelegen and Anregung.* But there has been no explanation of the nature of suggestion, that is, of the conditions under which influence without adequate logical foundation takes place. I should not avoid the task of supporting this statement by an analysis of the literature of the last thirty years, if I were not aware that an exhaustive inquiry is being undertaken close at hand which has in view the fulfilment of this very task.

Instead of this, I shall make an attempt at using the concept of *libido* for the purpose of throwing light upon group psychology, a concept which has done us such good service in the study of psychoneuroses.

Libido is an expression taken from the theory of the emotions. We call by that name the energy (regarded as a quantitative magnitude, though not at present actually mensurable) of those instincts which have to do with all that may be comprised under the word *love.* The nucleus of what we mean by love naturally consists (and this is what is commonly called love, and what the poets sing of) in sexual love with sexual union as its aim. But we do not separate from this—what in any case has a share in the name *love*—on the one hand, self-love, and on the other, love for parents and children, friendship, and love for humanity in general, and also

devotion to concrete objects and to abstract ideas. Our justification lies in the fact that psycho-analytic research has taught us that all these tendencies are an expression of the same instinctive activities; in relations between the sexes these instincts force their way towards sexual union, but in other circumstances they are diverted from this aim or are prevented from reaching it, though always preserving enough of their original nature to keep their identity recognizable (as in such features as the longing for proximity, and self-sacrifice).

We are of opinion, then, that language has carried out an entirely justifiable piece of unification in creating the word *love* with its numerous uses, and that we cannot do better than take it as the basis of our scientific discussions and expositions as well. By coming to this decision, psycho-analysis has let loose a storm of indignation, as though it had been guilty of an act of outrageous innovation. Yet psycho-analysis has done nothing original in taking love in this "wider" sense. In its origin, function, and relation to sexual love, the *"Eros"* of the philosopher Plato coincides exactly with the love force, the libido, of psycho-analysis, as has been shown in detail by Nachmansohn and Pfister;[3] and when the apostle Paul, in his famous epistle to the Corinthians, prizes love above all else, he certainly understands it in the same "wider" sense.[4] But this only shows that men do not always take their great thinkers seriously, even when they profess most to admire them.

Psycho-analysis, then, gives these love instincts the name of sexual instincts, *a potiori* and by reason of their origin. The majority of "educated" people have regarded this nomenclature as an insult, and have taken their revenge by retorting upon psycho-analysis with the reproach of "pan-sexualism." Anyone who considers sex as something mortifying and humiliating to human nature is at liberty to make use of the more genteel expressions "Eros" and "erotic." I might have done so myself from the first and thus have spared myself much opposition. But I did not want to, for I like to avoid concessions to faint-heartedness. One can never tell where that road may lead one; one gives way first in words, and then little by little in substance too. I cannot see any merit in being

---

[1] Literally: "Christopher bore Christ; Christ bore the whole world; Say, where did Christopher then put his foot?"—TR.

[2] Thus, McDougall: "A Note on Suggestion," *Journal of Neurology and Psychopathology,* 1920, Vol. I, No. 1.

[3] Nachmansohn, *"Freuds Libidotheorie verglichen mit der Eroslehre Platos," Internationale Zeitschrift für Psychoanalyse,* 1915, Vol. III; Pfister, "Plato: a Fore-Runner of Psycho-Analysis," *International Journal of Psycho-Analysis,* 1922, Vol. III.

[4] "Though I speak with the tongues of men and of angels, and have not love, I am become as sounding brass, or a tinkling cymbal."

ashamed of sex; the Greek word *Eros,* which is to soften the affront, is in the end nothing more than a translation of our German word *Liebe;* and finally, he who knows how to wait need make no concessions.

We will try our fortune, then, with the supposition that love relationships (or, to use a more neutral expression, emotional ties) also constitute the essence of the group mind. Let us remember that the authorities make no mention of any such relations. What would correspond to them is evidently concealed behind the shelter, the screen, of suggestion. Our hypothesis finds support in the first instance from two passing thoughts. First, that a group is clearly held together by a power of some kind: and to what power could this feat be better ascribed than to Eros, who holds together everything in the world? Secondly, that if an individual gives up his distinctiveness in a group and lets its other members influence him by suggestion, it gives one the impression that he does it because he feels the need of being in harmony with them rather than in opposition to them—so that perhaps after all he does it *ihnen zu Liebe.*[1]

V. Two Artificial Groups: the Church and the Army

We may recall from what we know of the morphology of groups that it is possible to distinguish very different kinds of groups and opposing lines in their development. There are very fleeting groups and extremely lasting ones; homogeneous ones, made up of the same sorts of individuals, and unhomogeneous ones; natural groups, and artificial ones, requiring an external force to keep them together; primitive groups, and highly organized ones with a definite structure. But for reasons which have yet to be explained we should like to lay particular stress upon a distinction to which the authorities have rather given too little attenion; I refer to that between leaderless groups and those with leaders. And, in complete opposition to the usual practice, we shall not choose a relatively simple group formation as our point of departure, but shall begin with highly organized, lasting, and artificial groups. The most interesting example of such structures are churches—communities of believers—and armies.

A church and an army are artificial groups,

[1] An idiom meaning "for their sake." Literally: "for love of them."—Tr.

that is, a certain external force is employed to prevent them from disintegrating and to check alterations in their structure. As a rule a person is not consulted, or is given no choice, as to whether he wants to enter such a group; any attempt at leaving it is usually met with persecution or with severe punishment, or has quite definite conditions attached to it. It is quite outside our present interest to enquire why these associations need such special safeguards. We are only attracted by one circumstance, namely that certain facts, which are far more concealed in other cases, can be observed very clearly in those highly organized groups which are protected from dissolution in the manner that has been mentioned.

In a church (and we may with advantage take the Catholic Church as a type) as well as in an army, however different the two may be in other respects, the same illusion holds good of there being a head—in the Catholic Church Christ, in an army its commander-in-chief—who loves all the individuals in the group with an equal love. Everything depends upon this illusion; if it were to be dropped, then both Church and army would dissolve, so far as the external force permitted them to. This equal love was expressly enunciated by Christ: "Inasmuch as ye have done it unto one of the least of these my brethren, ye have done it unto me." He stands to the individual members of the group of believers in the relation of a kind elder brother; he is their father surrogate. All the demands that are made upon the individual are derived from this love of Christ's. A democratic character runs through the Church, for the very reason that before Christ everyone is equal, and that everyone has an equal share in his love. It is not without a deep reason that the similarity between the Christian community and a family is invoked, and that believers call themselves *brothers in Christ,* that is, brothers through the love which Christ has for them. There is no doubt that the tie which unites each individual with Christ is also the cause of the tie which unites them with one another. The like holds good of an army. The commander-in-chief is a father who loves all his soldiers equally, and for that reason they are comrades among themselves. The army differs structurally from the Church in being built up of a series of such groups. Every captain is, as it were, the commander-in-chief and the father of his company, and so is every non-commissioned officer of his section. It is true that a similar hierarchy has been constructed in the Church, but it does not play the same part in it economically; for more knowledge and care about individuals may be attributed to Christ than to a human commander-in-chief.[1]

It is to be noticed that in these two artificial groups each individual is bound by libidinal ties on the one hand to the leader (Christ, the commander-in-chief), and on the other hand to the other members of the group. How these two ties are related to each other, whether they are of the same kind and the same value, and how they are to be described psychologically—these questions must be reserved for subsequent enquiry. But we shall venture even now upon a mild reproach against the authorities for not having sufficiently appreciated the importance of the leader in the psychology of the group, while our own choice of a first object for investigation has brought us into a more favourable position. It would appear as though we were on the right road towards an explanation of the principal phenomenon of group psychology—the individual's lack of freedom in a group. If each individual is bound in two directions by such an intense emotional tie, we shall find no difficulty in attributing to that circumstance the alteration and limitation which have been observed in his personality.

A hint to the same effect, that the essence of a group lies in the libidinal ties existing in it, is also to be found in the phenomenon of panic,

[1] An objection will justly be raised against this conception of the libidinal structure of an army on the ground that no place has been found in it for such ideas as those of one's country, of national glory, etc. which are of such importance in holding an army together. The answer is that that is a different instance of a group tie, and no longer such a simple one; for the examples of great generals, like Caesar, Wallenstein, or Napoleon, show that such ideas are not indispensable to the existence of an army. We shall presently touch upon the possibility of a leading idea being substituted for a leader and upon the relations between the two. The neglect of this libidinal factor in an army, even when it is not the only factor operative, seems to be not merely a theoretical omission but also a practical danger. Prussian militarism, which was just as unpsychological as German science, may have had to suffer the consequences of this in the Great War. We know that the war neuroses which ravaged the German army have been recognized as being a protest of the individual against the part he was expected to play in the army; and according to the communication of E. Simmel (*Kriegsneurosen und "Psychisches Trauma,"* Munich, 1918), the hard treatment of the men by their superiors may be considered as foremost among the motive forces of the disease. If the importance of the libido's claims on this score had been better appreciated, the fantastic promises of the American President's fourteen points would probably not have been believed so easily, and the splendid instrument would not have broken in the hands of the German leaders.

which is best studied in military groups. A panic arises if a group of that kind becomes disintegrated. Its characteristics are that none of the orders given by superiors are any longer listened to, and that each individual is only solicitous on his own account, and without any consideration for the rest. The mutual ties have ceased to exist, and a gigantic and senseless dread (*Angst*) is set free. At this point, again, the objection will naturally be made that it is rather the other way round; and that the dread has grown so great as to be able to disregard all ties and all feelings of consideration for others. McDougall has even (p. 24) made use of the case of panic (though not of military panic) as a typical instance of that intensification of emotion by contagion ("primary induction") upon which he lays so much emphasis. But, nevertheless, this rational method of explanation is here quite inadequate. The very question that needs explanation is why the dread has become so gigantic. The greatness of the danger cannot be responsible, for the same army which now falls a victim to panic may previously have faced equally great or greater danger with complete success; it is of the very essence of panic that it bears no relation to the danger that threatens, and often breaks out upon the most trivial occasions. If an individual in panic dread begins to be solicitous only on his own account, he bears witness in so doing to the fact that the emotional ties, which have hitherto made the danger seem small to him, have ceased to exist. Now that he is by himself in facing the danger, he may surely think it greater. The fact is, therefore, that panic dread presupposes a relaxation in the libidinal structure of the group and reacts to it in a justifiable manner, and the contrary view—that the libidinal ties of the group are destroyed owing to dread in the face of the danger—can be refuted.

The contention that dread in a group is increased to enormous proportions by means of induction (contagion) is not in the least contradicted by these remarks. McDougall's view meets the case entirely when the danger is a really great one and when the group has no strong emotional ties—conditions which are fulfilled, for instance, when a fire breaks out in a theatre or a place of amusement. But the really instructive case and the one which can be best employed for our purposes is that mentioned above, in which a body of troops breaks into a panic although the danger has not increased beyond a degree that is usual and has often been previously faced. It is not to be expected that the usage of the word *panic* should be clearly and unambiguously determined. Sometimes it is used to describe any collective dread, sometimes even dread in an individual when it exceeds all bounds, and often the name seems to be reserved for cases in which the outbreak of dread is not warranted by the occasion. If we take the word *panic* in the sense of collective dread, we can establish a far-reaching analogy. Dread in an individual is provoked either by the greatness of a danger or by the cessation of emotional ties (libidinal cathexes [*Libidobesetzungen*]); the latter is the case of neurotic dread.[1] In just the same way panic arises either owing to an increase of the common danger or owing to the disappearance of the emotional ties which hold the group together; and the latter case is analogous to that of neurotic dread.[2]

Anyone who, like McDougall *(op. cit.)*, describes a panic as one of the plainest functions of the "group mind," arrives at the paradoxical position that this group mind does away with itself in one of its most striking manifestations. It is impossible to doubt that panic means the disintegration of a group; it involves the cessation of all the feelings of consideration which the members of the group otherwise show one another.

The typical occasion of the outbreak of a panic is very much as it is represented in Nestroy's parody of Hebbel's play about Judith and Holofernes. A soldier cries out: "The general has lost his head!" and thereupon all the Assyrians take to flight. The loss of the leader in some sense or other, the birth of misgivings about him, brings on the outbreak of panic, though the danger remains the same; the mutual ties between the members of the group disappear, as a rule, at the same time as the tie with their leader. The group vanishes in dust, like a Bologna flask when its top is broken off.

The dissolution of a religious group is not so easy to observe. A short time ago there came into my hands an English novel of Catholic origin, recommended by the Bishop of London, with the title *When It Was Dark*. It gave a clever and, as it seems to me, a convincing picture of such a possibility and its consequences. The novel, which is supposed to relate to the present day, tells how a conspiracy of enemies of the figure of Christ and of the Christian faith succeed in arranging for a sepulchre to be discovered in Jerusalem. In this sepulchre is an inscription, in which Joseph of Arimathaea confesses that for reasons of piety he secretly removed the body of Christ from its grave on the third day after its entombment and buried it in this spot. The resurrection of Christ and his divine nature are by this means disposed of, and the result of this archaeological discovery is a convulsion in European civilization and an extraordinary increase in all crimes and acts of violence, which only ceases when the forgers' plot has been revealed.

The phenomenon which accompanies the dissolution that is here supposed to overtake a religious group is not dread, for which the occasion is wanting. Instead of it, ruthless and hostile impulses towards other people make their appearance, which, owing to the equal love of Christ, they had previously been unable to do.[3] But even during the kingdom of Christ those people who do not belong to the community of believers, who do not love him, and whom he does not love, stand outside this tie. Therefore a religion, even if it calls itself the religion of love, must be hard and unloving to those who do not belong to it. Fundamentally, indeed, every religion is in this same way a religion of love for all those whom it embraces; while cruelty and intolerance towards those who do not belong to it are natural to every religion. However difficult we may find it personally, we ought not to reproach believers too severely on this account; people who are unbelieving or indifferent are so much better off psychologically in this respect. If today that intolerance no longer shows itself so violent and cruel as in former centuries, we can scarcely conclude that there has been a softening in human manners. The cause is rather to be found in the undeniable weakening of religious feelings and the libidinal ties which depend upon them. If another group tie takes the place of the religious one—and the socialistic tie seems to be succeeding in doing so—then there will be the same intolerance towards outsiders as in the age of the Wars of Religion; and if differences between scientific opinions could ever attain a similar significance for groups, the same result would again be repeated with this new motivation.

---

[1] *General Introduction to Psycho-Analysis*, Lecture xxv, p. 607 above.

[2] Compare Bela v. Felszeghy's interesting though somewhat fantastic paper "*Panik und Pankomplex*," *Imago*, 1920, Vol. VI.

[3] Compare the explanation of similar phenomena after the abolition of the paternal authority of the sovereign given in P. Federn's *Die vaterlose Gesellschaft*, Vienna, Anzengruber-Verlag, 1919.

VI. FURTHER PROBLEMS AND LINES OF WORK

WE have hitherto considered two artificial groups and have found that they are dominated by two emotional ties. One of these, the tie with the leader, seems (at all events for these cases) to be more of a ruling factor than the other, which holds between the members of the group.

Now much else remains to be examined and described in the morphology of groups. We should have to start from the ascertained fact that a mere collection of people is not a group, so long as these ties have not been established in it; but we should have to admit that in any collection of people the tendency to form a psychological group may very easily become prominent. We should have to give our attention to the different kinds of groups, more or less stable, that arise spontaneously, and to study the conditions of their origin and of their dissolution. We should above all be concerned with the distinction between groups which have a leader and leaderless groups. We should consider whether groups with leaders may not be the more primitive and complete, whether in the others an idea, an abstraction, may not be substituted for the leader (a state of things to which religious groups, with their invisible head, form a transition stage), and whether a common tendency, a wish in which a number of people can have a share, may not in the same way serve as a substitute. This abstraction, again, might be more or less completely embodied in the figure of what we might call a *secondary* leader, and interesting varieties would arise from the relation between the idea and the leader. The leader or the leading idea might also, so to speak, be negative; hatred against a particular person or institution might operate in just the same unifying way, and might call up the same kind of emotional ties as positive attachment. Then the question would also arise whether a leader is really indispensable to the essence of a group—and other questions besides.

But all these questions, which may, moreover, have been dealt with in part in the literature of group psychology, will not succeed in diverting our interest from the fundamental psychological problems that confront us in the structure of a group. And our attention will first be attracted by a consideration which promises to bring us in the most direct way to a proof that libidinal ties are what characterize a group.

Let us keep before our eyes the nature of the emotional relations which hold between men in general. According to Schopenhauer's famous simile of the freezing porcupines, no one can tolerate a too intimate approach to his neighbour.[1]

The evidence of psycho-analysis shows that almost every intimate emotional relation between two people which lasts for some time—marriage, friendship, the relations between parents and children[2]—leaves a sediment of feelings of aversion and hostility, which have first to be eliminated by repression. This is less disguised in the common wrangles between business partners or in the grumbles of a subordinate at his superior. The same thing happens when men come together in larger units. Every time two families become connected by a marriage, each of them thinks itself superior to or of better birth than the other. Of two neighbouring towns, each is the other's most jealous rival; every little canton looks down upon the others with contempt. Closely related races keep one another at arm's length; the South German cannot endure the North German, the Englishman casts every kind of aspersion upon the Scotchman, the Spaniard despises the Portuguese. We are no longer astonished that greater differences should lead to an almost insuperable repugnance, such as the Gallic people feel for the German, the Aryan for the Semite, and the white races for the coloured.

When this hostility is directed against people who are otherwise loved, we describe it as *ambivalence* of feeling; and we explain the fact, in what is probably far too rational a manner, by means of the numerous occasions for conflicts of interest which arise precisely in such intimate relations. In the undisguised antipathies and aversions which people feel towards strangers with whom they have to do, we may recognize the expression of self-love—of narcissism. This self-love works for the self-assertion of the individual, and behaves as

[1] "A company of porcupines crowded themselves very closely together one cold winter's day so as to profit by one another's warmth and so save themselves from being frozen to death. But soon they felt one another's quills, which induced them to separate again. And now, when the need for warmth brought them nearer together again, the second evil arose once more. So that they were driven backwards and forwards from one trouble to the other, until they had discovered a mean distance at which they could most tolerably exist." *Parerga und Paralipomena*, Part II, xxxi, "*Gleichnisse und Parabeln.*"

[2] Perhaps with the solitary exception of the relation of a mother to her son, which is based upon narcissism, is not disturbed by subsequent rivalry, and is reinforced by a rudimentary attempt at sexual object-choice.

though the occurrence of any divergence from his own particular lines of development involved a criticism of them and a demand for their alteration. We do not know why such sensitiveness should have been directed to just these details of differentiation; but it is unmistakable that in this whole connection men give evidence of a readiness for hatred, an aggressiveness, the source of which is unknown, and to which one is tempted to ascribe an elementary character.[1]

But the whole of this intolerance vanishes, temporarily or permanently, as the result of the formation of a group, and in a group. So long as a group formation persists or so far as it extends, individuals behave as though they were uniform, tolerate other people's peculiarities, put themselves on an equal level with them, and have no feeling of aversion towards them. Such a limitation of narcissism can, according to our theoretical views, only be produced by one factor, a libidinal tie with other people. Love for oneself knows only one barrier—love for others, love for objects.[2] The question will at once be raised whether community of interest in itself, without any addition of libido, must not necessarily lead to the toleration of other people and to considerateness for them. This objection may be met by the reply that nevertheless no lasting limitation of narcissism is effected in this way, since this tolerance does not persist longer than the immediate advantage gained from the other people's collaboration. But the practical importance of the discussion is less than might be supposed, for experience has shown that in cases of collaboration libidinal ties are regularly formed between the fellow-workers which prolong and solidify the relation between them to a point beyond what is merely profitable. The same thing occurs in men's social relations as has become familiar to psycho-analytic research in the course of the development of the individual libido. The libido props itself upon the satisfaction of the great vital needs, and chooses as its first objects the people who have a share in that process. And in the development of mankind as a whole, just as in individuals, love alone acts as the civilizing factor in the sense that it brings a change from egoism to altruism. And this is true both of the sexual love for women, with all the obligations which it in-

volves of sparing what women are fond of, and also of the desexualised, sublimated homosexual love for other men, which springs from work in common.

If therefore in groups narcissistic self-love is subject to limitations which do not operate outside them, that is cogent evidence that the essence of a group formation consists in a new kind of libidinal ties among the members of the group.

But our interest now leads us on to the pressing question as to what may be the nature of these ties which exist in groups. In the psychoanalytic study of neuroses we have hitherto been occupied almost exclusively with ties that unite with their objects those love instincts which still pursue directly sexual aims. In groups there can evidently be no question of sexual aims of that kind. We are concerned here with love instincts which have been diverted from their original aims, though they do not operate with less energy on that account. Now we have already observed within the range of the usual sexual object-cathexis *(Objektbesetzung)* phenomena which represent a diversion of the instinct from its sexual aim. We have described them as degrees of being in love, and have recognized that they involve a certain encroachment upon the ego. We shall now turn our attention more closely to these phenomena of being in love, in the firm expectation of finding in them conditions which can be transferred to the ties that exist in groups. But we should also like to know whether this kind of object-cathexis, as we know it in sexual life, represents the only manner of emotional tie with other people, or whether we must take other mechanisms of the sort into account. As a matter of fact we learn from psycho-analysis that there do exist other mechanisms for emotional ties, the so-called *identifications,* insufficiently-known processes and hard to describe, the investigation of which will for some time keep us away from the subject of group psychology.

VII. IDENTIFICATION

IDENTIFICATION is known to psycho-analysis as the earliest expression of an emotional tie with another person. It plays a part in the early history of the Oedipus complex. A little boy will exhibit a special interest in his father; he would like to grow like him and be like him, and take his place everywhere. We may say simply that he takes his father as his ideal. This behaviour has nothing to do with a passive or feminine attitude towards his father (and towards males

---

[1] In a recently published study, *Beyond the Pleasure Principle* [p. 639 above], I have attempted to connect the polarity of love and hatred with a hypothetical opposition between instincts of life and death, and to establish the sexual instincts as the purest examples of the former, the instincts of life.

[2] See *On Narcissism: an Introduction,* p. 399 above.

in general); it is on the contrary typically masculine. It fits in very well with the Oedipus complex, for which it helps to prepare the way.

At the same time as this identification with his father, or a little later, the boy has begun to develop a true object-cathexis towards his mother according to the anaclitic type. He then exhibits, therefore, two psychologically distinct ties: a straightforward sexual object-cathexis towards his mother and a typical identification towards his father. The two subsist side by side for a time without any mutual influence or interference. In consequence of the irresistible advance towards a unification of mental life, they come together at last; and the normal Oedipus complex originates from their confluence. The little boy notices that his father stands in his way with his mother. His identification with his father then takes on a hostile colouring and becomes identical with the wish to replace his father in regard to his mother as well. Identification, in fact, is ambivalent from the very first; it can turn into an expression of tenderness as easily as into a wish for someone's removal. It behaves like a derivative of the first *oral* phase of the organization of the libido, in which the object that we long for and prize is assimilated by eating and is in that way annihilated as such. The cannibal, as we know, has remained at this standpoint; he has a devouring affection for his enemies and only devours people of whom he is fond.[1]

The subsequent history of this identification with the father may easily be lost sight of. It may happen that the Oedipus complex becomes inverted, and that the father is taken as the object of a feminine attitude, an object from which the directly sexual instincts look for satisfaction; in that event, the identification with the father has become the precursor of an object tie with the father. The same holds good, with the necessary substitutions, of the baby daughter as well.

It is easy to state in a formula the distinction between an identification with the father and the choice of the father as an object. In the first case, one's father is what one would like to *be;* and, in the second, he is what one would like to *have.* The distinction, that is, depends upon whether the tie attaches to the subject or to the object of the ego. The former is there-fore already possible before any sexual object-choice has been made. It is much more difficult to give a clear metapsychological representation of the distinction. We can only see that identification endeavours to mould a person's own ego after the fashion of the one that has been taken as a *model.*

Let us disentangle identification as it occurs in the structure of a neurotic symptom from its rather complicated connections. Supposing that a little girl (and we will keep to her for the present) develops the same painful symptom as her mother—for instance, the same tormenting cough. Now this may come about in various ways. The identification may come from the Oedipus complex; in that case it signifies a hostile desire on the girl's part to take her mother's place, and the symptom expresses her object love towards her father, and brings about a realization, under the influence of a sense of guilt, of her desire to take her mother's place: "You wanted to be your mother, and now you *are*—anyhow as far as the pain goes." This is the complete mechanism of the structure of an hysterical symptom. Or, on the other hand, the symptom may be the same as that of the person who is loved—(so, for instance, Dora in the "Fragment of an Analysis of a Case of Hysteria,"[2] imitated her father's cough); in that case we can only describe the state of things by saying that *identification has appeared instead of object-choice, and that object-choice has regressed to identification.* We have heard that identification is the earliest and original form of emotional tie; it often happens that under the conditions in which symptoms are constructed, that is, where there is repression and where the mechanisms of the unconscious are dominant, object-choice is turned back into identification—the ego, that is, assumes the characteristics of the object. It is noticeable that in these identifications the ego sometimes copies the person who is not loved and sometimes the one who is loved. It must also strike us that in both cases the identification is a partial and extremely limited one and only borrows a single trait from the person who is its object.

There is a third particularly frequent and important case of symptom formation, in which the identification leaves any object relation to the person who is being copied entirely out of account. Supposing, for instance, that one of the girls in a boarding school has had a letter from someone with whom she is secretly in

---

[1] See *Three Contributions to the Theory of Sex,* and Abraham's *"Untersuchungen über die früheste prägenitale Entwicklungsstufe der Libido," International Zeitschrift für Psychoanalyse,* 1916, Vol. IV; also included in his *Klinische Beiträge zur Psychoanalyse* (Internationale Psychoanalytische Bibliothek, No. 10, 1921).

[2] *Collected Papers,* III.

love which arouses her jealousy, and that she reacts to it with a fit of hysterics; then some of her friends who know about it will contract the fit, as we say, by means of mental infection. The mechanism is that of identification based upon the possibility or desire of putting oneself in the same situation. The other girls would like to have a secret love affair too, and under the influence of a sense of guilt they also accept the pain involved in it. It would be wrong to suppose that they take on the symptom out of sympathy. On the contrary, the sympathy only arises out of the identification, and this is proved by the fact that infection or imitation of this kind takes place in circumstances where even less pre-existing sympathy is to be assumed than usually exists between friends in a girls' school. One ego has perceived a significant analogy with another upon one point—in our example upon a similar readiness for emotion; an identification is thereupon constructed on this point, and, under the influence of the pathogenic situation, is displaced on to the symptom which the one ego has produced. The identification by means of the symptom has thus become the mark of a point of coincidence between the two egos which has to be kept repressed.

What we have learned from these three sources may be summarized as follows. First, identification is the original form of emotional tie with an object; secondly, in a regressive way it becomes a substitute for a libidinal object tie, as it were, by means of the introjection of the object into the ego; and thirdly, it may arise with every new perception of a common quality shared with some other person who is not an object of the sexual instinct. The more important this common quality is, the more successful may this partial identification become, and it may thus represent the beginning of a new tie.

We already begin to divine that the mutual tie between members of a group is in the nature of an identification of this kind, based upon an important emotional common quality; and we may suspect that this common quality lies in the nature of the tie with the leader. Another suspicion may tell us that we are far from having exhausted the problem of identification, and that we are faced by the process which psychology calls empathy (*Einfühlung*) and which plays the largest part in our understanding of what is inherently foreign to our ego in other people. But we shall here limit ourselves to the immediate emotional effects of identification, and shall leave on one side its significance for our intellectual life.

Psycho-analytic research, which has already occasionally attacked the more difficult problems of the psychoses, has also been able to exhibit identification to us in some other cases which are not immediately comprehensible. I shall treat two of these cases in detail as material for our further consideration.

The genesis of male homosexuality in a large class of cases is as follows. A young man has been unusually long and intensely fixated upon his mother in the sense of the Oedipus complex. But at last, after the end of his puberty, the time comes for exchanging his mother for some other sexual object. Things take a sudden turn: the young man does not abandon his mother, but identifies himself with her; he transforms himself into her, and now looks about for objects which can replace his ego for him, and on which he can bestow such love and care as he has experienced from his mother. This is a frequent process, which can be confirmed as often as one likes, and which is naturally quite independent of any hypothesis that may be made as to the organic driving force and the motives of the sudden transformation. A striking thing about this identification is its ample scale; it remoulds the ego in one of its important features—in its sexual character—upon the model of what has hitherto been the object. In this process the object itself is renounced—whether entirely or in the sense of being preserved only in the unconscious is a question outside the present discussion. Identification with an object that is renounced or lost as a substitute for it, introjection of this object into the ego, is indeed no longer a novelty to us. A process of the kind may sometimes be directly observed in small children. A short time ago an observation of this sort was published in the *Internationale Zeitschrift für Psychoanalyse.* A child who was unhappy over the loss of a kitten declared straight out that now he himself was the kitten, and accordingly crawled about on all fours, would not eat at table, etc.[1]

Another such instance of introjection of the object has been provided by the analysis of melancholia, an affection which counts among the most remarkable of its exciting causes the real or emotional loss of a loved object. A leading characteristic of these cases is a cruel self-depreciation of the ego combined with relentless

[1] Marcuszewicz: *"Beitrag zum autistischen Denken bei Kindern," Internationale Zeitschrift für Psychoanalyse,* (1920), Vol. VI.

self-criticism and bitter self-reproaches. Analyses have shown that this disparagement and these reproaches apply at bottom to the object and represent the ego's revenge upon it. The shadow of the object has fallen upon the ego, as I have said elsewhere.[1] The introjection of the object is here unmistakably clear.

But these melancholias also show us something else, which may be of importance for our later discussions. They show us the ego divided, fallen into two pieces, one of which rages against the second. This second piece is the one which has been altered by introjection and which contains the lost object. But the piece which behaves so cruelly is not unknown to us either. It comprises the conscience, a critical faculty (*Instanz*) within the ego, which even in normal times takes up a critical attitude towards the ego, though never so relentlessly and so unjustifiably. On previous occasions we have been driven to the hypothesis[2] that some such faculty develops in our ego which may cut itself off from the rest of the ego and come into conflict with it. We have called it the *ego ideal*, and by way of functions we have ascribed to it self-observation, the moral conscience, the censorship of dreams, and the chief influence in repression. We have said that it is the heir to the original narcissism in which the childish ego found its self-sufficiency; it gradually gathers up from the influences of the environment the demands which that environment makes upon the ego and which the ego cannot always rise to; so that a man, when he cannot be satisfied with his ego itself, may nevertheless be able to find satisfaction in the ego ideal which has been differentiated out of the ego. In delusions of observation, as we have further shown, the disintegration of this faculty has become patent, and has thus revealed its origin in the influence of superior powers, and above all of parents.[3] But we have not forgotten to add that the amount of distance between this ego ideal and the real ego is very variable from one individual to another, and that with many people this differentiation within the ego does not go further than with children.

But before we can employ this material for understanding the libidinal organization of groups, we must take into account some other examples of the mutual relations between the object and the ego.[4]

[1] "Mourning and Melancholia," *Collected Papers*, IV.—Tr.
[2] "On Narcissism: an Introduction" [p. 399 above], "Mourning and Melancholia."
[3] "On Narcissism: an Introduction,"
[4] We are very well aware that we have not ex-

VIII. BEING IN LOVE AND HYPNOSIS

EVEN in its caprices the usage of language remains true to some kind of reality. Thus it gives the name of *love* to a great many kinds of emotional relationship which we too group together theoretically as love; but then again it feels a doubt whether this love is real, true, actual love, and so hints at a whole scale of possibilities within range of the phenomena of love. We shall have no difficulty in making the same discovery empirically.

In one class of cases, being in love is nothing more than object-cathexis on the part of the sexual instincts with a view to directly sexual satisfaction, a cathexis which expires, moreover, when this aim has been reached; this is what is called *common, sensual love*. But, as we know, the libidinal situation rarely remains so simple. It was possible to calculate with certainty upon the revival of the need which had just expired; and this must no doubt have been the first motive for directing a lasting cathexis upon the sexual object and for *loving* it in the passionless intervals as well.

To this must be added another factor derived from the astonishing course of development which is pursued by the erotic life of man. In his first phase, which has usually come to an end by the time he is five years old, a child has found the first object for his love in one or other of his parents, and all of his sexual instincts with their demand for satisfaction have been united upon this object. The repression which then sets in compels him to renounce the greater number of these infantile sexual aims, and leaves behind a profound modification in his relation to his parents. The child still remains tied to his parents, but by instincts which

hausted the nature of identification with these examples taken from pathology, and that we have consequently left part of the riddle of group formations untouched. A far more fundamental and comprehensive psychological analysis would have to intervene at this point. A path leads from identification by way of imitation to empathy, that is, to the comprehension of the mechanism by means of which we are enabled to take up any attitude at all towards another mental life. Moreover there is still much to be explained in the manifestations of existing identifications. These result among other things in a person limiting his aggressiveness towards those with whom he has identified himself, and in his sparing them and giving them help. The study of such identifications, like those, for instance, which lie at the root of clan feeling, led Robertson Smith to the surprising result that they rest upon the recognition of a common substance (*Kinship and Marriage*, 1885), and may even therefore be brought about by a meal eaten in common. This feature makes it possible to connect this kind of identification with the early history of the human family which I constructed in *Totem and Taboo*.

must be described as being "inhibited in their aim [*zielgehemmte*]." The emotions which he feels henceforward towards these objects of his love are characterized as *tender*. It is well known that the earlier *sensual* tendencies remain more or less strongly preserved in the unconscious, so that in a certain sense the whole of the original current continues to exist.[1]

At puberty, as we know, there set in new and very strong tendencies with directly sexual aims. In unfavourable cases they remain separate, in the form of a sensual current, from the tender emotional trends which persist. We are then faced by a picture the two aspects of which certain movements in literature take such delight in idealizing. A man of this kind will show a sentimental enthusiasm for women whom he deeply respects but who do not excite him to sexual activities, and he will only be potent with other women whom he does not love but thinks little of or even despises.[2] More often, however, the adolescent succeeds in bringing about a certain degree of synthesis between the unsensual, heavenly love and the sensual, earthly love, and his relation to his sexual object is characterized by the interaction of uninhibited instincts and of instincts inhibited in their aim. The depth to which anyone is in love, as contrasted with his purely sensual desire, may be measured by the size of the share taken by the inhibited instincts of tenderness.

In connection with this question of being in love, we have always been struck with the phenomenon of sexual over-estimation—the fact that the loved object enjoys a certain amount of freedom from criticism, and that all its characteristics are valued more highly than those of people who are not loved, or than its own were at a time when it itself was not loved. If the sensual tendencies are somewhat more effectively repressed or set aside, the illusion is produced that the object has come to be sensually loved on account of its spiritual merits, whereas on the contrary these merits may really only have been lent to it by its sensual charm.

The tendency which falsifies judgment in this respect is that of *idealization*. But this makes it easier for us to find our way about. We see that the object is being treated in the same way as our own ego, so that when we are in love a considerable amount of narcissistic li-

bido overflows on to the object. It is even obvious, in many forms of love choice, that the object serves as a substitute for some unattained ego ideal of our own. We love it on account of the perfections which we have striven to reach for our own ego, and which we should now like to procure in this roundabout way as a means of satisfying our narcissism.

If the sexual over-estimation and the being in love increase even further, then the interpretation of the picture becomes still more unmistakable. The tendencies whose trend is towards directly sexual satisfaction may now be pushed back entirely, as regularly happens, for instance, with the young man's sentimental passion; the ego becomes more and more unassuming and modest, and the object more and more sublime and precious, until at last it gets possession of the entire self-love of the ego, whose self-sacrifice thus follows as a natural consequence. The object has, so to speak, consumed the ego. Traits of humility, of the limitation of narcissism, and of self-injury occur in every case of being in love; in the extreme case they are only intensified, and, as a result of the withdrawal of the sensual claims, they remain in solitary supremacy.

This happens especially easily with love that is unhappy and cannot be satisfied; for, in spite of everything, each sexual satisfaction always involves a reduction in sexual over-estimation. Contemporaneously with this *devotion* of the ego to the object, which is no longer to be distinguished from a sublimated devotion to an abstract idea, the functions allotted to the ego ideal entirely cease to operate. The criticism exercised by that faculty is silent; everything that the object does and asks for is right and blameless. Conscience has no application to anything that is done for the sake of the object; in the blindness of love, remorselessness is carried to the pitch of crime. The whole situation can be completely summarized in a formula: *The object has taken the place of the ego ideal.*

It is now easy to define the distinction between identification and such extreme developments of being in love as may be described as *fascination* or *infatuation*. In the former case, the ego has enriched itself with the properties of the object, it has *introjected* the object into itself, as Ferenczi expresses it. In the second case, it is impoverished, it has surrendered itself to the object, it has substituted the object for its most important constituent. Closer consideration soon makes it plain, however, that this

---

[1] See *Three Contributions to the Theory of Sex, op. cit.*

[2] "The Most Prevalent Form of Degradation in Erotic Life," *Collected Papers*, IV.

kind of account creates an illusion of contra-distinctions that have no real existence. Economically there is no question of impoverishment or enrichment; it is even possible to describe an extreme case of being in love as a state in which the ego has introjected the object into itself. Another distinction is perhaps better calculated to meet the essence of the matter. In the case of identification, the object has been lost or given up; it is then set up again inside the ego, and the ego makes a partial alteration in itself after the model of the lost object. In the other case, the object is retained, and there is a hyper-cathexis of it by the ego and at the ego's expense. But here again a difficulty presents itself. Is it quite certain that identification presupposes that object-cathexis has been given up? Can there be no identification with the object retained? And before we embark upon a discussion of this delicate question, the perception may already be beginning to dawn on us that yet another alternative embraces the real essence of the matter, namely, *whether the object is put in the place of the ego or of the ego ideal*.

From being in love to hypnosis is evidently only a short step. The respects in which the two agree are obvious. There is the same humble subjection, the same compliance, the same absence of criticism, towards the hypnotist just as towards the loved object. There is the same absorption of one's own initiative; no one can doubt that the hypnotist has stepped into the place of the ego ideal. It is only that everything is even clearer and more intense in hypnosis, so that it would be more to the point to explain being in love by means of hypnosis than the other way round. The hypnotist is the sole object, and no attention is paid to any but him. The fact that the ego experiences in a dream-like way whatever he may request or assert reminds us that we omitted to mention among the functions of the ego ideal the business of testing the reality of things.[1] No wonder that the ego takes a perception for real if its reality is vouched for by the mental faculty which ordinarily discharges the duty of testing the reality of things. The complete absence of tendencies which are uninhibited in their sexual aims contributes further towards the extreme purity of the phenomena. The hypnotic relation is the devotion of someone in love to an unlimited degree but with sexual satisfaction excluded; whereas in the case of being in love

[1] See "Metapsychological Supplement to the Theory of Dreams," *Collected Papers*, IV.

this kind of satisfaction is only temporarily kept back, and remains in the background as a possible aim at some later time.

But, on the other hand, we may also say that the hypnotic relation is (if the expression is permissible) a group formation with two members. Hypnosis is not a good object for comparison with a group formation, because it is truer to say that it is identical with it. Out of the complicated fabric of the group it isolates one element for us—the behaviour of the individual to the leader. Hypnosis is distinguished from a group formation by this limitation of number, just as it is distinguished from being in love by the absence of directly sexual tendencies. In this respect it occupies a middle position between the two.

It is interesting to see that it is precisely those sexual tendencies that are inhibited in their aims which achieve such lasting ties between men. But this can easily be understood from the fact that they are not capable of complete satisfaction, while sexual tendencies which are uninhibited in their aims suffer an extraordinary reduction through the discharge of energy every time the sexual aim is attained. It is the fate of sensual love to become extinguished when it is satisfied; for it to be able to last, it must from the first be mixed with purely tender components—with such, that is, as are inhibited in their aims—or it must itself undergo a transformation of this kind.

Hypnosis would solve the riddle of the libidinal constitution of groups for us straight away, if it were not that it itself exhibits some features which are not met by the rational explanation we have hitherto given of it as a state of being in love, with the directly sexual tendencies excluded. There is still a great deal in it which we must recognize as unexplained and mystical. It contains an additional element of paralysis derived from the relation between someone with superior power and someone who is without power and helpless—which may afford a transition to the hypnosis of terror which occurs in animals. The manner in which it is produced and its relationship to sleep are not clear; and the puzzling way in which some people are subject to it, while others resist it completely, points to some factor still unknown which is realized in it and which perhaps alone makes possible the purity of the attitudes of the libido which it exhibits. It is noticeable that, even when there is complete suggestive compliance in other respects, the moral conscience of the person hypnotized may show resistance. But this may be due to the fact that in hypnosis as it is usually practised some knowledge may be retained that what is happening is only a game, an untrue reproduction of another situation of far more importance to life.

But after the preceding discussions we are quite in a position to give the formula for the libidinal constitution of groups: or at least of such groups as we have hitherto considered, namely, those that have a leader and have not been able by means of too much *organization* to acquire secondarily the characteristics of an individual. *A primary group of this kind is a number of individuals who have substituted one and the same object for their ego ideal and have consequently identified themselves with one another in their ego.* This condition admits of graphic representation:

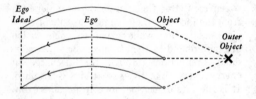

IX. THE HERD INSTINCT

WE cannot for long enjoy the illusion that we have solved the riddle of the group with this formula. It is impossible to escape the immediate and disturbing recollection that all we have really done has been to shift the question on to the riddle of hypnosis, about which so many points have yet to be cleared up. And now another objection shows us our further path.

It might be said that the intense emotional ties which we observe in groups are quite sufficient to explain one of their characteristics—the lack of independence and initiative in their members, the similarity in the reactions of all of them, their reduction, so to speak, to the level of group individuals. But if we look at it as a whole, a group shows us more than this. Some of its features—the weakness of intellectual ability, the lack of emotional restraint, the incapacity for moderation and delay, the inclination to exceed every limit in the expression of emotion and to work it off completely in the form of action—these and similar features, which we find so impressively described in Le Bon, show an unmistakable picture of a regression of mental activity to an earlier stage such as we are not surprised to find among savages

or children. A regression of this sort is in particular an essential characteristic of common groups, while, as we have heard, in organized and artificial groups it can to a large extent be checked.

We thus have an impression of a state in which an individual's separate emotion and personal intellectual act are too weak to come to anything by themselves and are absolutely obliged to wait till they are reinforced through being repeated in a similar way in the other members of the group. We are reminded of how many of these phenomena of dependence are part of the normal constitution of human society, of how little originality and personal courage are to be found in it, of how much every individual is ruled by those attitudes of the group mind which exhibit themselves in such forms as racial characteristics, class prejudices, public opinion, etc. The influence of suggestion becomes a greater riddle for us when we admit that it is not exercised only by the leader, but by every individual upon every other individual; and we must reproach ourselves with having unfairly emphasized the relation to the leader and with having kept the other factor of mutual suggestion too much in the background.

After this encouragement to modesty, we shall be inclined to listen to another voice, which promises us an explanation based upon simpler grounds. Such a one is to be found in Trotter's thoughtful book upon the herd instinct, concerning which my only regret is that it does not entirely escape the antipathies that were set loose by the recent Great War.[1]

Trotter derives the mental phenomena that are described as occurring in groups from a herd instinct (gregariousness), which is innate in human beings just as in other species of animals. Biologically this gregariousness is an analogy to multicellularity and as it were a continuation of it. From the standpoint of the libido theory, it is a further manifestation of the inclination, which proceeds from the libido, and which is felt by all living beings of the same kind, to combine in more and more comprehensive units.[2] The individual feels *incomplete* if he is alone. The dread shown by small children would seem already to be an expression of this herd instinct. Opposition to the herd is as good as separation from it, and is therefore anxiously avoided. But the herd turns

[1] W. Trotter: *Instincts of the Herd in Peace and War* Fisher Unwin, 1916.
[2] See *Beyond the Pleasure Principle*, p. 639 above.

away from anything that is new or unusual. The herd instinct would appear to be something primary, something *which cannot be split up*.

Trotter gives as the list of instincts which he considers as primary those of self-preservation, of nutrition, of sex, and of the herd. The last often comes into opposition with the others. The feelings of guilt and of duty are the peculiar possessions of a gregarious animal. Trotter also derives from the herd instinct the repressive forces which psycho-analysis has shown to exist in the ego, and from the same sources accordingly the resistances which the physician comes up against in psycho-analytic treatment. Speech owes its importance to its aptitude for mutual understanding in the herd, and upon it the identification of the individuals with one another largely rests.

While Le Bon is principally concerned with typical transient group formations, and McDougall with stable associations, Trotter has chosen as the centre of his interest the most generalized form of assemblage in which man, that $\zeta\tilde{\omega}o\nu$ $\pi o\lambda\iota\tau\iota\kappa\acute{o}\nu$,[1] passed his life, and he gives us its psychological basis. But Trotter is under no necessity of tracing back the herd instinct, for he characterizes it as primary and not further reducible. Boris Sidis's attempt, to which he refers, at tracing the herd instinct back to suggestibility is fortunately superfluous as far as he is concerned; it is an explanation of a familiar and unsatisfactory type, and the converse proposition—that suggestibility is a derivative of the herd instinct—would seem to me to throw far more light on the subject.

But Trotter's exposition, with even more justice than the other's, is open to the objection that it takes too little account of the leader's part in a group, while we incline rather to the opposite judgment, that it is impossible to grasp the nature of a group if the leader is disregarded. The herd instinct leaves no room at all for the leader; he is merely thrown in along with the herd, almost by chance; it follows, too, that no path leads from this instinct to the need for a God; the herd is without a herdsman. But besides this Trotter's exposition can be undermined psychologically; that is to say, it can be made at all events probable that the herd instinct is not irreducible, that it is not primary in the same sense as the instinct of self-preservation and the sexual instinct.

It is naturally no easy matter to trace the ontogenesis of the herd instinct. The dread which is shown by small children when they are left alone, and which Trotter claims as being already a manifestation of the instinct, nevertheless suggests more readily another interpretation. The dread relates to the child's mother, and later to other familiar persons, and it is the expression of an unfulfilled desire, which the child does not yet know how to deal with in any way except by turning it into dread.[2] Nor is the child's dread when it is alone pacified by the sight of any haphazard *member of the herd*, but on the contrary it is only brought into existence by the approach of a *stranger* of this sort. Then for a long time nothing in the nature of herd instinct or group feeling is to be observed in children. Something like it grows up first of all, in a nursery containing many children, out of the children's relation to their parents, and it does so as a reaction to the initial envy with which the elder child receives the younger one. The elder child would certainly like to put its successor jealously aside, to keep it away from the parents, and to rob it of all its privileges; but in face of the fact that this child (like all that come later) is loved by the parents in just the same way, and in consequence of the impossibility of maintaining its hostile attitude without damaging itself, it is forced into identifying itself with the other children. So there grows up in the troop of children a communal or group feeling, which is then further developed at school. The first demand made by this reaction-formation is for justice, for equal treatment for all. We all know how loudly and implacably this claim is put forward at school. If one cannot be the favourite oneself, at all events nobody else shall be the favourite. This transformation—the replacing of jealousy by a group feeling in the nursery and classroom—might be considered improbable, if the same process could not later on be observed again in other circumstances. We have only to think of the troop of women and girls, all of them in love in an enthusiastically sentimental way, who crowd round a singer or pianist after his performance. It would certainly be easy for each of them to be jealous of the rest; but, in face of their numbers and the consequent impossibility of their reaching the aim of their love, they renounce it, and, instead of pulling out one another's hair, they act as a united group, do homage to the hero of the occasion with their common actions, and would probably

---

[1] Political animal.—ED.

[2] See the remarks upon Dread in *General Introduction to Psycho-Analysis*, Lecture XXV, p. 607 above.

be glad to have a share of his flowing locks. Originally rivals, they have succeeded in identifying themselves with one another by means of a similar love for the same object. When, as is usual, a situation in the field of the instincts is capable of various outcomes, we need not be surprised if the actual outcome is one which involves the possibility of a certain amount of satisfaction, while another, even though in itself more obvious, is passed over because the circumstances of life prevent its attaining this aim.

What appears later on in society in the shape of *Gemeingeist, esprit de corps,* group spirit, etc., does not belie its derivation from what was originally envy. No one must want to put himself forward, every one must be the same and have the same. Social justice means that we deny ourselves many things so that others may have to do without them as well, or, what is the same thing, may not be able to ask for them. This demand for equality is the root of social conscience and the sense of duty. It reveals itself unexpectedly in the syphilitic's dread of infecting other people, which psychoanalysis has taught us to understand. The dread exhibited by these poor wretches corresponds to their violent struggles against the unconscious wish to spread their infection on to other people; for why should they alone be infected and cut off from so much? Why not other people as well? And the same germ is to be found in the pretty anecdote of the judgment of Solomon. If one woman's child is dead, the other shall not have a live one either. The bereaved woman is recognized by this wish.

Thus social feeling is based upon the reversal of what was first a hostile feeling into a positively-toned tie of the nature of an identification. So far as we have hitherto been able to follow the course of events, this reversal appears to be effected under the influence of a common tender tie with a person outside the group. We do not ourselves regard our analysis of identification as exhaustive, but it is enough for our present purpose that we should revert to this one feature—its demand that equalization shall be consistently carried through. We have already heard in the discussion of the two artificial groups, church and army, that their preliminary condition is that all their members should be loved in the same way by one person, the leader. Do not let us forget, however, that the demand for equality in a group applies only to its members and not to the leader. All the members must be equal to one another, but they all want to be ruled by one person. Many equals, who can identify themselves with one another, and a single person superior to them all—that is the situation that we find realized in groups which are capable of subsisting. Let us venture, then, to correct Trotter's pronouncement that man is a herd animal and assert that he is rather a horde animal, an individual creature in a horde led by a chief.

X. THE GROUP AND THE PRIMAL HORDE

IN 1912 I took up a conjecture of Darwin's to the effect that the primitive form of human society was that of a horde ruled over despotically by a powerful male. I attempted to show that the fortunes of this horde have left indestructible traces upon the history of human descent; and, especially, that the development of totemism, which comprises in itself the beginnings of religion, morality, and social organization, is connected with the killing of the chief by violence and the transformation of the paternal horde into a community of brothers.[1] To be sure, this is only a hypothesis, like so many others with which archaeologists endeavour to lighten the darkness of prehistoric times—a "Just-So Story," as it was amusingly called by a not unkind critic (Kroeger); but I think it is creditable to such a hypothesis if it proves able to bring coherence and understanding into more and more new regions.

Human groups exhibit once again the familiar picture of an individual of superior strength among a troop of similar companions, a picture which is also contained in our idea of the primal horde. The psychology of such a group, as we know it from the descriptions to which we have so often referred—the dwindling of the conscious individual personality, the focussing of thoughts and feelings into a common direction, the predominance of the emotions and of the unconscious mental life, the tendency to the immediate carrying out of intentions as they emerge—all this corresponds to a state of regression to a primitive mental activity, of just such a sort as we should be inclined to ascribe to the primal horde.[2]

[1] *Totem and Taboo.*

[2] What we have just described in our general characterization of mankind must apply especially to the primal horde. The will of the individual was too weak; he did not venture upon action. No impulses whatever came into play except collective ones; there was only a common will, there were no single ones. An idea did not dare to turn itself into a volition unless it felt itself reinforced by a perception of its general diffusion. This weakness of the idea is to be explained by the strength of the emotional tie which

Thus the group appears to us as a revival of the primal horde. Just as primitive man virtually survives in every individual, so the primal horde may arise once more out of any random crowd; in so far as men are habitually under the sway of group formation, we recognize in it the survival of the primal horde. We must conclude that the psychology of the group is the oldest human psychology; what we have isolated as individual psychology, by neglecting all traces of the group, has only since come into prominence out of the old group psychology, by a gradual process which may still, perhaps, be described as incomplete. We shall later venture upon an attempt at specifying the point of departure of this development.

Further reflection will show us in what respect this statement requires correction. Individual psychology must, on the contrary, be just as old as group psychology, for from the first there were two kinds of psychologies, that of the individual members of the group and that of the father, chief, or leader. The members of the group were subject to ties just as we see them today, but the father of the primal horde was free. His intellectual acts were strong and independent even in isolation, and his will needed no reinforcement from others. Consistency leads us to assume that his ego had few libidinal ties; he loved no one but himself, or other people only in so far as they served his needs. To objects his ego gave away no more than was barely necessary.

He, at the very beginning of the history of mankind, was the *Superman* whom Nietzsche only expected from the future. Even today the members of a group stand in need of the illusion that they are equally and justly loved by their leader; but the leader himself need love no one else, he may be of a masterly nature, absolutely narcissistic, but self-confident and independent. We know that love puts a check upon narcissism, and it would be possible to show how, by operating in this way, it became a factor of civilization.

The primal father of the horde was not yet immortal, as he later became by deification. If he died, he had to be replaced; his place was probably taken by a youngest son, who had up to then been a member of the group like any other. There must therefore be a possibility of transforming group psychology into individual psychology; a condition must be discovered under which such a transformation is easily accomplished, just as it is possible for bees in case of necessity to turn a larva into a queen instead of into a worker. One can imagine only one possibility: the primal father had prevented his sons from satisfying their directly sexual tendencies; he forced them into abstinence and consequently into the emotional ties with him and with one another which could arise out of those of their tendencies that were inhibited in their sexual aim. He forced them, so to speak, into group psychology. His sexual jealousy and intolerance became, in the last resort, the causes of group psychology.[1]

Whoever became his successor was also given the possibility of sexual satisfaction, and was by that means offered a way out of the conditions of group psychology. The fixation of the libido to woman and the possibility of satisfaction without any need for delay or accumulation made an end of the importance of those of his sexual tendencies that were inhibited in their aim, and allowed his narcissism always to rise to its full height. We shall return in a postscript to this connection between love and character formation.

We may further emphasize, as being specially instructive, the relation that holds between the contrivance by means of which an artificial group is held together and the constitution of the primal horde. We have seen that with an army and a church this contrivance is the illusion that the leader loves all of the individuals equally and justly. But this is simply an idealistic remodelling of the state of affairs in the primal horde, where all of the sons knew that they were equally persecuted by the primal father, and feared him equally. This same recasting upon which all social duties are built up is already presupposed by the next form of human society, the totemistic clan. The indestructible strength of the family as a natural group formation rests upon the fact that this necessary presupposition of the father's equal love can have a real application in the family.

But we expect even more of this derivation

---

is shared by all members of the horde; but the similarity in the circumstances of their life and the absence of any private property assist in determining the uniformity of their individual mental acts. As we may observe with children and soldiers, common activity is not excluded even in the excremental functions. The one great exception is provided by the sexual act, in which a third person is at best superfluous and in the extreme case is condemned to a state of painful expectancy. As to the reaction of the sexual need (for genital gratification) towards gregariousness, see below.

[1] It may perhaps also be assumed that the sons, when they were driven out and separated from their father, advanced from identification with one another to homosexual object love, and in this way won freedom to kill their father.

of the group from the primal horde. It ought also to help us to understand what is still incomprehensible and mysterious in group formations—all that lies hidden behind the enigmatic words *hypnosis* and *suggestion*. And I think it can succeed in this too. Let us recall that hypnosis has something positively uncanny about it; but the characteristic of uncanniness suggests something old and familiar that has undergone repression.[1] Let us consider how hypnosis is induced. The hypnotist asserts that he is in possession of a mysterious power which robs the subject of his own will, or, which is the same thing, the subject believes it of him. This mysterious power (which is even now often described popularly as animal magnetism) must be the same that is looked upon by primitive people as the source of taboo, the same that emanates from kings and chieftains and makes it dangerous to approach them *(mana)*. The hypnotist, then, is supposed to be in possession of this power; and how does he manifest it? By telling the subject to look him in the eyes; his most typical method of hypnotizing is by his look. But it is precisely the sight of the chieftain that is dangerous and unbearable for primitive people, just as later that of the Godhead is for mortals. Even Moses had to act as an intermediary between his people and Jehovah, since the people could not support the sight of God; and when he returned from the presence of God his face shone—some of the *mana* had been transferred on to him, just as happens with the intermediary among primitive people.[2]

It is true that hypnosis can also be evoked in other ways, for instance by fixing the eyes upon a bright object or listening to a monotonous sound. This is misleading and has given occasion to inadequate physiological theories. As a matter of fact, these procedures merely serve to divert conscious attention and to hold it riveted. The situation is the same as if the hypnotist had said to the subject: "Now concern yourself exclusively with my person; the rest of the world is quite uninteresting." It would of course be technically inexpedient for a hypnotist to make such a speech; it would tear the subject away from his unconscious attitude and stimulate him to conscious opposition. The hypnotist avoids directing the subject's conscious thoughts towards his own intentions, and makes the person upon whom he is experimenting sink into an activity in which

the world is bound to seem uninteresting to him; but at the same time the subject is in reality unconsciously concentrating his whole attention upon the hypnotist, and is getting into an attitude of *rapport*, of transference on to him. Thus the indirect methods of hypnotizing, like many of the technical procedures used in making jokes, have the effect of checking certain distributions of mental energy which would interfere with the course of events in the unconscious, and they lead eventually to the same result as the direct methods of influence by means of staring or stroking.[3]

Ferenczi has made the true discovery that when a hypnotist gives the command to sleep, which is often done at the beginning of hypnosis, he is putting himself in the place of the subject's parents. He thinks that two sorts of hypnosis are to be distinguished: one coaxing and soothing, which he considers is modelled upon the mother, and another threatening, which is derived from the father.[4] Now the command to sleep in hypnosis means nothing more nor less than an order to withdraw all interest from the world and to concentrate it upon the person of the hypnotist. And it is so understood by the subject; for in this withdrawal of interest from the outer world lies the psychological characteristic of sleep, and the kinship between sleep and the state of hypnosis is based upon it.

By the measures that he takes, then, the hypnotist awakens in the subject a portion of his archaic inheritance which had also made him compliant towards his parents and which had experienced an individual re-animation in his relation to his father; what is thus awakened is the idea of a paramount and dangerous personality, towards whom only a passive-

---

[1] "The Uncanny," *Collected Papers*, IV.
[2] See *Totem and Taboo* and the sources there quoted.

[3] This situation, in which the subject's attitude is unconsciously directed towards the hypnotist, while he is consciously occupied with monotonous and uninteresting perceptions, finds a parallel among the events of psycho-analytic treatment, which deserves to be mentioned here. At least once in the course of every analysis, a moment comes when the patient obstinately maintains that just now positively nothing whatever occurs to his mind. His free associations come to a stop and the usual incentives for putting them in motion fail in their effect. As a result of pressure, the patient is at last induced to admit that he is thinking of the view from the consulting-room window, of the wall-paper that he sees before him, or of the gas-lamp hanging from the ceiling. Then one knows at once that he has gone off into the transference and that he is engaged upon what are still unconscious thoughts relating to the physician; and one sees the stoppage in the patient's associations disappear, as soon as he has been given this explanation.

[4] Ferenczi: "*Introjektion und Übertragung*," *Jahrbuch der Psychoanalyse*, 1909, Vol. I (*Contributions to Psycho-Analysis*. Boston, Badger, 1916, chapter II).

masochistic attitude is possible, to whom one's will has to be surrendered—while to be alone with him, "to look him in the face," appears a hazardous enterprise. It is only in some such way as this that we can picture the relation of the individual member of the primal horde to the primal father. As we know from other reactions, individuals have preserved a variable degree of personal aptitude for reviving old situations of this kind. Some knowledge that, in spite of everything, hypnosis is only a game, a deceptive renewal of these old impressions, may however remain behind and take care that there is a resistance against any too serious consequences of the suspension of the will in hypnosis.

The uncanny and coercive characteristics of group formations, which are shown in their suggestion phenomena, may therefore with justice be traced back to the fact of their origin from the primal horde. The leader of the group is still the dreaded primal father; the group still wishes to be governed by unrestricted force; it has an extreme passion for authority; in Le Bon's phrase, it has a thirst for obedience. The primal father is the group ideal, which governs the ego in the place of the ego ideal. Hypnosis has a good claim to being described as a group of two; there remains as a definition for suggestion: a conviction which is not based upon perception and reasoning but upon an erotic tie.[1]

XI. A DIFFERENTIATING GRADE IN THE EGO

IF we survey the life of an individual man of today, bearing in mind the mutually complementary accounts of group psychology given by the authorities, we may lose the courage, in face of the complications that are revealed, to attempt a comprehensive exposition. Each individual is a component part of numerous groups, he is bound by ties of identification in many directions, and he has built up his ego ideal upon the most various models. Each individual, therefore, has a share in numerous group minds—those of his race, of his class, of his creed, of his nationality, etc.—and he can

also raise himself above them to the extent of having a scrap of independence and originality. Such stable and lasting group formations, with their uniform and constant effects, are less striking to an observer than the rapidly formed and transient groups from which Le Bon has made his brilliant psychological character sketch of the group mind. And it is just in these noisy ephemeral groups, which are as it were superimposed upon the others, that we are met by the prodigy of the complete, even though only temporary, disappearance of exactly what we have recognized as individual acquirements.

We have interpreted this prodigy as meaning that the individual gives up his ego ideal and substitutes for it the group ideal as embodied in the leader. And we must add, by way of correction, that the prodigy is not equally great in every case. In many individuals the separation between the ego and the ego ideal is not very far advanced; the two still coincide readily; the ego has often preserved its earlier self-complacency. The selection of the leader is very much facilitated by this circumstance. He need only possess the typical qualities of the individuals concerned in a particularly clearly marked and pure form, and need only give an impression of greater force and of more freedom of libido; and in that case the need for a strong chief will often meet him half-way and invest him with a predominance to which he would otherwise perhaps have had no claim. The other members of the group, whose ego ideal would not, apart from this, have become embodied in his person without some correction, are then carried away with the rest by *suggestion,* that is to say, by means of identification.

We are aware that what we have been able to contribute towards the explanation of the libidinal structure of groups leads back to the distinction between the ego and the ego ideal and to the double kind of tie which this makes possible—identification, and substitution of the object for the ego ideal. The assumption of this kind of differentiating grade *(Stufe)* in the ego as a first step in an analysis of the ego must gradually establish its justification in the most various regions of psychology. In my paper, "Narcissism: an Introduction," I have put together all the pathological material that could at the moment be used in support of this separation. But it may be expected that when we penetrate deeper into the psychology of the psychoses its significance will be discovered to be far greater. Let us reflect that the ego now

---

[1] It seems to me worth emphasizing the fact that the discussions in this section have induced us to give up Bernheim's conception of hypnosis and go back to the *naïf* earlier one. According to Bernheim, all hypnotic phenomena are to be traced to the factor of suggestion, which is not itself capable of further explanation. We have come to the conclusion that suggestion is a partial manifestation of the state of hypnosis, and that hypnosis is solidly founded upon a predisposition which has survived in the unconscious from the early history of the human family.

appears in the relation of an object to the ego ideal which has been developed out of it, and that all the interplay between an outer object and the ego as a whole, with which our study of the neuroses has made us acquainted, may possibly be repeated upon this new scene of action inside the ego.

In this place I shall only follow up one of the consequences which seem possible from this point of view, thus resuming the discussion of a problem which I was obliged to leave unsolved elsewhere.[1] Each of the mental differentiations that we have become acquainted with represents a fresh aggravation of the difficulties of mental functioning, increases its instability, and may become the starting-point for its breakdown, that is, for the onset of a disease. Thus, by being born we have made the step from an absolutely self-sufficient narcissism to the perception of a changing outer world and to the beginnings of the discovery of objects. And with this is associated the fact that we cannot endure the new state of things for long, that we periodically revert from it, in our sleep, to our former condition of absence of stimulation and avoidance of objects. It is true, however, that in this we are following a hint from the outer world, which, by means of the periodical change of day and night, temporarily withdraws the greater part of the stimuli that affect us. The second example, which is pathologically more important, is not subject to any such qualification. In the course of our development we have effected a separation of our mental existence into a coherent ego and into an unconscious and repressed portion which is left outside it; and we know that the stability of this new acquisition is exposed to constant shocks. In dreams and in neuroses what is thus excluded knocks for admission at the gates, guarded though they are by resistances; and in our waking health we make use of special artifices for allowing what is repressed to circumvent the resistances and for receiving it temporarily into our ego to the increase of our pleasure. Wit and humour, and to some extent the comic in general, may be regarded in this light. Everyone acquainted with the psychology of the neuroses will think of similar examples of less importance; but I hasten on to the application I have in view.

It is quite conceivable that the separation of the ego ideal from the ego cannot be borne for long either, and has to be temporarily undone. In all renunciations and limitations imposed

upon the ego, a periodical infringement of the prohibition is the rule; this indeed is shown by the institution of festivals, which in origin are nothing more nor less than excesses provided by law and which owe their cheerful character to the release which they bring.[2] The Saturnalia of the Romans and our modern carnival agree in this essential feature with the festivals of primitive people, which usually end in debaucheries of every kind and the transgression of what are at other times the most sacred commandments. But the ego ideal comprises the sum of all the limitations in which the ego has to acquiesce, and for that reason the abrogation of the ideal would necessarily be a magnificent festival for the ego, which might then once again feel satisfied with itself.[3]

There is always a feeling of triumph when something in the ego coincides with the ego ideal. And the sense of guilt (as well as the sense of inferiority) can also be understood as an expression of tension between the ego and the ego ideal.

It is well known that there are people the general colour of whose mood oscillates periodically from an excessive depression through some kind of intermediate state to an exalted sense of well-being. These oscillations appear in very different degrees of amplitude, from what is just noticeable to those extreme instances which, in the shape of melancholia and mania, make the most painful or disturbing inroads upon the life of the person concerned. In typical cases of this cyclical depression, outer exciting causes do not seem to play any decisive part; as regards inner motives, nothing more (or nothing different) is to be found in these patients than in all others. It has consequently become the custom to consider these cases as not being psychogenic. We shall refer later on to those other exactly similar cases of cyclical depression which can nevertheless easily be traced back to mental traumata.

Thus the foundation of these spontaneous oscillations of mood is unknown; we are without insight into the mechanism of the displacement of a melancholia by a mania. So we are free to suppose that these patients are people in whom our conjecture might find an actual application—their ego ideal might be tempo-

---

[1] "Mourning and Melancholia."

[2] *Totem and Taboo.*

[3] Trotter traces repression back to the herd instinct. It is a translation of this into another form of expression rather than a contradiction when I say in my "On Narcissism: an Introduction" that, on the part of the ego, the construction of an ideal is the condition of repression [see p. 408 above].

rarily resolved into their ego after having previously ruled it with especial strictness.

Let us keep to what is clear: On the basis of our analysis of the ego it cannot be doubted that in cases of mania the ego and the ego ideal have fused together, so that the person, in a mood of triumph and self-satisfaction, disturbed by no self-criticism, can enjoy the abolition of his inhibitions, his feelings of consideration for others, and his self-reproaches. It is not so obvious, but nevertheless very probable, that the misery of the melancholiac is the expression of a sharp conflict between the two faculties of his ego, a conflict in which the ideal, in an excess of sensitiveness, relentlessly exhibits its condemnation of the ego in delusions of inferiority and in self-depreciation. The only question is whether we are to look for the causes of these altered relations between the ego and the ego ideal in the periodic rebellions, which we have postulated above, against the new institution, or whether we are to make other circumstances responsible for them.

A change into mania is not an indispensable feature of the symptomatology of melancholic depression. There are simple melancholias, some in single and some in recurring attacks, which never show this development. On the other hand, there are melancholias in which the exciting cause clearly plays an aetiological part. They are those which occur after the loss of a loved object, whether by death or as a result of circumstances which have necessitated the withdrawal of the libido from the object. A psychogenic melancholia of this sort can end in mania, and this cycle can be repeated several times, just as easily as in a case which appears to be spontaneous. Thus the state of things is somewhat obscure, especially as only a few forms and cases of melancholia have been submitted to psycho-analytical investigation.[1] So far we only understand those cases in which the object is given up because it has shown itself unworthy of love. It is then set up again inside the ego, by means of identification, and severely condemned by the ego ideal. The reproaches and attacks directed towards the object come to light in the shape of melancholic self-reproaches.[2]

[1] Cf. Abraham: "Ansätze zur psychoanalytischen Erforschung und Behandlung des manisch-depressiven Irreseins," 1912, in Klinische Beiträge zur Psychoanalyse, 1921.

[2] To speak more accurately, they conceal themselves behind the reproaches directed towards the person's own ego, and lend them the fixity, tenacity, and imperativeness which characterize the self-reproaches of a melancholiac.

A melancholia of this kind may also end in a change to mania; so that the possibility of this happening represents a feature which is independent of the other characteristics in the symptomatology.

Nevertheless I see no difficulty in assigning to the factor of the periodical rebellion of the ego against the ego ideal a share in both kinds of melancholia, the psychogenic as well as the spontaneous. In the spontaneous kind, it may be supposed that the ego ideal is inclined to display a peculiar strictness, which then results automatically in its temporary suspension. In the psychogenic kind, the ego would be incited to rebellion by ill-treatment on the part of its ideal—an ill-treatment which it encounters when there has been identification with a rejected object.

XII. POSTSCRIPT

IN the course of the enquiry which has just been brought to a provisional end we came across a number of side-paths which we avoided pursuing in the first instance but in which there was much that offered us promises of insight. We propose now to take up a few of the points that have been left on one side in this way.

A. The distinction between identification of the ego with an object and replacement of the ego ideal by an object finds an interesting illustration in the two great artificial groups which we began by studying, the army and the Christian church.

It is obvious that a soldier takes his superior, that is, really, the leader of the army, as his ideal, while he identifies himself with his equals, and derives from this community of their egos the obligations for giving mutual help and for sharing possessions which comradeship implies. But he becomes ridiculous if he tries to identify himself with the general. The soldier in Wallensteins Lager laughs at the sergeant for this very reason:

> Wie er räuspert und wie er spuckt.
> Das habt ihr ihm glücklich abgeguckt![3]

It is otherwise in the Catholic Church. Every Christian loves Christ as his ideal and feels himself united with all other Christians by the tie of identification. But the Church requires more of him. He has also to identify himself with Christ and love all other Christians as Christ loved them. At both points, therefore, the Church requires that the position of the libido which is given by a group formation should be supplemented. Identification has to

[3] How he clears his throat and how he spits, that you have cleverly copied from him.—TR.

be added where object-choice has taken place, and object love where there is identification. This addition evidently goes beyond the constitution of the group. One can be a good Christian and yet be far from the idea of putting oneself in Christ's place and of having like him an all-embracing love for mankind. One need not think oneself capable, weak mortal that one is, of the Saviour's largeness of soul and strength of love. But this further development in the distribution of libido in the group is probably the factor upon which Christianity bases its claim to have reached a higher ethical level.

B. We have said that it would be possible to specify the point in the mental development of man at which the advance from group to individual psychology was also achieved by the individual members of the group.[1]

For this purpose we must return for a moment to the scientific myth of the father of the primal horde. He was later on exalted into the creator of the world, and with justice, for he had produced all the sons who composed the first group. He was the ideal of each one of them, at once feared and honoured, a fact which led later to the idea of taboo. These many individuals banded themselves together, killed him and cut him in pieces. None of the group of victors could take his place, or, if one of them did, the battles began afresh, until they understood that they must all renounce their father's heritage. They then formed the totemistic community of brothers, all with equal rights and united by the totem prohibitions which were to preserve and to expiate the memory of the murder. But the dissatisfaction with what had been achieved still remained, and it became the source of new developments. The persons who were united in this group of brothers gradually came towards a revival of the old state of things at a new level. Man became once more the chief of a family, and broke down the prerogatives of the gynaecocracy which had become established during the fatherless period. As a compensation for this, he may at that time have acknowledged the mother deities, whose priests were castrated for the mother's protection, after the example that had been given by the father of the primal horde. And yet the new family was only a shadow of the old one; there were numbers of fathers and each one was limited by the rights of the others.

[1] What follows at this point was written under the influence of an exchange of ideas with Otto Rank.

It was then, perhaps, that some individual, in the exigency of his longing, may have been moved to free himself from the group and take over the father's part. He who did this was the first epic poet; and the advance was achieved in his imagination. This poet disguised the truth with lies in accordance with his longing. He invented the heroic myth. The hero was a man who by himself had slain the father—the father who still appeared in the myth as a totemistic monster. Just as the father had been the boy's first ideal, so in the hero who aspires to the father's place the poet now created the first ego ideal. The transition to the hero was probably afforded by the youngest son, the mother's favourite, whom she had protected from paternal jealousy, and who, in the era of the primal horde, had been the father's successor. In the lying poetic fancies of prehistoric times the woman, who had been the prize of battle and the allurement to murder, was probably turned into the seducer and instigator to the crime.

The hero claims to have acted alone in accomplishing the deed, which certainly only the horde as a whole would have ventured upon. But, as Rank has observed, fairy tales have preserved clear traces of the facts which were disavowed. For we often find in them that the hero who has to carry out some difficult task (usually a youngest son, and not infrequently one who has represented himself to the father surrogate as being stupid, that is to say, harmless)—we often find, then, that this hero can carry out his task only by the help of a crowd of small animals, such as bees or ants. These would be the brothers in the primal horde, just as in the same way in dream symbolism insects or vermin signify brothers and sisters (contemptuously, considered as babies). Moreover, every one of the tasks in myths and fairy tales is easily recognizable as a substitute for the heroic deed.

The myth, then, is the step by which the individual emerges from group psychology. The first myth was certainly the psychological, the hero myth, the explanatory nature myth must have followed much later. The poet who had taken this step and had in this way set himself free from the group in his imagination, is nevertheless able (as Rank has further observed) to find his way back to it in reality. For he goes and relates to the group his hero's deeds which he has invented. At bottom this hero is no one but himself. Thus he lowers himself to the level of reality, and raises his hearers to the level of imagination. But his hearers understand the poet, and, in virtue of their having the same relation of longing towards the primal father, they can identify themselves with the hero.[1]

The lie of the heroic myth culminates in the deification of the hero. Perhaps the deified hero may have been earlier than the Father God and may have been a precursor to the return of the primal father as a deity. The series of gods, then, would run chronologically: Mother Goddess—Hero—Father God. But it is only with the elevation of the never forgotten primal father that the deity acquires the features that we still recognize in him today.[2]

C. A great deal has been said in this paper about directly sexual instincts and those that are inhibited in their aims, and it may be hoped that this distinction will not meet with too much resistance. But a detailed discussion of the question will not be out of place, even if it only repeats what has to a great extent already been said before.

The development of the libido in children has made us acquainted with the first but also the best example of sexual instincts which are inhibited in their aims. All the feelings which a child has towards its parents and those who look after it pass by an easy transition into the wishes which give expression to the child's sexual tendencies. The child claims from these objects of its love all the signs of affection which it knows of; it wants to kiss them, touch them, and look at them; it is curious to see their genitals, and to be with them when they perform their intimate excremental functions; it promises to marry its mother or nurse —whatever it may understand by that; it proposes to itself to bear its father a child, etc. Direct observation, as well as the subsequent analytic investigation of the residue of childhood, leave no doubt as to the complete fusion of tender and jealous feelings and of sexual intentions, and show us in what a fundamental way the child makes the person it loves into the object of all its incompletely centred sexual tendencies.[3]

This first configuration of the child's love,

which in typical cases is co-ordinated with the Oedipus complex, succumbs, as we know, from the beginning of the period of latency onwards, to a wave of repression. Such of it as is left over shows itself as a purely tender emotional tie, which relates to the same people, but is no longer to be described as *sexual*. Psycho-analysis, which illuminates the depths of mental life, has no difficulty in showing that the sexual ties of the earliest years of childhood also persist, though repressed and unconscious. It gives us courage to assert that wherever we come across a tender feeling it is the successor to a completely sensual object tie with the person in question or rather with that person's prototype (or *imago*). It cannot indeed disclose to us without a special investigation whether in a given case this former complete sexual current still exists under repression, or whether it has already been exhausted. To put it still more precisely: it is quite certain that it is still there as a form and possibility, and can always be charged with cathectic energy and put into activity again by means of regression; the only question is (and it cannot always be answered) what degree of cathexis and operative force it still has at the present moment. Equal care must be taken in this connection to avoid two sources of error—the Scylla of under-estimating the importance of the repressed unconscious, and the Charybdis of judging the normal entirely by the standards of the pathological.

A psychology which will not or cannot penetrate the depths of what is repressed regards tender emotional ties as being invariably the expression of tendencies which have no sexual aim, even though they are derived from tendencies which have such an aim.[4]

We are justified in saying that they have been diverted from these sexual aims, even though there is some difficulty in giving a representation of such a diversion of aim which will conform to the requirements of metapsychology. Moreover, those instincts which are inhibited in their aims always preserve some few of their original sexual aims; even an affectionate devotee, even a friend or an admirer, desires the physical proximity and the sight of the person who is now loved only in the "Pauline" sense. If we choose, we may recognize in this diversion of aim a beginning of the *sublimation* of the sexual instincts, or,

---

[1] Cf. Hanns Sachs: *"Gemeinsame Tagträume,"* a summary made by the lecturer himself of a paper read at the Sixth Psycho-analytical Congress, held at the Hague in 1920. *Internationale Zeitschrift für Psychoanalyse*, 1920, Vol. VI. ("Day-Dreams in Common," *International Journal of Psycho-Analysis*, 1920, Vol. I.)

[2] In this brief exposition, I have made no attempt to bring forward any of the material existing in legends, myths, fairy tales, the history of manners, etc., in support of the construction.

[3] See *Three Contributions to the Theory of Sex*.

[4] Hostile feelings, which are a little more complicated in their construction, offer no exception to this rule.

on the other hand, we may fix the limits of sublimation at some more distant point. Those sexual instincts which are inhibited in their aims have a great functional advantage over those which are uninhibited. Since they are not capable of really complete satisfaction, they are especially adapted to create permanent ties; while those instincts which are directly sexual incur a loss of energy each time they are satisfied, and must wait to be renewed by a fresh accumulation of sexual libido, so that meanwhile the object may have been changed. The inhibited instincts are capable of any degree of admixture with the uninhibited; they can be transformed back into them, just as they arose out of them. It is well known how easily erotic wishes develop out of emotional relations of a friendly character, based upon appreciation and admiration, (compare Molière's *"Embrassez-moi pour l'amour du grec"*[1]), between a master and a pupil, between a performer and a delighted listener, and especially in the case of women. In fact, the growth of emotional ties of this kind, with their purposeless beginnings, provides a much frequented pathway to sexual object-choice. Pfister, in his *Frömmigkeit des Grafen von Zinzendorf*,[2] has given an extremely clear and certainly not an isolated example of how easily even an intense religious tie can revert to ardent sexual excitement. On the other hand it is also very usual for directly sexual tendencies, short-lived in themselves, to be transformed into a lasting and purely tender tie; and the consolidation of a passionate love marriage rests to a large extent upon this process.

We shall naturally not be surprised to hear that the sexual tendencies that are inhibited in their aims arise out of the directly sexual ones when inner or outer obstacles make the sexual aims unattainable. The repression during the period of latency is an inner obstacle of this kind—or rather one which has become inner. We have assumed that the father of the primal horde, owing to his sexual intolerance, compelled all his sons to be abstinent, and thus forced them into ties that were inhibited in their aims, while he reserved for himself freedom of sexual enjoyment and in this way remained without ties. All the ties upon which a group depends are of the character of instincts that are inhibited in their aims. But here we have approached the discussion of a new subject, which deals with the relation between directly sexual instincts and the formation of groups.

D. The last two remarks will have prepared us for finding that directly sexual tendencies are unfavourable to the formation of groups. In the history of the development of the family there have also, it is true, been group relations of sexual love (group marriages); but the more important sexual love became for the ego, and the more it developed the characteristics of being in love, the more urgently it required to be limited to two people—*una cum uno*—as is prescribed by the nature of the genital aim. Polygamous inclinations had to be content to find satisfaction in a succession of changing objects.

Two people coming together for the purpose of sexual satisfaction, in so far as they seek for solitude, are making a demonstration against the herd instinct, the group feeling. The more they are in love, the more completely they suffice for each other. The rejection of the group's influence is manifested in the shape of a sense of shame. The extremely violent feelings of jealousy are summoned up in order to protect the sexual object-choice from being encroached upon by a group tie. It is only when the tender, that is, the personal, factor of a love relation gives place entirely to the sensual one, that it is possible for two people to have sexual intercourse in the presence of others or for there to be simultaneous sexual acts in a group as occurs at an orgy. But at that point a regression has taken place to an early stage in sexual relations, at which being in love as yet played no part, and all sexual objects were judged to be of equal value, somewhat in the sense of Bernard Shaw's malicious aphorism to the effect that being in love means greatly exaggerating the difference between one woman and another.

There are abundant indications that being in love only made its appearance later on in the sexual relations between men and women; so that the opposition between sexual love and group ties is also a late development. Now it may seem as though this assumption were incompatible with our myth of the primal family. For it was after all by their love for their mothers and sisters that the troop of brothers was, as we have supposed, driven to parricide; and it is difficult to imagine this love as being anything but unbroken and primitive—that is, as an intimate union of the tender and the sensual. But further consideration resolves this objection into a confirmation. One of the re-

---

[1] Embrace me for the love of the Greek.—ED.

[2] *Schriften zur angewandten Seelenkunde.* No. 8, Vienna, Deuticke 1910.—TR.

actions to the parricide was, after all, the institution of totemistic exogamy, the prohibition
of any sexual relation with those women of the
family who had been tenderly loved since
childhood. In this way a wedge was driven in
between a man's tender and sensual feelings,
one still firmly fixed in his erotic life today.[1]
As a result of this exogamy, the sensual needs
of men had to be satisfied with strange and
unloved women.

In the great artificial groups, the church and
the army, there is no room for woman as a
sexual object. The love relation between men
and women remains outside these organizations. Even where groups are formed which are
composed of both men and women, the distinction between the sexes plays no part. There is
scarcely any sense in asking whether the libido
which keeps groups together is of a homosexual or of a heterosexual nature, for it is not
differentiated according to the sexes, and particularly shows a complete disregard for the
aims of the genital organization of the libido.

Even in a person who has in other respects
become absorbed in a group, the directly sexual tendencies preserve a little of his individual
activity. If they become too strong, they dis-
integrate every group formation. The Catholic
Church had the best of motives for recommending its followers to remain unmarried and for
imposing celibacy upon its priests; but falling
in love has often driven even priests to leave
the church. In the same way, love for women
breaks through the group ties of race, of national separation, and of the social class system,
and it thus produces important effects as a
factor in civilization. It seems certain that
homosexual love is far more compatible with
group ties, even when it takes the shape of uninhibited sexual tendencies—a remarkable fact,
the explanation of which might carry us far.

The psycho-analytic investigation of the psychoneuroses has taught us that their symptoms
are to be traced back to directly sexual tendencies which are repressed but still remain
active. We can complete this formula by adding to it: or, to tendencies inhibited in their
aims, whose inhibition has not been entirely
successful or has made room for a return to
the repressed sexual aim. It is in accordance
with this that a neurosis should make its victim
asocial and should remove him from the usual
group formations. It may be said that a neurosis has the same disintegrating effect upon a

group as being in love. On the other hand, it
appears that where a powerful impetus has been
given to group formation neuroses may diminish and, at all events, temporarily disappear. Justifiable attempts have also been made
to turn this antagonism between neuroses and
group formation to therapeutic account. Even
those who do not regret the disappearance of
religious illusions from the civilized world of
today will admit that so long as they were in
force they offered those who were bound by
them the most powerful protection against the
danger of neurosis. Nor is it hard to discern in
all the ties with mystico-religious or philosophi-
co-religious sects and communities the manifestation of distorted cures of all kinds of neuroses. All of this is bound up with the contrast
between directly sexual tendencies and those
which are inhibited in their aims.

If he is left to himself, a neurotic is obliged
to replace by his own symptom formations the
great group formations from which he is excluded. He creates his own world of imagination for himself, his own religion, his own
system of delusions, and thus recapitulates the
institutions of humanity in a distorted way
which is clear evidence of the dominating part
played by the directly sexual tendencies.[2]

E. In conclusion, we will add a comparative
estimate, from the standpoint of the libido
theory, of the states with which we have been
concerned, of being in love, of hypnosis, of
group formation, and of the neurosis.

Being in love is based upon the simultaneous presence of directly sexual tendencies and
of sexual tendencies that are inhibited in their
aims, so that the object draws a part of the
narcissistic ego-libido to itself. It is a condition
in which there is only room for the ego and
the object.

Hypnosis resembles being in love in being
limited to these two persons, but it is based
entirely upon sexual tendencies that are inhibited in their aims and substitutes the object
for the ego ideal.

The group multiplies this process; it agrees
with hypnosis in the nature of the instincts
which hold it together, and in the replacement
of the ego ideal by the object; but to this it
adds identification with other individuals, which
was perhaps originally made possible by their
having the same relation to the object.

Both states, hypnosis and group formation,
are an inherited deposit from the phylogenesis

[1] See "The Most Prevalent Form of Degradation in
Erotic Life."

[2] See *Totem and Taboo*, towards the end of Part II,
"Totem and the Ambivalence of Emotions."

of the human libido—hypnosis in the form of a predisposition, and the group, besides this, as a direct survival. The replacement of the directly sexual tendencies by those that are inhibited in their aims promotes in both states a separation between the ego and the ego ideal, a separation with which a beginning has already been made in the state of being in love.

The neurosis stands outside this series. It also is based upon a peculiarity in the development of the human libido—the twice repeated start made by the directly sexual function, with an intervening period of latency.[1] To this extent it resembles hypnosis and group formation in having the character of a regression, which is absent from being in love. It makes its appear-

[1] Compare *Three Contributions to the Theory of Sex.*

ance wherever the advance from directly sexual instincts to those that are inhibited in their aims has not been completely successful; and it represents a *conflict* between those instincts which have been received into the ego after having passed through this development and those portions of the same instincts which, like other instinctive desires that have been completely repressed, strive, from the repressed unconscious, to attain direct satisfaction. The neurosis is extraordinarily rich in content, for it embraces all possible relations between the ego and the object—both those in which the object is retained and others in which it is abandoned or erected inside the ego itself—and also the conflicting relations between the ego and its ego-ideal.

The Ego and the Id

Introduction

In my essay, *Beyond the Pleasure Principle*, published in 1920, I began the discussion of a train of thought, my personal attitude towards which, as I mentioned there, might be described as a sort of benevolent curiosity; in the following pages this train of thought is developed further. I have taken up those ideas and brought them into connection with various facts observed in psycho-analysis and have endeavoured to draw fresh conclusions from the combination; in the present work, however, no further contributions are levied from biology, and it consequently stands in a closer relation to psycho-analysis than does *Beyond the Pleasure Principle*. The thoughts contained in it are synthetic rather than speculative in character and their aim appears to be an ambitious one. I am aware, however, that they do not go beyond the baldest outlines and I am perfectly content to recognize their limitations in this respect.

At the same time, the train of thought touches upon things not hitherto dealt with in the work psycho-analysis has done, and it cannot avoid concerning itself with a number of theories propounded by non-analysts or by former analysts on their retreat from analysis. I am, as a rule, always ready to acknowledge my debts to other workers, but on this occasion I feel myself under no such obligation. If there are certain things to which hitherto psycho-analysis has not given adequate consideration, that is not because it has overlooked their effects or wished to deny their significance, but because it pursues a particular path which had not yet carried it so far. And, moreover, now that these things have at last been overtaken, they appear to psycho-analysis in a different shape from that in which they appear to the other people.

I. Consciousness and the Unconscious

In this preliminary chapter there is nothing new to be said and it will not be possible to avoid repeating what has often been said before.

The division of mental life into what is conscious and what is unconscious is the fundamental premise on which psycho-analysis is based; and this division alone makes it possible for it to understand pathological mental processes, which are as common as they are important, and to co-ordinate them scientifically. Stated once more in a different way: psycho-analysis cannot accept the view that consciousness is the essence of mental life, but is obliged to regard consciousness as one property of mental life, which may co-exist along with its other properties or may be absent.

If I were to allow myself to suppose that every one interested in psychology would read this book, I should still be prepared to find that some of them would stop short even at this point and go no further; for here we have the first shibboleth of psycho-analysis. To most people who have had a philosophical education, the idea of anything mental which is not also conscious is so inconceivable that it seems to them absurd and refutable simply by logic. I believe this is only because they have never studied the mental phenomena of hypnosis and dreams, which—quite apart from pathological manifestations—necessitate this conclusion. Thus, their psychology of consciousness is incapable of solving the problems of dreams and hypnosis.

The term *conscious* is, to start with, a purely descriptive one, resting on a perception of the most direct and certain character. Experience shows, next, that a mental element (for instance, an idea) is not as a rule permanently conscious. On the contrary, a state of consciousness is characteristically very transitory; an idea that is conscious now is no longer so a moment later, although it can become so again under certain conditions that are easily brought about. What the idea was in the interval we do not know. We can say that it was *latent*, and by this we mean that it was *capable of becoming conscious* at any time. Or, if we say that it was *unconscious*, we are giving an equally correct description. Thus, *unconscious* in this sense of the word coincides with *latent and capable of becoming conscious*. The philosophers would no doubt object: "No, the term *unconscious* does not apply here; so long as the idea was in a state of latency, it was not a mental element at all." To contradict them at this point would lead to nothing more profitable than a war of words.

But we have arrived at the term or concept of *unconscious* along another path, by taking account of certain experiences in which mental dynamics play a part. We have found, that is, we have been obliged to assume, that very powerful mental processes or ideas exist—here a quantitative or *economic* factor comes into question for the first time—which can produce in the mind all the effects that ordinary ideas do (including effects that can in their turn become conscious as ideas) without themselves becoming conscious. It is unnecessary here to repeat in detail what has been explained so often before. We need only say that this is the point at which psycho-analytic theory steps in—with the assertion that such ideas cannot become conscious because a certain force is opposed to them, that, otherwise, they could become conscious, and that then one would see how little they differ from other elements which are admittedly mental. The fact that in the technique of psycho-analysis a means has been found by which the opposing force can be removed and the ideas in question made conscious renders this theory irrefutable. The state in which the ideas existed before being made conscious is called by us *repression*, and we assert that the force which instituted the repression and maintains it is perceived as *resistance* during the work of analysis.

We obtain our concept of the unconscious, therefore, from the theory of repression. The repressed serves us as a prototype of the unconscious. We see, however, that we have two kinds of unconscious—that which is latent but capable of becoming conscious, and that which is repressed and not capable of becoming conscious in the ordinary way. This piece of insight into mental dynamics cannot fail to affect terminology and description. That which is latent, and only unconscious in the descriptive and not in the dynamic sense, we call *preconscious;* the term *unconscious* we reserve for the dynamically unconscious repressed, so that we now have three terms, conscious (*Cs*), preconscious (*Pcs*), and unconscious (*Ucs*), which are no longer purely descriptive in sense. The *Pcs* is presumably a great deal closer to the *Cs* than is the *Ucs*, and since we have called the *Ucs* mental we shall with even less hesitation call the latent *Pcs* mental. But why do we not choose, instead of this, to remain in agreement with the philosophers and, in a consistent way, to distinguish the *Pcs* as well as the *Ucs* from what is conscious in the mind? The philosophers would propose that both the *Pcs* and

the *Ucs* should be described as two varieties or levels of *psychoid*, and harmony would be established. But endless difficulties in exposition would follow; and the one important fact, that the two kinds of *psychoid*, as thus defined, coincide in almost every other respect with what is admittedly mental, would be forced into the background in the interests of a prejudice dating from a period in which they, or the most important part of them, were still unknown.

We can now set to work comfortably with our three terms, *Cs, Pcs,* and *Ucs,* so long as we do not forget that, while in the descriptive sense there are two kinds of unconscious, in the dynamic sense there is only one. For purposes of exposition this distinction can in many cases be ignored, but in others it is, of course, indispensable. At the same time, we have become more or less accustomed to these two meanings of the term *unconscious* and have managed pretty well with them. As far as I can see, it is impossible to avoid this ambiguity; the distinction between conscious and unconscious is in the last resort a question of a perception which must be either affirmed or denied, and the act of perception itself tells us nothing of the reason why a thing is or is not perceived. No one has a right to complain because the actual phenomenon expresses the underlying dynamic factors ambiguously.[1]

[1] This may be compared with my "Note on the Unconscious in Psycho-Analysis" (1912), *Collected Papers*, IV. A new turn taken by criticisms of the unconscious deserves consideration at this point. Many investigators, who do not refuse to recognize the facts of psycho-analysis but who are unwilling to accept the unconscious, find a way out of the difficulty in the fact, which no one contests, that in consciousness (regarded as a phenomenon) it is possible to distinguish a great variety of gradations in intensity or clarity. Just as there are ideas which are very vividly, keenly, and definitely conscious, so we also entertain others which are but faintly, hardly even noticeably conscious; those that are most faintly conscious are, it is argued, the ones to which psycho-analysis wishes to apply the unsuitable name *unconscious*. These, however (the argument proceeds), are also conscious or *in consciousness* just as much as the others, and can be made fully and intensely conscious if sufficient attention is paid to them.

In so far as it is possible to influence by arguments the decision of a question of this kind which is based either on a convention or on emotional factors, we may make the following comments. The reference to gradations of clarity in consciousness is in no way conclusive and has no more evidential value than such analogous statements as: "There are so many gradations in illumination—from the brightest and most dazzling light to the dimmest glimmer—that we may conclude that there is no such thing as darkness at all", or, "There are varying degrees of vitality, consequently there is no such thing as death." Such statements may, in a certain sense, have a meaning, but for practical purposes they are worthless. This will be seen if one proceeds to draw certain conclusions

In the further course of psycho-analytic work, however, even these distinctions have proved to be inadequate and, for practical purposes, insufficient. This has become clear in more ways than one; but the decisive instance is as follows. We have formulated the idea that in every individual there is a coherent organization of mental processes, which we call his *ego*. This ego includes consciousness, and it controls the approaches to motility, i.e., to the discharge of excitations into the external world; it is this institution in the mind which regulates all its own constituent processes, and which goes to sleep at night, though even then it continues to exercise a censorship upon dreams. From this ego proceed the repressions, too, by means of which an attempt is made to cut off certain trends in the mind not merely from consciousness but also from their other forms of manifestation and activity. In analysis these trends which have been shut out stand in opposition to the ego and the analysis is faced with the task of removing the resistances which the ego displays against concerning itself with the repressed. Now we find that, during analysis, when we put certain tasks before the patient, he gets into difficulties; his associations fail when they ought to be getting near the repressed. We then tell him that he is dominated by a resistance; but he is quite unaware of the fact, and, even if he guesses from his feelings of discomfort that a resistance is now at work in him, he does not know what it is nor how to describe it. Since, however, there can be no question but that this resistance emanates from his ego and belongs to it, we find ourselves in an unforeseen situation. We

have come upon something in the ego itself which is also unconscious, which behaves exactly like the repressed, that is, which produces powerful effects without itself being conscious and which requires special work before it can be made conscious. From the point of view of analytic practice, the consequence of this piece of observation is that we land in endless confusion and difficulty if we cling to our former way of expressing ourselves and try, for instance, to derive neuroses from a conflict between the conscious and the unconscious. We shall have to substitute for this antithesis another, taken from our understanding of the structural conditions of the mind, namely, the antithesis between the organized ego and what is repressed and dissociated from it.[1]

For our conception of the unconscious, however, the consequences of our new observation are even more important. Dynamic considerations caused us to make our first correction; our knowledge of the structure of the mind leads to the second. We recognize that the *Ucs* does not coincide with what is repressed; it is still true that all that is repressed is *Ucs*, but not that the whole *Ucs* is repressed. A part of the ego, too—and Heaven knows how important a part—may be *Ucs,* undoubtedly is *Ucs.* And this *Ucs* belonging to the ego is not latent like the *Pcs;* for if it were, it could not be activated without becoming *Cs,* and the process of making it conscious would not encounter such great difficulties. When we find ourselves thus confronted by the necessity of postulating a third *Ucs* which is not repressed, we must admit that the property of being unconscious begins to lose significance for us. It becomes a quality which can have many implications, so that we are unable to make it, as we should have hoped to do, the basis of far-reaching and inevitable conclusions. Nevertheless, we must beware of ignoring this property, for, in the last resort, the quality of being conscious or not is the single ray of light that penetrates the obscurity of depth-psychology.

II. THE EGO AND THE ID

PATHOLOGICAL research has centred our interest too exclusively on the repressed. We wish to know more about the ego, now that we know that it, too, can be *unconscious* in the proper sense of the word. Hitherto, the only guide we have had while pursuing our investigations has been the distinguishing mark of

---

from them, such as, "it is not necessary, therefore, to strike a light," or, "therefore, all living things are immortal." Further, to include *what is unnoticeable* under the concept of *what is conscious* is simply to play havoc with the one and only piece of direct and certain knowledge that we have about the mind. And after all, a consciousness of which one knows nothing seems to me a good deal more absurd than an unconscious mind. Finally, this attempt to equate what is unnoticed with what is unconscious is obviously made without taking into account the dynamic conditions involved, which were the decisive factors in formulating the psycho-analytic view. For it ignores two facts: first, that it is exceedingly difficult and requires very great effort to concentrate enough attention on something unnoticed of this kind; and secondly, that when this has been achieved, the thought which was previously unnoticed is not recognized by consciousness, but often seems utterly alien and opposed to it and is promptly disavowed by it. Escaping from the unconscious in this way and taking refuge in what is scarcely noticed or unnoticed is, therefore, after all, only an expression of the preconceived belief which regards the identity of mental and conscious as settled once and for all.

[1] See *Beyond the Pleasure Principle,* p. 639 above.

being conscious or unconscious; and in the end we have come to see that this quality itself is ambiguous.

Now, all our knowledge is invariably bound up with consciousness. Even knowledge of the *Ucs* can only be obtained by making it conscious. But stop, how is that possible? What does it mean when we say "making it conscious"? How can that come about?

We already know the point from which we have to start in this connection. We have said that consciousness is the *superficies* of the mental apparatus; that is, we have allocated it as a function to the system which is situated nearest to the external world. Incidentally, on this occasion the topographical terminology does not merely serve to describe the nature of the function, but actually corresponds to the anatomical facts.[1] Our investigations too must take this surface organ of perception as a starting-point.

All perceptions which are received from without (sense-perceptions) and from within— what we call sensations and feelings—are *Cs* from the start. But how is it with those internal processes which we may—vaguely and inexactly—sum up under the name of *thought-processes*? They represent displacements of mental energy which are effected somewhere in the interior of the apparatus as this energy proceeds on its way towards action. Do they advance towards the superficies, which then allows of the development of consciousness? Or does consciousness make its way towards them? This is clearly one of the difficulties that spring up when one begins to take the spatial or *topographical* conception of mental life seriously. Both these possibilities are equally unimaginable; there must be a third contingency to meet the case.

I have already, in another place,[2] suggested that the real difference between a *Ucs* and a *Pcs* idea (thought) consists in this: that the former is worked out upon some sort of material which remains unrecognized, whereas the latter (the *Pcs*) has in addition been brought into connection with verbal images. This is the first attempt to find a distinguishing mark for the two systems, the *Pcs* and the *Ucs*, other than their relation to consciousness. It would seem, then, that the question, "How does a thing become conscious?" could be put more advantageously thus: "How does a thing become preconscious?" And the answer would be: "By

coming into connection with the verbal images that correspond to it."

These verbal images are memory-residues; they were at one time perceptions, and like all memory-residues they can become conscious again. Before we concern ourselves further with their nature, it dawns upon us like a new discovery that only something which has once been a *Cs* perception can become conscious, and that anything arising from within (apart from feelings) that seeks to become conscious must try to transform itself into external perceptions: this can be done by way of memory-traces.

We conceive of memory-residues as contained in systems which are directly adjacent to the system *Pcpt-Cs*, so that the cathexes pertaining to the memory-residues can readily extend outward on to the elements of the latter system. We are immediately reminded of hallucinations here, and of the fact that the most vivid memory is always distinguishable both from a hallucination and from an external perception; but it will also occur to us that when a memory is revived the cathexis in the memory-system will remain in force, whereas a hallucination which is not distinguishable from a perception can arise when the cathexis does not merely extend over from the memory-trace to the *Pcpt*-element, but passes over to it entirely.

Verbal residues are derived primarily from auditory perceptions, so that the system *Pcs* has, as it were, a special sensory source. The visual components of verbal images are secondary, acquired through reading, and may, to begin with, be left on one side; so may the sensory-motor images of words, which, except with deaf-mutes, play an auxiliary part. The essence of a word is, after all, the memory-trace of a word that has been heard.

We must not be led away, in the interests of simplification perhaps, into forgetting the importance of optical memory-residues—those of *things* (as opposed to *words*)—or to deny that it is possible for thought-processes to become conscious through a reversion to visual residues, and that in many people this seems to be a favourite method. The study of dreams and of preconscious phantasies on the lines of J. Varendonck's observations gives us an idea of the special character of this visual thinking. We learn that what becomes conscious is, as a rule, only the concrete subject-matter of the thought, and that the relations between the various elements of this subject-matter, which is what specially characterizes thought, cannot

---

[1] *Beyond the Pleasure Principle*, p. 639 above.
[2] *The Unconscious*, p. 428 above.

be given visual expression. Thinking in pictures is, therefore, only a very incomplete form of becoming conscious. In some way, too, it approximates more closely to unconscious processes than does thinking in words, and it is unquestionably older than the latter both ontogenetically and phylogenetically.

To return to our argument: if, therefore, this is the way in which something that is in itself unconscious becomes preconscious, the question how something that is repressed can be made (pre)conscious would be answered as follows. It is done by supplying through the work of the analysis *Pcs* connecting-links of the kind we have been discussing. Consciousness remains where it is, therefore; but, on the other hand, the *Ucs* does not rise up into the *Cs*.

Whereas the relation between external perceptions and the ego is quite perspicuous, that between internal perceptions and the ego requires special investigation. It gives rise once more to a doubt whether we are really justified in referring the whole of consciousness to the single superficial system *Pcpt-Cs*.

Internal perceptions yield sensations of processes arising in the most diverse and certainly also in the deepest strata of the mental apparatus. Very little is known about these sensations and feelings; the best examples we have of them are still those belonging to the pleasure-pain series. They are more fundamental, more elementary, than perceptions arising externally, and they can come into being even when consciousness is clouded. I have elsewhere expressed my views about their great economic significance and its metapsychological foundation. These sensations are multi-locular, like external perceptions; they may come from different places simultaneously and may thus have different or even opposite qualities.

Sensations of a pleasurable nature are not characterized by any inherently impelling quality, whereas "painful" ones possess this quality in a high degree. The latter impel towards change, towards discharge, and that is why we interpret "pain" as implying a heightening and pleasure a lowering of energic cathexis. Suppose we describe what becomes conscious in the shape of pleasure and "pain" as an undetermined quantitative and qualitative element in the mind; the question then is whether that element can become conscious where it actually is, or whether it must first be transmitted into the system *Pcpt*.

Clinical experience decides for the latter. It shows us that this undetermined element behaves like a repressed impulse. It can exert driving force without the ego noticing the compulsion. Not until there is resistance to the compulsion, and blocking of the discharge-reaction, does the undetermined element instantly become conscious as "pain." In the same way that tensions arising from physical need can remain unconscious, so also can physical pain—a thing intermediate between external and internal perception, which acts like an internal perception even when its source is in the external world. It remains true again, therefore, that sensations and feelings only become conscious through reaching the system *Pcpt*; if the way forward is barred, they do not come into being as sensations, although the undetermined element corresponding to them is the same as if they did. We then come to speak, in a condensed and not entirely correct manner, of *unconscious feelings*, keeping up an analogy with unconscious ideas which is not altogether justifiable. Actually the difference is that, whereas with *Ucs ideas* connecting-links must be forged before they can be brought into the *Cs*, with *feelings*, which are themselves transmitted directly, there is no necessity for this. In other words: the distinction between *Cs* and *Pcs* has no meaning where feelings are concerned; the *Pcs* here falls out of account, and feelings are either conscious or unconscious. Even when they are connected with verbal images, their becoming conscious is not due to that circumstance, but they become so directly.

The part played by verbal images now becomes perfectly clear. By their interposition, internal thought-processes are made into perceptions. It is like a demonstration of the theorem that all knowledge has its origin in external perception. It may sometimes happen that a hyper-cathexis of the process of thinking takes place, in which case thoughts are *perceived* in the literal sense of the word—as if they came from without—and are consequently held to be true.

After this clarifying of the relations between external and internal perception and the superficial system *Pcpt-Cs*, we can go on to work out our conception of the ego. It clearly starts out from its nucleus, the system *Pcpt*, and begins by embracing the *Pcs*, which is adjacent to the memory-residues. But the ego, as we have learnt, is also unconscious.

Now I think we shall gain a great deal by following the suggestion of a writer who, from personal motives, vainly insists that he has nothing to do with the rigours of pure science.

I am speaking of Georg Groddeck, who is never tired of pointing out that the conduct through life of what we call our ego is essentially passive, and that, as he expresses it, we are "lived" by unknown and uncontrollable forces.[1] We have all had impressions of the same kind, even though they may not have overwhelmed us to the exclusion of all others, and we need feel no hesitation in finding a place for Groddeck's discovery in the fabric of science. I propose to take it into account by calling the entity which starts out from the system *Pcpt* and begins by being *Pcs* the *ego,* and by following Groddeck in giving to the other part of the mind, into which this entity extends and which behaves as though it were *Ucs,* the name of *Id (Es).*[2]

We shall soon see whether this conception affords us any gain in understanding or any advantage for purposes of description. We shall now look upon the mind of an individual as an unknown and unconscious id, upon whose surface rests the ego, developed from its nucleus the *Pcpt*-system. If we make an effort to conceive of this pictorially, we may add that the ego does not envelop the whole of the id, but only does so to the extent to which the system *Pcpt* forms its surface, more or less as the germinal layer rests upon the ovum. The ego is not sharply separated from the id; its lower portion merges into it.

But the repressed merges into the id as well, and is simply a part of it. The repressed is only cut off sharply from the ego by the resistances

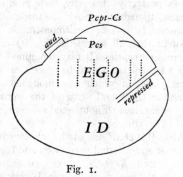

Fig. 1.

of repression; it can communicate with the ego through the id. We at once realize that almost all the delimitations we have been led into out-

[1] G. Groddeck, *Das Buch vom Es,* Vienna, 1923.
[2] Groddeck himself no doubt followed the example of Nietzsche, who habitually used this grammatical term for whatever in our nature is impersonal and, so to speak, subject to natural law.

lining by our study of pathology relate only to the superficial levels of the mental apparatus —the only ones known to us. The state of things which we have been describing can be represented diagrammatically (Fig. 1); though it must be remarked that the form chosen has no pretensions to any special applicability, but is merely intended to serve for purposes of exposition. We might add, perhaps, that the ego wears an auditory lobe—on one side only, as we learn from cerebral anatomy. It wears it crooked, as one might say.

It is easy to see that the ego is that part of the id which has been modified by the direct influence of the external world acting through the *Pcpt-Cs:* in a sense it is an extension of the surface-differentiation. Moreover, the ego has the task of bringing the influence of the external world to bear upon the id and its tendencies, and endeavours to substitute the reality-principle for the pleasure-principle which reigns supreme in the id. In the ego, perception plays the part which in the id devolves upon instinct. The ego represents what we call reason and sanity, in contrast to the id which contains the passions. All this falls into line with popular distinctions which we are all familiar with; at the same time, however, it is only to be regarded as holding good in an average or "ideal" case.

The functional importance of the ego is manifested in the fact that normally control over the approaches to motility devolves upon it. Thus in its relation to the id it is like a man on horseback, who has to hold in check the superior strength of the horse; with this difference, that the rider seeks to do so with his own strength while the ego uses borrowed forces. The illustration may be carried further. Often a rider, if he is not to be parted from his horse, is obliged to guide it where it wants to go; so in the same way the ego constantly carries into action the wishes of the id as if they were its own.

It seems that another factor, besides the influence of the system *Pcpt,* has been at work in bringing about the formation of the ego and its differentiation from the id. The body itself, and above all its surface, is a place from which both external and internal perceptions may spring. It is seen in the same way as any other object, but to the touch it yields two kinds of sensations, one of which is equivalent to an internal perception. Psychophysiology has fully discussed the manner in which the body attains its special position among other objects in the world of perception. Pain seems also to play a part in the process, and the way in which we gain new knowledge of our organs during painful illnesses is perhaps a prototype of the way by which in general we arrive at the idea of our own body.

The ego is first and foremost a body-ego; it is not merely a surface entity, but it is itself the projection of a surface.[1] If we wish to find an anatomical analogy for it we can easily identify it with the *cortical homunculus* of the anatomists, which stands on its head in the cortex, sticks its heels into the air, faces backwards and, as we know, has its speech-area on the left-hand side.

The relation of the ego to consciousness has been gone into repeatedly; yet there are still some important facts in this connection which remain to be described. Accustomed as we are to taking our social or ethical standard of values along with us wherever we go, we feel no surprise at hearing that the scene of the activities of the lower passions is in the unconscious; we expect, moreover, that the higher any mental function ranks in our scale of values, the more easily it will find access to consciousness assured to it. Here, however, psycho-analytic experience disappoints us. On the one hand, we have evidence that even subtle and intricate intellectual operations which ordinarily require strenuous concentration can equally be carried out preconsciously and without coming into consciousness. Instances of this are quite incontestable; they may occur, for instance, during sleep, as is shown when some one finds, immediately after waking, that he knows the solution of a difficult mathematical or other problem with which he had been wrestling in vain the day before.[2]

There is another phenomenon, however, which is far stranger. In our analyses we discover that there are people in whom the faculties of self-criticism and conscience—mental activities that is, that rank as exceptionally high ones—are unconscious and unconsciously produce effects of the greatest importance; the example of resistances remaining unconscious during analysis is therefore by no means unique. But this new discovery, which compels us, in spite of our critical faculties, to speak of an *unconscious sense of guilt*, bewilders us far more than the other and sets us fresh problems, especially when we gradually come to see that, in a great number of neuroses, this unconscious sense of guilt plays a decisive economic part and puts the most powerful obstacles in the way of recovery. If we come back once more to our scale of values, we shall have to say that not only what is lowest but also what is highest in the ego can be unconscious. It is as if we were thus supplied with a proof of what we have just asserted of the conscious ego: that it is first and foremost a body-ego.

III. THE EGO AND THE SUPER-EGO (EGO-IDEAL)

IF the ego were merely the part of the id that is modified by the influence of the perceptual system, the representative in the mind of the real external world, we should have a simple state of things to deal with. But there is a further complication.

The considerations that led us to assume the existence of a differentiating grade within the ego, which may be called the *ego-ideal* or *super-ego*, have been set forth elsewhere.[3] They still hold good.[4] The new proposition which must now be gone into is that this part of the ego is less closely connected with consciousness than the rest.

At this point, we must widen our range a little. We succeeded in explaining the painful disorder of melancholia by supposing that, in those suffering from it, an object which was lost has been reinstated within the ego; that is, that an object-cathexis has been replaced by an identification.[5] When this explanation was first proposed, however, we did not appreciate the full significance of the process and did not know how common and how typical it is. Since then we have come to understand that this kind of substitution has a great share in determining the form taken on by the ego and that it contributes materially towards building up what is called its *character*.

[1] *I.e.*, the ego is ultimately derived from bodily sensations, chiefly from those springing from the surface of the body. It may thus be regarded as a mental projection of the surface of the body, besides, as we have seen above, representing the superficies of the mental apparatus.—Authorized note by the Translator.

[2] I was quite recently told an instance of this which was, in fact, brought up as an objection against my description of the "dream-work."

[3] *On Narcissism: an Introduction* [p. 399 above]; and *Group Psychology and the Analysis of the Ego* [p. 664 above].

[4] Except that I seem to have been mistaken in ascribing the function of testing the reality of things to this super-ego—a point which needs correction. The view that the testing of reality is rather one of the functions of the ego itself would fit in perfectly with what we know of the relations of the ego to the world of perception. Some earlier suggestions about a "nucleus of the ego," never very definitely formulated, also require to be put right, since the system *Pcpt-Cs* alone can be regarded as the nucleus of the ego.

[5] "Mourning and Melancholia," (1917), *Collected Papers*, IV.

At the very beginning, in the primitive oral phase of the individual's existence, object-cathexis and identification are hardly to be distinguished from each other. We can only suppose that, later on, object-cathexes proceed from the id, in which erotic trends are felt as needs. The ego, which at its inception is still far from robust, becomes aware of the object-cathexes, and either acquiesces in them or tries to defend itself against them by the process of repression.[1]

When it happens that a person has to give up a sexual object, there quite often ensues a modification in his ego which can only be described as a reinstatement of the object within the ego, as it occurs in melancholia; the exact nature of this substitution is as yet unknown to us. It may be that, by undertaking this intro-jection, which is a kind of regression to the mechanism of the oral phase, the ego makes it easier for an object to be given up or renders that process possible. It may even be that this identification is the sole condition under which the id can give up its objects. At any rate the process, especially in the early phases of development, is a very frequent one, and it points to the conclusion that the character of the ego is a precipitate of abandoned object-cathexes and that it contains a record of past object-choices. It must, of course, be admitted from the outset that there are varying degrees of capacity for resistance, as shown by the extent to which the character of any particular person accepts or resists the influences of the erotic object-choices through which he has lived. In women who have had many love-affairs there seems to be no difficulty in finding vestiges of their object-cathexes in the traits of their character. We must also take into consideration the case of simultaneous object-cathexis and identification, i.e., in which the alteration in character occurs before the object has been given up. In such a case, the alteration in character would be able to survive the object-relation and, in a certain sense, to conserve it.

From another point of view it may be said that this transformation of an erotic object-

choice into a modification of the ego is also a method by which the ego can obtain control over the id and deepen its relations with it—at the cost, it is true, of acquiescing to a large extent in the id's experiences. When the ego assumes the features of the object, it forces itself, so to speak, upon the id as a love-object and tries to make good the loss of that object by saying, "Look, I am so like the object, you can as well love me."

The transformation of object-libido into narcissistic libido which thus takes place obviously implies an abandonment of sexual aims, a process of desexualization; it is consequently a kind of sublimation. Indeed, the question arises, and deserves careful consideration, whether this is not always the path taken in sublimation, whether all sublimation does not take place through the agency of the ego, which begins by changing sexual object-libido into narcissistic libido and then, perhaps, goes on to give it another aim.[2] We shall later on have to consider whether other instinctual vicissitudes may not also result from this transformation, whether, for instance, it may not bring about a defusion of the instincts that are fused together.

Although it is a digression from our theme, we cannot avoid giving our attention for a moment longer to the ego's object-identifications. If they obtain the upper hand and become too numerous, unduly intense and incompatible with one another, a pathological outcome will not be far off. It may come to a disruption of the ego in consequence of the individual identifications becoming cut off from one another by resistances; perhaps the secret of the cases of so-called *multiple personality* is that the various identifications seize possession of consciousness in turn. Even when things do not go so far as this, there remains the question of conflicts between the different identifications into which the ego is split up, conflicts which cannot after all be described as purely pathological.

But, whatever the character's capacity for resisting the influences of abandoned object-cathexes may turn out to be in after years, the effects of the first identifications in earliest childhood will be profound and lasting. This leads us back to the origin of the ego-ideal; for

---

[1] An interesting parallel to the replacement of object-choice by identification is to be found in the belief of primitive peoples, and in the taboos based upon it, that the attributes of animals which are assimilated as nourishment survive as part of the character of the persons who eat them. As is well known, this belief is one of the roots of cannibalism, and its effects can be traced throughout the series of customs derived from the totem feast down to the Holy Communion. The consequences ascribed by this belief to oral mastery of the object do, in fact, follow in the case of the later sexual object-choice.

[2] Now that we have distinguished between the ego and the id, we must recognize the id as the great reservoir of libido mentioned in my introductory paper *On Narcissism* (p. 399 above). The libido which flows into the ego owing to the identifications described above brings about its "secondary narcissism."

behind the latter there lies hidden the first and most important identification of all, the identification with the father,[1] which takes place in the prehistory of every person. This is apparently not in the first instance the consequence or outcome of an object-cathexis; it is a direct and immediate identification and takes place earlier than any object-cathexis. But the object-choices belonging to the earliest sexual period and relating to the father and mother seem normally to find their outcome in an identification of the kind discussed, which would thus reinforce the primary one.

The whole subject, however, is so complicated that is will be necessary to go into it more minutely. The intricacy of the problem is due to two factors: the triangular character of the Oedipus situation, and the constitutional bisexuality of each individual.

In its simplified form, the case of the male child may be described as follows. At a very early age the little boy develops an object-cathexis of his *mother*, which originally related to the mother's breast and is the earliest instance of an object-choice on the anaclitic model; his *father* the boy deals with by identifying himself with him. For a time these two relationships exist side by side, until the sexual wishes in regard to the mother become more intense and the father is perceived as an obstacle to them; this gives rise to the Oedipus complex.[2] The identification with the father then takes on a hostile colouring and changes into a wish to get rid of the father in order to take his place with the mother. Henceforward the relation to the father is ambivalent; it seems as if the ambivalence inherent in the identification from the beginning had become manifest. An ambivalent attitude to the father and an object-relation of a purely affectionate kind to the mother make up the content of the simple positive Oedipus complex in the boy.

Along with the dissolution of the Oedipus complex, the object-cathexis of the mother must be given up. Its place may be filled by one of two things: either an identification with

---

[1] Perhaps it would be safer to say "with the parents"; for before a child has arrived at definite knowledge of the difference between the sexes, the missing penis, it does not distinguish in value between its father and its mother. I recently came across the instance of a young married woman whose story showed that, after noticing the lack of a penis in herself, she had supposed it to be absent not in all women, but only in those whom she regarded as inferior, and had still supposed that her mother possessed one.
In order to simplify my presentment, I shall discuss only identification with the father.
[2] Cf. *Group Psychology and the Analysis of the Ego*, chap. VII [p. 678 above].

the mother or an intensified identification with the father. We are accustomed to regard the latter outcome as the more normal; it permits the affectionate relation to the mother to be in a measure retained. In this way the passing of the Oedipus complex would consolidate the masculinity in the boy's character. In a precisely analogous way, the outcome of the Oedipus attitude in the little girl may be an intensification of the identification with her mother (or such an identification may thus be set up for the first time)—a result which will stamp the child's character in the feminine mould.

These identifications are not what our previous statements would have led us to expect, since they do not involve the absorption of the abandoned object into the ego: But this alternative outcome may also occur; it is more readily observed in girls than in boys. Analysis very often shows that a little girl, after she has had to relinquish her father as a love-object, will bring her masculinity into prominence and identify herself with her father, that is, with the object which has been lost, instead of with her mother. This will clearly depend on whether the masculinity in her disposition —whatever that may consist of—is strong enough.

It would appear, therefore, that in both sexes the relative strength of the masculine and feminine sexual dispositions is what determines whether the outcome of the Oedipus situation shall be an identification with the father or with the mother. This is one of the ways in which bisexuality takes a hand in the subsequent vicissitudes of the Oedipus complex. The other way is even more important. For one gets the impression that the simple Oedipus complex is by no means its commonest form, but rather represents a simplification or schematization which, to be sure, is often enough adequate for practical purposes. Closer study usually discloses the more complete Oedipus complex, which is twofold, positive and negative, and is due to the bisexuality originally present in children: that is to say, a boy has not merely an ambivalent attitude towards his father and an affectionate object-relation towards his mother, but at the same time he also behaves like a girl and displays an affectionate feminine attitude to his father and a corresponding hostility and jealousy towards his mother. It is this complicating element introduced by bisexuality that makes it so difficult to obtain a clear view of the facts in connection with the earliest object-choices and identifications, and still more difficult to describe them intelligibly. It may even be that the ambivalence displayed in the relations to the parents should be attributed entirely to bisexuality and that it is not, as I stated just now, developed out of an identification in consequence of rivalry.

In my opinion, it is advisable in general, and quite especially where neurotics are concerned, to assume the existence of the complete Oedipus complex. Analytic experience then shows that in a number of cases one or the other of its constituents disappears, except for barely distinguishable traces, so that a series can be formed with the normal positive Oedipus complex at one end and the inverted negative one at the other, while its intermediate members will exhibit the complete type with one or other of its two constituents preponderating. As the Oedipus complex dissolves, the four trends of which it consists will group themselves in such a way as to produce a father-identification and a mother-identification. The father-identification will preserve the object-relation to the mother which belonged to the positive complex and will at the same time take the place of the object-relation to the father which belonged to the inverted complex: and the same will be true *mutatis mutandis*,[1] of the mother-identification. The relative intensity of the two identifications in any individual will reflect the preponderance in him of one or other of the two sexual dispositions.

The broad general outcome of the sexual phase governed by the Oedipus complex may, therefore, be taken to be the forming of a precipitate in the ego, consisting of these two identifications in some way combined together. This modification of the ego retains its special position; it stands in contrast to the other constituents of the ego in the form of an ego-ideal or super-ego.

The super-ego is, however, not merely a deposit left by the earliest object-choices of the id; it also represents an energetic reaction-formation against those choices. Its relation to the ego is not exhausted by the precept: "You *ought to be* such and such (like your father)"; it also comprises the prohibition: "You *must not be* such and such (like your father); that is, you may not do all that he does; many things are his prerogative." This double aspect of the ego-ideal derives from the fact that the ego-ideal had the task of effecting the repression of the Oedipus complex, indeed, it is to

[1] The necessary changes being made. —ED.

that revolutionary event that it owes its existence. Clearly the repression of the Oedipus complex was no easy task. The parents, and especially the father, were perceived as the obstacle to realization of the Oedipus wishes; so the child's ego brought in a reinforcement to help in carrying out the repression by erecting this same obstacle within itself. The strength to do this was, so to speak, borrowed from the father, and this loan was an extraordinarily momentous act. The super-ego retains the character of the father, while the more intense the Oedipus complex was and the more rapidly it succumbed to repression (under the influence of discipline, religious teaching, schooling and reading), the more exacting later on is the domination of the super-ego over the ego—in the form of conscience or perhaps of an unconscious sense of guilt. I shall later on bring forward a suggestion about the source of the power it employs to dominate in this way, the source, that is, of its compulsive character which manifests itself in the form of a categorical imperative.

If we consider once more the origin of the super-ego as we have described it, we shall perceive it to be the outcome of two highly important factors, one of them biological and the other historical: namely, the lengthy duration in man of the helplessness and dependence belonging to childhood, and the fact of his Oedipus complex, the repression of which we have shown to be connected with the interruption of libidinal development by the latency period and so with the twofold onset of activity characteristic of man's sexual life.[2] According to the view of one psycho-analyst, the last-mentioned phenomenon, which seems to be peculiar to man, is a heritage of the cultural development necessitated by the glacial epoch. We see, then, that the differentiation of the super-ego from the ego is no matter of chance; it stands as the representative of the most important events in the development both of the individual and of the race; indeed, by giving permanent expression to the influence of the parents, it perpetuates the existence of the factors to which it owes its origin.

Psycho-analysis has been reproached time after time with ignoring the higher, moral, spiritual side of human nature. The reproach is doubly unjust, both historically and methodologically. For, in the first place, we have

[2] This sentence represents a slight modification of the original text in accordance with direct instructions from the author.—TR.

from the very beginning attributed the function of instigating repression to the moral and aesthetic tendencies in the ego; and secondly, there has been a general refusal to recognize that psycho-analytic research could not produce a complete and finished body of doctrine, like a philosophical system, ready-made, but had to find its way step by step along the path towards understanding the intricacies of the mind by making an analytic dissection of both normal and abnormal phenomena. So long as the study of the repressed part of the mind was our task, there was no need for us to feel any agitated apprehensions about the existence of the higher side of mental life. But now that we have embarked upon the analysis of the ego, we can give an answer to all those whose moral sense has been shocked and who have complained that there must surely be a higher nature in man: "Very true," we can say, "and here we have that higher nature, in this ego-ideal or super-ego, the representative of our relation to our parents. When we were little children we knew these higher natures, we admired them and feared them; and later we took them into ourselves."

The ego-ideal, therefore, is the heir of the Oedipus complex and thus it is also the expression of the most powerful impulses and most important vicissitudes experienced by the libido in the id. By setting up this ego-ideal, the ego masters its Oedipus complex and at the same time places itself in subjection to the id. Whereas the ego is essentially the representative of the external world, of reality, the super-ego stands in contrast to it as the representative of the internal world, of the id. Conflicts between the ego and the ideal will, as we are now prepared to find, ultimately reflect the contrast between what is real and what is mental between the external world and the internal world.

Through the forming of the ideal, all the traces left behind in the id by biological developments and by the vicissitudes gone through by the human race are taken over by the ego and lived through again by it in each individual. Owing to the way in which it is formed, the ego-ideal has a great many points of contact with the phylogenetic endowment of each individual—his archaic heritage. And thus it is that what belongs to the lowest depths in the minds of each one of us is changed, through this formation of the ideal, into what we value as the highest in the human soul. It would be vain, however, to attempt to localize the ego-ideal, even in the sense in which we have localized the ego, or to work it into any of those analogies with the help of which we have tried to picture the relation between the ego and the id.

It is easy to show that the ego-ideal answers in every way to what is expected of the higher nature of man. In so far as it is a substitute for the longing for a father, it contains the germ from which all religions have evolved. The self-judgment which declares that the ego falls short of its ideal produces the sense of worthlessness with which the religious believer attests his longing. As a child grows up, the office of father is carried on by masters and by others in authority; the power of their injunctions and prohibitions remains vested in the ego-ideal and continues, in the form of conscience, to exercise the censorship of morals. The tension between the demands of conscience and the actual attainments of the ego is experienced as a sense of guilt. Social feelings rest on the foundation of identifications with others, on the basis of an ego-ideal in common with them.

Religion, morality, and a social sense—the chief elements of what is highest in man[1]— were originally one and the same thing. According to the hypothesis which I have put forward in *Totem and Taboo*, they were acquired phylogenetically out of the father-complex: religion and moral restraint by the actual process of mastering the Oedipus complex itself, and social feeling from the necessity for overcoming the rivalry that then remained between the members of the younger generation. It seems that the male sex has taken the lead in developing all of these moral acquisitions; and that they have then been transmitted to women by cross-inheritance. Even today the social feelings arise in the individual as a superstructure founded upon impulses of jealousy and rivalry against his brothers and sisters. Since the enmity cannot be gratified, there develops an identification with the former rival. The study of mild cases of homosexuality confirms the suspicion that in this instance, too, the identification is a substitute for an affectionate object-choice which has succeeded the hostile, aggressive attitude.[2]

With the mention of phylogenesis, however,

---

[1] I am at the moment putting science and art on one side.
[2] Cf. *Group Psychology and the Analysis of the Ego* [p. 664 above]; and "Certain Neurotic Mechanisms in Jealousy, Paranoia, and Homosexuality" (1922), *Collected Papers*, II.

fresh problems arise, from which one is tempted to shrink back dismayed. But there is no help for it, the attempt must be made; in spite of a fear that it will lay bare the inadequacy of the whole structure that we have so arduously built up. The question is: which was it, the ego of primitive man or his id, that acquired religion and morality in those early days out of the father-complex? If it was his ego, why do we not speak simply of these things being inherited by the ego? If it was the id, how does that agree with the character of the id? Or are we wrong in carrying the differentiation between ego, super-ego, and id back into such early times? Or should we not honestly confess that our whole conception of the processes within the ego is of no help in understanding phylogenesis and cannot be applied to it?

Let us answer first what is easiest to answer. The differentiation between ego and id must be attributed not only to primitive man but even to much simpler forms of life, for it is the inevitable expression of the influence of the external world. The super-ego, according to our hypothesis, actually originated from the experiences that led to totemism. The question whether it was the ego or the id that experienced and acquired these things soon ceases to have any meaning. Reflection at once shows us that no external vicissitudes can be experienced or undergone by the id, except by way of the ego, which is the representative of the outer world to the id. Nevertheless it is not possible to speak of direct inheritance by the ego. It is here that the gulf between the actual individual and the conception of the species becomes evident. Moreover, one must not take the difference between ego and id in too hard-and-fast a sense, nor forget that the ego is a part of the id which has been specially modified. The experiences undergone by the ego seem at first to be lost to posterity; but, when they have been repeated often enough and with sufficient intensity in the successive individuals of many generations, they transform themselves, so to say, into experiences of the id, the impress of which is preserved by inheritance. Thus in the id, which is capable of being inherited, are stored up vestiges of the existences led by countless former egos; and, when the ego forms its super-ego out of the id, it may perhaps only be reviving images of egos that have passed away and be securing them a resurrection.

The way in which the super-ego came into being explains how it is that the earlier conflicts of the ego with the object-cathexes of the id can be carried on and continued in conflicts with their successor, the super-ego. If the ego has not succeeded in mastering the Oedipus complex satisfactorily, the energic cathexis of the latter, springing from the id, will find an outlet in the reaction-formations of the ego-ideal. The very free communication possible between the ideal and these *Ucs* instinctual trends explains how it is that the ideal itself can be to a great extent unconscious and inaccessible to the ego. The struggle which once raged in the deepest strata of the mind, and was not brought to an end by rapid sublimation and identification, is now carried on in a higher region, like the Battle of the Huns which in Kaulbach's painting is being fought out in the sky.

IV. The Two Classes of Instincts

WE have already said that, if the differentiation we have made of the mind into an id, an ego, and a super-ego represents any advance in our knowledge, it ought to enable us to understand more thoroughly the dynamic relations within the mind and to describe them more clearly. We have also already reached the conclusion that the ego is especially affected by perception, and that, speaking broadly, perceptions may be said to have the same significance for the ego as instincts have for the id. At the same time, the ego is subject to the influence of the instincts, too, like the id, of which it is in fact only a specially modified part.

I have lately developed a view of the instincts[1] which I shall here hold to and take as the basis of further discussions. According to this view we have to distinguish two classes of instincts, one of which, Eros or the sexual instincts, is by far the more conspicuous and accessible to study. It comprises not merely the uninhibited sexual instinct proper and the impulses of a sublimated or aim-inhibited nature derived from it, but also the self-preservative instinct, which must be assigned to the ego and which at the beginning of our analytic work we had good reason for setting in opposition to the sexual object-instincts. The second class of instincts was not so easy to define; in the end we came to recognize sadism as its representative. As a result of theoretical considerations, supported by biology, we assumed the existence of a death-instinct, the task of which is to lead organic matter back into the

[1] *Beyond the Pleasure Principle*, p. 639 above.

inorganic state; on the other hand, we supposed that Eros aims at complicating life by bringing about a more and more far-reaching coalescence of the particles into which living matter has been dispersed, thus, of course, aiming at the maintenance of life. Acting in this way, both the instincts would be conservative in the strictest sense of the word, since both would be endeavouring to re-establish a state of things that was disturbed by the emergence of life. The appearance of life would thus be regarded as the cause of the continuance of life and also as the cause of the striving towards death; and life itself would be a conflict and compromise between these two trends. The problem of the origin of life would remain a cosmological one; and the problem of the purpose and goal of life would be answered dualistically.

On this view a special physiological process (of anabolism or katabolism) would be associated with each of the two classes of instincts; both instincts would be active in every particle of living substance, although in unequal proportions, so that some one substance might be the principal representative of Eros.

This hypothesis throws no light whatever upon the manner in which the two classes of instincts are fused, blended, and mingled with each other; but that this takes place regularly and very extensively is an assumption indispensable to our conception. It appears that, as a result of the combination of unicellular organisms into multicellular forms of life, the death-instinct of the single cell can successfully be neutralized and the destructive impulses be diverted towards the external world through the instrumentality of a special organ. This special organ would seem to be the musculature; and the death-instinct would thus seem to express itself—though probably only in part —as an instinct of destruction directed against the external world and other living organisms.

Once we have admitted the conception of a fusion of the two classes of instincts with each other, the possibility of a—more or less complete—*defusion* of them forces itself upon us. The sadistic component of the sexual instinct would be a classical example of instinctual fusion serving a useful purpose; and the perversion in which sadism has made itself independent would be typical of defusion, though not of absolutely complete defusion. From this point we obtain a new view of a great array of facts which have not before been considered in this light. We perceive that, for purposes of discharge, the instinct of destruction is habitu-

ally enlisted in the service of Eros; we suspect that the epileptic fit is a product and sign of instinctual defusion; and we come to understand that defusion and the marked emergence of the death-instinct are among the most noteworthy effects of many severe neuroses, e.g., the obsessional neuroses. Making a swift generalization, we might conjecture that the essence of a regression of libido, e.g., from the genital to the sadistic-anal level, would lie in a defusion of instincts, just as, conversely, the advance from an earlier to the definitive genital phase would be conditioned by an accession of erotic components. The question also arises whether ordinary ambivalence, which is so often unusually strong in the constitutional disposition to neurosis, should not be regarded as the product of a defusion; ambivalence, however, is such a fundamental phenomenon that it more probably represents a state of incomplete fusion.

It is natural that we should now turn with interest to inquire whether there may not be instructive connections to be traced between the formations we have assumed to exist in the mind—the ego, the super-ego, and the id—and the two classes of instincts; and, further, whether the pleasure-principle which dominates mental processes can be shown to have any constant relation both to the two classes of instincts and to these differentiations which we have drawn within the mind. But before we discuss this, we must clear away a doubt which arises concerning the terms of the problem itself. There can be no doubt about the pleasure-principle, and the differentiations within the ego have good clinical justification, but the distinction between the two classes of instincts does not seem sufficiently assured and it is possible that facts of clinical analysis may be found to conflict with it.

One such fact appears to exist. Instead of the opposition between the two classes of instincts let us consider the polarity of love and hate. (There is no difficulty in finding a representative of Eros; but we must be grateful that we can find a representative of the elusive death-instinct in the instinct of destruction, for which hate points the way.) Now, clinical observation shows not only that love is with unexpected regularity accompanied by hate (ambivalence), and not only that in human relationships hate is frequently a forerunner of love, but also that in many circumstances hate changes into love and love into hate. If this change is anything more than a mere succession in time, then clearly the ground is cut away from under a distinction so fundamental as that between erotic instincts and death-instincts, one which presupposes the existence of physiological processes running counter to each other.

Now the case in which someone first loves and then hates the same person (or the reverse), because that person has given him cause for doing so, has obviously nothing to do with our problem. Nor has the other case in which feelings of love that have not yet become manifest express themselves, to begin with, by enmity and aggressive tendencies; for it may be that here the destructive components in the object-cathexis have outstripped the erotic and are only later on joined by the latter. But we know of several instances in the psychology of the neuroses in which there are better grounds for assuming that a transformation does take place. In persecutory paranoia, the sufferer takes a particular way of defending himself against an unduly strong homosexual attachment to a given person, with the result that the person he once loved most is changed into a persecutor and then becomes the object of aggressive and often dangerous impulses on the part of the patient. Here we have grounds for interposing an intermediate phase in which the love is transformed into hate. Analytic investigation has only lately revealed that the sources of homosexuality and of desexualized social feelings include very intense feelings of rivalry giving rise to aggressive desires, which, after they have been surmounted, are succeeded by love for the object that was formerly hated or by an identification with it. The question arises whether in these instances we are to assume a direct transformation of hate into love. It is clear that here the changes are purely internal and an alteration in the behaviour of the object plays no part in them.

There is another possible mechanism, however, which we have come to know of by analytic investigation of the processes concerned in the change in paranoia. An ambivalent attitude is present from the outset and the transformation is effected by means of a reactive shifting of cathexis, by which energy is withdrawn from the erotic impulses and used to supplement the hostile energy.

Not quite the same thing but something like it happens when a hostile attitude of rivalry is overcome and leads to homosexuality. The hostile attitude has no prospect of gratification; consequently—i.e., as an economic measure—it is replaced by a loving attitude for which there is more hope of satisfaction, that is, possibility of discharge. So we see that we are not obliged in either of these cases to assume a direct transformation of hate into love which would be incompatible with a qualitative distinction between the two classes of instincts.

It appears, however, that by including in our calculations this other mechanism by means of which love can be changed into hate, we have tacitly made another assumption which deserves to be formulated explicitly. We have reckoned as though there existed in the mind—whether in the ego or in the id—a displaceable energy, which is in itself neutral, but is able to join forces either with an erotic or with a destructive impulse, differing qualitatively as they do, and augment its total cathexis. Without assuming the existence of a displaceable energy of this kind, we can make no headway. The only question is where it comes from, what it belongs to, and what it signifies.

The problem of the quality of instinctual impulses and of its persistence throughout their vicissitudes is still very obscure and has hardly been attacked up to the present. In the sexual component-instincts, which are especially accessible to observation, it is possible to perceive the working of processes which are in the same category as what we are discussing; e.g., we see that some degree of communication exists between the component instincts, that an instinct deriving from one particular erotogenic source can make over its intensity to reinforce another component-instinct originating in another source, that gratification of one instinct can take the place of gratification of another, and many more facts of the same nature—all of which must encourage us to venture upon certain assumptions.

In the present discussion, moreover, I am putting forward nothing but a supposition; I have no proof to offer. It seems a plausible view that this neutral displaceable energy, which is probably active alike in the ego and in the id, proceeds from the narcissistic reservoir of libido, i.e., that it is desexualized Eros. (The erotic instincts appear to be altogether more plastic, more readily diverted and displaced than the destructive instincts.) From this we can easily go on to assume that this displaceable libido is employed in the service of the pleasure-principle to obviate accumulations and to facilitate discharge. It is clear, incidentally, that there is a certain indifference about the path along which the discharge takes place, so long as it takes place somehow. We know this trait; it is characteristic of the cathetic processes in the id. It is found in erotic cathexes, where a peculiar indifference in regard to the object displays itself; and it is especially evident in the transferences arising in analysis, which develop inevitably no matter who the analyst may be. Rank has recently published some good examples of the way in which neurotic acts of revenge can be directed against the wrong people. Such behaviour on the part of the unconscious reminds one of the comic story of the three village tailors, one of whom had to be hanged because the only village blacksmith had committed a capital offence. The penalty must be exacted even if it does not fall upon the guilty. It was in studying dream-work that we first came upon this kind of looseness in the displacements brought about by the primary process. In that case it was the objects that were thus relegated to a position of no more than secondary importance, just as in the case we are now discussing it is the paths of discharge. It would seem to be characteristic of the ego to be more particular both about the choice of an object and about the path of discharge.

If this displaceable energy is desexualized libido, it might also be described as sublimated energy; for it would still retain the main purpose of Eros—that of uniting and binding—in so far as it helped towards establishing that unity, or tendency to unity, which is particularly characteristic of the ego. If the intellectual processes in the wider sense are to be classed among these displacements, then the energy for the work of thought itself must be supplied from sublimated erotic sources.

Here we arrive again at the possibility, which has already been discussed, that sublimation may take place regularly through the mediation of the ego. The other case will be recollected, in which the ego deals with the first object-cathexes of the id (and certainly with later ones too) by taking over the libido from them into itself and binding it to the ego-modification produced by means of identification. The transformation of erotic libido into ego-libido of course involves an abandonment of sexual aims, a desexualization. In any case this throws light upon an important function of the ego in its relation to Eros. By thus obtaining possession of the libido from the object-cathexes, setting itself up as sole love-object, and desexualizing or sublimating the libido of the id, the ego is working in opposition to the purposes of Eros and placing itself at the service of the oppos-

ing instinctual trends. It has to acquiesce in some of the other object-cathexes of the id; it has to go hand in hand with them, so to speak. We shall come back later to another possible consequence of this activity of the ego.

This would seem to imply an important amplification of the theory of narcissism. At the very beginning, all the libido is accumulated in the id, while the ego is still in process of formation or far from robust. Part of this libido is sent out by the id into erotic object-cathexes, whereupon the ego, now growing stronger, attempts to obtain possession of this object-libido and to force itself upon the id as a love-object. The narcissism of the ego is thus seen to be secondary, acquired by the withdrawal of the libido from objects.

Over and over again we find on tracing instinctual impulses back that they disclose themselves as derivatives of Eros. If it were not for the considerations put forward in *Beyond the Pleasure Principle*, and ultimately for the sadistic constituents which have attached themselves to Eros, we should have difficulty in holding to our fundamental dualistic point of view. But since we cannot escape that view, we are driven to conclude that the death-instincts are by their nature mute, and that the clamour of life proceeds for the most part from Eros.[1]

And from the struggle against Eros! It can hardly be doubted that the pleasure-principle serves the id as a compass in its struggle against the libido—the force that introduces such disturbances into the process of life. If it is true that life is governed by Fechner's principle of constant equilibrium, it consists of a continuous descent towards death; but the falling of the level is delayed, and fresh tensions are introduced, by the claims of Eros, of the sexual instincts, as expressed in instinctual needs. The id, guided by the pleasure-principle, that is, by the perception of "pain," guards itself against these tensions in various ways. It does so in the first place by complying as swiftly as possible with the demands of the non-desexualized libido, i.e., by striving for the gratification of the directly sexual trends. But it does so further, and in a far more comprehensive fashion, in relation to one particular form of gratification which subsumes all component claims—that is, by discharge of the sexual substances, which are saturated conductors, so to speak, of the erotic tensions. The ejection of sexual sub-

[1] In fact, according to our view it is through the agency of Eros that the destructive instincts that are directed towards the external world have been diverted from the self.

stances in the sexual act corresponds in a certain degree with the separation of soma and germ-plasm. This accounts for the likeness between dying and the condition that follows complete sexual satisfaction, and for the fact that death coincides with the act of copulation in some of the lower animals. These creatures die in the act of reproduction because, after Eros has been eliminated through the process of gratification, the death-instinct has a free hand for accomplishing its purposes. Finally, as we have seen, the ego, by sublimating some of the libido for itself and its purposes, assists the id in its work of mastering the tensions.

V. The Subordinate Relationships of the Ego

THE complexity of our subject-matter must be an excuse for the fact that none of the chapter-headings of this book correspond entirely to their contents, and that, in turning to new aspects of the problem, we constantly hark back to matters that have already been dealt with.

As has been said repeatedly, the ego is formed to a great extent out of identifications taking the place of cathexes, on the part of the id, which have been abandoned; the earliest of these identifications always fulfil a special office in the ego and stand apart from the rest of the ego in the form of a super-ego, while later on, as it grows stronger, the ego may become more able to withstand the effects of identifications. The super-ego owes its special position in the ego, or in regard to the ego, to a factor which must be considered from two sides: to the fact that on the one hand it was the first identification and one which took place while the ego was still feeble, and that on the other hand it was the heir to the Oedipus complex and thus incorporated into the ego objects of far greater significance than any others. The super-ego's relation to the subsequent modifications effected in the ego is roughly that of the primary sexual period in childhood to full-grown sexual activity after puberty. Although it is amenable to every later influence, it preserves throughout life the character given to it by its derivation from the father-complex, namely, the capacity to stand apart from the ego and to rule it. It is a memorial of the former weakness and dependence of the ego, and the mature ego remains subject to its domination. As the child was once compelled to obey its parents, so the ego submits to the categorical imperative pronounced by its super-ego.

The descent of the super-ego from the first object-cathexes of the id, from the Oedipus complex, however, signifies even more for it. This descent, as we have already described, connects it with the phylogenetic acquisitions of the id and makes it a reincarnation of former ego-structures which have left their precipitates behind in the id. Thus the super-ego is always in close touch with the id and can act as its representative in relation to the ego. It reaches deep down into the id and is for that reason farther from consciousness than the ego.[1]

We can best appreciate these relations by turning our attention to certain clinical facts, which have long since lost their novelty but which still await theoretical discussion.

There are certain people who behave in a quite peculiar fashion during the work of analysis. When one speaks hopefully to them or expresses satisfaction with the progress of the treatment, they show signs of discontent and their condition invariably becomes worse. One begins by regarding this as defiance and as an attempt to prove their superiority to the physician, but later one comes to take a deeper and truer view. One becomes convinced, not only that such people cannot endure any praise or appreciation, but that they react inversely to the progress of the treatment. Every partial solution that ought to result, and in other people does result, in an improvement or a temporary suspension of symptoms produces in them for the time being an exacerbation of their illness; they get worse during the treatment instead of getting better. They exhibit the so-called *negative therapeutic reaction*.

There is no doubt that there is something in these people that sets itself against their recovery and dreads its approach as though it were a danger. We are accustomed to say that the need for illness has got the upper hand in them over the desire for health. If we analyse this resistance in the usual way—then, even after we have subtracted from it the defiant attitude towards the physician and the fixation on the various kinds of advantage which the patient derives from the illness, the greater part of it is still left over; and this reveals itself as the most powerful of all obstacles to recovery, more powerful even than such fam-

---

[1] It may be said that the psycho-analytical or meta-psychological ego stands on its head no less than the anatomical ego—the *cortical homunculus*.

liar ones as narcissistic inaccessibility, the assumption of a negative attitude towards the physician, or a clinging to the advantages of he illness.

In the end we come to see that we are dealing with what may be called a "moral" factor, a sense of guilt, which is finding atonement in he illness and is refusing to give up the penalty of suffering. We are justified in regarding this rather disheartening explanation as conclusive. But, as far as the patient is concerned, this sense of guilt is dumb; it does not tell him he is guilty; he does not feel guilty, he simply feels ill. This sense of guilt expresses itself only as a resistance to recovery which it is extremely difficult to overcome. It is also particularly difficult to convince the patient that his motive lies behind his continuing to be ill; he holds fast to the more obvious explanation that treatment by analysis is not the right remedy for his case.[1]

The description we have given applies to the most extreme instances of this state of affairs, but in a lesser measure this factor has to be reckoned with in very many cases, perhaps in all severe cases of neurosis. In fact it may be precisely this element in the situation, the attitude of the ego-ideal, that determines the severity of a neurotic illness. We shall not hesitate, therefore, to discuss rather more fully the way in which the sense of guilt expresses itself under different conditions.

[1] The battle with the obstacle of an unconscious sense of guilt is not made easy for the analyst. Nothing can be done against it directly, and nothing indirectly but the slow procedure of unmasking its unconscious repressed roots, and of thus gradually changing it into a conscious sense of guilt. One has a special opportunity for influencing it when this Ucs sense of guilt is a "borrowed" one, i.e., when it is the product of an identification with some other person who was once the object of an erotic cathexis. When the sense of guilt has been adopted in this way, it is often the sole remaining trace of the abandoned love-relation and not at all easy to recognize as such. (The likeness between this process and what happens in melancholia is unmistakable.) If one can unmask this former object-cathexis behind the Ucs sense of guilt, the therapeutic success is often brilliant, but otherwise the outcome of one's efforts is by no means certain. It depends principally on the intensity of the sense of guilt; there is often no counteracting force of similar strength which the treatment can put in motion against it. Perhaps it may depend, too, on whether the personality of the analyst allows of the patient's putting him in the place of his ego-ideal, and this involves a temptation for the analyst to play the part of prophet, saviour, and redeemer to the patient. Since the rules of analysis are diametrically opposed to the physician's making use of his personality in any such manner, it must be honestly confessed that here we have another limitation to the effectiveness of analysis; after all, analysis does not set out to abolish the possibility of morbid reactions, but to give the patient's ego freedom to choose one way or the other.

An explanation of the normal conscious sense of guilt (conscience) presents no difficulties; it is due to tension between the ego and the ego-ideal and is the expression of a condemnation of the ego pronounced by its criticizing function. The feelings of inferiority so well known in neurotics are presumably closely related to it. In two very familiar maladies, the sense of guilt is over-strongly conscious; in them the ego-ideal displays particular severity and often rages against the ego with the utmost cruelty. The attitude of the ego-ideal in these two diseases, the obsessional neurosis and melancholia, presents, alongside of this similarity, differences that are no less significant.

In certain forms of the obsessional neurosis the sense of guilt expresses itself loudly but cannot justify itself to the ego. Consequently the patient's ego rebels against this imputation of guilt and seeks the physician's support in repudiating it. It would be folly to acquiesce in this, for to do so would have no effect. Analysis shows that the super-ego is being influenced by processes that have remained hidden from the ego. It is possible to discover the repressed impulses which really occasion the sense of guilt. The super-ego is thus proved to have known more than the ego about the unconscious id.

In melancholia, the impression that the super-ego has obtained a hold upon consciousness is even stronger. But in this case the ego ventures no objection; it admits the guilt and submits to the punishment. The explanation of this difference is plain. In the obsessional neurosis, the reprehensible impulses which are being criticized by the super-ego have never formed part of the ego; while in melancholia, the object of the super-ego's wrath has become part of the ego through identification.

It is certainly not clear why the sense of guilt reaches such an extraordinary intensity in these two neurotic disorders; and indeed, the main problem presented in this state of affairs lies in another direction. We shall postpone discussion of it until we have dealt with the other cases—in which the sense of guilt remains unconscious.

It is essentially in hysteria and in states of an hysterical type that this condition is found. The mechanism by which the sense of guilt is kept unconscious is easy to discover. The hysterical type of ego defends itself from the painful perception which the criticisms of its super-ego threaten to produce in it by the same means that it uses to defend itself from an unendurable object-cathexis—by an act of repression. It is the ego, therefore, that is responsible for the sense of guilt remaining unconscious. We know that, as a rule, the ego carries out repressions in the service and at the behest of its super-ego; but this is a case in which it has turned the same weapon against its harsh taskmaster. In the obsessional neurosis, as we know, the phenomena of reaction-formation predominate; but here the ego contents itself with keeping at a distance the material to which the sense of guilt refers.

One may go further and venture the hypothesis that a great part of the sense of guilt must normally remain unconscious, because the origin of conscience is closely connected with the Oedipus complex which belongs to the unconscious. If any one were inclined to put forward the paradoxical proposition that the normal man is not only far more immoral than he believes but also far more moral than he has any idea of, psycho-analysis, which is responsible for the first half of the assertion, would have no objection to raise against the second half.[1]

It was a surprise to find that exacerbation of this *Ucs* sense of guilt could turn people into criminals. But it is undoubtedly a fact. In many criminals, especially youthful ones, it is possible to detect a very powerful sense of guilt which existed before the crime, and is not therefore the result of it but its motive. It is as if it had been a relief to be able to fasten this unconscious sense of guilt on to something real and immediate.

In all these situations, the super-ego displays its independence of the conscious ego and the closeness of its relations with the unconscious id. And now, having regard to the importance we ascribed to preconscious verbal residues in the ego, the question arises whether the super-ego, if it is in part unconscious, can consist in such verbal images, or, if not, in what it does consist. Our answer, though it does not carry us very far, will be that it cannot possibly be disputed that the super-ego, no less than the ego, is derived from auditory impressions; it is part of the ego and remains to a great extent accessible to consciousness by way of these verbal images (concepts, abstractions), but the cathectic energy of these elements of the super-ego does not originate from the auditory

perceptions, instruction, reading, etc., but from sources in the id.

The question which we postponed answering runs thus: How is it that the super-ego manifests itself essentially as a sense of guilt (or rather, as criticism—for the sense of guilt is the perception in the ego which corresponds to the criticism) and at the same time develops such extraordinary harshness and severity towards the ego? If we turn to melancholia first, we find that the excessively strong super-ego which has obtained a hold upon consciousness rages against the ego with merciless fury, as if it had taken possession of the whole of the sadism available in the person concerned. Following our view of sadism, we should say that the destructive component had entrenched itself in the super-ego and turned against the ego. What is now holding sway in the super-ego is, as it were, a pure culture of the death-instinct, and in fact it often enough succeeds in driving the ego into death, if the latter does not protect itself from the tyrant in time by a revulsion into mania.

The reproaches of conscience in certain forms of obsessional neurosis are just as painful and tormenting, but here the situation is less perspicuous. It is remarkable that the obsessional neurotic, in contrast to the melancholiac, never takes the step of self-destruction; he is as if immune against the danger of suicide, and is far better protected from it than the hysteric. We can see that what guarantees the safety of the ego is the fact that the object has been retained. In the obsessional neurosis is has become possible, through a regression to the pre-genital organization, for the love-impulses to transform themselves into impulses of aggression against the object. Here again the instinct of destruction has been set free and it aims at destroying the object, or at least it appears to have this aim. These tendencies have not been adopted by the ego; it struggles against them with reaction-formations and pre-cautionary measures, and they remain in the id. The super-ego, however, behaves as if the ego were responsible for them and shows by its zeal in chastising these destructive intentions that they are no mere semblance evoked by regression, but an actual substitution of hate for love. Helpless in either direction, the ego defends itself vainly, alike against the instigations of the murderous id and against the reproaches of the punishing conscience. It succeeds in holding in check at least the most brutal actions of both sides; the first outcome

---

[1] This proposition is only apparently a paradox; it simply states that human nature has a far greater capacity, both for good and for evil, than it thinks it has, i.e., than it is aware of through the conscious perceptions of the ego.

is interminable self-torment, and eventually there follows a systematic torturing of the object, in so far as it is within reach.

The activity of the dangerous death-instincts within the individual organism is dealt with in various ways; in part they are rendered harmless by being fused with erotic components, in part they are diverted towards the external world in the form of aggression, while for the most part they undoubtedly continue their inner work unhindered. How is it then that in melancholia the super-ego can become a kind of gathering-place for the death-instincts?

From the point of view of morality, the control and restriction of instinct, it may be said of the id that it is totally non-moral, of the ego that it strives to be moral, and of the super-ego that it can be hyper-moral and then becomes as ruthless as only the id can be. It is remarkable that the more a man checks his aggressive tendencies towards others the more tyrannical, that is aggressive, he becomes in his ego-ideal. The ordinary view sees the situation the other way round: the standard set up by the ego-ideal seems to be the motive for the suppression of aggressiveness. The fact remains, however, as we have stated it: the more a man controls his aggressiveness, the more intense become the aggressive tendencies of his ego-ideal against his ego. It is like a displacement, a turning round upon the self. But even ordinary normal morality has a harshly restraining, cruelly prohibiting quality. It is from this, indeed, that the conception arises of an inexorable higher being who metes out punishment.

I cannot go further in my consideration of these questions without introducing a fresh assumption. The super-ego arises, as we know, from an identification with the father regarded as a model. Every such identification is in the nature of a desexualization or even of a sublimation. It now seems as though when a transformation of this kind takes place there occurs at the same time an instinctual defusion. After sublimation, the erotic component no longer has the power to bind the whole of the destructive elements that were previously combined with it, and these are released in the form of inclinations to aggression and destruction. This defusion would be the source of the general character of harshness and cruelty exhibited by the ideal—its dictatorial "Thou shalt."

Let us again consider the obsessional neurosis for a moment. The state of affairs is different here. The defusion of love into aggressiveness has not been effected by the agency of the ego, but is the result of a regression which has come about in the id. But this process has extended beyond the id to the super-ego, which now increases its tryanny over the innocent ego. It would seem, however, that in this case no less than in that of melancholia, the ego, having gained possession of the libido by means of identification, is punished for doing so by the super-ego through the instrumentality of the aggressiveness which had before been mixed with the libido.

Our ideas about the ego are beginning to clear, and its various relationships are gaining distinctness. We now see the ego in its strength and in its weaknesses. It is entrusted with important functions. By virtue of its relation to the perceptual system, it arranges the processes of the mind in a temporal order and tests their correspondence with reality. By interposing the process of thinking it secures a postponement of motor discharges and controls the avenues to motility. This last office is, to be sure, a question more of form than of fact, in the matter of action the ego's position is like that of a constitutional monarch, without whose sanction no law can be passed but who hesitates long before imposing a veto on any measure put forward by Parliament. All the experiences of life that originate from without enrich the ego; the id, however, is another outer world to it, which it strives to bring into subjection to itself. It withdraws libido from the id and transforms the object-cathexes of the id into ego-constructions. With the aid of the super-ego, though in a manner that is still obscure to us, it draws upon the experiences of past ages stored in the id.

There are two paths by which the contents of the id can penetrate into the ego. The one is direct, the other leads by way of the ego-ideal; which of these two paths they take may, for many mental activities, be of decisive importance. The ego develops from perceiving instincts to controlling them, from obeying instincts to curbing them. In this achievement a large share is taken by the ego-ideal, which, indeed, is partly a reaction-formation against the instinctual processes in the id. Psycho-analysis is an instrument to enable the ego to push its conquest of the id further still.

From the other point of view, however, we see this same ego as a poor creature owing service to three masters and consequently menaced by three several dangers: from the external world, from the libido of the id, and from the severity of the super-ego. Three kinds of anxiety correspond to these three dangers, since anxiety is the expression of a recoil from danger. Like the dweller in a borderland that it is, the ego tries to mediate between the world and the id, to make the id comply with the world's demands and, by means of muscular activity, to accommodate the world to the id's desires. In point of fact, it behaves like the physician during treatment by analysis; it offers itself to the id as a libidinal object in view of its power of adaptation to the real world, and aims at attaching the id's libido to itself. It is not only the ally of the id; it is also a submissive slave who courts the love of his master. Whenever possible, it tries to remain on good terms with the id; it draws the veil of its *Pcs* rationalizations over the id's *Ucs* demands; it pretends that the id is showing obedience to the mandates of reality, even when in fact it is remaining obdurate and immovable; it throws a disguise over the id's conflicts with reality and, if possible, over its conflicts with the super-ego too. Its position midway between the id and reality tempts it only too often to become sycophantic, opportunist, and false, like a politician who sees the truth but wants to keep his place in popular favour.

Towards the two classes of instincts the ego's attitude is not impartial. Its work of identification and sublimation gives the death-instincts in the id assistance in mastering the libido, but in so doing it incurs the risk of itself becoming the object of the death-instincts and of perishing. In order to be able to help in this way, it has to become flooded with libido itself; it thus becomes the representative of Eros and thenceforward desires to live and to be loved.

But since the ego's work of sublimation results in a defusion of the instincts and a liberation of the aggressive instincts in the super-ego, its struggle against the libido exposes it to the danger of maltreatment and death. In suffering under the attacks of the super-ego or perhaps even succumbing to them, the ego is meeting with a fate like that of the protozoa which are destroyed by the products of disintegration that they themselves have created. From the economic point of view, the morality that functions in the super-ego seems to be a similar product of disintegration.

Among the subordinate relationships in which the ego stands, that to the super-ego is perhaps the most interesting.

The ego is the true abode of anxiety. Threatened by dangers from three directions, it develops the flight-reflex by withdrawing its own cathexis from the menacing perception or from the equally dreaded process in the id, and discharging it as anxiety. This primitive reaction is later replaced by the introduction of protective cathexes (the mechanism of the phobias). What it is that the ego fears either from an external or from a libidinal danger cannot be specified; we know that it is in the nature of an overthrow or of extinction, but it is not determined by analysis. The ego is simply obeying the warning of the pleasure-principle. On the other hand, we can tell what lies hidden behind the ego's dread of the super-ego, its fear of conscience. The higher being which later became the ego-ideal once threatened the ego with castration, and this dread of castration is probably the kernel round which the subsequent fear of conscience has gathered; it is this dread that persists as the fear of conscience.

The high-sounding phrase, "Every fear is ultimately the fear of death," has hardly any meaning; at any rate, it cannot be justified. It seems to me, on the contrary, perfectly correct to distinguish the fear of death from dread of an external object (objective anxiety) and from neurotic libidinal anxiety. It presents a difficult problem to psycho-analysis, for death is an abstract concept with a negative content for which no unconscious correlative can be found. It would seem that the mechanism of the fear of death can only be that the ego relinquishes its narcissistic libidinal cathexis in a very large measure, that is, that it gives up itself, just as it gives up some *external* object in other cases in which it feels anxiety. I believe that the fear of death concerns an interplay between the ego and the super-ego.

We know that the fear of death makes its appearance under two conditions (which, moreover, are entirely analogous to the other situations in which anxiety develops), namely, as a reaction to an external danger and as an internal process, as for instance in melancholia. Once again a neurotic manifestation may help us to understand a normal one.

The fear of death in melancholia only admits of one explanation: that the ego gives itself up because it feels itself hated and persecuted by the super-ego, instead of loved. To the ego, therefore, living means the same as being loved —being loved by the super-ego, which here again appears as the representative of the id. The super-ego fulfils the same function of protecting and saving that was fulfilled in earlier days by the father and later by Providence or destiny. But, when the ego finds itself in overwhelming danger of a real order which it believes itself unable to overcome by its own strength, it is bound to draw the same conclusion. It sees itself deserted by all the forces of protection and lets itself die. Here, moreover, is once again the same situation as that which underlay the first great anxiety-state of birth and the infantile anxiety of longing for an absent person—the anxiety of separation from the protecting mother.

These considerations enable us to conceive of the fear of death, like the fear of conscience, as a development of the fear of castration. The great significance which the sense of guilt has in the neuroses makes it conceivable that ordinary neurotic anxiety is reinforced in severe cases by a development of anxiety between the ego and the super-ego (fear of castration, of conscience, of death).

The id, to which we finally come back, has no means of showing the ego either love or hate. It cannot say what it wants; it has achieved no unity of will. Eros and the death-instinct struggle within it; we have seen with what weapons the one group of instincts defends itself against the other. It would be possible to picture the id as under the domination of the mute but powerful death-instincts, which desire to be at peace and (as the pleasure-principle demands) to put Eros, the intruder, to rest; but that would be to run the risk of valuing too cheaply the part played by Eros.

Inhibitions, Symptoms, and Anxiety

CHAPTER I

In describing pathological phenomena, we are enabled by the ordinary usages of speech to distinguish symptoms from inhibitions, without, however, attaching much importance to the distinction. Indeed, we might hardly think it worthwhile to differentiate more exactly between the two, were it not for the fact that we meet with illnesses in which we observe the presence of inhibitions but not of symptoms and are curious to know the reason for this.

The two concepts are not upon the same plane. Inhibition has a special relation to function. It does not necessarily have a pathological implication. One can quite well call a normal restriction of a function an inhibition of it. A symptom, on the other hand, actually denotes the presence of some pathological process. Thus, an inhibition (among other things) may be a symptom. In ordinary speech, we should use the word *inhibition* when there is a simple lowering of function, and *symptom* when a function has undergone some unusual change or when a new phenomenon has arisen out of it. Very often it seems to be quite an arbitrary matter whether we emphasize the positive side of a pathological process and call its consequences a *symptom,* or its negative side and call them an *inhibition.* But all this is really of little interest; and the problem as we have stated it does not carry us very far.

Since the concept of inhibition is so intimately associated with that of function, we may perhaps proceed to examine the various functions of the ego with a view to discovering what forms any disturbance of those functions will assume in each of the different neurotic affections. Let us pick out for a comparative study of this kind the sexual function and those of eating, of locomotion, and of occupational work.

(*a*) The sexual function is liable to a great number of disturbances, most of which exhibit the characteristics of simple inhibitions. These are classed together as *psychical impotence.* The normal performance of the sexual function can only come about as the result of a very complicated process, and disturbances may appear at any point in it. In men the chief points at which inhibition occurs are shown by: a turning away of the libido at the very beginning of the process (psychological unpleasure[1]); abridgment of the sexual act *(ejaculatio praecox),* an occurrence which might equally well be regarded as a symptom; an arrest of the act before it has reached its natural conclusion (absence of ejaculation); or a non-appearance of the psychological results (lack of pleasure in orgasm). Other disturbances arise from the sexual function becoming dependent on special conditions of a perverse or fetishistic nature.

That there is a relationship between inhibition and anxiety is pretty evident. Many inhibitions obviously represent a relinquishment of a function whose exercise would produce anxiety. Many women are openly afraid of the sexual function. We class this anxiety under hysteria, just as we do the defensive symptom of disgust which, arising originally as a deferred reaction to the experiencing of a passive sexual act, appears later whenever the *idea* of such an act is presented. Furthermore, many obsessional acts turn out to be measures of precaution and security against sexual experiences and are thus of a phobic character.

This is not very illuminating. We can only note that disturbances of the sexual function are brought about by a great variety of means. (1) The libido may simply be turned away (this seems most readily to produce what we regard as an inhibition pure and simple); (2) the function may be less well carried out; (3) it may be hampered by having conditions attached to it, or modified by being diverted to other aims; (4) it may be prevented by measures of security; (5) if it cannot be prevented from starting, it may be immediately interrupted by the appearance of anxiety; and (6), if it is nevertheless carried out, there may be a subsequent reaction of protest against it and an attempt to undo what has been done.

(*b*) The function of nutrition is most frequently disturbed by a disinclination to eat, brought about by a withdrawal of libido. An

---

[1] Throughout this work, *Unlust* has been translated by the constructed word "unpleasure," while reserving "pain" for the German *Schmerz*.—Tr.

increase in the desire to eat is also a not uncommon thing. The compulsion to eat is attributed to a fear of starving; but this is a subject which has been but little studied. The hysterical defence against eating is known to us in the symptom of vomiting. Refusal to eat owing to anxiety is a concomitant of psychotic states (delusions of being poisoned).

(c) In many neurotic conditions, locomotion is inhibited by a disinclination to walk or a weakness in walking. In hysteria, there will be a paralysis of the motor apparatus, or this one special function of the apparatus will be abolished (abasia). Especially characteristic are the increased difficulties that appear in locomotion owing to the introduction of certain stipulations whose non-observance results in anxiety (phobia).

(d) In inhibition in work—a thing which we so often have to deal with as an isolated symptom in our therapeutic work—the subject feels a decrease in his pleasure in it or becomes less able to do it well; or he has certain reactions to it, like fatigue, giddiness, or sickness, if he is obliged to go on with it. If he is a hysteric he will have to give up his work, owing to the appearance of organic and functional impairments of activity which make it impossible for him to carry it on. If he is an obsessional neurotic, he will be perpetually being distracted from his work or losing time over it owing to delays and repetitions.

Our survey might be extended to other functions of the ego as well; but there would be nothing more to be learned by doing so, for we should not penetrate below the surface of the phenomena presented to us. Let us then proceed to describe inhibition in such a way as to leave very little doubt about what is meant by it, and say that inhibition is the *expression of a restriction of an ego-function.*

A restriction of this kind can itself have very different causes. Many of the mechanisms involved in a renunciation of function are well known to us, as is a certain general purpose which runs through it. This purpose is more easily recognizable in the specific inhibitions. Analysis shows that, when activities, like playing the piano, writing, or even walking, undergo neurotic inhibitions, it is because the physical organs brought into play—the fingers or the feet—have become too strongly eroticized. It has been discovered as a general fact that the ego-function of an organ is impaired if its erotogenicity—its sexual significance—is increased. It behaves, if I may be allowed a somewhat vulgar analogy, like a maid-servant who refuses to go on cooking because her master has started a love-affair with her. As soon as writing, which entails making a liquid substance flow on to a piece of white paper, assumes the significance of copulation, or as soon as walking becomes a symbolic substitute for treading upon the body of mother earth, both writing and walking are stopped because they represent the performance of a forbidden sexual act. The ego renounces these functions, which are within its sphere, in order not to have to undertake fresh measures of repression—in order to avoid coming into conflict with the id.

There are clearly also inhibitions which serve the purpose of self-punishment. This is often the case in inhibitions of occupational activities. The ego is not allowed to carry on those activities, because they would bring success and gain, and these are things which the severe super-ego has forbidden. So the ego gives them up too, in order to avoid coming into conflict with the super-ego.

The more generalized inhibitions of the ego obey a different mechanism of a simple kind. When the ego is faced with a particularly difficult mental task, as occurs in mourning or when there is some tremendous suppression of affect or when a continual flood of sexual phantasies is being kept down, it loses so much of the energy at its disposal that it has to cut down the expenditure of it at many points at once. It is in the position of a speculator whose money has become tied up in various enterprises. I came across an instructive example of this kind of intense, though short-lived, general inhibition. The patient, an obsessional neurotic, used to be overcome by a paralysing fatigue which lasted for one or more days whenever something occurred which should obviously have thrown him into a rage. We have here a point of departure from which we may hope to reach an understanding of the condition of general inhibition which characterizes states of depression, including the gravest form of them, melancholia.

As regards inhibitions, then, we may say in conclusion that they are restrictions of the functions of the ego which have either been imposed as a measure of precaution or brought about as a result of an impoverishment of energy; and we can see without difficulty in what respect an inhibition differs from a symptom: for a symptom cannot be described as a process that takes place within, or acts upon, the ego.

CHAPTER II

THE main characteristics of the formation of symptoms have long since been studied and, I hope, established beyond dispute. A symptom is a sign of, and a substitute for, an instinctual gratification which has remained in abeyance; it is a consequence of the process of repression. Repression proceeds from the ego when the latter—it may be at the behest of the super-ego —refuses to associate itself with an instinctual cathexis which has been aroused in the id. The ego is able by means of repression to keep the idea which is the vehicle of the reprehensible impulse from becoming conscious. Analysis shows that the idea often persists as an unconscious formation.

So far everything seems clear; but we soon come upon difficulties which have not as yet been solved. Up till now our account of what occurs in repression has laid great stress on this point of exclusion from consciousness. But it has left other points open to uncertainty. One question that arose was: what happened to the instinctual impulse which had been actuated in the id and which sought to be gratified? The answer was an indirect one. It was that, owing to the process of repression, the pleasure that would have been expected from gratification had been transformed into unpleasure. But we were then faced with the problem of how the gratification of an instinct could produce unpleasure. The whole matter can be clarified, I think, if we commit ourselves to the definite statement that, as a result of repression, the intended course of the excitatory process in the id does not occur at all; the ego succeeds in inhibiting or deflecting it. If this is so the problem of *transformation of affect* under repression disappears. At the same time, this view implies that the ego can exert a very extensive influence over processes in the id, and we shall have to find out in what way it is able to develop such astonishing powers.

It seems to me that the ego obtains this influence in virtue of its intimate connections with the perceptual system—connections which, as we know, constitute its essence and provide the basis of its differentiation from the id. In its function, the perceptual system, which we have called *Pcpt-Cs*, is bound up with the phenomenon of consciousness. It receives excitations not only from outside but from within and endeavours, by means of the pleasure-unpleasure sensations which reach it from these directions, to direct the course of every mental event in accordance with the pleasure-principle.

We are very apt to think of the ego as powerless against the id; but, when it is opposed to an instinctual process, it has only to give a *signal of unpleasure* in order to attain its object with the aid of that almost omnipotent institution, the pleasure-principle. To take this situation by itself for a moment, we can illustrate it by an example from another field. Let us imagine a country in which a certain small faction objects to a proposed measure the passage of which would have the support of the masses. This minority obtains command of the press and by its help manipulates the supreme arbiter, *public opinion*, and so succeeds in preventing the measure from being passed.

But this explanation opens up fresh problems. Whence does the energy come which is employed for giving the signal of unpleasure? Here we may be assisted by the idea that a defence against an unwelcome *internal* process will be modelled upon the defence adopted against an *external* stimulus, that the ego wards off internal and external dangers alike along identical lines. In the case of external danger, the organism has recourse to attempts at flight. The first thing it does is to withdraw cathexis from the perception of the dangerous object; later on it discovers that it is a better plan to perform muscular movements of such a sort as will render perception of the dangerous object impossible, even in the absence of any refusal to perceive it—that it is a better plan, that is, to remove itself from the sphere of danger. Repression is an equivalent of this attempt at flight. The ego withdraws its (preconscious) cathexis from the psychical representative of the impulse that is to be repressed and uses that cathexis for the purpose of releasing unpleasure (anxiety). The problem of how anxiety arises in connection with repression may be no simple one; but we may legitimately maintain the opinion that the ego is the actual seat of anxiety and give up our earlier view that the cathectic energy of a repressed impulse is automatically turned into anxiety. If I expressed myself in the latter sense on former occasions, I was giving a phenomenological description and not a metapsychological explanation of what was occurring.

This brings us to a further question: how is it possible, from an economic point of view, for a mere process of withdrawal and discharge, like the withdrawing of a pre-conscious ego-cathexis, to produce unpleasure or anxiety, seeing that, according to our assumptions, unpleasure and anxiety can only arise as a result of an *increase* in cathexis? The reply is that this causal sequence should not be explained from an economic point of view. In repression, anxiety is not newly created; it is reproduced as an affective state on the model of an already existing memory picture. If we go further and enquire into the origin of that anxiety—and of affects in general—we shall be leaving the realm of pure psychology and entering the confines of physiology. Affective states have become incorporated in the mind as precipitates of primeval traumatic experiences, and when a similar situation occurs they are revived in the form of memory symbols. I do not think I have been wrong in likening them to the more recent and individually acquired hysterical attack and in regarding them as normal prototypes of it. In man and the higher animals it would seem that the act of birth, as the individual's first experience of anxiety, has given the affect of anxiety certain characteristic forms of expression. But, while acknowledging this connection, we must not lay undue stress on it nor overlook the fact that biological necessity demands that a situation of danger should have an affective symbol, so that a symbol of this kind would have to be created in any case. Moreover, I do not think that we are justified in assuming that whenever there is an outbreak of anxiety something like a reproduction of the situation of birth goes on in the mind. It is not even certain whether hysterical attacks, though they were originally traumatic reproductions of this sort, permanently retain that character.

As I have shown elsewhere, most of the repressions with which we have to deal in our therapeutic work are cases of after-expulsion. They presuppose the operation of earlier, primal repressions which exert an attraction on the more recent situation. Far too little is known as yet about the background and preliminary stages of repression. There is a danger of over-estimating the part played in repression by the super-ego. We cannot at present say, for instance, whether it is the emergence of the super-ego which provides the line of demarcation between primal repression and after-expulsion. At any rate, the earliest outbreaks of anxiety, which are of a very intense kind, occur before the super-ego has become differentiated. It is highly probable that the precipitating causes of primal repression are quantitative factors such as an excessive degree of excitation and the breaking through of the protective barrier against stimuli.

This mention of the protective barrier sounds a note which recalls to us the fact that repressions occur in two different situations, namely, when an undesirable instinctual impulse is aroused by some external perception, and when it arises internally without any such provocation. We shall return to this difference presently. But the protective barrier only exists in regard to external stimuli, not in regard to internal instinctual demands.

So long as we direct our attention to the ego's attempt at flight, we shall get no nearer to the subject of symptom-formation. A symptom arises from an instinctual impulse which has been prejudicially affected by repression. If the ego, by making use of the signal of unpleasure, attains its object of completely suppressing the instinctual impulse, we learn nothing of how this has happened. We can only find out about it from those cases in which repression has to a greater or less extent failed. In this event the position, generally speaking, is that the instinctual impulse has found a substitute in spite of repression, but a substitute which is very much reduced, displaced, and inhibited, and which is no longer recognizable as a gratification. And when the impulse is carried out, there is no sensation of pleasure; its carrying out has, instead, the quality of a compulsion.

In thus degrading a gratificatory process to a symptom, repression displays its power in a further respect. The substitutive process is prevented, if possible, from finding discharge through motility; and even if this cannot be done the process is forced to expend itself in making alterations in the subject's own body and is not permitted to impinge upon the outer world. It may not be transformed into action. For, as we know, in repression the ego is operating under the influence of external reality and therefore it debars the substitutive process from having any effect upon that reality.

Just as the ego controls the path to action in regard to the outer world, so it controls access to consciousness. In repression it displays its power in both directions, acting, in the one manner, upon the instinctual impulse itself and, in the other, upon the psychical representative of that impulse. At this point it is relevant to ask how I can reconcile this acknowledgment of the might of the ego with the description of its position which I gave in *The Ego and the Id*. In that book I drew a picture of its dependence upon the id and upon the super-ego which revealed how powerless and apprehensive it was in regard to both and with what an effort it maintained its superiority over them. This view has been widely echoed in psycho-analytic literature. A great deal of stress has been laid on the weakness of the ego in relation to the id and of our rational elements in the face of the demonic forces within us; and there is a strong tendency to make what I have said into a foundation-stone of a psycho-analytic *Weltanschauung*. Yet surely the psycho-analyst, with his knowledge of the way in which repression works, should, of all people, be restrained from adopting such extreme and one-sided views.

I must confess that I am not at all partial to the fabrication of *Weltanschauungen*. Such activities may be left to philosophers, who avowedly find it impossible to make their journey through life without a Baedeker of that kind to tell them all about everything. Let us humbly accept the contempt with which they look down on us from the vantage-ground of their superior needs. But since we too cannot forego our narcissistic pride, we will draw comfort from the reflection that such "Guides to Life" soon grow out of date, and that it is precisely short-sighted, narrow, and finicky work like ours which obliges them to appear in new editions, and that even the most up-to-date of them are nothing but attempts to find a substitute for the ancient, useful, and all-embracing catechism. We know well enough how little light science has so far been able to throw on the problems that surround us. But however much ado the philosophers may make, they cannot alter the situation. Only patient, persevering research, in which everything is subordinated to the one requirement of certainty, can gradually bring about a change. The benighted traveller may sing aloud in the dark to deny his own fears; but, for all that, he will not see an inch further beyond his nose.

CHAPTER III

To return to this problem about the ego. The apparent contradiction is due to our having taken abstractions too rigidly and attended exclusively now to the one side and now to the other of what is in reality a complicated state of affairs. We were justified, I think, in dividing the ego from the id, for there were certain considerations which necessitated that step. On the other hand, the ego is identical with the id, and is merely a specially differentiated part of it. If we regard this part by itself, in contradistinction to the whole, or if a real split has occurred between the two, the weakness of the ego becomes apparent. But if the ego remains bound up with the id and indistinguishable from it, then it displays its power. The same is true of the relation between the ego and the super-ego. In many situations, the two are merged; and as a rule we can only distinguish one from the other when there is a tension or conflict between them. In repression, the decisive fact is that the ego is an organization and the id is not. The ego is, indeed, the organized portion of the id. We should be quite wrong in picturing the ego and the id as two opposing camps and in thinking that, when the ego tries to suppress a part of the id by means of repression, the remainder of the id comes to the rescue of the endangered part and measures its strength with the ego. This may often be what happens, but it is not the primary situation in repression. As a rule, the instinctual impulse which is to be repressed remains isolated. Although the act of repression demonstrates the strength of the ego, in one particular it reveals the ego's powerlessness and reveals, too, how impervious to influence are the separate instinctual impulses of the id. For the mental process, which has been turned into a symptom owing to repression, maintains its existence outside the organization of the ego and independently of it. Indeed, it is not the process alone but all its derivatives which enjoy, as it were, the privilege of extra-territoriality; and whenever they come into associative contact with a part of the ego-organization, it is not at all certain that they will not draw that part over to themselves and thus enlarge themselves at the expense of the ego. Long ago I compared a symptom to a foreign body which was keeping up a constant succession of stimuli and reactions in the tissue in which it was imbedded. It does sometimes happen that the defensive struggle against an unwelcome instinctual impulse is brought to an end with the formation of a symptom. As far as can be seen, this is most often possible in hysterical conversions. But usually the outcome is different. The initial act of repression is followed by tedious and often interminable manoeuvres in which the struggle against the instinctual impulse is prolonged into a struggle against the symptom.

In this secondary defensive struggle, the ego faces two ways. The one line of behaviour it adopts springs from the fact that its very nature obliges it to make what must be regarded as an attempt at restoration or reconciliation. The ego is an organization. It is based upon the maintenance of free intercourse and of the possibility of reciprocal influence between all its parts. Its de-sexualized energy still shows traces of its origin in its tendency to bind together and unify, and this necessity to synthetize grows stronger in proportion as the strength of the ego increases. It is therefore only natural that the ego should try to prevent symptoms from remaining isolated and foreign by using every possible method to bind them to itself in one way or another, and to incorporate them in its organization by means of those bonds. As we know, a tendency of this kind is already operative in the very act of forming a symptom. A classical instance of this are those hysterical symptoms which have been shown to be a compromise between the need for gratification and the need for punishment. Such symptoms participate in the ego from the very beginning, since they fulfil a requirement of the super-ego, while, on the other hand, they represent positions occupied by the repressed and points at which an irruption has been made by it into the ego-organization. They are a kind of frontier-position with a mixed cathexis. (Whether all primary hysterical symptoms are constructed on these lines would be worth enquiring into very carefully.) The ego now proceeds to behave as though it recognized that the symptom had come to stay and that the only thing to do was to accept the situation in good part and draw as much advantage from it as possible. It makes an adaptation to the symptom—to this piece of the internal world which is alien to it—just as it normally does to the objective, external world. It can always find plenty of opportunities for doing so. The presence of a symptom may entail a certain impairment of the capacities of the individual, and this can be exploited to appease some demand on the part of the super-ego or to refuse some requirement coming from the external world. In this way, the symptom gradually grows to be the representative of important interests; it is found to be useful for the maintenance of the self and becomes more and more closely merged with the ego and more and more indispensable to it. It is only very rarely that the physical process of *healing* round a foreign body follows such a course as this. There is a danger, too, of exaggerating the importance of a secondary adaptation of this kind to a symptom, and of saying that the ego has created the symptom merely in order to enjoy its advantages. It would be equally true to say that a man who had lost his leg in the war had got it shot away so that he might thenceforward live on his pension without having to work any more.

In obsessional neurosis and paranoia, the forms which the symptoms assume become very valuable to the ego because they obtain for it, not certain advantages, but a narcissistic gratification which it would otherwise forgo. The symptoms which the obsessional neurotic constructs flatter his self-esteem by making him feel that he is better than others because he is specially cleanly or specially conscientious. The delusional constructions of the paranoiac offer to his acute perceptive and imaginative powers a field of activity which he could not easily find elsewhere.

All of this results in what is known as the *epinosic gain* of a neurosis. This epinosic gain comes to the assistance of the ego in its endeavour to incorporate the symptom and increases the fixation of the latter. When the analyst tries to help the ego in its struggle against the symptom, he finds that these reconciliatory bonds between ego and symptom operate on the side of the resistances and that they are not easy to loosen.

The two lines of behaviour which the ego adopts towards the symptom are in fact directly opposed to each other. For the other line is less friendly in character, since it continues in the direction of repression. Nevertheless the ego, it appears, cannot be accused of inconsistency. Being of a peaceable disposition it would like to incorporate the symptom in its framework. It is from the symptom itself that the trouble comes. For the symptom, being the true substitute and derivative of the repressed impulse, carries on the rôle of the latter; it continually renews its demands for gratification and thus obliges the ego in its turn to give the signal of unpleasure and put itself in a posture of defence.

The secondary defensive struggle against the symptom is many-sided. It is fought out on many fields and makes use of a multitude of means. We shall not be able to say much about it until we have made an enquiry into individual cases of symptom-formation. In doing this we shall have an opportunity of going into the problem of anxiety—a problem which has long been looming in the background. The wisest plan will be, I think, to start from the symptoms produced by the hysterical neuroses; for we are not as yet in a position to consider the conditions in which the symptoms of obsessional neurosis, paranoia, and other neuroses are formed.

CHAPTER IV

LET us take as our first example an infantile hysterical phobia of animals. We will select the case of Little Hans,[1] whose phobia of horses was undoubtedly typical in all its main features. The first thing that is apparent is that in a concrete case of neurotic illness the state of affairs is much more complex than one would suppose so long as one was dealing with abstractions. It takes some time to orientate oneself and to decide which the repressed impulse is, what substitutive symptom it has found and where the motive for repression lies.

Little Hans refused to go out into the street because he was afraid of horses. This is the raw material of the case. Which part of it constitutes the symptoms? Is it his having the fear? Is it his choice of an object for his fear? Is it his giving up his freedom of movement? Or is it several of these combined? What is the gratification which he renounces? And why does he have to renounce it?

At a first glance one is tempted to reply that the case is not so very obscure. Little Hans's unaccountable fear of horses is the symptom, and his inability to go out into the streets is an inhibition, a restriction which his ego has imposed on itself so as not to arouse the anxiety-symptom. The second point is clearly correct; and in the discussion which follows I shall not concern myself any further with this inhibition. As regards what was presumably the symptom, a superficial acquaintance with the case does not even disclose its true formulation. For further investigation shows that what he was suffering from was not a vague fear of horses but a quite definite apprehension that a horse was going to bite him. This idea, indeed, was endeavouring to withdraw from consciousness and get itself replaced by an undefined phobia in which only the anxiety and its object still appeared. Was it perhaps this idea which was the nucleus of his symptom?

We shall not make any headway until we have reviewed the little boy's psychological situation as a whole as it came to light in the course of analytic treatment. He was at that time in the Oedipus position, with its attendant feelings of jealousy and hostility towards his father whom nevertheless—except in so far as his mother was the cause of estrangement—he dearly loved. Here, then, we have a conflict due to ambivalence: a firmly rooted love and a no less well grounded hatred directed against

one and the same person. Little Hans's phobia must be an attempt to solve this conflict. Conflicts of this kind due to ambivalence are very frequent and they can have another typical outcome, in which one of the two conflicting feelings (usually that of affection) becomes enormously enhanced and the other vanishes. Only the exaggerated degree and compulsive character of the feeling that remains betray the fact that it is not the sole one in existence but is continually on the alert to keep the opposite feeling under suppression, and enables us to postulate the operation of a process which we call *repression by means of reaction-formation* (in the ego). Cases like Little Hans's show no traces of a reaction-formation of this kind. There are clearly different ways of egress from a conflict of ambivalence.

Meanwhile we have been able to establish another point with certainty. The instinctual impulse which underwent repression in Little Hans was a hostile one against his father. Proof of this was obtained in his analysis while the idea of the biting horse was being followed up. Hans had seen a horse fall down and he had also seen a playmate, with whom he was playing at horses, fall down and hurt himself. Analysis justified the inference that he had a conative impulse that his father should fall down and hurt himself as his playmate and the horse had done. Moreover, his attitude towards someone's departure on a certain occasion makes it probable that his wish that his father should be out of the way found a less hesitating expression. But a wish of this sort is tantamount to an intention of putting the father out of the way oneself—is tantamount, that is, to the murderous impulse which is one component of the Oedipus complex.

So far there seem to be no connecting links between Little Hans's repressed instinctual impulse and the substitute for it which we suspect is to be seen in his phobia of horses. Let us simplify his psychological situation by setting on one side the elements of infancy and ambivalence. Let us imagine that he is a young servant who is in love with the mistress of the house and has received some tokens of her favour. He hates his master, who is more powerful than he, and he would like to have him out of the way. It would then be eminently natural for him to be afraid of his master and to dread his vengeance—just as Little Hans was frightened of horses. We cannot, therefore, describe the anxiety belonging to this phobia as a symptom. If Little Hans, being in love

[1] Freud, "Analysis of a Phobia in a Five-Year-Old Boy" (1909), *Collected Papers,* III.

with his mother, had shown fear of his father, we should have no right to say that he had a neurosis or a phobia. His emotional reaction would have been entirely comprehensible. What made it a neurosis was one thing alone: the replacement of his father by a horse. It is this displacement, then, which has a claim to be called a symptom, and which, incidentally, constitutes the alternative mechanism which enables a conflict due to ambivalence to be resolved without the aid of a reaction-formation. Such a displacement is made possible or facilitated at Little Hans's early age because the inborn traces of totemistic thought can still be easily revived. Children do not as yet recognize or, at any rate, lay such exaggerated stress upon the gulf that separates human beings from the animal world. In their eyes the grown man, the object of their fear and admiration, still belongs to the same category as the big animal who has so many enviable attributes but against whom they have been warned because he may become dangerous. As we see, the conflict of ambivalence is not dealt with in relation to one and the same person; it is circumvented, as it were, by one of the pair of conflicting impulses being directed to a vicarious figure.

So far everything is clear. But the analysis of Little Hans's phobia has been very disappointing in one respect. The distortion which constituted the symptom-formation was not applied to the psychical representative (the ideational content) of the instinctual impulse that was to be repressed; it was applied to a quite different representative and one which only corresponded to a *reaction* to the disagreeable instinct. It would be more in accordance with our expectations if Little Hans had developed, instead of a fear of horses, an inclination to ill-treat them and to beat them or if he had expressed in strong terms a wish to see them fall down or to be hurt or even die in agony ("make a row with their feet"). Something of the sort did in fact emerge in his analysis, but it was not by any means in the forefront of his neurosis. And, curiously enough, if he really had produced an animosity of this sort not against his father but against horses as his main symptom, we should not have said that he was suffering from a neurosis. There must be something amiss either with our view of repression or with our definition of a symptom. One thing strikes us at once: if Little Hans had really behaved in such a way to horses it would mean that repression had in no way altered the character of his objectionable and aggressive impulses themselves but only the object against which they were directed.

Undoubtedly there are cases in which this is all that repression does. But more than this has happened in the development of Little Hans's phobia—how much more can be guessed from another analysis.

As we know, Little Hans alleged that what he was afraid of was that a horse would bite him. Now sometime later I was able to learn something about the origin of another animal phobia. In this instance the dreaded animal was a wolf; it, too, had the significance of a father-substitute.[1] As a boy the patient in question—a Russian whom I did not analyse until he had reached his thirties—had had a dream (whose meaning was revealed in analysis) and immediately after it had developed a fear of being eaten up by a wolf, like the seven little goats in the fairy tale. In the case of Little Hans, the ascertained fact that his father used to play at horses with him doubtless determined his choice of a horse as his anxiety-animal. In the same way it appeared at least highly probable that the father of my Russian patient used, when playing with him, to pretend to be a wolf and jokingly threaten to eat him up. Since then I have come across a third instance. The patient was a young American who came to me for treatment. True, he had not developed an actual animal phobia, but it was precisely because of this omission that his case helped to throw light upon the other two. As a child he had been sexually excited by a fantastic children's story which had been read aloud to him about an Arab chief who pursued a gingerbread man so as to eat him up. He identified himself with this edible person, and the Arab chief was easily recognizable as a father-substitute. This phantasy formed the substratum of his auto-erotic phantasies.

The idea of being devoured by the father is typical, age-old and common to all children. It has familiar parallels in mythology (the myth of Cronos) and in the animal kingdom. Yet in spite of this, such an idea is so strange to us that we can hardly credit its existence in a child. Nor do we know whether it really means what it seems to, and we cannot understand how it can have become the subject-matter of a phobia. Analytic observation supplies the requisite information. It shows that the idea of being eaten by the father gives

[1] Freud, "From the History of an Infantile Neurosis" (1918), *Collected Papers*, III.

expression, in a form that has undergone regressive degradation, to a passive, tender impulse to be loved by him in a genital-erotic way.

Further research into the case-history of the Wolf Man leaves no doubt of the correctness of this explanation. The genital impulse, it is true, betrays no sign of its tender inclination when it is expressed in the language belonging to that transition phase between the oral and sadistic organization of the libido which has been left behind. Besides, is it merely a question of the replacement of a particular psychical representative by a regressive form of expression, or is it a question of the genuine regressive degradation of a genitally orientated impulse in the id? It is not at all easy to make certain. The case-history of the Wolf Man gives very definite support to the second, more serious, view, for, from the time of the decisive dream onward, the boy became naughty, tormenting, and sadistic, and soon after developed a regular obsessional neurosis. At any rate we can see that repression is not the only means which the ego can employ for the purpose of defence against an unwelcome instinctual impulse. If it succeeds in making an instinct regress, it will actually have done it much more injury than it could have by repressing it. Sometimes, indeed, after forcing an instinct to regress in this way, it goes on to repress it.

The case of the Wolf Man and the somewhat less complicated one of Little Hans raise a number of further considerations. But we already learn two unexpected facts. There can be no doubt that the instinctual impulse which was repressed in both phobias was a hostile one against the father. One might say that that impulse had been repressed by being reversed. Instead of aggressiveness *towards* the father there appeared aggressiveness *from* the father in the shape of revenge. Since this aggressiveness is in any case rooted in the sadistic phase of the libido, a certain degree of degradation of it is all that is needed to reduce it to the oral stage. This stage, while only adumbrated in Little Hans's fear of being bitten, was blatantly exhibited in the Wolf Man's terror of being devoured. But, besides this, the analysis has demonstrated, beyond a shadow of a doubt, the presence of another instinctual impulse of an opposite nature which had succumbed to repression. This was a loving, passive impulse directed towards the father, which had already attained the genital (phallic) level of libidinal organization. As regards the final outcome of

the process of repression, this impulse seems, indeed, to have been the more important of the two; it underwent a more far-reaching regression and had a decisive influence upon the content of the phobia. In following up a single current of instinctual repression, we have thus come upon a confluence of two. The two instinctual impulses that have been overtaken by repression—sadistic aggressiveness towards the father and passive affection for him—form a pair of opposites. Furthermore, a full comprehension of Little Hans's case shows that the formation of his phobia had had the effect of abolishing his affectionate object-cathexis of his mother as well, though the actual content of his phobia betrayed no sign of it. The process of repression had attacked almost all the components of his Oedipus complex—both his hostile and his tender impulses towards his father and his tender impulses towards his mother. In my Russian patient, this state of affairs was much less patent.

These are unwelcome complications, considering that we only set out to study simple cases of symptom-formation and with that intention selected the earliest and, to all appearances, most transparent neuroses of childhood. Instead of a single repression we have found a collection of them and have become involved with regression into the bargain. Perhaps we have added to the confusion by treating the two cases of animal phobia at our disposal— Little Hans and the Wolf Man—as though they were cast in the same mould. As a matter of fact, certain differences between them stand out. It is only with regard to Little Hans that we can positively assert that what his phobia disposed of were the two main impulses of the Oedipus complex, viz., his aggressiveness towards his father and his over-fondness for his mother. A tender feeling for his father was undoubtedly there too and played a part in repressing the opposite feeling; but we can prove neither that it was strong enough to draw repression upon itself nor that it subsided after his phobia appeared. Hans seems, in fact, to have been a normal boy with what is called a *positive* Oedipus complex. It is possible that those factors which seem not to have been present were actually at work in him, but we cannot demonstrate their existence. Even the most exhaustive analysis has gaps in its data and is insufficiently documented. In the case of the Wolf Man something different is lacking. His attitude to female objects had been disturbed by an early seduction, and his passive, feminine side was strongly developed. The analysis of his wolf-dream revealed very little intentional aggressiveness towards his father, but it brought forward unmistakable proof that his passive tender attitude to his father had been overtaken by repression. In his case, too, the other factors may have been operative as well; but they were not visible. How is it that, whereas these differences between the two cases almost amount to an antithesis, the final outcome—a phobia—was approximately the same? The answer must be sought in another quarter. I think it will be found in the second fact which emerges from our brief comparative examination. It seems to me that in both cases we can detect what the motive force of the repression was and can substantiate our view of its nature from the line of development which the two children subsequently pursued. This motive force was identical in both. It was the fear of impending castration. Little Hans gave up his aggressiveness towards his father from fear of being castrated. His fear that a horse would bite him can easily be extended into meaning a fear that a horse would bite off his genitals, would castrate him. But it was from fear of being castrated, too, that the little Russian relinquished his desire to be loved by his father, for he thought that a relation of that sort presupposed a sacrifice of his genitals—of the organ which distinguished him from women. As we see, both forms of the Oedipus complex, the normal, active form and the inverted one, are broken down by the castration complex. The Russian boy's anxiety-idea of being eaten up by a wolf contained, it is true, no suggestion of castration, for the oral regression it had undergone had removed it too far from the phallic stage. But the analysis of his dream rendered further proof superfluous. It was a triumph of repression that the form in which his phobia was expressed should no longer have contained any allusion to castration.

So now we have made the unexpected discovery that in both patients the motive force of the repression was a fear of castration. The ideational content of their anxiety—being bitten by a horse and being eaten up by a wolf—was a substitute by distortion for the idea of being castrated by their father. It was this idea which had undergone repression. In the Russian boy the idea was an expression of a desire which was not able to subsist in the face of his masculine revolt; in Little Hans it was the expression of a reaction in him which had

turned his aggressiveness into its opposite. But the *affect* of anxiety, which was the essence of their phobia, came, not from the process of repression, not from the libidinal cathexes of the repressed impulses, but from the repressing agency itself. The anxiety belonging to the animal phobias was an untransformed fear of castration. It was therefore an objective fear, a fear of a danger which actually was imminent or believed to be so. It was anxiety which produced repression, and not, as I formerly believed, repression which produced anxiety.

I cannot deny the fact, though it is not pleasant to recall it, that I have on many occasions asserted that in repression the psychical representative of the instinct is distorted, displaced, etc., while the libido belonging to the instinctual impulse is transformed into anxiety. But now an examination of phobias, which should be best able to provide confirmatory evidence, fails to bear out my assertion. The anxiety felt in animal phobias is the castration anxiety of the ego; while the anxiety felt in agoraphobia (a subject that has been less thoroughly studied) seems to be a fear of incurring sexual temptation—a fear which, after all, must be connected in its origins with the fear of castration. As far as can be seen at present, the majority of phobias go back to an anxiety of this kind felt by the ego in regard to the demands of the libido. It is always the ego's attitude of anxiety which is the primary thing and which sets repression going. Anxiety never arises from repressed libido. If I had formerly been content to say that·after the occurrence of repression there appeared, in place of the manifestation of libido that was to be expected, a certain amount of anxiety, I should have nothing to retract today. The description would be correct; and there does undoubtedly exist a correspondence of the kind asserted between the strength of the impulse that has to be repressed and the intensity of the resultant anxiety. But I must admit that I thought I was giving more than a mere description. I believed I had put my finger on a metapsychological process of direct transformation of libido into anxiety. I can now no longer maintain this view. And, indeed, I found it impossible at the time to explain how a transformation of that kind was carried out.

It may be asked how I arrived at this idea of transformation in the first instance. It was while I was studying the actual neuroses, at a time when analysis was still a very long way from distinguishing between processes in the ego and processes in the id. I found that outbreaks of anxiety and a general state of anxiety-preparedness were produced by certain sexual practices such as *coitus interruptus,* undischarged sexual excitement, or enforced abstinence—that is, whenever sexual excitement was inhibited, arrested, or deflected in its progress towards gratification. Since sexual excitement was an expression of libidinal instinctual impulses, it did not seem too rash to assume that the libido was turned into anxiety through the agency of these disturbances. The observations which I made at the time still hold good. Moreover, it cannot be denied that the libido belonging to the id-processes is subjected to interruption at the instigation of repression. We can still maintain, therefore, that in repression anxiety is produced from the libidinal cathexes of the instinctual impulses. But how can we reconcile this conclusion with our other conclusion that the anxiety felt in phobias is an ego anxiety and arises in the ego, and that it does not proceed out of repression but, on the contrary, sets repression in motion? There seems to be a contradiction here which is not at all simple to solve. It will not be easy to reduce the two sources of anxiety to a single one. We might attempt to do so by supposing that, when coitus is disturbed or sexual excitement interrupted or abstinence enforced, the ego scents certain dangers to which it reacts with anxiety. But this takes us nowhere. On the other hand, our analysis of the phobias seems to admit of no correction. *Non liquet.*[1]

CHAPTER V

WE set out to study the formation of symptoms and the secondary struggle waged by the ego against symptoms. But in picking on the phobias for this purpose we have clearly made an unlucky choice. The anxiety which predominates in them appears to complicate and obscure the picture. There are plenty of neuroses which exhibit no anxiety whatever. True conversion-hysteria is one of these. Even in its most severe symptoms no admixture of anxiety is found. This fact alone ought to warn us against making too close a connection between anxiety and symptom-formation. The phobias are so closely akin to conversion-hysteria in every other respect that I have felt justified in classing them with it under the name of *anxiety-hysteria.* But no one has as yet been able to say what it is that determines whether any given case shall take the form of a conversion-

[1] It is not clear.—ED.

hysteria or a phobia—has been able, that is to say, to establish how the production of anxiety in hysteria is conditioned.

The commonest symptoms of conversion-hysteria—motor paralyses, contractures, involuntary actions or discharges, pains, and hallucinations—are cathectic processes which are either permanently maintained or intermittent. But this puts fresh difficulties in the way. Not much is actually known about these symptoms. Analysis can show what the disturbed excitatory process is which the symptoms replace. It usually turns out that they themselves have a share in that process. It is as though they had concentrated in themselves the whole energy of the process. For instance, it will be found that the pains from which a patient suffers were present in the situation in which the repression occurred; or that his hallucination was, at that time, a perception; or that his motor paralysis stands for a defence against an action which he had meant to perform but which had been inhibited; or that his contracture is usually a displacement of an intended innervation of the muscles in some other part of his body; or that his convulsions are the equivalent of an outburst of affect which has been withdrawn from the normal control of the ego. The sensation of unpleasure which accompanies the appearance of the symptoms varies in a striking degree. In chronic symptoms which have been displaced on to motility, like paralyses and contractures, it is almost always entirely absent; the ego behaves towards the symptoms as though it had nothing to do with them. In intermittent symptoms and in those concerned with the sensory field, unpleasure is as a rule distinctly felt; and in symptoms of pain it may reach an extreme degree. The picture presented is so manifold that it is difficult to discover the factor which permits of all these variations and yet establishes a uniformity in them. There is, moreover, little to be seen in conversion-hysteria of the ego's struggle against the symptom after it has been formed. It is only when sensitivity to pain in some part of the body constitutes the symptom that that symptom is in a position to play a dual rôle. In that case the symptom of pain will appear no less regularly whenever the part of the body concerned is touched from outside than when the pathogenic situation which it represents is associatively activated from within; and the ego will take precautions to prevent the symptom from being aroused through external perceptions. Why the formation of symptoms in conversion-hysteria should be such a peculiarly obscure thing I do not know; but the fact provides us with a good reason for quitting such an unproductive field of enquiry.

Let us turn to the obsessional neuroses in the hope of learning more about the formation of symptoms. The symptoms belonging to this neurosis fall, in general, into two groups, each having an opposite bias. They are either prohibitions, precautions and expiations—that is, negative in character—or they are substitutive gratifications often appearing in symbolic disguise. The negative, defensive group of symptoms is the more primary of the two; but as the illness is prolonged the gratificatory group, overriding all defensive measures, gains the upper hand. The symptom-formation scores a triumph if it succeeds in combining the two by joining to what was originally a defensive command or prohibition the significance of a gratification; and in order to achieve this end it will often make use of the most ingenious associative paths. Such an achievement demonstrates the tendency of the ego to synthetization which it has already been seen to possess. In extreme cases the patient manages to make most of his symptoms have, in addition to their original meaning, a directly contrary one. This is a tribute to the power of ambivalence, which, no one knows why, plays such a large part in obsessional neuroses. In the crudest instance the symptom has two phases: an action which carries out a certain injunction is immediately succeeded by another action which stops or undoes the first one, even if it does not go quite so far as to carry out its opposite.

Two impressions at once emerge from this brief survey of obsessional symptoms. The first is that a ceaseless struggle is being waged against the repressed, in which the repressing forces steadily lose ground; the second is that the ego and the super-ego have a specially large share in the formation of the symptoms.

Obsessional neurosis is unquestionably the most interesting and repaying subject of analytic research. But as a problem it has not yet been mastered. It must be confessed that, if we endeavour to penetrate more deeply into its nature, we still have to rely upon doubtful assumptions and unconfirmed suppositions. Obsessional neurosis originates, no doubt, in the same situation as hysteria, namely, the necessity of warding off the libidinal demands of the Oedipus complex. Indeed, every obsessional neurosis seems to have a substratum of hysterical symptoms that have been formed at a very early stage. But it is subsequently shaped along quite different lines owing to a constitutional factor. The genital organization of the libido turns out to be weak and insufficiently resistant, so that when the ego begins its defensive actions the first thing it succeeds in doing is to throw back, in part or altogether, the genital organization (of the phallic phase) on to the earlier sadistic-anal level. This phenomenon of regression is decisive for all that follows.

Another possibility has to be considered. Perhaps regression is the result not of a constitutional factor but of a time-factor. It may be that regression is rendered possible not because the genital organization of the libido is too weak, but because the opposition of the ego begins too early, while the sadistic phase is at its height. I am not prepared to express an absolute opinion on this point, but I may say that analytic observation does not speak in favour of such an assumption. It rather tends to show that by the time an obsessional neurosis begins to show itself the phallic stage has already been attained. Moreover, the onset of this neurosis belongs to a later time of life than that of hysteria. It sets in in the second period of childhood, with the latency period. In a patient whose case I was able to study and who was overtaken by this disorder at a very late date, it became clear that the determining cause of his regression and of the emergence of his obsessional neurosis was a real occurrence that impaired a genital life which had up till then been intact.

As regards a metapsychological explanation of regression I am inclined to find it in a *defusion of instinct*, in a detachment of the erotic components which, at the beginning of the genital stage, had become joined to the destructive cathexes belonging to the sadistic phase.

In bringing regression about, the ego scores the first point in its defensive struggle against the demands of the libido. In this connection we shall find it advantageous to distinguish the more general notion of *defence* from *repression*. Repression is only one of the mechanisms which defence makes use of. It is perhaps in obsessional cases more than in normal or hysterical ones that we can most clearly recognize that the motive force of defence is the castration complex and that what is being warded off are the trends of the Oedipus complex. We are at present dealing with the beginning of the latency period, a period which is characterized by the passing away of the Oedipus complex, the

creation or consolidation of the super-ego and
the erection of ethical and aesthetic barriers in
the ego. In obsessional neuroses, these processes are carried further than is normal. In
order to effect the destruction of the Oedipus
complex, a regressive degradation of the libido
takes place as well, the super-ego becomes exceptionally severe and unkind, and the ego, in
obedience to the super-ego, produces strong reaction-formations in the shape of conscientiousness, pity, and cleanliness. Implacable, though
not therefore always successful, severity is
shown in putting down the temptation to continue early infantile masturbation which is now
attached to regressive (sadistic-anal) ideational
images but which still represents the unsub-
jugated part of the phallic organization. There
is an inherent contradiction about this state of
affairs, in which, precisely in the interests of
masculinity (castration anxiety), every activity
belonging to masculinity is stopped. But here,
too, obsessional neurosis is only overdoing the
normal method of abolishing the Oedipus complex. We once more find an illustration of the
truth that every exaggeration contains the seed
of its own destruction. For, under the guise of
obsessional acts, the masturbation that has
been suppressed approaches ever more closely
to gratification.

The reaction-formations in the ego of the
obsessional neurotic, which we have recognized
as exaggerations of normal character-formation,
should be regarded, I think, as yet another
mechanism of defence and placed on the same
level as regression and repression. They seem
to be absent or very much weaker in hysteria.
Looking back, we can now get an idea of what
is peculiar to the defensive process in hysteria.
It seems that in it the process is limited to
repression alone. The ego turns away from the
disagreeable instinctual impulse and leaves it to
pursue its course in the unconscious, taking no
further part in its lot. This view cannot be
absolutely correct, for we are acquainted with
the case in which a hysterical symptom is at
the same time a fulfilment of a penalty imposed by the super-ego; but it may describe a
general characteristic of the behaviour of the
ego in hysteria.

We can either simply accept it as a fact that
in obsessional neurosis a super-ego of this severe
kind emerges, or we can take the regression of
the libido as the fundamental characteristic of
the affection and attempt to relate the severity
of the super-ego to it. And indeed, the super-
ego, originating as it does in the id, cannot dis-

sociate itself from the regression and defusion
of instinct whch have taken place there. We
cannot be surprised if it becomes harsher, un-
kinder, and more tormenting than where development has been normal.

The chief task during the latency period
seems to be the warding off of the temptation
to masturbate. This struggle produces a series
of symptoms which appear in a typical fashion
in the most different individuals and which
bear the general character of ceremonial. It is
a great pity that no one has as yet collected
them and systematically analysed them. Being
the earliest products of the neurosis, they
should best be able to shed light on the mechanisms employed in its symptom-formation.
They already exhibit those features which are
destined to come to the fore so fatefully in the
serious illness that lies ahead—the manner in
which the symptoms are introduced into certain procedures (which later on become almost
automatic) in connection with going to sleep,
washing, dressing, and walking about, as well
as the tendency to repetition and delay. Why
this should be so is at present not at all clear;
but the sublimation of anal-erotic components
plays an unmistakable part.

The advent of puberty opens a new chapter
in the history of an obsessional neurosis. The
organization at the genital level which has been
stopped in childhood starts again with great
vigour. But, as we know, the sexual development of the child determines what direction
this new start will take. Not only will the early
aggressive impulses be reawakened; but a
greater or lesser proportion of the new libidinal
impulses—in bad cases the whole of them—
will have to follow the course prescribed for
them by regression and will emerge as aggressive and destructive tendencies. In consequence
of the erotic trends being disguised in this way
and owing to the powerful reaction-formations
in the ego, the struggle against sexuality will
henceforward be carried on under the banner
of ethical principles. The ego will recoil with
astonishment from promptings to cruelty and
violence which enter consciousness from the
id, and it has no notion that in them it is combating erotic wishes, including many which it
would otherwise not have taken exception to.
The super-ego, overstrict as it is, insists all the
more strongly on the suppression of sexuality,
seeing that the latter has assumed such repulsive forms. Thus in obsessional neurosis the
conflict is aggravated in two directions: the
defensive forces become more intolerant and

the forces that are to be kept off more intolerable. Both effects are due to one factor, namely, regression of the libido.

Much of what has been said may be objected to on the ground that the unpleasant obsessive ideas are themselves conscious. But there is no doubt that before becoming conscious they have been through a process of repression. In most of them the actual text of the aggressive instinctual impulse is altogether unknown to the ego, and it requires a good deal of analytic work to make it conscious. What does penetrate into consciousness is usually only a distorted substitute which is either of a vague, dream-like, and confused nature, or so travestied as to be unrecognizable. Even where repression has not encroached upon the content of the aggressive impulse, it has certainly abolished its accompanying affective quality, with the result that the aggressiveness appears to the ego not to be an impulsion but, as the patients themselves say, merely an *idea* which awakens no feeling. But the remarkable thing is that this is not the case. What happens is that the affect which has been left out when the obsessional idea is perceived appears in a different place. The super-ego behaves as though repression had not occurred and as though it knew the real formulation and full affective quality of the aggressive impulse, and it treats the ego accordingly. The ego which, on the one hand, knows that it is innocent must, on the other, accept a sense of guilt and carry a responsibility which it cannot account for. This state of affairs is, however, not so puzzling as it would seem at first sight. The behaviour of the super-ego is perfectly intelligible, and the contradiction in the ego merely shows that it has shut out the id by means of repression while remaining fully accessible to the influence of the super-ego.[1] If it is asked why the ego does not also attempt to withdraw itself from the painful criticism of the super-ego, the simple answer is that it does manage to do so in a great number of instances. There are obsessional neuroses in which no sense of guilt whatever is present. In them, as far as can be seen, the ego has avoided becoming aware of it by instituting a new set of symptoms, penances, or restrictions of a self-punishing kind. These symptoms represent at the same time a gratification of masochistic impulses which, in their turn, have been reinforced by regression.

Obsessional neurosis presents such a vast multiplicity of phenomena that we have never yet succeeded in making a coherent synthesis of all its variations. All we can do is to pick out certain typical correlations; but there is always the risk that we may have overlooked other uniformities of a no less important kind.

I have already described the general tendency of symptom-formation in obsessional neurosis. It is to give ever greater room to substitutive gratification at the expense of frustration. Symptoms which once stood for a restriction of the ego come later on to represent gratifications as well, thanks to the ego's inclination to synthetize, and it is quite clear that this second meaning gradually becomes the more important of the two. The result of this process, which approximates more and more to a complete failure of the original purpose of defence, is an extremely restricted ego which is reduced to seeking gratification in the symptoms. The displacement of the distribution of forces in favour of gratification may have the alarming outcome of paralysing the will of the ego, so that in every decision that it has to make it is almost as strongly impelled from the one side as from the other. The acute conflict between id and super-ego which has dominated the illness from the very beginning may assume such extensive proportions that the ego, unable to carry out its office of mediator, can undertake nothing which is not drawn into the sphere of that conflict.

CHAPTER VI

IN the course of these struggles, two activities of the ego of a symptom-forming kind are observable, which deserve special attention because they are obviously surrogates of repression and therefore well suited to illustrate its purpose and technique. The fact that such auxiliary and substitutive techniques emerge may argue that true repression has met with difficulties in its functioning. If one considers how much more the ego is the scene of action of symptom-formation in obsessional neurosis than it is in hysteria and with what tenacity it clings to its relations to reality, employing all its intellectual faculties to that end—so much so that the very process of thinking becomes hyper-cathected and eroticized—then one may perhaps get a closer idea of the importance of these variations of repression.

The two techniques I refer to are *undoing what has been done* and *isolating*. The first of these has a wide range of application and goes back very far. It is, as it were, a negative magic,

[1] Cf. Theodor Reik, *Geständniszwang und Strafbedürfnis*, 1925, p. 51.

and endeavours, by means of motor symbolism, to "blow away" not merely the consequence of some occurrence, experience, or impression, but those very events themselves. I choose the term "blow away" advisedly, so as to remind the reader of the part played by this technique not only in neuroses but in magical acts, popular customs, and religious ceremonies as well. In obsessional neurosis we first come across the technique of undoing what has been done in symptoms which occur in two phases—*dichronous* symptoms—in which one action is cancelled out by a second, so that it is as though neither action had taken place, whereas, in reality, both have. This aim of undoing is the second underlying motive of obsessional ceremonials, the first being to take precautions in order to prevent the occurrence or recurrence of some given event. The difference between the two is easily seen: the precautionary measures are rational, whilst the measures taken to abolish something by undoing it are irrational and magical. It is of course to be suspected that the latter is the earlier motive of the two and proceeds from an animistic attitude towards the environment. This endeavour to undo shades off into normal behaviour in the case in which a person decides to regard an event as not having happened. But whereas he will take no direct steps against the event, and will simply look away from it and its consequences, the neurotic person will try to make the past itself non-existent. He will try to repress it by motor means. The same aim may perhaps be present in and account for the compulsion to repeat actions which is so frequently met with in obsessional neuroses and which serves a number of contradictory purposes at once. When anything has not happened in the desired way, it can be undone by being repeated in a different way; and now all the motives that exist for lingering over such repetitions come into play as well. As the neurosis proceeds, we often find that one symptom-forming motive of first-rate importance is the endeavour to undo a traumatic experience. We thus unexpectedly discover a new, motor technique of defence, or (as we may say in this case with less inaccuracy) of repression.

The second of these techniques that we are setting out to describe for the first time, that of isolation, is characteristic for obsessional neurosis. It, too, takes place in the motor sphere. When the subject has done something which has a significance for his neurosis, or after something unpleasant has happened, he will interpolate an interval during which nothing further may happen—during which he may perceive nothing and do nothing. This behaviour, which seems so strange at first sight, is soon seen to have a relation to repression. We know that in hysteria a traumatic experience is able to be overtaken by amnesia. In obsessional neurosis this can often not be achieved. But, instead of being forgotten, the experience is deprived of its affect, and its associative connections are suppressed or interrupted so that it remains as though isolated and is not reproduced in the ordinary processes of thought. The effect of isolation is thus the same as the effect of repression with amnesia. This technique is, then, carried out in the isolations of obsessional neurosis. It is at the same time reinforced in a magical sense from the motor sphere. The elements that are held apart in this way are precisely those which belong together associatively. Motor isolation is meant to ensure an interruption of the connection in thought. The normal phenomenon of concentration provides a pretext for this kind of neurotic procedure. The normal person concentrates on what seems to him important in the way of an impression or a piece of work in order that it shall not be interfered with by the intrusion of any other mental processes or activities. But even he uses concentration to keep away not only what is irrelevant or unimportant to the matter in hand, but, above all, what is unsuitable because it is contradictory. He is most disturbed by those elements which once belonged to it but which have been discarded in the course of his development—as, for instance, by any manifestation of the ambivalence belonging to his father complex in his relation to God, or by any impulses attached to his excretory organs in his emotions of love. Thus, in the normal course of things, the ego has a great deal of isolating work to do in its function of directing the current of thought. And, as we know, in carrying out our analytic technique we have to train it to relinquish that function, eminently justified as it is in itself, for the time being.

All analysts have found that it is especially difficult for the obsessional neurotic to carry out the fundamental rule of psycho-analytic treatment. Probably his ego is more watchful and makes sharper isolations because of the high degree of tension due to conflict that exists between his super-ego and his id. While his thoughts are working, his ego has to keep off too much in the way of an intrusion of unconscious phantasies or a manifestation of am-bivalent trends. It must not relax, but is constantly prepared for a struggle. It fortifies its compulsion to concentrate and to isolate by the help of those magical acts of isolation which, in the form of symptoms, grow to be so noticeable and to have so much practical importance for the patient, but which are actually, of course, useless and in the nature of ceremonials.

But in thus endeavouring to prevent associations and connections of thought, the ego is obeying one of the oldest and most fundamental commands of obsessional neurosis, the taboo of touching. If one asks oneself why the avoidance of touching, contact, or contamination should play such a large part in this neurosis and should become the subject-matter of complicated systems, the answer is that touching and physical contact are the immediate aim of the aggressive as well as the loving object-cathexes. Eros desires contact because it strives to make the ego and the loved object one, to abolish all barriers of distance between them. But the first requisite of destructiveness, too, which (before the invention of long-range weapons) can only take effect at close quarters, is physical contact, a coming to grips. To *touch* a woman has become a euphemism for using her as a sexual object. No to *touch* one's genitals is the phrase employed for forbidding auto-erotic gratification. Since obsessional neurosis begins by persecuting touching in its erotic sense and then, after regression has taken place, goes on to persecute it in its new sense of aggressiveness, nothing is so strongly proscribed in this illness as touching nor so well suited to become the central point of a system of prohibitions. Now, to isolate a thing is to banish the possibility of its being touched, to withdraw it from any sort of contact. When a neurotic isolates an impression or an activity by interpolating an interval, he lets it be understood symbolically that he will not allow his thoughts about that impression or activity to come into associative contact with his other thoughts.

This is as far as our investigations into the formation of symptoms take us. It is hardly worth while summing them up, for the results they have yielded are scanty and incomplete and tell us scarcely anything that we do not already know. It would be fruitless to turn our attention to symptom-formation in other disorders besides phobias, conversion-hysteria, and obsessional neurosis, for too little is known about them. But in reviewing those three neuroses together we are brought up against a very serious problem the consideration of which can no longer be put off. All three have as their starting-point the destruction of the Oedipus complex; and in all three the motive force of the ego's opposition is, we believe, the fear of castration. Yet it is only in the phobias that this fear comes to the surface and is acknowledged as such. What has become of it in the other two neuroses? How has the ego spared itself this fear? The problem becomes accentuated when we recollect the possibility, already referred to, that anxiety arises directly, by a kind of fermentation, as it were, from a libidinal cathexis whose processes have been disturbed. Furthermore, is it absolutely certain that fear of castration is the only motive force of repression or defence? If we think of neuroses in women we are bound to doubt it. For though we can with certainty establish in them the presence of a castration *complex*, we can hardly speak with propriety of castration *anxiety* where castration has already taken place.

CHAPTER VII

LET us go back again to infantile phobias of animals; for we still know more about them than any others. In animal phobias, then, the ego has to oppose a libidinal object-cathexis coming from the id—a cathexis that belongs either to the positive or the negative Oedipus complex—because it believes that to give way to it would entail the danger of castration. This question has already been discussed, but there still remains a doubtful point to clear up. In Little Hans's case—that is, in the case of a positive Oedipus complex—was it his fondness for his mother or was it his aggressiveness towards his father which called out the defence of the ego? In practice it seems to make no difference, especially as each set of feelings implies the other; but the question has a theoretical interest, since it is only the feeling of affection for the mother which can count as a purely erotic one. The aggressive impulse flows mainly from the instinct of destruction; and we have always believed that in a neurosis it is against the demands of the libido and not against those of any other instinct that the ego is defending itself. In point of fact we know that, after Hans's phobia had been formed, his tender attachment to his mother seemed to disappear, having been completely disposed of by repression, while the symptom-formation (substitutive formation) took place in relation to his aggressive impulses. In the Wolf Man the situation was simpler. The impulse that was repressed was his feminine attitude towards his father, and that attitude was a genuinely erotic one. And it was in relation to that impulse, too, that the formation of his symptoms took place.

It is almost humiliating that, after working so long, we should still be having difficulty in understanding the most fundamental facts. But we are determined to simplify nothing and to hide nothing. If we cannot see things clearly, we will at least see clearly what the obscurities are. What is hampering us here is evidently some hitch in the development of our theory of the instincts. We began by tracing the organization of the libido through its successive stages—from the oral through the sadistic-anal to the genital—and in doing so placed all the components of the sexual instinct on the same footing. Later it appeared that sadism was the representative of another instinct which was opposed to Eros. This new view, that the instincts fell into two groups, seems to explode the earlier view of the successive stages of libidinal organization. But we do not have to break fresh ground in order to find a way out of the difficulty. The solution has been at hand for a long time and consists in the fact that what we are concerned with are scarcely ever pure instinctual impulses but mixtures in various proportions of the two groups of instincts. If this is so, there is no need to revise our view of the organizations of the libido. A sadistic cathexis of an object may legitimately claim to be treated as a libidinal one; and an aggressive impulse against the father can just as well be subjected to repression as a loving impulse towards the mother. Nevertheless we shall bear in mind for future consideration the possibility that repression is a process which has a special relation to the genital organization of the libido and that the ego resorts to other methods of defence when it has to secure itself against the libido on other levels of organization. A case like Little Hans's does not enable us to come to any clear conclusion. It is true that in him an aggressive impulse had been disposed of by repression, but this happened after the genital organization had been attained.

This time we will keep our attention on the question of anxiety. We have said that as soon as the ego recognized the danger of castration it gave the signal of anxiety and inhibited through the pleasure-unpleasure system (in a way which we cannot as yet understand more fully) the impending cathetic process in the id. At the same time the phobia became formed; and now the castration anxiety was directed to a different object and expressed in a distorted form, so that the patient was afraid, not of being castrated by his father, but of being bitten by a horse or eaten by a wolf. This substitutive formation had two obvious advantages. In the first place it avoided a conflict due to ambivalence (for the father had been a loved object, too), and in the second place it enabled the ego to cease producing anxiety. For the anxiety belonging to a phobia is conditional; it only emerges when the object of it is perceived, and rightly so, since it is only then that the danger-situation is present. There is no need to be afraid of being castrated by a father who is not there. On the other hand, one cannot get rid of a father; he can appear whenever he chooses. But if he is replaced by an animal, all one has to do is to avoid the sight of it—that is, its presence—in order to be free from danger and anxiety. Little Hans, therefore, imposed a restriction upon his ego. He produced the inhibition of not leaving the house so as not to come across any horses. The young Russian had an even easier time of it, for it was hardly a privation for him not to look at a particular picture-book any more. If his naughty sister had not always been showing him the book with the picture of the wolf standing upright in it, he would have been able to feel safe from his fears.

On a previous occasion I have stated that phobias have the character of a projection, in that they replace an internal, instinctual danger by an external, perceptual one. The advantage of doing this comes from the fact that the individual can protect himself against external dangers by fleeing from them and avoiding the perception of them, whereas it is useless to try to flee from dangers that arise from within. This statement of mine was not incorrect, but it did not go below the surface of things. For an instinctual demand is, after all, not dangerous in itself; it only becomes so inasmuch as it entails a real external danger, the danger of castration. Thus what happens in a phobia in the last resort is merely that one external danger is replaced by another. The view that in a phobia the ego is able to escape anxiety by means of avoidance or inhibitory symptoms fits in with the theory that that anxiety is only an affective signal and that no alteration has taken place in the economic situation.

The anxiety felt in animal phobias is, therefore, an affective reaction on the part of the ego to danger; and the danger which is being signalled in this way is the danger of castration. This anxiety differs in no respect from the anxiety which the ego normally feels in situations of danger except that its content remains unconscious and only becomes conscious in the form of a distortion.

The same is true, I think, of the phobias of grown-up persons, although the material that undergoes modification in their neuroses is much more abundant, and there are some additional factors in the formation of the symptoms. Fundamentally the position is identical. The agoraphobic patient imposes a restriction upon his ego so as to escape a certain instinctual danger, namely, the danger of giving way to his erotic desires. For, if he did so, the danger of being castrated, or some similar danger, would once more be conjured up as it was in his childhood. I may cite as an instance the case of a young man who became agoraphobic because he was afraid of yielding to the solicitations of prostitutes and of contracting a syphilitic infection from them as a punishment.

I am well aware that a great number of cases exhibit a much more complicated structure and that many other repressed instinctual impulses can enter into a phobia. But they are only tributary streams which have for the most part joined the main current of the neurosis at a later stage. The symptomatology of agoraphobia, for example, is complicated by the fact that the ego does not confine itself to making a renunciation. In order to rob the situation of danger it does more: it usually effects a temporal regression to infancy, or, in extreme cases, to pre-natal days, that is, to a time when the individual was in his mother's womb and protected against the dangers which beset him in the present. A regression of this kind now becomes a condition whose fulfilment exempts the ego from making its renunciation. For instance, an agoraphobic patient may be able to walk in the street provided he is accompanied, like a small child, by someone he knows and trusts; or, for the same reason, he may be able to go out alone, provided he remains within a certain distance of his own house and does not go to places which are not familiar to him or where people do not know him. What these stipulations are will depend in each case upon the infantile factors which dominate him through his neurosis. The phobia of being alone is unambiguous in its meaning, irrespective of any infantile regression: it is, ultimately, an endeavour to avoid the temptation to indulge in solitary masturbation. Naturally, infantile regression can only take place when the individual is no longer a child.

A phobia generally sets in only after a first anxiety attack has been experienced in specific circumstances, such as in the street or in a train or in solitude. Thereafter the anxiety is held in ban by the phobia, but it re-emerges whenever the protective stipulation cannot be fulfilled. The mechanism of phobia does good service as a means of defence and tends to be very stable. A continuation of the defensive struggle, in the shape of a struggle against the symptom, occurs frequently but not invariably.

What has been said about anxiety in phobias is true of obsessional neuroses as well. In this respect it is not difficult for us to put obsessional neuroses on a level with phobias. In the former, the mainspring of all later symptom-formation is clearly the ego's fear of the super-ego. The danger-situation from which the ego must get away is the hostility of the super-ego. There is no trace of projection here; the danger is completely internalized. But if we ask ourselves what it is that the ego fears from the super-ego, we cannot but think that the punishment threatened by the latter must be an extension of the punishment of castration. Just as the father has become depersonalized in the shape of the super-ego, so has the fear of castration at his hands become transformed into an undefined social or moral anxiety. But this anxiety is concealed. The ego escapes it by obediently carrying out the behests, precautions, and penances that have been enjoined on it. If it is impeded in doing so, it is at once overtaken by an acute feeling of discomfort which may, I think, be regarded as an equivalent of anxiety and which the patients themselves liken to anxiety.

The conclusion we have come to, then, is this. Anxiety is a reaction to a situation of danger. It is obviated by the ego's doing something to avoid that situation or to withdraw from it. It might be said that symptoms are created so as to prevent anxiety from emerging. But this does not go deep enough. It would be truer to say that symptoms are created so as to avoid a danger-situation whose approach has been signalled by the emergence of anxiety. In the cases that we have discussed, the danger concerned was the danger of castration or some off-shoot of castration.

If anxiety is a reaction of the ego to danger, we shall be tempted to regard the traumatic neuroses, which so often follow upon a narrow escape from death, as a direct result of a fear of death (or fear *for* life) and to dismiss from our minds the question of castration and the subordinate relations of the ego. Most physicians who observed the traumatic neuroses that occurred during the great war took this line and triumphantly announced that proof was now forthcoming that a threat to the instinct of self-preservation could by itself produce a neurosis without any admixture of sexual factors and without requiring any of the complicated hypotheses of psycho-analysis. It is in fact greatly to be regretted that not a single analysis of a traumatic neurosis of any value is extant. And it is to be regretted, not because such an analysis would contradict the aetiological importance of sexuality—for any such contradiction has long since been disposed of by the introduction of the concept of narcissism, which brings the libidinal cathexis of the ego into line with the cathexes of objects and emphasizes the libidinal character of the instinct of self-preservation—but because, in the absence of any analyses of this kind we have lost a precious opportunity of making decisive discoveries about the relations between anxiety and the formation of symptoms. In view of all that we know about the structure of the comparatively simple neuroses of everyday life, it would seem highly improbable that a neurosis could come into being merely because of the objective presence of danger without any participation of the deeper levels of the mental apparatus. But the unconscious seems to contain nothing that would lend substance to the concept of the annihilation of life. Castration can be pictured on the basis of the daily experience of the faeces being separated from the body or on the basis of losing the mother's breast at weaning. But nothing resembling death can ever have been experienced; or if it has, as in fainting, it has left no observable traces behind. I am therefore inclined to adhere to the view that the fear of death should be regarded as analogous to the fear of castration and that the situation to which the ego is reacting is one of being abandoned by the protecting super-ego—the powers of destiny—so that it has no longer any safeguard against all the dangers that surround it. In addition, it must be remembered that in those experiences which lead to a traumatic neurosis the protective barrier against external stimuli has been broken through and over-great quantities of excitation impinge upon the mental apparatus; so that we have here the second possibility, that anxiety is not only being signalled as an affect but is also being created anew out of the economic conditions of the situation.

The statement I have just made, to the effect that the ego has been prepared to expect castration by having undergone constantly repeated object-losses, places the question of anxiety in a new light. We have hitherto regarded it as an affective signal of danger. But now, since the danger is so often one of castration it appears to us as a reaction to a loss, a separation. Even though many considerations immediately arise which make against this view, we cannot but be struck by one very remarkable correlation. The first experience of anxiety through which the individual goes is (in the case of human beings, at all events) birth, and, objectively speaking, birth is a separation from the mother. It can be compared to a castration of the mother (by equating the child with a penis). Now it would be very satisfactory if anxiety, as a symbol of separation, were to be repeated on every subsequent occasion on which a separation took place. But unfortunately we are prevented from making use of this correlation by the fact that birth is not experienced subjectively as a separation from the mother, since the foetus, being a completely narcissistic creature, is totally unaware of her existence as an object. Another adverse argument is that we know what the affective reactions to separation are: they are pain and mourning, not anxiety. Incidentally, it may be remembered that in discussing the question of mourning[1] we also failed to discover why it should be such a painful thing.

CHAPTER VIII

THE time has come to pause and reflect. What we clearly want is some idea of what anxiety really is, some criterion that will enable us to distinguish true statements about it from false ones. But this is not easy to get. Anxiety is not so simple as all that. Up till now we have arrived at nothing but contradictory views about it, none of which can, to the unprejudiced eye, be given preference over the other. I therefore propose to adopt a different procedure. I propose to assemble, quite impartially, all the facts that we do know about anxiety and to give up the idea of making any immediate synthesis of them.

Anxiety, then, is in the first place something that is felt. We call it an affective state, although we are also ignorant of what an affect

[1] "Mourning and Melancholia" (1917), *Collected Papers*, IV.

is. As a feeling, anxiety has a very marked quality of unpleasure. But that is not the whole of its quality. Not every unpleasure is anxiety, for there are other sensations, such as tension, pain, or mourning, which have the quality of unpleasure. Thus anxiety must have other distinctive features besides this quality. Can we succeed in finding out what the differences are between these various unpleasurable affects?

We can at any rate note one or two things about the feeling of anxiety. Its unpleasurable quality seems to have a character of its own— something not very obvious, whose presence is difficult to prove yet which is in all likelihood there. But besides having this special character which is difficult to isolate, we notice that anxiety is accompanied by fairly definite physical sensations which can be referred to particular organs of the body. As we are not concerned here with the physiology of anxiety, we shall content ourselves with mentioning a few examples of these sensations. The clearest and most frequent ones are those connected with the respiratory organs and with the heart. They provide evidence that motor innervations, i.e., processes of discharge, play a part in the general phenomenon of anxiety.

Analysis of anxiety states therefore reveals the existence of (1) a specific quality of unpleasure, (2) acts of discharge, and (3) perceptions of those acts. The two last points indicate at once a difference between states of anxiety and other similar states, like those of mourning and pain. The latter do not have any motor manifestation; or if they have, the manifestation is not an integral part of the whole state but is distinct from it as being a result of it or a reaction to it. Anxiety, then, is a special state of unpleasure, with acts of discharge along particular channels. In accordance with our general views we should be inclined to think that anxiety is based upon an increase of excitation which, on the one hand, produces the quality of unpleasure and, on the other, finds relief through the channels of discharge mentioned above. But a purely physiological account of this sort is scarcely sufficient. We are tempted to assume the presence of a historical factor which binds the sensations of anxiety and its innervations firmly together; in other words, that an anxiety state is the reproduction of some experience which contains the necessary conditions for such an increase of excitation and a discharge along particular channels, and that from this circumstance the unpleasure of anxiety receives its specific

character. In man, birth is a prototypic experience of this kind, and one is therefore inclined to regard anxiety states as a reproduction of the trauma of birth.

This does not imply that anxiety occupies a different position from all the other affective states. In my opinion, the other affects are also reproductions of very early, perhaps even pre-individual, experiences of vital importance; and I should be inclined to regard them as universal, typical, and innate hysterical attacks, comparable with the recently and individually acquired attacks which occur in hysterical neuroses and whose origin and significance as memory symbols have been revealed by analysis. Of course it would be very desirable to be able to demonstrate the truth of this view in a number of such affects—a thing which is still very far from being the case.

Certain immediate objections to this view that anxiety goes back to the event of birth have to be met. It may be argued that anxiety is a reaction which, in all probability, is common to every organism, certainly every organism of a higher order, whereas birth is only experienced by the mammals; and it is doubtful whether in all of them, even, birth amounts to a trauma. Therefore, there can be anxiety without the prototype of birth. But this objection takes us beyond the barrier that divides psychology from biology. It may be precisely because anxiety has an indispensable biological function to fulfil as a reaction to a state of danger that it is differently fashioned in different living beings. We do not know, besides, whether anxiety involves the same sensations and innervations in creatures far removed from man as it does in man himself. Thus there is no good argument here against the view that, in man, anxiety is modelled upon the process of birth.

If the structure and origin of anxiety are as described, the next question is: what is the function of anxiety and on what occasions is it reproduced? The answer seems to be obvious and convincing: anxiety arose originally as a reaction to a state of danger, and it is reproduced whenever a state of that kind recurs.

This answer, however, raises further considerations. The innervations involved in the original state of anxiety probably had a meaning and purpose, just as have the muscular movements which accompany a first hysterical attack. In order to understand an hysterical attack, all one has to do is to look for a situation in which the movements in question would form part of an appropriate and expedient action. Thus in birth it is probable that the innervations, in being directed to the respiratory organs, are preparing the way for the activity of the lungs, and that in accelerating the heart-beat they are helping to keep the blood free from toxic substances. Naturally, when the anxiety state is reproduced later on as an affect, it will be lacking in any such expediency, just as the repetitions of a hysterical attack are. When the individual is placed in a new situation of danger, it may well be quite inexpedient for him to respond with an anxiety state (which is a reaction to an earlier danger) instead of initiating a reaction which is appropriate to the present danger. But his behaviour may become expedient once more if he recognizes the danger-situation before it has actually overtaken him and signals its approach by an outbreak of anxiety. In that case, he can at once get rid of his anxiety by having recourse to more suitable measures. Thus we see that there are two ways in which anxiety can emerge: in an expedient way, when a new situation of danger has occurred, or in an expedient way, in order to give a signal and prevent such a situation from occurring.

But what is a *danger?* In the act of birth there is a real danger to life. We know what this means objectively; but what it means in a psychological sense we have no idea. The danger of birth has as yet no mental content for the subject. One cannot possibly suppose that the foetus has any sort of knowledge that its life is in danger of being destroyed. It can only be aware of some vast upheaval in the economy of its narcissistic libido. Very large quantities of excitation crowd in upon it, giving rise to new sensations of unpleasure, and many organs acquire an increased cathexis, thus foreshadowing the object-cathexis which will soon set in. What elements in all this can be considered to be distinctive of a *danger-situation?*

Unfortunately, far too little is known about the mental constitution of the new-born child to make a direct answer possible. I cannot even vouch for the validity of the description I have just given. It is easy to say that the baby will repeat its affect of anxiety in every situation which recalls the event of birth. The important thing to know is what it is that recalls that event and what it is in that event that is recalled.

All we can do is to examine the occasions on which infants or rather older children show readiness to produce anxiety. In his book on the trauma of birth,[1] Rank has made a determined attempt to establish a relationship between the earliest phobias of children and the impressions made on them by the event of birth. But I do not think he has been successful. His theory is open to two objections. In the first place, he assumes that the infant has received certain sensory impressions, in particular of a visual kind, at the time of birth, the renewal of which can recall to its memory the trauma of birth and thus evoke a reaction of anxiety. This assumption is quite unfounded and extremely improbable. It is not credible that a child should retain any but tactile and general sensations relating to the process of birth. If, later on, children show fear of small animals that disappear into holes or emerge from them, this reaction, according to Rank, is due to their perceiving an analogy. But it is an analogy of which they cannot be aware. In the second place, in considering these later anxiety-situations Rank dwells, according as it suits him best, now on the child's recollection of its happy intra-uterine existence, now on its recollection of the traumatic disturbance which interrupted that existence; so that he is able to make almost any interpretation he pleases. There are, moreover, certain examples of childhood anxiety which directly traverse his theory. When, for instance, a child is left alone in the dark, one would expect it, according to his view, to welcome the re-establishment of the intra-uterine situation; yet it is precisely on such occasions that the child reacts with anxiety. And if this is explained by saying that the child is being reminded of the interruption which the event of birth made in its intra-uterine happiness, then one can no longer shut one's eyes to the far-fetched character of such explanations.

I am driven to the conclusion that the earliest phobias of infancy cannot be directly traced back to impressions of birth and that so far they have not been explained. A certain preparedness for anxiety is undoubtedly present in the infant. But this preparedness for anxiety, instead of being at its maximum immediately after birth and then slowly decreasing, does not emerge till later on, as the mental development of the infant proceeds. It lasts over a certain period of childhood. If the early phobias persist beyond that period, one is inclined to suspect the presence of a neurotic disturbance,

[1] Rank, *The Trauma of Birth and its Importance for Psycho-Analytic Therapy* (1924).

although here again it is not at all clear what their relation is to the undoubted neuroses that appear later on in childhood.

Only a few of the manifestations of anxiety in children are comprehensible to us, and we must confine our attention to them. They occur, for instance, when a child is alone or in the dark, or when it finds itself with an unknown person instead of one to whom it is used—such as its mother. These three instances can be reduced to a single condition, namely, that of missing someone who is loved and longed-for.

Here is the key, I think, to an understanding of anxiety and to a reconciliation of the contradictions that seem to beset it. The child's memory picture of the person longed-for is no doubt intensively cathected, probably in a hallucinatory way at first. But this has no effect; and now it seems as though the longing turns into anxiety. This anxiety has all the appearance of being an expression of the child's feeling of not knowing what to do, as though in its still undeveloped state it did not know how to cope with its cathexis of longing. Here anxiety seems to be a reaction to the felt loss of the object; and one is at once reminded of the fact that castration anxiety, too, is a fear of being separated from a highly valued object, and that the earliest anxiety of all—the primal anxiety of birth—is brought about on the occasion of a separation from the mother.

But our next reflection takes us a step beyond this question of loss of object. The reason why the infant in arms wants to perceive the presence of its mother is only because it already knows by experience that she gratifies all its needs without delay. The situation, then, that it regards as a *danger* and against which it wants to be safe-guarded is one of non-gratification, of a growing tension due to need, against which it is helpless. I think that if we adopt this view all the facts fall into place. The situation of non-gratification in which the amounts of stimulation rise to an unpleasurable height without the infant being able to master them by utilizing and discharging them psychologically must be analogous for it to the experience of being born—must be a repetition of that situation of danger. What both situations have in common is an economic disturbance caused by an accumulation of amounts of stimulation which require to be disposed of. It is this element which is the real essence of the danger. In both cases the same reaction of anxiety sets in.

(This anxiety reaction is still an expedient one in the child at the sucking stage, for, just as it activated the lungs of the new-born baby to get rid of the internal stimuli, so now, in being discharged into the respiratory and vocal muscular apparatus, it calls the mother to the child's side.) It is unnecessary to suppose that the child carries with it from the time of its birth anything more than this way of indicating the presence of danger.

When the child has found out by experience that an external, perceptible object can put an end to the dangerous situation which is reminiscent of birth, the nature of the danger it fears is displaced from the economic situation on to the condition which determined that situation, viz., the loss of object. It is the absence of the mother that is now the danger; and as soon as that danger arises the small child gives the signal of anxiety, before the dreaded economic situation has set in. This change constitutes a first important step forward in the provision made by the child for its self-preservation, and at the same time represents a transition from the automatic and involuntary new-creation of anxiety to the intentional reproduction of anxiety as a signal of danger.

In these two aspects, as an automatic phenomenon and as a rescue-signal, anxiety is seen to be a product of the infant's mental helplessness which is a natural counterpart of its biological helplessness. The striking coincidence by which the anxiety of the new born baby and the anxiety of the infant in arms both depend upon a separation from the mother does not need to be explained on psychological lines. It can be accounted for simply enough from a biological point of view; for, just as the mother originally satisfied all the needs of the foetus through her own body, so now, after its birth, she continues to do so, though partly through other means. There is much more continuity between intra-uterine life and earliest infancy than the impressive caesura of the act of birth allows us to believe. What happens is that the child's biological situation as a foetus is replaced for it by a psychological object-relation to its mother. But we must not forget that during its intra-uterine life the mother was not an object for the foetus, and that at that time there were no objects at all as far as it was concerned. It is obvious that in this scheme of things there is no room for the abreaction of the birth-trauma. We cannot find that anxiety has any other function except that of being a signal for the avoidance of a danger-situation.

The importance of the loss of object as a determinant of anxiety extends considerably further. For the next transformation of anxiety, viz., the castration anxiety belonging to the phallic phase, is also a fear of separation and is thus attached to the same determinant. In this case the danger is of being separated from one's genitals. Ferenczi has traced, quite correctly, I think, a clear line of connection between this fear and the fears contained in the earlier situations of danger. According to him, the high degree of narcissistic value which the penis possesses is due to the fact that this organ is a guarantee to its owner that he can be once more united to his mother—i.e., to a substitute for her—in the act of copulation. Being deprived of it amounts to a renewed separation from her and this in its turn means being helplessly exposed to an unpleasurable tension due to instinctual need, as was the case in birth. But this need whose increase is feared is now a specific one belonging to the genital libido and is no longer an indeterminate one, as in the period of infancy. It may be added that for a man who is impotent (that is, who is inhibited by the threat of castration) the substitute for copulation is a phantasy of returning into his mother's womb. Following out Ferenczi's line of thought, one might say that such a man, while endeavouring to return to his mother's womb vicariously—by means of his genital organ, proceeds to replace that organ regressively by his body as a whole.

The progress which the child makes in its development—its growing independence, the sharper division of its mental apparatus into several institutions, the advent of new needs—cannot fail to exert an influence upon the content of the danger-situation. We have already traced the change of that content from loss of the mother as an object to castration. The next change is enforced by the power of the super-ego. With the depersonalization of the parental institution from which castration was feared, the danger becomes less defined. Castration anxiety develops into moral anxiety—social anxiety—and it is not so easy now to know what the anxiety is about. The formula, *separation and expulsion from the horde,* only applies to that later portion of the super-ego which has been formed on the strength of social prototypes, not to the nucleus of the super-ego which corresponds to the introjected parental institution. Putting it more generally,

what the ego regards as the danger and responds to with an anxiety-signal is that the super-ego should be angry with it or punish it or cease to love it. The final transformation which the fear of the super-ego undergoes is, it seems to me, the fear of death (or fear for life) which is a fear of the super-ego projected on to the powers of destiny.

At one time I attached some importance to the view that what found discharge in anxiety was the cathexis which had been withdrawn in the process of repression. This view seems to me no longer of any interest. The reason for this is that whereas I formerly believed that anxiety invariably arose automatically through an economic process, my present conception of anxiety as a signal given by the ego in order to affect the pleasure-unpleasure institution does away with the necessity of considering the economic factor. Of course there is nothing to be said against the idea that it is precisely the energy that has been liberated by being withdrawn through repression which is used by the ego to arouse affect; but it is no longer of any importance which portion of the general energy is employed for this purpose.

This new view of things calls for an examination of another proposition of mine, namely, that the ego is the actual seat of anxiety. I think this proposition still holds good. There is, as far as can be seen, no reason to assign any manifestation of anxiety to the super-ego; while the expression *anxiety of the id* stands in need of correction, though rather as to its form than its substance. Anxiety is an affective state and as such can, of course, only be felt by the ego. The id cannot have anxiety as the ego can; for it is not an organization and cannot make a judgment about a situation of danger. On the other hand it very often happens that processes take place or begin to take place in the id which cause the ego to produce anxiety. Indeed, it is probable that the earliest repressions as well as most of the later ones are motivated by an ego-anxiety of this sort in regard to processes in the id. Here again one may rightly distinguish between the case in which something occurs in the id which activates a danger-situation for the ego and induces the latter to give the anxiety signal for inhibition to take place, and the case in which a situation analogous to the trauma of birth is established in the id and an automatic reaction of anxiety ensues. The two cases may be brought closer together if it is pointed out that the second case applies to the earliest and original danger-situation, while the first case applies to any one of the later determinants of anxiety that have been derived from it; or, with regard to psychological disorders, that the second case is operative in the aetiology of the actual neuroses, while the first remains typical for that of the psychoneuroses.

We see, then, that it is not so much a question of taking back our earlier findings as of bringing them into line with more recent discoveries. It is still an undeniable fact that, in sexual abstinence, improper interference with the processes of sexual excitation, or deflection of the latter from its psychological modification, anxiety arises directly out of libido; in other words, that the ego is reduced to a state of helplessness in the face of an excessive tension due to need, as it was in the situation of birth, and that anxiety is then produced. Here once more, though the matter is of little importance, it is very possible that what finds discharge in anxiety is precisely the surplus of unutilized libido. As we know, a psychoneurosis is especially liable to develop on the basis of an actual neurosis. This looks as though the ego were attempting to save itself from anxiety, which it has learned to keep in suspension for a while, and to bind it by the formation of symptoms. Analysis of the traumatic war-neuroses—a term which, by the way, covers a great variety of disorders—would probably have shown that a number of them possess the characteristics of actual neuroses.

In describing the evolution of the various danger-situations from their prototype, the act of birth, I have had no intention of asserting that every later determinant of anxiety completely invalidates the preceding one. It is true that as the development of the ego goes on the earlier danger-situations tend to lose their force and to be set aside, so that one might say that each period of the individual's life has its appropriate determinant of anxiety. Thus the danger of psychological helplessness is appropriate to the period of life when his ego is immature; the danger of loss of object, to early childhood when he is still dependent on others; the danger of castration, to the phallic phase; and the fear of his super-ego, to the latency period. Nevertheless, all these danger-situations and determinants of anxiety can persist side by side and cause the ego to react to them with anxiety at a later period than the appropriate one; or, again, several of them can come into operation at the same time. It is possible, moreover, that there is a close relationship between the danger-situation that is operative at a given

moment and the form taken by the ensuing neurosis.[1]

When, in an earlier part of this discussion, we found that the danger of castration was of importance in more than one neurotic affection, we put ourselves on guard against over-estimating that factor, since it could not be a decisive one for the female sex, and since women are undoubtedly more subject to neuroses than men. We now see that there is no danger of our regarding castration anxiety as the sole motive force of the defensive processes which lead to neurosis. I have shown elsewhere how the little girl, in the course of her development, is led to make a loving object-cathexis through her castration complex. It is precisely in women that the danger-situation of loss of object seems to have remained the most effective. All we need to do is to make a slight modification in our description of their determinant of anxiety, in the sense that it is no longer a matter of feeling the want of, or actually losing, the object itself, but of losing the object's love. Since there is no doubt that hysteria has a strong affinity with the nature of women, just as obsessional neurosis has with that of men, it appears probable that, as a determinant of anxiety, loss of love plays much

[1] Since the differentiation of the ego and the id, our interest in the problems of repression cannot fail to have received a fresh impetus. Up till then we had been content to confine our interest to those aspects of repression which concerned the ego—the keeping away from consciousness and from motility, and the formation of substitutes (symptoms). With regard to the instinctual impulses themselves, we assumed that they remained unaltered in the unconscious for an indefinite length of time. But now our interest is turned to the vicissitudes of the repressed, and we begin to suspect that it is not self-evident, perhaps not even the usual thing, that those impulses should remain unaltered and unalterable in this way. There is no doubt that the original impulses have been inhibited and deflected from their aim through repression. But has the unconscious portion of them maintained itself and been proof against the influences of life that tend to alter and depreciate them? In other words, are the old desires, about whose former existence analysis tells us, still there? The answer seems ready to hand and certain. It is that the old, repressed desires must still be present in the unconscious, since we still find their derivatives, the symptoms, at work. But this answer is not sufficient. It does not enable us to decide between two possibilities, either that the old desire is now operating only through its derivatives, having transferred the whole of its cathectic energy to them, or that it is itself still alive too. If its fate has been to exhaust itself in cathecting its derivatives, there is yet a third possibility. In the course of the neurosis it may have become reanimated by regression, anachronistic though it be. These are no idle speculations. There are many things about mental life, both normal and pathological, which seem to call for questions of this kind. In my paper, "The Passing of the Oedipus-Complex" (*Collected Papers*, II [1924]), I had occasion to notice the difference between mere repression and the real removal of an old conative impulse.

the same part in hysteria as the threat of castration does in phobias and fear of the super-ego in obsessional neurosis.

CHAPTER IX

WHAT we have now to do is to consider the relationship between the formation of symptoms and the production of anxiety.

There seem to be two very widely held opinions on this subject. One is that anxiety is itself a neurotic symptom. The other is that there is a much more intimate relation between the two. According to the second opinion, symptoms are only formed in order to avoid anxiety: they bind the mental energy which would otherwise be discharged as anxiety. Thus anxiety would be the fundamental phenomenon and main problem of neurosis.

That this latter opinion is at least in part true is shown by some striking examples. If an agoraphobic patient who has been accompanied into the street is left alone there, he will have an anxiety attack. Or if an obsessional neurotic is prevented from washing his hands after having touched something, he will become a prey to almost unbearable anxiety. It is plain, then, that the purpose and the result of having a companion in the street or of washing the hands were to obviate outbreaks of anxiety of this kind. In this sense, every inhibition which the ego imposes upon itself can be called a *symptom*.

Since we have traced back the production of anxiety to a situation of danger we should prefer to say that symptoms are created in order to remove the ego from a situation of danger. If the symptoms are prevented from being formed, the danger does in fact materialize; that is, a situation analogous to birth is established in which the ego is helpless in the face of a constantly increasing instinctual demand—the earliest and original determinant of anxiety. Thus in our view the relation between anxiety and symptom is less close than was supposed, for we have inserted the factor of the danger-situation between them. We can also add that the production of anxiety sets symptom-formation going and is, indeed, a necessary pre-requisite of it. For if the ego did not arouse the pleasure-unpleasure institution by developing anxiety, it would not have the power to arrest the process which is preparing in the id and which threatens danger. There is in all this an evident inclination to limit to a minimum the amount of anxiety developed and to employ it only as a signal; for to do more

would only be to feel in another place the unpleasure which the instinctual process was threatening to produce, and that would not be a good result from the standpoint of the pleasure-principle, although it is one that occurs often enough in the neuroses.

The formation of symptoms, then, does in effect put an end to the danger-situation. It has two aspects: one, hidden from view, brings about those alterations in the id in virtue of which the ego is removed from danger; the other presents to the world what the symptom-formation has created in place of the instinctual process which has been affected—namely, the substitutive formation.

It would, however, be more correct to ascribe to the defensive process what we have just said about symptom-formation and to use the latter term as synonymous with substitute-formation. It will then be clear that the defensive process is analogous to the method adopted by the ego for removing itself from a danger that threatens it from outside, that is, to flight. The defensive process is an attempt at flight from an instinctual danger. An examination of the weak points in this comparison should prove informative. One thing that can be said against it is that the loss of an object (or loss of love on the part of the object) and the threat of castration are just as much dangers coming from without as, say, a ferocious animal would be; they are not instinctual dangers. Nevertheless, the two cases are not the same. A wolf would probably attack a man irrespective of his behaviour towards it; but the loved person would not cease to love him, nor would he be threatened with castration if he did not entertain certain feelings and intentions in his mind. Thus such instinctual impulses are determinants of external dangers and so become dangerous in themselves; and the individual can proceed against the external dangers by taking measures against the internal ones. In phobias of animals, the danger seems to be still entirely felt as an external one, just as it has undergone an external displacement in the symptoms. In obsessional neuroses, the danger is much more internalized. That portion of anxiety in regard to the super-ego which constitutes social anxiety represents an internal substitute for an external danger, while the other portion—moral anxiety—is already completely endo-psychic.

Another objection is that in taking flight from an impending external danger all that the subject does is to increase the distance between himself and what is threatening him. He does not prepare to defend himself against it or attempt to alter anything about it, as would be the case if he attacked the wolf with a stick or shot at it with a gun. Now the defensive process seems to do something more than would correspond to an attempt at flight. It joins issue with the threatening instinctual process and somehow suppresses it or deflects it from its aims and thus renders it innocuous. This objection seems unimpeachable and must be given due weight. I think it is probable that there are some defensive processes which can truly be likened to an attempt at flight, while in others the ego takes a much more active line of self-protection and initiates vigorous counter-measures. But perhaps the whole analogy between defence and flight is invalidated by the fact that both the ego and the instinct in the id are parts of the same organization, not separate entities like the wolf and the child, so that any kind of behaviour on the part of the ego will result in an alteration in the instinctual process as well.

This study of the determinants of anxiety has, as it were, shown the defensive behaviour of the ego in a rational light. Each situation of danger corresponds to a particular period of life or developmental phase of the mental apparatus and appears to be justifiable for it. In early infancy the individual is really not fitted to master psychologically the large quantities of excitation that impinge upon him, whether from without or from within. Again, at a certain period of life his most important interest really is that the people he is dependent on should not withdraw their loving care of him. Later on in his boyhood, when he feels that his father is a powerful rival in regard to his mother and becomes aware of his own aggressive inclinations towards him and of his sexual intentions towards his mother, he really is justified in being afraid of his father; and his fear of being punished by him can find expression through phylogenetic reinforcement in the fear of being castrated. Finally, as he enters into social relationships, it really is necessary for him to be afraid of his super-ego, his conscience; for the absence of that factor would give rise for him to severe conflicts, dangers, and so on.

But this last point raises a new problem. Instead of the affect of anxiety, let us take, for a moment, another affect, say that of pain. It seems quite normal that at four years of age a girl should weep painfully if her doll is broken; or at six, if her schoolmistress reproves her; or at sixteen, if she is slighted by her young man; or at twenty-five, if a child of her own dies. Each of these determinants of pain has its own time and each passes away when that time is over. Only the final and definitive determinants remain throughout life. We should think it rather unusual if this same girl, after she had grown to be a wife and mother, were to cry over some worthless trinket that had been damaged. Yet that is how the neurotic behaves. Although all the institutions for mastering stimuli have long ago been developed within wide limits in his mental apparatus, and although he is sufficiently grown-up to gratify most of his needs for himself and has long ago learnt that castration is no longer practised as a punishment, he nevertheless behaves as though the old danger-situations still existed, and retains all the earlier determinants of anxiety.

Why this should be so requires a rather long answer. First of all, let us see what the facts are. In a great number of cases the old determinants of anxiety do really lapse, after having produced neurotic reactions. The phobias of infants, which consist in being afraid of being alone or in the dark or among strangers—phobias which can almost be called normal—usually pass off later on; the child "grows out of them," as we say about many other disturbances of childhood. Animal phobias, which are of such frequent occurrence, undergo the same fate, and many conversion-hysterias of early years find no continuation in later life. Ceremonial actions appear extremely often in the latency period but only a very small proportion of them develop later into a full obsessional neurosis. In general, so far as we can tell from our observations of town children belonging to the white races and living according to fairly high cultural standards, the neuroses of childhood are in the nature of regular episodes in a child's development, although too little attention is still being paid to them. Signs of childhood neuroses can be detected in all adult neurotics without exception; but by no means all children who show those signs become neurotic in later life. It must be, therefore, that certain determinants of anxiety are relinquished and certain danger-situations lose their significance as the individual becomes more mature. Moreover, some of these danger-situations manage to survive into later times by modifying their determinants of anxiety so as to bring them up to date. Thus, for instance, a man may retain his fear of castration in the guise of a syphilidophobia, after he has got to know that it is no longer customary to castrate people for indulging their sexual lusts, but that, on the other hand, severe diseases may overtake anyone who thus gives way to his instincts. Furthermore, some determinants of anxiety, such as fear of the super-ego, are destined not to disappear at all but to accompany the individual throughout his life. In that case the neurotic will differ from the normal person in that his reactions to the dangers in question will be unduly strong. Finally, being grown-up affords no absolute protection against a return of the original traumatic anxiety-situation. Each individual has in all probability a limit beyond which his mental apparatus fails in its function of mastering the quantities of excitation which require to be disposed of.

These minor rectifications cannot in any way alter the main fact that a great many people remain infantile in their behaviour in regard to danger and do not overcome age-old determinants of anxiety. To deny this would be to deny the existence of neurosis, for it is precisely such people whom we call neurotics. But how is this possible? Why are not all neuroses episodes in the development of the individual which come to a close when the next phase is reached? Whence comes the element of persistence in these reactions to danger? Why does the affect of anxiety alone seem to enjoy the advantage over all other affects of evoking reactions which are distinguished from the rest in being abnormal and which, through their inexpediency, run counter to the movement of life? In other words, we have once more unexpectedly come upon the riddle which has so often confronted us: whence does neurosis come—what is its ultimate, its own peculiar meaning? After whole decades of psycho-analytic work, we are as much in the dark about this problem as ever.

CHAPTER X

ANXIETY is the reaction to danger. One cannot help suspecting, however, that the reason why the affect of anxiety occupies a unique position in the economy of the mind has something to do with the essential nature of danger. Yet danger is a universal human experience; dangers are the same for everybody. What we need and cannot lay our finger on is some factor which will explain why some people are able to subject the affect of anxiety, in spite of its unique quality, to the ordinary workings of the mind, or why others are doomed to break down

over this task. Two attempts to find a factor of this kind have been made; and it is natural that such efforts should meet with a sympathetic reception, since they set out to fill a most urgent need. The two attempts in question are mutually complementary; they approach the problem at opposite ends. The first was made by Alfred Adler more than ten years ago.[1] He maintained in essence that it was those individuals who were too greatly impeded by some organic inferiority who failed to master the task set before them by danger. If it were true that *simplex sigillum veri*,[2] we should welcome this answer as a perfect solution of the problem. But on the contrary, our critical studies of the last ten years have effectively demonstrated the total inadequacy of such an explanation—an explanation, moreover, which sets aside the whole wealth of material that has been discovered by psycho-analysis.

The second attempt was made by Otto Rank in 1923 in his book, *The Trauma of Birth*. It would be unjust to put his attempt on the same level as Adler's except in this single point which concerns us here, for it remains upon psycho-analytic ground and pursues a psycho-analytic line of thought, so that it may be accepted as a legitimate endeavour to solve the problems of analysis. In this matter of the relation of the individual to danger, Rank moves away from the question of organic defect in the individual and concentrates on the variable degree of intensity of the danger.

The event of birth is the first situation of danger and the economic upheaval which it produces becomes the prototype of reaction to anxiety. We have already traced the line of development which connects this first danger-situation and determinant of anxiety with all the later ones, and we have seen that they all retain a common quality in so far as they signify in some way a separation from the mother—at first only in a biological sense, next as a direct loss of object and later as a loss of object indirectly incurred. The discovery of this extensive concatenation is an undoubted achievement of Rank's constructive work. Now the trauma of birth overtakes each individual with a different degree of intensity, and the violence of his anxiety-reaction varies with the strength of the trauma. According to Rank, whether the individual will ever learn to control his anxiety—whether he will become normal or neurotic—will depend upon the intensity

[1] Written in 1926.—TR.
[2] Simplicity is the seal of truth.—ED.

of the initial anxiety that is thus produced in him.

It is not our business to criticize Rank's hypothesis in detail here. All we need to do is to consider whether it helps to solve the particular problem before us. His proposition that those persons become neurotic in whom the trauma of birth was so strong that they have never been able completely to ab-react it is highly dubious from a theoretical point of view. We do not rightly know what is meant by ab-reacting a trauma. Taken literally, it implies that the more frequently and the more intensely a neurotic person reproduces affects of anxiety the more closely will he approach to mental health. This conclusion is not tenable. It was because it did not tally with the facts that I gave up the theory of ab-reaction which had played such a large part in the cathartic method. To lay so much stress on the variability in the strength of the birth trauma is to leave no room for the legitimate claims of hereditary constitution as an aetiological factor. For this variability is an organic factor which operates in an accidental fashion in relation to the constitution and is itself dependent on many influences which might be called accidental—as, for instance, upon timely assistance in child-birth. Rank's theory completely ignores constitutional factors as well as phylogenetic ones. If, however, we were to try to find a place for the constitutional factor by qualifying his statement with the proviso, let us say, that what is really important is the extent to which the individual reacts to the variable intensity of the trauma of birth, we should be depriving his theory of its significance and should be relegating the new factor introduced by him to a position of minor importance: the factor which decided whether a neurosis should supervene or not would lie in a different, and once more in an unknown, field.

Moreover, the fact that, while man has the process of birth in common with the other mammals, he alone is privileged to possess a special predisposition to neurosis is hardly favourable to Rank's theory. But the main objection to his theory is that it floats in the air instead of being based upon ascertained observations. No body of evidence has been collected to show that difficult and protracted birth does in fact coincide with the development of a neurosis, or even that children so born exhibit early infantile apprehensiveness more strongly and over a longer period than other children. It might be rejoined that pre-

cipitate labour and birth, that are easy for the mother quite possibly involve a severe trauma for the child. But we can still point out that births which lead to asphyxia would be bound to give clear evidence of the results which are supposed to follow. It should be one of the advantages of Rank's aetiological theory that it postulates a factor whose existence can be verified by observation. And so long as no such attempt at verification has been made it is impossible to assess the value of that theory.

On the other hand, I cannot identify myself with the view that Rank's theory contradicts the aetiological importance of the sexual instincts as hitherto recognized by psycho-analysis. For his theory only has reference to the position of the individual in regard to the danger-situation, so that it leaves it perfectly open to us to assume that, if a person has not been able to master his first dangers, he is bound to succumb to later situations involving sexual dangers and thus be driven into a neurosis.

I do not believe, therefore, that Rank's attempt has solved the problem of the causation of neurosis; nor do I believe that we can say as yet how much it may have contributed to such a solution. If an investigation into the effects of difficult birth upon the predisposition to neurosis should yield negative results, we shall rate the value of his contribution low. It is to be feared that our endeavours to find a single, tangible *ultimate cause* of neurotic illness will go unrewarded. The ideal solution, which the medical man no doubt still yearns for, would be to discover some bacillus which could be isolated and bred in a pure culture and which, when injected into a person, would invariably produce the same illness; or, to put it somewhat less fantastically, to demonstrate the existence of certain chemical substances the administration of which would create or abolish particular neuroses. But the probability of a solution of this kind seems slight.

Psycho-analysis leads to less simple and satisfactory conclusions. What I have to say in this connection is already long since known and contains nothing new. If the ego succeeds in protecting itself from a dangerous instinctual impulse, through, say, the process of repression, it has certainly inhibited and damaged the particular part of the id concerned; but it has at the same time given it a bit of independence and has renounced a bit of its own sovereignty. This is inevitable from the nature of repression, which is, fundamentally, an attempt at flight. The repressed is now, as it were, outlawed; it is excluded from the great organization of the ego and is only subject to the iaws which govern the realm of the unconscious. If, now, the danger-situation changes so that the ego has no reason for warding off a new instinctual impulse which resembles the repressed one, the consequence of the restriction of the ego which has taken place will become manifest. The new impulse will run its course under an automatic influence—or, as I should prefer to say, under the influence of the repetition-compulsion. It will follow the same path as the earlier, repressed impulse, as though the danger-situation that had been overcome still existed. The fixating factor in repression, then, is the repetition-compulsion of the unconscious id—a compulsion which in normal circumstances is only done away with by the mobile function of the ego. The ego may occasionally manage to break down the barriers of repression which it has itself put up and to recover its influence over the instinctual impulse and direct its course in accordance with the changed danger-situation. But in point of fact the ego very seldom succeeds in doing this: it cannot undo its repressions. It is possible that the way the struggle will go depends upon quantitative relations. In many cases one has the impression that the outcome is an enforced one: the regressive attraction exerted by the repressed impulse and the strength of the repression are so great that the new impulse has no choice but to obey the compulsion to repeat. In other cases the entrance of yet another element into the play of forces may be perceived: the attraction exerted by the repressed instinctual prototype is reinforced by a repulsion brought to bear by objective difficulties which are opposed to the new impulse taking a different course.

That this is the origin of fixation in repression and of the retention of danger-situations which are no longer present-day ones is confirmed by the fact of psycho-analytic therapy —a fact which is modest enough in itself but which can hardly be over-rated from a theoretical point of view. When, in the course of an analysis, we have given the ego assistance and have put it in a position to abolish its repressions, it recovers its power over the repressed id and can allow the instinctual impulses to run their course as though the old situations of danger no longer existed. What we can do in this way is in general accord with the therapeutic achievements of medicine; for as a rule we must be satisfied with bringing about more quickly, more certainly and with less expenditure of energy than would otherwise be the case a desired result which in favourable circumstances would have occurred of itself.

We see from what has been said that it is quantitative relations—relations which are not directly observable but can only be inferred— which determine whether or no old situations of danger shall be preserved, repressions on the part of the ego maintained,. and childhood neuroses find continuance. Among the factors that play a part in the causation of neuroses and that have created the conditions under which the forces of the mind are pitted against one another, three emerge into prominence: a biological, a phylogenetic, and a purely psychological factor.

The biological factor is the long period of time during which the young of the human species is in a condition of helplessness and dependence. Its intra-uterine existence seems to be short in comparison with that of most animals, and it is sent into the world in a less finished state. As a result the influence of the objective world upon it is intensified and it is obliged to make an early differentiation between the ego and the id. Moreover, the dangers of the outer world have a greater importance for it, so that the value of the object which can alone protect it against them and take the place of its former intra-uterine life is enormously enhanced. This biological factor, then, establishes the earliest situations of danger and creates the need to be loved which will accompany the child through the rest of its life.

The existence of the second, phylogenetic, factor, is based only upon inference. We have been led to assume its reality by a remarkable feature in the development of the libido. We have found that the sexual life of man, unlike that of most of the animals nearly related to him, does not make a steady advance from birth to maturity, but that, after an early expansion up till the fifth year, it undergoes a very decided interruption; and that it then starts on its course once more at puberty, beginning from the point at which it broke off in early childhood. This has led us to suppose that something momentous must have occurred in the vicissitudes of the human species which has left behind this interruption in the sexual development of the individual as a kind of historical precipitate. This factor owes its pathogenic significance to the fact that the majority of instinctual impulses belonging to infantile sexuality are treated by the ego as dangers and warded off as such, so that the later sexual impulses of puberty, which in the natural course of things would be ego-syntonic, run the risk of succumbing to the attraction of their infantile prototypes and following them into repression. It is here that we come upon the most direct aetiology of the neuroses. It is a curious thing that early contact with the demands of sexuality should have a similar effect on the ego as premature contact with the external world.

The third, psychological, factor resides in a defect of the mental apparatus which has to do with its differentiation into id and ego, and which is therefore ultimately attributable to the influence of the external world. In view of the dangers of objective reality the ego is obliged to guard against certain instinctual impulses in the id and to treat them as dangers. But it cannot protect itself from internal instinctual dangers as effectively as it can from some bit of objective reality that is not part of itself. Intimately bound up with the id as it is, it can only ward off an instinctual danger by restricting its own organization and by acquiescing in the formation of symptoms in exchange for having impaired the instinct. If the rejected instinct renews its attack, the ego is overtaken by all those difficulties which are known to us as neurotic illness.

Further than this, I believe, our knowledge of the nature and causes of neurosis has not as yet been able to go.

CHAPTER XI

APPENDICES

IN the course of this discussion various themes have had to be put aside before they had been fully dealt with. They have been brought together in this chapter in order to receive the attention they deserve.

A. *Modifications of Earlier Views*

(*a*) Resistance and Anti-Cathexis

An important element in the theory of repression is the view that repression is not an event that occurs once but that it requires a permanent expenditure of energy. If this expenditure of energy were to cease, the repressed impulse, which is being fed all the time from its sources of energy, would seize the next occasion to flow along the channels from which it has been forced aside, and the repression would either fail in its purpose or would have to be repeated an indefinite number of times. Thus it is because instincts are incessant in their nature that the ego has to make its defensive action secure by a permanent expenditure of energy. This action undertaken to protect repression is perceptible as *resistance* in analytic treatment. Resistance presupposes the existence of what I have called an *anti-cathexis*. An anti-cathexis of this kind is best seen in obsessional neurosis. It appears in the form of an alteration of the ego, as a reaction-formation in the ego, and is effected by the reinforcement of the attitude which is the opposite of the instinctual trend that has to be repressed, as is seen, for instance, in pity, conscientiousness, and cleanliness. These reaction-formations of obsessional neurosis are essentially exaggerations of the normal traits of character which develop during the latency period. The presence of an anti-cathexis in hysteria is much more difficult to detect, though theoretically it is equally indispensable. In hysteria, too, a certain amount of alteration of the ego through reaction-formation is unmistakable and in many circumstances becomes so marked that it forces itself on our attention as the principal symptom. The conflict of ambivalence in hysteria, for instance, is resolved by this means. The subject's hatred of a person whom he loves is kept down by an exaggerated amount of tenderness for him and apprehensiveness about him. But the difference between reaction-formations in obsessional neurosis and in hysteria is that in the latter they do not have the universality of a character-trait but are confined to particular relationships. An hysterical woman, for instance, may be specially affectionate with her own children whom at bottom she hates; but she will not be a more affectionate person than other women or even very fond of children in general. The reaction-formation of hysteria clings tenaciously to a particular object and never spreads over into a general disposition of the ego, whereas what is characteristic of obsessional neurosis is precisely a spreading over of this kind—a loosening of relations to the object and a great facility of displacement in the choice of object.

There is another kind of anti-cathexis, however, which seems more suited to the peculiar character of hysteria. A repressed instinctual impulse can be activated (newly cathected) from two directions: from within, through reinforcement from its internal sources of excitation, and from without, through the perception of an object that it desires. The hysterical anti-cathexis is mainly directed outwards, against dangerous perceptions. It takes the form of a special kind of vigilance which, by means of restrictions of the ego, causes situations to be avoided that would entail such perceptions, or if they do occur, manages to withdraw the subject's attention from them. Some French analysts, in particular Laforgue, have recently given this action of hysteria the special name of *scotomization*. This technique of anti-cathexis is still more noticeable in the phobias, where interest is concentrated on removing the subject ever further from the possibility of making the feared perception. The fact that anti-cathexis should be orientated in an op-posite direction in hysteria and the phobias from what it is in obsessional neurosis—though the difference is not an absolute one—seems to be significant. It suggests that there is an intimate connection between repression and external anti-cathexis on the one hand and between re-gression and internal anti-cathexis (i.e., altera-tions in the ego through reaction-formations) on the other. The task of defending against a dangerous perception is, incidentally, common to all neuroses. Various commands and pro-hibitions in obsessional neurosis have the same end in view.

As has already been seen, the resistance that has to be overcome in analysis proceeds from the ego clinging to its anti-cathexes. It is hard for the ego to direct its attention to percep-tions and ideas which it has up till now made a rule of avoiding, or to acknowledge as belong-ing to itself impulses that are the complete opposite of those which it has made its own. Our campaign against resistance in analysis is based upon this view of the facts. If the re-sistance is itself unconscious, as so often hap-pens owing to its connection with the repressed material, we make that resistance conscious. If it is conscious, or when it has become con-scious, we bring forward logical arguments against it; we promise the ego rewards and advantages if it will give up its resistance. There can be no doubt or mistake about the existence of this resistance on the part of the ego. But we have to ask ourselves whether it covers the whole state of affairs in analysis. For we find that, even after the ego has decided to relinquish its resistances, it still has difficulty in undoing the repressions; and we have called the period of strenuous effort which follows after its praiseworthy decision, the phase of *working through*. The dynamic factor which

makes a working through of this kind necessary and comprehensible is not far to seek. It must be that after the ego-resistance has been re-moved the power of the repetition-compulsion —the attraction exerted by the unconscious prototypes upon the repressed instinctual proc-ess—has yet to be overcome. This factor might well be described as the *resistance of the un-conscious*. There is no need to be discouraged by these emendations in our theory. They are to be welcomed if they do something towards furthering our knowledge, and they are no dis-grace to us so long as they enrich rather than invalidate our earlier views—by limiting some statement, perhaps, that was too general or by enlarging some idea that was too narrowly formulated.

It must not be supposed that these emenda-tions provide us with a complete review of all the varieties of resistance that are met with in analysis. Further investigation of the subject shows that the analyst has to combat no less than five varieties of resistance, emanating from three quarters—the ego, the id, and the super-ego. The id and the super-ego supply one variety apiece, while the ego is the source of three, each differing in its dynamic nature. The first of these three ego-resistances is the re-sistance due to repression, which we have al-ready discussed and about which there is least new to be added. Next there is the trans-ference resistance, which is of the same nature but has different and much clearer effects in analysis, since it succeeds in establishing a re-lation to the analytic situation or the analyst himself and thus re-animating a repression which should only have been recollected. The third resistance, though also an ego-resistance, is of quite a different nature. It proceeds from the epinosic gain and is based upon an assimila-tion of the symptom by the ego. It represents an unwillingness to renounce any gratification or relief that has been obtained. The fourth variety, belonging to the id, is the resistance which, as has just been seen, necessitates *work-ing through*. The fifth, belonging to the super-ego and the last to be discovered, is also the most obscure though not always the least powerful one. It seems to originate from the sense of guilt or the need for punishment; and it opposes every move towards success, in-cluding, therefore, the patient's own recovery through analysis.

(*b*) Anxiety from Transformation of Libido

The view of anxiety which I have put forward in these pages differs somewhat from the one I have hitherto held. Formerly I regarded anxiety as a general reaction of the ego to conditions of unpleasure. I always sought to account for its appearance on economic grounds and I assumed, on the strength of my investigations into the actual neuroses, that libido (sexual excitement) which was rejected or not utilized by the ego found direct discharge in the form of anxiety. It cannot be denied that these various assertions did not go very well together, or at any rate did not imply one another. Moreover, they gave the impression of there being a specially intimate connection between anxiety and libido and this did not accord with the general character of anxiety as a reaction to unpleasure.

The objection to this view arose from our coming to regard the ego as the sole seat of anxiety. It was one of the results of the attempt to subdivide the mental apparatus which I made in *The Ego and the Id*. Whereas the old view made it natural to suppose that anxiety arose from the libido belonging to the repressed instinctual impulses, the new one tended to make the ego the source of anxiety. Thus it is a question of id-anxiety (instinctual anxiety) versus ego-anxiety. Since the energy which the ego employed is desexualized, the new view tended to weaken the close connection between anxiety and libido. I hope I have at least succeeded in making the contradiction plain and in giving a clear idea of the point in doubt.

Rank's contention—which was originally my own—that the affect of anxiety is a consequence of the event of birth and a repetition of the situation then experienced, obliged me to review the problem of anxiety once more. But I could make no headway with his idea that birth is a trauma, states of anxiety a reaction of discharge to it, and all subsequent affects of anxiety an attempt to *ab-react* it more and more completely. I was obliged to go beyond the anxiety reaction to the situation of danger that lay behind it. The introduction of this element opened up new aspects of the question. Birth was seen to be the prototype of all later situations of danger which overtook the individual under the new conditions arising from a changed mode of life and a growing mental development. The significance of birth in regard to danger was, however, reduced to its occupying this rôle of a prototype. The anxiety felt at birth became the prototype of an affective state which had to undergo the same vicissitudes as the other affects. Two

things might happen to this affect of anxiety: it might reproduce itself automatically in situations which resembled the original situation and thus be an inexpedient form of reaction instead of an expedient one as it had been in the first situation; or the ego might acquire power over it and reproduce it on its own initiative, and employ it as a warning of danger and as a means of setting the pleasure-unpleasure mechanism in motion. We thus gave the biological aspect of the affect of anxiety its due importance by recognizing anxiety as the general reaction to situations of danger; while we endorsed the part played by the ego as the seat of anxiety by allocating to it the function of producing the affect of anxiety according to its needs. Thus we attributed two sources of origin to anxiety in later life. One was involuntary, automatic, and always due to economic causes and arose whenever a situation analogous to birth had established itself. The other was produced by the ego as soon as a situation of this kind merely threatened to occur, in order that it might be avoided. In the second case the ego subjected itself to anxiety as though to a sort of inoculation, willing to go through a slight attack of the illness in order to escape its full strength. It vividly imagined the danger-situation, as it were, with the unmistakable purpose of restricting the actual painful experience to a mere indication, a signal. We have already seen in detail how the various situations of danger arise one after the other, remaining at the same time connected in their origin.

We shall perhaps be able to proceed a little further in our knowledge of anxiety when we turn to the problem of the relation between neurotic anxiety and objective anxiety.

Our former hypothesis of a direct transformation of libido into anxiety possesses less interest for us now than it did. But if we do nevertheless consider this matter of transformation we shall have to distinguish different cases. As regards anxiety evoked by the ego as a signal, it does not come into consideration; nor does it, therefore, in any of those danger-situations which stimulate the ego to bring on repression. The libidinal cathexis of the repressed instinctual impulse is otherwise employed than in being transformed into anxiety and discharged as such, as is most clearly seen in conversion-hysteria. On the other hand, further enquiry into the question of the danger-situation will bring to our notice an instance of the production of anxiety which will, I think, have to be accounted for in a different way.

(c) Repression and Defence

In the course of discussing the problem of anxiety I have revived a concept or, to put it more modestly, a term, of which I made exclusive use thirty years ago when I first began to study the subject but which I later abandoned. I refer to the term *defensive process*.[1] I afterwards used the word *repression*, but the relation between the two remained uncertain. It will be an undoubted advantage, I think, to revert to the old term of *defence*, provided we employ it explicitly as a general designation for all the techniques which the ego makes use of in conflicts which may lead to a neurosis, while we retain the word *repression* for that special method of defence which the line of approach taken by our investigations made us better acquainted with in the first instance.

Even a terminological innovation ought to justify its adoption; it ought to reflect some new point of view or some extension of knowledge. The revival of the idea of defence and the restriction of that of repression takes into account a fact which has long since been known but which has received added importance owing to some new discoveries. Our first observations of repression and the formation of symptoms were made in connection with hysteria. We found that the perceptual content of excitatory experiences and the ideational content of pathogenic structures of thought were forgotten and debarred from being reproduced in memory, and we therefore concluded that the keeping away from consciousness was a main characteristic of hysterical repression. Later on, when we came to study the obsessional neuroses, we saw that in that illness pathogenic occurrences were not forgotten. They remained conscious; but they were isolated in some way that we could not as yet grasp, so that much the same result was obtained as in hysterical amnesia. Nevertheless, the difference was great enough to justify the belief that the process by which instinctual impulses were set aside in obsessional neurosis could not be the same as in hysteria. Further investigations have shown that in obsessional neurosis a regression of the instinctual impulses to an earlier libidinal stage takes place owing to the opposition of the ego, and that this regression clearly works in the same sense as repression although it does not make repression unnecessary. We have seen,

too, that in obsessional neurosis anti-cathexis, which is also presumably present in hysteria, plays a specially large part in protecting the ego by effecting a reactive alteration in it. Our attention has, moreover, been drawn to a process of *isolation* (whose technique cannot as yet be elucidated) which has direct symptomatic manifestations of its own, and to a procedure, that may be called magical, of *undoing* what has been done—a procedure about whose repudiating purpose there can be no doubt, but which has no longer any resemblance to the process of repression. These observations provide good enough grounds for re-introducing the old concept of defence, which can cover all of these processes with their same purpose—namely, the protection of the ego against instinctual demands—and for subsuming repression under it as a special instance. The importance of this nomenclature is heightened if we consider the possibility that further investigations may show that there is an intimate connection between special forms of defence and particular illnesses, as, for instance, between repression and hysteria. In addition we may look forward to the possible discovery of yet another important relationship. It may well be that before its sharp cleavage into an ego and an id, and before the formation of a super-ego, the mental apparatus makes use of different methods of defence from those which it employs after it has attained these levels of organization.

B. *Supplementary Remarks on Anxiety*

The affect of anxiety exhibits one or two features the study of which promises to throw further light on the subject. Anxiety has an unmistakable affinity with expectation: it is anxiety *about* something. It has a quality of indefiniteness and lack of object. In precise speech we use the word *fear* rather than *anxiety*, if the feeling has found an object. Moreover, in addition to its relation to danger, anxiety has a relation to neurosis which we have long been trying to elucidate. The question arises: why are not all reactions of anxiety neurotic—why do we accept so many of them as normal? And finally the problem of the difference between objective anxiety and neurotic anxiety awaits a thorough examination.

To begin with the last problem. The advance we have made is that we have gone behind reactions of anxiety to situations of danger. If we do the same thing with objective anxiety,

---

[1] Freud, "The Defence Neuro-Psychoses" (1894), see page 81 above.

we shall have no difficulty in solving the question. Objective danger is a danger that is known, and objective anxiety is anxiety about a known danger of this sort. Neurotic anxiety is anxiety about an unknown danger. Neurotic danger is thus a danger that has still to be discovered. Analysis has shown that it is an instinctual danger. By bringing this danger which is not known to the ego into consciousness, the analyst makes neurotic anxiety no different from objective anxiety, so that it can be dealt with in the same way.

There are two reactions to objective danger. One, an affective reaction, is an outbreak of anxiety. The other is a protective action. The same will presumably be true of instinctual danger. We know how the two reactions can co-operate in an expedient way, the one giving the signal for the other to appear. But they can also behave in an inexpedient way; paralysis due to anxiety may set in, and the one reaction spread at the cost of the other.

In some cases the characteristics of objective anxiety and neurotic anxiety are mingled. The danger is known and objective but the anxiety in regard to it is over-great, greater than seems proper. It is this surplus of anxiety which betrays the presence of a neurotic element. Such cases, however, contain no new principle; for analysis shows that to the known objective danger is attached an unknown instinctual one.

We can find out still more about this if, not content with tracing anxiety back to danger, we go on to enquire what the essence and meaning of a danger-situation is. Clearly, it consists in the subject's estimation of his own strength compared to the magnitude of the danger and in his admission of helplessness in the face of it—physical helplessness if the danger is objective and psychological helplessness if it is instinctual. In doing this he will be guided by the actual experiences he has had. (Whether he is wrong in his estimation or not is immaterial for the outcome.) Let us call a situation of helplessness of this kind that has been actually experienced a *traumatic situation*. We shall then have good grounds for distinguishing a traumatic situation from a danger-situation.

The individual will have made an important advance in his capacity for self-preservation if he can foresee and expect a traumatic situation of this kind entailing helplessness instead of simply waiting for it to happen. Let us call a situation which contains the determinant for an expectation of this kind a *danger-situation*. It is in this situation that the signal of anxiety is made. The signal announces: "I am expecting a situation of helplessness to set in," or: "The present situation reminds me of one of the traumatic experiences I have had before. Therefore I will anticipate the trauma and behave as though it had already come, while there is yet time to turn it aside." Anxiety is, therefore, on the one hand an expectation of a trauma, and on the other a repetition of it in a mitigated form. Thus the two features of anxiety which we have noted have a different origin. Its connection with expectation belongs to the danger-situation, whereas its indefiniteness and lack of object belong to the traumatic situation of helplessness—the situation which is anticipated in the danger-situation.

Taking this sequence—anxiety-danger-helplessness (trauma)—we can now summarize what has been said. A danger-situation is a recognized, remembered, and expected situation of helplessness. Anxiety is the original reaction to helplessness in the trauma and is reproduced later on in the danger-situation as a signal for help. The ego, which has undergone the trauma passively, now repeats it actively in a weakened version, hoping to have the direction of it in its own hands. It is certain that children behave in this fashion towards every painful impression they receive, by reproducing it in their play. In thus changing from passivity to activity they attempt to master it psychologically. If this is what is meant by *ab-reacting a trauma,* we can have nothing to urge against the phrase. But what is of decisive importance is the first displacement of the anxiety reaction from its origin in the situation of helplessness to an expectation of that situation, that is, to the danger-situation. After that come the later displacements, from the danger to the determinant of the danger—loss of the object and the modifications of that loss with which we are already acquainted.

The undesirable result of *spoiling* the small child is to increase the importance of the danger of losing the object (the object being a protection against every situation of helplessness) in comparison with every other danger. It therefore encourages the individual to remain in the state of childhood, the period of life which is characterized by motor and mental helplessness.

So far we have had no occasion to regard objective anxiety in any different light from neurotic anxiety. We know what the distinction is. An objective danger is a danger which threatens a person from an external object, and a neurotic danger is one which threatens him from an instinctual demand. In so far as the instinctual demand is something objective, his neurotic anxiety, too, can be admitted to have an objective basis. We have seen that the reason why there seems to be a specially close connection between anxiety and neurosis is that the ego defends itself against an instinctual danger with the help of the anxiety reaction just as it does against an external objective danger, but that this line of defensive activity eventuates in a neurosis, owing to an imperfection of the mental apparatus. We have also come to the conclusion that an instinctual demand often only becomes an (internal) danger because its gratification would bring on an external danger, i.e., because the internal danger represents an external one.

On the other hand, the external (objective) danger must have managed to become internalized if it is to be significant for the ego. It must have been recognized as related to some situation of helplessness that has been experienced.[1] Man does not seem to have been endowed, or has been endowed, in but small measure, with an instinctive recognition of the dangers that threaten him from without. Small children are constantly doing things which endanger their lives, and that is precisely why they cannot afford to be without a protecting object. With regard to the traumatic situation, in which the subject is helpless, external and internal dangers, objective dangers, and instinctual demands converge. Whether the ego is suffering from a pain which will not stop or experiencing an accumulation of instinctual needs which cannot obtain gratification, the economic situation is the same and the motor helplessness of the ego finds expression in psychological helplessness.

In this connection, the puzzling question of the phobias of early childhood deserves to be mentioned once again. Some of them, such as the fear of being alone or in the dark or with strangers, can be understood as reactions to the danger of losing the object. Others, like the fear of small animals, thunderstorms, etc.,

might perhaps be accounted for as vestigial traces of the congenital preparedness to meet objective dangers which is so strongly developed in other animals. In man only that part of this archaic inheritance is appropriate which has reference to the loss of object. If his childhood phobias become fixated and grow stronger and persist into later years, analysis shows that their content has become associated with instinctual demands and has come to stand for internal dangers as well.

C. *Anxiety, Pain, and Mourning*

So little is known about the psychology of processes of feeling that the tentative remarks I am about to make on the subject may claim a very lenient judgment. The problem before us arises out of the conclusion we have reached that anxiety comes to be a reaction to the danger of losing the object. Now we already know one reaction to the loss of an object, and that is mourning. The question therefore is: when does loss of object lead to anxiety and when to mourning? In discussing the subject of mourning on a previous occasion[2] I found that there was one feature about it which remained quite unexplained. This was its peculiar painfulness. And yet it somehow seems self-evident that separation from an object should be painful. Thus the problem becomes more complicated: when does separation from an object produce anxiety, when does it produce mourning, and when does it produce, it may be, only pain?

Let me say at once that there is no prospect of answering these questions at present. We must content ourselves with drawing certain distinctions and adumbrating certain possibilities.

Our starting-point will again be the one situation which we believe we understand—the situation of the infant when he is presented with a stranger instead of his mother. He will exhibit the anxiety which we have attributed to the danger of loss of object. But his anxiety is undoubtedly more complicated than this and merits a more thorough discussion. That he does have anxiety there can be no doubt; but the expression of his face and his reaction of crying indicate that he is feeling pain as well. Certain things seem to be confused in him which will later on be separated out. He cannot as yet distinguish between temporary absence and permanent loss. As soon as he misses his mother he behaves as if he were never going to

[1] It may also often happen that, although a danger-situation is correctly estimated in itself, a certain amount of instinctual anxiety is joined on to the objective anxiety. In that case the instinctual demand before whose gratification the ego recoils is a masochistic one: the instinct of destruction directed against the subject himself. Perhaps an addition of this kind explains cases in which reactions of anxiety are exaggerated, ineffectual, or paralysing. Phobias of heights (windows, towers, precipices, and the like) may have some such origin. Their hidden feminine significance is closely connected with masochism.

[2] "Mourning and Melancholia" (1917), *Collected Papers*, IV.

see her again; and repeated consolatory experiences to the contrary are necessary before he learns that her disappearance is usually followed by her reappearance. His mother encourages this piece of knowledge which is so vital to him by playing the familiar game of hiding her face from him with her hands and then, to his joy, uncovering it again. In these circumstances he can, as it were, feel longing unmixed with despair.

In consequence of the infant's misunderstanding of the facts, the situation of missing his mother is not a danger-situation but a traumatic one. Or, to put it more correctly, it is a traumatic situation if he happens at the time to be feeling a need which she is the one to gratify. It turns into a danger-situation if this need is not present at the moment. Thus, the first determinant of anxiety which the ego itself introduces is loss of perception of the object (which is equated with loss of the object itself). There is as yet no question of loss of love. It is only later on that experience teaches the child that the object can be present but angry with him; and then loss of love on the part of the object becomes a new and much more enduring danger and determinant of anxiety.

The traumatic situation of missing the mother differs in one important respect from the traumatic situation of birth. At birth no object existed and so no object could be missed. Anxiety was the only reaction that occurred. Since then repeated situations of gratification have resulted in setting up the mother as an object; and this object, whenever the infant feels a need, receives an intense cathexis of longing. It is to this new aspect of things that the reaction of pain is referable. Pain is thus the actual reaction to loss of object, and anxiety is the reaction to the danger which that loss entails and, in its further displacement, a reaction to the danger of the loss of object itself.

We know very little about pain either. The only fact we are certain of is that pain occurs in the first instance and as a regular thing whenever a stimulus which impinges on the periphery breaks through the protective barrier against stimuli and proceeds to act like a continual instinctual stimulus, against which muscular action, which is as a rule effective because it withdraws the place that is being stimulated from the stimulus, is powerless. If the pain does not proceed from a part of the skin but from an internal organ the situation is still the same. All that has happened is that a portion of the inner periphery has taken the place of the outer periphery. The child obviously has occasion to undergo experiences of pain of this sort, which have no relation to its experiences of need. This determinant of the development of pain seems, however, to have very little similarity with the loss of an object. And besides, the element which is essential to pain, peripheral stimulation, is entirely absent in the child's situation of longing. Yet it cannot be for nothing that the common usage of speech should have created the notion of internal mental pain and have treated the feeling of loss of object as equivalent to physical pain.

When there is physical pain, a high degree of what may be termed *narcissistic cathexis of the painful place* occurs. This cathexis continues to increase and tends, as it were, to empty the ego. It is well known that, when internal organs are giving pain, spatial and other images of the affected part of the body arise, though that part is not represented in conscious ideation on other occasions. Again, the remarkable truth that when the mind is diverted to some other interest by psychological means even the most intense physical pains fail to arise (I must not say "remain unconscious" in this case) can be accounted for by the fact that there is a concentration of cathexis on the psychical representative of the part of the body which is giving pain. I think it is here that we shall find the point of analogy which has enabled us to carry sensations of pain over to the mental sphere. For the economic conditions that are produced by the intense cathexis of longing which is concentrated on the missed or lost object (a cathexis which steadily mounts up because it cannot be appeased) are the same as the economic conditions that are produced by the cathexis of pain which is concentrated on the injured part of the body. Thus the element of the peripheral causation of physical pain can be left out of account. The transition from physical pain to mental pain corresponds to a change from narcissistic cathexis to object-cathexis. The object whose presentation is highly cathected by instinctual need plays the same rôle as the part of the body which is cathected by an increase of stimulus. The continuous nature of the cathectic process and the impossibility of inhibiting it produce the same state of mental helplessness. If the feeling of unpleasure which thus arises has the specific quality of pain (a quality which cannot be more exactly described) instead of manifesting itself in the reactive form of anxiety, this may very likely be due to a certain factor which we have not sufficiently made use of in our explanatory efforts. I refer to the high level of cathexis and attachment at which the unpleasurable processes we have been discussing take place.

We know of yet another reaction of feeling to the loss of an object, and that is mourning. But we have no longer any difficulty in accounting for it. Mourning occurs under the influence of reality-testing; for the latter function demands categorically from the bereaved person that he should separate himself from the object, since it no longer exists. Mourning is entrusted with the task of carrying out this retreat from the object in all those situations in which it was the recipient of a high degree of cathexis. That this separation should be painful fits in with what we have just said, in view of the high degree and insatiable nature of the cathexis of longing which is concentrated on the object by the bereaved person during the reproduction of the situations in which he must undo the ties that attach him to it.

Thoughts for the Times on
War and Death[1]

I. THE DISILLUSIONMENT OF THE WAR

SWEPT as we are into the vortex of this wartime, our information one-sided, ourselves too near to focus the mighty transformations which have already taken place or are beginning to take place, and without a glimmering of the inchoate future, we are incapable of apprehending the significance of the thronging impressions, and know not what value to attach to the judgments we form. We are constrained to believe that never has any event been destructive of so much that is valuable in the commonwealth of humanity, nor so misleading to many of the clearest intelligences, nor so debasing to the highest that we know. Science herself has lost her passionless impartiality; in their deep embitterment, her servants seek for weapons from her with which to contribute towards the defeat of the enemy. The anthropologist is driven to declare the opponent inferior and degenerate; the psychiatrist to publish his diagnosis of the enemy's disease of mind or spirit. But probably our sense of these immediate evils is disproportionately strong, and we are not entitled to compare them with the evils of other times of which we have not undergone the experience.

The individual who is not himself a combatant—and so a wheel in the gigantic machinery of war—feels conscious of disorientation, and of an inhibition in his powers and activities. I believe that he will welcome any indication, however slight, which may enable him to find out what is wrong with himself at least. I propose to distinguish two among the most potent factors in the mental distress felt by noncombatants, against which it is such a heavy task to struggle, and to treat of them here: the disillusionment which this war has evoked; and the altered attitude towards death which this —like every other war—imposes on us.

When I speak of *disillusionment*, everyone at once knows what I mean. One need not be a sentimentalist; one may perceive the biological and psychological necessity of suffering in the economics of human life, and yet condemn war both in its means and in its aims, and devoutly look forward to the cessation of all wars. True, we have told ourselves that wars can never cease so long as nations live under such widely differing conditions, so long as the value of individual life is in each nation so variously computed, and so long as the animosities which divide them represent such powerful instinctual forces in the mind. And we were prepared to find that wars between the primitive and the civilized peoples, between those races whom a colour-line divides, nay, wars with and among the undeveloped nationalities of Europe or those whose culture has perished—that for a considerable period such wars would occupy mankind. But we permitted ourselves to have other hopes. We had expected the great ruling powers among the white nations upon whom the leadership of the human species has fallen, who were known to have cultivated world-wide interests, to whose creative powers were due our technical advances in the direction of dominating nature, as well as the artistic and scientific acquisitions of the mind—peoples such as these we had expected to succeed in discovering another way of settling misunderstandings and conflicts of interest. Within each of these nations there prevailed high standards of accepted custom for the individual, to which his manner of life was bound to conform if he desired a share in communal privileges. These ordinances, frequently too stringent, exacted a great deal from him, much self-restraint, much renunciation of instinctual gratification. He was especially forbidden to make use of the immense advantages to be gained by the practise of lying and deception in competition with his fellow-men. The civilized state regarded these accepted standards as the basis of its existence; stern were its proceedings when an impious hand was laid upon them; frequent the pronouncement that to subject them even to examination by a critical intelligence was entirely impracticable. It could be assumed, therefore, that the state itself would respect them, nor would contemplate undertaking any infringement of what it acknowledged as the basis of its own existence. To be sure, it was evident

[1] *Collected Papers*, IV; first published early in 1915 in *Imago*, Vol. V; reprinted in *Sammlung*, 4th Series.

that within these civilized states were mingled remnants of certain other races who were universally unpopular and had therefore been only reluctantly, and even so not to the fullest extent, admitted to participation in the common task of civilization, for which they had shown themselves suitable enough. But the great nations themselves, it might have been supposed, had acquired so much comprehension of their common interests, and enough tolerance for the differences that existed between them, that *foreigner* and *enemy* could no longer, as still in antiquity, be regarded as synonymous.

Relying on this union among the civilized races, countless people have exchanged their native home for a foreign dwelling-place, and made their existence dependent on the conditions of intercourse between friendly nations. But he who was not by stress of circumstances confined to one spot, could also confer upon himself, through all the advantages and attractions of these civilized countries, a new, a wider fatherland, wherein he moved unhindered and unsuspected. In this way he enjoyed the blue sea, and the grey; the beauty of the snow-clad mountains and of the green pasture-lands; the magic of the northern forests and the splendour of the southern vegetation; the emotion inspired by landscapes that recall great historical events, and the silence of nature in her inviolate places. This new fatherland was for him a museum also, filled with all the treasures which the artists among civilized communities had in the successive centuries created and left behind. As he wandered from one gallery to another in this museum, he could appreciate impartially the varied types of perfection that miscegenation, the course of historical events, and the special characteristics of their mother-earth had produced among his more remote compatriots. Here he would find a cool inflexible energy developed to the highest point; there, the gracious art of beautifying existence; elsewhere, the sense of order and fixed law—in short, any and all of the qualities which have made mankind the lords of the earth.

Nor must we forget that each of these citizens of culture had created for himself a personal "Parnassus" and "School of Athens." From among the great thinkers and artists of all nations he had chosen those to whom he conceived himself most deeply indebted for what he had achieved in enjoyment and comprehension of life, and in his veneration had associated them with the immortals of old as well as with the more familiar masters of his own tongue. None

of these great figures had seemed to him alien because he had spoken another language—not the incomparable investigator of the passions of mankind, nor the intoxicated worshipper of beauty, nor the vehement and threatening prophet, nor the subtle mocking satirist; and never did he on this account rebuke himself as a renegade towards his own nation and his beloved mother-tongue.

The enjoyment of this fellowship in civilization was from time to time disturbed by warning voices, which declared that as a result of long-prevailing differences wars were unavoidable, even among the members of a fellowship such as this. We refused to believe it; but if such a war indeed must be, what was our imaginary picture of it? We saw it as an opportunity for demonstrating the progress of mankind in communal feeling since the era when the Greek Amphictyones had proclaimed that no city of the league might be demolished, nor its olive-groves hewn down, nor its water cut off. As a chivalrous crusade, which would limit itself to establishing the superiority of one side in the contest, with the least possible infliction of dire sufferings that could contribute nothing to the decision, and with complete immunity for the wounded who must of necessity withdraw from the contest, as well as for the physicians and nurses who devoted themselves to the task of healing. And of course with the utmost precautions for the non-combatant classes of the population—for women who are debarred from war-work, and for the children who, grown older, should be enemies no longer but friends and co-operators. And again, with preservation of all the international undertakings and institutions in which the mutual civilization of peace-time had been embodied.

Even a war like this would have been productive of horrors and sufferings enough; but it would not have interrupted the development of ethical relations between the greater units of mankind, between the peoples and the states.

Then the war in which we had refused to believe broke out, and brought—disillusionment. Not only is it more sanguinary and more destructive than any war of other days, because of the enormously increased perfection of weapons of attack and defence; but it is at least as cruel, as embittered, as implacable as any that has preceded it. It sets at naught all those restrictions known as International Law, which in peace-time the states had bound themselves to observe; it ignores the prerogatives of the wounded and the medical service, the distinction between civil and military sections of the population, the claims of private property. It tramples in blind fury on all that comes in its way, as though there were to be no future and no goodwill among men after it has passed. It rends all bonds of fellowship between the contending peoples, and threatens to leave such a legacy of embitterment as will make any renewal of such bonds impossible for a long time to come.

Moreover, it has brought to light the almost unbelievable phenomenon of a mutual comprehension between the civilized nations so slight that the one can turn with hate and loathing upon the other. Nay, more—that one of the great civilized nations is so universally unpopular that the attempt can actually be made to exclude it from the civilized community as *barbaric*, although it long has proved its fitness by the most magnificent co-operation in the work of civilization. We live in the hope that the impartial decision of history will furnish the proof that precisely this nation, this in whose tongue we now write, this for whose victory our dear ones are fighting, was the one which least transgressed the laws of civilization—but at such a time who shall dare present himself as the judge of his own cause?

Nations are in a measure represented by the states which they have formed; these states, by the governments which administer them. The individual in any given nation has in this war a terrible opportunity to convince himself of what would occasionally strike him in peacetime—that the state has forbidden to the individual the practice of wrong-doing, not because it desired to abolish it, but because it desires to monopolize it, like salt and tobacco. The warring state permits itself every such misdeed, every such act of violence, as would disgrace the individual man. It practises not only the accepted stratagems, but also deliberate lying and deception against the enemy; and this, too, in a measure which appears to surpass the usage of former wars. The state exacts the utmost degree of obedience and sacrifice from its citizens, but at the same time treats them as children by maintaining an excess of secrecy, and a censorship of news and expressions of opinion that renders the spirits of those thus intellectually oppressed defenceless against every unfavourable turn of events and every sinister rumour. It absolves itself from the guarantees and contracts it had formed with other states, and makes unabashed confession of its rapacity and lust for power, which the private individual is then called upon to sanction in the name of patriotism.

Nor may it be objected that the state cannot refrain from wrong-doing, since that would place it at a disadvantage. It is no less disadvantageous, as a general rule, for the individual man to conform to the customs of morality and refrain from brutal and arbitrary conduct; and the state but seldom proves able to indemnify him for the sacrifices it exacts. It cannot be a matter for astonishment, therefore, that this relaxation of all the moral ties between the greater units of mankind should have had a seducing influence on the morality of individuals; for our conscience is not the inflexible judge that ethical teachers are wont to declare it, but in its origin is *dread of the community* and nothing else. When the community has no rebuke to make, there is an end of all suppression of the baser passions, and men perpetrate deeds of cruelty, fraud, treachery, and barbarity so incompatible with their civilization that one would have held them to be impossible.

Well may that civilized cosmopolitan, therefore, of whom I spoke, stand helpless in a world grown strange to him—his all-embracing patrimony disintegrated, the common estates in it laid waste, the fellow-citizens embroiled and debased!

In criticism of his disillusionment, nevertheless, certain things must be said. Strictly speaking, it is not justified, for it consists in the destruction of—an illusion! We welcome illusions because they spare us emotional distress, and enable us instead to indulge in gratification. We must not then complain if now and again they come into conflict with some portion of reality, and are shattered against it.

Two things in this war have evoked our sense of disillusionment: the destitution shown in moral relations externally by the states which in their interior relations pose as the guardians of accepted moral usage, and the brutality in behaviour shown by individuals, whom, as partakers in the highest form of human civilization, one would not have credited with such a thing.

Let us begin with the second point and endeavour to formulate, as succinctly as may be, the point of view which it is proposed to criticize. How do we imagine the process by which an individual attains to a higher plane of morality? The first answer is sure to be: He is good and noble from his very birth, his very earliest beginnings. We need not consider this any further. A second answer will suggest that we are concerned with a developmental process, and will probably assume that this development consists in eradicating from him the evil human tendencies and, under the influence of education and a civilized environment, replacing them by good ones. From that standpoint it is certainly astonishing that evil should show itself to have such power in those who have been thus nurtured.

But this answer implies the thesis from which we propose to dissent. In reality, there is no such thing as *eradicating* evil tendencies. Psychological—more strictly speaking, psychoanalytic—investigation shows instead that the inmost essence of human nature consists of elemental instincts, which are common to all men and aim at the satisfaction of certain primal needs. These instincts in themselves are neither good nor evil. We but classify them and their manifestations in that fashion, according as they meet the needs and demands of the human community. It is admitted that all those instincts which society condemns as evil—let us take as representatives the selfish and the cruel—are of this primitive type.

These primitive instincts undergo a lengthy process of development before they are allowed to become active in the adult being. They are inhibited, directed towards other aims and departments, become commingled, alter their objects, and are to some extent turned back upon their possessor. Reaction-formations against certain instincts take the deceptive form of a change in content, as though egoism had changed into altruism, or cruelty into pity. These reaction-formations are facilitated by the circumstance that many instincts are manifested almost from the first in pairs of opposites, a very remarkable phenomenon—and one strange to the lay public—which is termed the *ambivalence of feeling*. The most easily observable and comprehensible instance of this is the fact that intense love and intense hatred are so often to be found together in the same person. Psychoanalysis adds that the conflicting feelings not infrequently have the same person for their object.

It is not until all these *vicissitudes to which instincts are subject* have been surmounted that what we call the character of a human being is formed, and this, as we know, can only very inadequately be classified as *good* or *bad*. A human being is seldom altogether good or bad; he is usually *good* in one relation and *bad* in another, or *good* in certain external circumstances and in others decidedly *bad*. It is interesting to learn that the existence of

strong *bad* impulses in infancy is often the actual condition for an unmistakable inclination towards *good* in the adult person. Those who as children have been the most pronounced egoists may well become the most helpful and self-sacrificing members of the community; most of our sentimentalists, friends of humanity, champions of animals, have been evolved from little sadists and animal-tormentors.

The transformation of *bad* instincts is brought about by two co-operating factors, an internal and an external. The internal factor consists in an influence on the bad—say, the egoistic—instincts exercised by erotism, that is, by the human need for love, taken in its widest sense. By the admixture of *erotic* components the egoistic instincts are transmuted into *social* ones. We learn to value being loved as an advantage for which we are willing to sacrifice other advantages. The external factor is the force exercised by upbringing, which advocates the claims of our cultural environment, and this is furthered later by the direct pressure of that civilization by which we are surrounded. Civilization is the fruit of renunciation of instinctual satisfaction, and from each newcomer in turn it exacts the same renunciation. Throughout the life of the individual, there is a constant replacement of the external compulsion by the internal. The influences of civilization cause an ever-increasing transmutation of egoistic trends into altruistic and social ones, and this by an admixture of erotic elements. In the last resort it may be said that every internal compulsion which has been of service in the development of human beings was originally, that is, in the evolution of the human race, nothing but an external one. Those who are born today bring with them as an inherited constitution some degree of a tendency (disposition) towards transmutation of egoistic into social instincts, and this disposition is easily stimulated to achieve that effect. A further measure of this transformation must be accomplished during the life of the individual himself. And so the human being is subject not only to the pressure of his immediate environment, but also to the influence of the cultural development attained by his forefathers.

If we give the name of *cultural adaptability* to a man's personal capacity for transformation of the egoistic impulses under the influence of the erotic, we may further affirm that this adaptability is made up of two parts, one innate and the other acquired through experience, and that the relation of the two to each other and to that portion of the instinctual life which remains untransformed is a very variable one.

Generally speaking, we are apt to attach too much importance to the innate part, and in addition to this we run the risk of overestimating the general adaptability to civilization in comparison with those instincts which have remained in their primitive state—by which I mean that in this way we are led to regard human nature as *better* than it actually is. For there is, besides, another factor which obscures our judgment and falsifies the issue in too favourable a sense.

The impulses of another person are naturally hidden from our observation. We deduce them from his actions and behaviour, which we trace to motives born of his instinctual life. Such a conclusion is bound to be, in many cases, erroneous. This or that action which is *good* from the civilized point of view may in one instance be born of a *noble* motive, in another not so. Ethical theorists class as *good* actions only those which are the outcome of good impulses; to the others they refuse their recognition. But society, which is practical in its aims, is little troubled on the whole by this distinction; it is content if a man regulates his behaviour and actions by the precepts of civilization, and is little concerned with his motives.

We have seen that the external compulsion exercised on a human being by his upbringing and environment produces a further transformation towards good in his instinctual life—a turning from egotism towards altruism. But this is not the regular or necessary effect of the external compulsion. Education and environment offer benefits not only in the way of love, but also employ another kind of premium system, namely, reward and punishment. In this way their effect may turn out to be that he who is subjected to their influence will choose to "behave well" in the civilized sense of the phrase, although no ennoblement of instinct, no transformation of egoistic into altruistic inclinations, has taken place within. The result will, roughly speaking, be the same; only a particular concatenation of circumstances will reveal that one man always acts rightly because his instinctual inclination compels him so to do, and the other is *good* only in so far and for so long as such civilized behaviour is advantageous for his own egoistic purposes. But superficial acquaintance with an individual will not enable us to distinguish between the two cases, and we are certainly misled by our optimism into grossly exaggerating the number of human beings who have been transformed in a civilized sense.

Civilized society, which exacts good conduct and does not trouble itself about the impulses underlying it, has thus won over to obedience a great many people who are not thereby following the dictates of their own natures. Encouraged by this success, society has suffered itself to be led into straining the moral standard to the highest possible point, and thus it has forced its members into a yet greater estrangement from their instinctual dispositions. They are consequently subjected to an unceasing suppression of instinct, the resulting strain of which betrays itself in the most remarkable phenomena of reaction and compensation formations. In the domain of sexuality, where such suppression is most difficult to enforce, the result is seen in the reaction-phenomena of neurotic disorders. Elsewhere the pressure of civilization brings in its train no pathological results, but is shown in malformations of character, and in the perpetual readiness of the inhibited instincts to break through to gratification at any suitable opportunity. Anyone thus compelled to act continually in the sense of precepts which are not the expression of instinctual inclinations, is living, psychologically speaking, beyond his means, and might objectively be designated a hypocrite, whether this difference be clearly known to him or not. It is undeniable that our contemporary civilization is extraordinarily favourable to the production of this form of hypocrisy. One might venture to say that it is based upon such hypocrisy, and that it would have to submit to far-reaching modifications if people were to undertake to live in accordance with the psychological truth. Thus there are very many more hypocrites than truly civilized persons—indeed, it is a debatable point whether a certain degree of civilized hypocrisy be not indispensable for the maintenance of civilization, because the cultural adaptability so far attained by those living today would perhaps not prove adequate to the task. On the other hand, the maintenance of civilization even on so questionable a basis offers the prospect of each new generation achieving a farther-reaching transmutation of instinct, and becoming the pioneer of a higher form of civilization.

From the foregoing observations, we may already derive this consolation—that our mortification and our grievous disillusionment regarding the uncivilized behaviour of our world-compatriots in this war are shown to be unjustified. They were based on an illusion to which we had abandoned ourselves. In reality our fellow-citizens have not sunk so low as we feared, because they had never risen so high as we believed. That the greater units of humanity, the peoples and states, have mutually abrogated their moral restraints naturally prompted these individuals to permit themselves relief for a while from the heavy pressure of civilization and to grant a passing satisfaction to the instincts it holds in check. This probably caused no breach in the relative morality within their respective national frontiers.

We may, however, obtain insight deeper than this into the change brought about by the war in our former compatriots, and at the same time receive a warning against doing them an injustice. For the evolution of the mind shows a peculiarity which is present in no other process of development. When a village grows into a town, a child into a man, the village and the child become submerged in the town and the man. Memory alone can trace the earlier features in the new image; in reality the old materials or forms have been superseded and replaced by new ones. It is otherwise with the development of the mind. Here one can describe the state of affairs, which is a quite peculiar one, only by saying that in this case every earlier stage of development persists alongside the later stage which has developed from it; the successive stages condition a co-existence, although it is in reference to the same materials that the whole series of transformations has been fashioned. The earlier mental state may not have manifested itself for years, but none the less it is so far present that it may at any time again become the mode of expression of the forces in the mind, and that exclusively, as though all later developments had been annulled, undone. This extraordinary plasticity of the evolution that takes place in the mind is not unlimited in its scope; it might be described as a special capacity for retroversion—for regression—since it may well happen that a later and higher stage of evolution, once abandoned, cannot be reached again. But the primitive stages can always be re-established; the primitive mind is, in the fullest meaning of the word, imperishable.

What are called *mental diseases* inevitably impress the layman with the idea of destruction of the life of mind and soul. In reality, the destruction relates only to later accretions and developments. The essence of mental disease lies in a return to earlier conditions of affective life and functioning. An excellent example of

the plasticity of mental life is afforded by the state of sleep, which every night we desire. Since we have learnt to interpret even absurd and chaotic dreams, we know that whenever we sleep we cast off our hard-won morality like a garment, only to put it on again next morning. This divestiture is naturally unattended by any danger because we are paralysed, condemned to inactivity, by the state of sleep. Only through a dream can we learn of the regression of our emotional life to one of the earliest stages of development. For instance, it is noteworthy that all our dreams are governed by purely egoistic motives. One of my English friends put forward this proposition at a scientific meeting in America, whereupon a lady who was present remarked that that might be the case in Austria, but she could maintain for herself and her friends that *they* were altruistic even in their dreams. My friend, although himself of English race, was obliged to contradict the lady emphatically on the ground of his personal experience in dream-analysis, and to declare that in their dreams high-minded American ladies were quite as egoistical as the Austrians.

Thus the transformations of instinct, on which our cultural adaptability is based, may also be permanently or temporarily undone by the experiences of life. Undoubtedly the influences of war are among the forces that can bring about such regression; therefore we need not deny adaptability for culture to all who are at the present time displaying uncivilized behaviour, and we may anticipate that the refinement of their instincts will be restored in times of peace.

There is, however, another symptom in our world-compatriots which has perhaps astonished and shocked us no less than the descent from their ethical nobility which has so greatly distressed us. I mean the narrow-mindedness shown by the best intellects, their obduracy, their inaccessibility to the most forcible arguments, their uncritical credulity for the most disputable assertions. This indeed presents a lamentable picture, and I wish to say emphatically that in this I am by no means a blind partisan who finds all the intellectual shortcomings on one side. But this phenomenon is much easier to account for and much less disquieting than that which we have just considered. Students of human nature and philosophers have long taught us that we are mistaken in regarding our intelligence as an independent force and in overlooking its dependence upon the emotional life. Our intelligence, they teach us, can function reliably only when it is removed from the influences of strong emotional impulses; otherwise it behaves merely as an instrument of the will and delivers the inference which the will requires. Thus, in their view, logical arguments are impotent against affective interests, and that is why reasons, which in Falstaff's phrase are "as plenty as blackberries," produce so few victories in the conflict with interests. Psycho-analytic experience has, if possible, further confirmed this statement. It daily shows that the shrewdest persons will all of a sudden behave like imbeciles as soon as the needful insight is confronted by an emotional resistance, but will completely regain their wonted acuity once that resistance has been overcome. The logical infatuations into which this war has deluded our fellow-citizens, many of them the best of their kind, are therefore a secondary phenomenon, a consequence of emotional excitement, and are destined, we may hope, to disappear with it.

Having in this way come to understand once more our fellow-citizens who are now so greatly alienated from us, we shall the more easily endure the disillusionment which the nations, those greater units of the human race, have caused us, for we shall perceive that the demands we make upon them ought to be far more modest. Perhaps they are reproducing the course of individual evolution, and still today represent very primitive phases in the organization and formation of higher unities. It is in agreement with this that the educative factor of an external compulsion towards morality, which we found to be so effective for the individual, is barely discernible in them. True, we had hoped that the extensive community of interests established by commerce and production would constitute the germ of such a compulsion, but it would seem that nations still obey their immediate passions far more readily than their interests. Their interests serve them, at most, as rationalizations for their passions; they parade their interests as their justification for satisfying their passions. Actually why the national units should disdain, detest, abhor one another, and that even when they are at peace, is indeed a mystery. I cannot tell why it is. It is just as though when it becomes a question of a number of people, not to say millions, all individual moral acquirements were obliterated, and only the most primitive, the oldest, the crudest mental attitudes were left. Possibly only future stages in development will be able in any way to alter this regrettable state of affairs. But a little more truthfulness and upright dealing on all sides, both in the personal relations of men to one another and between them and those who govern them, should also do something towards smoothing the way for this transformation.

II. Our Attitude Towards Death

The second factor to which I attribute our present sense of estrangement in this once lovely and congenial world is the disturbance that has taken place in our attitude towards death, an attribute to which hitherto we have clung so fast.

This attitude was far from straightforward. We were of course prepared to maintain that death was the necessary outcome of life, that everyone owes a debt to Nature and must expect to pay the reckoning—in short, that death was natural, undeniable, and unavoidable. In reality, however, we were accustomed to behave as if it were otherwise. We displayed an unmistakable tendency to "shelve" death, to eliminate it from life. We tried to hush it up; indeed we even have the saying, "To think of something as we think of death."[1] That is our own death, of course. Our own death is indeed unimaginable, and whenever we make the attempt to imagine it we can perceive that we really survive as spectators. Hence the psycho-analytic school could venture on the assertion that at bottom no one believes in his own death, or to put the same thing in another way, in the unconscious every one of us is convinced of his own immortality.

As to the death of another, the civilized man will carefully avoid speaking of such a possibility in the hearing of the person concerned. Children alone disregard this restriction; unabashed, they threaten one another with the eventuality of death, and even go so far as to talk of it before one whom they love, as for instance: "Dear Mamma, it will be a pity when you are dead, but then I shall do this or that." The civilized adult can hardly even entertain the thought of another's death without seeming to himself hard or evil-hearted; unless, of course, as a physician, lawyer or something of the sort, he has to deal with death professionally. Least of all will he permit himself to think of the death of another if with that event some gain to himself in freedom, means, or position

[1] The German saying is used as an equivalent for *incredible* or *unlikely*.—Tr.

is connected. This sensitiveness of ours is, of course, impotent to arrest the hand of death; when it has fallen, we are always deeply affected, as if we were prostrated by the overthrow of our expectations. Our habit is to lay stress on the fortuitous causation of the death —accident, disease, infection, advanced age; in this way we betray our endeavour to modify the significance of death from a necessity to an accident. A multitude of simultaneous deaths appears to us exceedingly terrible. Towards the dead person himself we take up a special attitude, something like admiration for one who has accomplished a very difficult task. We suspend criticism of him, overlook his possible misdoings, issue the command: *De mortuis nil nisi bene*,[1] and regard it as justifiable to set forth in the funeral-oration and upon the tombstone only that which is most favourable to his memory. Consideration for the dead, who no longer need it, is dearer to us than the truth, and certainly, for most of us, is dearer also than consideration for the living.

The culmination of this conventional attitude towards death among civilized persons is seen in our complete collapse when death has fallen on some person whom we love—a parent or a partner in marriage, a brother or sister, a child, a dear friend. Our hopes, our pride, our happiness, lie in the grave with him, we will not be consoled, we will not fill the loved one's place. We behave then as if we belonged to the tribe of the Asra, who must die too when those die whom they love.

But this attitude of ours towards death has a powerful effect upon our lives. Life is impoverished, it loses in interest, when the highest stake in the game of living, life itself, may not be risked. It becomes as flat, as superficial, as one of those American flirtations in which it is from the first understood that nothing is to happen, contrasted with a Continental love-affair in which both partners must constantly bear in mind the serious consequences. Our ties of affection, the unbearable intensity of our grief, make us disinclined to court danger for ourselves and for those who belong to us. We dare not contemplate a great many undertakings which are dangerous but quite indispensable, such as attempts at mechanical flight, expeditions to far countries, experiments with explosive substances. We are paralysed by the thought of who is to replace the son with his mother, the husband with his wife, the father with his children, if there should come dis-

[1] Say nothing but good of the dead.—Ed.

aster. The tendency to exclude death from our calculations brings in its train a number of other renunciations and exclusions. And yet the motto of the Hanseatic League declared: *"Navigare necesse est, vivere non necesse"!* (It is necessary to sail the seas, it is not necessary to live.)

It is an inevitable result of all this that we should seek in the world of fiction, of general literature, and of the theatre compensation for the impoverishment of life. There we still find people who know how to die, indeed, who are even capable of killing someone else. There alone, too, we can enjoy the condition which makes it possible for us to reconcile ourselves with death—namely, that behind all the vicissitudes of life we preserve our existence intact. For it is indeed too sad that in life it should be as it is in chess, when one false move may lose us the game, but with the difference that we can have no second game, no return-match. In the realm of fiction we discover that plurality of lives for which we crave. We die in the person of a given hero, yet we survive him, and are ready to die again with the next hero just as safely.

It is evident that the war is bound to sweep away this conventional treatment of death. Death will no longer be denied; we are forced to believe in him. People really are dying, and now not one by one, but many at a time, often ten thousand in a single day. Nor is it any longer an accident. To be sure, it still seems a matter of chance whether a particular bullet hits this man or that; but the survivor may easily be hit by another bullet; and the accumulation puts an end to the impression of accident. Life has, in truth, become interesting again; it has regained its full significance.

Here a distinction should be made between two groups—those who personally risk their lives in battle, and those who have remained at home and have only to wait for the loss of their dear ones by wounds, disease, or infection. It would indeed be very interesting to study the changes in the psychology of the combatants, but I know too little about it. We must stop short at the second group, to which we ourselves belong. I have said already that in my opinion the bewilderment and the paralysis of energies, now so generally felt by us, are essentially determined in part by the circumstance that we cannot maintain our former attitude towards death, and have not yet discovered a new one. Perhaps it will assist us to do this if we direct our psychological inquiry towards two other relations with death—the one which we may ascribe to primitive, prehistoric peoples, and that other which in every one of us still exists, but which conceals itself, invisible to consciousness, in the deepest-lying strata of our mental life.

The attitude of prehistoric man towards death is known to us, of course, only by inferences and reconstruction, but I believe that these processes have furnished us with tolerably trustworthy information.

Primitive man assumed a very remarkable attitude towards death. It was far from consistent, was indeed extremely contradictory. On the one hand, he took death seriously, recognized it as the termination of life and used it to that end; on the other hand, he also denied death, reduced it to nothingness. This contradiction arose from the circumstance that he took up radically different attitudes towards the death of another man, of a stranger, of an enemy, and towards his own. The death of the other man he had no objection to; it meant the annihilation of a creature hated, and primitive man had no scruples against bringing it about. He was, in truth, a very violent being, more cruel and more malign than other animals. He liked to kill, and killed as a matter of course. That instinct which is said to restrain the other animals from killing and devouring their own species we need not attribute to him.

Hence the primitive history of mankind is filled with murder. Even today, the history of the world which our children learn in school is essentially a series of race-murders. The obscure sense of guilt which has been common to man since prehistoric times, and which in many religions has been condensed into the doctrine of original sin, is probably the outcome of a blood-guiltiness incurred by primitive man. In my book *Totem and Taboo* (1913) I have, following clues given by W. Robertson Smith, Atkinson, and Charles Darwin, attempted to surmise the nature of this primal guilt, and I think that even the contemporary Christian doctrine enables us to deduce it. If the Son of God was obliged to sacrifice his life to redeem mankind from original sin, then by the law of the talion, the requital of like for like, that sin must have been a killing, a murder. Nothing else could call for the sacrifice of a life in expiation. And if the original sin was an offence against God the Father, the primal crime of mankind must have been a parricide, the killing of the primal father of the primitive human

horde, whose image in memory was later transfigured into a deity.[1]

His own death was for primitive man certainly just as unimaginable and unreal as it is for any one of us today. But there was for him a case in which the two opposite attitudes towards death came into conflict and joined issue; and this case was momentous and productive of far-reaching results. It occurred when primitive man saw someone who belonged to him die —his wife, his child, his friend, whom assuredly he loved as we love ours, for love cannot be much younger than the lust to kill. Then, in his pain, he had to learn that one can indeed die oneself, an admission against which his whole being revolted; for each of these loved ones was, in very truth, a part of his own beloved ego. But even so, on the other hand, such deaths had a rightfulness for him, since in each of the loved persons something of the hostile stranger had resided. The law of ambivalence of feeling, which to this day governs our emotional relations with those whom we love most, had assuredly a very much wider validity in primitive periods. Thus these beloved dead had also been enemies and strangers who had aroused in him a measure of hostile feeling.[2]

Philosophers have declared that the intellectual enigma presented to primitive man by the picture of death was what forced him to reflection, and thus that it became the starting-point of all speculation. I believe that here the philosophers think too philosophically, and give too little consideration to the primarily effective motives. I would therefore limit and correct this assertion: By the body of his slain enemy, primitive man would have triumphed, without racking his brains about the enigma of life and death. Not the intellectual enigma, and not every death, but the conflict of feeling at the death of loved, yet withal alien and hated persons was what disengaged the spirit of inquiry in man. Of this conflict of feeling, psychology was the direct offspring. Man could no longer keep death at a distance, for he had tasted of it in his grief for the dead; but still he did not consent entirely to acknowledge it, for he could not conceive of himself as dead. So he devised a compromise; he conceded the fact of death, even his own death, but denied it the significance of annihilation, which he had had no motive for contesting where the death of his enemy had been concerned. During his contemplation of his loved

[1] See "The Infantile Recurrence of Totemism," *Totem and Taboo.*
[2] See "Taboo and the Ambivalence of Emotions," *Totem and Taboo.*

one's corpse he invented ghosts, and it was his sense of guilt at the satisfaction mingled with his sorrow that turned these new-born spirits into evil, dreaded demons. The changes wrought by death suggested to him the disjunction of the individuality into a body and a soul—first of all into several souls; in this way his train of thought ran parallel with the process of disintegration which sets in with death. The enduring remembrance of the dead became the basis for assuming other modes of existence, gave him the conception of life continued after apparent death.

These subsequent modes of existence were at first no more than appendages to that life which death had brought to a close—shadowy, empty of content, and until later times but slightly valued; they showed as yet a pathetic inadequacy. We may recall the answer made to Odysseus by the soul of Achilles:

Erst in the life on the earth, no less than a god
we revered thee,
We the Achaeans; and now in the realm of the
dead as a monarch
Here dost thou rule; then why should death
thus grieve thee, Achilles?
Thus did I speak: forthwith then answering
thus he addressed me,
Speak not smoothly of death, I beseech, O fa-
mous Odysseus,
Better by far to remain on the earth as the
thrall of another;
E'en of a portionless man that hath means
right scanty of living,
Rather than reign sole king in the realm of the
bodiless phantoms.[1]

Or in the powerful, bitterly burlesque rendering by Heine, where he makes Achilles say that the most insignificant little Philistine at Stuckert-on-the-Neckar, in being alive, is far happier than he, the son of Peleus, the dead hero, the prince of shadows in the nether world.

It was not until much later that the different religions devised the view of this after-life as the more desirable, the truly valid one, and degraded the life which is ended by death to a mere preparation. It was then but consistent to extend life backward into the past, to conceive of former existences, transmigrations of the soul and reincarnation, all with the purpose of depriving death of its meaning as the termination of life. So early did the denial of death, which above we designated a convention of civilization, actually originate.

Beside the corpse of the beloved were generated not only the idea of the soul, the belief in immortality, and a great part of man's deep-rooted sense of guilt, but also the earliest inkling of ethical law. The first and most portentous prohibition of the awakening conscience was: Thou shalt not kill. It was born of the reaction against that hate-gratification which lurked behind the grief for the loved dead, and was gradually extended to unloved strangers and finally even to enemies.

This final extension is no longer experienced by civilized man. When the frenzied conflict of this war shall have been decided, every one of the victorious warriors will joyfully return to his home, his wife and his children, undelayed and undisturbed by any thought of the enemy he has slain either at close quarters or by distant weapons of destruction. It is worthy of note that such primitive races as still inhabit the earth, who are undoubtedly closer than we to primitive man, act differently in this respect, or did so act until they came under the influence of our civilization. The savage—Australian, Bushman, Tierra del Fuegan—is by no means a remorseless murderer; when he returns victorious from the war-path he may not set foot in his village nor touch his wife until he has atoned for the murders committed in war by penances which are often prolonged and toilsome. This may be presumed, of course, to be the outcome of superstition; the savage still goes in fear of the avenging spirits of the slain. But the spirits of the fallen enemy are nothing but the expression of his own conscience, uneasy on account of his blood-guiltiness; behind this superstition lurks a vein of ethical sensitiveness which has been lost by us civilized men.[2]

Pious souls, who cherish the thought of our remoteness from whatever is evil and base, will be quick to draw from the early appearance and the urgency of the prohibition of murder gratifying conclusions in regard to the force of these ethical stirrings, which must consequently have been implanted in us. Unfortunately this argument proves even more for the opposite contention. So powerful a prohibition can only be directed against an equally powerful impulse. What no human soul desires there is no need to prohibit;[3] it is automatically excluded. The very emphasis of the commandment *Thou shalt not kill* makes it certain that we spring from an endless ancestry of murderers, with

[1] *Odyssey*, XI, 484-491; translated by H. B. Cotterill.

[2] Cf. *Totem and Taboo*.

[3] Cf. the brilliant argument of Frazer quoted in *Totem and Taboo*.

whom the lust for killing was in the blood, as possibly it is to this day with ourselves. The ethical strivings of mankind, of which we need not in the least depreciate the strength and the significance, are an acquisition accompanying evolution; they have then become the hereditary possession of those human beings alive today, though unfortunately only in a very variable measure.

Let us now leave primitive man, and turn to the unconscious in our own mental life. Here we depend entirely upon the psycho-analytic method of investigation, the only one which plumbs such depths. We ask what is the attitude of our unconscious towards the problem of death. The answer must be: Almost exactly the same as primitive man's. In this respect, as in many others, the man of prehistoric ages survives unchanged in our unconscious. Thus, our unconscious does not believe in its own death; it behaves as if immortal. What we call our *unconscious* (the deepest strata of our minds, made up of instinctual impulses) knows nothing whatever of negatives or of denials— contradictories coincide in it—and so it knows nothing whatever of our own death, for to that we can give only a negative purport. It follows that no instinct we possess is ready for a belief in death. This is even perhaps the secret of heroism. The rational explanation for heroism is that it consists in the decision that the personal life cannot be so precious as certain abstract general ideals. But more frequent, in my view, is that instinctive and impulsive heroism which knows no such motivation, and flouts danger in the spirit of Anzengruber's Hans the Road-Mender: "Nothing can happen to *me*." Or else that motivation serves but to clear away the hesitation which might delay an heroic reaction in accord with the unconscious. The dread of death, which dominates us oftener than we know, is on the other hand something secondary, being usually the outcome of the sense of guilt.

On the other hand, for strangers and for enemies, we do acknowledge death, and consign them to it quite as readily and unthinkingly as did primitive man. Here there does, indeed, appear a distinction which in practise shows for a decisive one. Our unconscious does not carry out the killing; it merely thinks it and wishes it. But it would be wrong entirely to depreciate this psychical reality as compared with actual reality. It is significant and pregnant enough. In our unconscious we daily and hourly deport all who stand in our way, all who have offended or injured us. The expression: "Devil take him!" which so frequently comes to our lips in joking anger, and which really means "Death take him!" is in our unconscious an earnest, deliberate death-wish. Indeed, our unconscious will murder even for trifles; like the ancient Athenian law of Draco, it knows no other punishment for crime than death; and this has a certain consistency, for every injury to our almighty and autocratic ego is at bottom a crime of *lèse-majesté*.

And so, if we are to be judged by the wishes in our unconscious, we are, like primitive man, simply a gang of murderers. It is well that all these wishes do not possess the potency which was attributed to them by primitive men;[1] in the cross-fire of mutual maledictions, mankind would long since have perished, the best and wisest of men and the loveliest and fairest of women with the rest.

Psycho-analysis finds little credence among laymen for assertions such as these. They reject them as calumnies which are confuted by conscious experience, and adroitly overlook the faint indications through which the unconscious is apt to betray itself even to consciousness. It is, therefore, relevant to point out that many thinkers who could not have been influenced by psycho-analysis have quite definitely accused our unspoken thoughts of a readiness, heedless of the murder-prohibition, to get rid of anyone who stands in our way. From many examples of this I will choose one very famous one:

In *Le Père Goriot*, Balzac alludes to a passage in the works of J. J. Rousseau where that author asks the reader what he would do if— without leaving Paris and of course without being discovered—he could kill, with great profit to himself, an old mandarin in Peking by a mere act of the will. Rousseau implies that he would not give much for the life of this dignitary. *"Tuer son mandarin"*[2] has passed into a proverb for this secret readiness even on the part of ourselves today.

There is as well a whole array of cynical jests and anecdotes which testify in the same sense, such as, for instance, the remark attributed to a husband: "If one of us dies, I shall go and live in Paris." Such cynical jokes would not be possible unless they contained an unacknowledged verity which could not be countenanced if seriously and baldly expressed. In joke, as we know, even the truth may be told.

[1] See "The Omnipotence of Thought," *Totem and Taboo*.
[2] To kill his mandarin.—ED.

As for primitive man, so also for us in our unconscious, there arises a case in which the two contrasted attitudes towards death, that which acknowledges it as the annihilation of life and the other which denies it as ineffectual to that end, conflict and join issue—and this case is the same as in primitive ages—the death, or the endangered life, of one whom we love, a parent or partner in marriage, a brother or sister, a child or dear friend. These loved ones are on the one hand an inner possession, an ingredient of our personal ego, but on the other hand are partly strangers, even enemies. With the exception of only a very few situations, there adheres to the tenderest and closest of our affections a vestige of hostility which can excite an unconscious death-wish. But this conflict of ambivalence does not now, as it did then, find issue in theories of the soul and of ethics, but in neuroses, which afford us deep insight into normal mental life as well. How often have those physicians who practise psycho-analysis had to deal with the symptom of an exaggeratedly tender care for the well-being of relatives, or with entirely unfounded self-reproaches after the death of a loved person. The study of these cases has left them in no doubt about the extent and the significance of unconscious death-wishes.

The layman feels an extraordinary horror at the possibility of such feelings, and takes this repulsion as a legitimate ground for disbelief in the assertions of psycho-analysis. I think, mistakenly. No depreciation of our love is intended, and none is actually contained in it. It is indeed foreign to our intelligence as also to our feelings thus to couple love and hate, but Nature, by making use of these twin opposites, contrives to keep love ever vigilant and fresh, so as to guard it against the hate which lurks behind it. It might be said that we owe the fairest flowers of our love-life to the reaction against the hostile impulse which we divine in our breasts.

To sum up: Our unconscious is just as inaccessible to the idea of our own death, as murderously minded towards the stranger, as divided or ambivalent towards the loved, as was man in earliest antiquity. But how far we have moved from this primitive state in our conventionally civilized attitude towards death!

It is easy to see the effect of the impact of war on this duality. It strips us of the later accretions of civilization, and lays bare the primal man in each of us. It constrains us once more to be heroes who cannot believe in their own death; it stamps the alien as the enemy, whose death is to be brought about or desired; it counsels us to rise above the death of those we love. But war is not to be abolished; so long as the conditions of existence among the nations are so varied, and the repulsions between peoples so intense, there will be, must be, wars. The question then arises: Is it not we who must give in, who must adapt ourselves to them? Is it not for us to confess that in our civilized attitude towards death we are once more living psychologically beyond our means, and must reform and give truth its due? Would it not be better to give death the place in actuality and in our thoughts which properly belongs to it, and to yield a little more prominence to that unconscious attitude towards death which we have hitherto so carefully suppressed? This hardly seems indeed a greater achievement, but rather a backward step in more than one direction, a regression; but it has the merit of taking somewhat more into account the true state of affairs, and of making life again more endurable for us. To endure life remains, when all is said, the first duty of all living beings. Illusion can have no value if it makes this more difficult for us.

We remember the old saying: *Si vis pacem, para bellum*. If you desire peace, prepare for war.

It would be timely thus to paraphrase it: *Si vis vitam, para mortem*. If you would endure life, be prepared for death.

Civilization and Its Discontents

I

THE impression forces itself upon one that men measure by false standards, that everyone seeks power, success, riches for himself and admires others who attain them, while undervaluing the truly precious things in life. And yet, in making any general judgment of this kind, one is in danger of forgetting the manifold variety of humanity and its mental life. There are certain men from whom their contemporaries do not withhold veneration, although their greatness rests on attributes and achievements which are completely foreign to the aims and ideals of the multitude. One might well be inclined to suppose that after all it is only a minority who appreciate these great men, while the majority cares nothing for them. But the discrepancy between men's opinions and their behaviour is so wide and their desires so many-sided that things are probably not so simple.

One of these exceptional men calls himself my friend in his letters to me. I had sent him my little book which treats of religion as an illusion and he answered that he agreed entirely with my views on religion, but that he was sorry I had not properly appreciated the ultimate source of religious sentiments. This consists in a peculiar feeling, which never leaves him personally, which he finds shared by many others, and which he may suppose millions more also experience. It is a feeling which he would like to call a sensation of *eternity,* a feeling as of something limitless, unbounded, something "oceanic." It is, he says, a purely subjective experience, not an article of belief; it implies no assurance of personal immortality, but it is the source of the religious spirit and is taken hold of by the various Churches and religious systems, directed by them into definite channels, and also, no doubt, used up in them. One may rightly call oneself religious on the ground of this oceanic feeling alone, even though one reject all beliefs and all illusions.

These views, expressed by my friend whom I so greatly honour and who himself once in poetry described the magic of illusion, put me in a difficult position. I cannot discover this "oceanic" feeling in myself. It is not easy to deal scientifically with feelings. One may attempt to describe their physiological signs.

Where that is impossible—I am afraid the oceanic feeling, too, will defy this kind of classification—nothing remains but to turn to the ideational content which most readily associates itself with the feeling. If I have understood my friend aright, he means the same thing as that consolation offered by an original and somewhat unconventional writer to his hero, contemplating suicide: "Out of this world we cannot fall."[1] So it is a feeling of indissoluble connection, of belonging inseparably to the external world as a whole. To me, personally, I may remark, this seems something more in the nature of an intellectual judgment, not, it is true, without any accompanying feeling-tone, but with one of a kind which characterizes other equally far-reaching reflections as well. I could not in my own person convince myself of the primary nature of such a feeling. But I cannot on that account deny that it in fact occurs in other people. One can only wonder whether it has been correctly interpreted and whether it is entitled to be acknowledged as the *fons et origo*[2] of the whole need for religion.

I have nothing to suggest which could effectively settle the solution of this problem. The idea that man should receive intimation of his connection with the surrounding world by a direct feeling which aims from the outset at serving this purpose sounds so strange and is so incongruous with the structure of our psychology that one is justified in attempting a psycho-analytic, that is, genetic explanation of such a feeling. Whereupon the following lines of thought present themselves. Normally there is nothing we are more certain of than the feeling of our self, our own ego. It seems to us an independent unitary thing, sharply outlined against everything else. That this is a deceptive appearance, and that on the contrary the ego extends inwards without any sharp delimitation, into an unconscious mental entity which we call the *id* and to which it forms a façade, was first discovered by psycho-analytic research, and the latter still has much to tell us about the relations of the ego to the id. But towards the outer world, at any rate, the ego seems to keep

[1] Christian Grabbe, *Hannibal: "Ja, aus der Welt werden wir nicht fallen. Wir sind einmal darin."*
[2] Source and origin.—ED.

itself clearly and sharply outlined and delimited. There is only one state of mind in which it fails to do this—an unusual state, it is true, but not one that can be judged as pathological. At its height, the state of being in love threatens to obliterate the boundaries between ego and object. Against all the evidence of his senses, the man in love declares that he and his beloved are one, and is prepared to behave as if it were a fact. A thing that can be temporarily effaced by a physiological function must also of course be liable to disturbance by morbid processes. From pathology we have come to know a large number of states in which the boundary line between ego and outer world become uncertain, or in which they are actually incorrectly perceived—cases in which parts of a man's own body, even component parts of his own mind, perceptions, thoughts, feelings, appear to him alien and not belonging to himself; other cases in which a man ascribes to the external world things that clearly originate in himself, and that ought to be acknowledged by him. So the ego's cognizance of itself is subject to disturbance, and the boundaries between it and the outer world are not immovable.

Further reflection shows that the adult's sense of his own ego cannot have been the same from the beginning. It must have undergone a development, which naturally cannot be demonstrated, but which admits of reconstruction with a fair degree of probability.[1] When the infant at the breast receives stimuli, he cannot as yet distinguish whether they come from his ego or from the outer world. He learns it gradually as the result of various exigencies. It must make the strongest impression on him that many sources of excitation, which later on he will recognize as his own bodily organs, can provide him at any time with sensations, whereas others become temporarily out of his reach—amongst these what he wants most of all, his mother's breast—and reappear only as a result of his cries for help. Thus an *object* first presents itself to the ego as something existing *outside*, which is only induced to appear by a particular act. A further stimulus to the growth and formation of the ego, so that it becomes something more than a bundle of sensations, i.e., recognizes an *outside*, the external world, is afforded by the frequent, unavoidable and manifold pains and unpleasant sensations which the pleasure-principle, still in unre-

stricted domination, bids it abolish or avoid. The tendency arises to dissociate from the ego everything which can give rise to pain, to cast it out and create a pure pleasure-ego, in contrast to a threatening outside, not-self. The limits of this primitive pleasure-ego cannot escape readjustment through experience. Much that the individual wants to retain because it is pleasure-giving is nevertheless part not of the ego but of an object; and much that he wishes to eject because it torments him yet proves to be inseparable from the ego, arising from an inner source. He learns a method by which, through deliberate use of the sensory organs and suitable muscular movements, he can distinguish between internal and external —what is part of the ego and what originates in the outer world—and thus he makes the first step towards the introduction of the reality-principle which is to control his development further. This capacity for distinguishing which he learns of course serves a practical purpose, that of enabling him to defend himself against painful sensations felt by him or threatening him. Against certain painful excitations from within the ego has only the same means of defence as that employed against pain coming from without, and this is the starting-point of important morbid disturbances.

In this way the ego detaches itself from the external world. It is more correct to say: Originally the ego includes everything, later it detaches from itself the external world. The ego-feeling we are aware of now is thus only a shrunken vestige of a far more extensive feeling—a feeling which embraced the universe and expressed an inseparable connection of the ego with the external world. If we may suppose that this primary ego-feeling has been preserved in the minds of many people—to a greater or lesser extent— it would co-exist like a sort of counterpart with the narrower and more sharply outlined ego-feeling of maturity, and the ideational content belonging to it would be precisely the notion of limitless extension and oneness with the universe—the same feeling as that described by my friend as "oceanic." But have we any right to assume that the original type of feeling survives alongside the later one which has developed from it?

Undoubtedly we have: there is nothing unusual in such a phenomenon, whether in the psychological or in other spheres. Where animals are concerned, we hold the view that the most highly developed have arisen from the

---

[1] Cf. the considerable volume of work on this topic dating from that of Ferenczi (*Stages in the Development of the Sense of Reality*, 1913) up to Federn's contributions, 1926, 1927 and later.

lowest. Yet we still find all the simple forms alive today. The great saurians are extinct and have made way for the mammals, but a typical representative of them, the crocodile, is still living among us. The analogy may be too remote, and it is also weakened by the fact that the surviving lower species are not as a rule the true ancestors of the present-day more highly developed types. The intermediate members have mostly died out and are known to us only through reconstruction. In the realm of mind, on the other hand, the primitive type is so commonly preserved alongside the transformations which have developed out of it that it is superfluous to give instances in proof of it. When this happens, it is usually the result of a bifurcation in development. One quantitative part of an attitude or an impulse has survived unchanged while another has undergone further development.

This brings us very close to the more general problem of conservation in the mind, which has so far hardly been discussed, but is so interesting and important that we may take the opportunity to pay it some attention, even though its relevance is not immediate. Since the time when we recognized the error of supposing that ordinary forgetting signified destruction or annihilation of the memory-trace, we have been inclined to the opposite view that nothing once formed in the mind could ever perish, that everything survives in some way or other, and is capable under certain conditions of being brought to light again, as, for instance, when regression extends back far enough. One might try to picture to oneself what this assumption signifies by a comparison taken from another field. Let us choose the history of the Eternal City as an example.[1] Historians tell us that the oldest Rome of all was the *Roma quadrata*, a fenced settlement on the Palatine. Then followed the phase of the Septimontium, when the colonies on the different hills united together; then the town which was bounded by the Servian wall; and later still, after all the transformations in the periods of the republic and the early Caesars, the city which the Emperor Aurelian enclosed by his walls. We will not follow the changes the city went through any further, but will ask ourselves what traces of these early stages in its history a visitor to Rome may still find today, if he goes equipped with the most complete historical and topographical knowledge.

Except for a few gaps, he will see the wall of Aurelian almost unchanged. He can find sections of the Servian rampart at certain points where it has been excavated and brought to light. If he knows enough—more than present-day archaeology—he may perhaps trace out in the structure of the town the whole course of this wall and the outline of *Roma quadrata*. Of the buildings which once occupied this ancient ground-plan he will find nothing, or but meagre fragments, for they exist no longer. With the best information about Rome of the republican era, the utmost he could achieve would be to indicate the sites where the temples and public buildings of that period stood. These places are now occupied by ruins, but the ruins are not those of the early buildings themselves but of restorations of them in later times after fires and demolitions. It is hardly necessary to mention that all these remains of ancient Rome are found woven into the fabric of a great metropolis which has arisen in the last few centuries since the Renaissance. There is assuredly much that is ancient still buried in the soil or under the modern buildings of the town. This is the way in which we find antiquities surviving in historic cities like Rome.

Now let us make the fantastic supposition that Rome were not a human dwelling-place, but a mental entity with just as long and varied a past history: that is, in which nothing once constructed had perished, and all the earlier stages of development had survived alongside the latest. This would mean that in Rome the palaces of the Caesars were still standing on the Palatine and the Septizonium of Septimius Severus was still towering to its old height; that the beautiful statues were still standing in the colonnade of the Castle of St. Angelo, as they were up to its siege by the Goths, and so on. But more still: where the Palazzo Caffarelli stands there would also be, without this being removed, the Temple of Jupiter Capitolinus, not merely in its latest form, moreover, as the Romans of the Caesars saw it, but also in its earliest shape, when it still wore an Etruscan design and was adorned with terra-cotta antifixae. Where the Coliseum stands now, we could at the same time admire Nero's Golden House; on the Piazza of the Pantheon we should find out only the Pantheon of today as bequeathed to us by Hadrian, but on the same site also Agrippa's original edifice; indeed, the same ground would support the church of Santa Maria sopra Mi-

[1] According to *The Cambridge Ancient History*, Vol. VII. (1928) "The Founding of Rome," by Hugh Last.

nerva and the old temple over which it was built. And the observer would need merely to shift the focus of his eyes, perhaps, or change his position, in order to call up a view of either the one or the other.

There is clearly no object in spinning this fantasy further; it leads to the inconceivable, or even to absurdities. If we try to represent historical sequence in spatial terms, it can only be done by juxtaposition in space; the same space will not hold two contents. Our attempt seems like an idle game; it has only one justification; it shows us how far away from mastering the idiosyncrasies of mental life we are by treating them in terms of visual representation.

There is one objection, though, to which we must pay attention. It questions our choosing in particular the past history of a *city* to liken to the past of the mind. Even for mental life, our assumption that everything past is preserved holds good only on condition that the organ of the mind remains intact and its structure has not been injured by traumas or inflammation. Destructive influences comparable to these morbid agencies are never lacking in the history of any town, even if it has had a less chequered past than Rome, even if, like London, it has hardly ever been pillaged by an enemy. Demolitions and the erection of new buildings in the place of old occur in cities which have had the most peaceful existence; therefore a town is from the outset unsuited for the comparison I have made of it with a mental organism.

We admit this objection; we will abandon our search for a striking effect of contrast and turn to what is after all a closer object of comparison, the body of an animal or human being. But here, too, we find the same thing. The early stages of development are in no sense still extant; they have been absorbed into the later features for which they supplied the material. The embryo cannot be demonstrated in the adult; the thymus gland of childhood is replaced after puberty by connective tissue but no longer exists itself; in the marrow-bone of a grown man I can, it is true, trace the outline of the childish bone-structure, but this latter no longer survives in itself—it lengthened and thickened until it reached its final form. The fact is that a survival of all the early stages alongside the final form is only possible in the mind, and that it is impossible for us to represent a phenomenon of this kind in visual terms.

Perhaps we are going too far with this con-clusion. Perhaps we ought to be content with the assertion that what is past in the mind *can* survive and need not necessarily perish. It is always possible that even in the mind much that is old may be so far obliterated or absorbed—whether normally or by way of exception—that it cannot be restored or re-animated by any means, or that survival of it is always connected with certain favourable conditions. It is possible, but we know nothing about it. We can only be sure that it is more the rule than the exception for the past to survive in the mind.

Thus we are entirely willing to acknowledge that the "oceanic" feeling exists in many people, and we are disposed to relate it to an early stage in ego-feeling; the further question then arises: what claim has this feeling to be regarded as the source of the need for religion.

To me this claim does not seem very forcible. Surely a feeling can only be a source of energy when it is itself the expression of a strong need. The derivation of a need for religion from the child's feeling of helplessness and the longing it evokes for a father seems to me incontrovertible, especially since this feeling is not simply carried on from childhood days but is kept alive perpetually by the fear of what the superior power of fate will bring. I could not point to any need in childhood so strong as that for a father's protection. Thus the part played by the "oceanic" feeling, which I suppose seeks to reinstate limitless narcissism, cannot possibly take the first place. The derivation of the religious attitude can be followed back in clear outline as far as the child's feeling of helplessness. There may be something else behind this, but for the present it is wrapped in obscurity.

I can imagine that the "oceanic" feeling could become connected with religion later on. That feeling of oneness with the universe which is its ideational content sounds very like a first attempt at the consolations of religion, like another way taken by the ego of denying the dangers it sees threatening it in the external world. I must again confess that I find it very difficult to work with these intangible quantities. Another friend of mine, whose insatiable scientific curiosity has impelled him to the most out-of-the-way researches and to the acquisition of encyclopaedic knowledge, has assured me that the Yogi by their practices of withdrawal from the world, concentrating attention on bodily functions, peculiar methods of breathing, actually are able to produce new sensations and diffused feelings in themselves which he regards as regressions to primordial, deeply buried mental states. He sees in them a physiological foundation, so to speak, of much of the wisdom of mysticism. There would be connections to be made here with many obscure modifications of mental life, such as trance and ecstasy. But I am moved to exclaim, in the words of Schiller's diver:

Who breathes overhead in the rose-tinted light may be glad!

II

IN my *Future of an Illusion*[1] I was concerned much less with the deepest sources of religious feeling than with what the ordinary man understands by his religion, that system of doctrines and pledges that on the one hand explains the riddle of this world to him with an enviable completeness, and on the other assures him that a solicitous Providence is watching over him and will make up to him in a future existence for any shortcomings in this life. The ordinary man cannot imagine this Providence in any other form but that of a greatly exalted father, for only such a one could understand the needs of the sons of men, or be softened by their prayers and placated by the signs of their remorse. The whole thing is so patently infantile, so incongruous with reality, that to one whose attitude to humanity is friendly it is painful to think that the great majority of mortals will never be able to rise above this view of life. It is even more humiliating to discover what a large number of those alive today, who must see that this religion is not tenable, yet try to defend it inch by inch, as if with a series of pitiable rearguard actions. One would like to count oneself among the believers, so as to admonish the philosophers who try to preserve the God of religion by substituting for him an impersonal, shadowy, abstract principle, and say, "Thou shalt not take the name of the Lord thy God in vain!" Some of the great men of the past did the same, but that is no justification for us; we know why they had to do so.

We will now go back to the ordinary man and his religion—the only religion that ought to bear the name. The well-known words of one of our great and wise poets come to mind in which he expresses his view of the relation of religion to art and science. They run:

[1] 1927 (London: Hogarth Press, 1928).

He who has Science and has Art,
  Religion, too, has he;
Who has not Science, has not Art,
  Let him religious be![2]

On the one hand, these words contrast religion with the two highest achievements of man, and on the other, they declare that in respect of their value in life they can represent or replace each other. If we wish to deprive even the ordinary man, too, of his religion, we shall clearly not have the authority of the poet on our side. We will seek to get in touch with the meaning of his utterance by a special way. Life as we find it is too hard for us; it entails too much pain, too many disappointments, impossible tasks. We cannot do without palliative remedies. We cannot dispense with auxiliary constructions, as Theodor Fontane said. There are perhaps three of these means: powerful diversions of interest, which lead us to care little about our misery; substitutive gratification, which lessen it; and intoxicating substances, which make us insensitive to it. Something of this kind is indispensable.[3] Voltaire is aiming at a diversion of interest when he brings his *Candide* to a close with the advice that people should cultivate their gardens; scientific work is another deflection of the same kind. The substitute gratifications, such as art offers, are illusions in contrast to reality, but none the less satisfying to the mind on that account, thanks to the place which phantasy has reserved for herself in mental life. The intoxicating substances affect our body, alter its chemical processes. It is not so simple to find the place where religion belongs in this series. We must look further afield.

The question, "What is the purpose of human life?" has been asked times without number; it has never received a satisfactory answer; perhaps it does not admit of such an answer. Many a questioner has added that if it should appear that life has no purpose, then it would lose all value for him. But these threats alter nothing. It looks, on the contrary, as though one had a right to dismiss this question, for it seems to presuppose that belief in the superiority of the human race with which we are already so familiar in its other expressions. Nobody asks what is the

[2] Goethe, *Zahmen Xenien* IX (*Gedichte aus dem Nachlass*).
[3] Wilhelm Busch, in *Die fromme Helene*, says the same thing on a lower level: "The man who has cares has brandy too."

purpose of the lives of animals, unless perad-
venture they are designed to be of service to
man. But this, too, will not hold, for with
many animals man can do nothing—except
describe, classify, and study them; and countless species have declined to be put even to
this use, by living and dying and becoming
extinct before men had set eyes upon them.
So again, only religion is able to answer the
question of the purpose of life. One can hardly
go wrong in concluding that the idea of a
purpose in life stands and falls with the religious system.

We will turn, therefore, to the less ambitious problem: what the behaviour of men
themselves reveals as the purpose and object
of their lives, what they demand of life and
wish to attain in it. The answer to this can
hardly be in doubt: they seek happiness, they
want to become happy and to remain so.
There are two sides to this striving, a positive
and a negative; it aims on the one hand at
eliminating pain and discomfort, on the other
at the experience of intense pleasures. In its
narrower sense, the word *happiness* relates
only to the last. Thus human activities branch
off in two directions—corresponding to this
double goal—according to which of the two
they aim at realizing, either predominantly or
even exclusively.

As we see, it is simply the pleasure-principle
which draws up the programme of life's purpose. This principle dominates the operation
of the mental apparatus from the very beginning; there can be no doubt about its efficiency, and yet its programme is in conflict with
the whole world, with the macrocosm as much
as with the microcosm. It simply cannot be
put into execution, the whole constitution of
things runs counter to it; one might say the
intention that man should be *happy* is not
included in the scheme of *Creation*. What is
called *happiness* in its narrowest sense comes
from the satisfaction—most often instantaneous—of pent-up needs which have reached
great intensity, and by its very nature can
only be a transitory experience. When any
condition desired by the pleasure-principle is
protracted, it results in a feeling only of mild
comfort; we are so constituted that we can
only intensely enjoy contrasts, much less intensely states in themselves.[1] Our possibilities
of happiness are thus limited from the start

by our very constitution. It is much less
difficult to be unhappy. Suffering comes from
three quarters: from our own body, which is
destined to decay and dissolution, and cannot
even dispense with anxiety and pain as danger-
signals; from the outer world, which can rage
against us with the most powerful and pitiless
forces of destruction; and finally from our
relations with other men. The unhappiness
which has this last origin we find perhaps more
painful than any other; we tend to regard it
more or less as a gratuitous addition, although it cannot be any less an inevitable fate
than the suffering that proceeds from other
sources.

It is no wonder if, under the pressure of
these possibilities of suffering, humanity is
wont to reduce its demands for happiness, just
as even the pleasure-principle itself changes
into the more accommodating reality-principle
under the influence of external environment;
if a man thinks himself happy if he has merely
escaped unhappiness or weathered trouble; if
in general the task of avoiding pain forces
that of obtaining pleasure into the background.
Reflection shows that there are very different
ways of attempting to perform this task; and
all these ways have been recommended by the
various schools of wisdom in the art of life
and put into practice by men. Unbridled
gratification of all desires forces itself into
the foreground as the most alluring guiding
principle in life, but it entails preferring enjoyment to caution and penalizes itself after
short indulgence. The other methods, in which
avoidance of pain is the main motive, are differentiated according to the source of the
suffering against which they are mainly directed. Some of these measures are extreme
and some moderate, some are one-sided and
some deal with several aspects of the matter
at once. Voluntary loneliness, isolation from
others, is the readiest safeguard against the
unhappiness that may arise out of human relations. We know what this means: the happiness found along this path is that of peace.
Against the dreaded outer world one can defend oneself only by turning away in some
other direction, if the difficulty is to be solved
single-handed. There is indeed another and
better way: that of combining with the rest
of the human community and taking up the
attack on nature, thus forcing it to obey human will, under the guidance of science. One
is working, then, with all for the good of all.
But the most interesting methods for averting

[1] Goethe even warns us that "nothing is so hard to
bear as a train of happy days." This may be an exaggeration all the same.

pain are those which aim in influencing the organism itself. In the last analysis, all pain is but sensation; it only exists in so far as we feel it, and we feel it only in consequence of certain characteristics of our organism.

The crudest of these methods of influencing the body, but also the most effective, is the chemical one: that of intoxication. I do not think anyone entirely understands their operation, but it is a fact that there are certain substances foreign to the body which, when present in the blood or tissues, directly cause us pleasurable sensations, but also so change the conditions of our perceptivity that we become insensible of disagreeable sensations. The two effects not only take place simultaneously, they seem to be closely bound up with each other. But there must be substances in the chemical composition of our bodies which can do the same, for we know of at least one morbid state, that of mania, in which a condition similar to this intoxication arises without any drug being absorbed. Besides this, our normal mental life shows variations, according to which pleasure is experienced with more or less ease, and along with this goes a diminished or increased sensitivity to pain. It is greatly to be regretted that this toxic aspect of mental processes has so far eluded scientific research. The services rendered by intoxicating substances in the struggle for happiness and in warding off misery rank so highly as a benefit that both individuals and races have given them an established position within their libido-economy. It is not merely the immediate gain in pleasure which one owes to them, but also a measure of that independence of the outer world which is so sorely craved. Men know that with the help they can get from "drowning their cares" they can at any time slip away from the oppression of reality and find a refuge in a world of their own where painful feelings do not enter. We are aware that it is just this property which constitutes the danger and injuriousness of intoxicating substances. In certain circumstances they are to blame when valuable energies which could have been used to improve the lot of humanity are uselessly wasted.

The complicated structure of our mental apparatus admits, however, of a whole series of other kinds of influence. The gratification of instincts is happiness, but when the outer world lets us starve, refuses us satisfaction of our needs, they become the cause of very great suffering. So the hope is born that by influencing these impulses one may escape some measure of suffering. This type of defence against pain no longer relates to the sensory apparatus; it seeks to control the internal sources of our needs themselves. An extreme form of it consists in annihilation of the instincts, as taught by the wisdom of the East and practised by the Yogi. When it succeeds, it is true, it involves giving up all other activities as well (sacrificing the whole of life), and again, by another path, the only happiness it brings is that of peace. The same way is taken when the aim is less extreme and only control of the instincts is sought. When this is so, the higher mental systems which recognize the reality-principle have the upper hand. The aim of gratification is by no means abandoned in this case; a certain degree of protection against suffering is secured, in that lack of satisfaction causes less pain when the instincts are kept in check than when they are unbridled. On the other hand, this brings with it an undeniable reduction in the degree of enjoyment obtainable. The feeling of happiness produced by indulgence of a wild, untamed craving is incomparably more intense than is the satisfying of a curbed desire. The irresistibility of perverted impulses, perhaps the charm of forbidden things generally, may in this way be explained economically.

Another method of guarding against pain is by using the libido-displacements that our mental equipment allows of, by which it gains so greatly in flexibility. The task is then one of transferring the instinctual aims into such directions that they cannot be frustrated by the outer world. Sublimation of the instincts lends an aid in this. Its success is greatest when a man knows how to heighten sufficiently his capacity for obtaining pleasure from mental and intellectual work. Fate has little power against him then. This kind of satisfaction, such as the artist's joy in creation, in embodying his phantasies, or the scientist's in solving problems or discovering truth, has a special quality which we shall certainly one day be able to define metapsychologically. Until then we can only say metaphorically it seems to us *higher* and *finer*, but, compared with that of gratifying gross primitive instincts, its intensity is tempered and diffused; it does not overwhelm us physically. The weak point of this method, however, is that it is not generally applicable; it is only available to the few.

It presupposes special gifts and dispositions which are not very commonly found in a sufficient degree. And even to these few it does not secure complete protection against suffering; it gives no invulnerable armour against the arrows of fate, and it usually fails when a man's own body becomes a source of suffering to him.[1]

This behaviour reveals clearly enough its aim—that of making oneself independent of the external world, by looking for happiness in the inner things of the mind; in the next method the same features are even more marked. The connection with reality is looser still; satisfaction is obtained through illusions, which are recognized as such, without the discrepancy between them and reality being allowed to interfere with the pleasure they give. These illusions are derived from the life of phantasy which, at the time when the sense of reality developed, was expressly exempted from the demands of the reality-test and set apart for the purpose of fulfilling wishes which would be very hard to realize. At the head of these phantasy-pleasures stands the enjoyment of works of art which through the agency of the artist is opened to those who cannot themselves create.[2] Those who are sensitive to the influence of art do not know how to rate it high enough as a source of happiness and consolation in life. Yet art affects us but as a mild narcotic and can provide no more than a temporary refuge for us from the hardships of life; its influence is not strong enough to make us forget real misery.

Another method operates more energetically and thoroughly; it regards reality as the source of all suffering, as the one and only enemy, with whom life is intolerable and with whom, therefore, all relations must be broken off if one is to be happy in any way at all. The hermit turns his back on this world; he will have nothing to do with it. But one can do more than that; one can try to re-create it, try to build up another instead, from which the most unbearable features are eliminated and replaced by others corresponding to one's own wishes. He who in his despair and defiance sets out on this path will not as a rule get very far; reality will be too strong for him. He becomes a madman and usually finds no one to help him in carrying through his delusion. It is said, however, that each one of us behaves in some respect like the paranoiac, substituting a wish-fulfilment for some aspect of the world which is unbearable to him, and carrying this delusion through into reality. When a large number of people make this attempt together and try to obtain assurance of happiness and protection from suffering by a delusional transformation of reality, it acquires special significance. The religions of humanity, too, must be classified as mass-delusions of this kind. Needless to say, no one who shares a delusion recognizes it as such.

I do not suppose that I have enumerated all the methods by which men strive to win happiness and keep suffering at bay, and I know, too, that the material might have been arranged differently. One of these methods I have not yet mentioned at all—not because I had forgotten it, but because it will interest us in another connection. How would it be possible to forget this way of all others of practising the art of life! It is conspicuous for its remarkable capacity to combine characteristic features. Needless to say, it, too, strives to bring about independence of fate—as we may best call it—and with this object it looks for satisfaction within the mind, and uses the capacity for displacing libido which we mentioned before, but it does not turn away from the outer world; on the contrary, it takes a firm hold of its objects and obtains happiness from an emotional relation to them. Nor is it content to strive for avoidance of pain—that goal of weary resignation;

---

[1] When there is no special disposition in a man imperatively prescribing the direction of his life-interest, the ordinary work all can do for a livelihood can play the part which Voltaire wisely advocated it should do in our lives. It is not possible to discuss the significance of work for the economics of the libido adequately within the limits of a short survey. Laying stress upon importance of work has a greater effect than any other technique of living in the direction of binding the individual more closely to reality; in his work he is at least securely attached to a part of reality, the human community. Work is no less valuable for the opportunity it and the human relations connected with it provide for a very considerable discharge of libidinal component impulses, narcissistic, aggressive, and even erotic, than because it is indispensable for subsistence and justifies existence in a society. The daily work of earning a livelihood affords particular satisfaction when it has been selected by free choice, i.e., when through sublimation it enables use to be made of existing inclinations, of instinctual impulses that have retained their strength or are more intense than usual for constitutional reasons. And yet as a path to happiness work is not valued very highly by men. They do not run after it as they do after other opportunities for gratification. The great majority work only when forced by necessity, and this natural human aversion to work gives rise to the most difficult social problems.

[2] Cf. "Formulations regarding the Two Principles in Mental Functioning" (1911), *Collected Papers*, IV; and *General Introduction to Psycho-Analysis* (1915-17), Lecture XXIII, p. 593 above.

rather it passes that by heedlessly and holds fast to the deep-rooted, passionate striving for a positive fulfilment of happiness. Perhaps it really comes nearer to this goal than any other method. I am speaking, of course, of that way of life which makes love the centre of all things and anticipates all happiness from loving and being loved. This attitude is familiar enough to all of us; one of the forms in which love manifests itself, sexual love, gives us our most intense experience of an overwhelming pleasurable sensation and so furnishes a prototype for our strivings after happiness. What is more natural than that we should persist in seeking happiness along the path by which we first encountered it? The weak side of this way of living is clearly evident; and were it not for this, no human being would ever have thought of abandoning this path to happiness in favour of any other. We are never so defenceless against suffering as when we love, never so forlornly unhappy as when we have lost our love-object or its love. But this does not complete the story of that way of life which bases happiness on love; there is much more to be said about it.

We may here go on to consider the interesting case in which happiness in life is sought first and foremost in the enjoyment of beauty, wherever it is to be found by our senses and our judgment, the beauty of human forms and movements, of natural objects, of landscapes, of artistic and even scientific creations. As a goal in life, this aesthetic attitude offers little protection against the menace of suffering, but it is able to compensate for a great deal. The enjoyment of beauty produces a particular, mildly intoxicating kind of sensation. There is no very evident use in beauty; the necessity of it for cultural purposes is not apparent, and yet civilization could not do without it. The science of aesthetics investigates the conditions in which things are regarded as beautiful; it can give no explanation of the nature or origin of beauty; as usual, its lack of results is concealed under a flood of resounding and meaningless words. Unfortunately, psycho-analysis, too, has less to say about beauty than about most things. Its derivation from the realms of sexual sensation is all that seems certain; the love of beauty is a perfect example of a feeling with an inhibited aim. *Beauty* and *attraction* are first of all the attributes of a sexual object. It is remarkable that the genitals themselves, the sight of which is always exciting, are hardly ever regarded as beautiful; the quality of beauty seems, on the other hand, to attach to certain secondary sexual characters.

In spite of the incompleteness of these considerations, I will venture on a few remarks in conclusion of this discussion. The goal towards which the pleasure-principle impels us —of becoming happy—is not attainable; yet we may not—nay, cannot—give up the effort to come nearer to realization of it by some means or other. Very different paths may be taken towards it: some pursue the positive aspect of the aim, attainment of pleasure; others the negative, avoidance of pain. By none of these ways can we achieve all that we desire. In that modified sense in which we have seen it to be attainable, happiness is a problem of the economics of the libido in each individual. There is no sovereign recipe in this matter which suits all; each one must find out for himself by which particular means he may achieve felicity. All kinds of different factors will operate to influence his choice. It depends on how much real gratification he is likely to obtain in the external world, and how far he will find it necessary to make himself independent of it; finally, too, on the belief he has in himself of his power to alter it in accordance with his wishes. Even at this stage the mental constitution of the individual will play a decisive part, aside from any external considerations. The man who is predominantly erotic will choose emotional relationships with others before all else; the narcissistic type, who is more self-sufficient, will seek his essential satisfactions in the inner workings of his own soul; the man of action will never abandon the external world in which he can essay his power. The interests of narcissistic types will be determined by their particular gifts and the degree of instinctual sublimation of which they are capable. When any choice is pursued to an extreme, it penalizes itself, in that it exposes the individual to the dangers accompanying any one exclusive life-interest which may always prove inadequate. Just as a cautious businessman avoids investing all his capital in one concern, so wisdom would probably admonish us also not to anticipate all our happiness from one quarter alone. Success is never certain; it depends on the co-operation of many factors, perhaps on none more than the capacity of the mental constitution to adapt itself to the outer world and then utilize this last for obtaining pleasure. Any one who is born with a specially unfavourable instinctual constitution, and whose libido-components do not go through the transformation and modification necessary for successful achievement in later life, will find it hard to obtain happiness from his external environment, especially if he is faced with the more difficult tasks. One last possibility of dealing with life remains to such people and it offers them at least substitute-gratifications; it takes the form of the flight into neurotic illness, and they mostly adopt it while they are still young. Those whose efforts to obtain happiness come to nought in later years still find consolation in the pleasure of chronic intoxication, or else they embark upon that despairing attempt at revolt—psychosis.

Religion circumscribes these measures of choice and adaptation by urging upon everyone alike its single way of achieving happiness and guarding against pain. Its method consists in decrying the value of life and promulgating a view of the real world that is distorted like a delusion, and both of these imply a preliminary intimidating influence upon intelligence. At such a cost—by the forcible imposition of mental infantilism and inducing a mass-delusion—religion succeeds in saving many people from individual neuroses. But little more. There are, as we have said, many paths by which the happiness attainable for man can be reached, but none which is certain to take him to it. Nor can religion keep her promises either. When the faithful find themselves reduced in the end to speaking of God's *inscrutable decree*, they thereby avow that all that is left to them in their sufferings is unconditional submission as a last-remaining consolation and source of happiness. And if a man is willing to come to this, he could probably have arrived there by a shorter road.

III

OUR discussion of happiness has so far not taught us much that is not already common knowledge. Nor does the prospect of discovering anything new seem much greater if we go on with the problem of why it is so hard for mankind to be happy. We gave the answer before, when we cited the three sources of human sufferings, namely, the superior force of nature, the disposition to decay of our bodies, and the inadequacy of our methods of regulating human relations in the family, the community, and the state. In regard to the first two, our judgment cannot hesitate: it forces us to recognize these sources of suffering and to submit to the inevitable. We shall never completely subdue nature; our body, too, is an organism, itself a part of nature, and will always contain the seeds of dissolution, with its limited power of adaptation and achievement. The effect of this recognition is in no way disheartening; on the contrary, it points out the direction for our efforts. If we cannot abolish all suffering, yet a great deal of it we can, and can mitigate more; the experience of several thousand years has convinced us of this. To the third, the social source of our distresses, we take up a different attitude. We prefer not to regard it as one at all; we cannot see why the systems we have ourselves created should not rather ensure protection and well-being for us all. To be sure, when we consider how unsuccessful our efforts to safeguard against suffering in this particular have proved, the suspicion dawns upon us that a bit of unconquerable nature lurks concealed behind this difficulty as well—in the shape of our own mental constitution.

When we start to consider this possibility, we come across a point of view which is so amazing that we will pause over it. According to it, our so-called civilization itself is to blame for a great part of our misery, and we should be much happier if we were to give it up and go back to primitive conditions. I call this amazing because—however one may define culture—it is undeniable that every means by which we try to guard ourselves against menaces from the several sources of human distress is a part of this same culture.

How has it come about that so many people have adopted this strange attitude of hostility to civilization? In my opinion, it arose from a background of profound long-standing discontent with the existing state of civilization, which finally crystallized into this judgment as a result of certain historical happenings. I believe I can identify the last two of these; I am not learned enough to trace the links in the chain back into the history of the human species. At the time when Christianity conquered the pagan religions, some such antagonism to culture must already have been actively at work. It is closely related to the low estimation put upon earthly life by Christian doctrine. The earlier of the last two historical developments was when, as a result of voyages of discovery, men came into contact with primitive peoples and races. To the Europeans, who failed to observe them carefully and misunderstood what they saw, these people seemed to lead simple, happy lives—wanting for nothing —such as the travellers who visited them, with all their superior culture, were unable to achieve. Later experience has corrected this opinion on many points; in several instances the ease of life was due to the bounty of nature and the possibilities of ready satisfaction for the great human needs, but it was erroneously attributed to the absence of the complicated conditions of civilization. The last of the two historical events is especially familiar to us; it was when people began to understand the nature of the neuroses which threaten to undermine the modicum of happiness open to civilized man. It was found that men become neurotic because they cannot tolerate the degree of privation that society imposes on them in virtue of its cultural ideals, and it was supposed that a return to greater possibilities of happiness would ensue if these standards were abolished or greatly relaxed.

And there exists an element of disappointment, in addition. In the last generations, man has made extraordinary strides in knowledge of the natural sciences and technical application of them, and has established his dominion over nature in a way never before imagined. The details of this forward progress are universally known: it is unnecessary to enumerate them. Mankind is proud of its exploits and has a right to be. But men are beginning to perceive that all this newly-won power over space and time, this conquest of the forces of nature, this fulfilment of age-old longings, has not increased the amount of pleasure they can obtain in life, has not made them feel any happier. The valid conclusion from this is merely that power over nature is not the only condition of human happiness, just as it is not the only goal of civilization's efforts, and there is no ground for inferring that its technical progress is worthless from the standpoint of happiness. It prompts one to exclaim: Is it not then a positive pleasure, an unequivocal gain in happiness, to be able to hear, whenever I like, the voice of a child living hundreds of miles away, or to know directly a friend of mine arrives at his destination that he has come well and safely through the long and troublesome voyage? And is it nothing that medical science has succeeded in enormously reducing the mortality of young children, the dangers of infection for women in childbirth, indeed, in very considerably prolonging the average length of human life? And there is still a long list one could add to these benefits that we owe to the much-despised era of scientific and practical progress—but a critical, pessimistic voice makes itself heard, say-

ing that most of these advantages follow the model of those "cheap pleasures" in the anecdote. One gets this enjoyment by sticking one's bare leg outside the bedclothes on a cold winter's night and then drawing it in again. If there were no railway to make light of distances, my child would never have left home, and I should not need the telephone to hear his voice. If there were no vessels crossing the ocean, my friend would never have embarked on his voyage, and I should not need the telegraph to relieve my anxiety about him. What is the use of reducing the mortality of children, when it is precisely this reduction which imposes the greatest moderation on us in begetting them, so that taken all round we do not rear more children than in the days before the reign of hygiene, while at the same time we have created difficult conditions for sexual life in marriage and probably counteracted the beneficial effects of natural selection? And what do we gain by a long life when it is full of hardship and starved of joys and so wretched that we can only welcome death as our deliverer?

It seems to be certain that our present-day civilization does not inspire in us a feeling of well-being, but it is very difficult to form an opinion whether in earlier times people felt any happier and what part their cultural conditions played in the question. We always tend to regard trouble objectively, i.e., to place ourselves with our own wants and our own sensibilities in the same conditions, so as to discover what opportunities for happiness or unhappiness we should find in them. This method of considering the problem, which appears to be objective because it ignores the varieties of subjective sensitivity, is of course the most subjective possible, for by applying it one substitutes one's own mental attitude for the unknown attitude of other men. Happiness, on the contrary, is something essentially subjective. However we may shrink in horror at the thought of certain situations, that of the galley-slaves in antiquity, of the peasants in the Thirty Years' War, of the victims of the Inquisition, of the Jews awaiting a pogrom, it is still impossible for us to feel ourselves into the position of these people, to imagine the differences which would be brought about by constitutional obtuseness of feeling, gradual stupefaction, the cessation of all anticipation, and by all the grosser and more subtle ways in which insensibility to both pleasurable and painful sensations can be induced. Moreover, on occasions when the most extreme forms of suffering have to be endured, special mental protective devices come into operation. It seems to me unprofitable to follow up this aspect of the problem further.

It is time that we should turn our attention to the nature of this culture, the value of which is so much disputed from the point of view of happiness. Until we have learnt something by examining it for ourselves, we will not look round for formulas which express its essence in a few words. We will be content to repeat[1] that the word *culture* describes the sum of the achievements and institutions which differentiate our lives from those of our animal forebears and serve two purposes, namely, that of protecting humanity against nature and of regulating the relations of human beings among themselves. In order to learn more than this, we must bring together the individual features of culture as they are manifested in human communities. We shall have no hesitation in allowing ourselves to be guided by the common usages of language, or, as one might say, the *feeling* of language, confident that we shall thus take into account inner attitudes which still resist expression in abstract terms.

The beginning is easy. We recognize as belonging to culture all the activities and possessions which men use to make the earth serviceable to them, to protect them against the tyranny of natural forces, and so on. There is less doubt about this aspect of civilization than any other. If we go back far enough, we find that the first acts of civilization were the use of tools, the gaining of power over fire, and the construction of dwellings. Among these the acquisition of power over fire stands out as a quite exceptional achievement, without a prototype;[2] while the other two opened up paths

[1] Cf. *The Future of an Illusion*.

[2] Psycho-analytic material, as yet incomplete and not capable of unequivocal interpretation, nevertheless admits of a surmise—which sounds fantastic enough—about the origin of this human feat. It is as if primitive man had had the impulse, when he came in contact with fire, to gratify an infantile pleasure in respect of it and put it out with a stream of urine. The legends that we possess leave no doubt that flames shooting upwards like tongues were originally felt to have a phallic sense. Putting out fire by urinating—which is also introduced in the later fables of Gulliver in Lilliput and Rabelais's Gargantua—therefore represented a sexual act with a man, an enjoyment of masculine potency in homosexual rivalry. Whoever was the first to deny himself this pleasure and spare the fire was able to take it with him and break it in to his own service. By curbing the fire of his own sexual passion, he was able to tame fire as a force of nature. This great cultural victory was thus a reward for refraining from gratification of an instinct. Further, it is as if man had placed woman by the hearth as the guardian of the fire he had taken captive, because her anatomy makes it impossible for her to yield to such

which have ever since been pursued by man, the stimulus towards which is easily imagined. By means of all his tools, man makes his own organs more perfect—both the motor and the sensory—or else removes the obstacles in the way of their activity. Machinery places gigantic power at his disposal which, like his muscles, he can employ in any direction; ships and aircraft have the effect that neither air nor water can prevent his traversing them. With spectacles he corrects the defects of the lens in his own eyes; with telescopes he looks at far distances; with the microscope he overcomes the limitations in visibility due to the structure of his retina. With the photographic camera he has created an instrument which registers transitory visual impressions, just as the gramophone does with equally transient auditory ones; both are at bottom materializations of his own power of memory. With the help of the telephone he can hear at distances which even fairy-tales would treat as insuperable; writing to begin with was the voice of the absent; dwellings were a substitute for the mother's womb, that first abode, in which he was safe and felt so content, for which he probably yearns ever after.

It sounds like a fairy-tale, but not only that; this story of what man by his science and practical inventions has achieved on this earth, where he first appeared as a weakly member of the animal kingdom, and on which each individual of his species must ever again appear as a helpless infant—O inch of nature!— is a direct fulfilment of all, or of most, of the dearest wishes in his fairy-tales. All these possessions he has acquired through culture. Long ago he formed an ideal conception of omnipotence and omniscience which he embodied in his gods. Whatever seemed unattainable to his desires—or forbidden to him—he attributed to these gods. One may say, therefore, that these gods were the ideals of his culture. Now he has himself approached very near to realizing this ideal, he has nearly become a god himself. But only, it is true, in the way that ideals are usually realized in the general experience of humanity. Not completely; in some respects not at all, in others only by halves. Man has become a god by means of artificial limbs, so to speak, quite magnificent when equipped with all his accessory organs; but they do not grow on him and they still give him trouble at times.

a temptation. It is remarkable how regularly analytic findings testify to the close connection between the ideas of ambition, fire, and urethral erotism.

However, he is entitled to console himself with the thought that this evolution will not come to an end in A.D. 1930. Future ages will produce further great advances in this realm of culture, probably inconceivable now, and will increase man's likeness to a god still more. But with the aim of our study in mind, we will not forget, all the same, that the human being of today is not happy with all his likeness to a god.

Thus we recognize that a country has attained a high level of civilization when we find that everything in it that can be helpful in exploiting the earth for man's benefit and in protecting him against nature—everything, in short, that is useful to him—is cultivated and effectively protected. In such a country, the course of rivers which threaten to overflow their banks is regulated, their waters guided through canals to places where they are needed. The soil is industriously cultivated and planted with the vegetation suited to it; the mineral wealth is brought up assiduously from the depths and wrought into the implements and utensils that are required. The means of communications are frequent, rapid, and reliable; wild and dangerous animals have been exterminated, the breeding of tamed and domesticated ones prospers. But we demand other things besides these of civilization, and curiously enough, we expect to find them existing in the same countries. As if we wished to repudiate the first requisition we made, we count it also as proof of a high level of civilization when we see that the industry of the inhabitants is applied as well to things which are not in the least useful and, on the contrary seem to be useless, e.g., when the parks and gardens in a town, which are necessary as playgrounds and air-reservoirs, also bear flowering plants, or when the windows of dwellings are adorned with flowers. We soon become aware that the useless thing which we require of civilization is beauty; we expect a cultured people to revere beauty where it is found in nature and to create it in their handiwork so far as they are able. But this is far from exhausting what we require of civilization. Besides, we expect to see the signs of cleanliness and order. We do not think highly of the cultural level of an English country town in the time of Shakespeare when we read that there was a tall dungheap in front of his father's house in Stratford; we are indignant and call it "barbarous," which is the opposite of civilized, when we find the paths in the Wiener Wald littered with paper. Dirt of any kind seems to us incompatible with civilization; we extend our demands for cleanliness to the human body also, and are amazed to hear what an objectionable odour emanated from the person of the Roi Soleil; we shake our heads when we are shown the tiny washbasin on the Isola Bella which Napoleon used for his daily ablutions. Indeed, we are not surprised if anyone employs the use of soap as a direct measure of civilization. It is the same with order, which, like cleanliness, relates entirely to man's handiwork. But whereas we cannot expect cleanliness in nature, order has, on the contrary, been imitated from nature; man's observations of the great astronomical periodicities not only furnished him with a model, but formed the ground-plan of his first attempts to introduce order into his own life. Order is a kind of repetition-compulsion by which it is ordained once for all when, where and how a thing shall be done so that on every similar occasion doubt and hesitation shall be avoided. The benefits of order are incontestable: it enables us to use space and time to the best advantage, while saving expenditure of mental energy. One would be justified in expecting that it would have ingrained itself from the start and without opposition into all human activities; and one may well wonder that this has not happened, and that, on the contrary, human beings manifest an inborn tendency to negligence, irregularity, and untrustworthiness in their work, and have to be laboriously trained to imitate the example of their celestial models.

Beauty, cleanliness, and order clearly occupy a peculiar position among the requirements of civilization. No one will maintain that they are as essential to life as the activities aimed at controlling the forces of nature and as other factors which we have yet to mention; and yet no one would willingly relegate them to the background as trivial matters. Beauty is an instance which plainly shows that culture is not simply utilitarian in its aims, for the lack of beauty is a thing we cannot tolerate in civilization. The utilitarian advantages of order are quite apparent; with regard to cleanliness, we have to remember that it is required of us by hygiene, and we may surmise that even before the days of scientific prophylaxis the connection between the two was not altogether unsuspected by mankind. But these aims and endeavours of culture are not entirely to be explained on utilitarian lines; there must be something else at work besides.

According to general opinion, however, there

is one feature of culture which characterizes it better than any other, and that is the value it sets upon the higher mental activities—intellectual, scientific, and aesthetic achievement—the leading part it concedes to ideas in human life. First and foremost among these ideas come the religious systems with their complicated evolution, on which I have elsewhere endeavoured to throw a light; next to them come philosophical speculations; and last, the ideals man has formed, his conceptions of the perfection possible in an individual, in a people, in humanity as a whole, and the demands he makes on the basis of these conceptions. These creations of his mind are not independent of each other; on the contrary, they are closely interwoven, and this complicates the attempt to describe them, as well as that to trace their psychological derivation. If we assume as a general hypothesis that the force behind all human activities is a striving towards the two convergent aims of profit and pleasure, we must then acknowledge this as valid also for these other manifestations of culture, although it can be plainly recognized as true only in respect of science and art. It cannot be doubted, however, that the remainder, too, correspond to some powerful need in human beings—perhaps to one which develops fully only in a minority of people. Nor may we allow ourselves to be misled by our own judgments concerning the value of any of these religious or philosophical systems or of these ideals; whether we look upon them as the highest achievement of the human mind, or whether we deplore them as fallacies, one must acknowledge that where they exist, and especially where they are in the ascendant, they testify to a high level of civilization.

We now have to consider the last, and certainly by no means the least important, of the components of culture, namely, the ways in which social relations, the relations of one man to another, are regulated, all that has to do with him as a neighbour, a source of help, a sexual object to others, a member of a family or of a state. It is especially difficult in this matter to remain unbiased by any ideal standards and to ascertain exactly what is specifically cultural here. Perhaps one might begin with the statement that the first attempt ever made to regulate these social relations already contained the essential element of civilization. Had no such attempt been made, these relations would be subject to the wills of individuals: that is to say, the man who was physically strongest

would decide things in accordance with his own interests and desires. The situation would remain the same, even though this strong man should in his turn meet with another who was stronger than he. Human life in communities only becomes possible when a number of men unite together in strength superior to any single individual and remain united against all single individuals. The strength of this united body is then opposed as *right* against the strength of any individual, which is condemned as *brute force*. This substitution of the power of a united number for the power of a single man is the decisive step towards civilization. The essence of it lies in the circumstance that the members of the community have restricted their possibilities of gratification, whereas the individual recognized no such restrictions. The first requisite of culture, therefore, is justice—that is, the assurance that a law once made will not be broken in favour of any individual. This implies nothing about the ethical value of any such law. The further course of cultural development seems to tend towards ensuring that the law shall no longer represent the will of any small body—caste, tribe, section of the population—which may behave like a predatory individual towards other such groups perhaps containing larger numbers. The end-result would be a state of law to which all—that is, all who are capable of uniting—have contributed by making some sacrifice of their own desires, and which leaves none—again with the same exception—at the mercy of brute force.

The liberty of the individual is not a benefit of culture. It was greatest before any culture, though indeed it had little value at that time, because the individual was hardly in a position to defend it. Liberty has undergone restrictions through the evolution of civilization, and justice demands that these restrictions shall apply to all. The desire for freedom that makes itself felt in a human community may be a revolt against some existing injustice and so may prove favourable to a further development of civilization and remain compatible with it. But it may also have its origin in the primitive roots of the personality, still unfettered by civilizing influences, and so become a source of antagonism to culture. Thus the cry for freedom is directed either against particular forms or demands of culture or else against culture itself. It does not seem as if man could be brought by any sort of influence to change his nature into that of the ants; he will always, one imagines, defend his claim to individual freedom against the will of the multitude. A great part of the struggles of mankind centres round the single task of finding some expedient (i.e., satisfying) solution between these individual claims and those of the civilized community; it is one of the problems of man's fate whether this solution can be arrived at in some particular form of culture or whether the conflict will prove irreconcilable.

We have obtained a clear impression of the general picture presented by culture through adopting the common view as to which aspects of human life are to be called cultural; but it is true that so far we have discovered nothing that is not common knowledge. We have, however, at the same time guarded ourselves against accepting the misconception that civilization is synonymous with becoming perfect, is the path by which man is ordained to reach perfection. But now a certain point of view presses for consideration; it will lead perhaps in another direction. The evolution of culture seems to us a peculiar kind of process passing over humanity, of which several aspects strike us as familiar. We can describe this process in terms of the modifications it effects on the known human instinctual dispositions, which it is the economic task of our lives to satisfy. Some of these instincts become absorbed, as it were, so that something appears in place of them which in an individual we call a *character-trait*. The most remarkable example of this process is found in respect of the anal erotism of young human beings. Their primary interest in the excretory function, its organs and products, is changed in the course of their growth into a group of traits that we know well—thriftiness, orderliness, and cleanliness—valuable and welcome qualities in themselves, which, however, may be intensified till they visibly dominate the personality and produce what we call the anal character. How this happens we do not know; but there is no doubt about the accuracy of this conclusion.[1] Now, we have seen that order and cleanliness are essentially cultural demands, although the necessity of them for survival is not particularly apparent, any more than their suitability as sources of pleasure. At this point we must be struck for the first time with the similarity between the process of cultural development and that of the libidinal development in an individual. Other instincts have to be induced to change

[1] Cf. "Character and Anal Erotism" (1908), *Collected Papers,* II; also numerous contributions to the subject by Ernest Jones and others.

the conditions of their gratification, to find it along other paths, a process which is usually identical with what we know so well as sublimation (of the aim of an instinct), but which can sometimes be differentiated from this. Sublimation of instinct is an especially conspicuous feature of cultural evolution; this it is that makes it possible for the higher mental operations, scientific, artistic, ideological activities, to play such an important part in civilized life. If one were to yield to a first impression, one would be tempted to say that sublimation is a fate which has been forced upon instincts by culture alone. But it is better to reflect over this a while longer. Thirdly and lastly, and this seems most important of all, it is impossible to ignore the extent to which civilization is built up on renunciation of instinctual gratifications, the degree to which the existence of civilization presupposes the non-gratification (suppression, repression, or something else?) of powerful instinctual urgencies. This *cultural privation* dominates the whole field of social relations between human beings; we know already that it is the cause of the antagonism against which all civilization has to fight. It sets hard tasks for our scientific work, too; we have a great deal to explain here. It is not easy to understand how it can become possible to withhold satisfaction from an instinct. Nor is it by any means without risk to do so; if the deprivation is not made good economically, one may be certain of producing serious disorders.

But now, if we wish to know what use it is to us to have recognized the evolution of culture as a special process, comparable to the normal growth of an individual to maturity, we must clearly attack another problem and put the question: What are the influences to which the evolution of culture owes its origin, how did it arise, and what determined its course?

IV

THIS task seems too big a one; one may well confess oneself diffident. Here follows what little I have been able to elicit about it.

Once primitive man had made the discovery that it lay in his own hands—speaking literally —to improve his lot on earth by working, it cannot have been a matter of indifference to him whether another man worked with him or against him. The other acquired the value of a fellow-worker, and it was advantageous to live with him. Even earlier, in his ape-like prehistory, man had adopted the habit of forming families: his first helpers were probably the members of his family. One may suppose that the founding of families was in some way connected with the period when the need for genital satisfaction, no longer appearing like an occasional guest who turns up suddenly and then vanishes without letting one hear anything of him for long intervals, had settled down with each man like a permanent lodger. When this happened, the male acquired a motive for keeping the female, or rather, his sexual objects, near him; while the female, who wanted not to be separated from her helpless young, in their interests, too, had to stay by the stronger male.[1] In this primitive family one

[1] The organic periodicity of the sexual process has persisted, it is true, but its effect on mental sexual excitation has been almost reversed. This change is connected primarily with the diminishing importance of the olfactory stimuli by means of which the menstrual process produced sexual excitement in the mind of the male. Their function was taken over by visual stimuli, which could operate permanently, instead of intermittently as the olfactory ones. The *taboo of menstruation* has its origin in this *organic repression*, which acted as a barrier against a phase of development that had been surpassed; all its other motivations are probably of a secondary nature. (Cf. C. D. Daly, "*Hindumythologie und Kastrationskomplex*," *Imago*, Vol. XIII, 1927.) This process is repeated on a different level when the gods of a foregone cultural epoch are changed into demons in the next. The diminution in importance of olfactory stimuli seems itself, however, to be a consequence of man's erecting himself from the earth, of his adoption of an upright gait, which made his genitals, that before had been covered, visible and in need of protection and so evoked feelings of shame. Man's erect posture, therefore, would represent the beginning of the momentous process of cultural evolution. The chain of development would run from this onward, through the diminution in the importance of olfactory stimuli and the isolation of women at their periods, to a time when visual stimuli became paramount, the genitals became visible, further till sexual excitation became constant and the family was founded, and so to the threshold of human culture. This is only a theoretical speculation, but it is important enough to be worth checking carefully by the conditions obtaining among the animals closely allied to man.

There is an unmistakable social factor at work in the impulse of civilization towards cleanliness, which has been subsequently justified by considerations of hygiene but had nevertheless found expression before they were appreciated. The impulse towards cleanliness originates in the striving to get rid of excretions which have become unpleasant to the sense-perceptions. We know that things are different in the nursery. Excreta arouse no aversion in children; they seem precious to them, as being parts of their own bodies which have been detached from them. The training of children is very energetic in this particular; its object is to expedite the development that lies ahead of them, according to which the excreta are to become worthless, disgusting, horrible, and despicable to them. Such a reversal of values would be almost impossible to bring about, were it not that these substances expelled from the body are destined by their strong odours to share the fate that overtook the olfactory stimuli after man had erected himself from the ground. Anal erotism, therefore, is from the first subjected to the *organic repression* which opened up the way to culture. The social factor which has been active in the further modifications of anal erotism comes into play with the fact that in spite of all man's evolutionary progress the smell

essential feature of culture is lacking; the will of the father, the head of it, was unfettered. I have endeavoured in *Totem and Taboo* to show how the way led from this family-life to the succeeding phase of communal existence in the form of a band of brothers. By overpowering the father, the sons had discovered that several men united can be stronger than a single man. The totemic stage of culture is founded upon the restrictions that the band were obliged to impose on one another in order to maintain the new system. These taboos were the first *right* or law. The life of human beings in common therefore had a twofold foundation, i.e., the compulsion to work, created by external necessity, and the power of love, causing the male to wish to keep his sexual object, the female, near him, and the female to keep near her that part of herself which has become detached from her, her child. Eros and Ananke were the parents of human culture, too. The first result of culture was that a larger number of human beings could then live together in common. And since the two great powers were here co-operating together, one might have expected that further cultural evolution would have proceeded smoothly towards even greater mastery over the external world, as well as towards greater extension in the numbers of men sharing the life in common. Nor is it easy to understand how this culture can be felt as anything but satisfying by those who partake of it.

Before we go on to enquire where the disturbances in it arise, we will let ourselves digress from the point that love was one of the founders of culture and so fill a gap left in our previous discussion. We said that man, having found by experience that sexual (genital) love afforded him his greatest gratification, so that it became in effect a prototype of all happiness to him, must have been thereby impelled to seek his happiness further along the path of sexual relations, to make genital erotism the central point of his life. We went on to say that in so doing he becomes to a very dangerous degree dependent on a part of the outer world,

of his own excretions is scarcely disagreeable to him yet, but so far only that of the evacuations of others. The man who is not clean, i.e., who does not eliminate his excretions, therefore offends others, shows no consideration for them—a fact which is exemplified in the commonest and most forcible terms of abuse. It would be incomprehensible, too, that man should use as an abusive epithet the name of his most faithful friend in the animal world, if dogs did not incur the contempt of men through two of their characteristics, i.e., that they are creatures of smell and have no horror of excrement, and, secondly, that they are not ashamed of their sexual functions.

namely, on his chosen love-object, and this exposes him to most painful sufferings if he is rejected by it or loses it through death or defection. The wise men of all ages have consequently warned us emphatically against this way of life; but in spite of all it retains its attraction for a great number of people.

A small minority are enabled by their constitution, nevertheless, to find happiness along the path of love; but far-reaching mental transformations of the erotic function are necessary before this is possible. These people make themselves independent of their object's acquiescence by transferring the main value from the fact of being loved to their own act of loving; they protect themselves against loss of it by attaching their love not to individual objects but to all men equally, and they avoid the uncertainties and disappointments of genital love by turning away from its sexual aim and modifying the instinct into an impulse with an *inhibited aim*. The state which they induce in themselves by this process—an unchangeable, undeviating, tender attitude—has little superficial likeness to the stormy vicissitudes of genital love, from which it is nevertheless derived. It seems that Saint Francis of Assisi may have carried this method of using love to produce an inner feeling of happiness as far as anyone; what we are thus characterizing as one of the procedures by which the pleasure-principle fulfils itself has in fact been linked up in many ways with religion; the connection between them may lie in those remote fastnesses of the mind where the distinctions between the ego and objects, and between the various objects, become matters of indifference. From one ethical standpoint, the deeper motivation of which will later become clear to us, this inclination towards an all-embracing love of others and of the world at large is regarded as the highest state of mind of which man is capable. Even at this early stage in the discussion, I will not withhold the two principal objections we have to raise against this view. A love that does not discriminate seems to us to lose some of its own value, since it does an injustice to its object. And secondly, not all men are worthy of love.

The love that instituted the family still retains its power; in its original form it does not stop short of direct sexual satisfaction, and in its modified form, as aim-inhibited friendliness, it influences our civilization. In both these forms it carries on its task of binding men and women to one another, and it does this with greater intensity than can be achieved through the interest of work in common. The casual and undifferentiated way in which the word *love* is employed by language has its genetic justification. In general usage, the relation between a man and a woman whose genital desires have led them to found a family is called *love;* but the positive attitude of feeling between parents and children, between brothers and sisters in a family, is also called *love*, although to us this relation merits the description of *aim-inhibited love* or *affection*. Love with an inhibited aim was indeed originally full sensual love and in men's unconscious minds is so still. Both of them, the sensual and the aim-inhibited forms, reach out beyond the family and create new bonds with others who before were strangers. Genital love leads to the forming of new families; aim-inhibited love to *friendships*, which are valuable culturally because they do not entail many of the limitations of genital love—for instance, its exclusiveness. But the interrelations between love and culture lose their simplicity as development proceeds. On the one hand, love opposes the interests of culture; on the other, culture menaces love with grievous restrictions.

This rift between them seems inevitable; the cause of it is not immediately recognizable. It expresses itself first in a conflict between the family and the larger community to which the individual belongs. We have seen already that one of culture's principal endeavours is to cement men and women together into larger units. But the family will not give up the individual. The closer the attachment between the members of it, the more they often tend to remain aloof from others, and the harder it is for them to enter into the wider circle of the world at large. That form of life in common which is phylogenetically older, and is in childhood its only form, resists being displaced by the type that becomes acquired later with culture. Detachment from the family has become a task that awaits every adolescent, and often society helps him through it with pubertal and initiatory rites. One gets the impression that these difficulties form an integral part of every process of mental evolution—and indeed, at bottom, of every organic development, too.

The next discord is caused by women, who soon become antithetical to cultural trends and spread around them their conservative influence—the women who at the beginning laid the foundations of culture by the appeal of their love. Women represent the interests of the family and sexual life; the work of civilization has become more and more men's business; it confronts them with ever harder tasks, compels them to sublimations of instinct which women are not easily able to achieve. Since man has not an unlimited amount of mental energy at his disposal, he must accomplish his tasks by distributing his libido to the best advantage. What he employs for cultural purposes he withdraws to a great extent from women and his sexual life; his constant association with men and his dependence on his relations with them even estrange him from his duties as husband and father. Woman finds herself thus forced into the background by the claims of culture, and she adopts an inimical attitude towards it.

The tendency of culture to set restrictions upon sexual life is no less evident than its other aim of widening its sphere of operations. Even the earliest phase of it, the totemic, brought in its train the prohibition against incestuous object-choice, perhaps the most maiming wound ever inflicted throughout the ages on the erotic life of man. Further limitations are laid on it by taboos, laws, and customs, which touch men as well as women. Various types of culture differ in the lengths to which they carry this; and the material structure of the social fabric also affects the measure of sexual freedom that remains. We have seen that culture obeys the laws of psychological economic necessity in making the restrictions, for it obtains a great part of the mental energy it needs by subtracting it from sexuality. Culture behaves towards sexuality in this respect like a tribe or a section of the population which has gained the upper hand and is exploiting the rest to its own advantage. Fear of a revolt among the oppressed then becomes a motive for even stricter regulations. A high-water mark in this type of development has been reached in our Western European civilization. Psychologically it is fully justified in beginning by censuring any manifestations of the sexual life of children, for there would be no prospect of curbing the sexual desires of adults if the ground had not been prepared for it in childhood. Nevertheless, there is no sort of justification for the lengths beyond this to which civilized society goes in actually denying the existence of these manifestations, which are not merely demonstrable but positively glaring. Where sexually mature persons are concerned, object-choice is further narrowed down to the opposite sex and most of the extra-genital forms of satisfaction are in-

terdicted as perversions. The standard which declares itself in these prohibitions is that of a sexual life identical for all; it pays no heed to the disparities in the inborn and acquired sexual constitutions of individuals and cuts off a considerable number of them from sexual enjoyment, thus becoming a cause of grievous injustice. The effect of these restrictive measures might presumably be that all the sexual interest of those who are normal and not constitutionally handicapped could flow without further forfeiture into the channel left open to it. But the only outlet not thus censured, heterosexual genital love, is further circumscribed by the barriers of legitimacy and monogamy. Present-day civilization gives us plainly to understand that sexual relations are permitted only on the basis of a final, indissoluble bond between a man and woman; that sexuality as a source of enjoyment for its own sake is unacceptable to it; and that its intention is to tolerate it only as the hitherto irreplaceable means of muliplying the human race.

This, of course, represents an extreme. Everyone knows that it has proved impossible to put it into execution, even for short periods. Only the weaklings have submitted to such comprehensive interference with their sexual freedom, and stronger natures have done so only under one compensatory condition, of which mention may be made later. Civilized society has seen itself obliged to pass over in silence many transgressions which by its own ordinances it ought to have penalized. This does not justify anyone, however, in leaning towards the other side and assuming that, because it does not achieve all it aims at, such an attitude on the part of society is altogether harmless. The sexual life of civilized man is seriously disabled, whatever we may say; it sometimes makes an impression of being a function in process of becoming atrophied, just as organs like our teeth and our hair seem to be. One is probably right in supposing that the importance of sexuality as a source of pleasurable sensations, i.e., as a means of fulfilling the purpose of life, has perceptibly decreased.[1] Sometimes one imagines one perceives that it is not only the oppression of culture, but something in the nature of the function itself that denies us full satisfaction and urges us in other direc-

[1] There is a short story, which I valued long ago, by a highly sensitive writer, the Englishman, John Galsworthy, who today enjoys general recognition; it is called "The Apple Tree." It shows in a very moving and forcible way how there is no longer any place in present-day civilized life for a simple natural love between two human beings.

tions. This may be an error; it is hard to decide.[1]

[1] The following considerations would support the view expressed above. Man, too, is an animal with an unmistakably bisexual disposition. The individual represents a fusion of two symmetrical halves, of which, according to many authorities, one is purely male, the other female. It is equally possible that each half was originally hermaphroditic. Sex is a biological fact which is hard to evaluate psychologically, although it is of extraordinary importance in mental life. We are accustomed to say that every human being displays both male and female instinctual impulses, needs, and attributes, but the characteristics of what is male and female can only be demonstrated in anatomy, and not in psychology. Where the latter is concerned, the antithesis of sex fades away into that of activity and passivity, and we far too readily identify activity with masculinity and passivity with femininity, a statement which is by no means universally confirmed in the animal world. The theory of bisexuality is still very obscure, and in psycho-analysis we must be painfully aware of the disadvantage we are under as long as it still remains unconnected with the theory of instincts. However this may be, if we assume it to be a fact that each individual has both male and female desires which need satisfaction in his sexual life, we shall be prepared for the possibility that these needs will not both be gratified on the same object, and that they will interfere with each other, if they cannot be kept apart so that each impulse flows into a special channel suited for it. Another difficulty arises from the circumstance that so often a measure of direct aggressiveness is coupled with an erotic relationship, over and above its inherent sadistic components. The love-object does not always view these complications with the degree of understanding and tolerance manifested by the peasant woman who complained that her husband did not love her any more, because he had not beaten her for a week.

The conjecture which leads furthest, however, is that —and here we come back to the remarks in the footnote on p. 782—the whole of sexuality, and not merely anal erotism, is threatened with falling a victim to the organic repression consequent upon man's adoption of the erect posture and the lowering in value of the sense of smell; so that since that time the sexual function has been associated with a resistance not susceptible of further explanation, which puts obstacles in the way of full satisfaction and forces it away from its sexual aim towards sublimations and displacements of libido. I am aware that Bleuler (in *"Der Sexualwiderstand," Jahrbuch für psychoanalytische und psychopathologische Forschungen*, Vol. V, 1913) once pointed out the existence of a fundamental tendency of this kind towards rejecting sexual life. All neurotics, and many others too, take exception to the fact that *inter urinas et faeces nascimur* [We are born among urine and faeces]. The genitals, too, excite the olfactory sense strongly in a way that many people cannot tolerate and which spoils sexual intercourse for them. Thus we should find, as the deepest root of the sexual repression that marches with culture, the organic defence of the new form of life that began with the erect posture against the earliest type of animal existence— a result of scientific researches that coincides in a curious way with often expressed vulgar prejudices. At the present time, nevertheless, these results are but unconfirmed possibilities, not yet scientifically substantiated. Nor should we forget that, in spite of the undeniable diminution in the importance of olfactory stimuli, there exist even in Europe races who prize highly as aphrodisiacs the strong genital odours so objectionable to us and who will not renounce them. (Cf. the reports of folkloristic information obtained by Iwan Bloch's "Questionnaire," appearing under the title of *"Über den Geruchssinn in der vita sexualis"* in various volumes of Friedrich S. Krauss' *Anthropophyteia*.)

V

PSYCHO-ANALYTIC work has shown that these frustrations in respect of sexual life are especially unendurable to the so-called neurotics among us. These persons manufacture substitute-gratifications for themselves in their symptoms, which, however, are either painful in themselves or become the cause of suffering owing to the difficulties they create with the person's environment and society at large. It is easy to understand the latter fact, but the former presents us with a new problem. But culture demands other sacrifices besides that of sexual gratifications.

We have regarded the difficulties in the development of civilization as part of the general difficulty accompanying all evolution, for we have traced them to the inertia of libido, its disinclination to relinquish an old position in favour of a new one. It is much the same thing if we say that the conflict between civilization and sexuality is caused by the circumstance that sexual love is a relationship between two people, in which a third can only be superfluous or disturbing, whereas civilization is founded on relations between larger groups of persons. When a love-relationship is at its height, no room is left for any interest in the surrounding world; the pair of lovers are sufficient unto themselves, do not even need the child they have in common to make them happy. In no other case does Eros so plainly betray the core of his being, his aim of making one out of many; but when he has achieved it in the proverbial way through the love of two human beings, he is not willing to go further.

From all this we might well imagine that a civilized community could consist of pairs of individuals such as this, libidinally satisfied in each other, and linked to all the others by work and common interests. If this were so, culture would not need to levy energy from sexuality. But such a desirable state of things does not exist and never has existed; in actuality, culture is not content with such limited ties as these; we see that it endeavours to bind the members of the community to one another by libidinal ties as well, that it makes use of every means and favours every avenue by which powerful identifications can be created among them, and that it exacts a heavy toll of aim-inhibited libido in order to strengthen communities by bonds of friendship between the members. Restrictions upon sexual life are unavoidable if this object is to be attained. But we cannot see the necessity that forces culture along this path and gives rise to its antagonism to sexuality. It must be due to some disturbing influence not yet detected by us.

We may find the clue in one of the so-called *ideal standards* of civilized society. It runs: "Thou shalt love thy neighbour as thyself." It is world-renowned, undoubtedly older than Christianity which parades it as its proudest profession, yet certainly not very old; in historical times, men still knew nothing of it. We will adopt a naïve attitude towards it, as if we were meeting it for the first time. Thereupon, we find ourselves unable to suppress a feeling of astonishment, as at something unnatural. Why should we do this? What good is it to us? Above all, how can we do such a thing? How could it possibly be done? My love seems to me a valuable thing that I have no right to throw away without reflection. It imposes obligations on me which I must be prepared to make sacrifices to fulfil. If I love someone, he must be worthy of it in some way or other. (I am leaving out of account now the use he may be to me, as well as his possible significance to me as a sexual object; neither of these two kinds of relationship between us come into question where the injunction to love my neighbour is concerned.) He will be worthy of it if he is so like me in important respects that I can love myself in him; worthy of it if he is so much more perfect than I that I can love my ideal of myself in him; I must love him if he is the son of my friend, since the pain my friend would feel if anything untoward happened to him would be my pain—I should have to share it. But if he is a stranger to me and cannot attract me by any value he has in himself or any significance he may have already acquired in my emotional life, it will be hard for me to love him. I shall even be doing wrong if I do, for my love is valued as a privilege by all those belonging to me; it is an injustice to them if I put a stranger on a level with them. But if I am to love him (with that kind of universal love) simply because he, too, is a denizen of the earth, like an insect or an earthworm or a grass-snake, then I fear that but a small modicum of love will fall to his lot and it would be impossible for me to give him as much as by all the laws of reason I am entitled to retain for myself. What is the point of an injunction promulgated with such solemnity, if reason does not recommend it to us?

When I look more closely, I find still further difficulties. Not merely is this stranger on the whole not worthy of love, but, to be honest, I must confess he has more claim to my hostility, even to my hatred. He does not seem to have the least trace of love for me, does not show me the slightest consideration. If it will do him any good, he has no hesitation in injuring me, never even asking himself whether the amount of advantage he gains by it bears any proportion to the amount of wrong done to me. What is more, he does not even need to get an advantage from it; if he can merely get a little pleasure out of it, he thinks nothing of jeering at me, insulting me, slandering me, showing his power over me; and the more secure he feels himself, or the more helpless I am, with so much more certainty can I expect this behaviour from him towards me. If he behaved differently, if he showed me consideration and did not molest me, I should in any case, without the aforesaid commandment, be willing to treat him similarly. If the high-sounding ordinance had run: "Love thy neighbour as thy neighbour loves thee," I should not take objection to it. And there is a second commandment that seems to me even more incomprehensible, and arouses still stronger opposition in me. It is: "Love thine enemies." When I think it over, however, I am wrong in treating it as a greater imposition. It is at bottom the same thing.[1]

I imagine now I hear a voice gravely adjuring me: "Just because thy neighbour is not worthy of thy love, is probably full of enmity towards thee, thou shouldst love him as thyself." I then perceive the case to be like that of *Credo, quia absurdum*.[2]

Now it is, of course, very probable that my neighbour, when he is commanded to love me as himself, will answer exactly as I have done and reject me for the same reasons. I hope he will not have the same objective grounds for doing so, but he will hope so as well. Even so, there are variations in men's behaviour which ethics, disregarding the fact that they are determined, classifies as *good* and *evil*. As long as

---

[1] A great poet may permit himself, at least in jest, to give utterance to psychological truths that are heavily censured. Thus Heine: "Mine is the most peaceable disposition. My wishes are a humble dwelling with a thatched roof, but a good bed, good food, milk and butter of the freshest, flowers at my windows, some fine tall trees before my door; and if the good God wants to make me completely happy, he will grant me the joy of seeing some six or seven of my enemies hanging from these trees. With my heart full of deep emotion I shall forgive them before they die all the wrong they did me in their lifetime—true, one must forgive one's enemies, but not until they are brought to execution."—Heine, *Gedanken und Einfälle*.

[2] I believe it, because it is absurd.—ED.

these undeniable variations have not been abolished, conformity to the highest ethical standards constitutes a betrayal of the interests of culture, for it puts a direct premium on wickedness. One is irresistibly reminded here of an incident in the French Chamber when capital punishment was being discussed; the speech of a member who had passionately supported its abolition was being applauded with loud acclamation, when suddenly a voice was heard calling out from the back of the room, *"Que messieurs les assassins commencent!"*[1]

The bit of truth behind all this—one so eagerly denied—is that men are not gentle, friendly creatures wishing for love, who simply defend themselves if they are attacked, but that a powerful measure of desire for aggression has to be reckoned as part of their instinctual endowment. The result is that their neighbour is to them not only a possible helper or sexual object, but also a temptation to them to gratify their aggressiveness on him, to exploit his capacity for work without recompense, to use him sexually without his consent, to seize his possessions, to humiliate him, to cause him pain, to torture and kill him. *Homo homini lupus;*[2] who has the courage to dispute it in the face of all the evidence in his own life and in history? This aggressive cruelty usually lies in wait for some provocation, or else it steps into the service of some other purpose, the aim of which might as well have been achieved by milder measures. In circumstances that favour it, when those forces in the mind which ordinarily inhibit it cease to operate, it also manifests itself spontaneously and reveals men as savage beasts to whom the thought of sparing their own kind is alien. Anyone who calls to mind the atrocities of the early migrations, of the invasion by the Huns, or by the so-called Mongols under Jenghiz Khan and Tamurlane, of the sack of Jerusalem by the pious Crusaders, even indeed the horrors of the last World War, will have to bow his head humbly before the truth of this view of man.

The existence of this tendency to aggression which we can detect in ourselves and rightly presume to be present in others is the factor that disturbs our relations with our neighbours and makes it necessary for culture to institute its high demands. Civilized society is perpetually menaced with disintegration through this primary hostility of men towards one another.

Their interests in their common work would not hold them together; the passions of instinct are stronger than reasoned interests. Culture has to call up every possible reinforcement in order to erect barriers against the aggressive instincts of men and hold their manifestations in check by reaction-formations in men's minds. Hence its system of methods by which mankind is to be driven to identifications and aim-inhibited love-relationships; hence the restrictions on sexual life; and hence, too, its ideal command to love one's neighbour as oneself, which is really justified by the fact that nothing is so completely at variance with original human nature as this. With all its striving, this endeavour of culture's has so far not achieved very much. Civilization expects to prevent the worst atrocities of brutal violence by taking upon itself the right to employ violence against criminals, but the law is not able to lay hands on the more discreet and subtle forms in which human aggressions are expressed. The time comes when every one of us has to abandon the illusory anticipations with which in our youth we regarded our fellow-men, and when we realize how much hardship and suffering we have been caused in life through their ill-will. It would be unfair, however, to reproach culture with trying to eliminate all disputes and competition from human concerns. These things are undoubtedly indispensable; but opposition is not necessarily enmity, only it may be misused to make an opening for it.

The Communists believe they have found a way of delivering us from this evil. Man is whole-heartedly good and friendly to his neighbour, they say, but the system of private property has corrupted his nature. The possession of private property gives power to the individual and thence the temptation arises to ill-treat his neighbour; the man who is excluded from the possession of property is obliged to rebel in hostility against the oppressor. If private property were abolished, all valuables held in common and all allowed to share in the enjoyment of them, ill-will and enmity would disappear from among men. Since all needs would be satisfied, none would have any reason to regard another as an enemy; all would willingly undertake the work which is necessary. I have no concern with any economic criticisms of the communistic system; I cannot enquire into whether the abolition of private property is advantageous and expedient.[3] But I am able

---

[1] Let the murderers begin!— ED.
[2] Man is to man a wolf.— ED.

[3] Anyone who has been through the misery of poverty in his youth, and has endured the indifference **and**

to recognize that psychologically it is founded on an untenable illusion. By abolishing private property one deprives the human love of aggression of one of its instruments, a strong one undoubtedly, but assuredly not the strongest. It in no way alters the individual differences in power and influence which are turned by aggressiveness to its own use, nor does it change the nature of the instinct in any way. This instinct did not arise as the result of property; it reigned almost supreme in primitive times when possessions were still extremely scanty; it shows itself already in the nursery when possessions have hardly grown out of their original anal shape; it is at the bottom of all the relations of affection and love between human beings—possibly with the single exception of that of a mother to her male child. Suppose that personal rights to material goods are done away with, there still remain prerogatives in sexual relationships, which must arouse the strongest rancour and most violent enmity among men and women who are otherwise equal. Let us suppose this were also to be removed by instituting complete liberty in sexual life, so that the family, the germ-cell of culture, ceased to exist; one could not, it is true, foresee the new paths on which cultural development might then proceed, but one thing one would be bound to expect and that is that the ineffaceable feature of human nature would follow wherever it led.

Men clearly do not find it easy to do without satisfaction of this tendency to aggression that is in them; when deprived of satisfaction of it they are ill at ease. There is an advantage, not to be undervalued, in the existence of smaller communities, through which the aggressive instinct can find an outlet in enmity towards those outside the group. It is always possible to unite considerable numbers of men in love towards one another, so long as there are still some remaining as objects for aggressive manifestations. I once interested myself in the peculiar fact that peoples whose territories are adjacent, and are otherwise closely related, are always at feud with and ridiculing each other,

as, for instance, the Spaniards and the Portuguese, the North and South Germans, the English and the Scotch, and so on. I gave it the name of *narcissism in respect of minor differences*, which does not do much to explain it. One can now see that it is a convenient and relatively harmless form of satisfaction for aggressive tendencies, through which cohesion amongst the members of a group is made easier. The Jewish people, scattered in all directions as they are, have in this way rendered services which deserve recognition to the development of culture in the countries where they settled; but unfortunately not all the massacres of Jews in the Middle Ages sufficed to procure peace and security for their Christian contemporaries. Once the apostle Paul had laid down universal love between all men as the foundation of his Christian community, the inevitable consequence in Christianity was the utmost intolerance towards all who remained outside of it; the Romans, who had not founded their state on love, were not given to lack of religious toleration, although religion was a concern of the state and the state was permeated through and through with it. Neither was it an unaccountable chance that the dream of a German world-dominion evoked a complementary movement towards anti-semitism; and it is quite intelligible that the attempt to establish a new communistic type of culture in Russia should find psychological support in the persecution of the bourgeois. One only wonders, with some concern, however, how the Soviets will manage when they have exterminated their bourgeois entirely.

If civilization requires such sacrifices, not only of sexuality but also of the aggressive tendencies in mankind, we can better understand why it should be so hard for men to feel happy in it. In actual fact, primitive man was better off in this respect, for he knew nothing of any restrictions on his instincts. As a set-off against this, his prospects of enjoying his happiness for any length of time were very slight. Civilized man has exchanged some part of his chances of happiness for a measure of security. We will not forget, however, that in the primal family only the head of it enjoyed this instinctual freedom; the other members lived in slavish thraldom. The antithesis between a minority enjoying cultural advantages and a majority who are robbed of them was therefore most extreme in that primeval period of culture. With regard to the primitive human types living at the present time, careful in-

arrogance of those who have possessions, should be exempt from the suspicion that he has no understanding of or goodwill towards the endeavours made to fight the economic inequality of men and all that it leads to. To be sure, if an attempt is made to base this fight upon an abstract demand for equality for all in the name of justice, there is a very obvious objection to be made, namely, that nature began the injustice by the highly unequal way in which she endows individuals physically and mentally, for which there is no help.

vestigation has revealed that their instinctual life is by no means to be envied on account of its freedom; it is subject to restrictions of a different kind but perhaps even more rigorous than is that of modern civilized man.

In rightly finding fault, as we thus do, with our present state of civilization for so inadequately providing us with what we require to make us happy in life, and for the amount of suffering of a probably avoidable nature it lays us open to—in doing our utmost to lay bare the roots of its deficiencies by our unsparing criticisms, we are undoubtedly exercising our just rights and not showing ourselves enemies of culture. We may expect that in the course of time changes will be carried out in our civilization so that it becomes more satisfying to our needs and no longer open to the reproaches we have made against it. But perhaps we shall also accustom ourselves to the idea that there are certain difficulties inherent in the very nature of culture which will not yield to any efforts at reform. Over and above the obligations of putting restrictions upon our instincts, which we see to be inevitable, we are imminently threatened with the dangers of a state one may call *la misère psychologique* of groups. This danger is most menacing where the social forces of cohesion consist predominantly of identifications of the individuals in the group with one another, whilst leading personalities fail to acquire the significance that should fall to them in the process of group-formation.[1] The state of civilization in America at the present day offers a good opportunity for studying this injurious effect of civilization which we have reason to dread. But I will resist the temptation to enter upon a criticism of American culture; I have no desire to give the impression that I would employ American methods myself.

VI

NEVER before in any of my previous writings have I had the feeling so strongly as I have now that what I am describing is common knowledge, that I am requisitioning paper and ink, and in due course the labour of compositors and printers, in order to expound things that in themselves are obvious. For this reason, if it should appear that the recognition of a special independent instinct of aggression would entail a modification of the psycho-analytical theory of instincts, I should be glad enough to seize upon the idea.

[1] Cf. *Group Psychology*, etc., p. 664 above.

We shall see that this is not so, that it is merely a matter of coming to closer quarters with a conclusion to which we long ago committed ourselves and following it out to its logical consequences. The whole of analytic theory has evolved gradually enough, but the theory of instincts has groped its way forward under greater difficulties than any other part of it. And yet a theory of instincts was so indispensable for the rest that something had to be adopted in place of it. In my utter perplexity at the beginning, I took as my starting-point the poet-philosopher Schiller's aphorism that hunger and love make the world go round. Hunger would serve to represent those instincts which aim at preservation of the individual; love seeks for objects: its chief function, which is favoured in every way by nature, is preservation of the species. Thus first arose the contrast between ego instincts and object instincts. For the energy of the latter instincts, and exclusively for them, I introduced the term *libido;* an antithesis was thus formed between the ego instincts and the libidinal instincts directed towards objects, i.e., love in its widest sense. One of these object instincts, the sadistic, certainly stood out from the rest in that its aim was so very unloving; moreover, it clearly allied itself in many of its aspects with the ego instincts, and its close kinship with instincts of mastery without any libidinal purpose could not be concealed, but these ambiguities could be overcome; in spite of them, sadism plainly belonged to sexual life—the game of cruelty could take the place of the game of love. Neurosis appeared as the outcome of a struggle between the interests of self-preservation and the claims of libido, a struggle in which the ego was victorious, but at the price of great suffering and renunciations.

Every analyst will admit that none of this even now reads like a statement long since recognized as erroneous. All the same, modifications had to be made as our researches advanced from the repressed to the repressing, from the object instincts to the ego. A cardinal point in this advance was the introduction of the concept of narcissism, i.e., the idea that libido cathects the ego itself, that its first dwelling-place was in the ego, and that the latter remains to some extent its permanent headquarters. This narcissistic libido turns in the direction of objects, thus becoming object-libido, and can transform itself back into narcissistic libido. The concept of narcissism made it possible to consider the traumatic neuroses, as well as many diseases bordering on the psychoses, and also the latter themselves, from the psycho-analytic angle. It was not necessary to abandon the view that the transference-neuroses are attempts on the part of the ego to guard itself against sexuality, but the concept of the libido was jeopardized. Since the ego-instincts were found to be libidinal as well, it seemed for a time inevitable that libido should become synonymous with instinctual energy in general, as C. G. Jung had previously advocated. Yet there still remained in me a kind of conviction, for which as yet there were no grounds, that the instincts could not all be of the same nature. I made the next step in *Beyond the Pleasure Principle* (1920), when the repetition-compulsion and the conservative character of instinctual life first struck me. On the basis of speculations concerning the origin of life and of biological parallels, I drew the conclusion that, beside the instinct preserving the organic substance and binding it into ever larger units,[1] there must exist another in antithesis to this, which would seek to dissolve these units and reinstate their antecedent inorganic state. That is to say, a death instinct as well as Eros; the phenomena of life would then be explicable from the interplay of the two and their counteracting effects on each other. It was not easy, however, to demonstrate the working of this hypothetical death instinct. The manifestations of Eros were conspicuous and audible enough; one might assume that the death instinct worked silently within the organism towards its disintegration, but that, of course, was no proof. The idea that part of the instinct became directed towards the outer world and then showed itself as an instinct of aggression and destruction carried us a step further. The instinct would thus itself have been pressed into the service of Eros, in that the organism would be destroying something animate or inanimate outside itself instead of itself. Conversely, any cessation of this flow outwards must have the effect of intensifying the self-destruction which in any case would always be going on within. From this example one could then surmise that the two kinds of instincts seldom—perhaps never—appear in isolation, but always mingle with each other in different, very varying proportions, and so make themselves unrecognizable to us. Sadism,

long since known to us as a component-instinct of sexuality, would represent a particularly strong admixture of the instinct of destruction into the love impulse; while its counterpart, masochism, would be an alliance between sexuality and the destruction at work within the self, in consequence of which the otherwise imperceptible destructive trend became directly evident and palpable.

The assumption of the existence of a death instinct or a destruction instinct has roused opposition even in analytical circles; I know that there is a great tendency to ascribe all that is dangerous and hostile in love rather to a fundamental bipolarity in its own nature. The conceptions I have summarized here I first put forward only tentatively, but in the course of time they have won such a hold over me that I can no longer think in any other way. To my mind they are theoretically far more fruitful than any others it is possible to employ; they provide us with that simplification, without either ignoring or doing violence to the facts, which is what we strive after in scientific work. I know that we have always had before our eyes manifestations of the destruction instinct fused with erotism, directed outwards and inwards in sadism and masochism; but I can no longer understand how we could have overlooked the universality of non-erotic aggression and destruction, and could have omitted to give it its due significance in our interpretation of life. (It is true that the destructive trend that is directed inwards, when it is not erotically tinged, usually eludes our perceptions.) I can remember my own defensive attitude when the idea of an instinct of destruction first made its appearance in psycho-analytical literature and how long it took until I became accessible to it. That others should have shown the same resistance, and still show it, surprises me less. Those who love fairy-tales do not like it when people speak of the innate tendencies in mankind towards aggression, destruction, and, in addition, cruelty. For God has made them in his own image, with his own perfections; no one wants to be reminded how hard it is to reconcile the undeniable existence—in spite of all the protestations of Christian Science—of evil with His omnipotence and supreme goodness. The devil is, in fact, the best way out in acquittal of God; he can be used to play the same economic rôle of outlet as Jews in the world of Aryan ideals. But even so, one can just as well hold God responsible for the existence of the devil as for the evil he personifies. In view of

---

[1] The contradiction between the tireless tendency of Eros to spread ever further and the general conservative nature of the instincts here becomes very noticeable; it would serve as the starting-point of enquiries into further problems.

these difficulties, it is expedient for every man to make humble obeisance on suitable occasions in honour of the high-minded nature of men; it will assist him to become universally beloved and much shall be forgiven unto him on account of it.[1]

The name *libido* can again be used to denote the manifestations of the power of Eros in contradistinction to the energy of the death instinct.[2] We must confess that it is more difficult for us to detect the latter, and to a great extent we can merely conjecture its existence as a background to Eros, also that it eludes us wherever it is not betrayed by a fusion with Eros. In sadism, where it bends the erotic aim to its own will and yet at the same time gratifies the sexual craving completely, we can obtain the clearest insight into its nature and its relation to Eros. But even where it shows itself without any sexual purpose, even in the blindest frenzy of destructiveness, one cannot ignore the fact that satisfaction of it is accompanied by an extraordinarily intense narcissistic enjoyment, due to the fulfilment it brings to the ego of its oldest omnipotence-wishes. The instinct of destruction, when tempered and harnessed (as it were, inhibited in its aim) and directed towards objects, is compelled to provide the ego with satisfaction of its needs and with power over nature. Since the assumption of its existence is based essentially on theoretical grounds, it must be confessed that it is not entirely proof against theoretical objections. But this is how things appear to us now in the present state of our knowledge; future research and reflection will undoubtedly bring further light which will decide the question.

In all that follows, I take up the standpoint

that the tendency to aggression is an innate, independent, instinctual disposition in man, and I come back now to the statement that it constitutes the most powerful obstacle to culture. At one point in the course of this discussion, the idea took possession of us that culture was a peculiar process passing over human life and we are still under the influence of this idea. We may add to this that the process proves to be in the service of Eros, which aims at binding together single human individuals, then families, then tribes, races, nations, into one great unity, that of humanity. Why this has to be done we do not know; it is simply the work of Eros. These masses of men must be bound to one another libidinally; necessity alone, the advantages of common work, would not hold them together. The natural instinct of aggressiveness in man, the hostility of each one against all and of all against each one, opposes this program of civilization. This instinct of aggression is the derivative and main representative of the death instinct we have found alongside of Eros, sharing his rule over the earth. And now, it seems to me, the meaning of the evolution of culture is no longer a riddle to us. It must present to us the struggle between Eros and death, between the instincts of life and the instincts of destruction, as it works itself out in the human species. This struggle is what all life essentially consists of and so the evolution of civilization may be simply described as the struggle of the human species for existence.[3] And it is this battle of the Titans that our nurses and governesses try to compose with their lullaby-song of Heaven!

VII

WHY do the animals, kin to ourselves, not manifest any such cultural struggle? Oh, we don't know. Very probably certain of them, bees, ants, termites, had to strive for thousands of centuries before they found the way to those state institutions, that division of functions, those restrictions upon individuals, which we admire them for today. It is characteristic of our present state that we know by our own feelings that we should not think ourselves happy in any of these communities of the animal world, or in any of the rôles they delegate to individuals. With other animal species it may be that a temporary deadlock has been reached between the influences of their

---

[1] In Goethe's Mephistopheles we have a quite exceptionally striking identification of the principle of evil with the instinct of destruction:

> *All entities that be*
> *Deserve their end—nonentity.*

> *So all that you name sin, destruction—*
> *Wickedness, briefly—proves to be*
> *The native element for me.*

As his adversary, the devil himself cites not what is holy and good, but the power in nature working towards the creation and renewal of life—that is, Eros.

> *From air, from water, germs in thousands,*
> *As from the soil, break forth, break free,*
> *Dry, wet, warm, cold—a pullulation!*
> *Had I not laid on flame a reservation,*
> *Nothing were set apart for me.*

[2] Our present point of view can be roughly expressed in the statement that libido participates in every instinctual manifestation, but that not everything in that manifestation is libido.

[3] And we may probably add more precisely that its form was necessarily determined after some definite event which still remains to be discovered.

environment and the instincts contending within them, so that a cessation of development has taken place. In primitive man, a fresh access of libido may have kindled a new spurt of energy on the part of the instinct of destruction. There are a great many questions in all this to which as yet we have no answer.

Another question concerns us more closely now. What means does civilization make use of to hold in check the aggressiveness that opposes it, to make it harmless, perhaps to get rid of it? Some of these measures we have already come to know, though not yet the one that is apparently the most important. We can study it in the evolution of the individual. What happens in him to render his craving for aggression innocuous? Something very curious, that we should never have guessed and that yet seems simple enough. The aggressiveness is introjected, *internalized;* in fact, it is sent back where it came from, i.e., directed against the ego. It is there taken over by a part of the ego that distinguishes itself from the rest as a super-ego, and now, in the form of *conscience,* exercises the same propensity to harsh aggressiveness against the ego that the ego would have liked to enjoy against others. The tension between the strict super-ego and the subordinate ego we call the *sense of guilt;* it manifests itself as the need for punishment. Civilization, therefore, obtains the mastery over the dangerous love of aggression in individuals by enfeebling and disarming it and setting up an institution within their minds to keep watch over it, like a garrison in a conquered city.

As to the origin of the sense of guilt, analysts have different views from those of the psychologists; nor is it easy for analysts to explain it either. First of all, when one asks how a sense of guilt arises in anyone, one is told something one cannot dispute: people feel guilty (pious people call it "sinful") when they have done something they know to be *bad.* But then one sees how little this answer tells one. Perhaps, after some hesitation, one will add that a person who has not actually committed a bad act, but has merely become aware of the intention to do so, can also hold himself guilty; and then one will ask why in this case the intention is counted as equivalent to the deed. In both cases, however, one is presupposing that wickedness has already been recognized as reprehensible, as something that ought not to be put into execution. How is this judgment arrived at? One may reject the suggestion of an original—as one might say, natural—capacity for discriminating between good and evil. Evil is often not at all that which would injure or endanger the ego; on the contrary, it can also be something that it desires, that would give it pleasure. An extraneous influence is evidently at work; it is this that decides what is to be called good and bad. Since their own feelings would not have led men along the same path, they must have had a motive for obeying this extraneous influence. It is easy to discover this motive in man's helplessness and dependence upon others, it can best be designated the *dread of losing love.* If he loses the love of others on whom he is dependent, he will forfeit also their protection against many dangers, and above all he runs the risk that this stronger person will show his superiority in the form of punishing him. What is bad is, therefore, to begin with, whatever causes one to be threatened with a loss of love; because of the dread of this loss, one must desist from it. That is why it makes little difference whether one has already committed the bad deed or only intends to do so; in either case the danger begins only when the authority has found it out, and the latter would behave in the same way in both cases.

We call this state of mind a *bad conscience* but actually it does not deserve this name, for at this stage the sense of guilt is obviously only the dread of losing love, *social* anxiety. In a little child it can never be anything else, but in many adults too it has only changed in so far as the larger human community takes the place of the father or of both parents. Consequently, such people habitually permit themselves to do any bad deed that procures them something they want, if only they are sure that no authority will discover it or make them suffer for it; their anxiety relates only to the possibility of detection.[1] Present-day society has to take into account the prevalence of this state of mind.

A great change takes place as soon as the authority has been internalized by the development of a super-ego. The manifestations of conscience are then raised to a new level; to be accurate, one should not call them conscience and sense of guilt before this.[2] At this point

---

[1] One is reminded of Rousseau's famous mandarin!
[2] Every reasonable person will understand and take into account that in this descriptive survey things that in reality occur by gradual transitions are sharply differentiated and that the mere existence of a super-ego is not the only factor concerned, but also its relative strength and sphere of influence. All that has been said above in regard to conscience and guilt, moreover, is common knowledge and practically undisputed.

the dread of discovery ceases to operate and also once for all any difference between doing evil and wishing to do it, since nothing is hidden from the super-ego, not even thoughts. The real seriousness of the situation has vanished, it is true: for the new authority, the super-ego, has no motive, as far as we know, for ill-treating the ego with which it is itself closely bound up. But the influence of the genetic derivation of these things, which causes what has been outlived and surmounted to be re-lived, manifests itself so that on the whole things remain as they were at the beginning. The super-ego torments the sinful ego with the same feelings of dread and watches for opportunities whereby the outer world can be made to punish it.

At this second stage of development, conscience exhibits a peculiarity which was absent in the first and is not very easy to account for. That is, the more righteous a man is, the stricter and more suspicious will his conscience be, so that ultimately it is precisely those people who have carried holiness farthest who reproach themselves with the deepest sinfulness. This means that virtue forfeits some of her promised reward; the submissive and abstemious ego does not enjoy the trust and confidence of its mentor, and, as it seems, strives in vain to earn it. Now, to this some people will be ready to object that these difficulties are artificialities. A relatively strict and vigilant conscience is the very sign of a virtuous man, and though saints may proclaim themselves sinners, they are not so wrong, in view of the temptations of instinctual gratifications to which they are peculiarly liable—since, as we know, temptations do but increase under constant privation, whereas they subside, at any rate temporarily, if they are sometimes gratified. The field of ethics is rich in problems, and another of the facts we find here is that misfortune, i.e., external deprivation, greatly intensifies the strength of conscience in the super-ego. As long as things go well with a man, his conscience is lenient and lets the ego do all kinds of things; when some calamity befalls, he holds an inquisition within, discovers his sin, heightens the standards of his conscience, imposes abstinences on himself and punishes himself with penances.[1] Whole peoples have

acted in this way and still do so. But this is easily explained from the original infantile stage of conscience which, as we thus see, is not abandoned after the introjection into the super-ego, but persists alongside and behind the latter. Fate is felt to be a substitute for the agency of the parents: adversity means that one is no longer loved by this highest power of all, and, threatened by this loss of love, one humbles oneself again before the representative of the parents in the super-ego which in happier days one had tried to disregard. This becomes especially clear when destiny is looked upon in the strictly religious sense as the expression of God's will and nothing else. The people of Israel believed themselves to be God's favourite children, and when the great Father hurled visitation after visitation upon them, it still never shook them in this belief or caused them to doubt His power and His justice; they proceeded instead to bring their prophets into the world to declare their sinfulness to them and out of their sense of guilt they constructed the stringent commandments of their priestly religion. It is curious how differently a savage behaves! If he has had bad fortune, he does not throw the blame on himself, but on his fetish, who has plainly not done his duty by him, and he belabours it instead of punishing himself.

Hence we know of two sources for feelings of guilt: that arising from the dread of authority and the later one from the dread of the super-ego. The first one compels us to renounce instinctual gratification; the other presses over and above this towards punishment, since the persistence of forbidden wishes cannot be concealed from the super-ego. We have also heard how the severity of the super-ego, the rigour of conscience, is to be explained. It simply carries on the severity of external authority which it has succeeded and to some extent replaced. We see now how renunciation of instinctual gratification is related to the sense of guilt. Originally, it is true, renunciation is the consequence of a dread of external authority; one gives up pleasures so as not to lose its love. Having made this renunciation, one is quits with authority, so to speak; no feeling of guilt should remain. But with the dread of the super-ego the case is different. Renunciation of gratification does not suffice here, for the wish persists and is not capable of being hidden from the super-ego. In spite of the renunciations made, feelings of guilt will be experienced and this is a great disadvantage economically of the erection of the super-ego, or, as one may say,

---

[1] This increased sensitivity of morals in consequence of ill-luck has been illustrated by Mark Twain in a delicious little story: *The First Melon I ever Stole.* This melon, as it happened, was unripe. I heard Mark Twain tell the story himself in one of his lectures. After he had given out the title, he stopped and asked himself in a doubtful way: "Was it the first?" This was the whole story.

of the formation of conscience. Renunciation no longer has a completely absolving effect; virtuous restraint is no longer rewarded by the assurance of love; a threatened external unhappiness—loss of love and punishment meted out by external authority—has been exchanged for a lasting inner unhappiness, the tension of a sense of guilt.

These inter-relations are so complicated and at the same time so important that, in spite of the dangers of repetition, I will consider them again from another angle. The chronological sequence would thus be as follows: first, instinct-renunciation due to dread of an aggression by external authority—this is, of course, tantamount to the dread of loss of love, for love is a protection against these punitive aggressions. Then follows the erection of an internal authority, and instinctual renunciation due to dread of it—that is, dread of conscience. In the second case, there is the equivalence of wicked acts and wicked intentions; hence comes the sense of guilt, the need for punishment. The aggressiveness of conscience carries on the aggressiveness of authority. Thus far all seems to be clear; but how can we find a place in this scheme for the effect produced by misfortune (i.e., renunciations externally imposed), for the effect it has of increasing the rigour of conscience? How account for the exceptional stringency of conscience in the best men, those least given to rebel against it? We have already explained both these peculiarities of conscience, but probably we still have an impression that these explanations do not go to the root of the matter, and that they leave something still unexplained. And here at last comes in an idea which is quite peculiar to psycho-analysis and alien to ordinary ways of thinking. Its nature enables us to understand why the whole matter necessarily seemed so confused and obscure to us. It tells us this: in the beginning conscience (more correctly, the anxiety which later became conscience) was the cause of instinctual renunciation, but later this relation is reversed. Every renunciation then becomes a dynamic fount of conscience; every fresh abandonment of gratification increases its severity and intolerance; and if we could only bring it better into harmony with what we already know about the development of conscience, we should be tempted to make the following paradoxical statement: Conscience is the result of instinctual renunciation, or: Renunciation (externally imposed) gives rise to conscience, which then demands further renunciations.

The contradiction between this proposition and our previous knowledge about the genesis of conscience is not in actual fact so very great, and we can see a way in which it may be still further reduced. In order to state the problem more easily, let us select the example of the instinct of aggression, and let us suppose that the renunciation in question is always a renunciation of aggression. This is, of course, merely a provisional assumption. The effect of instinctual renunciation on conscience then operates as follows: every impulse of aggression which we omit to gratify is taken over by the super-ego and goes to heighten its aggressiveness (against the ego). It does not fit in well with this that the original aggressiveness of conscience should represent a continuance of the rigour of external authority, and so have nothing to do with renunciation. But we can get rid of this discrepancy if we presume a different origin for the first quantum of aggressiveness with which the super-ego was endowed.

When authority prevented the child from enjoying the first but most important gratifications of all, aggressive impulses of considerable intensity must have been evoked in it, irrespective of the particular nature of the instinctual deprivations concerned. The child must necessarily have had to give up the satisfaction of these revengeful aggressive wishes. In this situation, in which it is economically so hard pressed, it has recourse to certain mechanisms well known to us; by the process of identification it absorbs into itself the invulnerable authority, which then becomes the super-ego and comes into possession of all the aggressiveness which the child would gladly have exercised against it. The child's ego has to content itself with the unhappy rôle of the authority—the father—who has been thus degraded. It is, as so often, a reversal of the original situation, "If I were father and you my child, I would treat *you* badly." The relation between super-ego and ego is a reproduction, distorted by a wish, of the real relations between the ego, before it was subdivided, and an external object. That is also typical. The essential difference, however, is that the original severity of the super-ego does not—or not so much—represent the severity which has been experienced or anticipated from the object, but expresses the child's own aggressiveness towards the latter. If this is correct, one could truly assert that conscience is formed in the beginning from the suppression of an aggressive impulse and strengthened as time goes on by each fresh suppression of the kind.

Now, which of these two theories is the true one? The earlier, which seemed genetically so unassailable, or the new one, which rounds off our theories in such a welcome manner? Clearly, they are both justified, and by the evidence, too, of direct observation; they do not contradict each other, and even coincide at one point, for the child's revengeful aggressiveness will be in part provoked by the amount of punishing aggression that it anticipates from the father. Experience has shown, however, that the severity which a child's super-ego develops in no way corresponds to the severity of the treatment it has itself experienced.[1] It seems to be independent of the latter; a child which has been very leniently treated can acquire a very strict conscience. But it would also be wrong to exaggerate this independence; it is not difficult to assure oneself that strict upbringing also has a strong influence on the formation of a child's super-ego. It comes to this, that the formation of the super-ego and the development of conscience are determined in part by innate constitutional factors and in part by the influence of the actual environment; and that is in no way surprising—on the contrary, it is the invariable aetiological condition of all such processes.[2]

It may also be said that when a child reacts to the first great instinctual deprivations with an excessive aggressiveness and a corresponding strictness of its super-ego, it is thereby following a phylogenetic prototype, unheedful of what reaction would in reality be justified; for the father of primitive times was certainly terrifying, and one may safely attribute the utmost degree of aggressiveness to him. The differences between the two theories of the genesis of conscience are thus still further di-

minished, if one passes from individual to phylogenetic development. But then, on the other hand, we find a new important difference between the two processes. We cannot disregard the conclusion that man's sense of guilt has its origin in the Oedipus complex and was acquired when the father was killed by the association of the brothers. At that time the agression was not suppressed but carried out, and it is this same act of aggression whose suppression in the child we regard as the source of feelings of guilt. Now, I should not be surprised if a reader were to cry out angrily: "So it makes no difference whether one does kill one's father or does not, one gets a feeling of guilt in either case! Here I should think one may be allowed some doubts. Either it is not true that guilt is evoked by suppressed aggressiveness or else the whole story about the • father-murder is a romance, and primeval man did not kill his father any more often than people do nowadays. Besides this, if it is not a romance but a plausible piece of history, it would only be an instance of what we all expect to happen, namely, that one feels guilty because one has really done something which cannot be justified. And what we are all waiting for is for psycho-analysis to give us an explanation of this reaction, which at any rate is something that happens every day."

This is true, and we must make good the omission. There is no great mystery about it either. When one has feelings of guilt after one has committed some crime and because of it, this feeling should more properly be called *remorse*. It relates only to the one act, and clearly it presupposes that *conscience*, the capacity for feelings of guilt, was already in existence before the deed. Remorse of this kind can, therefore, never help us to find out the source of conscience and feelings of guilt in general. In these everyday instances the course of events is usually as follows: an instinctual need acquires the strength to achieve fulfilment in spite of conscience, the strength of which also has its limits, whereupon the inevitable reduction of the need after satisfaction restores the earlier balance of forces. Psycho-analysis is quite justified, therefore, in excluding the case of a sense of guilt through remorse from this discussion, however frequently it may occur and however great its importance may be practically.

But if man's sense of guilt goes back to the murder of the father, that was undoubtedly an instance of *remorse*, and yet are we to suppose

---

[1] As has rightly been emphasized by Melanie Klein and other English writers.

[2] In his *Psychoanalyse der Gesamtpersönlichkeit*, 1927, Franz Alexander has, in connection with Aichhorn's study of dissocial behaviour in children, discussed the two main types of pathogenic methods of training, that of excessive severity and of spoiling. The *unduly lenient and indulgent* father fosters the development of an over-strict super-ego because, in face of the love which is showered on it, the child has no other way of disposing of its aggressiveness than to turn it inwards. In neglected children who grow up without any love, the tension between ego and super-ego is lacking; their aggressions can be directed externally. Apart from any constitutional factor which may be present, therefore, one may say that a strict conscience arises from the co-operation of two factors in the environment: the deprivation of instinctual gratification which evokes the child's aggressiveness, and the love it receives which turns this aggressiveness inwards, where it is taken over by the super-ego.

that there were no conscience and feelings of guilt before the act on that occasion? If so, where did the remorse come from then? This instance must explain to us the riddle of the sense of guilt and so make an end of our difficulties. And it will do so, as I believe. This remorse was the result of the very earliest primal ambivalence of feelings towards the father: the sons hated him, but they loved him too; after their hate against him had been satisfied by their aggressive acts, their love came to expression in their remorse about the deed, set up the super-ego by identification with the father, gave it the father's power to punish as he would have done the aggression they had performed, and created the restrictions which should prevent a repetition of the deed. And since impulses to aggressions against the father were repeated in the next generations, the feelings of guilt, too, persisted, and were further reinforced every time an aggression was suppressed anew and made over to the super-ego. At this point, it seems to me, we can at last clearly perceive the part played by love in the origin of conscience and the fatal inevitableness of the sense of guilt. It is not really a decisive matter whether one has killed one's father or abstained from the deed; one must feel guilty in either case, for guilt is the expression of the conflict of ambivalence, the eternal struggle between Eros and the destructive or death instinct. This conflict is engendered as soon as man is confronted with the task of living with his fellows; as long as he knows no other form of life in common but that of the family, it must express itself in the Oedipus complex, cause the development of conscience, and create the first feelings of guilt. When mankind tries to institute wider forms of communal life, the same conflict continues to arise —in forms derived from the past—and intensified so that a further reinforcement of the sense of guilt results. Since culture obeys an inner erotic impulse which bids it bind mankind into a closely-knit mass, it can achieve this aim only by means of its vigilance in fomenting an ever-increasing sense of guilt. That which began in relation to the father ends in relation to the community. If civilization is an inevitable course of development from the group of the family to the group of humanity as a whole, then an intensification of the sense of guilt—resulting from the innate conflict of ambivalence, from the eternal struggle between the love and the death trends—will be inextricably bound up with it, until perhaps the sense of guilt may swell to a magnitude that individuals can hardly support. One is reminded of the telling accusation made by the great poet against the *heavenly forces:*

> *Ye set our feet on this life's road,*
> *Ye watch our guilty, erring courses,*
> *Then leave us, bowed beneath our load,*
> *For earth its every debt enforces.*[1]

And one may heave a sigh at the thought that it is vouchsafed to a few, with hardly an effort, to salve from the whirlpool of their own emotions the deepest truths, to which we others have to force our way, ceaselessly groping amid torturing uncertainties.

VIII

On reaching the end of such a journey as this, the author must beg his readers to pardon him for not having been a more skilful guide, not sparing them bleak stretches of country at times and laborious detours at others. There is no doubt that it could have been done better. I will now try to make some amends.

First of all, I suspect the reader feels that the discussion about the sense of guilt oversteps its proper boundaries in this essay and takes up too much space so that the rest of the subject-matter, which is not always closely connected with it, gets pushed to one side. This may have spoilt the composition of the work; but it faithfully corresponds to my intention to represent the sense of guilt as the most important problem in the evolution of culture, and to convey that the price of progress in civilization is paid in forfeiting happiness through the heightening of the sense of guilt.[2] What sounds puzzling in this statement, which is the final conclusion of our whole investigation, is probably due to the quite peculiar relation—as yet completely unexplained—

---

[1] Goethe, *Wilhelm Meister,* "The Song of the Harper."

[2] "Thus conscience does make cowards of us all. . . ." That the upbringing of young people at the present day conceals from them the part sexuality will play in their lives is not the only reproach we are obliged to bring against it. It offends too in not preparing them for the aggressions of which they are destined to become the objects. Sending the young out into life with such a false psychological orientation is as if one were to equip people going on a Polar expedition with summer clothing and maps of the Italian lakes. One can clearly see that ethical standards are being misused in a way. The strictness of these standards would not do much harm if education were to say: "This is how men ought to be in order to be happy and make others happy, but you have to reckon with their not being so." Instead of this the young are made to believe that everyone else conforms to the standard of ethics, i.e., that everyone else is good. And then on this is based the demand that the young shall be so too.

the sense of guilt has to our consciousness. In the common cases of remorse which we think normal, it becomes clearly perceptible to consciousness; indeed, we often speak of *consciousness of guilt* instead of sense of guilt. In our study of the neuroses, in which we have found invaluable clues towards an understanding of normal people, we find some very contradictory states of affairs in this respect. In one of these maladies, the obsessional neurosis, the sense of guilt makes itself loudly heard in consciousness; it dominates the clinical picture as well as the patient's life and lets hardly anything else appear alongside of it. But in most of the other types and forms of neurosis it remains completely unconscious, without its effect being any less great, however. Our patients do not believe us when we ascribe an *unconscious sense of guilt* to them; in order to become even moderately intelligible to them, we have to explain that the sense of guilt expresses itself in an unconscious seeking for punishment. But its connection with the form of the neurosis is not to be over-estimated; even in the obsessional neurosis there are people who are not aware of their sense of guilt or who perceive it only as a tormenting uneasiness or kind of anxiety and then not until they are prevented from carrying out certain actions. We ought some day to be able at last to understand these things; as yet we cannot. Here perhaps is the place to remark that at bottom the sense of guilt is nothing but a topographical variety of anxiety, and that in its later phases it coincides completely with the dread of the super-ego. The relation of anxiety to consciousness, moreover, is characterized by the same extraordinary variations. Somewhere or other there is always anxiety hidden behind all symptoms; at one moment, however, it sweeps into consciousness, drowning everything else with its clamour, and at the next it secretes itself so completely that we are forced to speak of unconscious anxiety—or if we want to have a cleaner conscience psychologically, since anxiety is after all only a perception—of possibilities of anxiety. Consequently it is very likely that the sense of guilt produced by culture is not perceived as such and remains to a great extent unconscious, or comes to expression as a sort of uneasiness or discontent for which other motivations are sought. The different religions, at any rate, have never overlooked the part played by the sense of guilt in civilization. What is more, they come forward with a claim,

which I have not considered elsewhere,[1] to save mankind from this sense of guilt, which they call *sin*. We indeed have drawn our conclusions, from the way in which in Christianity this salvation is won—the sacrificial death of one who therewith takes the whole of the common guilt of all upon himself—about the occasion on which this primal sense of guilt was first acquired, that is, the occasion which was also the inception of culture.[2]

It will not be very important, but it may be just as well to go more precisely into the meaning of certain words like *super-ego, conscience, sense of guilt, need for punishment, remorse*, which we have perhaps often used too loosely and in place of one another. They all relate to the same situation, but they denote different aspects of it. The *super-ego* is an agency or institution in the mind whose existence we have inferred: *Conscience* is a function we ascribe, among others, to the super-ego; it consists of watching over and judging the actions and intentions of the ego, exercising the functions of a censor. The *sense of guilt*, the severity of the super-ego, is therefore the same thing as the rigour of conscience; it is the perception the ego has that it is watched in this way, the ego's appreciation of the tension between its strivings and the standards of the super-ego; and the anxiety that lies behind all these relations, the dread of that critical institution, the *need for punishment*, is an instinctual manifestation on the part of the ego, which has become masochistic under the influence of the sadistic super-ego, i.e., which has brought a part of the instinct of destruction at work within itself into the service of an erotic attachment to the super-ego. We ought not to speak of conscience before a super-ego is demonstrable; as to consciousness of guilt, we must admit that it comes into being before the super-ego, therefore before conscience. At that time it is the direct expression of the dread of external authority, the recognition of the tension between the ego and this latter; it is the direct derivative of the conflict between the need for parental love and the urgency towards instinctual gratification, and it is the thwarting of this urgency that provokes the tendency to aggression. It is because these two different versions of the sense of guilt—one arising from dread of the external and the other from dread of the inner authority—are superimposed one on the other that our

[1] I mean in *The Future of an Illusion*.
[2] *Totem and Taboo* (1912).

insight into the relations of conscience has been hampered in so many ways. *Remorse* is a general term denoting the ego's reaction under a special form of the sense of guilt; it includes the almost unaltered sensory material belonging to the anxiety that is at work behind the sense of guilt; it is itself a punishment and may include the need for punishment; it too, therefore, may occur before conscience has developed.

Further, it will do no harm for us to review once more the contradictions which have confused us at times during our enquiries. The sense of guilt, we said at one point, was the consequence of uncommitted aggressions; but another time and, in particular, in the case of its historical beginning, the murder of the father, it was the consequence of an aggression that was carried out. We also found a way out of this difficulty. The development of the inner authority, the super-ego, was precisely what radically altered the whole situation. Before this, the sense of guilt coincided with remorse; we observe, in saying this, that the term *remorse* is to be reserved for the reaction after an actual performance of an aggressive deed. After this, the omniscience of the super-ego robbed the distinction between intended aggressions and aggressions committed of its significance; a mere intention to commit an act of violence could then evoke a sense of guilt— as psycho-analysis has found—as well as one which has actually been committed—as all the world knows. The conflict of ambivalence between the two primal instincts leaves the same impress on the psychological situation, irrespective of the change that has taken place in this. A temptation arises to look here for an explanation of the mystery of the varying relation between the sense of guilt and consciousness. The sense of guilt which is due to remorse for an evil deed must always have been conscious; that due to a perception of an evil impulse could have remained unconscious. But it cannot be as simple as that: the obsessional neurosis contradicts it emphatically. The second contradiction was that the aggressive energy with which one imagined the super-ego to be endowed was, according to one view, merely a continuation of the punitive energy belonging to external authority, preserved within the mind; whereas according to another view it consisted, on the contrary, of aggressive energy originating in the self, levelled against this inhibiting authority but not allowed to discharge itself in actions. The first view seemed to

accord better with the history of the sense of guilt, the second with the theory of it. More searching reflection has resolved this apparently irreconcilable contradiction almost too completely; what remained as essential and common to both was that in both cases we were dealing with an aggression that had been turned inward. Clinical observation, moreover, really permits us to distinguish two sources for the aggressiveness we ascribe to the super-ego, each of which in any given case may be operating predominantly, but which usually are both at work together.

This, I think, is the place to suggest that a proposal which I previously put forward as a provisional assumption should be taken in earnest. In the latest analytical literature,[1] a predilection has been shown for the view that any kind of privation, any thwarted instinctual gratification, results in a heightening of the sense of guilt, or may do so. I believe one obtains a great simplification of theory if one regards this as valid *only* for the aggressive instincts, and that little will be found to contradict this assumption. How then is it to be explained dynamically and economically that a heightening of the sense of guilt should appear in place of an unfulfilled erotic desire? This can surely only happen in a roundabout way: the thwarting of the erotic gratification provokes an access of aggressiveness against the person who interfered with the gratification, and then this tendency to aggression in its turn has itself to be suppressed. So then it is, after all, only the aggression which is changed into guilt, by being suppressed and made over to the super-ego. I am convinced that very many processes will admit of much simpler and clearer explanation if we restrict the findings of psycho-analysis in respect of the origin of the sense of guilt to the aggressive instincts. Reference to the clinical material here gives us no unequivocal answer, because, according to our own hypothesis, the two kinds of instincts hardly ever appear in a pure form, unmixed with each other; but the investigation of extreme cases would probably point in the direction I anticipate. I am tempted to extract our first advantage from this narrower conception by applying it to the repression-process. The symptoms of neurosis, as we have learned, are essentially substitutive gratifications for unfulfilled sexual wishes. In the course of our ana-

[1] In particular, in contributions by Ernest Jones, Susan Isaacs, Melanie Klein; also, as I understand, in those of Reik and Alexander.

lytic work we have found to our surprise that perhaps every neurosis masks a certain amount of unconscious sense of guilt, which in its turn reinforces the symptoms by exploiting them as punishment. One is now inclined to suggest the following statement as a possible formulation: when an instinctual trend undergoes repression, its libidinal elements are transformed into symptoms and its aggressive components into a sense of guilt. Even if this statement is only accurate as an approximation, it merits our interest.

Some readers of this essay, too, may be under the impression that the formula of the struggle between Eros and the death instinct has been reiterated too often. It is supposed to characterize the cultural process which evolves in humanity; but it has been related also to the development of the individual, and, besides this, is supposed to have revealed the secret of organic life in general. It becomes necessary for us to examine the relation of these three processes to one another. Now, the repetition of the same formula is vindicated by the consideration that the cultural processes, both in humanity and in the development of an individual, are life-processes; consequently they must both partake of the most universal characteristic of life. On the other hand, evidence of the presence of this universal characteristic does not help us to discriminate, unless it is further narrowed down by special qualifications. We can therefore set our minds at rest only if we say that the cultural process is the particular modification undergone by the life-process under the influence of the task set before it by Eros and stimulated by Ananke, external necessity; and this task is that of uniting single human beings into a larger unity with libidinal attachments between them. When, however, we compare the cultural process in humanity with the process of development or upbringing in an individual human being, we shall conclude without much hesitation that the two are very similar in nature, if not in fact the same process applied to a different kind of object. The civilizing process in the human species is naturally more of an abstraction than the development of an individual, and therefore harder to apprehend in concrete terms, nor should the discovery of analogies be pushed to extremes; but in view of the similar character of the aims of the two processes—in one the incorporation of an individual as a member of a group and in the other the creation of a single group out of

many individuals—the similarity of the means employed and of the results obtained in the two cases is not surprising. In view of its exceptional importance, we must no longer postpone mention of one feature differentiating the two processes. The development of the individual is ordered according to the program laid down by the pleasure-principle, namely, the attainment of happiness, and to this main objective it holds firmly; the incorporation of the individual as a member of a community, or his adaptation to it, seems like an almost unavoidable condition which has to be filled before he can attain this objective of happiness. If he could achieve it without fulfilling this condition, it would perhaps be better. To express it differently, we may say: Individual development seems to us a product of the interplay of two trends, the striving for happiness, generally called *egoistic,* and the impulse towards merging with others in the community, which we call *altruistic.* Neither of these descriptions goes far beneath the surface. In individual development, as we have said, the main accent falls on the egoistic trend, the striving for happiness; while the other tendency, which may be called the *cultural* one, usually contents itself with instituting restrictions. But things are different in the development of culture: here far the most important aim is that of creating a single unity out of individual men and women, while the objective of happiness, though still present, is pushed into the background; it almost seems as if humanity could be most successfully united into one great whole if there were no need to trouble about the happiness of individuals. The process of development in individuals must therefore be admitted to have its special features which are not repeated in the cultural evolution of humanity; the two processes only necessarily coincide in so far as the first also includes the aim of incorporation into the community.

Just as a planet circles round its central body, while at the same time rotating on its own axis, so the individual man takes his part in the course of humanity's development as he goes on his way through life. But to our dull eyes the play of forces in the heavens seems set fast in a never-varying scheme, though in organic life we can still see how the forces contend with one another and the results of the conflict change from day to day. So in every individual the two trends, one towards personal happiness and the other towards unity with the rest of humanity, must contend with each other; so must the two processes of individual and of cultural development oppose each other and dispute the ground against each other. This struggle between individual and society, however, is not derived from the antagonism of the primal instincts, Eros and death, which are probably irreconcilable; it is a dissension in the camp of the libido itself, comparable to the contest between the ego and its objects for a share of the libido; and it does eventually admit of a solution in the individual, as we may hope it will also do in the future of civilization—however greatly it may oppress the lives of individuals at the present time.

The analogy between the process of cultural evolution and the path of individual development may be carried further in an important respect. It can be maintained that the community, too, develops a super-ego, under whose influence cultural evolution proceeds. It would be an enticing task for an authority on human systems of culture to work out this analogy in specific cases. I will confine myself to pointing out certain striking details. The super-ego of any given epoch of civilization originates in the same way as that of an individual; it is based on the impression left behind them by great leading personalities, men of outstanding force of mind, or men in whom some one human tendency has developed in unusual strength and purity, often for that reason very disproportionately. In many instances the analogy goes still further, in that during their lives—often enough, even if not always—such persons are ridiculed by others, ill-used, or even cruelly done to death, just as happened with the primal father who also rose again to become a deity long after his death by violence. The most striking example of this double fate is the figure of Jesus Christ, if indeed it does not itself belong to the realm of mythology which called it into being out of a dim memory of that primordial event. Another point of agreement is that the cultural super-ego, just like that of an individual, sets up high ideals and standards, and that failure to fulfil them is punished by both with *anxiety of conscience*. In this particular, indeed, we come across the remarkable circumstance that the mental processes concerned here are actually more familiar to us and more accessible to consciousness when they proceed from the group than they can be in the individual. In the latter, when tension arises, the aggressions of the super-ego voicing its noisy reproaches are all that is perceived, while its injunctions themselves often remain unconscious in the background. If we bring them to the knowledge of consciousness, we find that they coincide with the demands of the prevailing cultural super-ego. At this point the two processes, that of the evolution of the group and the development of the individual, are always firmly mortised together, so to speak. Consequently many of the effects and properties of the super-ego can be more easily detected through its operations in the group than in the individual.

The cultural super-ego has elaborated its ideals and erected its standards. Those of its demands which deal with the relations of human beings to one another are comprised under the name of *ethics*. The greatest value has at all times been set upon systems of ethics, as if men had expected them in particular to achieve something especially important. And ethics does in fact deal predominantly with the point which is easily seen to be the sorest of all in any scheme of civilization. Ethics must be regarded, therefore, as a therapeutic effort: as an endeavour to achieve something through the standards imposed by the super-ego which had not been attained by the work of civilization in other ways. We already know—it is what we have been discussing—that the question is how to dislodge the greatest obstacle to civilization, the constitutional tendency in men to aggressions against one another; and for that very reason the commandment to love one's neighbour as oneself—probably the most recent of the cultural super-ego's demands—is especially interesting to us. In our investigations and our therapy of the neuroses we cannot avoid finding fault with the super-ego of the individual on two counts: in commanding and prohibiting with such severity it troubles too little about the happiness of the ego, and it fails to take into account sufficiently the difficulties in the way of obeying it—the strength of instinctual cravings in the id and the hardships of external environment. Consequently, in our therapy we often find ourselves obliged to do battle with the super-ego and work to moderate its demands. Exactly the same objections can be made against the ethical standards of the cultural super-ego. It, too, does not trouble enough about the mental constitution of human beings; it enjoins a command and never asks whether or not it is possible for them to obey it. It presumes, on the contrary, that a man's ego is psychologically capable of anything that is required of it—that his ego has unlimited power over his id. This is an error; even in so-called normal people the power of controlling the id cannot be increased beyond certain limits. If one asks more of them, one produces revolt or neurosis in individuals or makes them unhappy. The command to love our neighbours as ourselves is the strongest defence there is against human aggressiveness and it is a superlative example of the unpsychological attitude of the cultural super-ego. The command is impossible to fulfil; such an enormous inflation of love can only lower its value and not remedy the evil. Civilization pays no heed to all this; it merely prates that the harder it is to obey the more laudable the obedience. The fact remains that anyone who follows such preaching in the present state of civilization only puts himself at a disadvantage beside all those who set it at naught. What an overwhelming obstacle to civilization aggression must be if the defence against it can cause as much misery as aggression itself! *Natural* ethics, as it is called, has nothing to offer here beyond the narcissistic satisfaction of thinking oneself better than others. The variety of ethics that links itself with religion brings in at this point its promises of a better future life. I should imagine that as long as virtue is not rewarded in this life ethics will preach in vain. I too think it unquestionable that an actual change in men's attitude to property would be of more help in this direction than any ethical commands; but among the Socialists this proposal is obscured by new idealistic expectations disregarding human nature, which detract from its value in actual practice.

It seems to me that the point of view which seeks to follow the phenomena of cultural evolution as manifestations of a super-ego promises to yield still further discoveries. I am coming quickly to an end. There is one question, however, which I can hardly ignore. If the evolution of civilization has such a far-reaching similarity with the development of an individual, and if the same methods are employed in both, would not the diagnosis be justified that many systems of civilization—or epochs of it—possibly even the whole of humanity—have become *neurotic* under the pressure of the civilizing trends? To analytic dissection of these neuroses, therapeutic recommendations might follow which could claim a great practical interest. I would not say that such an attempt to apply psychoanalysis to civilized society would be fanciful or doomed to fruitlessness. But it behooves us

to be very careful, not to forget that after all we are dealing only with analogies, and that it is dangerous, not only with men but also with concepts, to drag them out of the region where they originated and have matured. The diagnosis of collective neuroses, moreover, will be confronted by a special difficulty. In the neurosis of an individual we can use as a starting-point the contrast presented to us between the patient and his environment which we assume to be *normal*. No such background as this would be available for any society similarly affected; it would have to be supplied in some other way. And with regard to any therapeutic application of our knowledge, what would be the use of the most acute analysis of social neuroses, since no one possesses power to compel the community to adopt the therapy? In spite of all these difficulties, we may expect that one day someone will venture upon this research into the pathology of civilized communities.

For various reasons, it is very far from my intention to express any opinion concerning the value of human civilization. I have endeavoured to guard myself against the enthusiastic partiality which believes our civilization to be the most precious thing that we possess or could acquire, and thinks it must inevitably lead us to undreamed-of heights of perfection. I can at any rate listen without taking umbrage to those critics who aver that when one surveys the aims of civilization and the means it employs, one is bound to conclude that the whole thing is not worth the effort and that in the end it can only produce a state of things which no individual will be able to bear. My impartiality is all the easier to me since I know very little about these things and am sure only of one thing, that the judgments of value made by mankind are immediately determined by their desires for happiness: in other words, that those judgments are attempts to prop up their illusions with arguments. I could understand it very well if anyone were to point to the inevitable nature of the process of cultural development and say, for instance, that the tendency to institute restrictions upon sexual life, or to carry humanitarian ideals into effect at the cost of natural selection, are developmental trends which it is impossible to avert or divert, and to which it is best for us to submit as though they were natural necessities. I know, too, the objection that can be raised against this: that tendencies such as these, which are believed to have insuperable power behind them, have often in the history of man been thrown aside and replaced by others. My courage fails me, therefore, at the thought of rising up as a prophet before my fellow-men, and I bow to their reproach that I have no consolation to offer them; for at bottom this is what they all demand—the frenzied revolutionary as passionately as the most pious believer.

The fateful question of the human species seems to me to be whether and to what extent the cultural process developed in it will succeed in mastering the derangements of communal life caused by the human instinct of aggression and self-destruction. In this connection, perhaps the phase through which we are at this moment passing deserves special interest. Men have brought their powers of subduing the forces of nature to such a pitch that by using them they could now very easily exterminate one another to the last man. They know this—hence arises a great part of their current unrest, their dejection, their mood of apprehension. And now it may be expected that the other of the two *heavenly forces*, eternal Eros, will put forth his strength so as to maintain himself alongside of his equally immortal adversary.

New Introductory Lectures on
Psycho-Analysis

Contents:
New Introductory Lectures on
Psycho-Analysis

New Introductory Lectures on Psycho-Analysis

PREFACE

MY *Introductory Lectures on Psycho-Analysis*[1] were delivered in the two winter terms of 1915-16 and 1916-17, in one of the lecture-rooms of the Vienna Psychiatrical Clinic, before an audience composed of members and students of every Faculty. The first half of the lectures were improvised, and written down immediately afterwards; the second half were composed during an intervening summer vacation in Salzburg, and were delivered word for word in the following winter. In those days I still possessed the gift of a phonographic memory.

In contradistinction to them, these new lectures have never been delivered. My age has in the meantime relieved me of the duty of marking my membership of the University—even though the relation is only a peripheral one—by giving lectures; and a surgical operation has rendered me incapable of addressing an audience. It is therefore only in imagination that I picture myself once more in the lecture-room as I write out what follows; it may help me not to forget my duty to the reader as I delve deeper into my subject.

The new lectures are in no way intended to take the place of the earlier ones. They do not compose an independent whole which could hope to find a circle of readers of its own; but they are continuations and supplements which fall into three groups in their relation to the earlier lectures. To the first group belong the new manipulations of themes which have already been dealt with fifteen years ago, but which demand further treatment on account of the deepening of our knowledge and the alteration of our views; this group consists, that is to say, of critical revisions. The two other groups contain actual enlargements of our field, in that they deal with matters which either did not exist in psycho-analysis at the time of the first lectures, or about which too little was known at that time to justify a special chapter-heading. It cannot be avoided, but it is also not to be deplored, that some of the new lectures unite the characteristics of these groups.

I have, moreover, emphasized the dependence of these new lectures on the *Introductory Lectures* by numbering them in continuation of the old ones. Thus the first lecture in this book is called the Twenty-ninth. Once more, they offer to the analytic specialist little that is new, and they are addressed to that large group of educated persons to whom, let us hope, one can ascribe a benevolent, if cautious, interest in the special nature and discoveries of this young science. And this time again it has been my guiding purpose to make no sacrifice in favour of apparent simplicity, completeness and finality; not to hide any problems and not to deny the existence of gaps and uncertainties. In no other field of scientific work would it be necessary to insist upon the modesty of one's claims. In every other subject this is taken for granted; the public expect nothing else. No reader of a work on astronomy would feel disappointed and contemptuous of that science, if he were shown the point at which our knowledge of the universe melts into obscurity. Only in psychology is it otherwise; here the constitutional incapacity of men for scientific research comes into full view. It looks as though people did not expect from psychology progress in knowledge, but some other kind of satisfaction; every unsolved problem, every acknowledged uncertainty is turned into a ground of complaint against it.

Anyone who loves the science of the mind must accept these hardships as well.

FREUD

VIENNA *Summer* 1932

LECTURE 29

REVISION OF THE THEORY OF DREAMS

LADIES AND GENTLEMEN: After a silence of more than fifteen years, I have brought you together again in order to discuss with you the new developments, or it may be improvements, which have taken place in psycho-analytic theory during the interval. From more than one point of view it is right and proper that we

[1] *A General Introduction to Psycho-Analysis*, p. 449 above.

should turn our attention, in the first place, to the theory of dreams. This theory occupies a peculiar position in the history of psycho-analysis; it marks a turning-point. With the theory of dreams, analysis passed from being a psycho-therapeutic method to being a psychology of the depths of human nature. Ever since then the theory of dreams has remained the most characteristic and the most peculiar feature of the young science, something which has no parallel in the rest of scientific knowledge, a new found land which has been reclaimed from the regions of Folklore and Mysticism. The strangeness of the ideas which are necessarily involved in it has made it into a shibboleth, the use of which distinguishes those who might become believers in psycho-analysis from those who are incapable of comprehending it. Speaking for myself, I always found it a thing I could hold on to during those difficult times when the unsolved problems of the neuroses used to confuse my inexperienced judgment. Whenever I began to have doubts about the correctness of my tentative conclusions, the moment I managed to translate a senseless and complicated dream into a clear and intelligible mental process in the dreamer, I felt, with renewed confidence, that I was on the right track.

It is therefore of especial interest for us to follow, in regard to this particular matter of the theory of dreams, what changes psycho-analysis has undergone during the interval I have mentioned, and what progress it has made in gaining appreciation and understanding from contemporary thought. I may as well tell you straight away that you will be disappointed in both directions.

Let us look through the volumes of the *Internationale Zeitschrift für (ärztliche) Psychoanalyse,* in which the most important work on our subject has appeared since 1913. In the earlier volumes you will find one recurring heading, "On the Interpretation of Dreams," under which will be a quantity of contributions on various points of dream-theory. But the further you go, the rarer such contributions become; this standing heading eventually disappears entirely. The analysts behave as though they had nothing more to say about the dream, as though the whole subject of dream-theory were finished and done with. If, on the other hand, you ask how much of the theory of dreams is accepted by outsiders, the numerous psychiatrists and psycho-therapeutists who warm their pot of soup at our fire—without indeed being very grateful for our hospitality—the so-called

educated people who are in the habit of appropriating the more startling of the conclusions of science, the literati and the general public, then the answer is not very satisfactory. A few formulae are generally known, and, among them, several which we have never put forward, such as the statement that all dreams are of a sexual nature; but even such important things as the fundamental distinction between the manifest dream-content and the latent dream-thoughts, the view that anxiety dreams do not contradict the wish-fulfilling function of the dream, the impossibility of interpreting a dream unless one knows the relevant associations of the dreamer, and, above all, the recognition of the fact that the most important part of the dream is the dream-work, seem, every one of them, to be as far removed from the consciousness of the generality of mankind as they were thirty years ago. I myself have every reason to say this, because during that period I have received an enormous number of letters, in which the writers inscribe their dreams for interpretation, or ask for information about the nature of dreams. They declare that they have read the *Interpretation of Dreams,* and yet in every sentence they betray their lack of understanding of our dream-theory. That will not prevent our once more giving an account of what we know about dreams. You will remember that last time we devoted a whole group of lectures to showing how we have come to understand this hitherto unexplained psychic phenomenon.

Supposing some one, say a patient under analysis, tells us one of his dreams; then we assume that he has made one of those communications to us to which he committed himself when he entered on his analytical treatment. It is, of course, a communication which is insufficiently communicative, because a dream is, in itself, not a social utterance; it is not a means for making oneself understood. We have not, indeed, the least idea what the dreamer wishes to say, and he himself knows no better than ourselves. At the outset, we have to make a quick decision. On the one hand, the dream may be, as the non-analytical physicians assure us, an indication that the dreamer has slept badly, that not all the parts of his brain achieved a uniform state of rest, that certain regions of it endeavoured to go on working under the influence of unknown stimuli and could only do so in a very incomplete way. If that is the case, then we are quite right not to bother ourselves any longer over this psychologically worthless product of nocturnal disturbance. For how could we expect from the investigation of such things to arrive at anything useful for our purposes? On the other hand, however—but it is clear that from the outset we have decided otherwise. We have—perhaps quite arbitrarily—made the assumption, put forward the postulate, that even this unintelligible dream must be a perfectly valid, sensible, and valuable psychic act, of which we can make use in the analysis, just like any other communication. Only the result of our attempt can show us whether we are right. If we are able to turn the dream into a valuable utterance of this kind, then we obviously have a chance of learning something new, and of obtaining information of such a sort as otherwise would remain inaccessible to us.

Now, however, the difficulties of our task, and the puzzling nature of our theme become apparent. How are we going to set about turning a dream into a normal communication, and how are we going to explain that a part of the utterance of our patient has taken on a form which is as unintelligible for him as for us?

You will observe, ladies and gentlemen, that this time I am not expounding the subject on genetic lines, but I am speaking dogmatically. The first thing we have to do is to lay the foundations of our new attitude towards the problem of the dream by introducing two new concepts and two new names. We call what one usually refers to as the dream, the dream-text or the *manifest* dream, and what we are looking for, what we, as it were, suspect to lie behind the dream, the *latent* dream-thoughts. Now we can express our two problems in the following way: we have got to turn the manifest dream into the latent dream, and we have to show how the latter became the former in the mental life of the dreamer. The first bit is a practical problem, it comes under the heading of *dream-interpretation,* and requires a technique; the second is a theoretical problem, its solution should be the explanation of the hypothetical *dream-work,* and can only be a theory. Both the technique of dream-interpretation and the theory of the dream-work have to be built up from the beginning.

Which bit shall we begin with? I think we should start with the technique of dream-interpretation. It has a clearer outline and will make a more vivid impression on you.

The patient, then, has described a dream which we have to interpret. We have listened quietly without making use of our powers of reflection. What do we do next? We determine to bother our heads as little as possible over what we have heard—over the *manifest* dream, that is to say. Naturally this manifest dream displays all sorts of characteristics to which we are not completely indifferent. It may be coherent, smoothly composed, like a literary work, or unintelligibly confused, almost like a delirium; it may have absurd elements, or jokes and apparently brilliant inferences; it may seem clear and well defined to the dreamer, or it may be dim and indefinite; the pictures in it may have the full sensuous force of a perception, or they may be as shadowy and vague as a mist. The greatest variety of characteristics can be found distributed in the various parts of the same dream. Finally, the dream may be attended by an indifferent feeling tone, or by a very strong pleasurable or painful affect. You must not think that we regard this endless variety as a matter of no importance; we shall come back to it later, and shall find in it much that is useful for our interpretation; but for the present we must put it aside, and travel along the main road which leads to the interpretation of the dream. This means that we ask the dreamer as well to free himself from the impression of the manifest dream, to switch his attention from the dream as a whole to individual parts of its content, and to tell us one after another the things that occur to him in connection with these parts, what associations come into his mind when he turns his mental eye on to each of them separately.

That is a curious technique, is it not? It is not the usual way to treat a communication or an utterance. You guess, of course, that behind this procedure there lie concealed assumptions which have not yet been mentioned. But let us proceed. In what order shall we get the patient to take the parts of his dream? Here we have a variety of courses open to us. We can simply follow the chronological order in which the dream has been presented to us in description. That is what one might call the strictest, the classical method. Or we can ask the dreamer to look for the *residue of the previous day* in his dream, because experience has taught us that in almost every dream is incorporated a memory trace of, or an allusion to, an event (or it may be several events) of the previous day; and if we follow up these links we often discover all of a sudden the bridge from the apparently remote dream-world to the real life of the patient. Or else we tell him to begin with those elements in the dream-content which have struck him on account of their clarity and sensuous force. We happen to know that it is particularly easy for him to obtain associations to such elements. It makes no difference by which of these ways we choose to reach the associations we are looking for.

And now let us consider these associations. They consist of the most varied material, memories of the day before, the "dream day," and memories of times long since passed, deliberations, arguments for and against, admissions and questionings. A great many of them are poured out by the patient with ease, while he hesitates when he reaches others. Most of them show a clear connection with one of the elements of the dream, and no wonder, because they have actually sprung from these elements; but it may also happen that the patient introduces them with the words: "That doesn't seem to have anything to do with the dream at all; I say it because it comes into my head."

When one listens to this flood of ideas, one soon notices that they have more in common with the content of the dream than the mere fact that it provided them with their origin. They throw an astonishingly clear light on all the parts of the dream, they fill in the gaps between them, and they make their odd juxtaposition intelligible. Finally, we must get clear the relation between them and the content of the dream. The dream seems to be an abridged extract from the associations, which has been put together in accordance with rules which we have not yet considered; its elements are like the representatives of a multitude which have been chosen by vote. There is no doubt that our technique has enabled us to discover what the dream has replaced, and wherein lies its psychological value; and what we have discovered displays no longer the bewildering peculiarities of the dream, its strangeness and its confused nature.

But let us have no misunderstanding. The associations to the dream are not the latent dream-thoughts. These are contained, but not completely contained, in the associations. On the one hand, the associations produce a great deal more than we require for the formulation of the latent dream-thoughts, namely, all the elaborations, the transitions, and the connecting links, which the intellect of the patient must produce on the road which leads to the dream-thoughts. On the other hand, the association has often stopped short immediately before it has reached the dream-thoughts themselves; it has only touched them allusively. We

now play a part ourselves: we follow up the indications, we draw inevitable conclusions and bring out into the open what the patient in his associations has only touched upon. That sounds as if we allow our cleverness and our arbitrary imagination to play with the material which the dreamer has placed at our disposal, and misuse it to the extent of reading into his utterances what we have no business to find there; and indeed it is no easy matter to show the propriety of our behaviour in an abstract exposition. But if you try a dream-analysis yourselves, or make yourselves familiar with a well-described example from our literature, you will be convinced of the compelling manner in which such a process of interpretation unfolds itself.

Although in dream-interpretation we are in general and predominantly dependent on the associations of the dreamer, nevertheless we treat certain elements of the content quite independently—mainly because we have to, because, as a rule, associations refuse to come. We noticed at an early stage that this happens always in connection with the same material; these elements are not very numerous, and long experience has taught us that they are to be taken as *symbols* for something else, and to be interpreted as such. In comparison with the other elements of the dream, one can give them a permanent meaning, which need not, however, be ambiguous, and the limits of which are determined by special laws, which are of an unusual kind. Since we understand how to translate these symbols, while the dreamer does not, although he himself has made use of them, it may very well be that the sense of the dream is immediately clear to us, even before we have begun the work of dream-interpretation, as soon as we have heard the text of the dream, while the dreamer himself is still puzzled by it. But in the earlier lectures I have already said so much about symbolism, about our knowledge of it, and about the special problems to which it gives rise, that I need not go over the same ground again today.

That, then, is our method of dream-interpretation. The next and very proper question is: Can we by these means interpret every dream? And the answer is: No, not every one; but so many that we can afford to be absolutely certain about the utility and correctness of our procedure. But why not all? The recent answer to this question will teach us something important, which has a bearing on the psychological conditions of dream formation. It is because the work of interpretation is carried on in the face of resistance, which may vary from an imperceptible amount to an amount so great that we cannot overcome it—at any rate with the means which are at present at our disposal. One cannot help observing the manifestation of this resistance during the interpretation. In many places the associations are given without hesitation, and the first or second of them already provides us with the explanation. In other places the patient pauses and hesitates before he utters an association, and then one often has to listen to a long chain of ideas before one gets anything which is of any use for the understanding of the dream. We are right in supposing that the longer and the more circuitous the chain of associations, the stronger is the resistance. And in the forgetting of dreams, too, we sense the same influence. Often enough it happens that, however much he may try, the patient cannot remember one of his dreams. But when, by a piece of analytical work, we have removed a difficulty which has been disturbing the patient in his relation to the analysis, the forgotten dream will come into his mind quite suddenly. Two more observations may be mentioned here. It very often happens that a piece of the dream is missing, which is eventually added as an afterthought. This is to be regarded as an attempt to forget that particular piece. Experience shows that it is this very piece of the dream which is the most valuable; we suppose that a stronger resistance stood in the way of its communication than was the case with the other parts. And, furthermore, we often find that a patient may try to combat the forgetting of his dreams by writing them down immediately after he wakes up. We may as well tell him that it is useless to do so, because the resistance from which he may have preserved the text of the dream will then transfer itself to the associations and render the manifest dream inaccessible for interpretation. This being the case, we need not be surprised if a further increase of the resistance suppresses the associations altogether, and thus frustrates the interpretation of the dream entirely.

From all this we draw the conclusion that the resistance which we come across during the process of dream-interpretation must play some part in the formation of the dream as well. One can actually distinguish between dreams which have been formed under low pressure of resistance and those in which the resistance has been high. But this pressure also changes within the same dream from one place

to another; it is responsible for the gaps, the obscurities and the confusion which may upset the coherence of the most beautiful dreams.

But what is the resistance doing here, and what is it resisting? Now for us a resistance is the sure sign of a conflict. There must be a force present which is trying to express something, and another which is striving to prevent its expression. What comes into being as the manifest dream may, therefore, be regarded as comprising all the solutions to which the battle between these two opposing forces can be reduced. At one point one of the forces may have been able to get through what it wanted to say, at another the counteracting force may have succeeded in abolishing the intended communication entirely, or may have substituted for it something which betrays no sign of it. The most usual cases, and those which are the most characteristic of the process of dream-formation, are those in which the conflict results in a compromise, so that the communicating force can indeed say what it wants to say, but not in the way it wants to say it; it is toned down, distorted, and made unrecognizable. If, therefore, the dream does not faithfully represent the dream-thoughts, if a process of interpretation is necessary to bridge the gulf between the two, this is the result of the counteracting, inhibiting, and restraining force whose existence we have inferred from perceiving the resistance in dream-interpretation. So long as we regarded the dream as an isolated phenomenon, independent of other psychological formations which are allied to it, we called this force the *dream-censor*.

You have long been familiar with the fact that this censorship is not a mechanism which is peculiar to dreams. You remember that the conflict of two psychic factors, which we—roughly—call the *repressed unconscious* and the *conscious,* dominates our lives, and that the resistance against the interpretation of dreams, the hall-mark of the dream-censorship, is none other than the repression-resistance which keeps these two factors apart. You also know that, under certain conditions, other psychological formations emerge from the conflict between these same factors, formations which are the result of compromises just as dreams are; and you will not require me to repeat all that is involved in my introduction to the theory of the neuroses in order to put before you what we know about the conditions under which such compromise formations come about. You will have realized that the dream is a pathological product, the first member of the series which includes the hysterical symptom, the obsession, and the delusion among its members; it is differentiated from the others by its transitoriness and by the fact that it occurs under conditions which are part of normal life. For we must never forget that the dream-life is, as Aristotle has already told us, the way our mind works during sleep. The state of sleep represents a turning away from the real external world, and thus provides a necessary condition for the development of a psychosis. The most penetrating study of serious cases of psychosis will reveal no characteristic which is more typical of these pathological conditions. In psychoses, however, the turning away from reality is brought about in two ways; either because the repressed unconscious is too strong, so that it overwhelms the conscious, which tries to cling on to reality, or because reality has become so unbearably painful that the threatened ego, in a despairing gesture of opposition, throws itself into the arms of the unconscious impulses. The harmless dream-psychosis is the result of a consciously willed, and only temporary, withdrawal from the external world; it ceases to operate when relations with the external world are resumed. While the sleeper is isolated, there is an alteration in the distribution of his psychic energy; part of the repressive expenditure, which is otherwise used to keep down the unconscious, can be saved, for if the unconscious makes use of its relative freedom and enters on some activity, it finds the avenue to motor expression stopped up, and only the innocent outlet of hallucinatory satisfaction open to it. It can now, therefore, form a dream, but the fact of dream-censorship shows that enough repressive resistance remains operative even during sleep.

Here we have an opportunity of answering the question whether the dream has also a function to perform, whether any useful task is entrusted to it. The condition of repose without stimuli, which the state of sleep attempts to bring about, is threatened from three sides: in a chance fashion by external stimuli during sleep, by interests of the day-before which have not yet abated, and, in an unavoidable manner, by the unsatisfied repressed impulses, which are ready to seize on any opportunity for expression. On account of the nightly reduction of the repressive forces, the risk is run that the repose of sleep will be broken every time the outer and inner disturbances manage to link up with one of the unconscious sources

of energy. The dream-process allows the result of such a combination to discharge itself through the channel of a harmless hallucinatory experience, and thus insures the continuity of sleep. There is no contradiction of this function in the fact that the dream sometimes wakes the sleeper in a state of anxiety; it is rather a sign that the watcher regards the situation as being too dangerous, and no longer thinks he can cope with it. Quite often, indeed, while we are still asleep, we are aware of the comforting thought, which is there to prevent our waking up: "After all, it is only a dream."

That is all, ladies and gentlemen, that I wanted to say about dream-interpretation, the business of which is to trace the manifest dream back to the latent dream-thoughts. When this has been done, the interest in the dream from the point of view of practical analysis fades. The analyst links up the communication which he has received in the form of a dream with the patient's other communications and proceeds with the analysis. We, however, wish to linger a little longer over the dream; we are tempted to study the process by means of which the latent dream-thoughts are transformed into the manifest dream. We call this the *dream-work*. You will remember that in the previous lectures I described it in such detail that, for today's review of the subject, I can confine myself to the briefest summary.

The process of dream-work is something quite new and strange, the like of which has never before been known. It has given us our first glimpse into those unconscious mental processes which go on in our unconscious mental system, and shows us that they are quite different from what we know about our conscious thought, and that to this latter they must necessarily appear faulty and preposterous. The importance of this discovery is increased when we realize that the same mechanisms—we hardly dare call them "thought processes"—are at work in the formation of neurotic symptoms as have turned the latent dream-thoughts into the manifest dream.

In what follows, I cannot avoid making my exposition a schematic one. Supposing we have before us in a given instance all the latent thoughts, more or less affectively toned, which have taken the place of the manifest dream after a complete interpretation. We shall then notice a distinction among them, and this distinction will take us a long way. Almost all these dream-thoughts will be recognized or acknowledged by the dreamer; he will admit that he thought thus at one time or another, or that he might very well have done so. But he may resist the acceptation of one single thought, it is foreign to him, perhaps even repellent; it may be that he will passionately repudiate it. Now it becomes clear to us that the other thoughts are bits of his conscious, or, more correctly, of his pre-conscious thought; they might very well have been thought during waking life, and have probably formed themselves during the day. This one rejected thought, or, better, this one impulse, is a child of the night; it belongs to the unconscious of the dreamer, and is therefore disowned and repudiated by him. It had to await the nightly relaxation of repression in order to achieve any sort of expression. In any case, the expression that it obtains is enfeebled, distorted, and disguised; without the work of interpretation we should never have discovered it. It is thanks to its connection with the other unobjectionable dream-thoughts that this unconscious impulse has had the opportunity of slipping past the barrier of the censorship in an unostentatious disguise; on the other hand, the pre-conscious dream-thoughts owe to the same connection their power of occupying the mental life, even during sleep. We can, indeed, have no doubt about this: the unconscious impulse is the real creator of the dream, it provides the psychic energy required for its formation. Just like any other instinctual impulse it can do no other than seek its own satisfaction, and our experience in dream-interpretation shows us, moreover, that this is the meaning of all dreaming. In every dream an instinctual wish is displayed as fulfilled. The nightly cutting-off of mental life from reality, and the regression to primitive mechanisms which it makes possible, enable this desired instinctual satisfaction to be experienced in a hallucinatory fashion as actually happening. On account of the same process of regression, ideas are turned into visual pictures in the dream; the latent dream-thoughts are, that is to say, dramatized and illustrated.

From this piece of dream-work we obtain information about some of the most striking and peculiar characteristics of the dream. Let me repeat the stages of dream-formation. The introduction: the wish to sleep, the voluntary withdrawal from the outside world. Two things follow from this: firstly, the possibility for older and more primitive modes of activity to manifest themselves, i.e., regression; and, secondly, the decrease of the repression-resistance which weighs on the unconscious. As a result of this latter feature, an opportunity for dream-

formation presents itself, which is seized upon by the factors which are the occasion of the dream; that is to say, the internal and external stimuli which are in activity. The dream which thus eventuates is already a compromise-formation; it has a double function: it is on the one hand in conformity with the ego (ego-syntonic), since it subserves the wish to sleep by draining off the stimuli which would otherwise disturb it, while on the other hand it allows to a repressed impulse the satisfaction which is possible in these circumstances in the form of an hallucinatory wish-fulfilment. The whole process of dream-formation, which is permitted by the sleeping ego, is, however, under the control of the censorship, a control which is exercised by what is left of the forces of repression. I cannot explain the process more simply; it is not in itself simpler than that. But now I can proceed with the description of the dream-work.

Let us go back once more to the latent dream-thoughts. Their dominating element is the repressed impulse, which has obtained some kind of expression, toned down and disguised though it may be, by associating itself with stimuli which happen to be there and by tacking itself on the residue of the day before. Just like any other impulse this one presses forward toward satisfaction in action, but the path to motor discharge is closed to it on account of the physiological characteristics of the state of sleep, and so it is forced to travel in the retrograde direction to perception, and content itself with an hallucinatory satisfaction. The latent dream-thoughts are therefore turned into a collection of sensory images and visual scenes. As they are travelling in this direction something happens to them which seems to us new and bewildering. All the verbal apparatus by means of which the more subtle thought-relations are expressed, the conjunctions and prepositions, the variations of declension and conjugation, are lacking, because the means of portraying them are absent: just as in primitive, grammarless speech, only the raw material of thought can be expressed, and the abstract is merged again in the concrete from which it sprang. What is left over may very well seem to lack coherence. It is as much the result of the archaic regression in the mental apparatus as of the demands of the censorship that so much use is made of the representation of certain objects and processes by means of symbols which have become strange to conscious thought. But of more far-reaching import are the other alterations to which the elements comprising the dream-thoughts are subjected. Such of them as have any point of contact are *condensed* into new unities. When the thoughts are translated into pictures, those forms are indubitably preferred which allow of this kind of telescoping, or condensation; it is as though a force were at work which subjected the material to a process of pressure or squeezing together. As a result of condensation, one element in a manifest dream may correspond to a number of elements of the dream-thoughts; but, conversely, one of the elements from among the dream-thoughts may be represented by a number of pictures in the dream.

Even more remarkable is the other process of *displacement* or transference of accent, which in conscious thinking figures only as an error in thought or as a method employed in jokes. For the individual ideas which make up the dream-thoughts are not all of equal value; they have various degrees of affective-tone attached to them, and corresponding to these, they are judged as more or less important, and more or less worthy of attention. In the dream-work these ideas are separated from their affects; the affects are treated separately. They may be transferred to something else, they may remain where they were, they may undergo transformation, or they may disappear from the dream entirely. The importance of the ideas which have been shorn of their affect reappears in the dream in the form of the sensuous vividness of the dream-pictures; but we notice that this accent, which should lie on important elements, has been transferred to unimportant ones, so that what seems to be pushed to the forefront in the dream, as the most important element in it, only plays a subsidiary rôle in the dream-thoughts, and, conversely, what is important among the dream-thoughts obtains only incidental and rather indistinct representation in the dream. No other factor in the dream-work plays such an important part in rendering the dream strange and unintelligible to the dreamer. Displacement is the chief method employed in the process of *dream-distortion,* which the dream-thoughts have to undergo under the influence of the censorship.

After these operations on the dream-thoughts, the dream is almost ready. There is still, however, a more or less non-constant factor, the so-called *secondary elaboration,* that makes its appearance after the dream has come into consciousness as an object of perception. When the dream has come into consciousness, we treat it in exactly the same way that we treat any content of perception; we try to fill in the gaps, we add connecting links, and often enough we let ourselves in for serious misunderstandings. But this, as it were, rationalizing activity, which at its best provides the dream with a smooth façade, such as cannot correspond to its real content, may be altogether absent in some cases, or only operate in a very feeble way, in which case the dream displays to view all its gaps and inconsistencies. On the other hand, one must not forget that the dream-work, too, does not always function with equal force; quite often it limits its activity to certain parts of the dream-thoughts, while others are allowed to come into the dream unaltered. In this event, one has the impression that one has carried out the most complicated and subtle intellectual operations during the dream, that one has made brilliant speculations or jokes, or that one has come to decisions or solved problems; really, however, all this is the result of our normal mental activity, and may just as well have happened during the day before the dream as during the night. It has nothing to do with the dream-work, nor does it display any feature which is characteristic of dreams. It is perhaps not superfluous once more to emphasise the distinction which subsists among the dream-thoughts themselves, between the unconscious impulse and the residues of the preceding day. While the latter exhibit the whole variety of our mental activity, the former, which is the real motive force of the dream, always finds its outlet in a wish-fulfilment.

I could have told you all that fifteen years ago; in fact I actually did tell it you at the time. Now let us bring together such modifications and new discoveries as have been made during the interval.

I have already told you that I am afraid you will find that there is very little to say; so you will not understand why I have obliged you to listen to the same thing twice over, and have obliged myself to say it. But fifteen years have passed, and I hoped that in this way I might most easily re-establish contact with you. And indeed these elementary matters are of such decisive importance for the understanding of psycho-analysis that it is a good thing to hear them for a second time, and the very fact that they have remained the same after fifteen years is in itself something worth knowing.

You will naturally find in the literature of these years a great deal of confirmatory material and exposition of details, of which I only intend to give you examples. I can also add to this a certain amount that was already known before. Most of it has to do with symbolism and the other methods of representation in dreams. Only quite recently the physicians at an American university refused to allow that psycho-analysis was a science, on the ground that it admits of no experimental proof. They might have raised the same objection against astronomy; experimentation with the heavenly bodies is, after all, exceedingly difficult. There one has to rely on observation Nevertheless, certain Viennese investigators have made a start on the experimental confirmation of our theory of dream-symbolism. Dr. Schrötter discovered as long ago as 1912 that when one orders a deeply hypnotized person to dream of sexual activities, the sexual material in the dream that is thus provoked is represented by the symbols which are familiar to us. For example, a woman is told to dream of sexual intercourse with a lady friend of hers. In her dream the friend appears with a travelling-bag, which has a label pasted on it: "Ladies only." Even more impressive are the experiments of Betlheim and Hartmann (1924), who worked with patients suffering from the so-called Korsakow's syndrome. They told the patient stories with a crude sexual content, and then noted the distortions which appeared when he was asked to reproduce what he had heard. Here again the symbols with which we are familiar as standing for the sexual organs and sexual intercourse cropped up, and among them the symbol of a staircase, with regard to which the authors very properly observe that it would be inaccessible to a conscious intention to distort.

Silberer performed a very interesting series of experiments in which he showed that one can surprise the dream-work, as it were, *in flagrante delicto*, and see how it translates the abstract thoughts into visual pictures. When he tried to force himself, in a very tired and sleepy condition, to perform an intellectual task, the thought itself would escape him, and in its place would come a visual image, which was often a substitute for it.

Here is a simple example. The thought which Silberer set before himself was that he must smooth out an uneven passage in an article. His visual image was that he saw himself planing a piece of wood. It often happened in these experiments that it was not the idea which was awaiting elaboration that formed the content of the visual image, but his own state of mind while he was trying to make the effort—the subjective condition rather than the objective content. This Silberer calls a *functional phenomenon*. An example will easily show you what is meant. The author is trying to make a comparison between the views of two philosophers about some problem, but in his drowsiness one of these views is always escaping him, and finally he has a vision of himself asking information of a cross-grained secretary, who is leaning over his desk and disregards him at first and then looks at him with a disagreeable expression, as if he would like to send him about his business. It is probably due to the conditions of the experiment itself that the visual images which are aroused in this way so often represent introspective material.

Let us consider symbols a little longer. There were some which we thought we had grasped, but about which we were nevertheless troubled because we could give no account of how that particular symbol got its particular meaning. In such cases any confirmation we could get from other sources, from philology, folklore, mythology or ritual, was particularly welcome. An example of this kind was the symbol of a cloak. We held that in a woman's dream a cloak stood for a man. I hope now you will be impressed when you hear that Reik (1920) tells us: "In the ancient marriage ceremony of the Bedouins, the bridegroom covers the bride with a special cloak which is called an 'aba,' and at the same time utters the ritual words: 'Let no man in the future cover thee but me'" (from Robert Eisler, *Weltenmantel und Himmelszelt*). We have also discovered a great many new symbols, of which I will give you two examples. According to Abraham (1922), a spider in a dream is a symbol of the mother; but it means the phallic mother, whom one fears, so that the fear of the spider expresses the horror of incest with the mother and the abhorrence felt towards the female genitals. You know, perhaps, that the mythological figure of the Medusa's head is to be traced back to the same motif of castration-fear. The other symbol of which I should like to speak is the symbol of the bridge. Ferenczi has explained it (1921-1922). It stands originally for the male genital organ, which connects the parents with each other during sexual intercourse; but it develops into a wider set of meanings, which spring out of the first. Since the male genital organ is responsible for the fact that one can emerge from the waters of birth into the world, the bridge depicts the passage from Yonder (not-yet-born-ness, the womb) to Here (life), and since mankind also represents death as the return into the mother's womb (into the water), the symbol of the bridge gets the meaning of something that brings about death; and finally, further removed from its original meaning, it indicates transition, or any change of condition whatever. That is why a woman who has not yet overcome her desire to be a man so frequently dreams of bridges which are too short to reach the other side.

Very often pictures and situations appear in the manifest content of the dream which remind one of well-known themes from fairy stories, legends and myths. The interpretation of such dreams throws light on the original motives which created these themes, though naturally we must not forget the change of meaning which this material has undergone during the passage of time. Our work of interpretation uncovers what one might call the raw material, which often enough may be regarded as sexual in the broadest sense of the word, but which has found the most varied application in later elaborations. When we trace things back like this, we very often arouse the rage of all investigators who do not share the analytical point of view, as though we were seeking to deny or underestimate all the later developments which the raw material has undergone. None the less, such ways of looking at things are instructive and interesting. The same is true of the tracing back of various motifs of plastic art—as, for example, when J. Eisler (1919), guided by the dreams of his patients, interprets analytically the young man playing with a little boy, portrayed in the *Hermes* of Praxiteles. Finally, I cannot help mentioning how often mythological themes find their explanation through dream-interpretation. The story of the Labyrinth, for example, is found to be a representation of anal birth; the tortuous paths are the bowels, and the thread of Ariadne is the umbilical cord.

The method of representation which the dream-work adopts, a fascinating and almost inexhaustible subject, is constantly becoming better known to us as we study it more closely. I will give you a few proofs of this. The notion of frequency, for instance, is expressed in dreams by means of the multiplication of similars. Listen to this remarkable dream of a young girl. She goes into a hall and finds there a person sitting on a chair; this figure is repeated six times, eight times, and even more, but every time the person is her father. This can easily be understood when one learns from the additional features which emerged in interpretation that the room represents the womb. The dream then becomes equivalent to the familiar fantasy of the young girl who believes that she met her father during her intra-uterine life, when he visited the womb during her mother's pregnancy. The fact that an element in the dream is turned the wrong way round, that the act of entry is transferred from the father to the dreamer herself, should not lead you astray; it has indeed a special meaning of its own. The multiplication of the father image can only mean that the procedure in question was frequently repeated. But then the dream always turns temporal relations into spatial ones whenever it has to deal with them. Thus, one may see in a dream a scene between people who look very small and far away, as if one were looking at them through the wrong end of a pair of opera glasses. The smallness and the spatial remoteness here mean the same; it is remoteness in time that is meant, the interpretation being that it is a scene from the far distant past. Besides this, you may remember that in my previous lectures I showed you, with the help of examples, that we had learnt to make use even of the purely formal characteristics of the manifest dream for purposes of interpretation; that is to say, to turn them into the content of the latent dream-thoughts. Now you know, of course, that all the dreams of one night belong to the same context; but it is by no means immaterial whether these dreams appear to the dreamer as a continuum, or whether they are organized in several pieces, and if so in how many. The number of pieces often corresponds to the same number of distinct nodal points in the chain of thoughts, which make up the latent dream-thoughts; or it may correspond to forces in the mental life of the dreamer which are struggling with one another, and each of which finds its main (though not its exclusive) expression in one particular part of the dream. A short introductory dream and a long main dream often stand to each other in the relation of condition and consequence; of this you will find a very clear example in the old lectures. A dream which the dreamer describes as "somehow interpolated" really corresponds to a dependent clause in the dream-thoughts. Franz Alexander in his essay on pairs of dreams that not infrequently two dreams which occur on the same night play separate parts in the fulfilment of the dream-function, so that taken together they provide a wish-fulfilment in two steps, a thing which each alone does not do. If a dream-wish has as its content some piece of forbidden behaviour towards a certain individual, then that person may appear in the first dream undisguised while the behaviour is only faintly indicated. In the second dream it will be the other way round. The behaviour will be openly shown, but the person will be made unrecognizable, or else some indifferent person will be substituted for him. It must be admitted that this gives one an impression of deliberate artfulness. A second and similar relation between two members of a pair of dreams is that in which the one represents the punishment and the other the sinful wish-fulfilment. It is just as if one said: "If I take the punishment on myself, then I can do the forbidden thing."

I must not detain you longer with such discoveries of matters of detail, nor with discussions of the uses of dream-interpretation in analytic work. I am sure you are impatient to hear what alterations have been made in our basic attitude towards the nature and meaning of dreams. You will be prepared to hear that there is little to tell. The most hotly disputed point of the whole theory was undoubtedly the assertion that all dreams are wish-fulfilments. The inevitable and ever-recurrent objection from the laity that there are so many anxiety-dreams has already been completely answered, I think, in my earlier lectures. We have kept our theory intact by dividing dreams into wish-dreams, anxiety-dreams, and punishment-dreams.

Even punishment-dreams are wish-fulfilments, but they do not fulfil the wishes of the instinctual impulses, but those of the critical, censuring, and punishing function of the mind. If we are faced with a pure punishment-dream, a simple mental operation will enable us to reinstate the wish-dream to which the punishment-dream was the proper rejoinder; on account of this repudiation, the punishment-dream has appeared in place of the wish-dream as the manifest one. You know, ladies and gentlemen, that the study of dreams was the first thing that helped us to understand the neuroses. And you will not be surprised to hear that our subsequent knowledge of the neuroses has influenced our conception of the dream. As you will learn presently, we have been forced to assume the existence in the mind of a special criticizing and forbidding function which we call the *super-ego*. Since we have now recognized the dream-censorship as an activity of this function, we have been led to consider the part which the super-ego plays in dream-formation in greater detail.

Only two serious difficulties face the wish-fulfilment theory of dreams, the examination of which leads us far afield and for which we have found no completely satisfactory solution. The first difficulty is presented by the fact that people who have had severe shocks or who have gone through serious psychic traumas (such as were frequent during the war, and are also found to lie at the back of traumatic hysteria) are continually being put back into the traumatic situation in dreams. According to our acceptation of the function of dreams, this ought not to be the case. What conative impulse could possibly be satisfied by this reinstatement of a most painful traumatic experience? It is indeed hard to guess. We meet with the second fact almost daily in our analytical work; it does not involve such a serious objection as the other. You know that it is one of the tasks of psycho-analysis to lift the veil of amnesia which shrouds the earliest years of childhood and to bring the expressions of infantile sexual life which are hidden behind it into conscious memory. Now these first sexual experiences of the child are bound up with painful impressions of anxiety, prohibition, disappointment, and punishment. One can understand why they have been repressed; but, if so, it is difficult to see why they should have such easy access to dream-life, why they should provide the pattern for so many dream-phantasies, and why dreams are full of reproductions of these infantile scenes and allusions to them. The pain that attaches to them and the wish-fulfilling tendency of the dream-work would seem to be incompatible. But perhaps in this case we exaggerate the difficulty. All the imperishable and unrealizable desires which provide the energy for the formation of dreams throughout one's whole life are bound up with these same childish experiences, and one can well trust to their ability with their powerful upward thrust to force even material of a painful nature to the surface. And, on the other hand, in the manner in which this material is reproduced the efforts of the dream-work are unmistakable; it disowns pain by means of distortion and turns disappointment into fulfilment. In the case of the traumatic neuroses it is quite different; here the dream habitually ends in anxiety. In my opinion we ought not to shirk the admission that in such cases the function of the dream fails. I will not have recourse to the saying that the exception proves the rule; the validity of this phrase seems to me very dubious. But at any rate the exception does not do away with the rule. If for the purposes of investigation one isolates from every other mental process a single psychic activity like the dream, one is enabled to discover the laws which govern it; if one then puts it back into its place, one must be prepared to find that one's discoveries are obscured and interfered with when they come into contact with other forces. We assert that the dream is a wish-fulfilment; in order to take these last objections into account, you may say that the dream is an *attempted* wish-fulfilment. But for those who have an understanding for the dynamics of the mind you will not be saying anything different. Under certain conditions the dream can only achieve its end in a very incomplete way, or has to abandon it entirely; an unconscious fixation to the trauma seems to head the list of these obstacles to the dream-function. The sleeper has to dream, because the nightly relaxation of repression allows the upward thrust of the traumatic fixation to become active; but sometimes his dream-work, which endeavours to change the memory traces of the traumatic event into a wish-fulfilment, fails to operate. In these circumstances, the result is that one becomes sleepless; one gives up all idea of sleep because of one's fear of the failure of the dream-function. The traumatic neurosis is an extreme case, but one must also attribute a traumatic character to infantile experiences as well; so one need not be surprised if lesser disturbances of the function of the dream occur in other circumstances.

LECTURE 30
DREAMS AND THE OCCULT

LADIES AND GENTLEMEN: Today we are to travel along a narrow path, but it may lead us to a wide prospect.

When you hear that I am going to talk about the connection between dreams and the occult, you need hardly feel surprised. Dreams are indeed often regarded as the portal to the world of mysticism, and even today seem to many to be in themselves an occult phenomenon. Even we, who have made them an object of scientific study, cannot deny that several strands link them up with those obscure regions. Mysticism —occultism—what is meant by these terms? Do not imagine that I shall attempt to provide you with a clear definition of such hazy concepts. In a general and vague way we all know what we mean by the terms. They refer to a kind of "other world" which lies beyond the clear world, with its inexorable laws, which science has built up for us.

Occultism assumes that there are in fact more things in heaven and earth than are dreamt of in our philosophy. Well, we need not be tied down by the narrow-mindedness of the Schools; we are ready to believe whatever is made plausible to us.

We intend to treat these things in just the same way as we treat any other material for scientific investigation. First, we have to establish whether these processes really occur, and then, but only then, when there is no doubt as to their actuality, we can set about their explanation. But we cannot hide from ourselves the fact that even the first step will be made difficult for us by intellectual, psychological, and historical factors. It is by no means the same as when we start on any other investigation.

Let us consider the intellectual difficulties first. Allow me to give you a crude, obvious explanation of what I mean. Supposing we are dealing with the constitution of the interior of the earth. Admittedly we know nothing certain about it. We suppose that it consists of heavy metals in a molten condition. Now let us imagine that some one asserts that the interior of the earth is made of water impregnated with carbonic acid; that is to say, a kind of soda-water. We shall certainly say that it is very improbable, that it runs counter to all our expectations, and that it does not take into consideration the scientific data which have led us to put forward the mental hypothesis. But for all that it is not unthinkable. If any one shows us the way to prove the soda-water hypothesis, we shall follow it without any resistance. But now another person comes along who seriously asserts that the centre of the earth is made of jam. We shall behave quite differently towards his theory. We shall say to ourselves that jam is not a product of Nature but of human cookery; moreover, the existence of that material presupposes the presence of fruit-trees and their fruit, and we cannot see our way to placing vegetation and human cookery in the centre of the earth. The result of this intellectual objection will be a diversion of our interests; instead of their being directed on to the investigation itself, as to whether the interior of the earth is really made of jam or not, we shall wonder what kind of man it must be who can get such an idea into his head, or at the most we shall ask him where he got the idea from. The unfortunate inventor of the jam hypothesis will be very much offended, and will complain that we are refusing to consider an objective evaluation of this theory out of what he calls scientific prejudice. But his complaints will be in vain. Prejudices, we feel, are not always to be deplored, but are sometimes justified; and they are useful in saving us unnecessary trouble. They are, indeed, nothing more than conclusions drawn by analogy from other well-founded judgments.

A whole number of occult theories make the same impression on us as the jam theory, so that we feel justified in putting them aside at the outset without testing them. But it is not quite such a simple matter. An analogy such as I have suggested—like all analogies—proves nothing. In any case it is doubtful whether it is a fair analogy, and it is obvious that it was our attitude of scornful rejection which in the first instance determined our choice of it. Prejudices are very often useful and justified, but sometimes they are erroneous and harmful, and one never knows when they will be the one or the other. The history of science is full of examples which should warn us against too hasty a condemnation. For a long time it was thought to be an absurd thesis that the stones which we now call meteorites should have reached the earth from outer space, or that mountains, the rocks of which contain remains of shells, should once have formed the bed of the sea. And, after all, not so very different a fate befell our psycho-analysis itself, when it brought forward the discovery of the unconscious. We analysts, therefore, have special reason to be cautious in making use of intellectual arguments in the rejection of new theories, and we must recognize that such arguments will not put us beyond the reach of feelings of aversion, doubt, and uncertainty.

I called the second factor psychological. By that I meant the general human inclination towards credulity and belief in the marvellous. From the very beginning, when life imposes its stern discipline upon us, there grows up in us a resistance against the restlessness and monotony of the laws of thought, and against the need for putting things to the test of reality. Reason becomes an enemy that keeps us from so many possibilities of pleasure. One discovers what a joy it is to escape from it at least for a moment, and give oneself up to the fascination of irrationality. The schoolboy amuses himself by making up ridiculous plays on words, the specialist makes fun of his own work after a scientific congress, and even the serious-minded man enjoys an occasional joke. More serious antagonism against "Wisdom and Science, man's most prized powers," awaits its opportunity; it is eager to prefer the miracle-man or the natural healer to the *trained* doctor, it makes us warm towards the theories of the occult, so long as its reputed facts can be taken as breaches of law and rule. It puts our critical faculty to sleep, falsifies our perception, and forces us to confirm and agree without real justification. Any one who takes these human weaknesses into consideration has every reason to discount the value of much of the information contained in occult literature.

In referring to the third obstacle as the historical one I had in mind the fact that nothing new is to be found in the world of the occult. On the contrary, we meet again in it with all the signs, wonders, prophecies, and apparitions which have been handed down to us from remote ages and in old books, and which we long ago thought we had done with as being the offspring of unbridled imagination or tendentious fraud, the product of a time when the ignorance of mankind was at its height and when the scientific spirit was still in its infancy. If we accept as true what we are told by the occultists of our own day, then we must be prepared to believe the accounts which have come down to us from the past. And then we remember that the traditions and sacred books of all races are packed with such marvels, and that religions base their claim to credibility precisely on such extraordinary and wondrous happenings, and find in them the proof of the operation of superhuman forces. At this point it is hard for us to avoid the suspicion that occult interests are really religious ones, and that it is one of the secret motives of the occultist movements to come to the aid of religious belief, threatened as it is by the progress of scientific thought. The discovery of a motive of this kind cannot fail to increase our mistrust and our disinclination to embark upon an investigation of these so-called occult phenomena.

But this disinclination must be overcome. The whole thing is really a question of fact: is what the occultists tell us true or not? It must be possible to decide this by observation. *Au fond,* we ought to be grateful to the occultists. The tales of wonderful happenings which have come down to us from ancient days are beyond our powers of testing. If we say that they cannot be proved, we must at least admit that, strictly speaking, they cannot be disproved. But about what happens in the present, about things which we can actually witness, we ought to be able to reach a definite conclusion. If we are convinced that such wonders do not occur nowadays, we need not fear the objection that they might have occurred in days gone by. Other explanations will then be far more plausible. We have, then, put aside our scruples and are ready to take part in the observation of occult phenomena.

Unfortunately, we come up against considerations which are highly unfavourable to our laudable intentions. The observations on which our judgments must depend have to be made under conditions which render our powers of perception insecure, and which blunt our faculty of attention; the phenomena take place in the dark or in the faint glimmer of a red light after long periods of fruitless waiting. We are told that even our sceptical—that is to say, our critical—attitude may very well prevent the hoped for phenomena from manifesting themselves. The situation which thus arises is simply a caricature of the conditions under which we are used to carrying out scientific investigations. The observations are made on so-called mediums, persons to whom are ascribed special "sensitive" gifts, who, however, do not display outstanding qualities of intelligence or character, and who are not moved, as the old wonder-workers were, by some great idea or by some serious purpose. On the contrary, they are regarded as particularly untrustworthy even by the people who believe in their mysterious powers; most of them have already been unmasked as frauds, and we are tempted to expect that the same will happen with the rest as well. Their performances remind us of the mischievous pranks of a child or of a conjuror's tricks. Nothing of any value has so far ever come out of these *séances* with mediums; no new source of energy has become accessible to us. And, to be sure, one does not expect any advances in our knowledge of pigeon-breeding from the tricks of a conjuror who produces pigeons out of an empty top-hat. I can easily put myself into the position of a man who wishes to fulfil the demands of objectivity and therefore takes part in these occult *séances,* but tires of them after a while, and, put off by what is required of him, gives up the whole business and returns to his prejudices no wiser than before. To such a man one might object that his behaviour is not right, and that

if one is going to investigate phenomena one cannot decide beforehand of what nature they shall be and under what conditions they shall manifest themselves. It is, on the contrary, his business to persevere and form some estimate of the precautionary measures of control which are used nowadays as a protection against the untrustworthiness of mediums. Unfortunately, the modern control technique puts an end to the easy accessibility of occult observations. The study of the occult has become a specialized and difficult pursuit, a form of activity which one cannot carry on side by side with one's other interests. And until the investigators who have given their minds to it have come to some conclusion, one is necessarily given over to doubts and to one's own conjectures.

Among these conjectures the most probable is, I think, that in occultism there is a core of facts which have hitherto not been recognized, and round which fraud and phantasy have woven a veil which it is hard to penetrate. But how can we even approach this core? at what point can we grasp the problem? It is here, it seems to me, that the dream comes to our aid by suggesting to us that we should pick out the theme of telepathy from all the confused material that surrounds it.

You know that by *telepathy* we mean the alleged fact that an event which occurs at a specific time comes more or less simultaneously into the consciousness of a person who is spatially distant, without any of the known methods of communication coming into play. The tacit assumption is that this event occurs to a person, in whom the receiver of the message has some strong emotional interest. Thus, for example, a person A has an accident, or dies, and a person B, some one closely connected with A, his mother or daughter or loved one, learns of it at about the time of its occurrence through a visual or auditory perception; in the latter case it is as though they were in telephonic communication, which, however, they are not; in fact, it is a kind of psychic parallel to wireless telegraphy. I need not emphasize to you the improbability of such processes, and anyway there are good grounds for rejecting the majority of such reports. Some of them are left over which cannot be rejected so easily. I must now ask you to allow me to leave out the precautionary word *alleged* for the purposes of what I have to tell you, and to let me continue as though I believed in the objective reality of telepathic phenomena. But you must remember all the time that this is not the case, that I have not committed myself to any conclusion on the subject.

As a matter of fact I have but little to tell you—only one modest fact. And I will further diminish your expectations by informing you that fundamentally the dream has but little to do with telepathy. Telepathy throws no new light on the nature of the dream, nor does the dream bear witness for the reality of telepathy. Telepathic phenomena are also by no manner of means confined to dreams; they can also manifest themselves during waking life. The only ground for mentioning the connection between dreams and telepathy is that the condition of sleep seems to be especially suitable for the reception of telepathic communications. If, then, one comes across a so-called *telepathic dream*, one can convince oneself by its analysis that the telepathic message has played the same rôle as any other residue of waking life, and as such has been altered by the dream-work and made to serve its purpose.

Now in the course of the analysis of a telepathic dream of this kind something occurred which seems to me of sufficient importance, in spite of its slightness, to serve as the starting-point for this lecture. When in the year 1922 I brought up this subject for the first time, I had only one observation at my disposal. Since then I have made several other observations; but I shall keep to the first example, because it is the easiest one to describe, and I shall proceed at once to the heart of the matter.

An obviously intelligent man, and one who according to his own estimation, was in no way "tainted with occultism" wrote to me about a dream which seemed to him to be remarkable. He prefaced his story with the information that his married daughter, who lived some distance from him, was expecting her first confinement in the middle of December. He was very much devoted to this daughter, and he knew that she was very much attached to him. Now he dreamed in the night between the 16th and 17th of November that his wife had had twins. There followed several details which I can pass over here, not all of which have found a satisfactory explanation. The woman who, in the dream, had become the mother of the twins, was his second wife, the daughter's step-mother. He did not wish to have children by this woman, whom he did not consider fitted for bringing up children in an understanding way, and at the time of the dream he had for a long time given up sexual

intercourse with her. What induced him to write to me was not a doubt about the validity of the theory of dreams, though the manifest dream would have justified him if that had been the case; for why does the dream, in flat contradiction to his wishes, depict this woman as bearing children? And according to his story he had no grounds for fearing that this un-wished-for occurrence might take place. What determined him to tell me about his dream was the fact that early in the morning of November 18th he received a telegram to say that his daughter had given birth to twins. The telegram had been handed in the day before, and the birth had taken place during the night between the 16th and 17th, at about the same time that he had dreamt that his wife had had twins. The dreamer asked me whether I thought that the simultaneity of the dream and the event was a mere coincidence. He did not go so far as to call the dream a telepathic one, because the difference between the content of the dream and the event itself concerned precisely what he considered to be the most important point, the person who had the children. But from one of his remarks it looked as though he would not have been surprised if he had had a real telepathic dream. His daughter, he felt certain, had "thought especially about him" during labour.

Ladies and Gentlemen, I am sure that you can already explain the dream, and that you understand why I have told it to you. Here is a man, dissatisfied with his second wife, who would prefer to have a wife like his daughter by his first marriage. In the unconscious this *like* is naturally omitted. Now during the night he receives the telepathic communication that his daughter has had twins. The dream-work seizes on this information, allows his unconscious wish that his daughter should replace his second wife to act upon it, and thus emerges the singular manifest dream in which the wish itself is veiled and the message distorted. We must admit that only dream-interpretation has shown us that this is a telepathic dream; psycho-analysis has discovered a telepathic event which we should not otherwise have recognized as such.

But do not let yourselves be led astray. In spite of all this, dream-interpretation has said nothing about the objective truth of telepathic phenomena. It may be only an appearance which can be explained in some other way. It is possible that the man's latent dream-thoughts ran like this: "Today is the day on which the confinement must take place, if my daughter, as I incidentally believe is the case, has been a month out in her calculations. And her appearance when I saw her last time was such that it looked as though she was going to have twins. And my dead wife was so fond of children: how delighted she would have been by twins!" (The last point is derived from associations of the dreamer which I have not yet mentioned.) In that case the stimulus for the dream would have been well-founded suspicions on the part of the dreamer and not a telepathic message; the result would have been the same in both cases. You notice that even this interpretation has told us nothing about the question of whether one should assign objective reality to telepathy. One could only come to a conclusion about that after making detailed enquiries into all the circumstances of the case, which unfortunately was impossible with this example, as it was with all the others in my experience. We may grant that the assumption of telepathy gives us by far the simplest explanation; but that does not carry us very far. The simplest explanation is not always the right one, truth is very often not simple, and one must act with the greatest caution before committing oneself to such a far-reaching assumption.

We can now leave the subject of dreams and telepathy; I have nothing more to say about it. But I want you to notice that it was not dreams that seemed to teach us something about telepathy, but the interpretation of the dreams, the psycho-analytic treatment of them. We can therefore leave dreams on one side in what follows, and we will examine further our suspicion that the application of psycho-analysis may throw a light on other so-called *occult facts*. There is, for example, the phenomenon of thought-transference, which is closely allied to telepathy and, indeed, can be identified with it without much difficulty. It is held that psychological processes, ideas, states of excitement, volitions, which occur in the mind of one person, can be transferred through space to another, without the usual means of communication (words or signs) being employed. Incidentally, it is remarkable that it is actually these phenomena which find the least mention in the old accounts of the miraculous.

During the psycho-analytic treatment of patients, I have had the impression that the activities of professional fortune-tellers provide an admirable opportunity for making really satisfactory observations of thought-transference. It is usually mediocre and even inferior people who carry on practices of this sort, deal out cards, study writing and the lines upon the hand, or make astrological reckonings, and foretell the future of their visitors, after having shown some knowledge of their past or present history. Their clients usually express themselves as satisfied by their performances, and bear them no ill-will if their prophecies do not come true in the end. I have come across a great many such cases and have been able to study them analytically. I will tell you the most remarkable instances of the kind. Unfortunately the evidential value of this information is reduced on account of the numerous omissions which are necessitated by the rules of professional secrecy. I have, however, carefully avoided any distortions. This is the story of one of my female patients, who had an experience of the kind we are discussing with a fortune-teller.

She was the eldest of a family of brothers and sisters, grew up with an extraordinarily strong attachment to her father, had married young, and had found entire satisfaction in her married life. There was only one thing wanting to make her happiness complete; she was childless, and thus the husband whom she loved could not wholly fill the place of her father. When after many years she decided to have a gynaecological operation, her husband disclosed to her the fact that the fault lay in him, that through an illness which had occurred before marriage he had been rendered incapable of procreating children. She took this disappointment very badly, became neurotic, and suffered unmistakably from dread of the husband's attempts. In order to cheer her up, her husband took her with him on a business visit to Paris. While they were there, they were sitting one day in the hall of the hotel when she noticed a stir among the hotel servants. She asked what was happening, and learnt that Monsieur le Professeur had arrived and was giving consultations in a certain room. She expressed her wish to see what the thing was like herself. Her husband tried to dissuade her, but when he was not looking she slipped into the room where the fortune-teller was giving his consultations. She was twenty-seven years old, but looked much younger, and she had taken off her wedding-ring. Monsieur le Professeur told her to rest her hand on a bowl filled with ashes, carefully studied the imprint, and, after telling her all sorts of things about severe troubles which lay before her, concluded with the comforting assurance that she would get married all the same and have two children by the time she was thirty-two years of age. When she told me this story she was forty-three, very ill, and with no expectation of ever having a child at all. The prophecy therefore had not come true, and yet she spoke of it with no bitterness whatever, but with an unmistakable expression of satisfaction, as though she were looking back with pleasure upon a happy experience. It was easy to assure oneself that she had not the slightest idea what the two numbers in the prophecy might mean, or whether they meant anything at all.

You will say that this is a stupid and incomprehensible story, and ask why I have related it to you. Now I should feel exactly as you do, but for the fact—and this is the important point—that the analysis enabled us to obtain an interpretation of the prophecy, which was actually most significant when it came to the details. For the two numbers have a place in the life of the *mother* of my patient. She had married late, when she was more than thirty, and her family had often remarked how successful she had been in making up for lost time. Her two first children—and our patient was the elder of these—had been born within a single calendar year with the smallest possible interval between them; and it was really true of her that by the time she was thirty-two she had two children. What Monsieur le Professeur told my patient meant this: "Cheer up, for you are still young! You will have the same experience as your mother, who also had to wait a long time for children, and you will have two children by the time you are thirty-two." But to have the same experience as her mother, to be in her position, to take her place with her father, was the strongest wish of her childhood, the wish whose non-fulfilment was beginning to make her ill. The prophecy promised her that it would be fulfilled, how could she feel otherwise than friendly towards the prophet? But do you think that Monsieur le Professeur could really have been familiar with the dates of the intimate family history of a chance client? It is impossible; whence, then, came the knowledge that enabled him to express in his prophecy the strongest and most secret wish of my patient by bringing in these two numbers? I can see only two possibilities. Either the story, as she told it to me, was not true and the events were different, or we must accept thought-transference as a real phenomenon. It could, no doubt, be argued that my patient, after the lapse of sixteen years, had carried over the two numbers we are discussing from her unconscious into her recollection. I have no evidence for this suggestion, but I cannot rule it out, and I imagine that you would prefer to believe in such an explanation rather than in the reality of thought-transference. If, however, you should accept the latter view, do not forget that it was only analysis that brought to light the occult element, which had been distorted out of all recognition.

If we had to deal with only *one* case like that of my patient, we should turn away from it with a shrug of the shoulders. It would not occur to any one to base a belief which has such far-reaching implications on an isolated observation. But I can assure you that this is not the only case in my experience. I have collected a whole set of such prophecies, and I have the impression that in every instance the fortune-teller has only given expression to the thoughts, and particularly to the secret wishes, of his clients; so that we are justified in analysing such prophecies as if they were the subjective productions, phantasies, or dreams of the people concerned. Naturally not all cases have equal evidential value, nor in all cases is it equally possible to rule out more rational explanations; but taking all the evidence together there remains a heavy weight of probability in favour of the reality of thought-transference. The importance of the matter would justify my putting all my cases before you; but I cannot do that because the material would be of inordinate length and would inevitably involve a breach of professional secrecy. I will try to salve my conscience as far as possible by giving you one or two more examples.

One day a very intelligent young man came to see me. He was a student, preparing for his final medical examination; but he was not in a condition to take it, because, as he complained, he had lost all his interests, all power of concentration, and even the faculty of a well-ordered memory. The history of this paralysing condition was soon unravelled: he had fallen ill after carrying through a line of conduct which had necessitated great self-discipline. He had a sister towards whom he felt, just as she did towards him, an intense but always restrained affection. They had often enough said to each other: "What a shame it is that we cannot marry!" An unobjectionable man had fallen in love with the sister, and she had returned his feeling, but her parents would not give their consent to the union. The couple had turned to my patient for help, and he had not refused it. He had enabled them to correspond with each other, and it had been due to his influence that the parents had eventually been persuaded to give their consent. While they were engaged, a chance occurrence had taken place, whose significance it is easy to guess. He and his future brother-in-law undertook a difficult climb without a guide; they lost their way and were in danger of never returning alive. Shortly after the marriage of his sister he had fallen into his present state of mental exhaustion.

When he had become able to work as a result of psycho-analysis, he left me to take his examination; but after he had got through it he came back to me in the autumn of the same year for a short period. He then told me of a remarkable experience which he had had before the summer. In his university town there lived a fortune-teller, who carried on a very successful practice there. Even the princes of the reigning house used to consult her regularly before undertaking any important step. The way in which she worked was very simple. She asked for the facts concerning the birth of the person involved, but wanted to know nothing else about him, not even his name. She then consulted her astrological books, made long calculations and in the end made a prophecy about him. My patient decided to make use of her secret arts in connection with his brother-in-law. He visited her and gave her the requisite data about him. After she had made her calculations she pronounced the following prophecy: "This person will die in July or August of this year of poison from eating crabs or oysters." My patient finished his story by explaining: "And that really was marvellous!"

From the very beginning, I had listened to his story without enthusiasm; and after this exclamation I permitted myself to ask: "What is it that makes you find this prophecy so marvellous? We have already reached the late autumn, and your brother-in-law is not dead yet, or you would have told me long ago. The prophecy therefore has not come true." "The prophecy—no," he said, "but the remarkable thing is this. My brother-in-law is passionately fond of crabs and oysters, and last summer, that is to say before my visit to the fortune-teller, he was poisoned by eating oysters, and nearly died of it." What could I say about it? I could only feel distressed that such an intelligent man, and, moreover, one who had a satisfactory analysis behind him, should not have

seen through the whole thing more clearly. For my part, before I believe that one can calculate the onset of shellfish-poisoning by consulting astrological tables, I would rather suppose that my patient had not yet overcome his hatred towards his rival, the repression of which had caused his own illness, and that the lady astrologer simply gave voice to his own hope: "People never give up such tastes, and one day they will really be the end of him." I admit that I can find no other explanation for this case, except perhaps that my patient was making a joke at my expense. But neither then nor later did he give me any grounds for such a suspicion, and he seemed to mean quite seriously what he said.

Here is another case. A young man of good position had a mistress, and showed a remarkable obsession in his relations with her. From time to time he was impelled to wound her feelings with insulting remarks till she was reduced to despair. When he had got her into this condition he felt relieved, made it up with her, and gave her presents. But now he wanted to free himself from her, for the obsession was becoming a worry to him: he noticed that his professional life was suffering from the relationship, and wanted to have a wife and family of his own. Since, however, he could not get away from his mistress by his own efforts, he came to analysis for help. After one of these scenes, which occurred during the analysis, he got her to write him a few words on a piece of paper and showed it to a graphologist. The information he received from him was to the effect that this was the handwriting of a person in the depths of despair, who would certainly commit suicide in the course of the next few days. That event did not indeed come about, for the lady remained alive, but the analytical treatment enabled him to free himself from his fetters; he left the lady and turned his attentions to a young girl who he thought would make him a good wife. Soon afterwards he had a dream which could only be explained as due to an incipient doubt about the young girl's worth. He obtained a specimen of her handwriting as well, which he placed before the same authority, and received a judgment on it which confirmed his anxieties. He therefore gave up his intention of making her his wife.

To estimate the reports of the handwriting expert, and particularly the first one, at their proper value, one must know something of the private history of our subject. In his early adolescent years he was madly in love with a young woman, some years older than himself, in the passionate way that was characteristic of him. She rejected him, and he thereupon attempted suicide; nor can we doubt the seriousness of his intention. It was only by a miracle that he escaped death, and it was only after careful nursing that he recovered. But this reckless act made a deep impression upon the woman he was in love with; she responded to his attentions, and became his mistress. From that time onwards he had a deep attachment to her, and served her in a truly devoted manner. After more than two decades, when they had both lost something of their youth, the woman naturally more than he, he felt the need of detaching himself from her; he wanted to be free, to lead his own life, and to have a house and family of his own. And at the same time that he felt this dissatisfaction, there sprang up in him the long-suppressed need for revenge upon her. Just as at first he had tried to commit suicide himself, because she rejected him, so now he wanted to have the satisfaction of seeing her seek destruction because he was leaving her. But his love was still too strong for this wish to become conscious; nor was he able to behave badly enough to her to drive her to commit suicide. In this frame of mind, he took on the mistress whom I first mentioned as a kind of whipping-boy, in order to satisfy his thirst for revenge *in corpore vili*, and inflicted on her all the injuries calculated to produce in her the effect he desired to produce in the woman he loved. The fact that the revenge was actually directed towards the latter was only betrayed by the circumstances that he made her a confederate and advisor in his love-affair, instead of hiding his lapse from her. The unfortunate woman, who had sunk from the position of giving favours to that of receiving them, probably suffered from his confidences more than the new mistress did from his brutality. The obsession of which he complained in reference to the latter, and which brought him under analytic treatment, had naturally been transferred from his first mistress to her; it was from his first mistress that he wanted to free himself and could not. I am no handwriting expert, and I do not think much of the art of guessing character from handwriting; still less do I believe in the possibility of foretelling the future of the writer in that way. You see, however, that, whatever one may think of the value of graphology, it is undeniable that the expert, when he promised that the writer of the specimen which had been brought to him would

commit suicide during the next few days, had once more only brought to light a very strong secret wish on the part of the person who was asking his opinion. Something similar happened in the case of the second report, only that here we are not concerned with an unconscious wish; here it was the incipient doubts and anxieties of the inquirer that found overt expression through the mouth of the handwriting specialist. I may add that my patient was able, with the help of analysis, to make a love-choice outside the magic circle within which he had been spell-bound.

Ladies and Gentlemen—You have now heard what dream-interpretation and psycho-analysis in general can do for occultism. You have seen by means of examples that, through the application of psycho-analytic theory, occult phenomena have been revealed which would otherwise have remained unrecognized. The question which doubtless interests you most, whether we ought to believe in the objective reality of the phenomena, is one which psycho-analysis cannot answer directly; but at least the material which it has helped to bring to light is favourable to an affirmative reply. But your interest will not stop there. You will want to know to what conclusion that far richer vein of material, with which psycho-analysis has nothing whatever to do, leads us. There, however, I cannot follow you; it is no longer my province. The only thing I can do is to tell you of some observations, which at any rate have something to do with psycho-analysis in the sense that they were made during analytical treatment, and were perhaps rendered possible by means of it. I will give you one example, the one which left the strongest impression with me; it will be long-winded, and you will have to keep a number of details in your minds, and even so a great deal will have to be omitted which increased the evidential value of the observation. It is an instance in which the phenomena in which we are interested came to light quite obviously and did not have to be brought out by analysis. In discussing it, however, we shall not be able to do without analysis. But I ought to warn you beforehand that even this example of apparent thought-transference in the analytic situation is not proof against all objections, and does not warrant unconditional acceptance of the reality of occult phenomena.

The story is this. One autumn day in the year 1919, at about 10.45 A.M., Dr. David Forsyth, who had just arrived from London, sent in his card while I was working with a patient. (My respected colleague from the University of London will, I feel sure, not think I am being indiscreet if I tell you that he came to me for some months to be initiated into the mysteries of psycho-analytical technique.) I had only time to say "How do you do?" and arrange an appointment for later on. Dr. Forsyth had a special claim upon my interest; for he was the first foreigner who came to me after the isolation of the war years, and seemed to be a harbinger of better times. Soon after this, at eleven o'clock, my next patient arrived, a Mr. P, an intelligent and charming man of between forty and fifty, who had come to me because he experienced difficulties in sexual intercourse with women. In his case there was no prospect of bringing about a cure, and I had long ago suggested that he should break off the treatment; but he had preferred to continue it, obviously because he felt comfortable in a well-tempered father-transference upon myself. Money played no part at this time, because there was too little of it about. The hours I spent with him were stimulating for me as well, and a relaxation, and so, setting aside the strict rules of medical etiquette, we were going on with the analytic treatment for a specified length of time.

On this particular day, P reverted to his attempts at sexual intercourse with women, and mentioned once more the pretty, piquante girl, in poor circumstances, with whom he might have been successful if only the fact of her virginity had not frightened him off from taking any serious steps. He had often spoken of her, but that day he told me for the first time that she, though naturally she had not the slightest idea of the real grounds of his difficulty, used to call him Mr. Foresight *(Vorsicht)*. I was much struck by this piece of information; Dr. Forsyth's card was beside me, and I showed it to him.

These are the facts. I dare say they will seem to you to be rather thin; but if you will have patience you will find that there is more to come.

P had spent some years of his youth in England, and had retained a lasting interest in English literature. He possessed a well-stocked library of English books, which he used to lend me, and it is to him that I owe my acquaintance with authors such as Arnold Bennett and Galsworthy, of whose works I had so far read but little. One day he lent me a novel by Galsworthy called *The Man of Property*, the sub-

ject of which is an imaginary family named Forsyte. Galsworthy's imagination was obviously captured by this creation of his, because in the later stories he repeatedly went back to members of this family, and eventually collected all the stories which had to do with them under the heading of *The Forsyte Saga*. Only a few days before the event I am telling you about, P had brought me a new volume out of this series. The name Forsyte, and all that it typified for the author, had played a part in my conversations with P; it had become a part of the private language which so easily grows up between two people who see each other regularly. Now the name *Forsyte* out of the novels is not very different from that of my visitor *Forsyth* (as pronounced by a German, indeed, they are hardly distinguishable), and the expressive English word *foresight*, which means *Voraussicht* or *Vorsicht*, would be pronounced in the same way. P had, therefore, produced from his own personal experiences a name that was in my mind at the same time on account of a circumstance quite unknown to him.

As you see, we are making some progress. But I think we shall be even more strongly impressed by this remarkable occurrence and get some sort of insight into the condition of its origin, if we turn the light of analysis on to two other associations which P brought up during the same hour.

First: One day in the preceding week I was expecting Mr. P at 11 o'clock, but he had not appeared, and I went out to pay a call on Dr. Anton von Freund at his pension. I was surprised to find that Mr. P lived on another floor of the same house in which the pension was. Referring to this later, I told P that I had in a sense paid him a visit at his house; but I am absolutely certain that I did not mention the name of the person whom I had visited in the pension, and now, soon after the mention of Mr. Foresight, he asked me the following question: "Is the lady called Freud-Ottorego who gives the English course at the Volks-universtät your daughter by any chance?" And for the first time in our long acquaintance he let slip the distorted form of my name, to which officials, clerks, and printers have accustomed me; instead of Freud, he said Freund.

Secondly: At the end of the hour he told me a dream out of which he had awakened with a feeling of anxiety, a regular *Alptraum (nightmare)* he called it. He added that he had recently forgotten the English word for it, and had told some one who had asked him, that the English for *Alptraum* was "a mare's nest." That is of course, absurd, because "a mare's nest" means nothing of the sort, and the correct translation of *Alptraum* is "nightmare." This association seemed to have nothing more in common with the others than the element of *English;* but he reminded me of a trivial occurrence which had happened about a month before. P was sitting in my room with me, when there appeared quite unexpectedly another welcome guest from London, Dr. Ernest Jones, whom I had not seen for a long time. I nodded to him to go into my other room until I had finished with P. The latter recognized him at once, however, from a photograph of him which hung in the waiting-room, and even asked to be introduced to him. Now Jones is the author of a monograph on the nightmare. I did not know whether P was acquainted with the book; he avoided reading analytical literature.

At this point I should like to consider what analytical understanding we can obtain of P's associations and their motivations. P had the same attitude towards the name Forsyte as I had; it meant the same to him as it did to me, and in fact it was to him that I owed my knowledge of the name. The remarkable thing was that he brought this name into the analysis immediately after it had acquired another meaning for me through a recent experience, namely the arrival of the physician from London. But perhaps not less interesting is the *way* in which the name came up in his analytical hour. He did not say: "Now the name Forsyte, out of the novels you have read, comes into my mind," but, without any conscious reference to this source, he managed to weave it into his own personal experiences and brought it to the surface in that way—a thing which might have happened long before, but which had not as a matter of fact occurred until now. At this juncture, however, he said: "I am a Forsyte, too, for that is what the girl called me." One cannot mistake the mixture of exacting jealousy and plaintive self-depreciation which finds expression in this utterance. We shall not go far wrong if we complete it thus: "I am hurt that your thoughts should be so much wrapped up in this newcomer. Come back to me; after all, I am a Forsyth too—or rather only a Mr. Foresight, as the girl called me." And now, starting from the idea of *English*, his train of thought worked back to two earlier situations, which might very well have aroused the same jealousy

in him. "A few days ago you paid a visit at my house, but, alas, it was not to me, it was to a Herr von Freund." This idea made him distort the name Freud into Freund. The name Freud-Ottorego from the lecture list came in, because as the name of a teacher of English it paved the way for the manifest association. And now the memory of another visitor of a few weeks back presented itself, a visitor towards whom he certainly felt just as jealous, this visitor (Dr. Jones) was at the same time in a superior position to him, because he could write a book about nightmares, while the best he could do was to have nightmares himself. The allusion to his mistake about the meaning of a "mare's nest" belonged to the same connection; it must mean: "I am not a proper Englishman after all, any more than I am a proper Forsyth."

Now it could not be said that his jealous feelings were either inappropriate or incomprehensible. He had already been made aware that his analysis, and with it our relations, would come to an end as soon as foreign pupils and patients began to return to Vienna; and this is actually what happened shortly afterwards. But what we have just been doing has been a piece of analytical work: the explanation of three ideas which were brought up in the same hour and were determined by the same motivation. This has not much to do with the question whether these ideas could have been produced without thought-transference or not. The latter question applies to each of the three ideas, and can thus be divided into three separate questions. Could P have known that Dr. Forsyth had just paid his first visit to me? Could he have known the name of the person whom I visited in his house? Did he know that Dr. Jones had written a book about nightmares? Or was it only my knowledge of these things which was displayed in the ideas that came into his head? Whether this observation of mine leads to a conclusion in favour of thought-transference depends on the answer which is given to these separate questions. Let us leave the first question aside for the moment, as the two others are easier to deal with. The case of the visit to the pension strikes one at first sight as being very convincing. I am quite sure that in my short humorous mention of my visit to his house I did not mention any name; I think it is most improbable that P made inquiries in the pension to discover the name of the person I had called on; in fact, I believe that he never knew of his existence. But the evidential value of this case is undermined by a chance factor.

The man whom I had been to see in the pension was not only *called* Freund, but was indeed a true friend to us all. It was he whose generosity had made possible the founding of our publishing-house. His early death, and that of Karl Abraham a few years later, were the most serious misfortunes which have befallen the development of psycho-analysis. It is possible, therefore, that I said to Mr. P: "I have been visiting a *friend* at your house," and with this possibility the occult interest of the second association evaporates.

The impression made by the third association, too, soon fades. Could P have known that Jones had published a monograph on the nightmare, seeing that he never read analytical literature? Yes, he could. He possessed books issued by our publishing-house, and he might certainly have seen the titles of new publications printed on the covers. It cannot be proved, but it cannot be disproved. Along this road, then, we can come to no decision. This example of mine, I regret to say, is open to the same objections as so many others. It was written down too late, and came up for discussion at a time when I was not seeing Mr. P any more, and could not ask him any further questions.

Let us return to the first association, which even by itself would support the alleged occurrence of thought-transference. Could P have known that Dr. Forsyth had been with me a quarter of an hour before him? Could he even have known of his existence or of his presence in Vienna? We must not give way to the temptation to answer both questions straight off in the negative. I might very well have told Mr. P I was expecting a physician from England for training in analysis, the first dove after the deluge. This might have happened in the summer of 1919; Dr. Forsyth had made arrangements with me by letter, months before his arrival. I may even have mentioned his name, though that is most improbable. In view of the other association which the name had for us both, the mention of it would inevitably have led to a conversation of which some trace at least would have been preserved in my memory. Nevertheless such a conversation may have taken place and I may have totally forgotten it, so that it became possible for the mention of Mr. Foresight in the analytical hour to strike me as miraculous. If one regards oneself as a sceptic, it is well from time to time to be sceptical about one's scepticism. Perhaps I too have that secret leaning towards the miraculous which meets the production of occult phenomena half-way.

Even if one part of this miraculous occurrence is thus explained away, we still have another part on our hands, and that the most difficult part of all. Granted that Mr. P knew that there was such a person as Dr. Forsyth and that he was expected in Vienna in the autumn, how was it that my patient became sensitive to him on the very day of his arrival and immediately after his first visit? We might say that it was chance, that is, we might leave it unexplained; but I have mentioned the two other ideas which occurred to Mr. P precisely in order to exclude chance, in order to show you that he really was occupied with jealous thoughts directed against people who visited me, and whom I visited. Or, if we are anxious not to overlook anything even remotely possible, we might suppose that P noticed that I was in a state of unusual excitement, a state of which I was certainly not aware, and that he drew his inference from that. Or that Mr. P, who after all had arrived only a quarter of an hour after the Englishman, had met him in the immediate neighbourhood of my house, that he had recognized him from his typically English appearance, and with his jealous feelings on the alert, had immediately thought: "Ah, there is Dr. Forsyth, whose arrival means the end of my analysis; and probably he has just left the Professor." I cannot go any further into these rationalistic hypotheses. We are left once more with a *non liquet,* but I must confess that here too I feel that the balance is in favour of thought-transference. For the matter of that, I am certainly not the only person who has met with *occult* phenomena in the analytic situation. Helene Deutsch in 1926 reported some observations of the same kind, and studied the way in which they were conditioned by the relation of transference between the patient and the analyst.

I am sure that you will not be satisfied with my position with regard to this problem—not completely convinced and yet ready to be convinced. Perhaps you will say to yourselves: "Here is another example of a person who has all his life been a steady-going man of science, and is now in his old age becoming weak-minded, religious, and credulous." I know that some great names belong in that category, but you must not reckon mine among them. At least I have not grown religious, and I hope I have not become credulous. If one has humbled oneself all one's life long in order to avoid painful conflict with facts, one tends to keep one's back bowed in one's old age before any new facts which may appear. No doubt you would far prefer that I should hold fast to a moderate theism, and turn relentlessly against anything occult. But I am not concerned to seek any one's favour, and I must suggest to you that you should think more kindly of the objective possibility of thought-transference and therefore also of telepathy.

You must not forget that I have only dealt with the problem here in so far as one can approach it from the direction of psycho-analysis. When I turned my thoughts towards it more than ten years ago, I too felt afraid lest our scientific outlook might be endangered and have to give way to spiritualism or mysticism if occult phenomena were proved to be true. I think otherwise now; it seems to me that one is displaying no great trust in science if one cannot rely on it to accept and deal with any occult hypothesis that may turn out to be correct. And as regards thought-transference in particular, it would seem actually to favour the extension of the scientific (or, as opponents would say, mechanistic) way of thinking on to the elusive world of the mind. For the telepathic process is supposed to consist in a mental act of one person giving rise to the same mental act in another. What lies between the two mental acts may very well be a physical process, into which the mental process transforms itself at one end and which is transformed back into the same mental process at the other. The analogy with other transformations, such as speaking and hearing across the telephone, is an obvious one. And think what it would mean if one could get hold of this physical equivalent of the mental act! I should like to point out that by inserting the unconscious between the physical and what has hitherto been regarded as the mental, psycho-analysis has prepared the way for the acceptance of such processes as telepathy. If one gets used to the idea of telepathy, one can account for a great deal by means of it, so far, of course, only in imagination. It is a familiar fact that we have no notion of how the communal will of the great insect states comes about. Possibly it works by means of mental transference of this direct kind. One is led to conjecture that this may be the original archaic method by which individuals understood one another, and which has been pushed into the background in the course of phylogenetic development by the better method of communication by means of signs apprehended by the sense organs. But such older methods may have persisted in the background, and may still manifest themselves under certain conditions: for example, in crowds roused to a state of passionate excitement. All of this is highly speculative and full of unsolved problems, but there is no need to be alarmed by it.

If telepathy is a real process, one may, in spite of the difficulty of proof, suppose that it is quite a common phenomenon. It would fit in with our expectations if we could show that it occurs particularly in the mental life of children. One is reminded of the frequent fear felt by children that their parents know all their thoughts without having been told them—a fear which is a complete parallel to, and perhaps the origin of, the belief of adults in the omniscience of God. A short time ago a trustworthy observer, Dorothy Burlingham, published some findings in a paper called "Child Analysis and the Mother," which, if they are confirmed, must put an end to any remaining doubts of the reality of thought transference. She took as her starting-point a number of those cases (now no longer rare) in which a mother and child are being analysed at the same time, and reported such remarkable phenomena as the following. One day in her analytic hour the mother was talking about a gold coin which had figured in one of her childhood experiences. Immediately afterwards, when she had returned home, her little ten-year-old boy came into her room and brought her a gold coin to keep for him. She was astonished and asked him where he had got it from. He had been given it on his birthday, but that was several months ago, and there was no reason why the child should have remembered the gold coin just then. The mother told the analyst about the coincidence, and asked her to try to find out from the child why he had behaved in this way. But the analysis of the child elicited nothing; the action had made its way into the child's life that day like a foreign body. A few weeks later the mother was sitting at her writing table, in order to make a note of the occurrence, as she had been asked to do. At that moment the boy came in and asked for the gold coin back, saying that he wanted to take it to show his analyst. Once more the child's analysis disclosed nothing that led up to the wish.

And with that we return to our starting-point—the study of psycho-analysis.

LECTURE 31

THE ANATOMY OF THE MENTAL PERSONALITY

LADIES AND GENTLEMEN: I am sure you all recognize in your dealings, whether with persons or things, the importance of your starting-point. It was the same with psycho-analysis: the course of development through which it has passed, and the reception which it has met with have not been unaffected by the fact that what it began working upon was the symptom, a thing which is more foreign to the ego than anything else in the mind. The symptom has its origin in the repressed; it is, as it were, the representative of the repressed in relation to the ego; the repressed is a foreign territory to the ego, an internal foreign territory, just as reality is—you must excuse the unusual expression—an external foreign territory. From the symptom the path of psycho-analysis led to the unconscious, to the life of the instincts, to sexuality, and it was then that psycho-analysis was met by illuminating criticisms to the effect that man is not merely a sexual being but has nobler and higher feelings. It might have been added that, supported by the consciousness of those higher feelings, he often allowed himself the right to think nonsense and to overlook facts.

You know better than that. From the very beginning our view was that men fall ill owing to the conflict between the demands of their instincts and the internal resistance which is set up against them; not for a moment did we forget this resisting, rejecting and repressing factor, which we believed to be furnished with its own special forces, the ego-instincts, and which corresponds to the ego of popular psychology. The difficulty was that, since the progress of all scientific work is necessarily laborious, psycho-analysis could not study every part of the field at once or make a pronouncement on every problem in one breath. At last we had got so far that we could turn our attention from the repressed to the repressing forces, and we came face to face with the ego, which seemed to need so little explanation, with the certain expectation that there, too, we should find things for which we could not have been prepared; but it was not easy to find a first method of approach. That is what I am going to talk to you about today.

Before I start, I may tell you that I have a suspicion that my account of the psychology of the ego will affect you differently than the introduction into the psychological underworld that preceded it. Why that should be the case, I cannot say for certain. My original explanation was that you would feel that, whereas hitherto I have been telling you in the main about facts, however strange and odd they might appear, this time you would be listening chiefly to theories, that is to say, speculations. But that is not quite true; when I weighed the matter more carefully I was obliged to conclude that the part played by intellectual manipulation of the facts is not much greater in our ego-psychology than it was in the psychology of the neuroses. Other explanations turned out to be equally untenable, and I now think that the character of the material itself is responsible, and the fact that we are not accustomed to dealing with it. Anyhow I shall not be surprised if you are more hesitant and careful in your judgment than you have been hitherto.

The situation in which we find ourselves at the beginning of our investigation will itself suggest the path we have to follow. We wish to make the ego the object of our study, our own ego. But how can we do that? The ego is the subject *par excellence*, how can it become the object? There is no doubt, however, that it can. The ego can take itself as object, it can treat itself like any other object, observe itself, criticize itself, and do Heaven knows what besides with itself. In such a case one part of the ego stands over against the other. The ego can, then, be split; it splits when it performs many of its functions, at least for the time being. The parts can afterwards join up again. After all that is saying nothing new; perhaps it is only underlining more than usual something that every one knows already. But on the other hand we are familiar with the view that pathology, with its magnification and exaggeration, can make us aware of normal phenomena which we should otherwise have missed. Where pathology displays a breach or a cleft, under normal conditions there may well be a link. If we throw a crystal to the ground, it breaks, but it does not break haphazard; in accordance with the lines of cleavage it falls into fragments, whose limits were already determined by the structure of the crystal, although they were invisible. Psychotics are fissured and splintered structures such as these. We cannot deny them a measure of that awe with which madmen were regarded by the peoples of ancient times. They have turned away from external reality, but for that very reason they know more of internal psychic reality and can tell us much that would otherwise be inaccessible to us. One group of them suffer what we call delusions of observation. They complain to us that they suffer continually, and in their most intimate actions, from the observation of unknown powers or persons, and they have hallucinations in which they hear these persons announcing the results of their observations: "Now he is going to say this; now he is dressing himself to go out," and so on. Such observation is not the same thing as persecution, but it is not far removed from it. It implies that these persons distrust the patient, and expect to catch him doing something that is forbidden and for which he will be punished. How would it be if these mad people were right, if we all of us had an observing function in our egos threatening us with punishment, which, in their case, had merely become sharply separated from the ego and had been mistakenly projected into external reality?

I do not know whether it will appeal to you in the same way as it appeals to me. Under the strong impression of this clinical picture, I formed the idea that the separating off of an observing function from the rest of the ego might be a normal feature of the ego's structure; this idea has never left me, and I was driven to investigate the further characteristics and relations of the function which had been separated off in this way. The next step is soon taken. The actual content of the delusion of observation makes it probable that the observation is only a first step towards conviction and punishment, so that we may guess that another activity of this function must be what we call conscience. There is hardly anything that we separate off from our ego so regularly as our conscience and so easily set over against it. I feel a temptation to do something which promises to bring me pleasure, but I refrain from doing it on the ground that *my conscience will not allow it*. Or I allow myself to be persuaded by the greatness of the expectation of pleasure into doing something against which the voice of my conscience has protested, and after I have done it my conscience punishes me with painful reproaches, and makes me feel remorse for it. I might simply say that the function which I am beginning to distinguish within the ego is the conscience; but it is more prudent to keep that function as a separate entity and assume that conscience is one of its activities, and that the self-observation which is necessary as a preliminary to the judicial aspect of conscience is another. And since the process of recognizing a thing as a separate entity involves giving it a name of its own, I will henceforward call this function in the ego the *super-ego*.

At this point I am quite prepared for you to ask scornfully whether our ego-psychology amounts to no more than taking everyday abstractions literally, magnifying them, and turning them from concepts into things—which would not be of much assistance. My answer to that is that in ego-psychology it will be difficult to avoid what is already familiar, and that it is more a question of arriving at new ways of looking at things and new groupings of the facts than of making new discoveries. I will not ask you, therefore, to abandon your critical attitude but merely to await further developments. The facts of pathology give our efforts a background for which you will look in vain in popular psychology. I will proceed. No sooner have we got used to the idea of this super-ego, as something which enjoys a certain independence, pursues its own ends, and is independent of the ego as regards the energy at its disposal, than we are faced with a clinical picture which throws into strong relief the severity, and even cruelty, of this function, and the vicissitudes through which its relations with the ego may pass. I refer to the condition of melancholia, or more accurately the melancholic attack, of which you must have heard often enough, even if you are not psychiatrists. In this disease, about whose causes and mechanism we know far too little, the most remarkable characteristic is the way in which the super-ego—you may call it, but in a whisper, the *conscience*—treats the ego. The melancholiac during periods of health can, like any one else, be more or less severe towards himself; but when he has a melancholic attack, his super-ego becomes over-severe, abuses, humiliates, and ill-treats his unfortunate ego, threatens it with the severest punishments, reproaches it for long forgotten actions which were at the time regarded quite lightly, and behaves as though it had spent the whole interval in amassing complaints and was only waiting for its present increase in strength to bring them forward, and to condemn the ego on their account. The super-ego has the ego at its mercy and applies the most severe moral standards to it; indeed it represents the whole demands of morality, and we see all at once that our moral sense of guilt is the expression of the tension between the ego and the super-ego. It is a very remarkable experience to observe morality, which was ostensibly conferred on us by God and planted deep in our hearts, functioning as a periodical phenomenon. For after a certain number of months the whole moral fuss is at an end, the critical voice of the super-ego is silent, the ego is reinstated, and enjoys once more all the rights of man until the next attack. Indeed in many forms of the malady something exactly the reverse takes place during the intervals; the ego finds itself in an ecstatic state of exaltation, it triumphs, as though the super-ego had lost all its power or had become merged with the ego, and this liberated, maniac ego gives itself up in a really uninhibited fashion, to the satisfaction of all its desires. Happenings rich in unsolved riddles!

You will expect me to do more than give a mere example in support of my statement that we have learnt a great deal about the formation of the super-ego, that is, of the origin of conscience. The philosopher Kant once declared that nothing proved to him the greatness of God more convincingly than the starry heavens and the moral conscience within us. The stars are unquestionably superb, but where conscience is concerned God has been guilty of an uneven and careless piece of work, for a great many men have only a limited share of it or scarcely enough to be worth mentioning. This does not mean, however, that we are overlooking the fragment of psychological truth which is contained in the assertion that conscience is of divine origin! but the assertion needs interpretation. Conscience is no doubt something within us, but it has not been there from the beginning. In this sense it is the opposite of sexuality, which is certainly present from the very beginning of life, and is not a thing that only comes in later. But small children are notoriously a-moral. They have no internal inhibitions against their pleasure-seeking impulses. The rôle, which the super-ego undertakes later in life, is at first played by an external power, by parental authority. The influence of the parents dominates the child by granting proofs of affection and by threats of punishment, which, to the child, mean loss of love, and which must also be feared on their own account. This objective anxiety is the forerunner of the later moral anxiety; so long as the former is dominant one need not speak of super-ego or of conscience. It is only later that the secondary situation arises, which we are far too ready to regard as the normal state of affairs; the external restrictions are introjected, so that the super-ego takes the place of the parental function, and thenceforward observes,

guides, and threatens the ego in just the same way as the parents acted to the child before.

The super-ego, which in this way has taken over the power, the aims and even the methods of the parental function, is, however, not merely the legatee of parental authority, it is actually the heir of its body. It proceeds directly from it, and we shall soon learn in what way this comes about. First, however, we must pause to consider a point in which they differ. The super-ego seems to have made a one-sided selection, and to have chosen only the harshness and severity of the parents, their preventive and punitive functions, while their loving care is not taken up and continued by it. If the parents have really ruled with a rod of iron, we can easily understand the child developing a severe super-ego, but, contrary to our expectations, experience shows that the super-ego may reflect the same relentless harshness even when the up-bringing has been gentle and kind, and avoided threats and punishment as far as possible. We shall return to this contradiction later, when we are dealing with the transmutation of instincts in the formation of the super-ego.

I cannot tell you as much as I could wish about the change from the parental function to the super-ego, partly because that process is so complicated that a description of it does not fit into the framework of a set of introductory lectures such as these, and partly because we ourselves do not feel that we have fully understood it. You will have to be satisfied, therefore, with the following indications. The basis of the process is what we call an *identification*, that is to say, that one ego becomes like another, one which results in the first ego behaving itself in certain respects in the same way as the second; it imitates it, and as it were takes it into itself. This identification has been not inappropriately compared with the oral cannibalistic incorporation of another person. Identification is a very important kind of relationship with another person, probably the most primitive, and is not to be confused with object-choice. One can express the difference between them in this way: when a boy identifies himself with his father, he wants to *be like* his father; when he makes him the object of his choice, he wants to *have* him, to possess him; in the first case his ego is altered on the model of his father, in the second case that is not necessary. Identification and object-choice are broadly speaking independent of each other; but one can identify oneself with a person, and alter one's ego accordingly, and take the same person as one's sexual object. It is said that this influencing of the ego by the sexual object takes place very often with women, and is characteristic of femininity. With regard to what is by far the most instructive relation between identification and object-choice, I must have given you some information in my previous lectures. It can be as easily observed in children as in adults, in normal as in sick persons. If one has lost a love-object or has had to give it up, one often compensates oneself by identifying oneself with it; one sets it up again inside one's ego, so that in this case object-choice regresses, as it were, to identification.

I am myself not at all satisfied with this account of identification, but it will suffice if you will grant that the establishment of the super-ego can be described as a successful instance of identification with the parental function. The fact which is decisively in favour of this point of view is that this new creation of a superior function within the ego is extremely closely bound up with the fate of the Oedipus complex, so that the super-ego appears as the heir of that emotional tie, which is of such importance for childhood. When the Oedipus complex passes away, the child must give up the intense object-cathexes which it has formed towards its parents, and to compensate for this loss of object, its identifications with its parents, which have probably long been present, become greatly intensified. Identifications of this kind, which may be looked on as precipitates of abandoned object-cathexes, will recur often enough in the later life of the child; but it is in keeping with the emotional importance of this first instance of such a transformation that its product should occupy a special position in the ego. Further investigation also reveals that the super-ego does not attain to full strength and development if the overcoming of the Oedipus complex has not been completely successful. During the course of its growth, the super-ego also takes over the influence of those persons who have taken the place of the parents, that is to say of persons who have been concerned in the child's upbringing, and whom it has regarded as ideal models. Normally the super-ego is constantly becoming more and more remote from the original parents, becoming, as it were, more impersonal. Another thing that we must not forget is that the child values its parents differently at different periods of its life. At the time at which the Oedipus complex makes way

for the super-ego, they seem to be splendid figures, but later on they lose a good deal of their prestige. Identifications take place with these later editions of the parents as well, and regularly provide important contributions to the formation of character; but these only affect the ego, they have no influence on the super-ego, which has been determined by the earliest parental imagos.

I hope you will by now feel that in postulating the existence of a super-ego I have been describing a genuine structural entity, and have not been merely personifying an abstraction, such as conscience. We have now to mention another important activity which is to be ascribed to the super-ego. It is also the vehicle of the ego-ideal, by which the ego measures itself, towards which it strives, and whose demands for ever-increasing perfection it is always striving to fulfil. No doubt this ego-ideal is a precipitation of the old idea of the parents, an expression of the admiration which the child felt for the perfection which it at that time ascribed to them. I know you have heard a great deal about the sense of inferiority which is said to distinguish the neurotic subject. It crops up especially in the pages of works that have literary pretensions. A writer who brings in the expression *inferiority-complex* thinks he has satisfied all the demands of psycho-analysis and raised his work on to a higher psychological plane. As a matter of fact the phrase *inferiority-complex* is hardly ever used in psycho-analysis. It does not refer to anything which we regard as simple, let alone elementary. To trace it back to the perception in oneself of some organic disability or other, as the school of so-called Individual Psychologists like to do, seems to us a short-sighted error. The sense of inferiority has a strong erotic basis. The child feels itself inferior when it peceives that it is not loved, and so does the adult as well. The only organ that is really regarded as inferior is the stunted penis—the girl's clitoris. But the major part of the sense of inferiority springs from the relationship of the ego to its super-ego, and, like the sense of guilt, it is an expression of the tension between them. The sense of inferiority and the sense of guilt are exceedingly difficult to distinguish. Perhaps we should do better if we regarded the former as the erotic complement to the sense of moral inferiority. We have paid but little attention to such questions of conceptual differentiation in psycho-analysis.

Seeing that the inferiority-complex has become so popular, I shall venture to treat you to a short digression. A historical personage of our own time, who is still living but who for the present has retired into the background, suffers from the mal-development of a limb caused by an injury at birth. A very well-known contemporary writer who has a predilection for writing the biographies of famous persons, has dealt with the life of the man to whom I am referring. Now if one is writing a biography, it is naturally very difficult to suppress the urge for psychological understanding. The author has therefore made an attempt to build up the whole development of his hero's character on the basis of a sense of inferiority, which was caused by his physical defect. While doing this he has overlooked a small but not unimportant fact. It is usual for mothers to whom fate has given a sickly or otherwise defective child to try to compensate for this unfair handicap with an extra amount of love. In the case we are speaking of, the proud mother behaved quite differently; she withdrew her love from the child on account of his disability. When the child grew up into a man of great power, he proved beyond all doubt by his behaviour that he had never forgiven his mother. If you will bear in mind the importance of mother-love for the mental life of the child, you will be able to make the necessary corrections in the inferiority-theory of the biographer.

But let us get back to the super-ego. We have allocated to it the activities of self-observation, conscience, and the holding up of ideals. It follows from our account of its origin that it is based upon an overwhelmingly important biological fact no less than upon a momentous psychological fact, namely the lengthy dependence of the human child on its parents and the Oedipus complex; these two facts, moreover, are closely bound up with each other. For us the super-ego is the representative of all moral restrictions, the advocate of the impulse towards perfection, in short it is as much as we have been able to apprehend psychologically of what people call the "higher" things in human life. Since it itself can be traced back to the influence of parents, teachers, and so on, we shall learn more of its significance if we turn our attention to these sources. In general, parents and similar authorities follow the dictates of their own super-egos in the upbringing of children. Whatever terms their ego may be on with their super-ego, in the education of the child they are severe and exacting. They have forgotten the difficulties of their own childhood, and are glad to be able to identify themselves

fully at last with their own parents, who in their day subjected them to such severe restraints. The result is that the super-ego of the child is not really built up on the model of the parents, but on that of the parents' super-ego; it takes over the same content, it becomes the vehicle of tradition and of all the age-long values which have been handed down in this way from generation to generation. You may easily guess what great help is afforded by the recognition of the super-ego in understanding the social behaviour of man, in grasping the problem of delinquency, for example, and perhaps, too, in providing us with some practical hints upon education. It is probable that the so-called materialistic conceptions of history err in that they underestimate this factor. They brush it aside with the remark that the *ideologies* of mankind are nothing more than resultants of their economic situation at any given moment or superstructures built upon it. That is the truth, but very probably it is not the whole truth. Mankind never lives completely in the present; the ideologies of the super-ego perpetuate the past, the traditions of the race and the people, which yield but slowly to the influence of the present and to new developments, and, so long as they work through the super-ego, play an important part in man's life, quite independently of economic conditions.

In 1921, I tried to apply the distinction between the ego and the super-ego to the study of group psychology. I reached a formula, which ran like this: A psychological group is a collection of individuals who have introduced the same person into their super-ego, and on the basis of this common factor have identified themselves with one another in their ego. This, naturally, only holds for groups who have a leader. If we could find more applications of this kind, the hypothesis of the super-ego would lose all its strangeness for us, and we should be entirely relieved of the embarrassment which we cannot help feeling when, used as we are to the atmosphere of the underworld, we make excursions into the more superficial and higher planes of the mental apparatus. Of course we do not for a moment think that the last word on ego-psychology has been spoken with the demarcation of the super-ego. It is rather the beginning of the subject, but in this case it is not only the first step that is difficult.

But now another task awaits us, as it were at the opposite end of the ego. This question is raised by an observation which is made during analytic work, an observation which is, indeed, an old one. As so often happens, it has taken a long time for its true value to be appreciated. As you are aware, the whole of psycho-analytic theory is in fact built up on the perception of the resistance exerted by the patient when we try to make him conscious of his unconscious. The objective indication of resistance is that his associations stop short or wander far away from the theme that is being discussed. He may also become subjectively aware of the resistance by experiencing painful feelings when he approaches the theme. But this last indication may be absent. In such a case, we say to the patient that we conclude from his behaviour that he is in a state of resistance, and he replies that he knows nothing about it and is only aware of a difficulty in associating. Experience shows that we were right, but, if so, his resistance too must have been unconscious, just as unconscious as the repressed material which we were trying to bring to the surface. Long ago we should have asked from which part of the mind such an unconscious resistance could operate. The beginner in psycho-analysis will be ready at once with the answer that it must be the resistance of the unconscious. An ambiguous and useless answer! If it means that the resistance operates from the repressed, then we must say: "Certainly not!" To the repressed we must rather ascribe a strong upward-driving force, an impulse to get through to consciousness. The resistance can only be a manifestation of the ego, which carried through the repression at one time or other and is now endeavouring to keep it up. And that, too, was our earlier view. Now that we have posited a special function within the ego to represent the demand for restriction and rejection, i.e., the super-ego, we can say that repression is the work of the super-ego—either that it does its work on its own account or else that the ego does it in obedience to its orders. If now we are faced with the case where the patient under analysis is not conscious of his resistance, then it must be either that the super-ego and the ego can operate unconsciously in quite important situations, or, which would be far more significant, that parts of both ego and super-ego themselves are unconscious. In both cases we should have to take account of the disturbing view that the ego (including the super-ego) does not by any means completely coincide with the conscious, nor the repressed with the unconscious.

Ladies and Gentlemen—I feel I must have a little breathing space, which I expect you will welcome with relief, and before I go on I must make an apology. Here am I giving you a supplement to the introduction to psycho-analysis which I started fifteen years ago, and I am behaving as though you yourselves had been doing nothing but psycho-analysis all that time. I know it is a monstrous supposition, but I am helpless, I have no alternative. The reason is that it is exceedingly difficult to give an insight into psycho-analysis to any one who is not himself a psycho-analyst. I assure you that we do not like to give the effect of being members of a secret society carrying on a secret science. And yet we have been obliged to recognize and state as our considered opinion that no one has a right to a say in psycho-analysis unless he has been through certain experiences which he can only have by being analysed himself. When I delivered my lectures to you fifteen years ago, I tried to let you off certain speculative parts of our theory, but it is with those very parts that are connected the new discoveries which I am going to speak of to-day.

Now let me return to my theme. With regard to the two alternatives—that the ego and the super-ego may themselves be unconscious, or that they may merely give rise to unconscious effects—we have for good reasons decided in favour of the former. Certainly, large portions of the ego and super-ego can remain unconscious, are, in fact, normally unconscious. That means to say that the individual knows nothing of their contents and that it requires an expenditure of effort to make him conscious of them. It is true, then, that ego and conscious, repressed and unconscious do not coincide. We are forced fundamentally to revise our attitude towards the problem of conscious and unconscious. At first we might be inclined to think very much less of the importance of consciousness as a criterion, since it has proved so untrustworthy. But if we did so, we should be wrong. It is the same with life: it is not worth much, but it is all that we have. Without the light shed by the quality of consciousness, we should be lost in the darkness of depth-psychology. Nevertheless we must try to orientate ourselves anew.

What is meant by *conscious*, we need not discuss; it is beyond all doubt. The oldest and best meaning of the word *unconscious* is the descriptive one; we call *unconscious* any mental process the existence of which we are obliged to assume—because, for instance, we infer it in some way from its effects—but of which we are not directly aware. We have the same relation to that mental process as we have to a mental process in another person, except that it belongs to ourselves. If we want to be more accurate, we should modify the statement by saying that we call a process *unconscious* when we have to assume that it was active *at a certain time*, although *at that time* we knew nothing about it. This restriction reminds us that most conscious processes are conscious only for a short period; quite soon they become *latent*, though they can easily become conscious again. We could also say that they had become unconscious, if we were certain that they were still something mental when they were in the latent condition. So far we should have learnt nothing, and not even have earned the right to introduce the notion of the unconscious into psychology. But now we come across a new fact which we can already observe in the case of errors. We find that, in order to explain a slip of the tongue, for instance, we are obliged to assume that an intention to say some particular thing had formed itself in the mind of the person who made the slip. We can infer it with certainty from the occurrence of the speech-disturbance, but it was not able to obtain expression; it was, that is to say, unconscious. If we subsequently bring the intention to the speaker's notice, he may recognize it as a familiar one, in which case it was only temporarily unconscious, or he may repudiate it as foreign to him, in which case it was permanently unconscious. Such an observation as this justifies us in also regarding what we have called *latent* as something *unconscious*. The consideration of these dynamic relations puts us in a position to distinguish two kinds of unconscious: one which is transformed into conscious material easily and under conditions which frequently arise, and another in the case of which such a transformation is difficult, can only come about with a considerable expenditure of energy, or may never occur at all. In order to avoid any ambiguity as to whether we are referring to the one or the other unconscious, whether we are using the word in the descriptive or dynamic sense, we make use of a legitimate and simple expedient. We call the unconscious which is only latent, and so can easily become conscious, the *preconscious*, and keep the name *unconscious* for the other. We have now three terms, *conscious*, *preconscious*, and *unconscious*, to serve our purposes in describing mental phenomena. Once again, from a purely descriptive point of view, the *preconscious* is also unconscious, but we do not give

it that name, except when we are speaking loosely, or when we have to defend in general the existence of unconscious processes in mental life.

You will, I hope, grant that so far things are not so bad and that the scheme is a convenient one. That is all very well; unfortunately our psycho-analytic work has compelled us to use the word *unconscious* in yet another, third, sense; and this may very well have given rise to confusion. Psycho-analysis has impressed us very strongly with the new idea that large and important regions of the mind are normally removed from the knowledge of the ego, so that the processes which occur in them must be recognized as unconscious in the true dynamic sense of the term. We have consequently also attributed to the word *unconscious* a topographical or systematic meaning; we have talked of *systems* of the preconscious and of the unconscious, and of a conflict between the ego and the *Ucs* system; so that the word *unconscious* has more and more been made to mean a mental province rather than a quality which mental things have. At this point, the discovery, inconvenient at first sight, that parts of the ego and super-ego, too, are unconscious in the dynamic sense, has a facilitating effect and enables us to remove a complication. We evidently have no right to call that region of the mind which is neither ego or super-ego the *Ucs* system, since the character of unconsciousness is not exclusive to it. Very well; we will no longer use the word *unconscious* in the sense of a system, and to what we have hitherto called by that name we will give a better one, which will not give rise to misunderstandings. Borrowing, at G. Groddeck's suggestion, a term used by Nietzsche, we will call it henceforward the *id*. This impersonal pronoun seems particularly suited to express the essential character of this province of the mind—the character of being foreign to the ego. Super-ego, ego and id, then, are the three realms, regions or provinces into which we divide the mental apparatus of the individual; and it is their mutual relations with which we shall be concerned in what follows.

But before we go on I must make a short digression. I have no doubt that you are dissatisfied with the fact that the three qualities of the mind in respect to consciousness and the three regions of the mental apparatus do not fall together into three harmonious pairs, and that you feel that the clarity of our conclusions is consequently impaired. My own view is that we ought not to deplore this fact but that we should say to ourselves that we had no right to expect any such neat arrangement. Let me give you an analogy; analogies prove nothing, that is quite true, but they can make one feel more at home. Let us picture a country with a great variety of geographical configurations, hills, plains and chains of lakes, and with mixed nationalities living in it, Germans, Magyars and Slovaks, who, moreover, are engaged upon a number of different occupations. Now the distribution might be such that the Germans lived in the hills and kept cattle, the Magyars on the plains and grew corn and vines, while the Slovaks lived by the lakes and caught fish and plaited reeds. If this distribution were neat and exact it would no doubt give great satisfaction to a President Wilson; it would also be convenient for giving a geography lesson. It is probable, however, that you would find a less orderly state of affairs if you visited the region. Germans, Magyars and Slovaks would be living everywhere mixed up together, and there would be cornfields, too, in the hills, and cattle would be kept on the plains as well. One or two things would be as you expected, for one cannot catch fish on the mountains, and wine does not grow in water. The picture of the region which you had brought with you might on the whole fit the facts, but in details you would have to put up with departures from it.

You must not expect me to tell you much that is new about the id, except its name. It is the obscure inaccessible part of our personality; the little we know about it we have learnt from the study of dream-work and the formation of neurotic symptoms, and most of that is of a negative character, and can only be described as being all that the ego is not. We can come nearer to the id with images, and call it a chaos, a cauldron of seething excitement. We suppose that it is somewhere in direct contact with somatic processes, and takes over from them instinctual needs and gives them mental expression, but we cannot say in what substratum this contact is made. These instincts fill it with energy, but it has no organization and no unified will, only an impulsion to obtain satisfaction for the instinctual needs, in accordance with the pleasure-principle. The laws of logic—above all, the law of contradiction—do not hold for processes in the id. Contradictory impulses exist side by side without neutralizing each other or drawing apart; at most they combine in compromise formations under the overpowering economic pressure towards discharging their energy. There is nothing in the id which can be compared to negation, and we are astonished to find in it an exception to the philosophers' assertion that space and time are necessary forms of our mental acts. In the id there is nothing corresponding to the idea of time, no recognition of the passage of time, and (a thing which is very remarkable and awaits adequate attention in philosophic thought) no alteration of mental processes by the passage of time. Conative impulses which have never got beyond the id, and even impressions which have been pushed down into the id by repression, are virtually immortal and are preserved for whole decades as though they had only recently occurred. They can only be recognized as belonging to the past, deprived of their significance, and robbed of their charge of energy, after they have been made conscious by the work of analysis, and no small part of the therapeutic effect of analytic treatment rests upon this fact.

It is constantly being borne in upon me that we have made far too little use of our theory of the indubitable fact that the repressed remains unaltered by the passage of time. This seems to offer us the possibility of an approach to some really profound truths. But I myself have made no further progress here.

Naturally, the id knows no values, no good and evil, no morality. The economic, or, if you prefer, the quantitative factor, which is so closely bound up with the pleasure-principle, dominates all its processes. Instinctual cathexes seeking discharge—that, in our view, is all that the id contains. It seems, indeed, as if the energy of these instinctual impulses is in a different condition from that in which it is found in the other regions of the mind. It must be far more fluid and more capable of being discharged, for otherwise we should not have those displacements and condensations, which are so characteristic of the id and which are so completely independent of the qualities of what is cathected. (In the ego we should call it an *idea*.) What would one not give to understand these things better? You observe, in any case, that we can attribute to the id other characteristics than that of being unconscious, and you are aware of the possibility that parts of the ego and super-ego are unconscious without possessing the same primitive and irrational quality. As regards a characterization of the ego, in so far as it is to be distinguished from the id and the super-ego, we shall get on better if we turn our attention to the relation between it and the most superficial portion of the mental apparatus; which we call the *Pcpt-Cs* (perceptual-conscious) system. This system is directed on to the external world, it mediates perceptions of it, and in it is generated, while it is functioning, the phenomenon of consciousness. It is the sense-organ of the whole apparatus, receptive, moreover, not only of excitations from without but also of such as proceed from the interior of the mind. One can hardly go wrong in regarding the ego as that part of the id which has been modified by its proximity to the external world and the influence that the latter has had on it, and which serves the purpose of receiving stimuli and protecting the organism from them, like the cortical layer with which a particle of living substance surrounds itself. This relation to the external world is decisive for the ego. The ego has taken over the task of representing the external world for the id, and so of saving it; for the id, blindly striving to gratify its instincts in complete disregard of the superior strength of outside forces, could not otherwise escape annihilation. In the fulfilment of this function, the ego has to observe the external world and preserve a true picture of it in the memory traces left by its perceptions, and, by means of the reality-test, it has to eliminate any element in this picture of the external world which is a contribution from internal sources of excitation. On behalf of the id, the ego controls the path of access to motility, but it interpolates between desire and action the procrastinating factor of thought, during which it makes use of the residues of experience stored up in memory. In this way it dethrones the pleasure-principle, which exerts undisputed sway over the processes in the id, and substitutes for it the reality-principle, which promises greater security and greater success.

The relation to time, too, which is so hard to describe, is communicated to the ego by the perceptual system; indeed it can hardly be doubted that the mode in which this system works is the source of the idea of time. What, however, especially marks the ego out in contra-distinction to the id, is a tendency to synthesize its contents, to bring together and unify its mental processes which is entirely absent from the id. When we come to deal presently with the instincts in mental life, I hope we shall succeed in tracing this fundamental characteristic of the ego to its source. It is this alone that produces that high degree of organization which the ego needs for its

highest achievements. The ego advances from the function of perceiving instincts to that of controlling them, but the latter is only achieved through the mental representative of the instinct becoming subordinated to a larger organization, and finding its place in a coherent unity. In popular language, we may say that the ego stands for reason and circumspection, while the id stands for the untamed passions.

So far we have allowed ourselves to dwell on the enumeration of the merits and capabilities of the ego; it is time now to look at the other side of the picture. The ego is after all only a part of the id, a part purposively modified by its proximity to the dangers of reality. From a dynamic point of view, it is weak; it borrows its energy from the id, and we are not entirely ignorant of the methods—one might almost call them "tricks"—by means of which it draws further amounts of energy from the id. Such a method, for example, is the process of identification, whether the object is retained or given up. The object-cathexes proceed from the instinctual demands of the id. The first business of the ego is to take note of them. But by identifying itself with the object, it recommends itself to the id in the place of the object and seeks to attract the libido of the id on to itself. We have already seen that, in the course of a person's life, the ego takes into itself a large number of such precipitates of former object-cathexes. On the whole, the ego has to carry out the intentions of the id; it fulfils its duty if it succeeds in creating the conditions under which these intentions can best be fulfilled. One might compare the relation of the ego to the id with that between a rider and his horse. The horse provides the locomotive energy, and the rider has the prerogative of determining the goal and of guiding the movements of his powerful mount towards it. But all too often in the relations between the ego and the id we find a picture of the less ideal situation in which the rider is obliged to guide his horse in the direction in which it itself wants to go.

The ego has separated itself off from one part of the id by means of repression-resistances. But the barrier of repression does not extend into the id; so that the repressed material merges into the rest of the id.

The proverb tells us that one cannot serve two masters at once. The poor ego has a still harder time of it; it has to serve three harsh masters, and has to do its best to reconcile the claims and demands of all three. These demands are always divergent and often seem quite incompatible; no wonder that the ego so frequently gives way under its task. The three tyrants are the external world, the super-ego, and the id. When one watches the efforts of the ego to satisfy them all, or rather, to obey them all simultaneously, one cannot regret having personified the ego, and established it as a separate being. It feels itself hemmed in on three sides and threatened by three kinds of danger, towards which it reacts by developing anxiety when it is too hard pressed. Having originated in the experiences of the perceptual system, it is designed to represent the demands of the external world, but it also wishes to be a loyal servant of the id, to remain upon good terms with the id, to recommend itself to the id as an object, and to draw the id's libido on to itself. In its attempt to mediate between the id and reality, it is often forced to clothe the *Ucs* commands of the id with its own *Pcs* rationalizations, to gloss over the conflicts between the id and reality, and with diplomatic dishonesty to display a pretended regard for reality, even when the id persists in being stubborn and uncompromising. On the other hand, its every movement is watched by the severe super-ego, which holds up certain norms of behaviour, without regard to any difficulties coming from the id and the external world; and if these norms are not acted up to, it punishes the ego with the feelings of tension which manifest themselves as a sense of inferiority and guilt. In this way, goaded on by the id, hemmed in by the super-ego, and rebuffed by reality, the ego struggles to cope with its economic task of reducing the forces and influences which work in it and upon it to some kind of harmony; and we may well understand how it is that we so often cannot repress the cry: "Life is not easy." When the ego is forced to acknowledge its weakness, it breaks out into anxiety: reality anxiety in face of the external world, normal anxiety in face of the super-ego, and neurotic anxiety in face of the strength of the passions in the id.

I have represented the structural relations within the mental personality, as I have explained them to you, in a simple diagram, which I here reproduce.

You will observe how the super-ego goes down into the id; as the heir to the Oedipus complex it has, after all, intimate connections with the id. It lies further from the perceptual system than the ego. The id only deals with the external world through the medium of the ego,

at least in this diagram. It is certainly still too early to say how far the drawing is correct; in one respect I know it is not. The space taken up by the unconscious id ought to be incomparably greater than that given to the ego or to the preconscious. You must, if you please, correct that in your imagination.

And now, in concluding this certainly rather exhausting and perhaps not very illuminating account, I must add a warning. When you think of this dividing up of the personality into ego, super-ego, and id, you must not imagine sharp dividing lines such as are artificially drawn in the field of political geography. We cannot do justice to the characteristics of the mind by means of linear contours, such as occur in a drawing or in a primitive painting, but we need rather the areas of colour shading off into one another that are to be found in modern pictures. After we have made our separations, we must allow what we have separated to merge again. Do not judge too harshly of a first attempt at picturing a thing so elusive as the human mind. It is very probable that the extent of these differentiations varies very greatly from person to person; it is possible that their function itself may vary, and that they may at times undergo a process of involution. This seems to be particularly true of the most insecure and, from the phylogenetic point of view, the most recent of them, the differentiation between the ego and the super-ego. It is also

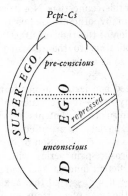

incontestable that the same thing can come about as a result of mental disease. It can easily be imagined, too, that certain practices of mystics may succeed in upsetting the normal relations between the different regions of the mind, so that, for example, the perceptual system becomes able to grasp relations in the deeper layers of the ego and in the id which would otherwise be inaccessible to it. Whether such a procedure can put one in possession of ultimate truths, from which all good will flow, may be safely doubted. All the same, we must admit that the therapeutic efforts of psychoanalysis have chosen much the same method of approach. For their object is to strengthen the ego, to make it more independent of the super-ego, to widen its field of vision, and so to extend its organization that it can take over new portions of the id. Where id was, there shall ego be.

It is reclamation work, like the draining of the Zuyder Zee.

LECTURE 32

ANXIETY AND INSTINCTUAL LIFE

LADIES AND GENTLEMEN: You will not be surprised to hear that I have a great deal of new information to give you about our hypotheses on the subject of anxiety and the fundamental instincts of the mind, and also that none of this information claims to provide a final solution of these doubtful problems. I speak purposely of *hypotheses*. This is the most difficult task that has been set us, but the difficulty does not lie in the incompleteness of our observations, for it is actually the commonest and most familiar phenomena that present us with such riddles; nor does it lie in the remoteness of the speculations to which these phenomena give rise, for speculation hardly comes into the picture in this connection. No, it is genuinely a question of hypotheses; that is to say, of the introduction of the right abstract ideas, and of their application to the raw material of observation so as to bring order and lucidity into it.

I devoted one lecture in my former series— the twenty-fifth—to the study of anxiety. I must recapitulate its contents in brief. We said then that anxiety is an affective condition— that is to say, a combination of certain feelings of the pleasure-pain series with their corresponding efferent innervations, and a perception of them—but we asserted that anxiety is probably also the trace of a certain important event, taken over by inheritance, and therefore comparable to the ontogenetically acquired hysterical attack. We suggested that the event which left this affective trace behind it was the process of birth, in which the modifications of the heart's action and of respiration, which are characteristic of anxiety, served a useful purpose. The first anxiety of all would thus have been a toxic one. We then started from the

distinction between objective anxiety and neurotic anxiety, the former being what seems to us an intelligible reaction to danger—that is, to anticipated injury from without—and the latter altogether puzzling and, as it were, purposeless. In our analysis of objective anxiety we explained it as a condition of increased sensory attention and motor tension, which we called *anxiety-preparedness*. Out of this the anxiety-reaction arises. The anxiety-reaction may run one of two courses. Either the *anxiety-development*, the repetition of the old traumatic experience, is restricted to a signal, in which case the rest of the reaction can adapt itself to the new situation of danger, whether by flight or defence; or the old experience gets the upper hand, and the whole reaction exhausts itself in anxiety-development, in which case the affective state is paralyzing and unadapted to the present situation.

We then turned our attention to neurotic anxiety, and pointed out that it could be observed in three forms. Firstly, we have freefloating, general apprehensiveness, ready to attach itself for the time being to any new possibility that may arise in the form of what we call *expectant dread*, as happens, for instance, in the typical anxiety-neurosis. Secondly, we find it firmly attached to certain ideas, in what are known as *phobias*, in which we can still recognize a connection with external danger, but cannot help regarding the anxiety felt towards it as enormously exaggerated. Thirdly and finally, we have anxiety as it occurs in hysteria and in other severe neuroses; this anxiety either accompanies symptoms or manifests itself independently, whether as an attack or as a condition which persists for some time, but always without having any visible justification in an external danger. We then asked ourselves two questions: "What are people afraid of when they have neurotic anxiety?" and: "How can one bring this kind of anxiety into line with objective anxiety felt towards an external danger?"

Our investigations were by no means unsuccessful, and we succeeded in reaching a few important conclusions. With regard to anxious expectation, clinical experience has taught us that there is a regular relationship between it and the disposition of the libido in the sexual life. The most frequent cause of anxiety-neurosis is undischarged excitation. A libidinal excitation is aroused, but is not satisfied or used; in the place of this libido which has been diverted from its use, anxiety makes its appearance. I even thought it was justifiable to say that this unsatisfied libido is directly transformed into anxiety. This view found some support in certain almost universal phobias of small children. Many of these phobias are altogether enigmatic, but others, such as the fear of being left alone and the fear of unfamiliar people, can be definitely explained. Being left alone or seeing strange faces stirs up the child's longing for the familiar presence of its mother; it cannot control this libidinal excitation; it cannot keep it in a state of suspension, but turns it into anxiety. This anxiety in children, therefore, is not objective anxiety, but must be classed among the neurotic anxieties. Children's phobias, and the anxious expectation in anxiety-neurosis, serve as two examples of one way in which neurotic anxiety comes about; i.e., through direct transformation of libido. In a moment we shall learn of a second method, and we shall see that it is not so very different from the first.

For it is to the process of repression that we attribute the appearance of anxiety in hysteria and other neuroses. We now believe that it is possible to give a fuller description of this process than before, if we separate the history of the idea that has to be repressed from that of the libido which is attached to it. It is the idea that undergoes repression and may be distorted so as to become unrecognizable; its associated affect is always turned into anxiety, regardless of its nature, whether, that is to say, it is aggression or love. Now it makes no essential difference on what grounds a given quantity of libido has become unusable, whether on account of the infantile weakness of the ego, as in the case of children's phobias, or on account of somatic processes in sexual life, as in the case of anxiety neuroses, or on account of repression, as in the case of hysteria. The two mechanisms which give rise to neurotic anxiety are therefore essentially the same.

While we were engaged in these investigations, we noticed a very important connection between anxiety-development and symptom-formation. It was that the two are interchangeable. The agoraphobiac, for example, begins his illness with an attack of anxiety in the street. This is repeated every time he walks along the street again. He now develops a symptom—a street phobia—which can also be described as an inhibition or a functional restriction of the ego, and thus he preserves himself from anxiety attacks. One can observe the reverse process if one interferes with the formation of symptoms, as is possible, for instance, in the case of obsessive acts. If one prevents a patient from carrying out his washing ceremonial, he is thrown into an intolerable state of anxiety, against which his symptom has obviously protected him. And, indeed, it seems as though anxiety-development is the earlier and symptom-formation the later of the two, as though the symptom were created in order to prevent the outbreak of a state of anxiety. And it is in keeping with this that the first neuroses of childhood are phobias—conditions, that is to say, in which one sees quite clearly how what began as anxiety-development is later replaced by symptom-formation: one gets an impression that this circumstance affords the best starting-point from which to approach an understanding of neurotic anxiety. At the same time, we succeeded in discovering the answer to the question of what it is that one fears in neurotic anxiety, and thus restoring the connection between neurotic anxiety and objective anxiety. What one fears is obviously one's own libido. The difference between this and objective anxiety lies in two points—that the danger is an internal instead of an external one, and that it is not consciously recognized.

In the case of phobias one can see clearly how this internal danger is transformed into an external one; how, that is to say, neurotic anxiety turns into apparent objective anxiety. Let us simplify a state of affairs which is often very complicated, and suppose that the agoraphobiac is always afraid of his impulses in connection with temptations aroused in him by meeting people in the street. In his phobia he makes a displacement and is now afraid of an external situation. What he gains thereby is obvious; it is that he feels he can protect himself better in that way. One can rescue oneself from an external danger by flight, whereas to attempt to fly from an internal danger is a difficult undertaking.

At the end of my original lecture on anxiety I expressed the opinion that, though these various results of our investigations did not actually contradict one another, they were nevertheless not entirely consistent. As an affective condition, anxiety is the reproduction of an old danger-threatening event; anxiety serves the purposes of self-preservation as being a signal of the presence of a new danger; it arises from libido that has become unusable for some reason or other, including the process of repression; it is replaced by symptom-formation, and is thus, as it were, psychically bound; in all of this one feels that something is missing which would combine these fragments into a unity.

Ladies and Gentlemen—The division of the mental personality into a super-ego, ego, and id, which I spoke about in the last lecture, has forced us to take up a new position with regard to the problem of anxiety. In assuming that the ego is the only seat of anxiety, and that only the ego can produce and feel anxiety, we have taken up a new and secure position, from which many facts take on a new aspect. And when you come to think of it, it is difficult to see what sense there could be in speaking of an *anxiety of the id,* or how we could ascribe a capacity for feeling anxiety to the super-ego. On the contrary, we have found a satisfactory confirmation of our theory in the fact that the three main varieties of anxiety—objective anxiety, neurotic anxiety, and moral anxiety— can so easily be related to the three directions in which the ego is dependent, on the external world, on the id, and on the super-ego. Our new position, too, has brought to the fore the function of anxiety as a signal indicating the presence of a danger-situation, a function with which we were already not unfamiliar. The question of the stuff out of which anxiety is made loses interest for us, and the relations between objective anxiety and neurotic anxiety are clarified and simplified in a surprising way. And, besides this, it is to be noticed that we now understand the apparently complicated cases of anxiety-formation better than we do those which seem to be simple.

We have recently investigated the manner in which anxiety comes about in certain phobias, which we class with anxiety-hysteria, and we have chosen for investigation cases in which we have to deal with the typical repression of desires proceeding from the Oedipus complex. We should have expected to find that it is the libidinal cathexis of the mother as object which, as a result of repression, is transformed into anxiety, and now manifests itself in the form of a symptom as attached to the father-substitute. I cannot tell you all the individual steps of an investigation of this kind; let it suffice to say that, to our astonishment, the result was the reverse of what we had expected. It is not the repression that creates the anxiety, but the anxiety is there first and creates the repression! But what sort of anxiety can it be? It can only be fear of a threatening external danger, that is to say, objective anxiety. It is true that the boy is afraid of the demands of his libido, in

this case of his love for his mother; so that this is really an instance of neurotic anxiety. But this being in love seems to him to be an internal danger, which he must avoid by renouncing his object, only because it involves an external danger-situation. And in every case we have investigated we have obtained the same result. It must, however, be confessed that we were not prepared to find that the instinctual danger was only a half-way house to an external and real danger-situation.

We have, however, not yet said what the real danger is that the child fears as a result of his being in love with his mother. It is the punishment of castration, the loss of his penis. Naturally, you will object that after all that is not a real danger. Our boys are not castrated because they are in love with their mothers during the phase of the Oedipus-complex. But the question cannot be so easily dismissed. It is not primarily a matter of whether castration is really performed; what is important is that the danger is one that threatens from without, and that the boy believes in it. He has some grounds for doing so, for, not infrequently, threats of his penis being cut off are made during his phallic phase, at the time of his early masturbation; and no doubt allusions to such a punishment will always find a phylogenetic reinforcement on his side. We have conjectured that, in the early days of the human family, castration really was performed on the growing boy by the jealous and cruel father, and that circumcision, which is so frequently an element in puberty rites, is an easily recognizable trace of it. We are aware of how far removed we are from the common point of view in saying this, but we must maintain our position that fear of castration is one of the most frequent and one of the strongest motive forces of repression, and therefore of the formation of neuroses. The analysis of cases in which, it is true, not castration itself, but circumcision, has been performed on boys as a cure or as a punishment for masturbation (a thing which was by no means of rare occurrence in English and American society) has provided us with conclusive proof that we are right. It is a great temptation at this juncture to go further into the castration-complex, but we will keep to our subject. Fear of castration is naturally not the only motive for repression; to start with, it has no place in the psychology of women; they have, of course, a castration-complex, but they cannot have any fear of castration. In its place, for the other sex, is found fear of the loss of love, obviously a continuation of the fear of the infant at the breast when it misses its mother. You will understand what objective danger-situation is indicated by this kind of anxiety. If the mother is absent or has withdrawn her love from the child, it can no longer be certain that its needs will be satisfied, and may be exposed to the most painful feelings of tension. There is no need to reject the idea that these conditions for anxiety fundamentally repeat the situation of the original birth-anxiety, which, to be sure, also implied separation from the mother. Indeed, if you follow a line of thought suggested by Ferenczi, you may add fear of castration, too, to this series, for the loss of the male genital organ results in the impossibility of a reunion with the mother, or with a substitute for her, in the sexual act. I might mention, incidentally, that the common phantasy of returning into the womb is a substitute for this desire for coitus. There are still a great number of interesting and surprising facts which I might tell you about in this connection; but I must not step beyond the bounds of an introduction to psycho-analysis. I will, therefore, merely draw your attention to the way in which, at this point, the findings of psychology take us to the frontiers of biological fact.

Otto Rank, to whom psycho-analysis owes many valuable contributions, has also the merit of having strongly emphasized the importance of the act of birth and of separation from the mother. It is true that the rest of us found it impossible to accept the extreme deductions that he drew from this factor with regard to the theory of the neuroses and even to analytical therapy. But before this he had already discovered the central feature of his doctrine, namely, that the anxiety-experience of birth is the prototype of all later danger-situations. If we pause for a moment at this point we can say that, as a matter of fact, every stage of development has its own particular conditions for anxiety; that is to say, a danger-situation appropriate to it. The danger of mental helplessness corresponds to the stage of early immaturity of the ego; the danger of loss of object or of love corresponds to the dependence of the early years of childhood; the danger of castration to the phallic phase; and finally, the fear of the super-ego, which occupies a special position, to the period of latency. As development proceeds, the old conditions for anxiety should vanish, since the danger-situations, which correspond to them, have lost their force

owing to the strengthening of the ego. But this only happens to a very incomplete degree. A great many people cannot overcome the fear of loss of love; they never become independent enough of the love of other people, and continue their infantile behaviour in this respect. The fear of the super-ego should normally never cease, since it is indispensable in social relations in the form of moral anxiety, and it is only in the rarest instances that an individual succeeds in becoming independent of the community. A few of the old danger-situations also manage to preserve their force in later life by giving their conditions for anxiety an up-to-date form. Thus, for instance, the danger of castration is preserved under the disguise of syphilidophobia. Grown-up people are well aware that castration is no longer practised as a punishment for indulging sexual desires, but, on the other hand, they have learned from experience that instinctual freedom in this direction involves the risk of severe illnesses. There is no doubt that persons whom we call *neurotic* remain infantile in their attitude towards danger and have not grown out of antiquated conditions for anxiety. Let us accept this as a factual contribution to our characterization of neurotics; why it should be so is not so easy to say.

I hope you have not lost the thread of our discourse, and that you remember that we are discussing the relations between anxiety and repression. We have discovered two new facts in doing so: first, that anxiety causes repression, and not the other way round as we used to think, and secondly, that frightening *instinctual* situations can in the last resort be traced back to *external* situations of danger. Our next question will be: How can we picture the process of repression carried out under the influence of anxiety? I think this is what happens: the ego becomes aware that the satisfaction of some nascent instinctual demand would evoke one among the well-remembered danger-situations. This instinctual cathexis must, therefore, somehow or other be suppressed, removed, made powerless. We know that the ego succeeds in this task if it is strong, and if it has assimilated the impulse in question into its organization. In the case of repression, however, the impulse is still a part of the id, and the ego feels weak. In such a contingency, the ego calls to its aid a technique, which is, at bottom, identical with that of normal thinking. Thinking is an experimental dealing with small quantities of energy, just as a general moves miniature figures about over a map before setting his troops in motion. In this way, the ego anticipates the satisfaction of the questionable impulse, and enables it to reproduce the painful feelings which are attached to the beginning of the dreaded danger-situation. Thereupon the automatic mechanism of the pleasure-pain principle is brought into play and carries through the repression of the dangerous impulse.

"Stop!" you will exclaim, "we cannot go so far as that with you." You are right; I shall have to add something to what I have said, to make it seem acceptable to you. First of all, I must admit that I have tried to translate into the language of our normal thought a process which is in fact certainly neither conscious nor preconscious, and which takes place between charges of energy at some deep level of the mind that it is hard to picture. But that is not a very serious objection; it could not be done in any other way. It is more important that we should clearly distinguish between what goes on in the ego and what goes on in the id during the process of repression. We have just explained what the ego does. It makes use of an experimental cathexis, and by means of a danger-signal sets in motion the automatic pleasure-pain mechanism. Several reactions then become possible, or a combination of them, in various proportions. Either the anxiety attack develops completely and the ego withdraws entirely from the objectionable excitation; or, in place of the experimental cathexis, the ego meets the excitation with an anti-cathexis (counter-charge) which then combines with the energy of the repressed impulse to form a symptom, or is taken up into the ego as a reaction-formation, as an intensification of certain dispositions, as a permanent alteration of the ego. The more the development of anxiety can be restricted to a mere signal, the more the ego can make use of defensive acts, which amount to a mental binding of the repressed, and the more the process approximates to the standard of a normal modification of the impulse, without of course ever reaching it. Here I shall digress for a moment or so. You will, no doubt, yourselves have assumed that the thing which is so hard to define but which we call *character* must be thought of as belonging entirely to the province of the ego. We have already learned something of what it is that creates this thing called character. The incorporation of the early parental function in the shape of the super-ego is no doubt the most important and decisive element; next come identifications with the par-

ents of a later date and with other persons in authority, and the same identifications as precipitates of abandoned object-relations. We can now add to this list, as contributions to character-formation which are never absent, the reaction-formations which the ego acquires, first in making its repressions, and later in a more normal way, in repudiating undesirable impulses.

Now let us go back to a consideration of the id. It is not so easy to discover what it is that happens during the process of repression to the impulses that are being opposed. The main question to which we want to know the answer is: What happens to the energy, to the libidinal charge of the impulse, and how is it used? You will remember that my earlier hypothesis was that it was precisely this energy that was turned into anxiety. We can, however, no longer venture to say that; we must content ourselves with a more modest answer. Its fate is probably not always the same. Probably there is a close correspondence between what happens in the ego and what happens in the id with respect to the repressed impulse, and it should be possible to learn something of its nature. For, since we have adopted the view that the pleasure-pain principle is brought into action in response to the danger-signal, and plays a part in repression, we are obliged to modify our anticipations. This principle has unrestricted sway over the processes in the id. We can credit it, too, with the power of bringing about very profound changes in the impulse in question. We are, therefore, prepared to believe that the effects of repression will be very varied, and sometimes more and sometimes less extensive. In many cases the repressed impulse may retain its libidinal cathexis, and continue to exist unaltered in the id, although under the perpetual pressure of the ego. In other instances it seems to undergo complete destruction, in which case its libido is finally diverted into other channels. I have suggested that this is what happens where the Oedipus complex is dealt with normally. In this desirable state of affairs, the Oedipus complex would thus not merely be repressed, but would be actually destroyed in the id. Clinical experience has further taught us that in a great many cases, instead of the usual result of repression, a degradation of the libido take place, a regression of the libidinal organization to an earlier stage of development. That can naturally only happen in the id, and when it does happen, it must be under the influence of the same conflict that was introduced by the danger-signal. The most remarkable example of this is to be found in the obsessional neurosis, where regression of libido and repression go hand in hand.

Ladies and Gentlemen—I am afraid that this account will seem to you very difficult to follow, and you will guess that it is by no means a complete one. I am sorry to have caused you annoyance. My only aim, however, must be to give you some impression of the nature of our findings, and of the difficulties we have to face in dealing with them. The deeper we probe in our study of mental processes, the more we become aware of the richness and complexity of their content. Many simple formulas which seemed to us at first to meet the case, turned out later to be inadequate. We are incessantly altering and improving them. In my lecture on the theory of dreams, I led you into a field of knowledge in which hardly a single new discovery has been made in the last fifteen years; here, where we are dealing with anxiety, everything is in a state of flux and change. These new findings have not yet been thoroughly worked over, and perhaps for that very reason their exposition is difficult. However, you must have patience; we shall soon be able to leave the problem of anxiety, though that does not mean that it will have been solved to our satisfaction. I hope, however, that we have advanced a step further. And incidentally we have acquired much fresh knowledge. Thus we are now able, through the study of anxiety, to add a fresh trait to our characterization of the ego. We have said that the ego is weak in relation to the id, that it is its faithful servant, and that it tries to carry out its orders and fulfil its requirements. We have no intention of withdrawing this assertion. But on the other hand the ego is the better organized part of the id, orientated as it is towards reality. We must not exaggerate too much the separation between the two, and we must not be surprised if the ego, too, on its side exerts an influence on the processes in the id. I think the ego exerts an influence of this kind when it sets the all-powerful pleasure-pain principle in motion by means of the danger-signal. It is true that immediately afterwards it displays its weakness again, for by the act of repression it renounces a portion of its organization, and is obliged to allow the repressed impulse to remain permanently withdrawn from its influence.

And now just one more point in regard to the problem of anxiety. Neurotic anxiety has, under our hands, turned into objective anxiety, into anxiety felt towards certain external danger-situations. But we cannot leave it at that; we must take a step further, though in a sense it will be a step backwards. What is it that is actually dangerous and actually feared in such a danger-situation? It is clearly not the objective injury, which need have absolutely no importance psychologically, but it is something which is set up in the mind by it. Birth, for example, our prototype for the state of anxiety, can hardly in itself be regarded as an injury, although it may involve a risk of injury. The fundamental thing about birth, as about every danger-situation, is that it evokes in mental experience a condition of tense excitation, which is felt as pain, and which cannot be mastered by discharge. Let us call such a situation, in which the efforts of the pleasure-principle come to nothing, a *traumatic* factor; in that way, by following the series—neurotic anxiety-objective anxiety-danger-situation—we can arrive at a simple formula: what is feared, the object of the anxiety, is always the emergence of a traumatic factor, which cannot be dealt with in accordance with the norms of the pleasure-principle. We can immediately see that the operation of the pleasure-principle does not guarantee us against objective injury, but only against a particular injury to our mental economy. From the pleasure-principle to the instinct of self-preservation is a long way; and the two tendencies are far from coinciding from the first. We can observe something else, however, and perhaps this is the solution for which we were looking. I have in mind the fact that all along we are dealing with questions of relative quantities. It is only the magnitude of the excitation which turns an impression into a traumatic factor, which paralyzes the operation of the pleasure-principle and gives significance to the danger-situation. And if this is really the case, if these problems admit of such a simple solution, why should it not be possible that traumatic factors of this kind should occur in the mental life without relation to the supposed danger-situations, traumatic factors in regard to which anxiety is not aroused as a signal, but manifests itself afresh and for new reasons? Clinical experience definitely tells us that this actually occurs. Only the later repressions display the mechanism which we have described, in which anxiety is called forth as a signal of an earlier danger-situation; the earliest and most fundamental repressions arise directly from traumatic factors, where the ego comes into contact with an excessive libidinal demand; these traumatic factors create their own anxiety anew, though in accordance with the pattern of the birth-situation. The same may be true of the development of anxiety in anxiety-neuroses, caused by somatic injury of the sexual function. We shall no longer maintain that it is the libido itself that is turned into anxiety in such cases. But I can see no objection to postulating twofold origin of anxiety, first as the direct effect of a traumatic factor, and secondly, as a signal that a traumatic factor of this kind threatens to recur.

Ladies and Gentlemen—I am sure you are delighted with the prospect of hearing no more about anxiety. But your delight will be short-lived, for what is to follow is no better. I propose to take you straight on to the subject of the theory of the libido or of the instincts, for there, too, many new developments have occurred. I cannot say that we have made any very great progress or that any trouble you may take in learning about it will be amply rewarded. No; it is a field in which we are struggling hard to get some sort of orientation and understanding; you will only be witnesses of the efforts we are making. Here, too, I shall have to repeat much that I put before you in my earlier lectures.

The theory of the instincts is, as it were, our mythology. The instincts are mythical beings, superb in their indefiniteness. In our work we cannot for a moment overlook them, and yet we are never certain that we are seeing them clearly. You know how popular thought deals with the instincts. It postulates as many different instincts as may be needed, an instinct of assertiveness, instincts of imitation and play, a social instinct and a great many more besides. It takes them up, as it were, lets each do its particular work, and then drops them again. We have always suspected that behind this multitude of small occasional instincts there lies something much more serious and powerful, which must be approached with circumspection. Our first step was tentative enough. We felt we should probably not go far wrong if we started by distinguishing two main instincts, or species or groups of instincts, corresponding to our two great needs—hunger and love. However jealously we may in other connections have defended the independence of psychology from all other sciences, nevertheless we are here overshadowed by the immutable biological fact that the living individual serves two purposes, self-preservation and the preservation of the species, which seem to be independent of each other, which we have not been able to trace back to a common source, and whose interests often conflict in animal life. Here we are really discussing biological psychology, we are studying the psychological concomitants of biological processes. In accordance with this view, we introduced the *ego-instincts* and the *sexual instincts* into psychoanalysis. Under the former heading we placed everything that had to do with the preservation, maintenance and advancement of the individual. To the latter we ascribed the rich content implied in infantile and perverse sexual life. Our investigation of the neuroses led us to regard the ego as the restricting and repressing force and the sexual impulses as the restricted and repressed ones, with the result that we thought we had firmly grasped not only the difference between the two groups of instincts, but the conflict between them. At first, the objects of our studies consisted only of the sexual impulses, whose energy we called the *libido*. From the study of them we tried to make out what an instinct was and what attributes it possessed. At this point we reach the theory of the libido.

An instinct differs from a stimulus in that it arises from sources of stimulation within the body, operates as a constant force, and is such that the subject cannot escape from it by flight as he can from an external stimulus. An instinct may be described as having a source, an object, and an aim. The source is a state of excitation within the body, and its aim is to remove that excitation; in the course of its path from its source to the attainment of its aim the instinct becomes operative mentally. We picture it as a certain sum of energy forcing its way in a certain direction. We speak of active and passive instincts, but we ought rather to speak of active and passive instinctual aims; for an expenditure of activity is required even in order to attain a passive aim. The aim can be attained in the subject's own body, but as a rule an external object is introduced, in which the instinct attains its external aim; its internal aim is always a somatic modification which is experienced as satisfaction. Whether the relation to a somatic source gives the instinct any specific characters, and if so which, is not at all clear. The evidence of analytic experience proves conclusively that instinctual impulses from one source can join on to instinctual impulses from another and share their further vicissitudes, and that in general the satisfaction of one instinct can be substituted for the satisfaction of another. It must be freely admitted, however, that we are not very clear about the explanation of this. The relations of an instinct to its aim and to its object are also susceptible to alterations; both can be exchanged for others, but the relation to the object is the more easily loosened of the two. There is a particular kind of modification of aim and change of object, with regard to which our social values come into the picture; to this we give the name of *sublimation*. We have also grounds for the differentiation of what we call *aim-inhibited* instincts; these proceed from familiar sources and have unambiguous aims, but come to a stop on their way to satisfaction, with the result that a permanent object-cathexis and an enduring driving force come into being. Of such a kind, for instance, is the feeling of affection, whose source undoubtedly lies in sexual needs but invariably renounces their gratification. We are, as you see, still in ignorance about many of the characteristics of the instincts and their history. We ought here to mention another distinction between the sexual instincts and the instincts of self-preservation which would be of the utmost theoretical importance, if it applied to the whole group. The sexual instincts are remarkable for their plasticity, for the facility with which they can change their aims, for their interchangeability—for the ease with which they can substitute one form of gratification for another, and for the way in which they can be held in suspense, as has been so well illustrated by the aim-inhibited instincts. It would be convenient if we could assert that these characteristics do not apply to the instincts of self-preservation, and that the latter are inflexible, do not allow of delay, are far more imperative and respond quite differently to repression and anxiety. On reflection, however, we see that this peculiarity does not apply to all the ego-instincts but only to those of hunger and thirst, and is clearly due to the special nature of their instinctual sources. A great deal of our perplexity also arises from the fact that we have not devoted any attention to the alterations which the instinctual impulses originally belonging to the id undergo under the influence of the organized ego.

We find ourselves on firmer ground when we turn to the question of how the instinctual life serves the sexual function. Here we have obtained decisive information; but you are already familiar with it. We do not, that is to say, believe that there is a single sexual instinct, which is from the first the vehicle of the impulse towards the aim of the sexual function, that is, the union of the two sex cells. On the contrary, we see a large number of component instincts, arising from various regions of the body, which strive for satisfaction more or less independently of one another, and find this satisfaction in something that may be called *organ-pleasure*. The genitals are the latest of these *erotogenic zones;* and their organ-pleasure must certainly be called *sexual*. Not all of these pleasure-seeking impulses are incorporated in the final organization of the sexual function. Many of them are put aside as useless, by means of repression or in some other way; some of them are deflected from their aims in the remarkable manner which we have already mentioned and used for the strengthening of other impulses; while others persist, but play minor parts, and serve the purpose of bringing about preliminary actions and of arousing fore-pleasure. You have heard that in this long-drawn-out course of development several phases of provisional organization are to be recognized, and that aberrations and maldevelopments of the sexual function are to be explained by reference to its history. The first of these *pregenital* phases is called the *oral* phase, because, in accordance with the fact that the infant is nourished through the mouth, the erotogenic zone of the mouth dominates what we may call the sexual activity of this period of life. At a second stage the *sadistic* and *anal* impulses come to the fore, obviously in connection with the cutting of the teeth, the strengthening of the musculature, and the control of the sphincters. We have learnt a great many interesting details about this remarkable stage of development in particular. Third comes the *phallic* phase, in which for both sexes the penis (and what corresponds to it in the girl) achieves an importance which can no longer be overlooked. We have reserved the name of *genital* phase for the final sexual organization, established after puberty, in which the female genitals receive for the first time the recognition which the male genitals have long since obtained.

So far all this has been mere recapitulation. And you must not suppose that the things which I have omitted to mention this time no longer hold true. This recapitulation was necessary so that we could have a starting-point for our account of the further advance in our knowledge. We can flatter ourselves that we have obtained a great deal of new information precisely about this matter of the early organizations of the libido and that we have a better understanding of what we already knew—in proof of which I will give you a few instances. In 1924, Abraham showed that we can differentiate two stages in the sadistic-anal phase. In the former of these the destructive tendencies to annihilate and to get rid of things have the upper hand, while in the latter those tendencies predominate which are friendly to the object, and seek to possess things and hold them fast. In the middle of this phase, then, there appears for the first time a consideration for the object which is a forerunner of a later relation of love towards the object. We are equally justified in assuming a similar subdivision in the first or oral phase. In the earlier stage of it, we only have oral incorporation, and there is no ambivalence in the relation to the object, i.e., the mother's breast. The second stage, which is distinguished by the onset of biting activities, may be called the *oral-sadistic* stage. It is here that we get the first manifestations of ambivalence, which become so much more obvious in the next, or sadistic-anal phase. The value of these new differentiations becomes especially clear when we want to discover the predispositional points of the libidinal development in the case of certain neuroses—such as obsessional neurosis and melancholia. I need only recall to you here what we have learnt on the subject of fixation of libido, predisposition, and regression.

Our attitude to the phases of libidinal organization has in general altered somewhat. We used formerly to emphasize the way in which one phase gives place to the next; nowadays, we direct our attention more to the facts which indicate how much of each earlier phase persists side by side with, and behind, later organizations, and obtains permanent representation in the economy of the libido and in the character of the individual. Even more important are those investigations which have shown us how frequently under pathological conditions regression to earlier phases takes place, and that certain regressions are characteristic of certain forms of illness. I cannot, however, go into that question here; it is a matter for a specialized treatise on the psychology of the neuroses.

We have been able to study the transformation of instincts and similar processes, especially with reference to anal-erotism, in which the impulses have their source in the erotogenic anal zone, and we are surprised to find the multiplicity of the channels along which these instinctual impulses can be directed. It is, perhaps, not easy to free oneself from the contemptuous attitude which we have come to adopt towards this particular zone during the course of our development. It is as well, therefore, to bear in mind Abraham's reminder that embryologically the anus corresponds to the primitive mouth, which has moved down to the end of the bowel. It appears, then, that when, in the course of development, the individual comes to feel disfavour for his own faeces cr excrement, his instinctual interest arising from anal sources passes over to objects which can be given away as gifts. And rightly so, for faeces were the first gift that the infant could make, and he parted with them out of love for the person who looked after him. Subsequently, the old interest in faeces turns into an appreciation of gold and money, and also makes a contribution to the affective cathexis attaching to the ideas of child and penis. It is the view of all children, who, as we know, cling to the cloaca-theory for a long time, that babies are born out of the bowel, like a piece of faeces; defecation is the prototype of the act of birth. But the penis, too, has its forerunner in the column of feaces, which fills the mucous membrane tube of the bowel and stimulates it. When the child has unwillingly imbibed the knowledge that there are human beings who do not possess a penis, that organ seems to him something which can be detached from the body, and an unmistakable analogy is drawn between it and the excrement which was the first piece of bodily substance that had to be given up. A large quantity of anal-erotism is thus transferred to the cathexis of the penis. But the interest in that part of the body has, besides an anal-erotic basis, a perhaps even more powerful root in oral erotism; for in accordance with the situation of sucking, the penis derives a great deal from the nipple of the mother's breast.

It is impossible to have any understanding of people's phantasies, or of associations which occur under the influence of the unconscious, or of the language of symptoms, if one does not know about these deep-lying connections. On this level, faeces-money-gift-child-penis are taken as having the same meaning, and can be represented by the same symbols. You must not forget that I can only give you very incomplete information on the subject. I will, however, add in passing that the late awakening interest in the vagina is mainly of anal-erotic derivation. This is not to be wondered at, since the vagina is, in the admirable phrase of Lou Andreas-Salomé, "hired out" from the rectum; and in the lives of homosexuals, who have not got beyond a certain stage in their sexual development, the vagina is once more represented by the anus. In dreams we often meet with a place which was formerly a single room, but is now divided into two by a partition wall, or vice versa. This always refers to the relation of the vagina to the rectum. We can also follow very clearly the way in which in a girl, the entirely unfeminine desire for the possession of a penis normally turns into the desire for a child, and then for a man as the bearer of the penis and the giver of the child, so that in this case, too, we can see how an element of what was originally an anal-erotic interest is taken up into the later genital organization.

In the course of these studies of the pregenital phases of the libido, we have gleaned some new pieces of information about the formation of character. We have been made aware of a triad of characteristics which are almost always to be found together: orderliness, parsimoniousness, and obstinacy, and we have concluded from the analysis of persons possessing them that these characteristics proceed from the dissipation of their anal-erotism and its employment in other ways. Where this remarkable combination is to be found, therefore, we speak of an *anal character*, and in a sense contrast it with unmodified anal-erotism. A similar and perhaps even firmer connection is to be found between ambition and urethral erotism. We have found a remarkable reference to this correlation in the legend that Alexander the Great was born on the same night that a certain Herostratus, from a craving for notoriety, set fire to the famous temple of Artemis at Ephesus. It seems that the ancients were well aware of the connection involved. You already know how close a connection there is between urination and fire and the putting out of fire. Naturally, we expect to find that other traits of character will also turn out to be derived from pregenital libidinal formations, either as precipitates or as reaction-formations; but we cannot as yet demonstrate this.

It is now time for me to turn back to an earlier stage of our problem, and again take up the question of instinctual life in its most general aspect. The contrast between ego-instincts and sexual instincts lay, to begin with, at the bottom of our theory of the libido. When, later on, we began to study the ego in greater detail, and came to understand the idea of narcissism,

this distinction itself lost its validity. In certain rare cases one observes that the ego takes itself as object, and behaves as if it were in love with itself. For this reason we have borrowed the name of *narcissism* from the Greek legend. But that is only an extreme exaggeration of the normal course of events. We must understand that the ego is always the main reservoir of libido, from which libidinal cathexes of objects proceed, and into which they return again, while the greater part of this libido remains perpetually in the ego. There is therefore a constant transformation of ego-libido into object-libido, and of object-libido into ego-libido. But if this is so, the two cannot differ from each other in their nature, and there is no point in distinguishing the energy of the one from that of the other; one can either drop the term *libido* altogether, or use it as meaning the same as psychic energy in general.

We did not keep to this point of view for long. The idea of contrasting forces within the instinctual life was soon given another and more precise meaning. I shall not go through the processes by which I arrived at this new point of view; it, too, rests essentially on biological considerations; I will put it before you as a finished article. We suppose that there are two fundamentally different kinds of instincts, the sexual instincts in the widest sense of the word (*Eros*, if you prefer that name) and the aggressive instincts, whose aim is destruction. When it is put like that, you will hardly think of it as anything new; it looks as though it were a theoretical glorification of the commonplace opposition between love and hate, which may perhaps coincide with the polarity of attraction and repulsion which physics postulates for the inorganic world. But it is remarkable that this hypothesis was nevertheless felt by many to be an innovation, and indeed a most undesirable one which ought to be got rid of as soon as possible. I think a strong emotional factor was responsible for this rejection. Why have we ourselves taken so long to bring ourselves to recognize the existence of an aggressive instinct? Why was there so much hesitation in using for our theory facts which lay ready to hand and were familiar to every one? One would probably meet with but little opposition if one were to ascribe to animals an instinct with such an aim as this. But to introduce it into the human constitution seems impious; it contradicts too many religious prejudices and social conventions. No, man must be by nature good, or at least good-natured. If he occasionally shows himself to be brutal, violent, and cruel, these are only passing disturbances of his emotional life, mostly provoked, and perhaps only the consequence of the ill-adapted social system which he has so far made for himself.

Unfortunately the testimony of history and our own experience do not bear this out, but rather confirm the judgment that the belief in the *goodness* of man's nature is one of those unfortunate illusions from which mankind expects some kind of beautifying or amelioration of their lot, but which in reality bring only disaster. We need not proceed with this polemic; for it is not on account of the teaching of history and of our own experience of life that we maintain the hypothesis of a special instinct of aggression and destructiveness in man, but on account of general considerations, to which we were led in trying to estimate the importance of the phenomena of *sadism* and *masochism*. You know that we use the word *sadism* when sexual satisfaction depends upon the sexual object suffering pain, ill-treatment, and humiliation, and the word *masochism,* when the subject himself has to suffer such treatment. You know, too, that there is a certain admixture of these two tendencies in normal sexual relations, and that we call them *perversions* when they thrust the other sexual aims into the background and substitute their own aims for them. It can hardly have escaped you that sadism has a close connection with masculinity, and masochism with femininity, as if there were some secret relationship between them. I must tell you at once that we have made no further progress along this path. Both of them, sadism and masochism, are very hard to account for by the theory of the libido, and especially masochism; and it is only right and proper that the stone which was an obstacle to the one theory should become the cornerstone of the other.

For we believe that in sadism and masochism we have two admirable examples of the fusion of the two kinds of instincts, Eros and aggressiveness, and we now put forward the hypothesis that this relationship is typical and that all the instinctual impulses that we can study are made up of such fusions or alloys of the two kinds of instincts. Naturally, they are to be found mixed in the greatest variety of proportions. To this mixture the erotic instincts will contribute the whole multiplicity of their sexual aims, while the others will admit only of mitigation and graduation of their uniform tendency. This hypothesis opens up a line of investigation which may some day be of great importance for the understanding of pathological processes. For fusions may be undone, and such defusions of instincts may be expected to bring about the most serious consequences to adequate functioning. But this point of view is still too new; no one has so far attempted to make practical use of it.

Let us return to the specific problem which is presented by masochism. If we put its erotic components on one side for a moment, it proves the existence of a tendency which has self-destruction as its aim. We have already stated that the ego (or rather, as we should here say, the id, the whole personality) originally includes all the instinctual impulses; if this applies equally to the destructive instinct, it will follow that masochism is older than sadism; and that sadism is the destructive instinct directed outwards, thereby acquiring the character of aggressiveness. Varying quantities of the original destructive instinct may still remain inside the organism; it seems as though we could only perceive it under two conditions, either when it is bound up with the erotic instincts so as to form masochism, or when it is turned on to the external world (with a greater or lesser erotic addition) in the shape of aggressiveness. We are now led to consider the important possibility of the aggression being unable to find satisfaction in the external world, because it comes up against objective hindrances. It may then perhaps turn back and increase the amount of self-destructiveness within. We shall see that this actually occurs, and that it is an event of great importance. It would seem that aggression when it is impeded entails serious injury, and that we have to destroy other things and other people, in order not to destroy ourselves, in order to protect ourselves from the tendency to self-destruction. A sad disclosure, it will be agreed, for the moralist.

But the moralist will, for a long time to come, console himself with the improbability of our speculations. It is indeed a strange instinct that is occupied with the destruction of its own organic home! It is true that the poets speak of things of this sort; but poets are irresponsible beings, they enjoy the privilege of poetic licence. But, after all, such ideas are not foreign to physiology, where we find, for instance, the mucous membrane of the stomach digesting itself. But it must be admitted that our instinct of self-destruction requires more confirmation. One cannot put forward a hypothesis that is so far-reaching, simply on the ground that a few poor fools have attached a curious condition to their sexual satisfaction. I think that a deeper study of the instincts will give us what we want. The instincts do not only dominate mental life, but vegetative life as well, and these organic instincts display a characteristic which merits our most serious attention. Whether it is a general characteristic of all instincts we shall only be able to decide later. They turn out to be directed towards the reinstatement of an earlier state of things. We may assume that, as soon as a given state of things is upset, there arises an instinct to re-create it, and phenomena appear which we may call *repetition-compulsion*. Embryology, for instance, is nothing but a repetition-compulsion; stretching far back in the animal series we find a capacity to form afresh organs which have been lost, and the instinct of recovery, to which, alongside of our therapeutic activities, we owe our power to get well, may be the remains of this capacity which is so wonderfully developed in the lower animals. The spawning migrations of fish and perhaps the migrations of birds, possibly all that we describe as a manifestation of *instinct* in animals, takes place under the domination of repetition-compulsion, which expresses the *conservative nature* of instincts. And in the realm of the mind, too, we shall not have far to seek for evidence of the presence of that compulsion. It has always surprised us that the forgotten and repressed experiences of early childhood should reproduce themselves in dreams and reactions during analytic treatment, especially in the reactions involved in the transference, although their reawakening runs counter to the interests of the pleasure-principle; and we have explained this by saying that in such cases repetition-compulsion has overcome even the pleasure-principle. Outside analysis, too, one can observe the same thing. There are people who, all their lives, repeat, to their own detriment, the same reactions, without any correction, or who seem to be dogged by a relentless ill-fortune, though a closer investigation shows that they are unwittingly bringing this ill-fortune upon themselves. Thus we explain what is called a *demonic* character as being due to the repetition-compulsion.

But how can this conservative quality of instincts help us to understand the self-destructive tendency? What is the earlier state of things that such an instinct is trying to rein-state? Now the answer to this question lies near at hand, and opens up a wide vista of possibilities. If it is true that once in an inconceivably remote past, and in an unimaginable way, life arose out of inanimate matter, then, in accordance with our hypothesis, an instinct must at that time have come into being, whose aim it was to abolish life once more and to re-establish the inorganic state of things. If in this instinct we recognize the impulse to self-destruction of our hypothesis, then we can regard that impulse as the manifestation of a *death instinct,* which can never be absent in any vital process. And now the instincts in which we believe separate themselves into two groups; the erotic instincts, which are always trying to collect living substance together into ever larger unities, and the death instincts which act against that tendency, and try to bring living matter back into an inorganic condition. The co-operation and opposition of these two forces produce the phenomena of life to which death puts an end.

You will perhaps shrug your shoulders and say: That is not natural science, that is the philosophy of Schopenhauer. But, Ladies and Gentlemen, why should not a bold thinker have divined something that a sober and painstaking investigation of details subsequently confirms? And after all, everything has been said already, and many people said the same thing before Schopenhauer. And besides, what we have said is not even true Schopenhauer. We do not assert that death is the only aim of life; we do not overlook the presence of life by the side of death. We recognize two fundamental instincts, and ascribe to each of them its own aim. How the two mingle in the vital process, how the death instinct is pressed into the service of Eros, especially when it is turned outwards in the form of aggressiveness—these are problems which remain for future investigation. We can go no further than the point at which this prospect opens up before us. The question whether all instincts without exception do not possess a conservative character, whether the erotic instincts also do not seek the reinstatement of an earlier state of things, when they strive towards the synthesis of living substance into larger wholes—this question, too, must be left unanswered.

We have wandered somewhat far from our thesis, but I will tell you the starting-point of these reflections upon the theory of the instincts. It was the same thing that led us to a revision of the relation between the ego and the unconscious: the impression we received from our analytical work that the patient who puts up a resistance very often knows nothing about it. But he is unconscious not only of the fact of his resistance but of the motives for it. It was necessary for us to look for these motives or this motive, and we found it, to our surprise, in a strong need for punishment, which we could not help associating with masochistic wishes. The practical value of this discovery is no less than its theoretical importance, for this need for punishment is the worst enemy of our therapeutic efforts. It is satisfied by the suffering which is bound up with the neurosis, and therefore holds fast to the state of illness. It seems as though this factor, the unconscious need for punishment, plays a part in every neurotic disease. The truth of this view is brought home to one in the most convincing way by cases in which we see neurotic suffering vanish at the appearance of suffering of another kind. I will give you an instance of this. I once succeeded in freeing a middle-aged spinster from a symptom-complex that had condemned her to a miserable existence for about fifteen years, and had quite prevented her from taking any part in life. She felt that she was now restored to health, and plunged into a whirl of activity in order to develop her talents, which were by no means small, and derive a little appreciation, enjoyment, and success from life before it was too late. But all her attempts ended in its being made clear to her, or in her seeing for herself, that she was too old to effect anything in that direction. Every time this happened, the next step for her would have been a relapse into her illness, but that she could no longer bring about; instead of it an accident would always befall her, which incapacitated her for some time and caused her suffering. She would fall down and sprain her foot, or injure her knee, or else hurt her hand while she was doing something or other. As soon as she saw how great a part she herself played in these apparently chance accidents, she altered her technique, as one might say. Instead of accidents she contracted on the same occasions slight illnesses, such as catarrhs, sore throats, influenzal conditions, or rheumatic swellings, until at last when she made up her mind to resign herself to inactivity, the whole business came to an end.

As to the origin of this unconscious need for punishment, there can be, I think, no doubt. It behaves like a part of the conscience, like the prolongation of conscience into the unconscious; and it must have the same origin as

conscience, that is to say, it will correspond to a piece of aggressiveness which has been internalized and taken over by the super-ego. If only the words were less incongruous, we should be justified, for all practical purposes, in calling it *an unconscious sense of guilt*. Theoretically, as a matter of fact, we are in doubt whether we ought to suppose that all aggressiveness that has turned back from the external world is bound by the super-ego, and so used against the ego, or whether a part of it carries on its silent sinister activity as a free destructive instinct in the ego and the id. Probably there is a division of this kind, but we know nothing further about it. When first the super-ego is set up, there is no doubt that that function is endowed with that part of the child's aggressiveness against its parents for which it can find no discharge outwards on account of its love-fixation and external difficulties; and, for this reason, the severity of the super-ego need not correspond to the severity of its upbringing. It is quite likely that when on subsequent occasions aggressiveness is suppressed, the instinct follows the path which was opened to it at that decisive period.

People in whom this unconscious sense of guilt is dominant, distinguish themselves under analytic treatment by exhibiting what is so unwelcome from the point of view of prognosis —a negative therapeutic reaction. In the normal course of events, if one gives a patient the solution of a symptom, at least the temporary disappearance of that symptom should result; with these patients, on the contrary, the effect is a momentary intensification of the symptom and the suffering that accompanies it. It often needs only a word of praise of their behaviour during the cure, the utterance of a few words of hope as to the progress of the analysis, to bring about an unmistakable aggravation of their condition. A non-analyst would say that they were lacking in the "will to recovery"; from the analytical point of view, their behaviour will appear as an expression of an unconscious sense of guilt, which favours illness with its attendant sufferings and handicaps. The problems raised by the unconscious sense of guilt, its relation to morality, education, criminality and delinquency, is at the present moment the favourite field of investigation for psycho-analysts. Here we have quite unexpectedly emerged into the open from the mental underworld. I cannot take you any further, but I will detain you for a few moments before I stop with one further consideration. We have got into the habit of saying that our civilization is built up at the cost of our sexual impulses, which are inhibited by society, being partly repressed, but partly, on the other hand, made use of for new aims. However proud we may be of our cultural achievements, we have admitted that it is by no means easy to satisfy the requirements of this civilization and to feel comfortable in its midst, because the restriction of the instincts which it involves lay a heavy psychological burden on our shoulders. Now what we have recognized as true of the sexual instincts holds to the same extent, and perhaps to an even greater extent, for the other instincts, for those of aggression. It is they above all that make communal existence difficult, and threaten its permanence. The limitation of aggression is the first and perhaps the hardest sacrifice which society demands from each individual. We have learnt in what an ingenious way this unruly element is tamed. The setting up of the super-ego, which makes the dangerous aggressive impulses its own, is like introducing a garrison into a province that is on the brink of rebellion. But, on the other hand, looking at it from a purely psychological point of view, one has to admit that the ego does not feel at all comfortable when it finds itself sacrificed in this way to the needs of society, when it has to submit itself to the destructive impulses of aggression, which it would have dearly liked itself to set in motion against others. It is like a carrying-over into the region of the mind of the dilemma—eat or be eaten—which dominates the organic world. Fortunately, the instincts of aggression are never alone, they are always alloyed with the erotic ones. In the cultural conditions which man has created for himself, the erotic instincts have much to mitigate and much to avert.

LECTURE 33

THE PSYCHOLOGY OF WOMEN

LADIES AND GENTLEMEN: The whole time that I have been preparing the lectures I am giving you, I have been struggling with an internal difficulty. I feel, as one might say, uncertain of the terms of my licence. It is quite true that in the course of fifteen years' work, psycho-analysis has altered and grown; but in spite of that, an introduction to psycho-analysis might be left unchanged and unexpanded. It is always at the back of my mind that there is no *raison d'être* for these lectures. For analysts I say too little and nothing at all that is new, while to

you I say too much and relate things which you are not in a position to understand and which are not for your ears. I have looked about for excuses, and have tried to justify each of my lectures on different grounds. The first, the one about the theory of dreams, was intended to put you back at once into the atmosphere of analysis, and to show you how durable our hypotheses have proved themselves to be. I was tempted to give the second, which traced the connection between dreams and the so-called occult, by the opportunity it afforded of saying something about a field of research in which at the present time prejudiced expectation is struggling against passionate opposition; and I allowed myself to hope that you would not refuse me your company on this expedition, but would follow me with a judgment educated to tolerance by example of psycho-analysis. The third lecture, which dealt with the anatomy of the personality, certainly made the severest demands upon you, so strange was its subject-matter; but it was quite impossible for me to withhold from you this first contribution to ego-psychology, and, if we had been in possession of the material fifteen years ago, I should have had to mention it then. Finally, the last lecture, which you have probably followed only with the greatest difficulty, contained some necessary emendations and new attempts at the solution of the most important problems; and my introduction would have been positively misleading if I had kept silent about them. You see how it is that when one tries to excuse oneself, it comes out in the end that everything was inevitable, that everything was pre-ordained. I submit to fate; and I beg that you will do the same.

Nor should today's lecture find a place in an introduction; but it may serve to give you an example of the detailed work of analysis, and there are two things I can add in its favour. It contains nothing but observed facts, with hardly any speculative additions, and it is concerned with a theme which claims your attention almost more than any other. Throughout the ages, the problem of woman has puzzled people of every kind—

> *Heads in hieroglyphic caps,*
> *Heads in turbans, and black bonnets,*
> *Heads bewigged and thousand other*
> *Poor and sweating heads of humans. . . .*
>   Heine, *Nordsee.*

You too will have pondered over this question in so far as you are men; from the women among you that is not to be expected, for you are the riddle yourselves. Male or female is the first differentiation that you make when you meet another human being, and you are used to making that distinction with absolute certainty. Anatomical science shares your certainty in one point, but not much more. Male is the male sexual secretion, the spermatozoon, and its carrier; female is the egg, and the organism that contains it. In each sex, organs have been formed which exclusively subserve the sexual functions; they have probably been developed from the same basis into two different formations. In both sexes, moreover, the other organs, the shape of the body and the tissues are influenced by sex (the so-called secondary sexual characters), but this influence is irregular and varying in degree. And then science tells you something that runs counter to your expectations, and is probably calculated to confuse your feelings. It points out to you that parts of the male sexual apparatus are also to be found in the body of the female, although in a rudimentary condition, and vice versa. Science sees in this phenomenon an indication of *bisexuality*, as though the individual were neither man nor woman, but both at the same time, only rather more the one than the other. It then expects you to make yourselves familiar with the idea that the proportions in which the masculine and the feminine mingle in an individual are subject to quite extraordinary variations. And even though, apart from very rare cases, only one kind of sexual product— ova or seminal cells—is present in any one individual, you will go wrong if you take this factor as being of decisive importance, and you must conclude that what constitutes masculinity or femininity is an unknown element which it is beyond the power of anatomy to grasp.

Can psychology do any better? We are used to consider masculine and feminine as mental qualities as well, and have also carried the notion of bisexuality over into mental life. We speak of a human being, whether male or female, behaving in a masculine or a feminine way. But you will at once observe that that is simply following the lead of anatomy and convention. You can give the concepts of masculine and feminine no new content. The difference is not a psychological one; when you say "masculine," you mean as a rule *active*, and when you say "feminine" you mean *passive*. Now it is quite true that there is such a correlation. The male sexual cell is active and mobile; it seeks out the female one, while the latter, the ovum, is stationary and waits passively. This behaviour of the elementary organisms of sex is more or less a model of the behaviour of the individuals of each sex in sexual intercourse. The male pursues the female for the purpose of sexual union, seizes her, and pushes his way into her. But with that you have, so far as psychology goes, reduced the quality of masculinity to the factor of aggressiveness. You will begin to doubt whether you have hit upon anything fundamental here, when you consider that in many classes of animals the female is the stronger and more aggressive party, and the male is only active in the single act of sexual intercourse. That is the case, for instance, with spiders. The functions of caring for the young, too, and of rearing them, which seems to us so essentially feminine, are not, among animals, always associated with the female sex. In some species of animals, quite high in the scale, one finds that the sexes share in the duties of looking after the young, or even that the male devotes himself to it alone. Even in the sphere of human sexual life, one soon notices how unsatisfactory it is to identify masculine behaviour with activity and feminine with passivity. The mother is in every sense of the word active in her relations with her child; it is just as true to say that she gives suck to the child, as that she lets it suck her breasts. The further you go from the sexual field in the narrower sense of the word the more apparent it becomes that the two ideas do not coincide. Women can display great activity in a variety of directions, while men cannot live together with their kind unless they develop a high degree of passive pliability. If you thereupon say that these facts precisely prove that men and women are psychologically bisexual, I shall infer that you have decided to identify activity with masculinity and passivity wth femininity. But I advise you not to do that. It seems to me to serve no good purpose and to give us no new information.

One might make an attempt to characterize femininity psychologically by saying that it involves a preference for passive aims. That is naturally not the same as passivity; it may require a good deal of activity to achieve a passive end. It may be that the part played by women in the sexual function leads them to incline towards passive behaviour and passive aims, and that this inclination extends into their ordinary life to a greater or less degree, according to whether the influence of her sexual life as a model is limited or far-reaching. But we must take care not to underestimate the influence of social conventions, which also force women into passive situations. The whole thing is still very obscure. We must not overlook one particularly constant relation between femininity and instinctual life. The repression of their aggressiveness, which is imposed upon women by their constitutions and by society, favours the development of strong masochistic impulses, which have the effect of binding erotically the destructive tendencies which have been turned inwards. Masochism is, then, as they say, truly feminine. But when, as so often happens, you meet with masochism in men, what else can you do but say that these men display obvious feminine traits of character?

You are now prepared for the conclusion that psychology cannot solve the riddle of femininity. The solution must, I think, come from somewhere else, and it cannot come until we have learned in general how the differentiation of living creatures into two sexes came about. We know nothing whatever about the matter, and yet sex-differentiation is a most remarkable characteristic in organic life, and one by which it is sharply cut off from inanimate nature. Meanwhile, we shall find plenty to occupy ourselves with in the study of those human individuals who are characterized as manifestly or preponderantly female by the possession of female genitals. It is in harmony with the nature of psycho-analysis that it does not try to describe what women are—that would be a task which it could hardly perform—but it investigates the way in which women develop out of children with their bisexual disposition. We have learnt a certain amount about this recently, thanks to the fact that several excellent women analysts have begun to work on the problem. A special piquancy has been lent to the discussion of this subject by the question of the difference between the sexes; for, whenever a comparison was made which seemed to be unfavourable to their sex, the ladies were able to express a suspicion, that we, the men analysts, had never overcome certain deeprooted prejudices against the feminine, and that consequently our investigations suffered from bias. On the other hand, on the basis of bisexuality, we found it easy to avoid any impoliteness. We had only to say: "This does not apply to you. You are an exception, in this respect you are more masculine than feminine."

In approaching the study of the sexual development of women we start with two preconceptions: firstly, that, as in the case of men, the constitution will not adapt itself to its function without a struggle; and secondly, that the decisive changes will have been set in motion or completed before puberty. Both of these preconceptions turn out to be justified. Further, a comparison with what happens in the case of the boy shows us that the development of the little girl into a normal woman is more difficult and more complicated; for she has two additional tasks to perform, to which there is nothing corresponding in the development of the man. Let us follow the parallel from the very beginning. Certainly the original material is different in the boy and the girl; it does not require psycho-analysis to find that out. The difference in the formation of their genital organs is accompanied by other bodily differences, which are too familiar for me to need to mention them. In their instinctual disposition, as well, there are differences which foreshadow the later nature of the woman. The little girl is as a rule less aggressive, less defiant, and less self-sufficient; she seems to have a greater need for affection to be shown her, and therefore to be more dependent and docile. The fact that she is more easily and more quickly taught to control her excretions is very probably only the result of this docility; urine and stool are, as we know, the first gifts that the child can offer to those who look after it, and control over them is the first concession which can be wrung from the instinctual life of the child. One gets the impression, too, that the little girl is more intelligent and more lively than the boy of the same age; she is more inclined to meet the external world half way, and, at the same time, she makes stronger object-cathexes. I do not know whether the view that she gets a start in development has been confirmed by more exact observations, but in any case it is quite clear that the little girl cannot be called intellectually backward. But these sexual differences are of no great importance; they can be out-balanced by individual variations. For the purposes which we have immediately in view they may be left on one side.

Both sexes seem to pass through the early phases of libidinal development in the same way. One might have expected that already in the sadistic-anal phase we should find that the girl showed less aggressiveness; but this is not the case. Women analysts have found from the analysis of children's play that the aggressive impulses of little girls leave nothing to be desired as regards copiousness and violence.

With the onset of the phallic phase the difference between the sexes becomes much less important than their similarities. We are now obliged to recognize that the little girl is a little man. As we know, in the boy this phase is characterized by the fact that he has discovered how to obtain pleasurable sensations from his little penis, and associates its state of excitation with his ideas about sexual intercourse. The little girl does the same with her even smaller clitoris. It seems as though, with her, all her masturbatory actions center round this penis-equivalent, and that the actual female vagina is still undiscovered by both sexes. It is true that, here and there, reports have been made that tell us of early vaginal sensations as well; but it cannot be easy to discriminate between these and anal sensations or from sensations of the vaginal vestibule; in any case they cannot play a very important rôle. We may assume that, in the phallic phase of the girl, the clitoris is the dominant erotogenic zone. But it is not destined to remain so; with the change to femininity, the clitoris must give up to the vagina its sensitivity, and, with it, its importance, either wholly or in part. This is one of the two tasks which have to be performed in the course of the woman's development; the more fortunate man has only to continue at the time of his sexual maturity what he has already practised during the period of early sexual expansion.

We shall return to the part played by the clitoris, but shall now pass on to the second task with which the girl's development is burdened. The first love-object of the boy is his mother, and she remains as such in the formation of his Oedipus-complex, and, ultimately, throughout his whole life. For the little girl, too, her mother must be her first object (together with figures of nurses and other attendants that merge into hers); the first object-cathexes, indeed, follow the lines of the satisfaction of the great and simple needs of life, and the circumstances in which the child is nursed are the same for both sexes. In the Oedipus situation, however, the father has become the little girl's love-object, and it is from him that, in the normal course of development, she should find her way to her ultimate object-choice. The girl has, then, in the course of time to change both her erotogenic zone and her object, while the boy keeps both of them unchanged. The question then arises of how this comes about. In particular, how does the little girl pass from an attachment to her mother to an attachment to her father? or, in other words, how does she pass from her masculine phase into the feminine phase which has been biologically marked out for her?

Now it would provide us with an ideally simple solution of the problem if we could assume that, from a certain age onwards, the elementary influence of heterosexual attraction makes itself felt, and draws the little girl towards men, while the same principle allows the boy to keep to his mother. One could even assume, further, that, in doing this, children are following a hint given them by the sexual preferences of their parents. But things are not so convenient as this. We hardly know whether we can seriously believe in the mysterious and unanalysable force, of which the poets sing so enthusiastically. Painstaking investigations have resulted in findings of quite a different kind, the material for which, at all events, was easily obtainable. You must know that the number of women who until late in life remain tenderly attached to father-objects, or indeed to their real fathers, is very large. We have made the most surprising discoveries about these women who display intense and prolonged father-fixations. We knew, of course, that there had been an earlier stage in which they were attached to their mother; but we did not know that it was so rich in content, that it persisted so long, and that it could leave behind it so many occasions for fixations and predispositions. During this time, their father is no more than an irksome rival. In many cases the attachment to the mother lasts beyond the fourth year; almost everything that we find later in the father-relation was already present in that attachment, and has been subsequently transferred on to the father. In short, we gain the conviction that one cannot understand women, unless one estimates this *pre-oedipal attachment to the mother* at its proper value.

Now we should very much like to know what the libidinal relations of the little girl to her mother are. The answer is that they are manifold. Since they pass through all the three phases of infantile sexuality, they take on the characteristics of each separate phase and express themselves by means of oral, sadistic-anal, and phallic wishes. These wishes represent active as well as passive impulses; if one relates them to the differentiation of the sexes which comes about later (which one should avoid doing as far as possible), one can speak of them as masculine and feminine. They are, in addition, completely ambivalent—both of a tender and of a hostile-aggressive nature. It often happens that the hostile wishes only become apparent after they have been turned into anxiety-ideas. It is not always easy to point out the way in which these early sexual wishes are formulated. What is most clearly expressed is the desire to get the mother with child as well as the corresponding one, to have a child by the mother; both belong to the phallic phase, and seem sufficiently strange, though their existence is established beyond all doubt by analytic observation. The attraction of these investigations lies in the extraordinary facts which they bring to light. Thus, for instance, one discovers the fear of being murdered or poisoned, which may later on form the nucleus of a paranoic disorder, already present in this pre-oedipal stage and directed against the mother. Or, to take another case. You will remember that interesting episode in the history of analytical research which caused me so many painful hours? At the time when my main interest was directed on to the discovery of infantile sexual traumas, almost all my female patients told me that they had been seduced by their fathers. Eventually, I was forced to the conclusion that these stories were false, and thus I came to understand that hysterical symptoms spring from phantasies and not from real events. Only later was I able to recognize in this phantasy of seduction by the father the expression of the typical Oedipus-complex in woman. And now we find, in the early pre-oedipal history of girls, the seduction-phantasy again; but the seducer is invariably the mother. Here, however, the phantasy has a footing in reality; for it must in fact have been the mother who aroused (perhaps for the first time) pleasurable sensations in the child's genitals in the ordinary course of attending to its bodily needs.

I dare say that you are prepared to suspect that this description of the richness and strength of the sexual relations of the little girl to her mother is very much exaggerated. One has, after all, plenty of opportunity of watching little girls, and one notices nothing of the sort. But the objection cannot be sustained. One can see enough of such things in children, if one understands how to observe them, and, besides this, you must consider how little the child is able to give preconscious expression to its sexual wishes, and how little it can communicate them. We are, therefore, acting entirely within our rights in studying the subsequent traces and consequences of this emotional field in persons in whom these developmental processes show a particularly clear, or even exaggerated, growth. Pathology, as you know, has always assisted us, by isolation and exaggeration, in making recognizable things which would normally remain hidden. And since our researches have been carried out on people who are by no means grossly abnormal, we may, I think, consider the results of them worthy of belief.

We will now turn our attention to the question of why this strong attachment of the girl to her mother comes to grief. We are aware that that is what usually happens to it; it is fated to give way to an attachment to her father. And here we stumble on a fact which points in the right direction. This step in development is not merely a question of a change of object. The turning away from the mother occurs in an atmosphere of antagonism; the attachment to the mother ends in hate. Such a hatred may be very marked and may persist throughout an entire lifetime; it may later on be carefully overcompensated; as a rule, one part of it is overcome, while another part persists. The outcome is naturally very strongly influenced by the actual events of later years. We will confine ourselves to studying this hatred at the actual time at which the turn towards the father takes place, and to inquiring into its motives. We are then met by a long list of complaints and grievances, levelled at the mother, which are intended to justify the antagonistic feelings of the child; they vary much in value, and we shall examine them further. Many are obvious rationalizations, and we have yet to find the true source of the antagonism. I hope you will bear with me, if on this occasion I conduct you through all the details of a psycho-analytical investigation.

The complaint against the mother that harks back furthest is that she has given the child too little milk, which is taken as indicating a lack of love. Now this complaint has a certain justification in the civilized human family. The mothers often have not enough nourishment for their children, and content themselves with nursing them for nine months or six or even less. Among primitive peoples, children remain at the breast for as long as two or three years. The figure of the wet-nurse is as a rule merged in that of the mother; where this does not take place, the complaint against the mother takes another form, namely, that she sent the nurse, who was so ready to feed the child, away too soon. But whatever may have been the true state of affairs, it is impossible that the child's complaint can be as often justified as it is met with. It looks far more as if the desire of the child for its first form of nourishment is altogether insatiable, and as if it never got over the pain of losing the mother's breast. I should not be at all surprised if an analysis of a member of a primitive race, who must have sucked the mother's breast when he could already run and talk, brought the same complaint to light. It is probable, too, that the fear of poisoning is connected with weaning. Poison is the nourishment that makes one ill. Perhaps, moreover, the child traces his early illnesses back to this frustration. It requires a good deal of intellectual training before we can believe in chance; primitive and uneducated people, and certainly children, can give a reason for everything that happens. Perhaps this reason was originally a motive (in the animistic sense). In many social strata, even to this day, no one can die, without having been done to death by some one else, preferably by the doctor. And the regular reaction of a neurotic to the death of some one intimately connected with him is to accuse himself of being the cause of the death.

The next accusation against the mother flares up when the next child makes its appearance in the nursery. If possible, this complaint retains the connection with oral frustration: the mother could not or would not give the child any more milk, because she needed the nourishment for the new arrival. In cases where the two children were born so close together that lactation was interfered with by the second pregnancy, this complaint has a real foundation. It is a remarkable fact that even when the difference between the children's ages is only eleven months, the older one is nevertheless able to take in the state of affairs. But it is not only the milk that the child grudges the undesired interloper and rival, but all the other evidences of motherly care. It feels that it has been dethroned, robbed, and had its rights invaded, and so it directs a feeling of jealous hatred against its little brother or sister, and develops resentment against its faithless mother, which often finds expression in a change for the worse in its behaviour. It begins to be naughty, irritable, intractable, and unlearns the control which it has acquired over its excretions. All this has been known for a long time, and is accepted as self-evident, but we seldom form a right idea of the strength of these jealous impulses, of the tenacious hold they have on the child, and the amount of influence they exert on its later development.

These jealous feelings are particularly important because they are always being fed anew during the later years of childhood, and the whole shattering experience is repeated with the arrival of every new brother or sister. Even if the child remains its mother's favourite, things are not very different; its demands for affection are boundless; it requires exclusive attention and will allow no sharing whatever.

A potent source of the child's antagonism against its mother is found in its many sexual wishes, which change with its libidinal phases. These cannot, for the most part, be satisfied. The strongest of these frustrations occurs in the phallic stage, when the mother forbids pleasurable activities centring round the genital organs—often with an accompaniment of harsh threats and every indication of disapproval—activities to which, after all, she herself stimulated the child. It might be thought that we had here motives enough for the little girl's alienation from her mother. In that case it might be our view that estrangement follows inevitably from the nature of infantile sexuality, from the child's unlimited demands for love and the unfulfillable nature of its sexual wishes. One might even believe that this first love relation of the child is doomed to extinction for the very reason that it is the first, for these early object-cathexes are always ambivalent to a very high degree; alongside the child's intense love there is always a strong aggressive tendency present, and the more passionately the child loves an object, the more sensitive it will be to disappointments and frustrations coming from it. In the end, the love is bound to capitulate to the accumulated hostility. Or, on the other hand, one might reject the idea of a fundamental ambivalence of this kind in the libidinal cathexes, and point to the fact that it is the peculiar nature of the mother-child relationship which leads, equally inevitably, to the disturbance of the child's love, since even the mildest form of education cannot avoid using compulsion and introducing restrictions, and every such encroachment on its freedom must call forth, as a reaction in the child, a tendency to rebellion and aggressiveness. A discussion of these possibilities might, I think, be very interesting, but at this point an objection suddenly arises, which forces our attention in another direction. All of these factors—slights, disappointments in love, jealousy, and seduction followed by prohibition—operate as well in the relationship between the boy and his mother, and yet are not sufficient to alienate him from the mother-object. If we do not find something which is specific for the girl, and which is not present at all, or not present in the same way, in the case of the boy, we shall not have explained the ending of the girl's attachment to her mother.

I think that we have discovered this specific factor, in a place where we might indeed have expected it, but in a surprising form. In a place where we might have expected it, I say, for it lies in the castration complex. The anatomical distinction between the sexes must, after all, leave its mark in mental life. It was a surprise, however, to discover from analyses that the girl holds her mother responsible for her lack of a penis, and never forgives her for that deficiency.

You will note that we ascribe a castration-complex to the female sex as well as to the male. We have good grounds for doing so, but that complex has not the same content in girls as in boys. In the boy, the castration-complex is formed after he has learnt from the sight of the female genitals that the sexual organ which he prizes so highly is not a necessary part of every human body. He remembers then the threats which he has brought on himself by his playing with his penis, he begins to believe in them, and thence forward he comes under the influence of *castration-anxiety,* which supplies the strongest motive force for his further development. The castration-complex in the girl, as well, is started by the sight of the genital organs of the other sex. She immediately notices the difference, and—it must be admitted—its significance. She feels herself at a great disadvantage, and often declares that she would "like to have something like that too," and falls a victim to *penis-envy,* which leaves ineradicable traces on her development and character-formation, and, even in the most favourable instances, is not overcome without a great expenditure of mental energy. That the girl recognizes the fact that she lacks a penis, does not mean that she accepts its absence lightly. On the contrary, she clings for a long time to the desire to get something like it, and believes in that possibility for an extraordinary number of years; and even at a time when her knowledge of reality has long since led her to abandon the fulfilment of this desire as being quite unattainable, analysis proves that it still persists in the unconscious and retains a considerable charge of energy. The desire after all to obtain the penis for which she so much longs may even contribute to the motives that impel a grown-up woman to come to analysis; and what she quite reasonably expects to get from analysis, such as the capacity to pursue an intellectual career, can often be recognized as a sublimated modification of this repressed wish.

One cannot very well doubt the importance of penis-envy. Perhaps you will regard the hypothesis that envy and jealousy play a greater part in the mental life of women than they do in that of men as an example of male unfairness. Not that I think that these characteristics are absent in men, or that they have no other origin in women except envy of the penis, but I am inclined to ascribe the greater amount of them to be found in women to this latter influence. Many analysts, however, tend to minimize the importance of this first wave of penis-envy in the phallic phase. They think that the signs one comes across of this attitude in women are in the main a secondary formation which has come about through regression to the early infantile impulse in question on the occasion of some subsequent conflict. Now this is one of the general problems of depth psychology. In the case of many pathological—or merely unusual—instinctual attitudes, for example with all sexual perversions, the question arises how much of their force is to be attributed to early infantile fixations and how much to the influence of later experiences and developments. It is almost always a question of complemental series, such as we have postulated when dealing with the aetiology of the neuroses. Both sets of factors share in the causation in a varying proportion; a less in the one set will be balanced by a more in the other. The infantile factor in every case paves the way; it is not always the decisive force, though it often is. But with regard to the particular case of penis-envy, I should like to come down decidedly in favour of the preponderance of the infantile factor.

The discovery of her castration is a turning-point in the life of the girl. Three lines of development diverge from it; one leads to sexual inhibition or to neurosis, the second to a modification of character in the sense of masculinity complex, and the third to normal femininity. We have learnt a good deal, though not everything, about all three. The fundamental content of the first is that the little girl, who has hitherto lived a masculine life, and has been able to obtain pleasure through the excitation of her clitoris, and has connected this behaviour with the sexual wishes (often of an active character) which she has directed towards her mother, finds her enjoyment of phallic sexuality spoilt by the influence of penis-envy. She is wounded in her self-love by the unfavourable comparison with the boy who is so much better equipped, and therefore gives up the masturbatory satisfaction which she obtained from her clitoris, repudiates her love towards her mother, and at the same time often represses a good deal of her sexual impulses in general. No doubt this turning away from her mother does not come to pass at one blow, for at first the girl looks on her castration as a personal misfortune, and only gradually extends it to other females, and eventually to her mother. Her love had as its object the phallic mother; with the discovery that the mother is castrated it becomes possible to drop her as a love-object, so that the incentives to hostility which have been so long accumulating, get the upper hand. This means, therefore, that, as a result of the discovery of the absence of a penis, women are as much depreciated in the eyes of the girl as in the eyes of the boy, and later, perhaps, of the man.

You all know what an overwhelming aetiological importance is attributed by neurotics to their masturbatory practices. They make them responsible for all their troubles, and we have the greatest difficulty in getting them to believe that they are wrong. But, as a matter of fact, we ought to admit that they are in the right, for masturbation is the executive agent of infantile sexuality, from the faulty development of which they are suffering. The difference is that what the neurotics are blaming is the masturbation of the pubertal stage; the infantile masturbation, which is the one that really matters, has for the most part been forgotten by them. I wish I could find an opportunity for giving you a circumstantial account of how important all the factual details of early masturbation are in determining the subsequent neurosis or character of the individual concerned—such details as whether it was discovered or not, how the parents combated it or whether they permitted it, and whether the subject succeeded in suppressing it himself. All these details will have left indelible traces upon his development. But, in fact, I am relieved that it is not necessary for me to do this; it would be a difficult and weary task, and at the end you would embarrass me because you would quite certainly ask for some practical advice as to how one should behave towards the masturbation of small children as a parent or educator. The history of the development of girls, which is the subject I am telling you

about, offers an instance of the child itself striving to free itself from masturbation. But it does not always succeed. Where penis-envy has aroused a strong impulse against clitoritic masturbation, but where the latter will not give way, there follows a fierce battle for freedom, in which the girl herself takes over, as it were, the rôle of the mother whom she has set aside, and expresses her whole dissatisfaction with the inferior clitoris, by striving against the gratification derived from it. Many years later, when her masturbatory activity has long ago been suppressed, we may find an interest persisting which we must interpret as a defence against the temptation, which she still fears. It finds expression in feelings of sympathy for persons to whom she ascribes similar difficulties; it may enter into her motives for marriage, and may indeed determine her choice of a husband or lover. The settling of the problem of infantile masturbation is truly no easy or unimportant task.

When the little girl gives up clitoritic masturbation, she surrenders a certain amount of activity. Her passive side has now the upper hand, and in turning to her father she is assisted in the main by passive instinctual impulses. You will see that a step in development, such as this one, which gets rid of phallic activity, must smooth the path for femininity. If in the process not too much is lost through repression, this femininity may prove normal. The wish with which the girl turns to her father, is, no doubt, ultimately the wish for the penis, which her mother has refused her and which she now expects from her father. The feminine situation is, however, only established when the wish for the penis is replaced by the wish for a child— the child taking the place of the penis, in accordance with the old symbolic equation. It does not escape us that at an earlier stage the girl has already desired a child, before the phallic phase was interfered with; that was the meaning of her playing with dolls. But this play was not really an expression of her femininity, it served, in identifying her with her mother, the purpose of substituting activity for passivity. She was the mother, and the doll was herself; now she could do everything to the doll that her mother used to do with her. Only with the onset of the desire for a penis does the doll-child become a child by the father, and, thence-forward, the strongest feminine wish. Her happiness is great indeed when this desire for a child one day finds a real fulfilment; but especially is this so if the child is a little boy, who brings the longed-for penis with him. In the idea of having a child by the father, the accent is often enough placed on the child, and not on the father. Thus the old masculine wish for the possession of a penis still shows under the completely developed femininity. But perhaps we should rather think of this desire for a penis as something essentially feminine in itself.

With the transference of the child-penis wish on to her father, the girl enters into the situation of the Oedipus-complex. The hostility against her mother, which did not require to be newly created, now receives a great reinforcement, for her mother becomes a rival, who gets everything from her father that she herself wants. The girl's Oedipus-complex has long concealed from us the pre-oedipal attachment to her mother which is so important and which leaves behind it such lasting fixations. For the girl, the Oedipus situation is the conclusion of a long and difficult period of development; it is a kind of temporary solution of her problem, a state of equilibrium which is not lightly to be given up, especially as the onset of the latency period is not far off. And here we notice a difference between the two sexes in the relation between the Oedipus-complex and the castration-complex, a difference which is probably a momentous one. The boy's Oedipus-complex, in which he desires his mother and wants to get rid of his father as a rival, develops naturally out of the phase of phallic sexuality. The threat of castration, however, forces him to give up this attitude. Under the influence of the danger of losing his penis, he abandons his Oedipus-complex; it is repressed and in most normal cases entirely destroyed, while a severe super-ego is set up as its heir. What happens in the case of the girl is almost the opposite. The castration-complex prepares the way for the Oedipus-complex instead of destroying it; under the influence of her penis-envy, the girl is driven from her attachment to her mother and enters the Oedipus situation, as though it were a haven of refuge. When the fear of castration disappears, the primary motive is removed, which has forced the boy to overcome his Oedipus-complex. The girl remains in the Oedipus situation for an indefinite period; she only abandons it late in life, and then incompletely. The formation of the super-ego must suffer in these circumstances; it cannot attain the strength and independence which give it its cultural importance, and feminists are not pleased if one points to the way in which this factor affects the development of the average feminine character.

Let us now go back a little. We have mentioned, as the second possible reaction after the discovery of female castration, the development of a strong masculinity complex. What is meant by this is that the girl refuses, as it were, to accept the unpalatable fact, and, in an outburst of defiance, exaggerates still further the masculinity which she has displayed hitherto. She clings to her clitoritic activities, and takes refuge in an identification either with the phallic mother, or with the father. What is the determinant which leads to this state of affairs? We can picture it as nothing other than a constitutional factor: the possession of a greater degree of activity, such as is usually characteristic of the male. The essential thing about the process is, after all, that at this point of development the onset of passivity, which makes possible the change over to femininity, is avoided. The most extreme achievement of this masculinity complex seems to occur when it influences the girl's object-choice in the direction of manifest homosexuality. Analytic experience teaches us, it is true, that female homosexuality is seldom or never a direct continuation of infantile masculinity. It seems to be characteristic of female homosexuals that they too take the father as love-object for a while, and thus become implicated in the Oedipus situation. Then, however, they are driven by the inevitable disappointments which they experience from the father into a regression to their early masculinity complex. One must not overestimate the importance of these disappointments; girls who eventually achieve femininity also experience them without the same results. The preponderance of the constitutional factor seems undeniable, but the two phases in the development of female homosexuality are admirably reflected in the behaviour of homosexuals, who just as often and just as obviously play the parts of mother and child towards each other as those of man and wife.

What I have been telling you is what one might call the pre-history of women. It is an achievement of the last few years, and you may have been interested in it as an example of detailed work in analysis. Since women are our theme, I am going to permit myself to mention by name a few women to whom this investigation owes important contributions. Dr. Ruth Mack Brunswick was the first to describe a case of neurosis which went back to a fixation in the pre-oedipal state, and in which the Oedipus situation was not reached at all. It took the form of paranoia with delusions of jealousy, and proved accessible to treatment. Dr. Jeanne Lamplde Groot has, from her own unequivocal observations, established the fact of the girl's phallic activities towards her mother which seem so hard to believe. Dr. Helene Deutsch has shown that the erotic behaviour of homosexual woman reproduces the mother-child relationship.

It is not my intention to trace the further course of femininity through puberty up to the time of maturity. Our views on the subject are indeed not complete enough for me to do so. In what follows, I will merely mention a few separate points. Bearing in mind the early history of femininity, I will emphasize the fact that its development remains open to disturbance from the traces left behind by the previous masculine period. Regressions to fixations at these pre-oedipal phases occur very often; in many women we actually find a repeated alternation of periods in which either masculinity or femininity has obtained the upper hand. What we men call "the enigma of woman" is probably based in part upon these signs of bisexuality in female life. But another question seems to have become ripe for discussion in the course of these investigations. We have called the motor force of sexual life *libido*. This sexual life is dominated by the polarity, masculine-feminine; one is therefore tempted to consider the relation of the libido to this polarity. It would not be surprising if it turned out that each form of sexuality had its own special form of libido, so that one kind of libido pursued the aims of the masculine sexual life, and the other those of the feminine. Nothing of the sort, however, is the case. There is only one libido which is as much in the service of the male as of the female sexual function. To it itself we can assign no sex; if, in accordance with the conventional analogy between activity and masculinity, we choose to call it masculine, we must not forget that it also includes impulses with passive aims. Nevertheless the phrase *feminine libido* cannot possibly be justified. It is our impression that more violence is done to the libido when it is forced into the service of the female function; and that—to speak teleologically—Nature has paid less careful attention to the demands of the female function than to those of masculinity. And—again speaking teleologically—this may be based on the fact that the achievement of the biological aim is entrusted to the aggressiveness of the

male, and is to some extent independent of the co-operation of the female.

The sexual frigidity of women, the frequency of which seems to confirm this last point, is still a phenomenon which is insufficiently understood. Sometimes it is psychogenic, and, if so, it is accessible to influence; but in other cases one is led to assume that it is constitutionally conditioned or even partly caused by an anatomical factor.

I have promised to put before you a few more of the mental characteristics of mature femininity, as we find them in our analytical observation. We do not claim for these assertions more than that they are true on the whole; and it is not always easy to distinguish between what is due to the influence of the sexual function and what to social training. We attribute to women a greater amount of narcissism (and this influences their object-choice) so that for them to be loved is a stronger need than to love. Their vanity is partly a further effect of penis-envy, for they are driven to rate their physical charms more highly as a belated compensation for their original sexual inferiority. Modesty, which is regarded as a feminine characteristic *par excellence*, but is far more a matter of convention than one would think, was, in our opinion, originally designed to hide the deficiency in her genitals. We do not forget that, later on, it takes over other functions. People say that women contributed but little to the discoveries and inventions of civilization, but perhaps after all they did discover one technical process, that of plaiting and weaving. If this is so, one is tempted to guess at the unconscious motive at the back of this achievement. Nature herself might be regarded as having provided a model for imitation, by causing pubic hair to grow at the period of sexual maturity so as to veil the genitals. The step that remained to be taken was to attach the hairs permanently together, whereas in the body they are fixed in the skin and only tangled with one another. If you repudiate this idea as being fantastic, and accuse me of having an *idée fixe* on the subject of the influence exercised by the lack of a penis upon the development of femininity, I cannot of course defend myself.

The conditions of object-choice in women are often enough made unrecognizable by social considerations. Where that choice is allowed to manifest itself freely, it often occurs according to the narcissistic ideal of the man whom the girl would have liked to be. If the girl has remained attached to her father, if, that is to say, she has remained in the Oedipus-complex, then she chooses according to a father-type. Since, when she turned from her mother to her father, the antagonistic part of her ambivalent feelings remained directed on to her mother, such a choice should ensure a happy marriage. But very often a factor emerges which in general imperils such solutions of the ambivalence-conflict. The antagonism which has been left behind may follow in the wake of the positive attachment, and extend to the new object. The husband, who had in the first instance inherited his position from the father, comes in the course of time to inherit the position of the mother as well. In this way it may easily occur that the second part of a woman's life is taken up with a struggle against her husband, just as the shorter earlier part was occupied with rebellion against her mother. After this reaction has been lived out, a second marriage may easily turn out far more satisfactorily. Another change in a woman's nature, for which neither husband nor wife are prepared, may come about after the first child has been born. Under the influence of her own motherhood, her identification with her mother may be revived (an identification against which she has struggled up to the time of her marriage) and may attract to itself all the libido that she has at her disposal, so that the repetition-compulsion may reproduce an unhappy marriage of the parents. That the old factor of lack of penis has not even yet forfeited its power is seen in the different reactions of the mother according to whether the child born is a son or a daughter. The only thing that brings a mother undiluted satisfaction is her relation to a son; it is quite the most complete relationship between human beings, and the one that is the most free from ambivalence. The mother can transfer to her son all the ambition which she has had to suppress in herself, and she can hope to get from him the satisfaction of all that has remained to her of her masculinity complex. Even a marriage is not firmly assured until the woman has succeeded in making her husband into her child and in acting the part of a mother towards him.

The mother-identification of the woman can be seen to have two levels, the pre-oedipal, which is based on the tender attachment to the mother and which takes her as a model, and the later one, derived from the Oedipus-complex, which tries to get rid of the mother and replace her in her relationship with the father. Much of

both remains over for the future. One is really justified in saying that neither is overcome to any adequate extent during the process of development. But the phase of tender pre-oedipal attachment is the decisive one; it paves the way for her acquisition of those characteristics which will later enable her to play her part in the sexual function adequately, and carry out her inestimable social activities. In this identification, too, she acquires that attractiveness for the man which kindles his oedipal attachment to his mother into love. Only what happens so often is that it is not he himself who gets what he wanted, but his son. One forms the impression that the love of man and the love of woman are separated by a psychological phase-difference.

It must be admitted that women have but little sense of justice, and this is no doubt connected with the preponderance of envy in their mental life; for the demands of justice are a modification of envy; they lay down the conditions under which one is willing to part with it. We say also of women that their social interests are weaker than those of men, and that their capacity for the sublimation of their instincts is less. The former is no doubt derived from the unsocial character which undoubtedly attaches to all sexual relationships. Lovers find complete satisfaction in each other, and even the family resists absorption into wider organizations. The capacity for sublimation is subject to the greatest individual variations. In spite of this I cannot refrain from mentioning an impression which one receives over and over again in analytic work. A man of about thirty seems a youthful, and, in a sense, an incompletely developed individual, of whom we expect that he will be able to make good use of the possibilities of development, which analysis lays open to him. But a woman of about the same age frequently staggers us by her psychological rigidity and unchangeability. Her libido has taken up its final positions and seems powerless to leave them for others. There are no paths open to her for further development; it is as though the whole process had been gone through and remained inaccessible to influence for the future; as though, in fact, the difficult development which leads to femininity had exhausted all the possibilities of the individual. As therapeutists, we deplore this state of affairs, even when we are successful in removing her sufferings by solving her neurotic conflict.

That is all I had to say to you about the

psychology of women. It is admittedly incomplete and fragmentary, and sometimes it does not sound altogether flattering. You must not forget, however, that we have only described women in so far as their natures are determined by their sexual function. The influence of this factor is, of course, very far-reaching, but we must remember that an individual woman may be a human being apart from this. If you want to know more about femininity, you must interrogate your own experience or turn to the poets, or else wait until science can give you more profound and more coherent information.

LECTURE 34
EXPLANATIONS, APPLICATIONS
AND ORIENTATIONS

LADIES AND GENTLEMEN: May I for once, tired, as one might say, of dry topics, speak to you about matters which have very little theoretical importance, but which will be of interest to you in so far as you are friendlily disposed towards psycho-analysis? Let us suppose that in a moment of idleness you take up a German or American or English novel, in which you expect to find a description of men and conditions as they are today. After reading a few pages you come upon the first mention of psycho-analysis, and then soon after upon another, even though the context does not seem to require it. You must not imagine that this has anything to do with the application of *depth-psychology*, with a view to a better understanding of the characters in the book or of their behaviour (though, of course, there are quite serious literary works in which this is attempted). No, such references are for the most part contemptuous remarks, by means of which the author seeks to display his wide reading or his intellectual superiority. And you will not always get the impression that he really knows what he is talking about. Or, again, you may go for your recreation to some social gathering; it need not necessarily be in Vienna. After a short time the conversation will turn on psycho-analysis, and you will hear a great variety of people giving their opinion upon it, usually in tones of dogmatic certainty. This judgment is nearly always a derogatory one, often abusive, and at the very least derisive. If you are so imprudent as to disclose the fact that you know something about the subject, every one rushes up to you, and asks for information and explanations, until after a little time you are convinced that all these severe judgments had been made in the absence of any knowledge; that hardly any of these adversaries have ever had a book about analysis in their hands, or, if they have, that they have never been able to overcome the first resistance which people experience on coming in contact with a new subject.

You may perhaps expect that an introduction to psycho-analysis should give you some indication of what arguments you should use in order to correct these vulgar errors about analysis, what books to recommend for those who want more knowledge, or even what examples from your reading and experience you should bring into the discussion in order to alter the attitude of your interlocutors. I beg you to do nothing of the sort. It would be quite useless, and your wisest course would be to hide your better knowledge altogether. If that is impossible, then restrict yourselves to saying that, so far as you know, psycho-analysis is a special branch of science, that it is exceedingly difficult to understand and to judge, that it is concerned with very serious matters, so that one cannot pass it off with a few jokes, and that it would be better to choose some other topic as a social pastime. Of course, you will not take part in any attempts at interpretation if imprudent people repeat their dreams, and you will resist the temptation to curry favour for analysis by giving accounts of cures that it has brought about.

You may, however, raise the question why these people, whether they write books or make conversation, should behave so badly, and you will incline to the view that the cause does not lie entirely with the people themselves, but with psycho-analysis as well. That is my opinion too; what you meet with in literature and conversation in the shape of prejudice is the after-effect of an earlier judgment, the judgment, namely, which the representatives of official science have passed upon the young science of psycho-analysis. I have already complained about it once before in a historical survey of the subject, and I shall not do so again—perhaps even that was once too often; but indeed there was no logical blunder, no offence against decency and good taste which the scientific opponents of psycho-analysis did not permit themselves in those days. It was a situation such as actually occurred in the middle ages, in which a wrong-doer, or even a mere political opponent, was put in the pillory and exposed to the ill-treatment of the mob. And perhaps you do not fully realize how high up in our society the mob spirit extends, and to what lengths people will go when they feel that they are a part of a crowd and superior to personal responsibility. At the beginning of those times I stood more or less alone, and I very soon saw that polemics would do no good, and that complaints and appeals to worthier minds were senseless, since there were no courts before which one could plead one's cause. That being so, I took another path; I made use of applied psycho-analysis for the first time by explaining the behaviour of the crowd as an expression of the same resistance which I had to struggle against in my individual patients. I kept off all polemics, and influenced my followers, as they gradually gathered, to do the same. This mode of behaviour was satisfactory. The ban under which analysis was placed in those days has since been lifted; but, just as a belief which has been given up lingers on as a superstition, just as a theory which science has abandoned is preserved as a popular belief, so today the original excommunication of psycho-analysis in scientific circles survives in the mocking contempt of the writers and conversationalists. You will therefore no longer be surprised at their behaviour.

You must not, however, expect the good news that the struggle is at an end, with the recognition of analysis as a science and its admission as a subject for university study. There is no question of that; the battle is still going on, but in a more respectable way. There is another new factor, and that is that in the scientific world a kind of buffer state has been formed between analysis and its opponents, consisting of people who will allow that there is something in analysis (and even believe in it, subject to the most diverting reservations), but who, on the other hand, reject other parts of it, as they are eager to let everyone know. What determines their choice is not easy to guess. It seems to be a matter of personal sympathies. Some take objection to sexuality, others to the unconscious; the existence of symbolism seems to be particularly disliked. The circumstance that the structure of psycho-analysis, although unfinished, nevertheless already possesses a unified organization from which one cannot select elements according to one's whim, seems not to enter the minds of these eclectics. When I consider these half or quarter followers I never get the impression from any of them that their rejections are based on an examination of the material. There are a great many distinguished men who fall

into this category. They are certainly to be excused on the ground that their time and their interests are devoted to other things, to the subjects, in fact, by the mastery of which they have achieved so much. But, that being so, would it not be better for them to reserve their judgments instead of taking sides so strongly? In the case of one of these great men, I once succeeded in making a rapid conversion. He was a world-famous critic, who had followed contemporary trends of thought with benevolent understanding and prophetic vision. I only got to know him when he had already passed his eightieth year, but he was still fascinating in conversation. You can easily guess to whom I am referring. And it was not I who raised the subject of psycho-analysis. He began it by comparing himself in the most modest way with myself, saying: "I am only a literary man, and you are a man of science and a discoverer. But there is one thing I should like to say to you: I have never had any sexual feeling for my mother." "But there's no need at all for you to have been conscious of it," was my reply, "such processes are unconscious in grown-up people." "Oh, so *that's* your idea," he said, greatly relieved, and pressed my hand. We went on talking for a few hours longer on the best of terms. I heard later that during the few remaining years of his life he repeatedly expressed himself in friendly terms about analysis, and liked to make use of what was for him a new word—*repression*.

A well-known saying enjoins us to learn from our enemies. I must own that I have never been able to manage it; but it occurred to me that it might be instructive for you if I were to call up all the reproaches and objections which the opponents of psycho-analysis have levelled at it, and then point out all the obvious misrepresentations and logical blunders which they contain. But on second thought I said to myself that it would not be at all interesting, but wearisome and disagreeable, and would, in fact, be precisely what I have taken such pains to avoid all these years. You will have to excuse me, therefore, if I refrain from following up this line of thought any further and spare you the judgments of our so-called scientific opponents. After all, we are here dealing almost exclusively with people whose sole claim to be heard rests on their impartiality— which they have preserved by keeping away from the facts of psycho-analysis. But I am aware that in other cases you will not let me get away so cheaply. You will point out that, after all, there are a great many people to whom my last remark does not apply. These people, you will say, have not kept away from analytical experience; they have analysed patients, they have perhaps even been analysed themselves, they were actually my colleagues for some time, and now they have come to other conclusions, and formed other theories, on the basis of which they have left me and have founded independent schools of psycho-analysis. You will expect me to give some explanation of the possibility and meaning of these dissenting movements which have occurred so frequently in the history of analysis.

Very well, then, I will try; but I shall only do it briefly, for it throws less light upon the nature of analysis than you might expect. I am sure that what you think of first will be Adler's Individual Psychology, which in America, for example, is looked on as being equal in importance to our psycho-analysis and as running on parallel lines, and is constantly mentioned in the same breath with it. In reality Individual Psychology has very little to do with analysis, but, for certain historical reasons, lives a sort of parasitic existence at its expense. The qualifications which we have predicated for this group of opponents only apply to the founders of Individual Psychology to a very limited extent. The name itself is unsuitable, and seems to be a product of embarrassment; we cannot assent to any interference with its correct application as meaning the opposite of Group Psychology; for the matter of that our own concern is, first and foremost, the psychology of the human individual. I am not going into an objective criticism of Adler's Individual Psychology today, for that is no part of my program in these lectures; besides which, I have already made such an attempt elsewhere, and I have little occasion for altering what I there said. I will, however, give you an illustration of the impression it makes, by telling you of a small incident which occurred to me in my pre-analytic years.

In the neighbourhood of the little Moravian town in which I was born and which I left as a child of three years old, there is a modest health resort, beautifully placed in a setting of green. During my school years I often spent my holidays there. Some twenty years later, the illness of a near relative of mine afforded me an opportunity of seeing the place again. In a conversation with the doctor in charge of the place, who had attended my relative, I enquired about his dealings with the—I believe

—Slovakian peasants, who were his only *clientèle* during the winter. He told me that his medical treatment was carried on in the following way. In his consulting hours the patients came into his room and formed up in a line. One after another they came forward and told him their complaints. One of them might have pains in the back, or a stomach-ache, or a feeling of tiredness in the legs, etc. The doctor then examined him and, when he had formed his conclusions, told him the diagnosis, which was in every case the same. He translated the word to me, and what it amounted to was: "bewitched." I was astonished, and asked whether the patients made no objection to his saying the same thing to all of his patients. "Oh, no!" he answered, "they are very much pleased; it is exactly what they expect. Each one as he goes back to his place in the line says to the others by his looks and gestures: 'There's a fellow who knows what's what!'" At that time I little thought in what circumstances I should meet with an analogous situation.

For whether a person is a homosexual, or a necrophilist, or an anxiety-ridden hysteric, or a shut-in obsessional, or a raving madman—in every case the Individual Psychologist of the Adlerian persuasion will assign as the motive force of his condition the fact that he wants to assert himself, to over-compensate for his inferiority, to be on top, and to move over from the feminine to the masculine line. We used to hear exactly the same kind of thing when we were young students at the hospital. Hysterics, we were told, produce their symptoms in order to make themselves interesting and to attract attention to themselves. It is extraordinary how these old profundities recur! But even at the time this little bit of psychology did not seem to us to cover the problem of hysteria; it left unexplained, for instance, why people who suffer from it do not make use of some means for the attainment of their ends. Some element of this doctrine of the Individual Psychologists must, of course, be correct, though they regard this fragmentary explanation as a complete one. The instinct of self-preservation will attempt to turn every situation to its own account; the ego will try to get some advantage even out of being ill. In psycho-analysis we call this the *secondary gain from illness*. But indeed, when one thinks of the facts of masochism, of the unconscious need for punishment, and of the neurotic tendency to self-injury, all of which seem to imply the existence of instinctual impulses which run counter to self-preservation, one comes to question even the general validity of the platitude on which the theoretical structure of Individual Psychology is built. But, to the mass of mankind, a theory like this must be exceedingly welcome, which takes no complications into account, which introduces no new and difficult concepts, which knows nothing of the unconscious, which removes at a single blow the problem of sexuality that weighs so heavily on everybody, and which confines itself to revealing the devices by means of which people try to make life comfortable. For the mass of mankind are themselves comfort-loving; they require only a single reason to serve as an explanation, they are not grateful to science for its intricacies, and they like to have simple answers given to their questions and to feel that their problems are settled once and for all. Once one sees how closely Individual Psychology approximates to the fulfilment of these requirements, one cannot help remembering a couplet from *Wallenstein:*

> *If the idea were not so deuced clever,*
> *One might be tempted just to call it stupid.*

Specialist criticism, which has been so uncompromisingly opposed to psycho-analysis, has, in general, handled Individual Psychology with a velvet glove. It is, indeed, true that in America one of the most distinguished psychiatrists published a paper against Adler, entitled *Enough*, in which he gave strong expression to his dissatisfaction with the *repetition-compulsion* of the Individual Psychologists. If others have behaved far more kindly, the opposition to analysis is largely responsible.

I need not say much about other schools that have split off from us. That such splits have occurred is no argument for or against the truth of psycho-analysis. You have only to think of the strong emotional factors which make it difficult for many people to co-operate with others or adopt a subordinate position, and of the still greater difficulty which is embodied in the proverb: *"Quot capita tot sensus."*[1] When the differences of opinion had gone beyond a certain limit, the best thing to do was to part company, and thenceforward to go different ways, especially if the theoretical difference involved an alteration in analytical technique. Let us take, for example, an analyst who thinks very little of the influence of the patient's past, and looks for the cause of a neurosis exclusively in contemporary motives and expectations directed towards the future.

[1] As many interpretations as heads.—Ed.

If that is so, he will also neglect the analysis of the patient's childhood and start on an altogether different technique; and he will have to make up for the absence of the effects of childhood-analysis by increasing his own didactic influence and by directly recommending the adoption of certain aims in life. We, for our part, would then say: "That may be a philosophy, but it is no longer analysis." Or another analyst may come to hold the view that the anxiety-experience of birth is the root of all later neurotic disturbances; in that case he may think it proper to restrict analysis to the effects of this one experience, and to promise therapeutic success after a three to four months' treatment. You will observe that I have chosen two examples which proceed from diametrically opposed premises. It is an almost universal characteristic of these *dissenting movements* that each of them seizes upon one fragment out of the wealth of motives found in psycho-analysis (such, for instance, as the instinct for the power, the ethical conflict, the mother, genitality, etc.), and, on the basis of this appropriation, makes itself independent. If it seems to you that such secessions are commoner today in the history of psycho-analysis than they are in any other movement of thought, I do not know whether I should agree with you. If it be so, we must attribute the responsibility to the close relationship between theoretical outlook and therapeutic practice, which is to be found in psycho-analysis. Mere differences of opinion would be borne with for far longer. People like to accuse us psycho-analysts of intolerance. The only evidence of this disagreeable characteristic was precisely our separation from people who thought differently from ourselves. Apart from that, we have taken no steps against them; on the contrary, they are now in clover; they are far better off than before, because, in parting company with us, they have in most cases got rid of one of the burdens under which we groan—the odium of infantile sexuality, for instance, or the ludicrousness of symbolism—and they are now regarded by the world at large as, at all events, semi-respectable, which we, who remain behind, cannot even yet claim to be. It was they themselves, moreover, who — excepting for one noteworthy example—effected the separation.

And what more do you ask of us in the name of tolerance? When any one has expressed an opinion that we hold to be fundamentally false, do you wish us to speak to him like this?

"Thank you so much for contradicting us. You have saved us from the danger of self-complacency, and have given us an opportunity of proving to the Americans that we really are as broadminded as they could possibly wish. We do not believe a word of what you say, but that does not matter. You are just as right as we are, in all probability. After all, who can ever know who is in the right? In spite of our disagreement, you must allow us to put forward your views in our publications. And we hope that you on your part will be so kind as to support ours although you disbelieve in them." This will obviously be the usage of the future in scientific circles, when the misapplication of Einstein's theory of relativity has completely won the day. It is true that, for the moment, we have not gone quite so far as that. We have confined ourselves, in the old-fashioned way, to putting forward only our own convictions; we expose ourselves to the danger of making mistakes, for no one can avoid that, and we reject anything that contradicts our views. As to the right to change our opinions, if we think we have found something better, we have made full use of it in psycho-analysis.

One of the first applications of psycho-analysis was that we were able to understand the opposition we had to meet on account of our psycho-analytic activities. Other applications, of an objective nature, can lay claim to a more general interest. Our first intention was, as you know, to understand the disturbances of the human mind, because an astonishing experience had shown us that in this case understanding and cure go almost hand in hand and that a practicable path leads from the one to the other. And for a long time this was our only intention. Then, however, we came to recognize the close relationship, in fact, the underlying identity, subsisting between pathological and so-called normal processes. So psycho-analysis became *depth-psychology;* and, since nothing that man makes or does can be understood without the aid of psychology, the applications of psycho-analysis to numerous fields of knowledge, and especially to the mental sciences, came about automatically, forced themselves on our attention and demanded elaboration. Unluckily, the tasks which we now undertook brought us up against obstacles, which, lying as they do in the very nature of the situation, have not yet been overcome. Such an application presupposes a technical knowledge which the analyst does not possess; while those who do possess the knowledge—the experts—do not know anything of analysis, and perhaps do not want to know anything. The result has been that analysts have entered the lists in such fields as those of mythology, the history of civilization, ethnology, the science of religion, etc., as amateurs, with a more or less adequate equipment, often collected in a hurry. In those fields they were treated by the specialists, who were established there, as no better than interlopers; and their methods, as well as their findings, in so far as they attracted any attention at all, were, to begin with, rejected. But the position is steadily improving; in every field, the number of people who study psycho-analysis with a view to making use of it in their special researches is growing, in the same way that colonists take the place of pioneers. Here we may expect a rich harvest of new knowledge. Applications of psycho-analysis are always confirmations of it as well. In regions where scientific work is more remote from practical activity, the inevitable differences of opinion will be less embittered.

I feel greatly tempted to take you through all the applications of psycho-analysis in the field of mental science. There are things which every one who has intellectual interests would think worth knowing, and to hear no more for a time about abnormalities and illness would give us a well-earned relief. But I must resist the temptation; it would once more take us too far outside the framework of these lectures, and, to tell you the truth, I should not be competent to do it. It is true that I took the first step along some of these lines, but today I no longer command a view over the whole field, and I should have to spend much time in study in order to grasp all that has been added since I made my first attempts. Those of you who are disappointed by my refusal can make up for it by reading our journal, *Imago,* which is devoted to the non-medical applications of analysis.

There is one subject, however, that I cannot pass by so easily, though this is not because I have any special understanding of it or have done much work on it myself. On the contrary, I have hardly ever occupied myself with it. But it is of immense importance, and rich in hopes for the future; perhaps, indeed, it is the most important of all the activities of analysis. I refer to the application of psycho-analysis to education, to the up-bringing of the next generation. I am at least glad to be able to say that my daughter, Anna Freud, has made this her life-work, and is in this way making good my own neglect of the subject. One can easily see the path that has led to this application of analysis. When, during the treatment of an adult neurotic, we tried to trace the determination of his symptoms, we were always led back into his early childhood. A knowledge of the later aetiological factors was not sufficient either for our understanding of his condition or to effect a cure. The result was that we were forced to acquaint ourselves with the psychological peculiarities of the years of infancy; and we learned a great many things which could not have been discovered except through analysis, and were in a position to set right a number of generally accepted beliefs about childhood. We came to see that the first years of infancy (up to about the age of five) are, for a number of reasons, of special importance. This is, in the first place, because they contain the first expansion of sexuality, which leaves behind decisive determinants for the sexual life of maturity; and, in the second place, because the impressions of this period come up against an unformed and weak ego, upon which they act like traumas. The ego cannot defend itself against the emotional storms which they call forth except by repression, and in this way it acquires in childhood all its predispositions to subsequent illnesses and disturbances of function. We have come to realize that the difficulty of childhood consists in the fact that the child has, in a short span of time, to make its own the acquisitions of a cultural development which has extended over tens of thousands of years; it has, that is, to attain instinctual control and social adaptation, or, at any rate, their first elements. It can only achieve a part of this alteration through its own development; a great deal must be forced upon it by education. We are not in the least surprised that the child often performs its task only incompletely. A great many children in these early years pass through conditions which may be compared with neuroses, and this is certainly true of all those who develop a manifest illness later on. In not a few cases the neurotic illness does not wait till they are grown up, but breaks out in childhood and is a source of great trouble to parents and doctors.

We have had no hesitation in applying analytic therapy to such children as either display unambiguous neurotic symptoms, or are on the way to an unfavourable character-development. The anxiety expressed by opponents of analysis, that the child might be harmed by the process, has turned out to be quite unfounded.

The advantage gained by this procedure is that we have been able to confirm in the living subject what we have only inferred, as though from historical documents, in the case of adults. But the advantages gained by the children themselves was most satisfactory. It turned out that the child is a most favourable subject for analytic therapy; successes were radical and permanent. Naturally, one has to make extensive alterations in the technique of treatment which has been developed for adults when one is dealing with children. The child is, psychologically, a different thing from the adult; it does not yet possess a super-ego, it cannot make much use of the method of free association, and transference plays a different part with it, since its real parents are still there. The internal resistances, against which we have to fight in the case of adults, are in the case of children for the most part replaced by external difficulties. If the parents make themselves into vehicles for the resistance, the aims of the analysis and even the process of the analysis itself, are often endangered. For this reason, it is often necessary to combine a certain amount of analytic influencing of the parents with the analysis of the children. On the other hand, the inevitable differences between child analysis and adult analysis are diminished by the fact that many of our patients have still kept so many of their infantile character-traits that the analyst, once more adapting himself to his patient, cannot avoid making use of certain parts of the technique of child analysis in their case too. It is in the nature of things that child analysis should have become the special field of women analysts, and this will no doubt continue to be so.

The view that the majority of our children pass through a neurotic phase in the course of their development automatically raises a hygienic question. It may be asked whether it would not be advantageous to come to the aid of a child with analysis even where there is no sign of a disturbance, as a precautionary measure in the interests of its health, just as nowadays one inoculates healthy children against diphtheria, without waiting for them to fall ill of the disease. The discussion of this question is today only a matter of academic interest. I can venture to speak about it to you; but the greater number of our contemporaries would regard the mere idea as nothing short of criminal, and, when one considers the attitude of most parents towards analysis, one must, as yet, give up any hope of its realization. Such a prophylactic against nervous disease, which would probably be very effective, presupposes an entirely different structure of society. The application of psycho-analysis to education must be looked for today in quite a different direction. Let us get a clear idea of what the primary business of education is. The child has to learn to control its instincts. To grant it complete freedom, so that it obeys all its impulses without any restriction, is impossible. It would be a very instructive experiment for child-psychologists, but it would make life impossible for the parents and would do serious damage to the children themselves, as would be seen partly at the time, and partly during subsequent years. The function of education, therefore, is to inhibit, forbid, and suppress, and it has at all times carried out this function to admiration. But we have learnt from analysis that it is this very suppression of instincts that involves the danger of neurotic illness. You will remember that we have gone into the question of how this comes about in some detail. Education has therefore to steer its way between the Scylla of giving the instincts free play and the Charybdis of frustrating them. Unless the problem is altogether insoluble, an optimum of education must be discovered, which will do the most good and the least harm. It is a matter of finding out how much one may forbid, at which times, and by what methods. And then it must further be considered that the children have very different constitutional dispositions, so that the same educational procedure cannot possibly be equally good for all children. A moment's consideration will show us that, so far, education has fulfilled its function very badly, and has done children serious injury. If we can find an optimum of education which will carry out its task ideally, then we may hope to abolish one of the factors in the aetiology of neurotic illness, viz., the influence of accidental infantile traumas. The other factor, the power of a refractory instinctual constitution, can never be got rid of by education. When, therefore, one comes to think of the difficult tasks with which the educator is confronted; when one reflects that he has to recognize the characteristic constitution of each child, to guess from small indications what is going on in its unformed mind, to give him the right amount of love and at the same time to preserve an effective degree of authority, then one cannot help saying to oneself that the only adequate preparation for the profession of educator is a good grounding in psycho-anal-

ysis. The best thing would be for him to be analysed himself, for, after all, without personal experience one cannot get a grasp of analysis. The analysis of teachers and educators seems to be a more practicable prophylactic measure than the analysis of children themselves; and there are not such great obstacles against putting it into practice.

I will only mention, in passing, an indirect advantage which analysis may bring to the education of children, an advantage which may eventually come to have considerable importance. Parents who have experienced an analysis themselves, and who have derived much benefit from it, among other things an insight into the mistakes in their own upbringing, will treat their children with better understanding, and will spare them a great deal which they were not spared themselves. Parallel with the efforts of the analyst to influence education, run other investigations into the cause and prevention of delinquency and criminology. Here again I shall only open the door and show you what lies behind it, but I shall not take you inside. If your interest in psycho-analysis is maintained, you will be able to learn a great deal that is both new and valuable on these subjects. I cannot, however, leave the theme of education without mentioning one particular point of view. It has been said—and no doubt with justice—that every education is partisan; it aims at making the child adapt itself to whatever social system is the established one, without consideration of how valuable or how stable that system may be. If, it is argued, one is convinced of the shortcomings of our present-day social arrangements, one cannot think it right to give them the added support of this psycho-analytical education of ours. We must place before it another and a higher aim, one which is emancipated from the social standards that are dominent today. I do not feel, however, that this argument is valid. It is demanding more of analysis than its functions can justify. The physician who is called in to treat a case of pneumonia has no need to consider whether the patient is a good man, a suicide, or a criminal; whether he deserves to remain alive, or whether it is for his advantage to do so. This other aim which it is sought to place before education would be a partisan one as well, and it is not the business of the analyst to decide between parties. I am not now considering the fact that people will refuse to allow psycho-analysis to have any influence at all on education if it confesses to aims which are incompatible with the existing social order. Psycho-analytic education will be assuming an unwarranted responsibility if it sets out to make its pupils into revolutionaries. It will have done its task if it sends them away as healthy and as efficient as possible. There are enough revolutionary elements contained within itself to ensure that no one brought up under its influence will in later life be on the side of reaction and suppression. I should go so far as to say that revolutionary children are not desirable from any point of view.

Ladies and Gentlemen—I shall conclude by saying a few words on the therapeutic aspect of psycho-analysis. I discussed the theoretical side of the subject fifteen years ago, and I cannot formulate it in any other way today; but I will say something about the practical experience which we have had with it during the interval. You know, of course, that psycho-analysis originated as a therapeutic procedure; it has gone far beyond that, but it has never given up its original field of work, and it still relies upon contact with clinical material for its further advances and development. The accumulation of empirical data upon which we base our theories can be obtained in no other way. Our therapeutic failures are constantly setting us new tasks, and the requirements of real life are an efficient protection against carrying to excess the speculation which we, nevertheless, cannot avoid in our work. I have already, in my former lectures, given an account of the means by which psycho-analysis helps the patient, and along what lines; today we will consider to what extent it succeeds.

You are perhaps aware that I have never been a therapeutic enthusiast; and there is no danger of my using this as an opportunity for ringing the praises of analysis in this respect. I would rather say too little than too much. At a time when I was still the only analyst, people who were apparently kindly disposed to my opinions used to say to me: "That is all very nice and clever; but show me a case that you have cured by analysis." This was one of the many formulas that succeeded one another, as time went on, whose function it was to put the inconvenient novelty on one side. Today it is as out of date as many others; the analyst, like any other therapeutist, has his collection of letters of gratitude from patients who have been cured. And the analogy does not end there. Psycho-analysis really is a form of therapy, just as other methods are. It has its triumphs, its defeats, its difficulties, its limitations, and its indications. There was a time when people attacked analysis with the accusation that it was not to be taken seriously as a therapy, because it did not venture to publish any statistics of its successes. Since then, the Institute of Psycho-Analysis in Berlin, which was founded by Dr. Max Eitingon, has published a report of its work during the first ten years of its existence. The proportion of recoveries which have been effected give us ground neither for boasting nor for feeling ashamed. But such statistics are not instructive, because the material with which they deal is so heterogeneous that it would need a very large number of cases to prove anything. It is better to examine one's own individual experience. As to that, I may say that I do not think our successes can compete with those of Lourdes. There are so many more people who believe in the miracles of the Blessed Virgin than in the existence of the unconscious. But if we disregard supernatural competition, we must compare psycho-analysis with other methods of psycho-therapy. Nowadays one need hardly take into consideration organic physical treatment of neurotic conditions. As a psycho-therapeutic method, analysis does not stand in opposition to other methods employed in this branch of medicine; it does not invalidate them nor does it exclude them. There would be no theoretical objection to a physician who described himself as a psycho-therapeutist using analysis upon his patients alongside other therapeutic methods, according to the peculiar character of the case and the favourable or unfavourable nature of the circumstances. In actual fact, it is the question of technique which renders necessary the specialization of medical practice. So, for example, it became necessary to separate surgery and orthopaedics. The practice of psycho-analysis is difficult and exacting! It cannot well be dealt with like a pair of spectacles, which can be put on for reading and taken off when one wants to go for a walk. As a rule, psycho-analysis either possesses the doctor entirely or not at all. The psycho-therapeutists who occasionally make use of analysis do not, as far as my experience goes, stand on a firm analytical basis; they have not accepted analysis as a whole, but have watered it down, and perhaps removed its sting; they cannot be counted as analysts. In my opinion this is to be regretted; but a co-operation in medical practice between an analyst and a psycho-therapeutist who limits himself to other methods, would be altogether advantageous.

Compared with other psycho-therapeutic procedures, psycho-analysis is far and away the most powerful. That is quite as it should be, since it costs the most trouble and time, and one would not make use of it for slight cases; in suitable cases, one can remove disturbances and bring about alterations which could not be hoped for in pre-analytic times. But it has also perfectly clearly felt limitations. The therapeutic ambitions of many of my followers have led them to be at great pains to remove such hindrances, so that all neurotic disturbances might be curable by means of psycho-analysis. They have attempted to compress the work of analysis into a shorter period, to intensify the transference so that it should be superior to any resistance, and to combine other methods of influence with analysis in order to obtain a cure. These enterprises are no doubt praiseworthy, but in my opinion they are in vain. They also involve the danger of oneself being drawn away from analysis and of drifting into a boundless sea of experimentation. The expectation that we shall be able to cure all neurotic symptoms is, I suspect, derived from the lay belief that neuroses are entirely superfluous things which have no right whatever to exist. As a matter of fact, they are serious, constitutionally determined affections, which are seldom restricted to a few outbreaks, but make themselves felt as a rule over long periods of life, or even throughout its entire extent. Our analytic experience that we can influence them to a far-reaching degree, if we can get hold of the historical precipitating causes and the incidental accessory factors, has made us neglect the constitutional factor in our therapeutic practice. And we are in fact powerless to deal with it; but in our theory we ought always to bear it in mind. In any case, the complete inaccessibility of the psychoses to analytic therapy should, in view of their close relationship to the neuroses, moderate our optimism in regard to the latter. The therapeutic efficiency of psycho-analysis is limited by a whole series of important factors, which can scarcely be dealt with at all. With children, where one might hope to have the greatest successes, there are the external difficulties of the parental situation; yet, after all, these are bound up with the very fact of being a child. With adults we are primarily concerned with two factors, the degree of their mental rigidity and the form of their disease with all the deeper-seated determinants that lie behind it. The former of these is often unjustifiably overlooked. However great the plasticity of mental life may be, and however great the possibility of reviving past states, not everything can be brought to life again. A great many alterations seem final, and correspond to scars left behind by processes which have run their course. In other cases one gets an impression of a general rigidity of the whole mind; mental processes, which one could very well redirect into other channels, seem incapable of leaving their old courses. But perhaps this is the same as what we have said already, but looked at from another point of view. Only too often one seems to see that the therapeutic process is merely lacking in the necessary motive force to enable it to bring about the alteration. Some specific tendency, some particular instinctual component, is too strong in comparison with the counter-forces that we can mobilize against it. This is quite generally so in the case of the psychoses. We understand them in so far as we know quite well where we ought to apply the levers, but they are not able to lift the weight. In this connection we may hope that in the future our knowledge of the action of hormones—you know, of course, what they are —will provide us with a means of coping successfully with the quantitative factors involved in these diseases; but today we are far from having reached that desirable goal. I can understand that the uncertainty prevailing in all these matters is a constant incentive towards perfecting the technique of analysis, especially in the matter of the transference. The beginner in analysis, in particular, will be in doubt, when he is unsuccessful, whether he ought to blame the peculiarity of the case or his own unskilful handling of the therapeutic procedure. But, as I have said already, I do not think that there is much to be gained by directing one's energies along these channels.

The other limitation to analytical successes is imposed by the form of the disease. You know already that the field in which analytical therapy can be applied is that of the transference-neuroses, phobias, hysterias, obsessional neuroses, and, besides these, such abnormalities of character as have been developed instead of these diseases. Everything other than these, such as narcissistic or psychotic conditions, is more or less unsuitable. Now it would be perfectly legitimate to save oneself from failures by carefully excluding such cases. If this precaution were taken, the statistics of analysis would be very much improved. Yes; but this is not so easy as it seems. Our diagnoses can very often only be made *ex post facto*. They are like the test for witch-finding applied by the Scottish king, of which I have read in one of Victor Hugo's books. This king declared that he had an infallible method for detecting witches. He put them to simmer in a cauldron of boiling water, and then tasted the soup. According to the taste he could say "that was a witch," or "that was not a witch." The same thing happens with us, except that it is we who are the sufferers. We cannot give an opinion about a patient who comes for treatment, or a candidate for training, until we have studied him analytically for some weeks or months. We are, in fact, always buying a pig in a poke. The subject comes to us with undefined, general troubles which do not allow of any certain diagnosis. After a period of probation, it may turn out that the case is an unsuitable one. Then, if he is a candidate, we send him away; or, if he is a patient, we keep him on a little while to see whether we cannot take a more favourable view of him. The patient has his revenge by swelling our list of failures, and the rejected candidate, it may be (if he is paranoid), by writing psycho-analytical books himself. You will observe that our caution has not been of much value to us.

I am afraid these details will have gone beyond the scope of your interests. But I should be even more distressed if you were to think that I intend to diminish your respect for psycho-analysis as a therapeutic procedure. Perhaps I have really set about the business clumsily. I wanted, you see, to achieve the opposite: to excuse the therapeutic limitations of analysis by indicating how unavoidable they are. With the same object in view, let me turn to another point, namely the complaint that analytic treatment takes up a disproportionately long time. The answer to that is that psychological changes only come about very slowly; if they occur quickly and suddenly it is a bad sign. It is true that the treatment of a serious neurosis may easily last several years, but, if a successful result is achieved, you must ask yourselves how long the illness itself would otherwise have lasted. It would probably have lasted a decade for every year of treatment, which means that the illness would never have passed off at all, as we so often find in untreated cases. In many instances we have reasons for resuming an analysis after an interval of many years; new events in the patient's life

have called out in him new pathological reactions, though in the meantime he has been perfectly healthy. The first analysis had not actually brought all his pathological dispositions to the surface, and it was natural that the analysis should have been broken off as soon as it was successful. There are also people who are so seriously afflicted that they have to be kept under analytic care throughout their whole lives and taken back into analysis from time to time; but such people would otherwise be incapable of carrying on their lives at all, and one must be thankful that they can be kept going by means of this intermittent and recurrent treatment. The analysis of characterological disturbances, too, involves a lengthy treatment but it is often successful; and it may be asked whether there is any other form of treatment that could even attempt to deal with this problem. Therapeutic ambition may make us feel unsatisfied with these results, but after all we have the examples of tuberculosis and lupus before us, which teach us that one can only meet with success if the treatment is adapted to the character of the disease.

I have told you that psycho-analysis began as a therapeutic procedure, but it is not in that light that I wanted to recommend it to your interest, but because of the truths it contains, because of the information it gives us about that which is of the greatest importance to mankind, namely his own nature, and because of the connections it has shown to exist between the most various of his activities. As a form of therapy it is one among many, though certainly *prima inter pares*.[1] If it had no therapeutic value, it would not have been discovered from clinical material and would not have continued to develop for more than thirty years.

LECTURE 35

A Philosophy of Life

Ladies and Gentlemen: In the last lecture we were occupied with trivial everyday affairs, with putting, as it were, our modest house in order. We will now take a bold step, and risk an answer to a question which has repeatedly been raised in non-analytic quarters, namely, the question whether psycho-analysis leads to any particular *Weltanschauung*, and if so, to what.

Weltanschauung is, I am afraid, a specifically German notion, which it would be difficult to

[1] Chief among equals.—Ed.

translate into a foreign language. If I attempt to give you a definition of the word, it can hardly fail to strike you as inept. By *Weltanschauung*, then, I mean an intellectual construction, which gives a unified solution of all the problems of our existence in virtue of a comprehensive hypothesis, a construction, therefore, in which no question is left open and in which everything in which we are interested finds a place. It is easy to see that the possession of such a *Weltanschauung* is one of the ideal wishes of mankind. When one believes in such a thing, one feels secure in life, one knows what one ought to strive after, and how one ought to organize one's emotions and interests to the best purpose.

If that is what is meant by a *Weltanschauung*, then the question is an easy one for psycho-analysis to answer. As a specialized science, a branch of psychology—depth-psychology or psychology of the unconscious—it is quite unsuited to form a *Weltanschauung* of its own; it must accept that of science in general. The scientific *Weltanschauung* is, however, markedly at variance with our definition. The *unified* nature of the explanation of the universe is, it is true, accepted by science, but only as a program whose fulfilment is postponed to the future. Otherwise it is distinguished by negative characteristics, by a limitation to what is, at any given time, knowable, and a categorical rejection of certain elements which are alien to it. It asserts that there is no other source of knowledge of the universe, but the intellectual manipulation of carefully verified observations, in fact, what is called *research*, and that no knowledge can be obtained from revelation, intuition, or inspiration. It appears that this way of looking at things came very near to receiving general acceptance during the last century or two. It has been reserved for the present century to raise the objection that such a *Weltanschauung* is both empty and unsatisfying, that it overlooks all the spiritual demands of man, and all the needs of the human mind.

This objection cannot be too strongly repudiated. It cannot be supported for a moment, for the spirit and the mind are the subject of scientific investigation in exactly the same way as any non-human entities. Psycho-analysis has a peculiar right to speak on behalf of the scientific *Weltanschauung* in this connection, because it cannot be accused of neglecting the part occupied by the mind in the universe. The contribution of psycho-analysis to science con-

sists precisely in having extended research to the region of the mind. Certainly without such a psychology, science would be very incomplete. But if we add to science the investigation of the intellectual and emotional functions of men (and animals), we find that nothing has been altered as regards the general position of science, that there are no new sources of knowledge or methods of research. Intuition and inspiration would be such, if they existed; but they can safely be counted as illusions, as fulfilments of wishes. It is easy to see, moreover, that the qualities which, as we have shown, are expected of a *Weltanschauung* have a purely emotional basis. Science takes account of the fact that the mind of man creates such demands and is ready to trace their source, but it has not the slightest ground for thinking them justified. On the contrary, it does well to distinguish carefully between illusion (the results of emotional demands of that kind) and knowledge.

This does not at all imply that we need push these wishes contemptuously aside, or underestimate their value in the lives of human beings. We are prepared to take notice of the fulfilments they have achieved for themselves in the creations of art and in the systems of religion and philosophy; but we cannot overlook the fact that it would be wrong and highly inexpedient to allow such things to be carried over into the domain of knowledge. For in that way one would open the door which gives access to the region of the psychoses, whether individual or group psychoses, and one would drain off from these tendencies valuable energy which is directed towards reality and which seeks by means of reality to satisfy wishes and needs as far as this is possible.

From the point of view of science we must necessarily make use of our critical powers in this direction, and not be afraid to reject and deny. It is inadmissible to declare that science is one field of human intellectual activity, and that religion and philosophy are others, at least as valuable, and that science has no business to interfere with the other two, that they all have an equal claim to truth, and that every one is free to choose whence he shall draw his convictions and in what he shall place his belief. Such an attitude is considered particularly respectable, tolerant, broad-minded, and free from narrow prejudices. Unfortunately it is not tenable; it shares all the pernicious qualities of an entirely unscientific *Weltanschauung* and in practice comes to much the same thing. The bare fact is that truth cannot be tolerant and cannot admit compromise or limitations, that scientific research looks on the whole field of human activity as its own, and must adopt an uncompromisingly critical attitude towards any other power that seeks to usurp any part of its province.

Of the three forces which can dispute the position of science, religion alone is a really serious enemy. Art is almost always harmless and beneficent, it does not seek to be anything else but an illusion. Save in the case of a few people who are, one might say, obsessed by Art, it never dares to make any attacks on the realm of reality. Philosophy is not opposed to science; it behaves itself as if it were a science, and to a certain extent it makes use of the same methods; but it parts company with science, in that it clings to the illusion that it can produce a complete and coherent picture of the universe, though in fact that picture must needs fall to pieces with every new advance in our knowledge. Its methodological error lies in the fact that it over-estimates the epistemological value of our logical operations, and to a certain extent admits the validity of other sources of knowledge, such as intuition. And often enough one feels that the poet Heine is not unjustified when he says of the philosopher:

With his night-cap and his night-shirt tatters,
He botches up the loop-holes in the structure of
the world.

But philosophy has no immediate influence on the great majority of mankind; it interests only a small number even of the thin upper stratum of intellectuals, while all the rest find it beyond them. In contradistinction to philosophy, religion is a tremendous force, which exerts its power over the strongest emotions of human beings. As we know, at one time it included everything that played any part in the mental life of mankind, that it took the place of science, when as yet science hardly existed, and that it built up a *Weltanschauung* of incomparable consistency and coherence which, although it has been severely shaken, has lasted to this day.

If one wishes to form a true estimate of the full grandeur of religion, one must keep in mind what it undertakes to do for men. It gives them information about the source and origin of the universe, it assures them of protection and final happiness amid the changing vicissitudes of life, and it guides their thoughts and actions by means of precepts which are backed by the whole force of its authority. It fulfils, therefore, three functions. In the first place, it satisfies man's desire for knowledge; it is here doing the same thing that science attempts to accomplish by its own methods, and here, therefore, enters into rivalry with it. It is to the second function that it performs, that religion no doubt owes the greater part of its influence. In so far as religion brushes away men's fear of the dangers and vicissitudes of life, in so far as it assures them of a happy ending, and comforts them in their misfortunes, science cannot compete with it. Science, it is true, teaches how one can avoid certain dangers and how one can combat many sufferings with success; it would be quite untrue to deny that science is a powerful aid to human beings, but in many cases it has to leave them to their suffering, and can only advise them to submit to the inevitable. In the performance of its third function, the provision of precepts, prohibitions, and restrictions, religion is furthest removed from science. For science is content with discovering and stating the facts. It is true that, from the applications of science, rules and recommendations for behaviour may be deduced. In certain circumstances they may be the same as those which are laid down by religion, but even so the reasons for them will be different.

It is not quite clear why religion should combine these three functions. What has the explanation of the origin of the universe to do with the inculcation of certain ethical precepts? Its assurances of protection and happiness are more closely connected with these precepts. They are the reward for the fulfilment of the commands; only he who obeys them can count on receiving these benefits, while punishment awaits the disobedient. For the matter of that, something of the same kind applies to science; for it declares that any one who disregards its inferences is liable to suffer for it.

One can only understand this remarkable combination of teaching, consolation, and precept in religion, if one subjects it to genetic analysis. We may begin with the most remarkable item of the three, the teaching about the origin of the universe—for why should a cosmogony be a regular element of religious systems? The doctrine is that the universe was created by a being similar to man, but greater in every respect, in power, wisdom, and strength of passion, in fact by an idealized superman.

Where you have animals as creators of the universe, you have indications of the influence of Totemism, which I shall touch on later, at any rate with a brief remark. It is interesting to notice that this creator of the universe is always a single god, even when many gods are believed in. Equally interesting is the fact that the creator is nearly always a male, although there is no lack of indication of the existence of female deities and many mythologies make the creation of the world begin precisely with a male god triumphing over a female goddess, who is degraded into a monster. This raises the most fascinating minor problems, but we must hurry on. The rest of our enquiry is made easy because this God-Creator is openly called Father. Psycho-analysis concludes that he really is the father, clothed in the grandeur in which he once appeared to the small child. The religious man's picture of the creation of the universe is the same as his picture of his own creation.

If this is so, then it is easy to understand how it is that the comforting promises of protection and the severe ethical commands are found together with the cosmogony. For the same individual, to whom the child owes its own existence, the father (or, more correctly, the parental function which is composed of the father and the mother), has protected and watched over the weak and helpless child, exposed as it is to all the dangers which threaten in the external world; in its father's care it has felt itself safe. Even the grown man, though he may know that he possesses greater strength, and though he has greater insight into the dangers of life, rightly feels that fundamentally he is just as helpless and unprotected as he was in childhood and that in relation to the external world he is still a child. Even now, therefore, he cannot give up the protection which he has enjoyed as a child. But he has long ago realized that his father is a being with strictly limited powers and by no means endowed with every desirable attribute. He therefore looks back to the memory-image of the overrated father of his childhood, exalts it into a deity, and brings it into the present and into reality. The emotional strength of this memory-image and the lasting nature of his need for protection are the two supports of his belief in God.

The third main point of the religious program, its ethical precepts, can also be related without any difficulty to the situation of childhood. In a famous passage, which I have already quoted in an earlier lecture, the philoso-pher Kant speaks of the starry heaven above us and the moral law within us as the strongest evidence for the greatness of God. However odd it may sound to put these two side by side—for what can the heavenly bodies have to do with the question whether one man loves another or kills him?—nevertheless it touches on a great psychological truth. The same father (the parental function) who gave the child his life and preserved it from the dangers which that life involves, also taught it what it may or may not do, made it accept certain limitations of its instinctual wishes, and told it what consideration it would be expected to show towards its parents and brothers and sisters, if it wanted to be tolerated and liked as a member of the family circle, and later on of more extensive groups. The child is brought up to know its social duties by means of a system of love-rewards and punishments, and in this way it is taught that its security in life depends on its parents (and, subsequently, other people) loving it and being able to believe in its love for them. This whole state of affairs is carried over by the grown man unaltered into his religion. The prohibitions and commands of his parents live on in his breast as his moral conscience; God rules the world of men with the help of the same system of rewards and punishments, and the degree of protection and happiness which each individual enjoys, depends on his fulfilment of the demands of morality; the feeling of security, with which he fortifies himself against the dangers both of the external world and of his human environment, is founded on his love of God and the consciousness of God's love for him. Finally, he has in prayer a direct influence on the divine will, and in that way insures for himself a share in the divine omnipotence.

I am sure that while you have been listening to me, a whole host of questions must have come into your minds which you would like to have answered. I cannot undertake to do so here and now, but I am perfectly certain that none of these questions of detail would shake our thesis that the religious *Weltenschauung* is determined by the situation that subsisted in our childhood. It is therefore all the more remarkable that, in spite of its infantile character, it nevertheless has a forerunner. There was, without doubt, a time when there were no religions and no gods. It is known as the *age of animism*. Even at that time the world was full of spirits in the semblance of men (demons, as we call them), and all the objects in the external world were their dwelling-place or perhaps identical with them, but there was no supreme power which had created them all, which controlled them, and to which it was possible to turn for protection and aid. The demons of animism were usually hostile to man, but it seems as though man had more confidence in himself in those days than later on. He was no doubt in constant terror of these evil spirits, but he defended himself against them by means of certain actions to which he ascribed the power to drive them away. Nor did he think himself entirely powerless in other ways. If he wanted something from nature—rain, for instance—he did not direct a prayer to the weather-god, but used a spell, by means of which he expected to exert a direct influence over nature; he himself made something which resembled rain. In his fight against the powers of the surrounding world, his first weapon was magic, the first forerunner of our modern technology. We suppose that this confidence in magic is derived from the overestimation of the individual's own intellectual operations, from the belief in the *omnipotence of thoughts,* which, incidentally, we come across again in our obsessional neurotics. We may imagine that the men of that time were particularly proud of their acquisition of speech, which must have been accompanied by a great facilitation of thought. They attributed magic power to the spoken word. This feature was later on taken over by religion. "And God said: Let there be light, and there was light." But the fact of magic actions shows that animistic man did not rely entirely on the force of his own wishes. On the contrary, he depended for success upon the performance of an action, which would cause Nature to imitate it. If he wanted it to rain, he himself poured out water; if he wanted to stimulate the soil to fertility, he offered it a performance of sexual intercourse in the fields.

You know how tenaciously anything that has once found psychological expression persists. You will, therefore, not be surprised to hear that a great many manifestations of animism have lasted up to the present day, mostly as what are called *superstitions,* side by side with and behind religion. But more than that, you can hardly avoid coming to the conclusion that our philosophy has preserved essential traits of animistic modes of thought, such as the overestimation of the magic of words and the belief that real processes in the external world follow the lines laid down by our thoughts. It

is, to be sure, an animism without magical practices. On the other hand we should expect to find that in the age of animism there must already have been some kind of morality, some rules governing the intercourse of men with one another. But there is no evidence that they were closely bound up with animistic beliefs. Probably they were the immediate expression of the distribution of power and of practical necessities.

It would be very interesting to know what determined the transition from animism to religion; but you may imagine in what darkness this earliest epoch in the evolution of the human mind is still shrouded. It seems to be a fact that the earliest form in which religion appeared was the remarkable one of totemism, the worship of animals, in the train of which followed the first ethical commands, the taboos. In a book called *Totem and Taboo,* I once worked out a suggestion, in accordance with which this change is to be traced back to an upheaval in the relationships in the human family. The main achievement of religion, as compared with animism, lies in the psychic binding of the fear of demons. Nevertheless, the evil spirit still has a place in the religious system as a relic of the previous age.

So much for the pre-history of the religious *Weltanschauung.* Let us now turn to consider what has happened since, and what is still going on under our own eyes. The scientific spirit, strengthened by the observation of natural processes, began in the course of time to treat religion as a human matter, and to subject it to a critical examination. This test it failed to pass. In the first place, the accounts of miracles roused a feeling of surprise and disbelief, since they contradicted everything that sober observation had taught, and betrayed all too clearly the influence of human imagination. In the next place, its account of the nature of the universe had to be rejected, because it showed evidence of a lack of knowledge which bore the stamp of earlier days, and because, owing to increasing familiarity with the laws of nature, it had lost its authority. The idea that the universe came into being through an act of generation or creation, analogous to that which produces an individual human being, no longer seemed to be the most obvious and self-evident hypothesis; for the distinction between living and sentient beings and inanimate nature had become apparent to the human mind, and had made it impossible to retain the original animistic theory. Besides this, one must not overlook the influence of the comparative study of different religious systems, and the impression they give of mutual exclusiveness and intolerance.

Fortified by these preliminary efforts, the scientific spirit at last summoned up courage to put to the test the most important and the most emotionally significant elements of the religious *Weltanschauung*. The truth could have been seen at any time, but it was long before any one dared to say it aloud: the assertions made by religion that it could give protection and happiness to men, if they would only fulfil certain ethical obligations, were unworthy of belief. It seems not to be true that there is a power in the universe, which watches over the well-being of every individual with parental care and brings all his concerns to a happy ending. On the contrary, the destinies of man are incompatible with a universal principle of benevolence or with—what is to some degree contradictory—a universal principle of justice. Earthquakes, floods, and fires do not differentiate between the good and devout man, and the sinner and unbeliever. And, even if we leave inanimate nature out of account and consider the destinies of individual men in so far as they depend on their relations with others of their own kind, it is by no means the rule that virtue is rewarded and wickedness punished, but it happens often enough that the violent, the crafty, and the unprincipled seize the desirable goods of the earth for themselves, while the pious go empty away. Dark, unfeeling, and unloving powers determine human destiny; the system of rewards and punishments, which, according to religion, governs the world, seems to have no existence. This is another occasion for abandoning a portion of the animism which has found refuge in religion.

The last contribution to the criticism of the religious *Weltanschauung* has been made by psycho-analysis, which has traced the origin of religion to the helplessness of childhood, and its content to the persistence of the wishes and needs of childhood into maturity. This does not precisely imply a refutation of religion, but it is a necessary rounding off of our knowledge about it, and, at least on one point, it actually contradicts it, for religion lays claim to a divine origin. This claim, to be sure, is not false if our interpretation of God is accepted.

The final judgment of science on the religious *Weltanschauung*, then, runs as follows. While the different religions wrangle with one another as to which of them is in possession of the truth, in our view the truth of religion may be altogether disregarded. Religion is an attempt to get control over the sensory world, in which we are placed, by means of the wish-world, which we have developed inside us as a result of biological and psychological necessities. But it cannot achieve its end. Its doctrines carry with them the stamp of the times in which they originated, the ignorant childhood days of the human race. Its consolations deserve no trust. Experience teaches us that the world is not a nursery. The ethical commands, to which religion seeks to lend its weight, require some other foundations instead, for human society cannot do without them, and it is dangerous to link up obedience to them with religious belief. If one attempts to assign to religion its place in man's evolution, it seems not so much to be a lasting acquisition, as a parallel to the neurosis which the civilized individual must pass through on his way from childhood to maturity.

You are, of course, perfectly free to criticise this account of mine, and I am prepared to meet you half way. What I have said about the gradual crumbling of the religious *Weltanschauung* was no doubt an incomplete abridgement of the whole story; the order of the separate events was not quite correctly given, and the co-operation of various forces towards the awakening of the scientific spirit was not traced. I have also left out of account the alterations which occurred in the religious *Weltanschauung* itself, both during the period of its unchallenged authority and afterwards under the influence of awakening criticism. Finally I have, strictly speaking, limited my remarks to one single form of religion, that of the Western peoples. I have, as it were, constructed a lay-figure for the purposes of a demonstration which I desired to be as rapid and as impressive as possible. Let us leave on one side the question of whether my knowledge would in any case have been sufficient to enable me to do it better or more completely. I am aware that you can find all that I have said elsewhere, and find it better said; none of it is new. But I am firmly convinced that the most careful elaboration of the material upon which the problems of religion are based would not shake these conclusions.

As you know, the struggle between the scientific spirit and the religious *Weltanschauung* is not yet at an end; it is still going on under our very eyes today. However little psycho-analysis may make use as a rule of polemical weapons, we will not deny ourselves the pleasure of look-

NEW INTRODUCTORY LECTURES ON PSYCHO-ANALYSIS

ing into this conflict. Incidentally, we may perhaps arrive at a clearer understanding of our attitude towards the *Weltanschauung*. You will see how easily some of the arguments which are brought forward by the supporters of religion can be disproved; though others may succeed in escaping refutation.

The first objection that one hears is to the effect that it is an impertinence on the part of science to take religion as a subject for its investigations, since religion is something supreme, something superior to the capacities of the human understanding, something which must not be approached with the sophistries of criticism. In other words, science is not competent to sit in judgment on religion. No doubt it is quite useful and valuable, so long as it is restricted to its own province; but religion does not lie in that province, and with religion it can have nothing to do. If we are not deterred by this brusque dismissal, but enquire on what grounds religion bases its claim to an exceptional position among human concerns, the answer we receive, if indeed we are honoured with an answer at all, is that religion cannot be measured by human standards, since it is of divine origin, and has been revealed to us by a spirit which the human mind cannot grasp. It might surely be thought that nothing could be more easily refuted than this argument; it is an obvious *petitio principii*, a "begging of the question." The point which is being called in question is whether there is a divine spirit and a revelation; and it surely cannot be a conclusive reply to say that the question cannot be asked, because the Deity cannot be called in question. What is happening here is the same kind of thing as we meet with occasionally in our analytic work. If an otherwise intelligent patient denies a suggestion on particularly stupid grounds, his imperfect logic is evidence for the existence of a particularly strong motive for his making the denial, a motive which can only be of an affective nature and serve to bind an emotion.

Another sort of answer may be given, in which a motive of this kind is openly admitted. Religion must not be critically examined, because it is the highest, most precious, and noblest thing that the mind of man has brought forth, because it gives expression to the deepest feelings, and is the only thing that makes the world bearable and life worthy of humanity. To this we need not reply by disputing this estimate of religion, but rather by drawing attention to another aspect of the matter. We

should point out that it is not a question of the scientific spirit encroaching upon the sphere of religion, but of religion encroaching upon the sphere of scientific thought. Whatever value and importance religion may have, it has no right to set any limits to thought, and therefore has no right to except itself from the application of thought.

Scientific thought is, in its essence, no different from the normal process of thinking, which we all, believers and unbelievers, alike, make use of when we are going about our business in everyday life. It has merely taken a special form in certain respects: it extends its interest to things which have no immediate obvious utility, it endeavours to eliminate personal factors and emotional influences, it carefully examines the trustworthiness of the sense perceptions on which it bases its conclusions, it provides itself with new perceptions which are not obtainable by everyday means, and isolates the determinants of these new experiences by purposely varied experimentation. Its aim is to arrive at correspondence with reality, that is to say with what exists outside us and independently of us, and, as experience has taught us, is decisive for the fulfilment or frustration of our desires. This correspondence with the real external world we call *truth*. It is the aim of scientific work, even when the practical value of that work does not interest us. When, therefore, religion claims that it can take the place of science and that, because it is beneficent and ennobling, it must therefore be true, that claim is, in fact, an encroachment which, in the interests of every one, should be resisted. It is asking a great deal of a man, who has learned to regulate his everyday affairs in accordance with the rules of experience and with due regard to reality, that he should entrust precisely what affects him most nearly to the care of an authority which claims as its prerogative freedom from all the rules of rational thought. And, as for the protection that religion promises its believers, I hardly think that any of us would be willing even to enter a motor-car, if the driver informed us that he drove without allowing himself to be distracted by traffic regulations, but in accordance with the impulses of an exalted imagination.

And indeed the ban which religion has imposed upon thought in the interests of its own preservation is by no means without danger both for the individual and for society. Analytic experience has taught us that such prohibitions, even though they were originally confined to some particular field, have a tendency to spread, and then become the cause of severe inhibitions in people's lives. In women, a process of this sort can be observed to follow from the prohibition against their occupying themselves, even in thought, with the sexual side of their nature. The biographies of almost all the eminent people of past times show the disastrous results of the inhibition of thought by religion. Intellect, on the other hand—or rather, to call it by a more familiar name, reason—is among the forces which may be expected to exert a unifying influence upon men —creatures who can be held together only with the greatest difficulty, and whom it is therefore scarcely possible to control. Think how impossible human society would be if every one had his own particular multiplication table and his own private units of weight and length. Our best hope for the future is that the intellect— the scientific spirit, reason—should in time establish a dictatorship over the human mind. The very nature of reason is a guarantee that it would not fail to concede to human emotions, and to all that is determined by them, the position to which they are entitled. But the common pressure exercised by such a domination of reason would prove to be the strongest unifying force among men, and would prepare the way for further unifications. Whatever, like the ban laid upon thought by religion, opposes such a development is a danger for the future of mankind.

The question may now be asked why religion does not put an end to this losing fight by openly declaring: "It is a fact that I cannot give you what men commonly call truth; to obtain that, you must go to science. But what I have to give you is incomparably more beautiful, more comforting and more ennobling than anything that you could ever get from science. And I therefore say to you that it is true in a different and higher sense." The answer is easy to find. Religion cannot make this admission, because if it did it would lose all influence over the mass of mankind. The ordinary man knows only one *truth*—truth in the ordinary sense of the word. What may be meant by a higher, or a highest, truth, he cannot imagine. Truth seems to him as little capable of having degrees as death, and the necessary leap from the beautiful to the true is one that he cannot make. Perhaps you will agree with me in thinking that he is right in this.

The struggle, therefore, is not yet at an end. The followers of the religious *Weltanschauung* act in accordance with the old maxim: the best

defence is attack. "What," they ask, "is this science that presumes to depreciate our religion, which has brought salvation and comfort to millions of men for many thousands of years? What has science for its part so far accomplished? What more can be expected of it? On it own admission, it is incapable of comforting or ennobling us. We will leave that on one side, therefore, though it is by no means easy to give up such benefits. But what of its teaching? Can it tell us how the world began, and what fate is in store for it? Can it even paint for us a coherent picture of the universe, and show us where the unexplained phenomena of life fit in, and how spiritual forces are able to operate on inert matter? If it could do that, we should not refuse it our respect. But it has done nothing of the sort, not one single problem of this kind has it solved. It gives us fragments of alleged knowledge, which it cannot harmonize with one another, it collects observations of uniformities from the totality of events, and dignifies them with the name of *laws* and subjects them to its hazardous interpretations. And with what a small degree of certitude does it establish its conclusions! All that it teaches is only provisionally true; what is prized today as the highest wisdom is overthrown tomorrow and experimentally replaced by something else. The latest error is then given the name of truth. And to this truth we are asked to sacrifice our highest good!"

Ladies and Gentlemen—in so far as you yourselves are supporters of the scientific *Weltanschauung*, I do not think you will be very profoundly shaken by this critic's attack. In Imperial Austria an anecdote was once current which I should like to call to mind in this connection. On one occasion the old Emperor was receiving a deputation from a political party which he disliked: "This is no longer ordinary opposition," he burst out, "this is factious opposition." In just the same way you will find that the reproaches made against science for not having solved the riddle of the universe are unfairly and spitefully exaggerated. Science has had too little time for such a tremendous achievement. It is still very young, a recently developed human activity. Let us bear in mind, to mention only a few dates, that only about three hundred years have passed since Kepler discovered the laws of planetary movement; the life of Newton, who split up light into the colours of the spectrum and put forward the theory of gravitation, came to end in 1727, that is to say a little more than two hundred years ago; and Lavoisier discovered oxygen shortly before the French Revolution. I may be a very old man today, but the life of an individual man is very short in comparison with the duration of human development, and it is a fact that I was alive when Charles Darwin published his work on the origin of species. In the same year, 1859, Pierre Curie, the discoverer of radium, was born. And if you go back to the beginnings of exact natural science among the Greeks, to Archimedes, or to Aristarchus of Samos (around 250 B.C.) the forerunner of Copernicus, or even to the tentative origins of astronomy among the Babylonians, you will only be covering a very small portion of the period which anthropology requires for the evolution of man from his original ape-like form, a period which certainly embraces more than a hundred thousand years. And it must not be forgotten that the last century has brought with it such a quantity of new discoveries and such a great acceleration of scientific progress that we have every reason to look forward with confidence to the future of science.

It has to be admitted that the other objections are valid within certain limits. Thus it is true that the path of science is slow, tentative and laborious. That cannot be denied or altered. No wonder that the gentlemen of the opposition are dissatisfied; they are spoilt, they have had an easier time of it with their revelation. Progress in scientific work is made in just the same way as in analysis. The analyst brings expectations with him to his work, but he must keep them in the background. He discovers something new by observation, now here and now there, and at first the bits do not fit together. He puts forward suppositions, he brings constructions to one's aid, and gives them up if they are not confirmed, he must have a great deal of patience, must be prepared for all possibilities, and must not jump at conclusions for fear of their leading him to overlook new and unexpected factors. And in the end the whole expenditure of effort is rewarded, the scattered discoveries fall into place, and he obtains an understanding of a whole chain of mental events; he has finished one piece of work and is ready for the next. But the analyst is unlike other scientific workers in this one respect, that he has to do without the help which experiment can bring to research.

But the criticism of science which I have quoted also contains a great deal of exaggeration. It is not true to say that it swings blindly from one attempt to another, and exchanges one error for the next. As a rule, the man of science works like a sculptor with a clay model, who persistently alters the first rough sketch, adds to it and takes away from it, until he has obtained a satisfactory degree of similarity to some object, whether seen or imagined. And, moreover, at least in the older and more mature sciences, there is already a solid foundation of knowledge, which is now only modified and elaborated and no longer demolished. The outlook, in fact, is not so bad in the world of science.

And finally, what is the purpose of all these passionate disparagements of science? In spite of its present incompleteness and its inherent difficulties, we could not do without it and could not put anything else in its place. There is no limit to the improvement of which it is capable, and this can certainly not be said of the religious *Weltanschauung*. The latter is complete in its essentials; if it is an error, it must remain one for ever. No attempt to minimize the importance of science can alter the fact that it attempts to take into account our dependence on the real external world, while religion is illusion, and it derives its strength from the fact that it falls in with our instinctual desires.

I must now go on to mention some other types of *Weltanschauung* which are in opposition to the scientific one; I do so, however, unwillingly, because I know that I am not competent to form a judgment upon them. I hope, therefore, that you will bear this confession in mind in listening to what I have to say, and that if your interest is aroused you will go elsewhere for more trustworthy information.

In the first place, I ought at this point to name the various philosophical systems which have ventured to draw a picture of the world, as it is reflected in the minds of thinkers whose eyes are as a rule turned away from it. But I have already attempted to give a general characterization of philosophy and its methods, and I believe I am more unfitted than almost any one to pass the individual systems under review. I shall ask you, therefore, instead to turn your attention to two other phenomena which, particularly in these days, cannot be ignored.

The *Weltanschauung* to which I shall first refer is, as it were, a counterpart of political anarchism, and may perhaps have emanated from it. No doubt there have been intellectual nihilists of this kind before, but at the present day the theory of relativity of modern physics seems to have gone to their heads. It is true that they start out from science, but they succeed in forcing it to cut the ground from under its own feet, to commit suicide, as it were; they make it dispose of itself by getting it to refute its own premises. One often has an impression that this nihilism is only a temporary attitude, which will only be kept up until this task has been completed. When once science has been got rid of, some kind of mysticism, or, indeed, the old religious *Weltanschauung,* can spring up in the space that has been left vacant. According to this anarchistic doctrine, there is no such thing as truth, no assured knowledge of the external world. What we give out as scientific truth is only the product of our own needs and desires, as they are formulated under varying external conditions; that is to say, it is illusion once more. Ultimately we find only what we need to find, and see only what we desire to see. We can do nothing else. And since the criterion of truth, correspondence with an external world, disappears, it is absolutely immaterial what views we accept. All of them are equally true and false. And no one has a right to accuse any one else of error.

For a mind which is interested in epistemology, it would be tempting to enquire into the contrivances and sophistries by means of which the anarchists manage to elicit a final product of this kind from science. One would no doubt be brought up against situations like the one involved in the familiar example of the Cretan who says that all Cretans are liars. But I am not desirous, nor am I capable, of going deeper into this. I will merely remark that the anarchistic theory only retains its remarkable air of superiority so long as it is concerned with opinions about abstract things; it breaks down the moment it comes in contact with practical life. Now the behaviour of men is guided by their opinions and knowledge, and the same scientific spirit which speculates about the structure of the atom or the origin of man is concerned in the building of a bridge that will bear its load. If it were really a matter of indifference what we believed, if there were no knowledge which was distinguished from among our opinions by the fact that it corresponds with reality, then we might just as well build our bridges of cardboard as of stone, or inject a tenth of a gramme of morphia into a patient instead of a hundredth, or take tear-gas as a narcotic instead of ether. But the intellectual anarchists themselves would strongly repudiate such practical applications of their theory.

The other opposing *Weltanschauung* is to be taken far more seriously, and in this case I very deeply regret the insufficiency of my knowledge. I dare say that you know more about this subject than I do and that you have long ago taken up your position for or against Marxism. The investigations of Karl Marx into the economic structure of society and into the influence of various forms of economic organization upon all departments of human life have, in our day, acquired an authority that cannot be denied. How far they are right or wrong in detail, I naturally do not know. I gather that it is not easy even for better informed people to decide. Some of the propositions in Marx's theory seem strange to me, such as that the evolution of forms of society is a process of natural history, or that the changes in social stratification proceed from one another in the manner of a dialectical process. I am by no means certain that I understand these statements rightly; moreover, they do not sound *materialistic* but like traces of the obscure Hegelian philosophy under the influence of which Marx at one time passed. I do not know how I can throw off the view which I share with other laymen, who are inclined to trace back the formation of classes in society to the struggles which went on from the beginning of history between various human hordes. These hordes differed to a slight degree from one another; and it is my view that social differences go back to these original differences of tribe or race. Psychological factors, such as the amount of constitutional aggressiveness and also the degree of cohesion within the horde, and material factors, such as the possession of better weapons, decided the victory. When they came to live together in the same territory, the victors became the masters and conquered the slaves. There is no sign in all this of natural laws or conceptual modifications; on the other hand, we cannot fail to recognize the influence which the progressive control over natural forces exerts on the social relationships between men, since men always place their newly won powers at the service of their aggressiveness, and use them against one another. The introduction of metals, of bronze and iron, put an end to whole cultural epochs and their social institutions. I really believe that gun-powder and fire-arms overthrew chivalry and the domination of the aristocracy, and that the Russian despotism was already doomed before the war was lost, since no amount of in-breeding among the ruling families of Europe could have produced a race of Tsars capable of withstanding the explosive force of dynamite.

It may be, indeed, that with the present economic crisis which followed upon the Great War, we are merely paying the price of our latest triumph over nature, the conquest of the air. This does not sound very convincing, but at least the first links in the chain of argument are clearly recognizable. The policy of England was based on the security guaranteed by the seas which encircle her coasts. The moment Blériot flew over the Channel in his aeroplane, this protective isolation was broken through; and on the night on which, in a time of peace, a German Zeppelin made an experimental cruise over London, war against Germany became a certainty.[1] Nor must the threat of submarines be forgotten in this connection.

I am almost ashamed of treating a theme of such importance and complexity in such a slight and inadequate manner, and I am also aware that I have not said anything that is new to you. I only wanted to call your attention to the fact that the factor of man's control over nature, from which he obtains his weapons for his struggle with his fellow-men, must of necessity also affect his economic arrangements. We seem to have travelled a long way from the problems of a *Weltanschauung*, but we shall soon come back to the point. The strength of Marxism obviously does not lie in its view of history, or in the prophecies about the future which it bases upon that view, but in its clear insight into the determining influence which is exerted by the economic conditions of man upon his intellectual, ethical, and artistic reactions. A whole collection of correlations and causal sequences were thus discovered which had hitherto been almost completely disregarded. But it cannot be assumed that economic motives are the only ones which determine the behaviour of men in society. The unquestionable fact that different individuals, races, and nations behave differently under the same economic conditions, in itself proves that the economic factor cannot be the sole determinant. It is quite impossible to understand how psychological factors can be overlooked where the reactions of living human beings are involved; for not only were such factors already concerned in the establishment of these economic conditions, but, even in obeying these conditions, men can do no more than set their original instinctual impulses in motion—their self-preservative instinct, their love of aggression, their need for love, and their impulse to attain

[1] I was informed of this in the first year of the war on trustworthy authority.

pleasure and avoid pain. In an earlier lecture, we have emphasised the importance of the part played by the super-ego, which represents tradition and the ideals of the past, and which will resist for some time the pressure exerted by new economic situations. And, finally, we must not forget that the mass of mankind, subjected though they are to economic necessities, are borne on by a process of cultural development—some call it civilization—which is no doubt influenced by all the other factors, but is certainly equally independent of them in its origin; it is comparable to an organic process, and is quite capable of itself having an effect upon the other factors. It displaces the aims of the instincts, and causes men to rebel against what has hitherto been tolerable; and, moreover, the progressive strengthening of the scientific spirit seems to be an essential part of it. If any one were in a position to show in detail how these different factors—the general human instinctual disposition, its racial variations, and its cultural modifications—behave under the influence of varying social organization, professional activities, and methods of subsistence, how these factors inhibit or aid one another—if, I say, any one could show this, then he would not only have improved Marxism but would have made it into a true social science. For sociology, which deals with the behaviour of man in society, can be nothing other than applied psychology. Strictly speaking, indeed, there are only two sciences—psychology, pure and applied, and natural science.

When at last the far-reaching importance of economic conditions began to be realized, the temptation arose to bring about an alteration in them by means of revolutionary interference, instead of leaving the change to the course of historical development. Theoretical Marxism, as put into effect in Russian Bolshevism, has acquired the energy, the comprehensiveness, and the exclusiveness of a *Weltanschauung;* but at the same time it has acquired an almost uncanny resemblance to what it is opposing. Originally it was itself a part of science, and, in its realization, was built up on science and technology; but it has nevertheless established a ban upon thought, which is as inexorable as was formerly that of religion. All critical examination of the Marxist theory is forbidden; doubts of its validity are as vindictively punished as heresy once was by the Catholic Church. The works of Marx, as the source of revelation, have taken the place of the Bible and the Koran, although they are no freer from contradictions and obscurities than these earlier holy books.

And although practical Marxism has remorselessly swept away all idealistic systems and illusions, it has nevertheless developed illusions itself, which are no less dubious and unverifiable than their predecessors. It hopes, in the course of a few generations, so to alter men that they will be able to live together in the new order of society almost without friction, and that they will do their work voluntarily. In the meantime, it moves elsewhere the instinctual barriers which are essential in any society, it directs outwards the aggressive tendencies, which threaten every human community, and finds its support in the hostility of the poor against the rich, and of the hitherto powerless against the former holders of power. But such an alteration in human nature is very improbable. The enthusiasm with which the mob follow the Bolshevist lead at present, so long as the new order is incomplete and threatened from outside, gives no guarantee for the future, when it will be fully established and no longer in danger. In exactly the same way as religion, Bolshevism is obliged to compensate its believers for the sufferings and deprivations of the present life, by promising them a better life hereafter, in which there will be no unsatisfied needs. It is true that this paradise is to be in this world; it will be established on earth, and will be inaugurated within a measurable time. But let us remember that the Jews, whose religion knows nothing of a life beyond the grave, also expected the coming of the Messiah here on earth, and that the Christian Middle Ages constantly believed that the Kingdom of God was at hand.

There is no doubt what the answer of Bolshevism to these criticisms will be. "Until men have changed their nature," it will say, "one must employ the methods which are effective with them today. One cannot do without compulsion in their education or a ban upon thinking or the application of force even to the spilling of blood; and if one did not awake in them the illusions you speak of, one would not be able to bring them to submit to this compulsion." And it might politely ask us to say how else it could be done. At this point we should be defeated. I should know of no advice to give. I should admit that the conditions of this experiment would have restrained me, and people like me, from undertaking it; but we are not the only ones concerned. There are also men of action, unshakable in their convictions,

impervious to doubt, and insensitive to the sufferings of anyone who stands between them and their goal. It is owing to such men that the tremendous attempt to institute a new order of society of this kind is actually being carried out in Russia now. At a time when great nations are declaring that they expect to find their salvation solely from a steadfast adherence to Christian piety, the upheaval in Russia—in spite of all its distressing features—seems to bring a promise of a better future. Unfortunately, neither our own misgivings nor the fanatical belief of the other side give us any hint of how the experiment will turn out. The future will teach us. Perhaps it will show that the attempt has been made prematurely, and that a fundamental alteration of the social order will have little hope of success until new discoveries are made that will increase our control over the forces of nature, and so make easier the satisfaction of our needs. It may be that only then will it be possible for a new order of society to emerge which will not only banish the material wants of the masses, but at the same time meet the cultural requirements of individual men. But even so, we shall still have to struggle for an indefinite length of time with the difficulties which the intractable nature of man puts in the way of every kind of social community.

Ladies and Gentlemen—Let me in conclusion sum up what I had to say about the relation of psycho-analysis to the question of a *Weltanschauung*. Psycho-analysis is not, in my opinion, in a position to create a *Weltanschauung* of its own. It has no need to do so, for it is a branch of science and can subscribe to the scientific *Weltanschauung*. The latter, however, hardly merits such a high-sounding name, for it does not take everything into its scope, it is incomplete, and it makes no claim to being comprehensive or to constituting a system. Scientific thought is still in its infancy; there are very many of the great problems with which it has as yet been unable to cope. A *Weltanschauung* based upon science has, apart from the emphasis it lays upon the real world, essentially negative characteristics, such as that it limits itself to truth and rejects illusions. Those of our fellow-men who are dissatisfied with this state of things and who desire something more for their momentary peace of mind may look for it where they can find it. We shall not blame them for doing so; but we cannot help them and cannot change our own way of thinking on their account.

GREAT BOOKS
OF THE WESTERN WORLD

••••••••••

Design and Typography by RUDOLPH RUZICKA

••••••••••

Cover Stamping Design for Founders' Edition by HENRY HARRINGER

Composition and Engravings by
THE LAKESIDE PRESS: R. R. DONNELLEY & SONS COMPANY
Chicago, Illinois, and Crawfordsville, Indiana

With these exceptions:

Volume 39: Adam Smith; Volume 54: Freud
Composition by POOLE BROS., INC.
Chicago, Illinois

Printing Plates by
ADVANCE INDEPENDENT ELECTROTYPE COMPANY, INC.
Indianapolis, Indiana

———

Further exceptions:

Volume 16: Ptolemy, Copernicus, Kepler;
Volume 17: Plotinus; Volume 21: Dante; Volume 42: Kant
Composition by DAYTON'S TYPOGRAPHICAL SERVICE
Dayton, Ohio

Volumes 26-27: Shakespeare
Composition by LINXWEILER PRINTING COMPANY
Decatur, Illinois

••••••••••

Printing and Binding by KINGSPORT PRESS, INC.
Kingsport, Tennessee

••••••••••

THE GREAT IDEAS, *Volumes 2 and 3*